McGraw-Hill Encyclopedia of

Environmental Science & Engineering

McGraw-Hill Encyclopedia of
Environmental Science & Engineering

Third Edition

EDITORS IN CHIEF
Sybil P. Parker
Robert A. Corbitt

McGraw-Hill, Inc.
New York   San Francisco   Washington, D.C.   Auckland   Bogotá
Caracas   Lisbon   London   Madrid   Mexico City   Milan   Montreal
New Delhi   San Juan   Singapore   Sydney   Tokyo   Toronto

2 3 4 5 6 7 8 9   DOW/DOW   9 8 7 6 5 4

Library of Congress Cataloging in Publication data

McGraw-Hill cncyclopedia of environmental science & engineering / editors
    in chief, Sybil P. Parker, Robert A. Corbitt. —3rd ed.
          p.   cm.
    Rev. ed. of: McGraw-Hill encyclopedia of environmental science,
2nd ed., c1980.
    ''Most of the material in this volume has been published previously
in the McGraw-Hill encyclopedia of science & technology, seventh
edition''—T.p. verso.
    Includes bibliographical references and index.
    ISBN 0-07-051396-1
    1. Environmental sciences—Encyclopedias.   2. Environmental
protection—Encyclopedias.   I. Parker, Sybil P.   II. Corbitt,
Robert A.   III. McGraw-Hill, Inc.   IV. Title: McGraw-Hill
encyclopedia of environmental science.   V. Title: McGraw-Hill
encyclopedia of science & technology.
GE10.M38   1993
628′.03—dc20   92-42118
                                                            CIP

ISBN 0-07-051396-1

McGraw-Hill Staff

Betty Richman, Editor
Patricia W. Albers, Editorial Administrator
Ron Lane, Art Director
Vincent Piazza, Assistant Art Director
Joe Faulk, Editing Manager
Frank Kotowski, Jr., Senior Editing Supervisor
Ruth W. Mannino, Editing Supervisor

Project Consultant

Robert A. Corbitt, P.E.
Associate, Metcalf & Eddy, Inc.
Atlanta, Georgia

Field Consultants

Prof. Lawrence Grossman
Department of Geophysical Science
University of Chicago

Prof. Edwin Kessler
Retired; formerly, Director
National Severe Storms Laboratory
Norman, Oklahoma

James B. Sullivan
Formerly, Executive Editor
''Engineering-News Record''
McGraw-Hill, Inc.
New York, New York

Prof. Richard G. Wiegert
Department of Zoology
University of Georgia

Suppliers

Typeset and composed by the Clarinda Company,
Clarinda, Iowa.

Printed and bound by R. R. Donnelley & Sons
Company, the Lakeside Press at Willard, Ohio.

Preface

Environmental science is concerned with the entire biosphere and with all the external influences to which organisms are exposed, both physical (abiotic) influences and those originating with other organisms (biotic). Environmental engineering is concerned with effects of human activities on the Earth's ecosystems, particularly those that result in pollution of the air, land, and water.

Environmental influences can be studied on various scales of space and time. For example, of global concern are possible changes in the world's climate resulting from natural causes, such as the spewing of sulfuric gases from a volcanic eruption into the atmosphere, or from human activities, such as the generation of massive volumes of carbon dioxide by burning fossil fuels. On a local scale, the problem of indoor air pollution is the subject of a great deal of study. Time scales can vary from the long time it takes for a fertile area to become a desert to the immediate effect of a drop of herbicide on the leaf of a plant.

Humans and other organisms are subjected to many environmental conditions; their responses are varied and range from fairly simple to extremely complex. Identifying and solving problems that may arise are the concerns of both scientists and engineers, using information from such diverse scientific fields as ecology, geophysics, geochemistry, forestry, public health, meteorology, agriculture, oceanography, soil science, as well as from engineering disciplines such as mechanical, mining, civil, petroleum, chemical, and power engineering. Problems range from smog and deforestation to dealing with hazardous and solid wastes that accumulate in industrialized countries. The consequences of perturbations of an ecosystem can be catastrophic and may extend beyond the system itself. Environmental science is concerned with identifying and characterizing the problems, while environmental engineering is concerned with finding the solutions.

The *Encyclopedia of Environmental Science & Engineering* has been published in two earlier editions (titled *Encyclopedia of Environmental Science*). It covers a great variety of topics in both multidisciplinary fields, giving valuable insights into the present state of knowledge, prospects for future developments, and relevant legislation, particularly in the United States. This third edition has been thoroughly revised to include the most recent aspects of all subjects. Some articles have been prepared especially for this volume, and the others have been taken from the authoritative and widely acclaimed *McGraw-Hill Encyclopedia of Science & Technology* (7th ed., 1992). The articles contain information that has been written and reviewed by experts in the field, supplemented by photographs, line drawings, diagrams, graphs, and useful bibliographies for readers seeking further information. In addition, there is a detailed analytical index for easy access to the extensive information in the Encyclopedia.

Sybil P. Parker
Editor in Chief

McGraw-Hill Encyclopedia of
Environmental Science & Engineering

A-Z

Acid rain

Precipitation that incorporates anthropogenic acids and acidic materials. The deposition of acidic materials on the Earth's surface occurs in both wet and dry forms as rain, snow, fog, dry particles, and gases. Although 30% or more of the total deposition may be dry, very little information is available that is specific to this dry form. In contrast, a large and expanding body of information exists related to the wet form, acid rain or acid precipitation. Acid precipitation, strictly defined, contains a greater concentration of hydrogen (H^+) than of hydroxyl (OH^-) ions, resulting in a solution pH less than 7. Under this definition, nearly all precipitation is acidic. The phenomenon of acid deposition, however, is generally regarded as resulting from human activity.

Sources. Theoretically, the natural acidity of precipitation corresponds to a pH of 5.6, which represents the pH of pure water in equilibrium with atmospheric concentrations of carbon dioxide. Atmospheric moisture, however, is not pure, and its interaction with ammonia, oxides of nitrogen and sulfur, and windblown dust results in a pH between 4.9 and 6.5 for most "natural" precipitation. The distribution and magnitude of precipitation pH in the United States (**Fig. 1**) suggest the impact of anthropogenic rather than natural causes. The areas of highest precipitation acidity (lowest pH) correspond to areas within and downwind of heavy industrialization and urbanization where emissions of sulfur and nitrogen oxides are high. It is with these emissions that the most acidic precipitation is thought to originate.

Atmospheric processes. The transport of acidic substances and their precursors, chemical reactions, and deposition are controlled by atmospheric processes. In general, it is convenient to distinguish between physical and chemical processes, but it must be realized that both types may be operating simultaneously in complicated and interdependent ways. The physical processes of transport by atmospheric winds and the formation of clouds and precipitation strongly influence the patterns and rates of acidic deposition, while chemical reactions govern the forms of the compounds deposited.

In midlatitude continental regions, such as eastern North America, most precipitation arises from cyclonic storms. As shown by the schematic representation of a typical storm (**Fig. 2**), rain tends to form along the surface cold and warm fronts that define the so-called warm sector of the storm. This characteristic structure, arising from prevailing north-south temperature gradients, simultaneously sets the stage for chemical transformations of pollutants and for incorporation of the compounds into precipitation. The motion of the cold front toward the southeast forces the moist warm-sector air to stream along the cold front toward the low-pressure region (L), as shown by the broad arrow in Fig. 2. At the same time, the air is gradually lifted out of the surface layer and into the colder, upper parts of the storm, which allows the supply of water vapor to condense out, forming the cloud and precipitation. *See Front; Storm.*

A number of chemical pathways exist by which the primary pollutants, sulfur dioxide (SO_2) from industry, nitric oxide (NO) from both industry and automobiles, and reactive hydrocarbons mostly from trees, are transformed into acid-producing compounds. Some of these pathways exist solely in the gas phase, while others involve the aqueous phase afforded by the cloud and precipitation. As a general rule, the volatile primary pollutants must first be oxidized to more stable compounds before they are efficiently removed from the atmosphere. Ironically, the most effective oxidizing agents, hydrogen peroxide (H_2O_2) and ozone (O_3), arise from photochemical reactions involving the primary pollutants themselves. *See Air pollution.*

All of the ingredients needed to form the strong mineral acids of sulfur and nitrogen [sulfuric acid (H_2SO_4) and nitric acid (HNO_3)], which constitute most of the acids found in rain, exist in the warm sector. Especialy in summertime, stagnant air conditions trap the pollutants under clear skies for several days, permitting photochemical reactions to initiate other gas-phase reactions. Nitrogen oxides (NO_x), in combination with ultraviolet light from the Sun, reactive hydrocarbons, atmospheric oxygen, and water vapor, simultaneously give rise to HNO_3 vapor, odd-hydrogen radicals (particularly OH), and the strong

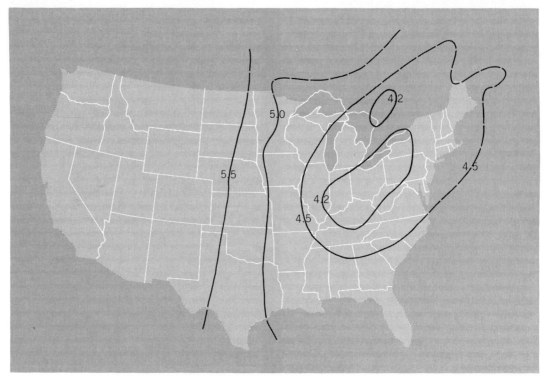

Fig. 1. Distribution of rainfall pH in the eastern United States.

oxidants H_2O_2 and O_3. Meanwhile, slow oxidation of sulfur dioxide (SO_2), initiated by reaction with the OH radical, leads to the gradual buildup of sulfate (SO_4^{2-}) aerosol, and hazy skies result from the highly condensible nature of H_2SO_4. While some dry deposition does occur under these conditions, the warm sector of midlatitude cyclones is a region conducive to the gradual accumulation of primary pollutants, ox-

idants, and acid-forming compounds in the lower atmosphere. *See Smog.*

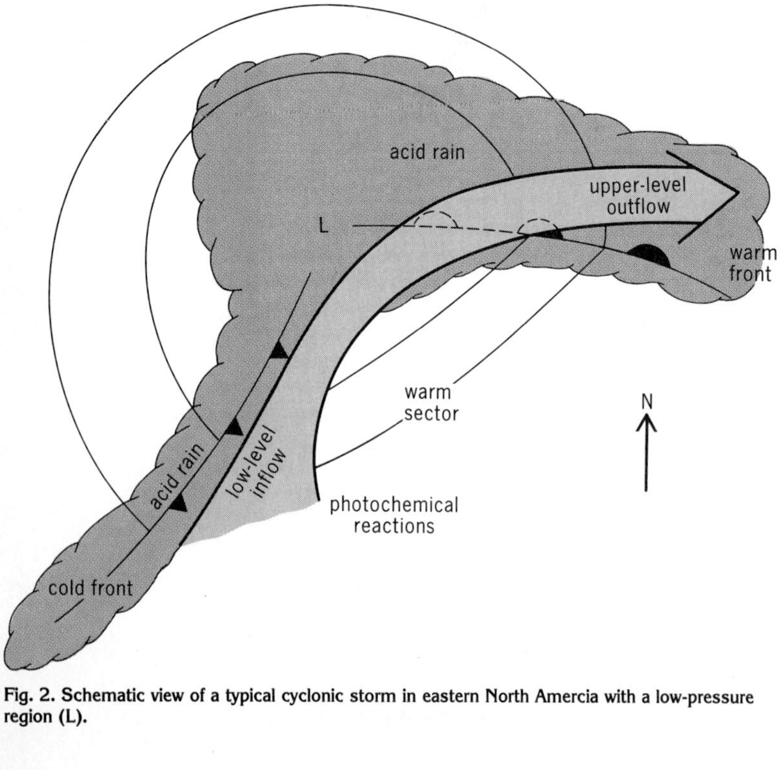

As the cold front approaches any given location in the warm sector, the airborne acids and their precursors are drawn into the circulations of the cyclone, particularly into the stream of moist air associated with the fronts. By this large-scale meteorological process, the pollutants become integrally associated with the frontal cloud systems, and attach to individual cloud particles by a variety of microphysical processes. Since most atmospheric sulfate particles are very soluble, they act as good centers (nuclei) for cloud drop formation. Thus, the process of cloud formation is itself a mechanism for scavenging particulate pollutants from the air. As the cloud drops grow by condensation, soluble gases will be absorbed by the cloud water. It is during this phase of the overall process that additional SO_2 will be oxidized to H_2SO_4 by the previously formed strong oxidants, particularly the H_2O_2.

The actual removal of pollutants from the atmosphere by wet deposition requires the formation of precipitation within the clouds. Without cloud elements greater than about 100 micrometers in diameter, the pollutant mass remains in the air, largely in association with the relatively small cloud drops, which have negligible rates of descent. Since most precipitation in midlatitude storms is initiated by the formation of ice particles in the cold, upper reaches of the clouds, pollutant fractionation between water phases inhibits the transfer of cloud water acidity to large particles, which do precipitate readily. Partly because of such microphysical phenomena and partly because of nonuniform distributions of pollutants within the clouds, the acidity of precipitation tends to be substantially less than that of the cloud water that remains aloft. The acidity of the precipitation appears to be acquired largely through collisions of the melted

Fig. 2. Schematic view of a typical cyclonic storm in eastern North Amercia with a low-pressure region (L).

ice particles with the relatively concentrated cloud drops in the lower portions of the storm clouds. The rate of wet deposition is thus governed by a complicated set of meteorological and microscale processes working in harmony to effect a general cleansing of the atmosphere. SEE ATMOSPHERIC CHEMISTRY; CLOUD PHYSICS.

Terrestrial and aquatic effects. The effect of acid deposition on a particular ecosystem depends largely on its acid sensitivity, its acid neutralization capability, the concentration and composition of acid reaction products, and the amount of acid added to the system. As an example, the major factors influencing the impact of acidic deposition on lakes and streams are (1) the amount of acid deposited; (2) the pathway and travel time from the point of deposition to the lake or stream; (3) the buffering characteristics of the soil through which the acidic solution moves; (4) the nature and amount of acid reaction products in soil drainage and from sediments; and (5) the buffering capacity of the lake or stream.

In many ecosystems, except for foliar effects, the impact of acid precipitation on aquatic and terrestrial ecosystems overlap. This is because soils are the key intermediate. They provide the root environment for terrestrial vegetation, and also control the water quality of runoff and soil drainage which supplies most of the water to the aquatic system. A number of acid-consuming reactions occur in soil which lessen the impact of acid additions on both the soil and soil drainage waters. In soils, indigenous or agriculturally amended carbonates (CO_3^{2-}) react with acid precipitation to raise the pH of soil drainage waters, while maintaining soil pH. Also, soils exhibit a cation-exchange capacity which can serve to neutralize acid precipitation. At neutral soil pH (6.0–8.0), most cations on the exchange are calcium (Ca) and magnesium (Mg). When acids are added, H^+ from solution exchange with the adsorbed Ca and Mg. Although this reduces the acidity of soil drainage waters, the soil acidity is increased. Eventually, when the neutralizing carbonates and exchangeable Ca and Mg supplies are exhausted, soil minerals react with the acid. At about a soil pH of 5.2 or less, substantial aluminum (Al) can be solubilized from the dissolution of clay minerals and coatings on soil particles. SEE SOIL CHEMISTRY.

Acid deposition directly into lakes and streams causes chemical reactions analogous to those in the soil system. However, instead of soil materials, the carbonate-bicarbonate (HCO_3^-) system buffers the solution. As with soils, waters of low pH and buffering capacities, in this case bicarbonate concentrations, are most sensitive. At solution pH of 4.5, bicarbonate is essentially depleted, and subsequent acid additions which reduce pH also mobilize metals from suspended solids and the lake or stream bed. Generally, lakes and streams that drain acid-susceptible soils are most susceptible to direct acid deposition as well. Shallow soils with low pH, low cation-exchange capacity, and high permeability not only are least able to neutralize acid flows but also are poor sources of the bicarbonate waters needed to buffer the aquatic system.

While the study of acid precipitation effects on terrestrial ecosystems is relatively new, soil acidification is a naturally occurring process in humid climates and has long been the subject of research, whose findings suggest acid precipitation effects. The generally ac-

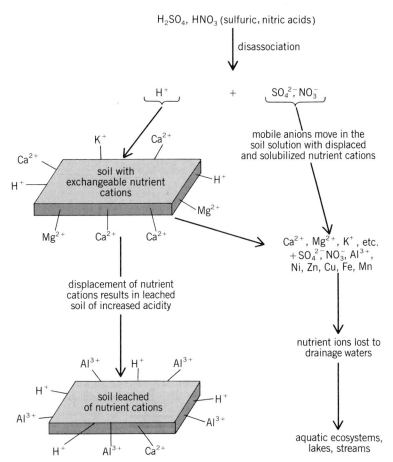

Fig. 3. Soil acidification and loss of soil nutrients following acid inputs.

cepted impact of soil acidification on the productivity of terrestrial plants is summarized as follows. As soil becomes more acidic, the basic cations (Ca, Mg) on the soil exchange are replaced by hydrogen ions or solubilized metals. The basic cations, now in solution, can be leached through the soil (**Fig. 3**). As time progresses, the soil becomes less fertile and more acidic. Resultant decreases in soil pH cause reduced, less-active populations of soil microorganisms, which in turn slow decomposition of plant residues and cycling of essential plant nutrients. The plant availability of phosphorus, now composed mostly of aluminum and iron (Fe) phosphates, decreases, while the plant availability of trace metal [aluminum, copper (Cu), iron, zinc (Zn), boron (B), manganese (Mn)] increases, sometimes to phytotoxic levels.

The rate and magnitude of acidification of aquatic systems depend upon the factors listed above. Predictable changes in water chemistry, as the pH of surface waters decreases, include decreased alkalinity, decreased buffering capacity, and increased concentrations of aluminum, magnesium, and iron, among other elements. Such changes in water chemistry generally result in decreased diversity of aquatic species and reduced productivity.

Many cases of important changes in the condition of forest trees have been reported in Europe and North America during the period of increasing precipitation acidity. These cases include injury to white pine in the eastern United States, red spruce in the Appalachian Mountains of eastern North America, and many economically important species in central

Europe. Despite documented damage to individual trees, no studies have shown losses in forest productivity, and in only a few cases is the cause of damage known with certainty. Forest trees are continuously stressed by competition for light, water, and nutrients, by disease organisms, by extremes in climate, and by atmospheric pollutants. Each of these sources of stress, singly or in combination, produces similar injury. Consequently, the extent to which acid precipitation harms forest ecosystems is as yet unclear. *SEE FOREST ECOSYSTEM; TERRESTRIAL ECOSYSTEM.*

The impact of acid deposition on terrestrial and aquatic ecosystems is not uniform. While increases in acid deposition may stress some ecosystems and reduce their stability and productivity, others may be unaffected. The degree and nature of the impact depend on the acid input load, organismal susceptibility, and buffering capacity of the particular ecosystem. *SEE BIOGEOCHEMISTRY; ECOSYSTEM.*

Ronald R. Schnabel; Dennis Lamb; Harry B. Pionke

Bibliography. *Acid Deposition: Atmospheric Processes in Eastern North America*, National Academy Press, 1983; *Acid Rain and Transported Air Pollutants: Implications for Public Policy*, U.S. Congress, Office of Technology Assessment, 1984; R. J. Charlson and H. Rohde, Factors controlling the acidity of natural rainwater, *Nature*, 195:683–685, 1982; F. M. D'Itri (ed.), *Acid Precipitation: Effects on Ecological Systems*, 1982; P. L. Haagenson et al., A relationship between acid precipitation and three-dimensional transport associated with synoptic-scale cyclones, *J. Climate Appl. Meteorol.*, 24:967–976, 1985; M. Havas, T. C. Hutchinson, and G. F. Likens, Red herrings in acid rain research, *Environ. Sci. Tech.*, 18:176A–186A, 1984; *Interim Assessment: The Causes and Effects of Acidic Deposition*, National Acid Precipitation Assessment Program, Washington, D.C., 1987; E. C. Krug and C. R. Frink, Acid rain on acid soil: A new perspective, *Science*, 221:520–525, 1983; J. N. Wordman and E. B. Cowling, Airborne chemicals and forest health, *Environ. Sci. Technol.*, 21:120–126, 1987.

Acoustic noise

Unwanted sound. Noise control is the process of obtaining an acceptable noise environment for people in different situations. These definitions and the words "unwanted" and "acceptable" suggest that criteria need to be established to determine when noise from different sources is unwanted and that these criteria could or should be used to decide on acceptable noise limits. Understanding noise and its control, then, requires a knowledge of the major sources of noise, sound propagation, human response to noise, and the physics of methods of controlling noise. The continuing increase in noise levels from many different human activities in industrialized societies led to the term noise pollution. Different governments have passed legislation and created regulations to control noise.

Noise as an unwanted by-product of an industrialized society affects not only the operators of machines and vehicles, but also other occupants of buildings in which machines are installed, passengers of vehicles, and most importantly the communities in which machines, factories, and vehicles are operated.

PROPAGATION OF SOUND

Sound is a three-dimensional wave motion in the atmosphere. The acoustic waves travel from the source with a speed independent of their amplitude (unless the latter is very large). This speed is then dependent only on the acoustic medium and is proportional to the square root of the absolute temperature for any given medium. For air at 68°F (20°C), the speed of sound c is 1117 ft/s (343 m/s).

Pure tones. The sources of sound may consist either of vibrating solid bodies (such as loudspeakers or vibrating metal panels on machines) or of random motion of air particles (such as when an air jet mixes with the atmosphere). If a loudspeaker cone is made to vibrate with simple harmonic motion at a given frequency f (in hertz or cycles per second), it gives rise to a sinusoidal disturbance in the atmosphere. This sound is known as a pure tone, of frequency f. At any instant there will be a sinusoidal variation of the atmospheric pressure with distance away from the source. The sound pressure p is defined as the difference in the pressure from the undisturbed pressure. For a pure tone, wave crests or wave troughs (maximum and minimum values of pressure) are separated by a distance called the wavelength λ. The relationship between the speed of sound c, wavelength λ, and frequency f is given by Eq. (1). Of course, at some

$$\lambda = c/f \qquad (1)$$

point in space the sound pressure p also varies sinusoidally with time. The period T between pressure maxima is related to the frequency by Eq. (2) for a

$$T = 1/f \qquad (2)$$

pure tone (**Fig. 1**).

Many sound sources, such as a singing voice or a musical instrument, contain strong pure-tone components. These sounds contain several simultaneous pure tones with a fundamental (or lowest-frequency tone) which is usually the strongest. Examples of noise sources which contain pure tones include fans, engine exhausts, pumps, compressors, gears, bearings, and electric motors.

Random noise. If a sound source is made to vibrate with a random motion, it also creates sound waves. However, the sound pressure–time history at some point in space then resembles **Fig. 2** rather than Fig. 1. This sound is called random noise, because it contains all frequencies instead of just one. Many noise sources, for example, jet engine exhausts, fans, flow noise in pipes, waterfalls, and wind, contain mostly random noise.

Although the strength of a pure tone can be de-

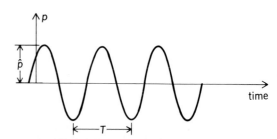

Fig. 1. Sound pressure p at one point in space, varying sinusoidally with time, in response to a source vibrating with simple harmonic motion.

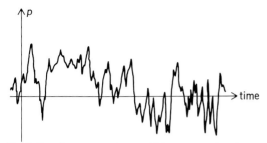

Fig. 2. Sound pressure p at one point in space, varying at random with time (random noise), in response to a source vibrating with random motion.

scribed by its amplitude or peak pressure $\hat{p}$ (Fig. 1), a random noise cannot, because the amplitude is never constant. Thus, noise signals are normally described by their time-averaged (effective or root-mean-square) values, P_{rms}, given by Eq. (3), where T

$$p_{rms} = (1/T)\int_0^T p^2 dt \qquad (3)$$

is the averaging time, which is allowed to approach infinity. Only in the case of pure tone does $p_{rms} = \hat{p}/\sqrt{2}$.

Sound pressure level. The value of effective sound pressure p_{rms} increases about 10^6 times from a pin drop to a thunderclap. Because of these large variations in sound magnitudes, and because the human hearing sensation seems to vary in a logarithmic way, logarithms are used in measurement of sound. The sound pressure level L_p of a sound of effective pressure p_{rms} is given by Eq. (4), where the units of

$$L_p = 10 \log (p_{rms}^2/p_{ref}^2) \qquad (4)$$

L_p are decibels (dB). The reference pressure is internationally accepted to be $p_{ref} = 2 \times 10^{-4}$ dyne/cm.

Sound power level and intensity. If a source is constantly pulsating, it will radiate acoustic energy at a rate that is called the acoustic power and is expressed as W, in watts (joules/s). Again, because acoustic powers vary from very small to very large values, logarithms are used. The sound power level L_w (in decibels) of such a source is given by Eq. (5),

$$L_w = 10 \log (W/W_{ref}) \qquad (5)$$

where the reference sound power is $W_{ref} = 10^{-12}$ W. In an ideal source, if it is assumed that there is no energy dissipation as the sound energy radiates away from the source, then the intensity I (power/unit area) is reduced by a factor of $(1/r^2)$ or $\frac{1}{4}$ every time the distance r from the source is doubled. This is the inverse-square law, Eq. (6). Because it is easily shown

$$I \propto 1/r^2 \qquad (6)$$

that the intensity I is proportional to p_{rms}^2, doubling the distance from the source reduces the sound pressure level L_p [Eq. (4)] by $10 \log (2)^2 = 20(0.30) \approx$ 6 dB, provided there are no reflections. One of the simplest noise control measures thus becomes evident; noise sources should be placed as far away from receivers as possible.

Frequency analysis. In order to determine the frequency distribution of a noise, the intensity or sound pressure level in different frequency bands is measured. The frequency analysis may be done by using electrical filters or fast Fourier transform (FFT) ana-

lyzers. The bands most commonly used are constant percentage bands of width one octave or one-third of one octave. (An octave is a doubling in frequency.) Constant-bandwidth bands such as 5, 20, or 50 Hz are also used, to obtain information on pure tones contained in a noise signal. The constant-percentage filter rapidly increases in bandwidth as the center frequency is raised. The range of hearing for most people is from about 20 to 16,000 Hz, and can be covered with 10 octave band filters with center frequencies: 31.5, 63, 125, 250, 500, 1000, 2000, 4000, 8000, and 16,000 Hz. The one-octave band has a bandwidth of 73% of the center frequency, while the one-third-octave band has a bandwidth of 23% of the center frequency.

HUMAN RESPONSE TO NOISE

Noise interferes with some human activities and if sufficiently intense can permanently damage the ear.

Hearing mechanism. The ear is a complicated transducer which converts acoustical energy into mechanical vibrations of the eardrum, the three auditory ossicles (bones), and the cochlear membrane, and eventually into electrical energy which triggers nerve impulses in the auditory nerve. The outer ear canal and the eustachian tube are filled with air, while the inner ear (the cochlea) is filled with fluid.

Loudness. Individual responses to pure tones of different frequencies vary a little. Equal-loudness level contours (**Fig. 3**) represent pure tones which appear equally loud to most people at various frequencies. The lowest curve in Fig. 3 represents the threshold of hearing or the softest sounds that can be heard. The top curve approximately represents the threshold of "pain" or "feeling." The equal-loudness level curves are given units of phons P, and are numerically equal to their sound pressure level value at 1000 Hz. Sounds must be increased about 10 phons in level before they double in loudness, and because of this nonlinear subjective response of the ear, a linear loudness scale with units of sones S, defined by Eq. (7), is used. Thus a sound level of 50 phons has a

$$S = 2^{(P - 40)/10} \qquad (7)$$

loudness of 2 sones; a sound of 60 phons, 4 sones; and so on. Equal-loudness curves for bands of noise resemble those shown in **Fig. 4** for pure tones, but with some differences. It follows from Fig. 4 that the low-frequency sounds must be much more intense than mid- and high-frequency sounds in order to seem equally loud. The greatest hearing sensitivity is in the range of about 1000 to 4000 Hz, which corresponds to the middle of the speech range.

Equal-loudness level contours have been used in acoustical instrumentation to produce useful single-number measures of the loudness or disturbing effect of noise. A-, B-, and C-weighting filters (**Fig. 5**), corresponding approximately to the inverse of the 40-, 70-, and 100-phon curves respectively, have been built into most sound level meters. The sound readings obtained using these filters are known as the A-weighted, B-weighted, or C-weighted sound levels. Although originally intended for low-level sounds, the A-weighted sound level is used for monitoring both low-level and intense sounds from almost all machine and vehicle noise sources. A-weighted levels are sometimes abbreviated as dB(A).

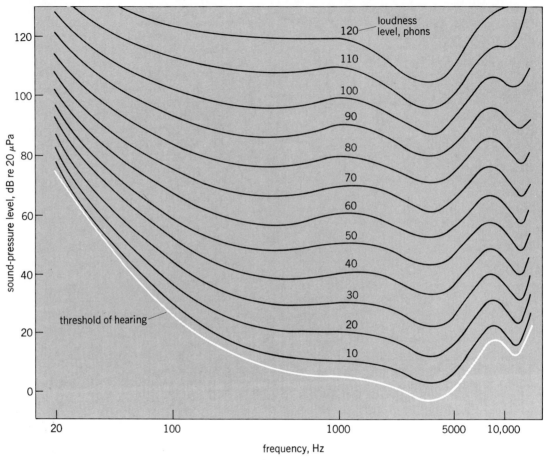

Fig. 3. Equal-loudness contours for pure tones. (*After D. W. Robinson and R. S. Dadson, A re-determination of the equal loudness relations for pure tones, Brit. J. Appl. Phys., 7:166, 1956*)

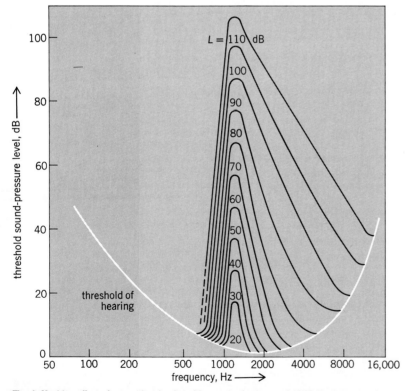

Fig. 4. Masking effect of narrow-band noise with a center frequency of 1200 Hz. Parameter L is root-mean-square value of sound pressure level of noise band. Curves show sound pressure level at threshold of hearing in presence of noise band. (*Data from E. Zwicker*)

Hearing damage. Immediate permanent hearing damage, normally to the eardrum or ossicles, can result from very intense sounds, above about 140 or 150 dB, such as those associated with nearby gunfire or explosions. Lower-level continuous intense noises about 90 to 110 dB(A) can cause temporary hearing loss, from which a person recovers after a period of rest in a quiet environment. However, if such lower-level intense noise is experienced every day over a period of years, permanent hearing damage occurs. The amount of hearing loss depends upon frequency and sound pressure level of noise, bandwidth of noise, duration of exposure each day, and number of years of exposures. A general criterion for specifying tolerable exposures to noise is that the noise should not exceed levels or durations that will cause the average person (after 10 years of exposure) a measurable loss in understanding normal conversation. The damage risk criteria given in **Fig. 6** are based primarily on industrial surveys, and many people can be exposed to greater intensities and durations than these criteria, particularly if the total duration is less than 8 hours per day.

Masking and speech interference. When two sounds contain the same frequency components, the more intense sound can normally be heard and it is difficult or impossible to detect the other. This phenomenon is known as masking. If the sounds are of different frequencies, the effect is more complicated and depends on the bandwidth and frequency separation of the two sounds. Figure 4 shows how the hear-

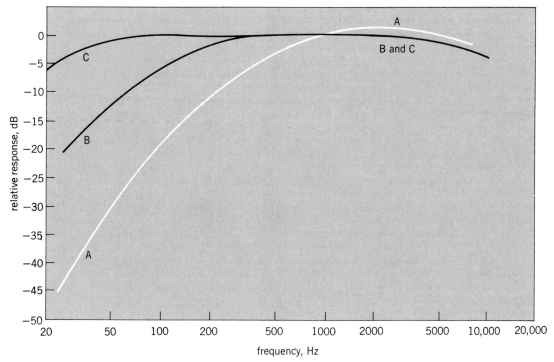

Fig. 5. A-, B-, and C-frequency weightings used with many sound-level meters.

ing threshold is changed for different levels of narrow band of noise centered at 1200 Hz. High-frequency sounds are masked easily by lower-frequency noise, while low-frequency sounds are not masked very easily by high-frequency noise.

Masking noise, sometimes called acoustic perfume, is supplied by loudspeakers in some buildings such as open-plan offices to try to mask unwanted sound such as conversation between other individuals at a distance. Noise in offices or workshops can become loud enough to mask wanted speech sounds, which normally have a sound pressure level of about 65 dB at the listener's ear. People do not become used to hearing speech above masking noises. One measure of the interference with speech of a steady broadband background noise is the preferred speech interference level (PSIL), the arithmetic average of the sound pressure levels of the background noise in the three octave bands centered at 500, 1000, and 2000 Hz (**Table 1**).

Annoyance. The louder the noise, the more annoying it tends to be. With continuing exposure to a noise, adaptation occurs as long as the noise is accepted as a part of the environment. Because of adaptation and the difficulty of separating noise annoyance from the effects of other environmental factors, it has not been possible to determine an acceptable annoyance criterion for noise.

Sleep interference. Sufficiently intense noise will awaken a person; less intense noise usually arouses a person from deep sleep to more shallow sleep. However, as with annoyance, people tend to adapt to noise during sleep, making it difficult to specify a noise criterion for sleep interference.

Work performance. Studies to find the effects (if any) of noise on work productivity, efficiency, concentration, incidents of errors and accidents, and so forth, have been inconclusive. Some researchers state that after a period of adaptation noise has little or no effect on work performance, provided it is not suffi-

ciently intense to interfere with speech communication, while others claim that noise can interfere particularly with those engaged in intellectual tasks.

Community reaction. The effect of noise on whole communities rather than individuals or relatively small groups has also been studied (**Fig. 7**). Several physical measures have been used to characterize the noise environment, including effective perceived noise level (EPNL), composite noise rating (CNR), noise and number index (NNI), and noise exposure forecast (NEF). Most of these measures were originally created to rate aircraft noise while others, such as equivalent sound level L_{eq} and day-night level L_{dn},

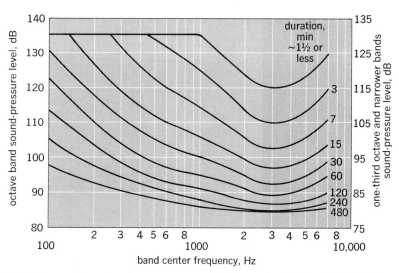

Fig. 6. Damage-risk contours for one exposure per day to one-octave (left-hand ordinate) and one-third-octave or narrower (right-hand ordinate) bands of noise. This graph can be applied to individual band levels which are present in broadband noise. (*After K. D. Kryter et al., Hazardous exposures to intermittent and steady state noise, J. Acoust. Soc. Amer., 39:451–463, 1966*)

Table 1. Preferred speech-interference levels (500–2000 Hz) that barely permit reliable conversation

Distance between talker and listener, ft (m)	Speech-interference level, dB			
	Normal vocal effort	Raised vocal effort	Very loud vocal effort	Shouting
0.5 (0.15)	72	77	83	89
1 (0.3)	66	71	77	83
2 (0.6)	60	65	71	77
3 (0.9)	56	61	67	73
4 (1.2)	54	59	65	71
5 (1.5)	52	57	63	69
6 (1.8)	50	55	61	67
12 (3.7)	44	49	55	61

were developed to characterize other sources such as traffic, factory, and construction noise.

NOISE REDUCTION METHODS

Most noise problems can be modeled as source–path–receiver systems. It is most desirable to reduce the strength or number of the sources. For example, the noise from the impact of two metal machine parts in a punch press might be reduced by replacing one or both of the metal contacts with softer material such as nylon or strong durable plastic. However, it is sometimes difficult to reduce the noise at a source without extensive redesign. For example, changes in some metal-cutting machines may affect the cutting process adversely. In such cases, it may be possible to reduce the source strength by substituting a quieter machine or using a different process.

When all possible ways of reducing the source

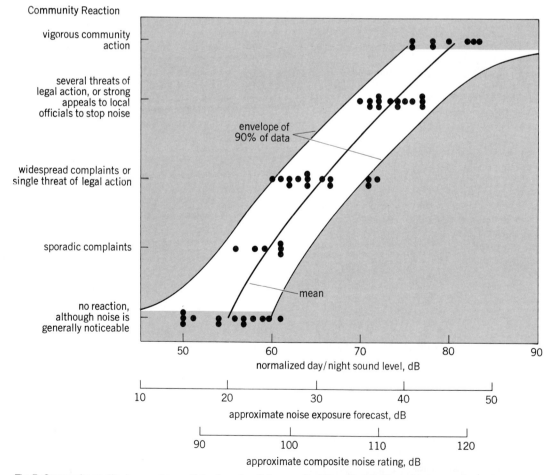

Fig. 7. Community reaction to many types of intrusive noise. Data normalized to residential urban noise, some prior exposure, windows partially open, no pure tones or impulses. (*After K. M. Eldred, Assessment of community noise, Noise Contr. Eng., 3(2):88–95, 1974*)

strength have been tried, ways of reducing noise propagation along paths from the sources to the receivers should be investigated. As a last resort, the receiver, which in most cases is the human ear, can be protected by using earplugs or earmuffs or by enclosure in a booth. However, the ear devices can interfere with communication and be uncomfortable, and booths can be inconvenient and expensive. In cases of community noise problems caused by traffic or aircraft, receiver noise control usually becomes socially unacceptable, extremely expensive, or even virtually impossible. It is usually necessary to control path noise propagation.

Planning. It is often possible to use distance and source directivity with advantage in noise reduction. Equation (6) shows that outdoors the sound pressure level theoretically decreases by 6 dB for each doubling of distance. Indoor sound behavior is described by Eq. (8), sometimes known as the room equation.

$$L_p = L_w + 10 \log \left(\frac{Q}{4\pi r^2} + \frac{4}{R} \right) \qquad (8)$$

Here, L_w is the sound power level of the noise source [Eq. (5)], Q is the directivity index of the noise source, r is the distance from source to receiver in meters, and R is the room constant defined as $R = S\bar{\alpha}/(1 - \bar{\alpha})$, where $\bar{\alpha}$ is the average absorption coefficient of the room walls of area S, in m². The sound pressure level L_p (in decibels) theoretically decreases at 6 dB per doubling of distance near to the source (where the term $Q/4\pi r^2$ dominates) and at a lower rate in the reverberant field (where the $4/R$ term and reflections dominate). Outdoors, one may assume no reflections, so that $\bar{\alpha} = 1$, $4/R = 0$, and Eq. (8) reduces to Eq. (6). If a source is omnidirectional (radiates equal sound energy to all directions), $Q = 1$. However, many noise sources are directional, making it advantageous in outdoor situations to position the receiver at locations relative to the source where the directivity index Q is small (directions in which the noise source radiates little energy). The same procedure is effective indoors but only close to the source, since the $4/R$ term dominates Eq. (8) in the reverberant field.

Absorbing materials. Although Eq. (8) is not accurate in rooms with low ceilings (such as factories), it can still be used for qualitative guidance with noise problems in irregularly shaped rooms. For example, in close proximity to a noise source, there is no reduction in sound pressure level L_p if the absorption coefficient of the materials on the walls is increased since the term $Q/4\pi r^2$ dominates; thus, it is not feasible to help the operator of a machine by using absorbing materials. However, far from a noise source in a room, a reduction of the reverberant noise level is achieved by increasing the absorption of the room walls. The absorption coefficient of a material α is defined as the fraction of incident acoustic intensity which is absorbed. Acoustic absorbing materials are usually made of porous materials such as fiberglass or open-celled foams. In environments where oil, water, or dirt can clog the pores of an absorbing material, a very thin impervious sheet of plastic may be placed over the absorbing material without substantially altering its sound-absorbing properties. The sheet (**Fig. 8**) increases the absorption at low frequencies but reduces it at high frequencies.

Enclosures. Noise may be reduced by enclosure of the source. If it is essential to have continuous access

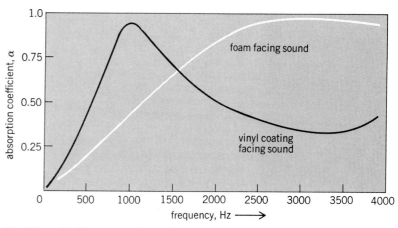

Fig. 8. Normal incidence absorption coefficient of a ¾-in.-thick (19-mm) porous foam material with vinyl coating facing sound and with foam facing sound.

to a noise source such as a machine used in mass production, or if cooling is necessary for a machine, a partial enclosure must be used. However, in the latter case noise leakage can be minimized by providing cooling vents, built from bent ducts, lined with absorbing material, and supplied with air from cooling fans, if necessary.

Transmission loss. The transmission loss TL in dB of a partition is defined by Eq. (9), where τ is the

$$\text{TL} \approx 10 \log (1/\tau) \qquad (9)$$

fraction of incident acoustic intensity transmitted by the wall. For random incidence sound, the transmission loss in dB of an enclosure wall, a wall in a building, or even an airplane cabin wall is given empirically by Eq. (10), where m is the wall mass per unit

$$\text{TL} \approx 20 \log mf - 48 \qquad (10)$$

area in kg/m². **Figure 9** shows a plot of Eq. (10). Enclosure walls are almost "transparent" to low-frequency sound, but for every doubling of frequency the transmission loss increases by 6 dB. Transmission loss also increases by 6 dB at any given frequency if mass per unit area is doubled. These increases are not always observed in practice; an increase of about 4 to 5 dB per octave is often found. If massive walls are used in buildings to obtain a high transmission loss, care must be used to prevent leaks since these will seriously reduce the sound insulation of the wall. Two walls with an air gap usually have a greater transmission loss than one wall of the same total mass.

Other measures of performance. Sometimes measures other than transmission loss are used to rate the effec-

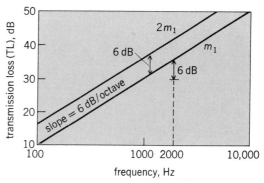

Fig. 9. Random incidence transmission loss for walls with mass per unit area m_1 and $2m_1$.

tiveness of enclosures, walls, or even mufflers. The noise reduction (NR) of an enclosure is the sound pressure level L_{p1} measured inside minus the sound pressure level L_{p2} at some point outside the enclosure, Eq. (11). The insertion loss (IL) of the enclosure is

$$NR = L_{p1} - L_{p2} \qquad (11)$$

the difference in sound pressure levels at some point with $[L_{p(w)}]$ and without $[L_{p(wo)}]$ the presence of the enclosure, Eq. (12).

$$IL = L_{p(wo)} - L_{p(w)} \qquad (12)$$

Although Eqs. (10), (11), and (12) have been defined for enclosures, very similar definitions can be used for walls in buildings and mufflers. In general, transmission loss, noise reduction, and insertion loss are not equal. Sometimes transmission loss is averaged throughout the important audible frequency range 125–4000 Hz to give a single-number rating of a wall. A more complicated scheme in which the transmission loss–against–frequency curve is compared with a set of standard curves yields a single number rating called sound transmission class (STC).

Vibration isolation. If a machine is rigidly attached to the floor or supporting structure of a building or vehicle, the structure or floor can act in a manner similar to the sounding board of a musical instrument, and radiate large amounts of noise. This problem can be overcome by placing vibration isolators between machines and their supports. Such isolators may be metal or elastomeric springs.

Forces on machines at discrete frequencies can be caused by magnetic forces (usually at 120 Hz and integer multiples in the United States), and out-of-balance forces in rotating machines such as engines, motors, pumps, and fans. Vibration isolators should be designed so that the natural frequency of the machine

on the isolators is very much less than any such forcing frequency. Such isolators will transmit much smaller forces to a support than those which act on the machine itself. However, isolators with this property generally must be very soft, and the machine may undergo static deflections when placed on them, resulting in misalignment of parts.

When a machine is started up, the forcing frequency increases and coincides briefly with the natural frequency before exceeding it. When the frequencies coincide, the machine will have a large vibration amplitude and transmit a large force to its support. To reduce this problem, during start-up, and during stopping, some damping is usually provided in isolators. Vibration and consequently noise can also be reduced by the application of viscous damping materials to the structures.

Barriers. Barriers are widely used in industry and alongside roads and railways to shield receivers from noise sources. For a given geometry, the insertion loss of a barrier depends on frequency, and can be calculated approximately from **Fig. 10** by first determining the Fresnel number N, given by Eq. (13).

$$N = \pm (2/\lambda)(a + b - d) \qquad (13)$$

Here λ = sound wavelength [Eq. (1)], $a + b$ = shortest path length of the sound wave over the barrier (Fig. 10), and d = straight-line distance between source S and receiver R. The positive sign is for the receiver in the shadow zone (receiver able to see source) and the negative sign for the receiver in the bright zone (receiver unable to see source). Figure 10 shows the theoretical insertion loss of a barrier as a function of N for a point source, under the assumption that the barrier is infinitely long and impervious to sound waves. If the sound source is composed of a line of sources (for example, closely spaced road vehicles), then the insertion loss is changed somewhat.

Obviously barriers for any given geometry are more effective at high frequencies, when λ is small, and are ineffective at low frequencies, when λ is large, and thus N is small. For any particular frequency, the insertion loss of the barrier can be made larger by increasing $a + b - d$, or equivalently by placing the barrier as near the source or receiver R as possible. If barriers are used in low factory-type buildings, the barrier effectiveness can be reduced by sound reflections from the ceiling and walls near the barrier, but this can be mitigated by adding absorbing materials to such ceilings and walls. Barriers will not reduce the noise on the receiver side, but will increase it, unless the barrier is also covered in absorbing material. If the source must be seen, a transparent barrier (made of Plexiglas) can be placed between a machine and operator.

Mufflers. Mufflers are used to reduce the sound from systems containing a noise source connected to a pipe or duct system such as air-conditioning systems, fans, and industrial blowers, gasoline and diesel engines, compressors, and jet engine inlets and exhausts. There are two main types of mufflers, reactive and dissipative. Reactive mufflers are usually composed of several chambers of different volumes and shapes connected together with pipes, and tend to reflect the sound energy back to the source. They are essentially sound filters. Dissipative mufflers are usually composed of ducts or chambers which are lined with acoustic absorbing materials that absorb the acoustic energy and turn it into heat. Some mufflers

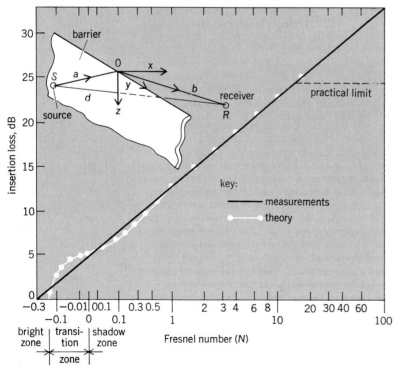

Fig. 10. Insertion loss of sound from a point source by a rigid barrier as a function of Fresnel number N. Negative N refers to the case where the receiver is able to see the source. (After L. L. Beranek, Noise and Vibration Control, McGraw-Hill, 1971)

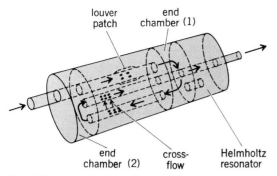

louver
patch

end
chamber (1)

end
chamber (2)

cross-
flow

Helmholtz
resonator

Fig. 11. Typical reverse flow automobile muffler.

are a combination of reactive and dissipative types. The type of muffler selected for any particular application will depend upon the noise source to be silenced and several environmental factors.

Reactive mufflers. Reactive types (**Fig. 11**) are most useful when the noise source to be reduced contains pure tones at fixed frequencies or when there is a hot, dirty, high-speed gas flow. Reactive mufflers for such purposes can be made quite inexpensively and require little maintenance. Such mufflers lose their effectiveness when used with large-diameter ducts and at high frequencies (that is, if 0.8 of the sound wavelength is less than the greatest diameter or lateral dimension of the muffler) due to the formation of lateral waves or cross modes in the muffler.

Dissipative mufflers. Dissipative types are useful when the source produces noise in a broad frequency band. They are particularly effective at high frequencies, but special precautions must be taken if the gas stream has a high speed and temperature and if it contains particles or is corrosive. If the speed of the gas stream is above about 15 m/s, the absorbing material (fiberglass or rock wool) should have surface bonding to prevent damage. At high speeds (up to 300 ft/s or 100 m/s), facing materials such as wire screens or perforated metal sheets are needed to prevent erosion of the absorbing material. If the gas stream has a high temperature (up to 1000°F or 550°C), materials such as Corten with special paints or stainless steel may be used for the facing material. Contamination of the absorbing material with oil, water, and dirt may be prevented by using a very thin surface sheet of impervious plastic material such as Mylar. The thin sheet causes a slight loss of acoustic absorption at high frequency but an increase at low frequency. Both parallel baffle and blocked line-of-sight mufflers are used. The latter tend to be better particularly at high frequency, although construction is more complicated.

Measures of performance. As with enclosures, the insertion loss, transmission loss, and noise reduction of a muffler can be defined and measured. The first two quantities are usually more useful. In general, the three quantities are not necessarily equal, although, in special cases, insertion loss can equal transmission loss. Insertion loss and transmission loss are sometimes loosely described interchangeably as attenuation.

Ear protectors. When all possible ways of reducing noise source strength and propagation along paths have been exhausted, the last resort is to protect the ear (the receiver). If a limited number of people are involved, this may sometimes be an attractive and economic approach (for example, to protect the sole operator of a large noisy machine). In many cases it is undesirable or impossible (for example, to protect thousands of residents living around airports).

There are three main types of ear protectors: earplugs that fit into the ear canal; earmuffs that fit over the external ear; and rigid helmets under which earmuffs or earplugs or both may be worn. There is some advantage in using more than one of these types simultaneously, although usually the attenuation is not strictly additive. Fortunately, both continuous unwanted sound and wanted sound are reduced by the same amount so that the ability to hear warning signals and speech is not adversely affected. This is because the signal-to-noise ratio is not changed.

In cases where only one or two people are involved, as in monitoring instrumentation near a large noisy machine, it may be desirable to build a special acoustic enclosure around the operators. The booth should be built as far as possible from the machine, vibration-isolated and acoustically sealed, with forced ventilation if necessary.

Noise Sources

The principal sources of noise may be classified as surface transportation noise, aircraft noise, industrial noise, noise in the community from industrial and construction sites, and noise at home.

Surface transportation noise. There are several sources of this noise: road traffic, railroads, off-road recreational vehicles, ships, and hovercraft.

Road traffic has become the dominant source of noise annoyance in most industrialized countries. The power/weight ratio of road vehicles has been continually increased to permit higher payloads, greater acceleration, and higher cruising speeds, resulting in more powerful engines which are usually more noisy than lower-power ones. The main effect of traffic noise is annoyance caused by interference with speech sounds. Traffic noise can also interfere with sleep, although (except for heavy truck traffic) it tends to decrease at night and people tend to adapt to it. Attempts have been made to devise special noise measures such as the traffic noise index and noise pollution level to account for the annoying effects of fluctuations in level, in addition to the overall level, but these measures are not universally accepted.

In many countries, there are government regulations for car and truck noise. In the United States there are federal regulations for the maximum sound levels permitted from trucks. In addition, some cities and states have regulations for maximum sound levels for automobiles. For new vehicles, peak A-weighted sound level limits at a distance of 50 ft (15 m) from the center of the road during maximum acceleration are normally specified. These limits have been progressively reduced.

The major sources of community noise from vehicles are exhaust, cooling fan, engine, and, at high speed [above about 50 mi/h (80 km/h)], tires. Exhaust and fan noise can be reduced fairly easily; engine and tire noise are more difficult to reduce. Heavy diesel engine trucks have become the major source of traffic noise in the United States, producing about four times as much acoustic energy each day as the total fleet of automobiles. In planning new cities or new highways, care should be taken to route heavy traffic far from residential areas and to locate light and heavy industry nearer to such highways. The double glazing of windows and ''soundproofing'' homes in some European cities are probably equally as cost-effective as reducing the vehicle noise. Barriers can also shield residential areas from highway and railroad noise.

The interior noise for passengers of cars and rail systems is not normally a major problem. However, some truck drivers are subject to noise which is potentially hazardous if experienced for long periods.

Aircraft noise. Aircraft noise is a much more localized problem than surface transportation noise, since it occurs only around major airports. In the United States and many other industrialized countries, only about 25% as many people are seriously disturbed by aircraft noise as by road traffic noise. However, because it is localized and more easily identifiable, it seems to receive more attention. Most of the noise is produced by scheduled airlines; the contribution from the large numbers of light general-aviation aircraft is relatively small.

Jet airliners produce more community noise than did the early propeller airliners, particularly at high frequency. However, jet airliners using fanjets, which bypass a considerable proportion of the inlet air past the main compressor and combustion chambers, are about 10 or 15 dB quieter than the earlier pure-jet airliners because their design results in a lower exhaust velocity. Exhaust noise is proportional to the eighth power of velocity, so that reducing this velocity results in much lower exhaust noise. Radiation through the fan inlet and noise from the exhaust of the fan and the compressor are still problems in fanjet airliners. However, extensive use of sound absorptive liners in the fan intake and exhaust ducts has effectively decreased this noise also.

Measures such as perceived noise level (PNL) and A-weighted sound level [dB(A)] are usually used to monitor the noise of individual aircraft, and since 1969 the United States has had federal regulations which set noise limits for new passenger airliners. In order to describe the effect of aircraft noise near an airport, more complicated measures have been created to allow not only for the noise of each event (takeoff and landing) but also for the number of aircraft movements and the time of day when each occurs. In the United States the noise exposure forecast (NEF) is widely used; in Britain, the noise and number index (NNI) is used. The International Civil Aviation Organization (ICAO) has recommended the use of the equivalent continuous perceived noise level (ECPNL).

Interior noise levels in early jet aircraft were sometimes very high. These resulted from transmission of the engine noise exhaust and from fuselage wall excitation by boundary-layer pressure fluctuations. Modern fanjet airliners have much lower interior noise levels. However, interior noise levels of commuter propeller-driven passenger airliners remain intolerably high in many cases. These interior levels can be reduced by using larger slower-rotating propellers and locating them further from the fuselage.

Industrial noise. Industrial noise is a widespread problem in the United States and other industrialized countries. However, unlike traffic and aircraft noise which are mainly annoyance problems, exposure to industrial noise each day or over a period of years can cause permanent hearing damage. Probably about 5 million people in the United States have varying degrees of such damage.

In 1969 the U.S. government created industrial noise regulations under the Walsh-Healey Act, and in 1971 these were extended to cover almost all workers

Table 2. Permissible noise exposures for occupational noise in the United States

Duration per day, h	Sound level, dB(A)
8	90
6	92
4	95
3	97
2	100
1½	102
1	105
½	110
¼ or less	115

under the Occupational Safety and Health Act (OSHA). For every 5-dB increase in A-weighted sound level, a halving in exposure time is allowed (**Table 2**). In most other countries, using energy considerations, the halving in exposure time occurs for a 3-dB(A) increase. In the United States a maximum peak overall level of 140 dB is allowed for impulsive noise.

Most metal-cutting, metal-forming, and woodcutting machines produce intense noise; many manufacturing industries are noisy. Noise reduction methods of enclosure, absorption, and vibration isolation and damping described previously can be used in many different cases; however, the cost of achieving significant noise reduction through such engineering means is very high.

Community site noise. In countries where cities are compact, factories have been built close to residential communities. Although community industrial noise can be reduced by some of the engineering methods already described, careful planning and zoning of new factories and cities constitute the best solution to such problems. There are no federal regulations governing exterior industrial noise in the United States, although some cities and states do have regulations. Some other countries have such regulations at the national level.

Construction noise is dissimilar to exterior industrial noise in that it is more temporary in nature and sometimes continues evenings, nights, and weekends. Several phases of construction are usually involved, including site clearing; demolition; excavation; placing of foundations; erection of floors, frames, walls, windows, and pipes; and finishing, filling, and paving. Often the initial and final phases of construction are the noisiest. Two different methods have been proposed to control construction noise: setting up acceptable noise limits at site or nearest residential boundaries; and specifying acceptable noise limits for each piece of equipment used. Both approaches are used in different countries, and a mixed approach is probably desirable in the control of both exterior industrial noise and construction noise.

Noise at home. Appliances used in and around houses can cause annoyance not only to the users but to others in adjoining rooms, apartments, and even separate houses. A few of the appliances that can cause noise include furnaces, plumbing, air conditioners, fans, water heaters, pumps, dishwashers, refrigerators, vacuum cleaners, blenders, mixers, electric razors, hair driers, saws, drills, sanders, typewriters, and lawnmowers. The problem can be reduced by manufacturers producing, and consumers purchasing, quieter appliances; by more carefully constructed houses which provide better sound insulation between walls and apartments; and by the use of acoustic tiles, drapes, and carpets.

Malcolm J. Crocker

FLOW NOISE

It is the ear's sensitivity to pressure variation that causes the sensation of sound. When those variations propagate through the air at the speed of sound, they are acoustical waves. But when the pressures heard by the ear are unsteady only because the ear is near to and buffeted by rough flow, then the ears sense flow noise, distinct from sound in its inability to propagate away from its turbulent source.

Unsteady flow always involves pressure fluctuations whose gradients produce the forces that accelerate the fluid particles. At large scale the motions tend to evolve slowly, as in the weather, but in smaller flows they have a shorter life, particularly when the flow is fast. The ratio of flow speed to the length scale of the eddying flow is the characteristic frequency of flow noise. The flow in a round jet of speed u and diameter L is very rough and unsteady, the associated pressure variations being flow noise. In fact, that noise is most energetic at frequency $0.3\ u/L$, and the buffeting effects on nearby parts of an aircraft structure can cause structural failure by acoustical fatigue.

A body moving through the air carries with it a thin boundary layer where the adjacent air tends to move with the body. Often that boundary layer is turbulent, and the rough unsteady pressures within and near that turbulence are another instance of flow noise. Such unsteady pressures cause vibration of the body structure, and that in turn causes noise in the interior, which can be a problem for passengers close to the fuselage surface in an aircraft; they hear the flow noise of the boundary layer. Similarly, the surface of a submarine is buffeted by the flow noise of its surrounding boundary layer, and that interferes with the sensitive sonar equipment used for underwater navigation. The same kind of flow noise is heard inside an automobile when the windows are open, or even on a rapidly moving bicycle as the wind causes flow noise at the ear.

The term flow noise is sometimes used for all noises generated by flow processes, even when that noise is organized in sound waves that propagate away from the flow. Indeed it is often very difficult to distinguish between the local field where unsteady pressure is simply a reflection of the local unsteady flow, and the acoustic elements that escape. Sometimes the term pseudosound is used for flow noise, on account of its inability to propagate as sound. Whenever the flow speed u is comparable with the sound speed c, the distinction is very hard to maintain; but in many common flows of small characteristic Mach number, that is, where u is much smaller than the speed of sound, the coupling between flow and sound is very weak. The sound proper is then very small, with most of the buffeting noise being flow noise whose characteristics are only weakly influenced by acoustic properties.

A microphone in a wind senses flow noise that is localized to the windy region. The compressibility of air is unimportant to that noise, and flow noise does not signify any energy or power transmission. Acoustic motions are ones that depend crucially on compressibility, and this is possibly the clearest distinction that can be made between the two kinds of noise.

John E. Ffowcs Williams

Bibliography. L. L. Beranek (ed.), *Noise and Vibration Control*, 1971; M. J. Crocker, A. J. Price, and F. M. Kessler (eds.), *Noise and Noise Control*, vol. 1, 1975, vol. 2, 1982; A. P. Dowling and J. E. Ffowcs Williams, *Sound and Sources of Sound*, 1983; C. M. Harris (ed.), *Handbook of Noise Control*, 2d ed., 1979; R. S. Jones, *Noise and Vibration Control in Buildings*, 1984; D. N. May (ed.), *Handbook of Noise Assessment*, 1978; R. G. White, J. B. Large, and J. G. Walter, *Noise and Vibration*, 1983.

Agricultural meteorology

A branch of meteorology that deals with the effects of weather and climate on agricultural activities. Agricultural meteorology is a discipline in which information from many fields is correlated. It is involved in all aspects of agricultural production, from farming, ranching, and forestry to the transportation of agricultural products as well as the delivery of water, fertilizer, and chemicals.

Agricultural meteorologists encounter a broad range of problems. Some problems require an understanding of the rapid energy exchange processes within a microenvironment, such as the deposition of spores onto a leaf or the movement of pollen to a flower. Other problems require an understanding of change that occur on a macroscale over many years in areas greater than several hundred square miles, such as the process of desertification or the impacts of climatic change on agricultural production. *See* CLIMATIC CHANGE; DESERTIFICATION.

Another function of this special branch of meteorology is the characterization of specific microclimates in order to develop sound management practices that will produce high yields with the most efficient utilization of energy. For example, changes in the microenvironment may occur as the result of tillage operations; these will have an impact on the degradation or persistence of pesticides in the soil. In another example, the absence or presence of dew has a significant effect on the development of diseases within the plant canopy; a successful agricultural operation will require an understanding of the life cycle of the disease and the changes that occur within the microclimate during a 24-h period. *See* CROP MICROMETEOROLOGY; MICROMETEOROLOGY.

Weather-related diseases and pests. Outbreaks of diseases or infestation by insects in agricultural settings have a strong weather component. The environment within a livestock barn, a greenhouse, or a plant canopy can be treated as a microclimate. Weather has significant effects on the life cycles of pathogens or insects, and these must be understood and defined in order to construct a mathematical model that will elucidate the dynamics within each specific microclimate. This is an important aspect of agricultural meteorology.

Meteorology can play an important role in reducing the large amount of agricultural production that is lost each year because of insects and diseases. Using information on the effect of the weather on the life cycle of pests, the agricultural meteorologist can predict the occurrence of outbreaks. Such predictions are usually issued in the form of special advisories that are included in agricultural weather forecasts. The projected direction of the movement of the insects and diseases and the areas in danger of infestation are determined by using their relationship with synoptic meteorology. Weather forecasters, agricultural meteorologists, climatologists, pathologists, and entomologists form scientific teams to address these problems. *See Entomology, economic*.

Weather and climate effects on production. Crop yields are affected by the weather throughout the growing season, while crop selection is determined by the climatic patterns of a region. Weather variables such as precipitation, temperature, solar radiation, wind speed, and carbon dioxide affect the growth of a plant during the season; deviations from the optimum conditions have an adverse impact on the final harvest. Computer models that integrate all of these factors have been developed for a number of crops, for example, wheat, cotton, soybeans, corn, alfalfa, peanuts, and rice. These models will allow the assessment of different management practices on production, such as irrigation regimes and fertilizer application. Climatic patterns, such as the length of the growing season (defined as the period between killing frosts), precipitation patterns (monthly distribution of rainfall and probability of rainfall), and evapotranspiration (water use by a crop) characterize the long-term environment in which crops are grown and the expected production levels of the crops.

Agricultural meteorologists collaborate with agronomists and agricultural economists to evaluate the effects of changes in patterns and economic levels of crop production that are associated with different farming practices. Another area of concern is prediction of the effects of introducing new crops or management practices into a region. Information on the crop production levels, anticipated within a growing season is utilized to estimate worldwide food reserves and patterns of crop production.

Climatic change and agricultural production. World-scale changes in temperature and precipitation can affect future levels of food supplies. Climatic change can be identified by climatologists, and the impact can be assessed in cooperation with agricultural meteorologists and agronomists. Decreases in water availability through reduced precipitation during the growing season or reductions in water being stored in irrigation reservoirs through lessened snowmelt would have adverse effects on crop production. Changing temperature patterns would affect the development of the crops currently grown in a specific region, while an increase in carbon dioxide levels would increase the rate of crop growth. The challenge for agricultural meteorologists is to assemble and interpret the facts so that the impact of climatic change can be assessed. *See Climatic change*.

Irrigation management and water-use efficiency. The efficient use of water by a crop is influenced by many cultural practices, including row spacing, cultivar selection, plant population densities, and tillage operations. An important area of concern in agricultural meteorology is the assessment of the rate of water used by a given crop (evapotranspiration) and the dry-matter production of that crop in order to calculate the water-use efficiency (dry matter produced per unit of water transpired by the crop). These studies are useful in evaluating the practices that may lead to more efficient water use, that is, better irrigation scheduling.

Agricultural meteorologists cooperate with crop geneticists to evaluate the response of germplasm to various weather factors. The purpose is to identify new germplasm that may use water more efficiently and hence adapt to specific conditions of water supply or be more tolerant of temperature extremes.

Pesticide application. Effective application of pesticides depends on an understanding of the field environmental conditions and the method of application. Aerial application of pesticides requires information about the effects of wind speed and thermal gradients on the movement of the pesticide once it is released from the aircraft. To address this problem, agricultural meteorologists cooperate with manufacturers of agricultural chemicals and operators of agricultural aircraft to define the limits of efficient pesticide application.

Frost. Agricultural meteorologists, in cooperation with synoptic meteorologists, predict the occurrence and severity of frosts. This information is extremely valuable in areas with high-cash crops, such as vegetables and citrus fruits. Climatologists utilize the historical weather records to define the temperature and frost patterns for a particular area. Microclimatologists synthesize this information with data on the topographic effects of cold air drainage and wind movement at night to suggest the most effective and economically feasible protection methods. Forecasters predict the possible occurrence of frost and temperature patterns at night and thereby help prevent the loss of millions of dollars annually. *See Frost*.

Wind. Each wind causes the loss of crop production by damage either to products or to plants. Agricultural meteorologists and plant physiologists attempt to determine the effects of wind on the processes of plant growth and on the development of fruit. Such studies have led to the design and construction of wind shelters for the protection of crops, particularly in areas subjected to high wind speeds. Using historical wind data, climatologists predict wind speed and wind direction, information valuable in determining the optimum placement of wind barriers. In cooperative studies with soil scientists, agricultural meteorologists have assessed wind erosion and have suggested preventive measures to reduce it.

Livestock management. Livestock production is also influenced by weather and climate. Understanding the nature of the environment within buildings used for animals has led to more efficient feed utilization in terms of meat and egg production and higher reproduction efficiency. Improvements in the environments of confined housing serve to reduce the stress on the animals and the occurrence of diseases which contribute to decreased production.

On the other hand, livestock raised in unconfined environments are exposed to the weather, and forecasts of severe winter storms can help in maintaining adequate supplies of hay and grain, thus reducing animal loss. In addition, the incidence of diseases or other stress effects in shipped animals caused by high temperatures or humidity can be reduced by appropriate use of weather forecasts.

Computer simulation models. Advances in computer technology have led to the development of computer simulation models that can improve management practices for crop and livestock production.

Expert systems and artificial intelligence are able to take into account the changing weather throughout the growing season and suggest management practices for achieving the best crop or animal production. This type of research has become more important as the available information collected by a number of disciplines is subjected to complex analysis for more efficient use.

Remote sensing. Remote sensing provided agricultural meteorologists with a new view of agricultural systems. Reflected visible and near-infrared wavebands have been related to the accumulation of dry matter by developing crops, increasing ground cover, and species differences. Thermal infrared wavebands have been incorporated into energy-exchange models and crop-stress indices. Micro- and radar wavebands have been related to the soil-water content in the upper soil surface and the water content of snow. *SEE REMOTE SENSING.*

Major agencies. Agricultural experiment stations on the state level and the Agricultural Research Service of the United States Department of Agriculture (USDA) are active in meteorological research for agriculture. The application of these research findings and dissemination of information to all public and private sectors is furnished by the Cooperative Extension Service. Special forecasts related to agriculture are issued through the agricultural weather offices of the National Oceanographic and Atmospheric Administration (NOAA). The World Agricultural Outlook Board is a joint facility between NOAA and USDA to track weather events and their effects on agricultural production in the United States and abroad. The NOAA Center for Climatic and Environmental Assessment is concerned with the relationships between weather, climate, and agriculture on a world scale.

The international exchange of information is handled by the Commission for Agricultural Meteorology of the World Meteorological Organization (WMO). This organization has been responsible for standardizing the observing techniques and the training of technicians in agricultural meteorology. Through the databases assembled by the WMO it has been possible to assess the large-scale impacts of drought in developing countries and to plan for the development of water resources. The Commission has also fostered the exchange of information by sponsoring technical conferences on the agricultural meteorology of each of the major world crops. *SEE CLIMATOLOGY; DROUGHT; METEOROLOGY; WEATHER FORECASTING AND PREDICTION.*

J. L. Hatfield

Bibliography. B. J. Barfield and J. F. Gerber (eds.), *Modification of the Aerial Environment of Crops*, 1979; G. S. Campbell, *An Introduction to Environmental Biophysics*, 1977; R. Geiger, *The Climate near the Ground*, 4th ed., 1965; J. L. Hatfield and I. J. Thomason (eds.), *Biometeorology and Integrated Pest Management*, 1982; J. L. Monteith, *Principles of Environmental Physics*, 1973; J. L. Monteith (ed.), *Vegetation and the Atmosphere*, vols. 1 and 2, 1977.

Agroecosystem

A model for the functionings of an agricultural system with all its inputs and outputs. Analyses of the basic biology of agriculture in which economic production is explained as only one aspect of biological responses to the environment and to inputs of energy and materials is called agroecosystem research. Un-

like the empirical disciplines of agronomy and animal science, which direct primary attention to increasing economic production, agroecosystem research considers all aspects of the biology of an agricultural system. This broader approach to agricultural systems becomes more useful with biotechnology, which may allow production to approach the limits of the biological processes. As these limits are approached, it becomes more important to know what biological processes determine yield and to learn how these processes act in determining the biological limits to yields. Nutrient cycling must also be considered, and recent research in sustainable agriculture directs attention to the management of nutrient cycles in order to maintain soil biota more like that of natural ecosystems. A stable biota with populations of the predators and parasites of crop pests may substantially contribute to maintaining yields without large increments of chemicals.

Models. The methods of ecosystem analysis are the basis for measuring the material and energy entering plant and animal populations and to explain how these inputs affect the physiological processes determining growth and maintenance. The general diagram for a biologically complete agroecosystem (see **illus.** *a*) shows three basic components and a pattern of en-

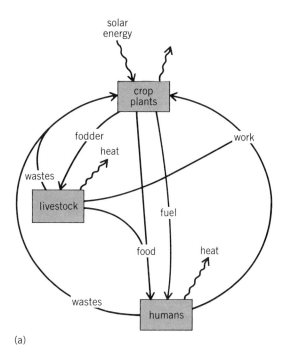

(a)

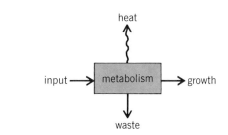

$$input = metabolism + growth + waste$$

(b)

Energy and material flow in agroecosystems. (*a*) A biologically complete agroecosystem. (*b*) Flows of a single species population, either a part of an agroecosystem or the extreme of a specialized agroecosystem.

Table 1. Measures of ecosystem and agronomic production

Crop	Growth rate, oz/ft² day (g/m² · day)		Aboveground net production, tons/acre (metric tons/ha)	Harvest index	Economic yield, tons/acre (metric tons/ha)
	Maximum	Average			
Wheat	>0.07 (>22)	0.03–0.06 (8–18)	4.0–5.7 (9–13)	0.45	1.8–5.3 (4–12)
Rice	0.18 (55)	0.02–0.06 (7–17)	3.5–5.3 (8–12)	0.50	1.8–2.6 (4–6)
Maize	0.17 (52)	0.06–0.07 (18–23)	8.8–1.3 (20–30)	0.43	4.0–5.7 (9–13)

ergy flow that is nearly the same in all agroecosystems. All ecosystems are driven by solar energy fixed as organic carbon by green plants. The accumulation of organic carbon fixed by plants in agroecosystems can be divided into three categories: (1) coarse materials, such as fodder, eaten by livestock; (2) grains, fruits, vegetables, and so on, eaten by humans and livestock; and (3) dense stems and leaves which may be used for fuel and constructing shelters or utensils. The patterns of energy and material flow between the plants and the two consumers, livestock and humans, follow simple and consistent patterns in most agricultural systems. Unlike other ecosystems, which have an immense variety of species with patterns of interaction that form complex food webs, agroecosystems have relatively simple cycles. Ecological generalizations can be directly applied to aboveground processes, but ecologists have not extended these models to cover the soil biota. This aspect of an ecosystem is being developed in agrosystem analysis. *SEE BIOLOGICAL PRODUCTIVITY; FOOD WEB*.

The development of specific agroecosystem models from this general scheme has been very rapid because the three components are biologically very uniform. Nearly 60% of all crop production is from three species of grasses (wheat, rice, and maize), while the livestock component is largely made up of cattle, swine, and chickens; one species, *Homo sapiens*, makes up the third component. The basic physiology of these seven species is understood in great detail, and the basic physiology, expressed as an energy budget (see illus. *b*), sets limits to the consumption and use of energy by a species. Thus the rates of energy flow through the three components of an agroecosystem can be determined from the general energy budget. *SEE ECOLOGICAL ENERGETICS*.

Crop growth rates. Independent estimates of crop metabolism and growth are extremely uncertain, and hence crop performance is given as net production, that is, organic carbon entering an agroecosystem. The three ways of measuring net production are given in **Table 1**. The maximum growth rate, an estimate of the physiological limit, is the highest short-term rate obtainable under the most favorable conditions. Crops grow from seeds under conditions that are rarely optimal for very long, so the average growth rates for a crop are well below the physiological potential. The average crop growth rate seems to be independent of the maximum photosynthetic potential, which leads some crop physiologists to argue that interactions within the crop community and between the plants of the community are fully as important as physiological processes of photosynthesis in determining the crop production. The early progress in agronomy was based on an evaluation of yields and selection for the highest yields. Economic yield is the fraction of aboveground net production represented by the grain, and is designated as the harvest index (Table 1). Progress in developing high-yielding varieties has been based on theoretical models for the ideal distribution of aboveground biomass, and the yields of newer varieties were increased by altering the harvest index from levels of 0.25 or 0.30 to nearly 0.50. The gain in yield resulting from an increased harvest index was developed through determination of how plants develop the most efficient canopies for the production of grain. *SEE BIOMASS*.

The production of plant biomass in agroecosystems can be converted to energy by using energy constants for grain and straw. The range of variation in these constants is much less than the year-to-year variation in yields. Therefore, general models can reasonably

Table 2. Energy budgets for the livestock in agroecosystems

Livestock	Energy budget in MJ/day (Mcal/day)				Feed efficiency (for dry weight)
	Intake =	Metabolism +	Growth +	Waste	
Meat					
Cattle	123.0	78.2	7.0	39.2	0.04
(at 660 lb or 300 kg)	(29.4)	(18.7)	(1.67)	(9.36)	
Swine	61.5	25.4	22.9	13.2	0.09
(at 176 lb or 80 kg)	(14.7)	(6.07)	(5.48)	(3.15)	
Chickens	2.15	0.65	1.04	0.45	0.05
(3.3 lb or 1.5 kg)	(0.51)	(0.16)	(0.25)	(0.11)	
Animal products per day					
Cow (1100 lb or 500 kg)	189.0	89.5	46.9	48.5	0.16
(33 lb or 15 kg milk)	(45.2)	(21.4)	(11.2)	(11.6)	
Hen (4.4 lb or 2 kg)	1.40	0.74	0.20	0.46	0.09
(0.6 egg)	(0.33)	(0.18)	(0.05)	(0.11)	

be based on extrapolations from the constants for energy per unit biomass given in standard agricultural references.

Animal energy budgets. The metabolism, food consumption, and growth of all domestic animals is so well known that reliable energy budgets can be specified for animals of any age or function in the agroecosystem (**Table 2**). The numbers from a simple census of livestock can be multiplied by the values in the energy budget to determine the energy flow in the system. Of course, the energy requirements of humans is easily determined from standard nutritional tables.

Structure. With data on crop production and standard energy equivalents, a reasonably accurate estimate of the energy and material flow can be determined for any agroecosystem. Some agricultural villages have all the attributes of an ecosystem, while specialized farms may be compared to a single species population in an ecosystem. Nearly all the farms in developed countries specialize in the production of a particular crop or animal; thus they are more like a single ecosystem component isolated from, and independent of, the rest of the ecosystem components.

Village agroecosystems. The farming villages in many less-developed countries are largely self-sustaining communities based on renewable (biological) resources with nonessential or minor links to other ecosystems. The agricultural systems of self-sufficient farming villages are closed, interdependent communities in which the number and kind of crops planted are determined by the local demands of livestock for fodder and of humans for food, fodder, and fuel. The work needed to manage the land and water resources and regulate the crops is developed by humans and animals from the energy stored in the harvest from earlier crops. The community may be an ecosystem functioning as a nearly closed economic unit. The primary economic goal is self-sufficiency, with profit as a secondary goal. The farmers are acutely aware of the biological relations that are schematized in illus. *a.* Long-term self-sufficiency can be achieved only by regulating the components of the agroecosystem. This management with its complex of intercrops (more than five crops grown together) and extensive recycling requires a large input of labor. Yields per area are higher than for monocrops, and these intercrops also resemble natural plant communities.

Specialized farms. The farms in a centralized economy tend to be large-scale production units for a few crops. Such specialization is possible if land is abundant relative to the demands of the local population, fossil carbon is a cheap source of energy and feedstock for chemicals, and there is an inexpensive transportation network for the exchange of products. While the consumption of products in a centralized agricultural economy follows the same paths as in a village agroecosystem, production is concentrated in areas determined by production and transportation costs so that the flow of materials and energy from compartment to compartment varies in response to commodity prices. For example, the economics of a national commodities market determines how much of the production of green plants will be diverted into cattle, hogs, chickens, or human food at any given time. Under such conditions, the decisions about what to plant or grow, and where to grow it, are largely independent of the biological linkages that must be observed in a village agroecosystem. The functional biological systems then become isolated populations, such as a flock of chickens or a farm producing wheat, and the physiology of growth for the population of one species is the principal, if not the only, biological factor affecting the viability of a farm.

Conclusion. The biological functions of a specialized farm are dependent on inputs of fossil carbon for fuel or chemicals, and it is uncommon for the food or fodder produced at the farm to be cycled within the farm. Even reproduction of the populations has become isolated from growth, as the seed for future crops and the sperm for animal reproduction is purchased from specialists. Dairy farming and grazing systems are the only major trophic-level agroecosystems commonly left in less developed countries, and much dairy production now comes from farms that produce little of the feed used in milk production. The agroecosystems in a centralized economy consist of a set of isolated populations regulated by economic factors and linked by a transportation network. *See Ecosystem.*

Rodger Mitchell

Bibliography. L. T. Evans, *Crop Physiology*, 1975; National Academy of Sciences, *Nutritional Energetics of Domestic Animals*, 1981; D. and M. Pimentel, *Food Energy and Future of Society*, 1980: C. R. W. Spedding, *The Biology of Agricultural Systems*, 1975.

Air mass

In meteorology, an extensive body of the atmosphere which is relatively homogeneous horizontally. An air mass may be followed on the weather map as an entity in its day-to-day movement in the general circulation of the atmosphere. The expressions air mass analysis and frontal analysis are applied to the analysis of weather maps in terms of the prevailing air masses and of the zones of transition and interaction (fronts) which separate them.

The relative horizontal homogeneity of an air mass stands in contrast to sharper horizontal changes in a frontal zone. The horizontal extent of important air masses is reckoned in millions of square miles. In the vertical dimension an air mass extends at most to the top of the troposphere, and frequently is restricted to the lower half or less of the troposphere. *See Front; Meteorology; Weather map.*

Development of concept. Practical application of the concept to the air mass and frontal analysis of daily weather maps for prognostic purposes was a product of World War I. A contribution of the Norwegian school of meteorology headed by V. Bjerknes, this development originated in the substitution of close scrutiny of weather map data from a dense local network of observing stations for the usual far-flung international network. The advantage of air-mass analysis for practical forecasting became so evident that during the three decades following World War I the technique was applied in more or less modified form by nearly every progressive weather service in the world. However, the rapid increase of observational weather data from higher levels of the atmosphere during and since World War II has resulted in a progressive tendency to drop the careful application of air-mass analysis techniques in favor of those involving the kinematical or dynamic analysis of upper-level air flow, usually involving numerical methods supported by large computers.

Origin. The occurrence of air masses as they appear on the daily weather maps depends upon the existence of air-mass source regions, areas of the Earth's surface which are sufficiently uniform so that the overlying atmosphere acquires similar characteristics throughout the region. *See Atmospheric general circulation.*

Weather significance. The thermodynamic properties of air mass determine not only the general character of the weather in the extensive area that it covers, but also to some extent the severity of the weather activity in the frontal zone of interaction between air masses. Those properties which determine the primary weather characteristics of an air mass are defined by the vertical distribution of water vapor and heat (temperature). On the vertical distribution of water vapor depend the presence or absence of condensation forms and, if present, the elevation and thickness of fog or cloud layers. On the vertical distribution of temperature depend the relative warmth or coldness of the air mass and, more importantly, the vertical gradient of temperature, known as the lapse rate. The lapse rate determines the stability or instability of the air mass for thermal convection and consequently, the stratiform or convective cellular structure of the cloud forms and precipitation. The most unstable moist air mass, in which the vertical lapse rate may approach 1°F/170 ft (1°C/100 m), is characterized by severe turbulence and heavy showers or thundershowers. In the most stable air mass there is observed an actual increase (inversion) of temperature with increase of height at low elevations. With this condition there is little turbulence, and if the air is moist there is fog or low stratus cloudiness and possible drizzle, but if the air is dry there will be low dust or industrial smoke haze. *See Temperature inversion.*

Classification. A wide variety of systems of classification and designation of air masses was developed by different weather services around the world. Most systems of air-mass classification are based on a designation of the character of the source region and the subsequent modifying influences to which the air mass is exposed. Probably the most effective and widely applied system of classification is a modification of the original Norwegian system that is based on the following four designations.

Polar versus tropical origin. All primary air-mass source regions lie in polar (*P* in **Figs. 1** and **2**) or in tropical (*T*) latitudes. In middle latitudes there occur the modification and interaction of air masses initially of polar or tropical origin. This difference of origin establishes the air mass as cold or warm in character.

Maritime versus continental origin. To be homogeneous, an air-mass source region must be exclusively maritime or exclusively continental in character. On this difference depends the presence or absence of the moisture necessary for extensive condensation forms. However, a long trajectory over open sea transforms a continental to a maritime air mass, just as a long land trajectory, particularly across major mountain barriers, transforms a maritime to a continental air mass. On Figs. 1 and 2, *m* and *c* are used with *P* and *T* (*mP*, *cP*, *mT*, and *cT*) to indicate maritime and continental character, respectively.

Heating versus cooling by ground. This influence determines whether the air mass is vertically unstable or stable in its lower strata. In a moist air mass it makes the difference between convective cumulus clouds with good visibility on the one hand and fog or low stratus clouds on the other. Symbols *W* (warm) and *K* (cold) are used on maps—thus, *mPK* or *mPW*.

Convergence versus divergence. Horizontal convergence at low levels is associated with lifting and hor-

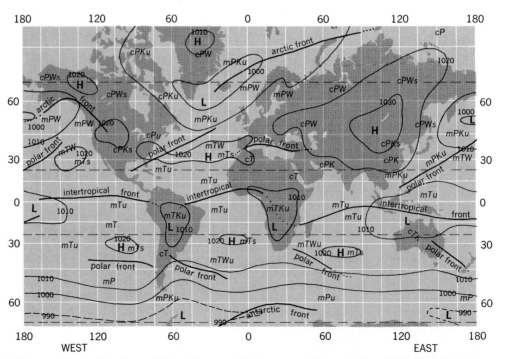

Fig. 1. Air-mass source regions, January. High- and low-atmospheric-pressure centers are designated *H* and *L* within average pressure lines numbered in millibars (such as 1010); 1 millibar = 10^2 Pa. Major frontal zones are labeled along heavy lines. (*After H. C. Willett and F. Sanders, Descriptive Meteorology, 2d ed., Academic Press, 1959*)

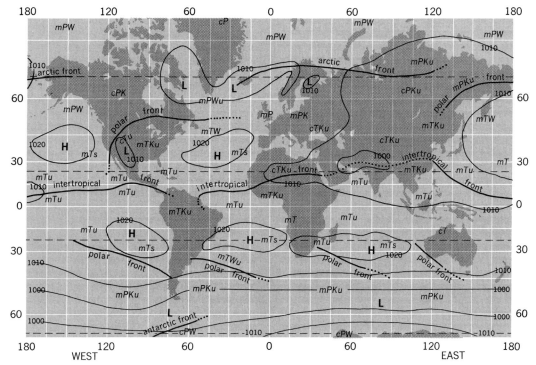

Fig. 2. Air-mass source regions, July. The symbols which are used in this figure are the same as those for Fig. 1. (*After H. C. Willett and F. Sanders*, Descriptive Meteorology, *2d ed., Academic Press, 1959*)

izontal divergence at low levels with sinking. Which condition prevails is dependent in a complex manner upon the large-scale flow pattern of the air mass. Horizontal convergence produces vertical instability of the air mass in its upper strata (*u* on maps), and horizontal divergence produces vertical stability (*s* on maps). On this difference depends the possibility or impossibility of occurrence of heavy air-mass showers or thundershowers or of heavy frontal precipitation. Examples of the designation of these tendencies and the intermediate conditions for maritime polar air masses are *mPWs*, *mPW*, *mPWu*, *mPs*, *mPu*, *mPKs*, *mPK*, and *MPKu*.

Hurd C. Willett; Edwin Kessler

Bibliography. L. J. Battan, *Fundamentals of Meteorology*, 2d ed., 1984; W. L. Donn, *Meteorology*, 4th ed., 1975; A. Miller and R. Anthes, *Meteorology*, 5th rev. ed., 1985.

Air pollution

The introduction of natural and artificial gaseous and particulate contaminants into the atmosphere. Most artificial impurities are injected into the atmosphere at or near the Earth's surface. For most pollutants, the lower atmosphere (troposphere) cleanses itself of these in a few hours or days because of its usually rapid vertical mixing. The rainfall sometimes associated with these conditions also assists in removing the impurities. Unfortunately, removal of some pollutants (for example, sulfates and nitrates) by rainfall results in acid rain, which may cause serious environmental damage. Also, mixing of the pollutants into the upper atmosphere may cause long-term changes in the ozone layer. *See* ATMOSPHERE.

All airborne particulate matter and contaminant gases exist in the atmosphere in variable amounts.

Typical natural contaminants are salt particles from the oceans or dust and gases from active volcanoes; typical artificial contaminants are waste smokes and gases formed by industrial, municipal, household, and automotive processes, and aircraft and rocket combustion processes. Pollens, spores, and rusts are natural aerosols augmented artificially by humans' land-use practices. *See* ATMOSPHERIC CHEMISTRY; SMOG.

Concern over air pollution has expanded so that many more gases besides those emitted by industrial and residential boilers are under study. It has been postulated, for example, that certain fluorocarbon compounds (gases) used as propellants in spray cans may significantly affect the ozone layer in the stratosphere. Also there is concern about trace gases and metals (for example, dioxin) that are emitted as by-products of industrial operations or refuse burning which can be quite toxic at low concentrations.

Because air pollution can affect health, can damage vegetation and structures, and may cause changes in climate, most countries have developed a set of air-pollution regulations. These regulations are implemented through engineering controls at the sources and through monitoring in the environment.

History. Air pollution has been a problem ever since fire was discovered by cave dwellers. With the Industrial Revolution, the intensive burning of coal and oil in centralized locations began. The problem was compounded because the population of the Earth had also been rapidly growing. The addition of motor vehicles in the twentieth century caused more and more serious problems, until finally a series of dangerous air-pollution episodes occurred.

The three most notorious episodes were all associated with light winds and reduced vertical mixing that persisted for several days. Many deaths were recorded in 1930 in the Meuse Valley in Belgium, in 1948 in Donora, Pennsylvania, and in 1952 in London, England. Smoke and sulfur dioxide (SO₂) concentrations measured during the episode in London were on the order of 10 times the current air quality standards, resulting in the passage of the British Clean Air Act. Through elimination of some sources and controls on others, the smoke concentration in London was cut by more than one-half in the decade following the Clean Air Act.

Types of sources. Sources may be characterized in a number of ways. First, a distinction may be made between natural and anthropogenic sources. Another frequent classification is in terms of stationary (power plants, incinerators, industrial operations, and space heating) and moving (motor vehicles, ships, aircraft, and rockets) sources. Another classification describes sources as point (a single stack), line (a line of stacks), or area (city).

Different types of pollution are conveniently specified in various ways: gaseous, such as carbon monoxide, or particulate, such as smoke, pesticides, and aerosol sprays; inorganic, such as hydrogen fluoride, or organic, such as mercaptans; oxidizing substances, such as ozone, or reducing substances, such as oxides of sulfur and oxides of nitrogen; radioactive substances, such as iodine-131, or inert substances, such as pollen or fly ash; or thermal pollution, such as the heat produced by nuclear power plants.

Air contaminants are produced in many ways and come from many sources; it is difficult to identify all the various producers. Also, for some pollutants such as carbon dioxide and methane, the natural emissions sometimes far exceed the anthropogenic emissions.

Both anthropogenic and natural emissions are variable from year to year, depending on fuel usage, industrial development, and climate. In some countries where pollution control regulations have been implemented, emissions have been significantly reduced. For example, in the United States sulfur dioxide emissions dropped by about 10% between 1970 and 1980 and carbon monoxide (CO) emissions were cut by over 20% in the same period. On the other hand, in some developing countries emissions continually rise as more cars are put on the road and more industrial facilities and power plants are constructed. In dry regions, natural emissions of nitrogen oxides (NO, NO₂), carbon dioxide (CO₂), and hydrocarbons can be greatly increased during a season with high rainfall and above-average vegetation growth.

Another overlooked source of air pollution is the inside of the typical home, office, or industrial building. Indoor air pollution has received increased attention since the discovery that concentrations of radon gas (naturally emitted from soils and structures) and household chemicals in indoor air can reach 5–10 times the levels in the dirtiest outside air. These high concentrations are caused by a lack of adequate ventilation. As an example of an attempt to control indoor air pollution, bans on cigarette smoking proliferated in the late 1980s.

The possibility of accidental release of toxic gases into the atmosphere was studied a great deal following the 1984 industrial accident in Bhopal, India, where over 2000 people died. There has been much research since then in order to better define the types of chemicals and source scenarios that might occur.

Effects. In order to design regulations for air pollution, first it is necessary to estimate the effects on humans and animals, vegetation, materials, and the atmospheric system. This assessment is not easy at low air-pollution levels where effects are marginal.

Humans and animals. The major concern with air pollution relates to its effects on humans. Since most people spend most of their time indoors, there has been increased interest in air-pollution concentrations in homes, workplaces, and shopping areas. Much of the early information on health effects came from occupational health studies completed prior to the implementation of general air quality standards.

Air pollution principally injures the respiratory system, and health effects can be studied through three approaches: clinical, epidemiological, and toxicological. Clinical studies use human subjects in controlled laboratory conditions, epidemiological studies use human subjects (health records) in real-world conditions, and toxicological studies are conducted on animals or simple cellular systems. Of course, epidemiological studies are the most closely related to actual conditions, but they are the most difficult to interpret because of the lack of control and the subsequent problems with statistical analysis. Another difficulty arises because of differences in response among different people. For example, elderly asthmatics are likely to be more strongly affected by sulfur dioxide than the teen-age members of a hiking club.

The response of humans and animals to air pollution also depends on the exposure time (**Fig. 1**). It is well known that survival at much higher concentrations is possible if exposure time is only a few seconds. These short averaging times are of interest for accidental release of toxic chemicals. Conversely, low levels of air pollution can be harmful if there is continual exposure to them over a period of a year or more.

Vegetation. Damage to vegetation by air pollution is

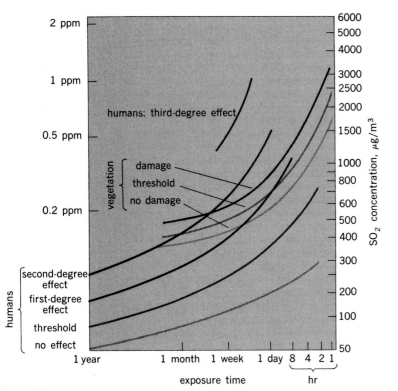

Fig. 1. Effects of sulfur dioxide on humans and vegetation. (*After L. J. Brasser et al., Sulphur Dioxide: To What Level Is It Acceptable?, Res. Inst. Pub. Health Eng. [Delft, Netherlands] Rep. G300, 1967*)

of many kinds. Sulfur dioxide may damage field crops such as alfalfa and trees such as pines, especially during the growing season; some general relations are presented in Fig. 1. Both hydrogen fluoride (HF) and nitrogen dioxide (NO_2) in high concentrations have been shown to be harmful to citrus trees and ornamental plants which are of economic importance in central Florida. Ozone and ethylene are other contaminants which cause damage to certain kinds of vegetation.

Since the early 1970s, long-term effects of acid rain (rain with low pH caused by regional sulfate and nitrate pollution) on vegetation and fishes have been recognized. Injury to conifer trees in Scandinavia and eastern North America have been documented, as well as fish kills in lakes in those regions. In most cases the damage is marginal and can be blamed on other causes, such as climate change.

Materials. Corrosion of materials by atmospheric pollution is a major problem. Damage occurs to ferrous metals; to nonferrous metals, such as aluminum, copper, silver, nickel, and zinc; to building materials; and to paint, leather, paper, textiles, dyes, rubber, and ceramics.

Atmospheric systems. Air pollution can affect the dynamics of the atmosphere through changes in long- and short-wave radiation processes. This may be the most serious aspect of air pollution in the long run. Layers of smog or particles can absorb or reflect short-wave solar radiation, keeping it from the Earth's surface during the day, and can keep long-wave radiation trapped near the surface at night.

Carbon dioxide also traps long-wave radiation near the surface, causing the temperature of the surface layer to increase (the greenhouse effect). Because the amount of carbon dioxide in the atmosphere is rising by about 0.3% per year (**Fig. 2**), some experts are worried that the temperature of the atmosphere will gradually rise, possibly resulting in severe climate changes over a time period of several generations. The carbon dioxide increase is primarily due to fossil fuel burning. It is very difficult to model this effect accurately, because of complicated atmospheric responses and unknown natural sources and sinks, but it is estimated that the global temperature may rise as much as 8°F (5°C) by 2040. This warming would result in significant environmental effects, such as a rise in mean sea level of a few meters due to the melting of ice sheets and a shift in vegetation patterns. *See* CLIMATIC CHANGE; GREENHOUSE EFFECT.

Researchers are also concerned with pollution of the stratosphere by aircraft and by broad surface sources. The stratosphere is important because there is little mixing at those elevations and because it contains the ozone layer, which blocks part of the Sun's short-wave radiation from reaching the surface. If the ozone layer is significantly depleted due to chemical reactions with nitrogen oxides and reactive hydrocarbons, an increase in skin cancer in humans is expected. Each 1% loss of ozone increases the skin cancer rate 3–6%. *See* ATMOSPHERIC OZONE.

Visibility is reduced as concentrations of aerosols or particles increase. The particles do not just affect visibility by themselves, but also act as condensation nucleii for cloud or smog formation. In each of the three serious air-pollution episodes above, smog (smoke and fog) were present with greatly reduced visibility. Before emissions controls were imposed in the United States, visibility in many urban areas was often less than 0.6 mi (1 km). There are urban visibility problems in several cities such as Mexico City and Los Angeles. Even with the reductions in emissions in urban areas, a study by the U.S. Department of the Interior found that visibility in the eastern United States has been cut more than 50% in 40 years. Visibility is also an issue in pristine areas where the air historically has been very clean, with visibilities as high as 60 mi (100 km). If a power plant is built in such an area, its plume can be visible over the entire region.

The energy released by anthropogenic activities is known to affect surface energy budgets and temperatures on urban scales. For example, near the surface in urban areas, temperatures are several degrees warmer than temperatures in nearby rural areas. Heat and moisture from large industrial plants and power plants are known to cause cloud formation on scales less than about 6 mi (10 km). Climate models have been used to estimate the global warming if current trends in energy usage continue into the next century, with the result that regional effects (increases in clouds and temperature) will be evident by the year 2050, with a total global temperature increase of a few tenths of a degree Celsius.

Meteorology. It is often important to understand the physical processes leading to an observed concentration at a given point, or to model the expected concentration at the given point based on future emission scenarios. In both cases it is necessary to estimate the fraction of the total emissions at the source that arrives at the receptor location in question. In general, the air-pollution concentration at the receptor will be greatest at low wind speeds. The physical processes relating to air quality are briefly described below.

Wind transport. For distance scales up to regional scales (about 600 mi or 1000 km), the key question in understanding air quality variations is the transport wind: in what direction and how fast the wind is blowing. Generally, the dilution of source material is inversely proportional to wind speed. For example, if

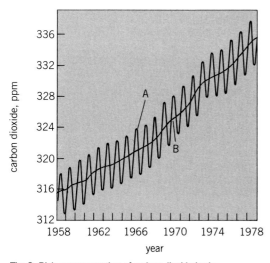

Fig. 2. Rising concentration of carbon dioxide in the atmosphere at Mauna Loa, Hawaii. The seasonal variation (curve A) arises because carbon dioxide is removed from the air by photosynthesis and is returned later by oxidation processes. Seasonal effect can be artificially suppressed (curve B). (*After R. Revelle, Carbon dioxide and world climate, Sci. Amer., 247:35–43, 1982*)

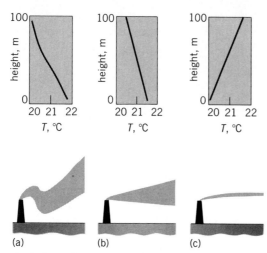

Fig. 3. Typical temperature variation with height and plume behavior for (a) unstable, (b) neutral, and (c) stable conditions. 1 m = 3.3 ft. °F = (°C × 1.8) + 32°.

the wind speed doubles, the volume of air passing over a given region also doubles.

It is best if winds are measured at several locations between the sources and the receptor, since the wind field is often highly variable over distances of 6 mi (10 km) or more. But the wind field can also be extrapolated or interpolated from limited measurements, or can be modeled by using fundamental meteorological laws. The principal concept in these procedures is that the wind field should conserve mass; that is, the amount of air blowing into an area must be balanced by an equal amount of air blowing out of the area. Usually it is safe to assume that the wind is constant over distances of about 6 mi (10 km), and it is necessary to account for the variability only in regional-scale models (say, for acid rain estimates).

Stability. The vertical dispersion or spread of air pollution near the ground can be very rapid on sunny afternoons (unstable conditions), or can be nearly nonexistent on calm, clear nights (stable conditions). In the first case the temperature decreases with height at a rate slightly greater than 0.55°F/100 ft (1°C/100 m), and in the second case the temperature can increase with height at a rate of 2.7°F/100 ft (5°C/100 m) or greater. Whenever the temperature increases with height, it is said than an inversion exists. Neutral stability occurs during high-wind, cloudy conditions, when the temperature decreases with height at a rate of 0.53°F/100 ft (0.98°C/100 m). **Figure 3** shows three temperature gradients and the vertical dispersion of a smoke plume that would be expected with each condition. The terms stable and unstable refer to

whether a parcel of air displaced upward adiabatically (with no exchange of heat with its environment) from its equilibrium level will tend to return to that level or will be accelerated upward, respectively.

If the wind is blowing, the air near the ground will be turbulent even during stable conditions at night, but the turbulence will drop off rapidly with height so that the atmosphere has little turbulence at heights above 330 ft (100 m). Gravity waves (smooth sinusoidal motions) can occur at these elevations, but they are not dispersive. During the day, the well-mixed turbulent layer adjacent to the ground is usually capped by an abrupt inversion at a height of about 3300 ft (1000 m), marking the tops of the thermals driven by surface heating. The atmosphere above this height shows little diurnal variability and is, in general, slightly stable. The depth of the turbulent air adjacent to the ground is commonly called the mixing depth, and is important because it marks the maximum vertical extent of diffusion in the mixed layer.

Dispersion. Dispersion is defined as the spread of pollutants caused by atmospheric turbulence, or random fluctuations in wind velocity. For hourly observations during the daytime, the fluctuations in wind speed are about 20% of the average value of speed. These fluctuations are caused by random whorls or eddies of air that cover a wide variety of scales, upward from a minimum of about 3.3×10^{-4} ft (10^{-4} m) to a maximum of about 3.3×10^4 ft (10^4 m) for vertical eddies and 3.3×10^7 ft (10^7 m) for horizontal eddies. The size of eddies is limited by the scale depth of the atmosphere in the vertical and by the size of the Earth in the horizontal. Any puff or plume of air pollution ultimately is affected by all scales in the atmosphere, but its concentration drops at some point to a level so low it cannot be measured.

Any air-pollution measurement or prediction is associated with a specific averaging time, such as 1 h or 24 h. A fundamental principle is that dispersion over that averaging time is caused only by eddies with sizes less than the distance that the wind will cover in that time period. Thus the apparent dispersion of a plume is greater, and the pollutant concentration at a given point is less, as the averaging time increases.

Turbulence and dispersion are enhanced over rough surfaces such as forests, hills, or urban areas, due to their larger surface friction. For a given wind speed, dispersion is about four times as great over a rough urban surface as over a smooth water surface. However, dispersion is even more strongly influenced by stability, and vertical plume spread can increase by a factor of 10 or more from night to day.

There has been much research to improve dispersion estimates in situations where maximum concentrations are observed for pollutants emitted from tall stacks. For example, highest short-term (1 h average) ground-level concentrations in flat terrain around tall stacks are observed during light-wind, sunny, daytime conditions when vigorous eddies frequently bring the plume to the ground near the stack. Another serious condition occurs in mountainous terrain where plumes during stable conditions may impact the terrain directly, leading to high concentrations in a narrow belt on the mountainside.

Air-pollution variability. The atmosphere is characterized by intense turbulence over a wide range of space or time scales. Just as instantaneous measurements of the wind speed will vary randomly about their long-term mean, so will air-pollution measurements. This

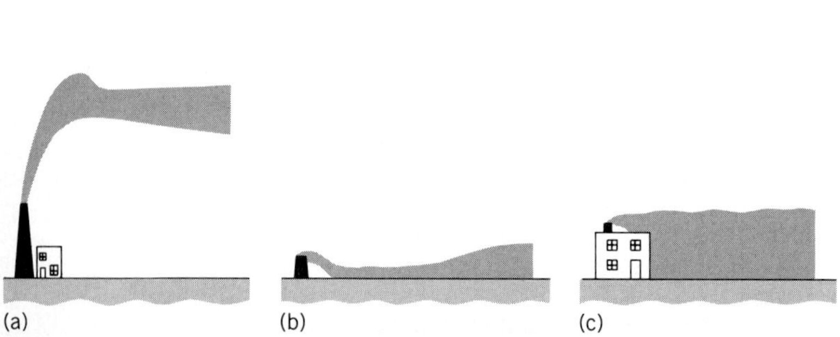

Fig. 4. Examples of the behavior of (a) a buoyant plume, (b) a dense gas plume, and (c) a plume being drawn into the aerodynamic wake of a building.

variability is greatest, of course, for instantaneous measurements, and slowly decreases as averaging time increases. For a given hourly average wind speed and stability, the hourly averaged concentration from a given source could vary by a factor of 2 from one day to the next, due to turbulence. This natural variability imposes a limit on the accuracy of any transport and dispersion model.

Source effects. Before atmospheric dispersion has a chance to act on a plume, there are sometimes significant source effects due to differences between the density and velocity of the effluent and the ambient air. Most stack plumes are much warmer and hence less dense than the ambient air, and also usually have a significant upward velocity (on the order of 33 ft/s or 10 m/s) out of the stack. In this case the plume can rise as much as several hundred feet above the stack before leveling off (**Fig. 4**). For constant source conditions, plume rise decreases as ambient stability and wind speed increase. For strongly buoyant plumes, the initial dispersion is due more to internal turbulence than to ambient turbulence.

Sometimes the effluent is more dense than the ambient air (for example, cold plumes or plumes containing gases with molecular weights greater than air), in which case the plume sinks toward the ground. Other dense gas sources may occur as a result of accidental rupturing of gas tanks. This situation is also pictured in Fig. 4, showing how the dense gas plume hugs the ground until it becomes sufficiently dilute to be dispersed by ambient turbulence.

At many short industrial stacks, the possibility exists that the plume may be drawn into the aerodynamic wake caused by the obstruction of the airflow by a nearby building. This may happen if the stack height is less than about 2.5 times the height of the structure (Fig. 4). The ground-level concentration of air pollutants will increase because the plume is "downwashed" to the ground, but the average concentration in the plume is less because of the increased ambient turbulence.

Chemistry. Air pollution can be divided into primary and secondary compounds, where primary pollutants are emitted directly from sources (for example, carbon monoxide, sulfur dioxide) and secondary pollutants are produced by chemical reactions between other pollutants and atmospheric gases and particles (for example, sulfates, ozone). Most of the chemical transformations are best described as oxidation processes. In many cases these secondary pollutants can have significant environmental effects, such as acid rain and smog.

Photochemistry. The Los Angeles smog is the best-known example of secondary pollutants formed by photochemical processes, as a result of primary emissions of nitric oxide (NO) and reactive hydrocarbons from automobiles. Energy from the Sun causes the formation of nitrogen dioxide, ozone (O_3), and peroxyacetalnitrate, which causes eye irritation and plant damage (**Fig. 5**).

Acid rain. The study of acid rain has grown from virtually none in the 1960s to a major component of air-pollution research. The reason for this rapid growth has been the discovery of damage to sensitive lakes in areas where the acidity of rain is the highest. Many scientists believe that when emissions of sulfur dioxide and nitrogen oxide from tall power plant and other industrial stacks are carried over great distances, and combine with emissions from other areas, acidic

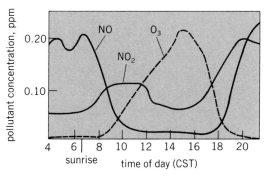

Fig. 5. The strong dependence of pollutant concentration on the intensity of sunlight. Note that ozone (O_3) concentration is a maximum in the afternoon, and is zero at night. (*After A. C. Stern et al., Fundamentals of Air Pollution, 2d ed., Academic, 1984*)

compounds are formed by complex chemical reactions. In the absence of anthropogenic pollution sources, the average pH of rain is 5.6 (slightly acidic). In the eastern United States, acid rain has a pH less than 5.0 and consists of about 65% dilute sulfuric acid, 30% dilute nitric acid, and 5% other acids (**Fig. 6**).

The chemistry of acid rain involves phase changes, catalysts, and aerosol formation, and is greatly influenced by cloud processes. It should be pointed out that a major component of sulfate deposition onto the surface is due to dry deposition, which occurs during all periods when precipitation is absent. Dry deposition is caused by impaction of particles or absorption of gases by the ground, water, or vegetation surface. Scientists have been debating whether the chemical reactions are such that sulfate deposition is linearly related to emissions, thus implying that a 50% cut in industrial sulfur emissions would result in a 50% decrease in sulfate deposition. SEE ACID RAIN.

Stratospheric ozone layer. The stratospheric ozone layer absorbs much of the Sun's ultraviolet radiation, and any depletion of this ozone could have serious effects on animals and vegetation. Several types of air pollutants may attack this ozone layer, including fluorocarbons from aerosol cans and nitrogen oxides in the exhaust of high-level planes and missiles. Photochemical reactions with hydrocarbons, nitrogen oxides, and ozone may lead to a new chemical balance in the stratosphere. The possibility of these changes was thought to have diminished because of a reduction in fluorocarbon use during the 1970s. However, in the mid-1980s, observations of ozone at great elevations in the atmosphere suggested that there has been a steady depletion, with major losses over Antarctica.

Accidental chemical releases. The chemical thermodynamics of some accidental releases are quite complicated. For example, if liquid chlorine is stored in a tank at high pressure and a nozzle ruptures, the release will consist of two phases—liquid chlorine and gaseous chlorine. The evaporation process can lead to extreme cooling of the cloud close to the source. As another example, the depolymerization of hydrogen fluoride and its reaction with atmospheric moisture can cause the relative buoyancy of the cloud to change sign.

Control. Air-pollution control is not an easy matter, because many issues are involved, including economics and social issues as well as purely technical

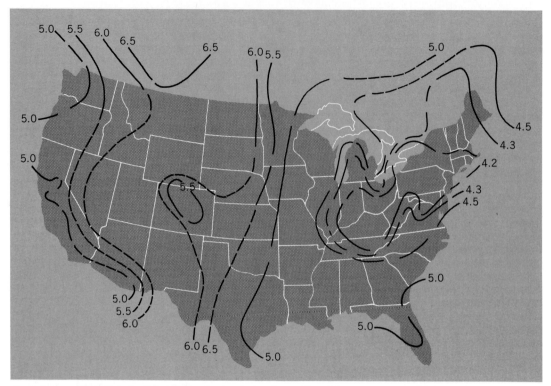

Fig. 6. Average pH of rain in the United States, showing the broad area of low pH in northeastern United States, downwind of the large power plants in the Ohio Valley. A change in pH of 1.0 indicates a factor-of-10 change in acidity. (*After J. Wisniewski and E. L. Keitz, Acid rain deposition patterns in the continental United States, Air Soil Pollut., 19:327–339, 1983*)

issues. Once the amount of control is decided upon, it is accomplished through ambient monitoring, source control engineering, and laws.

Ambient monitoring. An air quality monitor measures ambient air-pollution concentrations in order first to determine whether there is a problem in a given region, and then to determine whether control equipment is effective. Monitoring technology has improved greatly since the mid-1970s, so that concentrations can be measured with an accuracy of about 10%. A wide variety of techniques are available, depending on the particular pollutant.

An early method of measuring sulfur dioxide was to expose a lead peroxide candle and determine the amount of lead sulfate formed. Now it is usually measured by bubbling through a liquid or by a flame photometer. In the former case the sample must be sent to a laboratory for analysis, but in the latter case the concentration is displayed in close to real time. Other techniques are used to measure other gases, such as nondispersive infrared photometry for carbon monoxide, chemiluminescence for ozone and nitrogen dioxide, and flame ionization for methane. Other organic gases and several other gases are detected by a gas chromatograph–flame ionization technique. This system is used in experimental programs where the tracer material is a gas such as sulfur hexafluoride (SF_6).

Particle concentrations are measured by devices which depend on the mass, cross section, or chemical composition of the particle. The most straightforward device for measuring particles is the high-volume filter, where a large volume of air is pumped through a special filter and the filter is weighed to determine the particle concentration in air. A cascade impactor forces the particle-laden air to go around several sharp

corners, where particles of certain sizes are impacted on baffles. The number of particles of different diameters can also be detected by instruments which utilize light scattering. Advances in particle-monitoring include x-ray fluorescence spectroscopy and neutron-activation analysis. Lidars can be used to remotely detect both particles and gases.

Monitoring of odors and visibility is often done by human observers, since these characteristics are difficult to quantify. However, visibility can be measured directly by an integrating nephelometer or a transmissometer.

Acid rain is measured by the collection of rainwater and the subsequent analysis in the laboratory. Dry deposition of sulfate particles is sometimes measured by collection of particles on a plate or filter exposed during nonprecipitation periods. The dry-deposition flux of gases is more difficult to measure, due to the low gradients of concentration near the ground and the uncertainty of direct eddy-flux measurements.

Source control engineering. The amount of air pollution at the source can be reduced by process changes, fuel changes, or pollutant removal. An example of a process change is the installation of new recovery furnaces in a kraft paper mill. Examples of fuel changes are the use of coal, gas, or oil, with variations of sulfur and ash content within a given fuel type.

The most effective engineering controls have been applied to particles, with the result that particle emissions in the United States have been reduced by more than a factor of 2 since passage of the Clean Air Act (1968). Particles can be removed from the stack effluent by a variety of methods. For example, large filters can be effective. Inertial collectors rely on the impaction of particles on baffles as the air is forced around a corner. Electrostatic precipitators depend on

United States federal primary and secondary ambient air quality standards

Pollutant	Type of standard	Averaging time	Frequency parameter	Concentration	
				$\mu g/m^3$	ppm
Sulfur oxides (as sulfur dioxide)	Primary	24 h	Annual maximum*	365	0.14
		1 year	Arithmetic mean	80	0.03
	Secondary	3 h	Annual maximum*	1,300	0.5
Particular matter	Primary	24 h	Annual maximum*	260	—
		24 h	Annual geometric mean	75	—
	Secondary	24 h	Annual maximum*	150	—
		24 h	Annual geometric mean	60†	—
Carbon monoxide	Primary and secondary	1 h	Annual maximum*	40,000	35
		8 h	Annual maximum*	10,000	9
Ozone	Primary and secondary	1 h	Annual maximum*	235	0.12
Nitrogen dioxide	Primary and secondary	1 year	Arithmetic mean	100	0.05
Lead	Primary and secondary	3 months	Arithmetic mean	1.5	—

*Not to be exceeded more than once per year.
†As a guide to be used in assessing implementation plans for achieving the annual maximum 24-h standard.
SOURCE: 40 Code of Federal Regulations, Part 50.

the use of an electrical field to force the particles against a collector. In all these cases the industry has the problem of disposal of the solid material collected.

Gases can be removed by taking advantage of their particular chemical properties. For example, because sulfur dioxide is soluble in an alkaline solution, it is often removed by exposing it to drops of a scrubbing liquid. Light hydrocarbon gases can be removed by passing them through activated charcoal. Other hydrocarbons may be oxidized to relatively harmless carbon dioxide and water. Hydrogen sulfide gas is oxidized to sulfur dioxide, which is much less toxic, by means of an open flame with a fuel gas pilot.

Laws. In nearly all cases, pollution control is an added cost to an industry, and it is unlikely to be implemented unless there is an obvious problem (for example, occupational health or vegetative damage). Consequently, air-pollution laws are necessary in order to adequately protect the environment. The first wide-ranging air-pollution laws were passed in some European and North American countries during the early 1960s, following the serious air-pollution episodes described above. In succeeding years, more laws and amendments were put into effect, resulting in a complex network of requirements in some countries. These laws generally fall into two classes: ambient air standards and emission standards.

Laws defining ambient air quality standards are based on observed effects on humans, animals, vegetation, and the atmosphere. Primary standards are those that will protect health but not necessarily other parts of the environment, and secondary standards are those that will protect against all adverse effects of air pollutants. Standards are defined for various averaging times, and are found to vary from country to country. For example, in 13 countries the sulfur dioxide standard ranges from 0.30 to 0.75 mg/m^3 for a 30-min average and from 0.05 to 0.38 mg/m^3 for a 24-h average.

The United States has specific standards for "criteria" pollutants: lead, carbon monoxide, sulfur dioxide, nitrogen dioxide, ozone, and particles (see **table**). In general these standards are not permitted to be exceeded more than once per year.

The 1977 Amendments to the Clean Air Act de-

fined additional standards for specific geographical areas for "prevention of significant deterioration" (psd) of the air. These psd standards generally apply to areas such as national parks or forests, where more stringent rules on pollution increments are needed. For example, in a national park the psd increment for sulfur dioxide is 5 micrograms/m^3 for a 24-h average.

The best way to reduce air pollution is to reduce emissions, and many countries have put emission standards into law. There are subjective estimates of emissions, such as the darkness or opacity of the plume, a measure which has been used for decades. Objective new source performance standards (NSPS) were created for many source categories and air pollutants. In addition, best available control technology (BACT) is required of new major sources. In the United States, automotive emission standards for carbon monoxide, hydrocarbons, and nitrogen oxides were imposed on new cars. In addition, strict limits were set on lead in gasoline.

The Clean Air Act set a December 1987 deadline for federal standards to be met in United States cities. Some cities met the standards for criteria for air pollutants such as sulfur dioxide and ozone, but over 60 cities found it impossible to comply with the law. These cities made a serious effort to reduce air pollution by means of local emissions controls but were defeated in the long run by a combination of increased population (and hence automobiles and industries) and long-range transport of pollutants from sources in other regions. Consequently, instead of imposing strict penalties on these cities, the federal government has worked with them to achieve the optimum practical reductions in air pollution.

The Clean Air Act of 1990 represented the first new air-pollution legislation in the United States since the 1977 Amendments. The major requirement of the new act is an approximate 50% reduction in emissions of SO$_2$, which are known to be precursors for acid rain. In addition, air-quality and emissions standards are set for dozens of chemicals that were not mentioned in the 1968 Clean Air Act or its Amendments. For example, a schedule is set for the gradual phasing out of fluorocarbon production in the United States, since that chemical contributes toward depletion of the ozone layer.

Air-pollution control laws are complicated by differences in applications to new and existing sources, and to mobile and stationary sources. Furthermore, industries have discovered that they can reduce ground-level concentrations below ambient air quality standards in the neighborhood of the stack by building tall stacks. However, pollutants emitted high in the boundary layer can contribute to the acid rain problem hundreds of miles away. Governments have not yet decided how to control emissions to reduce acid rain. This could be done by an across-the-board reduction, or by a program where emissions are reduced more in one source region than in another. There are special problems created when air pollution crosses international boundaries. European countries and the United States and Canada have been involved in numerous meetings in order to resolve the acid rain problem. The policy of the government of the United States is that costly new regulations should not be imposed unless culpability can be shown without a doubt. *SEE AIR-POLLUTION CONTROL.*

Steven R. Hanna

Bibliography. L. J. Brasser et al., *Sulfur Dioxide: To What Level Is It Acceptable?*, Res. Inst. Pub. Health Eng. (Delft, Netherlands) Rep. G300, 1967; S. R. Hanna, G. A. Briggs, and R. P. Hosker, Jr., *Handbook on Atmospheric Diffusion*, DOE/TIC–11223, NTIS, U.S. Department of Commerce, 1982; G. M. Hidy, Source-receptor relationships for acid deposition: Pure and simple?, *J. Air Pollut. Control Ass.*, 34:518–531, 1984; M. Lipske, How safe is the air inside your house, *Nat. Wildlife*, 25:34–39, April-May 1987; F. Pasquill and F. B. Smith, *Atmospheric Diffusion*, 3d ed., 1984; A. C. Stern (ed.), *Air Pollution*, 6 vols., 1976; A. C. Stern et al., *Fundamentals of Air Pollution*, 2d ed., 1984.

Air-pollution control

Air-pollution control suggests in its simplest form a background knowledge concerning desirable criteria for clear air, the ability to relate air quality to levels of emissions, the development of emission limits or other control standards, the means to measure emissions and air quality, and the availability of practical techniques to reduce air-pollutant emissions. In actuality there are many complex relationships among the parameters listed above, and the air-pollution professional has become more concerned with scientific management of the air resource than with simple preventive measures.

While increasing attention has been directed to process alterations to reduce air-pollutant emissions, great reliance is still placed upon physical removal processes. Because of the significant contribution of vehicular emissions to carbon monoxide, nitrogen oxides, and hydrocarbons in the atmosphere, it is convenient to consider stationary sources apart from vehicular or mobile sources.

Stationary source controls. Air-cleaning devices for particulates are essentially based upon some form of aerodynamic capture such as inertial impaction, direct interception, and diffusion. Electrical and thermal forces are utilized in some equipment.

Cyclone collectors. Other than settling chambers for large particles, cyclone-type collectors are the most common of the inertial collector class. The particle-laden gas stream enters an upper cylindrical section

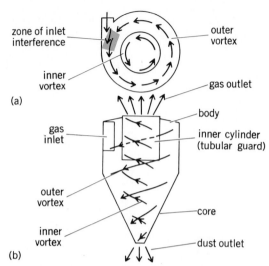

Fig. 1. Conventional reverse-flow cyclone. (*a*) Top view. (*b*) Side view. (*After Control Techniques for Particulate Matter, AP-51, USDHEW, PHS, NAPCA, 1969*)

tangentially and proceeds downward through a conical section. Particles migrate by centrifugal force to the wall and are removed through a seal at the apex of the inverted cone. A reverse-direction vortex moves upward through the cyclone and discharges through a top center opening (**Fig. 1**). Cyclones are often used as primary collectors because of their relatively low efficiency (50–90% is usual). Some small-diameter high-efficiency cyclones are utilized.

Fabric filters. These filters are in very extensive use and involve both direct interception and diffusional processes so that very high efficiencies can be obtained for small as well as large particles. Important parameters are the air volume–fabric area ratio, fabric material and construction, and method of cleaning. Most cloth filters are tubular in shape, with air flow being from inside to outside the tube (**Fig. 2**). Earlier fabric filters were cleaned by shaking, but many later ones use pulse-jet or reverse-flow action. This has permitted use of higher air volume–fabric area ratios, thus reducing size and cost. Many special weaves and finishes of natural and synthetic fibers are used in filter media construction. Fabrics capable of withstanding 150°F (66°C) have been produced. Many proprietary fabric coatings have been developed to enhance

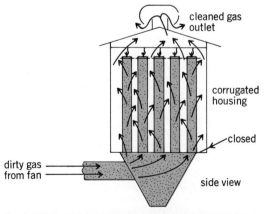

Fig. 2. Closed-pressure baghouse—side view. (*After Control Techniques for Particulate Matter, AP-51, USDHEW, PHS, NAPCA, 1969*)

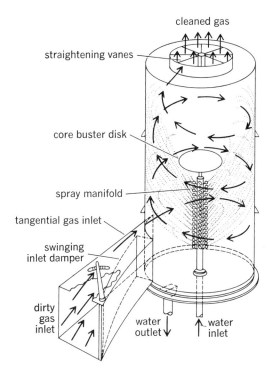

Fig. 3. Elements of a typical cyclonic spray scrubber. (*After W. L. Faith, Air Pollution Control, John Wiley and Sons, 1959*)

chemical and abrasion resistance. Some efforts have been made to enhance collection efficiencies through electrically charging the entering particles. Fabric filters operate with collection efficiencies up to 99.9 + %.

Wet scrubbers. These units for particulates operate by contacting the particles in the gas stream with a liquid. In principle the particles are incorporated in a liquid bath or in liquid particles which are much larger and therefore more easily collected (**Figs. 3** and **4**). Some simple direct-interception bath-type scrubbers are in use, but many other techniques have been developed to enhance particle-liquid contact. These include high-energy input venturi scrubbers, electro-

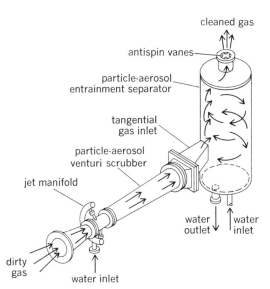

Fig. 4. Typical venturi scrubber. (*After W. L. Faith, Air Pollution Control, John Wiley and Sons, 1959*)

static scrubbers where particles or waterdroplets are charged, and flux force/condensation scrubbers where a hot humid gas is contacted with subcooled liquid or where steam is injected into saturated gas. In the latter scrubber the movement of water vapor toward the cold water surface carries the particles with it (diffusiophoresis), while the condensation of water vapor on the particles causes the particle size to increase, thus facilitating collection of fine particles. The foam scrubber is a modification of a wet scrubber in which the particle-laden gas is passed through a foam generator where the gas and particles are enclosed by small bubbles of foam.

Electrostatic precipitation. This is the third major technique for particulate collection. In general, particles in a gas stream are charged by a high-voltage discharge electrode and collected at collection plates of opposite polarity (**Fig. 5**). Particles of high resistivity create the most difficulty in collection. Because

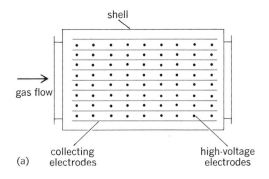

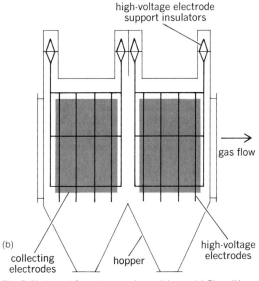

Fig. 5. Horizontal-flow electrostatic precipitator. (*a*) Plan. (*b*) Elevation. (*After W. L. Faith, Air Pollution Control, John Wiley and Sons, 1959*)

resistivity varies with temperature, this can be an important parameter. Conditioning agents such as sulfur trioxide have been used to lower resistivity. Other important parameters include design of electrodes, spacing of collection plates, minimization of air channeling, and collection-electrode rapping techniques (used to dislodge particles). Techniques under study include high-voltage pulse energization to enhance particle charging, electron-beam ionization, and wide plate spacing. Electrical precipitators are capable of high efficiencies of 99 + % under optimum conditions, but performance is still difficult to predict in new situations.

Gaseous contaminants. The control of gaseous pollutants involves the use of a variety of physical and physical-chemical techniques. Contaminants of most concern are the acid gases (mostly sulfur dioxide and hydrogen sulfide), volatile organic compounds, nitrogen oxides, hydrogen fluoride, and carbon monoxide. The most important gaseous contaminant historically is sulfur dioxide, primarily resulting from the burning of sulfur-containing fossil fuels and from the smelting of sulfide ores. When the sulfur dioxide concentration is high enough such as in copper smelter converters, direct conversion to sulfuric acid is possible. Most other sulfur dioxide control techniques involve some form of alkaline scrubbing. Stringent emission limits on coal-fired boilers have stimulated much research in this field. Both throwaway alkaline media such as $MgCO_3$ and $CaCO_3$ and regenerable media such as MgO are in use. There are major reliability and solid-waste disposal problems to be solved in the use of these scrubbers, but an increasing number of full-scale units have been placed in service. Much attention has been given to coal pretreatment to reduce sulfur content, such as washing and solvent refining. Hydrogen sulfide from catalytic petroleum crackers is controlled by partial oxidation to sulfur (Claus method). Tail gas alkaline scrubbers are used for a variety of acid gases.

Volatile organic compounds originate from gasoline storage and transfer, chemical manufacturing, and solvent loss from surface coatings, printing inks, and materials compounding. Transfer losses of gasoline vapors are collected by return vapor systems where they are adsorbed, combusted, or condensed by refrigeration. Solvent losses are controlled by afterburners and by solvent adsorption systems using activated carbon. The control of nitrogen oxides (NO and NO_2) from combustion operations is in the formative stage. Combustion modifications such as use of staged combustion, low excess air, and special burner and firebox designs have had much success, but are limited to control efficiencies of 40–70%. Control techniques using ammonia injection (which reacts with NO to form N_2) with or without selective catalysts have received widespread attention. *See* Dust and mist collection.

Mobile source controls. Most controls on mobile sources are limited to motor vehicles. Both evaporative emissions from fuel systems and crankcases and exhaust contaminants are regulated by the U.S. Environmental Protection Agency. Carbon monoxide and hydrocarbons are controlled by oxidation catalysts and by special fuel-injection and combustion-chamber design. Nitrogen oxides are controlled by spark timing, exhaust gas recirculation, and reduction catalysts in the exhaust.

Incineration. The need for municipalities to find a means of disposing of refuse when land values are high and little land is available for sanitary landfill has resulted in increased use of incineration for refuse disposal (**Fig. 6**). Incineration introduces problems of air pollution that are quite different from those of fuel-fired combustion. The refuse material is not homogeneous, and has a wide variation in fuel value ranging from 600 to 6500 Btu/lb (1.4 to 15.1 megajoules/kg) of refuse as fired. Volatiles are driven off

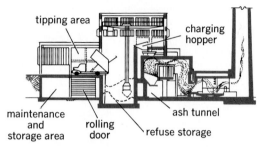

Fig. 6. An incinerator designed for refuse disposal. (*American Society of Civil Engineers*)

by destructive distillation and ignite from heat of the combustion chamber. Gases pass through a series of oxidation changes in which time-temperature relationship is important. The gases must be heated above 1200°F (650°C) to destroy odors. End products of refuse combustion pass out of the stack at 800°F (430°C) or less after passing through expansion chambers, fly ash collectors, wet scrubbers, and in some instances electrostatic precipitators. The end products include carbon dioxide; carbon monoxide; water oxides of nitrogen; aldehydes; unoxidized or unburned hydrocarbons; particulate matter comprising unburned carbon, mineral oxides, and unburned refuse; and unused or excess air. Particulates are reduced in quantity. Normally only particles of micrometer and submicrometer size should escape with the flue gases. Care in operation is required to hold down particulate loading. Increasingly stringent air-pollution control regulations have made it difficult to operate refuse incinerators without emission control equipment.

Much attention has been directed toward the use of refuse-derived fuel for steam and power generation. Refuse can be used in several different ways: in combination with other fuels, principally coal; as an independent fuel in a conventional boiler arrangement; in a matrix with a mineral media (such as limestone) using fluidized-bed combustion; and as a source for a synthetic fuel (using pyrolysis, for example).

Atmospheric processes. Ultimately, natural or anthropogenic air contaminants must settle out on the earth, react with surfaces, dissolve in water, be taken up by biologic systems, or accumulate in the atmosphere. The ultimate disposal sites have been described as sinks by scientists who study global pollution cycles. Except for any immediate deleterious effects caused by the pollutants, the cycles are sometimes thought of as atmospheric cleansing processes. This concept has long been utilized in the technique of minimizing immediate effects through atmospheric dilution. There has been increasing concern about longer-range effects such as possible reactions of fluorocarbons with the stratospheric ozone layer, accumulation of heavy metals and certain organic compounds in the surface soil and water, and the acid rain earlier mentioned. Nevertheless, atmospheric dilution has been and will continue to be used to reduce localized impacts of pollutant emissions.

Atmospheric dilution is most often utilized by increasing the height aboveground of pollutant discharges, although various approaches utilizing land use planning and impact analysis are being undertaken. Meteorological parameters, local topography, and shape and height of nearby structures are critical factors in determining suitability of the atmosphere as a dispersal, diffusion, and dilution medium. Basic meteorological conditions to consider are wind speed and direction, gustiness of wind, vertical temperature distribution, and solar insolation. Humidity is also important under certain circumstances.

In general, diffusion theories predict that the ground concentration of a gas or a fine-particle effluent with very low subsidence velocity is inversely proportional to the mean wind speed. Vertical temperature distribution is an important factor, determining the distance from a stack of known height at which maximum ground concentration occurs. Temperature of the stack gas has the effect of increasing stack height, as does stack gas velocity. Gas does not normally come to the ground under inversion conditions, but may accumulate aloft under calm or near-calm conditions and be brought down to the surface as the sun heats the ground in the early morning. Calculations of expected ground-level concentrations of contaminants are made by using various types of atmospheric dispersion models. The most common is the gaussian plume model, in which it is assumed that the plume spread has a gaussian distribution in both the horizontal and vertical planes (**Fig. 7**). SEE ATMO-SPHERIC CHEMISTRY; ATMOSPHERIC GENERAL CIRCULATION; ATMOSPHERIC OZONE.

Air-pollution measurement. Both source and ambient air-pollutant measurements are necessary to assess properly emission to the atmosphere and ambient air quality. Methods are generally classified into those for particulates and for gases. Procedures can be manual, automated-batch, or continuous analytical types. In the manual and some automated-batch types of sampling, contaminants are generally collected by filtration, impaction, absorption, or adsorption and removed to a laboratory for subsequent analysis. Continuous analyzers contain the analytical system within the instrument and produce results which can be recorded on site or even transmitted using telemetry. Meteorological data are often collected concurrently with ambient air sampling.

Most source measurements are still made utilizing extractive manual methods. This involves withdrawing a sample at a known rate through a probe while simultaneously measuring stack flow velocities and temperatures. Other data on flue gas composition and moisture control are necessary to make calculations of stack gas contaminant concentrations. Much attention has been devoted to using continuous stack gas analyzers. Such instruments utilize various principles such as transmissiometry for particulates (**Fig. 8**), ultraviolet and infrared spectrometry, chemiluminescence, fluorescence, and electrochemistry.

Ambient air sampling is conducted to determine exposure levels, to measure progress in pollution control, to obtain background levels, and to determine the air-quality impact of specific sources. Many manual samplers such as the high-volume filter for particulates are still being utilized, although many improvements have been made in flow control and in automated timing control. Various inertial devices such as virtual impactors are being used to obtain information on fine particles because of their health effects significance. Gaseous contaminants are still measured occasionally by manual liquid buffer techniques, but most sampling utilizes automatic analyzers. Ozone is measured by chemiluminescence and ultraviolet spectrometry, nitrogen oxides (NO and NO_2) are measured by chemiluminescence, sulfur

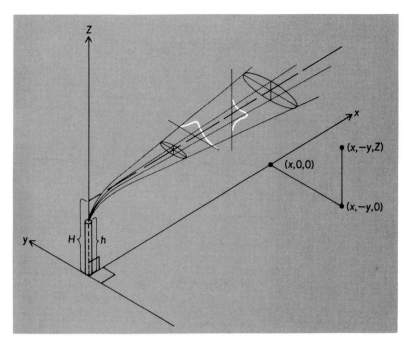

Fig. 7. Coordinate system showing gaussian distributions in the horizontal and vertical. (*After D. B. Turner, Workbook of Atmospheric Dispersion Estimates, USDEW, PHS, NAPCA, 1969*)

dioxide is measured by pulsed fluorescence and flame photometry, and carbon monoxide is measured by infrared spectrometry (**Fig. 9**). The location of sampling stations and instrument probes is critical in obtaining representative samples.

There are systems to record sampling instrument data in digital form either at the site or at a central location using telemetry. A data processor computes averages, identifies peak values, and carries out routine validity checks. This facilitates the generation of statistical air-quality data.

The Environmental Protection Agency developed mandatory reference methods for those air contaminants having natural ambient air-quality standards. The American Society for Testing and Materials and the Intersociety Committee on Air Pollution Methods of the American Public Health Association have also been active in producing standard analytical methods.

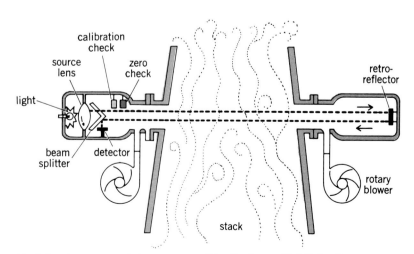

Fig. 8. Double-pass transmissiometer system. (*After Continuous Air Pollution Source Monitoring Systems, EPA 625/6-79-005, 1979*)

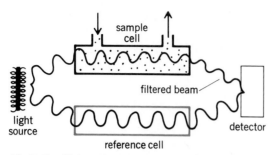

Fig. 9. Simplified nondispersive infrared analyzer. (*After Continuous Air Pollution Source Monitoring Systems, EPA 625/6-79-005, 1979*)

Air-quality management. The general approach to air-pollution control in the United States is directed toward managing the air resource. The first step is to develop air-quality standards which represent desirable or at least acceptable levels of air quality. National standards have been developed for ozone, carbon monoxide, nitrogen dioxide, sulfur dioxide, and suspended particulate matter. Some states have developed standards as well. Special standards have also been developed at the national level for hazardous pollutants such as beryllium, asbestos, and vinyl chloride. Air quality is then determined by monitoring, and a planning process is used which may include broad-scale atmospheric modeling to determine the extent of pollutant control necessary in various geographical regions. Following this implementation, plans are developed which include conventional regulatory approaches, such as emission standards and limitation of impurities or contaminating substances in fuels or raw materials. Permit processes are also used to determine whether, in critical locations, sources can be established at all without supplemental means of control. For very large industries of national importance, the federal government has adopted a number of emission standards which are applied nationwide. SEE AIR POLLUTION.

Robert J. Bryan

Bibliography. B. Bretschneider and J. Kurfurst, *Air Pollution Control Technology*, 1987; Chemical Engineering Magazine, *Industrial Air Pollution Engineering*, 1980; F. L. Cross and H. E. Hesketh (eds.), *Handbook on the Operation and Maintenance of Air Pollution Control Equipment*, 1975; J. A. Danielson (ed.), *Air Pollution Engineering Manual*, USEPA Publ. AP-40, May 1973; A. C. Stern et al., *Fundamentals of Air Pollution*, 2d ed., 1984.

Air pressure

The force per unit area that the air exerts on any surface in contact with it, arising from the collisions of the air molecules with the surface. It is equal and opposite to the pressure of the surface against the air, which for atmospheric air in normal motion approximately balances the weight of the atmosphere above, about 15 lb/in.^{2} at sea level. It is the same in all directions and is the force that balances the weight of the column of mercury in the torricellian barometer, commonly used for its precise measurement.

Units. The units of pressure traditionally used in meteorology are based on the bar, defined as equal to 1,000,000 dynes /cm^2. One bar equals 1000 millibars or 100 centibars.

In the meter-kilogram-second or International Sys-

tem of Units (SI), the unit of force, the pascal (Pa), is equal to 1 newton/m^2. One millibar equals 100 pascals. The normal pressure at sea level is 1013.25 millibars or 101.325 kilopascals.

Also widely used in practice are units based on the height of the mercury barometer under standard conditions, expressed commonly in millimeters or in inches. The standard atmosphere (760 mmHg) is also used as a unit, mainly in engineering, where large pressures are encountered. The following equivalents show the conversions between the commonly used units of pressure, where (mmHg)$_n$ and (in. Hg)$_n$ denote the millimeter and inch of mercury, respectively, under standard (normal) conditions, and where (kg)$_n$ and (lb)$_n$ denote the weight of a standard kilogram and pound mass, respectively, under standard gravity.

$$
\begin{aligned}
1 \text{ kPa} &= 10 \text{ millibars} = 1000 \text{ N/m}^2 \\
&= 7.50062 \text{ (mmHg)}_n \\
&= 0.295300 \text{ (in. Hg)}_n \\
1 \text{ millibar} &= 100 \text{ Pa} = 1000 \text{ dynes/cm}^2 \\
&= 0.750062 \text{ (mmHg)}_n \\
&= 0.0295300 \text{ (in. Hg)}_n \\
1 \text{ atm} &= 101.325 \text{ kPa} = 1013.25 \text{ millibars} \\
&= 760 \text{ (mmHg)}_n = 29.9213 \text{ (in. Hg)}_n \\
&= 14.6959 \text{ (lb)}_n/\text{in.}^2 \\
&= 1.03323 \text{ (kg)}_n/\text{cm}^2 \\
1 \text{ (mmHg)}_n &= 1 \text{ torr} = 0.03937008 \text{ (in. Hg)}_n \\
&= 1.333224 \text{ millibars} \\
&= 133.3224 \text{ Pa} \\
1 \text{ (in. Hg)}_n &= 33.8639 \text{ millibars} \\
&= 25.4 \text{ (mmHg)}_n \\
&= 3.38639 \text{ kPa}
\end{aligned}
$$

Variation with height. Because of the almost exact balancing of the weight of the overlying atmosphere by the air pressure, the latter must decrease with height, according to the hydrostatic equation (1),

$$dP = -g \, \rho \, dZ \tag{1}$$

where P is air pressure, ρ is air density, g is acceleration of gravity, Z is altitude above mean sea level, dZ is infinitesimal vertical thickness of horizontal air layers, and dP is pressure change which corresponds to altitude change dZ. Integration of Eq. (1) yields Eq. (2), where P_1 is pressure at altitude Z_1, and P_2 is

$$P_1 - P_2 = \int_{Z_1}^{Z_2} \rho g \, dZ \tag{2}$$

pressure at altitude Z_2. The expressions on the right-hand side of Eq. (2) represent the weight of the column of air between the two levels Z_1 and Z_2.

In the special case in which Z_2 refers to a level above the atmosphere where the air pressure is nil, one has $P_2 = 0$, and Eq. (2) yields an expression for air pressure P_1 at a given altitude Z_1 for an atmosphere in hydrostatic equilibrium.

By substituting in Eq. (1) the expression for air density based on the well-known perfect gas law and by integrating, one obtains the hypsometric equations for dry air under the assumption of hydrostatic equilibrium, Eqs. (3), valid below about 54 mi (90 km),

$$\log_e \left(\frac{P_1}{P_2} \right) = \frac{M}{R} \int_{Z_1}^{Z_2} \frac{g}{T} dZ \tag{3a}$$

$$Z_2 - Z_1 = \frac{R}{M} \int_{P_2}^{P_1} \frac{T}{g} \frac{dP}{P} \tag{3b}$$

where g is the gravitational acceleration; M is the gram-molecular weight, 28.97 for dry air; R is the gas constant for 1 mole of ideal gas, or 8.315×10^7 erg/(mole)(K); and T is the air temperature in K.

Equation (3) may be used for the real moist atmosphere if the effect of the small amount of water vapor on the density of the air is allowed for by replacing T by T_v, the virtual temperature given by Eq. (4),

$$T_v = T\left[1 - \left(1 - \frac{M_w}{M}\right)\frac{e}{P}\right]^{-1} \qquad (4)$$

in which e is partial pressure of water vapor in the air, M_w is gram-molecular weight of water vapor (18.016 g/mole), and $(1 - M_w/M) = 0.3780$.

Equations (3a) are used in practice to calculate the vertical distribution of pressure with height above sea level. The temperature distribution in a standard atmosphere, based on mean values in middle latitudes, has been defined by international agreement. The use of the standard atmosphere permits the evaluation of the integrals of Eqs. (3a) and (3b) to give a definite relation between pressure and height. This relation is used in all altimeters which are basically barometers of the aneroid type. The difference between the height estimated from the pressure and the actual height is often considerable; but since the same standard relationship is used in all altimeters, the difference is the same for all altimeters at the same location, and so causes no difficulty in determining the relative position of aircraft. Mountains, however, have a fixed height, and accidents have been caused by the difference between the actual and standard atmosphere.

Horizontal and time variations. In addition to the large variation with height discussed in the previous paragraph, atmospheric pressure varies in the horizontal and with time. The variations of air pressure at sea level, estimated in the case of observations over land by correcting for the height of the ground surface, are routinely plotted on a map and analyzed, resulting in the familiar "weather map" representation with its isobars showing highs and lows. The movement of the main features of the sea-level pressure distribution, typically from west to east in middle and high latitudes, and from east to west in the tropics, produces characteristic fluctuations of the pressure at a fixed point, which vary by a few percent within a few days.

Smaller-scale variations of sea-level pressure, some even too small to appear on the ordinary weather map, are also present. These are associated with various forms of atmospheric motion, including small-scale wave motion and turbulence. Relatively large variations in short distances are found in hurricanes and in intense winter storms, and in and near thunderstorms; the most intense is the low-pressure region in a tornado. The pressure drop within tornadoes and hurricanes can be extreme, about 10% of normal pressure. SEE WEATHER MAP.

It is a general rule that in middle latitudes at localities below 3280 ft (1000 m) in height above sea level, the air pressure on the continents tends to be slightly higher in winter than in other seasons; whereas at considerably greater heights on the continents and on the ocean surface, the reverse is true.

Various maps of climatic averages indicate certain regions where systems of high and low pressure predominate. Over the oceans there tend to be areas or bands of relatively high pressure, most marked during the summer, in zones centered near latitude 30°N and 30°S. The Asiatic landmass is dominated by a great high-pressure system in winter and a low-pressure system in summer. Deep low-pressure areas prevail during the winter over the Aleutian, the Icelandic-Greenland, and Antarctic regions. These and other centers of action produce offshoots which may travel for great distances before dissipating.

Thus during the winter, spring, and autumn in middle latitudes over the land areas, it is fairly common to experience the passage of a cycle of low- and high-pressure systems in alternating fashion over a period of about 6–9 days in the average, but sometimes in as little as 3–4 days, covering a pressure amplitude which ranges on the average from roughly 15–25 millibars less than normal in the low-pressure center to roughly 15–20 millibars more than normal in the high-pressure center. During the summer in middle latitudes the period of the pressure changes is generally greater, and the amplitudes are less than in the cooler seasons (see **table**).

Within the tropics, where there are comparatively few passages of major high- and low-pressure systems during a season, the most notable feature revealed by the recording barometer (barograph) is the characteristic diurnal pressure variation. In this daily cycle of pressure at the ground there are, as a rule though with some exceptions, two maxima, at approximately 10 A.M. and 10 P.M., and two minima, at approximately 4 A.M. and 4 P.M., local time.

The total range of the diurnal pressure variation is a function of latitude as indicated by the following approximate averages (latitude N): 0°, 3 millibars; 30°, 2.5 millibars; 35°, 1.7 millibars; 45°, 1.2 millibars; 50°, 0.9 millibars; 60°, 0.4 millibars. These results are based on the statistical analysis of thousands of barograph records for many land stations. Local peculiarities appear in the diurnal variation because of the influences of physiographic features and climatic factors. Mountains, valleys, oceans, elevations,

---

Mean atmospheric pressure and temperature in middle latitudes, for specified heights above sea level*

Altitude above sea level

Standard geopotential meters (m′)	Meters at latitude 45°32′40″	Air pressure, millibars	Assumed temperature, K‡
0	0	1.01325×10^3	288.15
11,000	11,019	2.2632×10^2	216.65
20,000	20,063	5.4747×10^1	216.65
32,000	32,162	8.6798×10^0	228.65
47,000	47,350	1.1090×10^0	270.65
52,000	52,429	5.8997×10^{-1}	270.65
61,000	61,591	1.8209×10^{-1}	252.65
79,000	79,994	1.0376×10^{-2}	180.65
88,743	90,000	1.6437×10^{-3}	180.65†

*Approximate annual mean values based on radiosonde observations at Northern Hemisphere stations between latitudes 40 and 49°N for heights below 105,000 ft (32,000 m) and on observations made from rockets and instruments released from rockets. Some density data derived from searchlight observations were considered. Values shown above 105,000 ft (32,000 m) were calculated largely on the basis of observed distribution of air density with altitude. In correlating columns 1 and 2, The acceleration of gravity, G, is taken to be 98,066.5 cm²/s² per standard geopotential meter (m′). Data on first three lines are used in calibration of aircraft altimeters. 1 m = 3.281 ft.

†Above 295,000 ft (90,000 m) there occurs an increase of temperature with altitude and a variation of composition of the air with height, resulting in a gradual decrease in molecular weight of air with altitude.

‡Temperature (°F) = 1.8 [temperature (K)] − 459.67.

ground cover, temperature variation, and season exert local influences; while current atmospheric conditions also affect it, such as amount of cloudiness, precipitation, and sunshine. Mountainous regions in the western United States may have only a single maximum at about 8–10 A.M. and a single minimum at about 5–7 P.M., local time, but with a larger range than elsewhere at the same latitudes, especially during the warmer months (for instance, about 4 millibars difference between the daily maximum and minimum).

At higher levels in the atmosphere the variations of pressure are closely related to the variations of temperature, according to Eq. (3*a*). Because of the lower temperatures in higher latitudes in the lower 6 mi (10 km), the pressures at higher levels tend to decrease toward the poles. The **illustration** shows a typical pattern at approximately 6 mi (10 km) above sea level. As is customary in representing pressure patterns at upper levels, the variation of the height of a surface of constant pressure, in this case 300 mb, is shown rather than the variation of pressure over a horizontal surface. SEE AIR TEMPERATURE.

Besides the latitudinal variation, the illustration also shows a wave pattern typical of the pressure field, and the midlatitude maximum in the wind field known as the jet stream, with its "waves in the westerlies." In the stratosphere the temperature variations are such as to reduce the pressure variations at higher levels, up to about 50 mi (80 km), except that in winter at high latitudes there are relatively large varia-

tions above 6 mi (10 km). At altitudes above 50 mi (80 km) the relative variability of the pressure increases again. Although the pressure and density at these very high levels are small, they are important for rocket and satellite flights, so that their variability at high altitudes is likewise important.

Relations to wind and weather. The practical importance of air pressure lies in its relation to the wind and weather. It is because of these relationships that pressure is a basic parameter in weather forecasting, as is evident from its appearance on the ordinary weather map.

Horizontal variations of pressure imply a pressure force on the air, just as the vertical pressure variation implies a vertical force that supports the weight of the air, according to Eq. (1). This force, if unopposed, accelerates the air, causing the wind to blow from high to low pressure. The sea breeze is an example of such a wind. However, if the pressure variations are on a large scale and are changing relatively slowly with time, the rotation of the Earth gives rise to geostrophic or gradient balance such that the wind blows along the isobars. This situation occurs when the pressure variations are due to the slow-moving lows and highs that appear on the ordinary weather map, and to the upper air waves shown in the illustration, in which the relationship is well illustrated.

The wind near the ground, in the lowest few hundred meters of the atmosphere, is retarded by friction with the surface to a degree that depends on the smoothness or roughness of the surface. This upsets

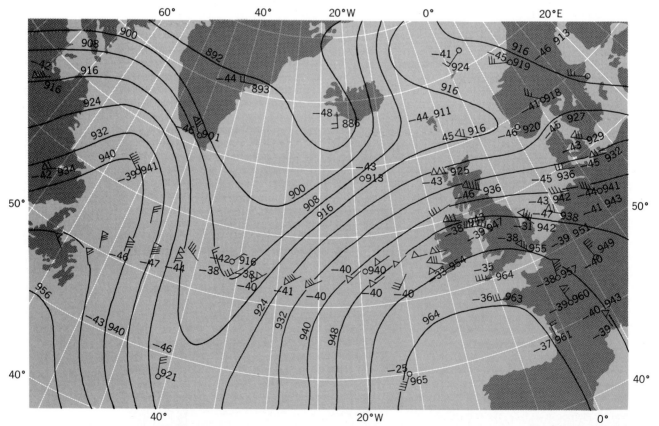

Contours of 300-millibar surface, in tens of meters, with temperature in °C [°F = (°C × 1.8) + 32°] and measured winds at the same level. Winds are plotted with arrow pointing in direction of the wind, with each bar of the tail representing 10 m/s (33 ft/s or 19.4 knots). Triangle represents 50 m/s (165 ft/s or 97 knots).

the balance mentioned in the previous paragraph, so that the wind blows somewhat across the isobars from high to low pressure.

The large-scale variations of pressure at sea level shown on a weather map are associated with characteristic patterns of vertical motion of the air, which in turn affect the weather. Descent of air in a high heats the air and dries it by adiabatic compression, giving clear skies, while the ascent of air in a low cools it and causes it to condense and produce cloudy and rainy weather. These processes at low levels, accompanied by others at higher levels, usually combine to justify the clear-cloudy-rainy marking on the household barometer.

Raymond J. Deland; Edwin Kessler

Bibliography. R. G. Fleagle, *An Introduction to Atmospheric Physics*, 2d ed., 1980; D. D. Houghton (ed.), *Handbook of Applied Meteorology*, 1985; A. Miller and R. A. Anthes, *Meteorology*, 4th ed., 1980.

Air temperature

The temperature of the atmosphere represents the average kinetic energy of the molecular motion in a small region, defined in terms of a standard or calibrated thermometer in thermal equilibrium with the air.

Measurement. Many different types of thermometer are used for the measurement of air temperature, the more common depending on the expansion of mercury or alcohol with temperature, the variation of electrical resistance with temperature, or the thermoelectric effect (thermocouple). The electrical methods are especially useful for the automatic recording of temperature. The basic problems of ensuring that the temperature of the thermometer be as close as possible to that of the air are the same for all methods of measurement. For the atmosphere, probably the most serious difficulty is the heating or cooling of the thermometer by radiation to and from other bodies at different temperatures, the most obvious being the Sun. The representativeness of temperature measurements, meaning the degree to which they provide information about the temperature of the air over a region much larger than the thermometer, is also an important practical requirement. The well-known standard meteorological measurement of the air temperature in a louvered shelter, about 6.5 ft (2 m) above a natural ground surface, with a mercury-in-glass thermometer that averages the temperature over a period of about 1 min because of its thermal inertia, is designed to satisfy the above requirements.

Causes of variation. The temperature of a given small mass of air varies with time because of heat added or subtracted from it, and also because of work done during changes of volume, according to alternate Eqs. (1) and (2). Here h represents heat added,

$$\frac{dT}{dt} = \frac{1}{C_v}\left(\frac{dh}{dt} - P\frac{d\alpha}{dt}\right) \qquad (1)$$

$$\frac{dT}{dt} = \frac{1}{C_p}\left(\frac{dh}{dt} + \frac{1}{\rho}\frac{dP}{dt}\right) \qquad (2)$$

P the pressure, ρ the density and α its reciprocal, and C_v and C_p the specific heat at constant volume and constant pressure, respectively. The heat added or subtracted may be due to many different physical processes, of which the most important are absorption and emission of radiation, heat conduction, and changes of phase of water involving latent heat of condensation and freezing. In the upper atmosphere, above about 12 mi (20 km), photochemical changes are also important; for example, those that occur when ultraviolet radiation dissociates oxygen molecules to atomic oxygen, which then recombines with molecular oxygen to form ozone. Because of the variation of air pressure with height, rising and sinking of air causes expansion and contraction and thus temperature changes due to the work of expansion, explicitly represented by the second term in parentheses in Eq. (1).

A spectacular example of temperature rise due to sinking of air from higher levels is the chinook, a warm wind that sometimes blows down the eastern slope of the Rocky Mountains in winter. The slower seasonal temperature changes are mainly due to a combination of radiational heat exchange and conduction to and from the ground surface, whose temperature itself changes in response to the varying radiational exchange with the Sun and the atmosphere. On a shorter time scale the diurnal variation of temperature throughout the day is caused by the same processes. *See* Air pressure; Atmospheric general circulation.

The rate at which the temperature changes at a particular point, that is, as measured by a fixed thermometer, depends on the movement of air as well as the physical processes discussed above. Large changes of air temperature from day to day are mainly due to the horizontal movement of air, bringing relatively cold or warm air masses to a particular point, as large-scale pressure-wind systems move across the weather map. *See* Air mass.

Temperature near the surface. Temperatures are read at one or more fixed times daily, and the day's extremes are obtained from special maximum and minimum thermometers, or from the trace (thermogram) of a continuously recording instrument (thermograph). The average of these two extremes, technically the midrange, is considered in the United States to be the day's average temperature. The true daily mean, obtained from a thermogram, is closely approximated by the mean of 24 hourly readings, but may differ from the mid-range by 1 or 2°F (0.6 or 1°C), on the average. In many countries temperatures are read daily at three or four fixed times, chosen so that their weighted mean closely approximates the true daily mean. These observational differences and variations in exposures complicate comparison of temperatures from different countries and any study of possible climatic changes.

Averages of daily maximum and minimum temperature for a single month for many years give mean daily maximum and minimum temperatures for that month. The average of these values is the mean monthly temperature, while their difference is the mean daily range for that month. Monthly means, averaged through the year, give the mean annual temperature; the mean annual range is the difference between the hottest and coldest mean monthly values. The hottest and coldest temperatures in a month are the monthly extremes; their averages over a period of years give the mean monthly maximum and minimum (used extensively in Canada), while the absolute extremes for the month (or year) are the hottest and coldest temperatures ever observed. The interdiurnal range or variability for a month is the average of the successive differences, regardless of sign, in daily temperatures.

Over the oceans the mean daily, interdiurnal, and annual ranges are slight, because water absorbs the insolation and distributes the heat through a thick layer. In tropical regions the interdiurnal and annual ranges over the land are small, because the annual variation in insolation is relatively small. The daily range also is small in humid tropical regions, but may be large (up to 40°F or 22°C) in deserts. Interdiurnal and annual ranges increase generally with latitude, and with distance from the ocean; the mean annual range defines continentality. The daily range depends on aridity, altitude, and noon sun elevation.

Extreme temperatures arouse much popular interest and often are cited uncritically, despite their possible instrumental, exposure, and observational errors of many kinds. The often given absolute maximum temperatures of 134°F (57°C) for the United States in Death Valley, California (July 10, 1913), and 136°F (58°C) for the world in Azizia, Tripoli (September 13, 1922) are both questionable; in the subsequent years, Death Valley's hottest reading has been only 127°F (53°C), and the Azizia reading was reported by an expedition, not a regular weather station. Lowest temperatures in the Northern Hemisphere are −90°F (−68°C) at Verkhoyansk (−89.7°F or −67.7°C on February 5 and 7, 1982) and Oimekon (−89.9°F or −67.7°C on February 6, 1933), Siberia; −87°F (−66°C) at Northice, Greenland (January 9, 1954); − 81°F (−63°C) at Snag, Yukon Territory, Canada (February 3, 1947); −70°F (−57°C) at Rogers Pass,

Montana (the current United States record, on January 20, 1954). The first winter at Vostok, 78°27′S, 106°52′E, encountered a minimum temperature of − 125°F (−87.2°C) on August 25, 1958, and the third winter a minimum of − 127°F (−88.3°C) on August 24, 1960, much lower than the lowest at the United States station at the South Pole. At Vostok on July 21, 1983, a new global minimum temperature record for Earth's surface was recorded, − 129°F (−89.4°C).

Vertical variation. The average vertical variation of temperature in the atmosphere is shown in the **illustration**. The atmosphere is seen to consist of layers, each of which has a characteristic variation of temperature with height. The decrease of temperature with height in the lowest layer, the troposphere, is basically due to the presence of a heat source resulting from the solar radiation absorbed at the Earth's surface, giving an excess of heat that is carried away from the surface mainly by convection currents and lost to space by reradiation. Heating a compressible fluid such as air from below results in a decrease in temperature with height because rising masses of air cool as they expand, according to Eq. (2). This is the main reason for the decrease of temperature with height in the troposphere. SEE ATMOSPHERE; HEAT BALANCE, TERRESTRIAL ATMOSPHERIC.

In the mesosphere and higher layers the exchange of heat energy between layers of air by emission and absorption of infrared radiation is the most important factor determining the distribution of temperature with height.

Raymond J. Deland; Edwin Kessler

Bibliography. R. G. Fleagle, *An Introduction to Atmospheric Physics*, 2d ed., 1980; D. D. Houghton (ed.), *Handbook of Applied Meteorology,* 1985; A. Miller and R. A. Anthes, *Meteorology,* 4th ed., 1980; H. Riehl, *Introduction to the Atmosphere*, 3d ed., 1978.

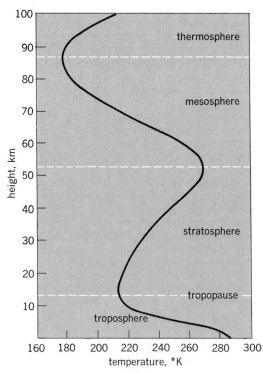

Average temperature distribution with height, from the International Reference Atmosphere. Note that the nomenclature for stratosphere and mesosphere varies, the upper part of the stratosphere being considered part of the mesosphere by some authorities. (*After R. G. Fleagle and J. A. Businger, An Introduction to Atmospheric Physics, Academic Press, 1963*)

Altitudinal vegetation zones

Intergrading regions on mountain slopes characterized by specific plant life forms or species composition, and determined by complex environmental gradients.

Along an altitudinal transect of a mountain, there are sequential changes in the physiognomy (growth form) of the plants and in the species composition of the communities. This sequential zonation of mountain vegetation has been recognized for centuries. Vertical zonation was fully developed as an ecological concept by the work of C. H. Merriam with the U.S. Biological Survey of 1889. He described a series of life zones on the slopes of the San Francisco Peaks in Arizona, based on characteristic species of the flora and fauna. Other patterns of plant physiognomic and community zonation have now been cataloged in mountain ranges throughout the world. SEE LIFE ZONES.

Merriam associated his life zones with temperature gradients present along mountain slopes. Later research on patterns of altitudinal zonation has centered on the response of species and groups of species to a complex of environmental gradients. Measurements of a species along a gradient, for example, the number of individuals, biomass, or ground coverage, generally form a bell-shaped curve. Peak response of a species occurs under optimum conditions and falls off at both ends of the gradient. The unique response of each species is determined by its physiological, reproductive, growth, and genetic characteristics.

Zones of vegetation along mountain slopes are formed by intergrading combinations of species that differ in their tolerance to environmental conditions. Zones are usually indistinct entities rather than discrete groupings of species. However, under some conditions of localized disjunctions, very steep sections of gradients, or competitive exclusion, discontinuities in the vegetation can create discrete communities. *See Ecological communities.*

Vegetation zones are often defined by the distributions of species having the dominant growth form, most frequently trees. For example, in the Cascade Mountains of Washington and Oregon, tundra above treeline has been called the sedge–grass zone, but successively lower zones are spruce–fir, arborvitae–hemlock, Douglas-fir, ponderosa pine, and finally several fescue–wheatgrass–sagebrush zones in which no trees grow. Another set of zones could be designated if other criteria were used. The boundaries of the middle elevation zones might be different if they had been defined instead by distributions of the dominant shrubs.

Environmental gradients in mountains. Altitudinal vegetation zonation, therefore, is an expression of the response of individual species to environmental conditions. Plants along an altitudinal transect are exposed, not to a single environmental gradient, but to a complex of gradients, the most important of which are solar radiation, temperature, and precipitation. Although these major environmental gradients exist in most mountain ranges of the world, the gradients along a single altitudinal transect are not always smooth because of topographic and climatic variability. This environmental variation can result in irregular vegetation zones.

The solar energy received by mountain surfaces increases with altitude, associated with decreases in air density and the amount of dust and water vapor. Global radiation levels in the European Alps have been shown to be 21% greater at 10,000 ft (3000 m) than at 650 ft (200 m) under a cloudless sky. An overcast sky is more efficient at reducing short-wave

energy reaching low elevations and can increase the difference in energy input to 160%. However, more frequent clouds over high elevations relative to sunnier lower slopes commonly reduces this difference.

Vegetation patterns are also strongly influenced by the decline in air temperature with increasing altitude, called the adiabatic lapse rate. Lapse rates are generally between 1.8°F to 3.6°F per 1000 ft (1°C to 2°C per 300 m), but vary with the amount of moisture present; wet air has a lower lapse rate. Thus, plants occurring at higher elevations generally experience cooler temperatures and shorter growing periods than low-elevation plants. Variation in the temperature gradient can be caused by differences in slope, aspect, radiation input, clouds, and air drainage patterns. *See Air temperature.*

The precipitation gradient in most mountains is the reverse of the temperature gradient: precipitation increases with altitude. Moist air from low elevations is forced upward by the blocking action of the mountains into regions of cooler temperatures. Air holds less moisture at low temperatures than at warmer ones. When the atmosphere reaches the point of saturation (the dew point), condensation occurs, forming clouds or precipitation. This moisture gradient is most pronounced on windward slopes and in ranges close to warm and moist oceanic winds. As the moving air passes over the peaks of the mountain range and moisture in the air is depleted, precipitation is reduced, creating a rain "shadow" on the lee side of the range.

Temperate, tropical, and high latitudes. General changes in vegetation with increases in altitude include reduction in plant size, slower growth rates, lower production, communities composed of fewer species, and less interspecific competition. However, many regional exceptions to these trends exist. In western North America, for example, the lowest zone is often a treeless shrubland or prairie, so plant size initially increases with altitude as trees become important. Above this zone, the trend toward smaller size prevails.

Characteristics of vegetation zones also vary with latitude (**Fig. 1**). Mountains at higher latitudes have predominantly seasonal climates, with major temper-

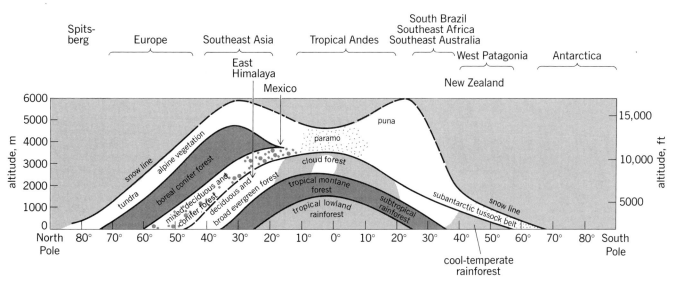

Fig. 1. Generalized patterns of altitudinal vegetation zonation in the Northern and Southern hemispheres. (*After L. W. Price, Mountains and Man, University of California Press, 1981*)

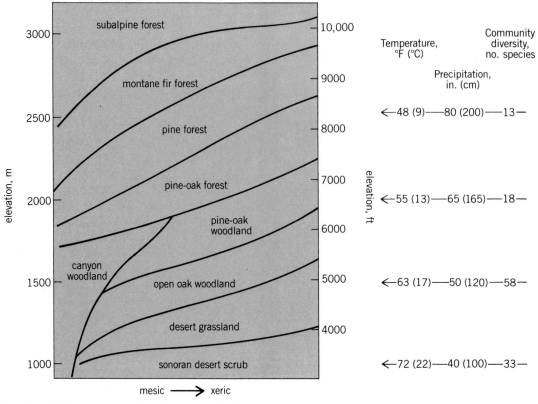

Fig. 2. Vegetation zones and gradients of mean annual soil temperature, annual precipitation, and community diversity on the south slopes of the Santa Catalina Mountains, Arizona, a temperate mountaiin range. *(After R. H. Whittaker, and W. A. Niering, Vegetation of the Santa Catalina Mountains: A gradient analysis of the south slope, Ecology, 46:429–451, 1965)*

ature and radiation extremes between summer and winter. Equatorial and tropical mountains have a strong diurnal pattern of temperature and radiation input with little seasonal variation. The upper altitudinal limit of trees, and the maximum elevation of plant growth generally, decreases with distance from the Equator, with the exception of a depression near the Equator.

The following examples of altitudinal zonation in temperate, tropical, and high-latitude regions illustrate patterns that exist in each region. These patterns are not comprehensive, and many others exist locally and worldwide.

Temperate. The vegetation of the Santa Catalina Mountains in Arizona illustrates the variety of zones found in a temperate mountain range (**Fig. 2**). Typically, precipitation increases with altitude, while air and soil temperatures decrease. Community diversity, the number of species present, decreases with altitude in all zones except the scrub desert, where arid conditions support fewer species. Biomass production is less at low elevations than on higher slopes, the reverse of the general trend, because of limitations to growth under arid conditions.

Hot and dry conditions at lower elevations support a treeless desert shrub and grassland, dominated by such shrubs as palo verde (*Cercidium microphyllum*) and mesquite (*Prosopis juliflora*). With increasing elevation, more moisture allows growth of broadleaf deciduous and evergreen oak trees (*Quercus* spp.). Needle-leaf evergreen trees, including ponderosa pine (*Pinus ponderosa*) and border limber pine (*P. strobiformis*), become increasingly important in the midelevation vegetation zones where temperatures are

cooler, moisture more readily available, and the growing season longer. Broadleaf trees decrease in importance in these zones. Finally, in the upper zones, where the coolest temperatures and highest moisture levels prevail, conifers that commonly extend farther north including Douglas-fir (*Pseudostuga menziesii*) and Engelmann spruce (*Picea engelmanni*) replace species better adapted to lower-elevation environments. At higher latitudes and where mountains are high enough, an alpine zone of grasses, forbs, cushion plants, and dwarf shrubs occurs above treeline. A similar sequential replacement of species in the altitudinal zones is repeated in both the herb and shrub layer.

The Southern Hemisphere has fewer mountains in the temperate regions than areas north of the Equator. The oceanic climate of these mountains is cooler and moister because of the small land mass relative to the nearby oceans. A prolonged cold season is absent. In New Zealand, broadleaf evergreen trees such as evergreen beech (*Nothofagus* spp.) dominate moist mountain forests, with needle-leaf evergreens such as *Podocarpus* spp. being of lesser importance. Zones at all elevations have a richer, more diverse flora than their Northern Hemisphere counterparts. Within each zone, shrubs are more luxurious, and epiphytes and hanging vines are common.

Tropical. Vegetation zones at all elevations in tropical mountains are dominated by a diurnal climate with little seasonality, because sun angles are high throughout the year. Growing seasons are determined by moisture availability rather than by temperature. At lower elevations in the Andes, tropical rainforests with a species-rich multilayered and luxurious canopy of broadleaf evergreen trees cover mountain slopes. These trees are accompanied by a lush mixture of hanging vines, epiphytes, shrubs, and flowering herbs. In the submontane and montane zones at higher elevations, the complexity of the forest is reduced. Trees are shorter and are adapted to drier conditions, and the canopy has fewer layers. Vines, epiphytes, and shrubs are present in fewer numbers, but mosses and lichens become more common.

The subalpine zone is an elfin woodland or cloud forest of short, stunted trees covered with an abundance of mosses and lichens. Vegetation is adapted to the higher moisture and lower light levels created by clouds, which almost continuously envelop the zone. Plant communities in this zone are less complex than those lower on the mountain; fewer species are present and canopy structure is simpler. In the northern Andes of Colombia, the alpine zone consists of a low vegetation called paramo, which is dominated by arborescent members of the sunflower family, Compositae. Growth forms consist of tall tussock grasses, dwarf shrubs, herbs, and two forms unique to the tropics of the Southern Hemisphere: dendroid or tufted-leaf stemmed plants, and woolly candlelike plants.

Farther from the Equator in the central and southern Andes, the climate is drier and lower zones are dominated by forests of deciduous trees or grassland savannas. The alpine zone consists of puna, a vegetation of smaller tussock grasses and many cushion and rosette plants. *See* Savanna.

High latitude. At high latitudes in both Northern and Southern hemispheres, fewer vegetation zones exist. Short growing seasons permit no tree growth, and shrubs and herbs are limited at higher elevations by a permanent cover of ice or snow, called the nival zone. Plant communities consist of fewer species than in temperate or tropical regions. In the Olgivie Mountains, Yukon Territory, Canada, valley bottoms are covered by willow (*Salix* spp.) and birch (*Betula* spp.) shrubs with a ground layer of grasses and forbs in drier sites, and tussock tundra dominated by cottongrass (*Eriophorum* spp.) in wet sites. At higher elevations, tall woody shrubs are absent, and this zone consists of a tundra of dwarf heath shrubs including mountain heather (*Cassiope* spp.) and mountain avens (*Dryas* spp.), grasses, forbs, and plants with cushion or rosette growth forms. *See* Terrestrial ecosystem.

John S. Campbell

Bibliography. E. W. Beals, Vegetational change along altitudinal gradients, *Science*, 165:981–985, 1969; W. Lauer, The altitudinal belts of the vegetation in the central Mexican highlands and their climatic condition, *Arctic Alpine Res.*, 5(pt. 2):A99–114, 1973; L. W. Price, *Mountains and Man*, 1981; C. Troll (ed.), *Geoecology of the Mountainous Regions of the Tropical Americas*, 1968; H. Walter, *Vegetation of the Earth and Ecological Systems of the Geo-Biosphere*, 1979; R. H. Whittaker and W. A. Niering, Vegetation of the Santa Catalina Mountains: A gradient analysis of the south slope, *Ecology*, 46:429–451, 1965.

Aquifer

A subsurface zone that yields economically important amounts of water to wells. The term is synonymous with water-bearing formation. An aquifer may be porous rock, unconsolidated gravel, fractured rock, or cavernous limestone. Economically important amounts of water may vary from less than a gallon per minute for cattle water in the desert to thousands of gallons per minute for industrial, irrigation, or municipal use.

Among the most productive are the sand and gravel formations of the Atlantic and Gulf Coastal plains of the southeastern United States. These layers extend for hundreds of miles and may be several hundred feet thick. Also highly productive are deposits of sand and gravel washed out from the continental glaciers in the northern United States; the outwash gravel deposits from the western mountain ranges; certain cavernous limestones such as the Edwards limestone of Texas and the Ocala limestone of Florida, Georgia, and South Carolina; and some of the volcanic rocks of the Snake River Plain in Idaho and the Columbia Plateau.

Aquifers are important reservoirs storing large amounts of water relatively free from evaporation loss or pollution. If the annual withdrawal from an aquifer regularly exceeds the replenishment from rainfall or seepage from streams, the water stored in the aquifer will be depleted. This "mining" of groundwater results in increased pumping costs and sometimes pollution from seawater or adjacent saline aquifers. Lowering the piezometric pressure in an unconsolidated artesian aquifer by overpumping may cause the aquifer and confining layers of silt or clay to be compressed under the weight of the overlying material. The resulting subsidence of the ground surface may cause structural damage to buildings, altered drainage paths, increased flooding, damage to wells, and other problems. Subsidence of 10 to 15 ft (3.0 to 4.6 m) has occurred in Mexico City and parts of the San Joaquin Valley of California. Careful management of aquifers is important to maintain their utility as a water source. *See* Artesian systems; Groundwater hydrology.

Ray K. Linsley

Arboriculture

A branch of horticulture concerned with the selection, planting, and care of woody perennial plants. Knowing the potential form and size of plants is essential to effective landscape planning as well as to the care needed for plants. Arborists are concerned primarily with trees since they become large, are long-lived, and dominate landscapes both visually and functionally.

Plants can provide privacy, define space, and progressively reveal vistas; they can be used to reduce glare, direct traffic, reduce soil erosion, filter air, and attenuate noise; and they can be positioned so as to modify the intensity and direction of wind. They also influence the microclimate by evaporative cooling and interception of the Sun's rays, as well as by reflection and reradiation. Certain plants, however, can cause human irritations with their pollen, leaf pubescence, toxic sap, and strong fragrances from flowers and fruit. Additionally, trees can be dangerous and costly: branches can fall, and roots can clog sewers and break paving.

Plant selection. A plant's growth habit and its size at maturity are important characteristics in the selection process. It is important to select plants with roots that are free from kinks or circling. It is also desirable that trees be able to stand without support and have small branches along the trunk to provide protection and nourishment during establishment. Whether the plant is to be used for shade, screening, privacy, accent, or protection will determine what kind is selected. Sturdy root systems protect plants from being uprooted during storms, and if the roots are tolerant of poor soil the plants will remain healthy and can resist pests more readily. Leaves, flowers, and fruit are another consideration; not only are they visually important, but they also can have a considerable impact on maintenance.

Most plants grow best in deep, loamy soils, although some are able to withstand unfavorable soil conditions such as poor drainage, strata of different textures, extreme acidity or alkalinity, or chemical toxicities. The lowest recorded temperatures in a given region will determine which plants can survive in that region. Long-lived plants in particular should be selected to withstand the lowest temperatures expected.

Species native to an area may not perform well, however, particularly around buildings where microclimate and soil can differ considerably from preconstruction conditions.

Planting and care. Unless the soil has been compacted, the planting hole should only be deep enough to take the roots. The soil around the roots should be firmed and watered to settle it and remove air pockets. Unless the plant is overgrown, the only pruning needed after planting is some thinning to begin tree structure development, to shape shrubs, or to select vine canes to trellis. Little pruning is necessary for central-leader trees, conifers, and some hardwoods to grow strong and be well shaped. Species that become round-headed, however, may need considerable pruning to ensure the desired height of branching and a strong branch structure.

The less a branch or tree is pruned, the larger it will become. Therefore, only large branches that are too low or will compete or interfere with more desirable branches should be removed. Permanent branches, particularly of large-growing trees, should be at least one-third smaller in diameter than the trunk where they arise and be vertically spaced at least 18 in. (45 cm) apart along the trunk.

A tree will be more open and better retain its natural form if branches are removed completely (thinned) in contrast to being headed or stubbed back (see **illus.**). Heading concentrates subsequent growth just below the pruning cut and results in dense foliage with weakly attached branches. In removing a branch the final cut should be just to the outside of the branch bark ridge in the crotch and the collar below. Such a cut minimizes the size of the wound and the possibility that the trunk will decay. Seldom is it advisable to paint pruning wounds.

Fertilization of young plants is necessary for rapid growth; mature plants, however, may need little or no added nutrients. Nitrogen is almost universally deficient in soils and usually is the only element to which trees and large shrubs will respond. Nitrogen fertilizers are water-soluble and can be applied to the soil or lawn surface and then watered in. In alkaline soils, the availability of iron or manganese may be so low for certain plants that they exhibit the typical pale leaves with narrow (due to iron deficiency) or wide (due to manganese deficiency) darker green bands along the veins. Increasing soil acidity or applying chelated nutrients usually ameliorates these problems.

Irrigation can ensure establishment of young plants, the attractive appearance of foliage, and even survival. Many mature plants can endure long periods without rain or irrigation, if a large volume of moist soil is present and the plants have extensive root systems. If the water supply is limited, it is important for the soil to be fully moist at the start of the growing season. A few heavy irrigations are more efficient than frequent light ones; more plants do poorly from too much water than not enough.

Mulch, that is, material placed on the soil surface, can control weeds, protect the soil from compaction and erosion, conserve moisture, moderate soil temperatures, provide an all-weather surface for walking, and allow plants to root in the most fertile and well-aerated surface soil. A wide range of organic and inorganic or synthetic materials can be used. Mulch should be kept 2 in. (5 cm) away from the trunks of plants to reduce trunk disease and rodent damage. See Landscape architecture.

Richard W. Harris

Bibliography. B. Ferguson, *All about Trees*, 1982; C. W. Harris and N. T. Dines (eds.), *Time-Saver Standards for Landscape Architecture*, 1988; R. W. Harris, *Arboriculture: Care of Trees, Shrubs, and Vines in the Landscape*, 1983; J. Hudak, *Trees for Every Purpose*, 1980; A. L. Shigo, *A New Tree Biology*, 1936; B. B. Wilson, *The Growing Tree*, 1984.

Artesian systems

Groundwater conditions formed by water-bearing rocks (aquifers) in which the water is confined above and below by impermeable beds. These systems are named after the province of Artois in France, where artesian wells were first observed.

Because the water table in the intake area of an artesian system is higher than the top of the aquifer in its artesian portion, the water is under sufficient head to cause it to rise in a well above the top of the aquifer. Many of the systems have sufficient head to cause the water to overflow at the surface, at least where the land surface is relatively low. Flowing artesian wells were extremely important during the early

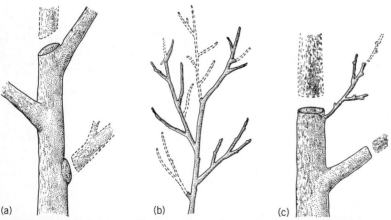

Methods of plant pruning. (a) Thinning (removing a branch at its origin) of a mature tree. (b) Thinning a young tree. (c) Heading (pruning to a small lateral branch or to a stub) of a mature tree. (*After R. W. Harris, Arboriculture: Care of Trees, Shrubs, and Vines in the Landscape, Prentice-Hall, 1983*)

days of the development of groundwater from drilled wells, because there was no need for pumping. Their importance has diminished with the decline of head that has occurred in many artesian systems and with the development of efficient pumps and cheap power with which to operate the pumps. When they were first tapped, many artesian aquifers contained water that was under sufficient pressure to rise 100 ft (30 m) or more above the land surface. Besides furnishing water supplies, many of the wells were used to generate electric power. With the increasing development of the artesian aquifers through the drilling of additional wells, the head in most of them has decreased and it is now from a few feet to several hundred feet below the land surface in many areas of former artesian flow. A majority of artesian wells are now equipped with pumps. SEE AQUIFER.

Perhaps the best-known artesian aquifer in the United States is the Dakota sandstone, of Cretaceous age, which underlies most of North Dakota, South Dakota, and Nebraska, much of Kansas, and parts of Minnesota and Iowa at depths ranging from 0 to 2000 ft (0 to 600 m). The water is highly mineralized, as a general rule, but during the latter part of the nineteenth century, when these areas were being settled, the Dakota sandstone provided a valuable source of water supply under high pressure. Few wells in this aquifer flow more than a trickle of water today. The St. Peter sandstone and deeper-lying sandstones of early lower Paleozoic age, which underlie parts of Minnesota, Wisconsin, Iowa, Illinois, and Indiana, form another well-known artesian system. Formerly, wells on low ground flowed abundantly, but now wells have to be pumped throughout most of the area. Some of the water is highly mineralized, but in many places it is of good quality. In New Mexico, in the Roswell artesian basin, cavernous limestone of Permian age provides water to irrigate thousands of acres of cotton and other farm crops. Although the head has been steadily declining, many wells still have large flows and others yield copious supplies by pumping. Among the most productive artesian systems are the

Cretaceous and Tertiary aquifers of the Atlantic and Gulf Coastal plains. These provide large quantities of water for irrigation and industrial use and supply large cities, such as Savannah, Georgia; Memphis, Tennessee; and Houston and San Antonio, Texas. Numerous artesian basins are found in intermontane valleys of the West. Some of the best known are in the Central Valley, California, where confined aquifers provide water to irrigate millions of acres of farmland, and the San Luis Valley, Colorado. Numerous other lesser artesian systems are found in all parts of the United States. SEE GROUNDWATER HYDROLOGY.

Albert N. Sayre/Ray K. Linsley

Atmosphere

A gaseous layer that envelops the Earth and most other planets in the solar system. Earth, Venus, Mars, Jupiter, Saturn, Uranus, Neptune, and Titan (Saturn's largest satellite) are all known to possess substantial atmospheres that are held by the force of gravity. The structure and properties of the various atmospheres are determined by the interplay of the various physical and chemical processes that are operating in each case. Structural features of Earth's atmosphere detailed below can often be identified in the atmospheres of other planetary bodies.

Composition. The composition of the Earth's atmosphere is primarily nitrogen (N_2), oxygen (O_2), and argon (Ar) [see **table**]. The concentration of water vapor (H_2O) is highly variable, especially near the surface, where volume fractions can vary from nearly 0% to as high as 4% in the tropics. There are many minor constituents or trace gases, such as neon (Ne), helium (He), krypton (Kr), and xenon (Xe), that are inert, and others, such as carbon dioxide (CO_2), methane (CH_4), hydrogen (H_2), nitrous oxide (NO), carbon monoxide (CO), ozone (O_3), and sulfur dioxide (SO_2), that play an important role in radiative and biological processes.

In addition to the gaseous component, the atmo-

Composition of the atmosphere*		
Molecule	Fraction volume near surface	Vertical distribution
Major constituents		
N_2	7.8084×10^{-1}	Mixed in homosphere; photochemical dissociation high in thermosphere
O_2	2.0946×10^{-1}	Mixed in homosphere; photochemically dissociated in thermosphere, with some dissociation in mesosphere and stratosphere
Ar	9.34×10^{-3}	Mixed in homosphere with diffusive separation increasing above
Important radiative constituents		
CO_2	3.5×10^{-4}	Mixed in homosphere; photochemical dissociation in thermosphere
H_2O	Highly variable	Forms clouds in troposphere; little in stratosphere; photochemical dissociation above mesosphere
O_3	Variable	Small amounts, 10^{-8}, in troposphere; important layer, 10^{-6} to 10^{-5}, in stratosphere; dissociated above
Other constituents		
Ne	1.82×10^{-5}	Mixed in homosphere with diffusive separation increasing above
He	5.24×10^{-6}	
Kr	1.14×10^{-6}	
CH_4	1.15×10^{-6}	Mixed in troposphere; dissociated in upper stratosphere and above
H_2	5×10^{-7}	Mixed in homosphere; product of H_2O photochemical reactions in lower thermosphere, and dissociated above
NO	$\sim 10^{-8}$	Photochemically produced in stratosphere and mesosphere

*Other gases, for example, CO, N_2O, NO_2, and many by-products of atmospheric pollution also exist in small amounts.

sphere suspends many solid and liquid particles. Aerosols are particulates usually less than 1 micrometer in diameter that are created by gas-to-particle reactions or are lifted from the surface by the wind. A portion of these aerosols can become centers of condensation or deposition in the growth of water and ice clouds. Cloud droplets and ice crystals are made primarily of water with some trace amounts of particles and dissolved gases. Their diameters range from a few micrometers to about 100 μm. Water or ice particles larger than about 100 μm begin to fall because of gravity and may result in precipitation at the surface. *See Cloud physics*.

One of the remarkable properties of the Earth's atmosphere is the large amount of free molecular oxygen in the presence of gases such as nitrogen, methane, water vapor, hydrogen and others that are capable of being oxidized. The atmosphere is in a highly oxidizing state that is far from chemical equilibrium. This is in sharp contrast to the atmospheres of Venus and Mars, the planets closest to the Earth, which are composed almost entirely of the more oxidized state, carbon dioxide. The chemical disequilibrium on the Earth is maintained by a continuous source of reactive gases derived from biological processes. Life plays a vital role in maintaining the present atmospheric composition. *See Atmospheric chemistry*.

Vertical structure. The total mass of the Earth's atmosphere is about 5.8×10^{15} tons (5.3×10^{15} metric tons). The vertical distribution of gaseous mass is maintained by a balance between the downward force of gravity and the upward pressure gradient force. The balance is known as the hydrostatic balance or the barometric law. Hence, the declining atmospheric pressure that is measured higher in the atmosphere is a result of gravity. The horizontally averaged pressure

at mean sea level is 1013.25 millibars (101,325 pascals).

Below about 60 mi (100 km) in altitude, the atmosphere's composition of major constituents is very uniform. This region is known as the homosphere to distinguish it from the heterosphere above 60 mi, where the relative amounts of the major constituents change with height. In the homosphere there are sufficient atmospheric motions and a short enough molecular free path to maintain uniformity in composition. Above the boundary between the homosphere and the heterosphere, known as the homopause or turbopause, the mean free path of the individual molecules becomes long enough so that gravity is able to partially separate the lighter molecules from the heavier ones. The mean free path is the average distance that a particle will travel before encountering a collision. Hence the average molecular weight of the heterosphere decreases with height as the lighter atoms dominate the composition.

Radiative transfer. The vertical structure of the atmosphere (**Fig. 1**) is in large part determined by the transfer properties of the solar and terrestrial radiation streams. The energy of the smallest unit of radiation, the photon, is directly proportional to its frequency. The type of interaction that occurs between photons and the atmosphere depends on the energy of the photons.

The most energetic of the photons are x-rays and extreme ultraviolet radiation of the eletromagnetic spectrum, which are capable of dissociating and ionizing the gaseous molecules. The less energetic near-ultraviolet photons are able to excite molecules and atoms into higher electronic levels. As a result, most of the ultraviolet and x-ray radiation is attentuated by the upper atmosphere. A cloudless atmosphere, however, is relatively transparent to visible light, where

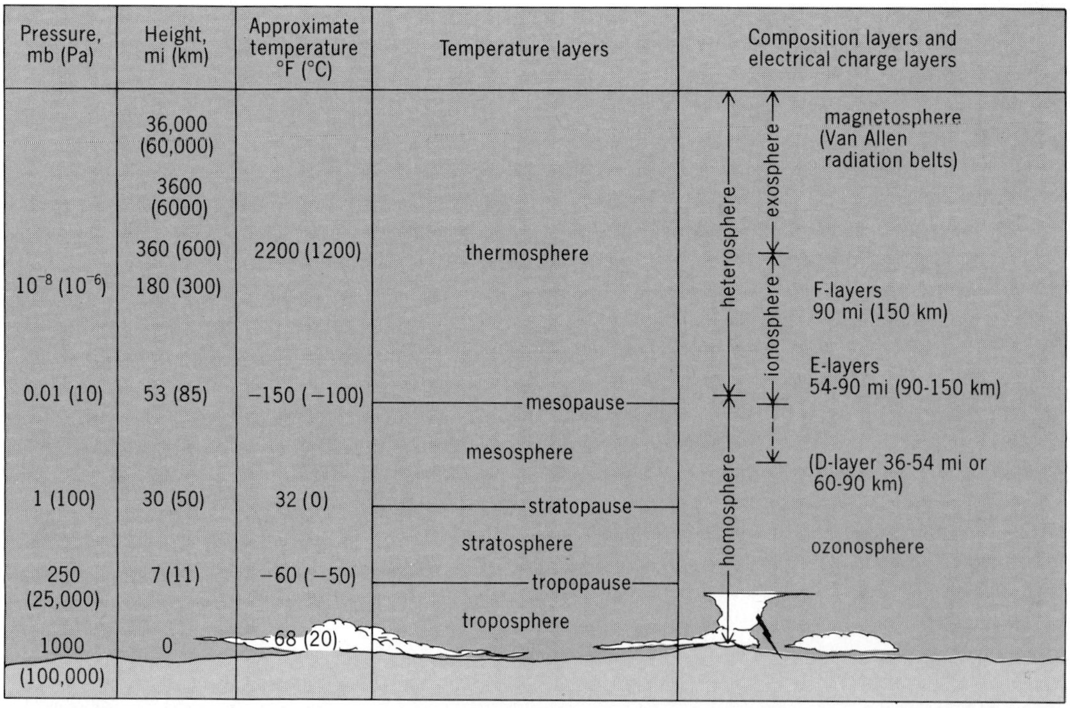

Pressure, mb (Pa)	Height, mi (km)	Approximate temperature °F (°C)	Temperature layers	Composition layers and electrical charge layers
	36,000 (60,000)			magnetosphere (Van Allen radiation belts)
	3600 (6000)			
10^{-8} (10^{-6})	360 (600)	2200 (1200)	thermosphere	
	180 (300)			F-layers 90 mi (150 km)
0.01 (10)	53 (85)	−150 (−100)	mesopause	E-layers 54-90 mi (90-150 km)
			mesosphere	(D-layer 36-54 mi or 60-90 km)
1 (100)	30 (50)	32 (0)	stratopause	
			stratosphere	ozonosphere
250 (25,000)	7 (11)	−60 (−50)	tropopause	
			troposphere	
1000 (100,000)	0	68 (20)		

Fig. 1. Layers of the atmosphere, shown in terms of pressure, height, temperature, and compositional properties. (*After M. Neiburger, J. G. Edinger, and W. D. Bonner, Understanding Our Atmospheric Environment, W. H. Freeman, 1973*)

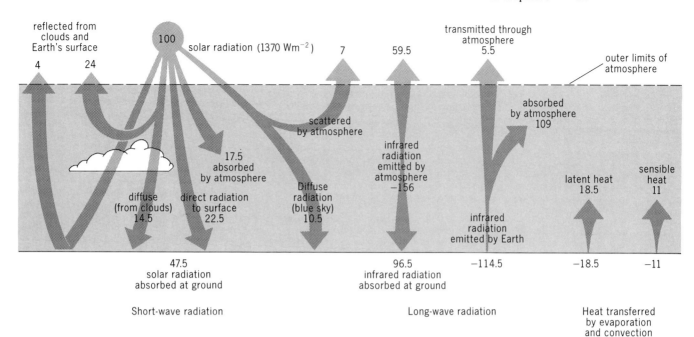

Fig. 2. Radiation energy budget of the Earth's atmosphere expressed as a percentage of the total incoming solar radiation; the numerical values sum to a net balance for the surface, atmosphere, and space separately. (*After M. Neiburger, J. G. Edinger, and W. D. Bonner, Understanding Our Atmospheric Environment, W. H. Freeman, 1973*)

most of the solar energy resides. At the opposite end of the spectrum toward the lower frequencies of radiation is the infrared part, which is capable of inducing various vibrational and rotational motions in triatomic and polyatomic molecules.

In order to maintain an energy balance, the Earth must emit about the same amount of radiation as it absorbs from the Sun. The terrestrial radiation occurs in the infrared part of the spectrum and hence is strongly affected by water vapor, clouds, carbon dioxide, and ozone and other trace gases. The ability of these gases to absorb and emit in the infrared allows them to effectively trap some of the outgoing radiation that is emitted by the surface, creating the so-called greenhouse effect. **Figure 2** shows the globally averaged annual radiation budget of Earth. *See* GREENHOUSE EFFECT.

Troposphere. The atmospheric layer that extends from the surface to about 7 mi (11 km) is called the troposphere. The tropopause, which is the top of the troposphere, has an average altitude that varies from about 11 mi (18 km) near the Equator to about 5 mi (8 km) near the poles. The actual tropopause height varies considerably on time scales from a few days to an entire year.

The troposphere contains about 80% of the atmospheric mass and exhibits most of the day-to-day weather fluctuations that are observed from the ground. Temperatures generally decrease with increasing altitude at an average lapse rate of about 17°F/mi (6°C/km), although this rate varies considerably depending on time and location (**Fig. 3**).

On average, about one-half of the total solar radiative flux is absorbed by the Earth's surface. This raises the surface temperature sufficiently to induce atmospheric circulations in the troposphere that redistribute the heat both vertically and horizontally throughout the troposphere. As air that is heated from contact with the surface is forced to rise, it becomes surrounded by lower pressure. As a result, the air ex-

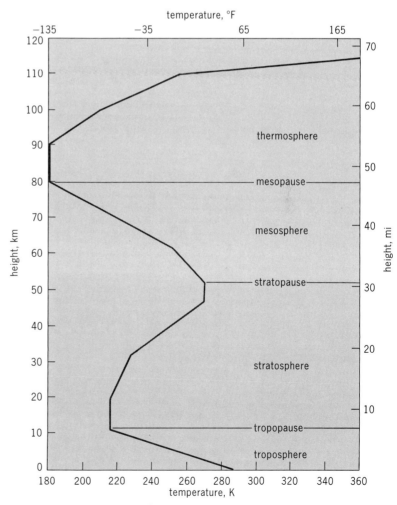

Fig. 3. Temperature of the United States standard atmosphere plotted as a function of height and showing the various thermal layers. The standard atmosphere is intended to be a global and annual representative average. (*After M. Neiburger, J. G. Edinger, and W. D. Bonner, Understanding Our Atmospheric Environment, W. H. Freeman, 1973*)

pands and must cool in order to conserve total energy, thereby creating the observed lapse rate.

In order to transfer heat from regions with a radiational surplus, such as the tropics, to regions with a radiational deficit, such as the high latitudes, the atmosphere goes into motion and produces the general circulation relative to the Earth's surface. The large-scale wind patterns are dominated by a balance between the horizontal pressure gradient force and the Coriolis force. The horizontal pressure gradients form when uneven solar heating creates horizontal temperature gradients. The Coriolis force is a fictitious force that arises because the rotating Earth is an accelerating body. The Coriolis force acts at right angles to the wind and is proportional to the wind speed. Winds that start moving from high to low pressure become deflected to the right in the Northern Hemisphere and to the left in the Southern Hemisphere, so that eventually the winds blow parallel to lines of constant pressure. This is called geostrophic balance and is responsible for the westerlies and the jet streams that are found in the mid and high latitudes and the easterlies in the tropics. *See Atmospheric general circulation; Jet stream; Wind.*

Superimposed on the basic westerly and easterly currents are numerous types of disturbances or waves that give the weather its complex character and dominate the transport of energy and momentum in the troposphere. Examples of such disturbances include (1) the Hadley cell, a thermally direct average circulation that transports heat and momentum away from the Equator; (2) the barotropic disturbance, a wave instability that forms in the presence of a very strong horizontal wind shear; (3) the baroclinic disturbance, a wave instability that grows in the presence of a strong horizontal temperature gradient and is responsible for the midlatitude cyclones; (4) hurricanes and typhoons, disturbances that convert the potential energy of the moist and warm sea surface air into kinetic energy; and (5) thunderstorms, disturbances that rapidly overturn highly localized regions of the atmosphere in which relatively cold, dry air overlays warm, moist air. *See Atmospheric electricity; Hurricane; Thunderstorm.*

The winds not only transport heat in a form that can be felt directly, namely sensible heat, but also transport latent heat, which is a form of heat that is carried by the water vapor. Latent refers to the fact that the heat which is absorbed when water is evaporated into the atmosphere is released only when the water condenses to form clouds and precipitation in the atmosphere. The global hydrological cycle that includes the clouds and precipitation is a major contributor to the global redistribution of heat. *See Hydrometeorology.*

The amount of water vapor present in a parcel of air can be measured by the partial vapor pressure that is exerted by those water molecules. Since the maximum water vapor pressure (saturation vapor pressure) decreases exponentially with decreasing temperature, most of the water vapor condenses out to form clouds as a moist air parcel ascends through the troposphere. It is sufficiently cold at the tropopause (-110 to $-40°F$ or -80 to $-40°C$) that very little water is able to escape above it, an effect known as the cold trap. As a result of the cold trap, the air is very dry and usually cloudfree above the tropopause.

Stratosphere. This is the atmospheric layer that extends from the tropopause up to the stratopause at about 30 mi (50 km) above the surface. It is characterized by a nearly isothermal layer in the first 6 mi (10 km) overlaid by a layer in which the temperature increases with height to a maximum of about 32°F (0°C) at the stratopause.

The reversal in the temperature lapse rate is a result of direct absorption of solar radiation, mainly by ozone and oxygen at the ultraviolet frequencies. Ozone, a molecule consisting of three oxygen atoms, is a poisonous and reactive gas. Most of the ultraviolet light is attenuated in the stratosphere by ozone and oxygen; hence the surface of the Earth is protected from receiving doses that are harmful to life. In spite of the great importance of stratospheric ozone, it is merely a trace gas with peak concentrations of about 10–15 parts per million by volume at an altitude of about 20 mi (33 km) in the tropics. Ozone concentrations are also influenced by stratospheric winds and hence are highly variable in space and time. Ozone photochemistry is highly complex and involves chemical cycles from the hydrogen, nitrogen, and chlorine groups. It is the chlorine chemistry that has received particular attention in light of the declining ozone concentrations over the Antarctic during spring in the Southern Hemisphere. There is strong evidence to suggest that the chlorofluorocarbons emitted by industrial activities may be contributing to this decline. *See Atmospheric ozone.*

The reversal of the temperature lapse rate makes the stratosphere vertically stable. This stability limits the amount of vertical mixing and results in molecular residence times of many months to years. Another consequence of a stable stratosphere is that it acts as a lid on the troposphere, which results in confining the strong vertical overturning and hence most of the surface-based weather phenomena. *See Weather.*

Occasionally a strong volcano is able to inject into the stratosphere large amounts of aerosols, commonly sulfate particles, that may remain several years before they are removed. While in the stratosphere, the sulfate particles can perturb the radiative balance slightly by increasing the stratospheric temperature and cooling the troposphere. A significant event of this type was the El Chichón eruption in 1982, in which about $13.2 × 10^6$ tons ($12 × 10^6$ metric tons) of material was injected into the stratosphere.

Mesosphere. This is the atmospheric layer extending from the stratopause up to the mesopause at an altitude of about 53 mi (85 km). The mesosphere is characterized by temperatures decreasing with height at a rate of about 12°F/mi (4°C/km). Although the mesosphere has less vertical stability than the stratosphere, it is still more stable than the troposphere and does not experience rapid overturning. The coldest temperatures of the entire atmosphere are encountered at the mesopause, with values as low as $-150°F$ ($-100°C$).

The temperature lapse rate found in the mesosphere is a result of the gradual weakening with height of the direct absorption of solar radiation by ozone. The radiative infrared cooling to space by the carbon dioxide molecules is responsible for the low temperatures near the mesopause.

Thermosphere. This part of the atmosphere is found above the mesopause. The thermosphere is characterized by rising temperatures with height up to an altitude of about 190 mi (300 km) and then is nearly isothermal above that. Although there is no clear upper limit to the thermosphere, it is convenient to consider it extending several thousand kilometers. Embedded within the thermosphere is the ionosphere, comprising those atmospheric layers in which the ionized molecules and atoms are dominating the processes.

Molecular species dominate the lower thermosphere, while atomic species are dominant above 190 mi (300 km). The distribution of the constituents is controlled by diffusive equilibrium in which the concentration of each constituent decreases exponentially with height according to its molecular weight. Hence the concentration of the heavier constituents such as nitrogen, oxygen, and carbon dioxide will decrease with height faster than the lighter constituents such as helium and hydrogen. At an altitude of 560 mi (900 km) helium becomes the dominant constituent while hydrogen dominates above 1900 mi (3000 km).

Diffusion becomes the dominant mode of transport in the thermosphere, because the low air densities allow the mean free path of the molecules and atoms to become very large, about 3 ft at 60 mi (1 m at 100 km), and it increases rapidly with height.

The thermosphere is exposed to the complete spectrum of radiation that is emitted by the Sun. This includes the extreme ultraviolet (wavelengths less than about 103 nanometers) and some x-ray radiation that is capable of dissociating and ionizing molecules. Although the amount of energy contained in these high-frequency (short-wavelength) radiation bands is small compared to the total solar flux in the visible band, they still dominate the radiative heating in the thermosphere.

Of the total absorbed solar energy in the thermosphere, about 35% goes into heating the neutral particles, raising the kinetic temperature, and about 45% is reradiated out of the thermosphere as ultraviolet airglow. Airglow occurs when molecules and atoms reemit temporarily absorbed single photons of solar radiation. The remainder of the incoming absorbed solar radiation (about 20%) is stored as chemical energy of oxygen atoms formed when an oxygen molecule is dissociated. This energy is released as heat when oxygen atoms recombine below 60 mi (90 km) in altitude.

In order to maintain thermal balance, the thermosphere must lose the heat it receives from the absorption of solar radiation. The emission of thermal, infrared radiation is weak, and so balance is achieved by thermal conduction of heat from the high temperatures of the upper thermosphere to the coldest temperatures at the mesopause. At the mesopause, there is sufficient carbon dioxide and ozone pressure to allow heat to be emitted radiatively to space. The reason that thermal conduction is such a good heat transfer mechanism in the thermosphere, and not in the lower atmospheric layers, is the large mean free path of the atoms and molecules at these heights.

The upper thermosphere, above 190 mi (300 km), is a very active region both thermally and dynamically; it exhibits large responses to changes in the solar radiative forcing and auroral particles. Temperatures can vary from about 600°F (300°C) at night to 2200°F (1200°C) during the day. A global circulation occurs in the thermosphere, with winds between 110 and 450 mi/h (50 and 200 m/s) blowing from the day to night side. This prevents the diurnal temperature change from becoming even larger. Also, auroral storms can induce a high- to low-latitude circulation in the thermosphere.

Ionosphere. This can be defined operationally as that part of the atmosphere that is sufficiently ionized to affect the propagation of radio waves. In the ionosphere, the dominant negative ion is the electron, and the main positive ions include O^+, NO^+, and O_2^+.

The ionosphere is classified into four subregions. The D region extends from 40 to 60 mi (60 to 90 km) and contains complex ionic chemistry; most of the ionization is caused by ultraviolet ionization of NO and by galactic cosmic rays. This region is responsible for the daytime absorption of radio waves, which prevents distant propagation of certain frequencies. The E region extends from 60 to 90 mi (90 to 150 km) and is caused primarily by the x-rays from the Sun. The F1 region from 90 to 125 mi (150 to 200 km) is caused by the extreme ultraviolet radiation from the Sun and disappears at night. Finally, the F2 region includes all the ionized particles above 125 mi (200 km), with the peak ion concentrations occurring near 190 mi (300 km).

Exosphere. The term exosphere is used to refer to the atmosphere above 300 mi (500 km) where the probability of interatomic collisions is so low that some of the atoms traveling upward with sufficient velocity can escape the Earth's gravitational field. The dominant escaping atom is hydrogen since it is the lightest constituent. Calculations of the thermal escape of hydrogen (also known as the Jeans escape) yield a value of about 3×10^8 atoms $\cdot$ cm$^{-2} \cdot$ s^{-1}. This is a very small amount since at this rate less than 0.5% of the oceans would disappear over the current age of the Earth.

The main source of the escaping hydrogen is water vapor that becomes dissociated by ultraviolet radiation above the tropopause. The importance of the cold water trap at the tropopause is evident, as this limits the availability of water for dissociation and hence provides a limit on the hydrogen escape. It is speculated that Venus may have lost all its water because such a cold trap did not limit the hydrogen escape.

Magnetosphere. This is the region surrounding the Earth where the movement of ionized gases is dominated by the geomagnetic field. The lower boundary of the magnetosphere, which occurs at an altitude of nearly 75 mi (120 km), can be roughly defined as the height where there are enough neutral atoms so that the ion-neutral particle collisions dominate the ion motion. The dynamics of the magnetosphere is dictated in part by its interaction with the plasma of ionized gases that blows away from the Sun, the solar wind. The solar wind interacts with the Earth's magnetic field and severely deforms it, producing a magnetosphere around the Earth. It extends about 40,000 mi (60,000 km) toward the Sun but extends beyond the orbit of the Moon away from the Sun.

Vertical energy transport. The division of the Earth's atmosphere into layers is based primarily on the thermal and chemical properties of each layer. Even though physical properties are found that distinguish the layers from each other, it is important to realize that interactions of mass and energy do occur between the layers.

The most obvious energy transfer is the outgoing terrestrial infrared radiation that escapes from the Earth. However, atmospheric dynamicists have also been studying the upward transfer of energy and momentum by the vertical propagation of waves. As a wave propagates upward, it encounters lower air densities, and the wave amplitude grows to conserve the total energy flux. Eventually the wave amplitude becomes so large that the wave is said to break, not unlike ocean waves breaking on the shoreline, and it deposits its energy and momentum at that height. The dissipation that occurs when a wave breaks is achieved by molecular conduction, viscosity, and ion drag.

It is believed that wave breaking may play an important role in the heating and circulation patterns of certain upper atmospheric regions. The two main wave types are atmospheric tides and gravity waves. Atmospheric tides are initiated in the stratosphere when ozone is heated, and can produce a vertically propagating wave. Gravity waves are oscillations produced by the stable buoyancy force; they also grow in amplitude as they move upward. SEE METEOROLOGY.

Glen B. Lesins

Bibliography. R. M. Goody and J. C. G. Walker, *Atmospheres*, 1972; J. T. Houghton, *The Physics of Atmospheres*, 1986; M. Neiburger, J. G. Edinger, and W. D. Bonner, *Understanding Our Atmospheric Environment*, 1973; J. M. Wallace and P. V. Hobbs, *Atmospheric Science: An Introductory Survey*, 1977; R. P. Wayne, *Chemistry of Atmospheres*, 1985.

Atmospheric chemistry

A subdivision of atmospheric science concerned with the chemistry and physics of atmospheric constituents, including studies of their sources, circulation, and sinks and their perturbations due to anthropogenic activity. SEE AIR POLLUTION.

Known gaseous constituents have mixing ratios with air by volume (or equivalently by number), f, ranging from 0.78 for N_2 to 6×10^{-20} for Rn. Known particulate constituents (solid or liquid) have mixing ratios with air by mass, χ, ranging from about 10^{-3} for liquid water in raining clouds to about 10^{-16} for large hydrated ions in otherwise clear air. These constituents are involved in cyclic processes of varying complexity which, in addition to the atmosphere, may involve the hydrosphere, biosphere, lithosphere, and even the deep interior of the Earth. The subject of atmospheric chemistry is of considerable importance because a number of the natural chemical cycles in the atmosphere may be particularly sensitive to perturbation by the industrial and related activities of humans.

Atmospheric composition. A summary of the important gaseous constituents of tropospheric air is given in the **table**. The predominance of N_2 and O_2 and the presence of the inert gases ^{40}Ar, Ne, ^{4}He, Kr, and Xe are considered to be the result of a very long-term evolutionary sequence in the atmosphere. These seven gases have extremely long atmospheric lifetimes, the shortest being 10^6 years for ^{4}He, which escapes from the top of the atmosphere. In contrast, all other gases in the table participate in relatively rapid chemical cycles and have atmospheric residence times of a few decades or less.

Particles in the atmosphere range in size from about 10^{-3} to more than 10^2 micrometers in radius. The term "aerosol" is usually reserved for particulate material other than water or ice. A summary of tropospheric aerosol size ranges and compositions is given in **Fig. 1**. Concentrations of the very smallest aerosol particles in the atmosphere are limited by coagulation to form larger particles, and the concentrations of the

Composition of tropospheric air	
Gas	Volume mixing ratio
Nitrogen, N_2	0.781 (in dry air)
Oxygen, O_2	0.209 (in dry air)
Argon, ^{40}Ar	9.34×10^{-3} (in dry air)
Water vapor, H_2O	Up to 4×10^{-2}
Carbon dioxide, CO_2	2 to 4×10^{-4}
Neon, Ne	1.82×10^{-5}
Helium, ^{4}He	5.24×10^{-6}
Methane, CH_4	1 to 2×10^{-6}
Krypton, Kr	1.14×10^{-6}
Hydrogen, H_2	4 to 10×10^{-7}
Nitrous oxide, N_2O	3.3×10^{-7}
Carbon monoxide, CO	1 to 20×10^{-8}
Xenon, Xe	8.7×10^{-8}
Ozone, O_3	Up to 5×10^{-8}
Nitrogen dioxide, NO_2	Up to 3×10^{-9}
Nitric oxide, NO	Up to 3×10^{-9}
Sulfur dioxide, SO_2	Up to 2×10^{-8}
Hydrogen sulfide, H_2S	2 to 20×10^{-9}
Ammonia, NH_3	Up to 2×10^{-8}
Formaldehyde, CH_2O	Up to 1×10^{-8}
Nitric acid, HNO_3	Up to 1×10^{-9}
Methyl chloride, CH_3Cl	6×10^{-10}
Hydrochloric acid, HCl	Up to 1.5×10^{-9}
Carbonyl sulfide, COS	5×10^{-10}
Freon-11, $CFCl_3$	1.7×10^{-10}
Freon-12, CF_2Cl_2	2.8×10^{-10}
Carbon tetrachloride, CCl_4	1.4×10^{-10}

larger aerosols are restricted by sedimentation, the rate of which increases as the square of the aerosol radius. In addition, the size distributions of water droplets and ice crystals are affected by evaporation, condensation, and coalescence processes. Some dry aerosols are water-soluble and can also grow by condensation. Aerosols are important in the atmosphere as nuclei for the condensation of water droplets and ice crystals, as absorbers and scatterers of radiation, and as participants in various chemical cycles.

Above the tropopause, the composition of the atmosphere begins to change, primarily because of the decomposition of molecules by ultraviolet radiation and the subsequent chemistry. For example, decomposition of O_2 produces an O_3 layer in the stratosphere. Although the peak value of f for O_3 in this layer is only about 10^{-5}, this amount is sufficient to shield the Earth from biologically lethal ultraviolet radiation. About 160 mi (100 km) above the surface, ultraviolet dissociation of O_2 is so intense that the predominant atmospheric constituents become N_2 and O. There is also a layer of aerosols in the lower stratosphere composed primarily of sulfuric acid and dust particles. The sulfuric acid is probably produced by oxidation and hydration of sulfur gases. This same process, strongly amplified, is the probable source of the much thicker clouds of sulfuric acid recently identified on Venus. SEE ATMOSPHERIC OZONE.

A number of radioactive nuclides are formed naturally in the atmosphere by decay of Rn and by cosmic radiation. Radon, produced by decay of U and Th in the crust, enters the atmosphere, where it in turn decays to produce a number of radioactive heavy metals. These metal atoms become attached to aerosol particles and sediment out. Cosmic rays striking N_2, O_2, and Ar principally in the stratosphere give rise to a number of radioactive isotopes, including ^{14}C, ^{7}Be, ^{10}Be, and ^{3}H. The incorporation of ^{14}C into organic matter, where it decays with a half-life of about 5600

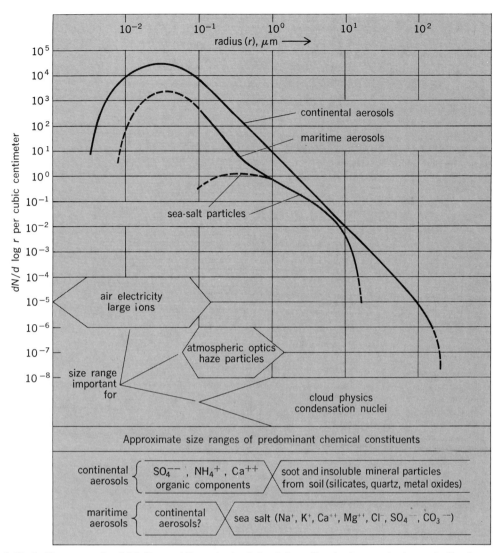

Fig. 1. Chart of the average size distributions and the predominant chemical constituents of some natural aerosols. The size ranges which are important for the various fields of meteorology are shown.

years, forms the basis of the radiocarbon dating method. In addition to naturally occurring radioactivity, large quantities of radioactive material have been injected into the atmosphere as a result of nuclear bomb tests. The most dangerous isotope is ^{90}Sr, which can be incorporated into human bones, where it radioactively decays with a half-life of about 28 years. Both natural and anthropogenic radioisotopes have been used as tracers for tropospheric and stratospheric motions.

Atmospheric chemical models. In order both to adequately understand the present chemistry of the atmosphere and to predict the effects of anthropogenic perturbations on this chemistry, it has been necessary to construct quantitative chemical models of the atmosphere. In general, gas and particle mixing ratios show considerable variation with space and time. This variability can be quantitatively analyzed using the continuity equation for the particular species. In terms of χ, time t, wind velocity $\mathbf{v}$, average particle sedimentation velocity W_p, and air density ρ, this equation is conveniently written as shown below, where

$$\frac{\partial \overline{\chi}}{\partial t} \approx -\overline{\mathbf{v}} \cdot \nabla \overline{\chi} - \frac{W_p}{\overline{\rho}} \frac{\partial (\overline{\rho}\overline{\chi})}{\partial z} - \frac{1}{\overline{\rho}} \nabla \cdot (\overline{\rho \chi' \mathbf{v}'}) + \frac{d\overline{\chi}}{dt}$$

an overbar denotes an average over a time scale that is long compared to that associated with turbulence, and a prime denotes an instantaneous fluctuation from this average value. The first term on the right-hand side of the equation describes the changes in $\overline{\chi}$ due to the mean atmospheric circulation; the second term gives the $\overline{\chi}$ alternation due to sedimentation which is, of course, zero for gases; the third term denotes fluctuations in $\overline{\chi}$ due to turbulence or eddies, and in this term the eddy flux $\overline{\rho} \; \overline{\chi' \mathbf{v}'}$ is often roughly approximated by $-K\overline{\rho}\nabla\overline{\chi}$, where K is a three-dimensional matrix of eddy diffusion coefficients; and the last term describes changes in $\overline{\chi}$ caused by chemical production or destruction which may involve simple condensation or evaporation or more complex chemical reactions.

From the equation above, it is seen that the variability of gas or aerosol concentrations is generally due to a combination of transport and true production or destruction. If a constituent has a destruction time T_0, then $d\overline{\chi}/dt = -\overline{\chi}/T_0$, and the equation then implies that the larger the T_0 value the less variability one expects to see in the atmosphere. A constituent for which $\overline{\chi}$ is completely independent of space and time is said to be well mixed. For example, the very long-lived gases N_2, O_2, ^{40}Ar, Ne, ^4He, Kr, and Xe are essentially well mixed in the lower atmosphere.

Atmospheric chemical models involve simultaneous solution of the above equation for each atmospheric constituent involved in a particular chemical cycle. Often, simplified versions of this equation can be utilized, for example, when chemical lifetimes are much shorter than typical atmospheric transport times, or vice versa. Models for the ozone layer have now progressed from historical one-dimensional models which neglected transport to sophisticated three-dimensional models which, in addition to solving the above equation, including transport, solve the equations of motion to obtain **v** as a function of position and time.

Chemical cycles. In studying the chemical cycles of atmospheric gases, it is important to consider both the overall budgets on a global scale and the kinetics of the elementary chemical reactions on a local scale. The study of chemical cycles is in its infancy. Some of the minor details in the cycles outlined below may be subject to change, but this present lack of definition does not detract from their importance.

Carbon cycle. The atmospheric cycle which is of primary significance to life on Earth is that of carbon, which is illustrated in **Fig. 2**. The CO_2 content of the oceans is about 60 times that of the atmosphere and is controlled by the temperature and acidity of sea water. Release of CO_2 into the atmosphere over tropical oceans and uptake by polar oceans result in a CO_2 residence time of about 5 years. On the other hand, the cycle of CO_2 through the biosphere has a turnover time of a few decades. The amount of CO_2 buried as carbonate in limestone, marble, chalk, dolomite, and related deposits is about 600 times that in the ocean-atmosphere system. If all this CO_2 were released to the atmosphere, a massive CO_2 atmosphere similar to that on the planet Venus would result. Because CO is a poisonous gas, its production from automobile engines in urban areas must be closely monitored. On a global scale, the principal sources of CO are combustion of oil and coal and oxidation of the CH_4 produced naturally during anaerobic decay, and oxidation of land plant emanations such as isoprene.

Sulfur cycle. The important aspects of the sulfur cycle are also illustrated in Fig. 2. Sulfur dioxide is pro-

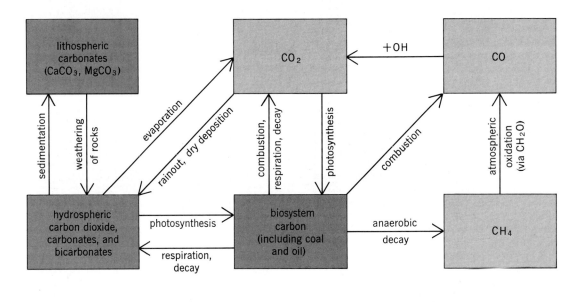

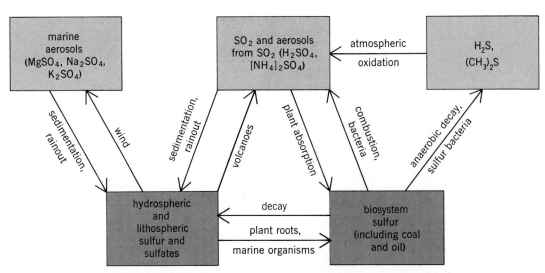

Fig. 2. Carbon and sulfur cycles.

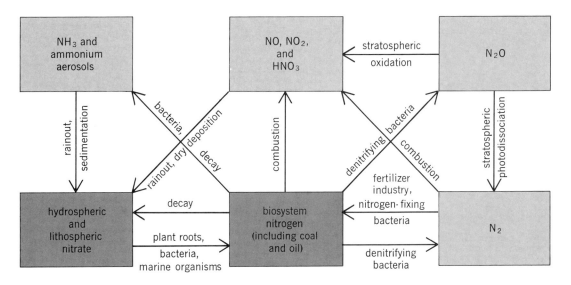

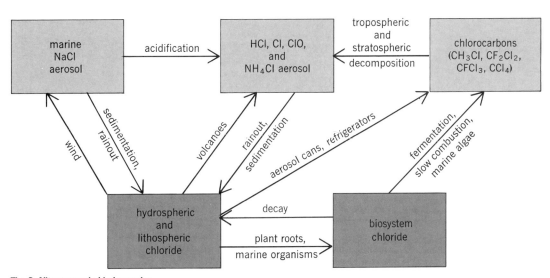

Fig. 3. Nitrogen and chlorine cycles.

duced in the atmosphere by combustion of high-sulfur fuels, by plants and bacteria, and by oxidation of H_2S introduced by anaerobic decay. On a global scale, the SO_2 budget is perturbed significantly by the anthropogenic source, and this perturbation is even more pronounced in urban localities. Oxidation of SO_2 produces sulfuric acid, which is a particularly noxious pollutant; thus regulation of high-sulfur fuel combustion, at least on the local scale, is now required.

Nitrogen cycle. The nitrogen cycle is shown in **Fig. 3**. The nitrogen oxides (NO, NO_2) are important because they are intimately involved in the chemistry of smog and of stratospheric ozone. The main source of smog NO_2 is fuel combustion. The main source of stratospheric NO and NO_2 is decomposition of the N_2O produced from soil nitrate ions (NO_2^-) by denitrifying bacteria. There had been considerable concern about injection of nitrogen oxides directly into the stratosphere by supersonic aircraft. Projected fleet levels for the year 2000 suggest a future anthropogenic source of these oxides comparable to their natural source. Initial studies suggested that such a perturbation would cause a very significant depletion of stratospheric ozone, but later studies suggest a much smaller impact.

Chlorine cycle. The main natural source for atmospheric chlorine is acidification of chloride aerosols producing HCl near the surface. The chlorine cycle (Fig. 3) has received considerable attention because any significant concentrations of Cl and ClO in the stratosphere will lead to depletion of ozone in a manner similar to that caused by NO and NO_2. Because the HCl produced at the ground is severely depleted by rain-out, it does not give rise to significant stratospheric chlorine concentrations.

However, the chlorocarbons CCl_4, $CFCL_3$, CF_2Cl_2, and CH_3Cl are relatively insoluble and are not rained out. They appear to decompose in the stratosphere, releasing chlorine; an unchecked buildup of these compounds could therefore conceivably lead to significant ozone depletion. The compounds CF_2Cl_2 and $CFCl_3$ are manufactured for use as propellants in aerosol cans, for use in refrigerators and air conditioners, and for manufacture of plastic foams. Methyl chloride is produced naturally by microbial fermentation and by combustion of vegetation, and CCl_4 is probably derived from both natural and industrial sources.

Ronald G. Prinn

Bibliography. M. M. Benarie, *Atmospheric Pollution, 1982*, 1982; C. E. Junge, *Air Chemistry and Radioactivity*, 1963; J. A. Logan et al., Atmospheric chemistry: Response to human influence, *Phil. Trans. Roy. Soc.*, 290:187–234, 1978; E. Meszaros, *Atmospheric Chemistry: Fundamental Aspects*, 1981; W. Strauss (ed.), *Air Pollution Control*, pt. 2, 1972.

Atmospheric electricity

The electrical processes constantly taking place in the lower atmosphere. This activity is of two kinds, the intense local electrification accompanying storms, and the much weaker fair-weather electrical activity over the entire Earth produced by the many electrified storms continuously in progress.

The relative importance of each of the various mechanisms that cause storms to accumulate electrically charged particles is unknown, and the role of atmospheric electricity in meteorology has not been determined. Some scientists believe that electrical processes may be of importance in precipitation formation and in severe tornadoes. SEE TORNADO.

Disturbed-weather phenomena. The usual height of a thunderstorm is about 6 mi (10 km); however, thunderstorms can be as low as 2.5 mi (4 km) or as high as 13 mi (20 km). A common feature of these storms is their strong updrafts and downdrafts, which often have speeds in excess of 65 mi/h (30 m/s).

As the result of various electrification processes, regions of charged water and ice particles are formed, positive in one part and negative in another part of the cloud. In over 90% of such clouds the positive charge accumulates in the upper part and the negative charge accumulates in the lower part, thus forming a positive, vertical dipole. In a small percentage, the polarity of the dipole may be inverted. When the electrified regions have dimensions of miles and contain charges of tens of coulombs, the electric field is of the order of several hundred kilovolts per meter, sufficient in intensity to cause dielectric breakdown in the form of lightning. A majority of these flashes, known as intracloud discharges, exchange charge between the upper positive and the lower negative charged regions within the cloud. A minority, the cloud-to-ground discharges, carry charge from the lower negatively charged region to the ground. An average thunderstorm generates a charging current of roughly an ampere and a potential of a hundred million volts that causes lightning flashes to occur every 10 s, each of which transports about 10 coulombs of charge. SEE LIGHTNING.

Because the atmosphere high above the cloud and the liquid and solid surface of the Earth beneath it are good conductors of electricity, the external electric fields produced by thunderclouds cause electric currents to flow between the Earth and its atmosphere over the entire planet. The atmosphere conducts electricity because it contains ions, that is, small electrically charged clusters of molecules, which move under the influence of an electric field. The upper level of the atmosphere above about 24 mi (40 km), known as the ionosphere, is a good conductor because of the high concentrations of electrons and ions produced by solar and extraterrestrial ionizing radiation. These move rapidly in the upper rarefied atmosphere under the influence of electrical forces. In this region the air is so conductive that the time required for a charge to leak away, the electrical relaxation time, may be as little as 10^{-7} s. At lower levels, because the atmosphere is more dense and there is much less ionizing radiation, it is a much poorer conductor. At sea level, where ions are produced at the low rate of about 10 ion pairs per cubic centimeter per second by cosmic rays and terrestrial radioactivity, the atmosphere has very little conductivity. Here the electrical relaxation time can be 10^3 s or longer. If suspended cloud or aerosol particles are present, the conductivity can be further reduced because many of the ions lose their mobility by becoming attached to these particles. In clouds, fog, or smoke the electrical relaxation time can become as much as 10^4 s.

During the half hour or more that an average thunderstorm is electrically active, it generates an electric current of about an ampere that deposits negative charge onto the Earth and an equal amount of positive charge into the atmosphere. Above the thundercloud the transfer of charge from the cloud to the conductive upper atmosphere is accomplished by the motion of positive ions away from the cloud and negative ions toward the cloud. At the upper cloud surface the transfer of charge is accomplished by downward-moving negative ions which become attached to the water particles in the top of the cloud. Although the details are not clear, the primary transfer of charge within the cloud occurs as the result of the downward motion of negatively charged cloud and precipitation particles and the upward motion of positively charged cloud particles. Beneath the cloud the charge is brought to the Earth by several processes. Cloud-to-ground lightning flashes bring down negative charges. Falling precipitation can transfer charge of either sign. Point discharge, a weak and usually invisible dielectric breakdown process, occurs from vegetation and other elevated points beneath the thundercloud under the influence of its strong electric field. This introduces positive charge into the atmosphere and deposits an equal negative charge on the Earth.

The combined effect of approximately a thousand thunderstorms in progress at any given time in the Earth's atmosphere provides an electric current of about a kiloampere that continuously deposits negative charge on the surface of the Earth and an equal and opposite charge in the atmosphere.

Fair-weather field. The potential of the upper conductive atmosphere reaches an equilibrium value of approximately 200 or 300 kV with respect to the surface of the Earth when the fair-weather electric current flowing from the atmosphere to the surface of the globe balances the generating electric currents being produced by the thunderstorms. Under these conditions, the Earth carries a negative charge of approximately 10^6 C, which creates a fair-weather electric field of a few hundred volts per meter at its surface. The resultant fair-weather current brings positive ions to Earth at a rate of approximately 2.6 microamperes/mi² ($1 \mu A/km^2$).

The fair-weather field at the Earth's surface is observed to fluctuate somewhat in space and time, largely as a result of air motions and local variations in atmospheric conductivity. However, in undisturbed locations far at sea or over the polar regions, the field is observed to have a diurnal variation of about 20%, independent of position or local time. According to

Greenwich Mean Time it is at a minimum a few hours after midnight and a maximum in the late afternoon. This corresponds to the similar diurnal variation of thunderstorm activity over the globe, which is at a minimum when the Sun is shining on the vast expanse of the Pacific Ocean and at a maximum when it is shining on Earth's large land masses.

Cloud electrification mechanisms. It is recognized that a variety of physical processes can contribute to the accumulation of charged cloud particles that cause lightning. However, the relative importance of these processes has not yet been established. Electrification is produced when falling precipitation particles collide with smaller, slower falling cloud particles and exchange charge. This may occur as the result of contact electrification between the colliding surfaces or by inductive charge transfer caused by the influence of the ambient electric field. Falling precipitation particles also may become charged under the influence of the ambient electric field, which causes them selectively to capture one polarity of the ions. Charge may be introduced into the cloud by conduction from the upper atmosphere, by the advection of ions released by point discharge, and by the charges deposited by lightning.

To form the large charged regions and the extensive electrical fields required for lightning, it is necessary that the charged particles be moved in opposition to electrical forces over large distances. Approximately 100 MW is required to maintain the electric field of the thundercloud. This power can be supplied by the action of gravitational forces on charged precipitation particles and by the movement of charged particles that results from the strong updrafts and downdrafts within the thundercloud. It will not be possible to have a satisfactory understanding of the origins of thunderstorm electricity until a great deal more is known about how the air moves within and around the cloud and about the details of the nature and location of various charged cloud particles. SEE CLOUD PHYSICS.

Effects of thunderstorm electricity. Electrical activity of a thunderstorm represents no more than a few percent of its total energy. It is probably for this reason that most meteorologists assume that atmospheric electricity plays a negligible role in weather processes. However, evidence has accumulated that electrical forces, particularly those generated as the result of lightning discharges, may play an important part by speeding up the growth of precipitation particles. Radar observations have shown that in the region of the cloud in which lightning occurs, heavy rain can form in less than a minute. Because the fall of precipitation is known to have large effects on the dynamics of clouds and storm systems, thunderstorm electricity may in this indirect way produce significant effects on meteorological processes.

If electrical forces can influence the behavior of clouds, it follows that whatever affects electrification may also affect the weather. For example, increases in conductivity of the atmosphere above thunderstorms caused by solar activity or decreases caused by aerosols from volcanic activity may be of importance.

It has been suggested that the relationship between thunderstorm and fair-weather electricity may be more complicated than just cause and effect. Experiments have been conducted to determine what would happen if the normal positive charge in air entering a growing cloud were reversed by negative charge released from a wire maintained at a high negative potential. The results showed that on more than four occasions when the clouds over the wire grew and became thunderstorms they were of abnormal polarity, with dominant positive charges instead of the usual negative charges in the lower part of the cloud. This finding suggests that in accord with various influence theories the electrification process in thunderclouds may be initiated and its polarity determined by the small fair-weather charges present in the atmosphere. Further evidence that fair-weather atmospheric electrical variables may affect thunderstorm electrification is provided by an analysis of lightning frequency during the summer of 1986 in northeastern Sweden, where there was a high level of ionization produced by radioactive fallout from the Chernobyl (Soviet Union) nuclear power plant disaster. The analysis showed that in this region, where the air conductivity in the lower levels was increased by over a factor of 10, there was an abnormal increase in the frequency of lightning. It is also suggestive that measurements above thunderstorms made in the southeastern United States from a high-altitude airplane show that the average rate at which lightning flashes in a storm are transferring charge is approximately equal to the conduction current that is flowing from the top of that storm to the global circuit.

Other discoveries have presented new challenges to the various explanations that have been proposed for thunderstorm electrification. Measurements of cloud-to-ground lightning that are made over very large areas with lightning-detection networks show that in the continental United States the fraction of cloud-to-ground flashes that bring positive charge to the Earth increases from a few percent in the summer to as much as 50% during the winter months. Space exploration discloses that intense electrical activity is also present in the very different atmospheres of other planets. Lightning has been reported on Venus, Jupiter, and Saturn. SEE THUNDERSTORM; WEATHER.

Bernard Vonnegut

Bibliography. J. A. Chalmers, *Atmospheric Electricity*, 1957; Geophysics Study Committee, Commission on Physical Sciences, Mathematics, and Resources, *The Earth's Electrical Environment*, 1986; C. Magono, *Thunderstorms*, 1980.

Atmospheric general circulation

The statistical description of atmospheric motions over the Earth, their role in transporting energy, and the transformations among different forms of energy. Through their influence on the pressure distributions that drive the winds, spatial variations of heating and cooling generate air circulations, but these are continually dissipated by friction. While large day-to-day and seasonal changes occur, the mean circulation during a given season tends to be much the same from year to year. Thus, in the long run and for the global atmosphere as a whole, the generation of motions nearly balances the dissipation. The same is true of the long-term balance between solar radiation absorbed and infrared radiation emitted by the Earth–atmosphere system, as evidenced by its relatively constant temperature. Both air and ocean currents, which are mainly driven by the winds, transport heat. Hence the atmospheric and oceanic general circulations form cooperative systems. *See Maritime Meteorology*.

Owing to the more direct incidence of solar radiation in low latitudes and to reflection from clouds, snow, and ice, which are more extensive at high latitudes, the solar radiation absorbed by the Earth–atmosphere system is about three times as great in the equatorial belt as at the poles, on the annual average. Infrared emission is, however, only about 20% greater at low than at high latitudes. Thus in low latitudes (between about 35°N and 35°S) the Earth–atmosphere system is, on the average, heated and in higher latitudes cooled by radiation. The Earth's surface absorbs more radiative heat than it emits, whereas the reverse is true for the atmosphere. Therefore, heat must be transferred generally poleward and upward through processes other than radiation. At the Earth–atmosphere interface, this transfer occurs in the form of turbulent flux of sensible heat and through evapotranspiration (flux of latent heat). In the atmosphere the latent heat is released in connection with condensation of water vapor. *See Climatology; Heat balance, terrestrial atmospheric*.

Considering the atmosphere alone, the heat gain by condensation and the heat transfer from the Earth's surface exceed the net radiative heat loss in low latitudes. The reverse is true in higher latitudes. The meridional transfer of energy, necessary to balance these heat gains and losses, is accomplished by air currents. These take the form of organized circula-

tions, whose dominant features are notably different in the tropical belt (roughly the half of the Earth between latitudes 30°N and 30°S) and in extratropical latitudes. *See Meteorology; Storm*.

Principal circulations. Characteristic circulations over the Northern Hemisphere are sketched in **Fig. 1**. In the upper troposphere, there are two principal jet-stream systems: the subtropical jet (STJ) near latitude 30°, and the polar-front jet (PFJ), with large-amplitude long waves and superimposed shorter waves associated with cyclone-scale disturbances. The long waves on the polar-front jet move slowly eastward, and the shorter waves move rapidly. At the Earth's surface, northeast and southeast trade winds of the two hemispheres meet at the intertropical convergence zone (ITCZ), in the vicinity of which extensive lines and large clusters of convective clouds are concentrated. Westward-moving waves and vortices form near the intertropical convergence zone and, in summer, within the trades. Heat released by condensation in convective clouds of the intertropical convergence zone, and the mass of air conveyed upward in them, drive meridional circulations (right of Fig. 1), whose upper-level poleward branches generate the subtropical jet stream at their poleward boundaries.

In extratropical latitudes, the circulation is dominated by cyclones and anticyclones. Cyclones develop mainly on the polar front, where the temperature contrast between polar and tropical air masses is concentrated, in association with upper-level waves on the

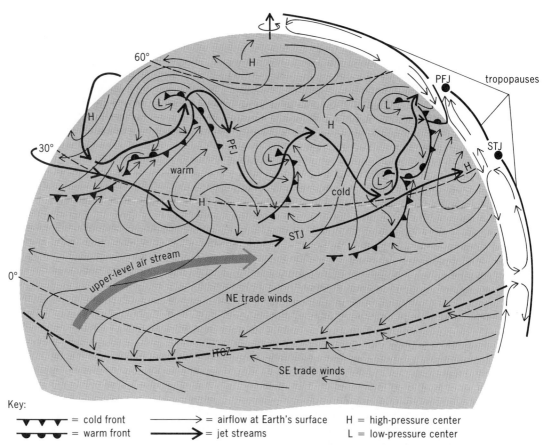

Key:

| ▼▼▼ = cold front | ——→ = airflow at Earth's surface | H = high-pressure center |
| ●●● = warm front | ➤ = jet streams | L = low-pressure center |

Fig. 1. Schematic circulations over the Northern Hemisphere in winter. The intertropical convergence zone (ITCZ) lies entirely north of the Equator in the summer. Eastward acceleration in the upper-level tropical airstream is due to Earth rotation and generates the subtropical jet stream (STJ). The vertical section (right) shows the dominant meridional circulation in the tropics and shows airstreams relative to the polar front in middle latitudes.

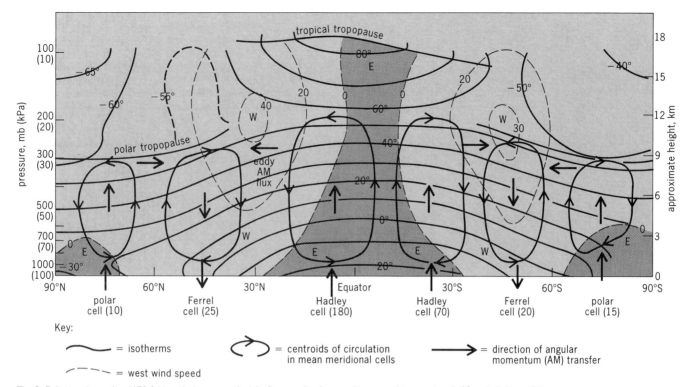

Fig. 2. Pole-to-pole section (450-fold vertical exaggeration) in January showing zonally averaged temperature in °C and wind speed in m/s; W and E denote westerlies and easterlies, respectively. Mean meridional cells are named and their intensities are given in terms of mass flow in megatons per second. °F = (°C × 1.8) + 32. 1 m/s = 2 knots. 1 km = 0.6 mi.

polar-front jet stream. In winter, cold outbreaks of polar air from the east coasts of continents over the warmer oceans result in intense transfer of heat and water vapor into the atmosphere. Outbreaks penetrating the tropics also represent a sporadic exchange in which polar air becomes transformed into tropical air. Tropical airstreams, poleward on the west sides of the subtropical highs, then supply heat and water vapor to the extratropical disturbances. *SEE FRONT.*

The characteristic flow in cyclones takes the form of slantwise descending motions on their west sides and ascent to their east in which extensive clouds and precipitation form. Heat that is released in condensation drives the ascending branch, and the descending branch consists of polar air that has been cooled by radiation in higher latitudes. When viewed relative to the meandering polar-front zone (right of Fig. 1), the combined sinking of cold air and ascent of warm air represents a conversion of potential energy into kinetic energy. This process maintains the polar jet stream. The branches of the circulation transfer heat both upward, to balance the radiative heat loss by the atmosphere, and poleward, to balance the radiative heat deficit in high latitudes.

Mean temperature and wind. A principal object of general circulation studies has been to explain the zonal mean (long-term average around latitude zones) structure of the atmosphere, shown for January in **Fig. 2**. The zonal (west-east) wind component is almost everywhere dominant and is in quasigeostrophic balance with the mean meridional pressure gradient. The pressure gradient changes with height in accordance with the distribution of air density, which at a given pressure is inverse to temperature. Hence the distribution of zonal wind is related to that of temperature, as expressed by Eq. (1), where u denotes zonal

$$\frac{\partial \overline{u}}{\partial z} = -\frac{g}{(2\Omega \sin \phi)\overline{T}} \frac{\partial \overline{T}}{\partial y} \qquad (1)$$

wind component; z, height above sea level; g, acceleration of gravity; Ω, angular velocity of the Earth; ϕ, latitude; T, Kelvin temperature; and y, distance northward. Overbars denote values averaged over longitude and time.

Only in the lowest kilometer or so, where surface friction disturbs the geostrophic balance, and in the vicinity of the Equator is the mean meridional (south-north) component comparable to the zonal wind. Because of the nature of the atmosphere as a shallow layer, the mean vertical wind component is weak. Whereas the magnitude of the mean zonal wind varies 100 mi/h (45 m/s), and the mean meridional wind up to 6.5 mi/h (3 m/s), the mean vertical wind nowhere exceeds 0.02 mi/h (1 cm/s). The vertical component cannot be observed directly, but can be calculated from the distribution of horizontal motions.

In the troposphere and lower stratosphere, the zonal circulation is similar in winter and summer, with easterlies in low latitudes and westerlies in higher latitudes, except in small regions of low-level easterlies around the poles. The strongest west winds are, in the winter hemispheres, observed near latitude 30° at about 7 mi (12 km). In summer, the west-wind maxima are weaker and located farther poleward.

In the troposphere, the zonal wind increases upward according to Eq. (1) and with a general poleward decrease in temperature. In the lower stratosphere over most of the globe, this temperature gradient is reversed, and the wind decreases with height. Above about 12 mi (20 km), separate wind systems exist, with prevailing easterly winds in summer and westerlies in winter that attain speeds up to

130–175 mi/h (60–80 m/s) near 40 mi (60 km) height in high latitudes. *See Jet stream*.

The much weaker meridional circulation consists of six separate cells. Their general locations and nomenclatures are shown in Fig. 2, along with the approximate circulations in terms of mass flux. For each cell, only central streamlines are shown, but these represent flows that are several kilometers deep in the horizontal branches, while each vertical branch represents gentle ascending or descending motions over latitude belts some thousands of kilometers wide. The tropical Hadley cells, best developed in the winter hemisphere, are mainly responsible for maintaining the westerly winds as described below.

Angular momentum balance. The motion of the atmosphere plus the eastward speed of a point on the Earth's surface represent the total motion relative to the Earth's axis. The angular momentum (M) of a unit mass of air is given by Eq. (2), where a represents

$$M = (u + \Omega a \cos \phi) \, a \cos \phi \qquad (2)$$

the radius of the Earth and the other terms are as defined for Eq. (1). Considering the mean value in a zonal ring, this quantity is conserved unless the ring is subjected to a torque.

The surface easterlies in low latitudes and westerlies in middle latitudes (Fig. 2) exert the principal torques upon the atmosphere, due to frictional drags that are opposite to the direction of the surface winds.

Since the torques would tend to diminish the westerlies and easterlies, and this is not observed to occur over the long run, it follows that angular momentum has to be transferred from the belts of surface easterlies to the zones of westerlies. Calculations show that this meridional flux occurs mainly in the upper troposphere. Hence angular momentum has to be brought upward from the surface layer in low latitudes, transferred poleward, and ultimately brought down to the Earth in the belt of westerlies (Fig. 2).

The vertical transfers are mainly accomplished by the mean meridional circulations, involving the second term on the right-hand side of Eq. (2), which is much larger than the first. Considering the $\cos^2 \phi$ factor in this term, there is a net upward transfer by the Hadley cells since their ascending branches are at lower latitudes than the descending branches. Similarly, the opposite Ferrel circulations bring angular momentum downward. With conservation of total angular momentum in the poleward upper branches of the Hadley cells, u in Eq. (2) increases at the expense of the Ω term. This process accounts for the generation of the strongest upper-level westerly winds in subtropical latitudes. From this source, eddies (waves in which poleward flow is associated with a stronger west-wind component than in equatorward flow) transfer angular momentum poleward to sustain the west winds at higher latitudes.

Heat energy balance. Maintenance of an average temperature distribution such as in Fig. 2 depends upon a balance between the effects of heat sources and sinks (for example, radiation) and of heat transport by air motion. The sources and sinks are largely a function of latitude and elevation, such that meridional and vertical fluxes of heat energy are required. Two methods by which these fluxes are calculated from different kinds of observations give results that offer a check upon one another.

In the first method estimates are made of the rate of change of any property X per unit area of the

Table 1. Sources of atmospheric properties

Different sources	$d\bar{X}/dt$
Atmospheric heat	$\bar{R}_a + \bar{Q}_s + L\bar{P}$
Latent heat	$L(\bar{E} - \bar{P})$
Heat of Earth's surface	$\bar{R}_e - \bar{Q}_s - L\bar{E}$
Heat of atmosphere and Earth	$\bar{R}_a + \bar{R}_e$

Earth's surface due to sources and sinks. To maintain an unchanged condition, their integrated value, over the area north of a latitude ϕ, must equal the northward flux F_ϕ of the property across the latitude circle. This requirement is expressed by Eq. (3), in which t denotes time.

$$F_\phi = -2\pi a^2 \int_\phi^{90°\text{N}} \frac{d\bar{X}}{dt} \cos \phi \, d\phi \qquad (3)$$

By employing this method, the energy balance may be calculated by substituting the quantities summarized in **Table 1** into Eq. (3). The listed heat sources comprise R_a, net (absorbed minus emitted) radiation of the atmosphere; R_e, net radiation at the Earth's surface; Q_s, flux of sensible heat from the surface to the atmosphere; LE, flux of latent heat from the surface (E denoting rate of evapotranspiration and L, heat of vaporization); and LP, release of latent heat in the atmosphere as estimated from the observed rate of precipitation P.

The second method is to compute the fluxes directly from aerological observations (made by balloon-borne radiosondes). If x denotes a given property per unit mass of air, the flux is given by Eq. (4),

$$F_\phi = \frac{2\pi a \cos \phi}{g} \int_0^{p_0} (\bar{x}\,\bar{v} + \overline{x'v'}) \, dp \qquad (4)$$

where v is the meridional wind component (positive northward). The integration, with pressure p as a vertical coordinate (related to height z as in Fig. 2), is extended from the bottom ($p = p_0$) to the top of the atmosphere ($p = 0$). Here $\bar{x}$ and $\bar{v}$ denote values averaged over time and longitude, and x' and v' are deviations from these mean values at a given pressure surface. A corresponding expression can be written for the vertical fluxes.

The forms of heat energy x are listed in **Table 2**. The atmospheric energy comprises the sum $c_p T + gz$, the two quantities being interchangeable during vertical air movement; decompression of rising air dimin-

Table 2. Atmospheric properties used for flux computations

Property	x (per unit mass)*
Atmospheric energy	
Sensible heat	$c_p T$
Potential energy	gz
Total atmospheric energy	$c_p T + gz$
Latent heat	Lq

*Here c_p is specific heat of air; q is specific humidity, or mass of water vapor per unit mass of air.

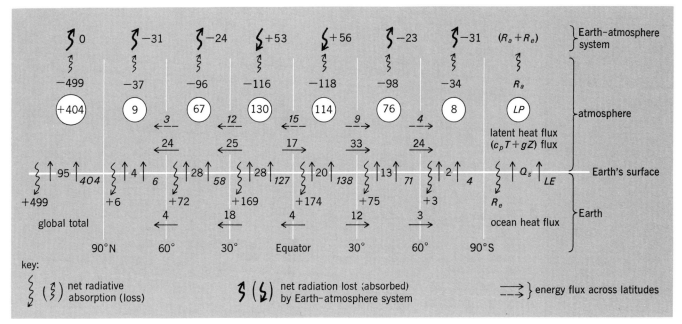

Fig. 3. Annual heat balance for the Earth as a whole and for each 30° latitude belt. Units are 10^{14} W. All values are keyed to the column at right. Italic numbers apply to water vapor (latent heat) flux.

ishes its sensible heat content by an amount equal to the increase of potential energy associated with change of elevation. Almost everywhere $c_pT + gz$ increases upward, and Lq generally but not always decreases upward.

The first term of Eq. (4) represents the mean meridional circulations in Fig. 2, which dominate in the tropical belt. Water vapor conveyed equatorward by the trade winds is condensed in tall convective clouds near the intertropical convergence zone. As a result of latent heat release, the atmospheric energy ($c_pT + gz$) is augmented, so that the upper-level flow of a Hadley cell carries more heat poleward than does the equatorward low-level flow. The second term represents eddy fluxes, dominant in subtropical and higher latitudes, associated with cyclones and anticyclones (Fig. 1) whose poleward flows are both warmest and richest in water vapor.

Various components of the energy balance are summarized, by 30° belts of latitude, in **Fig. 3**. Of the net radiation absorbed at the Earth's surface over the whole globe, 81% is expended in evaporation. Correspondingly, 81% of the net radiative loss by the atmosphere is compensated by release of latent heat when water vapor condenses and falls out as rain, snow, or hail, and 19% by transfer of sensible heat from the Earth. In the tropical belt 30°N–30°S, the Earth–atmosphere system gains heat by radiation; the excess is exported to higher latitudes as atmospheric heat and latent heat, and by ocean currents. Considering the tropical-latitude and temperate-latitude belts of the two hemispheres, significant differences in the apportionments of evaporation and sensible heat transfer from the Earth to the atmosphere, and of the meridional transports of energy in the various forms, arise from the greater dominance of continents in the Northern Hemisphere. On the annual average, water-vapor-laden trade winds (the lower branches of Hadley cells in Fig. 2) converge at about 5°N, where the greatest precipitation is observed. Minima of precipitation occur in the belts near 30°N, where mean descending motions occur. Secondary maxima of

precipitation, in latitudes 40–50°, are associated with frequent extratropical cyclones. SEE HYDROMETEOROLOGY.

The frequency and intensity of cyclones, and the contrasts between their cold and warm air masses, are much greater in winter than in summer in the Northern Hemisphere; these variations are much less pronounced in the oceanic Southern Hemisphere. Thus there is a fourfold greater poleward transport of sensible heat in middle latitudes of the Northern Hemisphere in winter than in summer, contrasted with only about a 30% seasonal variation in the Southern Hemisphere. In the tropics, large seasonal changes in the intensities of the Hadley circulation, together with a migration of the rain belt of the intertropical convergence zone (Fig. 1), are most pronounced in the monsoon regions of Asia-Australia and Africa.

Between late spring and early autumn a given hemisphere receives solar radiation far in excess of the amount it loses by infrared radiation. The excess heat is stored mainly in the oceans during the warm seasons and given up to the atmosphere as sensible and latent heat during the cooler seasons. Thus the oceans serve as an energy reservoir that tempers the seasonal changes of atmospheric temperature over them and over neighboring land areas invaded by marine air masses. SEE MARITIME METEOROLOGY.

C. W. Newton

Bibliography. J. R. Holton, *An Introduction to Dynamic Meteorology*, 2d ed., 1979; J. P. Peixóto and A. H. Oort, Physics of climate, *Rev. Mod. Phys.*, 56:365–429, 1984; S. Petterssen, *Introduction to Meteorology*, 3d ed., 1969.

Atmospheric ozone

Ozone is found in trace quantities throughout the atmosphere, the largest concentrations being located in a layer in the lower stratosphere between the altitudes of 9 and 18 mi (15 and 30 km) [**Fig. 1**]. This ozone

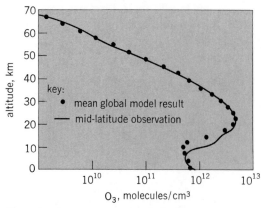

Fig. 1. The global average ozone concentrations predicted in the MIT Stratospheric Circulation Model are compared with midlatitude rocket observations of ozone. (*After D. Cunnold et al., A three-dimensional dynamical-chemical model of atmospheric ozone, J. Atmos. Sci., 32:170–194, 1975*)

results from the dissociation by solar ultraviolet radiation of molecular oxygen in the upper atmosphere and nitrogen dioxide in the lower atmosphere.

Although present in only trace quantities, this atmospheric ozone plays a critical role for the biosphere by absorbing the ultraviolet radiation with wavelength λ between 240 and 320 nanometers, which would otherwise be transmitted to the Earth's surface. This radiation is lethal to simple unicellular organisms (algae, bacteria, protozoa) and to the surface cells of higher plants and animals. It also damages the genetic material of cells (DNA) and is responsible for sunburn in human skin. In addition, the incidence of skin cancer has been statistically correlated with the observed surface intensities of the ultraviolet wavelengths between 290 and 320 nm, which are not totally absorbed by the ozone layer.

Ozone also plays an important role in photochemical smog and in the purging of trace species from the lower atmosphere. Furthermore, it heats the upper atmosphere by absorbing solar ultraviolet and visible radiation ($\lambda < 710$ nm) and thermal infrared radiation ($\lambda \approx 9.6$ micrometers). As a consequence, the temperature increases steadily from about $-60°F$ (220 K) at the tropopause (5–10 mi or 8–16 km altitude) to about 45°F (280 K) at the stratopause (30 mi or 50 km altitude). This ozone heating provides the major energy source for driving the circulation of the upper stratosphere and mesosphere. *See* ATMOSPHERE.

Chemistry of stratospheric ozone. Above about 19 mi (30 km), oxygen is dissociated during the daytime by ultraviolet photons, $h\nu$, as shown in reaction (1).

$$O_2 + h\nu \rightarrow O + O \quad \lambda < 240 \text{ nm} \quad (1)$$

The oxygen atoms produced then form ozone by reaction (2), where M is an arbitrary molecule required

$$O + O_2 + M \rightarrow O_3 + M \quad (2)$$

to conserve energy and momentum in the reaction. Ozone has a short lifetime during the day because of photodissociation, as shown in reaction (3). However, except above 54 mi (90 km), where O_2 begins to become a minor component of the atmosphere, reaction (3) does not lead to a net destruction of ozone. In-

$$O_3 + h\nu \rightarrow O_2 + O \quad \lambda < 7100 \text{ A or } 710 \text{ nm} \quad (3)$$

stead the O is almost exclusively converted back to O_3 by reaction (2). If the odd oxygen concentration is defined as the sum of the O_3 and O concentrations, then odd oxygen is produced by reaction (1). It can be seen that reactions (2) and (3) do not affect the odd oxygen concentrations but merely define the ratio of O to O_3. Because the rate of reaction (2) decreases with altitude while that for reaction (3) increases, most of the odd oxygen below 36 mi (60 km) is in the form of O_3 while above 36 mi (60 km) it is in the form of O.

Studies have disclosed that reaction (4) is respon-

$$O + O_3 \rightarrow O_2 + O_2 \quad (4)$$

sible for a small fraction of the odd oxygen removal rate. A significant fraction of the removal is caused by the trace gases nitric oxide, NO, and nitrogen dioxide, NO_2, which serve to catalyze reaction (4) by way of reactions (5) and (6).

$$NO + O_3 \rightarrow NO_2 + O_2 \quad (5)$$

$$NO_2 + O \rightarrow NO + O_2 \quad (6)$$

This catalytic destruction cycle is partially short-circuited in the daytime because reaction (5) can be followed by photodissociation, reaction (7), which re-

$$NO_2 + h\nu \rightarrow NO + O \quad \lambda < 395 \text{ nm} \quad (7)$$

generates odd oxygen. The gases NO and NO_2 constitute only about 3 parts per billion of the air in the ozone layer. They are produced naturally in this layer by the decomposition of atmospheric nitrous oxide, N_2O, with excited oxygen atoms, $O(^1D)$, derived from ozone, as shown in reactions (8) and (9). The

$$O_3 + h\nu \rightarrow O_2 + O(^1D) \quad \lambda < 310 \text{ nm} \quad (8)$$

$$O(^1D) + N_2O \rightarrow NO + NO \quad (9)$$

NO_2 is removed by reaction with hydroxyl radicals, OH, to form hydrogen nitrate, HNO_3, by reaction (10), and reformed by photodissociation of the HNO_3, in reaction (11). If the odd nitrogen family is defined

$$OH + NO_2 + M \rightarrow HNO_3 + M \quad (10)$$

$$HNO_3 + h\nu \rightarrow OH + NO_2 \quad \lambda < 345 \text{ nm} \quad (11)$$

to consist of the species NO, NO_2, and HNO_3, about half of the stratospheric odd nitrogen is present as HNO_3, and downward transport followed by rainout of this water-soluble HNO_3 is probably the main stratospheric odd nitrogen removal mechanism.

Another significant fraction of the total odd oxygen removal rate involves H atoms and OH and HO_2 (hydroperoxyl) radicals. These species are produced in the upper atmosphere by dissociation of water vapor (H_2O), methane (CH_4), and hydrogen peroxide (H_2O_2), and removed by various reactions which reform H_2O and H_2O_2. Of particular importance to ozone destruction are reactions (12) and (13). Finally,

$$HO_2 + O_3 \rightarrow OH + 2O_2 \quad (12)$$

$$HO_2 + O \rightarrow OH + O_2 \quad (13)$$

a somewhat smaller fraction of present ozone destruction involves Cl and ClO produced by decomposition in the stratosphere of chlorine species with industrial ($CFCl_3$, CF_2Cl_2, CH_3CCl_3, CCl_4) and biological

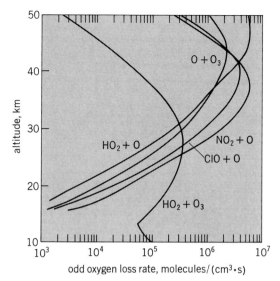

Fig. 2. The rates of reactions important in odd oxygen loss are given as a function of altitude. (*After R. P. Turco et al., SSTs, nitrogen fertilizer, and stratospheric ozone, Nature, 276: 805–807, 1978*)

(CH$_3$Cl) sources. Reactions (14)–(20) play roles sim-

$$Cl + O_3 \rightarrow ClO + O_2 \qquad (14)$$

$$ClO + O \rightarrow Cl + O_2 \qquad (15)$$

$$\begin{gathered} ClO + h\nu \rightarrow Cl + O \\ \lambda < 303.5 \text{ nm} \end{gathered} \qquad (16)$$

$$Cl + CH_4 \rightarrow HCl + CH_3 \qquad (17)$$

$$OH + HCl \rightarrow Cl + H_2O \qquad (18)$$

$$ClO + NO_2 + M \rightarrow ClNO_3 + M \qquad (19)$$

$$\begin{gathered} ClNO_3 + h\nu \rightarrow ClO + NO_2 \\ \lambda < 460 \text{ nm} \end{gathered} \qquad (20)$$

ilar to reactions (5)–(7), (10), and (11).

A summary of the main chemical destruction mechanisms for odd oxygen is given in **Fig. 2**. Measurements of O, O$_3$, NO, NO$_2$, N$_2$O, HNO$_3$, OH, CH$_4$, Cl, ClO, HCl, CF$_2$Cl$_2$, CFCl$_3$, and H$_2$O in the stratosphere have given support to these destruction mechanisms, although there are still some discrepancies. In addition to these chemical mechanisms, about 1% of the odd oxygen is removed by downward transport of ozone into the troposphere, where it is destroyed at or near the ground.

Circulation of stratospheric ozone. In a purely chemical model of stratospheric ozone with no transport, the maximum ozone concentrations would be obtained at altitudes and latitudes where reaction (1) is fastest; that is, in equatorial regions above 18 mi (30 km). However, the observed maximum ozone concentrations occur at about 11 mi (18 km) altitude in polar regions. A substantial poleward and downward transport of ozone must therefore occur in the lower stratosphere. This poleward transport is illustrated in **Fig. 3**, where it is seen that the column abundances of ozone are about 50% greater at the poles than at the Equator, with a maximum in polar ozone in the spring.

Most of the energy for driving the lower stratospheric circulation comes from planetary-scale waves which are generated in tropospheric air by ocean-land

temperature contrasts and topographic forcing, and then travel upward. As they ascend, these long waves are damped by emission and absorption of thermal radiation, and reflected downward when the stratosphere has easterly winds (as in summer) or strong westerly winds (as in the winter upper stratosphere). One would therefore expect the strongest circulation in the fall, spring, and lower winter stratospheres, where there are usually weak westerlies which do not cause downward reflection of the long waves. This period of maximum activity in the lower stratospheric forcing produces the observed spring maximum in ozone. Computations of ozone circulation and chemistry using the Massachusetts Institute of Technology (MIT) Three-Dimensional Stratospheric Circulation Model (MITSCM) have succeeded in simulating these observed seasonal ozone variations (Fig. 3). At a particular locality, daily variations of a few percent in total ozone are also observed, and these are probably associated with short-term variations in stratospheric motions.

Although the horizontal winds in the stratosphere can be quite large, the increase in temperature with altitude in this region makes it much more stable to vertical motions than the troposphere. Consequently, once destructive species such as Cl and ClO are introduced into the ozone layer, it takes roughly 3 years before they can be removed again by mixing down to the ground. This long stratospheric residence time, combined with the catalytic aspect of the ozone destruction caused by these and similar species, makes the ozone layer particularly sensitive to perturbations

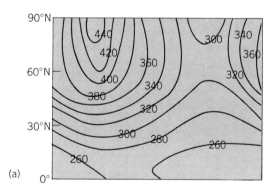

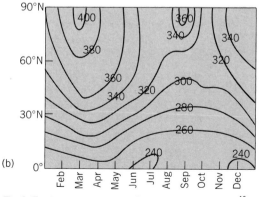

Fig. 3. Total ozone above the surface (in units of 2.7 × 10^{16} molecules per square centimeter) in the Northern Hemisphere as a function of season and latitude: (a) as determined from observations, and (b) as predicted by the MIT Stratospheric Circulation Model. (*After F. Alyea, D. Cunnold, and R. Prinn, Stratospheric ozone destruction by aircraft-induced nitrogen oxides, Science, 188:117–121, 1975*)

in their concentrations. SEE ATMOSPHERIC GENERAL CIRCULATION.

Perturbations to stratospheric ozone. Supersonic aircraft designed to fly in the lower stratosphere (such as the Anglo-French Concorde and Russian Tupolev-144) produce NO and NO_2 in their engines by thermal decomposition of air (N_2 and O_2). A fleet of about 3000 such aircraft would inject NO and NO_2 into the stratosphere at a rate some three times greater than that from the present N_2O source and would result in a significant perturbation to the atmospheric nitrogen cycle. Initial computations suggested that this large injection of nitrogen oxides would result in an 8–16% depletion of stratospheric ozone. Additional chemical reactions, combined with more accurate determination of some crucial rate constants, led to the conclusion that supersonic aircraft have a very much smaller effect on stratospheric ozone than originally predicted. This major change in an important environmental assessment gives an idea of the hazards associated with such predictions.

There has also been concern that industrial production of the chlorofluoromethanes $CFCl_3$ (Freon 11) and CF_2Cl_2 (Freon 12) may be significantly altering the natural chlorine cycle. These very inert species are principally used as refrigerants, as blowing agents for plastic foams, and as aerosol-can propellants. Once they are released into the atmosphere, their only presently recognized removal mechanism involves photodissociation in the stratosphere, as in reactions (21) and (22). The chlorine atoms released in these

$$CFCl_3 + h\nu \rightarrow CFCl_2 + Cl \qquad (21)$$
$$\lambda < 226 \text{ nm}$$

$$CF_2Cl_2 + h\nu \rightarrow CF_2Cl + Cl \qquad (22)$$
$$\lambda < 214 \text{ nm}$$

and subsequent reactions can catalytically destroy ozone by reactions (14) and (15). Computations in one-dimensional atmospheric chemical models imply that the chlorofluoromethanes are presently responsible for at most a 1% reduction in stratospheric ozone. However, when injection of $CFCl_3$ and CF_2Cl_2 into the atmosphere is continued at current rates, the models predict about a 7% decrease in ozone over the next 100 years. If reactions (21) and (22) are indeed the only atmospheric removal mechanisms for $CFCl_3$ and CF_2Cl_2, then their atmospheric lifetimes are about 80 and 180 years, respectively. Therefore, even if chlorofluoromethane production were halted, the effects would still be felt for several decades thereafter. Thus it is crucial to determine the actual lifetimes of these species. Results from a global program to measure the rate of increase of $CFCl_3$ and CF_3Cl with sufficient accuracy to determine their lifetimes indicate that the lifetime of $CFCl_3$ is indeed around 80 years.

A number of other potential ozone-altering processes with anthropogenic origins have also been identified. Increases in CO_2 due to fossil fuel combustion lead to a cooling of the stratosphere and thus a decrease in the rate of O_3 destruction. Atmospheric tests of thermonuclear weapons inject NO and NO_2, produced by thermal decomposition of air, into the stratosphere. Increased use of nitrate (NO_3^-) fertilizers may increase the rate of production of N_2O from soil nitrate by denitrifying bacteria, resulting in increased stratospheric N_2O concentrations. Solid-fuel rockets using ammonium perchlorate (NH_4ClO_4) as the oxidizer (Minuteman missiles, NASA space shuttle booster) inject small amounts of hydrogen chloride (HCl) into the stratosphere. Expanded production of methyl bromide (CH_3Br), an agricultural fumigant, may result in significant stratospheric bromine concentrations. Catalytic odd oxygen destruction by bromine is similar to but faster than that by chlorine. The global measurements of ozone which are required to ascertain the reality of all these possible long-term ozone depletions have become possible from satellites. Continuous ozone monitoring of this type is clearly mandatory for the future.

Chemistry of tropospheric ozone. Ozone is produced in polluted urban air during the NO-catalyzed oxidation of unburned hydrocarbons RH, where R is a hydrocarbon radical such as CH_3CO. The relevant reactions are (23)–(25), followed by reactions (7) and

$$RH + OH \rightarrow R + H_2O \qquad (23)$$
$$R + O_2 + M \rightarrow RO_2 + M \qquad (24)$$
$$RO_2 + NO \rightarrow RO + NO_2 \qquad (25)$$

(2). Ozone is also generated in "clean" nonurban air during oxidation of carbon monoxide through reactions (26)–(28), followed by reactions (7) and (2).

$$CO + OH \rightarrow CO_2 + H \qquad (26)$$
$$H + O_2 + M \rightarrow HO_2 + M \qquad (27)$$
$$HO_2 + NO \rightarrow OH + NO_2 \qquad (28)$$

Some tropospheric ozone is derived by injection of O_3 from the stratosphere. Tropospheric ozone is involved in the formation of photochemical smog, in the production of acid rain from SO_2 and NO_2, in agricultural productivity, and in the scavenging of a large number of trace pollutants injected into the atmosphere by industrial and biological processes. The importance of ozone in these processes derives from its oxidizing properties, its toxicity to plants, and its role as the source of tropospheric OH radicals by reaction (8) followed by reaction (29). The OH radical is a

$$O(^1D) + H_2O \rightarrow OH + OH \qquad (29)$$

primary oxidizing and scavenging agent in the atmosphere. SEE AIR POLLUTION; ATMOSPHERIC CHEMISTRY.

Ronald G. Prinn

Bibliography. B. J. Finlayson-Pitts and J. N. Pitts, *Atmospheric Chemistry: Fundamentals and Experimental Techniques*, 1986; National Research Council, *Causes and Effects of Stratospheric Ozone Reduction: An Update*, 1982; C. S. Zerefos and A. Ghazi (eds.), *Atmospheric Ozone*, 1985.

Avalanche

In general, a large mass of snow, ice, rock, earth, or mud in rapid motion down a slope or over a precipice. In the English language, the term avalanche is reserved almost exclusively for snow avalanche. Minimal requirements for the occurrence of an avalanche are snow and an inclined surface, usually a mountainside. Most avalanches occur on slopes between 30 and 45°.

Types. Two basic types of avalanches are recognized according to snow cover conditions at the point of origin. A loose-snow avalanche originates at a point and propagates downhill by successively dislodging increasing numbers of poorly cohering snow grains, typically gaining width as movement continues downslope. This type of avalanche commonly involves only those snow layers near the surface. The mechanism is analogous to dry sand. The second type, the slab avalanche, occurs when a distinct cohesive snow layer breaks away as a unit and slides because it is poorly anchored to the snow or ground below. A clearly defined gliding surface as well as a lubricating layer may be identifiable at the base of the slab, but the meteorological conditions which create these layers are complex. The thickness and areal extent of the slab may vary greatly, and those slab avalanches with larger dimensions pose the greatest threat to life and property. Both loose and slab types may occur in dry or wet snow. Dry avalanches often entrain large amounts of air within the moving mass of snow and are thus referred to as powder avalanches. Velocities for dry-snow avalanches may exceed 150 mi/h (67 m/s). Wet-snow avalanches occur when liquid water is present in the snow cover at the point of origin. While the wet avalanches move at lower velocities, they often involve greater masses of snow and therefore significant destructive forces. Theoretical calculations and empirical evidence indicate the general range of maximum impact forces to be between 7 and 70 lb/in.^{2} (5 and 50 metric tons/m^2), with extreme values reaching 142 lb/in.^{2} (100 metric tons/m^2). It is frequently the wet-snow avalanche which damages the soil and vegetation cover.

Release mechanism. In the case of the loose avalanche, release mechanisms are primarily controlled by the angle of repose, while slab releases involve complex strength-stress problems. A release may occur simply as a result of the overloading of a slope during a single snowstorm and involve only snow which accumulated during that specific storm, or it may result from a sequence of meteorological events and involve snow layers comprising numerous precipitation episodes. In the latter case, large avalanches may not necessarily be restricted to storms with large amounts of precipitation, but can result from lesser amounts of precipitation falling on older snow layers underlain by an extremely weak structure.

Defense methods. Where snow avalanches constitute a hazard, that is, where they directly threaten human activities, various defense methods have evolved. Attempts are made to prevent the avalanche from occurring by artificial supporting structures or reforestation in the zone of origin. The direct impact of an avalanche can be avoided by construction of diversion structures, dams, sheds, or tunnels. Hazardous zones may be temporarily evacuated while avalanches are released artificially, most commonly by explosives. Finally, attempts are made to predict the occurrence of avalanches by studying relationships between meteorological and snow cover factors. In locations where development has yet to occur, zones of known or expected avalanche activity can be mapped, allowing planners to avoid such areas entirely. Avalanche hazard is small when compared with certain other natural hazards such as floods and tornadoes, but it continues to rise as the popularity of wintertime mountain recreation increases.

Richard L. Armstrong

Bibliography. S. C. Colbeck, *Dynamics of Snow and Ice Masses*, 1980; C. Fraser, *Avalanches and Snow Safety*, 1978; E. R. La Chapelle, Snow avalanche: A review of current research and applications, *J. Glaciol.*, 19(81):313–324, 1977; R. I. Perla and M. Martinelli, Jr., *Avalanche Handbook*, USDA Forest Service, Agriculture Handb. 489, 1976; B. Voight (ed.), *Rockslides and Avalanches*, vol. 1 of *Natural Phenomena*, 1977; K. Williams, *Snowy Torrents: Avalanche Accidents in the United States, 1967–1971*, 1981.

Biogeochemistry

The study of the cycling of chemicals between organisms and the surface environment of the Earth. The chemicals either can be taken up by organisms and used for growth and synthesis of living matter or can be processed to obtain energy. The chemical composition of plants and animals indicates which elements, known as nutrient elements, are necessary for life. The principal element composition of land plants is shown in the **table**. The most abundant nutrient elements, carbon (C), hydrogen (H), and oxygen (O), supplied by the environment in the form of carbon dioxide (CO_2) and water (H_2O), are usually present in excess. The other nutrient elements, which are also needed for growth, may sometimes be in short supply; in this case they are referred to as limiting nutrients. The two most commonly recognized limiting nutrients are nitrogen (N) and phosphorus (P).

Biogeochemistry is concerned with both the biological uptake and release of nutrients, and the transformation of the chemical state of these biologically active substances, usually by means of energy-supplying oxidation-reduction reactions, at the Earth's surface. Emphasis is on how the activities of organisms affect the chemical composition of natural waters, the atmosphere, rocks, soils, and sediments. Thus, biogeochemistry is complementary to the science of ecology, which includes a concern with how the chemical composition of the atmosphere, waters, and so forth affects life. *SEE ECOLOGY.*

The two major processes of biogeochemistry are photosynthesis and respiration. Photosynthesis involves the uptake, under the influence of sunlight, of carbon dioxide, water, and other nutrients by plants

Elemental composition of plants*

Element	Concentration, % dry weight of tissue
Carbon	45
Oxygen	45
Hydrogen	6
Nitrogen	1.5
Potassium	1.0
Calcium	0.5
Phosphorus	0.2
Magnesium	0.2
Sulfur	0.1
Chlorine	0.01
Iron	0.01
Manganese	0.005
Zinc	0.002
Boron	0.002
Copper	0.0006
Molybdenum	0.00001

*From W. Stumm (ed.), *Global Chemical Cycles and Their Alterations by Man*, Dahlem Konferenzen, 1977.

to form organic matter and oxygen. A generalized expression is shown in reaction (1), where the expres-

$$CO_2 + H_2O + (xN + yP + \cdots) \rightarrow$$
$$CH_2ON_xP_y \ldots + O_2 \quad (1)$$

sion ($xN + yP + \cdots$) represents other nutrient elements in various chemical forms and $CH_2ON_xP_y \ldots$ represents organic matter. Respiration is the reverse of photosynthesis and involves the oxidation and breakdown of organic matter and the return of nitrogen, phosphorus, and other elements, as well as carbon dioxide and water, to the environment.

Biogeochemistry is usually studied in terms of biogeochemical cycles of individual elements. This gives rise to expressions such as the biogeochemical cycle of carbon and the terrestrial cycle of phosphorus. Time is an important consideration in such cycles: there are short-term cycles ranging from days to centuries and long-term (geological) cycles ranging from thousands to millions of years.

There has been increasing interest in biogeochemistry because the human influence on short-term biogeochemical cycling has become evident. Perhaps the best-known example is the changes in the biogeochemical cycling of carbon due to the burning of fossil fuels and the cutting and burning of tropical rainforests. The cycles of nitrogen and phosphorus have

been altered because of the use of fertilizer and the addition of wastes to lakes, rivers, estuaries, and the oceans. Acid rain, which results from the addition of sulfur and nitrogen compounds to the atmosphere by humans, affects biological systems in certain areas. A solid understanding of the biogeochemical cycles of the major nutrient elements is, therefore, basic to dealing with current and future problems caused by human impact on the environment. SEE HUMAN ECOLOGY.

Carbon cycle. Carbon is the basic biogeochemical element. The carbon cycle shown in **Fig. 1** provides a basis for understanding biogeochemical cycling. The atmosphere contains carbon in the form of carbon dioxide gas. There is a large annual flux of atmospheric carbon dioxide to and from forests and terrestrial biota, amounting to nearly 7% of total atmospheric carbon dioxide. This is because carbon dioxide is used by plants to produce organic matter through photosynthesis, and when the organic matter is broken down through respiration, carbon dioxide is released to the atmosphere. The concentration of atmospheric carbon dioxide shows a yearly oscillation (**Fig. 2**) because there is a strong seasonal annual cycle of photosynthesis and respiration in the Northern Hemisphere.

Photosynthesis and respiration in the carbon cycle can be represented by reaction (2), which is a simpli-

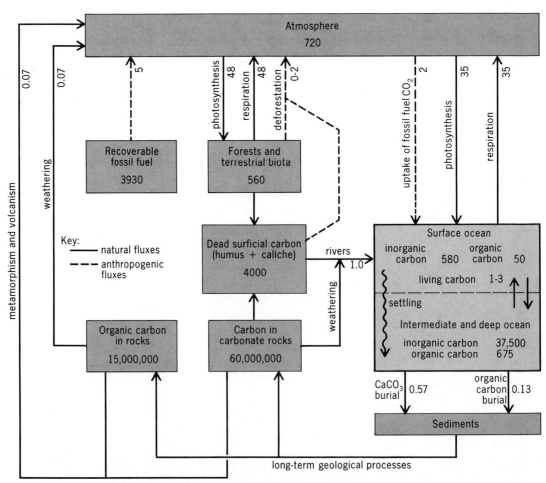

Fig. 1. Carbon cycle. Photosynthetic fluxes between the atmosphere and oceans, and the atmosphere and land, represent net primary productivity. Reservoir units, gigatons (10^{15} g) C; flux units, gigatons C/yr.

$$\text{CO}_2 + \text{H}_2\text{O} \underset{\text{respiration}}{\overset{\overset{\text{photo-}}{\text{synthesis}}}{\rightleftharpoons}} \text{CH}_2\text{O} + \text{O}_2 \qquad (2)$$

fied version of reaction (1). Breakdown of organic matter via respiration is accomplished mainly by bacteria that live in soils, sediments, and natural waters. As can be seen from Fig. 1, there is a very large reservoir of terrestrial carbon in carbonate rocks, which contain calcium carbonate (CaCO_3), and in rocks such as shales which contain organic carbon. Major exchange of carbon between rocks and the atmosphere is very slow, on the scale of thousands to millions of years, compared to exchange between plants and the atmosphere, which can even be seasonal. *See Microbial ecology; Soil microbiology*.

Organic carbon burial on land is not important now, but was important in the geologic past when coal deposits formed in swamps. Carbon is lost from the land by river transport of dissolved bicarbonate ion [$(\text{HCO}_3)^-$] and of dissolved and particulate organic carbon. Overall, about two-thirds of the river load is derived from the biological cycle and from atmospheric carbon dioxide, and the rest comes from the weathering of carbonate rocks. However, the river transport of carbon (1 gigaton or 10^{15} g per year) is small compared to the amount of carbon cycled between the atmosphere and the land (48 gigatons/yr) or the atmosphere and the oceans (35 gigatons/yr).

The oceans taken as a whole represent a major reservoir of carbon. Carbon in the oceans occurs primarily as dissolved $(\text{HCO}_3)^-$ and to a lesser extent as dissolved carbon dioxide gas and carbonate ion [$(\text{CO}_3)^{2-}$]. The well-mixed surface ocean (the top 250 ft or 75 m) rapidly exchanges carbon dioxide with the atmosphere. However, the deep oceans are cut off from the atmosphere and mix with it on a long-term time scale of about 1000–2000 years. Most of the biological activity in the oceans occurs in the surface (or shallow) water where there is light and photosynthesis can occur. *See Maritime meteorology*.

The main biological process in seawater is photosynthetic production of organic matter by phytoplankton. Some of this organic matter is eaten by animals, which are in turn eaten by larger animals farther up in the food chain. Almost all of the organic matter along the food chain is ultimately broken down by bacterial respiration, which occurs primarily in shal-

low water, and the carbon dioxide is quickly recycled to the atmosphere. However, some occurs in deeper waters which can accumulate excess dissolved carbon dioxide because of a lack of exchange with the atmosphere. Overall, of the large annual carbon flux (35 gigatons/yr) between the atmosphere and the oceans, only a small fraction (0.13 gigaton/yr) escapes destruction as organic matter that falls to the bottom and is buried in ocean sediments; part of this sedimentary organic matter is marine and part is transported by rivers from land. Most organic carbon is buried nearshore, for example, in marine deltas where the sediment deposition rate is high. *See Food web; Phytoplankton; Seawater*.

Another major biological process is the secretion of shells and other hard structures by marine organisms. Bicarbonate is removed from the water in the form of solid calcium carbonate (calcite and aragonite minerals), as shown in reaction (3).

$$\text{Ca}^{2+} + 2(\text{HCO}_3)^- \rightarrow \text{CO}_2 + \text{H}_2\text{O} + \text{CaCO}_3 \qquad (3)$$

A biogeochemical cycle of calcium and bicarbonate exists within the oceans, linking the deep and shallow water areas. Bottom dwellers in shallow water, such as corals, mollusks, and algae, provide calcium carbonate skeletal debris. Since the shallow waters are saturated with respect to calcium carbonate, this debris accumulates on the bottom and is buried, providing the minerals that form carbonate rocks such as limestone and dolomite. Calcium carbonate is also derived from the shells of organisms inhabiting surface waters of the deep ocean; these are tiny, floating plankton such as foraminiferans, pteropods, and coccoliths. Much of the calcium carbonate from this source dissolves as it sinks into the deeper ocean waters, which are undersaturated with respect to calcium carbonate. The undissolved calcium carbonate accumulates on the bottom to form deep-sea limestone. The calcium and the bicarbonate ions [Ca^{2+} and $(\text{HCO}_3)^-$] dissolved in the deep ocean water eventually are carried to surface and shallow water, where they are removed by planktonic and bottom-dwelling organisms to form their skeletons.

The long-term biogeochemical carbon cycle occurs over millions of years when the calcium carbonate and organic matter that are buried in sediments are returned to the Earth's surface. There, weathering occurs which involves the reaction of oxygen with sedimentary organic matter with the release of carbon dioxide and water (analogous to respiration), and the reaction of water and carbon dioxide with carbonate rocks with the release of calcium and bicarbonate ions. This latter process is the reverse of that shown in reaction (3).

Human perturbation of carbon cycle. Fossil fuels (coal and oil) represent a large reservoir of carbon (Fig. 1). Burning of fossil fuels releases carbon dioxide to the atmosphere, and an increase in the atmospheric concentration of carbon dioxide has been observed since the mid-1950s (Fig. 2). While much of the increase is attributed to fossil fuels, deforestation by humans accompanied by the decay or burning of trees is another possible contributor to the problem.

When estimates are made of the amount of fossil fuels burned from 1959 to 1980, only about 60% of the carbon dioxide released can be accounted for in the atmospheric increase in carbon dioxide. The remaining 40% is known as excess carbon dioxide. The

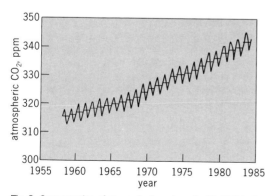

Fig. 2. Concentration of atmospheric carbon dioxide (CO_2) at Mauna Loa Observatory, Hawaii; ppm stands for parts per million volume fraction. Horizontal bars represent yearly averages. (*After J. R. Trabalka, ed., Atmospheric Carbon Dioxide and the Global Carbon Cycle, U. S. Department of Energy, DOE/ER-0239, 1985*)

surface oceans are an obvious candidate for storage of most of the excess carbon dioxide by the reaction of carbon dioxide with dissolved carbonate to form bicarbonate. Because the increase in bicarbonate concentration in surface waters due to excess carbon dioxide uptake would be small, it is difficult to detect whether such a change has occurred. Greater quantities of excess carbon dioxide could be stored as bicarbonate in the deeper oceans, but this process takes a long time because of the slow rate of mixing between surface and deep oceans.

An increase in atmospheric carbon dioxide is of concern because of the greenhouse effect. The carbon dioxide traps heat in the atmosphere; notable increases in atmospheric carbon dioxide should cause an increase in the Earth's surface temperature by as much as several degrees. This temperature increase would be greater at the poles, and the effects could include melting of polar ice, a rise in sea level, and changes in rainfall distribution, with droughts in interior continental areas such as the Great Plains of the United States. *See Climatic change; Drought; Greenhouse effect.*

Terrestrial nitrogen cycle. Nitrogen is dominantly a biogenic element and has no important mineral forms. It is a major atmospheric constituent with a number of gaseous forms, including molecular nitrogen gas (N_2), nitrogen dioxide (NO_2), nitric oxide (NO), ammonia (NH_3), and nitrous oxide (N_2O). As an essential component of plant and animal matter, it is extensively involved in biogeochemical cycling. On a global basis, the nitrogen cycle is greatly affected by human activities.

Nitrogen gas (N_2) makes up 80% of the atmosphere by volume; however, nitrogen is unreactive in this form. In order to be available for biogeochemical cycling by organisms, nitrogen gas must be fixed, that is, combined with oxygen, carbon, or hydrogen. There are three major sources of terrestrial fixed nitrogen: biological nitrogen fixation by plants, nitrogen fertilizer application, and rain and particulate dry deposition of previously fixed nitrogen. Biological fixation occurs in plants such as legumes (peas and beans) and lichens in trees, which incorporate nitrogen from the atmosphere into their living matter; about 30% of worldwide biological fixation is due to human cultivation of these plants. Nitrogen fertilizers contain industrially fixed nitrogen as both nitrate and ammonium.

Fixed nitrogen in rain is in the forms of nitrate [($NO_3)^-$] and ammonium [$(NH_4)^+$] ions. Major sources of nitrate, which is derived from gaseous atmospheric nitrogen dioxide (and nitric oxide), include (in order of importance) combustion of fossil fuel, especially by automobiles; forest fires (mostly caused by humans); and lightning. Nitrate in rain, in addition to providing soluble fixed nitrogen for photosynthesis, contributes nitric acid (HNO_3), a major component of acid rain. Sources of ammonium, which is derived from atmospheric ammonia gas (NH_3), include animal and human wastes, soil loss from decomposition of organic matter, and fertilizer release. *See Acid rain.*

The basic land nitrogen cycle (**Fig. 3**) involves the photosynthetic conversion of the nitrate and ammonium ions dissolved in soil water into plant organic material. Once formed, the organic matter may be stored or broken down. Bacterial decomposition of organic matter (ammonification) produces soluble ammonium ion which can then be either taken up again in photosynthesis, released to the atmosphere as ammonia gas, or oxidized by bacteria to nitrate ion (nitrification).

Nitrate ion is also soluble, and may be used in pho-

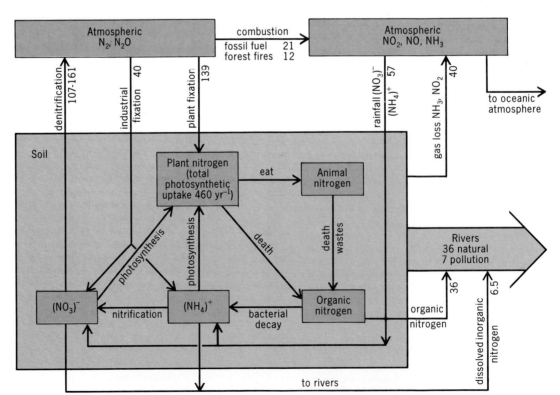

Fig. 3. Terrestrial nitrogen cycle; organic nitrogen includes both particulate and dissolved material. Flux units, teragrams (10^{12} g) N/yr.

tosynthesis. However, part of the nitrate may undergo reduction (denitrification) by soil bacteria to nitrogen gas or to nitrous oxide which are then lost to the atmosphere. Compared to the land carbon cycle, the land nitrogen cycle is considerably more complex, and because of the large input of fixed nitrogen by humans, it is possible that nitrogen is building up on land. However, this is difficult to determine since the amount of nitrogen gas recycled to the atmosphere is not known and any changes in the atmospheric nitrogen concentration would be too small to detect.

Oceanic nitrogen cycle. The oceans are another major site of nitrogen cycling (**Fig. 4**): the amount of nitrogen cycled biogenically, through net primary photosynthetic production, is about 13 times that on land. The main links between the terrestrial and the oceanic nitrogen cycles are the atmosphere and rivers. Nitrogen gases carried in the atmosphere eventually fall as dissolved inorganic (mainly nitrate) and organic nitrogen and particulate organic nitrogen in rain on the oceans. The flux of river nitrogen lost from the land is only about 9% of the total nitrogen recycled biogeochemically on land each year and only about 25% of the terrestrial nitrogen flux from the biosphere to the atmosphere.

River nitrogen is an important nitrogen source to the oceans; however, the greatest amount of nitrogen going into ocean surface waters comes from the upwelling of deeper waters, which are enriched in dissolved nitrate from organic recycling at depth. Dissolved nitrate is used extensively for photosynthesis by marine organisms, mainly plankton. Bacterial decomposition of the organic matter formed in photosynthesis results in the release of dissolved ammonium, some of which is used directly in photosynthesis. However, most undergoes nitrification to form nitrate, and much of the nitrate may undergo denitrification to nitrogen gas which is released to the atmosphere. A small amount of organic-matter nitrogen is buried in ocean sediments, but this accounts for a very small amount of the nitrogen recycled each year. There are no important inorganic nitrogen minerals such as those that exist for carbon and phosphorus, and thus there is no mineral precipitation and dissolution.

Phosphorus cycle. Phosphorus, an important component of organic matter, is taken up and released in the form of dissolved inorganic and organic phosphate. Phosphorus differs from nitrogen and carbon in that it does not form stable atmospheric gases and therefore cannot be obtained from the atmosphere. It does form minerals, most prominently apatite (calcium phosphate), and insoluble iron (Fe) and aluminum (Al) phosphate minerals, or it is adsorbed on clay minerals. The amount of phosphorus used in photosynthesis on land is large compared to phosphorus inputs to the land (**Fig. 5**). The major sources of phosphorus are weathering of rocks containing apatite and mining of phosphate rock for fertilizer and industry. A small amount comes from precipitation and dry deposition.

Phosphorus is lost from the land principally by river transport, which amounts to only 7% of the amount of phosphorus recycled by the terrestrial biosphere; overall, the terrestrial biosphere conserves phosphorus. Humans have greatly affected terrestrial phosphorus: deforestation and agriculture have doubled the amount of phosphorus weathering; phosphorus is added to the land as fertilizers and from industrial wastes, sewage, and detergents. Thus, about 75% of the terrestrial input is anthropogenic; in fact, phosphorus may be building up on the land.

In the oceans, phosphorus occurs predominantly as dissolved orthophosphates $[PO_4^{3-}$, $(HPO_4)^{2-}$ and $(H_2PO_4)^-]$. Since it follows the same cycle as do carbon and nitrogen, dissolved orthophosphate is depleted in surface ocean waters where both photosynthesis and respiration occur, and the concentration builds up in deeper water where organic matter is decomposed by bacterial respiration. The major phosphorus input to the oceans is from rivers, with about 5% coming from rain. However, 75% of the river phosphorus load is due to anthropogenic pollutants; humans have changed the ocean balance of phosphorus. Most of the dissolved oceanic orthophosphate is derived from recycled organic matter. The output of phosphorus from the ocean is predominantly biogenic: organic phosphorus is buried in sediments; a smaller amount is removed by adsorption on volcanic iron oxides. In the geologic past, there was a much greater inorganic precipitation of phosphorite (apatite) from seawater than at present, and this has resulted in the formation of huge deposits which are now mined.

Nutrients in lakes. Biogeochemical cycling of phosphorus and nitrogen in lakes follows a pattern that is similar to oceanic cycling: there is nutrient depletion in surface waters and enrichment in deeper waters. Oxygen consumption by respiration in deep water sometimes leads to extensive oxygen depletion with adverse effects on fish and other biota. In lakes, phosphorus is usually the limiting nutrient.

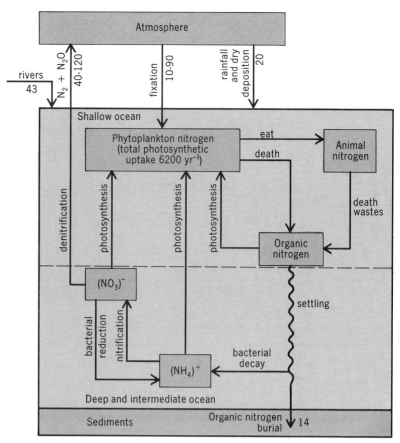

Fig. 4. Marine nitrogen cycle; organic nitrogen includes both particulate and dissolved material. Flux units, teragrams (10^{12} g) N/yr.

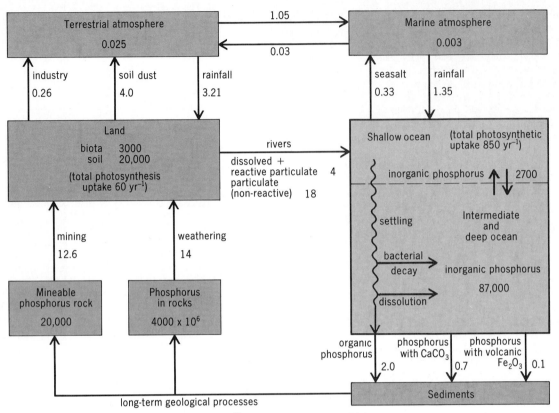

Fig. 5. Phosphorus cycle. Reservoir units, teragrams (10^{12} g) P; flux units, teragrams P/yr.

Many lakes have experienced greatly increased nutrient (nitrogen and phosphorus) input due to human activities. This stimulates a destructive cycle of biological activity: very high organic productivity, a greater concentration of plankton, and more photosynthesis. The result is more organic matter falling into deep water with increased depletion of oxygen and greater accumulation of organic matter on the lake bottom. This process, eutrophication, can lead to adverse water quality and even to the filling up of small lakes with organic matter. *See Eutrophication; Limnology.*

Biogeochemical sulfur cycle. A dominant flux in the global sulfur cycle (**Fig. 6.**) is the release of 65–70 teragrams of sulfur per year to the atmosphere from burning of fossil fuels. Sulfur contaminants in these fuels are released to the atmosphere as sulfur dioxide (SO_2) which is rapidly converted to aerosols of sulfuric acid (H_2SO_4), the primary contributor to acid rain. Forest burning results in an additional release of sulfur dioxide. Overall, the broad range of human activities contribute 75% of sulfur released into the atmosphere. Natural sulfur sources over land are predominantly the release of reduced biogenic sulfur gases [mainly hydrogen sulfide (H_2S) and dimethyl sulfide] from marine tidal flats and inland waterlogged soils and, to much lesser extent, the release of volcanic sulfur. The atmosphere does not have an appreciable reservoir of sulfur because most sulfur gases are rapidly returned (within days) to the land in rain and dry deposition. There is a small net flux of sulfur from the atmosphere over land to the atmosphere over the oceans.

Ocean water constitutes a large reservoir of dissolved sulfur in the form of sulfate ions [$(SO_4)^{2-}$].

Some of this sulfate is thrown into the oceanic atmosphere as sea salt from evaporated sea spray, but most of this is rapidly returned to the oceans. Another major sulfur source in the oceanic atmosphere is the release of oceanic biogenic sulfur gases (such as dimethyl sulfide) from the metabolic activities of oceanic organisms and organic matter decay. Marine organic matter contains a small amount of sulfur, but sulfur is not a limiting element in the oceans.

Another large flux in the sulfur cycle is the transport of dissolved sulfate in rivers. However, as much as 43% of this sulfur may be due to human activities, both from burning of fossil fuels and from fertilizers and industrial wastes. The weathering of sulfur minerals, such as pyrite (FeS_2) in shales, and the evaporite minerals, gypsum and anhydrite, make an important contribution to river sulfate. The major mechanism for removing sulfate from ocean water is the formation and burial of pyrite in oceanic sediments, primarily nearshore sediments. (The sulfur fluxes of sea salt and biogenic sulfur gases do not constitute net removal from the oceans since the sulfur is recycled into the oceans.)

Biogeochemical cycles and atmospheric oxygen. The main processes affecting atmospheric oxygen, as shown by reaction (2), are photosynthesis and respiration; however, these processes are almost perfectly balanced against one another and, thus, do not exert a simple effect on oxygen levels. Only the very small excess of photosynthesis over respiration, manifested by the burial of organic matter in sediments, is important in raising the level of oxygen. This excess is so small, and the reservoir of oxygen so large, that if the present rate of organic carbon burial were doubled, and the other rates remained constant, it

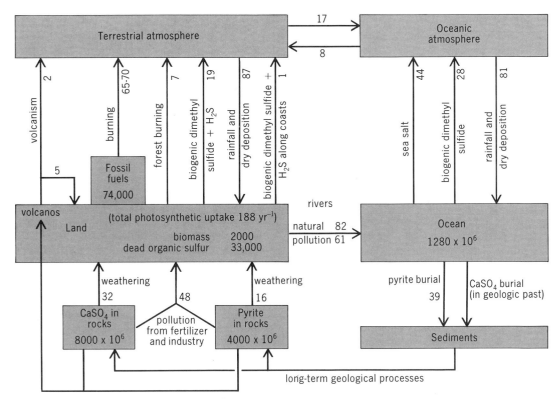

Fig. 6. Sulfur cycle. Reservoir units, teragrams (10^{12} g) S; flux units, teragrams S/yr.

would take 5–10 million years for the amount of atmospheric oxygen to double. Nevertheless, this is a relatively short time from a geological perspective. *SEE ATMOSPHERE; ATMOSPHERIC CHEMISTRY; BIOSPHERE; HYDROSPHERE.*

Elizabeth K. Berner; Robert A. Berner

Bibliography. E. K. Berner and R. A. Berner, *The Global Water Cycle: Geochemistry and Environment*, 1987; R. A. Berner (ed.), Geochemical cycles of nutrient elements, *Amer. J. Sci.*, 282:401–542, 1982; C. B. Gregor et al., *Chemical Cycles in the Evolution of the Earth*, 1988; G. E. Likens, F. H. Bormann, and N. M. Johnson, *Biogeochemistry of a Forested Ecosystem*, 1977; J. R. Trabalka (ed.), *Atmospheric Carbon Dioxide and the Global Carbon Cycle*, U. S. Department of Energy, DOE/ER-0239, 1985.

Biogeography

The science concerned with the distribution of life on the Earth. Biogeography is an ancient science that underwent significant development as early as the beginning of the nineteenth century. There has been a considerable burst of interest in this discipline since the late 1960s.

Nature of field. The field of biogeography can be divided into four major areas: descriptive biogeography, analytical (historical) biogeography, predictive biogeography, and experimental biogeography.

Descriptive biogeography. Descriptive biogeography, or areology, describes the distributional patterns of organisms, or sets of organisms, in the different parts of the Earth and establishes the phylogenetic relationships of floras and faunas between these regions. One aspect of this type of biogeography is to subdivide life zones according to geographical gradients such as latitude and altitude. Pioneers in this area of study have recognized five main biogeographical units over the Earth: Palearctic, Nearctic, Afrotropical, Neotropical, and Indo-Malayan. *SEE ALTITUDINAL VEGETATION ZONES; PLANT GEOGRAPHY; ZOOGEOGRAPHY.*

Analytical biogeography. Analytical, or historical, biogeography explains the causal factors for the spatial arrangement of organisms. It deals mainly with the history of biotas that are usually of the order of magnitude at a continental scale. Its aim is to reconstruct temporal patterns of species differentiation through the speciation processes using morphological clues, such as the variation of species within their distributional range. This approach proceeds through three steps: (1) the description of the modern variation of species, or groups of species, and the mapping of their different components; (2) the identification of historical events from paleobiological and paleogeographical records that could have produced past isolating barriers to gene flow, which eventually generated the splitting of a mother species into two or more daughter species; and (3) the comparison of modern data on the variation of species with the available evidence from paleobiology, and the reconstruction of the course of species differentiation. Whole faunas and floras have moved up and down land masses many times in the past in response to climatic changes, especially during the Pleistocene. These changes have resulted in many extinctions, speciation events, and distributional discontinuities. Modern distributional patterns of most faunas and floras over the Earth, including tropical regions, are the heritage of glacial times.

Predictive biogeography. This area of biogeography provides broad theories, such as ecosystem development or island biogeography, that allow the prediction of patterns and processes in the colonization of space, and the local turnover of species on a regional basis. These predictions may apply to changes in species composition of communities along ecological succession or to changes that occur on islands, for example, a woodlot isolated in a "sea" of cereals in a modern industrial farmland, or a true oceanic island. *See Eco-LOGICAL COMMUNITIES; ECOLOGY; ECOSYSTEM; ISLAND BIO-GEOGRAPHY.*

Experimental biogeography. As a result of the development of modern science, experimentation is more and more considered the best means to demonstrate scientific facts. For example, islets a short distance off the mainland coast may be defaunated of their small arthropod communities. Concerns in experimental biogeography at this scale might include such questions as: (1) How much time will be required for the species to recolonize the islets? (2) Will there be the same number of species after recolonization as before defaunation? (3) Will there be some relationship between the size of the islet and the number of new immigrants? (4) Will the new immigrant species be the same as those before the experiment? If not, why? (5) Will the trophic structure of the new communities be the same as those before defaunation? (6) Are the potential immigrants equally successful in colonizing abilities? If not, which species-specific attributes facilitate or prevent immigration? Such investigations have successfully provided tentative answers to some of these questions.

Hierarchical perspective. Biogeography is thus not restricted to a given scale of time or space, but is concerned with any point along and across hierarchical scales of space and time as well as with any level of biological integration. Modern biogeography is not just a study of the distribution of plants and animals. This discipline encompasses many ecological and evolutionary problems involved in the history, the structure, and the dynamics of populations, species, and communities. For this reason, a definition of modern biogeography could be: the study of the diversity of organisms and of the regulation of this diversity in heterogeneous and changing environments. Such a definition states nothing about either the levels of integration involved, or the time and space scales involved. The key words are diversity, heterogeneity, and change.

The diversity of floras and faunas can be studied from a continental scale to genetic systems on a molecular scale. Heterogeneity usually refers to spatial attributes of the environment, whatever the scale, from a mosaic of habitat patches within a landscape to the zonation of life around the Earth. Heterogeneity may also be concerned with local variation of populations and communities due to biological events, such as disease or predation. Change refers to time, and it is the main driving force of evolution. There are changes in climates, the position of land masses, and the distribution of habitat patches within a landscape. For this reason, the distribution of living organisms is never static. Distributional ranges of all species change through time because of changes in ecological conditions. Some species become extinct while new ones evolve.

The different time scales do not have the same effect on the diversities and the magnitude of change. At very long time scales (several tens of millions of years), such changes as plate tectonics had strong repercussions on the differentiation of biotas on a continental scale. For instance, the splitting of the Gond-

wana 150 million years ago into the major continents of the Southern Hemisphere gave rise to much speciation. The ancestor of the modern ratites (large flightless running birds) was probably widespread in open or semiopen habitats of Gondwana. Because of the fragmentation of this supercontinent, this ancestor was split into several populations which then evolved in isolation, for example, ostriches in Africa, rheas in South America, cassowaries and emus in the Australo-Papuan region, and kiwis in New Zealand. On the other hand, at very short time scales (years or tens of years) a treefall in a forest has large consequences on distributional patterns of many species within a forest block. Forest plant and animal communities include species that are narrowly dependent on such clearings in the forest. They could no longer survive if treefalls or other disturbance events did not occur.

A distinction was formerly made between so-called ecological time, which produces changes in communities by way of short-term processes such as ecological succession, and so-called evolutionary time, which is long enough to produce genetic changes in populations to occur through natural selection. Modern biogeography does not recognize this distinction because processes operate as a continuum along the scales of time, space, and change. For this reason, modern biogeography is also named evolutionary biogeography. Since biological systems are temporal systems as well as spatial systems, because they always reflect a history, and since time is a component of change, any study of biogeography must integrate these three components which are tautologically interrelated. An emerging view is that the organization of living systems is basically hierarchical. The basis of the assumption of a hierarchy theory is that each level of biological integration acts downstream as a filter, with only a fraction of its properties being transmitted to the lower level. Applied to biogeography, this hierarchical view indicates that problems involved with diversities and their regulation must be studied along three axes, namely space, time, and change. These three interdependent scales, along which biogeographical processes operate, define different fields of research or scientific disciplines that are actually much more interactive than formerly believed.

Case study. In a study of birds in the Mediterranean region, several levels of perception were designed through a zooming process going from large to smaller scales of investigation. As a whole, the Mediterranean region is about 1,200,000 mi^2 (3,000,000 km^2); at this scale, space is large and time is long. The level of biological organization involved is the whole fauna characterized by its own history. There are 335 bird species in this region. The numbers of species present in each subregion and the main islands has been estimated, for example, 207 in Iberia, 133 in Sicily, and 272 in Turkey and the Middle East. Plotting the numbers of species against area shows a relationship between species richness and area; islands are impoverished by comparison to areas of similar size on the nearby mainland. Analysis shows this fauna belonging to a Palearctic faunal stock; relationships with the Indo-Malayan and the Afrotropical regions are scanty. Analysis of floras and faunas since the beginning of the Pleistocene, using paleobiological records, has shown that during the most severe climatic episodes of glacial times entire European communities have been forced to find refugium in the Mediterranean region. Thus, Mediterranean forests have never been isolated from European forests, which explains why, except for a few cases, Mediterranean sylvatic bird faunas do not markedly differ from those farther north.

On a regional scale, the biogeographic patterns between two regions that differ in such important characteristics as the degree of isolation show striking biogeographical differences. A comparison of the bird faunas of the island of Corsica with those of three mainland areas of similar size shows striking differences; the insular bird fauna is heavily impoverished, with 119 breeding species instead of 172, on average, on the mainland. Many interesting biogeographical, ecological, and evolutionary questions arise from this impoverishment: What is the role of history and that of present-day immigration-extinction processes in these patterns? Are there differences between species for colonizing abilities? In other words, is the species composition of insular faunas a random sample of the nearby mainland fauna? The answer is definitely that it is not. This has been extensively studied by researchers for many kinds of organisms. SEE POPULATION DISPERSAL.

Continuing farther down along the space-time-change scales, an important question is the following: Given insular species impoverishment, does this impoverishment have repercussions on the structure, the organization, and the dynamics of communities? The best way to answer this question is to compare bird communities along two habitat gradients: one on the island, and the other on the mainland. Detailed studies at the community level have shown that the sharing of ecological space by species in species-poor island habitats is very different from that in species-rich mainland habitats.

Finally, whether or not differences in community organization and dynamics in species-poor versus species-rich habitats influence the functioning of populations is considered. This point is examined at a smaller scale by comparing population biology of selected species such as tits (*Parus* spp.) in two habitats that match each other, for instance, in the forests of the insular and of the mainland habitat gradients. Here again, large differences have been demonstrated for such life history traits as habitat selection, demography, and social structures. SEE TERRESTRIAL ECOSYSTEM.

Jacques Blondel

Bibliography. T. H. Allen and T. B. Starr, *Hierarchy: Perspectives for Ecological Complexity*, 1982; J. Blondel, From biogeography to life history theory: A multithematic approach illustrated by the biogeography of vertebrates, *J. Biogeogr.*, 14:405–422, 1987; J. H. Brown and A. C. Gibson, *Biogeography*, 1983; R. H. MacArthur and E. O. Wilson, *The Theory of Island Biogeography*, 1967; D. S. Simberloff and E. O. Wilson, Experimental zoogeography of islands: A two year record of colonization, *Ecology*, 51:934–937, 1970.

Biological productivity

The amount and rate of production which occur in a given ecosystem over a given time period. It may apply to a single organism, a population, or entire communities and ecosystems. SEE BIOMASS.

During the 1970s there was considerable study of biological productivity. This work was holistic, dealing with entire ecosystems. To understand how to optimize production of food and fiber, information on a wide array of organisms not usually harvested by humans is very important.

Productivity is best considered both in terms of dry matter produced (net production) and in terms of the thermodynamic cost of producing it (gross production, being respiration and heat losses plus net production). The following definitions are useful in calculating production. (1) Gross primary production (GPP) is the total energy fixed by photosynthesis. (2) Net primary production (NPP) is the gross production less losses due to plant respiration. (3) Secondary production is production by heterotrophs (animals, microorganisms), which feed on plant products or other heterotrophs. Note that human-associated terms, such as harvest or yield, refer to just that fraction of production of use to the plant harvester or animal husbander. Thus yield of a grain crop refers solely to the harvested seed portion of the aboveground net primary production. All energy units are presented in kilojoules; the outmoded, but frequently used, kilocalorie of the nutritionist is calculated by kJ/0.2388. SEE POPULATION ECOLOGY.

To illustrate productivity at an ecosystem level, an example of a terrestrial ecosystem is used (**Table 1**). For a lightly grazed shortgrass prairie, the gross rate of photosynthesis was 21,900 kJ/m^2 over 180 days. After accounting for respiration losses from the plants (7450 kJ), a net production of 14,455 kJ remained. This net primary production, partitioned above- and belowground, flows principally into the decomposition pathways. The predominant flow of energy of primary production thus goes to the saprophages, namely bacteria, fungi, and actinomycetes (compare saprophage assimiliation of 2930 kJ production plus 9640 kJ respiration with the input from NPP).

Animal heterotrophs, although accounting for only a small fraction (2–4%) of the total energy flow directly (as protoplasm synthesized from plant or microbial tissue) may play a synergistic or catalytic role in subsequent new plant production.

The concepts of net ecosystem production (net primary production minus respiration of heterotrophs) and ecosystem metabolism (GPP divided by net ecosystem respiration equals autotrophic plus heterotrophic respiration) are used to contrast agroecosystems and natural ecosystems. As shown in **Table 2**, the production and respiration components are

Table 1. Energy flow of autotrophic and heterotrophic production and respiration in lightly grazed shortgrass prairie at Pawnee Site, Colorado, 1972*

Energetic parameters	Production, kJ/m^2	Respiration, kJ/m^2
Gross primary production	21,900	
Net primary production	14,455	7445
Aboveground	2,165	5725
Belowground	12,290	1720
Heterotrophic activity		
Herbivory	99	242
Saprophages	2,930	9640

*"Lightly grazed" indicates 1 steer per 10.8 hectares or per 4.32 acres over 180 days.

SOURCE: Modified from D. C. Coleman et al., Energy flow and partitioning in selected man-managed and natural ecosystems, *Agro-Ecosystems*, 3:45–56, 1976.

Table 2. Annual production and respiration in growth-type and more mature ecosystems*

Energetic parameters	Types of ecosystems			
	Alfalfa field (U.S.)	Young pine plantation (U.K.)	Shortgrass prairie (Table 1)	80-year deciduous forest (Tennessee)
Gross primary production (GPP)	102,190	51,095	21,900	117,165
Autotrophic respiration (R_A)	38,530	19,685	7,445	76,220
Net primary production (NPP)	63,660	31,410	14,455	40,940
Heterotrophic respiration (R_H)	12,565	19,265	9,965	38,410
Net ecosystem production (NEP = NPP − R_H)	51,095	12,145	4,495	2,530
Net ecosystem respiration ($R_E = R_A + R_H$)	51,095	38,950	17,410	114,635
Ecosystem metabolism (GPP/R_E)	2.00	1.31	1.26	1.02

*Systems arranged in decreasing magnitudes of net ecosystem production (NEP). All values in kJ/m² per year.

nearly in balance in the more mature ecosystems, whereas there is more harvestable production in a thriving agroecosystem. Unfortunately, there is little information for many agroecosystems concerning belowground energy costs. Much of the existing information on production refers to readily harvested fibrous material, yet there may be considerable amounts of root exudates and sloughed cells produced in addition to the fibrous roots. These "exudates" represent an additional "cost of doing business" for plants in either old-growth forest or annual field crops. For example, it has been estimated that perhaps 23–25% of the carbon fixed by photosynthesis in a rice crop goes to furnish root exudates for rhizosphere (root-associated) microflora active in nitrogen fixation. This is an important intertie between carbon-energy flow and nutrient cycling. SEE AGROECOSYSTEM.

The production and activity of certain microflora may be of considerable importance to plant growth in a wide variety of terrestrial ecosystems. Thus various beneficial root-associated fungi (mycorrhizae) may facilitate uptake of a limiting nutrient, such as phosphorus, permitting a doubling of harvestable shoot production of such plants as clover. However, the net carbon or energy cost to the host plant is quite low, being estimated to be only about 1% of the total carbon allocation of the host plant.

It is apparent that one must define carefully the important aspects of biological productivity. Depending on management techniques, the amount and activity of beneficial microorganisms, such as mycorrhizae, may have an importance equal to that of the crop species of interest. A holistic approach, as outlined above, should pay great dividends in future years, in the endeavor to "manage" ecosystems with lowered inputs of fossil fuels for tillage and ever more costly fertilizers. SEE ECOLOGICAL ENERGETICS; ECOSYSTEM; FOOD WEB.

David C. Coleman

Bibliography. D. C. Coleman et al., Energy flow and partitioning in selected man-managed and natural ecosystems, *Agro-Ecosystems*, 3:45–54, 1976; W. F. Humphreys, Production and respiration in animal populations, *J. Animal Ecol.*, 48:427–453, 1979; H. F. Lieth (ed.), *Patterns of Primary Production in the Biosphere*, 1978; S. J. McNaughton, Serengeti migratory wildebeest: Facilitation of energy flow by grazing, *Science*, 191:92–94, 1976; F. R. Warembourg and R. A. A. Morrall, Energy flow in the plant-microorganism system, in Y. Dommergues and S. Krupa (eds.), *Interactions between Non-Pathogenic Soil Microorganisms and Plants*, pp. 205–242, 1978.

Biomass

The mass of living material present in an organism or organisms. Thus biomass may include some nonliving material, such as the hair and feathers of vertebrates or the heartwood of trees. The intent of the term is to provide a useful quantitative measure of the organism and not to make a sharp distinction between life and nonlife. It is typically referred to or calculated as dry weight. In a model, biomass can be a state variable, into and out of which several flows occur. For example, a heterotrophic organism, whether it is a bacterium, bird, or buffalo, ingests food or nutrients and in turn gives off respiratory gases (carbon dioxide) and waste products, and (at times) makes new body tissue (**Fig. 1**). Growth is an increase, and starvation a decrease, in biomass. SEE BIOLOGICAL PRODUCTIVITY.

To measure biomass, many ecologists express it in terms of an element, for example, biomass carbon, nitrogen, phosphorus, and sulfur. This mass is then expressed as grams per square meter ($g \cdot m^{-2}$), parts per million, or some other standard analytical units.

This approach focuses attention on the entire system, including microflora. Since the microflora and associated fauna may be a major part of the total labile pool (one which turns over rapidly) of nutrients in aquatic and terrestrial systems, it is important to know their biomass, as well as that of primary producers, grazers, predators, and so forth. Unfortu-

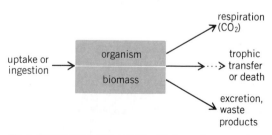

Fig. 1. Biomass as a state variable, with flows of energy and nutrients into and out of it.

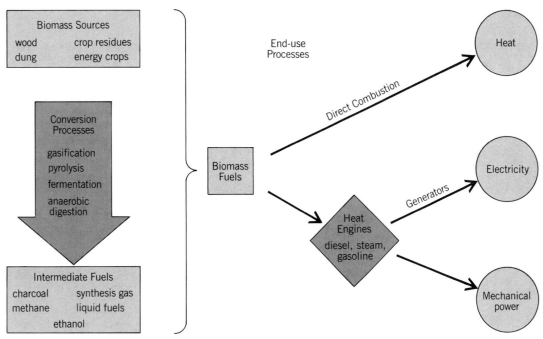

Fig. 2. Methods of using biomass for energy. (*After D. O. Hall, G. W. Barnard, and P. A. Moss, Biomass for Energy in the Developing Countries, Pergamon, 1982*)

nately, biomass of microbes in soils and sediments is difficult to determine. Much research has been done to correlate microbial biomass and total extractable adenosinetriphosphate (ATP), or adenylate pools.

Due to extensive losses of energy at each step in a food web (chain), going from primary producers on up the chain, there is a change in the amount of energy flowing to new biomass at each step in the chain. The change in amount of standing crop at each step is often represented as a horizontal bar. With the size of the bar usually decreasing as one ascends the food web, the shape of the histogram assumes a pyramidal form. This leads to the term biomass pyramid. There are many instances where one finds small standing crops (as with oceanic phytoplankton) and high turnover rates, so that one can describe inverted pyramids as well. SEE FOOD WEB.

Biomass offers several ways to provide relatively inexpensive fuel from a renewable source of energy (**Fig. 2**). Principal biomass sources include generation of alcohol by fermentation of agricultural materials (grain, straw, or other residues), or fermentation of sewage and feedlot wastes, producing biogas, which is mostly methane. The cost effectiveness of these processes is marginal, except in countries with a deficiency of foreign exchange and with considerable biomass production available. Thus, Brazil obtains approximately 80% of its automobile fuel needs from sugarcane and other ethanol crops, and China has over 500,000 biogas digesters using human and pig waste, which provide methane for on-farm use. Due to storage and transport problems, however, biogas will probably remain a localized, on-site source of fuel; many other third world countries, such as India, are rapidly developing this alternative energy source.

An important factor, often overlooked in fuels from biomass, is the quality (energy content) of the materials produced. Methanol or ethanol fermented from wood or agricultural wastes, respectively, has only half of the energy content of the ordinary car gasoline

it is meant to replace. An alternative approach is to raise certain species of unicellular algae in high-light and high-nutrient conditions, so that much of their primary production goes into a high-energy-content oil, which might become competitive with diesel fuel.

David C. Coleman

Bibliography. D. O. Hall, G. W. Barnard, and P. A. Moss, *Biomass for Energy in the Developing Countries*, 1982; D. N. Klass and G. H. Emert (eds.), *Fuels from Biomass and Waste*, 1981.

Biome

A major community of plants and animals having similar life forms or morphological features and existing under similar environmental conditions. The biome, which may be used at the scale of entire continents, is the largest useful biological community unit. In Europe the equivalent term for biome is major life zone, and throughout the world, if only plants are considered, the term used is formation. SEE ECOLOGICAL COMMUNITIES.

Each biome may contain several different types of ecosystems. For example, the grassland biome may contain the dense tallgrass prairie with deep, rich soil, while the desert grassland has a sparse plant canopy and a thin soil. However, both ecosystems have grasses as the predominant plant life form, grazers as the principal animals, and a climate with at least one dry season. Additionally, each biome may contain several successional stages. A forest successional sequence may include grass dominants at an early stage, but some forest animals may require the grass stage for their habitat, and all successional stages constitute the climax forest biome. SEE DESERT; ECOLOGICAL SUCCESSION; ECOSYSTEM; GRASSLAND ECOSYSTEM.

Distributions of animals are more difficult to map than those of plants. The life form of vegetation reflects major features of the climate and determines the structural nature of habitats for animals. Therefore, the life form of vegetation provides a sound basis for ecologically classifying biological communities. Terrestrial biomes are usually identified by the dominant plant component, such as the temperate deciduous forest. Marine biomes are mostly named for physical features, for example, for marine upwelling, and for relative locations, such as littoral. Many biome classifications have been proposed, but a typical one might include several terrestrial biomes such as desert, tundra, grassland, savanna, coniferous forest, deciduous forest, and tropical forest. Aquatic biome examples are fresh-water lotic (streams and rivers), fresh-water lentic (lakes and ponds), and marine littoral, neritic, upwelling, coral reef, and pelagic. *See* F*resh-water ecosystem;* M*arine ecology;* P*lants, life forms of;* T*errestrial ecosystem.*

Paul Risser

Bibliography. M. G. Barbour, J. H. Burk, and W. D. Pitts, *Terrestrial Plant Ecology*, 1980; S. J. McNaughton and L. L. Wolf, *General Ecology*, 1973; P. G. Risser et al., *The True Prairie Ecosystem*, 1981; R. H. Whittaker, Classification of natural communities, *Bot. Rev.*, 28:1–239, 1962.

Biometeorology

A branch of ecology that deals with the effects of the atmospheric environment on living organisms: humans, animals, and plants.

Radiation. The atmosphere forms a protective cover that shields the surface of the Earth from the cosmic radiation and the extreme cold of the universe. Solar radiation can penetrate and warm the atmosphere to a temperature conducive to life. The energetic, lethal, short-wave solar radiation is absorbed in the highest layers of the atmosphere, where it splits diatomic molecular oxygen (O_2) and leads to the formation of the triatomic species, ozone (O_3). This is a fortunate circumstance for living organisms, because ozone absorbs all radiation below the 290-nanometer wavelength. *See* A*tmosphere;* A*tmospheric ozone.*

Small amounts of solar radiation between 290 and 320 nm, ultraviolet-B, reaches the Earth's surface on clear days when the Sun is high above the horizon. This part of the radiation increases with elevation above the surface and can reach high intensities in the mountains. It causes sunburn, and repeated lengthy exposures can lead to skin cancers in persons with lightly pigmented skin. Protection is offered by ultraviolet-screening ointments containing *para*-aminobenzoic acid (PABA). A beneficial effect of ultraviolet-B

is the activation of ergosterol in the skin, which leads to the formation of vitamin D. Also, ultraviolet-B is fatal to bacteria; hence it has a disinfectant effect on outside air and surfaces.

Solar radiation in the 320–400-nm range, ultraviolet-A, is less dangerous but can also produce sunburn. In humans it is primarily melanogenic, that is, it produces tanning. All ultraviolet radiation can produce thickening (keratosis) and aging of the skin. Exposures of the human eye to ultraviolet, especially to shorter wavelengths, can lead to cataracts and to lesions of the cornea and the retina.

Altitude. Humans and animals need atmospheric oxygen for metabolism, hence survival. Although the relative proportion of atmospheric oxygen (21%) and nitrogen (78%) changes very little with elevation to about 40,000 ft (12.2 km) above sea level, the decreasing air density decreases the absolute amounts per unit volume (**Table 1**).

Individuals accustomed to pressure near sea level may suffer from hypoxia (lack of oxygen) at higher elevations (mountain sickness), especially upon exertion. For this reason, cabins of high-flying aircraft are pressurized, generally equivalent to an elevation of 5000–6000 ft (1500–1800 m). The human cardiopulmonary system can, however, become acclimated to higher elevations. For example, La Paz, Bolivia, and Lhasa, Tibet, both at an altitude of about 12,000 ft (3.6 km), are permanently settled regions, but oxygen amounts are about 30% less than at sea level. In some mines in the Andes heavy work is performed at 15,000 ft (4.5 km). Acclimatization is accomplished by large increases in the number of oxygen-carrying red blood corpuscles and in lung alveoli (natives of these altitudes have barrel chests). In mountainous areas there usually are gradual changes in faunal and floral composition with elevation. Although some individual animals can range at considerable differences of elevation, some species have adapted to the higher elevations, for example, pikas, marmot, llamas, and vicunas. Domestic cats seem to be unable to adapt to high elevations. Floral changes with elevation, from deciduous and flowering species to conifers, grasses, and mosses, are related to the variations in temperature and rainfall on mountain slopes. *See* A*ir pressure.*

Thermal equilibrium. The principal problem for living organisms is to achieve thermal equilibrium with the environment, and mechanisms for this adaptation vary widely. Adverse conditions are overcome by dormancy, by hibernation, and, in the case of humans, by technology.

Humans and warm-blooded animals have to main-

Table 1. U.S. standard atmosphere and oxygen content with elevation*				
Elevation, ft (m)	Temperature, °F (°C)	Total pressure, kPa (mb)	O_2 pressure, kPa (mb)	O_2 amount in percent of sea-level value
0 (0)	59.0 (15.0)	101.32 (1013.2)	21.2 (212.2)	100
5,000 (1,524)	41.2 (5.1)	84.89 (848.9)	17.66 (176.6)	86
10,000 (3,048)	23.3 (−4.2)	69.71 (697.1)	14.60 (146.0)	74
15,000 (4,572)	5.7 (−14.7)	57.14 (571.4)	11.97 (119.7)	63
20,000 (6,096)	−12.3 (−24.6)	46.50 (465.0)	9.75 (97.5)	53
30,000 (9,144)	−48.0 (−44.4)	30.09 (300.9)	6.31 (63.1)	37
40,000 (12,192)	−67.0 (−55.0)	18.74 (187.4)	3.87 (38.7)	25

*Temperature and pressure vary with season and geographic location.

Table 2. Insulating qualities of clothing

Environment	Sex	Garments	clo units
Tropical heat	m	Open-necked shirt, shorts, sandals	0.20
	f	Bra and panties, short-sleeved blouse, shorts, sandals	0.25
Warm summer	m	Open-necked shirt, slacks, shorts, ankle socks, shoes	0.40
	f	Bra and panties, short-sleeved blouse, light skirt, short stockings, shoes	0.30
Comfortable weather	m	Business suit, cotton underwear, long-sleeved shirt, socks, shoes	1.0
	f	Bra and panties, slip, dress, panty-hose, pumps	1.0
Cool weather	m	Business suit, light underwear, socks, shoes, light overcoat	1.5
	f	Bra and panties, stockings, slip, dress, sweater, shoes	1.5
Cold weather	m	Business suit, long underwear, woolen socks, shoes, hat, overcoat	2–2.5
	f	Warm underwear, skirt or slacks, slip, long-sleeved blouse, heavy sweater, hat, overcoat	2–2.5
		(For very cold weather, add lined gloves, fur or leather garment for both m & f)	3–3.5
Polar cold	m & f	Woolen underwear, coveralls, quilted parka with hood, fur mittens, fur-lined boots, face mask	4–4.5

tain a homeotherm condition; in humans the approximate equilibrium temperature is 98.6°F (37°C). The balance is provided by heat gain from metabolism and heat exchange with the environment, which must be a net loss. That exchange can take place by radiation, convection, and evaporation. Radiative exchange can be either a gain or a loss: the body surface radiates heat toward a colder region, such as a cold wall, and will gain radiative heat from the Sun or from a warm surface, such as a stove. Heat exchange by convection is generally a loss, with air moving around the body and carrying heat away from the skin. For heat gain from convection, air temperature must be higher than skin temperature. Evaporation always causes a heat loss, because the energy needed is taken from the body. The amount of heat generated by metabolism varies with activity. In humans it is measured in terms of the heat produced by a resting person, which is given the arbitrary value of 50 kilocalories/m^2 (5 kcal/ft^2) of body surface per hour. This is the value of the unit one MET. For a standing person doing light work the metabolic heat production doubles; for moderately hard work or brisk walking (3 mi/h or 5 km/h) it quadruples.

To regulate heat loss to the environment, warm-blooded animals developed fur and feathers, and humans invented clothing and shelter. The amount of insulation required to maintain equilibrium is governed by the conditions in the atmospheric environment. There are a limited number of physiological heat-regulatory mechanisms, controlled by the so-called master thermostat in the brain, the hypothalamus. In cold environments these mechanisms include the increase in metabolic heat production by shivering and a restriction of blood flow to the periphery, that is, the skin and the extremities; this lowers the temperature at the periphery and reduces the radiative heat loss. In warm environments the blood flow to the periphery is increased to raise the temperature and thus the radiative heat loss. In addition, the evaporative cooling process is enhanced by perspiration. There is always some evaporative heat loss by insensible perspiration and by water vapor carried from the lungs by respiration.

Primitive humans had only these natural defenses available against the atmospheric environment; hence their habitat was restricted to the warm climates of the tropics. The development of clothing permitted settlement of other climates. The insulating quality of clothing is measured by a unit (clo) derived from the metabolic heat losses and predicated on maintenance of skin temperature of 91.4°F (33°C), which is equivalent to optimal comfort. One clo permits a heat flux from the body through a garment of 1 kcal/m^2 (0.1 kcal/ft^2) per hour per square meter, with a temperature difference of 0.32°F (0.18°C) between the inner and outer surface of the fabric, as shown by the expression below, where n = number of degrees and

$$\text{Heat flux (kcal/m}^2) = \frac{n\,°C}{0.18(x\,\text{clo})}$$

x = number of clo units. **Table 2** shows a selection of clo values for a variety of atmospheric conditions. **Table 3** shows a few characteristic values of the insulating capacities of winter fur of various animals that have been obtained by laboratory experiments.

Hibernating mammals reduce their metabolism radically by reducing oxygen consumption and lowering heart rate, managing to maintain their body temperature at survival level even at low external temperatures.

Cold stress. Clothing, shelter, and artificial heat can largely compensate for environmental cold, but with extensive exposure to cold, vasoconstriction in the peripheral organs can lead to considerable damage, such as chilblains and frostbite on the nose, ears, cheeks, and toes. This exposure is expressed quantitatively as a wind chill equivalent temperature that is calculated by using an equation relating temperature and wind speed. The wind chill equivalent temperature is a measure of convective heat loss and describes a thermal sensation equivalent to a lower than ambient temperature but with calm conditions (**Table 4**).

Table 3. Insulating characteristic of winter fur of selected mammals

Species	Approximate thickness, in. (cm)	Relative insulation quality
Weasel	0.4 (1)	2
Squirrel	0.8 (2)	2.5
Rabbit	1.2 (3)	5
Dog	1.6 (4)	6
Beaver	1.6 (4)	5
Sheep	2.8 (7)	8

Table 4. Wind chill equivalent temperatures

Wind speed, mi/h (m/s)	Ambient air temperature, °F (°C)							
	50 (10)	41 (5)	32 (0)	23 (−5)	14 (−10)	−4 (−20)	−20 (−30)	−40 (−40)
Calm	50 (10)	41 (5)	32 (0)	23 (−5)	14 (−10)	−4 (−20)	−20 (−30)	−40 (−40)
5 (2.2)	48 (8.9)	38 (3.3)	27 (−1.7)	20 (−6.7)	10 (−12.2)	−9.0 (−22.8)	−28 (−33.3)	−47 (−43.9)
10 (4.5)	40 (4.4)	29 (−1.7)	18 (−7.8)	7 (−13.9)	−4 (−20)	−26.0 (−32.2)	−48 (−44.4)	−70 (−56.7)
15 (6.7)	36 (2.2)	24 (−4.4)	13 (−10.6)	−1 (−18.3)	−13 (−25.0)	−36.9 (−38.3)	−61 (−51.7)	−85 (−65.0)
25 (11.2)	30 (−1.1)	17 (−8.4)	3 (−16.1)	−10 (−23.2)	−24 (−31.1)	−50.1 (−45.6)	−77 (−60.6)	−104 (−75.5)

When the wind chill is below −67°F (−55°C), exposed flesh will freeze immediately. At 50°F (10°C), properly clothed persons can perform outdoor work with good dexterity; at −4°F (−20°C) efficiency is only 50%; and at −75°F (−60°C) no work can be done. Persons exposed to extreme cold develop hypothermia, which may be irreversible when the core temperature drops below 91°F (33°C). The term core temperature defines the temperature of the internal vital organs, for example the cardiopulmonary system, in contrast to that of the peripheral organs, for example, hands or skin. The fatality rate from cold exposure exceeds 450 cases per year in the United States. This number excludes tens of thousands of older individuals whose death indoors during sleep is attributed to cardiac arrest but is suspected to be caused by hypothermia as a result of inadequate heating. On the whole, there is a clear correlation between winter death rates and temperature: the colder the winter, the more deaths occur. Research findings seem to indicate that outdoor deaths may be caused by breathing cold air, which lowers the temperature of the cardiopulmonary system to a lethal level. When the ambient temperature is 68°F (20°C), exhaled air has a temperature of about 91°F (33°C); it has a lower value (73°F or 23°C) when the ambient air is at 23°F (−5°C). See Comfort temperatures.

Heat and humidity. The demands of cold climates are more readily overcome by technology than those of very hot conditions. Two categories of biometeorologically effective heat conditions are distinguished by either high or low humidities. See Humidity.

Low humidities exist principally in subtropical deserts, which have the highest daytime temperatures observed at the Earth's surface. Temperatures of 86 to 104°F (30 to 40°C) are common, and occasionally even 122°F (50°C) or higher temperatures are observed. Simultaneous relative humidities are usually below 10% and rarely exceed 30% in daytime. Human and animal bodies are also exposed to high val-

ues of solar radiation and reflected radiation from the surface of the sand. This combination makes extraordinary demands on the sweat mechanism. Water losses of 1.06 quarts (1 liter) per hour are common in humans and may be higher upon exertion. Unless the water is promptly replaced by fluid intake, dehydration sets in. Even moderate dehydration at tolerable temperatures during exertion causes body temperatures to rise 0.9 to 2.7°F (0.5 to 1.5°C). Extreme heat can cause panting initially, then an increased pulse rate and decreased urine volume, and will rapidly lead to heat exhaustion. In humans a 2% weight loss by dehydration is slight and causes no symptoms other than thirst. If the loss rises to 6%, scanty urine and a rapid pulse accompanying a temperature rise of 3.6°F (2°C) will ensue; a greater weight loss by dehydration will cause circulatory failure and brain damage. Death occurs when the weight loss reaches 10–15% of body weight. Desert populations use the cooler night hours with absence of incoming radiation for travel and other activities.

Similarly, animals that live in deserts are mostly nocturnal. Lizards and rodents spend the day in hollows and burrows because temperatures are 18–36°F (10–20°C) below the extreme heat of the top sand even an inch or so beneath the surface. Desert animals have also developed various mechanisms to maintain thermal equilibrium. Jackrabbits have large, highly vascularized ears that allow heat to radiate from the body. Heavy coats, panting, and some skin gland secretion permit dogs to survive. Carnivorous desert animals obtain the major part of their fluid needs from the body fluids of their prey. The most physiologically efficient desert animal is the camel. It can store fluid in its system and survive several days without water. The camel stores heat in its large body (1100 lb or 500 kg) rather than cooling it by evaporation. Its body temperature rises in the daytime from its normal of 99°F (37°C) to 104°F (40°C), while at night the excess heat is lost by radiation and convec-

Table 5. Conversion of outdoor relative humidity to indoor values (%) for various outdoor temperatures at 70°F (21°C) indoors

Relative humidity, %	Outdoor temperature				
	50°F (10°C)	41°F (5°C)	32°F (0°C)	23°F (−5°C)	14°F (−10°C)
100	46	32	23	16	10
90	41	29	21	14	9
80	37	26	19	13	8
70	32	23	16	11	7
60	28	20	14	9	6
50	23	17	11	8	5

Table 6. Humiture values, in °F (°C), for various combinations of temperatures and relative humidity

Relative humidity, %	77°F (25°C)	86°F (30°C)	95°F (35°C)	104°F (40°C)
30	76 (24)	87 (31)	97 (36)	110 (43)
40	77 (25)	89 (32)	102 (39)	120 (49)
50	78 (26)	93 (34)	108 (42)	132 (56)
60	80 (27)	95 (35)	116 (47)	
70	82 (28)	100 (38)	125 (52)	
80	85 (29)	106 (41)	135 (57)	

tion, dropping the body temperature to 95°F (35°C). If given water, only a small diurnal variation of body temperature will occur. Camels can survive a 25% weight loss by dehydration. In other species, 10–15% weight loss is the limit, with accompanying rapid temperature gain and ensuing death. *SEE DESERT.*

It is also possible for dehydration to occur in heated buildings during winter because the cold outside air has very little moisture and as it infiltrates into the building the relative humidity drops drastically and creates a desertlike climate. **Table 5** shows the indoor relative humidity for a room heated to 70°F (21°C) as a function of outdoor temperature and relative humidity.

For lower outdoor temperatures and relative humidities the indoor dryness is even more drastic. Household activities such as cooking, laundry, bathing, and growing house plants add moisture, but unless humidifiers are used, water losses of occupants can be substantial. At a room temperature of 70°F (21°C) and a relative humidity of 50%, a resting individual loses about 1.06 quarts (1 liter) of water in 24 h. At a relative humidity of 30% and the same temperature the water loss is about 1.16 quarts (1.1 liters), mostly from insensible perspiration and exhaled air.

Both outdoor and indoor comfort is governed by temperature and humidity combinations. However, there is a great variability among individuals in terms of comfort zones. Acclimatization plays a role, but in general older persons and infants require higher temperature values for comfort. On the average, there is a spread of 3.6–9°F (2–5°C) for comfort sensations for persons living in middle or higher latitudes compared with residents of subtropical or tropical climates, where there is a narrower spread of 2–5°F (1–3°C), but higher absolute comfort values of 5–7°F (3–4°C). There are a large number of indices describing comfort sensations as functions of ambient temperatures and humidities. One of these, the humiture value, is an equivalent temperature depicting the atmospheric comfort conditions that an individual would experience if temperature alone were governing (**Table 6**). Clearly the high temperature-humidity combinations are unbearable.

Wider technical use has been made of a measure called effective temperature, which is defined as the temperature of air at 100% relative humidity giving the same thermal sensation as the air at ambient temperature and relative humidity. The effective temperature can be conveniently approximated by a quantity known as temperature-humidity index (THI) or discomfort index. It is calculated from the observed dry- and wet-bulb temperatures (T_d and T_w, respectively) measured with a psychrometer, Eqs. (1) and (2).

For °F values, THI = $0.4(T_d + T_w) + 15$ (1)
For °C values, THI = $0.4(T_d + T_w) + 4.8$ (2)

Figure 1 shows a thermodynamic chart, combining all the temperature and humidity parameters. The solid curved lines represent the effective temperatures (THI). The shaded area represents the ranges of temperatures and humidities considered to be "comfortable" by healthy, appropriately dressed adult persons. Values up to effective temperatures of 88°F (31°C) are considered tolerable; above this level body temperatures rise from 99°F (37°C) to 100°F (38°C). At that point severe reactions begin, first noted as deterioration in performance of mental and physical tasks. Under exertion, even at lower effective temperatures, panting, high pulse rate, and cardiopulmonary symptoms develop. Observations of persons under severe physical stress, such as military personnel bearing heavy loads being drilled or joggers, have resulted in establishing limits for heat stroke (hyperpyrexia) and heat death (**Fig. 2**).

Statistics for the United States show increased mortality during summer heat waves. Older persons living in non-air-conditioned quarters are particularly afflicted. Death rates for persons over 80 years double

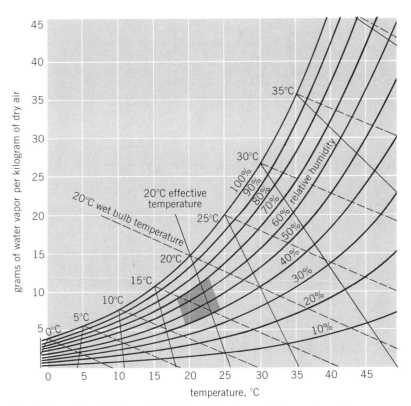

Fig. 1. Thermodynamic diagram showing the relations between air temperature, water vapor mixing ratio, wet-bulb temperature, effective temperature, and relative humidity. Shaded area shows comfort zone for most healthy adult persons in the United States. 1 g = 0.035 oz. 1 kg = 2.2 lb. °F = (°C × 1.8) + 32°.

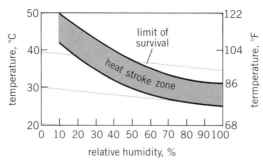

Fig. 2. Air temperature–relative humidity diagram, showing the danger zone for heat stroke and the upper limit for survival for various combinations of these elements.

when air temperatures exceed 99°F (37°C) compared with temperatures around 77°F (25°C). Individuals with congestive heart disease are particularly endangered by heat. Victims of multiple sclerosis also find their symptoms aggravated when exposed to a hot atmospheric environment.

The use of certain drugs is inadvisable during hot weather. For example, phenothiazines, which include several major tranquilizers, reduce the ability to sweat and can cause heat stroke. Similarly, the use of diuretics should be restricted, and drugs used to alleviate Parkinson's disease must be avoided during hot periods. Many drugs that inhibit sweating have been banned from use in the tropics. Coffee or caffeine-containing preparations should also be avoided because they constrict the peripheral blood vessels. Air conditioning can reduce the acute troubles caused by excessive heat.

Weather sensitivity. Both physiological and psychological responses to weather changes, known as meteorotropisms, are widespread and generally have their origin in some bodily impairment. A particularly common reaction to weather changes occurs in anomalous skin tissue such as scars and corns. This is induced by changes in atmospheric moisture which causes differential hygroscopic expansion and contraction between healthy and abnormal skin, leading to pain. Sufferers from rheumatoid arthritis are most commonly affected by weather changes; both pain and swelling of affected joints have been noted with increased atmospheric humidity. Sudden cooling can also trigger such symptoms. Clinical tests have shown that in these individuals the heat regulatory mechanism does not function well, but the underlying cause is not understood. High values of atmospheric humidity and heat leading to sweating can cause prickly heat, an itchy rash attributable to partial blocking of sweat glands.

Weather is also a significant factor in asthma attacks. Asthma as an allergic reaction may, in rare cases, be directly provoked by sudden changes in temperature that occur after passage of a cold front. More often, however, the weather effect is indirect, and attacks are caused by windblown allergens, such as air pollutants and pollen. An even more indirect relationship exists for asthma attacks in autumn, which often seem to be related to an early outbreak of cold air. This cold air initiates home or office heating, and dormant dust or fungi from registers and radiators are convected into rooms, irritating allergic persons. *SEE AIR POLLUTION.*

A variety of psychological effects have also been attributed to heat. They are vaguely described as las-

situde, decrease in mental and physical performance, and increased irritability. Similar reactions to weather have been described for domestic animals, particularly dogs.

Many of the physiological or pathological reactions to weather in the middle and higher latitudes have been related to the typical sequence of weather events that are common in the cold season. **Figure 3** is an idealized weather map with the associated changes in weather elements. There are six weather phases: (1) high pressure: clear, sunny sky, light wind, cool; (2) falling pressure: few clouds, subsidence (that is, descending air), solar warming; (3) approaching low pressure: increasing and lowering cloudiness (cirrostratus to altostratus to stratus); (4) passage of warm front: rain (or snow in winter), rising temperatures, fresh wind, occasional fog, high humidity; (5) passage of cold front: showers (thunderstorms in summer) or snow flurries (in winter), sharp drop in temperature, rapidly rising pressure, brisk winds; (6) high pressure. The map shows the phases changing from high pressure, approaching low pressure, passage of a warm front with rain or snow, a cold front with showers or flurries, and return to high pressure again. The weather system moves from left to right, passing over a locality in the sequence from right to left. A number of studies have shown that weather phase 4, the warm front passage, is the one most frequently related to meteorotropic symptoms. It also has an apparent relation to the frequency of industrial accidents. In schools, disciplinary infractions are higher

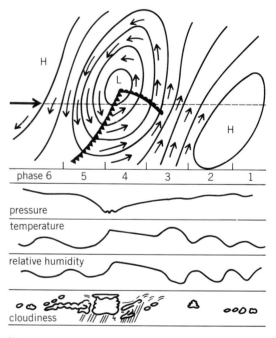

Key:

Fig. 3. Idealized weather map showing, from right to left, six biotropic weather phases, each depicting one day as the system moves from left to right over a locality. Lower panels show characteristic changes of weather elements.

and students' test scores are lower. In phases 4 and 5, weather elements change most rapidly, and there is an increase in cardiovascular deaths; also, phase 5 has been associated with the initiation of labor at the end of pregnancies. SEE WEATHER MAP.

It has been documented that lightning has killed more people (about 100 annually in the United States) in recent decades than tornadoes or hurricanes; the number of those injured is uncertain. Although it has been hypothesized that the broad spectrum of electromagnetic radiation associated with lightning discharges may have an influence on human brain waves, there is no proof. The many examples of the effects of thunderstorms on domestic animals seem mostly to be due to fright and thus may simply be caused by the noise of thunder. SEE THUNDERSTORM.

There has also been some speculation concerning biological effects of small atmospheric ions which are continuously created by cosmic radiation and by decay of natural radioactive substances. Their lifetime is very short, and they either recombine or attach themselves to larger aerosols, most of which, in settled regions, are air pollutants. These can, of course, cause allergic reactions. SEE ATMOSPHERIC CHEMISTRY.

Meteorological and seasonal changes in natural illumination have a major influence on animals. Photoperiodicity is widespread. The daily cycle of illumination triggers the feeding cycle in many species, especially birds. In insectivores this may result from the activities of the insects which themselves show temperature-influenced cycles of animation. Bird migration may likewise be initiated by light changes, but temperature changes and availability of food are also involved. In the process of migration, especially over long distances, birds have learned to take advantage of prevailing wind patterns. Occasional reactions to light changes have been observed in humans. Bright, dazzling sunshine is believed to initiate migraine headaches in some sufferers. Light deprivation, as is common in the cold weather season in higher latitudes, is suspected as a cause of depression.

Weather and flora. Unlike humans and animals, plants cannot move from one location to another and therefore must adapt genetically to their atmospheric environment. Plants are often characteristic for their climatic zone, such as palms in the subtropics and birches or firs in regions having cold winters. Whole systems of climatic classifications are based on the native floras: tropical rainforest, deciduous and coniferous forests, grassland, steppe, tundra, desert. SEE PLANT GEOGRAPHY.

In plants, photosynthesis, respiration, and transpiration are governed by the atmospheric environment. In these processes, water is usually the limiting element, and as a result, the ratio of rainfall to evapotranspiration is a governing factor in plant development. In addition, growth requires certain soil and air threshold temperatures; soil temperature and moisture regulate seed germination; and photosynthetic rates are also governed by temperature. Generally, there is no photosynthesis or growth at air temperature below 41°F (5°C). As temperature rises above this level, there is a rise in growth to an optimum, which in many plants is around 86°F (30°C); a drop in productivity occurs at high temperature, with cessation of growth at 113°F (45°C).

In the course of responding to the environment, plants experience typical cycles, so that at certain levels of temperature, specific growth responses take place, such as leaving, flowering, and fruit development. The seasonal phases can be disrupted by adverse weather conditions: drought causes wilting, and freezing temperatures destroy blossoms or other plant tissue.

Most available information relates to agricultural crop plants, which have been genetically altered to be able to withstand adverse weather. Examples are drought-resistant varieties and short-growth types that are less subject to wind damage. Protective measures that can be taken to modify local climatic conditions and benefit crop growth include irrigation, wind protection, and frost prevention. Adverse weather conditions can also cause disease outbreaks; for example, wind transports fungal spores from infected plants to healthy ones, and excessive moisture causes outbreaks of fungal diseases. SEE AGRICULTURAL METEOROLOGY.

Weather and farm animals. Much research has been devoted to the response of farm animals to the atmospheric environment because of their great economic importance. Many are kept in completely artificial surroundings where temperature, humidity, light, and ventilation are controlled to ensure optimal production. This applies particularly to chickens, with both egg and meat production maintained in completely regulated atmospheres. Many dairy farms are equipped with climate-controlled barns. For sheep, wool production is enhanced by cool temperatures, but very low temperatures during lambing and shearing can lead to losses. Even honey production is temperature-related: in years when there are many summer days with maximum temperatures above 77°F (25°C) honey production is higher than in the years when maximum daytime temperatures are lower. SEE ECOLOGY.

H. E. Landsberg

Bibliography. G. L. Campbell, *An Introduction to Environmental Biophysics,* 1977; Center for Occupational Research and Development, *Environmental Biology,* 1985; E. Flach, Human bioclimatology, *World Survey of Climatology,* vol. 2, pp. 1–187, 1981; G. E. Folk, *Introduction to Environmental Physiology,* 2d ed., 1974; E. Kessler (ed.), *The Thunderstorm in Human Affairs,* 2d ed., 1983; H. E. Landsberg, *The Assessment of Human Bioclimate,* World Meteorol. Org. Tech. Note 123, 1972; S. W. Tromp, *Biometeorology,* 1980; A. Y. M. Yao, Agricultural climatology, *World Survey of Climatology,* vol. 3, pp. 189–298, 1982.

Biosphere

The thin film of living organisms and their environments at the surface of the Earth. Included in the biosphere are all environments capable of sustaining life above, on, and beneath the Earth's surface as well as in the oceans. Consequently, the biosphere includes virtually the entire hydrosphere and portions of the atmosphere and outer lithosphere.

Neither the upper nor lower limits of the biosphere are sharp. Spores of microorganisms can be carried to considerable heights in the atmosphere, but these are resting stages that are not actively metabolizing. A variety of organisms inhabit the ocean depths, including the giant tube worms and other creatures that were discovered living around hydrothermal vents. Evidence exists for the presence of bacteria in oil reservoirs at depths of about 6600 ft (2000 m) within the Earth. The bacteria are apparently metabolically active, utilizing the paraffinic hydrocarbons of the oils as an energy source. These are extreme limits to the biosphere; most of the mass of living matter is within the upper 330 ft (100 m) of the lithosphere and hydrosphere, although there are places even within this zone that are too dry or too cold to support much life. Most of the biosphere is within the zone which is reached by sunlight and where liquid water exists.

Origin. For over 50 years after Louis Pasteur disproved the theory of spontaneous generation, scientists believed that life was universal and was transplanted to other planets and solar systems by the spores of microorganisms. This is the theory of panspermia. In the 1920s the modern theory of chemical evolution of life on Earth was proposed independently by A. I. Oparin, a Soviet biochemist, and J. B. S. Haldane, a British biochemist. The basic tenet of the theory is that life arose through a series of chemical steps involving increasingly complex organic substances that had been chemically synthesized and had accumulated on the prebiotic Earth. The first organisms originated under anaerobic conditions in an atmosphere devoid of free molecular oxygen. Because they were incapable of aerobic photosynthesis, a complex process which evolved undoubtedly after life originated, the oxygen in the present atmosphere arose as a secondary addition.

The first organisms appeared probably prior to 3.5 billion years (b.y.) and possibly earlier than 3.8 b.y. ago. One piece of evidence pinpointing the time of emergence of the first cells is the presence of stromatolites in rocks of the Warrawoona Group in Australia and the Onverwacht Group in South Africa, both deposited about 3.5 b.y. ago. Stromatolites are distinctive, thinly laminated deposits formed by layers of bacterial or cyanobacterial mats alternating with sedimentary deposits, usually calcium carbonate or chert. Carbon (C) isotopes also provide supporting evidence for the origin of life about this time. The $^{13}C/^{12}C$ ratio of the insoluble organic carbon, or kerogen, in sedimentary rocks extending back 3.5 b.y. ago is within the range of reduced carbon found in all younger rocks, an indication that organisms, which are responsible for the isotopic fractionation of carbon, had already appeared.

Of greater antiquity are the approximately 3.8-b.y.-old sedimentary rocks from the Isua region of western Greenland. While these rocks contain no convincing evidence that life existed at this time, they demonstrate that liquid water was present and that the processes of erosion, transportation, and deposition of sediments were occurring, all indicative of conditions on the Earth conducive to life-forms. If life did exist by this time, the preceding period of chemical evolution leading up to the first cells lasted for about 0.3–0.5 b.y., or about the time span between 3.8 b.y. and the cooling of the Earth's surface sufficiently to contain liquid water, an event that may have occurred within a few hundred million years of the formation of the Earth about 4.6 b.y. ago.

Evolution. The changes wrought during the evolution of the biosphere had profound effects on the atmosphere, hydrosphere, and outer lithosphere.

Photosynthesis. Probably the first significant event in the evolution of the biosphere was the development of photosynthesis, a process that led to autotrophic organisms capable of synthesizing organic matter from inorganic constituents. This evolutionary advance freed the early organisms from a dependence on the coexisting abiogenic organic matter, which was being depleted by heterotrophic anaerobes. These autotrophs were anaerobic organisms similar to modern photosynthetic bacteria, and they did not release oxygen as a by-product. Some time later, probably by about 2.9 b.y. ago with the appearance of cyanobacteria, oxygen-releasing photosynthesis, another major milestone in the development of the biosphere, evolved.

Eukaryotes. A profound evolutionary event was the emergence of eukaryotic organisms. All early lifeforms were prokaryotic, as are modern bacteria and cyanobacteria; all other organisms are eukaryotic, characterized by the presence of a nucleus and capable of reproducing by meiosis and mitosis. The origin of eukaryotic organisms was an important evolutionary event, as it represented the emergence of sexual reproduction and set the stage for the later evolution of multicellular organisms. The time of first appearance of eukaryotic organisms is thought to be as early as 1.6 b.y. ago.

Geochemical cycles. Organisms have had an effect on the geochemistry of their environment for at least 3.5 b.y. Prior to the development of oxygen-releasing photosynthesis, the Earth's surface was anoxic, all organisms were anaerobic, and chemical elements existed in their reduced forms. The gradual release of free oxygen permanently changed the Earth's surface from a reducing environment to an oxidizing one. Elements such as iron and sulfur were converted to an oxidized state, and a great amount of reduced carbon was converted to carbon dioxide (CO_2). This increased the bicarbonate (HCO_3^-) and carbonate (CO_3^{2-}) concentrations in the oceans and resulted in the precipitation of calcium carbonate ($CaCO_3$) to form the massive limestones and dolomites of the later Precambrian. Major events in Precambrian evolution are shown in the **illustration.** *See Biogeochemistry.*

Organisms. Although the biosphere is the smallest in mass, it is one of the most reactive spheres. In the course of its reactions, the biosphere has important influences on the outer lithosphere, hydrosphere, and atmosphere. *See Atmosphere; Hydrosphere.*

Ecosystem. The biosphere is characterized by the interrelationship of living things and their environments. Communities are interacting systems of organisms tied to their environments by the transfer of energy and matter. Such a coupling of living organisms and the nonliving matter with which they interact defines an ecosystem. An ecosystem may range in size from a small pond to a tropical forest to the entire biosphere. Ecologists group the terrestrial parts of the biosphere into about 12 large units called biomes. Examples of biomes include tundra, desert, grassland and boreal forest. *See Biome; Ecological communities; Ecosystem.*

Metabolic processes. The major metabolic processes occurring within the biosphere are photosynthesis and respiration. Green plants, through the process of photosynthesis, form organic compounds composed essentially of carbon (C), hydrogen (H), oxygen (O), and nitrogen (N) from carbon dioxide and water (H_2O), and nutrients, with O_2 being released as a by-product. The O_2 and organic compounds are partially reconverted into CO_2 and H_2O through respiration by plants and animals. Driving this cycle is energy from

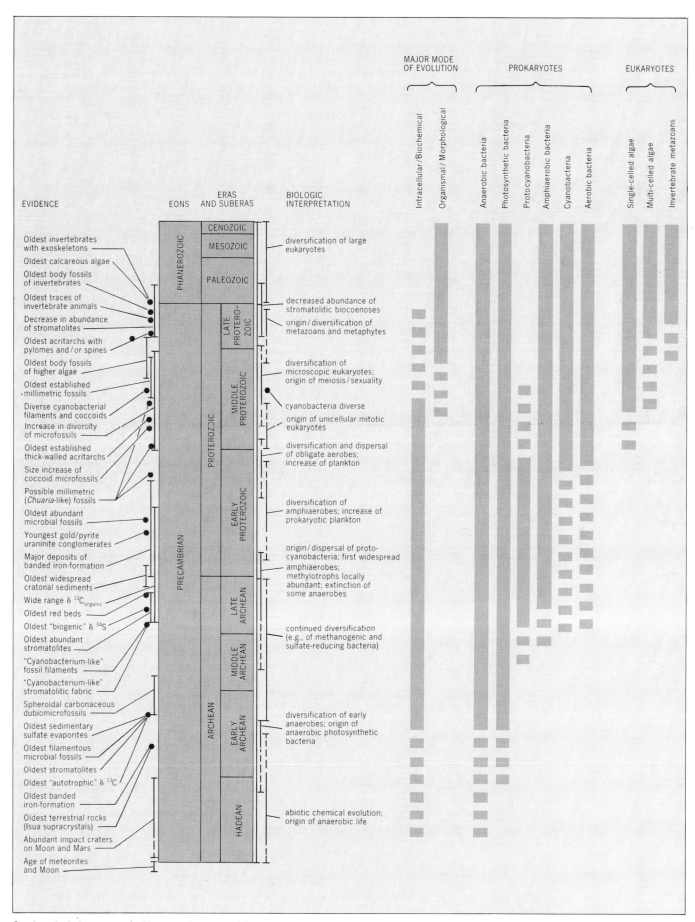

Geochronological summary of evidence relating to the origin and evolution of the earliest biosphere. (*After J. W. Schopf et al., eds., Earth's Earliest Biosphere: Its Origin and Evolution, Princeton University Press, 1983*)

the Sun; respiration releases the Sun's energy which has been stored by photosynthesis.

Types. The fundamental types of organisms engaged in these activities are producers, or green plants that manufacture their food through the process of photosynthesis and respire part of it; consumers, or animals that feed on plants directly or on other animals by ingestion of organic matter; and decomposers, or bacteria that break down organic substances to inorganic products.

Productivity, the rate of formation of living tissue per unit area in a given time, is one of the fundamental attributes of an ecosystem. All organisms in the community are dependent on the energy obtained through gross primary productivity. The productivity of an ecosystem is determined by a number of environmental variables, particularly temperature and the availability of water and nutrients. In marine environments, availability of nutrients is the limiting factor, while the productivity in terrestrial environments is limited by the availability of water. The productivity of different ecosystems is given in the **table**. The biomass, or the total mass of living organisms at one time in an ecosystem, may or may not correlate with productivity. The productivities of tropical rain forests and reefs are nearly identical, but their biomasses differ by a factor of about 650. *See Biological productivity.*

The portion of gross primary productivity that is not respired by green plants is the net primary productivity that is available to consumer and reducer organisms. Organic matter and energy are passed from one organism to another along food chains. The steps, or groupings of organisms, in a chain are trophic levels. Green plants, the producers, occupy the first trophic level, followed by herbivores (primary consumers), primary carnivores, secondary carnivores, and tertiary carnivores. The number of links in a food chain is variable, but three to five levels are common. Only about 10% or less of the matter and energy is passed from one trophic level to the next because of the utilization of energy in respiration at each level. *See Food web.*

Living and dead organic matter that is not consumed by higher trophic levels is decomposed as dead tissue through bacterial action. Decomposers play a major role in the flow of matter and energy in ecosystems because they are the final agents to release the photosynthetic energy from the organic compounds that they utilize. Decomposers recycle the chemical components, but not energy, back into the ecosystem. *See Population ecology.*

Human impact. Human beings, of course, are part of the biosphere. Some of their activities have an adverse impact on many ecosystems and on themselves by the addition of toxic or harmful substances to the outer lithosphere, hydrosphere, and atmosphere. Many of these materials are eventually incorporated into or otherwise affect the biosphere. The major types of environmental pollutants are sewage, trace metals, petroleum hydrocarbons, synthetic organic compounds, and gaseous emissions.

Sewage. Bulk sewage is generally disposed of satisfactorily and is normally not a problem unless it contains one or more of the other types of substances. Under certain conditions, either when the load of organic matter is at a high level or nutrients lead to eutrophication, dissolved oxygen is depleted, creating

Primary production and plant biomass estimates for the Earth*

Ecosystem type	Area, 10^6 km²	Net primary productivity per unit area, (g/m²)/yr Normal range	Mean	World net primary production, 10^9 dry metric tons/yr	Biomass per unit area, kg/m² Normal range	Mean	World biomass, 10^9 dry metric tons
Tropical rainforest	17.0	1000–3500	2200	37.4	6–80	45	765
Tropical seasonal forest	7.5	1000–2500	1600	12.0	6–60	35	260
Temperate evergreen forest	5.0	600–2500	1300	6.5	6–200	35	175
Temperate deciduous forest	7.0	600–2500	1200	8.4	6–60	30	210
Boreal forest	12.0	400–2000	800	9.6	6–40	20	240
Woodland and shrubland	8.5	250–1200	700	6.0	2–20	6	50
Savanna	15.0	200–2000	900	13.5	0.2–15	4	60
Temperate grassland	9.0	200–1500	600	5.4	0.2–5	1.6	14
Tundra and alpine	8.0	10–400	140	1.1	0.1–3	0.6	5
Desert and semidesert scrub	18.0	10–250	90	1.6	0.1–4	0.7	13
Extreme desert, rock, sand, and ice	24.0	0–10	3	0.07	0–0.2	0.02	0.5
Cultivated land	14.0	100–3500	650	9.1	0.4–12	1	14
Swamp and marsh	2.0	800–3500	2000	4.0	3–50	15	30
Lake and stream	2.0	100–1500	250	0.5	0–0.1	0.02	0.05
Total continental	149.0		773	115		12.3	1837
Open ocean	332.0	2–400	125	41.5	0–0.005	0.003	1.0
Upwelling zones	0.4	400–1000	500	0.2	0.005–0.1	0.02	0.008
Continental shelf	26.6	200–600	360	9.6	0.001–0.04	0.01	0.27
Algal beds and reefs	0.6	500–4000	2500	1.6	0.04–4	2	1.2
Estuaries	1.4	200–3500	1500	2.1	0.01–6	1	1.4
Total marine	361		152	55.0		0.01	3.9
Full total	510		333	170		3.6	1841

*10^6 km² = 3.86 × 10^5 mi². 1 g/m² = 2.048 × 10^{-4} lb/ft². 10^9 dry metric tons = 1.1 × 10^9 short tons. 1 kg/m² = 0.2048 lb/ft².
SOURCE: R. H. Whittaker, *Communities and Ecosystems*, 2d ed., Macmillan, 1975.

undesirable stagnation of the water. *See Eutrophication; Sewage treatment*.

Trace metals. Some metals are toxic at low concentrations, while other metals that are necessary for metabolic processes at low levels are toxic when present in high concentrations. Examples of metals known to be toxic at low concentrations are lead, mercury, cadmium, selenium, and arsenic. Industrial uses and automobile exhaust are the chief sources of these metals. Additions of these metals through human activity are, in some cases, about equal to the natural input. Great increases of metals are observed near major sources. Plants and soils near highways or lead-processing facilities contain as much as 100 times the unpolluted value of lead. Introduction of unleaded gasoline and passage of legislation requiring safer disposal practices and clean-up of contaminated land should reduce the danger from trace-metal contamination.

Petroleum hydrocarbons. Petroleum hydrocarbons from runoff, industrial and ship discharges, and oil spills pollute coastal waters and may contaminate marine organisms. Oil slicks smother marine life by preventing the diffusion of oxygen into the water or by coating the organisms with a tarry residue. Aromatic constituents of petroleum are toxic to all organisms. Large doses can be lethal, while sublethal quantities can have a variety of physiological effects, especially carcinogenicity. The hydrocarbons are lipophilic and, because they are not metabolized or excreted, tend to accumulate in fatty tissues. Even when marine life has not been subjected to massive contamination by an oil spill, the organisms may be gradually contaminated by accumulating the hydrocarbons to which they have been continuously exposed at low concentrations. Contamination of shellfish, in particular, is of concern because they are consumed in great quantities by humans. *See Water pollution*.

Synthetic organic compounds. Manufacture and use of synthetic organic compounds, such as insecticides and plasticizers, are commonplace worldwide. Many of these chemicals are chlorinated hydrocarbons, a category of substances that is known to be generally toxic to organisms. Of even greater concern is that chlorinated hydrocarbons are carcinogenic and long-term exposure to sublethal doses increases the risk of cancer. The widespread use of chlorinated hydrocarbons in industrial society leads to an increasing background of these compounds in natural waters, including drinking water.

Synthetic organic compounds and petroleum hydrocarbons are generally not metabolized or excreted by organisms. Both groups tend to be retained in the fatty tissues and passed on to other organisms in the next level of the food chain. Consequently, predators high in the food chain are exposed to much greater concentrations of toxic or carcinogenic substances through their ingested food than is present at background levels in the environment. Prior to banning its widespread use in the United States (use is still legal in many other countries), DDT was found in concentrations as high as tens of parts per million in fish-eating birds such as gulls and grebes, even though the concentration of DDT in the lower organisms of their food chain and in the bottom sediment was as low as 0.01 ppm. The high concentrations led to thinning of egg shells and decline in reproduction rate in many predator bird populations. *See Insecticide; Mutagens and carcinogens*.

Gaseous emissions. Gaseous emissions to the atmosphere from industrial sources and automobiles represent both short-term and long-term hazards. Short-term problems include the addition of sulfurous gases, leading to more acidic rainfall, the emission of nitrogen oxides which form smog, and carbon monoxide from automobile exhaust which leads to impairment of breathing in cities. *See Smog*.

Of more long-term concern is the increase in CO_2, methane, chlorofluorocarbons, and nitrous oxide in the atmosphere. These gases absorb heat radiated from the Earth—the so-called greenhouse effect—which will lead to a gradual warming of the Earth's surface and the attendant problems of shifting of climatic zones, upsetting of ecosystem balances, partial melting of polar icecaps, and possibly other unanticipated effects. Combustion of fossil fuels and deforestation are the major sources of the CO_2, the concentration of which has been increasing at the rate of about 1 part per million by volume each year since measurements began in the late 1950s. Since the early 1960s the increase in CO_2 correlates precisely with the growth of world population.

Atmospheric methane, another so-called greenhouse gas, has doubled during the last few hundred years. Methane is produced naturally by bacterial decomposition of organic matter in the absence of oxygen, with major sources being rice paddies, natural wetlands, and animal digestive tracts (termites, for example, are a significant source). Like that of CO_2, the increase in atmospheric methane may also be due to population-related environmental pressures as forests are cleared and rice paddies are expanded.

The synthetic organic compounds called chlorofluorocarbons, also known as the freons, used in aerosol sprays and refrigeration equipment, are both greenhouse gases and a threat to the Earth's ozone layer, which shields organisms from lethal ultraviolet radiation. Scientists predict that a partial depletion of the ozone layer will cause an increase in the incidence of skin cancer and decrease in crop and seafood yields due to the increased dosage of damaging ultraviolet radiation. Concern about the potential destruction of the ozone layer has escalated with the discovery of a large hole in it centered over Antarctica. Although world production of chlorofluorocarbons has decreased slightly because of the ban on their use in aerosol sprays in the United States, production in the rest of the world has increased.

Nitrous oxide (N_2O), derived by nitrification and denitrification reactions in fertilized soils, sewage, and animal wastes, is another agent leading to depletion of ozone. Increasing reliance on chemical fertilizers to increase crop productivity is generating a larger N_2O flux to the atmosphere.

Most, if not all, of the additions of potentially harmful substances to the environment are a result of the population growth and the technological advances of industrial society. The impact of these pollutants will be felt by future generations. Humans are conducting a global ecological experiment with uncertain consequences by altering the fragile equilibrium between the biosphere and its environment. *See Acid rain; Air pollution; Atmospheric chemistry; Atmospheric ozone; Greenhouse effect; Human ecology*.

Richard M. Mitterer

Bibliography. National Academy of Sciences, *Protection Against Depletion of Stratospheric Ozone by Chlorofluorocarbons*, 1979; N. D. Newell and

L. Marcus, Carbon dioxide and people, *Palaios*, 2:101–103, 1987; M. Schidlowski, A 3,800-million-year isotopic record of life from carbon in sedimentary rocks, *Nature*, 333:313–318, 1988; J. W. Schopf et al. (eds.), *Earth's Earliest Biosphere: Its Origin and Evolution*, 1983; R. H. Whittaker, *Communities and Ecosystems*, 2d ed., 1975.

Climate modeling

Construction of a mathematical model of the climate system of the Earth capable of simulating its behavior under present and altered conditions. The Earth's climate is continually changing over time scales ranging from millions of years to a few years. Since the climate is determined by the laws of classical physics, it should be possible in principle to construct such a model. The advent of a worldwide weather observing system capable of gathering data for validation and the development and widespread routine use of digital computers have made this undertaking possible, starting in the mid-1970s. SEE CLIMATIC CHANGE.

The first attempts at modeling the planetary climate showed that the Earth's average temperature is determined mainly by the balance of radiant energy absorbed from sunlight and the radiant energy emitted by the Earth system. About 30% of the incoming radiation is reflected directly to space, and 72% of the remainder is absorbed at the surface (**Fig. 1**). The incoming solar radiation is divided among reflection, absorption by the atmospheric constituents, and absorption by the surface of the planet. The outgoing infrared radiation comes from the surface, atmospheric gases, and clouds. In addition, the atmosphere radiates down to the surface, and the surface gives energy to the atmosphere in the forms of latent and sensible heat. The radiation is absorbed unevenly over the Earth, which sets up thermal contrasts that in turn induce convective circulations in the atmosphere and oceans. Climate models attempt to calculate from mathematical algorithms the effects of these contrasts and the resulting motions in order to understand better and perhaps predict future climates in some probabilistic sense.

Climate models differ in complexity, depending upon the application. The simplest models are intended for describing only the surface thermal field at a fairly coarse resolution. These mainly thermodynamical formulations are successful at describing the seasonal cycle of the present climate, and have been used in some simulations of past climates, for example, for different continental arrangements that occurred millions of years ago. At the other end of the spectrum are the most complex climate models, which are extensions of the models used in weather forecasts. These models aim at simulating seasonal and even monthly averages just shortly into the future, based upon conditions such as the temperatures of the tropical-sea surfaces. Intermediate to these extremes are models that attempt to model climate on a decadal basis, and these are used mainly in studies of the impact of hypothesized anthropogenically induced climate change. SEE CLIMATE MODIFICATION; WEATHER FORECASTING AND PREDICTION.

Anatomy of models. Since the main interest of climate modelers is in computing the thermal field over the Earth, their primary goal is to represent the conservation of energy at each location in the system. This must include accurate formulations of the absorption and reflection of solar radiation as it passes through the atmosphere and strikes surfaces. It must also include the radiation emitted from each mass element in the Earth–atmosphere system. Conversions of heat from latent to sensible must be taken into account as water changes its phase in the system. Clouds must be included since they participate in the radiation transfer and in the changes of water phase. Similarly, snow and ice cover enter both energy disposal accounts. The thermodynamic expression of the conservation of energy is not complete until allowance is made for the flow of matter of a different temperature into a given region. To include this effect, a model of the circulation must be considered, and this in turn is governed by the same thermal contrasts given by the thermodynamic equation.

The circulation of atmospheric and oceanic material is governed by Newton's second law: local acceleration of a fluid element is proportional to total forces on it. In fluid mechanics this is known as the Navier-Stokes equation. It is a nonlinear partial differential equation that is exceedingly complex. Climate models that include a detailed attempt to solve the fluid dynamics equations must be approached by computer simulation. Even here the solutions are known to differ in detail from nature after only a few weeks at most. However, it is thought that statistics, for example, long-term means for the climate of the numerical model and those of nature, should agree; and this has been borne out in numerous tests.

In order to simulate the climate system, the problem must be cast onto a three-dimensional grid in the global ocean-atmosphere volume. The intermediate-sized models typically being used for decadal simulations have a horizontal resolution of about 300 to 600 mi (500 to 1000 km) and vertical resolutions of about 0.6 to 1.8 mi (1 to 3 km). This implies about 25,000 grid points, at each of which the model is keeping track of about six meteorological variables. The system is solved by numerically advancing in time at each grid point, updating at each time step (typically about intervals of 1 h of so-called model time). Simulation of 15 years of model time, which is typical of models that include only simple formulations of the oceanic interaction, may take tens of hours on the fastest computers. About a half dozen

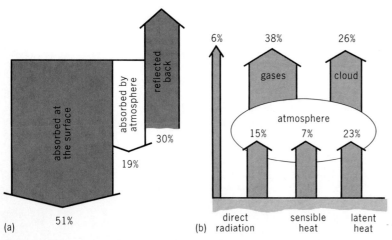

Fig. 1. Schematic diagram of the budget of incoming and outgoing radiation affecting the Earth's climate. (*a*) Solar radiation. (*b*) Terrestrial radiation.

models of this type are being investigated around the world. The models as a group simulate the present seasonal cycle of different geographical regions with remarkable fidelity, considering the short time that has passed since the inception of this field. The models are best at simulating the thermal surface field and weakest in modeling such secondary features as precipitation.

Feedback mechanisms and sensitivity. Attempts at modeling climate have demonstrated the extreme complexity and subtlety of the problem. This is due largely to the many feedbacks in the system. One of the simplest and yet most important feedbacks is that due to water vapor. If the Earth is perturbed by an increase in the solar radiation, for example, the first-order response of the system is to increase its temperature. But an increase in air temperature leads to more water vapor evaporating into the air; this in turn leads to increased absorption of space-bound radiation from the ground (greenhouse effect), which leads to an increased equilibrium temperature. This effect, known as a positive feedback mechanism, is illustrated in **Fig. 2**. It roughly doubles the response to most perturbations. Water vapor feedback is not the only amplifier in the system. Another important one is snow-cover: a cooler planet leads to more snow and hence more solar radiation reflected to space, since snow is more reflecting of sunlight than soil or vegetation. Other, more subtle mechanisms that are not yet well understood include those involving clouds and the biosphere. SEE GREENHOUSE EFFECT.

While water vapor and snowcover feedback are fairly straightforward to model, the less understood feedbacks differ in their implementations from one climate model to another. These differences as well as the details of their different numerical formulations have led to slight differences in the sensitivity of the various models to such standard experimental perturbations as doubling carbon dioxide in the atmosphere. All models agree that the planetary average temperature should increase if carbon dioxide concentrations are doubled. However, the predicted response in planetary temperatures ranges, from 4.5 to 9°F (2.5 to 5.0°C). Regional predictions of temperature or precipitation are not reliable enough for detailed response policy formulation. Many of the discrepancies are expected to decrease as model resolution increases (more grid points), since it is easier to include such complicated phenomena as clouds in finer-scale formulations. Similarly, it is anticipated that some observational data (such as rainfall over the oceans) that are needed for validation of the models will soon be available from satellite sensors.

Applications. Climate models are being used in a large variety of applications that aid in the understanding of Earth history. Many simple climate model simulations have been used to sort out the mechanisms responsible for climate change in the past. For example, although not yet fully understood, the astronomical theory of the ice ages states that the waxing and waning of the great continental ice sheets has been forced by the periodic changes in the Earth's elliptical orbit parameters in the past. Similarly, the onset of glaciation in Antarctica and Greenland has been studied by such means.

A problem that has received considerable attention is that of the greenhouse effect. Models are being studied to attempt to achieve better understanding of how the increase of atmospheric carbon dioxide and other trace gases from anthropogenic sources are likely to change the climate in the coming decades. The models are being compared to past climates ranging from the ice ages to the records of the last hundred years, for which an instrumental record exists. SEE CLIMATOLOGY.

Gerald R. North

Bibliography. T. J. Crowley et al., Role of seasonality in the evolution of climate during the last 100 million years, *Science*, 231:579–584, 1986; S. H. Schneider, Climate modeling, *Sci. Amer.*, 256 (5):72–80, 1987; S. H. Schneider and R. E. Dickinson, Climate modeling, *Rev. Geophys. Space Phys.*, 12:447–493, 1974; M. Washington and C. L. Parkinson, *An Introduction to Three-Dimensional Climate Modeling*, 1986.

Climate modification

Alteration of the Earth's climate by human activities; humans have the capacity to modify the Earth's climate in several important ways.

Local and regional scale. Conventional agriculture alters the microclimate in the lowest few meters of air, causing changes in the evapotranspiration and local heating characteristics of the air-surface interface. These changes lead to different degrees of air turbulence over the plants and to different moisture and temperature distributions in the local air.

Another example of human influence on climate at a larger scale is that the innermost parts of cities are several degrees warmer than the surrounding countryside, and they have slightly more rainfall as well. These changes are brought about by the differing surface features of urban land versus natural countryside and the unique ways that cities dispose of water (for example, storm sewers). The altered urban environment prevents evaporation cooling of surfaces in the city. The modified surface texture of cities (that is, horizontal and vertical planes of buildings and streets versus gently rolling surfaces over natural forest or grassland) leads to a more efficient trapping of solar heating of the near-surface air. The characteristic scales of buildings and other structures also lead to a different pattern of atmospheric boundary-layer turbulence modifying the stirring efficiency of the atmosphere. SEE MICROMETEOROLOGY.

At the next larger scale, human alteration of regional climates is caused by changes in the Earth's

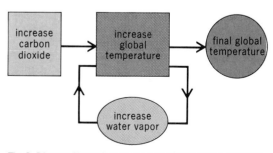

Fig. 2. Diagram illustrating the concept of water vapor feedback in amplifying the sensitivity of the Earth's climate to increases in atmospheric carbon dioxide concentration. Increases in the Earth's temperature cause an increase in water vapor. This in turn causes a warming of the surface because of the greenhouse effect. The net effect is to amplify the response to increases of carbon dioxide.

average reflectivity to sunlight. For example the activities of building roads and highways and deforestation change the reflectivity characteristics of the Earth's surface and alter the amount of sunshine that is reflected to space, as opposed to its being absorbed by the surface and thereby heating the air through contact. Such contact heating leads to temperature increases and evaporation of liquid water at the surface. Vapor wakes from jet airplanes are known to block direct solar radiation near busy airports by up to 20%.

Human activities also inject dust, smoke, and other aerosols into the air, causing sunlight to be scattered back to space. Dust particles screen out sunlight before it can enter the lower atmosphere and warm the near-surface air. An extreme case is popularly referred to as the nuclear winter scenario, where a massive injection of smoke particles into the upper atmosphere occurs during a hypothetical exchange of nuclear blasts. The resulting smoke veil theoretically remains in the atmosphere for up to 6 months and leads to a shading of the world and a resulting cooling of continental interiors by as much as 90°F (50°C) for several months. Ocean and coastal regions would experience less than about 18°F (10°C) of cooling. *See* Air pollution; Smog.

Global scale and greenhouse effect. Humans are inadvertently altering the atmospheric chemical composition on a global scale, and this is likely to lead to an unprecedented warming of the global atmosphere during the next generation. It comes about by anthropogenic injection into the atmosphere of relatively inert trace gases that perturb the radiation balance of the globe as a whole. Most of this gaseous waste comes from burning fuels that contain carbon and nitrogen. Other sources include inert gases used in aerosol spray cans and cooling devices. *See* Atmospheric chemistry.

It has been known for over 150 years that some gases act as so-called greenhouse veils and can lead to increased temperatures of the planet if their concentration in the atmosphere is increased. Greenhouse gases such as carbon dioxide have the property of permitting sunlight to pass through volumes containing them but they strongly absorb the surface-originated infrared radiation that would normally pass through a "clean" atmospheric column out to space. The Earth–atmosphere system is balanced on an annual basis between sunlight absorbed by the system and terrestrial infrared radiation emitted to space. When a greenhouse gas is present throughout the column of air over the ground, that gas absorbs some of the surface-originated radiation, and, as a warm body itself, the gas reradiates half of its own emission downward, eventually raising the surface temperature. Increasing the atmospheric concentration of a greenhouse gas invariably raises the temperature of near-surface air and lowers the temperature in the stratosphere. *See* Greenhouse effect; Heat balance, terrestrial atmospheric.

For every carbon atom burned in fossil fuels such as coal, oil, wood, or gasoline, there is one molecule of carbon dioxide (CO_2) released into the global atmospheric system. The relative chemical inertness and water insolubility of CO_2 means that it has a long residence time in the atmosphere. It does eventually react with chemicals and life forms at the Earth's surface and is partially removed by oceanic processes. Currently about 11×10^{12} lb/yr (5.2×10^{12} kg/yr)

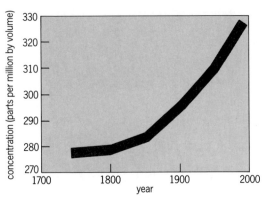

Fig. 1. History of atmospheric CO_2 concentrations as inferred from an analysis of bubbles taken from ice cores in the Antarctic. (*After E. M. Neftel, H. Oeschger, and B. Stauffer, Evidence from polar ice cores for the increase in atmospheric CO_2 in the past two centuries, Nature, 315:45–47, 1985*)

of carbon are being added to the atmosphere from fossil fuel burning, and another 2×10^{12} lb/yr (10^{12} kg/yr) are being added from the decay of tropical forests that have been cut down and are decaying or being burned. About half of this anthropogenic production remains in the atmosphere as CO_2, with the remainder being taken up by plants and the oceans. This accounts for the observed 0.3% increase in atmospheric CO_2 every year. The 1988 level was 345 parts per million by volume, fully 25% higher than it was in the preindustrial atmosphere as inferred from gas bubbles in ice cores taken from Greenland and Antarctica (**Fig. 1**). A doubling of atmospheric CO_2 is expected to occur by the year 2050. Climate model simulations of the Earth with twice as much atmospheric CO_2 as the present value suggest that the Earth may warm by 5 to 11°F (3 to 6°C) with considerable regional variation. For example, the equatorial regions would warm only by about half of this amount, and the polar regions would warm by two or three times the global average amount. Agriculturally favorable climatic bands might be expected to migrate to new positions. Glacial melting could result in a raising of sea level by as much as 3 ft (1 m). *See* Climate modeling.

An equally important group of greenhouse gases being pumped regularly into the atmosphere are the chlorofluorocarbons, popularly known as freons (CCl_3F and CCl_2F_2); with respect to impact on climate change, one freon molecule is equivalent to 10^4 CO_2 molecules. These gases are produced in industrial processes and are widely used in aerosol cans and air-conditioning equipment. They are relatively more inert and less water-soluble and therefore have an even longer residence time than CO_2. It is believed that they may have a significant potential impact on the ozone layer in the stratosphere. However, they also have an effect on climate, since they are particularly strong greenhouse gases. Two other important greenhouse gases, methane and nitrous oxide, are known to be increasing. Their origins are thought to be connected with anthropogenic activities, although their precise sources are not well understood. The concentrations of these gases increased by 11 and 3.5%, respectively, between 1975 and 1985, and they are projected to continue increasing into the next century.

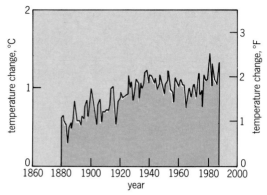

Fig. 2. Global average temperature variations from 1880 to 1988 as inferred from many types of observations. Superimposed on a long-term warming trend are fluctuations that are attributable to volcanic and oceanic activity. The values are relative to an arbitrary baseline.

Climate-modeling groups estimate that the contributions of all these minor trace gases contribute about as much toward anthropogenically induced global climate change as does the most publicized greenhouse gas, CO_2. SEE ATMOSPHERIC OZONE.

Since alteration of the atmospheric composition by human activities has taken place for more than 150 years, it is important to ask whether the climate system has started to respond to the forcing. While no definitive answer exists, globally averaged temperature data suggest that on the whole the Earth has been warming over the last 100 years (**Fig. 2**), and the observed warming is consistent with the greenhouse hypothesis. SEE ATMOSPHERE; CLIMATIC CHANGE; CLIMATIC PREDICTION; CLIMATOLOGY; WEATHER MODIFICATION.

Gerald R. North

Bibliography. R. E. Dickinson and R. J. Cicerone, Future global warming from atmospheric trace gases, *Nature,* 319:109–115, 1986; J. Hansen and S. Lebedeff, Global trends of measured surface air temperature, *J. Geophys. Res.,* D11:13345–13372, 1987; P. D. Jones et al., Evidence for global warming in the past decade, *Nature,* 332:790, 1988; E. M. Neftel, H. Oeschger, and B. Stauffer, Evidence from polar ice cores for the increase in atmospheric CO_2 in the past two centuries, *Nature,* 315:45–47, 1985; V. Ramanathan, The greenhouse theory of climate change: A test by an inadvertent global experiment, *Science,* 240:293–299, 1988.

Climatic change

The long-term fluctuations in precipitation, temperature, wind, and all other aspects of the Earth's climate. The climate, like the Earth itself, has a history extending over several billion years. Climatic fluctuations have occurred at time scales ranging from the longest observable (10^8–10^9 years) to interdecadal variability (10^1 years) and interannual variability (10^0 years). Processes in the atmosphere, oceans, cryosphere (snow cover, sea ice, continental ice sheets), biosphere, and lithosphere, and certain extraterrestrial factors (such as the Sun), are part of the climate system.

The present climate can be described as an ice age climate, since large land surfaces are covered with ice sheets (Antarctica, Greenland). The origins of the present ice age may be traced, at least in part, to movement of the continental plates. With the gradual movement of Antarctica toward its present isolated polar position, ice sheets began to develop about 30,000,000 years ago. Within the past several million years, the Antarctic ice sheet reached approximately its present size, and ice sheets appeared on the lands bordering the northern North Atlantic Ocean. During the past million years of the current ice age, about 10 glacial-interglacial fluctuations have been documented. The most recent glacial period came to an end between about 15,000 and 6000 years ago with the rapid melting of the North American and European ice sheets and the associated rise in sea level. The present climate is described as interglacial. The scope of this article is limited to a discussion of climatic fluctuations within the present interglacial period and, in particular, the climatic fluctuations of the past 100 years—the period of instrumental records. A more complete discussion of past climates is found in other articles.

Evidence. Instrumental records of climatic variables such as temperature and precipitation exist for the past 100 years in many locations and for as long as 200 years in a few locations. These records provide evidence of year-to-year and decade-to-decade variability but are completely inadequate for the study of century-to-century and longer-term variability. Even for the study of short-term climatic fluctuations, instrumental records are of limited usefulness, since most observations were made from the continents (only 29% of the Earth's surface area) and limited to the Earth's surface. Aerological observations which permit the study of atmospheric mass, momentum and energy budgets, and the statistical structure of the large-scale circulation are available for only about 20 years. Again there is a bias toward observations over the continents. It is only with the advent of satellites that global monitoring of the components of the Earth's radiation budget (planetary albedo, from which the net incoming solar radiation can be estimated; and the outgoing terrestrial radiation) has begun. SEE HEAT BALANCE, TERRESTRIAL ATMOSPHERIC.

There remain important gaps in the ability to describe the present state of the climate. For example, precipitation estimates, especially over the oceans, are very poor. Oceanic circulation, heat transport, and heat storage are only crudely estimated. Also, the solar irradiance is not being monitored to sufficient accuracy to permit estimation of any variability and evaluation of the possible effect of fluctuations in solar output upon the Earth's climate. Thus, although climatic fluctuations are found in instrumental records, the task of defining the scope of these fluctuations and diagnosing potential causes is at best difficult and at worst impossible.

In spite of the inadequacy of the instrumental records for assessing global climate, there is considerable evidence of regional climatic variations. For example, there is evidence of climatic warming in the polar regions of the Northern Hemisphere during the first four to five decades of the twentieth century. During the 1960s, on the other hand, there is evidence of cooling in the polar and mid-latitude regions of the Northern Hemisphere; and, especially in the early 1970s, there were drier conditions along the northern margin of the monsoon lands of Africa and Asia.

Under the auspices of the World Meteorological Organization and the International Council of Scientific Unions, the Global Atmospheric Research Program (GARP) was charged with developing plans for detailed observation and study of the global climate system—especially the atmosphere, the oceans, the sea ice, and the changeable features of the land surface.

Causes. Many extraterrestrial and terrestrial processes have been hypothesized to be possible causes of climatic fluctuations. A number of these processes are listed and described below.

Solar irradiance. It is possible that variations in total solar irradiance could occur over a wide range of time scales (10^0–10^9 years). If these variations did take place, they would almost certainly have an influence on climate. Radiance variability in limited portions of the solar spectrum has been observed, but not linked clearly to climate variability. SEE SOLAR ENERGY.

Orbital parameters. Variations of the Earth's orbital parameters (eccentricity of orbit about the Sun, precession, and inclination of the rotational axis to the orbital plane) lead to small but possibily significant variations in incoming solar radiation with regard to seasonal partitioning and latitudinal distribution. These variations occur at times scales of 10^4–10^5 years.

Lithosphere motions. Sea-floor spreading and continental drift, continental uplift, and mountain building operate over long time scales (10^5–10^9 years) and are almost certainly important factors in long-term climate variation.

Volcanic activity. Volcanic activity produces gaseous and particulate emissions which lead to the formation of persistent stratospheric aerosol layers. It may be a factor in climatic variations at all time scales.

Internal variability of climate system. Components of the climate system (atmosphere, ocean, cryosphere, biosphere, land surface) are interrelated through a variety of feedback processes operating over time scales from, say, 10^0 to 10^9 years. These processes could, in principle, produce fluctuations of sufficient magnitude and variability to explain any observed climate change. For example, atmosphere-ocean interactions may operate over time scales ranging from 10^0 to 10^3 years, and atmosphere-ocean-cryosphere interactions may operate over time scales ranging from 10^0 to 10^5 years. Several hypotheses have been proposed to explain glacial-interglacial fluctuations as complex internal feedbacks among atmosphere, ocean, and cryosphere. (Periodic buildup and surges of the Antarctic ice sheet and periodic fluctuations in sea ice extent and deep ocean circulation provide examples.) Atmosphere-ocean interaction is being studied intensively as a possible cause of short-term climatic variations. It has been observed that anomalous ocean temperature patterns (both equatorial and mid-latitude) are often associated with anomalous atmospheric circulation patterns. Although atmospheric circulation plays a dominant role in establishing a particular ocean temperature pattern (by means of changes in wind-driven currents, upwelling, radiation exchange, evaporation, and so on), the anomalous ocean temperature distribution may then persist for months, seasons, or longer intervals of time because of the large heat capacity of the oceans. These anomalous oceanic heat sources and sinks may, in turn, produce anomalous atmospheric motions.

Human activities. Forest clearing and other large-scale changes in land use, changes in aerosol loading, and the changing CO_2 concentration of the atmosphere are often cited as examples of possible mechanisms through which human activities may influence the large-scale climate. Because of the large observational uncertainties that exist in defining the state of the climate, it has not been possible to establish the relative importance of human activities (as compared to natural processes) in recent climatic fluctuations. There is, however, considerable concern that future human activities may lead to large climatic variations (for example, continued increase in atmospheric CO_2 concentration due to burning of fossil fuels) within the next several decades. SEE AIR POLLUTION; ATMOSPHERIC OZONE; CLIMATE MODIFICATION; GREENHOUSE EFFECT.

It is likely that at least several of the above-mentioned processes have played a role in past climatic fluctuations (that is, it is unlikely that all climatic fluctuations are due to one factor). In addition, certain processes may act simultaneously, or in various sequences. Also, the climatic response to some causal process may depend on the particular initial climatic state, which, in turn, depends upon previous climatic states because of the long time constants of oceans and cryosphere. True equilibrium climates may not exist, and the climate system may be in a continual state of transience.

Modeling. Because of the complexity of the real climate system, simplified numerical models of climate are being used to study particular processes and interactions. Some models treat only the global-average conditions, whereas others, particularly the atmospheric models, simulate detailed patterns of climate. These models are still in early stages of development but will undoubtedly be of great importance in attempts to understand climatic processes and to assess the possible effects of human activities on climate. SEE CLIMATOLOGY.

John E. Kutzbach

Ocean-atmosphere interaction. The atmosphere and the oceans have always jointly participated in climatic change, past and contemporary. Some of the contemporary changes can be investigated in the modern records of climatic anomalies in the atmosphere and the oceans.

The most important source of the climatic change surpassing 1-year duration seems to be located along the equatorial zone of the Pacific Ocean. The prevailing winds there are easterly and maintain a westward wind drift of the surface water which diverges, under influence of the Earth's rotation, to the right of the wind direction north of the Equator and the left south of the Equator. The resulting equatorial upwelling of cold water, and subsequent lateral mixing, ordinarily maintains a belt of cold surface water several hundred kilometers wide straddling the Equator from the coast of South America about to the dateline, about one earth quadrant farther west.

Analogous processes are found in the equatorial belt of the Atlantic, but the upwelling water there covers a much smaller area and is also less cold than in the Pacific. The Indian Ocean has no steady easterlies and thus no equatorial upwelling.

The equatorial process varies in intensity with the equatorial easterlies. Since that wind system is mostly fed by way of the southerlies along the west coasts of South Africa and South America, it is likely that anomalies in the Southern Hemisphere atmospheric circulation frequently are transmitted to the tropical belt. Once an impulse, for example, a strengthening of the Pacific equatorial easterlies, has occurred, the new anomaly has a built-in tendency of self-amplification, because it makes the upwelling strengthen too and thus increases the temperature deficit of the Pacific compared to the persistently warm Indonesian and Indian Ocean tropical waters. This in turn feeds back into further strengthening of the easterlies which started the anomaly in the first place.

The observational proof of this feedback system can be seen in the statistically well-substantiated "southern oscillation," which exhibits opposite contemporaneous anomalies of atmospheric pressure over the tropical parts of the Pacific Ocean on the one side and the Indonesian and Indian Ocean tropical waters on the other (nodal line on the average at 165°E). The periodicity is rather irregular, so the term oscillation should not be taken too literally. The average length of the cycles is 2–3 years.

The cycles of tropical precipitation of more than a year's length by and large agree with those of pressure wherever special local conditions do not interfere. Satellite photos confirm that in the phase of the southern oscillation with positive pressure anomaly over the Pacific, along with strong equatorial easterlies and strong upwelling, most of the Pacific equatorial belt is arid; while in the opposite phase the western and central part of that belt experiences heavy rainfall. In extreme "El Niño" years this rainfall can also extend to the normally arid coast of northern Peru.

When there is more than normal rainfall at the Equator, the general circulation of the atmosphere is supplied with more-than-normal total heat convertible into kinetic energy. The remote effect of this phenomenon, particularly in the winter hemisphere, is the occurrence of stronger-than-normal tradewinds and midlatitude westerlies. At the opposite extreme, the tradewinds are weak and the westerlies meandering. This produces cold winters in the longitude sectors with winds out of high latitudes and mild winters interspersed at longitudes where wind components from low latitudes prevail. Again, it is in the Pacific longitude sector that these teleconnections are most clearly seen, because the interannual variability of sea temperature up to a range of 5.4°F (3°C) over a large equatorial area is found only in the Pacific sector. SEE ATMOSPHERIC GENERAL CIRCULATION; MARITIME METEOROLOGY.

Jacob Bjerknes

Bibliography. H. P. Berlage, *The Southern Oscillation and World Weather*, Kon. Ned. Meteorol. Inst. Meded. Verh. 88, 1966; J. Bjerknes, A possible response of the Hadley circulation to variations of the heat supply from the equatorial Pacific, *Tellus*, 18:820–829, 1966; H. H. Lamb, *Climate, History, and the Modern World*, 1982; H. H. Lamb, *Climate: Present, Past and Future*, vol. 1: *Fundamentals and Climate Now*, 1972; S. H. Schneider and R. E. Dickinson, Climate modelling, *Rev. Geophys. Space Phys.*, 12:447–493, 1974; H. Shapley (ed.), *Climatic Change*, 1953; B. J. Skinner (ed.), *Climate Past and Present*, 1981; Study of man's impact on climate, in *Inadvertent Climate Modification*, 1971; UNESCO, *Changes of Climate*, Arid Zone Research, 1963; U.S. National Academy of Sciences, *Understanding Climatic Change: A Program for Action*, 1975.

Climatic prediction

Prediction of the response of the Earth-atmosphere system to changes in one of the variables involved, or prediction of future climate from observed present conditions. It is useful to distinguish between these two types of climatic prediction.

First type. Studies of the first type attempt to determine the response of the Earth-atmosphere system to small changes in one of the many variables involved—for example, the solar constant or the atmospheric carbon dioxide content. The most useful results have been obtained by using mathematical models of various degrees of complexity. These range from zero-dimension models, which consider only the radiation balance of the complete global system, to three-dimensional (3-D) models which couple the circulation of the atmosphere and oceans with the hydrologic cycle to reproduce the climatic sequence at several levels in the atmosphere and oceans and at points 130–300 mi (200–500 km) apart.

Sensitivity tests with this hierarchy of models indicate, among other things, that the climate system responds almost identically to a 2% increase in the solar constant and a doubling of the atmospheric carbon dioxide concentration. This is rather surprising considering the differences in the natures of these two forcings. In both cases the globally averaged annual surface temperature rises by 5 to 9°F (3 to 5°C), with increases of almost 36°F (20°C) occurring at high latitudes in both hemispheres in winter.

Various attempts have been made to use paleoclimatic and historical data to predict the regional climatic changes that will occur with changes in the global climate. An interesting approach, used in the Soviet Union is to correlate the local historical temperature record, for example, with that averaged for the hemisphere or globe. The regression coefficient (or slope of the regression line) gives the ratio of the local temperature change to that for the hemisphere or globe. This method could be applied to any variable for which the necessary data are available.

More and more, climatologists realize that the source of climatic variability lies in the tropics, even though the largest climatic changes occur in polar latitudes. The atmosphere is heated primarily by the absorption of infrared radiation emitted by the Earth's surface. However, all of this heat, and more, is radiated away, either back to the surface or to space. This leaves the atmosphere with a net loss of infrared radiation, equivalent to a cooling rate of about 2.3°F (1.3°C) per day. To offset this, the atmosphere is heated by the absorption of solar radiation (0.9°F or 0.5°C/day), the condensation of water vapor (1.3°F or 0.7°C/day), and, to a smaller extent, the convection of heat from the Earth's surface (0.2°F or 0.1°C/day). Between 20°N and 20°S the heat generated by these processes far exceeds the cooling by infrared radiation. The excess heat is transferred to higher latitudes as either potential energy or sensible heat—equatorward of about 30°, by the Hadley cells of the two hemispheres, and poleward of 30°, primarily by moving low- and high-pressure systems. Almost half of the heat added to the atmosphere is added in the 34% of the globe between 20°N and 20°S. Since more than half of this heat is added by condensation, small variations in tropical precipitation, for example, those associated with El Niño, can have a strong impact on the poleward heat transport and, hence, on climatic conditions in middle and high latitudes. *See Green-house effect*.

Second type. This type of climatic prediction deals with actually predicting the future state of the climate, given the observed present conditions. Forecasts can be made for periods ranging from a month to a millennium or more in the future. Eventually, numerical models may be used for this purpose, but so far this type of prediction, with one exception, involves primarily the application of various statistical techniques.

The exception occurs where the climate-forcing function itself is predictable. A good example is systematic variations in the Earth's orbit about the Sun which produce changes in the seasonal incidence of solar radiation. These changes are completely predictable and can be fed into a climate model to determine the response.

Extremely popular among the statistical approaches are attempts to isolate climatic cycles, especially those which can be related to solar activity. So far the results have not been especially encouraging, partly because more often than not the phase of a significant cycle changes abruptly and randomly.

Statistically derived interrelationships have been observed between sea-surface temperatures and certain subsequent atmospheric circulation features in the tropics and middle latitudes. These have already been useful in seasonal climatic prediction and may eventually provide a strong base for the numerical prediction of climate. *See Climatic change; Climatology; Weather forecasting and prediction*.

W. D. Sellers

Bibliography. W. Bach, H.-J. Jung, and H. Knottenberg, *Modeling the Influence of Carbon Dioxide on the Global and Regional Climate*, 1985; S. Manabe (ed.), *Issues in Atmospheric and Oceanic Modeling*: pt. A, *Climate Dynamics*, pt. B, *Weather Dynamics*, 1985; M. E. Schlesinger and J. F. B. Mitchell, Climate model simulations of the equilibrium climatic response to increased carbon dioxide, *Rev. Geophys.*, 25:760–798, 1987.

Climatology

The scientific study of climate. Climate is the expected mean and variability of the weather conditions for a particular location, season, and time of day. The climate is often described in terms of the values of meteorological variables such as temperature, precipitation, wind, humidity, and cloud cover. A complete description also includes the variability of these quantities, and their extreme values. The climate of a region often has regular seasonal and diurnal variations, with the climate for January being very different from that for July at most locations. Climate also exhibits significant year-to-year variability and longer-term changes on both a regional and global basis.

Climate has a central influence on many human needs and activities, such as agriculture, housing, human health, water resources, and energy use. The influence of climate on vegetation and soil type is so strong that the earliest climate classification schemes were often based more on these factors than on the meteorological variables. While technology can be used to mitigate the effects of unfavorable climatic conditions, climate fluctuations that result in significant departures from normal cause serious problems

for modern industrialized societies as much as for primitive ones. The goals of climatology are to provide a comprehensive description of the Earth's climate, to understand its features in terms of fundamental physical principles, and to develop models of the Earth's climate that will allow the prediction of future changes that may result from natural and human causes. *See Climate modeling; Climatic prediction*.

Physical basis of climate. The global mean climate and its regional variations can be explained in terms of physical processes. For example, the temperature is warmer near the Equator than near the poles (**table** and **Figs. 1** and **2**). This is because the source of heat for the Earth is the radiant energy coming from the Sun, and the Sun's rays fall more directly on the Equator than on the poles. The circulations in the atmosphere and the oceans transport heat poleward and thereby reduce the Equator-to-pole temperature difference that is continually forced by insolation. The energy released by the rising of warm air in the tropics and the sinking of cold air in high latitudes drives the great wind systems of the atmosphere, such as the trade winds in the tropics and the westerlies of middle latitudes. *See Atmospheric general circulation; Wind*.

The flux of solar energy at the mean distance of the Earth from the Sun is about 1365 W · m^{-2}. The supply of energy per unit of the Earth's surface area is controlled by geometric and astronomical factors. Because the axis of rotation of the Earth is inclined at an oblique angle to the plane of the Earth's orbit, the declination angle of the Sun undergoes a seasonal variation as the Earth makes its annual circuit around it. The declination angle is equivalent to the latitude at which the Sun is directly overhead at noon. The declination angle varies between 23.5° N at northern summer solstice (June 21) and 23.5° S at northern winter solstice (December 22), for the current alignment of the Earth's orbit. The approximate sphericity of the Earth and the annual variation of the declination angle of the Sun cause the incoming solar radiation to be a function of latitude and season (**Fig. 3**). Annual mean insolation is largest at the Equator and decreases toward the poles. Seasonal variation is largest at high latitudes. At the poles 6 months of daylight alternate with 6 months of darkness. The Earth is closer to the Sun during summer in the Southern Hemisphere, so this region receives about 7% more insolation at this time than the Northern Hemisphere.

About half of the energy from the Sun that is incident at the top of the atmosphere is transmitted through the atmosphere and absorbed at the Earth's surface (**Fig. 4**). About 30% is reflected directly to space, and another 20% is absorbed in the atmosphere. The fraction of the incoming solar radiation that is reflected to space is called the albedo. The albedo increases where clouds or surface ice are present. It increases toward the poles because cloud cover and surface ice increase and because the Sun is closer to the horizon. The albedo of desert areas is generally higher than that of heavily vegetated areas or oceans. The solar energy that reaches the surface may raise the surface temperature, or the energy can be used to evaporate water. The energy that is used to evaporate water is later released into the atmosphere when the water vapor condenses and returns to the surface in the form of precipitation (**Fig. 5**).

Greenhouse effect. In order to achieve an energy balance, the solar energy that is absorbed by the Earth

Temperature (T) and precipitation (P) for selected stations in North America, South America, and Antarctica*

Station	Latitude, degrees	T_{annual}	T_{Jan}	T_{July}	P_{annual}	P_{Jan}	P_{July}
Alert	82.50 N	−18.0	−32.1	3.9	156	8	18
Barrow	71.30 N	−12.5	−26.8	3.9	109	5	20
Fairbanks	64.80 N	−3.4	−23.9	15.4	287	23	47
Baker Lake	64.30 N	−12.3	−33.6	10.7	213	7	36
Anchorage	61.17 N	1.8	−10.9	13.9	373	20	47
Juneau	58.37 N	4.5	−3.8	12.9	1288	102	114
Edmonton	53.57 N	2.8	−14.7	17.5	447	25	83
Seattle	47.45 N	10.8	3.9	18.2	980	153	19
Montreal	45.50 N	7.2	−8.9	21.6	999	80	93
Des Moines	41.53 N	10.5	−5.2	25.2	789	32	77
Salt Lake City	40.78 N	10.7	−2.1	24.7	353	34	15
Washington, D.C.	38.85 N	13.9	2.7	25.7	1087	82	107
San Francisco	37.62 N	13.8	9.2	17.1	475	102	t
Nashville	36.12 N	15.6	4.4	26.8	1146	139	94
Los Angeles	33.93 N	18.0	13.2	22.8	373	78	t
Birmingham	33.57 N	17.8	8.1	27.6	1349	128	131
Phoenix	33.43 N	21.4	10.4	32.9	184	19	20
New Orleans	29.95 N	20.0	12.3	27.3	1369	98	171
Havana	23.17 N	24.6	21.8	27.0	1126	54	108
Acapulco	16.83 N	27.6	26.1	28.7	1401	8	230
Caracas	10.60 N	26.1	24.4	26.4	545	42	72
Guayaquil	02.18 S	25.5	26.5	24.2	811	199	0.3
Manaus	03.13 S	27.5	26.7	27.6	2294	279	65
Brazilia	15.78 S	20.4	21.2	18.0	1643	248	6
Rio de Janeiro	22.90 S	23.7	26.1	20.9	1218	211	52
Antofagasta	23.47 S	16.2	19.8	13.2	1.9	0.0	0.3
Santiago	33.45 S	14.4	21.2	8.1	264	0.1	69
Buenos Aires	34.58 S	16.9	23.7	10.6	1029	104	61
Puerto Aisen	45.50 S	9.2	13.9	3.9	3001	203	331
Comodoro Rivadavia	45.78 S	12.6	18.6	6.9	216	16	21
Punta Arenas	53.00 S	6.0	10.4	1.3	362	40	24
Melchior	64.32 S	−3.6	1.0	−9.3	1116	42	90
Byrd Station	80.02 S	−27.9	−14.6	−35.1	39	7	2.5
Amundsen Scott	90.00 S	−49.4	−28.7	−60.3	1.5	t	t

*Temperature is in degrees Celsius; $°F = (°C × 1.8) + 32$. Precipitation is in millimeters; 1 mm = 0.04 in. t indicates trace of precipitation.

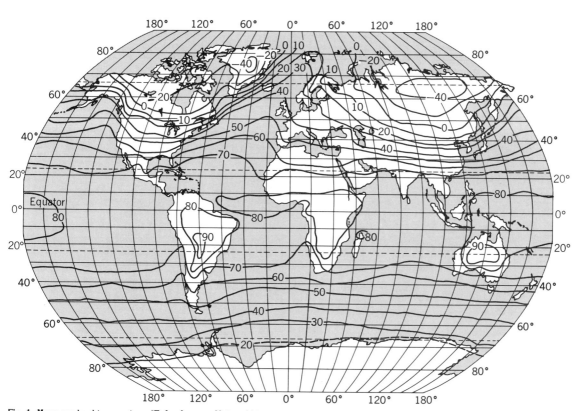

Fig. 1. Mean sea-level temperature, °F, for January. Note cold temperatures near centers of northern land masses. $°C = (°F − 32) ÷ 1.8$.

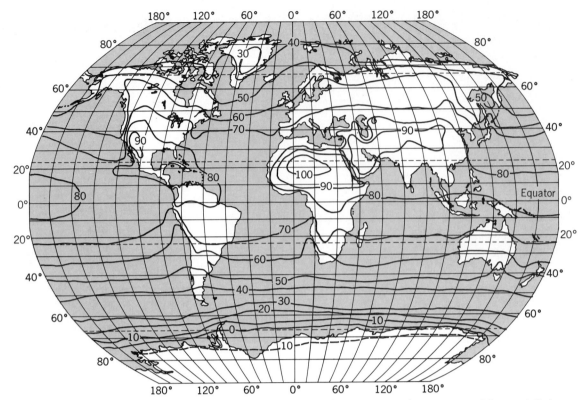

Fig. 2. Mean sea-level temperature, °F, for July. Note that northern continents are warmer than ocean areas at the same latitude. °C = (°F − 32) ÷ 1.8.

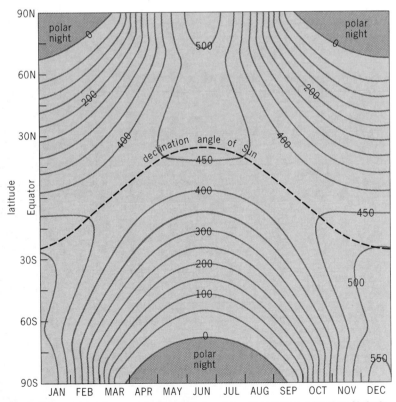

Fig. 3. Daily-average solar energy incident at the top of the atmosphere as a function of latitude and season in watts per square meter of surface area.

must be returned to space. The Earth emits radiative energy at frequencies that are substantially different from those of the Sun because of the Earth's colder temperature. The Earth emits primarily thermal infrared radiation (wavelengths from 4 to 200 micrometers), whereas most of the energy from the Sun arrives in the form of visible and near-infrared radiation (0.4–4 μm). The atmosphere is much less transparent to thermal radiation than to solar radiation, because water vapor, clouds, and carbon dioxide in the atmosphere absorb thermal radiation. Because the atmosphere prevents thermal radiation emitted from the surface from escaping to space, the surface temperature is warmer than it would be in the absence of the atmosphere. The combination of the relative transparency of the atmosphere to solar radiation and the blanketing effect of the gases in the atmosphere that absorb thermal radiation is referred to as the greenhouse effect. *SEE* ATMOSPHERE; GREENHOUSE EFFECT.

Clouds affect the energy emission of the Earth. The thermal emission is low over tropical regions where high, cold clouds are present, such as the major precipitation regions of equatorial Africa, South America, southern Asia, Indonesia, and the band of cloudiness along the Equator. Because the albedo is higher, the solar energy absorbed is decreased when clouds are present. Since clouds decrease both the solar energy absorbed and the terrestrial energy emitted to space, the net effect of tropical convective clouds on the energy balance of the Earth is less than their individual effects on solar and terrestrial energy. As a result, the distribution of the net radiative energy ex-

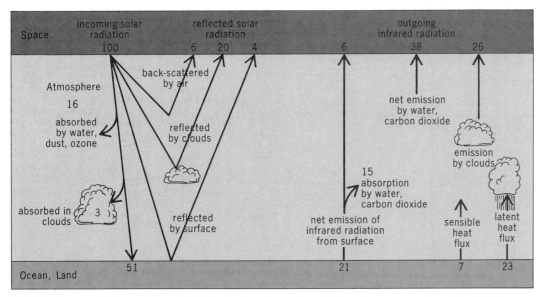

Fig. 4 Annual-mean global energy balance for the Earth–atmosphere system. Numbers given are percentages of the globally averaged solar energy incident upon the top of the atmosphere. (*After J. M. Wallace and P. V. Hobbs, Atmospheric Science: An Introductory Survey, Academic Press, 1977*)

change at the top of the atmosphere does not show the tall cloud signature so clearly. The net radiation shows a strong influx of energy at those latitudes where the insolation is strongest.

A striking feature of the distribution of net radiation during July is the low values over the Sahara and Arabian deserts compared with the surrounding ocean and moist land areas. This is because desert sand has a relatively high albedo, so that less solar radiation is absorbed there. In addition, few clouds and little water vapor are present in the atmosphere over the deserts to absorb the thermal radiation emitted by the very hot surface. Since the emitted thermal radiation is high and the absorbed solar radiation is low, desert

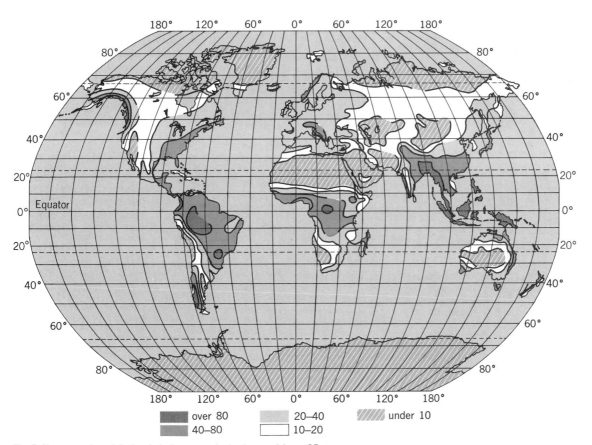

Fig. 5. Mean annual precipitation, in inches, on major land areas. 1 in. = 25 mm.

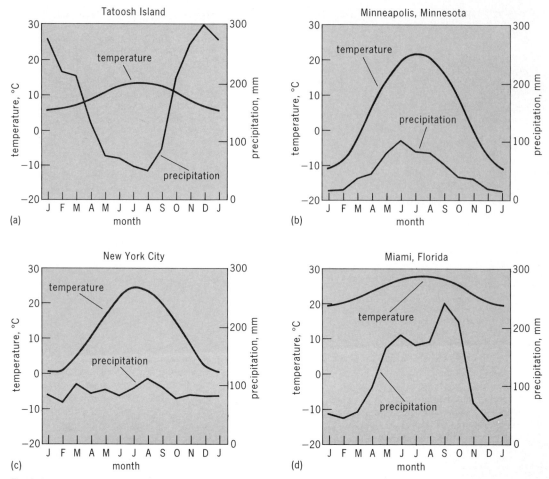

Fig. 6. Annual variation of monthly mean temperature and precipitation at (*a*) Tatoosh Island, Washington; (*b*) Minneapolis, Minnesota; (*c*) New York, New York; and (*d*) Miami, Florida. °F = (°C × 1.8) + 32; 1 mm = 0.04 in.

areas often show a net loss of radiative energy. This fact plays a central role in the maintenance of desert dryness. The loss of energy requires a continual transport of energy into the desert regions by the atmosphere. This results in downward motion of dry air, which flows outward near the ground and prevents the moist surface air of surrounding regions from reaching the desert interior. *SEE DESERT*.

Influences of land and ocean. Land and ocean areas have very different seasonal variations because of their different capacities for strong heat. Because the ocean is a fluid, 160–320 ft (50–100 m) of the surface ocean depth are generally in direct thermal communication with the surface. Therefore solar energy incident on the surface can be absorbed in this large heat sink without raising the surface temperature very much. In addition, over the oceans it is possible for solar energy to evaporate water and thus never be realized as heat. In contrast, over land only about the first meter of soil is in thermal contact with the surface, and much less water is available for evaporation. During the winter, the ocean can return heat stored during the summer to the surface, keeping it relatively warm. The land cools off very quickly in winter, warms up rapidly in summer, and experiences large day-night differences. Continental climates in middle latitudes are characterized by hot summers and cold winters, whereas climates that are over or near the oceans are more equable with milder seasons (Figs. 1 and 2).

The distinction between maritime and continental climates can be seen by comparing the annual variations of temperature and precipitation for Tatoosh Island, Washington, with those for Minneapolis, Minnesota (**Fig. 6**). The temperature at Tatoosh Island varies between a mean of 42°F (5.6°C) for January and a mean of 56°F (13.3°C) for August. This narrow temperature range results from the strong influence of the ocean, which is adjacent to and upwind of the Pacific coast and has a small seasonal variation in temperature because of its large capacity to store and release heat. Although it is at nearly the same latitude, Minneapolis has a much larger annual variation of monthly-mean temperatures, with readings of 12°F (−10.9°C) for January and 72°F (22.4°C) for July. Figures 1 and 2 show the large annual variation of temperature near the centers of the continents.

The annual variation of precipitation is also very different in the two climate regimes (Fig. 6). At Tatoosh Island the precipitation peaks in the winter season in association with rainfall produced by the cyclones and fronts of wintertime weather. In Minneapolis the precipitation peaks in the summer season. Most of this precipitation is associated with thunderstorms. Adequate precipitation during the warm summer season is an essential ingredient of the agricultural productivity of the American Midwest.

New York City shows an annual variation of temperature and precipitation that is a combination of maritime and continental. It is near the Atlantic

Ocean, but because the prevailing winds are out of the west, it also comes under the influence of air that has been over the continent. It has a fairly large annual variation of temperature (Fig. 6). Monthly-mean precipitation is almost constant through the year. It receives precipitation both from winter storms and summer thunderstorms. Miami, Florida is in the subtropics at 26°N. The annual variation of insolation is weak, so that the seasonal variation of temperature is rather small. The precipitation shows a strong seasonal variation, with maximum precipitation during the summer half-year associated primarily with thunderstorm activity.

General circulation of atmosphere and climate. Many aspects of the Earth's climate are determined by the nature of the circulation that results from the radiative heating of the tropics and cooling of the polar regions. In the belt between the Equator and 30° latitude the bulk of the poleward atmospheric energy transport is carried by a large circulation cell, in which air rises in a narrow band near the Equator and sinks at tropical and subtropical latitudes. The upward motion near the Equator is associated with intense rainfall and wet climates, while the downward motion away from the Equator results in the suppression of rainfall and very dry climates (see Fig. 5). Most of the world's great deserts, including the Sahara, Australian, Arabian, Kalahari, and Atacama, are in the belts between 10 and 30° latitude.

In middle latitudes the poleward flow of energy is produced by extratropical cyclones rather than by a mean circulation cell. These storms are thousands of miles across and are characterized by poleward motion of warm, moist air and equatorward motion of cold, dry air. Most of the wintertime precipitation in middle latitudes is associated with weather disturbances of this type.

Surface features are also of importance in determining local climate. Mountain ranges can block the flow of moist air from the oceans, resulting in very low rainfall. The dryness of the Great Basin of North America and the Gobi Desert of Asia is maintained in this way. On the upwind side of mountain ranges, forced ascent of moist air can result in very moist climates; this occurs, for example, on the west slope of the coastal mountains of western America and the south slope of the Himalayas during the summer monsoon. The downwind sides of such mountains are often very dry, since the moisture precipitates out on the upwind side. Two locations which show the effect of topography on local climates are Puerto Aisen, Chile, and Comodoro Rivadavia, Argentina, which are both located near a latitude of 45° (see table). Puerto Aisen is on the westward and upwind side of the Andes mountains in a deep valley that is exposed to the midlatitude westerly winds coming off the Pacific Ocean. It receives more than 10 ft (3 m) of precipitated water annually. Only a few hundred miles downwind of the Andes on the Atlantic seaboard, Comodoro Rivadavia receives only about 8 in. (0.2 m) of precipitation each year.

Complete climate system. The climate of the Earth results from complex interactions among externally applied parameters, like the distribution of insolation, and internal interactions among the atmosphere, the oceans, the ice, and the land (**Fig. 7**). The composition of the atmosphere, which plays a key role in determining the surface temperature through the greenhouse effect, has been radically changed by the life-forms that have developed, and continues to be modified and maintained by them. The atmosphere and the oceans exchange heat, momentum, water, and important constituent gases such as oxygen and carbon dioxide. The exchange of constituent gases is

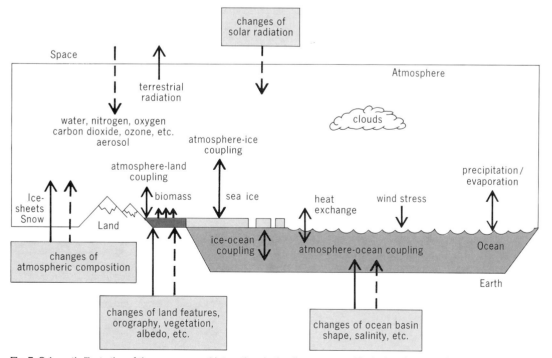

Fig. 7. Schematic illustration of the processes and interactions in the climate system. The broken-line arrows indicate externally applied conditions, and the solid arrows show internal processes that act to influence climate change. (*After J. G. Lockwood, Causes of Climate, Halstead Press, 1979*)

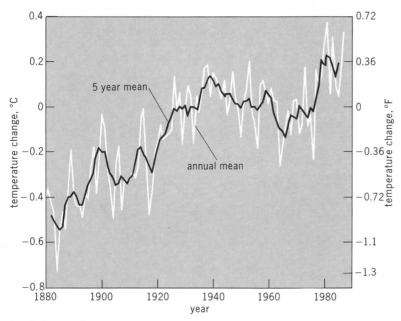

Fig. 8. Global surface air temperature change over the last century inferred from measurements. (*After J. Hansen and S. Lebedeff, Global surface air temperatures: Update through 1987, Geophys. Res. Lett., 15(4):323, April 1988*)

more solar energy per unit area and are thus much hotter than the Earth. The surface of Venus is sufficiently hot that water vapor cannot condense. Venus has a very thick atmosphere composed mostly of carbon dioxide. On Mars, which is farther from the Sun than the Earth and therefore colder, water freezes, leaving a very thin atmosphere of carbon dioxide. Thus the basic climatic conditions of a relatively circular orbit at a favorable distance for the Sun led to a drastically different evolutionary history for the Earth than for the neighboring planets.

History of Earth's climate. Direct measurements allow the estimation of global mean surface temperature of the Earth for only about the last 100 years (**Fig. 8**). Global surface air temperature rose by about 0.9°F (0.5°C) between 1880 and 1940 and then declined slightly in the following three decades. The decade of the 1980s contained some of the warmest years on record.

Evidence of climate variations in prehistoric times must be obtained from proxy indicators in dated sediments, such as pollen spores, the shells of small animals, or isotopic abundances, or from geologic features such as terminal moraines of glaciers or dry lake beds. A wealth of geological evidence exists to indicate that the Earth underwent a great glaciation as recently as 20,000 years ago. During this period, ice sheets nearly 2 mi (3 km) thick covered parts of North America and western Europe. Variations in the relative abundance of oxygen isotopes in deep-sea cores indicate that a succession of these major glaciations separated by relatively warm, ice-free periods called interglacials has occurred during the last million years of Earth history (**Fig. 9**).

Analyses of time series show a relationship between global ice volume and known variations in the Earth's orbit. The parameters of the Earth's orbit include the eccentricity, which measures the departure from a circular orbit to a more elliptical one; the obliquity, which measures the magnitude of the annual variation in the declination angle of the Sun; and the longitude of perihelion, which measures the season at which the Earth makes its closest approach to the Sun. These parameters control the seasonal and latitudinal distribution of insolation. Because ice sheets form primarily on land and much of the land area is in high northern latitudes, ice sheets form more readily when the summertime insolation is relatively low, which allows some of the winter snow accumulation to survive the summer season. The global climate responds to the presence of the ice sheets through a process called ice-albedo feedback. Ice sheets are more reflective to solar radiation than other surfaces, so that their presence tends to reduce the amount of solar heat absorbed by the Earth. This in turn leads to a cooling of the planet and a greater tendency for the ice sheets to grow.

Evidence from air bubbles trapped in glacial ice indicates that there were lower atmospheric concentrations of greenhouse gases such as carbon dioxide and methane during past glacial ages than there is at present. The concentration of carbon dioxide 20,000 years ago during the last glacial age was only about 190 parts per million by volume (ppmv), compared with the preindustrial level of 280 ppmv and the current concentration of 350 ppmv. During past glacial periods, the rather low values of carbon dioxide are thought to have been produced by changes in ocean chemistry and biology. Such low greenhouse gas con-

strongly influenced by life in the ocean. The hydrologic cycle of evaporation, cloud formation, and precipitation as rain or snow is intimately connected to the climate through the effects of water vapor, clouds, and surface ice on the radiation balance of the planet. Vegetation interacts strongly with the hydrologic cycle over land to determine the soil moisture, surface albedo, evaporation, precipitation, and surface water runoff. *SEE HYDROLOGY.*

Evolution of Earth's climate. The climate of the Earth is unique among the planets in the solar system. All of them evolved out of material in the rotating cloud from which the solar system was formed. The subsequent evolution of the planets' atmospheres depended critically on the mass of each planet and its distance from the Sun.

The mass of the Earth and its distance from the Sun are such that water can exist in liquid form rather than being frozen or escaping to space. The liquid water formed the oceans and led to the development of photosynthetic life, which reduced the carbon dioxide content and increased the molecular oxygen content of the atmosphere. Planets closer to the Sun receive

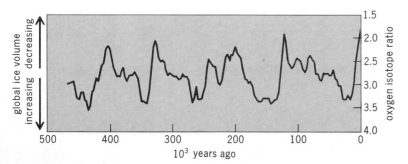

Fig. 9. Climate of the past half-million years. Oxygen isotope ratios are from ocean sediments, which reflect variations in the global volume of ice in glaciers and ice sheets. (*After J. Imbrie and K. P. Imbrie, Ice Ages: Solving the Mystery, Enslow Publishers, 1979*)

centrations contribute significantly to the cooling associated with glacial advances.

Future climate changes. Past relationships between the Earth's orbital parameters and global ice volume indicate that the Earth will undergo another major glacial age about 23,000 years from now. Currently, however, the composition of the Earth's atmosphere is changing rapidly as a result of human influences. Of climatic interest are industrial gases that are transparent to solar radiation entering the Earth's atmosphere, but are opaque to the thermal radiation emitted by the Earth. Gases with these characteristics are called greenhouse gases. In order to achieve an energy balance in the presence of increased concentration of greenhouse gases, the Earth's surface must warm, so that its thermal emission will increase to offset increasing downward emission of thermal energy from an atmosphere that is becoming more effective at intercepting outgoing thermal radiation, it other factors remain the same. The principal greenhouse gases are carbon dioxide, which is increasing principally because of the burning of coal and oil; methane or natural gas, whose increase is related to agriculture and coal and gas mining; nitrous oxide, which is a product of the decay of fixed nitrogen in plants or artificial fertilizer; and chlorofluorocarbons, which are gases used in industry for refrigeration, foam-blowing, and cleaning, and as aerosol propellants. Carbon dioxide is expected to contribute about half of the increase in atmospheric thermal opacity due by the year 2030.

Within the next 100 years, if current trends continue, climate models indicate that human activities will result in a climate that is 4–8°F (2.2–4.4°C) warmer than it is today. The magnitude of this increase is similar to that between the present climate and the last glacial age, and would represent an extremely rapid warming by the standards of natural climate variability and change. Studies also suggest increased probability of drought during the summer growing season in midlatitude agricultural areas and rising sea levels that may be 27 in. (70 cm) higher than present levels by the year 2080. SEE CLIMATE MODIFICATION; CLIMATIC CHANGE; DROUGHT; METEOROLOGY; MICROMETEOROLOGY.

Dennis L. Hartmann

Bibliography. B. Bolin, B. R. Doos, and J. Jager, *The Greenhouse Effect, Climatic Change and Ecosystems,* 1986; J. F. Griffiths and D. M. Driscoll, *Survey of Climatology,* 1982; J. Imbrie and K. P. Imbrie, *Ice Ages: Solving the Mystery,* 1979; J. G. Lockwood, *Causes of Climate,* 1979; G. T. Trewartha and L. Horn, *An Introduction to Climate,* 1980; W. M. Washington and C. L. Parkinson, *An Introduction to Three-Dimensional Climate Modeling,* 1986.

Cloud

Suspensions of minute droplets or ice crystals produced by the condensation of water vapor. This article presents an outline of cloud formation upon which to base an understanding of cloud classifications. For a more technical consideration of the physical character of atmospheric clouds, including the condensation and precipitation of water vapor, SEE CLOUD PHYSICS.

Rudiments of cloud formation. A grasp of a few physical and meteorological relationships aids in an understanding of clouds. First, if water vapor is cooled sufficiently, it becomes saturated and is in equilibrium with a plane surface of liquid water (or ice) at the same temperature. Further cooling in the presence of such a surface causes condensation upon it; in the absence of any surfaces, no condensation occurs until a substantial further cooling provokes condensation upon ions or random large aggregates of water molecules. In the atmosphere, even in the apparent absence of any surfaces, nuclei always exist upon which condensation proceeds at barely appreciable cooling beyond the state of saturation. Consequently, when atmospheric water vapor is cooled sufficiently, condensation nuclei swell into minute water droplets and form a visible cloud. The total concentration of liquid in the cloud is controlled by its temperature and the degree of cooling beyond the state in which saturation occurred, and in most clouds approximates to 1 g/m³ (0.001 oz/ft³) of air. The concentration of droplets is controlled by the concentrations and properties of the nuclei and the speed of the cooling at the beginning of the condensation. In the atmosphere these are such that there are usually about 100,000,000 droplets/m³ (2,800,000 droplets/ft³). Because the cloud water is at first fairly evenly shared among them, these droplets are necessarily of microscopic size, and an important part of the study of

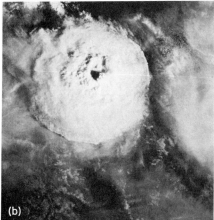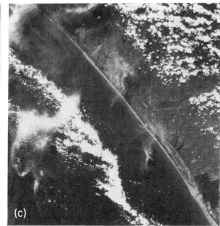

Fig. 1 Clouds as photographed by meteorological satellites. (*a*) A garden of thunderstorms, showing the anvils, forming at the tropopause inversion. (*b*) A hurricane, showing the eye. (c) Convective cloud over land and sea-breeze clouds.

Fig. 2. Cirrus, with trails of slowly falling ice crystals at a high level. (*F. Ellerman, U.S. Weather Bureau*)

gions temperatures below 0°C (32°F) are encountered a few kilometers above the ground, and clouds of frozen particles prevail at higher levels. Of the abundant nuclei which facilitate droplet condensation, very few cause direct condensation into ice crystals or stimulate the freezing of droplets, and especially at temperatures near 0°C (32°F) their numbers may be vanishingly small. Consequently, at these temperatures, clouds of unfrozen droplets are not infrequently encountered (supercooled clouds). In general, however, ice crystals occur in very much smaller concentrations than the droplets of liquid clouds, and may by condensation alone become large enough to fall from their parent cloud. Such ice nuclei are particles of clay, or sometimes bacteria, mixed upward from the Earth's surface. All cloud droplets freeze by self-nucleation (ice crystal formation by random motion of the water molecules) at temperatures below -35 to -40°C (-31 to -40°F). Even small high clouds may produce or become trails of snow crystals, whereas droplet clouds are characteristically compact in appearance with well-defined edges, and produce rain only when well developed vertically (2 km or 1.5 mi, or more, thick).

Classification of clouds. The contrast in cloud forms mentioned above was recognized in the first widely accepted classification, as well as in several succeeding classifications. The first was that of L. Howard in 1803, recognizing three fundamental types: the stratiform (layer), cumuliform (heap), and cirriform (fibrous). The first two are indeed fundamental, representing clouds formed respectively in stable and in convectively unstable atmospheres, whereas the clouds of the third type are the ice clouds which are in general higher and more tenuous and less clearly reveal the kind of air motion which led to their

clouds concerns the ways in which they become aggregated into drops large enough to fall as rain.

The cooling which produces clouds is almost always associated with the upward movements of air which carry heat from the Earth's surface and restore to the atmosphere that heat lost by radiation into space. These movements are most pronounced in storms, which are accompanied by thick, dense clouds, but also take place on a smaller scale in fair weather, producing scattered clouds or dappled skies. *SEE STORM.*

Rising air cools by several degrees Celsius for each kilometer of ascent, so that even over equatorial re-

Fig. 3. Small cumulus. (*U.S. Weather Bureau*)

Fig. 4. Overcast of stratus, with some fragments below the hilltops. (*U.S. Weather Bureau*)

Fig. 5. View from Mount Wilson, California. High above is a veil of cirrostratus, and below is the top of a low-level layer cloud. (*F. Ellerman, U.S. Weather Bureau*)

Fig. 6. Cirrocumulus, high clouds with a delicate pattern. (*A. A. Lothman, U.S. Weather Bureau*)

Fig. 7. Altocumulus, which occurs at intermediate levels. (*G. A. Lott, U.S. Weather Bureau*)

Fig. 8. Altostratus, a middle-level layer cloud. Thick layers of such cloud, with bases extending down to low levels, produce prolonged rain or snow, and are then called nimbostratus. (*C. F. Brooks, U.S. Weather Bureau*)

formation. Succeeding classifications continued to be based upon the visual appearance or form of the clouds, differentiating relatively minor features, but later in the nineteenth century increasing importance was attached to cloud height, because direct measurements of winds above the ground were then very difficult, and it was hoped to obtain wind data on a great scale by combining observations of apparent cloud motion with reasonably accurate estimates of cloud height, based solely on their form. With the advent of satellite and rocket observations in the 1970s, a broader perspective became available for examination of clouds on a global basis. Such pictures readily show the distribution of clouds from systems such as a midlatitude cyclone, hurricane, or the intertropical convergence zone; they show the influence of land and ocean in initiating convective motion; and they show dramatically the relationship of lenticular clouds to mountain and island topography (**Fig. 1**).

WMO cloud classification. The World Meteorological Organization (WMO) uses a classification which, with minor modifications, dates from 1894 and represents a choice made at that time from a number of competing classifications. It divides clouds into low-level (base below about 2 km or 1.5 mi), middle-level (about 2 to 7 km or approximately 1 to 4.5 mi), and high-level (between roughly 7 and 14 km or approximately 4 to 8.5 mi) forms within the middle latitudes. The names of the three basic forms of clouds are used in combination to define 10 main characteristic forms, or genera.

1. Cirrus are high white clouds with a silken or fibrous appearance (**Fig. 2**).

2. Cumulus are detached dense clouds which rise in domes or towers from a level low base (**Fig. 3**).

3. Stratus are extensive layers or flat patches of low clouds without detail (**Fig. 4**).

4. Cirrostratus is cirrus so abundant as to fuse into a layer (**Fig. 5**).

Fig. 9. Cumulonimbus clouds photographed over the upland adjoining the upper Colorado River valley. (*Lt. B. H. Wyatt, U.S.N., U.S. Weather Bureau*)

Cloud classification based on air motion and associated physical characteristics

Kind of motion	Typical vertical speeds, cm/s*	Kind of cloud	Name	Characteristic dimensions, km†		Characteristic precipitation
				Horizontal	Vertical	
Widespread slow ascent, associated with cyclones (stable atmosphere)	10	Thick layers	Cirrus, later becoming: cirrostratus altostratus altocumulus	10^3	1–2	Snow trails
			nimbostratus	10^3	10	Prolonged moderate rain or snow
Convection, due to passage over warm surface (unstable atmosphere)	10^2	Small heap cloud	Cumulus	1	1	None
	10^3	Shower- and thundercloud	Cumulonimbus	10	10	Intense showers of rain or hail
Irregular stirring causing cooling during passage over cold surface (stable atmosphere)	10	Shallow low layer clouds, fogs	Stratus Stratocumulus	$<10^2$ $<10^3$	<1	None, or slight drizzle or snow

*1 cm = 0.4 in.   †1 km = 0.62 mi.

5. Cirrocumulus is formed of high clouds broken into a delicate wavy or dappled pattern (**Fig. 6**).

6. Stratocumulus is a low-level layer cloud having a dappled, lumpy, or wavy structure. See the foreground of Fig. 5.

7. Altocumulus is similar to stratocumulus but lies at intermediate levels (**Fig. 7**).

8. Altostratus is a thick, extensive, layer cloud at intermediate levels (**Fig. 8**).

9. Nimbostratus is a dark, widespread cloud with a low base from which prolonged rain or snow falls.

10. Cumulonimbus is a large cumulus which produces a rain or snow shower (**Fig. 9**).

Classification by air motion. Modern studies of clouds have been stimulated by the need to know their composition from the viewpoint of aircraft and rocket penetration, which gives rise to icing, turbulence, and lightning hazards, and by the discovery that seeding of supercooled clouds could, on occasion, give rise to enhanced precipitation. *See Weather modification*.

These studies show that the external form of clouds gives only indirect and incomplete clues to the physical properties which determine their evolution. Throughout this evolution the most important proper-

ties appear to be the air motion and the size-distribution spectrum of all the cloud particles, including the condensation and ice-forming nuclei. These properties vary significantly with time and position within the cloud, so that cloud studies demand the intensive examination of individual clouds with aircraft, radar, and satellites. Nevertheless, the overall cloud shape does give information on the formation process. Lenticular clouds with smooth tops may form from smooth air flow with little environmental mixing (**Fig. 10**); clouds with irregular tops (Fig. 9) show that mixing is strong. The former has nonturbulent, laminar air motions and give a smooth flight; the mixing clouds give modest to strong turbulence and a bumpy flight. An observer of clouds can readily see motions of convective clouds; motions in other systems can be viewed by time-lapse photography at 5–50-s intervals, or sequential satellite pictures at intervals of several hours. From a general meteorological point of view, a classification can be based upon the kind of air motion associated with the cloud, as shown in the **table**.

Frank H. Ludlam; John Hallett

Fig. 10. A cloud formed by moist air flowing over a mountain. Note the smooth upper profile, indicating low-turbulence flow. (*Courtesy of John Hallet*)

Cloud physics

The study of the physical and dynamical processes governing the structure and development of clouds and the release from them of snow, rain, and hail (collectively known as precipitation).

The factors of prime importance are the motion of the air, its water-vapor content, and the number and properties of the particles in the air which act as centers of condensation and freezing. Because of the complexity of atmospheric motions and the enormous variability in vapor and particle content of the air, it seems impossible to construct a detailed, general theory of the manner in which clouds and precipitation develop. However, calculations based on the present conception of laws governing the growth and aggregation of cloud particles and on simple models of air

motion provide reasonable explanations for the observed formation of precipitation in different kinds of
clouds.

Cloud formation. Clouds are formed by the lifting
of damp air which cools by expansion under continuously falling pressure. The relative humidity increases until the air approaches saturation. Then condensation occurs (**Fig. 1**) on some of the wide variety
of aerosol particles present; these exist in concentrations ranging from less than 2000 particles/in.^{3}
(100/cm^3) in clean, maritime air to perhaps 10^7/in.^{3}
(10^6/cm^3) in the highly polluted air of an industrial
city. A portion of these particles are hygroscopic and
promote condensation at relative humidities below
100%; but for continued condensation leading to the
formation of cloud droplets, the air must be slightly
supersaturated. Among the highly efficient condensation nuclei are the salt particles produced by the evaporation of sea spray, but it appears that particles produced by human-made fires and by natural
combustion (for example, forest fires) also make a
major contribution. Condensation onto the nuclei continues as rapidly as the water vapor is made available
by cooling of the air and gives rise to droplets of the
order of 0.0004 in. (0.01 mm) in diameter. These
droplets, usually present in concentrations of several
thousand per cubic inch, constitute a nonprecipitating
water cloud.

Mechanisms of precipitation release. Growing
clouds are sustained by upward air currents, which
may vary in strength from about an inch per second
to several yards per second. Considerable growth of
the cloud droplets (with falling speeds of only about
0.4 in./s or 1 cm/s) is therefore necessary if they are
to fall through the cloud, survive evaporation in the
unsaturated air beneath, and reach the ground as drizzle or rain. Drizzle drops have radii exceeding 0.004
in. (0.1 mm), while the largest raindrops are about
0.24 in. (6 mm) across and fall at nearly 30 ft/s (10
m/s). The production of a relatively few large particles from a large population of much smaller ones
may be achieved in one of two ways.

Coalescence process. Cloud droplets are seldom of

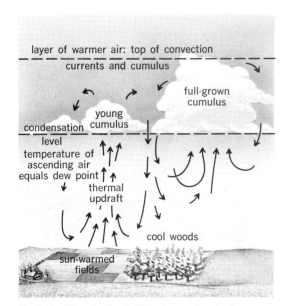

Fig. 1. Conditions leading to birth of a cumulus cloud.

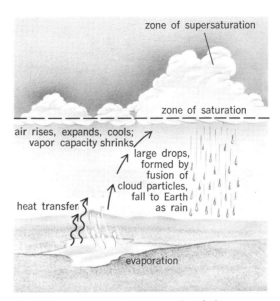

Fig. 2. Diagram of the steps in the formation of rain.

uniform size for several reasons. Droplets arise on
nuclei of various sizes and grow under slightly different conditions of temperature and supersaturation in
different parts of the cloud. Some small drops may
remain inside the cloud for longer than others before
being carried into the drier air outside.

A droplet appreciably larger than average will fall
faster than the smaller ones, and so will collide and
fuse (coalesce) with some of those which it overtakes
(**Fig. 2**). Calculations show that, in a deep cloud containing strong upward air currents and high concentrations of liquid water, such a droplet will have a sufficiently long journey among its smaller neighbors to
grow to raindrop size. This coalescence mechanism is
responsible for the showers that fall in tropical and
subtropical regions from clouds whose tops do not
reach the 32°F (0°C) level and therefore cannot contain ice crystals which are responsible for most precipitation. Radar evidence also suggests that showers
in temperate latitudes may sometimes be initiated by
the coalescence of waterdrops, although the clouds
may later reach to heights at which ice crystals may
form in their upper parts.

Initiation of the coalescence mechanism requires
the presence of some droplets exceeding 20 micrometers in diameter. Over the oceans and in adjacent
land areas they may well be supplied as droplets of
sea spray, but in the interiors of continents, where so-
called giant salt particles of marine origin are probably scarce, it may be harder for the coalescence
mechanism to begin.

Ice crystal process. The second method of releasing
precipitation can operate only if the cloud top reaches
elevations where temperatures are below 32°F (0°C)
and the droplets in the upper cloud regions become
supercooled. At temperatures below −40°F (−40°C)
the droplets freeze automatically or spontaneously; at
higher temperatures they can freeze only if they are
infected with special, minute particles called ice nuclei. As the temperature falls below 32°F (0°C), more
and more ice nuclei become active, and ice crystals
appear in increasing numbers among the supercooled
droplets. But such a mixture of supercooled droplets
and ice crystals is unstable. The cloudy air, being

usually only slightly supersaturated with water vapor as far as the droplets are concerned, is strongly oversaturated for the ice crystals, which therefore grow more rapidly than the droplets. After several minutes the growing crystals will acquire definite falling speeds, and several of them may become joined together to form a snowflake. In falling into the warmer regions of the cloud, however, the snowflake may melt and reach the ground as a raindrop.

Precipitation from layer-cloud systems. The deep, extensive, multilayer-cloud systems, from which precipitation of a usually widespread, persistent character falls, are generally formed in cyclonic depressions (lows) and near fronts. Such cloud systems are associated with feeble upcurrents of only a few centimeters per second, which last for at least several hours. Although the structure of these great raincloud systems, which are being explored by aircraft and radar, is not yet well understood, it appears that they rarely produce rain as distinct from drizzle, unless their tops are colder than about 10°F (-12°C). This suggests that ice crystals may be responsible. Such a view is supported by the fact that the radar signals from these clouds usually take a characteristic form which has been clearly identified with the melting of snowflakes.

Production of showers. Precipitation from shower clouds and thunderstorms, whether in the form of raindrops, pellets of soft hail, or true hailstones, is generally of greater intensity and shorter duration than that from layer clouds and is usually composed of larger particles. The clouds themselves are characterized by their large vertical depth, strong vertical air currents, and high concentrations of liquid water, all these factors favoring the rapid growth of precipitation elements by accretion.

In a cloud composed wholly of liquid water, raindrops may grow by coalescence with small droplets. For example, a droplet being carried up from the cloud base would grow as it ascends by sweeping up smaller droplets. When it becomes too heavy to be supported by the vertical upcurrents, the droplet will then fall, continuing to grow by the same process on its downward journey. Finally, if the cloud is sufficiently deep, the droplet will emerge from its base as a raindrop.

In a dense, vigorous cloud several kilometers deep, the drop may attain its limiting stable diameter (about 0.2 in. or 5 mm) before reaching the cloud base and thus will break up into several large fragments. Each of these may continue to grow and attain breakup size. The number of raindrops may increase so rapidly in this manner that after a few minutes the accumulated mass of water can no longer be supported by the upcurrents and falls out as a heavy shower. The conditions which favor this rapid multiplication of raindrops occur more readily in tropical regions.

The ice crystals grow initially by sublimation of vapor in much the same way as in layer clouds, but when their diameters exceed about 0.004 in. (0.1 mm), growth by collision with supercooled droplets will usually predominate. At low temperatures the impacting droplets tend to freeze individually and quickly to produce pellets of soft hail. The air spaces between the frozen droplets give the ice a relatively low density; the frozen droplets contain large numbers of tiny air bubbles, which give the pellets an opaque, white appearance. However, when the growing pellet traverses a region of relatively high air temperature or high concentration of liquid water or both, the trans-

fer of latent heat of fusion from the hailstone to the air cannot occur sufficiently rapidly to allow all the deposited water to freeze immediately. There then forms a wet coating of slushy ice, which may later freeze to form a layer of compact, relatively transparent ice. Alternate layers of opaque and clear ice are characteristic of large hailstones, but their formation and detailed structure are determined by many factors such as the number concentration, size and impact velocity of the supercooled cloud droplets, the temperature of the air and hailstone surface, and the size, shape, and aerodynamic behavior of the hailstone. Giant hailstones, up to 4 in. (10 cm) in diameter, which cause enormous damage to crops, buildings, and livestock, most frequently fall not from the large tropical thunderstorms, but from storms in the continental interiors of temperate latitudes. An example is the Nebraska-Wyoming area of the United States, where the organization of larger-scale wind patterns is particularly favorable for the growth of severe storms.

The development of precipitation in convective clouds is accompanied by electrical effects culminating in lightning. The mechanism by which the electric charge dissipated in lightning flashes is generated and separated within the thunderstorm has been debated for more than 200 years, but there is still no universally accepted theory. However, the majority opinion holds that lightning is closely associated with the appearance of the ice phase, and the most promising theory suggests that the charge is produced by the rebound of a small fraction of the supercooled cloud droplets that collide with the falling hail pellets.

Basic aspects of cloud physics. The various stages of the precipitation mechanisms raise a number of interesting and fundamental problems in classical physics. Worthy of mention are the supercooling and freezing of water; the nature, origin, and mode of action of the ice nuclei; and the mechanism of ice-crystal growth which produces the various snow crystal forms.

It has been established how the maximum degree to which a sample of water may be supercooled depends on its purity, volume, and rate of cooling. The freezing temperatures of waterdrops containing foreign particles vary linearly as the logarithm of the droplet volumes for a constant rate of cooling. This relationship, which has been established for drops varying between 0.0004 and 0.4 in. (10 μm and 1 cm) in diameter, characterizes the heterogeneous nucleation of waterdrops and is probably a consequence of the fact that the ice-nucleating ability of atmospheric aerosol increases logarithmically with decreasing temperature.

When extreme precautions are taken to purify the water and to exclude all solid particles, small droplets, about 0.00004 in. (1 μm) in diameter, may be supercooled to -40°F (-40°C) and drops of 0.04 in. (1 mm) diameter to -31°F (-35°C). Under these conditions freezing occurs spontaneously without the aid of foreign nuclei.

The nature and origin of the ice nuclei, which are necessary to induce freezing of cloud droplets at temperatures about -40°F (-40°C), are still not clear. Measurements made with large cloud chambers on aircraft indicate that the most efficient nuclei, active at temperatures above 14°F (-10°C), are present in concentrations of only about 30/ft³ (10/m³) of air, but as the temperature is lowered, the number of ice crystals increases logarithmically to reach concentrations of about 25/ft^3 (1/liter) at $-4°F$ ($-20°C$) and 2500/ft^3 (100/liter) at $-22°F$ ($-30°C$). Since these measured concentrations of nuclei are less than one-hundredth of the number that apparently is consumed in the production of snow, it seems that there must exist processes by which the original number of ice crystals are rapidly multiplied. Laboratory experiments suggest the fragmentation of the delicate snow crystals and the ejection of ice splinters from freezing droplets as probable mechanisms.

The most likely source of atmospheric ice nuclei is provided by the soil and mineral-dust particles carried aloft by the wind. Laboratory tests have shown that, although most common minerals are relatively inactive, a number of silicate minerals of the clay family produce ice crystals in a supercooled cloud at temperatures above $-0.4°F$ ($-18°C$). A major constituent of some clays, kaolinite, which is active below $16°F$ ($-9°C$), is probably the main source of highly efficient nuclei.

The fact that there may often be a deficiency of efficient ice nuclei in the atmosphere has led to a search for artificial nuclei which might be introduced into supercooled clouds in large numbers. Silver iodide is a most effective substance, being active at $25°F$ ($-4°C$), while lead iodide and cupric sulfide have threshold temperatures of $21°F$ ($-6°C$) for freezing nuclei.

In general, the most effective ice-nucleating substances, both natural and artificial, are hexagonal crystals in which spacings between adjacent rows of atoms differ from those of ice by less than 16%. The detailed surface structure of the nucleus, which is determined only in part by the crystal geometry, is of even greater importance. This is strongly indicated by the discovery that several complex organic substances, notably steroid compounds, which have apparently little structural resemblance to ice, may act as nucleators for ice at temperatures as high as $30°F$ ($-1°C$).

The collection of snow crystals from clouds at different temperatures has revealed their great variety of shape and form. By growing the ice crystals on a fine fiber in a cloud chamber, it has been possible to reproduce all the naturally occurring forms and to show how these are correlated with the temperature and supersaturation of the environment. With the air temperature along the length of a fiber ranging from 32 to $-13°F$ (0 to $-25°C$), the following clear-cut changes of crystal habit are observed (**Fig. 3**):

hexagonal plates–needles–hollow prisms–
plates–stellar dendrites–plates–prisms.

This multiple change of habit over such a small temperature range is remarkable and is thought to be associated with the fact that water molecules apparently migrate between neighboring faces on an ice crystal in a manner which is very sensitive to the temperature. Certainly the temperature rather than the supersaturation of the environment is primarily responsible for determining the basic shape of the crystal, though the supersaturation governs the growth rates of the crystals, the ratio of their linear dimensions, and the development of dendritic forms.

Artificial stimulation of rain. The presence of either ice crystals or some comparatively large waterdroplets (to initiate the coalescence mechanism) appears essential to the natural release of precipitation.

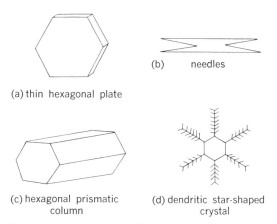

Fig. 3. Ice crystal types formed in various temperature ranges: (a) 32 to 27°F (0 to $-3°C$), 18 to 10°F (-8 to $-12°C$), 3 to $-13°F$ (-16 to $-25°C$); (b) 27 to 23°F (-3 to $-5°C$); (c) 23 to 18°F (-5 to $-8°C$), below $-13°F$ ($-25°C$); (d) 10 to 3°F (-12 to $-16°C$).

Rainmaking experiments are conducted on the assumption that some clouds precipitate inefficiently, or not at all, because they are deficient in natural nuclei; and that this deficiency can be remedied by seeding the clouds artificially with dry ice or silver iodide to produce ice crystals, or by introducing waterdroplets or large hygroscopic nuclei. In the dry-ice method, pellets of about 0.4-in. (1-cm) diameter are dropped from an aircraft into the top of a supercooled cloud. Each pellet chills a thin sheath of air near its surface to well below $-40°F$ ($-40°C$) and produces perhaps 10^{12} minute ice crystals, which subsequently spread through the cloud, grow, and aggregate into snowflakes. Only a few pounds of dry ice are required to seed a large cumulus cloud. Some hundreds of experiments, carried out mainly in Australia, Canada, South Africa, and the United States, have shown that cumulus clouds in a suitable state of development may be induced to rain by seeding them with dry ice on occasions when neighboring clouds, untreated, do not precipitate. However, the amounts of rain produced have usually been rather small.

For large-scale trials designed to modify the rainfall from widespread cloud systems over large areas, the cost of aircraft is usually prohibitive. The technique in this case is to release a silver iodide smoke from the ground and rely on the air currents to carry it up into the supercooled regions of the cloud. In this method, with no control over the subsequent transport of the smoke, it is not possible to make a reliable estimate of the concentrations of ice nuclei reaching cloud level, nor is it known for how long silver iodide retains its nucleating ability in the atmosphere. It is usually these unknown factors which, together with the impossibility of estimating accurately what would have been the natural rainfall in the absence of seeding activities, make the design and evaluation of a large-scale operation so difficult.

Little convincing evidence can be found that large increases in rainfall have been produced consistently over large areas. Indeed, in temperate latitudes most rain falls from deep layer-cloud systems whose tops usually reach to levels at which there are abundant natural ice nuclei and in which the natural precipitation processes have plenty of time to operate. It is therefore not obvious that seeding of these clouds would produce a significant increase in rainfall, although it is possible that by forestalling natural processes some redistribution might be effected.

Perhaps more promising as additional sources of rain or snow are the persistent supercooled clouds produced by the ascent of damp air over large mountain barriers. The continuous generation of an appropriate concentration of ice crystals near the windward edge might well produce a persistent light snowfall to the leeward, since water vapor is continually being made available for crystal growth by lifting of the air. The condensed water, once converted into snow crystals, has a much greater opportunity of reaching the mountain surface without evaporating, and might accumulate in appreciable amounts if seeding were maintained for many hours.

Trials carried out in favorable locations in the United States and Australia suggest that in some cases seeding has been followed by seasonal precipitation increases of about 10%, but rarely have the effects been reproduced from one season to the next, and overall the evidence for consistent and statistically significant increases of rainfall is not impressive. Indeed, as the experiments have been subjected to stricter statistical design and evaluation, the claims have steadily became more modest, and the difficulty of improving on natural processes has become increasingly apparent.

During the 1960s and 1970s, remaining trials were carried out in some 75 countries, and at one time about 25% of the land area of the United States was being seeded. However, by the late 1980s the activity was much reduced and had virtually ceased in Australia and many other countries. Nevertheless, China and Israel persevered. The Israeli experiments were unique in that they appeared to have produced rainfall increases on the order of 15% year after year for about 15 years. No convincing explanation for this has yet emerged. SEE CLOUD; WEATHER MODIFICATION.

Basil J. Mason

Bibliography. E. M. Agee and T. Assai (eds.), *Cloud Dynamics*, 1982; L. J. Battan, *Cloud Physics and Cloud Seeding*, 1962, reprint 1979; B. J. Mason, *Clouds, Rain and Rainmaking*, 1975; H. R. Pruppacher and J. D. Klett, *Microphysics of Atmospheric Clouds and Precipitation*, 1980.

Coastal engineering

A branch of civil engineering concerned with the planning, design, construction, and maintenance of works in the coastal zone. The purposes of these works include control of shoreline erosion; development of navigation channels and harbors; defense against flooding caused by storms, tides, and seismically generated waves (tsunamis); development of coastal recreation; and control of pollution in nearshore waters. Coastal engineering usually involves the construction of structures or the transport and possible stabilization of sand and other coastal sediments.

The successful coastal engineer must have a working knowlege of oceanography and meteorology, hydrodynamics, geomorphology and soil mechanics, statistics, and structural mechanics. Tools that support coastal engineering design include analytical theories of wave motion, wave-structure interaction, diffusion in a turbulent flow field, and so on; numerical and physical hydraulic models; basic experiments in wave and current flumes; and field measurements of basic processes such as beach profile response to wave attack, and the construction of works. Postconstruction monitoring efforts at coastal projects have also contributed greatly to improved design practice.

Environmental forces. The most dominant agent controlling coastal processes and the design of coastal works is usually the waves generated by the wind. Wind waves produce large forces on coastal structures, they generate nearshore currents and the alongshore transport of sediment, and they mold beach profiles. Thus, a primary concern of coastal engineers is to determine the wave climate (statistical distribution of heights, periods, and directions) to be expected at a particular site. This includes the annual average distribution as well as long-term extreme characteristics. In addition, the nearshore effects of wave refraction, diffraction, reflection, breaking, and runup on structures and beaches must be predicted for adequate design.

Other classes of waves that are of practical importance include the astronomical tide, tsunamis, and waves generated by moving ships. The tide raises and lowers the nearshore water level and thus establishes the range of shoreline over which coastal processes act. It also generates reversing currents in inlets, harbor entrandes, and other locations where water motion is constricted. Tidal currents which often achieve a velocity of 3–6 ft/s (1–2 m/s) can strongly affect navigation, assist with the maintenance of channels by scouring sediments, and dilute polluted waters.

Tsunamis are quite localized in time and space but can produce devastating effects. Often the only solution is to evacuate tsunami-prone areas or suffer the consequences of a surge that can reach elevations in excess of 33 ft (10 m) above sea level. Some attempts have been made to design structures to withstand tsunami surge or to plant trees and construct offshore works to reduce surge velocities and runup elevations. SEE TSUNAMI.

The waves generated by ships can be of greater importance at some locations than are wind-generated waves. Ship waves can cause extensive bank erosion in navigation channels and undesirable disturbance of moored vessels in unprotected marinas.

On coasts having a relatively broad shallow offshore region (such as the Atlantic and Gulf coasts of the United States), the wind and lower pressures in a storm will cause the water level to rise at the shoreline. Hurricanes have been known to cause storm surge elevations of as much as 16 ft (5 m) for periods of several hours to a day or more. Damage is caused primarily by flooding, wave attack at the raised water levels, and high wind speeds. Defense against storm surge usually involves raising the crest elevation of natural dune systems or the construction of a barrier-dike system. SEE STORM SURGE.

Other environmental forces that impact on coastal works include earthquake disturbances of the sea floor and static and dynamic ice forces. Direct shaking of the ground will cause major structural excitations over a region that can be tens of kilometers wide surrounding the epicenter of a major earthquake. Net dislocation of the ground will modify the effect of active coastal processes and environmental forces on structures. SEE EARTHQUAKE.

Ice that is moved by flowing water and wind or raised and lowered by the tide can cause large and often controlling forces on coastal structures. However, shore ice can prevent coastal erosion by keeping wave action from reaching the shore.

Coastal processes. Wind-generated waves are the dominant factor that causes the movement of sand parallel and normal to the shoreline as well as the resulting changes in beach morphology. Thus, structures that modify coastal zone wave activity can strongly influence beach processes and geometry.

Active beach profile zone. **Figure 1** shows typical beach profiles found at a sandy shoreline (which may be backed by a cliff or a dune field). The backshore often has one or two berms with a crest elevation equal to the height of wave runup during high tide. When low swell, common during calm conditions, acts on the beach profile, the beach face is built up by the onshore transport of sand. This accretion of sand adds to the seaward berm. However, storm waves will attack the beach face, cut back the berm, and carry sand offshore. This active zone of shifting beach profiles occurs primarily landward of the 33-ft (10-m) depth contour. If the storm tide and waves are sufficiently high, the berms may be eroded away to expose the dunes or cliff to erosion. The beach profile changes shown in Fig. 1 are superimposed on any longer-term advance or retreat of the shoreline caused by a net gain or loss of sand at that location.

Any structure constructed along the shore in the active beach profile zone may retain the sand behind it and thus reduce or prevent erosion. However, wave attack on the seaward face of the structure causes increased turbulence at the base of the structure, and usually increased scour which must be allowed for or prevented, if possible, by the placement of stone or some other protective material.

It is desirable to keep all construction of dwellings, recreational facilities, and such landward of the active beach profile zone, which usually means landward of the frontal dunes or a good distance back from retreating cliffs. It is also desirable to maintain and encourage the growth of the frontal dune system by planting grass or installing sand fencing.

In addition to constructing protective structures and stabilizing the dune system, it is common practice to nourish a beach by placing sand on the beach face and nearshore area. This involves an initial placement of sand to develop the desired profile and periodic replenishment to make up for losses to the profile. A common source for sand, which should be clean and at least as coarse as the native sand, is the offshore area near the nourishment site.

Alongshore current and transport. Waves arriving with their crest oriented at an angle to the shoreline will generate a shore-parallel alongshore current in the nearshore zone. The current flows in the direction of the alongshore component of wave advance and has the highest velocity just inside the breaker line. It may be assisted or hindered by the wind and by tidal action, particularly along sections of the shore adjacent to tidal inlets and harbor entrances. There is a continuous accumulation of flow in the downcoast direction which may be relieved by seaward-flowing jets of water known as rip currents.

The alongshore current transports sand in suspension and as bed load, and is assisted by the breaking waves, which place additional sand in suspension. Also, wave runup and the return flow transports sand particles in a zigzag fashion along the beach face.

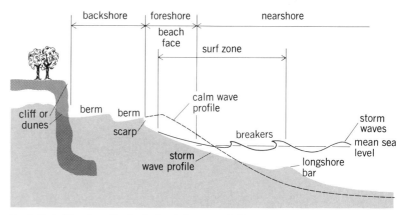

Fig. 1. Typical beach profiles (vertical scale is exaggerated).

Coastal structures that obstruct these alongshore transport processes can cause the deposition of sand. They do this by blocking wave action from a section of the shore and thus removing the wave energy required to maintain the transport system; by interfering with the transport process itself; or by directly shutting off a source of sand that feeds it (such as a structure that protects an eroding shoreline).

The design of most coastal works requires a determination of the volumetric rate of alongshore sand transport at the site—both the gross rate (upcoast plus downcoast transport) and the net rate (upcoast minus downcoast transport). The most reliable method of estimating transport rates is by measuring the rate of erosion or deposition at an artificial or geomorphic structure that interrupts the transport. Also, field studies have developed an approximate relationship between the alongshore transport rate and the alongshore component of incident wave energy per unit time. With this, net and gross transport rates can be estimated if sufficient information is available on the annual wave climate. Typical gross transport rates on exposed ocean shorelines often exceed 500,000 yd^3 (382,000 m^3) per year.

Primary sources of beach sediment include rivers discharging directly to the coast, beach and cliff erosion, and artificial beach nourishment. Sediment transported alongshore from its sources will eventually be deposited at some semipermanent location or sink. Common sinks include harbors and tidal inlets; dune fields; offshore deposition; spits, tombolos, and other geomorphic formations; artificial structures that trap sand; and areas where beach sand is mined.

By evaluating the volumetric transports into and out of a segment of the coast, one can develop a sediment budget for the coastal segment. If the supply exceeds the loss, shoreline accretion will occur, and vice versa. When a coastal project modifies the supply or loss to the segment, geomorphic changes can be expected. For example, when a structure that traps sediment is constructed upcoast of a point of interest, the shoreline at the point of interest can be expected to erode as it resupplies the longshore transport capacity of the waves.

Harbor entrance and tidal inlet control structures built to improve navigation conditions, stabilize navigation channel geometry, and assist with the relief of flood waters will often trap a large portion of the alongshore transport. This can result in undesirable deposition at the harbor or inlet entrance and subse-

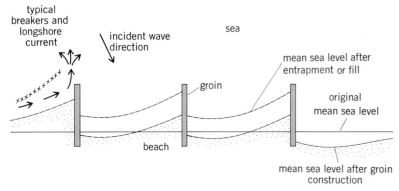

Fig. 2. Groin system and beach response.

quent downcoast erosion. The solution usually involves designing the entrance structures to trap the sediment at a fixed and acceptable location and to provide protection from wave attack at this location so a dredge can pump the sand to the downcoast beach.

Coastal structures. Coastal structures can be classified by the function they serve and by their structural features. Primary functional classes include seawalls, revetments, and bulkheads; groins; jetties; breakwaters; and a group of miscellaneous structures including piers, submerged pipelines, and various harbor and marina structures.

Seawalls, revetments, and bulkheads. These structures are constructed parallel or nearly parallel to the shoreline at the land-sea interface for the purpose of maintaining the shoreline in an advanced position and preventing further shoreline recession. Seawalls are usually massive and rigid, while a revetment is an armoring of the beach face with stone rip-rap or artificial units. A bulkhead acts primarily as a land retaining structure and is found in a more protected environment such as a navigation channel or marina.

A key factor in the design of these structures is that erosion can continue on adjacent shores and flank the structure if it is not tied in at the ends. Erosion on adjacent shores also increases the exposure of the main structure to wave attack. Structures of this class are prone to damage and possible failure caused by wave-induced scour at the toe. In order to prevent this, the toe must be stabilized by driving vertical sheet piling into the beach, laying stone on the beach seaward of the toe, or maintaining a protective beach by artificial nourishment. Revetments that are sufficiently porous will allow leaching of sand from below the structure. This can lead to structure slumping and failure. A proper stone or cloth filter system must be developed to prevent damage to the revetment.

Groins. A groin is a structure built perpendicular to the shore and usually extending out through the surf zone under normal wave and surge-level conditions. It functions by trapping sand from the alongshore transport system to widen and protect a beach or by retaining artificially placed sand. The resulting shoreline positions before and after construction of a series of groins and after nourishment is placed between the groins are shown schematically in **Fig. 2**. Typical groin alongshore spacing-to-length ratios vary from 1.5:1 up to 4:1.

There will be erosion downcast of the groin field, the volume of erosion being approximately equal to the volume of sand removed by the groins from the alongshore transport system. Groins must be sufficiently tied into the beach so that downcoast erosion superimposed on seasonal beach profile fluctuations does not flank the landward end of a groin. Even the best-designed groin system will not prevent the loss of sand offshore in time of storms.

Jetties. Jetties are structures built at the entrance to a river or tidal inlet to stabilize the entrance as well as to protect vessels navigating the entrance channel. Stabilization is achieved by eliminating or reducing the deposition of sediment coming from adjacent shores and by confining the river or tidal flow to develop a more uniform and hydraulically efficient channel. Jetties improve navigation conditions by eliminating bothersome crosscurrents and by reducing wave action in the entrance.

At many entrances there are two parallel (or nearly parallel) jetties that extend approximately to the seaward end of the dredged portion of the channel. However, at some locations a single updrift or downdrift jetty has been used, as have other arrangements such as arrowhead jetties (a pair of straight or curved jetties that converge in the seaward direction). Jetty layouts may also be modified to assist sediment-bypassing operations. A unique arrangement is the weir-jetty system in which the updrift jetty has a low section or weir (crest elevation about mean sea level) across the surf zone. This allows sand to move over the weir section and into a deposition basin for subsequent transport to the downcoast shore by dredge and pipeline.

Breakwaters. The primary purpose of a breakwater is to protect a shoreline or harbor anchorage area from wave attack. Breakwaters may be located completely offshore and oriented approximately parallel to shore, or they may be oblique and connected to the shore where they often take on some of the functions of a jetty. At locations where a natural inland site is not available, harbors have been developed by the construction of shore-connected breakwaters that cover two or three sides of the harbor.

Figure 3 shows the breakwater and jetty system at the entrance to Channel Islands Harbor in southern California. The offshore breakwater intercepts incident waves, thus trapping the predominantly southeastern longshore sand transport; it provides a protected area where a dredge can operate to bypass sediment; and it provides protection to the harbor en-

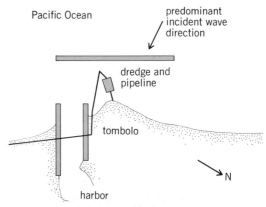

Fig. 3. Overhead view of breakwater and jetty system of Channel Islands Harbor, California.

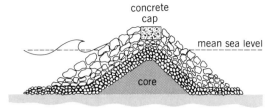

Fig. 4. Rubble mound breakwater cross section.

trance. A series of shore-parallel offshore breakwaters (with or without artificial nourishment) has been used for shore protection at a number of locations. If there is sufficient fill or trapped material, the tombolo formed in the lee of each breakwater may grow until it reaches the breakwater.

Breakwaters are designed to intercept waves, and often extend into relatively deep water, so they tend to be more massive structures than are jetties or groins. Breakwaters constructed to provide a calm anchorage area for ships usually have a high crown elevation to prevent overtopping by incident waves and subsequent regeneration of waves in the lee of the breakwater.

Groins, jetties, and breakwaters are most commonly constructed as rubble mound structures. **Figure 4** shows the cross section of a typical rubble mound breakwater placed on a sand foundation. The breakwater has an outer armor layer consisting of the largest stones or, if sufficiently large stones are not available, the armor units may be molded of concrete with a special shape. Stone sizes decrease toward the core and base in order to develop a filter system so that the fine core stone and base sand are not removed by wave and current action. The core made of fine stone sizes is provided to diminish wave transmission through the structure. Jetties and groins have a simpler cross section, consisting typically of only armor and core layers. Breakwaters, groins, and jetties have also been constructed of steel or concrete caissons with sand and gravel fill; wood, steel, and concrete sheet piles; and sand-filled bags.

A different type of breakwater that can be effective where incident wave periods are short and large water-level fluctuations occur (as in a reservoir marina) is the moored floating breakwater. This type has been constructed of hollow concrete prisms, scrap tires, logs, and a variety of other materials.

In an attempt to develop low-cost shore protection, a number of novel materials have been used for shoreline revetments, including cinder blocks, tires, sand-filled rubber tubes, woven-fiber mattresses, and soil-cement paving.

Robert M. Sorensen

Bibliography. American Society of Civil Engineers, *Journal of the Waterway, Port, Coastal and Ocean Engineering Division* and *Proceedings of the International Conferences on Coastal Engineering*; P. Braun, *Design and Construction of Mounds for Breakwater and Coastal Protection*, 1985; B. L. Edge (ed.), *Coastal Engineering: 1982*, 1983; P. D. Komar, *Beach Processes and Sedimentation*, 1976; A. D. Quinn, *Design and Construction of Ports and Marine Structures*, 1972; R. Silvester, *Coastal Engineering*, 2 vols., 1974; U.S. Army Coastal Engineering Research Center, *Shore Protection Manual*, 3 vols., 1977.

Comfort heating

The maintenance of the temperature in a closed volume, such as a home, office, or factory, at a comfortable level during periods of low outside temperature. Two principal factors determine the amount of heat required to maintain a comfortable inside temperature: the difference between inside and outside temperatures and the ease with which heat can flow out through the enclosure.

Heating load. The first step in planning a heating system is to estimate the heating requirements. This involves calculating heat loss from the space, which in turn depends upon the difference between outside and inside space temperatures and upon the heat transfer coefficients of the surrounding structural members.

Outside and inside design temperatures are first selected. Ideally, a heating system should maintain the desired inside temperature under the most severe weather conditions. Economically, however, the lowest outside temperature on record for a locality is seldom used. The design temperature selected depends upon the heat capacity of the structure, amount of insulation, wind exposure, proportion of heat loss due to infiltration or ventilation, nature and time of occupancy or use of the space, difference between daily maximum and minimum temperatures, and other factors. Usually the outside design temperature used is the median of extreme temperatures.

The selected inside design temperature depends upon the use and occupancy of the space. Generally it is between 66 and 75°F (19 and 24°C).

The total heat loss from a space consists of losses through windows and doors, walls or partitions, ceiling or roof, and floor, plus air leakage or ventilation. All items but the last are calculated from $H_l = UA(t_i - t_o)$, where heat loss H_l is in British thermal units per hour (or in watts), U is overall coefficient of heat transmission from inside to outside air in Btu/(h)(ft^2)(°F) (or J/s · m^2 · °C), A is inside surface area in square feet (or square meters), t_i is inside design temperature, and t_o is outside design temperature in °F (or °C).

Values for U can be calculated from heat transfer coefficients of air films and heat conductivities for building materials or obtained directly for various materials and types of construction from heating guides and handbooks.

The heating engineer should work with the architect and building engineer on the economics of the completed structure. Consideration should be given to the use of double glass or storm sash in areas where outside design temperature is 10°F (−12°C) or lower. Heat loss through windows and doors can be more than halved and comfort considerably improved with double glazing. Insulation in exposed walls, ceilings, and around the edges of the ground slab can usually reduce local heat loss by 50–75%. **Table 1** compares two typical dwellings. The 43% reduction in heat loss of the insulated house produces a worthwhile decrease in the cost of the heating plant and its operation. Building the house tight reduces the large heat loss due to infiltration of outside air. High heating-energy costs may now warrant 4 in. (10 cm) of insulation in the walls and 8 in. (20 cm) or more in the ceiling.

Humidification. In localities where outdoor temperatures are often below 36°F (2°C), it is advisable to provide means for adding moisture in heated spaces

Table 1. Effectiveness of double glass and insulation*

Heat-loss members	Area, ft² (m²)	Heat loss, Btu/h[†]	
		With single-glass weather-stripped windows and doors	With double-glass windows, storm doors, and 2-in. (5.1-cm) wall insulation
Windows and doors	439 (40)	39,600	15,800
Walls	1952 (181)	32,800	14,100
Ceiling	900 (84)	5,800	5,800
Infiltration		20,800	20,800
Total heat loss		99,000	56,500
Duct loss in basement and walls (20% of total loss)		19,800	11,300
Total required furnace output		118,800	67,800

*Data are for two-story house with basement in St. Louis, Missouri. Walls are frame with brick veneer and 25/32-in. (2.0-cm) insulation plus gypsum lath and plaster. Attic floor has 3-in. (7.5-cm) fibrous insulation or its equivalent. Infiltration of outside air is taken as a 1-h air change in the 14,400 ft³ (408 m³) of heating space. Outside design temperature is −5°F (−21°C); inside temperature is selected as 75°F (24°C).
[†]1 Btu/h = 0.293 W.

to improve comfort. The colder the outside air is, the less moisture it can hold. When it is heated to room temperature, the relative humidity in the space becomes low enough to dry out nasal membranes, furniture, and other hygroscopic materials. This results in discomfort as well as deterioration of physical products.

Various types of humidifiers are available. The most satisfactory type provides for the evaporation of the water to take place on a mold-resistant treated material which can be easily washed to get rid of the resultant deposits. When a higher relative humidity is maintained in a room, a lower dry-bulb temperature or thermostat setting will provide an equal sensation of warmth. This does not mean, however, that there is a saving in heating fuel, because heat from some source is required to evaporate the moisture.

Some humidifiers operate whenever the furnace fan runs, and usually are fed water through a float-controlled valve. With radiation heating, a unitary humidifier located in the room and controlled by a humidistat can be used.

Insulation and vapor barrier. Good insulating material has air cells or several reflective surfaces. A good vapor barrier should be used with or in addition to insulation, or serious trouble may result. Outdoor air or any air at subfreezing temperatures is comparatively dry, and the colder it is the drier it can be. Air inside a space in which moisture has been added from cooking, washing, drying, or humidifying has a much higher vapor pressure than cold outdoor air. Therefore, moisture in vapor form passes from the high vapor pressure space to the lower pressure space and will readily pass through most building materials. When this moisture reaches a subfreezing temperature in the structure, it may condense and freeze. When the structure is later warmed, this moisture will thaw and soak the building material, which may be harmful. For example, in a house that has 4 in. (10 cm) or more of mineral wool insulation in the attic floor, moisture can penetrate up through the second floor ceiling and freeze in the attic when the temperature there is below freezing. When a warm day comes, the ice will melt and can ruin the second floor ceiling. Ventilating the attic helps because the dry outdoor air readily absorbs the moisture before it condenses on the surfaces. Installing a vapor barrier in insulated outside walls is recommended, preferably on the room side of the insulation. Good vapor barriers include asphalt-impregnated paper, metal foil, and some plastic-coated papers. The joints should be sealed to be most effective.

Thermography. Remote heat-sensing techniques evolved from space technology developments related to weather satellites can be used to detect comparative heat energy losses from roofs, walls, windows, and so on. A method called thermography is defined as the conversion of a temperature pattern detected on a surface by contrast into an image called a thermogram (see **illus.**). Thermovision is defined as the technique of utilizing the infrared radiation from a surface, which varies with the surface temperatures, to pro-

(a)

(b)

(c)

(d)

Thermograms of building structures: (*a-c*) masonry buildings; (*d*) glass-faced building. Black indicates negligible heat loss; gray, partial loss; and white, excessive loss. (*Courtesy of A. P. Pontello*)

duce a thermal picture or thermogram. A camera can scan the area in question and focus the radiation on a sensitive detector which in turn converts it to an electronic signal. The signal can be amplified and displayed on a cathode-ray tube as a thermogram.

Normally the relative temperature gradients will vary from white through gray to black. Temperatures from -22 to $3540°F$ (-30 to $2000°C$) can be measured. Color cathode-ray tubes may be used to display color-coded thermograms showing as many as 10 different isotherms. Permanent records are possible by using photos or magnetic tape.

Infrared thermography is used to point out where energy can be saved, and comparative insulation installations and practices can be evaluated. Thermograms of roofs are also used to indicate areas of wet insulation caused by leaks in the roof.

Infiltration. In **Table 2**, the loss due to infiltration is large. It is the most difficult item to estimate accurately and depends upon how well the house is built. If a masonry or brick-veneer house is not well caulked or if the windows are not tightly fitted and weather-stripped, this loss can be quite large. Sometimes, infiltration is estimated more accurately by measuring the length of crack around windows and doors. Illustrative quantities of air leakage for various types of window construction are shown in Table 2. The figures given are in cubic feet of air per foot of crack per hour.

Design. Before a heating system can be designed, it is necessary to estimate the heating load for each room so that the proper amount of radiation or the proper size of supply air outlets can be selected and the connecting pipe or duct work designed.

Heat is released into the space by electric lights and equipment, by machines, and by people. Credit to these in reducing the size of the heating system can be given only to the extent that the equipment is in use continuously or if forced ventilation, which may be a big heat load factor, is not used when these items are not giving off heat, as in a factory. When these internal heat gain items are large, it may be advisable to estimate the heat requirements at different times during a design day under different load conditions in order to maintain inside temperatures at the desired level.

Cost of operation. Design and selection of a heating system should include operating costs. The quan-

tity of fuel required for an average heating season may be calculated from

$$F = \frac{Q \times 24 \times DD}{(t_i - t_o) \times Eff \times H}$$

where F = annual fuel quantity, same units as H
Q = total heat loss, Btu/h (or J/s)
t_i = inside design temperature, °F (or °C)
t_o = outside design temperature, °F (or °C)
Eff = efficiency of total heating system (not just the furnace) as a decimal
H = heating value of fuel
DD = degree-days for the locality for 65°F (19.3°C) base, which is the sum of 65 (19.3) minus each day's mean temperature in °F (or °C) for all the days of the year

If a gas furnace is used for the insulated house of Table 1, the annual fuel consumption would be

$$F = \frac{56,500 \times 24 \times 4699}{[75 - (-5)] \times 0.80 \times 1050}$$

$$= 94,800 \text{ ft}^3 \text{ (2684 m}^3)$$

For a 5°F (3°C), 6–8-h night setback, this consumption would be reduced by about 5%.

Gayle B. Priester

Bibliography. American Society of Heating, Refrigerating, and Air Conditioning Engineers, *Handbook of Fundamentals*, 1977; A. P. Pontello, Thermography: Bringing energy waste to light, *Heat. Piping Air Condit.*, 50(3):55–61, 1978.

Comfort temperatures

Air temperatures adjusted to represent human comfort or discomfort under prevailing conditions of temperature, humidity, radiation, and wind. Theoretical formulas attempt to compare the rate of heat loss to surroundings with rate of heat production by work and metabolism. Most modern empirical relations, based on relative comfort expressed by human subjects under differing atmospheric combinations, attempt to indicate the temperature at which air at some standard humidity, air motion, and radiation load would be just as uncomfortable (or comfortable). Many former indices, however, had arbitrary scales.

Heat is produced constantly by the human body at a rate depending on muscular activity. For body heat balance to be maintained, this heat must be dissipated by conduction to cooler air, by evaporation of perspiration into unsaturated air, and by radiative exchange with surroundings. Air motion (wind) affects the rate of conductive and evaporative cooling of skin, but not of lungs; radiative losses occur only from bare skin or clothing, and depend on its temperature and that of surroundings, as well as sunshine intensity.

As air temperatures approach body temperature, conductive heat loss decreases and evaporative loss increases in importance. Hence, at warmer temperature, humidity is the second-most important atmospheric property controlling heat loss and hence comfort, and the various sensible temperature formulas incorporate some humidity measure.

Temperature and humidity. Almost a century ago, wet-bulb temperature was thought to indicate human comfort under warm conditions, especially in deep

Table 2. Infiltration loss with 15-mi/h (24 km/h) outside wind

Building item	Infiltration, ft³/(ft)(h)
Double-hung unlocked wood sash windows of average tightness, non-weather-stripped including wood frame leakage	39
Same window, weather-stripped	24
Same window poorly fitted, non-weather-stripped	111
Same window poorly fitted, weather-stripped	34
Double-hung metal windows unlocked, non-weather-stripped	74
Same window, weather-stripped	32
Residential metal casement, ¹⁄₆₄-in. (0.4-mm) crack	33
Residential metal casement, ¹⁄₃₂-in. (0.8-mm) crack	52

mines, ship engine rooms, and steel mills and other factories, on the assumption that sweaty skin approximated a wet bulb. It was superseded after 1923 by the effective temperature, which combined dry- and wet-bulb temperatures, at constant low-ventilation rate, as evaluated by 300 trained subjects walking between controlled-environment rooms. In the 1950s this was approximated by the discomfort index, soon renamed temperature-humidity index (THI) and used by the Weather Bureau (now National Weather Service) for several years. In Canada it was called humidity index. It is calculated by either Eq. (1) or Eq. (2), where the dry-bulb (air) and wet-bulb tempera-

$$THI = 15 - 0.4\,(t_a + t_w) \qquad (1)$$

$$THI = t_a - 0.55(1 - RH)(t_a - 58) \qquad (2)$$

tures—t_a and t_w respectively—are expressed in °F, and relative humidity (RH) is expressed as a decimal fraction. Except in saturated air (RH = 1.0, that is, 100%), the temperature-humidity index is usually lower than air temperature. A different temperature-humidity index was used in 1980 by another National Weather Service office to compute a heat wave index, ranging from 0 (mild) to 15 (extreme).

A simple average of air temperature in °F and relative humidity in percent was called humiture in 1937, changed in 1959 to a simple average of dry- and wet-bulb temperatures in °F. Later, this was further changed to an average of air temperature in °F and excess vapor pressure e, above 10 millibars, with the saturation vapor pressure at 45°F. This index is called humidex in Canada. The originator of humidex opposed raising the threshold to 21 mb (saturation at 65°F), which was being used by at least one television weatherperson. No two of these formulations are equivalent, but each is usually less than air temperature. *See* AIR TEMPERATURE; HUMIDITY.

Wind and radiation. Meanwhile, more refined measurements led to more elaborate formulas involving all aspects of heat loss. Operative temperature

modifies effective temperature to include radiation at constant wind speed, and standard operative temperature considers also temperature and heat conduction of skin. The 1955 heat stress index, essentially the ratio of evaporation needed to maintain a stable body temperature to the evaporation possible under existing conditions and working rate, has been evaluated by a detailed computer program. The 1979 apparent temperature, a very complete formulation, is calculated by use of a nomograph or computer as the heat index of the National Oceanic and Atmospheric Administration (see **illus.**). It is a nonlinear combination of air temperature and relative humidity, adjusted for wind.

A less detailed graphic computation yields a similar but not equivalent value known as humisery. Another approach uses the shaded comfort-factor thermometer, which is a large bulb half-covered by a wetted cloth so that air temperature, wet-bulb temperature, wind, and radiation are integrated into a single number similar to a Fahrenheit temperature; most people are said to be comfortable at values from 63 to 72.

Cold conditions. Under cold conditions, atmospheric moisture is negligible and wind becomes important in heat removal. Wind chill, given by Eq. (3),

$$H = (10.45 + 10\sqrt{v} - v)(33 - t) \qquad (3)$$

where H represents heat loss in kcal/(m²)(h²), does not estimate sensible temperature as such, but rather heat loss in kcal/(m²)(h) for wind speed v in m/s and air temperature t in °C.

The formula was based on the rate of freezing, at various temperature-wind combinations during the Antarctic winter, of water in a plastic cylinder, not on responses of human subjects. It has never been validated by the latter approach. Nevertheless, the temperature of which the estimated heat loss at some reference wind speed equals that at the existing temperature-wind combination is the wind chill temperature. The reference wind speed is variously 3 mi/h, 3 knots, or 4 mi/h, and in a revised formulation is 0.

Arnold Court

Bibliography. P. O. Fanger, *Thermal Comfort,* 1972, reprint 1982; H. Landsberg (ed.), *World Survey of Climatology,* vol. 3: *General Climatology,* 1981.

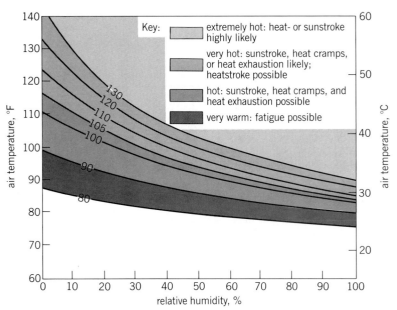

Heat index used by the National Weather Service, National Oceanographic and Atmospheric Administration. The numerical values on each curve represent a heat index, that is, apparent temperature in °F.

Conservation of resources

Management of natural resources to prevent overexploitation or destruction. Natural resources (sunlight, water, plants, animals, soil, and minerals) help support life. Many natural resources must be utilized to maintain the quality of human life, yet some are needlessly wasted or destroyed, diminishing the heritage of future generations. Direct effects on humans are not the only or the highest standard for conservation decisions, but actions affecting any natural system eventually affect human systems because of the interrelations of all parts of the biosphere. Renewable natural resources, such as forests and fisheries, are to be preserved while providing the maximum benefit. Others, such as fossil fuels, are nonrenewable except over geologic time scales and should be used cautiously with a view to eventual replacement by other resources. Conservation sometimes requires unconditional protection, in the belief that natural systems are important in themselves rather than for exploitation. *See Biosphere*.

Historically, conservation measures came into being after an adequate supply of material goods was available to an organized population; until that time, the meeting of material needs took precedence, and the long-term health of the environment was considered secondary to human needs.

The emerging recognition among ecologists that seemingly local environmental concerns interact with larger-scale problems has created an awareness that decisions affecting localized systems will eventually affect other systems in a regional or global sense. For example, air pollution from fossil fuel–burning electric power plants was at first considered a normal and acceptable by-product of a growing economy; health effects, scenic damage, or objections to odors were consigned to local nuisance lawsuits. Eventually government regulations forced the development of modern pollution-control technologies. Within a few years it was discovered that air pollution was damaging water bodies hundreds of miles from the source through acid deposition. These effects have become international problems. Today the scale is global, as climate alterations caused by gases, partly produced by power-generating plants, are challenging human societies to alter basic technologies. It is rare to find an environmental action affecting only local concerns. *See Acid rain; Air pollution*.

The purpose of natural resource conservation is to maintain valuable and essential resources in a condition of good health that will allow development of the necessary resources for maximum long-term benefits. The human responsibility is to manage the environment in such a way as to ensure that there will be adequate supplies of natural resources for future generations.

An ecological perspective on the conservation of natural resources looks to a sustained optimum yield of the resources that can be continually utilized without depletion. This is not necessarily the same as maximum yield. Additionally, this perspective recognizes that there are certain sensitive systems and species from which humans must no longer seek direct benefit, either to avoid destruction of the resource or to allow time for recovery from past use. Historically, the pattern was to deplete local resources, then move to more bountiful areas that had yet to be developed. This allowed depleted areas adequate time for natural recovery. This process is still practiced in some undeveloped countries, but with the rapid growth of human population in these areas, adequate recovery is no longer possible. Moreover, intensive use over a short time can create soil erosion and plant destruction. Problems of uneven distribution of natural resources exacerbate problems of overutilization; when a scarce resource is available in a growing economy, efforts to restrict use are difficult to establish and enforce. *See Human ecology*.

Wildlife conservation. The first conservation efforts in the United States focused on forestry and wildlife preservation and management. The term wildlife includes all undomesticated animals, birds, and fish living in their natural environments. Wildlife populations historically were regulated by natural processes, including catastrophes such as fire, flood, and drought, and biological controls such as predation, disease, and food limitations. The increasing influence of human populations has caused extensive wild-

life species extinctions, which came about first through overhunting and later through agricultural and building practices and environmental pollution. In the past, uncontrolled hunting was the principal single cause of species loss (for example, the extinction of the passenger pigeon, which once covered North America with a population in the billions). Today, hunting laws protect rare or endangered species. With the exception of threats to the whales from hunting, habitat destruction is the largest single cause of species loss and endangerment today. Human activities that cause habitat degradation or destruction include the development of land for human habitation, transportation, or farming, leading to deforestation and wetlands draining; sewage and solid-waste disposal; decreased streamside vegetative cover and stream channelization; clear-cutting of forested areas; improper applications of pesticides and fertilizers; increased sedimentation in waters; and air and water pollution.

Food, water, and shelter requirements vary greatly among species, even in the same ecosystem. Actions affecting one part of an ecosystem can have unforeseen and deleterious effects in another part. The classic example is the application of DDT for mosquito control, which led to eggshell thinning and population reductions of pelicans and other carnivorous birds. The disturbed animals cannot simply move to a less affected area. Yet often the degradation is too rapid for species to adapt. Over 90% of the original wetlands in the United States have disappeared because of human activities. Some elements of an ecosystem can remain stable only if large contiguous land areas are undisturbed; this is the reason for the decline in grizzly bear populations outside Alaska. Other types of habitats are disturbed by activities upstream, as rivers and estuaries receive pollutants transported by water. Upwind activities harm forests and lakes with acid precipitation or air pollution.

Wildlife has greatly decreased in importance as a food and clothing source even in undeveloped countries. Consequently, hunting and fishing control must be based on current information. Properly controlled hunting benefits game species, especially large animals, keeping them within the carrying capacity of the area. Hunting and fishing are normally regulated through licenses, with limits on open seasons and numbers taken; ecologists urge the harvesting of wildlife populations that exceed the carrying capacity of the natural area to prevent damage to habitats from excess population pressures and to avoid disease and starvation.

Other wildlife habitat conservation activities encourage wild strips left along cultivated fields; clean farming practices remove food and shelter used by indigenous species that are often beneficial for the farmers, especially in pest control. Proper use of fertilizers and pesticides avoids problems of chemical persistence and runoff to water sources. Wildlife conservation encourages good forest management practices such as selective cutting and underbrush clearing.

Rangeland conservation. Grass-covered lands, also known as grasslands, grazing lands, and rangelands, represent the optimum growth in areas where low to moderate precipitation is too little to support farming or forests. Rangelands provide food and shelter for a wide variety of wildlife and forage for livestock (cattle, horses, and sheep). The native nonwoody plants enhance soil stability, maintain soil productivity, and assure replenishment of underground water sources. The balance between soil stability and plant cover in rangeland areas is delicate, although rangelands seem to be boundless, hardy, and easily replaceable. They often recover rapidly from fire, even with improved productivity; however, they are very sensitive to overgrazing, which can cause rapid deterioration.

Grazing domestic animals on rangelands was an early practice. Some areas are still grazed in a fully nomadic manner, though this is very rare in the United States. Under these circumstances, there is little incentive for conservation, since the users do not own or permanently occupy the land. As the human population grew, overgrazing became an increasing problem. When the number of animals exceeds the carrying capacity of the ecosystem, desirable grasses give way to weeds and brush, which are less nutritious and provide less protection to soils against water erosion and wind damage. Bare soil areas destroy habitats of indigenous species. Overgrazed slopes cannot hold moisture, and the soil-laden runoff pollutes streams and reservoirs and aggravates flooding. Sedimentation reduces the storage capacity of reservoirs. SEE EROSION.

When vast areas of the rangelands began to be farmed, plows turned over the grasses, eventually creating near-desert conditions because the soil's ability to hold moisture and resist wind erosion was destroyed and the fields were left barren after crops were harvested. The dust bowl seen in the 1930s in the midwestern United States is being repeated today in marginal agricultural areas in sub-Saharan Africa. In both cases, the combination of overexploitation of the environment and extreme climatic conditions was much worse than either alone. The combined adverse effects of human and natural stresses on the environment will be felt increasingly as the population grows and the Earth's climate changes.

Overgrazing damage is reduced by properly located watering facilities to decrease daily travel by livestock. Rotation of grazing areas allows time for recovery of grass. Proper positioning of fences and salt lures also reduces damage. Rangelands can be restored, as was done in the late 1930s in response to the dust bowl conditions in the United States. Reseeding of grasses and the installation of irrigation or water storage tanks were of value. Grazing was avoided in marginal areas. Some land can be easily restored if grazing is allowed only during one season; some rangelands should be grazed only during nongrowth seasons. Some advocate the use of herbicides and burning to destroy weeds and poisonous plants. The goal of rangeland conservation is to rehabilitate mismanaged areas and adopt sound practices.

Most rangeland in the United States is owned by the federal government and administered by the U.S. Bureau of Land Management or the U.S. Forest Service. Ranchers are issued permits to use public grazing lands; these permits limit the number of animals that can be grazed and prescribe their movements. The management of rangelands is intended to protect wildlife, the economic value of grazing animals, and recreational uses.

Plant and animal conservation   Natural resource conservation requires the preservation of species and the genetic diversity of life. The growth of human populations assures that, despite all measures taken, some species will be lost. Scientists do not know how many species exist on the Earth today; estimates range from 2 to 30 million or more. It is agreed that species are being lost at alarming rates, especially in the tropics as a result of large-scale deforestation. At these rates, virtually all tropical forests will be lost in a few decades, and with them millions or tens of millions of species. But loss of diversity is not limited to the tropics, and temperate regions of the world have already been remade almost totally into human-affected environments.

For most species that become extinct, the costs of this loss will never be assessed, as their possible value cannot be estimated. The loss of so-called keystone species can result in a cascading effect, in which many other species disappear because of associated changes in the food chains that define ecosystems. Other species or groups of species perform critical functions such as nutrient cycling. The loss of these functional groups of species can undermine entire ecosystems. SEE ECOSYSTEM; FOOD WEB.

Some species that were almost eliminated through intensive hunting and fishing or through habitat destruction have survived in zoos, fish hatcheries, and captive breeding programs (California condor, bison, and wildebeest). However, management of species and habitats is much preferable, benefiting many more species for the same effort and cost. National parks, nature reserves, national forests, wildlife refuges, biosphere reserves, and similar areas have been established in many parts of the world. They create opportunities for scientific research and recreational activities. Some communities should be left undisturbed to act as genetic reserves, where ecological knowledge can be gained through the study of undisturbed systems.

Biological reserves can provide for the preservation of seeds, seedlings, and shoots that could be used in the future as lost habitats are reestablished. The purpose of natural resource conservation should be to maintain the biosphere in a healthy condition. Ensuring the long-term security of natural resources in an increasingly stressed global environment will secure a vital heritage for future generations. SEE FISHERY CONSERVATION; FOREST MANAGEMENT; LAND-USE PLANNING; MINERAL RESOURCES; SOIL CONSERVATION; WATER CONSERVATION.

Christine C. Harwell; Mark A. Harwell

Crop micrometeorology

Crop micrometeorology deals with the interaction of crops and their immediate physical environment. Especially, it seeks to measure and explain net photosynthesis (photosynthesis minus respiration) and water use (transpiration plus evaporation from the soil) of crops as a function of meteorological, crop, and soil moisture conditions. These studies are complex because the intricate array of leaves, stems, and fruits modifies the local environment and because the processes of energy transfers and conversions are interrelated. As a basic science, crop micrometeorology is related to plant anatomy, plant physiology, meteorology, and hydrology. Expertise in radiation exchange theory, boundary-layer and diffusion processes, and turbulence theory is needed in basic crop micrometeorological studies. A practical goal is to provide improved plant designs and cropping patterns for light interception, for reducing infestations of diseases, pests, and weeds, and for increasing crop water-use efficiency. Shelter belts are modifications that have been used in arid or windy areas to protect crops and seedlings from a harsh environment. SEE AGRICULTURAL METEOROLOGY; MICROMETEOROLOGY.

Unifying concepts. Conservation laws for energy and matter are central to crop micrometeorology. Energy fluxes involved are solar wavelength radiation, consisting of photosynthetically active radiation (0.4–0.7 micrometer) and near-infrared radiation (0.7–3 μm); far-infrared radiation (3–100 μm); convection in the air; molecular heat conduction in and near the plant parts and in the soil; and the latent heat carried by water vapor. The main material substances transported to and from crop and soil surfaces are water vapor and carbon dioxide. However, fluxes of ammonia, sulfur dioxide, pesticides, and other gases or pollutants to or from crop or soil surfaces have been measured. These entities move by molecular diffusion near the leaves and soil, but by convection (usually turbulent) in the airflow. During the daytime generally, and sometimes at night, airflow among and above crops is strongly turbulent. However, often at night a stable air layer forms because of surface cooling caused by emission of far-infrared radiation back to space, and the air flow becomes nonturbulent. Fog or radiation frosts may result. The aerodynamic drag and thermal (heat-absorbing) effects of plants contribute to the pattern of air movement and influence the efficiency of turbulent transfer.

Both field studies and mathematical simulation models have dealt mostly with tall, close-growing crops, such as maize and wheat, which can be treated statistically as composed of infinite horizontal layers. Downward-moving direct-beam solar and diffuse sky radiation are partly absorbed, partly reflected, and partly transmitted by each layer. Less photosynthetically active radiation than near-infrared radiation is transmitted to ground level and reflected from the crop canopy because photosynthetically active radiation is strongly absorbed by the photosynthetic pigments (chlorophyll, carotenoids, and so on) and near-infrared radiation is only weakly absorbed. The plants act as good emitters and absorbers of far-infrared radiation. Transfers of momentum, heat, water vapor, and carbon dioxide can be considered as composed of two parts; a leaf-to-air transfer and a turbulent vertical transfer. As a bare minimum, two mean or representative temperatures are needed for each layer: an average air temperature and a representative plant surface temperature. Because some leaves are in direct sunlight and some are shaded, a representative temperature is difficult to obtain. Under clear conditions, traversing solar radiation sensors show a bimodal frequency distribution of irradiances in most crop communities; that is, most points in space and time are exposed to either high irradiances of direct-beam radiation or low irradiances characteristic of shaded conditions. Models of radiation interception have been developed which predict irradiance on both shaded leaves and on exposed leaves, depending on the leaf inclination angle with respect to the rays. The central concept of both experimental studies and simulation models is that radiant energy fluxes, sensible heat fluxes, and latent heat fluxes are coupled physically and can be expressed mathematically. This interdependence applies to a complex crop system as well as to a single leaf.

Photosynthesis. Studies of photosynthesis of crops using micrometeorological techniques do not consider the submicroscopic physics and chemistry of photosynthesis and respiration, but consider processes on a microscopic and macroscopic scale. The most important factors are the transport and diffusion of carbon dioxide in air to the leaves and through small ports called stomata to the internal air spaces. Thence it diffuses in the liquid phase of cells to chloroplasts, where carboxylation enzymes speed the first step in the conversion of carbon dioxide into organic plant materials. Solar radiation provides the photosynthetically active radiant energy to drive this biochemical conversion of carbon dioxide. Progress has been made in understanding the transport processes in the bulk atmosphere, across the leaf boundary layer, through the stomata, through the cells, and eventually to the sites of carboxylation. Transport resistances have been identified for this catenary process: bulk aerodynamic resistance, boundary-layer resistance, stomatal diffusion resistance, mesophyll resistance, and carboxylation resistance. All these resistances are plant factors which control the rate of carbon dioxide uptake by leaves of a crop; however, boundary-layer resistance and especially bulk aerodynamic resistance are determined also by the external wind flow.

Carbon dioxide concentration and photosynthetically active radiation are two other factors which control the rate of crop photosynthesis. Carbon dioxide concentration does not vary widely from about 315 microliters per liter (0.0315 vol %). Experiments have revealed that it is not practical to enrich the air with carbon dioxide on a field scale because the carbon dioxide is rapidly dispersed by turbulence. Therefore carbon dioxide concentration can be dismissed as a practical variable. Solar radiation varies widely in quantity and source distribution (direct-beam or diffuse sky or cloud sources). Many species of crop plants have leaves which can utilize solar radiation having flux densities greater than full sunlight (tropical grasses such as maize, sugarcane, and Burmuda grass, which fix carbon dioxide through the enzyme phosphoenolpyruvate carboxylase). Other species have leaves which may give maximum photosynthesis rates by individual leaves at less than full sunlight (such as soybean, sugarbeet, and wheat, which fix carbon dioxide through the enzyme ribulose 1,5-diphosphate carboxylase). However, in general, most crops show increasing photosynthesis rates with increasing irradiances for two reasons. First, more solar energy would become available to the shaded and partly shaded leaves deep in the crop canopy. Second, many of the well-exposed leaves at the top of a crop canopy are exposed to solar rays at wide angles of inclination so that they do not receive the full solar flux density. These leaves will respond to increasing irradiance also. Furthermore, increased diffuse to direct-beam ratios of irradiance (which could be caused by haze or thin clouds) may increase the irradiance on shaded leaves and hence increase overall crop photosynthesis.

If crop plants lack available soil water, the stomata may close and restrict the rate of carbon dioxide uptake by crops. Stomatal closure will protect plants against excessive dehydration, but will at the same time decrease photosynthesis by restricting the diffusion of carbon dioxide into the leaves.

Transpiration and heat exchange. Transpiration involves the transport of water vapor from inside leaves to the bulk atmosphere. The path of flow of water vapor is from the surfaces of cells inside the leaf through the stomata, through the leaf aerodynamic boundary layer, and from the boundary layer to the bulk atmosphere. Sensible heat is exchanged by convection directly from plant surfaces; therefore there is no stomatal diffusion resistance associated with this exchange. Stomatal diffusion resistance does affect heat exchange from leaves, however, because when stomata are open wide (low resistance) much of the heat exchanged from leaves is in the form of latent heat of evaporation of water involved in transpiration.

Small leaves, such as needles, convect heat much more rapidly than large leaves, such as banana leaves. Engineering boundary-layer theory suggests that boundary-layer resistance should be proportional to the square root of a characteristic dimension of a leaf and inversely proportional to the square root of the airflow rate past a leaf. Experiments support these relationships.

Under high-irradiance conditions, low air humidity, high air temperature, and low stomatal diffusion resistance will favor high transpiration, whereas high air humidity, low air temperature, and high stomatal diffusion resistance will favor sensible heat exchange from leaves. The function of wind is chiefly to enhance the transport rather than determine which form of convected energy will be most prominent. In arid environments, the latent energy of transpiration from crops may exceed the net radiant energy available, because heat from the dry air may actually be conducted to crops which will cause transpiration to increase. In those areas, crop temperature is lower than air temperature.

Flux methods. At least three general methods have been employed to measure flux density of carbon dioxide, water vapor, and heat to and from crop surfaces on a field scale. These methods are restricted to use in the crop boundary layer immediately above the crop surface, and they require a sufficient upwind fetch of a uniform crop surface free of obstructions. Flux densities obtained by these methods will reflect the more detailed interactions of crop and environment, but will not explain them.

The principle of the energy balance methods is to partition the net incoming radiant energy into energy associated with latent heat of transpiration and evaporation, sensible heat, photochemical energy involved in photosynthesis, heat flux into the soil, and heat stored in the crop. Measurement of net input of radiation to drive these processes is obtained from net radiometers, which measure the total incoming minus the total outgoing radiation. The most important components—latent heat, sensible heat, and photochemical energy—are determined by average vertical gradients of water vapor concentration (or vapor pressure), air temperature, and carbon dioxide concentration.

The principle of the bulk aerodynamic methods is to relate the vertical concentration gradients of those transported entities to the vertical gradient of horizontal wind speed. The transports are assumed to be related to the aerodynamic drag (or transport of momentum) of the crop surface. Corrections are required for thermal instability or stability of the air near the crop surface.

The eddy correlation methods are direct methods which correlate the instantaneous vertical components of wind (updrafts or downdrafts) to the instantaneous values of carbon dioxide concentration, water vapor concentration, or air temperature. Under daytime conditions, turbulent eddies, or whorls, transport air from the crop in updrafts, which are slightly depleted in carbon dioxide, and conversely, turbulence transports air to the crop in downdrafts which are representative of the atmospheric content of these entities. More basic and applied research is being done on eddy correlation methods because they measure transports through direct transport processes.

Plant parameters. The stomata are the most important single factor in interactions of plant and environment because they are the gateways for gaseous exchange. Soil-to-air transfers are also very important while crops are in the seedling stage until a large degree of ground cover is attained. Coefficients of absorption, transmission, and reflection by leaves of photosynthetically active, near-infrared, and long-wavelength infrared radiation are not very different among crop species, but the geometric arrangement and stage of growth of plants in a crop may affect radiation exchange greatly. The crop geometry also interacts with radiation-source geometry (diffuse to direct-beam irradiance, solar elevation angle). Crop micrometeorology attempts to show how the plant parameters interact with the environmental factors in crop production and water requirements of crops under field conditions. SEE PHYSIOLOGICAL ECOLOGY (PLANT).

L. H. Allen, Jr.

Bibliography. J. Goudriaan, *Crop Micrometeorology*, 1977; E. Lemon, D. W. Stewart, and R. W. Shawcroft, The sun's work in a cornfield, *Science*, 174:371–378, 1971; J. L. Monteith (ed.), *Vegetation and the Atmosphere*, vol. 1, 1975; vol. 2, 1976; R. E. Munn, *Biometeorological Methods*, 1971; N. J. Rosenberg and B. L. Blad, *Microclimate: The Biological Environment*, 2d ed., 1983; W. D. Sellars, *Physical Climatology*, 1965; L. P. Smith (ed.), *The Application of Micrometeorology to Agricultural Problems*, 1972; O. G. Sutton, *Micrometeorology*, 1977.

Dam

A barrier or structure across a stream, river, or waterway for the purpose of confining and controlling the flow of water. Dams vary in size from small earth embankments for farm use to high, massive concrete structures for water supply, hydropower, irrigation, navigation, recreation, sedimentation control, and flood control. As such, dams are cornerstones in the water resources development of river basins. Dams are now built to serve several purposes and are therefore known as multipurpose (**Fig. 1**). The construction of a large dam requires the relocation of existing highways, railroads, and utilities from the river valley to elevations above the reservoir. The two principal types of dams are embankment and concrete. Appurtenant structures of dams include spillways, outlet works, and control facilities; they may also include structures related to hydropower and other project purposes. SEE ELECTRIC POWER GENERATION; WATER SUPPLY ENGINEERING.

Dams have been built since ancient times, and improvements were made at varying intervals as engineering technology developed. However, very rapid advances occurred in the twentieth century as a result of developments in the use of concrete, soil mechan-

Fig. 1. John Day Lock and Dam, looking upstream across the Columbia River at Washington shore. In the foreground the navigation lock is seen, then the spillway beyond it, and then the powerhouse. The John Day multiple-purpose project has the highest single-lift navigation lock in the United States. (*U.S. Army Corps of Engineers*)

ics, construction equipment. In the early 1900s, concrete dams became thinner, and a new era of thin arch dams began. Earth and rock–fill embankment dams became economical during and after World War II. In 1980, an innovative method of using earth-moving and compacting equipment to place dry concrete (roller-compacted concrete) greatly improved the economics of concrete dams. Numerous dams have been constructed in various countries worldwide (**Table 1**). Many dams possess considerable height, volume, and reservoir capacity (**Table 2**).

Purposes. Dams are built for specific purposes. In ancient times, they were built only for water supply or irrigation. Early in the development of the United States, rivers were a primary means of transportation, and therefore navigation dams with locks (**Fig. 2**) were constructed on the major rivers. Dams have become more complex to meet large power demands and other needs of modern countries (**Figs. 3** and **4**). Although recreation is a popular purpose of small private dams, it is planned as a benefit with an assigned monetary value in federal projects in the United States. A typical summary of purposes of nonfederal dams is shown in **Table 3**.

Features. In addition to the standard impounded reservoir and the appurtenant structures of a dam (spillway, outlet works, and control facility), a dam with hydropower requires a powerhouse, penstocks, generators, and switchyard. The inflow of water into the reservoir must be monitored continuously, and the outflow must be controlled to obtain maximum benefits. Under normal operating conditions, the reservoir is controlled by the outlet works, consisting of a large tunnel or conduit at stream level with control gates. Under flood conditions, the reservoir is maintained by both the spillway and outlet works.

The reservoir level of a flood control dam is maintained as low as possible to create the maximum amount of storage space for use in the flood season. For an irrigation project, the reservoir is filled as high as possible in the winter and early spring, and it is maintained at that level for maximum release of water during the dry season. The reservoir level of a hydropower dam is maintained as constant as feasible to create a uniform head for power generation. Water quality is an important ingredient in sustaining a balance in nature and is taken into account in modern dam design, construction, and operation. The chemical quality and temperature of the water are monitored in the reservoir. Intake ports at various depths allow selective withdrawal and mixing to produce the desired temperature and oxygen content, in order to en-

Table 1. Countries with the largest number of dams*	
Country	Number of dams†
China	18,595
United States	5,338
Japan	2,142
India	1,085
Spain	690
Republic of Korea	628
Canada	580
United Kingdom	529
Brazil	489
Mexico	487
France	432
Italy	408
Australia	374

*From "ICOLD Register of Dams," updated 1986.
†Dams at least 50 ft (15 m) high.

Table 2. Landmark dams of the world*

HIGHEST DAMS

Order	Name	River	Country	Type[†]	Height ft	Height m	Year completed
1	Rogun	Vakhsh	Commonwealth of Independent States	E-R	1099	335	UC
2	Nurek	Vakhsh	Commonwealth of Independent States	E	984	300	1980
3	Grand Dixence	Dixence	Switzerland	G	935	285	1961
4	Inguri	Inguri	Commonwealth of Independent States	A	892	272	1980
5	Chicoasen	Grijalva	Mexico	R	856	261	1980
6	Tehri	Bhagirathi	India	E-R	856	261	UC
7	Kishau	Tons	India	E-R	830	253	UC
8	Sayano-Shushensk	Yenisei	Commonwealth of Independent States	A	804	245	UC
9	Guavio	Guavio	Colombia	R	797	243	UC
10	Mica	Columbia	Canada	E	794	242	1972
11	Mauvoisin	Drance de Bangnes	Switzerland	A	777	237	1957
12	Chivor	Bata	Colombia	R	777	237	1975
13	El Cajon	Comayagua	Honduras	A	768	234	1984
14	Chirkei	Sulak	Commonwealth of Independent States	A	764	233	1978
15	Oroville	Feather	United States	E	754	230	1968
16	Bhakra	Sutlej	India	G	741	226	1963
17	Hoover	Colorado	United States	G-A	725	221	1936
18	Contra	Verzasca	Switzerland	A	722	220	1965
19	Mratinje	Piva	Yugoslavia	A	722	220	1976
20	Dworshak	Clearwater, N. Fork	United States	G	718	219	1973

LARGEST EMBANKMENT DAMS BY VOLUME

Order	Name	River	Country	Type	Volume 10^3 yd^3	Volume 10^3 m^3	Year completed[‡]
1	Chapeton	Paraná	Argentina	E-G	387,400	296,200	UC
2	Pati	Paraná	Argentina	E-G	311,411	238,100	UC
3	Tarbella	Indus	Pakistan	E-R	19³4,223	148,500	1967
4	Fort Peck	Missouri	United States	E	125,624	96,050	1937
5	Lower Usuma	Usuma	Nigeria	E	121,635	93,000	UC
6	Cipasang	Cimanuk	Indonesia	E-R	117,842	90,100	1984
7	Tucurui	Tocantis	Brazil	E-R	84,098	85,200	UC
8	Ataturk	Firat	Turkey	R	111,172	85,000	UC
9	Rogun	Vakhsh	Commonwealth of Independent States	E-R	98,746	75,500	1986
10	Guri	Caroni	Venezuela	R-G	92,716	70,889	1958
11	Oahe	Missouri	United States	E	91,996	70,339	1967
12	Parambikulam	Parambikulam	India	E-G	90,461	69,165	1967
13	Mangla	Jhelum	Pakistan	E	85,497	65,370	1968
14	Gardiner	S. Saskatchewan	Canada	E	85,014	65,000	1932
15	Afsluitdijk	Zuiderzee	Netherlands	E	82,921	63,400	1967
16	Mangla	Jhelum	Pakistan	E	82,893	63,379	1968
17	Oroville	Feather	United States	E	77,997	59,635	1967
18	San Luis	San Luis	United States	E	77,897	59,559	1980
19	Nurek	Vakhsh	Commonwealth of Indepedent States	E	75,858	58,000	1967
20	Tanda	Kohat Toi	Pakistan	E	74,887	57,250	

LARGEST ARTIFICIAL RESERVOIRS IN TERMS OF CAPACITY

Order	Name	River	Country	Capacity 10^3 acre ft[§]	Capacity 10^5 m^3	Year completed
1	Owen Falls	Victoria Nile	Uganda	166,033	204,800	1954
2	Kariba	Zambezi	Zimbabwe/Zambia	146,090	180,200	1959
3	Bratsk	Angara	Commonwealth of Independent States	137,010	169,000	1964
4	High Aswan	Nile	Egypt	131,335	162,000	1970
5	Akosombo	Volta	Ghana	119,952	147,960	1965
6	Daniel Johnson	Manicouagan	Canada	115,000	141,851	1968
7	Guri	Caroni	Venezuela	109,446	135,000	1986
8	Krasnoyarsk	Yenisei	Commonwealth of Independent States	59,425	73,300	1967
9	WAC Bennett	Peace	Canada	57,000	70,309	967
10	Zeya	Zeya	Commonwealth of Independent States	55,452	68,400	1978
11	Cabora Bassa	Zambezi	Mozambique	51,075	63,000	1974
12	La Grande 2	La Grande	Canada	50,033	61,715	1978
13	Chapeton	Paraná	Argentina	49,129	60,600	UC
14	La Grande 3	La Grande	Canada	48,659	60,020	1981
15	Ust-Ilim	Angara	Commonwealth of Independent States	48,075	59,300	1977
16	Boguchany	—	Commonwealth of Independent States	47,183	58,200	UC
17	Kuibyshev	Volga	Commonwealth of Independent States	47,021	58,000	1955
18	Serra da Mesa	—	Brazil	44,103	54,400	UC
19	Caniapiscau Barrage KA 3	Caniapiscau	Canada	43,608	53,790	1980
20	Upper Wainganga	Wainganga	India	41,103	50,700	UC

*As of January 1988.
[†]E = embankment, earth-fill. R = embankment, rock-fill. E-R = embankment, earth and rock–fill. G = gravity. A = arch.
[‡]UC = under construction.
[§]1 acre foot = 1 acre of water 1 foot deep.

Table 3. Primary purpose of nonfederal dams in the United States*

Purpose	Percent of total
Recreation	35
Flood control	15
Water supply	15
Irrigation	13
Farm and livestock water	9
Power	3
Other	10

*From "National Dam Inventory," 1984 update.

Fig. 2. Lock and Dam 1 on the Mississippi River between St. Paul and Minneapolis, Minnesota. Built in 1917 with a single lock to provide barge traffic to Minneapolis, the dam failed in 1929 and was rebuilt with twin locks in 1932. (*U.S. Army Corps of Engineers*)

hance downstream environmental conditions. Fish ladders, that is, stepped series of elevated pools, are provided at many dams to allow free passage of fish upstream and downstream. Screens are used to keep fish out of the turbines.

The discharge from modern dams must be managed carefully and continuously. During floods, reservoir inflows may exceed maximum discharges and cause reservoir levels to rise. To prevent dams from overtopping and possibly failing, spillways are provided to pass floodwater safely. They are commonly built at elevations just below dam crests and without gates. These uncontrolled, ungated spillways are designed to allow all of the excess water to pass. In other cases, spillways are constructed at even lower levels and contain gates that are operated from the control facilities. The tops of these gates are lower than the dam crests, thus allowing some control of floodwater.

Penstocks (usually steel pipes or concrete-lined tunnels) are used to convey water from the reservoir through or around the dam to the powerhouse. The penstocks are connected to the turbines, and the water flow is controlled by valves. The number and size of the penstocks vary, depending on the number of gen-

Fig. 3. Guri Dam, Venezuela, showing construction under way on the second stage of the concrete gravity dam. Embankment dams are shown on the left and right abutments. The concrete batch plant is shown at left with a trestle for transporting concrete shown on the downstream face of the dam. The second powerhouse with an excavated outlet channel is shown at the center of the photo. (*C.V.G. Electrification del Caroni, C. A. EDELCA, Caracas, Venezuela*)

Fig. 4. Itaipu Dam, on the Paraná River between Brazil and Paraguay. An operating spillway with a flip bucket on the Paraguay side of the river is shown at left. The hollow concrete gravity dam with powerhouse construction at the downstream toe is shown at center. (*G. S. Sarkaria, International Engineering Company, Inc.*)

erators and amount of water needed.

All the features of a dam are monitored and operated from a control room. The room contains the necessary monitors, controls, computers, emergency equipment, and communications systems to allow project personnel to operate the dam safely under all conditions. Standby generators and backup communications equipment are necessary to operate the gates and other reservoir controls in case of power failure. Weather conditions, inflow, reservoir level, discharge, and downstream river levels are also monitored. In addition, the control room monitors instru-

mentation located in the dam and appurtenant features that measures their structural behavior and physical condition.

Requirements. All dams are designed and constructed to meet specific requirements. First, a dam should be built from locally available materials when possible. Second, the dam must remain stable under all conditions, during construction, and ultimately in operation, both at the normal reservoir operating level and under all flood and drought conditions. Third, the dam and foundation must be sufficiently watertight to control seepage and maintain the desired reservoir level. Finally, it must have sufficient spillway and outlet works capacity as well as freeboard to prevent floodwater from overtopping it.

Types. Dams are classified by the type of material from which they are constructed. In early times, the materials were earth, large stones, and timber, but as technology developed, other materials and construction procedures were used. Most modern dams fall into two categories: embankment and concrete. Embankment dams are earth or rock-fill; other gravity dams and arch and buttress dams are concrete.

Earth-fill dam. Earth is the predominant material in this type of embankment dam. Earth dams are further classified by the construction method: hydraulic-fill or rolled-fill. A hydraulic-fill dam is one in which the soil is excavated, transported, and placed by flowing water. A large dredge operating in the river or other borrow area pumps a slurry of earth and water to the damsite. Here the coarse-grained materials settle on the outside portion of the embankment, and the remaining slurry is allowed to pond at the center, where the very fine-grained clay-size particles settle to form the impervious portion of the dam.

Advances in earth-moving construction equipment during World War II led to widespread construction of rolled-earth-fill dams. Economic advantages of this

Fig. 5. Aerial view of North Fork Dam, a combination earth-and-rock embankment of the North Fork of Pound River, Virginia. The channel-type spillway (left center) has a simple overflow weir. (*U.S. Army Corps of Engineers*)

type of embankment often include the use of material available from the site excavation as embankment material, and the ready availability of fill material at or near the damsite. Other advantages of earth-fill dams include their adaptability to a wide variety of site configurations and their tolerance of weak foundations.

At various stages during excavation and placement of the fill, the moisture content of the soil may be adjusted by wetting or drying in order to optimize its performance in the finished embankment. The soil is spread on the embankment in uniform layers 8–12 in. (20–30 cm) thick and compacted with sheepsfoot or rubber-tired rollers. The rollers make from four to eight passes, depending on the desired density. Typical dry densities for rolled earth fill range 100–130 lb/ft^3 (1602–2083 kg/m^3).

Seepage control is an important aspect of earth-dam design. In early times, earth embankments were homogeneous, and seepage would emerge on the downstream slope just above ground level. If uncontrolled, such seepage can move soil particles and cause failure. In 1940, filter criteria were developed after careful scientific tests on all types of soil and on the sands and gravel to be used as filter material. These criteria allow engineers to design internal drains to collect and remove seepage. When an earth dam is built on a site where the bedrock is at a considerable depth, the foundation must be treated to control seepage. Typical treatment includes one or a combination of several things: upstream impervious blanket, cutoff wall, drainage blanket, gravel drains that are excavated into the foundation at the downstream toe, and relief wells.

Earth-fill dams are by far the most popular type in the world. They make up 78%, or 27,260, of all those dams at least 50 ft (15 m) high. The earth dam's spillway is usually located in adjacent terrain rather than in the dam itself. The outlet works are either a conduit in the valley or a tunnel in one of the abutments (**Figs. 5** and **6**). Excavation for the spillway and outlet works usually produces large quantities of rock. As a result, the use of both earth and rock in an embankment is a common practice.

Rock-fill dam. A rock-fill dam is a rolled fill embankment composed of fragmented rock with an impervious zone or membrane located on the upstream face or incorporated in the center of the embankment. The impervious membrane is typically a concrete slab or asphalt layer on the upstream face. The impervious zone is typically a thin internal core of earth fill. The earth core is separated from the rock shell (the structural mass of the dam) by zones of small rock fragments or gravel, to prevent the earth from washing into the rock fill, and a drain to control seepage. In Europe, it is common to use asphalt for the impervious zone.

Rock-fill dams require solid rock foundations and sites where large quantities of rock are available. Seepage through rock foundations is prevented or minimized by grout curtains. Rock-fill dams are usually more economical than concrete gravity dams at sites having wide valleys and adequate foundations. Spillways and outlet works are at locations similar to those of earth-fill dams. The primary advantage of rock-fill dams is that they require less material. Rock fill has a higher shear strength than earth fill and therefore permits steeper exterior slopes.

Rock for the embankment is normally excavated by drilling and blasting. Hole spacing and powder charges are set to produce a particular gradation of rock fragments for the dam. The rock is placed and spread in the same manner as earth but in thicker layers, 18–36 in. (45–90 cm). The material is normally compacted by weighted or vibratory steel drum rollers. Dry densities of rock fill are normally in the range 110–145 lb/ft^3 (1762–2323 kg/m^3).

Rock-fill dams became popular in the United States during the California gold rush in the 1860s and 1870s, when many dams were built in remote locations to store water for use in hydraulic sluicing. Of the 34,780 dams in the world that are at least 50 ft (15 m) high, 1590 are rock-fill embankments.

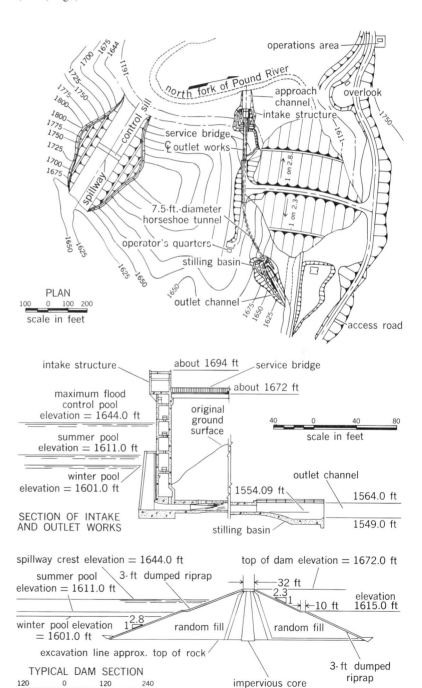

Fig. 6. Plan and sections of North Fork of Pound Dam, Virginia. 1 ft = 0.3 m. (*U.S. Army Corps of Engineers*)

Concrete gravity dam. Concrete gravity dams are massive structures, characterized by vertical or near-vertical upstream faces and steep downstream faces (**Figs. 7** and **8**). They are designed with enough weight to resist being overturned or moved by the force of the water in the reservoirs. They are economical only at sites with shallow, high-strength rock foundations. Because of the large volumes of concrete involved, adequate sources of high-quality aggregates must be available near the sites. Concrete is composed of water, cement, pozzolan, aggregates, and entrained air. These ingredients are proportioned to produce concrete of the desired workability, durability, and strength as economically as possible. The density of concrete in dams typically ranges 140–160 lb/ft^3 (2243–2563 kg/m^3). An important feature of gravity dams is the simplicity with which safe spillways and outlet works can be provided.

The design of a concrete gravity dam is controlled by stability considerations and internal stresses. The structure must be able to resist water, sediment, and ice pressures from the reservoir, as well as earthquake forces. Computers permit rapid solutions of complex equations for determining the magnitude and distribution of internal stresses. These dams are built in monolithic units by using the block method of construction (**Fig. 9**). This promotes dissipation of heat produced by hydration of the cement (chemical combination with the water) and thus helps minimize the volume changes associated with overheating that cause tensile stresses and cracking. The blocks are separated by construction joints. In building a block, the concrete is placed in horizontal layers and vibrated to eliminate voids. The monoliths are cast on top of firm rock foundations that have been cleaned with water and treated by placement of cement and water slurry or grout in the cracks and joints.

A concrete gravity dam usually contains an internal gallery large enough to allow for physical inspection and for collection of drainage from downstream drain holes drilled into the foundation. Grout holes to reduce seepage in the foundation are also drilled from the gallery in the vertical or upstream direction. The grout is injected under pressure to force it into all joints and openings encountered at depth.

Arch dam. The arch dam is a thin concrete dam that curves upstream from each abutment (**Figs. 10** and **11**). Such dams are classified as thin, medium, or thick arch, depending on the ratio of structural height to base thickness. The ratio is 0.2 or less for a thin arch, 0.25 for a medium arch, and 0.3 or greater for a thick arch. The arch transmits the water pressure and other loads directly to the abutments and foundation. It contains significantly less concrete than a concrete gravity dam of the same height and length. Relatively narrow canyons favor the use of arch dams.

The shape of early arch dams was controlled by construction materials available at the time, and by less sophisticated understanding of structural behavior and the way that loads were transmitted through the curved structures to the foundations. As a result, arches were simple masonry structures with curved alignments and near-vertical upstream faces. This type was popular among water companies supplying domestic and irrigation water.

Beginning in the 1900s, improved structural analysis and actual performance records led to the use of variable-thickness arch dams. Varying the thickness can reduce the volume of concrete required. Measurement of the physical properties of concrete began in the late 1920s. This led to improved design procedures and measurement of actual performance with such instruments as strain gages. The concept of working stresses emerged in the late 1920s. The double-curvature shape (curved top to bottom as well as transversely) emerged in the mid-1950s. Vertical curving and shaping of the arch improves stress distribution. Making the compressive stresses levels throughout the dam as close as possible to the maximum allowable stress results in the minimum volume of concrete. A symmetrical profile is desirable. This may require excavation on one abutment if the canyon is not symmetrical. The economic upper limit of the length-to-height ratio of an arch dam lies between 4:1 and 6:1.

Buttress dam. The buttress dam consists of two principal structural elements: a sloping upstream deck that retains the water, and buttress walls that support the deck and transmit the loads to the foundation. Traditionally, buttress dams have been classified into three categories: flat slab, multiple arch, and massive head. The flat-slab type consists of a reinforced concrete flat slab inclined at about 45° and connected to buttresses. The multiple-arch type is a series of concrete arches spanning the buttresses. The massive-head type has a large mass of concrete in the section upstream from the buttresses.

In 1918, the flat-slab design was patented in the United States. About 200 buttress dams of all three categories have been built in the United States. Many are less than 150 ft (15 m) high. Some landmark buttress dams are the Daniel Johnson in Canada (1986),

Fig. 7. Green Peter Dam, a concrete gravity type on the Middle Santian River, Willamette River Basin, Oregon. A gate-controlled overflow-type spillway is constructed through the crest of the dam; the powerhouse is at the downstream toe of the dam. (*U.S. Army Corps of Engineers*)

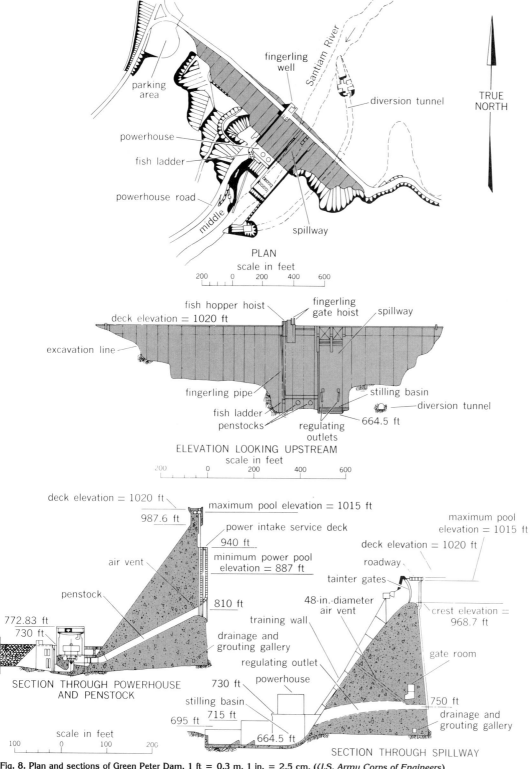

Fig. 8. Plan and sections of Green Peter Dam. 1 ft = 0.3 m, 1 in. = 2.5 cm. (*U.S. Army Corps of Engineers*)

702 ft (214 m) high, the world's highest multiple-arch buttress dam; and the José M. Oriol in Spain (1969), 426 ft (130 m), the world's highest flat-slab buttress dam.

Site and type selection. The type of dam for a particular site is selected on the basis of technical and economic data and environmental considerations. In the early stages of design, several sites and types are considered. Drill holes and test pits at each site provide soil and rock samples for testing physical properties. In some cases, field pumping tests are performed to evaluate seepage potential. Preliminary designs and cost estimates are prepared and reviewed by hydrologic, hydraulic, geotechnical, and structural

Fig. 9. Block method of construction on a typical concrete gravity dam. (*U.S. Army Corps of Engineers*)

engineers, as well as geologists. Environmental quality of the water, ecological systems, and cultural data are also considered in the site-selection process.

Factors that affect the type are topography, geology, foundation conditions, hydrology, earthquakes, and availability of construction materials. The foundation of the dam should be as sound and free of faults as possible. Narrow valleys with shallow sound rock favor concrete dams. Wide valleys with varying rock depths and conditions favor embankment dams.

Fig. 10. East Canyon Dam, a thin-arch concrete structure on the East Canyon River, Utah. There is an uncontrolled overflow-type spillway through the crest of the dam at the right. (*U.S. Bureau of Reclamation*)

Earth dams are the most common type.

Construction process. Hydraulic-fill operations over a 4-year period at Fort Peck Dam, on the Missouri River, the largest embankment by volume in the United States (**Fig. 12**), dredged 156,000,000 yd^3 (119,340,000 m^3) of material. Of this volume, 122,000,000 yd^3 (93,333,000 m^3) was retained in the embankment. Large conventional excavation operations can produce hourly volumes of 2000–3000 yd^3 (1530–2293 m^3). Processing, hauling, placement, and compaction operations for earth or rock result in daily placement rates that vary from as low as 2500 yd^3 (1911 m^3) on small dams to 6500 yd^3 (4969 m^3) on larger dams.

The materials and construction procedures for concrete dams evolved gradually from the early dams in Asia and Europe to the modern massive concrete dams. Prior to 1900, portland cement used in the United States was imported from England. Thus, the early concrete dams built in the United States were masonry. Generally, the concrete was mixed and transported in wheelbarrows. In the case of cyclopean masonry, large irregular blocks of rock with mortar, small derricks were erected, and the maximum rate of placement approached a few hundred cubic yards a day. There was no attempt to cure the concrete. Between 1900 and 1930, concrete was placed by towers and chutes. Portland cement had become available in the United States, and placement rates improved. However, little attention was given to the mix design, and wet mixes that could easily flow in chutes were widely used.

Hoover Dam, on the Colorado River, was a major turning point in both the design and construction of concrete dams. Its unprecedented size, 4,400,000 yd^3 (3,363,800 m^3), led to the introduction of mass concrete placement. Average placement rates of 10,000 yd^3 (7645 m^3) per day were achieved. Advances in design resulting from the Hoover project led to the construction of Grand Coulee, on the Columbia River, 10,585,000 yd^3 (8,099,000 m^3). Two large concrete plants were used that supported a maximum placement of 20,680 yd^3 (15,810 m^3) per day and an

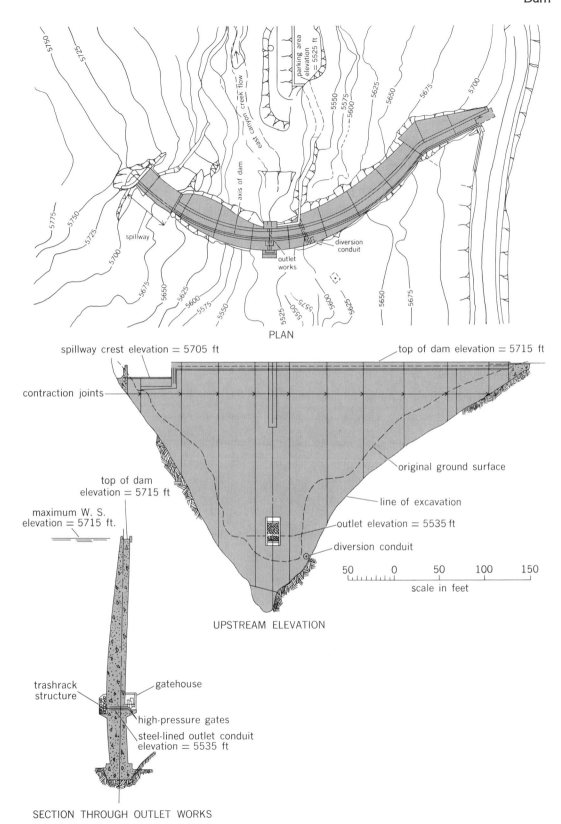

PLAN

spillway crest elevation = 5705 ft

top of dam elevation = 5715 ft

contraction joints

original ground surface

line of excavation

top of dam
elevation = 5715 ft

maximum W. S.
elevation = 5715 ft.

outlet elevation = 5535 ft

diversion conduit

| 50 | 0 | 50 | 100 | 150 |

scale in feet

UPSTREAM ELEVATION

trashrack
structure

gatehouse

high-pressure gates

steel-lined outlet conduit
elevation = 5535 ft

SECTION THROUGH OUTLET WORKS

Fig. 11. Plan and sections of East Canyon Dam, Utah. 1 ft = 0.3 m. (*U.S. Army Corps of Engineers*)

average rate over the construction period of 6000 yd³ (4587 m³) per day.

Since 1980, the technology of placing dry concrete with paving equipment and compacting it with rollers has gained wide acceptance (**Fig. 13**). This construction method is known as roller-compacted concrete.

By 1987, 21 dams at least 50 ft (15 m) high had been constructed by using the roller-compacted concrete method. This method produces the high placement rates usually associated with earth-fill construction and results in economical structures. It was initially used in 1975 in the tunnel repairs at Tarbela Dam,

Fig. 12. Fort Peck Dam, Missouri River, Montana, the largest embankment dam by volume in the United States, 125,628,000 yd³ (95,625,000 m³). A hydraulic-fill dam, it was built between 1935 and 1939 for flood control, hydropower, irrigation, and navigation. (*U .S. Army Corps of Engineers*)

Pakistan, and placement reached a maximum rate of 24,000 yd³ (18,343 m³).

An outstanding example of the rapid construction achieved by using roller-compacted concrete is Copperfield Dam in Australia. This 131-ft-high (40 m) dam contains 183,000 yd³ (140,000 m³) and required only 10 months from initial design to completion. The project was originally designed as an earth- and rock-fill dam, but it was switched to roller-compacted concrete for greater economy.

River diversion during construction. The designers of a dam must consider the stream flow around or through the damsite during construction. Stream flow records provide the information for use in determining the largest flood to divert during the selected con-

struction period. One common practice for diversion involves constructing the permanent outlet works, which may be a conduit or a tunnel in the abutment, along with portions of the dam adjacent to the abutments, in the first construction period. In some cases, a temporary channel is built at a preferred diversion location, and levees are built to control the flow of water through the damsite. After the outlet works and main dam are completed to an appropriate level, the stream is diverted into the outlet works by a cofferdam high enough to prevent overtopping during construction. A downstream cofferdam is also required to keep the damsite dry. In the final construction period, the entire dam is brought to full height.

Operation and maintenance. Personnel responsible for operation and maintenance of the dam become involved during the final design and construction to become familiar with design details that relate to operation. The operating instructions and maintenance schedule are published in a formal document for each dam. A schedule is established for collection and reporting of data for climatic conditions, rainfall, snow cover, stream flows, and water quality of the reservoir, as well as the downstream reaches. All these data are evaluated for use in reservoir regulation. Another schedule is established for the collection of instrumentation data used to determine the structural behavior and physical condition of the dam. These data are evaluated frequently.

Routine maintenance and inspection of the dam and appurtenant structures are ongoing porocesses. The scheduled maintenance is important to preserve the integrity of the mechanical equipment.

Periodic inspection and evaluation. Upon completion of construction, the project is inspected in detail by a team made up of the designers, construction managers, operations personnel, and other experts. The purpose is to ensure that the dam has been built as designed and can safely impound water and that all systems are ready for the initial reservoir filling and operation. In addition, the same team conducts an in-depth inspection once a year for about 5 years after completion and at 5-year intervals thereafter. Design criteria and performance of the dam as measured by instruments are reviewed during the life of the dam, and structural reanalyses are made when necessary. Photographs are taken to record rates of deterioration.

The intake structure, trash racks, emergency gates, outlet conduit or tunnel, and stilling basin are normally under water and therefore require special procedures such as dewatering prior to the inspection. At normal velocity, the flowing water can severely erode soil and rock in the approach and discharge channels. High-velocity flow over small irregularities can cause a phenomenon known as cavitation, which can lead to rapid erosion of metal and concrete and can threaten the safety of the outlet works.

Instrumentation. As the technology of dam design and construction progressed, the need to measure performance and structural behavior became important in order to verify the design. Advances in instruments starting in the 1950s gave the designer a valuable tool. Instrumentation gave the engineer knowledge of how the temperatures from hydration in concrete varied and the effect on strength. Pressure cells were developed that gave information about the interaction between soil backfill and a concrete wall or structure as well as the actual load distribution. Piezometers (devices to measure water level), settlement plates,

Fig. 13. Galesville Dam, Oregon, showing roller-compacted concrete construction; completed in 1985, it has a height of 157 ft (48 m) and a volume of 161,000 yd³ (123,100 m³).

and slope indicators are used in measuring the performance of embankment dams. Plumb lines, strain gages, and uplift cells are used for the same purpose in concrete dams. In addition, instruments are used to measure vertical and horizontal movement, alignment and plumb, stresses, strains, water pressure, seismic effects, and the quantity and clarity of seepage.

Instrumentation for a dam is installed at first in the design phase to establish baseline data, then during construction and throughout the life of the dam as conditions warrant. The frequency with which instrumentation data are obtained is an extremely important issue and depends on operating conditions. Timely collection and evaluation of data are critical for periods when the loading changes, such as during floods and after earthquakes. Advances in applications of remote sensing to instrumentation have made real-time data collection possible. This is a significant improvement for making dam safety evaluations.

Safety.   Throughout history there have been instances of dam failure and discharge of stored water, sometimes causing considerable loss of life and great damage to property. Failures have generally involved dams that were designed and constructed to engineering standards acceptable at the time.

As dam technology advanced with increasing knowledge of design principles and better understanding of foundation and material properties, dams became safer. There is no question that they can be built and operated safely. The major issue is to monitor deterioration as the structures and equipment get older. In earlier times, the sizes of spillways and outlet pipes had to be determined by judgment. As a result, overtopping was the main cause of dam failure. Little was known about soil mechanics and slope stability, and so slides and slope failures were common. Beginning in the 1930s, statistical methods were used to predict floods. Advances in soil mechanics in the later 1930s and early 1940s produced new methods of stability analysis that revolutionized the slope design for excavations and earth embankment dams. Historical data indicate that the causes of failure (in the order of their significance) are piping, overtopping, slope instability, conduit leakage (outlet works), and foundatin failures.

It is estimated that about 150,000 dams around the world present a potential hazard to life or property; there have been 200 failures since 1900. Many of these have involved small dams. **Table 4** lists some major failures that resulted in considerable loss of life.

Dam failures cause loss of life and property damage in downstream reaches that are beyond the control of the dam owner or local government. For this reason, and because dam safety practices should apply to all dams, national governments have become involved in order to provide supervision and standardize regulations. The United States government published "Federal Guidelines for Dam Safety" in June 1979. This initiated a coordinated effort in management practices among federal agencies and set an example for private organizations that own dams. The International Commission on Large Dams (ICOLD) was formed in 1928 by 6 countries with the purpose of developing and exchanging dam design experience, and it has grown to 76 member countries. In 1982 ICOLD established a committee on dam safety to define common safety principles, integrate efforts, and develop guidelines, and in 1987 ICOLD published "Dam Safety Guidelines."

Arthur H. Walz, Jr.

Bibliography.   W. P. Creager, J. D. Justin, and J. Hinds, *Engineering for Dams*, 1945; Federal Emergency Management Agency, *Federal Guidelines for Dam Safety*, FEMA 93, June 1979; A. R. Golze, *Handbook of Dam Engineering*, 1977; International Commission on Large Dams, *Dam Safety Guidelines*, Bull. 59, ICOLD, 1987; International Commission on Large Dams, *World Register of Dams*, 1984; R. B. Jansen, *Dams and Public Safety*, U.S. Department of the Interior, 1980; E. B. Kollgaard and W. L. Chadwick (eds.), *Development of Dam Engineering in the United States*, 1988; J. Sherard et al., *Earth and Earth-Rock Dams*, 1967; U.S. Army Corps of Engineers, *Gravity Dam Design*, EM 1110-2-2200, September 25, 1958; U.S. Bureau of Reclamation, *Design of Small Dams*, 3d ed., 1987.

Decontamination of radioactive materials

The removal of radioactive contamination which is deposited on surfaces or may have spread throughout a work area. Personnel decontamination is also included. The presence of radioactive contamination is a potential health hazard, and in addition, it may interfere with the normal functioning of plant processes, particularly in those plants using radiation detection instruments for control purposes. Thus, the detection and removal of radioactive contaminants from unwanted locations to locations where they do not create a health hazard or interfere with production are the basic purposes of decontamination. The objective of a good decontamination operation is to remove the radioactive contamination permanently from the human environment, with minimum radiation exposure.

There are four ways in which radioactive contaminants adhere to surfaces, and these limit the decontamination procedures which are applicable. The contaminant may be (1) held more or less loosely by such

Table 4. Some major dam failures in history

Dam	Country	Year
San Ildefonso	Bolivia	1626
Puentes	Spain	1802
Bradfield	England	1864
Johnstown	United States	1889
Walnut Grove	United States	1890
Bouzey	France	1895
Austin	United States	1911
Bila Densa	Czechoslovakia	1916
Tigra	India	1917
Glenco	Italy	1923
St. Francis	United States	1928
Alla S. Zerbimo	Italy	1935
Fred Burr	United States	1948
Malpasset	France	1959
Kuala Lumpur	Malaya	1961
Babi Yar	Soviet Union (now Commonwealth of Independent States)	1961
Baldwin Hills	United States	1963
Vaiont	Italy	1963
Buffalo Creek	United States	1972
Teton	United States	1976
Kelly Barnes	United States	1977
Machhu II	India	1979

physical forces as electrostatic or surface tension, (2) absorbed in porous materials, (3) adsorbed on or by the surface in the form of ions, atoms, or molecules, or (4) mechanically bonded to surfaces through oil, grease, tars, paint, and so on.

Methods. Decontamination methods follow two broad avenues of attack, mechanical and chemical. Commonly used mechanical methods are vacuum cleaning, sand blasting, blasting with other abrasives, flame cleaning, scraping, ultrasonic radiation, and surface removal (for example, removal of concrete floors with an air hammer). The principal chemical methods of decontamination are water washing, steam cleaning, and scrubbing with detergents, acids, caustics, and solvents.

Another important method of handling contamination is to store the contaminated object, or temporarily abandon the contaminated space. This can be done when the use of the material or space is not necessary for a period of time and the half-life of the contaminant is relatively short. For example, tools contaminated with short-lived fission products may be stored, or a building contaminated with such material may be sealed off and barred from use, until the natural radioactive decay has reduced the contamination to an acceptable level.

Other methods used involve covering the contamination by some means, such as painting, and disposing of part or all of the contaminated equipment or facility. Considerations which determine the methods used for decontamination or removal of contamination include (1) the hazards involved in the decontamination procedure, (2) the cost of removal of the contamination, and (3) the permanency of removal of the contamination (for example, painting over a surface contaminated with a long-lived radioactive material only postpones ultimate disposal considerations, while painting a surface contaminated with a short-lived, alpha-emitting radionuclide may provide a permanent solution).

Personnel. Personnel decontamination methods differ from those used for materials primarily because of the possibilities of injury to the person being decontaminated. Procedures used for normal personal cleanliness usually will remove radioactive contaminants from the skin, and the method used will depend upon its form and associated dirt (grease, oil, soil, and so on). Soap and water (sequestrants and detergents) normally remove more than 99% of the contaminants. If it is necessary to remove the remainder, chemical methods which remove the outer layers of skin upon which the contamination has been deposited can be used. These chemicals—citric acid, potassium permanganate, and sodium bisulfite are examples—should be used with caution and preferably under medical supervision, because of the increased risk of injury to the skin surface. The use of coarse cleansing powders should be avoided for skin decontamination, because they may lead to scratches and abraded skin which can permit the radioactive material to enter the body. Similarly, the use of organic solvents should be avoided for skin decontamination because of the probability of penetration through the pores of the skin. It is very difficult to remove radioactive material once it is fixed inside the body, and the ensuing hazard depends very little on the method of entry into the body, that is, through wounds, through pores of the skin, by injection, by ingestion, or by inhalation. When certain of the more dangerous

radioactive materials, such as radium or plutonium, have been taken into the body, various chemical treatments have been attempted to increase the body elimination, but the results of these treatments are not very encouraging. With plutonium and certain other heavy metals, the most effective treatment for removal from the body is the administration of chelating agents, such as calcium ethylenediaminetetraacetate (CaEDTA) or a sodium citrate solution of zirconyl chloride. Chelating agents must be used with caution because of the possibility of harmful side effects. In any case, the safest and most reliable way to prevent internal exposure from radioactive material is the application of health physics procedures to prevent entry of radioactive material into the body.

Air and water. Air contaminants frequently are eliminated by dispersion into the atmosphere. Certain meteorological conditions, such as prevailing wind velocities, wind direction, and inversion layers, seriously limit the total amount of radioactive material that may be released safely to the environment. Consequently, decontamination of the airstream by filters, cyclone separators, scrubbing with caustic solutions, cryogenic removal, and entrapment on charcoal beds is often resorted to. The choice of method is guided by such things as the volume of airflow, the cost of heating and air conditioning, the hazards associated with the airborne radioactive material, and the isolation of the operation from other populated areas.

Water decontamination processes can use one or both of the two opposing philosophies of maximum dilution or maximum concentration (and subsequent removal) of the contaminant. Water concentration methods involve the use of water purification processes, that is, ion exchange, chemical precipitation, flocculation, filtration, and biological retention.

Certain phases of radioactive decontamination procedures are potentially hazardous to personnel. Health physics decontamination practices include the use of protective clothing, respiratory devices, localized shielding, isolation or restriction of an area, provisions for the proper disposal of the attendant wastes, and application of the recommended rules and procedures for limiting the internal and external doses of ionizing radiation. For decontamination of high levels of radioactivity, remotely controlled equipment, local hood enclosures, closed-circuit television, and so forth reduce exposure of the worker. SEE RADIOACTIVE WASTE MANAGEMENT.

Karl Z. Morgan

Bibliography. DOE Technical Information Center Staff, *Radioactive Waste Management: Decontamination and Decommissioning: A Bibliography*, 1982, suppl. 1, 1985; M. Eisenbud, *Environmental Radioactivity*, 2d ed., 1973; W. R. Hendee, *Radioactive Isotopes in Biological Research*, 1973, reprint 1984; International Atomic Energy Agency, *Manual on Decontamination of Surfaces: Procedures and Data*, 1979; K. Z. Morgan and J. E. Turner, *Principles of Radiation Protection*, 1967, reprint 1973; J. Shapiro, *Radiation Protection*, 2d ed., 1981.

Defoliant and desiccant

Defoliants are chemicals that cause leaves to drop from plants; defoliation facilitates harvesting. Desiccants are chemicals that kill leaves of plants; the leaves may either drop off or remain attached; in the harvesting process the leaves are usually shattered and blown away from the harvested material. Defoliants are desirable for use on cotton plants because dry leaves are difficult to remove from the cotton fibers. Desiccants are used on many seed crops to hasten harvest; the leaves are cleaned from the seed in harvesting.

True defoliation results from the formation of an abscission layer at the base of the petiole of the leaf. Most of the chemicals bring about this type of defoliation, and the leaves abscise and drop from the plant. Certain chemicals kill plant leaves at low application rates, resulting in desiccation but not abscission.

The most common agency of defoliation in nature is frost; frosted leaves of cotton dry up and fall off after a few days. With the rapid increase in mechanical harvesting of crops, new chemicals and new processes have been introduced; these are termed harvest aids. Most harvest-aid chemicals are growth regulators that function at low concentrations or at low application rates; in some way they stimulate or inhibit growth. Some of the chemicals serve to hold fruits such as apples and pears upon the trees, thus preventing preharvest drop. Others cause loosening of fruits, facilitating harvest by shaking; examples are sour cherries and grapes.

Because of the advantages of harvest aids, much effort has gone into the search for new chemicals.

A list of active ingredients in some harvest aids includes (trade names are given in parentheses) ametryn, (Evik), amino triazole, ammonia gas, ammonium nitrate, ammonium thiocyanate, arsenic acid, cacodylic acid, calcium cyanamide, diethyl dithio-bis-thionoformate, diquat, endothal (Accelerate, Des-I-Cate), ethephon (Ethrel), 4,6-dinitro-*o-sec*-butyl-phenos, hexachloroacetone, magnesium chlorate, nitrophen, oxyfluorfen, paraquat, pentachlorophenol, petroleum solvents, sodium borate, sodium cacodylate (Bollseye), sodium chlorate (Tumbleleaf), sodium *cis*-3-chloroacrylate, sodium naphthalene acetate (Fruitone N), tributylphosphorothioate (Folex), tributylphosphorotrithioate (Def-6), 2,4,5-TP (Silvex), triethanolamine salt of Silvex (Fruitone T).

Crops upon which harvest aids are used include alfalfa, apples, blackberries, blueberries, clovers (Alsike, Ladino), cantaloupes, castor beans, cherries, cranberries, flax, figs, filbert nuts, grapes, guar, hops, lemons, onions, oranges, peas, potatoes, rice, safflower, sudan grass, sorghum, soybeans, sunflowers, tangerines, tomatoes, walnuts, and wheat. Tomato plants are sometimes cut below the soil surface and allowed to dry out; this brings the fruits to a uniform ripeness for mechanical harvesting.

Modern agricultural technology, which has greatly increased production in the United States, is dependent upon harvest-aid chemicals. These aids bring fruits to uniform ripeness for harvest by machinery or by well-managed crews. They reduce or eliminate much labor, save time, and make for reliable management of harvest. They, along with fertilizers and improved crop varieties, are responsible for the great abundance of foods in developed countries.

It was in an effort to find such chemical agents that 2,4-D was discovered in 1942 by E. J. Kraus. For more than 30 years 2,4-D and 2,4,5-T have been important compounds used for weed control.

Defoliants and desiccants have also been used during war to destroy crops. *See Herbicide.*

Alden S. Crafts

Desert

No precise definition of a desert exists. From an ecological viewpoint the scarcity of rainfall is all important, as it directly affects plant productivity which in turn affects the abundance, diversity, and activity of animals. It has become customary to describe deserts as extremely arid where the mean precipitation is less than 2.5–4 in. (60–100 mm), arid where it is 2.5–4 to 6–10 in. (60–100 to 150–250 mm), and semiarid where it is 6–10 to 10–20 in. (150–250 to 250–500 mm). However, mean figures tend to distort the true state of affairs because precipitation in deserts is unreliable and variable. In some areas, such as the Atacama in Chile and the Arabian Desert, there may be no rainfall for several years. It is the biological effectiveness of rainfall that matters and this may vary with wind and temperature, which affect evaporation rates. The vegetation cover also alters the evaporation rate and increases the effectiveness of rainfall. Rainfall, then, is the chief limiting factor to biological processes but intense solar radiation, high temperatures, and a paucity of nutrients (especially of nitrogen) may also limit plant productivity, and hence animal abundance.

The main desert regions of the world are shown in the **illustration**. Most lie within the tropics and hence are hot as well as arid. The Namib and Atacama coastal deserts are kept cool by the Benguela and Humboldt ocean currents, and many desert areas of central Asia are cool because of high latitude and altitude.

Plant production. As a consequence of unreliable rainfall, plant productivity is much more variable than in most ecosystems. It may vary from none to 880 dry lb/acre · yr (1000 dry kg/ha · yr) although in most places there is usually some productivity even when there is no rainfall. The average biomass is generally low at 0.004–0.144 dry lb/ft^2 (0.02–0.7 dry kg/m^2) compared to 9.25 dry lb/ft^2 (45 dry kg/m^2) in tropical forest and 6.17 dry lb/ft^2 (30 dry kg/m^2) in temperate forest. Another feature of desert vegetation is the low percentage of green, photosynthetic plant biomass. There is also about three times as much dead as living plant material, a high figure compared to most other ecosystems. *See Biological productivity; Biomass.*

Between 10 and 20% of the living plant material is eaten by consumers, a figure typical of terrestrial ecosystems, where the level of consumption may be as low as 5% (compared to over 90% in ocean ecosystems). Much desert vegetation tends to be hard and prickly and hence unpalatable to many consumers. Dead plant material does not accumulate and is utilized by the decomposers, particularly wood-eating termites. Seeds are abundant and can survive a long time without germinating. Many animals, including rodents, ants, and birds, depend heavily upon them for food. There is evidence of both intra- and interspecific competition for seeds, the production of which varies markedly with variations in rainfall.

A common viewpoint is that desert plants and animals live in a harsh environment and as a consequence have evolved many morphological and behavioral adaptations that enable them to "escape" the rigors of their surroundings. Certainly extreme aridity coupled with extreme heat seems a stressful environment, but whether desert organisms really possess more escape adaptations than, say, rainforest organisms is a matter for conjecture. Nevertheless, specific

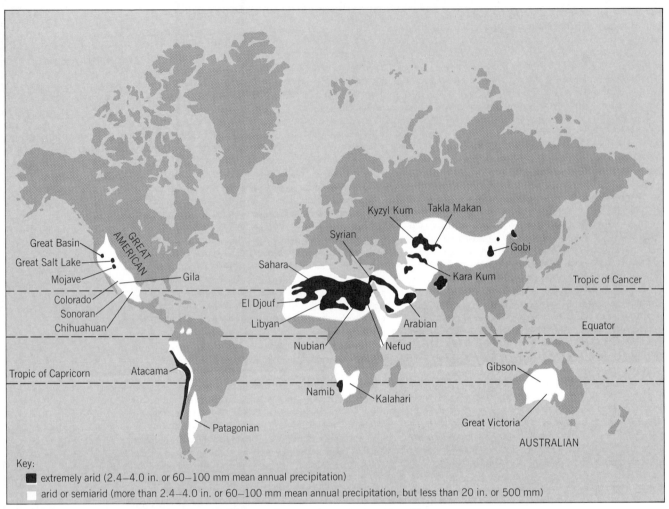

The deserts of the world; those within the tropics are hot as well as arid.

adaptations to drought and heat can be readily identified.

Adaptations in plants. In many deserts, annual rather than perennial plants form the bulk of the climax vegetation, quite unlike the situation in most terrestrial ecosystems where perennial plants dominate. Deserts, especially those within the tropics, periodically "bloom" with flowering annuals soon after a significant rainfall. In general, the more unreliable the rainfall in a desert, the greater the abundance and diversity of annual plants. Estimates vary, but these annuals account for up to half the primary production in a year, although for a given site they may fail altogether if there is no rain. Many annuals last for only a very short time. They tend to have the C_4 photosynthetic pathway, which means they grow quickly and opportunistically. It is these plants in particular that produce the vast quantities of seed which under extreme aridity can last for years, providing a "seed bank" until conditions are right for germination. Most ephemeral annuals do not have special drought-resistant or drought-tolerant adaptations: they are simply opportunists, much like the annuals of wetter communities which, however, tend to be successional rather than climax species.

Succulent plants occur in all deserts but nowhere as conspicuously as in the Sonoran Desert of North America. These fleshy plants store water in their tissues, and tend to be especially prickly, a defense against browsers which need water as well as food. In American deserts the obvious succulents are members of the Cactaceae; in Africa where cactus is almost absent, many species of Euphorbiaceae have the same types of growth form and occupy essentially the same ecological niches.

Other perennial plants include trees and shrubs with long tap roots that can reach underground water, making them independent of scarce and unreliable rainfall. Some perennials burst into leaf only after there has been rain, and are hence leafless most of the time. Yet others retain leaves throughout dry periods; the leaves tend to be small and narrow and require relatively little water to photosynthesize. These plants, mostly small shrubs and grasses, invariably have an extensive root system which enables them to maximize their acquisition of water. *See Physiological ecology (plant); Plants, life forms of.*

Adaptations in animals. A majority of terrestrial invertebrates are cryptic in coloration, matching almost exactly components of the background on which they normally live. Many invertebrates and small vertebrates, such as rodents and snakes, spend the day in holes and burrows, and become active at night, when it is cooler. In all environments there

are many small animals that escape by hiding, in most places to escape from predators; but in deserts escape from high daytime temperatures and radiation appears to be the chief adaptive response. The burrow constructed by the New World kangaroo rat, *Dipodomys*, protects the animal from daytime heat and radiation and also from predatory snakes and birds. The entrance of the burrow is sealed with soil which allows a high (30%) relative humidity to develop which helps the animal maintain its water budget. Kangaroo rats do not drink but exist on water derived from the seeds they eat; their urine is the most concentrated of all mammals, another antidesiccation adaptation. Desert birds also shelter and avoid the heat of the day. In the Kalahari, the social weaverbird, *Philetarius socius*, builds a gigantic communal nest in an acacia or other suitable tree. The insulation within such a nest protects the birds from both the heat of the day and the cold of the night.

The largest of all birds, the ostrich, *Struthio camelus*, is an inhabitant of arid regions of Africa. The birds are too large to retreat into hiding during the day, although they may seek the shade of a big tree. With a high ambient temperature (95°F or 35°C or more) and no wind an ostrich loses heat by panting and by erecting the sparsely distributed feathers on its back. If there is wind, panting ceases and heat is lost by convection across the erect back feathers. At night when it is cool or even cold (below 64°F or 18°C), the back feathers are flattened and an insulating layer of air is trapped which reduces heat loss.

Soon after heavy rainfall, holes and depressions in sand or rock fill with water and within a few hours teem with microscopic life, chiefly algae, bacteria, and protozoa. After a few days countless small crustaceans appear, such as fairy and tadpole shrimps. These grow and reproduce with great rapidity. They can tolerate high water temperatures and also the high salinity which often builds up in temporary desert pools. The pools soon disappear and the land may then remain dry for months, even years, before the next downpour. The shrimps and other organisms diapause in the soil, usually as eggs which are remarkably resistant to high temperatures and extreme desiccation. *SEE PHYSIOLOGICAL ECOLOGY (ANIMAL).*

Aestivation. The term aestivation is used to describe a lengthy period of dormancy during which metabolism is much reduced. Many desert animals are capable of prolonged aestivation which enables them to survive during periods of food and water scarcity. In insects such as butterflies, which have a complete metamorphosis (clear-cut egg, larval, pupal, and adult stages), aestivation can occur at any stage of the life cycle but is almost invariably confined to a particular stage for a given species. Before entering aestivation, most animals seek out a secluded place that provides the best protection from temperature fluctuations and solar radiation, as well as from predators. Many species, ranging from lungfish to insect larvae, construct some form of protective cocoon in which to aestivate.

Migration and movement. An alternative to aestivation is migration or other movement away in search of better feeding and breeding conditions. Some of the African antelopes, such as the oryx, *Oryx gazella*, undertake long-distance movements which are correlated with changes in the quality and quantity of grass upon which they feed. These grass characteristics in turn are determined by rainfall, so there may be regular movements to and from areas where the rainfall is predictable and regular, or much more erratic movements in areas of unpredictable rainfall.

The semiregular migrations of several species of African weaverbirds (Ploceidae) are strongly associated with the seeding of wild grasses. The birds may form flocks of thousands or even tens of thousands of individuals and descend on and devour ripening seeds before moving on. Some of these birds, including the black-faced dioch, *Quelea quelea*, have become serious pests of millet and other cereals grown on land irrigated from underground water.

The blooming of desert annuals and the leafing out of trees and shrubs soon after rainfall often result in a dramatic increase in abundance of leaf-eating insects. Eggs that have remained dormant for months produce larvae which can be so numerous as to defoliate vegetation. In Africa, white butterflies, *Belenois*, may migrate in vast numbers from areas where the larval food plants have been defoliated to areas where there is fresh growth. Pastoral people and their livestock undertake similar movements in response to changes in the availability of graze and browse for their animals, and to some extent, in response to changes in the risk of diseases such as trypanosomiasis, which affects both humans and domestic animals.

One of the most successful groups of desert animals is the grasshoppers. In many deserts there is a considerable variety of species, some of which are abundant. A few species are able to build up suddenly in numbers, often in response to unseasonal rain which has promoted a rapid growth of vegetation. They then undertake long-distance irruptive movements, followed by further breeding until they reach such numbers that they invade higher-rainfall areas and devastate crops. One of these grasshoppers, the desert locust, *Schistocerca gregaria*, can invade and seriously affect the vegetation of an area extending through 110° of longitude from West Africa to Assam, north to Turkey and south to southern Tanzania. Plagues of desert locusts may last for years and then suddenly stop, the locust reverting to a normal desert grasshopper.

Species diversity. The diversity of species of animals in a desert is generally correlated with the diversity of plant species, which to a considerable degree is correlated with the predictability and amount of rainfall. There is a rather weak latitudinal gradient of diversity with relatively more species nearer the Equator than at higher latitudes. This gradient is much more conspicuous in wetter ecosystems, such as forests, and in deserts appears to be overridden by the manifold effects of rainfall. Animals, too, may affect plant diversity: the burrowing activities of rodents create niches for plants which could not otherwise survive, and mound-building termites tend to concentrate decomposition and hence nutrients, which provide opportunities for plants to colonize.

Convergent evolution. Each desert has its own community of species, and these communities are repeated in different parts of the world. Very often the organisms that occupy similar niches in different deserts belong to unrelated taxa. The overall structural similarity between American cactus species and African euphorbias is an example of convergent evolution, in which separate and unrelated groups have evolved almost identical adaptations under similar environmental conditions in widely separated parts of the world. Convergent structural modification occurs in many organisms in all environments, but is especially noticeable in deserts where possibly the small number of ecological niches has necessitated greater specialization and restriction of way of life. The face and especially the large ears of desert foxes of the Sahara and of North America are remarkably similar, and there is an extraordinary resemblance between North American sidewinding rattlesnakes and Namib sidewinding adders.

Desert community. Ecological change in deserts seems to occur slowly. Plant and animal succession is much less obvious than in other communities, although there is some evidence of cyclical change in which species replace one another. In the Chihuahuan Desert of North America, the shrub *Larrea tridentata* reduces the wind speed enough to cause accumulation of soil and organic nutrients around the bottom of the trunk. This enables other plants to establish themselves, including the cactus *Opuntia leptocaulis*, whose seeds are introduced into the accumulated soil via the feces of rodents and birds which eat the fruit. The cactus grows and its roots overrun and outcompete those of the *Larrea* shrub, which then dies and falls over. Wind and water erosion then dislodge the rather shallow roots of the cactus, which itself dies and topples over. The vacant space is eventually filled by another *Larrea*, and the cycle starts again. No one has witnessed the complete cycle, which is believed to take many years to complete, but all stages can be identified and the presumed sequence of events drawn together. *See Ecological communities; Ecological succession; Ecology; Ecosystem.*

Denis F. Owen

Bibliography. G. N. Louw and M. K. Seely, *Ecology of Desert Organisms*, 1982; G. M. O. Maloiy (ed.), *Comparative Physiology of Desert Animals*, 1972; K. Schmidt-Nielsen, *Desert Animals: Physiological Problems of Heat and Water*, 1964; F. H. Wagner, *Wildlife of the Deserts*, 1980.

Desertification

Desertification is the spread of desertlike conditions in arid and semiarid areas, due to human influence or climatic change. Natural vegetation is being lost over increasingly larger areas because of overgrazing, especially in Africa and southwestern Asia. Where the original state of vegetation has been retained, for example, in military compounds, the contrast is dramatic. In such a case, near Nefta in southern Tunisia, the coverage of vegetation inside an area fenced for 60 years is 85%, in contrast to 5% outside the area; here the original dry steppe has changed into a semidesert, without any appreciable variation of precipitation (about 3.15 in. or 80 mm per year). Another dramatic example of this type is revealed in a NASA *Earth Resources and Technology Satellite* (*ERTS*) photograph of the Sinai-Negev desert region. The political boundary established in the 1948 armistice between these two regions is clearly visible, with the lighter Sinai region to the west of the boundary and the darker Negev region to the east. The sharp demarcation is due to the fact that Bedouin Arabs' goats in the Sinai have defoliated enough land on the Egyptian side to make the boundary visible from space. Similar conditions have been observed in India.

In many areas the deserts seem to be spreading, with an apparent speed of about one or more kilometers per year. During the 1968–1973 drought, as a consequence of overgrazing (especially goats), the Sahara Desert appeared to be advancing into the Sahel (Mauritania, Senegal, Mali, Upper Volta, Niger, and Chad) at an average rate of 31 mi (50 km) per year, which varied somewhat with the density of the population. However, recent desertification is the result of the interaction of naturally recurring drought with unwise land-use practices. To understand to what extent each factor plays a part in the total desertification process, and to consider whether the process can be slowed down or reversed, it is helpful to review natural causes and human causes of deserts, as follows.

Natural causes of deserts. The world distribution of dry climates depends mainly on the subsidence associated with the subtropical high-pressure belts, which migrate poleward in summer and equatorward in winter. These migrations are connected with the atmospheric general circulation. There results a threefold structure in the arid zone: a Mediterranean fringe, with rains occurring only in winter; a desert core (in about 20–30° latitude), with little or no rain; and a tropical fringe, with rains mainly in the high sun season. Throughout the arid zone, rainfall variability is high. Aridity arises from persistent widespread subsidence or from more localized subsidence in the lee of mountains. In some regions, such as the northern Negev, the combination of widespread and local subsidence is clearly visible as clouds on the windward side of mountains form and immediately dissipate on the leeward side. Aridity may also be caused by the absence of humid airstreams and of rain-inducing disturbances. Clear skies and low humidities in most regions give the dry climates very high solar radiation (averaging over 200 W/m²), which leads to high soil temperatures. The light color and high reflectivity (albedo) of many dry surfaces cause large reflectional losses, and long-wave cooling is also severe. Hence net radiation incomes are relatively low—of the order of 80–90 W/m².

Climatic variation takes place on many time scales. The processes that may cause climatic variation, plotted against their characteristic time scale, are shown in the **illustration**, in which autovariation means internal behavior. The world's deserts and semideserts are very old, although they have shifted in latitude and varied in extent during geological history. The modern phase of climate began with a major change about 10,000 years before present, when a rapid warming trend removed most of the continental ice sheets. The Sahara and Indus valleys were at first moist, but since about 4000 years before present, when severe natural desiccation took place, aridity has been profound.

Recent climatic variations, such as the Sahelian drought, are natural in origin, and are not without precedent. Statistical analysis of rainfall shows a distinct tendency for abnormal wetness or drought to persist from year to year, especially in the Sahel. Prolonged desiccation, lasting a decade and more, is common and often ends abruptly with excessive rainfall. This persistence suggests that feedback mechanisms may be operating, whereby drought feeds drought and rain feeds rain.

Human causes of deserts. Recent desertification has resulted from the spatially uneven pressure exerted by humans on soil and vegetation, especially at times of drought or excessive rainfall. The Dust Bowl

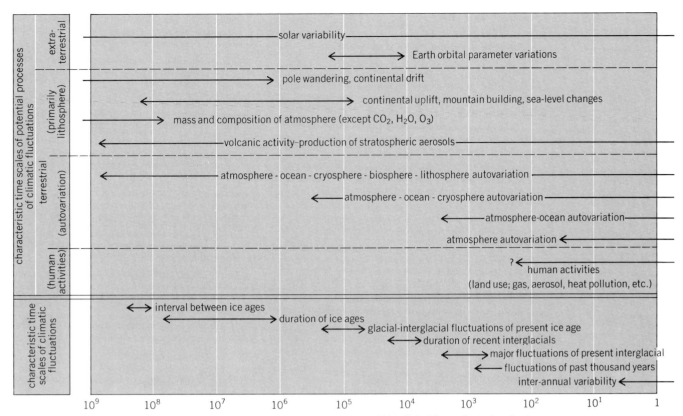

Processes that may cause climatic variation, plotted against their characteristic time scale. (*After United States Committee for the Global Atmospheric Research Program, Understanding Climatic Change: A Program for Action, National Academy of Sciences, 1975*)

in the Great Plains of the United States and the degeneration in the Sahel, the Ethiopian plateaus, and Mendoza Province of Argentina are all manifestations of human misuse of the land at times of climatic stress.

A common mechanism of desertification includes the following steps: (1) expansion and intensification of land use in marginal dry lands during wet years, including increased grazing, plowing and cultivation of new lands, and wood collection around new camps or settlements; and (2) wind erosion during the next dry year, or water erosion during the next maximum rainstorm.

This desertification process has the following climatological implications: (1) Increased grazing during wet years tends to compact the soil near water holes, and increased livestock numbers cause pressure on perennial plants during dry seasons. The result is to expose surface soil to erosion by wind. Runoff may be increased, and so may albedo (that is, reflectivity of the ground with respect to solar radiation). (2) Increased cultivation during wet years greatly improves the chances of wind erosion of fine soil materials during the dry season, and possibly increases evapotranspiration (in the case of water-demanding crops). (3) Removal of wood increases direct solar heating and may considerably decrease evapotranspiration. (4) In the ensuing dry years, the acceleration of wind erosion by the above processes further reduces water storage capacity by removal of topsoil. The loss of some or all perennial plant cover lowers infiltration rates and hence the potential percolation. During subsequent rains, surface runoff is increased, with an at-tendant loss of water for subsequent use by shrubs, herbage, or crops.

In order to test hypotheses of both natural and human-caused effects on the climate, one must have effective mathematical models of the dry climate.

Modeling attempts. In the mathematical model, the particular physical phenomenon to be studied is described in mathematical terms, and the equations are then solved by means of high-speed computers. In this way, predictions may be made of the effects of changes in external forcing, including the inadvertent or intentional changes caused by humans. Experiments thus far comprise:

1. General circulation models (GCMs) applied to the specific problems of the causes of climatic fluctuations in the dry climates. These models simulate in three dimensions the general circulation of the hemisphere or globe, and can be subjected to chosen perturbations, such as sea surface temperature anomalies, to determine the effects.

2. Investigations of specific feedback processes, such as changed albedo or variations of soil moisture storage. The models seek to predict the effect of feedbacks on circulation and precipitation over the arid zone. One recent experiment of this type was carried out in the United Kingdom. A model investigation tested the speculation that rainfall variations over north and central Africa were related to sea surface temperature anomalies over the tropical Atlantic. The experiment showed that introduction of an extensive sea surface temperature anomaly over the tropical Atlantic was related to higher precipitation amounts over North Africa. While the experiment did not actually

prove the causal relationship, it changed the speculation into a credible hypothesis.

Most recent modeling attempts have been related to specific feedback processes that may augment or retard naturally induced climatic variations along the desert margin, especially the effect of changed albedo and other consequences of the degradation of vegetation cover.

The albedo feedback hypothesis argues that the destruction of vegetation and exposure of soil increase albedo and hence lower surface temperatures and suppress convective shower formation. This hypothesis has been considered to be a mechanism for desertification. Since certain regions of the central and northern Sahara, eastern Saudi Arabia, and southern Iraq have a negative radiation balance at the top of the atmosphere on hot summer days, in spite of the intense input of solar radiation through the cloudless atmosphere, the following argument has been advanced: Since the ground stores little heat, it is the air that loses heat radiatively. In order to maintain thermal equilibrium, the air must descend and compress adiabatically. Since the relative humidity then decreases, the desert increases its own dryness. A biogeophysical feedback mechanism of this type could lead to instabilities or metastabilities in borders themselves, which might conceivably be set off or maintained by anthropogenic influences.

This hypothesis has been tested by means of a dynamical model, in which the surface albedo was increased over large desert regions. Sharp reductions of cloud and rain followed the increase in albedo. Possible mechanisms by which albedo is changed are removal of vegetation by drought, overstocking, cultivation, or all of these, or by desiccation of the soil itself, soil albedo being related to soil water content. In practice, the three mechanisms are likely to occur simultaneously, so that soil moisture content may itself serve as a positive feedback for drought, a wet soil favoring renewed rainfall which is derived from local evapotranspiration.

All of the above hypotheses work by influencing the overall dynamics of the desert margin climates, essentially via their effect on rates of subsidence and hence stability. There is also the possibility that cloud microphysics may be affected by surface conditions. It has been suggested that cumulus and cumulonimbus clouds of the Sahelian and Sudanian belts of western Africa are "seeded" by organic ice nuclei raised from the vegetated surface below. Removal of the vegetation destroys the local source of organic nuclei. Hence, well-formed clouds remain unseeded and rainless, accelerating the decay of surface vegetation.

In summary, modeling experiments suggest that there may well be a positive feedback process along the desert margin, operating via the increase of surface albedo attendant upon the destruction of the surface vegetation layer, and possibly also upon the decrease of soil moisture and surface organic litter. It thus appears possible that widespread destruction of the vegetation cover of the dry world may tend to further reduce rainfall over these areas.

Possible solutions. Suggestions for solution of the desertification problem include weather and climate modification, control of surface cover, and maximum application of modern technology.

Weather and climate modification. Cloud seeding, establishing green belts, and flooding of desert basins are a few of the weather and climate modification techniques under consideration.

Special conditions are required for rainfall augmentation by cloud seeding. If the proper type of seedable cloud exists, it may be possible to increase the rainfall locally by this method.

Establishment of green belts along the northern and southern margins of the Sahara is considered to be of dubious value climatologically, inasmuch as desertification does not spread outward from the desert. Thus the green belt would not serve as a "shelter belt." However, this hypothesis should be tested by means of a model.

Precipitation depends largely on water vapor which has traveled great distances, along with upward motion of the air. The experience with artificial oases to date has shown little or no change of climate in their vicinity. Modeling experiments carried out by simulating the "flooding" of Lake Sahara predicted no significant change of rainfall around the lake, although rainfall was increased over an isolated mountain region 560 mi (900 km) from the shore. However, these results do indicate the possibility of creating artificial bodies of water judiciously with respect to the areas where rainfall augmentation is desired. This hypothesis may also be tested by model experiments.

Control of surface cover. The key to the control of the desertification process is the control of surface cover. If the relatively secure wind-stable surfaces of some desert areas, or a reasonably complete vegetation cover (even if dead) can be maintained, soil drifting and deflation are minimized. Overstocking, unwise cultivation, and the use of overland vehicles weaken and ultimately destroy these protective covers. The proposed green belt is of value because of the added protection it affords the soil.

The usefulness of land depends on the surface microclimate. The ability to conserve this microclimate rests on the transformation of desert technology, rather than on transformation of climate. The ability of the surface to respond quickly and generously to renewed abundance of rainfall depends on the soil's capacity to retain nutrients, organic substances, and fine materials; on high infiltration capacity; and, of course, on viable seeds as well as a surviving root system. A surface litter of organic debris may also be important for precipitation mechanisms, and has some effect on surface radiation balance.

Use of modern technology. Satellite data could be used in tracking the major rainstorms of the rainy season to study their habits and, if possible, to predict their displacement. Other important satellite data, for example, radiation, could be collected and used in connection with feedback studies. SEE CLIMATE MODIFICATION; CLIMATIC CHANGE; DESERT; DROUGHT.

Louis Berkofsky

Bibliography. F. El-Baz and M. H. Hassan (eds.), *Physics of Desertification*, 1986; M. H. Glantz, *Desertification*, 1977; F. K. Hare, T. Gal-Chen, and K. Hendrie, *Climate and Desertification*, Institute for Environmental Studies, University of Toronto, 1976; Massachusetts Institute of Technology, *Inadvertent Climate Modification: Report of the Study of Man's Impact on Climate* (SMIC), 1971; S. H. Schneider and L. E. Mesirow, *The Genesis Strategy*, 1976; F. G. Sulman, *Short and Long Term Changes in Climate*, 2 vols., 1982.

Dew point

The temperature at which air becomes saturated when cooled without addition of moisture or change of pressure. Any further cooling causes condensation; fog and dew are formed in this way.

Frost point is the corresponding temperature of saturation with respect to ice. At temperatures below freezing, both frost point and dew point may be defined because water is often liquid (especially in clouds) at temperatures well below freezing; at freezing (more exactly, at the triple point, $+.01°C$ or $32.02°F$) they are the same, but below freezing the frost point is higher. For example, if the dew point is $-9°C$ ($16°F$), the frost point is $-8°C$ ($17.5°F$). Both dew point and frost point are single-valued functions of vapor pressure.

Determination of dew point (or frost point) can be made directly by cooling a flat polished metal surface until it becomes clouded with a film of water or ice; the dew point is the temperature at which the film appears. In practice, the dew point is usually computed from simultaneous readings of wet- and dry-bulb thermometers. *See* Humidity.

J. R. Fulks

Drought

A general term implying a deficiency of precipitation of sufficient magnitude to interfere with some phase of the economy. Agricultural drought, occurring when crops are threatened by lack of rain, is the most common. Hydrologic drought, when reservoirs are depleted, is another common form. The Palmer index has been used by agriculturalists to express the intensity of drought as a function of rainfall and hydrologic variables.

The meteorological causes of drought are usually associated with slow, prevailing, subsiding motions of air masses from continental source regions. These descending air motions, of the order of 600 or 900 ft/day (200 or 300 m/day), result in compressional warming of the air and therefore reduction in the relative humidity. Since the air usually starts out dry, and the relative humidity declines as the air descends, cloud formation is inhibited—or if clouds are formed, they are soon dissipated. In the United States, the area over which such subsidence prevails may involve several states, as in the 1977 drought over much of the Far West, the 1962–1966 Northeast drought, or the dust bowl of the 1930s over the Central Plains.

The atmospheric circulations which lead to this subsidence are the so-called centers of action, like the Bermuda High, which are linked to the planetary waves of the upper-level westerlies. If these centers are displaced from their normal positions or are abnormally developed, they frequently introduce anomalously moist or dry air masses into regions of the temperate latitudes. More important, these long waves interact with the cyclones along the Polar Front in such a way as to form and steer their course into or away from certain areas. In the areas relatively invulnerable to the cyclones, the air descends, and if this process repeats time after time, a deficiency of rainfall and drought may occur. In other areas where moist air is frequently forced to ascend, heavy rains occur. Therefore, drought in one area, say the north-eastern United States, is usually associated with abundant precipitation elsewhere, like over the Central Plains.

After drought has been established in an area, there seems to be a tendency for it to persist and expand into adjacent areas. Although little is known about the physical mechanisms involved in this expansion and persistence, some circumstantial evidence suggests that numerous ''feedback'' processes are set in motion which aggravate the situation. Among these are large-scale interactions between ocean and atmosphere in which variations in ocean-surface temperature are produced by abnormal wind systems, and these in turn encourage further development of the same type of abnormal circulation. Atmospheric interactions called teleconnections can then establish drought-producing upper-level high-pressure areas over North America. Then again, if an area, such as the Central Plains, is subject to dryness and heat in spring, the parched soil appears to influence subsequent air circulations and rainfall in a drought-extending sense.

A theory supported by numerical modeling studies suggests that over very dry areas, particularly deserts, the loss of heat by radiation relative to the surroundings creates a slow descending motion. This results in compressional warming, lowered relative humidity in the descending air, and inhibition of rain. These processes are probably partly responsible for the tropical droughts observed in various parts of the Sahel (sub-Saharan) region during the 1970s. Of course, interactions with other parts of the atmosphere's prevailing circulation as indicated earlier also play a role in tropical droughts.

Finally, it should be pointed out that some of the most extensive droughts, like those of the 1930s dust bowl era, require compatibly placed centers of action over both the Atlantic and the Pacific. *See* Climatic change.

Another type of drought came to light in Indonesia and the surrounding area, sometimes extending as far westward as India. These droughts may last a couple of years and are associated with the wind systems which create El Niño, an abnormally warm mass of water near the Equator, which can have an east-west extent of hundreds, sometimes thousands, of miles. This water, as much as a few degrees above normal temperature, interacts with the overlying atmosphere to produce rising air motion with more clouds and rainfall in the eastern Pacific (from Peru westward) but sinking air motion with inhibition of rainfall over the western Pacific including Indonesia. While occurring on average every five or so years, El Niño is not periodic and is difficult to predict.

The Sahel (sub-Saharan) droughts are the most long-lasting, sometimes persisting for more than a decade. These droughts impact on agriculture and cattle production to the extent that hundreds of thousands of people starve to death in countries such as Ethiopia. These Sahel droughts are associated with abnormal displacements of the Intertropical Convergence Zone, a west-to-east-oriented area where the trade winds of both hemispheres converge. This is a zone of enhanced rainfall, so that its variable latitudinal position often determines how much rain occurs in parts of the sub-Saharon region. Once desiccation sets in, air-land feedbacks help to perpetuate the drought.

In view of the immense scale and complexity of

drought-producing systems, it will be difficult to devise methods of eliminating or ameliorating them.

Jerome Namias

Bibliography. J. G. Charney, Dynamics of deserts and drought in the Sahel, *Quart. J. Roy. Meteorol. Soc.,* 101(428):193–202, 1975; C. K. Folland, T. N. Palmer, and D. E. Parker, Sahel rainfall and worldwide sea temperatures, 1901–85, *Nature,* 320:602–607, 1986; J. Namias, *Factors in the Initiation, Perpetuation and Termination of Drought,* Int. Union Geod. Geophys. Ass. Sci. Hydrol. Publ. 51, 1960; J. Namias, Multiple causes of the North American abnormal winter 1976–77, *Mon. Weath. Rev.,* 106(3):279–295, March 1978; W. C. Palmer, *Meterological Drought,* U. S. Weather Bur. Res. Pap. 45, 1965; N. J. Rosenberg (ed.), *Drought in the Great Plains: Research on Impact and Strategies,* 1980; UNESCO-WMO, *Hydrological Aspects of Drought,* Studies Rep. Hydrol. 39, 1985.

Dune vegetation

Plants occupying sand dunes and the slacks, or swales, and flats between them. The density and diversity of dune vegetation are greater on coastal dunes than on desert dunes.

Zonation. A zonation pattern is evident in the vegetation of the coastal dunes (**Fig. 1**). A wrack, or debris, line occurs at the upper limit of the beach. Seeds caught in decaying plant material and other debris washed in on the high tides germinate here and trap windblown sand, initiating the formation of a dune. Small mounds formed in this way may eventually become foredunes as more sand accumulates and as the foredune grasses invade these mounds. Decomposing plant material (detritus) washed in on the tides provides additional nourishment for the young plants.

The foredunes, also called the primary dunes, are those closest to the water and lie behind the wrack line. The plants on these dunes, mostly grasses, are tolerant to sea spray, high winds, and sand accretion. By a system of underground stems called rhizomes, they overcome burial by sand and spread throughout the dune with new shoots arising from buds on the rhizomes. The roots and rhizomes of these dune grasses are important in stabilizing the dune sand and preventing wind erosion. The foredune plants participate in dune formation; by slowing the wind, they favor sand deposition.

Behind the primary dunes are the secondary dunes, sometimes called the dune field. In this more favorable environment, the vegetation is denser and more diverse; the foredunes block sea spray and reduce wind velocity. Here are found plants adapted to dry land and those tolerant of flooding, which often occurs in the dune slacks. The dune slacks are the low areas between dunes and are frequently a result of a blowout, an area where sand has been blown away down to where the sand is moist and close to the water table. Plants typical of wetlands often vegetate these areas. Shrub communities also inhabit the dune field and often form dense patches of vegetation.

A maritime forest may be found behind the secondary dunes. In coastal barrier beach or island locations, a salt marsh adjacent to a bay or sound may lie behind the forest.

Plant communities. Not all the plant species occupying the sand dunes of the United States can be described here. Although the names of the plants vary from coast to coast, their functions and adaptations are essentially the same. Sea rocket (*Cakile maritima*), probably the most widely distributed wrackline beach plant, can be found in many coastal regions. It is an annual plant that initiates dune formation by trapping sand and debris.

The foredune species are primarily responsible for forming and stabilizing the seaward-facing row of dunes. American beachgrass (*Ammophila breviligulata*) is the dominant pioneer plant on the dunes of the North Atlantic and mid-Atlantic coast. This plant and prairie sandreed (*Calamovilla longifolia*) dominate the dunes along the shores of the Great Lakes. Sea oats (*Uniola paniculata*) dominates the foredunes of the South Atlantic coast (**Fig. 2**) and, with bitter panicum (*Panicum amarum*), is the pioneer species on the Gulf of Mexico dunes. On the northern west coast, European beachgrass (*Ammophila arenaria*) and American dunegrass (*Elymus mollis*) dominate. On the southern west coast, species of *Carpobrotus, Artemisia, Ambrosia,* and *Abrona* are most abundant.

In the secondary dunes the diversity increases. On the Atlantic coast, shrub communities include bayberry (*Myrica pensylvanica*), wax myrtle (*Myrica cerifera*), beach plum (*Prunus maritima*), and poison ivy (*Rhus radicans*). In the south, saw palmetto (*Serenoa repens*) and yucca (*Yucca filamentosa*) are common. On the Pacific coast, the shrub community includes salal (*Gaultheria shallon*), evergreen huckleberry (*Vaccinium ovatum*), chaparral broom (*Baccharis pilularis*), California figwort (*Schrophularia californica*), hooker willow (*Salix hookeriana*), and Pacific wax myrtle (*Myrica californica*). Seaside goldenrod (*Solidago sempervirens*), running beach grass (*Panicum amarum*), sand bur (*Cenchrus tribuloides*), beach heather (*Hudsonia tomentosa*), and beach pea

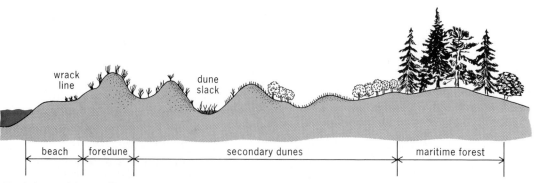

Fig. 1. A coastal dune profile.

(*Lathyrus maritimus*) are common on Atlantic and Gulf coast dunes. On the Pacific coast, common herbaceous plants are red fescue (*Festuca rubra*), dune goldenrod (*Solidago spathulata*), beach sagewort (*Artemisia pycnocephala*), and seashore lupine (*Lupinus littoralis*). On the dunes of the Great Lakes, blue joint (*Calamagrostis canadensis*), beach bea (*Lathyrus maritimus*), tansy (*Tanacetom huronense*), scouring rush (*Equisetum hyemale*), and beach heather (*Hudsonia tomentosa*) are common. Dune slacks of the Atlantic coast contain sedges such as American three-square (*Scirpus americanus*), rushes (*Juncus*), and grasses such as salt grass (*Distichlis spicata*). In the Pacific dune slacks, Douglas's spirea (*Spiraea douglasii*), slough sedge (*Carex obnupta*), Pacific silverweed (*Potentilla pacifica*), and common cattail (*Typha latifolia*) are common.

Forest species of the Atlantic and Gulf coast dunes include pitch pine (*Pinus rigida*), loblolly pine (*Pinus taeda*), sassafras (*Sassafras albidum*), wild black cherry (*Prunus serotina*), live oak (*Quercus virginiana*), and red cedar (*Juniperus virginiana*). Pacific dune forests include lodgepole pine (*Pinus contorta*), Douglas-fir (*Pseudotsuga menziesii*), western hemlock (*Tsuga heterophylla*), and sitka spruce (*Picia sitchensis*). Balsam poplar (*Populus balsamifera*) is the most common forest species of the Great Lakes dunes.

Ecology. Plants growing on sand dunes are adapted to the environment. The plants closest to the sea are usually the most tolerant of salt spray. The plants in the wrack line must be tolerant to salinity, wind, and burial by sand. Succulence helps sea rocket to tolerate the salty environment of the beach. It stores water in its fleshy stems and leaves, helping to dilute the salt taken up by its roots. Its tough cuticle withstands sand abrasion.

The foredune plants must be tolerant of sand burial, sea spray, and a nutrient-poor substrate. American beachgrass, for example, grows more vigorously in a location of accreting sand than in a more stable area. Its rhizomes, like those of other foredune grasses, can grow and spread rapidly as new sand is added to a dune. Once buried, these plants send a vertical rhizome to the surface, where a new shoot develops. Furthermore, some of these plants, such as American beachgrass, have specialized bacterium named *Azotobacter* associated with their roots, which fix atmospheric nitrogen into a form usable by the plant. These bacteria enable the plants to grow in an otherwise nitrogen-poor environment. Young roots secrete carbohydrates which may nourish the nitrogen-fixing bacteria.

The plants in the dune slacks have morphological and physiological adaptations for growth in flooded areas. For example, the sedge American three-square contains large air spaces (aerenchyma) in its stems and roots, which provide an oxygen pathway from the shoots above the water to the oxygen-deprived roots in the flooded soil. When these plants are flooded, they increase their production of the hormone ethylene, which may stimulate the production of aerenchymatous tissue.

Management. Sand dunes form a natural defense against the sea; vegetation holds the sand in place and favors its accretion. Although dune vegetation is very tolerant of wind, windblown sand, and salt, it is sensitive to many human activities. Coastal areas are highly populated, especially in summer. The protec-

Fig. 2. Sea oats are abundant on the foredunes of the Atlantic coast of the southeastern United States. Wrack, decomposing plant material, can be seen on the beach in the zone seaward of the sea oats.

tion of these valuable ecosystems requires good management practices. Access to the beach through the dunes is controlled, and damaged areas are restored with the help of porous fencing, such as snow fence, to trap and accumulate sand in eroded areas. Such fencing can increase the height and width of dunes. The new sand is planted with dune vegetation (**Fig. 3**) growing nearby or in commercial nurseries. These practices have been very successful.

Human disturbances include pedestrian and vehicular traffic, which can cause serious damage. In one typical area that was walked over less than 200 times in a year, more than half of the vegetation disappeared, leaving barren ground.

Off-road vehicular traffic is another serious threat. At the wrack line, it prevents the formation of new dunes by destroying organic matter and causing the

Fig. 3. After one growing season, this planting of American beachgrass is already helping to stabilize this dune. Snow fence was used to trap and hold sand prior to planting.

loss of nutrients, water, and the seedlings themselves. Traffic behind the foredunes is equally destructive. Plants such as beach heather can be completely destroyed, needing years to recover. Tire tracks may remain visible for many seasons. Laws help but may be difficult to enforce. The complete abolition of beach vehicles may become necessary.

The protection of vegetation on the remaining dunes is important for several reasons. Dunes not stabilized by vegetation are highly susceptible to wind and water erosion and threatened with destruction. Their disappearance means a loss of nesting areas for many seabirds, other wildlife habitat, and valuable recreational areas. It would also leave settled areas, now protected by coastal dunes, open to erosion by wind and sea. *SEE EROSION.*

Denise M. Seliskar

Bibliography. V. J. Chapman, *Coastal Vegetation*, 2d ed., 1976; P. J. Godfrey and M. M. Godfrey, Ecological effects of off-road vehicles on Cape Cod, *Oceanus*, 23:56–67, 1980/1981; R. R. Lewis III (ed.), *Creation and Restoration of Coastal Plant Communities*, 1982; D. S. Ranwell, *Ecology of Salt Marshes and Sand Dunes*, 1972; D. S. Ranwell and R. Boar, *Coast Dune Management Guide*, 1986; D. M. Seliskar, Waterlogging stress and ethylene production in the dune slack plant, *Scirpus americanus*, *J. Exper. Bot.*,39:1639–1648, 1988; G. M. Silberhorn, *Common Plants of the Mid-Atlantic Coast*, 1982; A. M. Wiedemann, *The Ecololgy of Pacific Northwest Coastal Sand Dunes: A Community Profile*, 1984.

Dust and mist collection

The physical separation and removal of particles, either solid or liquid, from a gas in which they are suspended. Such separation is required for one or more of the following purposes: (1) to collect a product which has been processed or handled in gas suspension, as in spray-drying or pneumatic conveying; (2) to recover a valuable product inadvertently mixed with processing gases, as in kiln or smelter exhausts; (3) to eliminate a nuisance, as in fly-ash removal; (4) to reduce equipment maintenance, as in engine intake air filters; (5) to eliminate a health, fire, explosion, or safety hazard, as in bagging operations or nuclear separations plant ventilation air; and (6) to improve product quality, as in cleaning of air used in processing pharmaceutical or photographic products. Achievement of these objectives involves primarily gas-handling equipment, but the design must be concerned with the properties and relative amounts of the suspended particles as well as with those of the gas being handled.

All particle collection systems depend upon subjecting the suspended particles to some force which will drive them mechanically to a collecting surface. The known mechanisms by which such deposition can occur may be classed as gravitational, inertial, physical or barrier, electrostatic, molecular or diffusional, and thermal or radiant. There are also mechanisms which can be used to modify the properties of the particles or the gas to increase the effectiveness of the deposition mechanisms. For example, the effective size of particles may be increased by condensing water vapor upon them or by flocculating particles through the action of a sonic vibration. Usually, larger particles simplify the control problem. To function successfully, any collection device must have an adequate means for continuously or periodically removing collected material from the equipment.

Devices for control of particulate material may be considered, by structural or application similarities, in eight categories, which follow.

Gravity settling chamber. In this, the simplest type of device but not necessarily the least expensive, the velocity of the gas is reduced to permit particles to settle out under the action of gravity. Normally, settling chambers are useful for removing particles larger than 50 micrometers in diameter, although with special configurations they may be used to remove particles as small as 10 μm.

Inertial device. The basis of this type of device is that the particles have greater inertia than the gas. The cyclone separator, typical of this type of equipment, is one of the most widely used and least expensive types of dust collector. In a cyclone, the gas usually enters a conical or cylindrical chamber tangentially and leaves axially. Because of the change of direction, the particles are flung to the outer wall, from which they slide into a receiving bin or into a conveyor, while the gases whirl around to the central exit port (**Fig. 1**). A large variety of configurations is available. For large air-handling capacities, an arrangement of multiple small-diameter units in parallel is often used to attain high collection efficiencies and

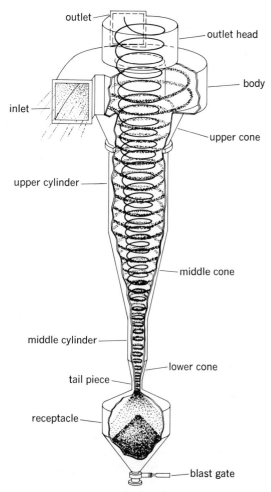

Fig. 1. Cyclone dust separator, an inertial device. (*American Standard Industrial Division*)

to permit lower headroom requirements than a single unit would.

Mechanical inertial units are similar to cyclones except that the rotational motion of the gas is induced by the action of a rotating member. Some such units are designed to act as fans in addition to their dust-collecting function. There are also a wide variety of other units; many are called impingement separators. Most separators that are used to remove entrained liquids from steam or compressed air fall into this category.

Packed bed. A particle-laden gas stream may be cleaned by passing it through a bed or layer of packing composed of granular materials such as sand, coke, gravel, and ceramic rings, or fibrous materials such as glass wool, steel wool, and textile staples. Depending on the application, the bed depth may range from a fraction of an inch to several feet. Coarse packings, which are used at relatively high throughput rates (1–15 ft/s or 0.3–4.5 m/s superficial velocity) to remove large particles, rely primarily on the inertial mechanism for their separating action. Fine packings, operated at lower throughput rates (1–5 ft/min or 0.3–15 m/min superficial velocity) to remove relatively small suspended particles, usually depend on a variety of deposition mechanisms for their separating effect. Packed beds, because of a gradual plugging caused by particle accumulation, are usually limited in use to collecting particles present in the gas at low concentration, unless some provision is made for removing the dust—for example, by periodic or continuous withdrawal of part of the packing for cleaning. Depending on the application and design, the collection efficiencies of packed beds range widely (50–99.999%).

Cloth collector. In such a collector, also known as a bag filter, the dust-laden gas is passed through a woven or felted fabric upon which the gradual deposition of dust forms a precoat, which then serves as a filter for the subsequent dust. These units are analogous to those used in liquid filtration and represent a special type of packed bed. Because the dust accumulates continuously, the resistance to gas flow gradually increases. The cloth must, therefore, be periodically vibrated or flexed, or back-flushed with a stream or pulse of air to dislodge accumulated dust (**Fig. 2**). A wide variety of filter media is available. Cotton or wool sateen or felts are usually used for temperatures below 212°F (100°C). Some of the synthetic fibers may be used at temperatures up to 500°F (260°C). Glass and asbestos or combinations thereof have been used for temperatures up to 650°F (343°C). For special high-temperature applications, metallic screens and porous ceramics or stainless steel have been employed. Collection efficiencies of over 98% are attained readily with cloth collectors, even with very fine dusts.

Scrubber. A scrubber uses a liquid, usually water, to assist in the particulate collection process. An extremely wide variety of equipment is available, ranging from simple modifications of corresponding dry units to permit liquid addition, to devices specifically designed for wet operation only (**Fig. 3**). When properly designed for a given application, scrubbers can give very high collection efficiency, although the mere addition of water to a gas stream is not necessarily effective. For a given application, collection efficiency is primarily a function of the amount of power supplied to the gas stream, in the form of gas

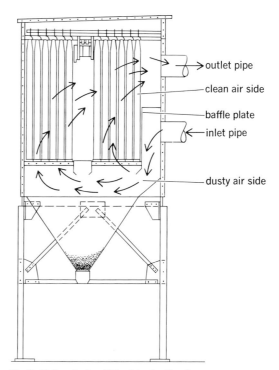

Fig. 2. Cloth collector. (*Wheelabrator Corp.*)

outlet pipe
clean air side
baffle plate
inlet pipe
dusty air side

pressure drop, water pressure, or mechanical energy. With scrubbers it is important that proper attention be given to liquid entrainment separation in order to avoid a spray nuisance. Consideration must also be given to the liquid-sludge disposal problem.

Electrostatic precipitator. Particles may be charged electrically by a corona discharge and caused to migrate to a collecting surface. The single-stage unit, which is commonly known as a Cottrell precipitator, and in which the charging and collecting proceed simultaneously, is the type generally used for industrial or process applications. These units normally employ direct current at voltages ranging from 30,000 to 100,000 V. The two-stage unit, in which charging and collection are carried out successively, is commonly used for air conditioning applications. These units also employ direct current, ranging from 5000 to 13,000 V, and involve close internal clearances (0.25–0.5 in. or 6–12 mm). Electrical precipitators are capable of high collection efficiency of fine particles.

In dry precipitators, collected dust is dislodged by intermittent rapping or vibration of the collection plates with possible dust reentrainment. Another problem arises from high dust resistivity, which causes collected dust to be reentrained by back-ionization because the dust particles are not discharged electrically upon collection. The reentrainment of collected material as flocs in the exhaust gas, a phenomenon known as snowing, must be avoided to prevent a possible accentuated nuisance or vegetation damage problem.

In "wet" electrostatic precipitators, a film of water is allowed to flow over the collecting surface. This serves to minimize problems of dust reentrainment either by mechanical means or by the process of back-ionization. It also provides a means of removing collected dust.

Air filter. This is a unit used to eliminate very small quantities of dust from large quantities of air, as in air conditioning applications. Although units in

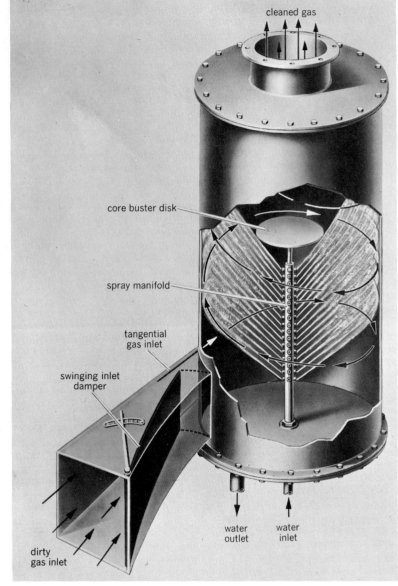

cleaned gas

core buster disk

spray manifold

tangential
gas inlet

swinging inlet
damper

dirty
gas inlet

water
outlet

water
inlet

Fig. 3. Cyclonic liquid scrubber. (*Chemical Construction Corp.*)

precipitation, suspended particles are caused to migrate toward a cold surface or away from a heated surface by the action of a temperature gradient in the gas stream. This principle has found extensive use in atmospheric sampling work. SEE AIR POLLUTION; AIR-POLLUTION CONTROL.

Charles E. Lapple

Bibliography. L. T. Buonicore and A. J. Buonicore, *Air Pollution Control Equipment: Selection Design, Operation,* and *Maintenance,* 1982; R. H. Perry and D. Green (eds.), *Perry's Chemical Engineer's Handbook,* 6th ed., 1984; *Kirk-Othmer Encyclopedia of Chemical Technology,* 3d ed., vol. 1, 1978; C. E. Lapple, Elements of dust and mist collection, *Chem. Eng. Progr.,* 50(6):283–287, 1954; K. E. Lunde and C. E. Lapple, Dust and mist collection, *Chem. Eng. Progr.,* 53(8):385–391, 1957; G. Nonhebel, *Processes for Air Pollution Control,* 1972; W. Strauss and S. J. Mainwaring, *Air Pollution,* 1984.

Dust storm

A strong, turbulent wind bearing large clouds of dust. The suspended dust consists predominantly of mineral particles with diameters less than 100 micrometers. Sand storms differ from dust storms in that the particles are much larger and have high settling speeds. When the wind and turbulence weaken, the larger particles settle out rapidly, leaving behind a cloud of dust with diameters mainly under 20 μm. Wind systems can carry these clouds many thousands of miles, in some cases across oceans.

Sources of dust. Dust storms can occur where the soils are loosely consolidated and poorly protected by vegetation. Soil moisture is critically important, since water binds the soil particles together and supports the growth of plants. Consequently, storms occur most frequently in arid and semiarid regions (**Fig. 1**), with the maximum frequency in regions having an annual rainfall of $4–8 \times 10^{-3}$ in. (100–200 mm). Hyperarid areas such as deep deserts are not particularly good sources, because the surface is often covered with rock and sand, neither of which contains an abundance of fine particles.

Marginal agricultural lands are especially susceptible to storms in the spring when the soils, loosened by plowing and overgrazing, are easily blown away. Extended periods of drought have the same effect, for example, the periodic dust bowl conditions in the Great Plains of the United States. SEE DROUGHT.

Most of the global dust storm activity is concentrated in a belt of arid lands that extends from the west coast of North Africa, through the Middle East and across Central Asia, almost to the Pacific coast. Many locations in this region experience dust storms 30 to 60 days a year.

Soil factors. In typical soils, dust generation begins when winds become strong enough to dislodge particles with diameters of several millimeters and larger (**Fig. 2**). These particles roll across the surface and bounce into the air, where they pick up speed from the wind. When they fall back to the surface, they strike other particles, blasting them into the air. This process is known as saltation. These new particles continue the process, producing an avalanche effect that rapidly sets the entire surface of the soil into motion. Particles larger than about 0.2 in. (5 mm) move in a shallow layer within a few feet of the

this class actually fall into one of the previous classes, they are given a special category because of wide usage and common special features. In this category are viscous-coated fiber-mat filters and dry filters. These are actually a form of packed bed and are frequently known as unit filters. The domestic furnace filter is an example of a viscous-coated unit filter. Automatic filters provided with continuous and automatic cleaning arrangements are available in both the viscous-coated and dry forms, as well as with electrostatic provisions.

Miscellaneous equipment. Electrostatic fields have been used with packed beds, scrubbers, and air filters to improve collection efficiency, and with cloth collectors to dislodge dust from the cloth. Acoustic or sonic vibrations imparted to a gas stream cause particulates to collide and flocculate, forming larger particles that are more readily collected in conventional apparatus. This principle has been employed, but has had extremely limited application because of economic and other practical considerations. In thermal

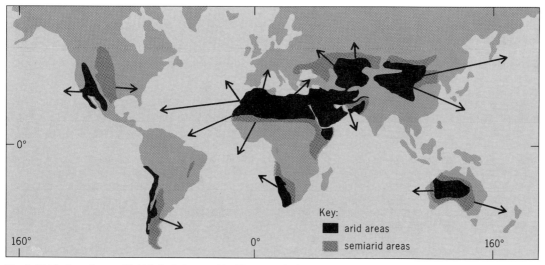

Fig. 1. Distribution of areas with high dust storm activity. The arrows indicate the major trajectories that dust storms follow. (*After K. Pye, Aeolian Dust and Dust Deposits, Academic Press, 1987*)

ground. Smaller particles will be blasted into the air with the large particles; because of their smaller settling velocity, they will not fall back to the surface so rapidly. In this manner, a cloud of dust particles rapidly fills the turbulent atmospheric boundary layer. The depth of this boundary layer can vary greatly, depending on meteorological conditions.

Dust generation can be impeded in a number of ways. Vegetation reduces the force of the wind on the surface, and roots tend to hold the soil together. Soil cohesiveness is increased if the soil surface is minimally disturbed. Improper tilling and overgrazing are prime factors in wind erosion. *See Erosion.*

Meteorological factors. The wind speed required to generate dust varies widely according to soil characteristics. Typical values are 9–29 mi/h (4–13 m/s) for poorly sorted river sediments; 11–36 mi/h (5–16 m/s) for various desert environments including the deep Sahara; and 25–36 mi/h (11–16 m/s) for areas in Colorado and Arizona.

The area covered by the dust cloud and its height will depend on the meteorological conditions that generate the winds. Dust devils normally have a diameter of a few meters at most, and the height of the vortex is usually in the range of 10–300 ft (3–100 m). Although dust devils are small, they are commonplace, and in many areas they are probably responsible for much of the low-level dust generated under normal wind conditions.

In some areas, dust is commonly generated by cold downdrafts from cumulonimbus clouds. Known as haboobs, these generally last for 30 min to an hour, and they typically carry dust to heights of several hundred yards, at times to several thousand yards. The dust-generating area is confined to the region of the cloud and usually covers an area of tens to a few hundred square miles.

Major dust storms are associated with large-scale atmospheric features. The close positioning of high- and low-pressure centers produces a tight pressure gradient and strong winds. This situation is responsible for many dust events in the Middle East and for the Santa Ana in the western United States. Dust generated under these conditions is usually confined to the lower mile of the atmosphere. *See Air pressure; Wind.*

Cold fronts are responsible for truly large dust events that can be carried great distances. The vigorous winds associated with fronts are effective in generating dust over large areas. Moreover, the stronger atmospheric lifting ahead of the front can carry the dust to great altitudes, 10,000–23,000 ft (3–7 km). The high winds found at these altitudes can transport the dust thousands of miles in a few days. In China, storms of this type produce heavy dust over thousands of square miles and subsequently carry the dust over large areas of the North Pacific Ocean. The movement of these large dust clouds can be readily observed in satellite imagery. *See Air mass; Atmosphere; Front.*

Effects of dust. Dust plays a further role in weather in that mineral particles serve as condensation and freezing nuclei which are essential for the formation of clouds. Dust clouds typically contain particle concentrations of 10^{-7} to 10^{-4} oz/ft^3 (10^2 to 10^5 micrograms/m^3). These amounts can severely reduce visibility, causing problems for air, ship, and ground traffic over large areas. *See Cloud physics.*

Dust can alter the distribution of solar energy in the Earth–atmosphere system, reducing the amount reaching the Earth's surface and producing heating in the troposphere. These effects can alter the dynamics

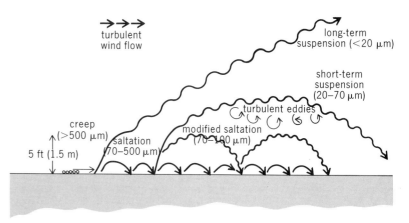

Fig. 2. Dust generation and transport near the soil surface. The bouncing dislodges both large particles, which continue the saltation process, and small particles, which can go into suspension. (*After K. Pye, Aeolian Dust and Dust Deposits, Academic Press, 1987*)

of the atmosphere. Large amounts of dust as hypothesized in the nuclear winter scenarios would dramatically alter climate. SEE ATMOSPHERIC GENERAL CIRCULATION; CLIMATE MODIFICATION.

The impact of windblown dust on surfaces can produce large electrostatic charges that can affect the operation of electronic equipment. The inhalation of large quantities of dust can result in a variety of lung damage, the degree of damage depending on the composition of the dust (for example, asbestos). Organisms associated with the soil particles can also cause diseases, some of them quite serious.

Bibliography. R. A. Bagnold, *The Physics of Blown Sand and Desert Dunes*, 1941; D. A. Gillette et al., Threshold friction velocities and rupture moduli for crushed desert soils for input of soil particles into air, *J. Geophys. Res.*, 87:9003–9015, 1982; T. L. Pewe, *Desert Dust: Origin, Characteristics, and Effect on Man*, Geol. Soc. Amer. Spec. Pap. 186, 1981; J. M. Prospero, Aeolian transport to the world ocean, in *The Sea*, vol. 7: *Oceanic Lithosphere*, ed. by C. Emiliani, 1981; K. Pye, *Aeolian Dust and Dust Deposits*, 1987.

Earth resource patterns

The physical character and distribution of natural resources at the face of the Earth. No section of the Earth is exactly like any other in its resource endowment. Nevertheless, the fundamental differences between land and ocean, latitudinal differences in insolation, spatial variations in receipts of precipitation, and patterns of geological composition and deformation of the Earth's crust together provide the basis for distinguishing definite geographical patterns of resource availability over the world.

Delineation of the Earth's resource patterns begins with differentiation between continental and marine resources. Although the resources of the oceans and seas have been used by people since earliest times, the more than 4,000,000,000 on the Earth today are primarily dependent upon the resources of the land for their existence.

Five principal resources associated with the land are soils, forests, grasslands, fresh-water resources, and minerals. Although other resources such as native animal life may be of local importance, and although the very concept of "resources" has been extended to include such complexes as recreation resources, these five land resources remain of fundamental importance for the material support of human life.

Two sets of underlying causes in particular engender the spatial patterns of resources over the Earth. One set of causes consists of the basic climatic controls, including latitude, distribution of land and water, the wind and pressure system of the rotating Earth, the major landforms of the continents, and the elevation of the land surface above sea level. A second, independent set of causes consists of the tectonic and rock-forming processes which have operated over the Earth. The climatic controls account for a system of regional climates over the continents, and these climates in turn provide keys for understanding the spatial distribution of forests, grasslands, and fresh-water resources, as well as some of the fundamental attributes of soils and the agriculture they support. The second set of causes may be regarded as even more fundamental since the movements of the Earth's plates and their associated continents in conjunction

with the Earth's plate tectonics account not only for the position on the Earth and hence the latitudinal location of each continent, but also for the global distribution of land and water and continental landforms, all with consequences for regional climatic patterns. Moreover, rock composition and surface configuration also produce overlays of difference on forests, grasslands, water resources, and soils which alter the patterns within the climatic regions, and they are fundamental to an understanding of the global patterns of minerals on and beneath the Earth's surface.

Climatic types. Eleven regional climatic types (numbered consecutively in the **illustration**) in four groups are recognized in describing the Earth's resource patterns of forests, grasslands, soils, and fresh water. This number of types is fewer than that normally employed to describe regional climates, but is considered adequate to outline the basic global patterns of each of these four major renewable resources. Distinction is made between the so-called humid climates and the water-deficient climates, with subtypes as follows:

Humid microthermal
 1. Polar and ice cap
 2. Tundra
 3. Taiga
 4. Puna
Humid mesothermal
 5. Upper midlatitude
 6. Humid subtropical
Humid macrothermal
 7. Wet-and-dry
 8. Rainforest
Water-deficient
 9. Desert
 10. Semiarid
 11. Mediterranean

Humid microthermal regions. These areas of predominantly low temperature are so unfavorable to soil formation and use in agriculture that under present techniques their population-carrying capacity is low even in those regions with the warmest summers.

1. In polar and ice cap areas where soils and vegetative growth are essentially absent, available resources necessarily are dominantly marine and land animal life, on which the sparse native human settlement is almost wholly dependent. Despite the enormous size of the Antarctic, settlements are exclusively in the Arctic, except for special government-supported Antarctic stations.

2. Tundra, except for minor alpine locations, is entirely within the Northern Hemisphere. The principal renewable resources are lichens and the native animal life, such as reindeer and caribous, which can use these as food. Parts of the tundra may be considered a grazing land, as managed herds of reindeer are pastured nomadically. The natural resource significance of tundra lands for the larger world may be greatly enhanced locally where minerals are being extracted, such as the oil field adjacent to Prudhoe Bay on Alaska's North Slope. SEE TUNDRA.

3. Millions of acres of boreal coniferous forest, or taiga, located in a broad curving zone from Scandinavia across the northern, European part of the former Soviet Union, and Siberia, and, east of the Bering Sea, across much of Alaska and northern Canada, has given its name to this climatic belt. Varieties of spruce, fir, and larch, which are of particular signifi-

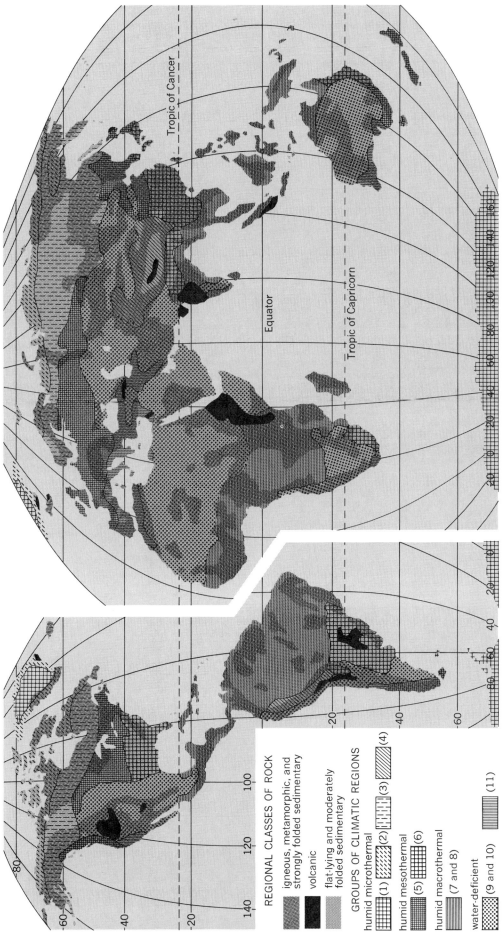

REGIONAL CLASSES OF ROCK

igneous, metamorphic, and
strongly folded sedimentary

volcanic

flat-lying and moderately
folded sedimentary

GROUPS OF CLIMATIC REGIONS

humid microthermal

(1)   (2)   (3)   (4)

humid mesothermal

(5)   (6)

humid macrothermal

(7 and 8)

water-deficient

(9 and 10)   (11)

Map showing predominant Earth resource patterns. Climate types identified as: (1) polar and ice cap, (2) tundra, (3) taiga, (4) puna, (5) upper midlatitude, (6) humid subtropical, (7 and 8) wet-and-dry and rainforest, (9 and 10) desert and semiarid, (11) mediterranean. The map is a flat polar quartic equal-area projection.

cance to the pulping industries, constitute the most valuable known renewable resource of the humid microthermal regions. The zone of taiga climate is of scant importance for agriculture; soils are predominantly thin, stony, and infertile, and development for agriculture is further discouraged by the possible incidence of frost in every month of the year and by the short growing season of 80 days or less. As in the case of the areas of tundra climate, the resource significance of particular localities within the taiga zone is locally enhanced by deposits of minerals, including gold, iron, and uranium. Fresh-water resources are large, and some hydroelectric power is developed. *See Taiga.*

4. The puna type of climate is found at much lower latitudes but at elevations generally 10,000 ft (3048 m) or more above sea level, and is characteristically cold. Certain plateaus, particularly the high plateau of Tibet and the intermontane Andean plateau (Altiplano) of southeastern Peru and western Bolivia, belong to this group. Low temperatures preclude tree growth, and the principal renewable resource is low-productivity grazing land. Thin, stony soils are limited in production to hardy small grains and root crops. The resource significance of the South American puna is greatly enhanced by metal deposits, particularly those of copper, tin, lead, and zinc.

Humid mesothermal regions. Considered in the light of present-day technology, the heart of the world's renewable natural resource base is in the humid mesothermal regions with their generally adequate precipitation and generally intermediate temperatures. They contain a large share of the world's most productive soils which support both crop and pasture lands. Some productive coniferous and broad-leaf forests occur in these climatic regions. Concentrated surface and subsurface fresh-water supplies are relatively abundant, but owing to the high population densities and major urban and industrial complexes in these regions, the water resources are often intensively developed to the point where both quantitative and qualitative problems develop.

5. Upper midlatitude climate contains most of the lands adapted to the raising of wheat, barley, rye, and oats. In addition, certain areas within this climatic type, and particularly the North American corn belt and the Middle Danube Basin and the North Italian Plain, also produce maize. Further crops, including soybeans, are also important, and extensive forage cropping supports dairying and meat animal raising in east-central North America, western and central Europe, and the nonarid part of the southern European Soviet Union. The lands which support the agricultural types of this climatic region possess the most extensive areas of superior soils on Earth. They are relatively deep and are often moderately to highly endowed with plant nutrients and humus. Some of the best soils have developed from glacial drift; others have benefited from the deposition of fine-grained windblown loess deposits during the glacial period. Extensive preagricultural grasslands also contributed high humus content to some of the soils. Finally, the extensive plains under which these soils are deployed, and the generally favorable growing season conditions of temperature and rainfall, also underlie the present high productivity of the agriculture supported by the soils in this climatic type. It is within the upper midlatitude climate that the region of greatest surplus food production (the North American interior) at present exists.

6. Humid subtropical areas have an ample water supply and relatively long growing season (200 days or longer), making the best of these lands potentially very productive for crops or for forest products. Soils other than in floodplains tend to be less fertile than those of upper midlatitudes, however, owing to the effects of relatively high rainfall and temperatures on the removal of plant nutrients, and generally require fertilization for sustained cultivation over long periods. Where cropping is on alluvial soils of floodplains large and small, as in central and southern China and in southern Japan, and in the Ganges Plain of India, soils are more easily maintained at high levels of productivity. High rural population densities generally preclude the generation of large exportable food surpluses from regions with the best soils. Although the favorable combination of temperature and moisture can result in high timber growth, as on the best-managed tracts of forest in the American South, the potential is not realized in other areas of the Earth having this type of climate, owing to previous large-scale deforestation. Water resources are generally abundant; in part of southern and eastern Asia, fresh-water resources underlie the most extensive humid land irrigation in the world—namely, for paddy rice.

Humid macrothermal regions. These predominantly winterless regions of warm to hot temperatures are divided according to the regime of rainfall: (7) wet-and-dry, with a pronounced dry season, and (8) rainforest, with year-round growing seasons, but over extensive areas their soils are lateritic with a high iron content, and harden irreparably under use for cropping. Problems induced by fungal growth, bacterial disease, and insect abundance also handicap the use of the soil resources. Within the great alluvial valleys, flooding may also be disruptive. Owing to these adverse factors, shifting cultivation is common, and much land is not in production at any particular time. Within the rainforest regions, extensive and rapid-growing forests occur, including the largest such forest area on the Earth in the Amazon Basin, but are mostly unexploited commercially in the twentieth-century economy. Extensive clearing of the Amazon forest for agricultural development appears likely during the last two decades of the twentieth century. Sites of enormous potential hydroelectric generation are largely undeveloped. *See Rainforest.*

Water-deficient regions. Receipts of moisture are scant or lacking during much of the year. Except where exotic water supplies are available for irrigation, soils inherently are less productive than those of any humid region with comparable land surface. There are three major subdivisions.

9. Deserts differ strikingly in their form and in temperature conditions, but everywhere present meager resources for agriculture. Where water is available, desert oases blossom, but vast areas contain only scrub growth, ephemerals, or virtually no vegetation. Livestock-carrying capacity of desert scrub is meager. Sparsity of vegetation has made mineral prospecting and exploration somewhat easier than in vegetation-covered humid areas, and in this century desert occupancy often started with mineral discoveries. *See Desert.*

10. The semiarid regions are basically grasslands, which have grazing as their characteristic resource use. Because of cyclic rainfall variability, people have converted the inherently fertile soils, as in China and the United States, to cereal growing during periods of higher rainfall. Rainfall fluctuations, however,

make the soils unstable under cultivation. For this reason, these regions have suffered consistently from unsuited cultivation and overgrazing. Semiarid lands are responsive to and most productive under irrigation, but neither surface-water nor groundwater resources are adequate to irrigate more than a fraction of the area. *See Grassland ecosystem.*

11. Regions of mediterranean climate, because of their winter rainfall, generally are classed as humid lands. However, the greater part of the gowing season is water-deficient, and the most productive agricultural lands depend on irrigation. Soils are the major resource since water deficiency is pronounced enough to discourage forest productivity. Major mineral deposits may complement agricultural lands in a few areas. *See Climatology.*

Rock composition and surface configuration. Imposed on the basic resource pattern induced by climatic differences are variations in rock composition and surface configuration which cause intraregional differences within the pattern. Although not exactly the same in their effects, the variations caused by these two geographical elements are often concomitant and may be treated together as follows:

1. Rock composition and structure
   a. Flat-lying and moderately folded sedimentary rocks
   b. Igneous, metamorphic, strongly folded sedimentary rocks
   c. Volcanic rocks
2. Surface configuration
   a. Floodplains and other flat or gently sloped surfaces
   b. Mountains and maturely dissected hill lands, plateau faces, or faces of cuestas

These elements of crustal variation produce the six following geographical differences in resource endowment:

First, all major agricultural lands are on flat-lying or moderately folded sediments and have gentle slopes, well exemplified in such alluvial valleys as the Mississippi, Nile, Huang, and Ganges-Brahmaputra, and such other outstanding agricultural areas as the North American corn belt or the Paris Basin.

Second, productive secondary agricultural lands, particularly in the tropics, are located on volcanic areas where soils have been formed through weathering or wind action. Examples include the Deccan Plateau in west-central peninsular India, and volcanic soils fringing much of the central mountain backbone of Java.

Third, agricultural lands are extremely limited on igneous rock areas, no matter what the surface configuration, in regions north of 40°N latitude, as illustrated in the Laurentian Shield area of Canada and the Fenno-Scandian Shield in northern Europe. In the humid tropical and subtropical climates, however, where weathering has proceeded long enough to produce a substantial soil mantle as on the Piedmont of the southeastern United States, underlying igneous rocks do not have the same negative effect on agricultural development.

Fourth, forest lands are not limited in their extent (although limited in productivity) by either crustal rock composition or surface configuration.

Fifth, mountains are important catchment areas and sources of fresh water and the services which may be derived from water. Most hydroelectric generation, or

generation potential, is associated with mountains. In arid and semiarid regions, mountains are sources of water for irrigation, domestic and industrial supply, wood products, and warm-season grazing lands.

Sixth, mineral resources have definite patterns which are associated with rock structure and composition. Major deposits of coal and lignite, petroleum, and natural gas are, with few exceptions, found in flat-lying or gently folded and faulted sedimentary rocks, as in Texan oil fields and the coal fields of the Allegheny Plateau. Sedimentary nonmetallics (the phosphates, potash, sulfur, nitrates, and limestone) as well as bauxite and uranium (carnotite) also are associated with sedimentary rocks.

Associated with the igneous and metamorphic rock areas are most metals, for example, iron (usually), lead, copper, tin, the ferroalloys, gold, and silver. Most gems and some nonmetallic minerals (mica and asbestos) are found in the same associations. Uranium (pitchblende) occurs in these rocks.

Whereas these associations are well recognized, the mineral deposits themselves have a highly erratic geographical occurrence owing to the great variety of processes involving both mineral enrichment and dispersal which have occurred. The broad global pattern of rock classes with which minerals are related is delineated on the accompanying map.

Employed and potential resources. Resources have meaning insofar as they are placed in use or are available for future exploitation. Distinction must be made between the employed and the potential resources. In practice this distinction is complex, but here only the simple geographical distinction will be noted. Employed resources are those which are significant to the present support of humans, at least locally. In general, the denser the population and the more advanced the technical arts of an area, the greater the need for production from resources, and employed resources become more nearly synonymous with all known resources. Thus, the recognized resources of the European peninsula and of the northeastern United States are mainly employed resources. On the other hand, the natural resources of the Amazon Basin or of much of Siberia are still largely potential resources.

Marine resources. Although the physical and biotic geography of the oceans is much less fully explored than that of the continents, enough is known to indicate that both living and mineral resources extend far beyond those presently exploited. The employed resources are rather sharply localized. The principal exploitation of marine animals and vegetation occurs: over the continental shelves; in the vicinity of the mixing of warm and cold currents; near large upwellings which occur particularly off the west coast of continents in lower middle latitudes; and adjacent to densely populated countries. Thus, the North Atlantic near Europe and from New England to Newfoundland contains heavily exploited fishing grounds, as do the seas near Japan, Korea, and southern California, and also waters of the Gulf of Mexico.

Minerals are derived from three separate types of marine sources: from sedimentary deposits underlying the continental shelves; from inshore deposits on the surface of the continental shelves; and from seawater. By far the most valuable of the mineral resources exploited from marine environments is petroleum; there has been an expansion of exploration, drilling, and pumping from beneath continental shelf waters, as off the Gulf coast of Louisiana and in the middle of the

North Sea between Scotland and Norway. Offshore placer deposits on the surface of the continental shelves yield gold, platinum, and tin. Common salt, magnesium, and bromine are derived directly from seawater.

Potential marine resources include: the population of life-forms now exploited in some parts of the world, but not in others; animal and vegetative species now unused; fresh water from desalted seawater; and minerals so far unexploited which are in solution, are precipitated to the ocean bottom, or lie within rock below the surface of the continental shelf. One of the interesting speculative resources appears in the large quantities of so-called manganese nodules that cover some sections of sea bottoms at intermediate depths. SEE MARINE RESOURCES.

Resources of the continents.
The resource pattern of the Earth may be summarized in a brief description of that for each continent and its neighboring waters.

Eurasian continent. As the largest landmass in the world, the Eurasian continent has the largest area of agricultural land in use, a very extensive total forest land area in which the softwood coniferous forest belt from Scandinavia to eastern Siberia predominates, and a wide variety of mineral resources. Great differences mark the major sections of the continent. The most productive agricultural areas are generally near the edge of the landmass, in western and central Europe and extending eastward into much of the central and southern sections of the former Soviet Union in Europe; in the Indian subcontinent; and in mainland east Asia from the Red River valley in Vietnam northward to the Great Wall of China. The aggregate mineral endowment is outstanding and includes the largest known aggregate iron ore reserves in the world within the former Soviet Union, located particularly in districts adjacent to the Urals; very substantial coal deposits, including the Ruhr field and the extensive coal beds in northern China and Manchuria; and what increasingly appears to be one of the two great concentrations of petroleum fields on Earth, namely, the Persian Gulf fields shared by a number of separate states in the Middle East. The southeastern and eastern borders of the Eurasian heartland, moreover, have some of the great, but still undeveloped, hydroelectric generation sites of the world. Off the coasts of western Europe and Japan are the two most productively employed fisheries of the world.

Africa and Australia. Much of the entire area of Africa north of approximately 12°N must be classed as desert or semiarid, with few exotic water sources other than the Nile. Much of the remainder of the continent has wet-and-dry or rainforest climates, with the former predominating greatly in area. Seasonal drought, soil infertility, and widespread problems of laterization handicap agricultural exploitation. The east African highlands from Ethiopia southward, the high veld in South Africa, and the loftier sections of Zimbabwe Rhodesia and the Nile Valley and Delta are noteworthy exceptions. Except along the Nile there are still potential agricultural land resources, but they are comparatively minor. Associated with the extensive areas of igneous and metamorphic rocks which underlie much of the continent and particularly its southern half are outstanding deposits of metalliferous minerals, such as the copper ores astride the Zaire-Zambia boundary, the chrome-bearing ores of Zimbabwe Rhodesia, and the gold deposits of the Witwatersrand in South Africa. Other mineral resources include diamonds, uranium, and, in Nigeria and the far north of the continent (Libya, Algeria), petroleum and natural gas. The water resources of mid-Africa include the largest potential hydroelectric power on Earth.

Similar general remarks may be made about Australia, whose much smaller area is covered mostly by desert, semiarid, and tropical wet-and-dry environments. Most agricultural productivity is peripheral, especially in the southeast. Metallic minerals at currently exploitable levels of size and richness support a substantial number of mining operations on the continent.

South America. The land resource is dominated by the unbroken extent of rainforest and wet-and-dry climates stretching east of the Andes from Colombia to northern Argentina and by substantial areas of water-deficient territory along the west coast and in the south and northeast of the South American continent. Some highly fertile soils in flat humid subtropical lands both west and east of the Paraná–La Plata river system are of minor extent by comparison with the whole. The Amazon Basin contains the largest stand of tropical hardwood forest on Earth. Metallic mineral resources are abundant in three general regions: the Andes, the largely crystalline rock highlands of eastern and southeastern Brazil, and the low plateau south of the lower Orinoco River. The Caribbean coast of Venezuela has the most productive petroleum reserves on the continent.

North America. Large sections of North American lands benefit from the advantages which characterize midlatitude humid-land resources under present technology. Disadvantages of desert and semiarid environments in much of the western half of the North American continent are tempered somewhat by the interspersal of mountain ranges throughout these drier regions. Taiga and other northern climatic environments are in considerable part coincident with the igneous and metamorphic rocks of the Laurentian Shield; and tropical environments are of small extent. In sum, this continent may be considered to have one of the best-balanced sets of resources, considering its substantial endowment in minerals of many different kinds, extensive forest lands, large annually renewed fresh-water supplies, great and varied agricultural lands, and the productive fisheries off both Atlantic and Pacific coasts. In addition, evidence has accumulated that in the southern, Latin American section of the continent there may exist a major concentration of petroleum and natural gas resources extending southeastward from eastern Mexico and the contiguous continental shelf beneath the waters of the Gulf of Mexico to the fringes of the western Caribbean, with eventual productivity on the order of magnitude of the cluster of fields in the Middle East. Finally, North America has the highest ratio of employed resources to land area of all continents. In addition, it still contains considerable potential resources.

Summary comment.
The Earth's resource pattern has certain general characteristics. (1) Minerals usable under present technology are found in every environment, although mineral types differ according to location in sedimentary or igneous and metamorphic rock areas. Mineral exploration will continue indefinitely in all land areas, but the mineral resource possibilities of North America and the European part of the Eurasian continent have been examined in greater detail than those of any other large area. Ocean basins

are the least-known part of the world as to mineral possibilities. (2) Agricultural lands and forest lands usable under present technology are dominated by those lying in midlatitudes. Sections of the taiga are important as forest resources. (3) The great potential agricultural and forest resources, if some technological improvement is assumed, lie within the humid tropical environments.

Donald J. Patton

Bibliography. P. R. Cresson and K. D. Frederick, *The World Food Situation: Resource and Environmental Issues in the Developing Countries and the United States*, 1977; S. L. Cutter et al., *Exploitation, Conservation, Preservation: A Geographic Perspective on Natural Resource Use*, 1985; J. F. McDivitt and G. Manners, *Minerals and Men: An Exploration of the World of Minerals and Metals, Including Some of the Major Problems That Are Posed*, 1974; I. G. Simmons, *The Ecology of Natural Resources*, 2d ed., 1981.

Earth sciences

Sciences that involve attempts to understand the nature, origin, evolution, and behavior of the Earth or of its parts and to comprehend Earth's place in the universe and especially in the solar system. Geophysics is the study of the physics of the Earth, emphasizing its physical structure and dynamics. Geochemistry is the study of the chemistry of the Earth, dealing with its composition and chemical change. Geology is the study of the solid Earth and of the processes that have formed and modified it throughout its 4.5-billion-year history.

Geology can also be defined simply as the study of the Earth, and by that definition it includes all of the earth sciences. Geologists seek to determine the origin, history, and processes of the Earth from study of rocks. Each of the following major branches of geology is considered a separate science by many. Mineralogy is the study of the composition, structure, and properties of minerals, Petrography is the description and classification of rocks. Petrology is more inclusive and includes the origin of rocks. Many specialties are possible in petrology and petrography, such as sedimentology and volcanology. Stratigraphy is the interpretation of the origin and age of layered, generally sedimentary rocks. Paleontology is the study of ancient (fossil) life. Historical geology is the study of the evolution of the Earth and its life. Geomorphology is the study of landscapes and their evolution. Hydrology is the study of water on the continents. Seismology is the study of earthquakes and their effects. Structural geology is the study of deformed rocks. Engineering geology is geology applied to design of structures and the like. *See* GEOMORPHOLOGY; HYDROLOGY.

Oceanography is the study of the oceans; limnology, the study of lakes; hydrology, the study of underground and surface water; and glaciology, the study of glaciers and ice caps. Together, these disciplines embrace the study of the aqueous parts of the Earth. The gaseous outer regions of the Earth are the province of the atmospheric sciences, including meteorology, which is concerned with the weather and weather forecasting; climatology, which deals with longer-term and regional variations; and aeronomy, which, because it deals with the outermost ionized parts of the atmosphere, is much concerned with solar terrestrial relationships, including such features as the Aurora Borealis and Aurora Australis. The biosphere embodies all life on Earth, and its study includes zoology, botany, and ecology. Geography, the study of all aspects of the Earth's surface, is distinctive because it includes not only aspects of the physical and biological sciences but also the social sciences, especially political science and economics. *See* BIOSPHERE; CLIMATOLOGY; HYDROLOGY; LIMNOLOGY; METEOROLOGY; OCEANOGRAPHY.

A great deal of overlap exists among the earth sciences, and all are divided into many subdisciplines. However, in the latter half of the twentieth century, and especially since the International Geophysical Year (IGY) in 1957, a trend has developed toward integration of the geosphere–biosphere system. For example, the rise in so-called greenhouse gases related to the burning of fossil fuel and the destruction of forests can be expected to lead to warming of the troposphere (the lower atmosphere) and indirectly to a rise in sea level. However, because the biogeochemical processes and the climatic–biotic reactions involved are not yet completely understood, it is not possible to predict either how large these changes may be or what other changes (for example changes in desert extent and agricultural productivity) may accompany them. Concern that unprecedented changes in the global environment may occur early in the twenty-first century has given both scientists and politicians a new interest in the science of the Earth system. *See* BIOGEOCHEMISTRY; GREENHOUSE EFFECT.

Another change that began with the IGY has been that Earth-observing instruments are regularly deployed on satellites both in geostationary and in low Earth orbit. These devices have revolutionized such earth sciences as meteorology and oceanography, and the introduction of this capability for monitoring changes in the behavior of the Earth system from space came just when continuing global observation was recognized to be a basic requirement.

The coming of the space age has given earth scientists yet another perspective, because the exploration of the Moon and planets has led to comparisons that have helped in understanding the origin of the Earth as well as its structure, composition, and evolution. These studies have led to ideas such as that the Moon originated as the result of a collision between the Earth and an object approximately the size of Mars (0.1 of the Earth's mass) very early in Earth history. The application of geological concepts and methods to the study of the terrestrial planets and to the rocky and icy satellites of the giant planets is known as planetology, a discipline that has grown rapidly.

Kevin Burke

Bibliography. National Aeronautics and Space Administration, *Earth System Science: A Program for Global Change*, 1988; F. Press and R. Siever, *Earth*, 4th ed., 1986.

Earthquake

A phenomenon during the occurrence of which the Earth's crust is set shaking for a period of time. The shaking is caused by the passage through the Earth of seismic waves—low-frequency sound waves that are emanated from a point in the Earth's interior where a

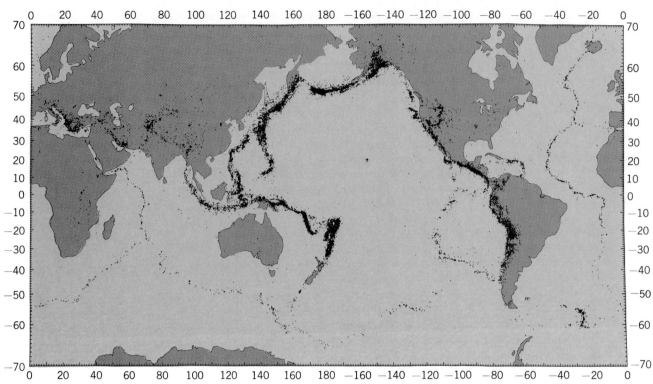

Fig. 1. Seismicity of the Earth from 1961 to 1967; depths to 700 km. The earthquake belts mark the plate boundaries. The number scales indicate latitude and longitude. (*After M. Barazangi and J. Dorman, World seismicity maps compiled from ESSA, Coast and Geodetic Survey, Epicenter Data, 1961–1967, Bull. Seis. Soc. Amer., 59:369–380, 1969*)

sudden, rapid motion has taken place. It is more appropriate to use the term earthquake to refer to the source of seismic waves, rather than the shaking phenomenon, which is an effect of the earthquake.

CHARACTERISTICS

Earthquakes vary immensely in size, from tiny events that can be detected only with the most sensitive seismographs, to great earthquakes that can cause extensive damage over widespread areas. Although thousands of earthquakes occur every day, and have for billions of years, a truly great earthquake occurs somewhere in the world only once every 2 or 3 years. When a great earthquake occurs near a highly populated region, tremendous destruction can occur within a few seconds. In 1976, 600,000 people were killed in Tangshan, China, by a single earthquake. The city

of Lisbon, one of the principal capitals of that day, was utterly destroyed, with high loss of life, in 1755. In the twentieth century such cities as Tokyo and San Francisco have been leveled by earthquakes. In these more modern cases, much of the damage was not due to the shaking of the earthquake itself, but was caused by fires originating in the gas and electrical lines which interweave modern cities, and by damage to fire-fighting capability which rendered the cities helpless to fight the conflagrations.

Cause. The locations of earthquakes which occurred between 1961 and 1967 are shown on the map in **Fig. 1**. The map shows that earthquakes are not distributed randomly over the globe but tend to occur in narrow, continuous belts of activity. These earthquake belts link up so that they encircle large regions, known as plates, which are relatively quiet, although no region is immune. The plates are in continuous motion with respect to one another at rates on the order of centimeters per year; this plate motion is responsible for most geological activity.

Plate motion occurs because the outer cold, hard skin of the Earth, the lithosphere, overlies a hotter, soft layer known as the asthenosphere. Heat from decay of radioactive minerals in the Earth's interior sets the asthenosphere into thermal convection. This convection has broken the lithosphere into plates which move about in response to the convective motion in a manner shown schematically in **Fig. 2**. The plates move apart at oceanic ridges. Magma wells up in the void created by this motion and solidifies to form new sea floor. This process, in which new sea floor is continually created at oceanic ridges, is called sea-floor spreading. Since new lithosphere is continually being created at the oceanic ridges by sea-floor spreading, a like amount of lithosphere must be destroyed some-

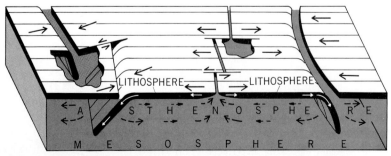

Fig. 2. Movement of the lithosphere over the more fluid asthenosphere. In the center, the lithosphere spreads away from the oceanic ridges. At the edges of the diagram, it descends again into the asthenosphere at the trenches. (*After B. Isacks, Oliver, and L. R. Sykes, Seismology and the new global tectonics, J. Geophys. Res., 73:5855–5899, American Geophysical Union, 1968*)

where. This occurs at the oceanic trenches, where plates converge and the oceanic lithosphere is thrust back down into the asthenosphere and remelted. The melting of the lithosphere in this way supplies the magma for the volcanic arcs which occur behind the trenches. Where two continents collide, however, the greater bouyancy of the less dense continental material prevents the lithosphere from being underthrust, and the lithosphere buckles under the force of the collision, forming great mountain ranges such as the Alps and Himalayas. Where the relative motion of the plates is parallel to their common boundary, slip occurs along great faults which form that boundary, such as the San Andreas fault in California.

According to the theory of plate tectonics, the motion of the plates is very similar to the movement of ice floes in arctic waters. Where floes diverge, leads form and waters. Where floes diverge, leads form and water wells up, freezing to the floes and producing new floe ice. The formation of pressure ridges where floes converge is analogous to the development of mountain ranges where plates converge.

Stick-slip friction and elastic rebound. As the plates move past each other, the motion at their boundaries does not occur by continuous slippage but in a series of rapid jerks. Each jerk is an earthquake. This happens because, under the pressure and temperature conditions of the shallow part of the Earth's lithosphere, the frictional sliding of rock exhibits a property known as stick-slip, in which frictional sliding occurs in a series of jerky movements, interspersed with periods of no motion—or sticking. In the geologic time frame, then, the lithospheric plates chatter at their boundaries, and at any one place the time between chatters may be hundreds of years.

The periods between major earthquakes is thus one during which strain slowly builds up near the plate boundary in response to the continuous movement of the plates. The strain is ultimately released by an earthquake when the frictional strength of the plate boundary is exceeded. This pattern of strain buildup and release was discovered by H. F. Reid in his study of the 1906 San Francisco earthquake. During that earthquake, a 250-mi-long (400-km) portion of the San Andreas fault, from Cape Mendocino to the town of Gilroy, south of San Francisco, slipped an average of 12 ft (3.6 m). Subsequently, the triangulation network in the San Francisco Bay area was resurveyed; it was found that the west side of the fault had moved northward with respect to the east side, but that these motions died out at distances of 20 mi (32 km) or more from the fault. Reid had noticed, however, that measurements made about 40 years prior to the 1906 earthquake had shown that points far to the west of the fault were moving northward at a slow rate. From these clues, he deduced his theory of elastic rebound, illustrated schematically in **Fig. 3**. The figure is a map view, the vertical line representing the fault separating two moving plates. The unstrained rocks in Fig. 3a are distorted by the slow movement of the plates in Fig. 3b. Slippage in an earthquake, returning the rocks to an unstrained state, occurs as in Fig. 3c.

Classification. Most great earthquakes occur on the boundaries between lithospheric plates and arise directly from the motions between the plates. Although these may be called plate boundary earthquakes, there are many earthquakes, sometimes of substantial size, that cannot be related so simply to the movements of the plates.

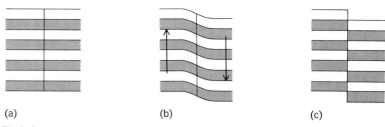

Fig. 3. Schematic of elastic rebound theory. (a) Unstrained rocks (b) are distorted by relative movement between the two plates, causing strains within the fault zone that finally become so great that (c) the rocks break and rebound to a new unstrained position. (*After C. R. Allen, The San Andreas Fault, Eng. Sci. Mag., Calif. Inst. Technol., pp. 1–5, May 1957*)

Near many plate boundaries, earthquakes are not restricted to the plate boundary itself, but occur over a broad zone—often several hundred miles wide—adjacent to the plate boundary. These earthquakes, which may be called plate boundary–related earthquakes, do not reflect the plate motions directly, but are secondarily caused by the stresses set up at the plate boundary. In Japan, for example, the plate boundaries are in the deep ocean trenches offshore of the Japanese islands, and that is where the great plate boundary earthquakes occur. Many smaller events occur scattered throughout the Japanese islands, caused by the overall compression of the whole region. Although these small events are energetically minor when compared to the great offshore earthquakes, they are often more destructive, owing to their greater proximity to population centers.

Although most earthquakes occur on or near plate boundaries, some also occur, although infrequently, within plates. These earthquakes, which are not related to plate boundaries, are called intraplate earthquakes, and can sometimes be quite destructive. Although intraplate earthquakes are probably caused by the same convective forces which drive the plates, their immediate cause is not understood. Some of them can be quite large. One of the largest earthquakes known to have occurred in the United States was one of a series of intraplate earthquakes which took place in the Mississippi Valley, near New Madrid, Missouri, in 1811 and 1812. Another intraplate earthquake, in 1886, caused moderate damage to Charleston, South Carolina.

In addition to the tectonic types of earthquakes described above, some earthquakes are directly associated with volcanic activity. These volcanic earthquakes result from the motion of undergound magma that leads to volcanic eruptions.

Sequences. Earthquakes often occur in well-defined sequences in time. Tectonic earthquakes are often preceded, by a few days to weeks, by several smaller shocks (foreshocks), and are nearly always followed by large numbers of aftershocks. Foreshocks and aftershocks are usually much smaller than the main shock. Volcanic earthquakes often occur in flurries of activity, with no discernible main shock. This type of sequence is called a swarm.

Size. Earthquakes range enormously in size, from tremors in which slippage of a few tenths of an inch occurs on a few feet of fault, to the greatest events, which may involve a rupture many hundreds of miles long, with tens of feet of slip. Accelerations as high as 1 g (acceleration due to gravity) can occur during an earthquake motion. The velocity at which the two sides of the fault move during an earthquake is only

1–10 mi/h (10–100 cm/s), but the rupture front spreads along the fault at a velocity of nearly 5000 mi/h (3 km/s). The earthquake's primary damage is due to the generated seismic waves, or sound waves which travel through the Earth, excited by the rapid movement of the earthquake. The energy radiated as seismic waves during a large earthquake can be as great as 10^{12} cal ($10^{12} \times 4.19$ joules), and the power emitted during the few hundred seconds of movement as great as a billion megawatts.

The size of an earthquake is given by its moment: average slip times the fault area that slipped times the elastic constant of the Earth. The units of seismic moment are dyne-centimeters. An older measure of earthquake size is magnitude, which is proportional to the logarithm of moment. Magnitude 2.0 is about the smallest tremor that can be felt. Most destructive earthquakes are greater than magnitude 6; the largest shock known was the 1960 Chile earthquake, with a moment of 10^{30} dyne-centimeters (10^{23} newton-meters) or magnitude 9.6. It involved a fault 600 mi (1000 km) long slipping 30 ft (10 m). The magnitude scale is logarithmic, so that a magnitude 7 shock is about 30 times more energetic than one of magnitude 6, and 30 × 30, or 900 times, more energetic than one of magnitude 5. Because of this great increase in size with magnitude, only the largest events (greater than magnitude 8) significantly contribute to plate movements. The smaller events occur much more often but are almost incidental to the process.

The intensity of an earthquake is a measure of the severity of shaking and its attendant damage at a point on the surface of the Earth. The same earthquake may therefore have different intensities at different places. The intensity usually decreases away from the epicenter (the point on the surface directly above the onset of the earthquake), but its value depends on many factors and generally increases with moment. Intensity is usually higher in areas with thick alluvial cover or landfill than in areas of shallow soil or bare rock. Poor building construction leads to high intensity ratings because the damage to structures is high. Intensity is therefore more a measure of the earthquake's effect on humans than an innate property of the earthquake.

Effects. Many different effects are produced by earthquake shaking. Although the fault motion that produced the earthquake is sometimes observed at the surface, often other earth movements, such as landslides, are triggered by earthquakes. On rare occasions the ground has been observed to undulate in a wavelike manner, and cracks and fissures often form in soil. The flow of springs and rivers may be altered, and the compression of aquifers sometimes causes water to spout from the ground in fountains. Undersea earthquakes often generate very long-wavelength water waves, which are sometimes called tidal waves but are more properly called seismic sea waves, or tsunami. These waves, almost imperceptible in the open ocean, increase in height as they approach a coast and often inflict great damage to coastal cities and ports. *See Tsunami.*

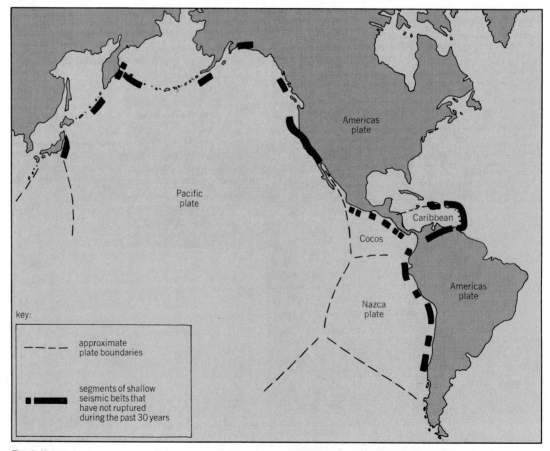

Fig. 4. Major seismic gaps, western Pacific. (*After J. Kelleher et al., J. Geophys. Res., 78:2547–2585, American Geophysical Union, 1973*)

PREDICTION

The elastic rebound theory of earthquakes has been verified by detailed long-term geodetic measurements in Japan. Consequently, it has become possible, where such measurements are available, to make long-range predictions of future earthquakes along major plate boundaries. Thus, a portion of a plate boundary that has not ruptured in a major earthquake for a long time is known as a seismic gap (**Fig. 4**). These are the regions that are next expected to experience great earthquakes. Where data permit, rough estimates of the occurrence times and size of these expected earthquakes can now be made decades in advance. Short-term prediction, in the sense of warnings months or weeks in advance, however, is still entirely in the realm of ongoing research and no method is known to be reliable.

Christopher H. Scholz

Bibliography. G. L. Berlin, *Earthquakes and the Urban Environment*, 3 vols., 1980; B. Bolt, *Earthquakes*, 2d ed., 1987; *Earthquake Information Bulletin*, U.S. Geological Survey, Reston, Virginia, published six times yearly; *Facing Geological Hazards*, U.S. Geol. Surv. Prof. Pap. 1240-B, 1981; T. Rikitaki, *Earthquake Forecasting*, 1982.

Ecological communities

Assemblages of living organisms that occur together in an area. The nature of the forces that knit these assemblages into organized systems and those properties of assemblages that manifest this organization have been topics of intense debate among ecologists since the early years of this century. On the one hand, there are those who view a community as simply consisting of species with similar physical requirements, such as temperature, soil type, or light regime. The similarity of requirements dictates that these species be found together, but interactions between the species are of secondary importance and the level of organization is low. On the other hand, there are those who conceive of the community as a highly organized, holistic entity, with species inextricably and complexly linked to one another and to the physical environment, so that characteristic patterns recur, and properties arise that one can neither understand nor predict from a knowledge of the component species. In this view, the ecosystem (physical environment plus its community) is as well organized as a living organism, and constitutes a superorganism. Between these extremes are those who perceive some community organization but not nearly enough to invoke images of holistic superorganisms. *See* ECOSYSTEM.

Emergent and collective properties. The crux of this debate is whether communities have emergent properties, a concept that itself is sufficiently confused, so that part of the ecological debate may be semantic. Some denote by emergent property any property of a group that is not a property of the component individuals. Others call any group trait a collective property, and reserve as emergent only those collective properties that do not derive trivially from properties of component individuals or from the very definition of the group. An emergent property, in this conception, represents a new level of organization, and cannot be predicted even with complete knowledge of all properties of individuals in the group. Thus, the number of species in a community is a property that is not defined for any particular species, but once one knows all the species in a community one can easily measure the property "number of species" for that community. In the restricted view of emergent property, the number of species in a community is a collective property, but not an emergent one.

Whether any properties of communities are emergent is debatable, but all ecologists agree that communities have collective properties that are significant both biologically and practically. For example, it is not a trivial matter to understand why the number of species in a given community is S and not $2S$, and what the consequences are of having S species. Also, human exploitation of ecological communities often rests on a thorough knowledge of certain collective properties, such as biomass produced per unit time, or rate of cycling of certain nutrients. *See* BIOMASS.

Size. Every community comprises a given group of species, and their number and identities are distinguishing traits. Most communities are so large that it is not possible to enumerate all species; microorganisms and small invertebrates are especially difficult to census. However, particularly in small, well-bounded sites such as lakes or islands, one can find all the most common species and estimate their relative abundances. The number of species is known as species richness, while species diversity refers to various statistics based on the relative numbers of individuals of each species in addition to the number of species. The rationale for such a diversity measure is that some communities have many species, but most species are rare and almost all the individuals (or biomass) in such a community can be attributed to just a few species. Such a community is not diverse in the usual sense of the word. Patterns of species diversity abound in the ecological literature; for example, pollution often effects a decrease in species diversity. The most popular species diversity statistic is given in the equation below, where S is the number of spe-

$$H' = \sum_{i=1}^{s} p_i \log (p_i)$$

cies, and p_i is the fraction of all the individuals (or all the biomass) in the community contributed by species i. For many sets of data on diversities of groups of communities (or parts of communities, such as all birds or all plants), values of H' are highly correlated with species richness, suggesting that H' may not be the ideal expression of biotic diversity.

The main patterns of species richness that have been detected are area and isolation effects, successional gradients, and latitudinal gradients. Larger sites tend to have more species than do small ones, and isolated communities (such as those on oceanic islands) tend to have fewer species than do less-isolated ones of equal size. Later communities in a temporal succession tend to have more species than do earlier ones, except that the last (climax) community often has fewer species than the immediately preceding one. Tropical communities tend to be very species-rich, while those in arctic climates tend to be species-poor. This observation conforms to a larger but less precise rule that communities in particularly stressful environments tend to have few species.

Composition. Species composition is important, largely in assisting in the classification of communities. If the complete species list for each community and the proportional representation of each species in it were known, no two communities would be found to be identical. The criteria are arbitrary for how similar these lists must be before two communities are viewed as the same.

Communities are usually denoted by the presence of species, known as dominants, that contain a large fraction of the community's biomass, or account for a large fraction of a community's productivity. Dominants are usually plants. Determining whether communities at two sites are truly representatives of the "same" community requires knowledge of more than just the dominants, however. "Characteristic" species, which are always found in combination with certain other species, are useful in deciding whether two communities are of the same type, though the designation of "same" is arbitrary, just as is the designation of "dominant" or "characteristic."

Although there is no objective answer to the question of whether two communities are the same, the question bears heavily on the matter of whether communities are in fact integrated superorganisms with emergent properties. One would not expect a superorganismic entity to have an infinite variety of representations, for the same cohesive forces that bind it into a holistic unit should constrain it to a limited number of forms. Organisms for the most part do not form a continuous gradient of all conceivable phenotypes, but rather are constrained by a number of physiological and morphological relationships (such as allometry). Thus there is generally no trouble in saying that individual X is a human, individual Y is a longleaf pine, and so on. Although there is phenotypic variation in all species, it is limited and centered on recognizable modes.

An active area of research among animal ecologists has been the search for limits to how similar two species can be and still occur in the same community. That there exists some limiting similarity beyond which coexistence is impossible is a theoretical consequence of conceptions of the ecological niche; but clear evidence, in any instance, that such limiting similarity is the reason why a given species is absent from a given community is exceedingly difficult to amass. There are two main difficulties. First, it must be demonstrated that some resource is limiting so that species that are too similar will find it in short supply. Second, an appropriate index of a species' use of the resource (its niche) must be determined. Much attention has been focused on the size of an animal or of its trophic appendages as such an index, though there is much evidence that many other forces affect these sizes. For few, if any, animal communities has it been shown that size similarity restricts species composition or that patterns of size differences among species are highly predictable or regular.

Spatial distribution patterns. A related matter bearing on the aptness of the superorganismic community metaphor is that most organisms have clear spatial boundaries; communities often do not. There is no difficulty discerning where one human ends and another begins, but there are not always clear boundaries to communities. Occasionally, very sharp limits to a physical environmental condition impose similarly sharp limits on a community. For example, serpentine soils are found sharply delimited from adjacent soils in many areas, and have mineral concentrations strikingly different from those of the neighboring soils. Thus they support plant species that are very different from those found in nearby nonserpentine areas, and these different plant species support animal species partially different from those of adjacent areas. Here two different communities are sharply bounded from each other.

Usually, however, communities grade into one another more gradually, through a broad intermediate region (an ecotone) that includes elements of both of the adjacent communities, and sometimes other species as well that are not found in either adjacent community. One has little difficulty telling when one is in the center of either of the adjacent communities A and B, but exactly when one passes from A to B is not easily discerned. The reason is that, though each species in a community is adapted to its physical environment and to some extent to other species in the community, the adaptations to the physical environment are usually not identical, and most of the adaptations to one another are not obligatory.

The environment created by the dominant species, by their effects on temperature, light, humidity, and other physical factors, and by their biotic effects, such as allelopathy and competition, may entrain some other species so that these other species' spatial boundaries coincide with those of the dominants. The mangrove skipper, *Phocides pygmalion*, can feed only on red mangrove, *Rhizophora mangle*, so whatever aspects of the physical environment limit the mangrove (especially temperature), the skipper will also be limited to the same sites. However, many other species that feed on the mangrove (for example, the io moth, *Automeris io*) also feed on other plants, and their spatial boundaries do not coincide with those of the mangrove. Nor do most of the species in a community share identical physical requirements. Black mangrove (*Avicennia germinans*) co-occurs with red mangrove in most sites, and the two are normal constituents of a community often termed mangrove swamp. But *Avicennia* can tolerate much colder weather than can *Rhizophora*, and so it is found much farther north in the Northern Hemisphere. Eventually it too ceases, and the mangrove community is replaced in more northerly areas by salt marsh communities. In some intermediate regions, salt marsh grasses and black mangrove are found together. There is no clear boundary between the two communities.

This continuous intergradation of most communities argues against the superorganism concept, but there are aspects of the spatial arrangement within communities that suggest that the component species are far from independent, and indicate, if not complete holism, at least that some community properties are not easily predicted from exhaustive knowledge of the component species. One example is stratification, the vertical arrangement of canopy layers in most forests. Individuals of the different species do not have heights that are independently and continuously distributed from the ground to the top of the tallest tree. Instead, there are a few rather distinct strata, with each species at maturity characteristically occupying one of these. Tropical forests from all parts of the world, even though they may have completely different species compositions, usually contain five fairly clear strata: a topmost layer composed of the tallest tree species, two lower layers of smaller trees, a shrub layer, and a ground layer. There are doubtless good physical reasons why the diffusion of light can explain this characteristic structure given a knowledge of evolution and plant physiology (though no completely compelling explanation has yet surfaced), so it may be that this is an elaborate collective property rather than an emergent one. In either case, there is clearly a high degree of multispecies organization in this spatial arrangement. *SEE PHYSIOLOGICAL ECOLOGY (PLANT).*

In addition to vertical arrangement, horizontal locations of individuals of different species are usually not random. Usually, individuals of a given species are clumped; they are found on average closer to one another than one would have predicted. Probably the major reason for this is response to habitat heterogeneity: conspecific individuals tend to favor more similar habitats than do heterospecific individuals. Individuals of different species may also be nonrandomly arranged with respect to one another. Competitive interactions may cause two species typically to be found in different microsites, while mutualistic interactions or preference for a similar physical habitat may cause two species to be associated spatially. *SEE POPULATION ECOLOGY.*

Succession. More or less distinct communities tend to follow one another in rather stylized order. As with recognition of spatial boundaries, recognition of temporal boundaries of adjacent communities within a sere is partly a function of the expectations that an observer brings to the endeavor. Those who view communities as superorganisms are inclined to see sharp temporal and spatial boundaries, and the perception that one community does not gradually become another community over an extended period of time confirms the impression that communities are highly organized entities, not random collections of species that happen to share physical requirements. In this superorganismic view, ecological succession of communities in a sere is analogous to the life cycle of an organism, and follows a quite deterministic course. That secondary succession following a disturbance often leads to a community resembling the original one is the analog in the superorganism to wound repair in an organism. The driving force for succession, in this conception, is that the community or its dominant species modify the environment so that these dominant species are no longer favored, and when the dominant species are replaced, the bulk of the community, complexly linked to the dominant species and to one another, disappears as well, to be relaced by the next community in the sere.

This superorganismic conception of succession has been replaced by an individualistic succession. Data on which species are present at different times during a succession show that there is not abrupt wholesale extinction of most members of a community and concurrent simultaneous colonization by most species of the next community. Rather, most species within a community colonize at different times, and as the community is replaced most species drop out at different times. Thus, though one can usually state with assurance that the extant community is of type A or type B, there are extended periods when it is difficult to assign the assemblage of species at a site to any recognizable community.

That successsion is primarily an individualistic process does not mean that there are not characteristic changes in community properties as most successions proceed. Species richness usually increases through most of the succession, for example, and stratification becomes more highly organized and well defined. A number of patterns are manifest in aspects of energy flow and nutrient cycling. *SEE ECOLOGICAL SUCCESSION.*

Functional organization. Living organisms are characterized not only by spatial and temporal structure but by an apparent purpose or activity. In short, they are ''doing something,'' and this activity has been termed teleonomy. In humans, for example, various physiological functions are continuously under way until death intervenes. Communities have functions analogous to physiology.

In the first place, the various species within a community have different trophic relationships with one another. One species may eat another, or be eaten by another. A species may be a decomposer, living on dead tissue of one or more other species. Some species are omnivores, eating many kinds of food; others are more specialized, eating only plants or only animals, or even just one other species. These trophic relationships certainly unite the species in a community into a common endeavor, the transmission of energy through the community. This energy flow is patently analogous to an organism's mobilization and transmission of energy from the food it eats.

One aspect of energy flow is a candidate for an emergent property: the topology of the food web. Examination of this topology for a number of webs suggests that they are highly constrained in structure. For example, the maximum number of trophic levels in a web rarely exceeds five. One reason may be that the total amount of energy that has not already been degraded by the time the energy has passed through three or four levels may not be enough to sustain a viable population of a species that would feed at still higher levels. An alternative explanation is that the population dynamics of a web with so many levels would probably confer mathematical instability on the web, so that one or more species would be eliminated. Other properties of food webs that have been discerned include a low number of omnivore species (those feeding on more than one level), and a tendency for the number of predator species and the number of prey species to be in the ratio of 4:3. No explanation is forthcoming for the latter observation. The former observation is held to reflect mathematical instability that arises from the presence of omnivores in a web. Other workers contend that neither pattern will be maintained when much more comprehensive data are available on what paths calories actually follow as they flow through a community. If these patterns do not turn out to be artifacts of incomplete knowledge, they would appear to be emergent properties reflecting a high degree of organization. *SEE FOOD WEB.*

Just as energy flows through the communities, so do nutrients move. A calorie of energy does not move in the abstract from organism to organism; rather, the calorie is bound up in a molecule that moves when one organism eats (or decomposes) another. Or the calorie may be respired away as a result of the metabolism of the organism that ingests it. A calorie of energy, once respired by some member of the community, is no longer available to the community. But the molecule associated with that calorie, or a new molecule produced from it, is still present and can go through the food web again. Thus nutrients can cycle within a community, while energy flow, once the energy is transformed to heat, is one-way. Nutrient cycling is analogous to circulation in an organism, and combines with energy flow to support the superorganism metaphor. Different nutrients cycle at different rates, and for several nutrients the cycle within the community is linked to cycles in other communities. Nutrients exist in abiotic entities, as well as biotic organisms, so nutrient cycling is as much an ecosystem trait as a community one. A number of properties of nutrient cycling (such as rate, turnover times, and sizes of different pools or compartments) have been measured. Whether any of these are emergent as opposed to collective properties has yet to be determined.

Productivity. By virtue of differing rates of photosynthesis by the dominant plants, different communities have different primary productivities. Tropical forests are generally most productive, while extreme environments such as desert or alpine conditions harbor rather unproductive communities. Agricultural communities are intermediate. Algal communities in estuaries are the most productive marine communities, while open ocean communities are usually far less productive. The efficiency with which various animals ingest and assimilate the plants and the structure of the trophic web determine the secondary productivity (production of organic matter by animals) of a community. Marine secondary productivity generally exceeds that of terrestrial communities. *See* Agroecosystem; Biological productivity.

Reproduction. A final property that any organism must have is the ability to reproduce itself. Communities may be seen as possessing this property, though the sense in which they do so does not support the superorganism metaphor. A climax community reproduces itself through time simply by virtue of the reproduction of its constituent species, and may also be seen as reproducing itself in space by virtue of the propagules that its species transmit to less mature communities. For example, when a climax forest abuts a cutover field, if no disturbance ensues, the field undergoes succession and eventually becomes a replica of the adjacent forest. Both temporally and spatially, then, community reproduction is a collective rather than an emergent property, deriving directly from the reproductive activities of the component species. *See* Altitudinal vegetation zones; Desert; Ecology; Grassland ecosystem; Mangrove.

Daniel Simberloff

Bibliography. T. F. H. Allen and T. B. Starr, *Hierarchy: Perspectives for Ecological Complexity*, 1988; M. Begon and M. Mortimer, *Population Ecology: A Unified Study of Animals and Plants*, 2d rev. ed., 1986; P. G. Digby and R. A. Kempton, *Multivariate Analysis of Ecological Communities*, 1987; J. R. Trabalka and D. E. Reichle (eds.), *The Changing Carbon Cycle*, 1986.

Ecological energetics

The study of the flow of energy within an ecological system from the time the energy enters the living system until it is ultimately degraded to heat and irretrievably lost from the system. It is also referred to as production ecology, because ecologists use the word production to describe the process of energy input and storage in ecosystems.

Ecological energetics provides information on the energetic interdependence of organisms within ecological systems and the efficiency of energy transfer within and between organisms and trophic levels.

Nearly all energy enters the biota by green plants' transformation of light energy into chemical energy through photosynthesis; this is referred to as primary production. This accumulation of potential energy is used by plants, and by the animals which eat them, for growth, reproduction, and the work necessary to sustain life. The energy put into growth and reproduction is termed secondary production. As energy passes along the food chain to higher trophic levels (from plants to herbivores to carnivores), the potential energy is used to do work and in the process is degraded to heat. The laws of thermodynamics require the light energy fixed by plants to equal the energy degraded to heat, assuming the system is closed with respect to matter. An energy budget quantifies the energy pools, the directions of energy flow, and the rates of energy transformations within ecological systems. *See* Biological productivity; Food web.

The peak of studies in ecological energetics occurred in the 1960s and early 1970s largely because a

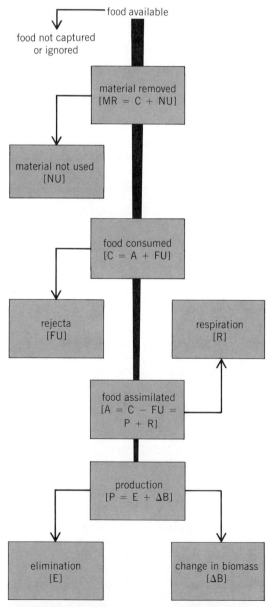

Fig. 1. Diagrammatic representation of energy flow through an ecological unit; abbreviations are explained in the text.

major concern of the International Biological Program was an appraisal of the biological productivity of terrestrial and aquatic communities in relation to human welfare. Initially considered to have the potential of becoming a unifying language in ecology—an ecological Rosetta Stone—the subject has yielded little in the way of general theory.

The essentials of ecological energetics can be most readily appreciated by considering the schema (**Fig. 1**) of energy flowing through an individual; it is equally applicable to populations, communities, and ecosystems. Of the food energy available, only part is harvested (MR) in the process of foraging. Some is wasted (NU), for example, by messy eaters, and the rest consumed (C). Part of the consumed food is transformed but is not utilized by the body, leaving as fecal material (F) or as nitrogenous waste (U), the by-product of protein metabolism. The remaining energy is assimilated (A) into the body, part of which is used to sustain the life functions and to do work—this is manifest as oxygen consumption. The remainder of the assimilated energy is used to produce new tissue, either as growth of the individual or as development of offspring. Hence production is also the potential energy (proteins, fats, and carbohydrates) on which other organisms feed. Production (P) leads to an increase in biomass (B) or is eliminated (E) through death, migration, predation, or the shedding of, for example, hair, skin, and antlers.

Pathways. Energy flows through the consumer food chain (from plants to herbivores to carnivores) or through the detritus food chain. The latter is fueled by the waste products of the consumer food chain, such as feces, shed skin, cadavers, and nitrogenous waste. Most detritus is consumed by microorganisms such as bacteria and fungi, although this food chain includes conspicuous carrion feeders like beetles and vultures. In terrestrial systems, more than 90% of all primary production may be consumed by detritus feeders. In aquatic systems, where the plants do not require tough supporting tissues, harvesting by herbivores may be efficient with little of the primary production passing to the detrivores.

Pyramids of biomass are used to depict the amount of living material, or its energetic equivalent, present at one time in the different trophic levels (**Fig. 2**). Although the energy flow cannot increase at higher trophic levels, pyramids of biomass may be inverted, especially in aquatic systems. This occurs because the index P/B is inversely related to the size of the organisms. Hence a small biomass may support a high level of production if the biomass is composed of small individuals (**Fig. 3**).

Units. Traditionally the calorie, a unit of heat energy, has been used, but this has been largely replaced by the joule. Confusion is possible, especially in the field of nutrition, because with an initial capital, Calorie may denote kilocalories. Biomass or standing crop is expressed as potential energy per unit area, but the other compartments in Fig. 1, for example P and R, are expressed in terms of energy flux or rates. The efficiency values such as P/A are dimensionless, but the ratio P/B is a rate—the inverse of the turnover time.

Measurement of energy flow. For illustrative purposes some general methods for assessing biological productivity are described here in the context of energy flow through a population. Production is measured from individual growth rates and the reproductive rate of the population to determine the turnover time. The energy equivalent of food consumed, feces, and production can be determined by measuring the heat evolved on burning a sample in an oxygen bomb calorimeter, or by chemical analysis—determining the amount of carbon or of protein, carbohydrate, and lipid and applying empirically determined caloric equivalents to the values. The latter three contain, respectively, 16.3, 23.7, and 39.2 kilojoules per gram of dry weight. Maintenance costs are usually measured indirectly as respiration (normally the oxygen consumed) in the laboratory and extrapolated to the field conditions. Error is introduced by the fact that animals have different levels of activity in the field and are subject to different temperatures, and so uncertainty has surrounded these extrapolations. Oxygen consumption has been measured in animals living in

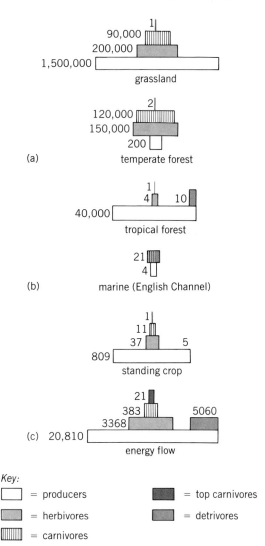

Fig. 2. Trophic levels of a number of ecosystems represented in different units. (*a*) As numbers of individuals per 1000 m² of grassland and temperate forest community in summer; microorganisms and soil animals excluded. (*b*) The standing crop or biomass (grams dry weight per meter squared) of terrestrial (Panamanian tropical rainforest) and marine (English Channel) communities; note the inversion of the marine pyramid. (*c*) The aquatic community of Silver Springs, Florida, represented as standing crop (kilocalorie per meter) and energy flow (kilocalories per meter per year). (*After E. P. Odum, Fundamentals of Ecology, 3d ed., W. B. Saunders, 1971*)

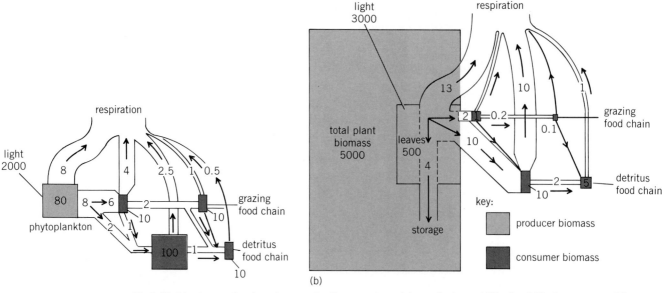

Fig. 3. Models of energy flow through two contrasting ecosystems: (*a*) a marine bay and (*b*) a forest. The boxes represent the biomass in kilocalories per meter and the flow lines show the energy flux (kilocalories per meter per day) along the various pathways. The boxes and the flux lines are scaled to indicate their relative magnitudes. (*After E. P. Odum, Relationships between structure and function in the ecosystem, Jap. J. Ecol., 12:108–118, 1962*)

the wild by using the turnover rates of doubly labeled water (D_2O).

Levels of inquiry. Ecological energetics is concerned with several levels of inquiry: the partitioning of energy between the compartments denoted in Fig. 1; the pathways traced by the energy as it passes through the trophic levels; and the efficiency of energy transfer between trophic levels. The ratio of energy flux through one compartment in Fig. 1 to any previous compartment is referred to as an efficiency. Numerous efficiencies can be calculated both within and between trophic levels. The most common are the assimilation efficiency (A/C), namely the proportion of energy assimilated by the body from the food consumed, and the production efficiency (P/A), which denotes the proportion of energy assimilated which ends up as new tissue. These various efficiencies combine to limit the energy available to the higher trophic levels. The ratio of food consumed or ingested at one trophic level to that ingested by the next lower

level is termed ecological efficiency. A value of 10% for this efficiency is often cited; consideration of the A/C and P/A efficiencies of most organisms shows that it could seldom exceed 15–20%. However, the effect of heat losses at each trophic level in limiting the length of food chains in nature remains controversial.

Factors affecting efficiency. Respiration rate of organisms is scaled as the three-quarters power of body weight. Hence larger organisms have proportionately slower rates of respiration. This scaling factor seems to affect many rate processes in the body so that size does not influence those efficiencies which are the focus of ecological energetics. However, different types of organisms of the same size have different metabolic rates. For example, warm-blooded animals have much higher weight-specific respiration rates than cold-blooded ones. Analysis of energy budgets derived for wild-living animals shows that a number of taxonomic and trophic groups can be distinguished according to characteristic production efficiencies (see **table**). Production efficiency appears to be related to the general level of metabolic activity—animals with high rates of metabolism generally having low production efficiency.

Due to the loss of usable energy with each transformation, in an area more energy can be diverted into production by plants than by consumer populations. For humans this means that utilizing plants for food directly is energetically much more efficient than converting them to eggs or meat. See BIOMASS; ECOLOGICAL COMMUNITIES; ECOSYSTEM.

W. F. Humphreys

Bibliography. S. Brody, *Bioenergetics and Growth*, 1945; R. M. May, Production and respiration in animal communities, *Nature*, 282:443–444, 1979; E. P. Odum, *Fundamentals of Ecology*, 3d ed., 1971; K. Petrusewicz and A. Macfadyen, *Productivity of Terrestrial Animals: Principles and Methods*, 1970; J. Phillipson, *Ecological Energetics*, 1966; S. L. Pimm, *Food Webs*, 1982.

Production efficiency of populations of various classes of animals living in the wild*	
Animal group	Production efficiency (P/A), %
Shrews	0.9
Birds	1.3
Other mammals	3.1
Fish, ants, and termites	9.8
Invertebrates other than insects	25.0
Herbivores	20.8
Carnivores	27.6
Detrivores	36.2
Insects except ants and termites	40.7
Herbivores	38.8
Detrivores	47.0
Carnivores	55.6

*After W. F. Humphreys, Production and respiration in animal populations, *J. Anim. Ecol.*, 48:427–454, 1979.

Ecological methods

The methods required for the measurement of features of plant and animal populations or for quantifying energy flow or other aspects of ecological communities. Ecologists are concerned with such a wide range of variables that they may use many other techniques, including in particular those for the measurement of weather conditions or for determining features and composition of air, water, and soil. SEE ECOLOGICAL COMMUNITIES.

Patterns of distribution. Ecologists often attempt to describe the way that individual plants or animals are distributed in the habitat. One pattern is the clumping of organisms. This may occur because only part of the habitat is suitable for them (as when rushes occur in the damp patches of a field) or because they represent the offspring of an original colonist and have not moved far from the parent. Another pattern is known as random distribution because each organism is independent of the other (as when thistledown settles on a plowed field). A regular pattern describes the situation when organisms are virtually equidistant from each other. It is often a reflection of competition.

Such patterns are normally determined by sampling the organisms from unit areas—generally squares known as quadrats. For vegetation sampling, long pins resembling knitting needles are dropped into the ground and plants that touch them are recorded. These pins are regarded as infinitely small quadrats and are termed point quadrats. Various statistics, such as the mean ($\bar{x}$) and the variance (s^2), may be calculated from the results of such sampling, and their magnitudes and relationships to each other will show whether the pattern is clumped, random, or regular: if the ratio $s^2/\bar{x} \sim 1$ the individuals are randomly distributed; if the ratio is greater than 1 they are clumped; but if less than 1 they are in a regular pattern.

Estimation of populations. For plants, individuals (such as trees) may be counted directly, and the main problem is often (as with grasses) deciding what is a plant. However, the populations of only a few animals can be estimated by direct counting; in these cases, the organism is either sessile (like barnacles) or the individuals are very large, and all the individuals in an area can be seen (or at least recorded on a photograph) at the same time. Aerial photography and remote sensing techniques have provided powerful approaches for the estimation of the numbers of large animals (such as cattle or elephants) over wide areas or the extent and type of vegetation cover. However, most animals are active and small, and only a part (sample) of the population can be seen at any one time. Alternatively, it may be tedious and time-consuming to count the animals; therefore, only those in small parts (samples) can be counted (for example, mites per leaf rather than per tree). SEE REMOTE SENSING.

One approach to estimating population size is to mark a number of the animals (a), perhaps with a colored dye or paint, and release these into the population. If it can be assumed that they have mixed completely (and the marking has not affected their behavior), the proportion that they constitute of the next sample will be the same as the proportion that the original number marked constitutes of the total population (N). This is shown in the equation below,

$$\frac{r}{n} = \frac{a}{N} \quad \text{or} \quad N = \frac{an}{r}$$

where r is the number of marked individuals recaptured, n is the total number in the sample after marking, a is the number originally marked, and N is the population. This calculation also assumes that there are no births or deaths, or any migration in the period between the samples. Often these assumptions are not justified, and many more complex systems, of both sampling and marking (on several occasions) and of calculation, have been devised.

An alternative approach is to take a number of samples and determine the total number of animals in them. The average number per sample is then multiplied by the total number of sample units in the habitat (for example, leaves on a tree) to obtain the population for that habitat. Special techniques are often needed to determine the total animals in a sample. For example, mites and insects in samples of soil (or litter) are usually extracted by placing the soil in a special apparatus, the Berlese-Tüllgren funnel, where a light bulb or other heat source slowly dries out the soil so that the animals move down and eventually drop through the funnel to a collecting tube. Other soil animals (for example, many types of worms) require moist conditions, and they can be driven out of wet samples by lowering the oxygen level (again by heat) or by chemicals. There is a wide variety of methods for different organisms and for various habitats. Special methods may also be necessary to take the samples: a common method of sampling insects from grassland is the D-vac sampler, basically a large, specially designed vacuum cleaner.

Population dynamics. The aim of population estimation is often to contribute toward an understanding of how the population is changing over time, such as to determine trends or the major mortalities. Methods are devised to measure the amount of mortality (for example, the remains of dead animals or plants can be found, or the level of parasitism assessed), the numbers born (natality), and the organisms moving in (immigration) and out (emigration) of the habitat. Special computational techniques are used to estimate the numbers of individuals in a population and to construct life tables. All these methods make certain assumptions, but since these are not always justified, there is great value in making population estimates by a number of different methods. SEE POPULATION ECOLOGY.

Energy flow. The contribution of organisms of different sizes to the functioning of an ecosystem may be best compared in terms of their total weight—the biomass. The biomass in a habitat is termed the standing crop. It is measured in wet weight or dry weight, the latter obtained by freeze drying. The dynamics of an ecosystem, that is, the exchanges between the different components, may be expressed in terms of energy transfers to form a picture of the energy flow. The energy content of a given biomass is often determined by burning a sample in a bomb calorimeter; the heat rise is a measure of the calorific value of the sample. Then it is possible to determine the amount of animal or plant material produced (the production) and, for animals, the amount of food consumed. SEE BIOLOGICAL PRODUCTIVITY; BIOMASS.

Two equations are particularly useful for determining the energy relationships of organisms:

Consumption − (fecal and urinary waste)
= assimilation
Assimilation = respiration and production

Consumption and production can usually be measured in terms of biomass and calorific value. Respiration is often measured with special respirometers, and assimilation can sometimes be measured directly by using an inert marker in the food.

Other methods are used to measure the flow of specific nutrients in ecosystems; special computational methods are used to calculate indices to describe the diversity of animal and plant communities; many types of traps or similar devices are used to capture animals; and radioactive isotopes can be used as markers for organisms or materials. Ecologists are always devising new methods for the many and varied problems they encounter. SEE ECOLOGICAL ENERGETICS; ECOLOGY; ECOSYSTEM.

T. R. E. Southwood

Bibliography. J. G. Blower, L. M. Cook, and J. A. Bishop, *Estimating the Size of Animal Populations*, 1981; R. Clarke (ed.), *The Handbook of Ecological Monitoring*, 1986; P. A. Erickson, *Environmental Impact Assessment: Principles and Applications*, 1987; T. R. E. Southwood, *Ecological Methods*, 3d ed., 1988; *Statistical Ecology: Primer on Methods and Computing*, 1988; H. Walter and S. W. Breckle, *Ecological Systems of the Geobiosphere*, 1985.

Ecological modeling

The conceptualization and implementation of computer simulations of the behavior of living systems. In contrast to systems ecology, with which it somewhat overlaps, ecological modeling focuses on the predictions derived from models of particular systems rather than on the general behavior of entire classes of systems. The living systems that are modeled range from a single population to an entire ecosystem, including models of global processes. The models may be causal or correlative. Causal models, also known as mechanistic models, are constructed by incorporating hypothesized rules of interaction. The resulting behavior of such models can be compared to the behavior of real systems by way of validation. Correlative, or empirical, models, which are constructed by fitting observed system behavior with some appropriate mathematical functions, are more properly the domain of statistical ecology. They have great utility as predictors, provided an adequate database is available, but they offer no explanation of why the system behaves as it does. SEE SYSTEMS ECOLOGY.

Purpose. An emphasis on explanation is one of the distinguishing marks of ecological modeling. The models are designed and used to provide insight into the rules governing the interaction of system structure with system function to produce system behavior. The terms system structure and system function denote groupings of ecological attributes different from those used by many ecologists. Such models can be used as aids to ecological research, as guides to the development of ecological theory, or as predictors of system behavior outside the range of observed perturbations.

Constructing a model. Most ecological model builders begin by defining the system of interest: the boundaries must be delineated, the abstract system structure must be described, and the specific functional components to be modeled must be added. The steps in the process of conceptualization and construction of the model are as follows.

1. Describe the boundaries of the system in space and time.

2. Choose those components of the system that are to be included as variables of state in the model.

3. Choose those pathways of transfer of matter-energy that are to be included in the model.

4. Decide on the units of flow (individuals, biomass, nutrient, joules, and so on).

5. Verbalize the determined limits to each rate of transfer in the model and the operation of the factors responsible for controlling the rates within those limits.

6. Translate the verbal model into a set of mathematical expressions, usually a set of differential equations.

7. Rewrite the model in a form that can be simulated by the digital computer.

8. Choose parameter values and initial conditions of the variables of state, simulate model behavior by numerical integration on the computer, then compare the output with observational or experimental data.

9. Revise the model to more closely mimic the observed system behavior on the basis of further data collection or new insight.

10. Repeat steps 6–9.

Traditionally, ecological models consist of a set of nonlinear, often discontinuous differential equations. The discontinuities that result from the incorporation of threshold behavior preclude global analytical solutions to these sets of equations, although the large number of interactions and nonlinear processes that are present in all but the simplest ecological systems would make analytical solutions impossible in any case. Ecological modelers are fortunate in that the systems they simulate normally are relatively stationary or else oscillate around some long-term mean. Thus errors in the numerical integration of sets of differential equations tend to cancel each other, with the only result being decreases in the predicted peaks and increases in the predicted troughs.

When an ecological model is being constructed according to the algorithm of the steps listed above, a number of issues must be decided, particularly when the nature and form of the controls in step 5 are to be exercised and they are to be translated into mathematical expressions, step 6. Living organisms are faced with choices. Thus any system that contains organisms must be subject to some uncertainty apart from that attributable to physical factors in the environment. The decision about what amount of that uncertainty, if any, should be incorporated into the model depends on the level of uncertainty and the goals of the model. For example, in modeling the behavior of an individual, the level of uncertainty is high because of randomness, and the result of the choices made is a major objective of the model. To accommodate those factors, such a model must be highly stochastic. Modeling the growth of a population in response to changes in one or more life-history characteristics, however, presents a much different picture. First, although the time of reproduction of each individual in the population cannot be known exactly, a mean based on large numbers of individuals might very well suffice. Furthermore, the stochasticity in this case is irrelevant to the goals of the model, which is to evaluate the quantitative effect of a change in life history with the remainder of the system held the same. Adding a stochastic term to such a model to increase its realistic simulation of a real population would only serve to obscure the result. It is analogous to setting up an experiment to test the law of diffusion and then deliberately introducing some external stirring of the system.

In mechanistic models of the kind discussed here, a good rule is to use no mathematical function or parameter that cannot be explained or defined in biological terms. Similarly, the linearity or nonlinearity of an equation must depend on the process it is mimicking. Many physiological processes, such as respiration, excretion, and individual growth, can often be well represented by linear or stepwise-linear equations, where linearity refers to the multiplication of a variable of state by a constant, and stepwise linearity to results from multiplication with a time-varying parameter. However, most of the processes involved in the transfer of matter or energy into a biotic component of the model, as through some kind of ingestion, must be modeled with nonlinear terms.

Because of the propensity of organisms to switch behaviors, as often occurs in feeding behavior, the equations, in addition to being nonlinear, must incorporate thresholds. For example, a predator's switching from one prey to another very often does not take place in a smooth transition that reflects the densities of the alternate prey, but instead more closely resembles a unit step function in which one prey is eaten until its density or that of the alternate prey reaches some critical point. Then the predator may begin to eat only the alternate.

In addition to thresholds, the distribution of components and the interactions within even the simplest of ecological systems form a mosaic in space and time. Temporal heterogeneity is more easily handled, since the model will generally be simulated in time. Spatial heterogeneity can be incorporated explicitly by constructing and running several models simultaneously, with transfer between spatial divisions, or patches. Less satisfactory—but less laborious and less expensive—are models in which the spatial heterogeneity is implied, in part, by averaging parameter values and initial conditions across patches. The latter method can be very useful for a special case of heterogeneity in which the patches are fixed in space. An example is the high marsh–creek bank heterogeneity in a tidal salt marsh. *SEE SALT MARSH.*

Central to any ecological model is the way in which the determination and control of the transfer rates are viewed. Consider, for example, the rate of flow of energy from the plant to its consumer (see **illus.**). The determination of the maximum rate of ingestion for the population under optimum conditions will be a function of the genotypic and phenotypic characteristics of the consumer within the specified environment. For example, one may consider only the two factors associated with the plant or with the consumer, resource control versus intraspecific competition, and may assume that as the plant component becomes more abundant, exceeding some threshold of availability, consumption by the herbivore increases in a linear fashion. At some maximum value of plant abundance, the growth capabilities of the herbivore are saturated, a point known as the satiation threshold. Similarly, as the herbivore popula-

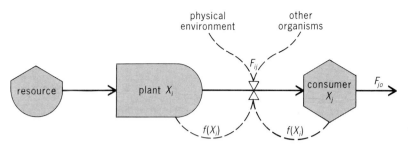

An example of a single trophic transfer pathway showing four possible sources of information that could affect the flow of energy from a plant (X_i) to a consumer, the herbivore (X_j). The broken lines, which show information transfer, indicate that four different sets of factors may operate to control the realized rate of intake within the determined limits of zero and a maximum.

tion exceeds some lower response threshold, its overall ingestion decreases linearly with increasing density until some upper carrying capacity is reached. There, ingestion is reduced by intraspecific interference to be just equal to physiological losses from such factors as respiration, nonpredatory mortality, and excretion.

A maximum transfer rate at which all are optimal—plus four thresholds and two linear control functions—can be expressed in mathematical form using Eq. (1), where X_j is the recipient density and X_i

$$\frac{dX_j}{dt} = F_{ij} - F_{j0} = X_j\,[\tau_{ij}\,f(X_i)\,f(X_j) - \lambda_j] \quad (1)$$

is the donor density. When the product of $f(X_i)$ and $f(X_j)$ is unity, the population is ingesting at the maximum rate, τ_{ij}. If λ_j is the specific rate of loss (in units over time), ingestion balances loss and the population is at steady state when the product of $f(X_i)$ and $f(X_j)$ equals λ_j/τ_{ij}, assuming no predatory losses. (For clarity of discussion, the example also assumes 100% assimilation by the herbivore.)

The two linear control functions that incorporate the rules necessary to quantify that interaction are shown in Eqs. (2) and (3). In Eqs. (2) and (3), γ_{ij} is

$$f(X_i) = \left[1 - \left(\frac{\gamma_{ij} - X_i}{\gamma_{ij} - \alpha_{ij}}\right)_+\right]_+ \quad (2)$$

$$f(X_j) = 1 - \left(\frac{X_j - \alpha_{jj}}{\gamma_{jj} - \alpha_{jj}}\right)_+ \quad (3)$$

where

$$(a - b)_+ \begin{cases} = 0 & \text{if } (a - b) \le 0 \\ = (a - b) & \text{if } (a - b) > 0 \end{cases}$$

the satiation concentration of X_i, α_{ij} is the refuge level of X_i, γ_{jj} is the carrying capacity of X_j, and α_{jj} is the response threshold of X_j. Thus, whenever $X_i \ge \gamma_{ij}$, then $f(X_i) = 1$; the change in $f(X_i)$ for changing X_i is linear, and when $X_i \le \alpha_{ij}$, then X_i is unavailable and $f(X_i) = 0$. A similar relationship applies for the interference function. Whenever $X_j \le \alpha_{jj}$, the value of $f(X_j) = 1$ (no control) and when $X_j = \gamma_{jj}$, the population is at steady state.

Uses. Such an equational structure generates models that combine useful aspects of reality as well as generality and precision with any degree of functional complexity desired. Models so constructed reflect all the relevant ecological information available for the system under consideration. An important use of such models is to aid ongoing research programs. Because it contains all information, a model constructed at the start of research can quickly reveal serious gaps in existing information. Repeated simulation can help identify sensitive parameters where further effort at refining values could be productive. Another use of such models is that they can provide, via "what-if" simulations, insight into the behavior of whole classes of systems that are similar to the one modeled. That can lead to a more general theory about a class of systems, thus tying ecological modeling to systems ecology.

The use of such causal, or mechanistic, models as predictors of the consequences of perturbation is the least common, because they are much more information-intensive than the correlative models. Within the range of observed data, correlative models, such as those constructed by using the techniques of multiple regression, are more reliable predictors. But in some situations there may be no alternative, as in the absence of an existing body of information on the behavior of similar systems to a range of perturbation intensity. The system of interest may be so large or so rare that a body of data cannot be gathered, or the possible consequences of the proposed perturbation may be so serious or long-lasting that pilot experiments are not advisable. Under those conditions a carefully constructed mechanistic ecological model may be necessary to predict the consequences of an environmental perturbation. SEE ECOLOGICAL ENERGETICS; ECOLOGY, APPLIED; ECOSYSTEM.

Richard G. Wiegert

Ecological succession

A directional change in an ecological community. Populations of animals and plants are in a dynamic state. Through the continual turnover of individuals, a population may expand or decline depending on the success of its members in survival and reproduction. As a consequence, the species composition of communities typically does not remain static with time. Apart from the regular fluctuations in species abundance related to seasonal changes, a community may develop progressively with time through a recognizable sequence known as the sere. Pioneer populations are replaced by successive colonists along a more or less predictable path toward a relatively stable community. This process of succession results from interactions between different species, and between species and their environment, which govern the sequence and the rate with which species replace each other. The rate at which succession proceeds depends on the time scale of species' life histories as well as on the effects species may have on each other and on the environment which supports them. SEE ECOLOGICAL COMMUNITIES; POPULATION ECOLOGY.

The course of ecological succession depends on initial environmental conditions. Primary succession occurs on novel areas such as volcanic ash, glacial deposits, or bare rock, areas which have not previously supported a community. In such harsh, unstable environments, pioneer colonizing organisms must have wide ranges of ecological tolerance to survive. In contrast, secondary succession is initiated by disturbance such as fire, which removes a previous community from an area. Pioneer species are here constrained not by the physical environment but by their ability to enter and exploit the vacant area rapidly.

As succession proceeds, many environmental factors may change through the influence of the community. Especially in primary succession, this leads to more stable, less severe environments. At the same time interactions between species of plant tend to intensify competition for basic resources such as water, light, space, and nutrients. Successional change results from the normal complex interactions between organism and environment which lead to changes in overall species composition. Whether succession is promoted by changing environmental factors or competitive interactions, species composition alters in response to availability of niches. Populations occurring in the community at a point in succession are those able to provide propagules (such as seeds) to invade the area, being sufficiently tolerant of current environmental conditions, and able to withstand competition from members of other populations present at the same stage. Species lacking these qualities either become locally extinct or are unable to enter and survive in the community.

Primary succession. In some cases, seres may take hundreds of years to complete, and direct observation at a given site is not possible. Adjacent sites may be identified as successively older stages of the same sere, if it is assumed that conditions were similar when each seral stage was initiated.

Table 1. Successional changes in vegetation and soils observed on an aged series of moraines at Glacier Bay, Alaska		
Years	Vegetation	Soil environment
0	Initial colonizers: mosses, fireweed, horsetail, *Dryas*, dwarf willows; later, willows form dense scrub	Initially pH 8.0–8.4 due to CaCO₃: soil N and organic matter lacking
50	Alder invades, forming dense thickets less than 33 ft (10 m) tall	pH falls to 5.0 in 30–50 years due to acidic products of alder leaf decomposition; marked increase in soil N due to fixation in alder root nodules; soil organic matter accumulates
170	Sitka spruce invades, forming dense forest	Reduction in soil N by incorporation in forest biomass; progressive increase in soil organic matter
250+	Western and mountain hemlock enter (climax forest on well-drained slopes) *Sphagnum* bog with occasional pines replaces forest in poorly drained areas	Soil becomes waterlogged, deoxygenated, acidified

Table 2. Succession on sand dunes of Lake Michigan

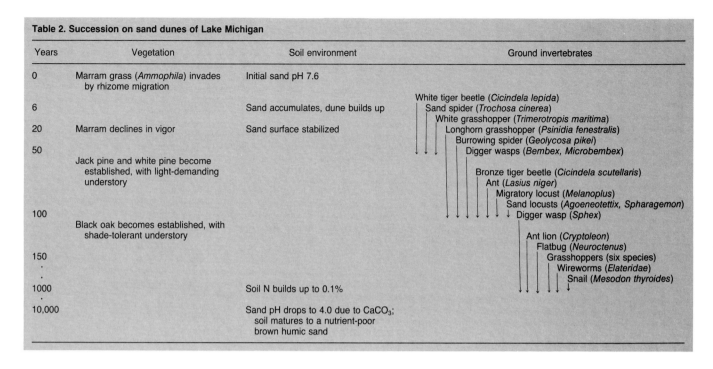

Years	Vegetation	Soil environment	Ground invertebrates
0	Marram grass (*Ammophila*) invades by rhizome migration	Initial sand pH 7.6	
6		Sand accumulates, dune builds up	White tiger beetle (*Cicindela lepida*) / Sand spider (*Trochosa cinerea*)
20	Marram declines in vigor	Sand surface stabilized	White grasshopper (*Trimerotropis maritima*) / Longhorn grasshopper (*Psinidia fenestralis*) / Burrowing spider (*Geolycosa pikei*)
50	Jack pine and white pine become established, with light-demanding understory		Digger wasps (*Bembex, Microbembex*) / Bronze tiger beetle (*Cicindela scutellaris*) / Ant (*Lasius niger*) / Migratory locust (*Melanoplus*) / Sand locusts (*Agoeneotettix, Spharagemon*) / Digger wasp (*Sphex*)
100	Black oak becomes established, with shade-tolerant understory		Ant lion (*Cryptoleon*) / Flatbug (*Neuroctenus*) / Grasshoppers (six species) / Wireworms (*Elateridae*) / Snail (*Mesodon thyroides*)
150			
·			
·			
1000		Soil N builds up to 0.1%	
·			
10,000		Sand pH drops to 4.0 due to CaCO₃; soil matures to a nutrient-poor brown humic sand	

Glacier Bay. In the Glacier Bay region of Alaska, glaciers have retreated, in phases, some 61 mi (98 km) since 1750, leaving a series of moraines of known ages supporting a range of seral vegetational types. Soil factors become modified by vegetation, enabling new species to become established (see **Table 1**). Acidic decomposition products of alder leaves sharply reduce soil pH, whereas virtually no change occurs on bare glacial till or under other vegetation. Pioneer species must tolerate low nitrogen levels, but alder is able to fix atmospheric nitrogen (N) by the presence of microbial symbionts in root nodules and is correlated with a rapid increase in soil nitrogen by way of leaf fall. After invasion by spruce, levels of accumulated nitrogen fall as nitrogen becomes incorporated in forest biomass, and the annual additions from alder are reduced. Soil organic matter increases progressively, and influences the structural development of the soil. The mature forest remains only on well-drained slopes. In areas of poorer drainage, invasion by *Sphagnum* moss leads to replacement of trees by wet acidic bog or muskeg.

Lake Michigan. Another example of primary succession has been recorded on a sequence of dune ridges bordering Lake Michigan, ranging in age to 12,000 years. Succession is initiated on a bare sand surface either following a fall in lake level, as occurred in phases since the last glaciation, or due to wind erosion of an existing dune redepositing sand (see **Table 2**). Marram grass impedes the transport of sand across bare dune surfaces and so promotes accretion of sand. At the same time, it grows and branches vigorously, thus maintaining cover on the expanding dune (**Fig. 1**).

Succession on Lake Michigan dunes demonstrates that local factors may modify the typical pattern (**Fig. 2**). In damp depressions with impeded drainage, a grassland community develops. Sheltered pockets on lee slopes have a moister microclimate and tend to accumulate leaf litter from more exposed parts of the dunes, as well as receiving protection from frequent fires. As a result, a more nutrient-rich soil can de-

velop, and succession proceeds via basswood to more nutrient-demanding oak-hickory and finally maple-beech woodland, typical of normal soils of the region. The black oak association appears to be stable on dune soils, since it is tolerant of low nutrients and water limitation, and tends to maintain these conditions by returning few nutrients in the leaf litter.

Climax community. Early stages of succession tend to be relatively rapid, whereas the rates of species turnover and soil changes become slower as the community matures. Eventually an approximation to the steady state is established with a relatively stable community, the nature of which has aroused considerable debate. Earlier, the so-called climax vegetation was believed to be determined ultimately by regional climate and, given sufficient time, any community in a region would attain this universal condition. This unified concept of succession, the monoclimax hypothesis, implies the ability of organisms progressively to

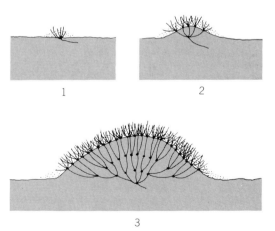

Fig. 1. Dune formation by the gradual deposition of wind-carried sand particles around aerial shoots of *Ammophila arenaria*. 1, 2, and 3 indicate successive periods of time. *(After K. A. Kershaw, Quantitative and Dynamic Ecology, 2d ed., Arnold, 1973)*

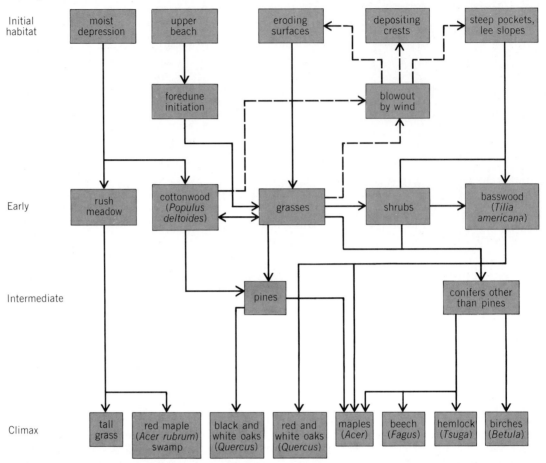

Fig. 2. Alternative patterns of primary plant succession on Lake Michigan dunes, depending on initial conditions, extrinsic variables, and colonization-invasion patterns. (*After S. J. McNaughton and L. L. Wolf, General Ecology, 2d ed., Holt, Reinhart, and Winston, 1979*)

modify their environment until it can support the climatic climax community. Although plants and animals do sometimes ameliorate environmental conditions, evidence suggests overwhelmingly that succession has a variety of stable end points. This hypothesis, known as the polyclimax hypothesis, suggests that the end point of a succession depends on a complex of environmental factors that characterize the site, such as parent material, topography, local climate, and human influences.

In the Lake Michigan sand dunes, the course of succession and its climax appear to be determined by physiographic conditions at the start (Fig. 2). Similarly, the transformation of glacial moraine forest to muskeg depends on local drainage. In the tropical rainforest of Moraballi Creek, Guyana, five apparently stable vegetation types have been distinguished on different soil types under the same climate. A mixed forest is present on red loam, whereas the Wallaba forest occurs on bleached sand, with the Mora forest type in areas liable to flooding.

Autogenic vs. allogenic factors. In the examples of succession discussed above, the chief agent in modifying the environment is the community itself: thus marram stabilizes the sand dune surface, and alder increases the soil nutrient status of moraine soil. These actions of the community on the environment, termed autogenic, provide an important driving force

promoting successional change, and are typical of primary succession where initial environments are inhospitable. Alternatively, changes in species composition of a community may result from influences external to the community called allogenic. For example, in aquatic ecosystems (the hydrosere) the community commonly develops from open water with submerged and floating aquatic plant species toward a swamp community in which rooted emergent plants dominate in shallower water, until finally the marsh is colonized by land plants from the surrounding area as sediment deposition continues and the soil dries out. Reduction in water depth, enabling colonization by marsh species and finally terrestrial species, occurs with input of waterborne and airborne sediments—thus the aquatic phase of the hydrosere is controlled by input of materials from outside the system. Similarly, lakes are typically subject to enrichment of nutrients from surrounding areas, resulting in increased productivity. Extremely high production occurs in culturally eutrophic lakes, which receive nutrient inputs from human activities. In aquatic systems where the influence of allogenic factors such as siltation are apparently minimal, vegetation tends to develop via a series of productive intermediate steps toward an oligotrophic community, that is, one with low productivity, dominated by *Sphagnum* moss (**Fig. 3**). See EUTROPHICATION.

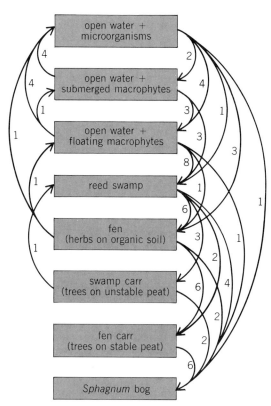

Fig. 3. Transitions between vegetation "stages" free from obvious allogenic influences derived from 20 pollen diagrams for lake sediments and peat. Figures show numbers of observed transitions.

Whereas intrinsic factors often result in progressive successional changes, that is, changes leading from simple to more complex communities, external (allogenic) forces may induce retrogressive succession, that is, toward a less mature community. For example, if a grassland is severely overgrazed by cattle, the most palatable species will disappear. As grazing continues, the grass cover is reduced, and in the open areas weeds characteristic of initial stages of succession may become established.

Heterotrophic succession. In the preceding examples of succession, the food web was based on photosynthetic organisms and there was a slow accumulation of organic matter, both living and dead. This is termed autotrophic succession. In some instances, however, addition of organic matter to an ecosystem initiates a succession of decomposer organisms which invade and degrade it. Such a succession is called heterotrophic. In an Illinois pasture, cow dung is degraded by a seral community of some 40 to 60 invertebrate species over a period of 30 days. The newly deposited cow pat is immediately visited by the horn fly (*Haematobia irritans*), which quickly lays eggs and returns to the cow. It is followed by several other dung flies whose larvae are eaten by beetles such as *Sphaeridium scaraboides* which burrow through the dung and lay their eggs. A parasitic wasp (*Xyalophora quinquelinata*) deposits eggs inside maggots of *Sarcophaga* flies. As the dung ages and dries out, it is inhabited by a wider variety of species. Little is known in detail of the importance of the various saprovores in degrading the dung and in modifying the microhabitat, or of their dependence on the activities of saprophytic fungi.

Discharge of organic effluent into a river is detectable downstream by a progression in chemical factors and in the biota. Succession in time is here equivalent to the change in species composition resulting from the decline in organic effluent that corresponds to the distance from the discharge. Marked reduction in dissolved oxygen directly below an outfall results from respiration of microorganisms as they degrade organic matter. Detritivores tolerant of low oxygen concentrations, such as *Tubificidae* and *Chironomidae,* attain high population densities in the bottom sediments. Subsequently, a bloom of algae is typical, utilizing released nitrate and phosphate. As the river flows downstream, the aquatic food web progressively changes from a heterotrophic to an autotrophic basis and productivity declines to its normal level as the "clean water" community returns. SEE BIOLOGICAL PRODUCTIVITY; FOOD WEB.

Secondary succession. Following the partial or complete destruction of an established community by disturbing events such as fire or clearfelling, and similarly on the cessation of grazing or tillage, a sequence of species invasion and replacement ensues. Compared to the slow initial progress of primary succession in which amelioration of the environment plays an important part, secondary succession is characterized initially by rapid turnover of typically opportunist species which invade relatively congenial habitats.

Piedmont. Abandoned fields in the Piedmont area of North Carolina show a rapid sequence of replacement of herbaceous species, apparently related to the life histories of the plants (**Table 3**). Horseweed produces seeds in late summer which germinate immediately so that the plant overwinters as a juvenile, grows rapidly the following year, and dies after seeding in the summer. Aster seeds do not germinate until the following spring, and seedlings grow slowly due to shading by established horseweed plants. In addition, decaying horseweed roots inhibit its own growth and, to a greater extent, that of aster. Horseweed attains dominance in the first year by efficient seed dispersal and rapid establishment. Being a perennial, aster is able to outcompete horseweed in the second year despite the inhibitory effect of the latter. Seedlings of aster

Table 3. Secondary succession on abandoned fields in the Piedmont area of North Carolina*

Years after last cultivation	Dominant plant	Other common species
0 (autumn)	Crabgrass (*Digitaria sanguinalis*) ↓	
1	Horseweed (*Erigeron canadensis*) ↓	Ragweed (*Ambrosia elatior*)
2	Aster (*Aster pilosus*) ↓	Ragweed
3	Broomsedge (*Andropogon virginicus*) ↓	
5–15	Shortleaf pine (*Pinus echinata*) ↓	Loblolly pine
50–150	Hardwoods (oaks)	Hickory

*From C. Krebs, *Ecology,* 2d ed., Harper and Row, 1978.

are present in abundance in third-year fields but are less drought-resistant than those of broomsedge, which outcompetes aster except in fields with more available water, where aster survives the competition longer.

Broomsedge seeds are not available to colonize initially because seeds are not produced until the end of the plant's second year and require a period of cold dormancy before germination. Seedling growth is apparently enhanced by decomposition products of the previous colonists. The late establishment of broomsedge in the succession is dependent not on changes brought about by earlier colonists but on the life history of the plant.

After broomsedge, shortleaf pine invades the herb community. Pine seeds require mineral soil and minimal root competition to become established, and the seedlings are not shade-tolerant. Hence after about 20 years, under a dense pine canopy, reproduction of pines is almost lacking. Accumulation of litter and shade under pines causes the old-field herbs to die out.

Oak seedlings become established after about 20 years, when the depth of litter is adequate to prevent desiccation of acorns. Organic matter in the soil surface layer also increases, improving its water-holding capacity. After about 50 years, several oak species become established and gradually assume dominance as the pines fail to reproduce. Unlike pine, which is capable of germinating on bare soil, oaks and other hardwoods require changes in the soil resulting from pine litter before their seedlings can establish successfully.

While plant species are the main indicators of succession, it is important to note that animal species are also changing over time. In the Piedmont, the changes in bird species as succession proceeds have been well documented. Just a few species, such as meadowlarks and grasshopper sparrows, are found in the initial stages, while more complicated assemblages of species are common in the latter forest stages.

Nova Scotia forest. Following clearfelling in a Nova Scotia forest, the course of secondary succession involves invasion by shrubs (raspberry) followed by understory trees (pincherry, aspen), followed by shade-intolerant species (red maple, paper birch), and finally a shade-tolerant community (hard maple, yellow birch, white ash). Perhaps shade-tolerant species such as red maple, which are of low commercial value, could be inhibited if strip felling were practiced by the forestry industry as an alternative to clearfelling in large blocks. Commercially desirable shade-tolerant species such as white ash would be favored where there was greater local shading of the regenerating community.

Mechanisms of species replacement. Observed changes in the structure and function of seral communities result from natural selection of individuals within their current environment. Three mechanisms by which species may replace each other have been proposed; the relative importance of each apparently depends on the nature of the sere and stage of development.

1. The facilitation hypothesis states that invasion of later species depends on conditions created by earlier colonists. Earlier species modify the environment so as to increase the competitive ability of species which are then able to displace them. Succession thus proceeds because of the effects of species on their environment.

2. The tolerance hypothesis suggests that later successional species tolerate lower levels of resources than earlier occupants and can invade and replace them by reducing resource levels below those tolerated by earlier occupants. Succession proceeds despite the resistance of earlier colonists.

3. The inhibition hypothesis is that all species resist invasion of competitors and are displaced only by death or by damage from factors other than competition. Succession proceeds toward dominance by longer-lived species.

None of these models of succession is solely applicable in all instances; indeed most examples of succession appear to show elements of all three replacement mechanisms. In secondary succession on North Carolina croplands, stimulation of broomsedge growth by decomposition products of previous colonists, and the requirement of oak seedlings for a deep litter layer in which to germinate, exemplify facilitation. The ability of broomsedge to displace aster in competition for water suggest the tolerance mechanism, whereas the inhibition hypothesis is supported by the greater tolerance of horseweed seedlings than aster seedlings to horseweed decomposition products.

Deterministic vs. stochastic succession. Succession has traditionally been regarded as following an orderly progression of changes toward a predictable end point, the climax community, in equilibrium with the prevailing environment. This essentially deterministic view implies that succession will always follow the same course from a given starting point and will pass through a recognizable series of intermediate states (such as in Fig. 2). In contrast, a more recent view of succession is based on adaptations of independent species. It is argued that succession is disorderly and unpredictable, resulting from probabilistic processes such as invasion of propagules and survival of individuals which make up the community. Such a stochastic view reflects the inherent variability observed in nature and the uncertainty of environmental conditions. In particular, it allows for succession to take alternative pathways and end points dependent on the chance outcome of interactions among species and between species and their environment.

Consideration of community properties such as energy flow supports the view of succession as an orderly process. Early in autotrophic succession gross primary productivity (P_g) increases rapidly with community biomass (B), whereas community respiration (R) increases more slowly (**Fig. 4**). As a result, net primary productivity (P_n, where $P_n = P_g - R$) builds

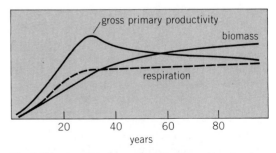

Fig. 4. The energetics of ecosystem development in a forest. The difference between gross primary productivity and respiration is the net primary productivity. (*After E. P. Odum, Ecology, 2d ed., Holt, Reinhart, and Winston, 1975*)

up early in succession, and the ratio P_g/B is at its highest in the initial stages. As the community increases in biomass and complexity over time, more complete overall utilization of basic resources such as light limits further increase in primary productivity, whereas R continues to increase because of the increase in tissue to support. Hence P_n declines toward zero and the biomass of a mature forest community no longer accumulates. The rate of gross primary productivity typically becomes limited also by the availability of nutrients, now incorporated within the community biomass, and declines to a level sustainable by release from decomposer organisms. Species di-

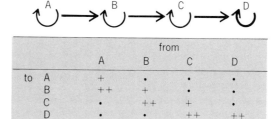

		from			
		A	B	C	D
to	A	+	•	•	•
	B	++	+	•	•
	C	•	++	+	•
	D	•	•	++	++

(a)

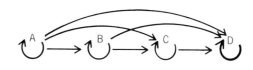

		from			
		A	B	C	D
to	A	+	•	•	•
	B	+	+	•	•
	C	+	+	+	•
	D	+	+	+	++

(b)

		from			
		A	B	C	D
to	A	+	•	•	•
	B	+	++	•	•
	C	+	•	+	•
	D	+	•	+	++

(c)

Fig. 5. Schematic representation of three postulated mechanisms for species replacement in succession: (a) facilitation, (b) tolerance, and (c) inhibition. Arrows indicate the direction in which the systems tend to move between different states, A–D. Relative probabilities of movement are indicated by thickness of arrows and by symbols in the accompanying transition matrix, where • = close to zero, + = moderate, and + + = high.

Table 4. Proposed successional trends in ecosystem structural and functional organization, species characteristics, evolutionary factors, and homeostasis*

Ecosystem property	Ecosystem stage	
	Successional (immature)	Climax (mature)
Energy Flow		
Gross productivity/ respiration (P_g/R)	Autotrophic >1 Heterotrophic <1	Approaches 1
Biomass supported/unit energy flow (B/P_g)	Low	High
Net productivity (P_n)	High	Low
Type of food chains	Linear, grazing	Webs, detritus
Nutrient Flow		
Mineral cycles	Open	Closed
Flow rate: organism-environment	Rapid	Slow
Role of detritus	Unimportant	Important
Community Structure		
Total organic matter	Little	Much
Location of chemicals	Habitat pools	Biotic pools
Species richness	Low	High
Species evenness	Low	High
Biochemical diversity	Low	High
Spatial heterogeneity	Low	High
Species Life History Characteristics		
Niche breadth	Broad	Narrow
Organism size	Small	Large
Life cycles	Short, simple	Long, complex
Selection Pressure		
Growth form	Rapid growth (r-selection)	Feedback control (K selection)
Production	Quantity	Quality
Overall Homeostasis		
Internal symbiosis	Undeveloped	Developed
Nutrient conservation	Poor	Good
Resistance to perturbations	Poor	Good
Entropy	High	Low
Information	Low	High

*After Odum, 1976.

versity tends to rise rapidly at first as successive invasions occur, but declines again with the elimination of the pioneer species by the climax community.

Trends in community function, niche specialization, and life history strategy are summarized in **Table 4**. As the community acquires increasing maturity, P_n declines to zero, nutrients become incorporated in biotic pools, broad-niched species are replaced by those with more specific requirements, and the structural organization of the community increases.

Regeneration of an area of subtropical rainforest in Queensland was observed after the vegetation and surface litter were removed with a bulldozer. Because of small environmental differences in the 10 quadrats observed, succession took four directions after the demise of the first ubiquitous colonizing species, resulting in four apparently stable plant associations. This divergence may result merely from small-scale variation in topography within the 65 × 130 ft (20 × 40 m) experimental site and from differing efficiencies of removal of surface litter between the quadrats. Hence the different plant associations detected could be interpreted as divergent products of succession or as phases within a larger-scale vegetation unit.

Stochastic aspects of succession can be represented in the form of models which allow for transitions between a series of different "states." Such models, termed Markovian models, can apply at various levels: plant-by-plant replacement, changes in tree size categories, or transitions between whole communities. A matrix of replacement probabilities defines the direction, pathway, and likelihood of change, and the model can be used to predict the future composition of the community from its initial state. With alternative transition matrices, this simple model could represent a linear progression toward a stable end state, or a cyclical, recursive sequence of communities. The three postulated mechanisms for species replacement discussed above can be illustrated by the topology of alternative Markovian models (**Fig. 5**). The facilitation model of succession is represented as a linear sequence with greater probabilities of progression toward the final state (D) than maintenance of intermediate states. In the tolerance model, later stages may develop from earlier stages depending on the availability of propagules of subsequent stages and their competitive ability. Again, only state D has a high probability of self-replacement. In the inhibition model, there is a high probability that an intermediate state (in this case, B) will persist by strong self-replacement, thereby truncating the normal succession toward state D. A very low probability that B will change to C or D is assumed. Hence, a high degree of realism can be achieved with a simple model system, and alternative predictions of successional changes can be compared with observed data. SEE ECOLOGY.

Peter Randerson

Bibliography. D. H. Boucher (ed.), *The Biology of Mutualism: Ecology and Evolution*, 1985; R. E. Ricklefs, *Ecology*, 3d ed., 1988; P. Yodis, *Introduction to Theoretical Ecology*, 1988.

Ecology

The subdiscipline of biology that concentrates on the relationships between organisms and their environments; it is also called environmental biology. Ecology is concerned with patterns of distribution (where organisms occur) and with patterns of abundance (how many organisms occur) in space and time. It seeks to explain the factors that determine the range of environments that organisms occupy and that determine how abundant organisms are within those ranges. It also emphasizes functional interactions between co-occurring organisms. In addition to its character as a unique component of the biological sciences, ecology is both a synthetic and an integrative science since it often draws upon information and concepts in other sciences, ranging from physiology to meteorology, to explain the complex organization of nature.

Environment is all of those factors external to an organism that affect its survival, growth, development, and reproduction. It can be subdivided into physical, or abiotic, factors and biological, or biotic, factors. The physical components of the environment include all nonbiological constituents, such as temperature, wind, inorganic chemicals, and radiation. The biological components of the environment include the organisms. A somewhat more general term is habitat, which refers in a general way to where an organism occurs and the environmental factors present there. SEE ENVIRONMENT.

A recognition of the unitary coupling of an organism and its environment is fundamental to ecology; in fact, the definitions of organism and environment are not separate. Environment is organism-centered since the environmental properties of a habitat are determined by the requirements of the organisms that occupy that habitat. For example, the amount of inorganic nitrogen dissolved in lake water is of little immediate significance to zooplankton in the lake because they are incapable of utilizing inorganic nitrogen directly. However, because phytoplankton are capable of utilizing inorganic nitrogen directly, it is a component of their environment. Any effect of inorganic nitrogen upon the zooplankton, then, will occur indirectly through its effect on the abundance of the phytoplankton that the zooplankton feed upon. SEE PHYTOPLANKTON; ZOOPLANKTON.

Just as the environment affects the organism, so the organism affects its environment. Growth of phytoplankton may be nitrogen-limited if the number of individuals has become so great that there is no more nitrogen available in the environment. Zooplankton, not limited by inorganic nitrogen themselves, can promote the growth of additional phytoplankton by consuming some individuals, digesting them, and returning part of the nitrogen to the environment.

Ecology is concerned with the processes involved in the interactions between organisms and their environments, with the mechanisms responsible for those processes, and with the origin, through evolution, of those mechanisms. It is distinguished from such closely related biological subdisciplines as physiology and morphology because it is not intrinsically concerned with the operation of a physiological process or the function of a structure, but with how a process or structure interacts with the environment to influence survival, growth, development, and reproduction.

Scope. There are a wide variety of approaches to ecology because of its broad, comprehensive character. Ecological studies can be characterized by the type of organisms studied, the habitat where studies take place, the level of organization that is of interest, and the methodology used. These are nonexclusive categories, and ecologists combine them in various ways while doing research. Major subdivisions by organism include plant ecology, animal ecology, and microbial ecology. Subdivisions by habitat include terrestrial ecology, the study of organisms on land; limnology, the study of fresh-water organisms and habitats; and oceanography, the study of marine organisms and habitats.

The levels of organization studied range from the individual organism to the whole complex of organisms in a large area. Autecology is the study of individuals, population ecology is the study of groups of individuals of a single species or a limited number of species, synecology is the study of communities of several populations, and ecosystem, or simply systems, ecology is the study of communities of organisms and their environments in a specific time and place.

Higher levels of organization include biomes and the biosphere. Biomes are collections of ecosystems with similar organisms and environments and, therefore, similar ecological properties. All of Earth's coniferous forests are elements in the coniferous forest biome. Although united by similar dynamic relationships and structural properties, the biome itself is more abstract than a specific ecosystem. The biosphere is the most inclusive category possible, including all regions of Earth inhabited by living things. It extends from the lower reaches of the atmosphere to the depths of the oceans. *See Biome; Biosphere*.

The principal methodological approaches to ecology are descriptive, experimental, and theoretical. Much of ecology through the first half of the twentieth century was descriptive, concentrating on describing the variety of populations, communities, and habitats throughout Earth. Experimental ecology, which involves manipulating organisms or their environments to discover the underlying mechanisms governing distribution and abundance, has become of increasing importance since the mid-1960s. Theoretical ecology uses mathematical equations based on assumptions about the properties of organisms and environments to make predictions about patterns of distribution and abundance. It also has become of increasing importance. All of these approaches, however, are evident in the origins of ecology. The science was more descriptive in its early phases and has become more experimental and theoretical in recent decades.

Ecosystem. An ecosystem is the organisms and physical factors in a specific location that are interrelated through the flow of energy and chemicals to form a characteristic trophic structure (**Fig. 1**). The concept of the ecosystem is fundamental to ecology and may be applied at various levels of organization, although it commonly encompasses several different species. The trophic structure of an ecosystem characterizes organisms according to their feeding level and how those feeding relationships of species result in specific patterns of energy flow and chemical cycling. The living mass of a given population or trophic level at any given time is called biomass. A change in mass with time is referred to as net productivity. *See Biological productivity; Biomass*.

Primary producers, largely green photosynthetic plants, utilize the energy of the Sun and inorganic molecules from the environment to synthesize organic molecules. Those organic molecules serve as food for higher trophic levels. Primary consumers, or herbivores, feed on the producers. Secondary consumers, or carnivores, feed on other consumers, while omnivores feed at several trophic levels. Decomposers feed on the dead tissues of other organisms.

Each single pathway of energy and chemical flow is referred to as a food chain; the entire collection of food chains in an ecosystem is a food web, or trophic web. Since energy is expended to do work and chemicals are released back into the environment at each step of the trophic web, energy flow in ecosystems is unidirectional, constantly diminishing up the trophic web, while chemicals are recycled to the environment where they can be reutilized in organic syntheses. *See Food web*.

The ultimate energy source of all ecosystems is the radiant energy of photons from the Sun. Two major types of ecosystems can be distinguished, however, by their proximate energy sources. Autotrophic ecosystems have primary producers as a principal component and sunlight as the major initial energy source. Heterotrophic ecosystems depend upon preformed or-

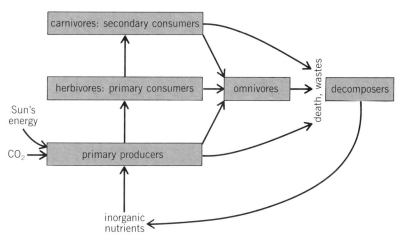

Fig. 1. Generalized trophic levels of ecosystems. Arrows indicate flow of energy and chemicals.

ganic matter that is imported from autotrophic ecosystems elsewhere. The organisms in a stream, for example, may be highly dependent upon organic matter which has eroded from surrounding terrestrial ecosystems.

The ecosystem concept is flexible in application, but the way that it is applied must be clearly specified. An ecosystem study might concentrate on all the organisms and their environments in a specified forest. Alternatively, it might confine itself to the forest floor and soil, concentrating on trophic relationships within that more restricted habitat. *See Ecosystem*.

AUTECOLOGY

Autecology is the study of particular organisms, typically directed toward determining the traits they possess, and the traits they lack, that allow them to occupy, or be excluded from, certain environments. Early in the twentieth century, autecology placed considerable emphasis upon the morphology and anatomy of organisms, but the field has become diversified in the last few decades into a variety of different approaches. Autecology now also includes physiological ecology, which emphasizes the role of physiological processes, and chemical ecology, which emphasizes the role of biochemical traits. *See Physiological ecology (plant)*.

One of the earliest generalizations of ecology was the principle of limiting factors, which states that organisms are limited by the factor or combination of factors that are farthest from the requirements of the organism. It was first stated by Liebig based on his studies of soil fertility. He recognized that there usually was a single chemical that would promote yield when it was added to the soil. When that initial limiting factor had been enriched, he found that addition of another nutrient might promote yield even more. The British physiologist Blackman restated the principle in its modern form based on his studies of photosynthesis revealing that the process sometimes could be limited simultaneously by more than one factor.

Though autecology is concerned with individual organisms, that information is often used to contrast the traits of organisms that occupy different environments. Thus there is a strong comparative character to autecological studies; two major habitat comparisons, discussed below, are marine vs. fresh-water, and terrestrial vs. aquatic.

Marine vs. fresh-water habitats. Life first evolved in the sea; the colonization of fresh-water habitats that followed was accompanied by the evolution of traits associated with exploiting the more dilute solutions of fresh-water habitats. Seawater is over 3.6% dissolved solids, largely sodium chloride, while fresh water contains 0.01–0.05% dissolved solids. Colonization of fresh water was coupled with the evolution of relatively impervious body surfaces, mechanisms allowing organisms to accumulate ions against a concentration gradient, and the production of large quantities of very dilute urine or other excretory waste. For example, many marine invertebrates are isotonic (equal in osmotic pressure) to seawater so they have no tendency to either lose or gain water. Elasmobranchs have high concentrations of urea in the blood, and although the concentrations of ions is lower than is seawater, the concentrations of urea plus ions is isotonic. Marine teleosts have blood osmotic concentrations well below that of seawater, and they therefore tend to lose water to the sea. They counteract this loss by drinking large quantities of seawater, absorbing it through the gut, and secreting the salt from special cells in the gills. Most fresh-water animals are hypotonic (lower osmotic concentration) to the solution that bathes them so they tend to gain water.

Terrestrial vs. aquatic habitats. The colonization of terrestrial habitats was accompanied by the evolution of a large number of traits that allowed organisms to occupy habitats where water was a comparatively rare component of the environment and the atmosphere and soils became principal media surrounding organisms.

Since the body was no longer bathed in fluid, plants and animals both evolved traits allowing them to conserve water and obtain it when it was scarce. Plants developed extensive absorptive surfaces which allowed them to grow into moist regions of the soil and obtain both water and nutrients from the soil solution. Animals often drank water directly and developed outer tissue layers that were extremely impervious to water. The evolution of vascular systems in both animals and plants allowed them to transport water from limited sites of acquisition to the rest of the body. Since the atmosphere is a much less dense and buoyant medium than water, terrestrial plants and animals also evolved traits providing rigid support, such as the skeletons of vertebrates and the strengthened woody stems of vascular plants.

Terrestrial habitats are also characterized by much greater temperature fluctuations than occur in aquatic habitats. Animals therefore evolved physiological traits that allowed them to maintain their body temperatures constant, as well as behavioral traits that involved the ability to move into habitats where favorable temperatures occurred. Physiologically, evolution culminated in homeothermy in birds and mammals; these organisms expend energy to maintain body temperature within narrow limits. Other animals, called heterotherms, which are incapable of maintaining their body temperature over a wide range of environmental temperatures, often move into localized environmental areas providing appropriate temperatures, and spend unfavorable seasons in quiescent metabolic states.

Finally, the colonization of terrestrial habitats was associated with many changes in reproductive methods due to the inability of organisms to effectively disperse gametes through the surrounding medium.

Such adaptations include the behavioral mating systems of birds and mammals that allow mates to find one another, and the elaborate pollination mechanisms of flowering plants that may involve specific transfer of pollen between individuals of the same species by animal vectors.

Physiological and chemical ecology. The postwar development of analytical instrumentation that was much more sensitive to many chemicals than previous analytical techniques led directly to the development of physiological and chemical ecology, which applies that instrumentation to studying organisms in their natural environments. The development of infrared gas analyzers that detect carbon dioxide and water vapor at concentrations that occur in nature led to many studies of photosynthesis, respiration, and transpiration by plants. Those studies have revealed two different types of photosynthesis that occur in plants occupying different types of environments. C_3 plants, so named because the initial stable product of carbon fixation is a three-carbon molecule, are characteristic of almost all aquatic habitats and of terrestrial environments with lower temperatures, less arid climates, and lower solar radiation intensities. C_4 plants, so named because the initial stable product of photosynthesis is a four-carbon molecule, are more common in arid, hotter environments with more intense solar radiation. Those differences are due to the fact that C_3 photosynthesis is intrinsically more efficient but is also more temperature-sensitive and generally more likely to be light-saturated well below the intensity of full sunlight. Thus, C_4 plants are common in tropical and subtropical, arid terrestrial ecosystems, while C_3 plants are more common in most other ecosystems.

Chemical ecology studies have been largely devoted to studying rare molecules that have major biological effects. Many animals, for example, produce pheromones that are extremely dilute in the environment but can attract mates, repel predators, or kill pathogens. Many plants also produce organic molecules that are present in their tissues in very small concentrations but act to deter herbivores and pathogens. The evolution of highly toxic molecules by plants sometimes has led to the evolution of specific mechanisms of avoidance or detoxification by a limited number of animals. That type of coupled evolution in which populations change genetically in response to the properties of each other is called coevolution. For example, some animals, such as the monarch butterfly whose larvae feed on milkweeds, have even appropriated aspects of their food plant's chemistry to protect them from predators. Milkweeds produce cardiac glycosides, chemicals that poison the heart muscles of vertebrates. The larvae of the monarch sequester those chemicals in their body, which protects them from such potential predators as birds and small mammals.

POPULATION ECOLOGY

Population ecology is the study of the vital statistics of populations, and the interactions within and between populations that influence survival and reproduction. Population ecologists are concerned with the balances between births and deaths that determine the rate of change of population size through time. When births exceed deaths, of course, population size increases, and when deaths exceed births, population size declines. Vital statistics are often expressed on a per capita basis or, in human populations, on a per-10,000-persons basis. Density, the number of organisms per unit area, is a fundamental property of populations.

One of the principal concerns of population ecologists is identifying and determining the importance of factors that control population densities. Since A. van Leeuwenhoek first calculated the massive potential of flies to reproduce—that is, one pair of flies could produce 746,496 flies after only 3 months of breeding—population ecology has been concerned with the factors that limit the complete realization of this reproductive potential. There are two fundamentally different types of factors limiting population density. Density-independent factors are environmental factors that reduce reproduction or increase death rate independently of the number of organisms in the population. Weather is believed to be a major density-independent factor that often affects populations in a catastrophic way to reduce density. Severely cold winters, deep snowfalls, exceptionally wet growing seasons, and extreme drought occur with a frequency and intensity that are independent of population size. Although these factors can determine population density, they cannot regulate that density since regulation involves maintaining density within certain limits. Density-dependent factors influence the survival or reproduction of individuals in a way that is proportional to density. They can, therefore, regulate population density. Food supply, predators, disease, and such behavioral interactions as territoriality can limit survival and reproduction with increasing intensity as population density increases.

Two vital statistics of populations of principal interest to population ecology are survivorship and reproductive schedules (**Fig. 2**): It is the balance between the probability that an individual will live to reach a certain age, and the average number of offspring produced by individuals of that age that determine population growth rate.

Population growth. One of the earliest quantitative expressions in ecology was a description of density-dependent population growth called the logistic equation. It was first described by P. F. Verhulst in 1838, but it was completely forgotten until its rediscovery by R. Pearl and L. Reed in 1920. Population growth rate is a consequence of population size (N) and per capita birth (b) and death (d) rates, as shown by Eq. (1), where dN/dt is rate of change of population size.

$$\frac{dN}{dt} = (b - d)N \qquad (1)$$

If the symbol r is used to represent the realized per capita reproductive rate, that is, $b - d$, then Eq. (1) can be written in the form of Eq. (2). If r is a con-

$$\frac{dN}{dt} = rN \qquad (2)$$

stant, a population described by Eq. (2) would grow exponentially with time. The logistic equation recognizes two factors lacking in Eq. (2) that can influence population growth: the maximum per capita reproductive potential of the population, r_m, and the carrying capacity of the environment, K. Maximum reproductive potential would only be realized in the most favorable environment when population density was low enough that individuals did not make simulta-

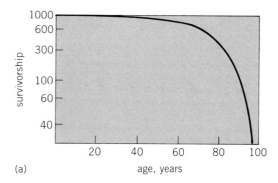

(a)

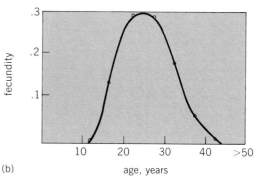

(b)

Fig. 2. Demographic statistics of females in the United States. (a) Survivorship, where the vertical axis is the number surviving, of 1000 born alive (on a logarithmic scale). (b) Reproductive schedule, where the vertical axis is the number of female offspring per female of given age, at 5-year intervals.

neous demands on the same resources. Carrying capacity is a measure of both the amount of resources in the environment and the efficiency with which organisms use those resources. A population is at its carrying capacity when no additional individuals can be supported by an environment. Incorporating those constants into the growth equation above gives Eq. (3), the logistic equation. Maximum per capita reproductive potential is determined by the genetic ability

$$\frac{dN}{dt} = r_m N \left(1 - \frac{N}{K} \right) \qquad (3)$$

ductive potential is determined by the genetic ability to reproduce in an unlimited environment. A population growing according to this equation has a sigmoid, or S-shaped, pattern of population size through time (**Fig. 3**). The maximum population growth rate, which, again, is the product of population size and per capita reproductive rate, is reached when the population is halfway to K.

Dividing Eq. (3) through by N and rearranging gives Eq. (4). Plotting r against N gives a straight line

$$\frac{dN}{Ndt} = r_m - \left(\frac{r_m}{K} \right) N \qquad (4)$$

with an intercept on the y axis that is equal to r_m and an intercept on the x axis that is equal to K.

An equation as simple as the logistic equation provides merely a yardstick against which the growth of real populations can be compared since it contains a number of assumptions that will not be met in nature. Principal among those assumptions in the logistic equation are that carrying capacity is a constant; that each individual in the population is equivalent enough

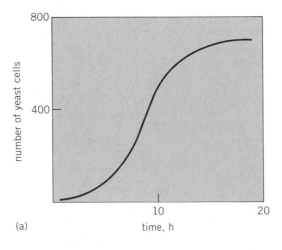

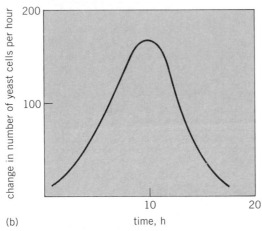

Fig. 3. A yeast population growing according to the logistic equation. (*a*) Population size. (*b*) Growth rate.

and in population growth in nature. Competition occurs when the resources in the environment are in short supply relative to the demands that individuals make on those resources. In the logistic equation, that competition is expressed in the decline of r as N increases. This type of competition between members of the same species population is called intraspecific competition.

Population interactions. Competition also is a principal type of interaction between the members of different species, when it is termed interspecific competition. Another important type of interaction between populations is predation, when the individuals of one population feed on the individuals of another population. Both of these interactions were described mathematically in the 1920s by two ecologists working independently, A. Lotka and V. Volterra. The Lotka-Volterra competition equations are Eq. (5) and the exact equivalent, Eq. (6), where 1 and 2 refer to

$$\frac{dN_1}{dt} = r_{m1}N_1\frac{K_1 - N_1 - \alpha_{12}N_2}{K_1} \qquad (5)$$

$$\frac{dN_2}{dt} = r_{m2}N_2\frac{K_2 - N_2 - \alpha_{21}N_1}{K_2} \qquad (6)$$

the different species, with α_{12} being the competitive effect of an individual of species 2 on species 1, and α_{21} being the competitive effect of an individual of species 1 on species 2. These Lotka-Volterra competition equations recognize that each species depresses the growth rate and carrying capacity of the other. Depending upon the respective competition coefficients, carrying capacities, and maximum per capita reproductive rates, there are four potential outcomes of competition: (1) species 1 may go extinct; (2) species 2 may go extinct; (3) the species may have an unstable equilibrium in which they coexist for a while until chance events allow one species to increase a bit above the equilibrium and the other species then goes extinct; or (4) there may be a stable equilibrium in which both species coexist at some population size below the carrying capacity for either species alone.

The Lotka-Volterra predation equations describe population ecology when members of a predator population, P, feed on members of a prey population, H. The prey equation is Eq. (7), where k_1 is a constant

$$\frac{dH}{dt} = r_mH\left(1 - \frac{H}{K}\right) - k_1PH \qquad (7)$$

that is the predation rate per capita of predator. The equation for the predator is Eq. (8), where k_2 is the

$$\frac{dP}{dt} = k_2PH - k_3P \qquad (8)$$

efficiency with which predators convert their food into more offspring and k_3 is the per capita predator death rate. Unlike the logistic and Lotka-Volterra competition equations, which predict that populations will reach some final constant size, the Lotka-Volterra predator-prey equations predict that predator and prey populations will tend to oscillate through time. At low densities of both predator and prey, the values of H/K and k_1PH in the prey population equation will both approach zero, and the prey will grow according to the unmodified logistic, approaching the maximum per capita reproductive rate. As the prey population

to all other individuals to be represented in the average population statistic, r_m; that all individuals have an equal probability of mating; and that there are no time lags so that birth and death rates are adjusted immediately for each increment of N as population size increases to K. Much of the study of the ecology of real populations involves understanding how those assumptions are violated.

Competition is inherent in the logistic equation,

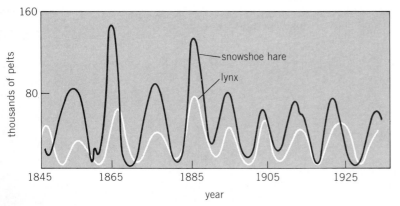

Fig. 4. Oscillations of predator and prey populations. Data are from pelt records of lynx and snowshoe hare of the Hudson's Bay Company, in Canada.

increases, the predator population also can increase, and there is a tendency for predator density to over-shoot prey density, leading to oscillations through time. Such oscillations are, in fact, often observed in nature, with a classic example being Canadian populations of snowshoe hare, the prey, and predators, such as lynx (**Fig. 4**). Whether such oscillations in real populations are due to the instability of predator-prey relations inherent in the Lotka-Volterra predation equations, or to the fluctuations of other factors such as weather or food supply available to the hares, has not yet been proven. *SEE POPULATION ECOLOGY*.

Parasitism and disease are additional types of population interactions involving detrimental effects on one participant and beneficial effects on the other participant. A parasite is an organism that grows, feeds on, and is sheltered by another organism, the host. Disease is an abnormal condition of an organism, often due to infection, that impairs normal physiological activity. Parasitism and disease often are described mathematically by equations similar to the Lotka-Volterra predation equations, although they are commonly modified to account for the dispersal of parasites or pathogens between different hosts. These population interactions have been of growing interest in ecology, although they have been the subject of the entire field of epidemiology, an important aspect of medicine. The importance of parasitism and disease in natural ecosystems is evident from the extinctions of two important tree species, the American chestnut (*Castanea dentata*) and American elm (*Ulmus americana*), from the forests of eastern North America during this century. Those extinctions were caused, respectively, by chestnut blight and Dutch elm disease, both due to pathogens introduced into North America from Europe.

Symbiosis is a type of interaction between populations in which a participant is promoted by the interaction. There are two types of symbiosis: commensalism, which occurs when one participant is promoted by the interaction and the other is unaffected, and mutualism, which occurs when both participants are promoted by the interaction. Mutualism often involves organisms that are very different and have coevolved such a strong mutual interdependence that neither can exist in natural environments in the absence of the other. Symbiosis commonly is described mathematically by variations of the Lotka-Volterra competition equations in which the sign preceding the α becomes positive for one (commensalism) or both (symbiosis) populations. This transforms the competition coefficients into mutualism coefficients.

Mutualism is an extremely important type of ecological interaction since it often allows the symbionts to perform functions that have proven impossible for any single organism to accomplish with the same efficiency. Lichens are symbiotic associations between fungi and algae. They are capable of colonizing some of the most inhospitable environments on Earth, such as the bare faces of boulders and extremes of drought, cold, and heat. The fungal and algal species are so closely integrated that lichens have been classified by the binomial systems that are applied to other true species.

An example of the functional importance of symbiosis to ecology is the digestion of cellulose, which is accomplished largely by symbiotic associations.

Cellulose is the most abundant organic molecule on Earth, but this vast energy source is largely inaccessible to living organisms except to symbionts. Among the most important symbiotic associations capable of digesting cellulose are ruminant animals and their gut flora, and termites and their gut protozoa. In the absence of these symbiotic associations, Earth would be covered with vast residues of undecomposed cellulose.

SYNECOLOGY

Synecology is the study of groups of populations co-occurring in time and space; it is also called community ecology. Synecology is concerned with factors controlling the species composition of communities and why species composition changes in different environments and with time in the same habitat. Species composition of a community may include density, biomass, or productivity of individuals of different species.

The study of communities is one of the oldest branches of ecology, arising strongly in the studies of naturalists in the sixteenth to nineteenth century, and one of the most descriptive. Only since the mid-1960s have ecologists begun to turn significantly to experimental studies that manipulate either the environment or the species composition of communities. Those experiments are designed to understand mechanisms responsible for the species compositions of communities and the interactions that occur between different species in the community. *SEE ECOLOGICAL COMMUNITIES*.

Community organization. A principal concern of community ecology is the life forms of organisms, the taxonomic composition of co-occurring species groups, and the spatial arrangement of species. Plant life forms are relatively easy to characterize, and communities in widely separated geographic areas but similar environments commonly have a similar life-form composition. Most of the species in tropical rainforests, for example, are trees and shrubs, while most of the species in grasslands are small shrubs, and perennials with buds belowground. Although the species compositions of communities in different geographic areas may be quite different, the life forms are often quite similar in similar environments.

Another aspect of community organization that is a concern of synecology is spatial patterns, or dispersion. Ecologists typically distinguish between dispersal, the process of movement, and dispersion, the arrangement of individuals in space. The three types of dispersion patterns are random, regular, and clumped (aggregated). In a random distribution, the probability of an individual occupying a given location in a community is not influenced by the presence of another individual at a nearby location, which implies that no important factor, such as environment or parental proximity, has influenced the dispersion of individuals. In a regular distribution, the probability of an individual occupying a location is reduced if another individual occupies a nearby location; this distribution may be due to competition for an evenly spread environmental resource. In a clumped distribution, which may be due to proximity to seed source, or environmental heterogeneity, the probability of an individual occupying a location increases if another individual occupies a nearby location. *SEE POPULATION DISPERSAL; POPULATION DISPERSION*.

Temporal distributions are also a concern of synecology. By substituting the phrase ''at a given time'' for the phrase ''at a given location'' in the above definitions, temporal distributions are judged by the same criteria. Spatial and temporal patterns of individuals are important aspects of community ecology because they can provide insight into the underlying distributions of limiting factors in the environments and how species are related to those factors. Species with distributions in which individuals are clumped in space or time often utilize resources that also are clumped in space or time. Limited dispersal also can lead to a clumped distribution due to the clustering of offspring around their parents. Regular distributions can often result from competition between individuals for a resource that is evenly distributed in space or time. Desert plants, for example, frequently have a regular distribution pattern because they compete for soil moisture, and each individual must utilize the moisture available in a certain minimum soil volume if it is to survive.

Niche. The niche concept refers to the environmental factors that control a species, and its distribution in relation to those factors. A species' niche is a consequence of the genetic properties of the individuals of that species, the environmental factors that affect it, and interactions with other species. G. E. Hutchinson described the niche as an *n*-dimensional hypervolume occupied by a population, where *n* is the number of environmental factors affecting it. He also distinguished between a fundamental niche, which is the genetic potential of the species, and a realized niche, which is the range of environmental factors occupied in the presence of other organisms.

Species are often distributed along environmental gradients as a series of bell-shaped curves (**Fig. 5**). Those curves represent the realized niches of species. Removal of other species, a type of experiment that is becoming increasingly common in synecology, would be required to reveal a species' fundamental niche. A species that is narrowly distributed has a narrow niche and is often referred to as an ecological specialist, while a widely distributed species has a broad niche and is often referred to as an ecological generalist. It is often inferred that intense interspecific competition will lead to specialization, restricting a species' realized niche to only that portion of the fundamental niche where it is a strong competitor. Conversely, intense intraspecific competition will tend to lead to a broader niche that reduces the effects of different members of the same species upon each other. However, there are as yet insufficient experimental studies to strongly support either of these inferences.

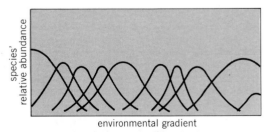

Fig. 5. A continuum of species distributions along an environmental gradient, where each line represents a different species. Note that peaks of species abundance do not overlap, and that breadth of curves differs between species.

Species diversity. Species diversity is a property of a community that encompasses both the number of species present (species richness) and the equality of relative abundances of the species present (equitability of evenness). One of the principal concerns of synecology since its origin has been why communities differ so dramatically in the number of species present and the similarities of their relative abundances. Naturalists attached to exploratory expeditions during the historical colonial period were particularly overwhelmed by the variety of plant and animal life in the wet tropics. Tropical forests seemed to consist of an almost countless number of plant and animal species compared with communities in the temperate climates with which the naturalists were familiar. Indeed, there is a general gradient of increasing diversity from the poles to the Equator.

Various explanations for the latitudinal differences in biotic diversity have been proposed, but none is wholly satisfactory and none has gained prominence. Chief among those explanations are: (1) Nontropical habitats have been subject to severe climatic fluctuations, including glaciation, that lead to repeated species extinctions. (2) The moderate climates of tropical locations allow species to become more specialized for narrow ranges of climate and other environmental factors. (3) Biological interactions, such as competition and predation, are stronger in tropical locations, leading to a proliferation of different adaptive types. (4) Productivity is higher in tropical locations, allowing more species to coexist due to greater available food. (5) Spatial variation of environments is greater in the tropics, leading to a proliferation of specialists in different areas. (6) There is greater environmental complexity in the tropics, partly because of more species, leading to greater specialization among species in a sort of positive feedback. *See Biogeography.*

Community: reality vs. abstraction. One of the most contentious issues throughout the history of ecology has been the degree to which the species that co-occur in space and time represent an organized, meaningful biological unit and to what extent they are merely a fortuitous collection of individuals. Two of the principal ecologists in American ecology in the early decades of the twentieth century argued these points. F. Clements referred to communities as being like an organism, while H. A. Gleason said that communites were merely a happenstance collection of species with similar ecological tolerances. Clements's view prevailed until the middle of the twentieth century, and then Gleason's view gained ascendency, largely because of quantitative studies of community composition revealing that species distributions along environmental gradients were commonly the type of bell-shaped curves in Fig. 5. Those bell-shaped curves suggested that each species population had its own, individualistic response to the environment, and that the species that occurred at a given point on the gradient did so fortuitously.

Still, there is no gainsaying that similar communities occur in similar habitats. Although the species compositions of communities may vary considerably in different geographic areas, the occurrence of communities with very similar life forms in geographically separated locations with similar environments suggests that a community is not merely a random collection of species. Many experiments in marine intertidal communities indicate that the removal of one species has a cascading effect that alters the abundances of many other species, even leading to the extinction of some species and invasion of the community by other species that were previously absent. These results indicate that the species in a community are interconnected through the functional processes of competition, predation, and symbiosis in ways producing a community that is not just a random collection of species.

Succession. Succession is the process of change in community composition and environmental properties over time on a site. Primary succession occurs in newly formed habitats, such as glacial moraines, river levees, or volcanic ash. Secondary succession occurs in habitats where the previous community has been destroyed or severely disturbed, such as following forest fire, abandonment of agricultural fields, or epidemic disease or pest attack.

A general consequence of succession is an amelioration of physical factors and a reduction of their importance as controlling factors, and an increase in the complexity and importance of biological factors. In newly formed ash fields or newly abandoned fields, sunlight is intense, nutrients are often in poor supply, winds are strong, and evaporative stress is severe. As such sites are colonized by plants, all of these physical factors tend to be modified and trophic webs develop that depend upon the plants. Species diversity increases as more species colonize, and increasingly complex trophic patterns develop. There often is an increase in the stature of the vegetation, which reduces sunlight, wind, and evaporative stress below the canopy. That creates new conditions that allow species to invade that were incapable of withstanding the physically harsh conditions early in succession.

Early in succession, there is directional change in both environmental factors and species composition of the community. Ultimately a relatively constant environment is reached and species composition no longer changes in a directional fashion but, instead, fluctuates about some mean, or average, community composition. That stage is called the climax.

As in the nature of the community itself, there is disagreement among ecologists about the exact nature of succession, and of the climax. Nevertheless, there is a general tendency for communities to become more complex and for biological factors to increase in importance and the effects of physical factors to be reduced as time passes. *See Ecological succession.*

Systems Ecology

Systems ecology is the study of dynamic relationships between the units of the ecosystem, particularly those relationships that influence rates of energy flow and chemical cycling. The ecosystem concept, as pointed out above, can be applied to many different levels of organization and varying degrees of complexity. Ecosystem science, or systems ecology, can be broadly divided into approaches concerned with relationships between trophic levels and those that employ with specific details of population dynamics of community organization within trophic levels. In both approaches the goal is to develop mechanistic explanations for the observed behavior of the system as a whole. Often this goal is accomplished through simulation modeling.

Simulation modeling involves the use of mathematical equations to characterize the state and dynamics of a system. Mathematical approaches to population dynamics, as seen earlier in this article, commonly use simplified equations, such as the logistic, to model the dynamics of one or a few populations. Simulation modeling differs principally in using a set of coupled equations to characterize the processes occurring in ecosystems. Those models often have much more detail than the simplified models of population dynamics, and require numerical solution using digital computers. A simulation model typically begins with a conceptual model or diagram consisting of boxes that represent components of system state and connecting arrows representing processes that interconnect the components. Simulation modeling uses rate equations to describe the processes and evaluate the mechanisms that are important to understanding both the dynamics and functional properties of ecosystems. Simulation models have as goals both isolating the general features of a broad range of similar ecosystems and providing sufficient detail to accurately predict how a specified system will respond to perturbations.

A system can be defined as a group of interacting and interdependent elements that form a collective entity. An ecosystem, therefore, is a collection of environmental factors and organisms that interact through specific, dynamic relationships defined by the food web of which they are members. Systems may be open or closed. A closed system is completely self-contained and does not interact with any other system; an example would be molecules of a gas enclosed in a container that was a perfect insulator. Those molecules would function independently of all other things. An open system interacts with other systems. All ecosystems are open systems. In particular, they are open to energy, whose ultimate source is the Sun. Proximally, however, energy can be imported into an ecosystem from some other system where the energy of photons from the Sun is converted into organic energy by photosynthesis.

Energy flow. Energy flow in ecosystems is approached in a way closely related to the laws of thermodynamics, that branch of physics that deals with the relationships among different forms of energy. The first law of thermodynamics states that the energy input to a system either is stored or is used to do work. It is generally given as Eq. (9), where Q is

$$Q = \Delta E + W \tag{9}$$

energy input, ΔE is a change in the energy content of the recipient system, and W is work done by that system. Ecologists restate the law as Eq. (10), where P_g

$$P_g = P_n + R \tag{10}$$

is gross productivity, P_n is net productivity, and R is respiration. The change in energy content, P_n, is therefore equal to the energy input minus the work done. That work has two components: one is maintenance respiration, the cost of maintaining the structure of the system at the time of energy input, and the other is growth respiration, the cost of synthesizing new biomass.

The second law of thermodynamics also is important to energy balance in ecosystems. That law states that the entropy of isolated systems always tends to increase. Entropy (S) is a measure of the randomness, disorder, or lack of organization of a system. In energy terms it is measured as the heat capacity of the system (joules · degree^{-1} · mole^{-1}) at a particular temperature (T). In isolated systems, entropy always increases. Because ecosystems are open systems, they are able to maintain their organization and avoid decaying to a state of maximum entropy and zero free energy. The maintenance component of respiration is the cost of maintaining present structure, that is, replacing the free energy degraded to heat. The growth component of respiration is the cost, that is, the free energy intake necessary to build structure and organization. Those costs are expressed both as an increase in the entropy (thus an increase in heat content) of the environment to which organisms in an ecosystem are coupled as well as the loss of heat produced by "friction" representing the degree of thermodynamic inefficiency of the metabolic energy transformations.

A fundamental generalization of systems ecology is that net productivity diminishes about one order of magnitude at each level in the trophic web. If primary P_n averaged 100 g/m^2 · yr, secondary P_n at the herbivore level would be about 10 g/m^2 · yr, and at the carnivore level would be about 1 g/m · yr. This so-called energy pyramid has two causes. First, the above-mentioned maintenance costs of respiration at each trophic level diminish the energy available to higher levels. Second, the ecological harvest of energy by any trophic level is not fully efficient. Therefore, the energy flow must diminish at each successive trophic level in an ecosystem.

In most ecosystems, certainly, the biomass of primary producers is greater than that of the herbivores which, in turn, is greater than carnivore biomass. Sometimes, however, particularly in aquatic habitats, biomass increases up the trophic web. That is possible only when lower trophic levels consist of organisms with very high rates of net productivity per unit of biomass. The ratio of energy flow to biomass is referred to as turnover time. If turnover time is short, as it is for small organisms with rapid life cycles, it is possible for the biomass pyramid to be inverted; that is probably most common in the open ocean where large, long-lived organisms are at upper trophic levels and small, short-lived organisms are at lower trophic levels. *See Ecological energetics.*

Chemical cycling. Another fundamental concern of systems ecology is the pattern of chemical flow that is coupled to the process of energy flow. Each time that energy is used to do work, some chemicals are released back into the environment. Death also releases chemicals back into the environment.

There are two different types of trophic webs in ecosystems. The grazing food web is based on the consumption of the tissues of living organisms. The detritus food web is based on the consumption of dead organic material, called detritus in aquatic systems and sometimes referred to as litter in terrestrial ecosystems. Chemicals are recycled to the environment from the grazing food web each time that work is done, and as the excretory wastes of living organisms. Chemicals are recycled to the environment from the detritus food web as organisms utilize excretory wastes and the dead tissues of organisms.

Decomposition is the process of degrading the energy content of dead tissues and simultaneously releasing chemicals back into the environment. When those chemicals are released in inorganic forms, the process is called mineralization. Decomposition and

mineralization typically involve many steps and take place in a trophic web fully as complex as those of the grazing food web. There is a size-dependent hierarchy as particles are broken into progressively smaller particles; that subdivision increases surface-volume ratios, exposing progressively more of the substance to decay. There also typically is a chemical hierarchy. Fats, proteins, and simple carbohydrates are the most easily utilized organic chemicals, and they generally are rapidly attacked. Wood, chitin, and bones are only slowly decomposed. More resistant substances accumulate in terrestrial ecosystems as soil humus or in aquatic ecosystems as sediments, or ooze, beneath the water. In geological time, those sediments were transformed into the hydrocarbon deposits that serve as sources of coal, oil, and gas for modern industrial society.

Microorganisms are exceptionally important in the processes of decomposition and mineralization. The final steps of mineralization are almost invariably accomplished by microorganisms. For example, the cycling of nitrogen in ecosystems involves microorganisms at several critical steps (**Fig. 6**). The only significant pathway introducing nitrogen into trophic webs is the process of nitrogen fixation in which gaseous, molecular nitrogen is converted into organic nitrogeneous compounds by nitrogen-fixing bacteria and blue-green algae. Some of these bacteria and algae are free-living, and some participate in symbiotic associations with other organisms. The organic molecules are degraded in the detritus food web by ammonifying bacteria that release ammonium ion or ammonia. Nitrite bacteria convert the ammonia into nitrite, and nitrate bacteria oxidize the nitrogen further into nitrate; those conversions are referred to collectively as nitrification. Both nitrate and ammonium ion can reenter the food web via uptake by plants. Denitrifying bacteria convert the nitrate into nitrogen gas, a process called denitrification that releases gaseous nitrogen back into the atmosphere. *See Biogeochemistry.*

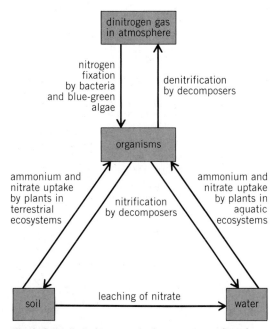

Fig. 6. Generalized nitrogen cycle. Arrows represent flow of nitrogen.

APPLIED ECOLOGY

Applied ecology is that branch of ecology dealing with practical problems of immediate social importance. Ecology is often confused in the minds of laypersons with the environmental movement, a social interest group concerned with environmental degradation and problems of resource supply to human societies. Applied ecology makes a fundamental contribution to those social and political concerns by identifying environmental problems, gaging their significance, and suggesting potential solutions. Among the environmental issues to which ecology has made an important contribution have been problems of population growth and resource supply, acid rain, eutrophication, consequences of pollution, biological control of crop pests, range management, forestry, and the ecological consequences of nuclear war. From T. R. Malthus's essay on human population growth to scientific evaluations of nuclear war, ecology has always been concerned with problems that are important to human affairs. SEE ECOLOGY, APPLIED.

Samuel J. McNaughton

Bibliography. B. Glaeser (ed.), *The Green Revolution Revisited*, 1987; H. Howe and L. Westley, *Ecological Relationships of Plants and Animals*, 1988; J. Keating, *Interdependence in the Natural World*, 1987; R. P. McIntosh, *The Background of Ecology: Concept and Theory*, 1985; M. B. Rambler et al. (eds.), *Global Ecology: Towards a Science of the Biosphere*, 1988.

Ecology, applied

The application of ecological principles to the solution of human problems and the maintenance of a quality life. It is assumed that humans are an integral part of ecological systems and that they depend upon healthy, well-operating, and productive systems for their continued well-being. For these reasons, applied ecology is based on a knowledge of ecosystems and populations, and the principles and techniques of ecology are used to interpret and solve specific environmental problems and to plan new management systems in the biosphere. Although a variety of management fields, such as forestry, agriculture, wildlife management, environmental engineering, and environmental design, are concerned with specific parts of the environment, applied ecology is unique in taking a view of whole systems, and attempting to account for all inputs to and outputs from the systems—and all impacts. In the past, applied ecology has been considered as being synonymous with the above applied sciences. SEE SYSTEMS ECOLOGY.

Ecosystem ecology. Ecological systems, or ecosystems, are complexes of plants, animals, microorganisms, and humans, together with their environment. Environment includes all those factors, physical, chemical, biological, sociocultural, which affect the ecosystem. The complex of life and environment exists as an interacting system and is unique for each part of the Earth. The unique geological features, soils, climate, and availability of plants, animals, and microorganisms create a variety of different types of ecosystems, such as forests, fields, lakes, rivers, and oceans. Each ecological system may be composed of hundreds to thousands of biological species which interact with each other through the transfer of energy, chemical materials, and information. The interconnecting networks which characterize ecosystems are often called food webs (**Fig. 1**). It is obvious from this structural feature of interaction that a disturbance to one population within an ecosystem could potentially affect many other populations. From another point of view, ecosystems are composed of chemical elements, arranged in a variety of organic complexes. There is a continual process of loss and uptake of chemicals to and from the environment as populations are born, grow and die, and are decomposed. Ecosystems operate on energy derived from photosynthesis (called primary production) and from other energy exchanges. The functional attributes of ecosystems, such as productivity, energy flow, and cycling of chemical elements, depend upon the biological species in the ecosystem and the limiting conditions of the environment. SEE BIOLOGICAL PRODUCTIVITY; ECOLOGICAL ENERGETICS; FOOD WEB.

Ecological systems develop in accord with the regional environment. Although these systems have evolved to resist the normal expected perturbations encountered in the environment, unusual disturbances and catastrophic events can upset and even destroy the system. In this case, recovery can occur after the disturbance stops. Recovery is termed ecological succession since it comprises a sequence of communities which succeed each other until a dynamic steady state is reestablished. SEE ECOLOGICAL SUCCESSION.

Populations in these ecosystems fill a variety of structural and functional roles within the system. Often, groups of populations coevolve, so that they form a more or less isolated subunit. For example, the pollinators of a plant species, and their predators and parasites, form such a guild. Populations continually adapt and develop through natural selection, expanding to the limit of their resources. Population growth is, therefore, due to an increase in resources or a relaxation of limiting factors. SEE ECOSYSTEM; POPULATION ECOLOGY.

Ecosystem management theory. The objective of applied ecology management is to maintain the system while altering its inputs or outputs. Often, ecology management is designed to maximize a particular output or the quantity of a specific component. Since outputs and inputs are related (**Fig. 2**), maximization of an output may not be desirable; rather, the management objective may be the optimum level. Optimization of systems can be accomplished through the use of systems ecology methods which consider all parts of the system rather than a specific set of components. In this way, a series of strategies or scenarios can be evaluated, and the strategy producing the largest gain for the least cost can be chosen for implementation.

The applied ecology management approach has been partially implemented through the U.S. National Environmental Policy Act. This act requires that an environmental-impact analysis be carried out by an interdisciplinary team of specialists representing the subjects necessary for an ecosystem analysis. This team is required to evaluate a project on the basis of its environmental, social, and cultural features. One alternative that must be considered is that of no alteration of the system.

A variety of general environmental problems within the scope of applied ecology relate to the major components of the Earth: the atmosphere, water, land,

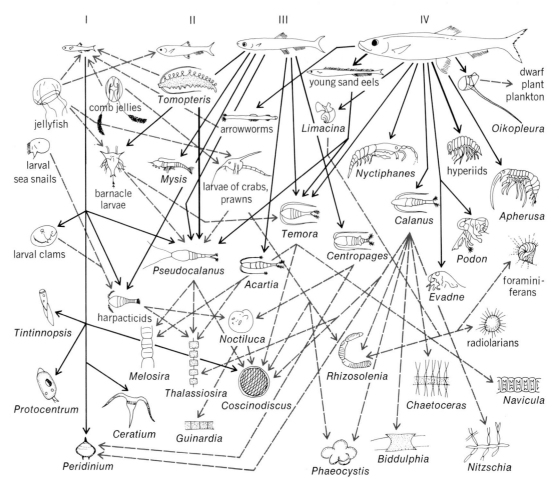

Fig. 1. The food relations of the herring at different stages in its life. Sizes of herring are (I) 0.6 to 1.3 cm, (II) 1.3 to 4.5 cm, (III) 4.5 to 12.5 cm, and (IV) over 1.25 cm. Solid lines indicate food eaten directly by herring. 1 cm = 0.4 in.

and the biota. The ecological principles used in applied ecology are discussed elsewhere; a sequence of environmental problems of special importance to applied ecology is discussed below.

Atmospheric problems. The atmosphere is one of the most important components of the environment to consider from the viewpoint of applied ecology since it connects all portions of the Earth into one ecosystem. The atmosphere is composed of a variety of gases, of which oxygen and nitrogen make up the largest percentage. It is not uniform in its depth or its composition, but is divided into several layers or zones which differ in density and composition. Although most interaction with humans occurs in the zone nearest Earth, the most distant parts of the atmosphere are also important since they affect the heat balance of the Earth and the quality of radiant energy striking the surface. Disturbances to these portions of the atmosphere could affect the entire biosphere. *See* Atmosphere.

The composition of the atmosphere varies according to location. The qualities of minor gases such as carbon dioxide, the amounts of various metallic elements, and the quantity of water vapor and dust all may differ, depending on the relative distance from land or sea. But, in addition, the atmospheric composition may change in time. For example, over the history of the planet, the percentage composition of oxygen has changed from a very oxgen-poor environment to the present atmosphere, with 20.95% oxygen by volume. *See* Atmospheric chemistry.

Human activities may introduce a variety of pollutants into the atmosphere. The principal pollutants are carbon dioxide, sulfur compounds, hydrocarbons, nitrogen oxides, solid particles (particulates), and heat. The amounts of pollutants that are produced may be quite large, especially in local areas, and have increased in amount as industrialization has become more widespread. Industrial and domestic activities have also been estimated to put 2.18×10^8 tons (1.96×10^8 metric tons) of sulfur into the atmo-

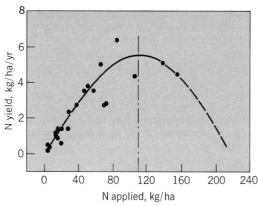

Fig. 2. The relationship between N yield and N consumption (1964–1969).

sphere per year. In most cases, these pollutants have increased during the recent past, and in many areas have become a serious problem. *SEE AIR POLLUTION.*

Atmospheric problems can have a variety of impacts on humans. Numerous observers have attributed climatic change to atmospheric alteration, since any change in the gaseous envelope of the Earth could alter the heat balance and the climate. The Earth's climate is not constant, and it is difficult to establish an exact correlation between pollution and variation in temperature or solar radiation at the Earth's surface. The pollutants most likely to have an effect on climate are carbon dioxide and solid particles. Pollution may also affect the chemical balance of regions of the Earth. These effects may be extremely complicated. For example, it has been reported that sulfur oxides produced in the industrial districts of northern Europe have moved north in the atmosphere over Scandinavia. The sulfur oxides react with water to form sulfuric acid, which rains out in precipitation. The acid rain changes the acidity of the soil in this region and may depress the activity of blue-green algae, which fix nitrogen from the atmosphere. Acid rain appears to cause reduction in the growth of trees. Other pollutants may act in a similar complicated fashion through the network of interactions in the Earth ecosystem. *SEE ACID RAIN.*

Finally, atmospheric pollution has direct effects on plants and animals and human activities. Pollutants, like other materials, can act as limiting influences on the growth, reproduction, and survival of plants and animals. A variety of plants, such as lichens and mosses, that are extremely sensitive to pollution can be used to indicate the degree of atmospheric deterioration. In some severe cases, all vegetation and animal life may be destroyed in the vicinity of the polluting industry. Gases and solids are taken into the lungs of humans, and cause disease or discomfort. In cities, such pollutants as asbestos and lead are exceedingly dangerous to the population. And finally, the impact of pollutants on buildings, clothes, artwork, and machines is costly.

Control of atmospheric pollution requires interception of pollutants at the point of discharge. Industrial control can be achieved by the use of special filters, precipitators, and other devices. Control of pollution for automobiles also may involve special equipment, as well as redesign of engines and fuel. Reduction in dust and similar general sources of air pollution may demand a change in the operation producing the problem. *SEE AIR-POLLUTION CONTROL.*

Water problems. The aquatic environment is of equal importance to applied ecology since most of the Earth's surface is covered by the oceans, and the land is connected to the oceans by streams and rivers. Thus, like the atmosphere, the waters are a connection between distant parts of the biosphere and can carry a disturbance from its origin to another region.

The composition of waters varies widely, and it is essential in evaluating aquatic health to establish the base-line conditions which are stable under the normal or undisturbed conditions. Water pollution arises from a variety of sources—industry, domestic sewage, agricultural fertilizers and feedlots, construction activities, and forest practices. Principal pollutants are sediments, organic pollutants containing nitrites, and phosphates, lead, mercury, hydrocarbons, pesticides, and various synthetic chemicals. The impact of the pollutant depends both on its chemical nature and on the quantity released. All water bodies receive quantities of chemicals and solid materials; a variety of organisms which break down and utilize these inputs have evolved. Serious problems arise when the inputs to the water body become unusually large or contain synthetic materials which cannot be decomposed by the extant organisms. Further problems may develop through concentrations of pollutants in the food web of the aquatic system. For example, if a chemical is not metabolized by organisms, but is concentrated in their tissues, as are some pesticides, then as each organism is eaten by another, the body burden of chemicals can increase. In this way, predators may obtain very large and dangerous amounts of pollutants. The decline in population of certain fish-eating birds has been attributed to this process of transfer and concentration.

Aquatic pollution has many consequences of significance to humans. An excess of chemical materials which enrich plant and animal growth can cause rapid increase in life. This process, termed eutrophication, may entail dramatic increases in the algal, planktonic, or rooted aquatic plant populations, with the result that the water body appears green in color or becomes clogged with vegetation. Toxic chemicals released to water bodies may directly kill aquatic life or, if present in sublethal amounts, may change the species of plants and animals present. Often aquatic pollution is not a dramatic either-or proposition, with all fish or other aquatic life killed; rather, more commonly a trend toward an increase in the more resistant species is seen, with the elimination of those forms which are especially susceptible to the pollutant. Aquatic pollution also involves heat, especially that derived from industrial activities, including nuclear power and fossil fuel plants. In these instances, water is used to cool the machines or reactors and is exhausted to the environment at elevated temperatures. Since all metabolic and chemical processes are influenced by heat, thermal pollution should have a significant effect on aquatic systems, but thus far it has been difficult to prove that such an impact occurs.

Other aquatic problems of interest to applied ecology concern alteration of water channels by impoundments or channelization and irrigation. In each instance the natural pattern of water movement is altered, and deterioration of the environment may result. Impoundments limit the natural movement of sediment and chemical elements; production patterns in the water and lands below the impoundment may be altered, and other changes may occur. But, on the plus side, impoundments often provide fisheries, electrical energy, recreation, and other advantages. Irrigation problems may involve the movement of salts from depths in the soil, with deposition near the surface. Disturbance of the chemical equilibrium of the soil, in turn, interferes with plant growth. *SEE WATER POLLUTION.*

Terrestrial and soil problems. Terrestrial environments constantly undergo a degrading and decomposing process owing to the action of water, frost, wind, and other environmental processes on the surface which involve the linkages joining land, water, and atmosphere. Human activities may accelerate these natural processes. In addition, the use of chemical materials on the land may have effects similar to those resulting from their addition to water. Most terrestrial environmental problems are caused by agricultural, grazing, or forest practices. Probably the most serious effect concerns practices which increase the rate of surface erosion. Only a small percentage of the Earth's surface is suitable for agriculture, and the loss of soil from these areas is extremely serious. As a consequence, certain regions have been denuded and are no longer productive. Overgrazing may also remove the cover of vegetation and allow water and wind to erode the soil. Deserts have increased in extent almost everywhere because of overgrazing, and in India the increase in the Rajasthan Desert can be measured in feet per year. Dust from this desert blows as far east as Thailand. Overcutting trees and lack of reforestation programs also may increase soil erosion and nutrient losses in forest regions. These impacts are not solely the mark of modern civilization. Misuse of the land has been noted in many past civilizations and can even be a problem for present-day primitive societies. SEE DESERTIFICATION; EROSION; FOREST AND FORESTRY.

However, modern agriculture has added new problems to those of the primitive farmer. Various chemicals such as fertilizers, pesticides, and herbicides are used to increase agricultural production. These chemicals may be needed because of past misuse of the land or because of economic demands in a society that does not recognize the need to maintain and protect terrestrial resources. Organic and ecological agricultural practices seek to reestablish a pattern of land use without causing deterioration of the soil and biotic resources. Although reestablishment of the pattern may result in somewhat lower productivity, proponents of ''ecoagriculture'' argue that high productivity can be maintained without loss of soil through erosion and without a reduction in fertility.

Probably the most serious short-term impact arises from the use of chemicals on the land. In the most extreme cases, the health of the agriculturalist may be affected by the materials. But more commonly, the pesticide or chemical in the soil is taken up by the crop and then enters the human food chain. Many modern governments maintain agencies to advise farmers on the proper amounts of chemicals to apply so that buildup does not occur; other agencies periodically sample and analyze foodstuffs for residues. In this way, the consumer can be protected from misuse of chemicals or from excessive concentrations. Unfortunately, these agencies seldom consider the impacts of agricultural chemicals on other animal food chains. For example, the soil fauna and the natural nitrogen-fixing organisms present in the soil, as well as the terrestrial faunas living near the agricultural or forest plantations, can be significantly affected; and populations of animals, even beneficial species, may be reduced through misuse of chemical materials. However, extinction of plants and animals, which is also a serious applied ecology problem, usually is due to the destruction of their habitat. Pollution, disturbance of the land, and overhunting may provide the final cause of the destruction of a particular living species.

Nuclear energy. Industrialized societies require large quantities of energy. Energy production from nuclear reactors has been enthusiastically developed in many regions of the biosphere. However, nuclear energy also has environmental consequences that are of concern to applied ecology and that must be considered when these facilities are designed and operated, so that negative impacts on the environment do not occur.

Nuclear energy has three primary environmental consequences: the storage of radioactive products, release of radioactive material to the environment, and, as mentioned above, release of heat.

There are various kinds of radioactivity associated with the particular elements used in the reactor. In the process of the generation of energy, these fuel elements are changed into a suite of radioactive materials. Although these materials, in turn, form a new source of chemicals, the process of separation and concentraton is very costly and dangerous. In either case, however, the processes result in radioactive waste that must be stored for periods of hundreds, even thousands of years. The fact that the potential danger of these wastes will require technical attention for periods of time longer than the histories of many modern societies is a prime argument against the widespread use of nuclear energy. However, proponents of the use of nuclear energy state that certain geological structures such as salt mines can be safely used for storage indefinitely.

A second environmental problem concerns the loss of relatively small quantities of radioactive materials to the environment during chemical processing in reactors or chemical plants. If these materials enter the body, they can cause disease and death. Like pesticides, radioactive chemical materials may be concentrated in food chains and can appear in relatively large concentrations. In certain fragile environments such as the arctic tundra, the food chains are very short. Thus, radioactive chemicals derived from testing atomic weapons pass through lichens or reindeer or caribou to humans. Concentrations in certain localities may be high enough to cause concern to public health authorities.

Population problems. Applied ecology also is concerned with the size of the human population, since many of the impacts of human activities on the environment are a function of the number and concentration of people. The human population on Earth has increased exponentially, and in many countries this increase poses almost insurmountable problems. Control of environmental degradation, even a concern for environment, is nonexistent when the population is undernourished, starving, ill-housed, and underemployed. Social disorder, alienation, psychological disturbances, physical illness, and other problems have been correlated with overpopulation. Population also places demands on the resources of the Earth; as the standard of living rises, these demands increase.

The human population problem is exceedingly complicated because the growth of population is controlled largely by the decisions of individual families. The family may visualize several different strategies—the number of children that is best for the family, best for their social group or tribe, or best for the human race—or have no strategy at all. Families may decide that a large family is best even under serious conditions of overpopulation. Considerable evidence indicates that the size of the family declines as the population becomes less rural and more industrial. Thus, some specialists urge economic development, regardless of environmental impact, as a means of solving the population problem. Others urge that the family be more directly influenced to reduce the number of children. Direct action might entail birth control advice, medical abortion and sterilization, and taxation. Yet others argue that no measures such as these can be significant and that the human population will be controlled by famine, war, or disease. Each of these positions leads toward a set of social policies, all of which have an environmental impact which, in turn, affects the human society. *See Human ecology.*

Environmental planning and design. The foregoing discussion suggests that there is an optimum environment for the human race which is influenced by a variety of population densities and activities. Thus, although the population of the United States is relatively sparse, it has a large environmental impact. This, in turn, suggests that the human environment and society could be designed in such a way to minimize the negative impacts and provide a satisfactory productive life for the population. Environmental design considers economic and social policy, as well as the impact of designed rural, urban, transport, industrial, and other systems. It also considers the design of the individual environment of house, furniture, clothes, and so on. Considering the often violent impact modern society has had on the environment, a design revolution is required to reorganize the environment created by society so that these impacts can be reduced.

Environmental planning and design obviously have a deep political component, since the methods used to redesign society depend upon the control of individual demands. At one extreme, individual demand is allowed to express itself without limit, and education is used to create in the individual a realization that environmental constraints must be recognized. At the other extreme, the government or party controls demand through regulation. Most societies operate somewhere between these extremes.

Throughout human history, utopian designs have been developed for human societies and environments. Today these designs pay more attention to environmental features of society and are often labeled as ecological. Applied ecology, thus, considers not only the alteration of specific features of the modern industrial society to correct some environmental defect but also the fundamental reorientation of society to achieve a balance between humans and the natural world on which they depend. *See Ecology.*

Frank B. Golley

Ecosystem

The functional system created by the interaction of a living unit with its habitat or surroundings. The term, a contraction of ecological system, was coined in 1935 by the British plant ecologist A. G. Tansley to emphasize the dynamic nature of the mutual relationships between organisms and their physical-chemical environment. It was initially, and is most commonly, applied to the higher levels of biological organization, such as community, biome, and biosphere, and to relatively large habitat units such as lakes, forests, or watersheds. It is, however, equally applicable to much smaller interaction systems such as that of an individual plant in its particular microenvironment or that of the organisms of a decomposing log. At all levels, the concept of ecosystem implies the integration of living things and their nonliving environments through a set of processes involving the circulation, transformation, and accumulation of both matter, especially nutrient materials, and energy. Because ecology is the study of relations between organisms and their environments, the ecosystem concept is basic to

a quantitative analysis in that science. *See Biome; Biosphere; Ecological communities; Environment.*

If not unduly disturbed, ecosystems continue to function as productive units for long periods of time—hundreds, if not thousands, of years in the case of the redwood (*Sequoia sempervirens*) forests of California. Some of them, like the tropical rainforests of the Amazon Basin, contain many thousands of species of both plants and animals, and are marked by extremely complex structure and organization. They can rarely be studied in their entirety, and their analysis often requires many years of monitoring and research.

Organization and structure. The major parts of an ecosystem include (1) the physical envelope of air or water that surrounds the living unit and provides its climate; (2) the substrate on which the living unit rests or is anchored, that is, the soil, rock, or bottom sediments; and (3) the assemblage of organisms—plants, animals, and microorganisms—living within the given habitat. For analytical purposes, these organisms are conventionally grouped into components according to their major roles in the handling of matter and energy. Those which are able to manufacture their own food from simple inorganic substances with energy obtained from sunlight (photosynthetic green plants) or from the chemical oxidation of inorganic compounds (chemosynthetic bacteria) are autotrophic and classed as producers, while those which depend on already-synthesized organic matter as the source of their food energy (all animals, many fungi, and bacteria) are heterotrophic and classed as consumers. A special and very important group of consumers are the decomposers or reducers, which break up the complex organic substances of dead matter, incorporating some of the decay products in their own protoplasm and making available simple organic substances to the producers. Decomposers consist chiefly of fungi and bacteria, which absorb their food through cell membranes and thus differ significantly from the larger (animal) consumers, which ingest plant and animal tissue into an alimentary tract. Heterotrophic consumer organisms can alternatively be classified on the basis of their energy resources, for example, as biophages, if they obtain their energy from living matter, or as saprophages if they derive energy from dead and decaying materials **(Fig. 1)**.

Food webs. A hierarchy of relationships is formed as green plants or their products are eaten by animals and these in turn are eaten by other animals. Thus, the organisms of an ecosystem are functionally related as links in a food chain, that is, as successive components in the transfer of nutrient materials and associated energy. Consumer organisms that are one, two, or three links removed from the base of producer organisms are referred to as primary, secondary, or tertiary consumers, respectively. Primary consumers subsist on green plants or their products and are broadly termed herbivores, in contrast to the secondary or higher-order consumers, termed carnivores. Many animals and humans eat both plant and animal tissues and qualify as omnivores. Food chains generally do not involve more than four or five links from the producer base to the ultimate larger consumer, for example, from grass to a grasshopper to a sparrow to an owl. However, food chains are usually connected with other food chains at almost every link—the grass is eaten by numerous species of herbivores, each of which has its own set of predators, and so on, and

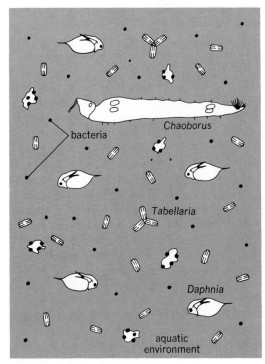

Fig. 1. Simplified ecosystem consisting of water and plankton organisms. Components of this ecosystem are environment, or water and its dissolved material; green plants, or producers (*Tabellaria*, diatom); herbivorous animals, or primary consumers (*Daphnia*, water flea); carnivorous animals, or secondary consumers (*Chaoborus*, fly larva); and bacteria, or decomposers. The various organisms are not drawn in correct size relations.

the result is an interlocking and highly complex food web. Food webs are made up of two principal types of food chains: grazing food chains, based on the consumption of green plant material, and detritus food chains, based on consumption of decomposing organic matter. *SEE FOOD WEB.*

Pyramids. Organisms which occupy similar positions in their food chains are seen as belonging to the same trophic level. The number of individuals, or the total biomass (weight of tissue), or the energy content of the organisms of successive trophic levels generally decreases with increasing remoteness of the level from the producer base. Thus these relations between trophic levels often take the form of ecological pyramids—a pyramid of numbers, a pyramid of biomass, or a pyramid of energy. Such pyramids are often used to summarize the trophic structure of ecosystems. *SEE BIOMASS.*

Niches. Each species of organism is, by definition, different from all other species, having its own distinct set of life processes and being limited in its distribution by its own particular tolerances to environmental conditions. It also has its own unique set of relationships to other species and its own characteristic functional role in the dynamics of the community; in other words, it has its own ecological niche. Some requirements and tolerances of a species usually overlap with those of other species, as in the food web, and the degree to which niche overlap can occur without the exclusion of one species by another is a significant factor in the diversity and complexity of the system. Competition and cooperation, then, are regarded as important forces in ecosystem structure and function. *SEE POPULATION ECOLOGY.*

Guilds. Species that exploit a common resource base in similar fashion, for example, the aphids, spittlebugs, moth larvae, and other insects that feed on plant juices, may usefully be grouped into guilds, and the community of organisms in an ecosystem can be viewed as an assembly of interacting guilds. Each guild can be studied as a subunit in its own right, and the complexity of the whole system can thereby be more easily handled.

Dominants. Ecosystems frequently contain a small number of species that, at any given time by virtue of their numerical abundance or overwhelming biomass, exert a powerful influence over the occurrence or behavior of other species and are therefore considered as dominants. For example, the sugar maple (*Acer saccharum*) is a dominant tree species in part of the climax forest in eastern North America; because it is so abundant there, it determines to a considerable degree the physical conditions of the forest community. Identification of the dominant species of an ecosystem is an important first step in ecological analysis.

Keystone species. Ecosystems are also often characterized by the presence of keystone species, whose presence may be critical to the community. In rocky intertidal areas of the coast of western North America, a predaceous starfish (*Pisaster ochraceus*) has been found to be such a species. When it was removed experimentally, mussels (*Mytilus californianus*) were able to monopolize the space and exclude other invertebrates and algae from attachment sites; as a result, the nature of the intertidal community was significantly altered. Thus a single species, by virtue of its own life-style, can exert a disproportionate degree of influence within its community.

Functioning. Ecosystems are integrated by the flow of nutrient material and energy between organisms and their environments. They are open systems (in that matter and energy enter from outside the system) through such physical means as rainfall or loess deposition, and by such biological phenomena as photosynthesis and colonization, and leave it by such processes as evaporation, respiration, and emigration. At any given moment, an ecosystem contains a quantity (standing crop) of living matter, but through time this is subject to more or less continuous replacement (turnover), and the balance between the additions and losses determines the degree of stability in the system. Ecological theory holds that in a stable ecosystem there is a stable supply of available free energy of organic compounds, and the flow of energy into this supply by photosynthesis is offset by the outward flow in respiration, by which energy is lost to the environment; such an ecosystem is said to be in a steady state. It is unlikely, however, that such a balance is often, if ever, attained in nature, and it is probably more appropriate to use the term dynamic equilibrium. *SEE ECOLOGICAL ENERGETICS.*

Biogeochemical cycles. Unlike energy, which is sooner or later dissipated as heat and thus lost from ecosystems, the chemical materials present in the system may circulate through it more or less indefinitely. Carbon, oxygen, hydrogen, nitrogen, and the other elements that make up the bodies of plants and animals are moved through the various components of the system in a predictable cycle, the general nature of which is shown in **Fig. 2**. When the pathways along which particular substances are moved are examined closely, they are often seen to be extremely complex. For example, an experiment was carried out by R. H. Whittaker, who used a radioactive phospho-

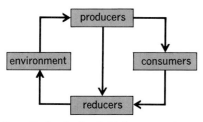

Fig. 2. Generalized cycle of materials in an ecosystem.

rus (^{32}P) tracer to ascertain the pattern of phosphate movement in a pond (**Fig. 3**). The quantity of ^{32}P in the water at a given time was found to depend not only on the total amount of phosphorus in the system but also on the various flux rates at which the element moved from component to component. Such circulation is a small-scale version of the large biogeochemical cycles that characterize the movement of water, nitrogen, sulfur, and other materials through the ecosystem of the Earth as a whole. *See BIOGEOCHEMISTRY*.

Productivity. One of the most important functional characteristics of an ecosystem is its productivity, generally measured as the rate at which energy is bound or matter is combined into organic compounds. Such productivity depends not only on the rate at which new tissue is added as growth to the bodies of already existing organisms but also on the rate at which new individuals are reproduced. Rates of growth and reproduction are influenced by many factors, such as temperature and availability of water and nutrients, and various broad correlations between environmental factors and plant productivity have been observed; for example, there is a gradient in temperature from tropical rainforest through the temperate zone to the treeless arctic tundra, and moisture follows a similar decrease along the gradient from rainforest to desert.

Disturbance. That portion of the productivity that can be diverted to use by humans is known as the yield or harvest. Ecosystems vary widely in respect

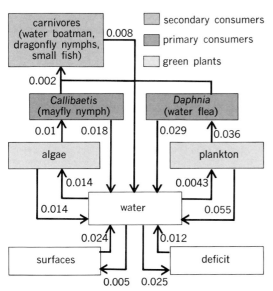

Fig. 3. Simplified pattern of phosphate movement in pond, based on an experiment by R. H. Whittaker with radioactive phosphorus (^{32}P) tracer. Numbers are transfer rates (that fraction of ^{32}P in box at tail of arrow moving in direction indicated per hour). Surface is film of bacteria and other microorganisms on rock surfaces; deficit refers to ^{32}P, mainly in depths of rocky substrate, not otherwise accounted for.

to their efficiency of production, and many of those that are exploited recover slowly, if at all, from disturbance. It has long been evident that agricultural practices developed in temperate regions are poorly adapted for use in the tropics; the apparent success with monocultures and animal husbandry in the temperate zone has generally been achieved only with much hidden cost in the manufacture of fertilizers and the energy expenditures of modern farm implements. Large-scale destruction of tropical forests and other habitats is likely to bring about a rapid extinction of many plant and animal species, thus drastically reducing the diversity of these ecosystems.

When an ecosystem's functioning is disturbed, however, as by a fire or a flood, it will frequently show some degree of resilience in returning to its normal state, provided that the disturbance has not been too severe or long-lasting. For example, Lake Washington near Seattle was disturbed for many years by the discharge of sewage into the lake, producing a heavy growth of phytoplankton, but since 1963, when the discharge began to be diverted to the ocean, the lake water has become much clearer and there has been a rapid drop in phosphorus in the surface waters, with a consequent decrease in the standing crop of phytoplankton. An ecosystem's capacity for resilience may depend in part on the sort of structure and organization it has developed, such as in the degree of patchiness or spatial heterogeneity. For example, the mosaic structure produced by forest fires in the Boundary Waters Canoe Area of northern Minnesota and Canada has apparently enhanced the ability of these forests to recover from fresh burns. In contrast, many extensive ecosystems which are currently being exploited, for example, marshlands, deserts, and the tropical rainforests, are proving very fragile and greatly lacking in resilience.

Development and evolution. When an uninhabited environment is first colonized by plants and animals, there is little evidence of organization in the community, but with the passage of time distinct patterns appear: aggregations and clumps of individuals, assemblages of different species, their partitioning into distinct layers or strata, their incorporation into food chains and food webs, and their temporal separation into components with differing seasonal or daily rhythms of activity. If such developing ecosystems are left undisturbed, theory holds that they will become increasingly integrated and self-controlled, eventually reaching the steady-state conditions in which the structure and function of the system remain constant with time. This ultimate stage is referred to as the climax, and the process of development to it as succession. Throughout the course of succession there is usually increasing productivity, more diversity of species, greater conservation of nutrient material within the system, an increasing quantity of matter in circulation, and an increasing modification of the abiotic environment by the biotic community. By the time climax has been attained, these properties will generally have reached maximal values (some may decline prior to climax) and the community will have become more or less self-supporting as long as environmental conditions do not change significantly. The course of organic evolution has been accompanied by, and has contributed to, the evolution of many new ways of life that have resulted in more complex and better-integrated biotic communities and in more efficient and presumably stable ecosystems. *See ECOLOGICAL SUCCESSION*.

Control. Many of the interactions between the components, both biotic and abiotic, of ecosystems appear to serve a regulatory function in limiting or controlling the input, flux, and output, and thus to help maintain the balance of the system. Light, temperature, moisture, and other factors may determine whether particular species can exist in particular systems, and may also influence the rates of metabolism of organisms in a given system. Some interactions behave essentially as feedback mechanisms, influencing rates in the manner of a household thermostat. This can be illustrated by the spring and fall overturns of water masses in many temperate-zone lakes, and by the density-dependent limitation of numbers of mice or lemmings by their predators. The effectiveness of regulatory control mechanisms and the relative importance of density-dependent and density-independent limitation vary greatly from ecosystem to ecosystem, and are not as yet predictable with much certainty.

Humans have learned how to exploit natural ecosystems to a degree unexcelled by any other species, and their influence at all levels of biological organization, including that of the biosphere, has already resulted in widespread destruction. Methods to dispose safely of the waste products, including nuclear ones, whose toxic potential continues to increase, are not yet mastered. Nor have humans been able to achieve population control. Pollution of the environment and overpopulation of the human species are widely seen as the greatest threats to the stability and resilience of the world ecosystem. *SEE AIR POLLUTION; CONSERVATION OF RESOURCES; ECOLOGY, APPLIED; HAZARDOUS WASTE; HUMAN ECOLOGY, WATER POLLUTION.*

F. C. Evans

Bibliography. E. E. Herricks, *The Effects of Contaminants on Ecological Systems*, 1988; C. J. Krebs, *Ecology: The Experimental Analysis of Distribution and Abundance*, 3d ed., 1984; R. V. O'Neill et al., *A Hierarchical Concept of Ecosystems*, 1986; T. Pickett and P. S. White (eds.), *The Ecology of Natural Disturbances and Patch Dynamics*, 1986; E. Polunin, *Ecosystem Theory and Application*, 1986; H. Walter and S. W. Breckle, *Ecological Systems of the Geobiosphere*, 1985; R. H. Whittaker, *Communities and Ecosystems*, 2d ed., 1975; D. Worster, *Nature's Economy: A History of Ecological Ideas*, 1985.

Electric power generation

The production of bulk electric power for industrial, residential, and rural use. Although limited amounts of electricity can be generated by many means, including chemical reaction (as in batteries) and engine-driven generators (as in automobiles and airplanes), electric power generation generally implies large-scale production of electric power in stationary plants designed for that purpose. The generating units in these plants convert energy from falling water, coal, natural gas, oil, and nuclear fuels to electric energy. Most electric generators are driven either by hydraulic turbines, for conversion of falling water energy; or by steam or gas turbines, for conversion of fuel energy. Limited use is being made of geothermal energy, and developmental work is progressing in the use of solar energy in its various forms. Electric power generating plants are normally interconnected by a transmission and distribution system to serve the electric loads in a given area or region.

Fossil-fuel and hydroelectric plants, and various types of advanced power sources, are discussed in detail below.

GENERAL CONSIDERATIONS

An electric load (or demand) is the power requirement of any device or equipment that converts electric energy into light, heat, or mechanical energy, or otherwise consumes electric energy as in aluminum reduction, or the power requirement of electronic and control devices. The total load on any power system is seldom constant; rather, it varies widely with hourly, weekly, monthly, or annual changes in the requirements of the area served. The minimum system load for a given period is termed the base load or the unity load-factor component. Maximum loads, resulting usually from temporary conditions, are called peak loads, and the operation of the generating plants must be closely coordinated with fluctuations in the load. The peaks, usually being of only a few hours' duration (**Figs. 1** and **2**), are frequently served by gas or oil combustion-turbine or pumped-storage hydro generating units. The pumped-storage type utilizes the most economical off-peak (typically 10 P.M. to 7 A.M.) surplus generating capacity to pump and store water in elevated reservoirs to be released through hydraulic turbine generators during peak periods. This type of operation improves the capacity factors or relative energy outputs of base-load generating units and hence their economy of operation.

Actual variations in the load with time are recorded, and from these data load graphs are made to forecast the probable variations of load in the future. A study of hourly load graphs (Figs. 1 and 2) indicates the generation that may be required at a given hour of the day, week, or month, or under unusual weather conditions. A study of annual load graphs and forecasts indicates the rate at which new generating stations must be built; they are an inseparable part of utility operation and are the basis for decisions that profoundly affect the financial requirements and overall development of a utility.

Generating unit sizes. The size or capacity of electric utility generating units varies widely, depending upon type of unit; duty required, that is, base-, intermediate-, or peak-load service; and system size and degree of interconnection with neighboring systems. Base-load nuclear or coal-fired units may be as large as 1200 MW each, or more. Intermediate-duty generators, usually coal-, oil-, or gas-fueled steam units, are of 200 to 600 MW capacity each. Peaking units, combustion turbines or hydro, range from several tens of megawatts for the former to hundreds of megawatts for the latter. Hydro units, in both base-load and intermediate service, range in size up to 825 MW.

The total installed generating capacity of a system is typically 20 to 30% greater than the annual predicted peak load in order to provide reserves for maintenance and contingencies.

Power-plant circuits. Both main and accessory circuits in power plants can be classified as follows:

1. Main power circuits to carry the power from the generators to the step-up transformers and on to the station high-voltage terminals.

2. Auxiliary power circuits to provide power to the motors used to drive the necessary auxiliaries.

3. Control circuits for the circuit breakers and other equipment operated from the plant's control room.

4. Lighting circuits for the illumination of the plant and to provide power for portable equipment required in the upkeep and maintenance of the plant. Sometimes special circuits are installed to supply the portable power equipment.

5. Excitation circuits, which are so installed that they will receive good physical and electrical protection because reliable excitation is necessary for the operation of the plant.

6. Instrument and relay circuits to provide values of voltage, current, kilowatts, reactive kilovoltamperes, temperatures, pressures, flow rates, and so forth, and to serve the protective relays.

7. Communication circuits for both plant and system communications. Telephone, radio, transmission-line carrier, and microwave radio may be involved.

It is important that reliable power service be provided for the plant itself, and for this reason station service is usually supplied from two or more sources. To ensure adequate reliability, auxiliary power supplies are frequently provided for start-up, shutdown, and communication services.

Generator protection. Necessary devices are installed to prevent or minimize other damage in cases of equipment failure. Differential-current and ground relays detect failure of insulation, which may be due to deterioration or accidental overvoltage. Overcurrent relays detect overload currents that may lead to excessive heating; overvoltage relays prevent insulation damage. Loss-of-excitation relays may be used to warn operators of low excitation or to prevent pulling out of synchronism. Bearing and winding overheating may be detected by relays actuated by resistance devices or thermocouples. Overspeed and lubrication failure may also be detected.

Not all of these devices are used on small units or

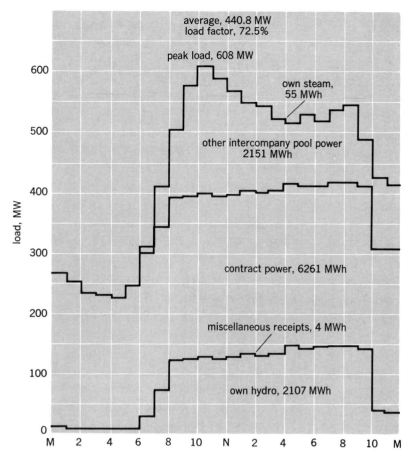

Fig. 1. Load graph indicates net system load of a metropolitan utility for typical 24-h period (midnight to midnight), totaling 10.578 MWh. Such graphs are made to forecast probable variations in power required.

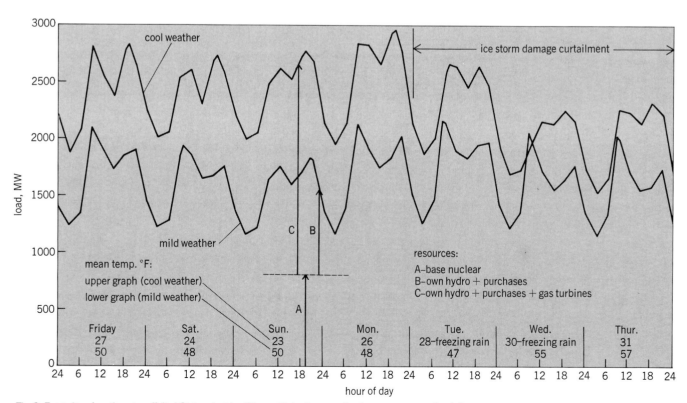

Fig. 2. Examples of northwestern United States electric utility weekly load curves showing same-year weather influence.

in every plant. The generator is immediately deenergized for electrical failure and shut down for any over-limit condition, all usually automatically.

Voltage regulation. This term is defined as the change in voltage for specific change in load (usually from full load to no load) expressed as percentage of normal rated voltage. The voltage of an electric generator varies with the load and power factor; consequently, some form of regulating equipment is required to maintain a reasonably constant and predetermined potential at the distribution stations or load centers. Since the inherent regulation of most alternating-current (ac) generators is rather poor (that is, high percentagewise), it is necessary to provide automatic voltage control. The rotating or magnetic amplifiers and voltage-sensitive circuits of the automatic regulators, together with the exciters, are all specially designed to respond quickly to changes in the alternator voltage and to make the necessary changes in the main exciter or excitation system output, thus providing the required adjustments in voltage. A properly designed automatic regulator acts rapidly, so that it is possible to maintain desired voltage with a rapidly fluctuating load without causing more than a momentary change in voltage even when heavy loads are thrown on or off.

In general, most modern synchronous generators have excitation systems that involve rectification of an ac output of the main or auxiliary stator windings, or other appropriate supply, using silicon-controlled rectifiers or thyristors. These systems enable very precise control and high rates of response.

Generation control. Computer-assisted (or on-line controlled) load and frequency control and economic dispatch systems of generation supervision are being widely adopted, particularly for the larger new plants. Strong system interconnections greatly improve bulk power supply reliability but require special automatic controls to ensure adequate generation and transmission stability. Among the refinements found necessary in large, long-distance interconnections are special feedback controls applied to generator high-speed excitation and voltage regulator systems.

Synchronization of generators. Synchronization of a generator to a power system is the act of matching, over an appreciable period of time, the instantaneous voltage of an alternating-current generator (incoming source) to the instantaneous voltage of a power system of one or more other generators (running source), then connecting them together. In order to accomplish this ideally the following conditions must be met:

1. The effective voltage of the incoming generator must be substantially the same as that of the system.

2. In relation to each other the generator voltage and the system voltage should be essentially 180° out of phase; however, in relation to the bus to which they are connected, their voltages should be in phase.

3. The frequency of the incoming machine must be near that of the running system.

4. The voltage wave shapes should be similar.

5. The phase sequence of the incoming polyphase machine must be the same as that of the system.

Synchronizing of ac generators can be done manually or automatically. In manual synchronizing an operator controls the incoming generator while observing synchronizing lamps or meters and a synchroscope, or both. The operator closes the connecting switch or circuit breaker as the synchroscope needle slowly approaches the in-phase position.

Automatic synchronizing provides for automatically closing the breaker to connect the incoming machine to the system, after the operator has properly adjusted voltage (field current), frequency (speed), and phasing (by lamps or synchroscope). A fully automatic synchronizer will initiate speed changes as required and may also balance voltages as required, then close the breaker at the proper time, all without attention of the operator. Automatic synchronizers can be used in unattended stations or in automatic control systems where units may be started, synchronized, and loaded on a single operator command.

Eugene C. Starr

FOSSIL-FUEL PLANTS

Fossil fuels are of plant or animal origin and consist of hydrogen and carbon (hydrocarbon) compounds. The most common fossil fuels are coal, oil, and natural gas. The less common ones include peat, oil shale, and biomass (wood and so forth), as well as various waste or by-products such as steel mill blast furnace gas, coke-oven gas, and refuse-derived fuels. Fossil-fuel electric power generation uses the combustion heat energy from these fuels to produce electricity.

Steam power plants. A fossil-fuel steam power plant operation essentially consists of four steps (**Fig. 3**): (1) Water is pumped at high pressure to a boiler, where (2) it is heated by fossil-fuel combustion to produce steam at high temperature and pressure. (3) This steam flows through a turbine, rotating an electric generator (connected to the turbine shaft) which converts the mechanical energy to electricity. (4) The turbine exhaust steam is condensed by using cooling water from an external source to remove the heat rejected in the condensing process. The condensed water is pumped back to the boiler to repeat the cycle. Figure 3 also shows features to increase cycle efficiency, including preheating of the boiler feedwater by using steam extracted from the turbine, and reheating the high-pressure turbine exhaust steam before it enters the intermediate-pressure turbine.

Steam cycle. Modern fossil-fuel power plants are based on a steam cycle first proposed by W. J. M. Rankine in 1908. The basic Rankine cycle underwent conceptual evolution through the 1950s that improved cycle efficiency to current levels but which also increased the complexity of building and operating a fossil-fuel power plant. Commercial development lagged behind conceptual cycle development because of the unavailability of suitable materials and fabrication techniques to accommodate the higher steam pressures and temperatures required to increase cycle efficiency. **Table 1** summarizes this steam cycle evolution with respect to turbine inlet steam pressure, turbine heat rate, and turbine cycle and overall thermal efficiencies, along with related available main steam piping materials from the 1930s through the 1950s.

During the 1960s and 1970s, there was no significant cycle efficiency improvement, primarily due to the advent of nuclear power and the abundant supply of low-cost fossil fuel. In the 1980s, the interest in cycle efficiency improvement was renewed due to the uncertain future of nuclear energy and escalating fossil-fuel costs.

Plant size and facilities. A given power plant's size is determined by the utility company's need for power as dictated by the electrical demand growth forecast.

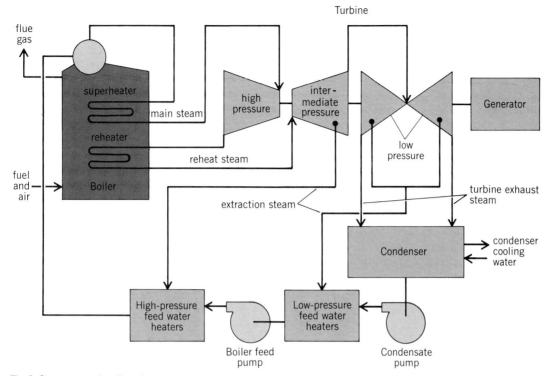

Fig. 3. Steam power plant flow diagram.

The additional generating capacity needed is matched to commercially available turbine-generator capacity sizes. The boiler is selected to suit the turbine steam flow requirements, and the remaining accessory equipment is sized to serve the needs of the resulting boiler-turbine steam cycle.

A typical large fossil-fuel power plant consists of several major facilities and equipment (**Fig. 4**), including fuel handling and processing, boiler (including furnace), turbine and electric generator, condenser and condenser heat removal system, feedwater heating and pumping system, flue gas–cleaning system, and plant controls and control system.

1. Fuel handling. Fuel type determines the fuel-handling system requirements. Natural gas is normally delivered by pipeline directly and fired in the furnace, needing no special handling or storage. For coal and oil, which are usually delivered by rail, ship, or pipelines, the fuel-handling system includes fuel unloading, storage, reclaiming from storage, and fuel preparation for combustion (such as coal pulverizing and pneumatic conveying to the burners, and oil heating and atomizing). Coal is usually stored in open stockpiles and oil in closed tanks. Normally, 30 to 180 days of fuel requirement is stored at the plant site to maintain operation during fluctuations in fuel delivery.

2. Boiler. The fuel type also determines the size, design, and operation of the furnace and boiler, which become larger and more complex (in ascending order) for gas, oil, and coal. For coal, the size and complexity also increase with the decline in coal rank and quality (in ascending order) for bituminous, subbituminous, lignite, and brown coal. Specialized boiler

Table 1. Steam cycle development in fossil-fuel power plant

Years	Steam cycle, psig/°F/°F* (MPa/°C/°C)	Main steam piping material	Turbine cycle[†] heat rate, Btu/kWh (MJ/kWh)	Thermal efficiency (%) Turbine cycle[†]	Overall[‡]
Late 1930s	1250/950 (8.7/510)	Chromium-molybdenum alloy (0.2% C, 0.5% Cr, 0.5% Mo)	9350 (9.86)	36.50	29.2
Mid 1940s	1450/1000/1000 (10.1/538/538)	Chromium-molybdenum alloy (0.2% C, 1.0% Cr, 0.5% Mo)	8150 (8.60)	41.9	33.5
Late 1940s	2000/1050/1050 (13.9/566/566)	Chromium-molybdenum alloy (0.2% C, 1.0% Cr, 0.5% Mo)	7700 (8.12)	44.3	35.5
Early 1950s	2400/1100/1050 (16.6/593/566)	Chromium-molybdenum alloy (0.2% C, 1.0% Cr, 0.5% Mo)	7500 (7.91)	45.5	36.4
Late 1950s	4500/1200/1050 (31.1/649/566)	Nickel-chromium-molybdenum-manganese alloy (0.8% C, 13% Ni, 16% Cr, 2% Mo, 2% Mn)	7100 (7.49)	48.1	38.5

*Main steam pressure/main steam temperature/reheat steam temperature.
[†]Cycle heat rate and thermal efficiency are at rated load for a condenser backpressure of 1.43 in. Hg (36.3 mmHg or 4.84 kPa) absolute and a condensate temperature of 90°F (32.2°C).
[‡]Based on a boiler efficiency of 85% and a power plant auxiliary power requirement of 5% of plant output.

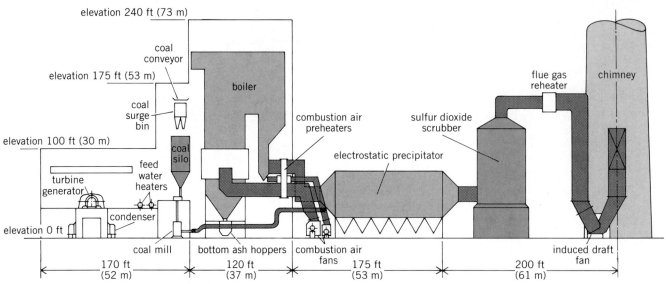

elevation 240 ft (73 m)

elevation 175 ft (53 m)

elevation 100 ft (30 m)

elevation 0 ft

Fig. 4. Schematic cross section of a 600-MW coal-fired steam power plant.

170 ft (52 m)   120 ft (37 m)   175 ft (53 m)   200 ft (61 m)

designs are required to handle peat, shale, and the various waste fuels. One evolving technology, fluidized-bed boilers, can effectively burn a wide range of low-quality solid fuels in the same boiler, but only relatively small industrial-scale units presently are commercially proven and available.

3. *Turbines.* Modern power plants, depending on the size and steam conditions, have single or multiple-casing turbines with high-, intermediate-, and low-pressure sections. High-pressure steam from the boiler after expanding through one or more turbines is exhausted to a condenser under vacuum, where the steam is condensed by cooling water.

4. *Condenser.* About 50% of the fuel heat input to the boiler is ultimately rejected as waste heat in the condenser. Condenser heat-removal-system selection depends on the geography, climatology, and water availability at each plant site. There are basically two types of heat rejection systems: open (or once-through) cooling and closed cooling. The open system is the most simple and normally used where water is abundantly available. It takes water from an ocean, lake, or river and discharges the heated water to a downstream location. The closed system is used when it is determined not to return heated water to the water source due to environmental or other constraints. The closed system rejects heat to the atmosphere by using a secondary heat rejection system such as a cooling tower or pond. However, closed-system operation involves evaporating a portion of the water circulated, requiring a water supply capable of restoring the quantity of water evaporated. Dry cooling (with air condensers) is less efficient, but is used in arid areas where the water supply is limited. The temperature of the cooling medium (water or air) at the condenser inlet determines the cycle thermal efficiency by establishing the steam condensation temperature.

5. *Feedwater heating.* The condensed steam is pumped back to the boiler inlet to complete the cycle, with heat from turbine extraction steam transferred along the way to increase cycle efficiency. Condensate pumps deliver feedwater from the condenser through low-pressure feedwater heaters to the boiler feed pumps, which increase the feedwater pressure and pump it through high-pressure feedwater heaters

to the boiler inlet. A modern power plant typically has six feedwater heaters, which can be increased in number to improve cycle efficiency, but with offsetting increases in plant complexity and cost.

6. *Flue gas and liquid waste.* Fossil-fuel power plants produce gaseous and liquid wastes which are treated prior to discharge to minimize effects on the environment. In many countries, environmental regulations define the extent of flue gas and liquid waste treatment required.

Major pollutants in the flue gas include particulates (except for natural gas fuel), sulfur dioxide, and nitrogen oxides. Incombustible matter in coal and oil yields particulates upon combustion which are collected in devices such as electrostatic precipitators and fabric filters (baghouses). These devices are capable of removing more than 99% of the particulate matter.

A variety of chemical processes is available for the removal of sulfur dioxide from the flue gas. Flue gas desulfurization systems use alkaline chemicals such as lime, limestone, sodium, or magnesium compounds in solution, slurry, or dry form to react with and remove sulfur dioxide. The choice depends on the fuel sulfur content, performance requirement, capital and operating costs, and market for the desulfurization by-products. The throw-away wet limestone slurry process is the most widely used in the United States due to the limited market for by-products. A similar process producing gypsum as the by-product is common in Europe and Japan. *See* AIR-POLLUTION CONTROL.

Nitrogen oxides emission can be reduced by combustion modifications which limit their formation during combustion. These techniques involve reduction of flame temperature by prolonging the combustion time (staged combustion) and reducing the combustion air quantity (low–nitrogen oxides burners).

Processes to remove nitrogen oxides after their formation have been developed and demonstrated. They involve injection of ammonia into the hot flue gas in the presence or absence of catalysts. They are referred to as the selective catalytic reduction and noncatalytic reduction processes, respectively. The selective catalytic reduction process is widely used in Japan and Europe, particularly in Germany, in both large-scale electric utilities and in small-scale industrial boilers. The noncatalytic reduction process is used in the United States in some small-scale industrial boilers. Typical nitrogen oxide reductions with the selective catalytic reduction process range from 70 to 90% and with the noncatalytic reduction process from 30 to 70%.

Waste liquid pollutants include suspended solids, toxic metal compounds, dissolved chlorine, and high-acidity or high-alkalinity, high-temperature, and oily compounds. Treatment prior to discharge or reuse usually involves one or more of the following: neutralization, sedimentation, clarification, filtration, dechlorination, and incineration.

7. Plant controls. The power plant size and steam cycle pressure and temperature determine plant controls and control systems requirements. In ascending order of complexity and sophistication, these include pneumatic analog controls, electronic analog controls, hard-wired digital controls, and distributed digital control with microprocessors and minicomputers. Modern power plants typically use pneumatic local controls and electronic analog remote controls with electromechanical or solid-state interlocking devices and variable-speed motor drives.

A typical cost distribution by major systems and equipment for a coal-fired steam power plant is given in **Table 2**.

Gas turbine plants. Power plants with gas turbine–driven electric generators are often used to meet short-term peaks in electrical demand. They are generally small (less than 50 MW), have a low thermal efficiency, require clean fuels such as natural gas or light oils, and consequently are more expensive to operate. However, these plants have a relatively low capital cost and can be used in areas with low power demand and limited water availability. Diesel engine–driven electric generators are also used under similar conditions.

Gas turbine power plants use atmospheric air as the working medium, operating on an open cycle where air is taken from and discharged to the atmosphere and is not recycled. In a simple gas turbine plant (**Fig. 5**), air is compressed and fuel is injected into the compressed air and burned in a combustion chamber. The combustion products expand through a gas turbine and exhaust to the atmosphere. Variations of this basic operation to increase cycle efficiency include regeneration (where exhaust from the turbine is used to preheat the compressed air before it enters the

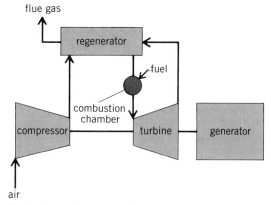

Fig. 5. Gas turbine plant flow diagram.

combustion chamber) and reheating (where the combustion gases are expanded in more than one stage and are reheated between stages).

Combined-cycle plants use both gas and steam turbines and offer some overall thermal efficiency improvement and operating economy. The gas turbine exhaust heat is used to generate steam for operating steam turbine generators. Cogeneration is another method of improving overall thermal efficiency, where steam exhausted from the steam turbine generator is used in industrial processes. Substantial energy is saved as heat rejected in the condenser is put to use.

Advanced concepts. Advanced fossil-fuel power generation concepts such as integrated coal gasification combined cycle and magnetohydrodynamics offer the promise of significant overall thermal efficiency improvement. In the integrated coal gasification combined cycle, gas produced from coal (after proper purification) is burned and expanded through a gas turbine, with the exhaust heat used to generate steam for a steam turbine generator. In the magnetohydrodynamic process, an electrically conducting medium such as hot flue gas from a coal combustor (seeded with alkali metal salts to increase the flue gas electrical conductivity) is passed through a magnetic field (magnetohydrodynamic channel) to produce electricity. The magnetohydrodynamic channel exhaust gas is then used to generate steam in a conventional steam power plant. The alkali salts are recovered and reused. Power generation based on these concepts can reach a thermal efficiency of 48–52%, whereas a steam turbine plant has an efficiency of 30–40% and a conventional gas turbine plant 22–28%.

Maris T. Fravel; Natarajan Sekhar

HYDROELECTRIC PLANTS

Hydroelectric generation is an attractive source of electric power because it is a renewable resource and a nonconsumptive use. In the broadest sense, hydroelectric power is a form of solar power; the resource is renewed by the solar cycle in which water is evaporated from the oceans, transported by clouds, and falls as precipitation on the land masses, and returns through rivers to the ocean, generating power on the way. Hydroelectric power can be defined as the generation of electricity by flowing water; potential energy from the weight of water falling through a vertical distance is converted to electrical energy. The amount of electric power P that can be generated is

Table 2. Typical cost distribution of major systems and equipment for a coal-fired steam power plant*

Systems and equipment	% of capital cost
Boiler (including furnace)	30
Turbine and electric generator	18
Flue gas desulfurization system	16
Particulate collection system	7
Coal-handling equipment	5
Condenser and cooling tower	5
Ash-handling equipment	3
Pumps	3
Chimney	2
Water treatment	1
Other mechanical equipment	10

*Excluding land, site preparation, and building costs.

given by the equation below, where Q is the volume

$$P = \frac{Qh}{k} \quad \text{kW}$$

flow of water, h is the height through which the water falls, and k is a constant equal to 11.8 when Q is given in cubic feet and h in feet (English units), and equal to 0.102 when Q is in cubic meters and h is in meters (SI units).

Development. In the United States, the first hydroelectric generating station was built in 1882 in Appleton, Wisconsin. The total power output was sufficient to operate some 250 electric lights. Rapid expansion followed, and by 1900 about 300 hydroelectric plants were in operation worldwide. This rapid expansion was a consequence of the development in the nineteenth century of the hydraulic reaction turbine. Also, by the same date, the concept of pumped storage had been introduced in Switzerland, but extensive development in the United States did not occur until the advent of the reversible pump–turbine design in the early 1950s.

Major components. A typical hydroelectric development consists of a dam to divert or store water; waterways such as a forebay, canals, tunnels, and penstocks to deliver the water to the hydraulic turbine and a draft tube, tunnel, or tailrace to return the water to the stream; hydraulic turbines and governors; generators and exciters; electrical controls to provide protection and to regulate frequency, voltage, and power flow; a powerhouse to enclose the machinery and equipment; transformers and switching equipment;

and a transmission line to deliver the power to the load center for ultimate distribution (**Fig. 6**).

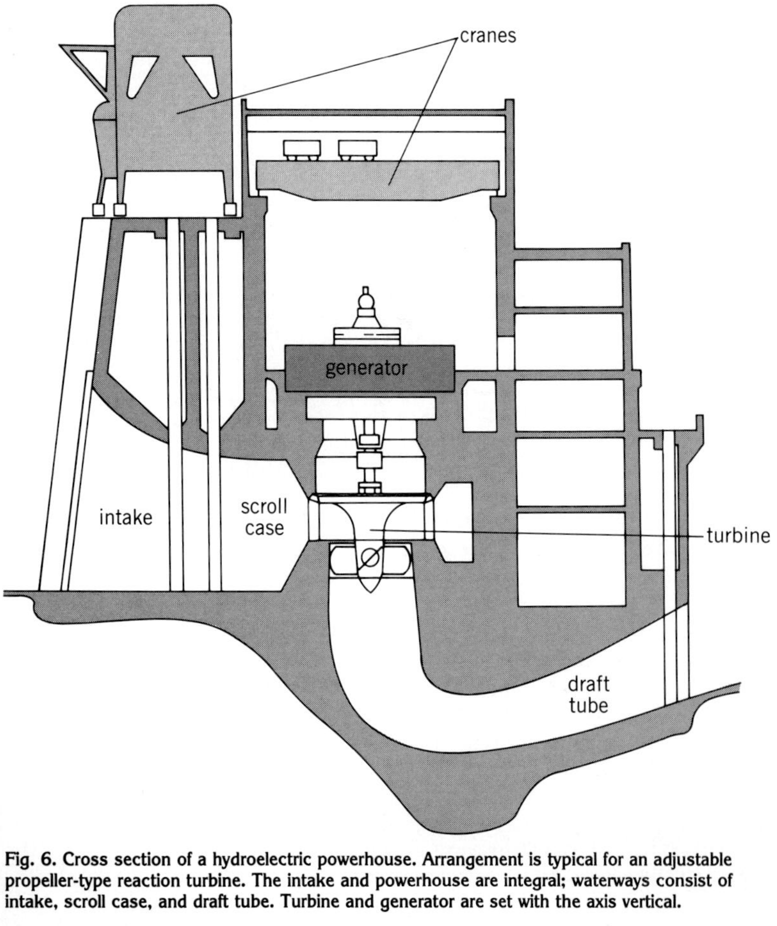

Dam. Dams are functionally important as they regulate the water supply to the plant and also are frequently the largest single element of cost in a hydroelectric development. Dams may be classified according to materials or type of construction, height, or use. SEE DAM.

Waterways. Waterways may be very short or as much as 10 mi (16 km) or more in length. The type of waterway is selected on the basis of length, pressure, plant arrangement, and economy. Very short waterways are required in installations where the powerhouse and the dam are integral structures; then the waterway is short and the length dictated by the plant arrangement. In other low-head plants, canals and forebays are frequently used. Conversely, very long waterways are also common in the developments where the head is great. Tunnels and penstocks are commonly used in high-head developments to deliver the water to a powerhouse some distance from the impoundment.

Some of the important aspects of the hydraulic design of waterways are provision for dewatering to facilitate inspection and maintenance, provision for water hammer resulting from surges caused by sudden start-up or shutdown, and optimization of hydraulic losses for an economic design.

An intake structure may be provided at the entrance to the waterway to reduce the hydraulic losses and to provide a closure gate for dewatering the waterway. Surge chambers are required at abrupt vertical changes in the direction of the waterways to provide relief of surges on shutdown and to prevent separation of the water column on start-up. When tunnels are used for the tailrace, surge chambers may be required for surge suppression.

Penstocks are defined as large-diameter pipelines for delivering water to the turbine or the steel-lined part of a tunnel adjacent to the powerhouse. Materials other than steel have been used in penstock construction; in the past, wood staves were common; and fiber glass is now used selectively.

Turbines. Hydraulic turbines are used to drive an electric generator, thereby converting the potential energy of the water to electrical energy. Reaction- or impulse-type turbines are used depending upon the head available, with a reaction turbine being used for heads under 1200 ft (365 m) and an impulse turbine for greater heads. Reaction turbines operate in a closed system from headwater to tailwater. For impulse turbines, only the portion to the turbine is closed and under pressure; from that point, flow is by gravity. As water passes through the reaction turbine, conversion from potential to mechanical energy takes place and, through a shaft, drives the generator. For an impulse turbine, the potential energy of the water is first converted to kinetic energy in high-velocity jets which impinge on buckets at the circumference of the impulse wheel. There the kinetic energy is converted to mechanical energy for driving the generator. Reaction turbines are classified as Francis or propeller types, and propeller types are further categorized as fixed-blade and adjustable-blade, or Kaplan-type. Both classes of reaction turbines are normally installed with the axis vertical.

Generator. In vertical installations, the generator is located above the turbine. When the turbine rotates, so does the rotor of the synchronous generator which produces electrical energy in a conventional way. An

Fig. 6. Cross section of a hydroelectric powerhouse. Arrangement is typical for an adjustable propeller-type reaction turbine. The intake and powerhouse are integral; waterways consist of intake, scroll case, and draft tube. Turbine and generator are set with the axis vertical.

operating speed is chosen, as well as a generator with the correct number of poles to develop the desired frequency. From the generator, electricity is carried by buses to switching apparatus and then to transformers, where the voltage is stepped up for transmission.

Bulb units. Bulb units, which take their name from their shape, are an adaptation of the propeller unit and differ from the conventional unit in two significant respects: the alignment is horizontal, and the generator is totally enclosed within the bulb and mounted in the water passage. Water flows to the unit in a horizontal conduit and passes in the annular space between the bulb and the walls of the conduit. As the water passes the bulb, it drives the propeller and exits from the unit through a divergent horizontal water passage. Flow is controlled in a manner similar to the vertical units by wicket gates.

Classification of developments. Hydroelectric developments may be classified according to purpose, use, location of powerhouse, and head. The descriptive classifications commonly used are the run-of-river or storage, high- or low-head, base- or peak-load, multipurpose or single-purpose, and conventional or pumped-storage. Powerhouses may be indoor or outdoor, aboveground (surface) or underground. A number of these classifications may apply to any specific project such as conventional, run-of-river with surface, outdoor powerhouse, or pumped-storage with an underground powerhouse.

Multipurpose projects. A multipurpose project has a number of uses, some of which may be governed by competing criteria. Hydroelectric generation is generally compatible with other uses because it is nonconsumptive. Such projects normally require large reservoirs to accommodate the multiple uses. The most frequent purposes are irrigation, power, flood control, navigation, water supply, and recreation. Some adjustment must be made in either the amount of or the timing of the generation for compatibility with other uses. On major river systems in the United States, multipurpose projects have been developed in conjunction with navigation, flood control, and power. In the semiarid states, irrigation has played a dominant role in multipurpose developments.

Pumped storage. Pumped storage is a process for converting large quantities of electrical energy to potential energy by pumping water to a higher elevation where it can be stored indefinitely, then released to pass through hydraulic turbines and generate electrical energy on demand. Storage is desirable, as the consumption of electricity is highly variable according to the time of day or week, as well as seasonally. Consequently, there is excess generating capacity at night and on weekends. This excess capacity can be used to generate energy for pumping, hence storage. Normally, pumping energy can be obtained cheaply at night or on weekends, and its value will be upgraded when used for daytime peak loads.

In a typical operation, water is pumped at night or on weekends from a lower to an upper reservoir, where it is stored. The water can be retained indefinitely without deterioration or significant loss. During the daylight hours when the loads are greatest, stored water is released to flow from the upper to the lower reservoir through hydraulic turbines which generate electricity. No water is consumed in either the pumping or the generating cycles. A hydroelectric pumped-storage development is similar to a typical hydro installation, except that it has two reservoirs of essen-

tially equal size situated to maximize their difference in elevation. Also, since it is a closed system, it need not be located directly on a large stream but must have a source for initial filling and to make up for the losses of evaporation and seepage. The second principal difference is the pump-turbine which is capable of rotation in either direction and acts as a pump in one direction and a turbine in the other.

Dwight L. Glasscock

ADVANCED POWER SOURCES

Interest has developed in alternative or advanced power sources. Most of this attention has focused on solar or solar-related technologies, although several additional options including geothermal and fusion have been examined. Genuine interest in alternatives developed following the oil embargo in 1973.

The supplies of fossil and nuclear fuels are classified as nonrenewable and therefore are gradually being depleted. The advanced power sources of interest are those which are renewable and linked to the Sun, naturally occurring steam or hot water in the Earth's crust, or fusion. Since all solar sources suffer from intermittent availability, they require special consideration. As these various options are considered, three significant problems must be addressed. First, availability and the primary form of occurrence of the resource must be assessed. Second, a conversion system must be developed to transform the source into a usable form of energy, typically electricity. Third, the electricity production source must be effectively and efficiently appended to the existing electrical supply system. **Figure 7** shows the predicted development of advanced power sources.

Solar power. The solar options consisting of photovoltaics, wind, solar thermal process, and biomass

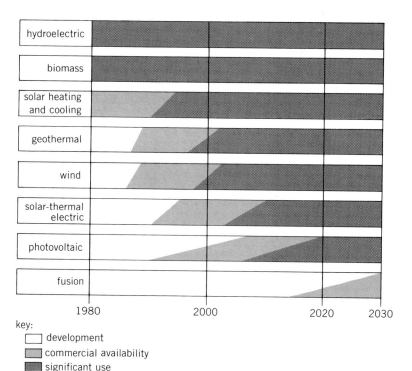

key:
☐ development
▨ commercial availability
▩ significant use

Fig. 7. Predicted development of advanced power sources. Commercial availability refers to the time when a commercial system can be ordered. Significant use is defined as equal to or greater than the equivalent of 1% of total United States electric power generation. Pitched lines cover uncertainty of time estimates that divide the three phases. (*After Earth's renewable resources, EPRI J., December 1981*)

will be discussed below. Other solar alternatives, including solar ponds, passive solar, and ocean-thermal energy conversion, and other ocean power systems such as tide and wave power will not be treated.

Photovoltaics. The collection of solar energy takes many forms, but one of its most desirable configurations is direct conversion to electricity. The device configurations are modular in form, making them convenient from a mass-production viewpoint.

The heart of the photovoltaic system is a thin flat layer of semiconductor material. When the material is struck by sunlight, electrons are freed, producing an electric current. The direct-current (dc) power is passed through a dc load, into a storage battery, or converted to alternating current (ac) for general use in electric utility grids. Typically, individual solar cells are ganged together to form photovoltaic modules that are about 5 ft^2 (0.5 m^2) in size with a generating capacity of about 50 W. Typically, about half the cost of a solar system lies with the solar cell modules, and the remainder is directed toward power conditioning, electrical wiring, installation, and site preparation.

Typically, silicon or gallium arsenide is used to fabricate solar cells, although other semiconductor materials are being developed. Silicon technology is the most advanced because it is the least expensive, and takes many different forms including single-crystal, polycrystal, and amorphous configurations. The efficiency of these configurations ranges from about 6 to about 14% in module form. Amorphous silicon offers significant potential because of low manufacturing cost.

One way to advance the power yield from photovoltaics is to use concentrator systems. Special lenses and mirrors are used to focus sunlight on the cells, thereby raising the output of a module. Concentrator systems result in larger electric current which increases cell losses but improves overall economic efficiency of the system. Concentrator technology can raise module efficiencies to about 20%. Photovoltaic systems have potential application at the household level; however, the best near-term application is in array configurations for utility application.

Wind. The use of wind energy dates back to sailing ships and windmills. Today the interest in wind is for electricity generation by wind turbines. Wind energy conversion systems consist of several major subsystems. Among the most important is the mechanical system and electromechanical rotary converter. A wind energy conversion system is designed to rotate at either constant or variable speed as the wind varies. The variable-speed system usually offers high wind-collection efficiency; however, constant-speed units permit simpler electrical systems.

There are a multitude of aeroturbine designs available, with each striving to enhance the wind to mechanical power conversion effectiveness. A measure of this effectiveness is the power coefficient (C_p). The power coefficient is expressed as a function of the tip speed ratio, that is, the ratio of the blade tip speed to the wind speed. In variable-speed systems, C_p is tuned to its optimum value, whereas constant-speed systems cannot operate at optimum C_p over the entire wind speed range. This does not suggest that variable speed is a panacea, since it exposes the mechanical drive train and tower to potential resonance problems and requires more power conditioning of the electrical output.

The characteristics of the aeroturbine and the electric generator are not totally compatible; therefore, an element is required to effectively tie these two components. The mechanical interface has two major assignments. First, aeroturbines usually rotate at low speeds, which are not desirable for electrical production. Typically, a transmission is used to convert low-speed, high-torque mechanical power into high-speed, low-torque mechanical power for electrical conversion. Second, the mechanical interface can be used to regulate the drive train shaft stiffness, and thus shape its dynamic performance.

Ultimately the mechanical energy that has been produced by the aeroturbine and conditioned by the mechanical interface must be converted to an electrical form. In general, the type of wind system, constant- or variable-speed, determines the type of electric generator—synchronous, induction, or dc. Variable-speed systems tend to produce initially poor-quality ac or dc electric power, and then use power conditioners in the electrical interface to enhance it. Usually, constant-speed systems produce high-quality electric power at the generator terminals.

Further development of wind turbine technology is required to provide economical systems; however, wind electric systems show promise. Systems under development will produce as much 4–5 MW per machine. Typically, units larger than 200 kW are used by utilities (**Fig. 8**).

Solar thermal. The process of collecting and concentrating solar energy at a focal point is known as solar thermal. There are two broad classes of solar thermal collection systems: power tower and point- and line-focus. The power tower is a large central power-generating system which shows significant promise, while the point- and line-focus systems are smaller and would be deployed as so-called dispersed sources. In both cases, solar energy is focused at a point or a line and heat is transferred to a working fluid.

The power tower concept has received significant attention because of its potentially large power production capability. A 10-MW demonstration plant, called Solar One, developed by the U.S. Department of Energy near Barstow, California, consists of 1818 heliostats, each containing 12 separate mirror facets designed to aim their energy at a central receiver on top of a structural steel tower. The heliostats are computer-controlled and adjust during the day to track the Sun so that optimal collection efficiency is maintained. The working fluid in this system is water, which is converted to steam and then passed through a conventional steam turbine for eventual conversion to electricity. One significant application for the solar thermal system is as a repowering plant. Repowering is a term applied to the concept of adding a solar thermal plant to a conventional power plant to supplement steam production.

The point- and line-focus systems are smaller facilities which produce power at lower temperatures (200–600°F or 100–300°C). A typical point system is a parabolic dish which concentrates sunlight on a receiver a few feet away. Line-focus or trough systems consist of a series of cylindrical or parabolic trough lines with mirrors to collect and concentrate the Sun's radiation. Both the point- and line-focus systems could be used in smaller cogeneration facilities for commercial and industry electric power systems. *See* SOLAR ENERGY.

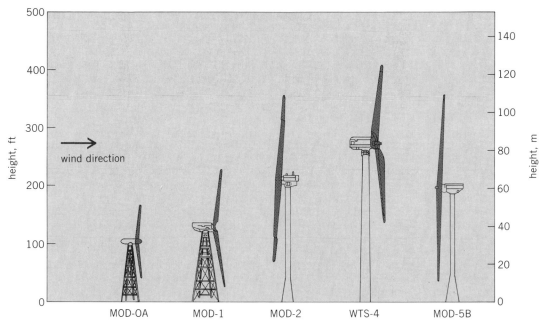

Fig. 8. Large horizontal-axis wind turbines under development for utility application. Values for annual electrical output assume 90% machine availability, wind speed average at 30 ft (9 m) above sea level, and Weibull wind speed distribution. Relative performance of specific designs is dependent on site wind characteristics. (*After Earth's renewable resources, EPRI J., December 1981*)

Biomass. Biofuel applications, involving consumption of wood products and garbage, have existed for many years. Perhaps the single largest hurdle for this application of wood and other products is the creation of effective distribution and supply systems. In general, these materials are low-density, thus causing significant transportation problems in delivering them to the chosen site for consumption.

An alternative to direct burning of biofuels is conversion to combustible liquids, gases, and solids. One process is classified as thermochemical—pyrolysis and gasification. Pyrolysis is a low-temperature process for forming gases, liquids, and solids by heating them in the absence of air, while gasification is a high-temperature process for producing gaseous fuels in the presence of an oxidant (air). A second class of processes for converting biomass to an alternative form is biochemical, which is better known as fermentation, that is, microbial transformation of organic feed materials that takes place without oxygen and produces alcohols and organic chemicals, such as methane, ethanol, acetic acid, and acetone.

The typical process of converting solar radiation to electricity by using vegetation as the collector is very inefficient (**Table 3**). It is clear that direct conversion by means other than vegetation is desirable. *See Biomass.*

Geothermal power. The natural emissions of steam (geysers), hot springs, and volcanoes represent potential sources of electricity production and are indicative of the steam and hot water potential embedded in the Earth's crust. Geothermal energy manifests itself in three basic types: hydrothermal, geopressured, and petrothermal. Hydrothermal is the natural production of steam when water is vaporized by coming into contact with hot rock. In geopressured systems, hot water is generated in deep reservoirs embedded in sand and shale formations within the Earth. The hot water is trapped and pressurized and is saturated with natural gas. Petrothermal systems consist of hot rock at the Earth's surface which could have a fluid injected into it and pumped out again, to extract thermal energy. The amount of geothermal potential for electricity production is estimated at 220×10^{15} Btu $(2.3 \times 10^{20}$ joules), which is about three times the United States' energy consumption in 1980.

Presently, most geothermal power-producing facilities are limited to application of geysers or so-called dry steam sources. Since dry steam represents less than 1% of the total geothermal potential, other systems are under development to harness the Earth's natural heat. The largest near-term potential appears to be the hydrothermal resource. The present approach of converting high-temperature (above 410°F or 210°C) water is direct-flash technology. Hot water is extracted from the earth and its pressure is dropped, causing the water to vaporize (flash-boil). The steam is applied to conventional steam turbine technology. The overall efficiency of this process requires improvement since significant energy is lost when flashing the hydrothermal fluid. Since the hot water arrives from the geothermal well as a two-phase mixture of steam and water, a centrifugal process is under development to separate steam and water, capturing natural

Table 3. Typical energy losses in using vegetation for generation of electricity	
Energy losses	% of energy in incident solar radiation
Due to leaf reflection and ineffective absorption	9
Due to invisible light, unusable for photosynthesis	55
Due to photosynthetic conversion	31
Due to plant respiration and metabolism	2
Due to conversion to electricity	2
Available as electricity	1

steam and optimizing conversion of the hot water to steam.

Since much of the geothermal potential occurs at lower temperatures, below 410°F (210°C), a process is being developed to capture this energy. The process is called binary since hot geothermal energy is used to vaporize a secondary fluid such as a hydrocarbon like isobutane or isopentain which boils at a lower temperature. The heat from the geothermal source is transferred to the secondary fluid through a heat exchanger, which in turn produces steam for a conventional steam cycle.

Although the various geothermal sources follow different paths to the production of steam, several common problems exist. Most hydrothermal fluids contain dissolved minerals. As the temperature of the fluid drops, the minerals precipitate out causing scaling in most flow channels and thus reducing the efficiency and effectiveness of the system. The corrosive nature of the brine hydrothermal fluids is a general problem. Perhaps the other general problem is the noncondensable gases found dissolved in the hydrothermal fluids. These gases reduce thermal efficiency, accelerate equipment wear, and cause environmental concerns. SEE GEOTHERMAL POWER.

Fusion power. The use of nuclear energy as a power source has been confined to nuclear fission or the splitting of atomic nuclei for energy production. In the process of fusion, atomic nuclei merge by overcoming their normal electrostatic repulsion. When the nuclei fuse, energy is released as a result of the freeing of fast-moving nuclear particles. The Sun is a natural fusion reactor and is indicative of the potential from this source of energy.

Atomic mixtures used in fusion, called plasmas, consist of positively and negatively charged particles resulting from heating a gas to a high temperature. Fusion requires that the working plasma have not only extreme temperature to free the nuclei but also a sufficiently dense or compact environment to merge them. As a gas heats up, it will expand unless confined, resulting in a very low-density mixture that will not allow nuclear fusion. A successful fusion effort must therefore combine both high temperature and confinement.

The Sun accomplishes the process of fusion with its own high temperature (15×10^6°C) and its enormous mass which holds the plasma by gravity at proper densities. On Earth, such gravitational systems are not possible and thus higher temperatures will be necessary. The development of fusion reactors has concentrated on the two problems of temperature and confinement. Heating appears a less formidable problem than confinement. Electric currents, radio-frequency waves, and neutral-beam heaters have been effective approaches to the heating problem. Containment systems have focused on two approaches: magnetic and inertial.

The leading contender in magnetic confinement is a doughnut-shaped device called a tokamak. A magnetic field is used to control the plasma by deflecting the charged particles into a cylindrical or magnetic bottle and preventing them from striking the walls of the containment vessel. Such an occurrence would drop the temperature of the plasma, preventing the fusion process. In inertial confinement, a pulsed-energy source, called a drive, is used to compact and heat the fusion fuel in a single step. This results in

rapid burning of the fuel to yield energy release. SEE ELECTRIC POWER SYSTEMS.

Thomas W. Reddoch

Bibliography. Babcock and Wilcox Co., *Steam: Its Generation and Use*, 39th ed., 1978; P. N. Cheremisinoff and R. A. Young, *Pollution Engineering Practice Handbook*, 1981; Earth's renewable resources, special issue, *EPRI J.*, vol. 6, no. 10, December 1981; D. G. Fink and H. W. Beaty (eds.), *Standard Handbook for Electrical Engineers*, 12th ed., 1987; L. L. Freris, *Principles of Wind Energy Conversion Systems*, 1990; General Electric Co., *Updating Excitation Systems*, Publ. GET-6675B, 1986; T. G. Hicks, *Power Plant Evaluation and Design Reference Guide*, 1986; K. W. Li and A. P. Priddy, *Power Plant System Design*, 1985; N. M. Lipman (ed.), *Alternative Energy Sources for the Centralised Generation of Electricity*, 1983; P. Longrigg and E. H. Buell, *Electric Power from Renewable Energy Technologies*, Solar Energy Research Institute, May 1983; P. H. Nowill, *Productivity and the Technological Change in Electric Power Generating Plants*, 1979; J. G. Singer, *Combustion-Fossil Power Systems*, 3d ed., 1981; G. Van Overstraeten and R. P. Mertens, *Physics, Technology and Use of Photovoltaics*, 1986; J. Vardi and B. Avi-Itzhak, *Electrical Energy Generation: Economics, Reliability and Rates*, 1980; C. L. Wadhwa, *Generation, Distribution and Utilization of Electrical Energy*, 1989; J. H. Willenbrock and H. R. Thomas (eds.), *Planning, Engineering and Construction of Electric Power Generation Facilities*, 1980; A. J. Wood and B. J. Wollenberg, *Power Generation, Operation, and Control*, 1984.

Electric power systems

Complex assemblages of equipment and circuits for generating, transmitting, and distributing electrical energy. Principal elements of a typical power system are shown in **Fig. 1**. These elements form complex networks which require energy control centers to monitor and regulate their operation.

Since electrical energy plays a central role in industrialized societies, the reliability of electric power systems is a critical factor in their planning, design, and operation, and considerable effort is directed toward quantifying performance. In addition to the provision of electrical energy, attention is given to the myriad of items that consume this energy, that is, the power system load.

PRINCIPAL ELEMENTS

Electrical systems require generating stations to produce electric power, transmission systems to carry it to areas of consumption, substations to transform it for use in industrial and residential areas, and distribution systems to carry it to customers (Fig. 1). Coordinated interconnections between power systems play a critical role in ensuring an acceptable degree of reliability.

Generation. Electricity in the large quantities required to supply electric power systems is produced in generating stations, commonly called power plants. Such generating stations, however, should be considered as conversion facilities in which the chemical or

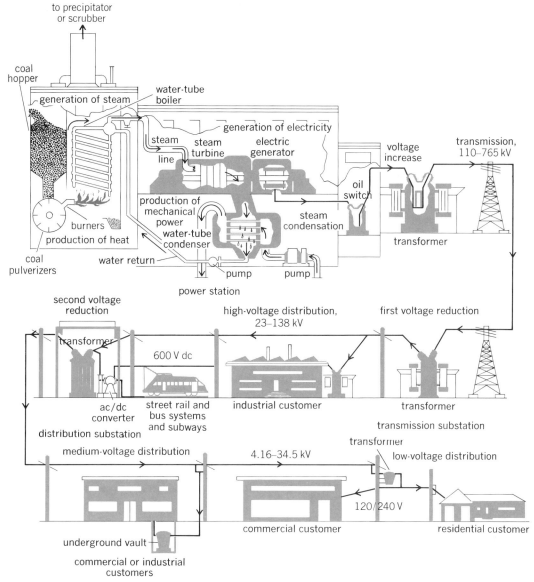

Fig. 1. Major steps in the generation, transmission, and distribution of electricity.

nuclear energy of fuel (coal, oil, gas, or uranium) or the kinetic energy of falling water is converted to electricity. *See* Electric power generation.

Steam stations. Most of the electric power used in the United States is obtained from generators driven by steam turbines. Units of 650, 800, and 950 MW are commonplace for new fossil-fuel-fired stations, with 1100 MW the largest in service. The most commonly installed units in nuclear stations are 1150–1300 MW.

Coal is an important fuel for more than half of steam turbine generation. Other fuels include natural gas and heavy fuel oil; the remainder is generated from the nuclear energy of slightly enriched uranium. As nuclear units have come into commercial operation, the contribution of uranium to the electrical energy supply has risen to about 15% of the total fuel generated. However, uranium's share should decrease, because no additional nuclear plants are slated for service.

Combustion of coal produces sulfur dioxide and nitrogen oxides in the stack gases. To reduce these emissions below those permitted by the Environmental Protection Agency, modern coal-fired stations use either low-sulfur coal (that is, less than 0.3% sulfur by weight) or scrubbers that react the sulfur dioxide with a reagent to permit its removal. Nitrogen oxides are controlled by controlling combustion temperatures. *See* Air-pollution control.

Nuclear steam stations used by United States utilities are mostly of the water-cooled and moderated types in which the heat of a controlled nuclear reaction is used to convert ordinary or ''light'' water into steam to drive a conventional turbine generator.

Hydroelectric plants. Waterpower supplies about 10% of the electric power consumed in the United States, but this share will decline because very few sites remain undeveloped where sufficient water drops far enough in a reasonable distance to drive large hydraulic turbines. Much of the very small share of the planned additional hydroelectric capability will be used at existing plants to increase their effectiveness in supplying peak power demands, and as a quickly available source of emergency power. Special incentives from the federal government have made development of small hydroelectric plants of 15 MW or less financially attractive to private developers.

Some hydroelectric plants actually draw power from other generating facilities during light system-load periods, to drive their turbines in a reverse mode to pump water from a river or lake into an artificial reservoir at a higher elevation. From there, the water can be released through the hydraulic turbines when the power system needs additional generation. These pumped-storage installations consume about 35% more energy than they return to the power system and, accordingly, cannot be considered as primary energy sources. Their use is justified, however, by their ability to convert surplus power that is available during low-demand periods into prime power to serve system needs during peak-demand intervals, a need that otherwise would require building more generating stations for operation during the relatively few hours of high system demand.

Combustion turbine plants. Gas-turbine–driven generators, now commonly called combustion turbines because of the use of light oil as fuel, have gained wide acceptance as an economical source of additional power for heavy-load periods. In addition, they offer the fastest erection time and the lowest investment cost per kilowatt of installed capability. Offsetting these advantages, however, is their relatively less efficient consumption of more costly fuel. Combustion turbine units, even in the largest rating (100 MW), offer extremely flexible operation and can be started and run up to full load in as little as 10 minutes. Thus they are useful as emergency power sources, as well as for operating during the few hours of daily load peaks.

Combustion turbines have an additional role besides applying peaking or emergency power. Some installations use their exhaust gases to heat boilers that generate steam to drive steam turbine generators. Such combined-cycle units offer fuel economy comparable to that of modern steam plants and at considerably less cost per kilowatt. In addition, because only part of the plant uses steam, the requirement for cooling water is considerably reduced. However, wide acceptance is inhibited by the government's restrictions on light fuel oil for them. This barrier will be resolved by the development of systems for fueling combustion-turbine installations with gas derived from coal or by direct firing with pulverized coal.

Internal combustion plants. Internal combustion engines of the diesel type drive generators in many small power plants. In addition, they offer the ability to start quickly for operation during peak loads or emergencies. However, their small size, commonly about 2 MW per unit (although a few approach 10 MW), has limited their use. Such installations account for less than 1% of the total power-system generating capability in the United States, and make an even smaller contribution to total electric energy consumed.

Renewable resources. Utilities actively seek to develop generating resources that do not consume fuel, including geothermal steam, wind, Sun, and biomass-powered capacity. Of these, geothermal is by far the major category. *See* Biomass; Energy sources; Geothermal power; Solar energy.

Three-phase output. Because of their simplicity and efficient use of conductors, three-phase 60 Hz alternating-current systems are used almost exclusively in the United States. Consequently, power-system generators are wound for three-phase output at a voltage usually limited by design features to a range from about 11 kW for small units to 30 kW for large ones. The output of modern generating stations is usually stepped up by transformers to the voltage level of transmission circuits used to deliver power to distant load areas.

Transmission. The transmission system carries electric power efficiently and in large amounts from generating stations to consumption areas. Such transmission is also used to interconnect adjacent power systems for mutual assistance in case of emergency and to gain for the interconnected power systems the economies possible in regional operation. Interconnections have so expanded that most of the generation east of the Rocky Mountains regularly operates in parallel and in synchronism. More than 90% of all generation in the United States and Canada, exclusive of Alaska and Hawaii, is or can be linked.

Transmission circuits are designed to operate up to 765 kV, depending on the amount of power to be carried and the distance to be traveled. The permissible power loading of a circuit depends on many factors, such as the thermal limit of the conductors and their clearances to ground, the voltage drop between the sending and receiving end and the degree to which system service reliability depends on it, and how much the circuit is needed to hold various generating stations in synchronism. A widely accepted approximation to the voltage appropriate for a transmission circuit is that the permissible load-carrying ability varies as the square of the voltage. Typical ratings are listed in **Table 1**.

Transmission as a distinct function began about 1886 with a 17-mi (27-km) 2 kV line in Italy. Transmission began at about the same time in the United States, and by 1891 a 10-kV line was operating (**Fig. 2**). In 1896, an 11-kV three-phase line brought electrical energy generated at Niagara Falls to Buffalo, New York, 20 mi (32 km) away. Subsequent lines were built at successively higher levels until 1936, when the Los Angeles Department of Water and Power energized two lines at 287 kV to transmit 240 MW the 266 mi (428 km) from Hoover Dam on the Colorado River to Los Angeles. A third line was completed in 1940.

For nearly two decades these three 287-kV lines were the only extra-high-voltage (EHV) lines in North America, if not in the entire world. But in 1946 the American Electric Power (AEP) System inaugurated, with participating manufacturers, a test program for equipment up to 500 kV. From this came the basic design for a 345-kV system, the first link of which

Table 1. Power capability of typical three-phase open-wire transmission lines

Line-to-line voltage, kV	Capability, MVA
115 ac	60
138 ac	90
230 ac	250
345 ac	600
500 ac	1200
765 ac	2500
800 dc*	1500

*Bipolar line with grounded neutral.

went into commercial operation in 1953 as part of a system overlay that finally extended from Roanoke, Virginia to the outskirts of Chicago. By the late 1960s, the 345-kV level had been adopted by many utilities interconnected with the AEP System, as well as others in Illinois, Wisconsin, Minnesota, Kansas, Oklahoma, Texas, New Mexico, Arizona, and across New York State into New England.

The development of 500-kV circuits began in 1964, even as the 345-kV level was gaining wide acceptance. One reason for this was that many utilities had already adopted 230 kV, and could gain only about 140% in capability by switching to 345 kV. The jump to 500 kV, however, gave them nearly 400% more capability per circuit. The first line energized at this new level was by Virginia Electric and Power Company, to carry the output of a new mine mouth station in West Virginia to its service area. A second line completed the same year provided transmission for a 1500-MW seasonal interchange between the Tennessee Valley Authority and a group of utilities in the Arkansas-Louisiana area. Lines at this voltage level now extend from New Jersey to Texas and from New Mexico via California to British Columbia, comprising almost 20,000 circuit miles (32,000 km).

The next and latest step-up occurred in 1969, when the AEP System, after another cooperative test program, completed the first line of an extensive 765-kV system to overlay its earlier 345-kV system. The first installation in this voltage class, however, at 735 kV, was by the Quebec Hydro-Electric Commission to carry the output from a vast hydro project to its load center at Montreal, some 375 mi (604 km) away. The very high capacity of lines at this voltage limits their use, but 2000 mi (3200 km) are now in service in the United States alone.

Transmission engineers have anticipated even higher voltages, of 1100 to 1500 kV, but they are fully aware that this objective may prove too costly in space requirements and funds to gain wide acceptance. Experience already gained at 500 and 765 kV verifies that the prime requirement no longer is insulating the lines to withstand lightning discharges, but insulating them to tolerate voltage surges caused by the operation of circuit breakers. Audible noise levels, especially in rain or humid conditions, are high, requiring wide buffer zones. Environmental challenges have been brought on the basis of possible negative biological effects of the electrostatic field produced under EHV lines, although research has not shown any such effects.

Experience has indicated that, within about 10 years after the introduction of a new voltage level for overhead lines, it becomes necessary to begin connecting underground cable. This has already occurred for 345 kV; the first overhead line was completed in 1953, and by 1967 about 100 mi (160 km) of pipe-type cable had been installed to take power received at this voltage level into metropolitan areas. The first 500-kV cable in the United States was placed in service in 1976 to take power generated at the enormous Grand Coulee hydroelectric station to a major switch-yard several thousand feet away.

Another approach to high-voltage long-distance transmission is high-voltage direct current (HVDC), which offers the advantages of less costly lines, lower transmission losses, and insensitivity to many system problems that restrict alternating-current systems. Its greatest disadvantage is the need for costly equipment

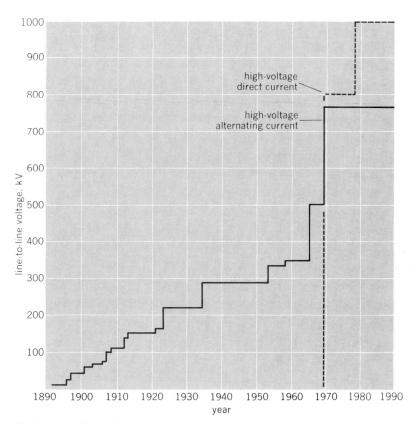

Fig. 2. Growth of alternating-current transmission voltages from 1890.

for converting the sending-end power to direct current, and for converting the receiving-end direct-current power to alternating current for distribution to consumers. However, the development of solid-state converter valves made overhead HVDC economical for distances more than about 400 mi (650 km), but only 25–30 mi (40–50 km) in underground construction. Where systems that are out of synchronism must be interconnected, much shorter distances may be economic. An extreme example of this is at Eel River, New Brunswick, Canada, where back-to-back converters connect Canadian and United States systems. Starting in the late 1950s with a 65-mi (105-km) 100-kV system in Sweden, HVDC has been applied successfully in a series of special cases around the world, each one for a higher voltage and greater power capability. The first such installation in the United States was put into service in 1970. It operates at 800 kV line to line, and is designed to carry a power interchange of 1440 MW over an 841-mi (1354-km) overhead tie line between the winter-peaking Northwest Pacific coastal region and the summer-peaking southern California area. These HVDC lines perform functions other than power transfer, however. The Pacific Intertie is used to stabilize the parallel alternating-current transmission lines, permitting an increase in their capability; and back-to-back converters with no tie line between them are used to tie together two systems in Nebraska that otherwise could not be synchronized. The first urban installation of this technology was energized in 1979 in New York.

In addition to these high-capability circuits, every large utility has many miles of lower-voltage transmission, usually operating at 110 to 345 kV, to carry bulk power to numerous cities, towns, and large industrial plants. These circuits often include extensive lengths of underground cable where they pass through densely populated areas.

Interconnections. As systems grow and the number and size of generating units increase, and as transmission networks expand, higher levels of bulk-power-system reliability are attained through properly coordinated interconnections among separate systems. This practice began around 1930.

Most of the electrical utilities in the contiguous United States and a large part of Canada operate as members of power pools, and these pools in turn are interconnected into one gigantic power grid, known as the North American Power Systems Interconnection. The operation of this interconnection, in turn, is coordinated by the operating committee of the North American Electric Reliability Council (NERC). Each individual utility in such pools operates independently, but has contractual arrangements with other members in respect to generation additions and scheduling of operation. Their participation in a power pool affords a higher level of service reliability and important economic advantages.

The Northeast blackout of November 9, 1965, stemmed from the unexpected trip-out of a key transmission circuit carrying emergency power into Canada and cascaded throughout the northeastern states to cut off electrical service to some 30,000,000 people. It spurred the utilities into a chain reaction affecting the planning, construction, operation, and control procedures for their interconnected systems. They soon organized regional coordination councils, eventually nine in number, to cover the entire contiguous United States and four Canadian provinces (**Fig. 3**). Their objective was to further improve reliability of the planning and operation of their generation and transmission facilities.

Then, in 1968, the North American Electric Reliability Council (NERC) was established to serve as an effective body for the collection, unification, and dissemination of various reliability criteria for use by individual utilities in meeting their planning and operating responsibilities (Fig. 3).

Increased interconnection capability among power systems reduces the required generation reserve of each of the individual systems. In most utilities the loss-of-load probability (LOLP) is used to measure the reliability of electrical service, and it is based on the application of probability theory to unit-outage statistics and load forecasts. A common LOLP criterion is 1 day in 10 years when load may exceed generating capability. The LOLP decreases (that is, reliability increases) with increased interconnection between two areas until a level is reached which depends upon the amount of reserve, unit sizes, and annual load shape in each area.

Traditionally, systems were planned to withstand all reasonably probable contingencies, and operators seldom had to worry about the possible effect of unscheduled outages. Reserve margin, which is the excess of capacity over load at maximum annual peak, while difficult for every system, is generally considered acceptable at 25%. Operators' normal security functions were to maintain adequate generation online and to ensure that such system variables as line flows and station voltages remained within the limits specified by planners. However, stronger interconnections, larger generating units, and rapid system growth spread the transient effects of sudden disturbances and increased the responsibilities of operators for system security.

System security is concerned with service continuity at standard frequency and voltage levels. The system is said to be insecure if a contingency would result in overloading some system components, in abnormal voltage levels at some stations, in change of system frequency, or in system instability, even if there is adequate capability as indicated by some reliability index. The concepts of power system reliability and security are discussed in more detail below.

Substations. Power delivered by transmission circuits must be stepped down in facilities called substations to voltages more suitable for use in industrial and residential areas. On transmission systems, these facilities are often called bulk-power substations; at or near factories or mines, they are termed industrial substations; and where they supply residential and commercial areas, distribution substations.

Basic equipment in a substation includes circuit breakers, switches, transformers, lightning arresters and other protective devices, instrumentation, control devices, and other apparatus related to specific functions in the power system.

Distribution. That part of the electric power system that takes power from a bulk-power substation to customers' switches, commonly about 35% of the total plant investment, is called distribution. This category includes distribution substations, subtransmission circuits that feed them, primary circuits that extend from distribution substations to every street and alley, distribution transformers, secondary lines, house service drops or loops, metering equipment, street and highway lighting, and a wide variety of associated devices.

Primary distribution circuits usually operate at 4160 to 34,500 V line to line, and supply large commercial institutional and some industrial customers directly. Since about 1950, by far the majority of lines constructed have been in the 15-kV class. Primary lines may be overhead open wire on poles, spacer or aerial cable, or underground cable. Legislation in more than a dozen states requires that all new services to developments of five or more residences be put underground. The bulk of existing lines are overhead, however, and will remain so for the indefinite future.

At conveniently located distribution transformers in residential and commercial areas, the line voltage is stepped down to supply low-voltage secondary lines, from which service drops extend to supply the customers' premises. Most such service is at 120/240 V, but other common voltages are 120/208 and 125/216 V, and for larger commercial and industrial buildings, 240/480, 265/460, or 277/480 V. These are classified as utilization voltages.

Electrical utility industry. In the United States, which has the third highest per capita use of electricity in the world and more electric power capability than any other nation, electrical systems as measured by some criteria are the country's largest industry.

The utility industry in the United States is pluralistic in the nature of its ownership. Investor-owned utilities comprise about 78% of total installed capacity, and about the same percentage of customers served. Publicly owned utilities (that is, municipal, state, and power-district utilities) own and operate about 10% of the installed capacity and serve almost 14% of the customers; cooperatives own 3% of the capacity and serve about 10% of the customers; and

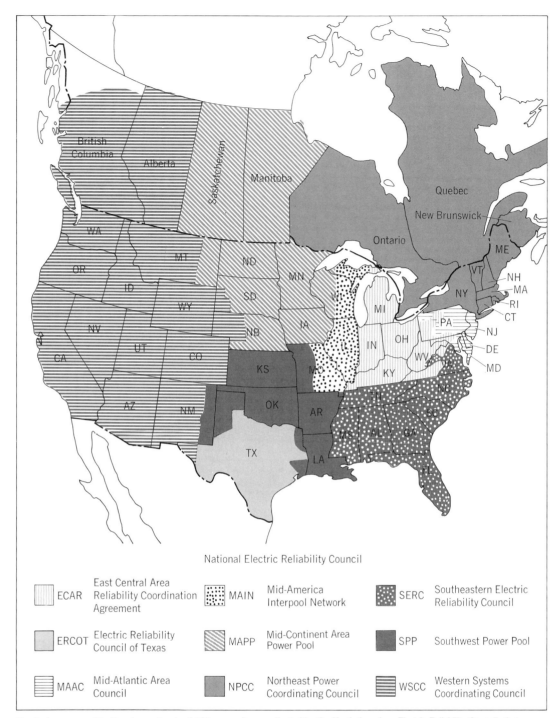

National Electric Reliability Council

ECAR	East Central Area Reliability Coordination Agreement	MAIN	Mid-America Interpool Network	SERC	Southeastern Electric Reliability Council
ERCOT	Electric Reliability Council of Texas	MAPP	Mid-Continent Area Power Pool	SPP	Southwest Power Pool
MAAC	Mid-Atlantic Area Council	NPCC	Northeast Power Coordinating Council	WSCC	Western Systems Coordinating Council

Fig. 3. Areas served by the nine regional reliability councils, coordinated by the North American Electric Reliability Council, that guide the planning, coordination, and operation of generation and transmission facilities.

federal agencies, while serving no measurable percentage of customers, own almost 10% of installed capacity. Electrical utilities are among the most capital-intensive of industries, primarily because of the huge investment in generating units.   *William C. Hayes*

ENERGY CONTROL CENTERS

The monitoring and control of a power system from a centralized control center became desirable quite early in the development of electric power systems, when generating stations were connected together to supply the same loads. As electrical utilities interconnected and evolved into complex networks of gener-

ators, transmission lines, distribution feeders, and loads, the control center became the operations headquarters for each utility. Since the generation and delivery of electrical energy is controlled from this center, it is referred to as the energy control center or energy management system.

Although these centers have advanced in technology from hard-wired metering and supervisory control to sophisticated computer systems connected by microwave communication links, their basic control objectives of economy and security remain the same. The economic goal has always been clearly defined to minimize the cost of supplying the electrical demand.

Security, on the other hand, is broadly defined to include minimum requirements for reliability and quality of service. (The concepts of power system reliability and security are discussed in more detail below.) The tools to achieve these goals have become more sophisticated, especially since the advent of the digital computer, and better economy and security are possible today despite the increasing complexity of power systems.

Evolution. The early control center monitored the power system by bringing in measurements of important power flows, voltages, and currents. These were displayed on banks of meters, and if permanent records had to be kept, strip-chart recorders were used. The circuit breaker and switch positions were sometimes monitored and displayed by the switching of lights which were placed appropriately on a wall map of the power system. Hard-wired control switches were used to open or close breakers remotely from the control centers. These supervisory control and data acquisition (SCADA) functions became more versatile and flexible with the computerization of the control center.

Automatic generation control (AGC), which adjusts the generator outputs to follow the load changes, became absolutely necessary when utilities started to interconnect with each other, and customized controllers were initially built for the purpose. The use of first the analog computer and then the digital computer greatly improved the capabilities of automatic generation control. For example, the problem of meeting the load with the cheapest combination of generating sources requires a multistep calculated solution, and the digital computer is ideal for this.

The digital computer–based SCADA-AGC control centers became common in the 1960s. They could handle more information, provide the information to the operator more efficiently, and provide monitoring and control of the power system more reliably. Also, the availability of unprecedented computational power made it possible to develop new functions for better control. Since the mid-1970s, security analysis and scheduling functions have become available to the control center operator. The computer programs needed for these functions previously could only be run prior to application on batch computers, but their on-line availability to the power system operator can provide more economic and secure control.

Configuration. The control center computers are connected through communication channels, usually microwave links, although telephone lines are also used, to remote terminal units. A remote terminal unit is placed at each substation and generating station, and it can gather all the measurements at that station and execute the control commands sent from the control center.

At the control center itself, redundant computers are used to provide reliability. If a computer fails, another can automatically take over its functions. This redundancy has to be carefully designed into the control center configuration so that the probability of losing the critical functions is very small. Thus, backup is usually provided for communication channels, remote terminal unit circuits, operator consoles, and other equipment in addition to backup computers. *See* M*ULTIPROCESSING*.

Quite often, several computers need to be linked together to accomplish all the control center functions. For example, one computer may handle the

SCADA-AGC functions, while another may be dedicated to the security analysis and scheduling tasks. Such distributed processing configurations (**Fig. 4**) have become common.

Control centers are often designed for particular applications. For example, within a given utility, one control center may have jurisdiction over the distribution circuits and another over the transmission network and generating plants. It is common for a large utility to have several distribution-level control centers which are connected to one transmission and generation control center. Such hierarchical arrangements are also common in power pools, where the pool control center directs the control centers of the member utilities. Automatic data exchange between control centers of neighboring utilities is also becoming common, because such information is very useful when their power systems are strongly interconnected.

The human-machine interface. The banks of control panels have been replaced by operator consoles which typically consist of color semigraphic cathode-ray tubes, a keyboard with extra function buttons, logging printers, and telephones. All the measured and calculated data can be viewed at the cathode-ray tube, and all control can be initiated and monitored from these consoles. A control center will usually have several consoles (**Fig. 5**), each being dedicated to a particular aspect of system operation, like generation dispatch or transmission control. Because the consoles are computer-controlled, their responsibilities can be changed at any time to accommodate changing procedures or availability of operators. The use of wall-mounted maps of the power system is quite common. Sometimes indicators on the mapboard are driven by the computers to denote breaker positions, line overloading, or out-of-limit voltages.

Since the main interaction of the operators with the power system is through the cathode-ray tube displays, the control center computers must handle thousands of displays, many of which are continually accessed and updated. This imposes a high demand on the computers, especially during emergencies, when the operator has to absorb and react to rapidly changing power-system conditions.

Formerly, the creation or modification of the cathode-ray-tube displays required computer programming changes. Since the mid-1970s, however, control centers have been using display generator programs that allow the on-line creation of displays by the users themselves. Since the usefulness of all the sophisticated functions is determined largely by the ease with

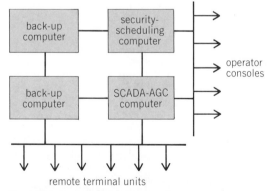

remote terminal units

Fig. 4. Typical computer configuration for an energy control center.

Fig. 5. Layout of an energy control center. (*Courtesy of Control Data Corp. and Delmarva Power and Light Co.*)

which the operators can interface with them, allowing the operators to design and update their own displays was a major step forward.

Logging and accounting. The computers have largely automated the logging and accounting functions. This has resulted in more comprehensive record keeping while saving labor costs. Other than historical record keeping, programs are used to produce daily, weekly, and monthly reports automatically.

Supervisory control and data acquisition. All measurement data are scanned periodically by the computers, usually every 2 to 4 s. These data and others calculated from them are available to the operators through the displays. The data are checked for limit violations, and alarms are generated if necessary. Computerization has made it feasible for a control center to handle tens of thousands of information points, which could not be done with banks of meters. Good database management programs have enabled the efficient handling of such large amounts of data.

The supervisory control for switching of circuit breakers is usually done by using the displays and the function keys on the keyboard, with automatic checking and verification by the computers.

Automatic generation control. To match the load at all times by controlling generation, an automatic feedback control called load frequency control is used. The errors in frequency and scheduled power interchanges with neighboring utilities are continually checked, and control signals are sent to the generating units to adjust their generation levels. Since the different units may use different fuels and have different efficiencies, their costs must be considered in apportioning the total generation so that the total production cost of electricity is minimized. The cost characteristics of generators are complex but can be stored in the computer, and the most economical dispatch of generation can be calculated by using a multistep algorithm. The digital computer updates the load frequency calculations every few seconds to balance generation with load and updates economical dispatch calculations every few minutes to maintain economy (**Fig. 6**).

The generation control functions also include reserve monitoring to ensure adequate generation reserve, interchange scheduling to automatically schedule contracted sales and purchases of energy with neighboring companies, and interchange evaluation to set sale prices or evaluate purchase prices of power quoted by other utilities.

Security analysis functions. This set of functions (**Fig. 7**) is the direct result of the availability of large digital computers at control centers. It is now possible to store a mathematical model of the power system in the computer. This model of the power grid can be automatically updated in real time by using the measurements that are being continually monitored by the data acquisition system. A program called the state estimator can track the real-time conditions of the power system with the stored model.

This real-time model can be used to provide the operator with answers to security questions. The contingency analysis program can analyze the effect of all probable contingencies on this model. If equipment failures at particular locations are determined to

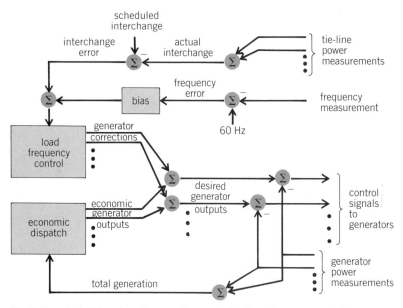

Fig. 6. Flow chart of the automatic generation control functions of an energy control center.

billing for energy that was sold to neighboring utilities.

Operator training simulator. As the control center has become more sophisticated, the training of the operator has also become more important. The use of simulation training, like that used to train airline pilots, is very desirable because there are no good alternatives for learning to handle emergency situations. The capability of the present-day computers to model the power system in real time has made this simulation training possible. In the latest control centers it is possible to use the backup computers to control a model of the power system instead of the real one. The instructor can simulate special scenarios on the model so that the operator can be trained in particular procedures for different system conditions.

Future developments. The major advances in energy control centers have all been due to the technological breakthroughs in digital computers. This trend will continue as long as the price of computation power continues to fall. As the power system grows, bigger and more responsive control centers will be used. More importantly, the development of new functions will help the operators to control the power system more economically and securely. The use of optimal power flows will enable better economics without sacrificing security. Security analysis programs that take into account transient phenomena on the power system will be feasible with bigger computers and better analytical tools.

The main motivation for these new operating tools is that the power system can be operated closer to its limits without sacrificing reliability. This means that the safety factors required in planning and designing the power system can be less conservative, resulting in tremendous savings in capital costs.　　*Anan Bose*

cause unacceptable operating conditions, the operator is alerted. The operator may choose to change the present operating conditions so that these contingencies are no longer threatening to the system.

By using a power flow program, the operator can also study this model for other purposes. If changes to the operating condition are contemplated by the operator, they can be first studied on this model to determine if they produce the desired results. An enhanced version, called the optimal power flow, can even determine the best operating strategies that should be tried to get the desired results.

Scheduling functions. Steam-generating units have limits on how fast they can be started up or shut down. Hydroelectric units have limited energy depending on the storage capacity of their reservoirs. These and other constraints affect the commitment and decommitment of generating units to meet the daily and weekly cycles of load. Unit commitment and hydrothermal coordination programs are available to determine the most economic scheduling pattern. With the availability of large computers at the control center, these programs can now be integrated with the center database so that the operator can update the results conveniently for changing conditions.

Similar programs can be used to determine the cost of producing electricity and automatically calculate the

RELIABILITY EVALUATION

The basic function of a modern electric power system is to satisfy the system load requirement as economically as possible and with a reasonable assurance of continuity and quality. The concern regarding the ability of the system to provide an adequate supply of electrical energy is usually designated by the word reliability. The concept of power system reliability is therefore an extremely broad one and covers all aspects of the ability of the system to satisfy the customer requirements. The word reliability has a wide range of meaning and cannot be associated with a single specific definition. It is therefore often used to indicate the overall ability of the power system to perform its function.

The utilization of electrical energy is closely related to the quality of life, particularly in a heavily industrialized society. Reliability of this service is therefore a primary consideration in the planning, design, and operation of an electric power system. Effort has been directed for many years toward quantifying both past and future performance. The advent of relatively cheap and universal computing capability has accelerated developments in quantitative assessment and in the utilization of the resulting indices in economic assessment and decision making.

Adequacy and security. The concern designated as system reliability may be subdivided into two basic aspects of system planning and operation: system adequacy and system security.

Adequacy relates to the existence of sufficient fa-

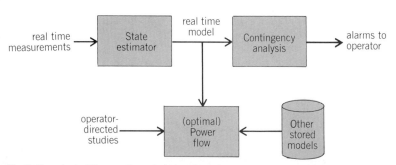

Fig. 7. Flow chart of the security analysis functions of an energy control center.

cilities within the system to satisfy the customer load requirement. This therefore includes the facilities necessary to generate sufficient energy and the associated transmission and distribution facilities required to transport the energy to the actual customer load point. The concept of adequacy can therefore be generally associated with static system conditions which do not include disturbances such as those considered under security.

Security involves the ability of the system to suitably respond to disturbances arising within that system. The concept of security can therefore be associated with the response of the system to whatever perturbations it is subjected to. This includes the conditions associated with both local and widespread disturbances and the loss of major generation and transmission facilities.

Quantitative and qualitative evaluation. The techniques used to assess the adequacy and security aspects of a power system are quite different. The main thrust has been to attempt to express reliability in quantitative terms rather than as a qualitative requirement. The term quantitative is used to denote a numerical assessment which incorporates a probabilistic interpretation of risk. A qualitative assessment involves the utilization of fixed criteria which do not respond or only partially respond to the actual factors that affect reliability. Significant gains have been made in this regard in the area of adequacy assessment, particularly in the context of planning generating capacity. Application in the areas of transmission and distribution systems has been slow to develop but is now part of system planning and design. The utilization of probabilistic techniques in security evaluation has not developed to the same extent. Apart from some extensive work in the area of operating capacity reserves and research work in the area of stability assessment, virtually all security evaluation is done by using fixed or deterministic criteria.

Hierarchical level evaluation. The techniques available and their applications to power system reliability evaluation can be illustrated by dividing the power system into three basic functional zones, namely generation facilities, transmission facilities, and distribution facilities. This division is somewhat simplistic, but it is one that is used in many situations such as organization, operation, planning, and analysis. These functional zones can be combined for the purposes of reliability evaluation and expressed in the form of hierarchical levels as shown in **Fig. 8**.

Hierarchical level I (HLI) is concerned only with the generation facilities. HLII includes both generation and transmission, while HLIII includes all three functional zones in an assessment of customer load-point reliability. Quantitative reliability evaluation is quite extensive at the HLI level but becomes mostly qualitative at the HLII and HLIII levels. Approximately 80% of all the interruptions an individual customer in North America experiences arise from the distribution system; therefore, extensive quantitative and qualitative analysis is done in this functional zone which does not include HLII considerations. Security evaluation is normally conducted at the HLI and HLII levels, because distribution system difficulties do not normally lead to widespread system disturbances.

HLI. In the case of adequacy evaluation at HLI, the total system generation is examined to determine its adequacy to satisfy the total system load requirement.

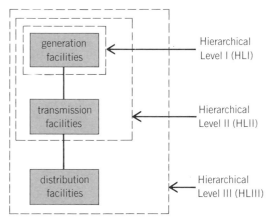

Fig. 8. Hierarchical levels in reliability evaluation.

The basic concern is the ability of the system to satisfy the total system demand and also have sufficient capacity to perform corrective and preventive maintenance of the generating facilities. The system in this case may include random assistance from neighboring interconnected facilities, together with firm purchases involving contractual obligations.

A standard qualitative technique used in the past for determining the total required capacity was the percentage reserve method. In this approach, a fixed percentage of either the installed capacity or the load was designated as the reserve necessary for an adequate supply. This technique did not respond to changes in unit size or availability, and was often modified to include a reserve margin at least equal to the largest unit on the system. These techniques have been largely replaced by probabilistic or quantitative techniques which incorporate the actual factors that influence generating-system adequacy. The most common techniques are loss of load expectation, loss of energy expectation, and frequency and duration evaluation. Direct analytical techniques are most popular in North America, both for single-system and interconnected-system appraisals. Monte Carlo or simulation techniques are not often used in North America but are popular in Europe, particularly France and Italy.

The adequacy or inadequacy of a particular generating configuration is most often expressed in terms of an expectation index, such as the expected megawatt-hours of energy not supplied or the expected number of days that the daily peak load will exceed the available capacity. These are long-run average indicators which reflect important factors such as generating unit size, availability, maintenance requirements, load characteristics and uncertainty, and the potential assistance available from neighboring systems. They are relative, not absolute, indices, and cannot be used to measure supply adequacy at a given consumer load point.

Security evaluation at the HLI level is usually performed to determine the amount of operating capacity which must be synchronized, or immediately available, to the system to meet the changing system load. This is most often done using the quantitative criterion that the operating capacity must equal the greatest single risk of outage. This problem has been analyzed by using probabilistic analysis, but most utilities appear to prefer a qualitative approach.

Reliability evaluation at the HLI level does not normally involve transmission considerations. Interconnections between interconnected facilities and the transmission required to connect remote generating facilities to a major system are sometimes included, but intraconnections within a given system are usually assumed to be both fully reliable and capable of moving the generated energy to the customer load points.

HLII. Reliability evaluation at the HLII level, that is, both generation and major transmission, is usually done by using a fixed set of qualitative criteria. The system is considered to be reliable if it can withstand a designated contingency such as a three-phase or single-phase fault, or the loss of one (or more) major facilities. This could include a line out for maintenance and the failure of another line. These criteria have been shown by experience to lead to reliable systems, but do not reflect the likelihood (or probability or risk) of these events happening. The power industry at large has expended considerable effort to develop quantitative techniques which incorporate the risk of inadequate supply and the likelihood of widespread system disturbances. Quantitative techniques have been under development for adequacy evaluation in composite generation and transmission systems. These techniques provide quantitative indices, which respond to the actual factors that influence adequacy, at individual load points and for the system as a whole. They require considerable input data in terms of component outage and repair data, and the electric power industry is responding by setting up comprehensive reporting procedures. The ability to calculate responsive adequacy indices has provided the power-system planner and manager with a potentially powerful aid in the decision-making process. Data collected on the monetary costs associated with electric-power-supply interruptions for different customer classes have been directed toward the consideration of the cost of reliability in relation to the worth of reliability. This form of economic analysis cannot be conducted with qualitative indicators, and requires a numerical evaluation of the risks associated with supply deficiencies.

Quantitative evaluation is often conducted within the transmission functional zone to compare changes in system configuration, particularly in connection with alternate transmission and switching-station configurations. Similar techniques are also utilized for assessment of distribution-system configurations.

HLIII. The distribution system provides the last link in the connection between the electric energy sources (generating units) and the actual customer load points. In many situations, the distribution system does not contain the redundancy present in the generation or bulk transmission system. Outages, however, tend to be local in nature and affect a relatively small number of customers compared to disturbances created at the HLII level.

Reliability evaluation in the distribution system functional zone is composed of two parts. The first of these, and by far the most common, is a quantitative assessment of the system performance. Most utilities in North America maintain a historical record of customer interruptions and determine annual statistics which reflect the total system performance. One subset of these data is simply designated as loss of supply and represents the contribution from the HLII level. The service reliability in most locations in North America has, on the average, been excellent for many years. This is illustrated by the annual service availability index (ASAI), which is normally in the order of 99.95% or better. (ASAI is the ratio of customer-hours of service supplied to customer-hours requested expressed as a percentage.)

The second aspect of a distribution-system reliability evaluation is the prediction of future performance. This requires extensive component outage data, which up to the present time have not been generally available. This situation seems to be slowly changing as electric power utilities take advantage of mainframe and remote computer terminals and facilities to record and analyze all aspects of system operations.

R. Billinton

POWER SYSTEM LOAD

Electric power system load can be defined as any item that consumes electricity. Therefore, while electric toothbrushes, razors, and can openers consume very little electricity, they are considered electrical loads, as are other components like air conditioning, large industrial motors, and lighting, which consume substantial amounts of electrical energy.

Most power system loads require not only real energy, which is measured in kilowatt-hours, but also reactive energy, which is measured in kilovar-hours. Some loads, like water heaters and ranges, require no reactive power, but small motors require about the same amount of reactive energy as they do real energy. For residential loads, utility companies charge according to the use of real energy, although the rate structure already includes an average expected reactive energy consumption. For industrial and commercial loads, utilities meter both real and reactive energy and include both in the charge.

Composition of total load. In the utility industry, power system loads have been classified according to the area of their use: residential, commercial, or industrial. Incandescent lights, fluorescent lights, air conditioners, dryers, refrigerators, electric ranges,

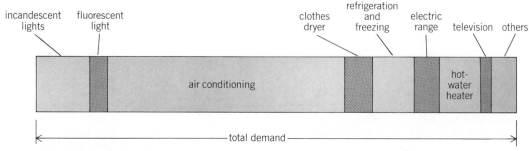

Fig. 9. Typical summer residential load window.

Table 2. Characteristics of typical lamps

Classification	Typical size and type	Color rendering index (CRI)*	Range of life, h	Efficiency, %
Incandescent	40 W, general service	92	1000–1500	11
Incandescent	100 W, general service	89	750–1000	22
Fluorescent	20 W, 24 in. (0.6 m)	55–75	9000–15000	50
Fluorescent	40 W, 48 in. (1.2 m)	55–75	12000–20000	70
Fluorescent	75 W, 96 in. (2.4 m)	55–75	12000–20000	73
High-intensity discharge	400 W, coated mercury	47–51	16000–24000	50
High-intensity discharge	400 W, metal halide	53–72	12000–18000	77
High-intensity discharge	400 W, high pressure sodium	21	12000–18000	100

*CRI is a measure of how much a lamp shifts the color of an object, as compared to the shift caused by a standard fluorescent lamp at 3000 K (5000 °F). All shifts are relative to the colors under an incandescent reference lamp at 3000 K (5000 °F). CRI ratings run from zero to a maximum of 100 (best).

water heaters, and televisions are typical elements in a summer residential load (**Fig. 9**). The percentage of these individual elements in the total demand depends on time of year, time of day, geographical location, socioeconomic conditions, and variations in the elements themselves. Commercial load is composed of many of the same elements as residential load, except for a much larger percentage of fluorescent lights. In industrial loads, induction motors usually account for the highest percentage of load, but in special cases, such as the steel industry, the arc furnace may be the dominant load element.

Characteristics of load components. Power system loads that consume notable amounts of electrical energy include electric lighting, electric motors, air conditioning, electrical appliances, and special industrial loads.

Lamps. **Table 2** compares the characteristics of different lamps; relative efficiency varies over a wide range.

Induction motors. Induction motors can be either single-phase or three-phase. In the United States, the supplied sources are 60 Hz.

Induction motors may be the most important of all power system loads; approximately two-thirds of the electrical energy generated is consumed in motor-oriented loads. Single-phase motors are used widely in various kinds of home electrical appliances such as sewing machines, refrigerators, washing machines, dish washers, fans, disposals, heating and air-conditioning units, and various power tools. These single-phase motors usually have built-in, split-phase capacitor-connected windings for starting purposes. Three-phase induction motors are much more efficient than single-phase motors and are most commonly used in industry for such loads as centrifugal pumps, fans, machine tools, lathes, saws, millers, compressors, reciprocating pumps, loaded conveyors, high-speed punch presses, draw presses, bending brakes, cranes, hoists, and extractors.

The standard voltage ratings for single-phase motors are 115 and 230 V, fractional horsepower motors being rated 115 V and motors of 1 to 10 (0.75 to 7.5 kW) being rated 230 V. When they are operating under light load conditions, induction motors operate at higher efficiency at reduced voltage levels (**Fig. 10**).

All three-phase motors are either squirrel-cage motors or round-rotor motors, and either type may be single-speed or multispeed. The standard voltage ratings for three-phase motors are given in **Table 3**.

Typical full-load efficiency for motors rated less than 1 hp (0.75 kW) is between 65 and 70%, whereas the efficiency of 5-hp (3.7 kW) motors is about 80%, of 10-hp (7.5 kW) motors about 85%, of 100-hp (75-kW) motors about 90%, and of 500-hp (370-kW) motors about 93%. Common synchronous speeds for induction motors are 1800, 1200, 900, 720, 600, and 514 revolutions per minute; generally, the larger the motor and the higher its operating speed, the higher the efficiency of the machine.

An induction motor should be selected for use according to the starting and running characteristics of the load. Too often, oversized motors are chosen for small industrial applications, which usually results in costs for higher starting current, in lower efficiency, and in a poor power factor. The percent of voltage imbalance can be defined by the equation below.

Percent voltage imbalance

$$= 100 \times \frac{\text{maximum voltage deviation from average}}{\text{average voltage}}$$

If the percentage of voltage imbalance is above 2%, not only will efficiency decrease significantly, but also the machine will overheat. In many distribution systems in the United States, open-wye and open-delta connections are used to supply electricity for small industrial loads. These connections allow two transformers to supply three-phase power to a grow-

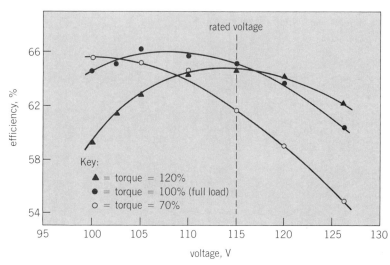

Fig. 10. Efficiency as a function of applied voltage for a ¾-hp (560-W) single-phase motor with constant-torque loads.

Table 3. Standard voltage ratings and preferred powers for three-phase induction motors

Voltage, V	Preferred power
110–115–120	Up to 15 hp (11 kW)
200–208	Up to 200 hp (150 kW)
220–230–240	
440–460	1 hp to 1000 hp (0.75 to 750 kW)
550–575	
2300	50 hp–6000 hp (37–4500 kW)
4000–4160	100 hp–7500 hp (75–5600 kW)
4600	250 hp–8000 hp (190–6,000 kW)
6600	400 hp (300 kW) and up
13,200	No maximum
15,000	No maximum

ing load. When the load requires it, a third transformer can readily be added. Because a two-transformer open-wye to open-delta connection is unsymmetrical with respect to the three phases, any unbalance loading causes voltage imbalance. Thus, in such systems, voltage imbalance always exists.

Synchronous motors. Unlike induction motors, the speed of synchronous motors is constant regardless of load conditions. Synchronous motors have a direct-current (dc) field winding and can be operated at either a leading or a lagging power factor. They are also much more costly to operate than induction motors. Large industrial plants often employ one or two synchronous motors along with many induction motors because such a mix allows a certain amount of control over reactive power. SEE SYNCHRONOUS MOTOR.

Air conditioners. Energy efficiency ratio is the amount of heat removed per unit of electricity used; an air-conditioning unit with a high energy efficiency ratio is a very efficient unit. The efficiency of an air-conditioning unit is drastically affected by ambient temperature (**Fig. 11**).

Special industrial loads. Besides the residential, commercial, and general industrial loads, industries and businesses involved in areas such as electrical transit systems, textiles, petroleum, chemicals, agriculture, coal mining, steel, paper, welding, machine tools, news and printing, laundry and dry cleaning,

excavating, and elevators also consume significant amounts of electrical energy. These industries also include some special load components, such as arc furnaces in steel mills and rectifiers in chemical plants.

Effects of computers. Residential, commercial, and industrial loads are all affected by computers and automation. The reduced cost of microprocessors allows virtually all important industrial, commercial, and residential loads to be controlled through process computers; for instance, air-conditioning and heating systems can be regulated by a microprocessor to conserve energy. Solid-state and microprocessor devices control virtually all the processes and the use of electricity in the special industrial loads discussed above. The computer itself requires very little energy, but it demands constant supplied voltage and a high quality of electricity because harmonics can be extremely harmful to process computers, sometimes causing malfunctions that can shut down an entire industrial plant. Since power electronic devices are widely used and many such devices produce some harmonics, they act as a source of pollution to power distribution systems and to computers. With computers as an integral part of load management, effort must be exerted to filter harmonics from computer and computer-oriented equipment. Computers will continue to affect the pattern of electricity use and to facilitate more efficient use of electrical energy.

M. S. Chen

Bibliography. Annual electric utility industry forecast, *Elec. World*, September; Annual statistical report, *Elec. World*, March; R. Billinton and R. N. Allan, *Reliability Evaluation of Power Systems*, 1983; A. Bose and P. M. Anderson, Impact of new energy technologies on generation scheduling, *IEEE Transactions on Power Apparatus and Systems*, 103:66–71, 1984; M. S. Chen, *Determining Load Characteristics for Transient Performances*, EPRI Final Rep. (EL-849), vols. 1–3, 1979; M. S. Chen, R. R. Shoults, and J. Fitzer, *Effects of Reduced Voltage on the Operation and Efficiency of Electric Loads*, EPRI Final Rep. (EL-2036), vol. 1, 1981, and vol. 2, 1984; T. Y. DyLiacco, Real-time computer control of power systems, *Proceedings of the IEEE*, 62:884–891, 1974; *Electricity Supply and Demand, 1989–1998*, North American Electric Reliability Council, 1989; D. G. Fink and H. W. Beaty (eds.), *Standard Handbook for Electrical Engineers*, 12th ed., 1987; L. H. Fink and K. Carlsen, Operating under stress and strain, *IEEE Spectrum*, 15(3):48–53, March 1978; G. F. Friedlander, Steam station design survey, *Elec. World*, November of even years; H. Glavitsch, Computer control of electric-power systems, *Sci. Amer.*, 231(5):34–44, November 1974; J. E. Kaufman (ed.), *IES Lighting Handbook—1984: Reference Volume*, Illuminating Engineering Society, 1984; *Transmission Line Reference Book, 345 kV and Above*, Rep. EL-2500, Electric Power Research Institute, 2d ed., 1987; *Year-End Electric Power Survey*, Edison Electric Institute, annually; A. J. Wood and B. F. Wollenberg, *Power Generation, Operation, and Control*, 1984.

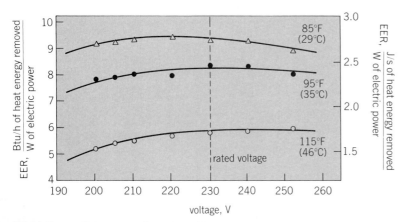

Fig. 11. Energy efficiency ratio (EER) as a function of applied voltage for single-phase central air conditioner, rated 32,600 Btu/h (9550 joules/s).

Energy sources

Sources from which energy can be obtained to provide heat, light, and power. The term energy is used to describe an amount of work perfomed. There are

two kinds of energy, kinetic energy, meaning work performed by the movement of matter, and potential energy, meaning work that is stored or at rest in matter.

ENERGY CONCEPTS AND NEEDS

In the kinetic or potential state, energy takes on one of five forms: (1) Chemical energy results from changes in the chemical structure of substances, such as during combustion of fuel. (2) Electrical energy results from electrons and protons in motion in a stream called an electric current, or in temporary storage as in a battery or fuel cell. (3) Mechanical energy results from force applied or about to be applied to liquid, solid, or gaseous matter. (4) Thermal energy results from heat being applied to matter. (5) Nuclear fission is the splitting of the nucleus of an atom into two or more parts by collision with neutrons, with the consequent release of the force that binds protons and neutrons of the nucleus together. All living things on Earth depend on one or more of these forms of energy and must look to a wide variety of energy sources.

The Sun. The ultimate source of energy on Earth is the Sun, which produces energy sources in two ways on a daily basis and a stored-over-time basis (see **Figs. 1** and **2**).

The Sun provides radiant heat on a daily basis to the Earth which drives many reactions. For example, solar heat evaporates water from the sea and the lakes, providing the moisture for cloud formations which break into rain in mountainous regions. The rain runs off into constructed reservoir lakes which feed water through hydroelectric dams, thus rotating electric generators that produce the kinetic electrical energy supplied through power lines to industrial plants, commercial buildings, and residential homes. Tidal power, wave power, solar power, and wind power are additional examples of daily energy sources.

On a stored-over-time basis, radiant heat from the Sun striking the Earth over millions of years provided the necessary energy input to convert vegetable matter into coal, petroleum, and natural gas. This phenomenon is still taking place, but the conversion process is so slow that it is meaningless in terms of its replacement capability, especially when compared to the enormous rate at which modern industrial society is consuming these resources.

Capital energy. Scientists refer to the stored-over-time energy sources collectively as capital energy, and this is subdivided into six categories: primary energy, secondary energy, renewable energy, nonrenewable energy, combustion process, and noncombustion process.

Primary. This classification includes all forms of potential energy created mainly by the Sun in the Earth's crust that need no processing or treatment to transform them into usable energy (Fig. 1).

Secondary. This classification includes the forms of potential energy manufactured from primary energy forms generally by mechanical, chemical, thermal, or nuclear reaction means to transform them into usable energy.

Renewable. This term refers to forms of potential energy that constantly and rapidly renew themselves for steady, reliable use. This is a somewhat ambiguous definition, particularly when the word ''rapidly'' is added. Coal, crude petroleum, and natural gas are listed as nonrenewable in Fig. 1, but this is not totally accurate. These forms of potential energy are, in fact, constantly being created. However, modern industrialized societies are utilizing these energy sources so rapidly compared to the geological time period required for the formation of additional sources as to render the concept of renewable useless within any reasonable time frame. On the other hand, such energy forms as solar and wind power are clearly renewed on a timely basis and are labeled as renewable energy.

Nonrenewable. Any form of potential energy that does not fall within the definition accepted for renewable energy is considered nonrenewable. For example, the fossil fuels may be defined in specific considerations as nonrenewable energy sources.

Combustion process. Many of the forms of potential energy shown in Figs. 1 and 2 must be utilized in a combustion process before they will release their stored energy into a work process. This is part of the process of conversion that will be discussed below.

Noncombustion process. There are also ways to release energy without a combustion process, such as river water turning a waterwheel. This was an important source of energy for nineteenth-century factories.

Energy needs. Human use of energy, particularly capital energy, has accelerated over time due to an increase in the human population and the discovery of

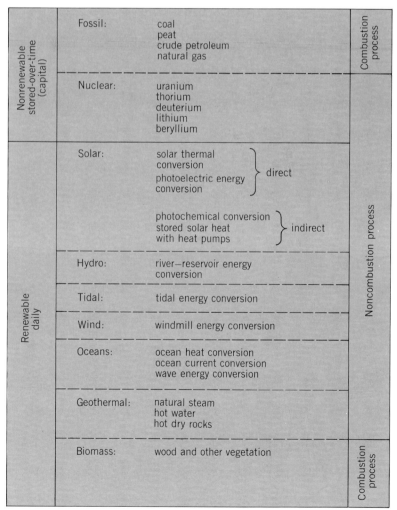

Fig. 1. Primary energy sources.

Electric:	electric power generation fuel cells	Noncombustion process
Nuclear:	tritium plutonium	
Fossil: (coal- derived)	coke char tar blast furnace gas water gas and carbureted water gas producer gas town gas briquetting coal slurries coal gasification coal methanol	Combustion process
Fossil: (petroleum- derived)	gasoline kerosine petroleum coke oil shale petroleum tar sands petroleum fuel oils (No. 1, 2, 4, 5, and 6) liquefied natural gas (LNG) liquefied petroleum gas (LPG) propane butane recycled lubricants and solvents	
Biomass:	wood waste and bark bagasse hulls (grain, rice, cottonseed) peanut shells coffee grounds sugarbeets tobacco stems citrus rinds corncobs garbage and trash methane gas alcohol (ethanol, methanol)	

Nonrenewable (left margin spanning Electric through petroleum-derived Fossil)
Renewable (left margin spanning Biomass)

Fig. 2. Secondary energy sources.

new technologies for utilizing energy. This acceleration took on exponential proportions during the Industrial Revolution of the nineteenth and twentieth centuries (see **table**). As the utilization of, and therefore the demand for, energy rose, scientists and engineers discovered ways to utilize new forms of energy. The availability and technical feasibility of many energy forms yielded a proliferation of energy choices, so that decisions had to be reached on the selection of energy sources. The need to make energy decisions has resulted in the development of an energy choice system (see **Fig. 3**). This system involves an economic analysis which compares the cost of input versus the benefit of output for two specific energy sources. Among the factors included in this analysis are depletion cost, the cost of using nonrenewable energy; social cost, the health and environmental issues; availability cost, the cost of utilizing energy sources subject to interruptions of supply; and switching or conversion cost, converting plant and equipment to other energy uses.

TECHNICAL ASPECTS

Certain technical aspects must be considered in order that energy users can make intelligent decisions regarding energy sources.

Fossil fuels. Crude petroleum, natural gas, and coal were formed in the Earth's crust over the course of millions of years and exist today in subsurface locations. For instance, coal usually exists in seams ranging from 3 to 6 ft (0.9 to 1.8 m), although one seam in Wyoming averages 100 ft (30 m) thick with a maximum thickness of 220 ft (67 m). Crude petroleum is found trapped in the pores of rock (sandstone, limestone, or dolomite) or sand overlain with some kind of impervious cap rock that prevents the liquid from dispersing. Natural gas is normally found trapped in the Earth alongside or with crude petroleum.

The specific ways in which fossil fuels were formed is not known. The theory most dominant since the 1920s, and the one accepted by the United States oil, gas, and coal industry, is that they were formed as a result of the fossilization and carbonization of trees, ferns, and other vegetable matter under intense pressure and temperature over exceedingly long periods of time in the Earth's crust.

Another theory about the formation of fossil fuels is based on the deep-earth gas hypothesis formulated by T. Gold of Cornell University. According to Gold, incredibly huge quantities of methane gas (CH_4), the principal constituent of natural gas, may be trapped deep inside Earth. Tapping into this reserve would require wells drilled several miles below Earth's surface. According to this model, the known deposits of crude oil, natural gas, and coal were formed as a result of the mixing of the deep methane gas with deposits of vegetable and animal remains as the methane rose up through the earth.

Coal. This complex mineral substance is located principally in 29 of the 50 states of the United States and is actively and economically mined in 12 states in meaningful commercial quantities.

The principal chemical constituents of coal are water, carbon, hydrogen, sulfur, nitrogen, oxygen, and ash (noncombustible mineral residue). However, coal is not a uniform substance. It is almost infinitely variable in its composition from one location to the next, even within the same mine location. Nevertheless, 31 tests for defining coal have been established by the American Society for Testing and Materials. Different coals can be ranked according to the degree to which they have progressed from lignite through the bituminous stage to anthracite. This progression is roughly equivalent to the geologic time of development, although the other variables of depth-pressure, heat, and vegetable matter constituents play an important part.

Coal is used in the United States for generating electric power, metallurgical production, general industrial processes, residential-commercial uses, and synthetic fuels. For the most part, coal is burned in fire-tube or water-tube boilers for raising steam that is used to generate electricity, provide heat for factories and buildings, and provide steam for production processes.

Peat. In the very early stages of coal formation, accumulations of decomposed and partially decomposed vegetation, trees, ferns, and mosses located in a wet, cold, and anaerobic (oxygen-deficient) environment are very likely to turn to peat at the rate of about 3 in. (7.5 cm) per 100 years. Only after hundreds or even millions of years would this material graduate to the status of coal.

Energy consumption in the United States*

Item	1982	2000
Key energy use factors		
U.S. population, $\times 10^6$	232	268
Dwellings, $\times 10^6$	83	107
Passenger cars, $\times 10^6$	128	148
Other cars, $\times 10^6$	11	14
Buses and trucks, $\times 10^6$	20	25
Gross national product (1972\$), $\times 10^9$	1476	2426
Fuel consumption		
Petroleum (total), 10^3 bbl (m^3)/day	15,254 (2425)	12,940 (2057)
Gasoline, 10^3 bbl (m^3)/day	6538 (1039)	4890 (778)
Jet fuel, 10^3 bbl (m^3)/day	1009 (160)	1400 (220)
Aviation gasoline, 10^3 bbl (m^3)/day	26 (4.1)	10 (2)
Diesel, 10^3 bbl (m^3)/day	1298 (206)	1800 (290)
Other distillates, 10^3 bbl (m^3)/day	1506 (239)	500 (80)
Petrochemical chemical feed, 10^3 bbl (m^3)/day	507 (80.6)	940 (150)
LNG/LPG, 10^3 bbl (m^3) day	1537 (244)	1000 (200)
Residual fuels, 10^3 bbl (m^3) day	1694 (269)	1640 (260)
Still gas, 10^3 bbl (m^3)/day	554 (88.1)	360 (57)
Asphalts/road oils, 10^3 bbl (m^3)/day	343 (54.5)	200 (30)
Lubricating waxes, 10^3 bbl (m^3)/day	154 (24.5)	200 (30)
Petroleum coke, 10^3 bbl (m^3)/day	247 (39.3)	100 (20)
Miscellaneous, 10^3 bbl (m^3)/day	91 (14)	—
Fuel alcohol, 10^3 bbl (m^3)/day	3 (0.5)	300 (50)
Natural gas, 10^3 ft^3 (m^3)	17.9 (0.5)	17.9 (0.5)
Coal (not including exports), 10^6 tons (metric tons)	678 (615)	1160 (1053)
Solar, $\times 10^6$ units	0.1	3.0
Hydro electricity, 10^9 kWh (megajoules)	310 (1122)	340 (1224)
Nuclear, 10^9 kWh (megajoules)	283 (1019)	589 (2120)
Electricity from wind-waste, 10^9 kWh (megajoules)	2 (7.)	18 (65)
Geothermal, 10^9 kWh (megajoules)	4 (14)	52 (187)
Electricity from geothermal, quad (joules)	—	1 (1.055×10^{18})
TOTALS, quad (joules)	70.9 (74.8×10^{18})	84.7 (89.4×10^{18})

*Based on U.S. Department of Commerce, statistics, July 1983.

Since the vegetable matter in peat, consisting of cellulose and other organic compounds, becomes only partially converted to carbon and hydrocarbons, peat has only one-third to one-half of the heating value of coals. It is used in very limited quantities for fuel after it is cut from the earth and formed into briquettes. Peat is harvested and sold mainly as a soil conditioner.

Crude petroleum. Oil is also a complex substance derived from the carbonized remains of trees, ferns, mosses, and other types of vegetable matter. Like coal there is doubt about the exact nature of its origin. The principal chemical constituents of oil are carbon, hydrogen, and sulfur. Crude petroleum extracted from the earth will burn and produce thermal energy, but virtually all crude oil is processed in refineries, where it is converted into several useful fuels and special products (for example, feedstock for chemicals, plastics, food products, medicines, and tires, plus tar, asphalts, and lubricating oils). The various fuels made from crude oil are jet fuel, gasoline, kerosine, diesel fuel (or No. 2 fuel oil), and heavy fuel oils (or No. 4, 5, and 6 fuel oils).

Major oil comsumption in the United States is in the following areas: transportation, residential-commercial, industry boilers and other industrial uses, and generating electric power.

Natural gas. This energy source is 83–93% methane (CH_4), so that its principal chemical constituents are carbon and hydrogen. Natural gas is usually found in the immediate vicinity of crude petroleum, although

some natural gas wells do not yield oil.

Of all the chemical or mineral sources of energy, natural gas may well be the most desirable because it can be pipelined directly to the customer, requires no

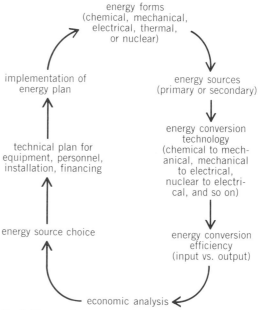

Fig. 3. Diagram of an energy choice system.

storage vessels, is clean-burning, requires no air-pollution control equipment, produces no ash for disposal, and mixes with air easily to provide complete combustion at low excess air.

The principal uses for natural gas are residential, commercial buildings, industrial, transportation, and generating electric power.

Nuclear energy. The two ways to utilize radioactive fuel as an energy source are fission and fusion. In fission, heavy atoms are split into two principal elements that form the nucleus of two new, smaller atoms. In fusion, the nuclei of two small atoms fuse together into a single, larger nucleus. In both cases large quantities of energy are released.

Nuclear fission. The splitting of atoms cannot be effectively accomplished with electrically charged matter such as alpha particles, beta particles, or protons, which tend to be diverted or slowed down as they approach other charged matter. Neutrons, however, are not deflected by positive or negative electrical charges, and this fact makes them ideal candidates for atom smashing. The fission process, therefore, involves the bombardment of atoms with neutrons so that a sufficient number of collisions will take place on a statistically predictable basis and split those atoms into two or more separate nuclei while releasing massive quantities of thermal energy.

Nuclear fusion. The fusion process is the opposite of fission. Instead of splitting atoms into two or more pieces, the fusion process causes two atoms to collide with such force that their natural electronic repulsion is overcome and their nuclei fuse into one.

The most suitable fuels for fusion are hydrogen isotopes (hydrogen atoms with the same number of protons but different numbers of neutrons). In particular, deuterium and tritium are thought to be ideal for fusion reactions. The former is relatively abundant and can be found in ordinary seawater. The latter is scarce.

Although this energy source offers tremendous potential for the twenty-first century, there are formidable problems that must be overcome before it can be utilized. The temperature in a fusion reactor should be between 1.0 and 2.5×10^8 K, and no solid material has been developed for a container for such a reaction. A solution to this problem may be found by setting up an extremely powerful magnetic field around the reacting materials. However, conventional magnets may consume more energy than the fusion reaction puts out. This could be solved by using superconducting magnets that operate at very low temperatures to decrease their resistance to electrical flow, except that it will be difficult to operate such magnets adjacent to the heat of a fusion reactor.

At any rate, fusion power is still an important potential source of continuous low-cost energy, provided that the technical problems can be solved.

Solar energy. By far the most attractive energy source is the Sun itself because it is free, is clean and nonpolluting, and does not involve the use of dwindling, finite reserves of capital energy. The problem with solar energy is its cost, particularly for large industrial uses. Roughtly 50% of the sunlight approaching Earth is reflected or absorbed by the atmosphere and the other 50% strikes Earth's surface. In the tropical and temperate zones, the Sun provides the equivalent of, on average, about 622 MW of energy per square mile (240 MW/km²). Unfortunately, technology is able to convert only about 15% of the Sun's radiant heat to usable work, so that a typical large electric generating station capable of producing 1000 MW would require an array of solar head collector-converters covering an area of at least 11 mi² (28 km²). *SEE SOLAR ENERGY.*

The collector-converters are made of silicon, which produces electricity when it is exposed to light. The high cost of these devices derives from the cost of growing and cutting large crystals into thin slices of silicon. The more this process becomes automated, the lower the price and the more the process is likely to be employed.

Another idea is the solar power tower. This type of technology was demonstrated by an Italian scientist, G. Francia, in 1976. A 10-MW electric generating station is in operation in Daggett, California; it utilizes a 72-acre (29-hectare) field of mirrors to concentrate sunlight at the top of a central tower. The thermal energy from the sunlight superheats steam that is used to power electricity-generating turbines.

Finally, the concept of solar ponds has received attention in many parts of the world. These are artificial, salt-gradient ponds. They are derived from the work of a Russian scientist, A. Von Kaleczinsky, who in 1902 found that the temperature of the water in Lake Medve in Transylvania a few feet below the surface was 185°F (85°C) due to the variation in salinity of the water. Experiments have been conducted with ponds in which layers of different salinity allow the water to trap and hold solar heat. The hot brine can be used for space heating or for producing electricity with a thermoelectric device or organic Rankine cycle engine.

Hydro energy. One of the oldest energy-producing mechanisms uses water flowing in a river or falling from a height to rotate work devices, ranging from the waterwheels of the past to the massive modern hydroelectric dams that employ gigantic electricity-generating turbines. Internationally only 7% of the total potential hydroelectric power estimated at 2.9×10^6 MW is being used. Much of that potential, unfortunately, is located in remote places from which lengthy transmission lines would be prohibitively expensive. Furthermore, environmental protectionists are resisting new projects that might threaten natural resources. *SEE ELECTRIC POWER GENERATION.*

Tidal energy. The only major tidal energy project in operation is the Rance River project in Brittany, France; however, estimates indicate a worldwide potential for producing 3×10^6 MW of electric power from tidal movement. The French project employs a barrage type of dam across the estuary of a river. Turbines located in this barrage pump water into the estuary when the tide is rising. When a sufficient head of water is built up in the estuary, the water is permitted to flow back through the turbines to produce electricity.

Wind energy. This is also a form of energy that can be used to generate electrical or mechanical energy. Rotating devices known as windmills can convert the mechanical energy of wind to useful work.

The largest known wind generator has a 300-ft (90-m) span to produce 2.5 MW of electricity for a local electric power grid in Goldendale, Washington. This installation employs huge aircraft propeller-type blades which must always be facing into the wind; a more efficient design might be the Darrieus vertical-axis windmill that rotates regardless of the direction of the wind. Such a device was erected at Sandia Laboratories, Albuquerque, New Mexico, with funds from the U. S. Energy Research and Development Administration. It measures 61 ft (19 m) in height and produces 60 kW of electric power in a 28 mi/h (45 km/h) wind.

In other parts of the United States (such as California and Hawaii), the concept of wind farms is being developed that involves the erection and operation of perhaps dozens of windmills for the production of significant amounts of electric power.

Ocean energy. Ocean power may become an energy source in the future, either as wave power or as ocean temperature differential. Both forms are highly experimental and may require many years to become significant energy sources.

Wave power. Many different devices have been proposed and tested for exploiting the wave motion of the sea. In Scandinavia, one device is designed so that ocean waves cause massive quantities of water to flow into the confines of the device which then generates electricity as the water tries to escape back to the sea. In England, S. Salter demonstrated his so-called nodding duck device, which is a floating device that rotates due to the motion of waves rolling over it. The float is capable of driving a hyraulic pump that, in turn, can drive an electrical generating device.

Ocean temperature. An energy-producing system known as ocean thermal energy conversion (OTEC) is based on the temperature differential in the oceans near the Equator where the surface water is about 40°F (20°C) warmer than the water a few thousand feet down. This temperature difference can be utilized to vaporize a working fluid (such as ammonia) that can be run through an electricity-producing turbine.

Geothermal energy. As with ocean power, the geothermal energy source may be exploited in either or both of two ways: hot rocks and hydrothermal.

Hot rocks. It is known that hot granite rock (up to 400°F or 200°C) exists almost everywhere on Earth. The heat is generated, for the most part, by a slow radioactive decay process deep within the earth. According to one estimate, a 40-mi^3 (170-km^3) chunk of granite at 350°F (177°C) would yield the equivalent energy output of 1.2×10^{10} barrels (2×10^9 m^3) of oil, which is approximately the total yearly energy consumption in the United States. According to another estimate, the continental United States is underlain by hot rock with thermal energy amounting to 1.3×10^7 quad (1 quad = 10^{15} Btu) at a depth of just under 6 mi (10 km).

The technique (still experimental) for tapping this energy source involves conventional oil or gas drilling expertise. The first hole drilled is used for injecting water pressurized to 5000 lb/in.^{2} (35 megapascals) that will cause the hot granite to fracture vertically. Once the rock is fractured, the amount of pressure is decreased to a normal pumping pressure. The next hole drilled and any subsequent holes must follow the fracture line so that the water heated by the hot granite can be brought back up to the surface and utilized for raising steam and generating electricity for space heating or for industrial process steam.

Hydrothermal. The earth emits steam in many locations, such as Iceland, the United States, the Philipines, and New Zealand, where it is captured and employed for space heating, generating electricity, or industrial process steam applications. Hydrothermal steam now provides the equivalent of about 1200 MW

of electric power. It is believed that only about 1% of the total potential hydrothermal energy can be utilized in the world and converted to electricity at a 25% efficiency factor for a total contribution of only 3 × 10^6 MW. *See Geothermal power.*

Biomass energy. As applied to the field of energy, the term biomass energy encompasses a broad selection of energy sources: Any and all types of living matter that can be converted to a form of energy can be said to be biomass. Hence, scientists tend to think of such items as wood, wood waste, coffee grounds, corn husks, peanut shells, rice hulls, garbage, animal and human waste, sugarcane waste (bagasse), and organic effluent from streams and ponds as biomass.

The biomass considered to be most significant in terms of energy sources is wood and wood waste. There are approximately 9.6×10^9 acres (3.9×10^9 hectares) of forest land in the world, of which about 4×10^9 acres (1.6×10^9 hectares) are economically accessible. Up until the end of the nineteenth century, when coal took over as the leading energy source, wood was a preeminent provider of energy to the world. Wood is again being used on a limited scale at the residential level. The lumber, furniture, plywood, and pulp-and-paper industries all utilize wood waste items (for example, bark, shavings, sawdust, slabs, and end pieces) for raising steam that, in turn, is employed for space heating and industrial processes. *See Biomass.*

CONSERVATION

An energy source that is being increasingly considered to be significant is energy conservation. Better insulation of buildings and homes could slash heating and air-conditioning requirements in half. More people could travel by public transportation than by using private vehicles. There could be greater use of smaller, fuel-efficient automobiles, bicycles, or low-gas-consumption ''mopeds,'' motorcycles, and such. Greater use could be made of fluorescent lighting in homes and industry. Government agencies, businesses, and individuals could lower their thermostats in winter and raise them in summer. In fact, this movement was already quietly under way in the late 1970s until its effects were dramatically felt in the early 1980s in terms of mass decreases in total energy consumption. Conservation, coupled with the worldwide economic recession of 1982, resulted in the so-called oil glut in the mid 1980s. Therefore, conservation may acquire a major role in establishing energy source security. *See Conservation of resources.*

William K. Fox

Bibliography. R. C. Dorf, *The Energy Factbook*, 1981; J. H. Harker and J. R. Backhurst, *Fuel and Energy*, 1981; V. D. Hunt, *Handbook of Energy Technology: Trends and Perspectives*, 1982; D. Marier and L. Stolaken (eds.), *Alternative Sources of Energy*, 1988; J. T. McMullen, R. Morgan, and R. B. Murray, *Energy Resources and Supply*, 1976; A. Petrick, Jr., *Energy Resource Assessment*, 1985; T. N. Veziroğlu, *Alternate Energy Sources: An International Compendium*, 1978.

Engineering

Most simply, the art of directing the great sources of power in nature for the use and the convenience of humans. In its modern form engineering involves people, money, materials, machines, and energy. It is differentiated from science because it is primarily concerned with how to direct to useful and economical ends the natural phenomena which scientists discover and formulate into acceptable theories. Engineering therefore requires above all the creative imagination to innovate useful applications of natural phenomena. It is always dissatisfied with present methods and equipment. It seeks newer, cheaper, better means of using natural sources of energy and materials to improve the standard of living and to diminish toil.

Types of engineering. Traditionally there were two divisions or disciplines, military engineering and civil engineering. As knowledge of natural phenomena more grew and the potential civil applications became more complex, the civil engineering discipline tended to become more and more specialized. The practicing engineer began to restrict operations to narrower channels. For instance, civil engineering came to be concerned primarily with static structures, such as dams, bridges, and buildings, whereas mechanical engineering split off to concentrate on dynamic structures, such as machinery and engines. Similarly, mining engineering became concerned with the discovery of, and removal from, geological structures of metalliferous ore bodies, whereas metallurgical engineering involved extraction and refinement of the metals from the ores. From the practical applications of electricity and chemistry, electrical and chemical engineering arose.

This splintering process continued as narrower specialization became more prevalent. Civil engineers had more specialized training as structural engineers, dam engineers, water-power engineers, bridge engineers; mechanical engineers as machine-design engineers, industrial engineers, motive-power engineers; electrical engineers as power and communication engineers (and the latter divided eventually into telegraph, telephone, radio, television, and radar engineers, whereas the power engineers divided into fossil-fuel and nuclear engineers); mining engineers as metallic-ore mining engineers and fossil-fuel mining engineers (the latter divided into coal and petroleum engineers).

As a result of this ever-increasing utilization of technology, people and their environments have been affected in various ways—some good, some bad. Sanitary engineering has been expanded from treating the waste products of humans to also treating the effluents from technological processes. The increasing complexity of specialized machines and their integrated utilization in automated processes has resulted in physical and mental problems for the operating personnel. This has led to the development of bioengineering, concerned with he physical effects upon humans, and management engineering, concerned with the mental effects.

Integrating influences. While the specialization was taking place, there were also integrating influences in the engineering field. The growing complexity of modern technology called for many specialists to cooperate in the design of industrial processes and even in the design of individual machines. Interdisciplinary activity then developed to coordinate the specialists. For instance, the design of a modern structure involves not only the static structural members but a vast complex including moving parts (elevators, for example); electrical machinery and power distribu-

tion; communication systems; heating, ventilating, and air conditioning; and fire protection. Even the structural members must be designed not only for static loading but for dynamic loading, such as for wind pressures and earthquakes. Because people and money are as much involved in engineering as materials, machines, and energy sources, the management engineer arose as another integrating factor.

Typical modern engineers go through several phases of activity during their careers. Formal education must be broad and deep in the sciences and humanities underlying the particular field. Then comes an increasing degree of specialization in the intricacies of the discipline, also involving continued postscholastic education. Normal promotion thus brings interdisciplinary activity as the engineer supervises various specialists. Finally, the engineer enters into the management function by interweaving workers, money, materials, machines, and energy sources into completed processes for the use of humankind.

Joseph W. Barker

Engineering, social implications of

The rapid development of human ability to bring about drastic alterations of the environment has added a new element to the responsibilities of the engineer. Traditionally, the ingredients for sound engineering have been sound science and sound economics. Today, sound sociology must be added if engineering is to meet the challenge of continued improvement in the standard of living without degradation of the quality of the environment.

Despite the fact that present and evolving engineering practices must meet the criteria of scientific and economic validity, these same practices generally cause societal problems of new dimensions. Consider, for example, exhaust gases emitted from tens of millions of internal combustion engines, both stationary and moving; stack gases from fossil-fuel-burning plants generating steam or electric power; gaseous and liquid effluents and solid waste from incinerators and waste-treatment systems; strip mining of coal and mineral ores; noise issuing from automotive vehicles, aircraft, and factory and field operations; toxic, nondegradable or long-lived chemical and particulate residues from ore reduction, chemical processing, and a broad spectrum of factory and mill operations; dust storms, soil erosion, and disruption of groundwater quality and quantity accompanying intensified mechanized farming in conjunction with massive irrigation and fresh-water diversion. SEE ECOLOGY, APPLIED.

Progress often results in the substitution of one set of problems for another. For example, in nuclear electric power generating plants, replacement of fossil fuels by nuclear fuels relieves the burden of atmospheric pollution from stack gas emissions. Lower thermal efficiency of a nuclear plant, however, results in higher heat rejection rates and increased thermal pollution of sources of cooling water or air. The attendant consequences on atmospheric conditions or on the viability of aquatic life in the affected water are of great concern in the short and long terms. Ultimately, the cost and benefit considerations of nuclear power must be all-inclusive; in addition to usual considerations of economic length of plant life and so forth, one must account for all the economic and societal costs of the entire fuel cycle, from mining and refinement through use and ultimate recycling or safe disposal. The long-term effects of very low levels of radiation exposure (as such studies become available) will be an additional factor to consider.

The modern engineer must be increasingly conscious of the societal consequences of technological innovation. *See* ENGINEERING.

Eugene A. Avallone

Entomology, economic

The study of insects that have a direct influence on humanity. Though this includes beneficial as well as harmful species, most attention is devoted to the latter and how they become pests and are controlled. The emphasis on managing harmful insects reflects the immediacy and seriousness of pest problems, particularly the destruction of agricultural products and the transmission of disease. These are highly visible problems, whereas the benefits gained from useful insects are, in most cases, not so clearly understood or so well documented economically.

Economic thresholds. Central to the definition of a pest is determination of the economic threshold. Any insect population, when introduced into a favorable environment, increases numbers until reaching an environmental carrying capacity (see **illus.**). In pest insects, there exists a density above which the insect population interferes with human health, comfort, convenience, or profits. When this economic threshold is reached, a decision must be made to utilize some control measure to prevent further increase in numbers. Precise estimation of the economic threshold is difficult, since it depends on a myriad of factors such as weather, crop conditions, stage in the life cycle of the insect, market value of the crop, and cost of control, each of which varies. Often, the presence of even a single insect is sufficient to warrant control measures, for instance, when that insect is a flea harboring the plague bacillus, or a mosquito transmitting malaria. Also, consumer expectations in most markets of the United States, Canada, and western Europe are for insect-free produce, so the economic threshold is very low on items that people eat. However, some crops, such as field corn or forest trees, have a higher threshold since they can tolerate a low amount of insect damage before yield is reduced. Economic thresholds may also be higher for insects that damage

only the inedible portions of crop plants such as the leaves of beans, tomatoes, and apple trees. In any case, knowledge of the amount of injury which is due to different densities of insects is an important prerequisite for efficient management.

Harmful insects. Insects cause damage in various ways. Direct damage occurs when insects eat foods destined for human consumption or otherwise decrease resource yields. Direct damage to crops by locusts has been a major factor limiting grain production in some semiarid countries of Asia and Africa. Damage to structures by termites and other wood-chewing insects runs to billions of dollars annually. Indirect damage may occur when an insect, feeding on nonedible portions of a crop plant, reduces yield of the edible portion. Red mites and aphids respectively feed on leaves and sap of apple trees, which results in lowered yield of fruit. Many of the most serious insect pests are those that affect humans indirectly by transmitting pathogens. Mosquitoes transmit malaria, yellow fever, viral encephalitis, and filarial roundworms. Such vectors (transmitters) are number one among insect pests. Fleas, ticks, lice, houseflies, cockroaches, and many others are capable of transmitting diseases to humans, while many aphids and leafhoppers are major vectors of plant virus diseases. Indirect damage may also occur from the mere inclusion of insects or their fragments in fresh or processed foods, especially when prohibited by law. Some persons exhibit extreme psychological reaction to a real or imagined insect infestation, and this, too, is damaging.

Pest management. Management of insect pests begins with prevention. Many of the United States' most noxious insects have been imported from overseas: most domestic cockroaches, the gypsy moth, Japanese beetle, corn borer, housefly, cabbageworm, and codling moth are just a few. Most major pests of foreign origin were introduced accidentally during the nineteenth century. Some North American insects have spread elsewhere, for example—the Colorado potato beetle to Europe and the fall webworm to Japan. To stem the flow of insect invasions, the federal government's Animal and Plant Health Inspection Service maintains inspection facilities for the examination of all incoming shipments of plant or other material that may harbor pests in order to intercept infested items.

Once a pest is established, its spread can sometimes be slowed by an efficient system of local quarantines, early detection, and local eradication. The gypsy moth, long an established defoliator of forests in New England, is slowly extending its range into the midwestern United States, with isolated individuals as distant as Oregon and California. States outside the infested region maintain a vigorous program of detection: sticky traps baited with sex attractant lure male moths, and when several are located at one site, a thorough inspection is followed by application of insecticide. Gypsy moths lay their eggs on the undersides of vehicles, so that inspection and treatment of autos and trucks that have traveled in the infested area slows the westward spread of this pest.

Insecticides. Once noxious insects are firmly established in a region, there are many techniques to reduce their numbers below the economic threshold. The most widely used method is the application of synthetic chemical insecticides. Insecticides are probably the only efficient control technique for insects

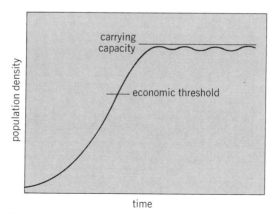

Growth of an insect population continues until reaching the environmental carrying capacity.

with an exceedingly low economic threshold such as occurs on commercial floral crops, fresh and processed fruits and vegetables, or nursery stock. There are scores of available insecticides which vary greatly in their characteristics; extension specialists at the county level or state university should be consulted for the latest information on available compounds. Most insecticides are poisonous to other animals, and handling requires appropriate caution. Insecticides were once regarded as a panacea for pest problems, but the development of resistant strains of major insect pests, together with the rising cost of materials and application and legal restrictions has led to recognition that insecticides are more efficiently utilized in a program that integrates them with other techniques in a framework of total crop management. Research has been directed toward development of insecticides that minimize hazards to people and their environment. *SEE INSECTICIDE*.

Biological control. For insects whose economic threshold lies somewhat higher than the artificially low demands of "clean" produce, there is a wider choice of control techniques. Insects introduced into a new homeland where they become numerous sometimes have had their numbers checked in their old homeland by natural enemies. Economic entomologists have effectively reduced densities of several pests by releasing parasites or predators. Imported natural enemies have had major impact in controlling scale insects, aphids, whiteflies, alfalfa weevils, and many others. Natural enemies that are mobile and relatively restricted in diet are most effective in biological control. Diseases of insects often are important in halting outbreaks by killing large numbers in a short time. A few pathogens of caterpillars, mosquito larvae, Japanese beetle larvae, and others are formulated as biological rather than chemical insecticides and are applied commercially. *SEE INSECT CONTROL, BIOLOGICAL*.

Cultural practices. All populations are limited by their environment, and much can be done to augment the activity of natural control by manipulation of cultural practices. Crop rotation is a standard agronomic practice that often reduces damage due to insects. Rotation of alfalfa or soybeans with corn reduces populations of corn rootworms, wireworms, and white grubs. The physical disruption of autumnal plowing and disking destroys many insects, such as the corn borer, wheat stem sawfly, and cereal leaf beetle, that could overwinter in stubble or on the soil surface. Plant breeders and entomologists have cooperated to produce varieties of corn, wheat, soybeans, alfalfa, and other crops which retain high yields but which resist attacks from some of their more serious pests. The action of natural enemies can be enhanced by cultural practices such as leaving fencerows or other preserves for refuges at harvest. Strip cutting of alfalfa in the southwestern states has been particularly valuable in preserving predators of alfalfa aphids and caterpillars.

Sanitation. The cleanup of breeding and gathering sites is useful, especially in management of medically important insects, many of which have evolved resistance to the commoner insecticides. Housefly larvae feed in decaying vegetable compost and dung; efficient disposal of garbage, manure, and sewage brings enormous relief from fly problems and associated diseases. Similarly, draining standing water with its crop of mosquito larvae reduces their numbers near human habitations. Personal hygiene and proper care of pets virtually eliminate problems with lice and fleas.

Special programs. Rarely, a unique program is developed to control a single pest insect. The screwworm fly, whose larvae infest open wounds of livestock, has been controlled in the United States and much of Mexico by weekly release of 180,000,000 sterile males. These mate with wild females (who only mate once), and the ensuing eggs do not hatch. Obviously, this technique is limited to species in which males are undamaging, though despite technical problems it is being developed for use against codling moths. The method is also being developed to control some species of mosquitoes, in which only females bite.

Integrated control. Most successful programs of insect pest management rely on integrated control or the use of several methods in concert to control a complex of pests. Apples, for example, are attacked by a host of insect pests, led by species such as the codling moth and apple maggot that attack the fruit directly and consequently have a low economic threshold (1/100 apples). Other pests, notably aphids and European red mites, feed on leaves and sap and are only pests when their numbers become enough to reduce yield of fruit.

Application of chemical insecticides to control codling moths killed predators of red mites and caused these creatures to become damaging secondary pests. Eventually, both the red mite and its major predators become partially resistant to most conventional insecticides. In the integrated control program, reduced dosages of insecticides conserve predators of the red mite while still yielding acceptable control of the fruit eaters.

The alfalfa weevil, whose larvae eat alfalfa tips in spring, is usually managed by use of resistant plant varieties and judiciously planned cutting times, with some additional control from six species of introduced parasites. Occasionally, the economic threshold is exceeded enough for an insecticide to be applied. Farmers must watch carefully as populations increase, or the crop may also be inspected by an agricultural consultant. The consultant's pest management scouts observe the fields regularly, and the farmers receive weekly (or more frequent) reports on the status of their crops. Pest management programs involving crop scouting are now operational for corn, cotton, soybeans, fruits, tomatoes, tobacco, alfalfa, and other crops. *SEE FOREST PEST CONTROL*.

Beneficial insects. It has been estimated that the dollar value gained from a single insect, the honeybee, equals the loss from damage plus cost of control for all pests combined. Honeybees are managed for their honey and beeswax, but their most valued service is pollination of crop plants. Nearly all fruits and many vegetables, ornamental plants, and seed crops require pollination by honeybees or other insects. Bees of many species are the chief pollinators, though wasps, flies, moths, butterflies, and beetles pollinate as well.

Silk is produced by larvae of the silkworm, an insect so thoroughly domesticated that it cannot climb its food plant, mulberry, with its degenerated legs. The silkworm apparently no longer survives in the wild. In many uses, silk has been more recently replaced by less expensive synthetic materials.

The economic value of silkworms and honeybees is rather easily estimated from the cash value of their products. Other insects may be equally beneficial, but their value is not so easily calculated. Foremost among these are predatory insects of several orders.

Some, chiefly parasitic wasps and predatory beetles, have been imported specifically for control of noxious pests. Others, such as dragonflies, mantises, lacewings, and such, are voracious predators and doubtless are a factor determining the environmental carrying capacity for many pests. These predators may prevent other insects from ever reaching an economic threshold and thus from becoming pests, as was demonstrated when predators of the European red mite were destroyed by chemical insecticides, allowing the mite population to reach damaging numbers on apple crops.

Innumerable insect species are scavengers, quietly but efficiently breaking down the remains of dead plants and animals. Their economic activity goes unnoticed, save when scavengers such as termites forsake logs on the forest floor for sills and siding on a summerhouse, or when flies invade a home. A lack of scavenging insects would, however, result in a great increase of decomposing organic material lying about.

Plant-eating insects have been set to beneficial use when their diets consist mainly of unwanted weeds. Alligatorweed in the southeastern United States and klamath weed in the northwestern states have been controlled by imported beetles, while prickly-pear cactus was similarly eliminated from Australian rangeland by larvae of moths from South America. Pasture thistles may soon be controlled by beetles in the eastern United States and adjacent Canada.

In many parts of the world, particularly the tropics and subtropics, termites, grubs, locusts, and other insects are routinely eaten by people, and for some they are a major source of dietary protein. In places like the United States, human consumption of insects is limited to expensive novelty items such as chocolate-covered ants, fried grasshoppers, and the like.

Certain rare and showy butterflies and beetles are sought after so that they have considerable economic worth. Conservation of rare and endangered insects incurs some expense as well. Habitat management to conserve rare insects is a valid and growing concern of economic entomologists.

Finally, insects have rendered invaluable service to science, and thus to humanity, as easily reared experimental animals for investigation of basic principles of genetics, biochemistry, development, and behavior. Pomace flies (genus *Drosophila*) have been extremely useful in this regard, and even cockroaches and houseflies are helpful in testing the effectiveness of new chemical insecticides and other insect control methods.

David J. Horn

Bibliography. R. H. Davidson and W. F. Lyon, *Insect Pests of Farm, Garden, and Orchard*, 8th ed., 1987; D. J. Horn, *Ecological Approach to Pest Management*, 1988; R. L. Metcalf and W. H. Luckmann, *Introduction to Insect Pest Management*, 2d ed., 1982; R. E. Pfadt, *Fundamentals of Applied Entomology*, 4th ed., 1985.

Environment

All external influences, abiotic (physical factors) and biotic (actions of other organisms), to which an organism is exposed. The environment affects basic life functions, growth, and reproductive success of organisms, and determines their local and geographic distribution patterns. A fundamental idea in ecology is that the environment changes in time and space and living organisms respond to these changes. *See Ecology.*

The influence of the environment on organisms can be viewed on scales of space and time. On a large spatial scale is the relationship between regional climate and geographic distribution of organisms. Researchers such as L. R. Holdridge have attempted to classify patterns of geographic distribution on the basis of climate. In the southern United States, a regional pattern is the east-to-west transition from forest to grassland to desert, which correlates with a decline in precipitation. On the microenvironmental scale, highly localized conditions determine the precise location and activity of individual organisms. The microscale can range from distribution of tree species along an environmental gradient on a mountain slope (temperature and precipitation vary with elevation) to the influence of moisture on bacteria on the surface of a single dead leaf. *See Altitudinal vegetation zones; Life zones.*

Temporally, organisms may respond differently to the frequency and duration of a given environmental change. For example, a plant exposed to increasing temperature and decreasing soil moisture immediately closes its stomates (leaf pores) to reduce water loss. If the higher temperatures and lower moisture levels persist for several hours or days, the plant may wilt temporarily. If such conditions persist for weeks or months, the plant may die. Long-term (years) shifts in environmental conditions could cause the extinction of a local population. If some individuals in the population have adaptations which allow them to survive and to reproduce under new environmental conditions (for example, more efficient physiological functions with low moisture), the local population will continue, but the genetic composition will have changed. Some organisms have the ability to acclimate, that is, to adjust their physiology or morphology in response to intermediate or long-term environmental changes, so that the new environmental conditions are no more stressful than the previous conditions. *See Physiological ecology (animal); Physiological ecology (plant).*

Two important ecological concepts are (1) environmental factors restrict or limit an organism's activities (limiting factors), and (2) the environment is highly complex with many interacting variables (factor interaction).

Limiting factors. Justus von Liebig's law of the minimum states, in a generalized form, that the essential environmental factor most closely approaching the minimum requirement of an organism tends to be the limiting factor. We now know that two or more limiting factors may operate simultaneously. Victor Shelford added the concept of limiting maxima in his law of tolerance which indicates that there is a range for any given factor within which an organism can survive with varied success. A species may have a wide range of tolerance for one factor (for example, eurythermal for temperature) and a narrow range for another factor (for example, stenohydric for moisture). A small change in an environmental factor may have little effect on a euryspecies (wide-range) but may be critical for a stenospecies (narrow-range). A stenoorganism may be tolerant at the low range of a factor (for example, oligothermal), at the high range (for example, polythermal), or in between (**Fig. 1**). Species with wide tolerance ranges for all factors are most likely to be widely distributed. For most spe-

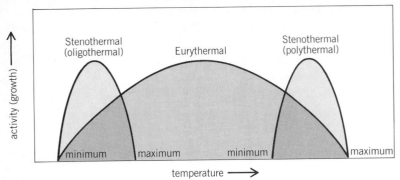

Fig. 1. Relative tolerance limits of stenothermal and eurythermal organisms. The three shaded areas approximate optimal zones for the organisms. (*After E. P. Odum , Basic Ecology, Saunders College Publishing, 1983*)

cies, optimum conditions are more realistically identified as a range than as a single point. Tolerance ranges traditionally have been derived from experimental data by the single-factor approach. Typically, an organism is placed in a controlled environmental chamber where a single factor, such as temperature, is manipulated while all other factors are held constant. Then the response is measured by observing the organism's activity through a range of values for each factor of interest.

Factor interaction. Single-factor experiments and tolerance ranges are useful in evaluating the relationship between an organism and its environment because they focus on the critical factors. However, environmental relationships are much more complex than indicated by these approaches. The environmental complex is highly interactive (holocoenotic); that is, environmental factors do not act independently on organisms. All factors operate simultaneously and interdependently, and the environment is in turn modified by the organism's activities and responses. For example, plants change soil conditions by removing mineral nutrients and adding organic matter. Regional rainfall can be altered by cutting forests. W. D. Billings's "yarn ball" depiction of environmental relationships (**Fig. 2**) exemplifies the complexity involved. This scheme illustrates the difficulties researchers face when attempting to clarify these relationships. Real-world responses to environmental change cannot be precisely predicted from knowledge of single-factor responses. Most organismal responses are synergistic; that is, the overall effect of the environment is different from the sum of the effects of individual factors. The concept of limiting factors is complicated by environmental complexity. A limiting factor, as defined by Liebig's law, may not actually be limiting to an organism if compensating factors exist. A compensating factor allows an organism to exceed its tolerance range for a potentially limiting factor. For example, many plants survive low soil moisture conditions when the temperature is cool to moderate. Cool temperatures, resulting in less water loss from the plant, compensate for low soil moisture.

Abiotic Factors

The abiotic environment consists of all physical factors which affect an organism. The quantitative range and importance of each abiotic factor vary considerably among different habitat types. This variation is accentuated in comparing aquatic and terrestrial habitats.

Light radiation. Visible light enters the Earth's atmosphere as electromagnetic waves in the range 390–760 nanometers. Light is required to drive the photosynthetic process in green plants and serves as an optic or visual cue for orientation to many animals. Photoperiod (day-night cycle) triggers hormone production and many activities in plants and animals. The quality (wavelength), intensity, and duration of light are all important to organisms. Light is limiting to plants when the intensity is below the compensation point (the level at which photosynthesis just balances respiration). Also, some plants grow poorly in full sunlight. In aquatic habitats, both light intensity and quality are altered by absorption or refraction. The energy content of visible light is reduced by 50% after passage through 33 ft (10 m) of seawater and by 93% after 330 feet (100 m); the photosynthetically active reds and blues absorbed by chlorophyll are filtered out. Light intensity, quality, and duration vary with latitude on the macroenvironmental scale, and are affected by slope position (north- or south-facing), cloudiness, and shading by large plants on the microenvironmental scale.

Ionizing radiation. All organisms are exposed to natural background radiation in the form of cosmic rays from outer space and ionizing radiation from radioactive materials in soil, water, and air. These radiations cause a very small number of mutations in natural populations, and thus add to genetic variability. There are three major types of ionizing radiation: alpha particles, beta particles, and gamma rays. Alpha particles (helium nucleii) do not travel far (they can be stopped by human skin), but produce a great amount of local ionization. Beta particles (high-speed electrons) penetrate farther (a few inches in tissue). Gamma rays (electromagnetic radiations) travel long distances through tissue and may generate a long path of ionization. Natural radiation is highest at high altitudes and near granitic rocks. The amount of ionizing radiation in the environment has increased due to human use of atomic energy (for example, nuclear weapons testing and the operation of nuclear power plants). *See Radiation biology.*

Temperature. The tolerance ranges of most species are within a narrow band from 0 to 113°F (−17.8 to 45°C). Some thermal eukaryotic organisms live at temperatures up to 122°F (50°C), and some prokaryotic thermal bacteria are found at any temperature at which liquid water is present. A few rotifers and nematodes have the ability to enter a cryptobiotic state (suspended animation) by excreting water from their bodies, and thereby remain viable at temperatures over 302°F (150°C) for several minutes and near absolute zero (−459.5°F or −273°C) for several days. Temperature alters metabolic and growth processes in most organisms and frequently is a limiting factor. Physiological and behavioral reactions to temperature change are strikingly different in homeotherms (warm-blooded animals, that is, birds and mammals) and poikilotherms (cold-blooded animals, such as amphibians and reptiles). Homeotherms adjust their metabolic rates in response to temperature changes and thus are able to maintain constant body temperatures; poikilotherms, unable to do this, may control body temperature through behavioral responses (for example, snakes sun themselves on rocks). Temperature varies with latitude on the macroenvironmental scale and drops 11°F (6°C) with each 500-mi (800-km) increase in latitude. On the microenvironmental scale, south-facing slopes are warmer than north-facing

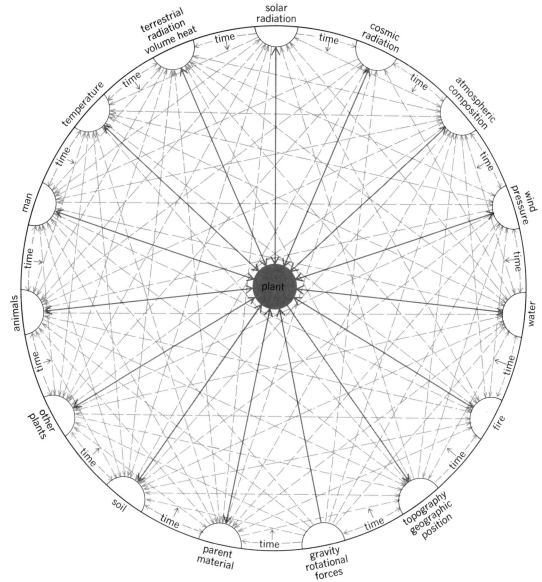

Fig. 2. "Yarn ball" concept of environmental complexity.

slopes and there is an 11°F (6°C) drop with each 3300-ft (1000-m) increase in elevation.

Water. Water, essential to all living organisms, is often a limiting factor. Precipitation and evaporation rates, humidity, and available soil moisture are factors governing water availability for terrestrial organisms. Precipitation varies in relation to the position and movement of air masses and weather systems, location relative to mountain ranges (rain shadow effect), and altitude. Seasonal distribution of rainfall is as important as the total amount; rainfall evenly distributed throughout the year usually results in greater availability.

Evaporative losses of water from a particular microenvironment are determined primarily by air temperature, wind speed, and the dominant plants. Annual evapotranspiration (evaporative loss through leaf stomates) is greater from an evergreen conifer forest than a deciduous hardwood forest because the conifers have greater leaf surface area and retain their leaves all year. Humidity, the amount of water vapor in the air, is affected by temperature and barometric pressure, and in turn can modify the effects of tem-

perature. Some organisms require high humidity; for example, redwood trees on the west coast of the United States are associated primarily with foggy areas where they obtain a large amount of moisture directly from the air.

Available soil moisture is critically important to rooted plants and is affected by topography (steep slopes drain rapidly) and soil particle size (sandy soils drain more rapidly than silts or clays). Plants and animals residing in low-moisture habitats have adaptations to store water internally or to reduce water loss. For example, cacti have modified leaves and stems. The nocturnal kangaroo rat avoids the drying heat of the day, extracts water from seeds it eats and from its own metabolic processes, and produces a highly concentrated urine. Because high salinity in soil or water can dehydrate organisms by osmosis, plants and animals that live in salty soils or marine habitats must have adaptations which allow them to osmoregulate under such conditions. On the other hand, excess water is a problem for terrestrial organisms in flooded habitats. The pneumatophores (air tubes) of mangrove trees are an adaptation which permits gas exchange in the roots when submerged. *See GROUNDWATER HYDROLOGY*.

Atmospheric gases. Oxygen is essential to aerobic organisms for respiration, and carbon dioxide is required by green plants for photosynthesis. Increases in concentrations of carbon dioxide in the atmosphere (0.03 vol %) and decreases in oxygen (21 vol %) increase photosynthesis rates in many plants. Low levels of oxygen in aquatic habitats are limiting to aerobic organisms. Oxygen levels in water are affected by temperature, salinity, and current (still water contains less oxygen than flowing water).

Air and water currents. Wind influences evapotranspiration and photosynthesis rates in plants by affecting gas exchange via the stomates, and can damage plants, especially when associated with low temperatures. Wind speeds vary with altitude and topography. Water currents have an impact on aquatic organisms because flow rates affect oxygen level, nutrient levels, and the ability of an organism to navigate and maintain position in the current.

Soil. Soils are formed from physically and chemically weathered bedrock and organic matter contributed by plants. Edaphic (soil-related) factors have a major influence on rooted plants and soil-dwelling organisms. The soil serves as a support medium and provides water and nutrients for these organisms. The most important factors include texture (particle-size composition), salinity, moisture content, organic matter content, pH (which affects nutrient availability), and ion-exchange capacity [the amount of exchangeable (available) nutrients]. Nutrients required in relatively large amounts by most living organisms (macronutrients) include potassium, calcium, magnesium, sulfur, nitrogen, and phosphorus, with the last two most commonly limiting. Some of the nutrients required in relatively small amounts (micronutrients) are iron, manganese, boron, copper, zinc, and silicon. The major factors responsible for variation in soil conditions are temperature, precipitation, chemical nature of the bedrock, local topography, and type of vegetation. *See SOIL; SOIL CHEMISTRY; SOIL MICROBIOLOGY*.

Catastrophic disturbances. Knowledge of average day-to-day and year-to-year environmental conditions makes it possible to predict the species that will live in a given habitat and how well they will live. However, such predictions may be invalidated by the occurrence of stochastic (random) events. These usually unpredictable and infrequent disturbances, such as fire, hurricanes, volcanic activity, landslides, and major floods, may drastically alter the environment of an area and thus change the species composition and activity patterns of the inhabitants. Many species and even whole communities of organisms actually require such disturbances for their maintenance. For example, pines in the forests of the southeastern United States and giant redwoods of California are adapted for fire and require it to burn away competing hardwoods. If fire is prevented, the pines and redwoods will not replace themselves. Many such fire-adapted communities have been mismanaged by humans as a result of fire prevention policies.

BIOTIC FACTORS

The primary biotic influences on an organism are direct interactions with other organisms, which in turn are affected by the physical environment and biotic interactions.

Natural interactions. Major forms of interaction include predation and parasitism (consumption of an organism or a portion of an organism's blood or tissue), competition (two or more organisms contesting for a limited resource), and mutualism [beneficial, cooperative interaction between different species, for example mycorrhizal (root-associated) fungi increase nutrient uptake efficiency of plants and receive photosynthetically produced sugars in return]. *See POPULATION ECOLOGY*.

Anthropogenic stress. The effects of human activity on other organisms are viewed as being different from natural biotic interactions because of their extraordinary nature and magnitude. Some of the major stresses humans inflict on natural populations are chemical pollution (such as pesticides, industrial compounds, radioisotopes, heavy metals, fertilizers, oil, acid rain, and smog), thermal pollution (such as warm water discharged from power plants), noise pollution, and habitat alteration and destruction. *See AIR POLLUTION; BIOSPHERE; HUMAN ECOLOGY; WATER POLLUTION*.

Frank P. Day, Jr.

Bibliography. T. F. H. Allen and T. B. Starr, *Hierarchy: Perspectives for Ecological Complexity*, 1988; R. Brewer, *Principles of Ecology*, 1979; J. Cairns, Jr. (ed.), *Rehabilitating Damaged Ecosystems*, 2 vols., 1988; D. M. Gates, *Energy and Ecology*, 1985; D. Pepper, *The Roots of Modern Environmentalism*, 1984; H. Walter and S. W. Breckle, *Ecological Systems of the Geobiosphere*, 1985; P. Yodzis, *Introduction to Theoretical Ecology*, 1988.

Environmental assessment

The systematic identification and evaluation of the potential impacts of proposed projects, plans, programs, policies, or legislative actions upon the physical-chemical, biological, cultural, and socioeconomic components of the environment. Also known as environmental impact assessment (EIA), it includes as well the consideration of measures to mitigate undesirable impacts. The primary purpose of environmental impact assessment is to encourage consideration of the environment in planning and decision making and ultimately to arrive at actions that are more environmentally compatible.

The practice of environmental assessment was initiated on January 1, 1970, the effective date of the National Environmental Policy Act (NEPA) in the United States. Since that time, more than 100 developing and developed nations either have passed specific analogous laws or have adopted procedures used elsewhere. NEPA is applicable to all federal agencies in the United States. In addition, over 30 states have the equivalent of NEPA or other requirements, with many of these laws, regulations, or executive orders being closely patterned after the requirements for environmental impact assessment of NEPA. The Council on Environmental Quality (CEQ) was created by this federal legislation.

Analysis. A key concept of the CEQ regulations establishes three levels of analysis. Level 1 relates to a categorical exclusion determination, level 2 to the preparation of an environmental assessment report and a finding of no significant impact (FONSI), and level 3 to the preparation of an environmental impact statement. Federal actions fall within one of the following categories: adoption of official policy (such as rules, regulations, and interpretations), treaties and international conventions or agreements, and formal documents establishing an agency's policies; adoption of formal plans; adoption of programs, such as a group of concerted actions to implement a specific policy or plan; and approval of specific projects, such as construction or management activities located in a defined geographical area (projects include actions approved by permit or other regulatory decision, as well as federal and federally assisted activities).

Categorical exclusions refer to a category of actions that do not individually or cumulatively have a significant effect on the human environment; therefore, neither an environmental assessment report nor an environmental impact statement is required. An environmental assessment report is a concise public document that provides sufficient evidence and analysis for determining whether to prepare an environmental impact statement or a finding of no significant impact; aids an agency's compliance with NEPA when no environmental impact statement is necessary; and facilitates preparation of a statement when one is necessary. The FONSI document briefly presents the reasons why an action, not otherwise excluded, will not have a significant effect on the human environment, and entails that an environmental impact statement will not be prepared.

Human environment. The National Environmental Policy Act indicated that for major federal actions significantly affecting the human environment an environmental impact statement would be required. The human environment can be considered in terms of descriptors for the physical-chemical, biological, cultural, and socioeconomic environments. The physical-chemical environment includes such major areas as soils, geology, topography, surface-water and groundwater resources, water quality, air quality, and climatology. The biological environment refers to the flora and fauna of the area, including species of trees, grasses, fish, herpetofauna, birds, and mammals. Specific consideration must be given to threatened or endangered plant or animal species and their habitats. General biological features such as species diversity and overall ecosystem stability should be considered. The cultural environment includes historical and archeological sites, and esthetic resources such as visual quality. The socioeconomic environment refers to considerations related to people in the environment, including population trends and distributions; economic indicators of human welfare; educational systems; transportation networks and other infrastructure concerns such as water supply, wastewater disposal, and solid-waste management; public services such as police and fire protection and medical facilities; and many others. *See* Ecological methods; Ecology, applied; Ecosystem.

Significant effect. The key factor is significant effect or impact. The term "significant" in the NEPA process requires consideration of both context and intensity. The significance of an action must be analyzed in several contexts such as society as a whole (human, national), the affected region, the affected interests, and the affected locality. Impact characteristics such as duration, reversibility, and mitigability should be considered. Intensity refers to the severity of either direct or indirect impacts. Direct impacts are caused by the action and occur at the same time and place. Indirect impacts are later in time or farther removed in distance but are still reasonably foreseeable. Indirect impacts may include growth effects related to

changes in the pattern of land use and in population, and effects on air and water and other natural systems, including ecosystems.

The Council on Environmental Quality has established ten specific considerations in evaluating intensity, divisible into two groups: those related to environmental laws, regulations, policies, and executive orders, and those in other categories, having implications for the first group. If it is determined that a federal action has a significant impact based on the environmental assessment, or if the pertinent federal agency has previously listed the action as one typically requiring an environmental impact statement, then the statement should be prepared.

Determination of impacts. A flexible approach comprising five activities can be used for planning and conducting impact studies. The focus herein will be on projects, although the approach could also be applied to plans, programs, policies, and regulatory actions.

First activity. The features of the proposed project, the need for it, and the alternatives that have been or could be considered are determined. Key information includes (1) the type of project and how it functions; (2) the proposed location; (3) the time period required for construction; (4) the potential environmental outputs (stresses) during the operational phase; (5) an identified need for the project in the proposed location; and (6) the alternatives that have been considered.

Second activity. Pertinent regulatory requirements for the environmental categories that would be related to the construction and operation of the proposed project are considered. Over 50 federal environmental statutes may have relevance; in addition, statutes exist at state and local levels. Scoping, which is an early and open process to identify significant environmental issues and impacts relative to proposed projects, can aid this activity. In the scoping process, which would include contacts with regulatory agencies and other interested public groups, the identification of pertinent regulatory information would be expected. This information can be used in the interpretation of existing conditions and of the anticipated impacts of the project.

Third activity. Potential impacts of the subject project are identified. An appropriate task is a computer-based literature review to identify generic impacts related to the project type. Another task could be the identification of potential impacts via the preparation of simple interaction matrices. A matrix basically consists of a list of project actions compared against a list of environmental factors (resources), so that the interaction points can be systematically studied.

Fourth activity. The affected environment is described. This activity enables the selective identification of pertinent environmental factors for the study in progress. There is considerable baseline information available in computerized information storage and retrieval systems; examples include databases on air quality, water quality, soils, habitat types in geographical areas, threatened and endangered species, historical and archeological properties in geographical areas, and multiple socioeconomic factors such as population density, income levels, and infrastructure characteristics.

Fifth activity. Technically the most challenging activity, this involves impact prediction. Basically impact prediction refers to the quantification of (where possible), or at least the qualitative description of, the anticipated impacts of the proposed project on various environmental factors. The range of techniques for impact prediction is broad and encompasses the use of analogies through sophisticated mathematical models. In a specific study, several techniques may be required because of the availablitiy or nonavailability of data and of specific mathematical models. In addition, as greater attention is being given to the global environment, it is increasingly necessary to consider mesoscale environmental consequences of large-scale projects.

Impact prediction. The simplest technique for impact prediction is to utilize analogies or comparisons to the effects experienced from existing projects. In this look-alike technique, information from similar types of projects in similar environmental settings could be utilized to address anticipated impacts qualitatively (descriptively).

Inventory technique. Environmental resources can be inventoried by using either existing data or baseline monitoring, with the presumption being that the particular resources, or portions thereof, will be lost as a result of the proposed project. This loss could be perceived as a worst-case prediction.

Checklists and interaction matrices. An often-used technique for impact prediction is incorporation of checklists or interaction matrices in the study. Checklists range from simple lists of anticipated impacts by project type to lists incorporating a series of detailed questions that could provide a structure to the impact prediction activity. Some checklists include the use of scaling/rating/ranking of the anticipated impacts of alternatives, and of relative importance weights for the individual environmental factors; such checklists can be utilized to aggregate the impacts of a project into a final index or score, which can then be used for comparisons of conditions that would prevail with and without the project. Interaction matrices include simple x-y matrices to identify impacts and to provide a basis for further evaluation of such impacts in terms of magnitude and importance. Stepped matrices have been developed wherein secondary and tertiary consequences of project actions can be delineated. The most sophisticated matrices are networks or impact trees in which systematic approaches are utilized to trace out the consequences of a project. The key point in both checklist and matrix methods is that they tend to be qualitative in terms of the actual predicted impacts; however, they do represent useful tools for impact prediction.

Environmental indices. An environmental index refers to a mathematical or descriptive presentation of information on a series of factors that can be used for classification of environmental quality and sensitivity and for prediction of the impacts of a proposed project. The basic concept for impact prediction would be to anticipate and quantify (if possible) the change in the environmental index as a result of the project, and then to consider this difference in the index as one measure of impact. Indices have been developed for air quality, water quality, noise, visual quality, and quality of life (a socioeconomic index that can include many specific factors). One type of index that has been widely used is based on habitat considerations. A key advantage of indices for impact prediction is that they represent approaches that can be related to available information; in addition, they provide a systematic basis upon which to consider potential consequences of a project.

Experimental methods. These can include specific laboratory experiments to develop coefficients for mathematical models or large-scale field experiments to measure changes in environmental features as a result of system perturbations. In addition, physical models have been utilized to examine impacts related to hydrodynamics and ecological changes within microcosms of environmental settings. Experimental methods are primarily useful in dealing with physical/chemical components and biological features of the environmental setting.

Mathematical models. The most sophisticated prediction techniques involve mathematical models. Numerous models have been developed for pollutant transport and fate within the environmental setting. Some models exist for describing the features and the functioning of ecosystems. With regard to air-quality dispersion, models exist for addressing elevated stacks, highways, and area sources of air pollution and the results of dispersion from the sources. Models also exist for long-range transport of pollution and for atmospheric reactions leading to photochemical smog formation and acid rain. *See* ECOLOGICAL MODELING.

Models for the quality and quantity of surface water and groundwater are plentiful; major research developments have occurred in the realm of solute transport in subsurface systems. Surface-water quality and quantity models range from one-dimensional steady-state models to three-dimensional dynamic models that can be utilized for rivers, lakes and estuarine systems. Groundwater flow models have been modified to include subsurface processes such as adsorption and biological decomposition. *See* GROUND-WATER HYDROLOGY; HYDROLOGY.

Noise impact prediction models have been developed for single location, highways, and area sources of noise generation. These models range from simple calculations involving the use of nomographs to sophisticated computer models for airport operations. The technology for noise impact prediction is well developed as a result of numerous research studies related to highways and airports.

Biological impact prediction models typically involve habitat approaches. The habitat evaluation procedures developed by the U.S. Fish and Wildlife Services and the Army Corps of Engineers are widely used. These models involve the calculation of an index that incorporates both qualitative and quantitative information. Prediction of impacts involves determination of the index under baseline as well as future conditions. Species population models based on empirical approaches involving statistical correlations have been developed. The most sophisticated models involve energy system diagrams. *See* ECOLOGICAL ENERGETICS.

Predictive modeling is also possible for ascertaining the potential for archeological resources in geographical study areas. Such modeling is primarily based upon evaluating a series of factors to indicate the likelihood of archeological resources being found; the factors are related to existing information, the likelihood for early occupations in the area, and other environmental and sociological factors. Such modeling is often used to determine the necessity for conducting archeological field surveys.

Visual quality has also been a subject of some importance in selected impact studies. Visual impact modeling approaches have been developed by several federal agencies. These models typically involve the evaluation of a series of factors, either quantitatively or descriptively, with the assemblage of the information into an overall visual quality index for the study area.

Impact prediction related to the socioeconomic environment often begins with the use of human population and econometric models. Population forecasting can range from simple projections of historical trends to complicated cohort analysis models. Econometric models relate the population and economic characteristics of study areas so that interrelationships between changes in population and changes in economic features can be depicted. Other impact predictions for the socioeconomic environment can be addressed by the use of multiplier factors applied to population or economic indicator changes.

A common ingredient in the various techniques for impact prediction is that decisions have to be made for a specific project to utilize the best available predictive technology in view of the location, size, and type of project, as well as the available budget for the study. Therefore, sophisticated mathematical models may not be appropriate because they require extensive data input and model calibration. Accordingly, a range of techniques will probably be necessary in conducting an impact study in relation to a specific project.

Impact assessment. Assessment refers to the interpretation of the significance of anticipated changes related to the proposed project. Impact interpretation can be based upon the systematic application of the definition of significance, as described earlier. For some types of anticipated impacts, there are specific numerical standards or criteria that can be used as a basis for impact interpretation. Examples include air-quality standards, environmental noise criteria, surface-water and groundwater quality standards, and wastewater discharge standards for particular facilities. Professional judgment will also be needed. One example of such professional judgment is the context of impacts related to the biological environment: the biological scientist in a study team renders judgments as to the potential significance of the loss of particular habitats, including wetland areas. Another basis for assessment is public input, which could be received through the scoping process or through public participation programs.

Mitigation measures. Identifying and evaluating potential impact mitigation measures should also be an activity in the process of environmental impact assessment. Mitigation has been defined by the CEQ as the sequential consideration of the following measures: (1) avoiding the impact altogether by not taking a certain action or parts of an action; (2) minimizing impacts by limiting the degree or magnitude of the action and its implementation; (3) rectifying the impact by repairing, rehabilitating, or restoring the affected environment; (4) reducing or eliminating the impact over time by preservation and maintenance operations during the life of the action; and (5) compensating for the impact by replacing or providing substitute resources or environments.

Examples of mitigation measures include pipeline routing to avoid archeological resources, inclusion of pollution-control equipment on airborne and liquid discharges, reductions in project size, revegetation programs, wildlife protection plans, erosion control measures, remediation activities, and creation of artificial wetlands.

Evaluation of alternatives. A key activity in environmental impact assessment is associated with selecting the proposed action from alternatives that have been evaluated. In public projects, there is considerable emphasis on the evaluation of alternatives; in fact, the CEQ regulations indicate that the analysis of alternatives represents the heart of the impact assessment process. Conversely, for many private developments, the range of alternatives may be limited. Even so, there are still potential alternative measures that could be evaluated, including those relating to project size and design features even if location alternatives are not available.

Environmental impact studies need to address a minimum of two alternatives, and can include more than fifty alternatives. Typical studies address three to five alternatives. The minimum number usually represents a choice between construction and operation of a project versus project nonapproval. The alternatives may encompass a wide range of considerations such as site location alternatives; design alternatives for a site; construction, operation, and decommissioning alternatives for a design; project size alternatives; phasing alternatives for size groupings; no project or no action alternatives; and timing alternatives relative to project construction, operation, and decommissioning.

In order to achieve systematic decision making among alternatives, it is desirable to use a trade-off analysis, which typically involves the comparison of a set of alternatives relative to a series of decision factors. A trade-off matrix is used for systematically comparing alternatives relative to a series of decision factors. A number of options that can be used in the trade-off matrix include (1) the qualitative approach, in which descriptive information on each alternative relative to each decision factor is presented in the matrix cells; (2) the quantitative approach, in which quantitative information on each alternative relative to each decision factor is displayed in the matrix cells; (3) a combination of the qualitative and quantitative approaches; (4) an approach in which the qualitative or quantitative information on each alternative is summarized by assigning a rank, rating, or scale value relative to each decision factor (the rank or rating or scale value is presented in the matrix cells); (5) the weighting approach, in which the importance weight of each decision factor relative to each other decision factor is considered, with the resultant discussion of the information on each alternative being presented in view of the relative importance of the decision factors; and (6) an approach in which the importance weight for each decision factor is multiplied by the ranking/rating/scale of each alternative, and then the resulting products for each alternative are summed to develop an overall composite index or score for each alternative.

Decision making that involves the comparison of a set of alternatives relative to a series of decision factors is not unique to impact studies. This is a classic decision-making problem, which is often referred to as multiattribute or multicriteria decision making or decision analysis.

Content of impact statement. An environmental impact statement is a detailed written statement as required by NEPA. The primary purpose of the impact statement is as an action-forcing device to ensure that the policies and goals defined in NEPA are infused into the ongoing programs and actions of the federal government. The impact statement must provide full and fair discussion of significant environmental impacts, and must inform decision makers and the public of the reasonable alternatives that would avoid or minimize adverse impacts or enhance the quality of the human environment.

The approach used to prepare a draft, final, or supplemental environmental impact statement should be interdisciplinary, systematic, and reproducible. A degree of organization and uniformity should be utilized in the assessment process. An interdisciplinary approach requires that the environment be considered in its broadest sense; thus the input of persons trained in a number of technical fields needs to be included. The disciplines represented in a specific environmental assessment must be oriented to the unique features of the proposed action and the environmental setting; however, at a minimum it is necessary to have input from a physical scientist or engineer, a biologist, and a person who can address cultural and socioeconomic impacts.

During the 1970s, approximately 1200 final environmental impact statements were produced annually by various federal agencies. During the 1980s the number decreased, and in the early 1990s 400 to 500 environmental impact statements were produced annually. However, there has been a corresponding significant increase in the number of environmental assessments that have been prepared. While no statistics are available, it is estimated that well over 10,000 environmental assessments are prepared annually in the United States. In addition, concepts such as scoping and mitigation are now being included in initial project planning and decision making, thus reducing the need for subsequent preparation of environmental impact statements.

Focused studies. In the process of environmental impact assessment in the United States, within recent years there has been a growing usage of focused environmental documentation to address specific needs. Thus the principles of environmental impact assessment are being incorporated in documents that have been targeted for specific issues. Examples of focused studies include the documentation necessary to procure air-quality permits or wastewater discharge and nonpoint source discharge permits from state or federal regulatory agencies, and documents prepared in conjunction with property transfers to establish liability for site contamination.

Larry W. Canter

Bibliography. L. W. Canter, *Environmental Impact Assessment,* 1977; L. W. Canter, Interdisciplinary teams in environmental impact assessment, *Environ. Impact Assess. Rev.,* 11(4):375–387, 1991; Council on Environmental Quality, *Environmental Quality,* 22d Annual Report, March 1992; Council on Environmental Quality, 40 Code of Federal Regulations, July 1, 1987; E. D. Smith, *Future Challenges of NEPA: A Panel Discussion,* CONF-891098-10, Oak Ridge National Laboratory, 1989; U.S. Army Corps of Engineers, *A Habitat Evaluation System for Water Resources Planning,* Lower Mississippi Valley Division, August 1980; U.S. Congress, National Environmental Policy Act, PL 91-190, S. 1075, 91st Congress, 1970; U.S. Environmental Protection Agency, *Facts about the National Environmental Policy Act,* LE-133, September 1989; U.S. Fish and Wildlife Service, *Habitat Evaluation Procedures (HEP),* ESM 102, March 1980.

Environmental engineering

A branch of engineering concerned with the environment and its proper management. Formerly known as sanitary engineering, environmental engineering originally developed as a subdiscipline of civil engineering. However, it has evolved to include aspects of chemical engineering, microbiology, hydrology, and chemistry as they can be applied to solve environmental problems.

Environmental engineering practice includes surveys, reports, designs, reviews, management, operation and investigation of works or programs for (1) water supply, treatment, and distribution; (2) sewage collection, treatment, and disposal; (3) control of pollution in surface and underground waters; (4) collection, treatment, and disposal of refuse; (5) sanitary handling of milk and food; (6) housing and institutional sanitation; (7) rodent and insect control; (8) recreational place sanitation; (9) control of atmospheric pollution and air quality in both the general air of communities and in industrial work spaces; (10) control of radiation hazards exposure; and (11) other environmental factors affecting health, comfort, safety, and well-being of people.

The development of civilization has caused perturbation of much of the Earth's ecosystem, resulting in pollution of the air, land, and water. It is the task of the environmental engineer not only to design systems to assuage this pollution but also to educate people in protecting their surroundings from additional pollution. The practice of environmental engineering is divided into various subdisciplines.

Wastewater treatment and disposal. In many cases, rivers, lakes, and oceans have become polluted from discharges of liquid wastes from residential, commercial, and industrial sources. Many of these bodies of water have been reclaimed because of a movement in the 1970s to construct new wastewater treatment facilities and to improve old ones. Both physical-chemical and biological processes are used to remove organic matter from the liquid wastewater stream. It is this organic matter that causes a depletion of oxygen in rivers and lakes, with consequent anaerobic conditions leading to fish kills and noxious odors.

The physical-chemical and biological processes remove an abundance of the organic matter, along with floatable scum and grease from the waste stream. Chemical disinfection inactivates bacteria, viruses, and protozoa in the waste stream. The physical and chemical processes used for removing solids from the waste stream include screening, sand and grit separation, chemical coagulation, and plain sedimentation. Biological processes include activated sludge, contact towers, and biological discs. *See* Sewage.

The application of these treatment processes to residential, commercial, and industrial wastewaters has reduced the pollutional load on many rivers, lakes, and harbors. There do remain, however, cases of large metropolitan areas that have not completed their clean-up campaigns, and in many other regions discharges of untreated mixtures of sanitary wastes and stormwaters occur during heavy rains. These discharges emanate from large conduits that carry both sanitary and storm wastes. The impurities that run off the land during a storm mix with the sanitary wastes in the pipes, and the quantity of wastewater overtaxes the carrying capacity of the conduits; a portion of this mixture flows into the nearest body of water before it can reach the wastewater treatment facility. It is usually too expensive to construct a whole new set of separate sanitary conduits; however, some cities, like Chicago, have begun to solve the problem by constructing a system of deep underground tunnels that store the large quantities of discharges during the storm, following which the wastewaters can be bled into the treatment facilities at reasonable rates. *SEE SEWAGE COLLECTION SYSTEMS; SEWAGE TREATMENT.*

Where wastewater must be discharged into lakes and dry streams, a higher level of treatment must be employed, including removal of nutrients and colloidal matter. Physical-chemical and biological treatment processes are employed as for wastewater treatment. In addition, chemicals are introduced for precipitation of nutrients, followed by coagulation and filtration for removing solids remaining after biological treatment; and in some cases granular activated carbon or membrane filtration is used for additional purification of the waste stream. This higher level of treatment is advisable because of the damage that any visual traces of wastes can do to the appearance of the waters. In addition, the treatment may combat the potential eutrophic effect that the nutrients phosphorus and nitrogen can have on the receiving waters. *SEE EUTROPHICATION.*

Where wastewater discharges into rivers from which drinking water is taken downstream, special attention is given not only to the removal of organic matter from the wastes but also to the disinfection processes that inactivate microorganisms. Also of concern are discharges of organic chemical contaminants from industry or runoff from farm lands along the river contaminated by pesticides and herbicides.

The indirect reuse of wastewater that has been discharged into rivers is common around the world, and it is acceptable as long as the discharges are treated properly and contamination from organic chemicals is avoided. Less acceptable is the direct reuse of wastewater for potable use, even after a high level of treatment. Of most concern here is the possibility of outbreak of disease. However, some nations, such as Israel, do practice, out of necessity, reuse by storing wastewaters for long periods of time in maturation ponds prior to chemical and physical treatment. It has become quite common and acceptable, especially in drier climates, to reuse wastewater, following a respectable level of treatment, for irrigation of crops and for watering golf courses. In addition, certain communities such as Naples, Florida, and Irvine, California, have constructed dual water systems, using treated wastewater for outdoor residential and commercial use and for fire fighting, while saving higher-quality water for potable use. In other cases, large industries take waters directly from rivers for the cooling of industrial processes. *SEE SALINE WATER RECLAMATION; WATER POLLUTION.*

Wastewater solids treatment and disposal. The organic and inorganic solids that are removed from wastewater by the physical-chemical and biological processes must be dewatered, stabilized biologically or chemically, and then placed in a controlled landfill, burned, or composted for return to the land. There are some circumstances in which the solids do not have to be dewatered but can be applied directly to the land, following biological stabilization. There are also instances, such as in Milwaukee, Wisconsin, where the solids are processed into a fertilizer.

Unfortunately, in many parts of the world, including the east coast of the United States, the waste solids are neither reclaimed to the land nor burned as a source of energy. They are barged or piped out to sea and then dumped into the water. It is anticipated that this practice will be discontinued, and incineration for energy recovery along with composting for reuse on the land will replace ocean dumping. Where the solids are composted, heavy and toxic metals must be removed at their source.

The processes employed for treating wastewater solids include dewatering presses, belts, and centrifuges, as well as fluid-bed furnaces. Another process that has received considerable attention is in-vessel composting. *SEE SEWAGE DISPOSAL.*

Refuse disposal. The indiscriminate dumping of trash and garbage on land has caused serious pollution problems. Refuse disposal can be controlled in a well-designed and -operated landfill, and this can be a suitable process for certain small communities. However, land for the disposal of refuse for mid- and large-size communities is being seriously reduced, and composting of refuse for reuse on the land may have limited application. The appropriate system for the majority of communities appears to be incineration of the refuse, with recovery of energy from the burning of organic materials. The air emission systems from these thermal reactors, as well as from the furnaces that burn solids emanating from wastewater plants, must be designed to prevent chemical and particulate air pollution. These air emission systems include electrostatic precipitators and afterburners.

Hazardous waste disposal. Unfortunately, countrysides and groundwaters have become cluttered and polluted by long-term illegal dumping and washings from industrial and commercial activities, as well as from public agencies. The removal of stored containers of wastes from the dumping grounds is necessarily a slow process, and an approved disposal site must be developed and contained. The cleaning of contaminated soils and groundwaters is an even slower process, and the technology for decontamination must be properly designed and put into place. For example, waters contaminated with organic chemicals are slowly pumped from the aquifer, and then the contaminants are removed either by air-stripping or adsorption onto granular activated carbon. The cleansed water is injected back into the aquifer, and this process can take years to accomplish. This can be inconvenient and, in some cases, a danger to health for communities that must use these groundwaters for their potable water supply. *SEE GROUNDWATER HYDROLOGY; HAZARDOUS WASTE.*

Air-pollution control. To the environment has been added smoke from diesel-driven trucks, uncontrolled gasoline engine emissions, and pollution from industrial smoke stacks. In the United States, statistics published by the Environmental Protection Agency in 1987 revealed that 2.4×10^9 lb $(1.1 \times 10^9$ kg) of toxic chemicals are released into the air annually, while 100 million people live where other air pollutants, chiefly from automobiles, exceed federal standards. Local smog in metropolitan areas, such as Los Angeles, is caused by the activities of the respective communities. Acid rain caused by the emissions of gases from the industrial smokestacks of the midwestern United States falls on the forests and lakes of the Northeast and Canada. *See Acid rain; Smog*.

There have been attempts at cleaning up the air, but the action toward solution has been limited. The technology is available (for example, multiple-hearth and fluid-bed reactors along with sophisticated air emissions technology) for removing the particulate matter and the contaminating chemicals from the air emissions; but the processes are expensive, and the progress is slow. *See Air pollution; Air-pollution control*.

Potable management. The availability of drinking water that is safe and of good quality is an important factor in modern civilization.

Sources. Indirect use of wastewater by withdrawing drinking water from rivers is a viable and economical way to supply communities with potable water, especially those located on waterfronts. The water must be disinfected for the inactivation of microbiological pollutants, and physical and chemical treatment must be provided for the removal of organic and inorganic impurities.

Other sources of drinking water are natural lakes and impoundments of rivers. These are usually of better quality than river waters, and they can be used for multiple purposes such as water supply and hydroelectric power. Controlled recreational use of sections of these lakes is not unusual.

Underground aquifers are a common source of drinking water, and their quality is very high, except where chemical contamination has occurred. In some parts of the world, aquifers can be recharged with reclaimed surface waters. *See Aquifer*.

A serious problem in many parts of the world is the shortage of pure drinking water during periods of low rainfall and snow. A major drought occurred on the eastern seaboard of the United States in the spring of 1989. There appear to be two reasons for water shortages during droughts: many drinking-water supply systems have not been planned to deal adequately with droughts, and water is wasted because of its relatively low price. *See Drought*.

Quality. It is prudent to select the purest water available for drinking purposes. This can be underground water, springs, or upland lakes. It then becomes imperative to protect that source. Prevention of chemical contamination of groundwaters is extremely important, as is the judicious control of the use of the banks of a surface water. Lakes can be used for recreation as well as for a water source; however, such mixed use requires good planning.

The purification of the water supply is just as important as watershed planning and control. Where the quality of the source is decent to start with, chemical disinfection, coagulation, and filtration are adequate. If water is being taken from a river supply that is muddy and subject to organic pollution, additional treatment is required. Great strides were made in the 1980s in the development of water purification technology. Ozone has become the chemical disinfectant of choice because it is the most potent disinfectant for bacteria, viruses, and protozoa; and unlike chlorine, it does not form carcinogenic by-products when there is organic matter present in the water. Economic inline or direct filtration can be employed to purify many upland supplies. Combined with ozone, this process is adaptable to many unfiltered water supplies. Granular activated carbon removes substances that form tastes and odors from the waters, and it adsorbs harmful organic chemicals. *See Water treatment*.

The final barrier to contamination of the water supply is careful management of the water distribution system. Chemicals can be added to the purified water to offset corrosive conditions in the system, thus greatly reducing the leaching of lead from the joints of plumbing systems; and the water pipes can be lined with cement mortar and kept flushed to prevent dirty water. *See Water supply engineering*.

Other aspects. Environmental engineering can be applied to the solution of regional problems. Ponds and lakes that become eutrophic and have massive algae blooms cannot be used for recreation, and the water, if used for drinking, may be noxious. These conditions can be prevented by trapping the runoff of nutrients into the lakes and by aerating the lakes. The indiscriminate disposal of water into harbors and consequent contamination of beaches can be prevented by proper regulations and enforcement. Finally, better ways of dealing with disposal of wastes on landscapes must be developed.

Paul W. Prendiville

Bibliography. American Water Works Research Foundation, *Res. News*, December 1988; R. A. Corbitt, *Standard Handbook of Environmental Engineering*, 1990; V. M. Ehlers and E. W. Steel, *Municipal and Rural Sanitation*, 6th ed., 1965; G. M. Fair, J. C. Geyer, and D. A. Okun, *Water and Wastewater Engineering*, vol. 2: *Water Purification and Wastewater Treatment and Disposal*, 1968; *J. Amer. Water Works Ass.*, March 1989; *J. Water Pollut. Control Federat.*, February 1989; J. M. Kalbermatten et al., *Appropriate Sanitation Alternatives: A Planning and Design Manual*, 1983; R. K. Linsley, Jr., *Water Resource Engineering*, 1990; F. S. Merritt (ed.), *Standard Handbook for Civil Engineers*, 1990; G. G. Patry, *Dynamic Modeling and Expert Systems in Wastewater Engineering*, 1989; E. W. Steel, *Water Supply and Sewerage*, 5th ed., 1979; H. H. Uhlig, *Corrosion and Corrosion Control*, 3d ed., 1985; M. Willrich and R. K. Lester, *Radioactive Waste Management and Regulation*, 1977.

Environmental radioactivity

Radioactivity that originates from natural and anthropogenic sources, including radioactive materials in food, housing, and air, radioactive materials used in medicine, nuclear weapon tests in the open atmosphere, and radioactive materials used in industry and power generation.

Natural radioactivity, which is by far the largest component to which humans are exposed, is of both terrestrial and extraterrestrial (cosmic) origin. About 340 nuclides are known in nature, of which 70 are radioactive and are found mainly among the heavy elements. Three nuclides which are responsible for most of the terrestrial component are potassium-40, uranium-238, and thorium-232.

Terrestrial nuclides. Potassium-40 has a half-life of 1.3×10^9 years and decays, through calcium-40, to stable argon-40. This nuclide is present to the extent of about 0.01% in natural potassium, thereby imparting a specific activity of approximately 800 picocuries per gram (3.0×10^4 becquerels per kilogram) of potassium. Potassium is of course an essential element of the human body, which contains about 0.1 microcurie (3.7×10^3 Bq) of the radioactive form of the element.

Uranium-238, the most abundant uranium isotope, decays through a chain of 18 nuclides to stable lead-206. This chain includes radionuclides of 10 heavy elements, the half-lives ranging from 4.5×10^9 years (uranium-238) to 1.64×10^{-4} s (polonium-214).

An important characteristic of the uranium-238 chain is that it includes a radioactive noble gas, radon-222, with a half-life of 3.8 days. Radon emanates from the Earth's crust, diffuses into the atmosphere, and eventually decays to radionuclides of lead and polonium that attach themselves electrically to the dust normally present in the atmosphere. The dose of the lung from radon daughter products attached to atmospheric dust is much higher than the dose received from natural sources by any other part of the body.

The radon daughters are also a source of natural "fallout" which, when released into the soil, results in broad-leaved plants having relatively high concentrations of both lead-210 and polonium-210. In the case of tobacco, the polonium is volatized in the course of smoking and delivers a higher-than-normal dose to the lung. It has been suggested that this phenomenon may play a role in the production of lung cancer from tobacco smoking, but this suggestion must be regarded as highly speculative.

Thorium-232 has a half-life of 1.4×10^9 years and decays through a series of 12 nuclides to a stable isotope of lead (lead-208). Human exposure from this series results mainly from the energetic gamma radiation from thallium-208. Internal irradiation results from absorption of radium-228 (6.7-year half-life) which finds its way into food.

Dose rates. The average person in the United States receives 80–180 mrem/year (0.8–1.8 millisieverts/year) from natural sources of ionizing radiation, depending on the organ considered (see **table**). Most of this dose originates from radioactive materials in the Earth's crust. The external dose due to cosmic rays is an average of about 28 mrem/year (0.28 mSv/year), a value that increases with altitude due to reduced shielding of cosmic radiation by the atmosphere. At Denver, which is located 1 mi (1.6 km) above sea level, the annual dose from cosmic radiation is more than 50 mrem/year (0.5 mSv/year), or about twice the average dose.

The human body is also exposed to radionuclides in food and water. Potassium-40 is the most important of these, with radium-226 and radium-228 of perhaps less importance from the point of view of the dose delivered.

A number of radionuclides are produced in nature by the interaction of cosmic rays with atmospheric gases, and these add slightly to the exposure received from natural sources. Carbon-14 is the most important of these nuclides which, like potassium-40, is present in the body to the extent of about 0.1 microcurie (3.7×10^3 Bq), but which delivers a dose of only about 1 mrem/year (10 µSv/year) because of the unusual softness (low energy) of its beta emission.

There are wide deviations from the average doses shown in the table. Thus, at one extreme, miners working underground in the presence of radioactive ore can be exposed to such high levels of atmospheric radon that they develop lung cancer. This was observed in mines in central Europe that were worked for precious metals long before radioactivity was discovered. Uranium miners in the southwestern United States have also been subject to a high incidence of lung cancer because of lack of control of radon.

Radioactive anomalies. There are also geographical areas where the levels of natural radioactivity are unusually high. Six types of anomalies that can be important from the point of view of population exposure are: monazite sands and other placers, alkaline intrusives and granites of the Conway type in New Hampshire, bauxites and intensely weathered soils, uraniferous phosphate rock (and soils), groundwaters enriched in radium and radon, and black shales and related organic accumulations.

There are two locations, in India and in Brazil, where the external radiation levels are greatly elevated by the presence of thorium-bearing monazite sands on or near ocean beaches. The local inhabitants are thus exposed to doses several times those received under normal circumstances. In Kerala, India, more than 25% of the 70,000 people living in the monazite area receive a dose greater than 500 mrem/year (5 mSv/year), and a small percentage receive between 1000 and 2000 mrem/year (10 and 20 mSv/year). In Guarapari, Brazil, the 6000 residents receive a mean dose of about 600 mrem/year (6 mSv/year).

Another type of anomaly, of which the outstanding example is the Morro do Ferro near Pocos de Caldas, Brazil, is found in regions of alkaline intrusives. The Morro do Ferro is a hill located in the state of Minas Gerais. The plants absorb so much radioactivity that they autoradiograph themselves when placed on radiation-sensitive film (see **illus.**). It has been estimated that the lungs of rodents living underground on the Morro do Ferro receive as much as 3000 mrem/year (30 mSv/year) from inhalation of a short-lived (53 s) radon isotope found in the thorium chain. The source

Average dose equivalent rates from various sources of natural background radiation in the United States

Source	Dose, mrem/year*				
	Gonads	Lung	Bone surfaces	Bone marrow	Gastrointestinal tract
Cosmic radiation	28	28	28	28	28
Cosmogenic radionuclides	0.7	0.7	0.8	0.7	0.7
External terrestrial	26	26	26	26	26
Inhaled radionuclides	—	100	—	—	—
Radionuclides in the body	27	24	60	24	24
Rounded totals	80	180	120	80	80

*1 mrem/year = 10^{-2} mSv/year.

Autoradiograph of plant from the Morro do Ferro, Brazil, made by the plant's natural radioactivity.

of the radioactivity on the Morro do Ferro is a deposit of about 13,000 tons (12,000 metric tons) of thorium located near the summit of the hill. The deposit has been in place for perhaps as long as 80,000,000 years, and is in an advanced state of weathering. Rainfall averages about 67 in./year (170 cm/year).

Because of marked chemical similarities between thorium and plutonium, a study of the history of the deposit and the manner in which it has been mobilized by hydraulic and other forces will provide useful information for predicting the behavior over geologic time of plutonium and other actinides in a radioactive waste repository that has been breached.

It is known that water from deep wells may have high concentrations of radium. About 1,000,000 people in northern Illinois and southern Iowa drink water with abnormally high radium concentrations.

Technological modification. The natural radioactive environment can also be altered by human activities, as described below.

Building construction. The radon concentration within buildings is influenced by the materials of construction. Construction materials that often have high concentrations of radium (the parent of radon) include pumice, concrete containing alum shale, and granite. Tailings from uranium and phosphate mining have been particularly troublesome in this regard, and it

has been necessary to place restrictions on the use of these materials in construction of buildings. In Grand Junction, Colorado, the use of uranium mine tailings in home construction resulted in such high indoor radon concentrations that remedial action was necessary.

It is ironic that the need to conserve energy is resulting in higher exposures to radon. Weather stripping and other measures that reduce the rate of building ventilation cause less dilution of the radon that diffuses from the materials of construction, and hence tend to increase the radon concentration of the air within such buildings.

Combustion of fossil fuels. All fossil fuels contain naturally occurring radionuclides. Natural gas contains radon, which is sometimes present in detectable concentrations at the place of combustion.

Both oil and coal contain uranium and thorium and their daughter products. The radionuclides are discharged into the atmosphere in measurable amounts that are probably not significant to public health. It has been found that the radioactivity disseminated by burning coal is greater than that discharged into the atmosphere during normal operation of nuclear power reactors.

Aircraft travel. Flying at high altitudes increases the exposure from cosmic rays, and it is estimated that the dose received during a transcontinental trip across the United States is about 2 mrem (20 μSv).

Medical procedures. Procedures in which x-rays or radionuclides are used for diagnostic or therapeutic purposes are also a major source of radiation exposure, second in importance only to natural radioactivity. Doses of iodine-131 and iodine-125 are administered the most frequently. Other important nuclides include phosphorus-32, cobalt-60, gold-198, iron-59, and technetium-99. These nuclides are usually administered internally.

The use of diagnostic x-rays subjects the general population to far more exposure than radiopharmaceuticals. Estimates of the per capita dose from diagnostic x-rays range from 75 mrem/year (0.75 mSv/year) in New Orleans and 50 mrem/year (0.5 mSv/year) in New York to as little as 1.25 mrem/year (12.5 μSv/year) in Thailand. The per capita dose tends to increase with the general level of economic development of the country and the availability of medical services. However, in all countries, developed and developing, the per capita dose can be minimized by improving the techniques used.

Nuclear weapons testing. Environmental radioactivity from the testing of nuclear weapons diminished after the major nuclear powers declared a moratorium on atmospheric testing in 1963. Relatively small-scale tests have been conducted by France, China, and India, but these have not added significantly to the levels of radioactivity previously disseminated from tests by the United States, Soviet Union, and United Kingdom prior to the moratorium.

The residual radioactivity from weapons tests is largely from cesium-137 and strontium-90. Cesium-137 is chemically similar to potassium and tends to be distributed more or less uniformly throughout the soft tissues. The dose commitment (the mean lifetime dose from cesium-137 already deposited) was about 27 mrem (0.27 mSv) in the United States in 1976. Cesium-137 has a half-life of 30 years.

Strontium-90, which has a half-life of 38 years, is chemically similar to calcium and therefore tends to deposit in the skeleton. The dose from strontium-90 is highest in individuals whose skeletons were formed during the period of heavy weapons testing, from about 1954 to 1962. Among this segment of the population, the bone dose was annually about 2 mrem (20 μSv), and the 50-year dose in the temperate zone was estimated to have been about 87 mrem (0.87 mSv) in 1976. *See Radioactive fallout.*

Nuclear power plants. Although various national and international regulatory organizations have proposed guidelines that limit the per capita dose received by individuals in the general population to 170 mrem/year (1.7 mSv/year), it has become evident that nuclear power plants can be routinely operated so that the general population will not be exposed to more than 1% of this limit. The U.S. Nuclear Regulatory Commission requires that the reactors be operated so that the dose to the maximum exposed individual, usually a hypothetical person located at the fenceline, is not more than 10 mrem/year (0.1 mSv/year).

The radioactive wastes discharged into the environment by a normally operated nuclear power reactor are minimal. As noted above, it has been shown that, at least so far as airborne radioactivity is concerned, coal- and oil-fired power plants discharge higher quantities of radioactivity into the environment.

Two of the oldest privately operated power reactors in the United States are Dresden I, a boiling water reactor operated by Commonwealth Edison Company near Chicago, and Yankee Rowe, a pressurized water reactor operated by the Yankee Atomic Electric Company in Rowe, Massachusetts. Surveys made by the U.S. Public Health Service after the reactors were in operation for about 10 years showed that there was no detectable residual radioactivity in the environs. Other reactors that have been studied have been found to expose people in the vicinity to no more than a few mrem per year, and these small levels should be reduced even further as the technology of reactor operation is improved.

A serious accident at the Three Mile Island Unit Two nuclear reactor early in 1979 resulted in worldwide concern about the danger from exposure of nearby Pennsylvania populations. Fortunately, despite extensive damage to the reactor core brought about by a series of mechanical and human errors, the radioactivity was well contained and exposures to the general population were minimal. The average dose, due to the accident, to the population in a 50-mi (80-km) radius was less than 2 mrem (20 μSv).

The principal source of this low-level radiation exposure in the past was gaseous plumes from boiling water reactors. It was at one time permissible to discharge the waste gases after only a 30-min holdup, and this permitted the discharge of short-lived noble gases in copious amounts, thereby accounting for the dose from the plume. However, in order to meet the more stringent standards set by the Nuclear Regulatory Commission in 1975, it is now necessary to provide longer holdup times to permit essentially complete decay of the shorter-lived noble gases.

The most significant nuclides in the liquid wastes are cesium-137 and cesium-134. The former is produced in both weapons tests and nuclear reactors. However, cesium-134 is produced only in nuclear reactors and provides a label by which it is possible to differentiate environmental cesium due to weapons testing from that due to reactors.

The standard methods of treating the low-level radioactive wastes are sufficient to limit the maximum dose to humans who consume fish or shellfish to a few mrem per year. The Environmental Protection Agency has forecast that by the year 2000 the per capita dose from the operation of the several hundred reactors (and associated fuel-reprocessing services) will be 0.4 mrem/year (4 μSv/year), which is less than 1% of the average dose people receive from nature and well within the range of variability in the natural radiation background. *See Radioactive waste management.*

Merril Eisenbud

Bibliography. M. Eisenbud, *Environmental Radioactivity*, 3d ed., 1987; R. L. Kathren, *Radioactivity in the Environment*, 1984; *Report of the President's Commission on the Accident at Three Mile Island*, 1979; V. Schultz and F. W. Whicker (eds.), *Radioactivity: Nuclear Energy and the Environment*, 2 vols., 1982; United Nations Scientific Committee on the Effects of Atomic Radiation, *Report to the General Assembly*, 1977.

Environmental toxicology

A broad field of study encompassing the production, fate, and effects of natural and synthetic pollutants in the environment. The breadth of this field depends on the definition of environment. It can be defined as narrowly as the home and workplace or as broadly as the entire Earth and its biosphere. Environmental toxicology is truly an interdisciplinary science. The effects of a pollutant on the environment depend on the amount released (the dose) and its chemical and physical properties. Pollutants can be grouped according to their origin and effects.

Nutrients. Pollution from nutrients is generally a problem of aquatic systems. Carbon, nitrogen, and phosphorus are essential nutrients and, when present in excess, can result in an overstimulation of microbial and plant growth. Nutrients enter the environment in runoff from fertilized agricultural areas, in effluents from municipal and industrial wastewater treatment facilities, and in dead and decaying plant material. Excess microbial growth can result in deoxygenation of a body of water. The overstimulation of algae and plant growth in aquatic systems due to excess nutrients of human origin is called cultural eutrophication. Decreased clarity of water, overgrowth of emergent vegetation, increased rate of sedimentation and filling-in of lake basins, and greatly shortened lifespan of an aquatic system are all characteristics of cultural eutrophication. *See Eutrophication.*

Microbial pollution. Pathogenic bacteria and protozoa can be a major source of pollution in areas that receive untreated sewage, items from ocean dumping, and improperly discarded hospital waste. Toxic metabolites of fungal origin (mycotoxins) are also potential pollutants. Most important of the broad range of mycotoxins are those that contaminate human food and the feed of domestic animals. These contaminants include the ergot alkaloids, tricothecins, and aflatoxins. Ergot alkaloids are produced by *Claviceps* spp. and are strong neurotoxic and vasoconstrictive agents. Tricothecins are produced by a variety of species of the genus *Fusarium* and are potent inflammatory agents and tissue irritants. Aflatoxins are produced by species of the genus *Aspergillus* and contaminate improperly stored grains and nuts. Aflatoxins have been implicated in a variety of diseases in poultry and humans, have caused cancer in experimental animals, and have been linked epidemiologically to cancer in humans. Aflatoxins are the only mycotoxins that have been regulated by the U.S. Food and Drug Administration.

Suspended solids. Forest fires, volcanic eruptions, and dust storms can be major sources of suspended materials. These materials can also originate in runoff from agricultural areas, construction and mining sites, and roads and other paved areas. Truck and automobile exhaust and industrial discharge to the atmosphere are also sources of suspended solids. These materials reduce the amount of light in the atmosphere and bodies of water, interfering with photosynthesis. Physical irritation and abrasion, and obliteration of habitat by silting are the primary toxic effects of suspended solids.

Atmospheric pollutants. Metabolic processes and natural combustion and thermal activity (such as forest fires and volcanoes) can release large amounts of gaseous by-products to the atmosphere. However, natural inputs are minor compared to atmospheric pollutants due to human activity. Although most anthropogenic air pollution is produced by the various forms of transportation, emissions from stationary sources of fuel combustion (for example, factories and power plants) are responsible for the greatest amount of hazardous materials released.

Sulfur oxides, a primary combustion product of coal, are converted to acids in the atmosphere and precipitated in rain. In areas of limited buffering capacity such as northeastern North America and Scandinavia, pH levels are known to be greatly reduced, with loss of forests and aquatic life. *See Acid rain*.

Nitrogen oxides are formed during high-temperature combustion of petroleum products in refining operations and internal combustion engines. As with sulfur oxides, nitrogen oxides can form acid precipitation. They can also react with hydrocarbons and sunlight to form ozone and peroxyacetyl nitrates, the major constituents of photochemical smog.

Chlorofluorocarbons are important refrigerants and aerosol propellants. These gases accumulate in the upper atmosphere and have been implicated in a decrease in the protective ozone layer surrounding the Earth. Because the ozone layer absorbs harmful ultraviolet radiation from the Sun, it has been predicted that a decrease in this layer will result in an increase in skin cancer. In addition, the biological structures of aquatic and terrestrial ecosystems are strongly influenced by solar ultraviolet radiation, and most organisms exist very near their threshold of tolerance. *See Atmospheric ozone*.

Carbon monoxide, formed by the incomplete combustion of fossil fuels, is primarily derived from transportation sources. It interferes with the oxygen-carrying function of hemoglobin in the bloodstream. The effects of carbon monoxide are acute but reversible, and thus pose a relatively small health hazard compared to other forms of atmospheric pollution. However, repeated anoxic episodes due to carbon monoxide can permanently damage the blood–brain barrier and the white matter of the brain.

Carbon dioxide is a by-product of respiration and fossil fuel combustion. Increasing amounts of carbon dioxide in the atmosphere have caused concern over a global warming trend, the so-called greenhouse effect. *See Air pollution; Greenhouse effect*.

Metals. All living organisms require certain metals for physiological processes. These elements, when present at concentrations above the level of homeostatic regulation, can be toxic. In addition, there are metals that are chemically similar to, but higher in molecular weight than, the essential metals (heavy metals). Metals can exert toxic effects by direct irritant activity, blocking functional groups in enzymes, altering the conformation of biomolecules, or displacement of essential metals in metalloenzymes.

Solvents. Organic solvents are used widely and in large amounts in industries, laboratories, and homes (see **table**). They are released to the atmosphere as vapor and can pose a significant inhalation hazard. Improper storage, use, and disposal have resulted in the contamination of surface and groundwaters and drinking water. *See Water pollution*.

Pesticides. The pesticides represent an important group of materials that can enter the environment as pollutants. They are highly toxic, and many nontarget organisms can suffer harmful effects if misuse or unintended release occurs. *See Pesticide*.

Insecticides. The most diverse group of pesticides is the insecticides and acaricides. Insecticides have been used for hundreds of years, but it has only been since World War II that synthetic insecticides have been widely used.

The chlorinated hydrocarbons include dichlorodiphenyl trichloroethane (DDT) and its analogs, the cyclodienes and related compounds, and the benzene hexachlorides (BHCs). Beginning in the 1940s, chlorinated hydrocarbons were used extensively in mosquito control and agriculture. These compounds exert their toxic effect by interfering with the transmission of nerve impulses, inhibiting the transport of ions across the axonal membrane. Many are very persistent in the environment and undergo biomagnification in food chains. Toxic effects on top predators such as birds and the contamination of human food supplies raised concern over their use. After the 1960s, most were replaced with other, less persistent compounds. *See Food web*.

Organophosphates inhibit the enzyme acetylcholinesterase, resulting in an overstimulation and excitation of nerves. Because of their mode of action, organophosphates are toxic not only to target insects but also to nontarget insects (bees and aquatic insects), birds, wildlife, and fish and other aquatic life. With few exceptions (malathion), organophosphates are toxic to mammals and humans. They are easily degraded and do not persist in the environment. However, because of their high nontarget organism toxicity, their use is limited to areas where undesired exposure can be minimized.

Carbamate insecticides exhibit neurotoxic action similar to the organophosphates, by inhibiting acetylcholinesterase. However, this action is more readily reversible than that of the organophosphates.

Botanical insecticides are natural and synthetic derivatives of toxic plant materials and have been used for hundreds of years. Nicotine and its analogs are neuroactive agents. Rotenones are electron-transport inhibitors and are used as insecticides and pesticides. Pyrethroid insecticides were originally derived from chrysanthemum plants; however, most pyrethroids in use today are synthetic derivatives of natural plant toxins. Pyrethroids are nerve poisons, acting through interference of ion transport along the axonal membrane. The pyrethroids are the most widely used in-

Uses and effects of selected organic solvents

Solvent	Uses	Effects
Aliphatic hydrocarbons		
Pentane, hexanes, heptanes, octanes	Commercial products and solvents	Depression of central nervous system and liver pathology
Halogenated aliphatic hydrocarbons		
Methylene chloride	Paint remover, aerosol solvent	Depression of central nervous system, respiratory poison
Chloroform	Chemical intermediate, solvent	Liver pathology, carcinogen
Carbon tetrachloride	Industrial and laboratory solvent	Lipid peroxidation, liver and renal pathology
Aromatic hydrocarbons		
Benzene	Organic synthesis, solvent, printing	Hematopoietic toxicity, immunosuppression, leukemia
Toluene	Solvent, chemical intermediate, paints, rubber	Narcotic, central nervous system pathology
Xylene	Solvent, chemical intermediate, pesticides, adhesives	Central nervous system pathology
Alcohols		
Methanol	Commercial and laboratory solvent, paints, fuel additive	Toxic metabolites (formaldehyde), optic nerve damage
Isopropyl alcohol	Cosmetics, glass cleaning solutions	Central nervous system depressant
Glycols		
Ethylene glycol	Heat exchangers, antifreeze, hydraulic fluids	Toxic metabolites

secticides, primarily because of their low mammalian toxicity. Although not very toxic to mammals, pyrethroids are extremely toxic to nontarget arthropods, such as bees, aquatic insects, and crustaceans, and to nonmammalian vertebrates such as fish.

Fumigants are volatile substances used as soil pesticides and to control insects in stored products and scale insects on citrus. Common fumigants include ethylene dibromide, ethylene dichloride, ethylene oxide, carbon disulfide, methyl bromide, hydrogen cyanide, phosphine, and chloropicrin. Because they are nonselective and toxic to humans, many fumigants are now restricted or banned.

Organic thiocyanate insecticides are mild general poisons, and have been used as fly sprays and fumigants that are also toxic to nontarget animals and plants. Dinitrophenols were important as early insecticides and acaricides and still have limited use as dormant acaricides. They are toxic to mammals and plants. Fluoroacetate derivatives are general toxicants that form lethal metabolic products.

Inorganic insecticides are general toxicants and have been largely replaced with synthetic organic insecticides. However, two classes of inorganic insecticides are still being used, arsenicals and fluorides. Common arsenicals include lead and calcium arsenates and sodium arsenite. Sodium fluoride, sodium fluoraluminate, and sodium fluorosilicate are common fluorides. Both groups are stomach poisons, increasing in toxicity with increasing metal content. *See In-secticide.*

Herbicides. These chemicals are selectively toxic to plants. Examples include the chlorophenoxy growth stimulators 2,4-dichlorophenoxyacetic acid (2,4-D) and 2,4,5-trichlorophenoxyacetic acid (2,4,5-T), the protein synthesis–inhibiting alachlor, the defoliant paraquat, and the chlorophenolic contact herbicides. Although herbicides have in large part not been an environmental problem because of their selectivity and low persistence, some can be very toxic to nontarget

organisms. Paraquat, for example, can cause severe pulmonary symptoms. *See Herbicide.*

Fungicides. Fungicidal compounds are used widely to treat seed grains and wood. Common ones are pentachlorophenol and the organomercurials.

Fossil fuels. Coal and pretroleum-derived materials and by-products are major environmental pollutants. The world's economy is highly dependent on fossil fuels in energy production, industry, and transportation. Widespread use has led to enormous releases to the environment of distillate fuels, crude oils, runoff from coal piles, exhaust from internal combustion engines, emissions from coal-fired power plants, industrial emissions, and emissions from municipal incinerators. Point-source leaks and spills, and non-point-source emissions have resulted in environmental contamination with millions of tons of petroleum hydrocarbons each year. Spills of crude oil and fuels have caused wide-ranging damage in the marine and fresh-water environments. Oil slicks and tar in shore areas and beaches can ruin the esthetic value of entire regions.

The toxicity of polycyclic aromatic hydrocarbons is perhaps one of the most serious long-term problems associated with the use of petroleum. They comprise a large class of petroleum compounds containing two or more benzene rings. They are present in fossil fuels and are formed in the incomplete combustion of organic materials. Polycyclic aromatic hydrocarbons are formed in nature by long-term, low-temperature chemical reactions in sedimentary deposits of organic materials and in high-temperature events such as volcanoes and forest fires. The major source of this pollution is, however, human activity. Polycyclic aromatic hydrocarbons accumulate in soil, sediment, and biota. At high concentrations, they can be acutely toxic by disrupting membrane function. Many cause sunlight-induced toxicity in humans and fish and other aquatic organisms. In addition, long-term, chronic toxicity has been demonstrated in a wide variety of organisms. Through metabolic activation, some polycyclic aromatic hydrocarbons form reactive intermediates that bind to deoxyribonucleic acid (DNA). For this reason, many of these hydrocarbons are mutagenic, teratogenic, or carcinogenic. They are also suspected of interfering in the reproduction of aquatic life. Low rates of reproduction and high rates of larval deformities and mortality have been observed in fish exposed to polycyclic aromatic hydrocarbons. *See Mutagens and carcinogens.*

Other synthetic organic compounds. Polychlorinated biphenyls (PCBs) are produced by the chlorination of biphenyl, giving rise to mixtures of up to 210 possible products. They have been used worldwide in electrical equipment, vacuum pumps, hydraulic fluids, heat-transfer systems, lubricants, and inks. The related polybrominated biphenyls (PBBs) have been used as fire retardants. Major sources of polychlorinated biphenyls have included leaks from waste disposal facilities, vaporization during combustion, and disposal of industrial fluids. They have been identified in environments and organisms worldwide. Being lipid-soluble, they accumulate in the biota, and biomagnification in food chains can be demonstrated. They induce activity in hepatic enzymes and cause long-term liver damage, including cancer. Their use has been largely restricted or eliminated. Environmental concentrations are decreasing, but with their persistence they remain significant pollutants. *See Polychlorinated biphenyls.*

Chlorinated dibenzo-*p*-dioxins and dibenzofurans are formed during the heating of chlorophenols, and have been identified as potential contaminants in the herbicide 2,4,5-T. They can be formed during the incineration of municipal wastes, polychlorinated biphenyls, or plant materials treated with chlorophenols. In certain organisms (guinea pig) they are some of the most toxic known substances, exhibiting hepatotoxic, carcinogenic, and immunosuppressive activity. The dioxins and dibenzofurans have been implicated in several spectacular incidents, including the spraying of Agent Orange during the Vietnam War, the Yusho disease in Japan, the Seveso herbicide plant explosion in Italy, and the discovery of contamination at Love Canal, New York, at Times Beach, Missouri, and in the Great Lakes region of North America. *See Environmental engineering.*

James T. Oris

Bibliography. D. W. Connell and G. J. Miller, *Chemistry and Ecotoxicology of Pollution,* 1984; J. Doull, C. D. Klaassen, and M. O. Amdur (eds.), *Casarett and Doull's Toxicology: The Basic Science of Poisons,* 2d ed., 1980; F. E. Guthrie and J. J. Perry (eds.), *Introduction to Environmental Toxicology,* 1980; E. Hodgson and P. E. Levi, *A Textbook of Modern Toxicology,* 1987; F. Matsumura, *Toxicology of Insecticides,* 1975; T. N. Veziroglu (ed.), *The Biosphere: Problems and Solutions,* 1984.

Eolian landforms

Topographic features generated by the wind. The most commonly seen eolian landforms are sand dunes created by transportation and accumulation of windblown sand. Blankets of wind-deposited loess, consisting of fine-grained silt, are less obvious than dunes, but cover extensive areas in some parts of the world.

Movement of particles by wind. Although wind is not capable of moving large particles, it can transport large amounts of sand, silt, and clay, especially in desert or coastal areas where loose sand and finer particles are exposed at the surface as a result of the scarcity of vegetation or the continuous supply of loose material.

The size of particles which can be moved by wind depends primarily on wind velocity. Swirls and eddies associated with wind turbulence have upward components of movement which pick up loose material. The velocity of upward gusts is usually not very constant, but generally averages about 20% of mean wind velocity. Where turbulence is strong enough to overcome the force of gravity, the particles remain suspended in the air and are carried downwind. Because the maximum size of a particle suspended in the air varies with the square of its radius, wind is generally limited to the movement of material of sand size or smaller, and suspended particles are quite sensitive to changes in wind velocity. Thus, the wind is an effective winnowing agent, separating finer from coarser material, and grain size of eolian deposits is typically quite uniform.

Windblown sand seldom rises more than a few feet above the ground. However, fine silt and dust may rise to altitudes of hundreds or thousands of feet during desert windstorms. Individual sand grains rise and fall as they are blown downwind and travel in a bouncing fashion known as saltation. Sand grains bouncing along the ground within a few feet of the surface abrade materials with which they collide. Such natural sand blasting produces polished, pitted, grooved, and faceted rocks known as ventifacts, and mutual abrasion of the sand results in highly rounded, spherical grains. *See Desert.*

Silt- and clay-sized particles can be held in suspension much longer than sand grains, and thus may travel long distances before settling out.

Sand dunes. Where abundant loose sand is available for the wind to carry, sand dunes develop. As soon as enough sand accumulates in one place, it interferes with the movement of air and a wind shadow is produced which contributes to the shaping of the pile of sand. Sand grains bounce up the windward side of the sand pile until they reach the crest, then tumble down the lee side in the wind shadow behind the crest. Sand trapped in the wind shadow accumulates until the slope reaches the angle of repose for loose sand, where any additional increase in slope causes sliding of the sand and development of a slip face. Dunes advance downwind by erosion of sand on the windward side and redeposition on the slip face. Dunes may have various shapes, depending on wind conditions, vegetation, and sand supply.

Fine-grained deposits. The fine silt and clay winnowed out from coarser sand is often blown longer distances before coming to rest as a blanket of loess mantling the preexisting topography. Thick deposits of loess are most often found in regions downwind from glacial outwash plains or alluvial valleys such as the Mississippi Valley, southeastern Washington, and portions of Europe, China, and the former Soviet Union.

Don J. Easterbrook

Bibliography. R. A. Bagnold, *The Physics of Blown Sand and Desert Dunes,* 1971; R. V. Cooke, *Geomophology in Deserts,* 1974; S. D. Tuttle, *Landforms and Landscapes,* 1980.

Erosion

The loosening and transportation of rock debris at the Earth's surface. Erosion is one of the most important geologic processes at the surface and operates to move earth materials to lower levels. Agents of erosion include moving surface, ground, and ocean waters; ice; wind; organisms; temperature changes; and gravity. They work by moving earth materials in two ways: physically, that is, without change in chemical composition of the earth materials; and chemically, in which the rock materials have been dissolved or decomposed. The energies driving the forces of erosion are dominantly solar (which includes temperature change, raising moisture for precipitation, wind, and waves); gravitational, aided by rotation of the Earth; and chemical. Counteracting the effects of erosion are geologic processes which raise the Earth's surface, such as volcanism (volcanoes and intrusions) and diastrophism (folding, faulting, plate tectonics).

Erosion develops and alters landscapes and scenery, and modifies agricultural practice and human habitats. It slowly lowers the surface of the Earth, on the average 3 ft (1 m) in the order of several thousands of years; but local movements, such as landslides and mud slumps, may occur very rapidly. As a high region is lowered by erosion, it gradually progresses through an erosion cycle in topographic stages conceptually characterized by distinctive groups of landforms. These stages were named youthful, mature, and old age by W. M. Davis. He considered the lowering to be simultaneously effective over the whole region. Alternatively, W. Penck and L. King described the erosional process as one in which laterally directed planation and parallel retreat of slopes were the most prominent mechanisms.

Within a given region, distinctive landforms, enjoyed as scenery, are produced by stream erosion, mountain glaciation, continental glaciation, wind (desert) erosion, landslides and mass wastage, and groundwater solution (karstic) features. SEE STREAM TRANSPORT AND DEPOSITION.

Not only does erosion affect human beings, but the human race in turn is an almost violent agent of erosion, with its practices of agriculture, overgrazing, lumbering, and urban development on continental land slopes and coastal topographic features. For ages—from ancient Greece, Egypt, Babylonia, and China, to modern nations with their dust bowls and intensive tillage practices—the human race has been the cause of rapid (in geologic time) and sometimes disastrous episodes of erosion. SEE SOIL CONSERVATION.

In long enough time, erosion would tend to reduce the Earth's surface to a subdued plain—except that geologic processes driven by internal earth energy presumably will reactivate the geomorphic cycle by reelevating the land. SEE GEOMORPHOLOGY.

W. D. Keller

Estuarine oceanography

The study of the physical, chemical, biological, and geological characteristics of estuaries. An estuary is a semienclosed coastal body of water which has a free connection with the sea and within which the seawater is measurably diluted by fresh water derived from land drainage. Many characteristic features of estuaries extend into the coastal areas beyond their mouths, and because the techniques of measurement and analysis are similar, the field of estuarine oceanography is often considered to include the study of some coastal waters which are not strictly, by the above definition, estuaries. Also, semienclosed bays and lagoons exist in which evaporation is equal to or exceeds fresh-water inflow, so that the salt content is either equal to that of the sea or exceeds it. Hypersaline lagoons have been termed negative estuaries, whereas those with precipitation and river inflow equaling evaporation have been called neutral estuaries. Positive estuaries, in which river inflow and precipitation exceed evaporation, form the majority.

Topographic classification. Embayments are the result of fairly recent changes in sea level. During the Pleistocene ice age, much of the seawater was locked up in continental ice sheets, and the sea surface stood about 300 ft (100 m) below its present level. In areas not covered with ice, the rivers incised their valleys to this base level; and during the ensuing Flandrian Transgression, when the sea level rose at about 3 ft (1 m) per century, these valleys became inundated. Much of the variation in form of the resulting estuaries depends on the volumes of sediment that the river or the nearby coastal erosion has contributed to fill the valleys.

Where river flow and sediment discharge were high, the valleys have become completely filled and even built out into deltas. Generally, deltas are best developed in areas where the tidal range is small and where the currents cannot easily redistribute the sediment the rivers introduce. They occur mainly in tropical and subtropical areas where river discharge is seasonally very high. The distributaries, or passes, of the delta are generally shallow, and often the shallowest part is a sediment bar at the mouths of the distributaries. The Mississippi and the Niger are examples of this type of delta.

Where sediment discharge was less, the estuaries are unfilled, although possibly they are still being filled. These are drowned river valleys or coastal plain estuaries, and they still retain the topographic features of river valleys, having a branching, dendritic, though meandering, outline and a triangular cross section, and widening regularly toward the mouth, which is often restricted by spits. River discharge tends to be reasonably steady throughout the year, and sediment discharge is generally small. These estuaries occur in areas of high tidal range, where the currents have helped to keep the estuaries clear of sediment. They are typical of temperate regions such as the east coast of North America and northwestern Europe, examples being the Chesapeake Bay system, the Thames, and the Gironde.

In areas where glaciation was active, the river valleys were overdeepened by glaciers, and fiords were created. A characteristic of these estuaries is the rock bar or sill at the mouth that can be as little as a few tens of meters deep. Inside the mouth, however, they can be at least 1800 ft (600 m) deep and can extend hundreds of kilometers inland. Fiords are typical of Norway and the Canadian Pacific coast.

There is another estuarine type, called the bar-built estuary. These are formed on low coastlines where extensive lagoons have narrow connecting passages or inlets to the sea. Within the shallow lagoons the tidal currents are small, but the deep inlets have higher currents. Again, a sediment bar is generally present across the entrance. In tropical areas the lagoons can be hypersaline during the hot season. They are typical of the southern states of the United States and of parts of Australia.

Estuaries are ephemeral features since great alterations can be wrought by small changes in sea level. If the present ice caps were to melt, the sea level would rise an estimated 90 ft (30 m), and the effect on the form and distribution of estuaries would be drastic.

Physical structure and circulation. Within estuaries, the river discharge interacts with the seawater, and river water and seawater are mixed by the action of tidal motion, by wind stress on the surface, and by the river discharge forcing its way toward the sea. The difference in salinity between river water and seawater—about 35 parts per thousand—creates a difference in density of about 2%. Even though this difference is small, it is sufficient to cause horizontal pressure gradients within the water which affect the way it flows. Density differences caused by temperature variations are comparatively smaller. Salinity is consequently a good indicator of estuarine mixing and the patterns of water circulation. Obviously, there are likely to be differences in the circulation within estuaries of the same topographic type which are caused by differences in river discharge and tidal range. The action of wind on the water surface is an important mixing mechanism in shallow estuaries, particularly in lagoons; but generally its effect on estuarine circulation is only temporary, although it can produce considerable variability and thus make interpretation of field results difficult. *See Seawater.*

Salt-wedge estuaries. Fresh water, being less dense than seawater, tends to flow outward over the surface of seawater, which penetrates as a salt wedge along the bottom into the estuary (**Fig. 1**). This creates a vertical salinity stratification, with a narrow zone of sharp salinity change, called a halocline, between the two water masses which can reach 30 parts per thousand in 1½ ft (0.5 m). If the sea is tideless, the water in the salt wedge is almost motionless. However, if the surface layer flowing toward the sea has a sufficiently high velocity, it can create interfacial waves on the halocline. These waves break, ejecting small parcels of salt water into the fresher surface layer; this process is called entrainment, and it occurs all along the halocline. No fresh water is mixed downward; thus the salinity within the salt wedge is almost constant along the estuary. However, the salt wedge loses salt water which is mixed into the surface layer and discharged into the sea. Consequently, for this loss to be replaced, there must be a compensatory flow of salt water toward the head of the estuary within the salt wedge, but of a magnitude much less than that of the flow in the surface layer. There is a considerable velocity gradient near the halocline as a result of the friction between the two layers. Consequently, the position of the salt wedge will change according to the magnitude of the flow in the surface layer, that is, according to the river discharge. The Mississippi River is an example of a salt-wedge estuary. When the flow in the Mississippi is low, the salt wedge extends more than 100 mi (160 km) inland, but with high discharge, the salt wedge only extends a mile or so above the river mouth. Some bar-built estuaries, in areas of restricted tidal range and at times of high river discharge, as well as deltas, are typical salt-wedge types.

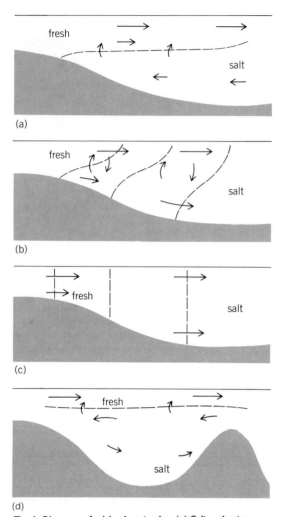

Fig. 1. Diagrams of mixing in estuaries. (a) Salt-wedge type. (b) Partially mixed type. (c) Well-mixed type. (d) Fiord.

Partially mixed estuaries. When tidal movements are appreciable, the whole mass of water in the estuary moves up and down with a tidal periodicity of about 12½ h. Considerable friction occurs between the bed of the estuary and the tidal currents, and this causes turbulence. The turbulence tends to mix the water column more thoroughly than entrainment does, although little is known of the relationship of the exchanges to the salinity and velocity gradients. However, the turbulent mixing not only mixes the salt water into the fresher surface layer but also mixes the fresher water downward. This causes the salinity to decrease toward the head of the estuary in the lower layer and also progressively increase toward the sea in the surface layer. As a consequence, the vertical salinity gradient is considerably less than that in salt-wedge estuaries. In the surface, seaward-flowing layer, the river discharge moves toward the sea; but because the salinity of the water has been increased by mixing during its passage down the estuary, the discharge at the mouth can be several times the river discharge. To provide this volume of additional water, the compensating inflow must also be much higher than that in the salt-wedge estuary. The velocities involved in these movements are only on the order of a few centimeters per second, but the tidal velocities can be on the order of a hundred centimeters per second. Consequently, the only way to evaluate the effect of turbulent mixing on the circulation pattern is to average out the effect of the tidal oscillation, which requires considerable precision and care. The resulting residual or mean flow will be related to the river discharge, although the tidal response of the estuary can give additional contributions to the mean flow. The tidal excursion of a water particle at a point will be related to the tidal prism, the volume between high- and low-tide levels upstream of that point; and the instantaneous cross-sectional velocity at any time will be related to the rate of change of the tidal prism upstream of the section. In details, the velocities across the section can differ considerably. It has been found that in the Northern Hemisphere the seaward-flowing surface water keeps to the right bank of the estuary, looking downstream, and the landward-flowing salt intrusion is concentrated on the left-hand side (**Fig. 2**). This is caused by the Coriolis force, which deflects the moving water masses toward the right. Of possibly greater importance, however, is the effect of topography, because the curves in the estuary outline tend to concentrate the flow toward the outside of the bends. Thus, in addition to a vertical circulation, there is a horizontal one, and the halocline slopes across the estuary. Because the estuary has a prismatic cross section, the saline water is concentrated in the deep channel and the fresher water is discharged in the shallower areas. Examples of partially mixed estuaries are the rivers of the Chesapeake Bay system.

Well-mixed estuaries. When the tidal range is very large, there is sufficient energy available in the turbulence to break down the vertical salinity stratification completely, so that the water column becomes vertically homogeneous. In this type of estuary there can be lateral variations in salinity and in velocity,

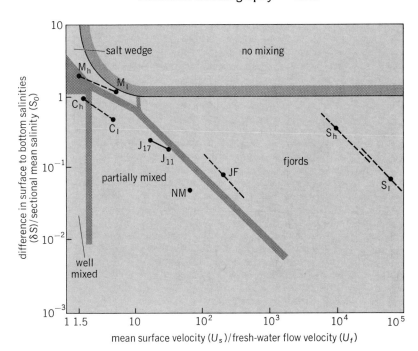

Fig. 3. Classification diagram for estuaries. An estuary appears as a line on the diagram; the upper reaches are less well mixed than the lower sections. Subscript letters refer to high (h) and low (l) river discharge; subscript numbers are distances from the mouth. J = James River; M = Mississippi; C = Columbia River; NM = Narrows of the Mersey; S = Silver Bay; JF = Strait of Juan de Fuca. (*After D. V. Hansen and M. Rattray, Jr., New dimensions in estuary classification, Limnol. Oceanogr., 11:319–326, 1966*)

with a well-developed horizontal circulation; or if the lateral mixing is also intense, the estuary can become sectionally homogeneous (also called a one-dimensional estuary). Because there is no landward residual flow in the sectionally homogeneous estuary, the upstream movement of salt is produced during the tidal cycle by salty water being trapped in bays and creeks and bleeding back into the main flow during the ebb. This mechanism spreads out the salt water, but it is probably effective only for a small number of tidal excursions inland.

Fiords. Because fiords are so deep and restricted at their mouths, tidal oscillation affects only their near-surface layer to any great extent. The amount of turbulence created by oscillation is small, and the mixing process is achieved by entrainment. Thus fiords can be considered as salt-wedge estuaries with an effectively infinitely deep lower layer. The salinity of the bottom layer will not vary significantly from mouth to head, and the surface fresh layer is only a few tens of meters deep. When the sill is deep enough not to restrict circulation, the inflow of water occurs just below the halocline, with an additional slow outflow near the bottom. When circulation is restricted, the replenishment of the deeper water occurs only occasionally, sometimes on an annual cycle; and between the inflows of coastal water, the bottom layer can become anoxic.

The descriptive classification of estuaries outlined above depends on the relative intensities of the tidal and river flows and the effect that these flows have on stratification. A quantitative comparison between estuaries can be made using the diagram of **Fig. 3**, which is based on a stratification and a circulation parameter.

Flushing and pollution-dispersal prediction. Much research into estuarine characteristics is aimed at pre-

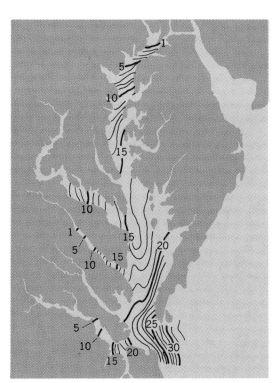

Fig. 2. Typical surface salinity distribution in Chesapeake Bay. (*After H. E. Landsberg, ed., Advances in Geophysics, vol. 1, Academic Press, 1952*)

dicting the distribution of effluents discharged into estuaries. Near the mouth of a partially mixed estuary, the salt water is only slightly diluted, and in order for a volume of fresh water equivalent to the river flow to be discharged, a much greater volume of mixed water must flow seaward. Consequently, estuaries are more effective in diluting and removing pollutants than rivers. It has been observed that increased river flow causes both a downstream movement of the saline intrusion and a more rapid exchange of water with the sea. The latter effect occurs because increased river discharge increases stratification; increased stratification diminishes vertical mixing and enhances the flow toward the sea in the surface layer. Thus, increased river discharge has the effect of increasing the volume of fresh water accumulated in the estuary, but to a lesser extent than the increase of the discharged volume. Obviously, it takes some time for the fresh water from the river to pass through the estuary. The flushing time can be determined by dividing the total volume of fresh water accumulated in the estuary by the river flow. For most estuaries the flushing time is between 5 and 10 days.

If a conservative, nondecaying pollutant is discharged at a constant rate into an estuary, the effluent concentration in the water moving past will vary with the tidal current velocity, and will spread out by means of turbulent mixing. The concentrations will be increased during the next half cycle as the water passes the discharge point again. After several tidal cycles a steady-state distribution will be achieved, with the highest concentration near the discharge point. Concentrations will decrease downstream, but not as quickly as they decrease upstream. However, the details of the distribution will depend largely on whether the discharge is of dense or light fluid and whether it is discharged into the lower or upper layer. Since its movement will be modified by the estuarine circulation, the effluent will be more concentrated in the lower layer upstream of the discharge point, and it will be more concentrated in the upper layer downstream. To obtain maximum initial dilution, a light effluent would have to be discharged near the estuary bed so that it would mix rapidly as it rose.

For nonconservative pollutants, such as coliform sewage bacteria, prediction becomes more difficult. The population of bacteria dies progressively through the action of sunlight, and concentrations diminish with time as well as by dilution. The faster the mixing, the larger the populations at any distance from the point of introduction, since less decay occurs.

Because of the poor mixing of fresh water into a salt-wedge estuary, an effluent introduced in the surface layer will be flushed from the estuary before it contaminates the lower layer, provided that it is not too dense.

Mathematical modeling. Increasingly, mathematical modeling is being used, with reasonable success in many instances, to predict effluent dispersal with the minimum amount of field data. Although the governing mathematical equations can be stated, they cannot be solved in their full form because there are too many unknowns. Consequently, to reduce the number of unknowns, various assumptions are made, including some form of spatial averaging to reduce a three-dimensional problem to two dimensions or even one dimension. The exchange ratios, about which little is known, are assumed constant, or are considered as a simple variable in space, and are altered so that the model fits the available prototype data.

The first step is usually to model the flow and salinity distribution. Because the density field is important in determining the flow characteristics, density and flow are interlinked problems. Then, for pollutant studies, the pollutant is assumed to act in the same manner as fresh or salt water, or the flow parameters are used with appropriate exchange coefficients to predict the distribution. Simple models consider the mean flow to be entirely the result of river discharge, and tidal flow to be given by the tidal prism. Segmentation is based on simple mixing concepts and crude exchange ratios. Salinity and pollutant concentrations can then be calculated for cross-sectionally averaged and vertically homogeneous conditions by using the absolute minimum of field data. These models are known as tidal prism models. One-dimensional models are very similar, but use a finer grid system and need better data for validation. Two-dimensional models either assume vertical homogeneity and allow lateral variations, or vice versa. There are difficulties in including the effects of tidally drying areas and junctions; the models become increasingly costly and require extensive prototype data, but they are more realistic. The ideal situation of modeling the flow and salinity distribution accurately simply on the basis of knowledge about the topography, the river discharge, and the tidal range at a number of points is still a long way off.

Estuarine environments. Estuarine ecological environments are complex and highly variable when compared with other marine environments. They are richly productive, however. Because of the variability, fewer species can exist as permanent residents in this environment than in some other marine environments, and many of these species are shellfish that can easily tolerate short periods of extreme conditions. Motile species can escape the extremes. A number of commercially important marine forms are indigenous to the estuary, and the environment serves as a spawning or nursery ground for many other species.

River inflow provides a primary source of nutrients such as nitrates and phosphates which are more concentrated than in the sea. These nutrients are utilized by plankton through the photosynthetic action of sunlight. Because of the energetic mixing, production is maintained throughout, in spite of the high levels of suspended sediment which restrict light penetration to a relatively thin surface layer. Plankton concentrations can be extremely high, and when they are, higher levels of the food web—filter-feeding shellfish and young fish—have an ample food source. The rich concentrations provide large quantities of organic detritus in the sediments which can be utilized by bottom-feeding organisms and which can be stirred up into the main body of the water by tidal action. For a more complete treatment of the ecology of estuarine environments from the biological viewpoint *SEE MARINE ECOLOGY.*

There is a close relationship between the circulation pattern in estuaries and the faunal distributions. Several species of plankton peculiar to estuaries appear to confine their distribution to the estuary by using the water-circulation pattern; pelagic larvae of oysters are transported in a similar manner. The fingerling fish (*Micropogon undulatus*), spawned in the coastal waters off the eastern coast of the United States, are carried into the estuarine nursery areas by the landward residual bottom flow.

Estuarine sediments. The patterns of sediment distribution and movement depend on the type of estuary and on the estuarine topography. The type of sediment brought into the estuary by the rivers, by erosion of the banks, and from the sea is also important; and the relative importance of each of these sources may change along the estuary. Fine-grained material will move in suspension and will follow the residual water flow, although there may be deposition and re-erosion during times of locally low velocities. The coarser-grained material will travel along the bed and will be affected most by high velocities and, consequently, in estuarine areas, will normally tend to move in the direction of the maximum current.

Fine-grained material. Fine-grained clay material, about 2 micrometers in size, brought down the rivers in suspension, can undergo alterations in its properties in the sea. Base (cation) exchange with the seawater can alter the chemical composition of some clay minerals; also, because the particles have surface ionic charges, they are attracted to one another and can flocculate. Flocculation depends on the salinity of the water and on the concentration of particles. It is normally complete in salinities in excess of 4 parts per thousand, and with suspended sediment concentrations above about 300 ppm (1 mg/liter), and has the effect of increasing the settling velocities of the particles. The flocs have diameters larger than 30 μm, but effective densities of about 1.1 g/cm^3 because of the water closely held within. If the material is carried back into regions of low salinity, the flocculation is reversed, and the flocs can be disrupted by turbulence. In sufficiently high concentrations, the suspended sediment can suppress turbulence. The sediment then settles as layers which can reach concentrations as high as 300,000 ppm and which are visible as a distinctive layer of ''fluid mud'' on echo-sounder recordings. At low concentrations, aggregation of particles occurs mainly by biological action.

Turbidity maximum. A characteristic feature of partially mixed estuaries is the presence of a turbidity maximum. This is a zone in which the suspended sediment concentrations are higher than those either in the river or farther down the estuary. This zone, positioned in the upper estuary around the head of the salt intrusion and associated with mud deposition in the so-called mud reaches, is often related to wide tidal mud flats and saltings. The position of the turbidity maximum changes according to changes in river discharge, and is explained in terms of estuarine circulation. Suspended sediment is introduced into the estuary by the residual downstream flow in the river. In the upper estuary, mixing causes an exchange of suspended sediment into the upper layer, where there is a seaward residual flow causing downstream transport. In the middle estuary, the sediment settles into the lower layer in areas of less vigorous mixing to join sediment entering from the sea on the landward residual flow. It then travels in the salt intrusion back to the head of the estuary. This recirculation is very effective for sorting the sediment, which is of exceedingly uniform mineralogy and settling velocity. Flocs with low settling velocities tend to be swept out into the coastal regions and onto the continental shelf. The heavier or larger flocs tend to be deposited.

The concentrations change with tidal range and during the tidal cycle, and fluid muds can occur within the area of the turbidity maximum if concentrations become sufficiently high. During the tidal cycle, as the current diminishes, individual flocs can settle and adhere to the bed, or fluid muds can form. The mud consolidates slightly during the slack water period, and as the current increases at the next stage of the tide, erosion may not be intense enough to remove all of the material deposited. A similar cycle of deposition and erosion occurs during the spring-neap tidal cycle. Generally, there is more sediment in suspension in the turbidity maximum than is required to complete a year's sedimentation on the estuary bed.

Mud flats and tidal marshes. The area of the turbidity maximum is generally well protected from waves, and there are often wide areas of mud flats and tidal marshes (**Fig. 4**). These areas also exchange considerable volumes of fine sediment with sediment in suspension in the estuary. At high water the flats are covered by shallow water, and there is often a long stand of water level which gives the sediment time to settle and reach the bottom, where it adheres or is trapped by plants or by filter-feeding animals. The ebb flow is concentrated in the winding creeks and channels. At low water there is not enough time for the sediment to settle, and it is distributed over the tidal flats during the incoming tide. Thus there is a progressive movement of the fine material onto the mud flats by a process that depends largely on the time delay between sediment that is beginning to settle and sediment that is actually reaching the bed. The tidal channels migrate widely, causing continual erosion. Thus, there is a constant exchange of material between one part of the marshes and another by means of the turbidity maximum. As the muds that are eroded are largely anaerobic, owing to their very low permeability, the turbidity maximum is an area with reduced amounts of dissolved oxygen in the water.

Coarse-grained material. Coarser materials such as quartz sand grains that do not flocculate travel along the bed. Those coming down the river will stop at the tip of the salt intrusion, where the oscillating tidal

Fig. 4. Aerial photograph of tidal flats showing the areas of pans, marshes, and vegetation between the channels, Scolt Head Island, England. (*Photograph by J. K. St. Joseph, Crown copyright reserved*)

velocities are of equal magnitude at both flood and ebb. Ideally, coarser material entering from the sea on the landward bottom flow will also stop at the tip of the salt intrusion, which becomes an area of shoaling, with a consequent decrease of grain size inland. However, normally the distribution of the tidal currents is too complex for this pattern to be clear. Especially in the lower part of the estuary, lateral variations in velocity can be large. The flood and ebb currents preferentially take separate channels, forming a circulation pattern that the sediment also tends to follow. The channels shift their positions in an apparently consistent way, as do the banks between them. This sorts the sediment and restricts the penetration of bed-load material into the estuary.

Salt-wedge patterns. In salt-wedge estuaries the river discharge of sediment is much larger, though generally markedly seasonal. Both suspended and bed-load material are important. The bed-load sediment is deposited at the tip of the salt wedge, but because the position of the salt wedge is so dependent on river discharge, the sediments are spread over a wide area. At times of flood, the whole mass of accumulated sediment can be moved outward and deposited seaward of the mouth. Because of the high sedimentation rates, the offshore slopes are very low, and the sediment has a very low bearing strength. Under normal circumstances, the suspended sediment settles through the salt wedge, and there is a zonation of decreasing grain size with distance down the salt wedge, but changes in river flow seldom allow this process to occur.

Fiord patterns. Sedimentation often occurs only at the heads of fiords, where river flow introduces coarse and badly sorted sediment. The sediment builds out into deltalike fans, and slumping on the slopes of the fan carries the sediment into deep water. Much of the rest of the fiord floor is bare rock or only thinly covered with fine sediment.

Bar-built estuary patterns. Bar-built estuaries are a very varied sedimentary environment. The high tidal currents in the inlets produce coarse lag deposits, and sandy tidal deltas are produced at either end of the inlets, where the currents rapidly diminish. In tropical areas, the muds that accumulate in the lagoons can be very rich in chemically precipitated calcium carbonate.

K. R. Dyer

Bibliography. R. S. K. Barnes and J. Green (eds.), *The Estuarine Environment*, 1972; K. R. Dyer, Coastal and Estuarine Sediment Dynamics, 1988; K. R. Dyer, *Estuaries: A Physical Introduction*, 1973; K. R. Dyer (ed.), *Estuarine Hydrography and Sedimentation*, 1980; B. J. Neilson and E. L. Cronin (eds.), *Estuaries and Nutrients*, 1981; D. A. Wolfe (ed.), *Estuarine Variability*, 1986.

Eutrophication

The deterioration of the esthetic and life-supporting qualities lakes and estuaries, caused by excessive fertilization from effluents high in phosphorus, nitrogen, and organic growth substances. Algae and aquatic plants become excessive, and when they decompose, a sequence of objectional features arises. Water for consumption from such lakes must be filtered and treated. Diversion of sewage, better utilization of manure, erosion control, improved sewage treatment and harvesting of the surplus aquatic crops alleviate the symptoms. Prompt public action is essential. *See Water conservation.*

Extent of problem. In inland lakes this problem is due in large part to excessive but inadvertent introduction of domestic and industrial wastes, runoff from fertilized agricultural and urban areas, precipitation, and groundwaters. The interaction of the natural process with the artificial disturbance caused by human activities complicates the overall problem and leads to an accelerated rate of deterioration in lakes. Since population increase necessitates an expanded utilization of lakes and streams, cultural eutrophication has become one of the major water resource problems in the United States and throughout the world. A more thorough understanding must be obtained of the processes involved. Without this understanding and the subsequent development of methods of control, the possibility of losing many of the desirable qualities and beneficial properties of lakes and streams is great. *See Water pollution.*

Cultural eutrophication is reflected in changes in species composition, population sizes, and productivity in groups of organisms throughout the aquatic ecosystem. Thus the biological changes which are caused by excessive fertilization are of considerable interest from both the practical and academic viewpoints. *See Fresh-water ecosystem; Lake; Limnology.*

Phytoplankton. One of the primary responses to eutrophication is apparent in the phytoplankton, or suspended algae, in lakes. The nature of this response can be examined by comparing communities in disturbed and undisturbed lakes or by following changes in the community over a period of years during which nutrient input is increased. *See Ecological communities; Phytoplankton.*

The former approach was utilized in studies at the University of Wisconsin, in which the overall structure of the phytoplankton communities of the eutrophic Lake Mendota, at Madison, and the oligotrophic Trout Lake, in northern Wisconsin, was analyzed. These investigations showed that in the eutrophic lake the population of species is slightly lower, although the average size of organisms is considerably larger, indicating higher levels of production than in the oligotrophic lake. When compared in terms of an index of species diversity, the community of the eutrophic lake displayed values lower than those observed in the oligotrophic lake. Seasonal changes and bathymetric differences in the index of diversity were also more apparent in the eutrophic lake.

Often the low species diversity of the phytoplankton in eutrophic lakes is a result of high populations of blue-green algae, such as *Aphanizomenon flosaquae* and *Anabaena spiroides* in Lake Mendota. Frequently, however, species of diatoms such as *Fragillaria crotonensis* and *Stephanodiscus astrae* also attain high degrees of dominance in the community. Dense populations of the blue-green algae *Oscillatoria rubescens* were indicative of the deteriorating conditions in Lake Zurich (Switzerland) and Lake Washington (Seattle), but since diversion of sewage from these lakes, they are no longer a problem. The same species has been observed in several other lakes that have undergone varying degrees of cultural eutrophication. The relatively high nutrient concentrations in eutrophic waters appear to be capitalized on by one or two species that outcompete other species and periodically develop extremely high population levels. Because of the formation of gas vacuoles during metabolism, senescent forms of the blue-green algae rise to the surface of the lake and cause nuisance blooms.

In addition to nuisance scums in the pelagial, or open-water regions, the rooted aquatic plants and the attached algae of the littoral, or shoreward, region often prove to be equally troublesome in eutrophic lakes. Species of macrophytes, such as *Myriophyllum* and *Ceratophyllum*, and algal forms, such as *Cladophora*, frequently form dense mats of vegetation, making such areas unsuited for both practical and recreational uses.

Bottom fauna. Often in eutrophic lakes the bottom fauna display characteristics similar to those observed in the algal community. Changing environmental conditions appear to allow one or two species to attain high degrees of dominance in the community. Generally higher levels of production are associated with the change in structure of the community—the result being nuisance populations of organisms. In Lake Winnebago, in Wisconsin, for example, the lake fly or midge *Chironomus plumosus* develops extremely high populations, which as adults create an esthetic as well as an economic problem in nearby cities.

Great Lakes. It was generally thought that eutrophication would not be a major problem in large lakes because of the vast diluting effect of their size. However, there has been evidence that eutrophication is occurring in the lower Great Lakes. Furthermore, the undesirable changes in the biota appear to have been initiated in relatively recent years. Utilizing long-term records from Lake Erie, qualitative and quantitative changes have been observed in phytoplankton of that large body of water owing to cultural eutrophication. Total numbers of phytoplankton have increased more than threefold since 1920, while the dominant genera have changed from *Asterionella* and *Synedra* to *Melosira*, *Fragillaria*, and *Stephanodiscus*.

Other biological changes usually associated with the eutrophication process in small lakes have also been observed in the Great Lakes. Of the five lakes, Lake Erie has undergone the most noticeable changes due to eutrophication. In terms of annual harvests, commercially valuable species of fish, such as the lake herring or cisco, sauger, walleye, and blue pike, were replaced by less desirable species, such as the freshwater drum or sheepshead, carp, and smelt. Similarly, in the organisms living in the bottom sediments of Lake Erie, drastic changes in species composition have been observed.

Oxygen demand. It is apparent that the increase in organic matter production by the algae and plants in a lake undergoing eutrophication has ramifications throughout the aquatic ecosystem. Greater demand is placed on the dissolved oxygen in the water as the organic matter decomposes at the termination of life cycles. Because of this process, the deeper waters in the lake may become entirely depleted of oxygen, thereby destroying fish habitats and leading to the elimination of desirable species. The settling of particulate organic matter from the upper, productive layers changes the character of the bottom muds, also leading to the replacement of certain species by less desirable organisms. Of great importance is the fact that nutrients inadvertently introduced to a lake are for the most part trapped there and recycled in accelerated biological processes. Consequently, the damage done to a lake in a relatively short time requires a many-fold increase in time for recovery of the lake.

Action programs. Lake eutrophication represents a complex interaction of biological, physical, and chemical processes. The problem, therefore, necessitates basic research in a wide variety of scientific disciplines. Moreover, to be profitable, such research must be coordinated into well-integrated team-research efforts requiring extensive monetary support.

Studies are needed in such areas as monitoring the amount of those nutrients that reach critical levels in lake waters and lead to the development of nuisance growths of plants and algae. Nitrogen and phosphorus are undoubtedly important.

Sewage effluent is the major contributor of nitrogen and phosphorus to lakes, followed by runoff from manured and fertilized land. Considering nitrogen alone, rain adds more than any single source. Its nitrogen content comes from combustion engines and smokestacks. Where sewage effluent and agricultural drainage have been diverted from lakes, an improvement in nuisance conditions occurs. Dead lakes become alive again; hence this treatment is the first step in alleviation.

The conditions observed in lakes and streams reflect not only the processes operating within the body of water but also the metabolism and dynamics of the entire watershed or drainage basin. After precise identification of the critical nutrient compounds, it is necessary to determine the nutrient budget of the whole drainage basin before acting to alleviate the undesirable fertilization of a lake or stream.

Methods of treating sewage plant effluent are being explored, and further support for these efforts is justified. Agricultural practices such as low tillage reduces erosion, hence the amount of fertilizer in the runoff. *See* Erosion; Sewage treatment.

It is known that aquatic plants concentrate nutrients from the lake waters in their tissues. The removal or harvesting of aquatic plants in eutrophic lakes, consequently, is a good potential method for reducing nutrient levels in these lakes. Similarly, significant amounts of nitrogen and phosphorus are concentrated in fish flesh. Efficient methods of harvesting these organisms are important in impoverishing a well-fertilized lake.

Utilization or land disposal of farm manure is a major problem. Animal manures are largely unsewered, yet in the Midwest it is equivalent to the sewage of 350,000,000 people.

In addition to improvements in waste disposal, more research and development are needed on the profitable utilization of surplus algae, aquatic plants, fish, manure, and sewage. The overfertilized lake needs to be impoverished of its nutrients as well as protected from inflowing sources. Chemicals have been used to poison the plants and algae, but this is not a good conservation practice because the plants and algae rot and provide more nutrients. Moreover, eventual harm to other species has not been assessed.

It would seem desirable to set aside certain lake areas for research purposes. More information is needed to decide upon the best plans for allowing the domestic development of these areas with the least disturbance to the water resources. Steps will be necessary to devise optimum zoning laws and multiple-use programs in light of the intense economic and recreational uses made of water resources. Legislation and law enforcement in relation to public interactions undoubtedly will be a complex problem to overcome in this respect.

Cultural eutrophication is a paradoxical condition, since it is in large part due to human economic, agricultural, and recreational activities and at the same time eventually conflicts with these same activities of society in general.

Arthur D. Hasler

Bibliography. C. R. Goldman, *Limnology*, 1983; A. D. Hasler, *Causes and Correctives of Man-Made Eutrophication*, in *Ökologie und Lebensshutz in Internationaler Sicht*, 2d ed., 1983; G. E. Hutchinson, *A Treatise on Limnology*, vol. 1: *Geography and Physics of Lakes*, and vol. 2: *Chemistry of Lakes* 1975; J. R. Vallentyne, *The Algal Bowl*, 1974.

Fishery conservation

The supervision, management, or protection of the catching or taking of fishes or other aquatic organisms from lakes, rivers, or seas. Although it encompasses marine and fresh-water fisheries, the term is more often used in reference to fresh-water environments. Fishery conservation has been practiced for at least 2000 years, but the emphasis and technology associated with it have changed drastically, evolving from a concentration on species, geographic regulations, or prohibitions to a concept of total environmental management. Attempts to manage isolated species or specific fisheries have been replaced by efforts that consider the complex biological interactions and social and economic consequences of conservation and management. SEE MARINE FISHERIES.

Development of modern approach. Few advances in fishery conservation took place until the nineteenth century. Fishery resources were abundant, harvest technology was primitive, and demand was relatively low, and so the need to conserve was minimal. In the nineteenth century, however, increased demand accompanied by improved harvest technology and increased pollution caused by urbanization, industrialization, and changing agricultural practices prompted an increase in fishery conservation. Fishery resources had declined rapidly, especially in the large rivers and streams of developed countries. In the northeastern United States, commercial and recreational fisheries such as those for sturgeon and shad were reduced to the point that they ceased to be economically feasible. Concern about the extent and rate of decline of fishery resources led to the formation of international, federal, and state fishery conservation agencies. The U.S. Commission on Fish and Fisheries (now the Fish and Wildlife Service) was established in 1871, and state conservation agencies were created throughout the United States. They conducted surveys and proposed regulations to protect wildlife and fishery resources, including prohibitions against taking fish below a minimum size, limits on the number taken, limits on the number of persons allowed to engage in commercial fishing, and restrictions on fishing seasons. Government-built hatcheries and publicly sponsored stocking of fishes were popular conservation efforts. During the peak of the stocking popularity, millions of fishes were stocked directly from specially constructed railroad cars. At the same time, popular game and commercial species were introduced throughout the world. In most cases, indiscriminate stocking did little good. Habitat degradation, exploitation, and the stocking of inappropriate species lim-

ited the success of these efforts much more than reproduction and recruitment. In some cases, such as the introduction of the common carp in North America, stocking of an exotic species reduced native populations.

A better understanding of the dynamics of aquatic populations and the interactions of all components of the aquatic community led to significant changes in fishery conservation from the 1930s to the 1960s. There was a general move away from strict regulations and stocking, which appeared to have accomplished relatively little. The trend was particularly evident in inland fresh-water recreational fisheries. Many local conservation agencies did away with seasons, and size and creel limits were eliminated or made less restrictive. Large reservoirs constructed during that period were believed to hold virtually unlimited recreational fishery resources. Even professional fishery biologists believed it was impossible to deplete recreational fisheries in large reservoirs through hook-and-line harvest. Increases in the numbers of anglers and improved technology led to the rejection of that idea. Angler harvest reduced or altered the size structure of the most popular sport fisheries in reservoirs. Sports groups became highly vocal in favor of the conservation movement. In organized tournaments, they advocated catch-and-release for heavily exploited fishes such as largemouth bass and trout.

Environmental awareness and concern in the 1960s influenced fishery conservation. Public and private environmental groups were formed at the local, national, and international level. Legislation to stop pollution, improve water quality, and protect endangered species was enacted. As a result, the improved water quality in the streams and rivers of developed countries increased fishery resources.

The demand on commercial and recreational fisheries has grown rapidly. Consumption of fish and fisheries products per person has reached all-time highs and is expected to continue to increase. The supply of wild fishes has stabilized or in some cases declined. Conservation agencies are again turning to regulations in order to manage, protect, and enhance fishery resources. Conservation efforts are based on sound scientific data, and modern fishery conservation considers all of the components of the aquatic community and habitat, including consideration of the biological, social, and economic aspects of aquatic resources.

Conservation and management. Current fishery conservation and management practices evolved from concerns about overharvesting accompanied by rapid declines in fishery resources. Overharvesting seldom exterminates a species, but it can reduce populations so seriously that decreases in return per unit effort make the fishery unattractive for commercial or recreational purposes. Lack of harvesting may also affect the quality of a fishery. For example, failure to remove species that have high a reproductive potential may deplete the food supply and lead to an abundance of small fishes unsuitable for harvest. Selective or excessive harvest, especially of predator species, may result in an increase of less desirable species. Fishery conservation efforts often are attempts to manage exploitation of the resource. Although exploitation is an obvious and easily measured characteristic of a fishery, it may not be the limiting factor. Exploitation regulations may or may not accomplish the desired conservation aim.

Conservation efforts for individual species have had limited success. Increases in one species are often accompanied by declines in another. Aquatic communities are limited by their basic productivity and will support only a limited biomass. Successful species-directed conservation efforts have usually involved introductions of species to areas that have an underutilized food source. *See Biomass.*

The creation of a coho salmon fishery in the Great Lakes is an example of a successful species-directed fishery conservation effort. The native lake trout fishery had been decimated by parasitic lampreys, and contamination and industrial pollution had reduced other desirable fishes in the Great Lakes. Biologists introduced an exotic Pacific coast fish, the coho salmon, to feed on the alewife, whose population had developed rapidly without predators. The introduction resulted in creation of a multimillion-dollar recreational fishery in an area that had been described as biologically dead. The introduction of striped bass on the west coast of the United States and the use of hybrid striped bass (the progeny of a striped bass and a white bass) in reservoirs have produced very successful fisheries. In reservoirs, these fish feed in open waters where other predators did not exist.

Management of populations rather than species is more difficult because of the complexity of aquatic ecosystems. Successful population management has been achieved in simple systems such as small recreational ponds, which are stocked at specified rates with only three or four species. A predator species such as largemouth bass is stocked with forage species such as bluegill and red-ear sunfish. Other species, usually with limited reproductive abilities in the pond environment or feeding habits that do not detract from production of the primary species, may be added. The most commonly used secondary species are the channel catfish, which usually do not reproduce in ponds, and the grass carp, which feed on aquatic vegetation. If the appropriate predator-to-prey ratio is achieved, the predators will eat enough of the prey species to reduce their numbers to the point that predators have enough food to grow to a harvestable size. The prey species, for their part, will reproduce enough to provide sufficient food for individual predators to grow to a harvestable size. The quantity of fish that are produced will be limited primarily by the nutrients available. In warm-water recreational ponds, the quantity of fish can be increased by the addition of nutrients that are contained in organic or inorganic fertilizers. These populations may be harvested indefinitely at specified rates and continue to provide satisfactory fishing. *See Fresh-water ecosystem.*

Fishery conservation requires management of human as well as natural resources. People management is an integral part of human impact in the form of exploitation, introductions, habitat alterations, or other direct effects on water quality. Human destruction or alteration of aquatic habitat also affects fishery resources. Deforestation, land development, construction, and agricultural practices that can result in soil erosion can cause excessive warming of the water, altering the physical and biological characteristics of streams and rivers and changing productivity and species composition. Sewage and industrial waste pollutes the water and can make it unsuitable for desirable aquatic life. Organic pollutants such as sewage may remove dissolved oxygen from the water and re-

sult in massive fish kills. Nutrients from industrial, agricultural, and domestic sources can cause the eutrophication of streams, rivers, lakes, and ponds. *See Eutrophication; Water pollution.*

The construction of dams on waterways can interfere with the movements of fishes, as by acting as a barrier to salmon and other species migrating upriver to spawn. However, fish ladders have been used with moderate success to aid fish in their migration around dams. Impounded waters may cover shallow- or flowing-water spawning habitats. Some species, including the striped bass, require long runs of flowing water to keep their eggs buoyant while they develop. If a dam impedes water flow, the eggs will sink to the bottom and become smothered in the silt. Channelization of streams and rivers can also alter spawning habitats by reducing riffle areas. Channelization is often accompanied by removal of trees along the stream banks, resulting in warming of the water.

Pesticides and contaminants. Public concern about the safety of foods has grown, in part because various pesticides, metals, and other contaminants have been reported in the flesh of some fishes. Some contaminants do not kill the fish directly but accumulate in the flesh. Governments have set standards for these contaminants and are increasing monitoring efforts. In some instances, governments have banned the taking of fish from an area or advised the public to limit consumption of certain fish or fish products. The impact of some pesticides and other contaminants can be dramatic, even killing entire aquatic communities. Persistent contaminants can confound efforts at repopulation of the aquatic habitat for years or can selectively eliminate certain species, which results in an undesirable species composition. *See Pesticide.*

Exotic and introduced species. An exotic animal or plant is a species that is not native to a geographical area. Exotic fishes may be highly desirable, but most have the potential to displace or seriously harm native species. Still, undesirable exotic fishes have been stocked throughout the world. A species that is desirable in one geographic area may be a pest in another. Many species of aquatic organisms have become established in waters far removed from their native ranges or in newly created waters. In some cases, species have been introduced in waters ill-suited to their habitat or reproductive requirements and soon disappeared. They may introduce new diseases or parasites into native populations. The introduction of exotic species was once a significant form of fishery conservation, but introductions are now considered cautiously and are controlled through a stringent permit system. *See Conservation of resources; Population ecology; Water conservation.*

Ronnie J. Gilbert; George W. Lewis

Bibliography. W. H. Everhart and D. Youngs, *Principles of Fishery Science*, 2d ed., 1981; H. B. N. Hynes, *The Ecology of Running Waters*, 1970; P. B. Moyle and J. Cech, Jr., *Fishes: An Introduction to Ichthyology*, 1982; G. C. Radonski and G. Martin, Fisheries advances since the thirties, *Fisheries*, 10(3):2–4, 1985; R. A. Rosen, The role of fish culture in fishery management: Politics, policies and future directions, *Fisheries*, 10(1):2–4, 1985; D. Saults, M. Walker, and R. G. Schmidt (eds.), *Sport Fishing USA*, U. S. Department of the Interior; H. M. Smith, America's surpassing fisheries: Their present condition and future prospects, and how the federal government fosters them, *Fisheries*, 11(1):2–13, 1986.

Food web

A diagram of the trophic (feeding) interrelationships within a community or ecosystem. The basic data constitute a catalog of the known diet of each community member. Each node of the diagram, representing a single species or an aggregation of ecologically similar species, is connected to at least one other node (see **illus.**). The community web therefore represents the connection, or the coalescing, of a number of individual food chains (diatom → zooplankton → fish → fish; or, rosebush → aphid → warbler → hawk). [The arrows point in the direction of the species or ecological unit doing the consuming.]

The base of almost all food webs, the first trophic level, is autotrophic, usually comprising photosynthetically active plants. Two different kinds of webs derive from these primary producers. In grazing food webs, each additional trophic level is, on the average, one link further removed from the first level: producers → herbivores → primary canivores → secondary carnivores. Usually there are no more than five levels, or four links, in such communities. Omnivores are represented by connections to two or more lower levels. In detrital food webs, the majority of the photosynthetically fixed energy goes directly to saprophages or decomposers, organisms feeding on dead or dying organisms or their products. Their activities bear important implications for ecosystem functioning, especially nutrient cycling. All natural communities are characterized by the presence of both consumer and detrital food webs.

Two major foci of ecological research are derived from food web relationships. Ecosystem studies focus on the rates of transfer of energy or nutrients between species or blocks (often whole trophic levels). The preferred rate units are mass of some substance or energy transferred per unit area per time. The blocks are connected by arrows or conduits which indicate both direction and amount. These energy-flow diagrams can illustrate the amount of energy or material imported from, or exported to, other systems; the rate of supply of fecal matter or corpses to decomposers; and the loss of energy as heat (due to respiratory oxidation) at each transfer. The emphasis is on the fate of energy entering the ecosystem and the construction of balanced budgets for each trophic level. *See Eco-*
Logical Energetics.

Studies on community organization employ food web patterns as a measure of complexity. Assemblages in which there are both more species and more links per species are more complex. Other web attributes, such as the ratio of prey to predators, the proportion of omnivores, or consideration of the ecological importance of the link (interaction strength) between two species, can be related to community stability. Food web diagrams permit the pattern of community change, observed following human-induced perturbations, to be modeled. Thus, removal of sea otters from the North Pacific resulted in increased biomass of algae, because otters controlled the numbers of sea urchins (grazers), which in turn controlled the algae (primary producers).

Not all trophic interactions involve harm to one participant. Food web diagrams can indicate the presence of symbioses (mutually beneficial interactions), the trophic position of cannibalism (where a species eats a conspecific), or the existence of compartments or subwebs, groups of species interacting more frequently or strongly with themselves than with other species within the same community. *See Ecological*
communities; Ecosystem; Population ecology.

Robert Paine

Bibliography. R. M. May, *Model Ecosystems*, 1974; S. L. Pimm, *Food Webs*, 1982.

A typical food web characteristic of the protected rocky shore community of southern New England. Solid lines suggest major trophic interactions, broken lines minor ones. Such webs provide useful but incomplete biological descriptions, since not all prey are listed, and certain categories of consumers (birds, snails) and prey (detritus, benthic algae) can include many individual species. (*After D. C. Edwards et al., Mobile predators and the structure of marine intertidal communities, Ecology, 63(4):1175–1180, 1982*)

Forest and forestry

A forest is a community of trees, other plants, and animals which live in and thrive on the forest environment. Trees are the dominant form of vegetation. The forest community or ecosystem also includes shrubs, herbs, mosses, fungi, insects, reptiles, birds, and mammals. All these organisms live on or in the soil, water, and air of the forest. Each is a part of the community, and each reacts with all the other parts, but all require the warmth and energy provided by the Sun to survive. A knowledge and understanding of the complex nature of the forest and the manner in which its many organisms interact with each other and their environment is called forest ecology and is essential to the practice of forestry. *See Forest ecosystem; Forest soil*.

Forest influences. Environmental factors within the forest determine its nature. The forest, as it develops, tends to affect these same environmental factors and adjacent areas. For example, the microclimate, that is, the local climate, is appreciably affected by forests. They reduce the force of the wind over land horizontally for as much as 10 to 40 times the vertical height of the trees. The air in forests is cooler and more humid in the summer and warmer and drier in the winter as compared to open land. The difference may range from 3 to 10°F (2 to 6°C) aboveground and as much as 20°F (11°C) in the soil. Forests may not, however, have much impact on the macroclimate or major weather patterns over the surface of the Earth.

In the spring, melting snow and rain tend to remain on the ground longer under the trees than in the open. This causes the runoff of water under the trees to be extended over a longer period of time than in open spaces, providing a more even flow of water from forested areas than from grassy areas or bare soil. The severity of flooding is thus reduced in the lowland areas.

The cooling effect above forests may increase rainfall by as much as 2–3% above that of nonforested areas. On the other hand, evaporation and transpiration from the trees may exceed that which takes place over open areas. This action plus the great retention of water in forest soils may actually result in less runoff from forested watersheds than from clear-cut or open grasslands.

The spongelike nature of organic matter on the forest ground also protects the more mineral soils below from erosion and provides for cleaner and clearer water in the streams which drain the forested areas. This is an essential aspect of keeping the water from large watershed areas in a healthy condition for human and wildlife consumption. In short, forests represent natural ground cover that provides a maximum yield in environmental protection for both human and animal life.

These qualities of forests, together with forest management, have resulted in the development of urban forestry. One objective is to enhance the well-being of urban people through recreation and esthetics in a forest environment. Urban forestry also contributes to noise abatement (as much as 6 to 8 decibels) and to the reduction of air pollution—two serious problems in larger cities.

Tree groups. The natural affiliation of some trees for specific environmental conditions in the forests of the United States has resulted in hundreds of groupings of trees known as forest types and subtypes. These can be classified into six major forests or natural forest regions. Three are east of the Great Plains: the Northern Forest, the Central Hardwood Forest, and the Southern Forest. The Rocky Mountain, Pacific Coast, and Alaskan Forests are west of the prairie states.

To facilitate forest management, foresters have arbitrarily classified forest trees into several groups. One classification, based on the size of the individual trees, refers to them as seedlings, saplings, poles, standards, or veterans. A forest containing trees ranging from small seedlings to poles to large veterans is said to be all-aged. Forests with trees essentially the same size and age are called even-aged. Foresters talk of a pure forest if it is composed mainly of one species, and of a mixed forest if it contains several species. Botanists and foresters refer to tolerant trees as those which can grow in the shade of other trees. Species which cannot survive in shade are said to be intolerant.

The trees in a forest compete with each other for soil, water, and light on any given site. Some tree species may grow better on hills facing north, while others do better on slopes facing south. This forest competition may result in one combination of trees being more successful than another for a given type of environment. As new species invade a site, others may decline in importance and bring about a forest community change called forest succession. *See Eco-* *logical communities; Ecological succession.*

Fig. 1. Rangeland providing forage for cattle grazing in Sawtooth National Forest, Idaho. (*U. S. Forest Service*)

Fig. 2. Foresters studying terrain for its suitability for skiing. (*U. S. Forest Service*)

Forest uses and ownership. The uses of forest land are myriad. Originally forests were found to be essential as a source of food for hunting or grazing animals and as a source of shelter or building materials. These are still the major uses of forests, but the utility of forests in regulating streamflow, improving navigation, maintaining water quality, and providing a host of outdoor recreations is also of major significance.

The demands for use of the many resources of any specific forest are frequently in conflict. The coordination or resolution of these conflicting demands can give rise to multiple-use, dominant-use, or single-use forestry. The coordination of multiple uses is the goal sought by the U.S. Forest Service in managing national forests. The dominant use of most industrial forests is that of growing timber or other wood products or fiber for industrial use. Other uses may be developed or tolerated. The wilderness areas of the National Park Service and of other government administrations are clearly devoted to the single use of esthetic and wilderness enjoyment, such as hiking, back-packing, camping, or canoeing.

The ownership, management, or location of a forest may provide a form of classifying forests that should be understood. Forests administered by the U.S. Forest Service are referred to as national forests. Some of the latter may have more acres of rangelands than forests (**Fig. 1**). There are also state forests, county forests, industrial forests, and other private forests.

The policies of the owners of forest lands may call for other designations of forests. Some forest lands involving unique natural features or scenic values may be set aside by acts of Congress as wilderness areas. Some forests are designated for recreational use as national or state parks. Others may be devoted to the management or protection of wildlife and are referred to as wildlife refuges. It is evident that the policy of the owners must determine whether the use of the forest shall be limited to one or a few of its total natural resources, or whether all of them shall be used and managed under a multiple-use policy. Such decisions will determine the type of forestry practiced on any specific unit of forest land. *SEE FOREST RESOURCES.*

Forestry. In 1971 the Society of American Foresters defined forestry as "the science, the art and practice of managing and using for human benefit the natural resources that occur on and in association with forest lands." Other definitions might note specifically that the basic "natural resources" are wood, forage, water, wildlife, and recreation. The practice of forestry requires knowledge of the complex biological nature of the forest. It also requires some knowledge of geology, biology, mathematics, physics, chemistry, economics, and sociology. The forester's technical training in forestry at colleges or universities includes basic courses in some of these subjects.

The science of forestry itself requires intensive study of more than a dozen subjects which may be required in the practice of forestry. The need or choice of the divisions of forestry as a science depends upon the field of specialization or interest of the student or practicing forester (**Fig. 2**). Four major fields of interest seem to cover most forestry subjects. They involve biological, management, administrative, or utilization considerations.

The major divisions of forestry which deal specifically with biological fields are forest soils, dendrology, silvics, and silviculture. Forest pathology, forest zoology, and forest entomology also fall into this category. The part that forest soils play in providing growth and support of forest trees is essential. Soil composition, physical and chemical character, and the behavior of soils under different forest conditions must be studied and understood.

Dendrology covers the description, classification, and identification of the numerous species of trees with which foresters must work. Silvics deals with the manner in which environmental factors such as climate, slope, soil, fire, and biological conditions affect forest sites.

Silviculture deals with the technical problems of establishing new forests, naturally or artificially, making thinnings or cuttings to stimulate growth on the remaining trees, and making harvest cuts of forest stands in such a way as to assure their perpetuation.

Studies of the life cycles of living organisms of the forests other than trees and plants are needed. Forest pathology concerns the study of fungi, forest zoology deals with animal life, and forest entomology reviews the important insects affecting trees and wood.

Management considerations. The fact that forest crops of timber take from 20 to 100 years to mature makes it essential that planning and decision making be based on the best facts and forecasts available. Planning for use of resources other than timber also requires careful long-term planning and integration with all the environmental factors of the forest. Forest management refers to the practical application of scientific, economic, and social principles affecting the administration and working of a forest estate for specified objectives. Forest management includes mensuration (forest measurement), regulation, and preparation of working plans. The working plans also involve forest finance, forest economics, and forest policy, and should meet the requirements of an environmental impact statement. This statement, which is now a prerequisite of all management plans of national forests, must show the probable impact that the management plan will have on the wildlife, watershed, and recreational resources. The statement may even include integration with range (grazing of livestock) management resources and, in some cases, with municipal and utility plans and resources. Management planners and policy makers for forests or public lands may have to submit their plans and environmental impact statements to a series of public hearings and amendments before they are finally adopted.

The adaptation of mathematics to the measurement of timbered areas or whole forests, of single trees and logs, and of other pieces and units of forest products is called mensuration (**Fig. 3**). Foresters must now include in their inventories and plans for the forest the ways of measuring the significant wildlife, watershed and recreational resources, and needs for their development and use.

After the volume of timber resources and their annual growth have been measured and estimated, it may be necessary to provide for annual or periodic cuttings to improve growth conditions or to remove overmature timber, that is, to harvest surplus growing stock or growth. The planning for or regulation of such cuttings is referred to as forest regulation.

In regarding forestry as a business, it is necessary to develop values of one course of action as compared with another. The financial, economic, and statistical considerations involved in such comparisons are known as forest valuation. *See* F*orest management*.

Policy and administration. Forest policy is the term applied to the process of decision making as de-

Fig. 3. Measuring pulpwood cut from a red pine plantation. (*U. S. Forest Service*)

termined by laws and regulations established by the government, and by rules and procedures set up by the administrators of a specific forest.

The selection, training, assignment, compensation, and use of workers and executives in carrying out forest policies and procedures make up an array of knowledge referred to as forest administration. One forest of 100,000 to 500,000 acres (40,000 to 200,000 hectares) may be administered by one forest supervisor or forest manager who may have several staff assistants. The subdivisions of the forest may be administered as districts, each headed by a district ranger who runs a separate office and district but is responsible to the forest supervisor. The operation of such an organization must be clear-cut, as the district managers carry out all phases of their management plans. This is particularly true of the protection of the forest from fire, insects, and disease—and in some cases from wind, animals, and humans themselves as they make use of the recreational resources of the forest (**Figs. 4** and **5**). These resources include places for hunting and fishing, picnicking and camping, walking, hiking and mountain climbing, driving vehicles in forest settings, boating, swimming, winter sports, painting, photography, and nature study.

Fig. 4. Fire detection tower in the Olympic National Forest, Washington. (*U. S. Forest Service*)

Fig. 5. Airplane spraying insecticide, a modern technique to control insect epidemics in the forest, Boise National Forest, Idaho. (*U. S. Forest Service*)

Utilization. Forests cannot be used or timber harvested without a system of roads, bridges, culverts, and some administrative structures. Their planning and construction and the planning and conduct of logging operations make up a body of knowledge called forest engineering. In terms of volume and dollar value, the greatest direct product of most forests is wood. Study of its variations of structure, physical and mechanical properties, and behavior of wood under varying conditions is labeled wood technology. Utilization also includes the manufacture, transportation, and marketing of forest products, and it most certainly includes the utilization of all wood (and bark) materials left over after logging operations in the woods and manufacturing at the mills. The use of leftovers is resulting in a minimum of waste in the woods and provides a major source of increased yields of products and fuel for the forest.

Conclusion. In short, forestry is a highly complex activity requiring sound judgment in the formulation and interpretation of policy, and great managerial and administrative skills in its implementation. Professional competence in a wide variety of interdisciplinary fields is essential.

Willard S. Bromley

Bibliography. J. Buongiorno and J. K. Gilless, *Forest Management; A Primer in Qualitative Methods*, 1987; R. T. Deacon and M. Bruce Johnson, *Forestlands: Public and Private*, 1985; B. Husch, *Guidelines for Forestry Policy Formulation*, 1987; G. W. Sharpe and C. Hendes, *Introduction to Forestry*, 5th ed., 1986.

Forest ecosystem

An ecological community found in the world's forest environments. The continents cover 5.8×10^7 mi^2 (1.5×10^8 km^2), or nearly one-third of the Earth's surface. Forests occupy as much as 38% of the land and surpass any other landscape type in surface area, biological diversity, and biomass. Forests grow under diverse climatic conditions. The average annual number of growing-season days of forests ranges from 106 to 365, average annual temperature from 32.5 to 79.7°F (0.25 to 26.5°C), and average annual precipitation from 20 to 104 in. (514 to 2630 mm). Seasonal patterns of climate and soil conditions are important influences on forest development. *See ECOSYSTEM.*

The three principal types of the Earth's forests are the equatorial evergreen forest, the temperate deciduous forest, and the northern coniferous forest (taiga) of the highest latitudes. Dry tropical woodlands and woodland mosaics are found in the mid-latitudes. Within these forested regions, or biomes, an array of forest ecosystems occurs. Many forest types have been identified and include conifers (evergreen and deciduous) and hardwoods (broadleaf evergreen and deciduous). Forests may occupy high mountain sites, coastal regions of high precipitation, floodplains, hot dry lowlands, or cold northern regions. The occurrence of specific forest types may be determined by soil drainage and nutrients, precipitation, exposure, and length of growing season. Each forest is in itself a complex ecological entity. The global distribution and productivity of forests are summarized in the **table**. *See BIOGEOGRAPHY; BIOME.*

Ecosystem processes. Forests, like all ecosystems, are assemblages of self-sustaining plant (autotroph) and animal (heterotroph) species with many coevolved interdependencies for sustenance and perpetuation. Ecosystems are characterized by their primary producers, consumers, and decomposers. The primary producers are the autotrophic green, chlorophyll-containing plants that convert solar energy by photosynthesis to biomass and organic molecules needed by animal (heterotrophic) consumers. Primary producers are the energy and nutrient base supporting all other organisms in the ecosystem. Successive levels of animal consumers, beginning with plant-eating herbivores and ending with several levels of carnivorous predators, form food chains. Because of the respiratory costs of producing carbohydrates by photosynthesis, the metabolic demands of consumers, and the inefficiencies of their digestive processes, less than 10% of the energy content of one trophic level (autotrophs) is passed to the next level (heterotrophs) in most food chains.

Interconnected food chains form complex food webs, and predator–prey relationships regulate both producer and consumer populations. Primary producers and consumers eventually die, their remains decompose, and their nutrients are recycled. The decomposers are saprophytic organisms, which feed upon detritus and release degradation products. Complex biogeochemical and hydrologic cycles have developed within forest ecosystems to recycle nutrients for reuse by the primary producers. Trees modify and regulate the environment, making it suitable for varied plant and animal populations. *See FOOD WEB; POPULATION ECOLOGY.*

Biomass and productivity. Trees are the primary component of forest ecosystems. With their woody support structures, trees extend and stratify their leaves to provide efficient photosynthetic conversion of atmospheric carbon dioxide and water to organic molecules. In typical forests, autotrophic (leaf) mass may make up only a small percentage of the biomass above the ground, but the flat shape and vertical distribution of leaves give forests a photosynthetic surface three to ten times greater than the ground area. The ratio of leaf-to-ground area is called the leaf-area index and is a measure of the photosynthetic potential of a forest. Vertical stratification also allows for a large mass of living tissue, or biomass, and dead wood, which create a variety of arboreal habitats and a biotic reservoir of nutrients. About 80% of the total biomass of forests is visible above the ground; the remaining 20% is invisible, that is, below the ground. In most forests, in fact, nearly half the total organic matter lies beneath the soil surface in roots, soil organisms, and humus. *See BIOMASS; FOREST SOIL.*

Biomass and productivity of forest biomes

Type	Area covered,* 10^6 mi^2	Total carbon, 10^9 tons[†]	Productivity of biomass, 10^9 tons/year[†]
Northern and southern taiga	2.77	68	3.3
Other conifers	1.36	65	2.3
Temperate broadleaf forest	0.58	17	1.0
Midlatitude mixed woods, deciduous and evergreen	1.32	39	2.3
Broadleaf tropical humid forest	4.00	172	9.1
Dry tropical forest and woodland	1.83	36	3.0
Tropical savanna or montane	2.83	28	—
Dry tropical woods mosaics with scrub and grass	3.29	39	—
Northern maritime subalpine taiga	1.69	24	1.4
Second-growth woods and field mosaics	2.79	37	—
Total forests and woods	22.46	525	—

*Total continental land surface minus lakes, 5.7×10^7 mi^2 (1.48×10^8 km^2). 1 mi^2 = 2.59 km^2.
[†]1 ton = 0.907 metric ton.

Roots are important for structural integrity and for the absorption of nutrients and water. Detritus decomposed by soil organisms provides a fertile substrate for plant growth and a reservoir of nutrients.

Their large woody structures (both living and dead) make forests a major repository of organic matter and nutrient elements. It is easy to understand their importance as chemical reservoirs and modifiers of the Earth's biologic and hydrologic cycles. *See* Hydrology.

Productivity. Research has produced few comprehensive sets of metabolic data for forest ecosystems, but relationships are becoming clearer. Forests can have higher gross primary production (total photosynthetic carbon fixation) and net ecosystem production than any other type of ecosystem because of their large biomass. Typical total standing-crop (biomass) values for carbon would be 1.8 lb/ft^2 (8.76 kg/m^2) in a second-growth *Liriodendron* or *Quercus* forest, 3.1 lb/ft^2 (15.9 kg/m^2) in an old-growth coniferous forest, and 1.4 lb/ft^2 (7.0 kg/m^2) in a rapidly growing pine plantation. (The carbon content of forest biomass is approximately 50% of dry weight.) Gross primary production values for carbon greater than 0.4 lb/ft^2 (2 kg/m^2) are common for forests and may be three times that of native prairies and ten times that of tundra. Highly productive managed pine plantations may have gross primary production carbon values that exceed 0.8 lb/ft^2 (4 kg/m^2) per year. Photosynthetic carbon fixation is offset by respiratory costs and the metabolism of animal consumers. The difference between carbon fixation and total respiratory loss is the net accumulation of carbon in the ecosystem. Carbon may accumulate in stem wood and organic soil matter (humus). In a rapidly growing pine plantation, for example, the net accumulation of carbon is typically high because silvicultural techniques encourage high yields, and early successional stages (seres) of forest development enrich the soil with humus. In mature forests, the net accumulation of carbon may approach zero.

The production of an ecosystem can be expressed by the ratio of losses (respiration) to gains (primary production). Since wood biomass is not photosynthetically active, autotrophic respiration is useful in describing the metabolic cost of gross primary production. As measured by the ratio of gross primary production to autotrophic respiration, forests have low production efficiencies (25–50%) because they have the highest standing crop of biomass and because nonphotosynthetic autotrophic respiration (stems and roots) makes up a larger percentage of total respiration in forests than in other ecosystems. On the other hand, forests have lower heterotrophic respiration rates than grasslands, where foliage grazers may equal the primary producers in respiration rates. The overall productivity of an ecosystem is defined as the ratio of net-to-gross production, which for forests is between 5 and 25%. *See* Biological productivity; Grassland ecosystem.

Succession and competition. A forest ecosystem is dynamic in its growth and development. Species composition and biomass reach a steady state only in very old, mature forests, and tree death and replacement continue even there. Forests develop in regular sequential stages; classical succession begins on exposed sites such as abandoned farms or newly formed dunes, or after a fire or tornado. Each location has a characteristic sere dominated by edaphic features and the presence of regional species. The first woody plants to inhabit a site are pioneers, tolerant of hot, dry, exposed conditions. Typically, they require abundant sunlight but grow on poor soils. This first stand of woody vegetation ameliorates the microclimate and builds up organic matter that retains moisture and nutrients in the soil. The site becomes richer, damper, and shadier. Successive species develop under the canopy of the pioneer, each more shade-tolerant and taller, to replace its predecessor.

A mature forest thus may develop on abandoned farmland by passing through successive stages: first, blackberry, then eastern red cedar and sumac, followed by dogwoods, cherry, gum, and tulip poplar, and finally oak and hickory forest. Animals and the wind assist the process by dispersing seed. Some early succession species, such as jack pine near the Great Lakes, begin with a fire that clears vegetation, opens pine cones, and permits reseeding. Another form of succession, gap-phase replacement, occurs in mature forests when trees die and fall, creating openings through which light penetrates to the forest floor and releases seedlings of previously repressed species. Young trees compete to fill the canopy. *See* Ecological succession; Population dispersal.

The success of a species depends upon two criteria. First, the site must be established by seed dispersal and germination. Rapid growth may, of course, be an advantage: persistence of the seedling is essential in gap-phase replacement. Second, the species must compete effectively for water, nutrients, and light. Many species play different roles in different stages of forest development, contributing to the rich diver-

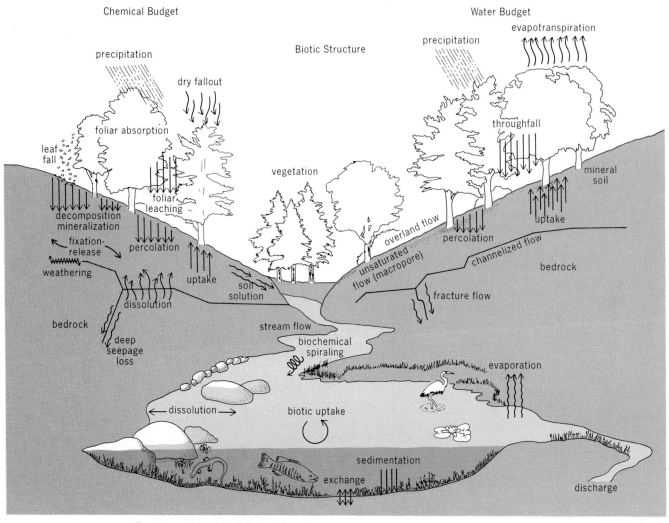

Forest ecosystem and hydrologic drainage (watershed) illustrating the major biotic components and the chemical and hydrologic processes. (*U.S. Department of Agriculture*)

sity of tropical and temperate forests. What appears tranquil to the untrained eye is actually a dynamic population of growing and competing trees. Many early forest stages can be managed for their economic value (for example, Douglas-fir in the northwestern United States or loblolly pine in the Southeast).

Products. Forest products have great economic value in the pulp and paper and construction industries. However, nearly half of the timber consumed in the world is used for fuel.

Replanting after lumbering is an important investment for the future. In most regions, forest management concentrates on conifers or other rapidly growing species early in the succession. Lumbering can be costly in economic and environmental terms; clearcutting is controlled to avoid damage to habitat, water resources, and scenic beauty. Research is concentrating on the short-rotation, intensive culture of hardwoods for fuel, with the objective of producing fast-growing systems (often with mixed species) that offer high energy yields in less than 10 years. Self-fertilizing, coppicing (root-sprouting), and disease-resistant varieties that are noncompetitive with agriculture on marginal lands are needed.

Forests enhance water resources in both quantity and quality, because of their storage capacity and ecological cleansing action. The integrity of hydrologic cycles depends upon ecosystems that encourage absorption rather than runoff of precipitation, thus avoiding flash discharges from drainage basins. Forests harbor wildlife and fish. Each stage of the forest succession may offer its own features, which can be exploited by good management. SEE FOREST MANAGEMENT.

Forests also represent an important pathway for the exchange and regulation of atmospheric gases, water, and trace chemicals. For example, it is estimated that every 7½ years the global biosphere processes an amount of carbon dioxide equal to that present in the entire atmosphere. The forest biomass above ground efficiently intercepts atmospheric particles and aerosols. Atmospheric pollutants move through leaves into forest ecosystems, which are important to the balance of life on Earth and should be of wide concern. SEE AIR POLLUTION; FOREST RESOURCES.

Environmental issues. Forests are central to a number of modern environmental problems, including atmospheric pollution and acid rain effects on leaves and soil chemistry. Increased concentrations of soluble aluminum have been found to be toxic to trees and to biota in streams that drain acidified forest watersheds. The complex biogeochemical cycles (see **illus.**) of nutrients and pollutants in forest ecosystems are under investigation. These cycles must be understood in order to protect forests from harm. SEE ACID RAIN; BIOGEOCHEMISTRY.

Before human beings began burning large quantities of fossil fuel and clearing forests for agriculture, the metabolic exchange of carbon dioxide by the biosphere was in rough equilibrium with that in the atmosphere, with about 1.2×10^{11} metric tons of carbon exchanged annually by terrestrial vegetation. Today, industrial emissions of carbon dioxide have raised the atmospheric concentration of carbon dioxide from past values of 280 ppm to nearly 345 ppm, an increase of about 5×10^9 metric tons of carbon. That is significant, because a doubling of atmospheric carbon dioxide is expected to raise global temperatures and modify precipitation. Such climatic changes could seriously affect the biosphere, including forest and agricultural ecosystems. The clearing of forests on a large scale also adds carbon (1.3×10^9 metric tons/year) to the atmosphere. This destruction limits the Earth's ability to deal with the increases of atmospheric carbon that have already occurred. SEE CLIMATIC CHANGE; FOREST AND FORESTRY; GREENHOUSE EFFECT; HEAT BALANCE, TERRESTRIAL ATMOSPHERIC.

David Reichle

Bibliography. Office of Technology Assessment, *Wood Use*: *U.S. Competitiveness and Technology*, 1983; J. S. Olson, J. S. Watts, and L. J. Allison, *Carbon in Live Vegetation of Major World Ecosystems*, Oak Ridge National Laboratory, ORNL-5862, 1983; D. E. Reichle, Advances in ecosystem analysis, *BioScience*, 25(4):257–264, 1975; D. E. Reichle (ed.), *Dynamic Properties of Forest Ecosystems*, 1981; J. R. Trabalka and D. E. Reichle, *The Changing Carbon Cycle*: *A Global Analysis*, 1986; U.S. Department of Agriculture, Forest Service, *An Analysis of the Timber Situation in the United States 1952–2030*, For. Res. Rep. 23, 1982.

Forest fire control

The term wildfire refers to all uncontrolled fires that burn surface vegetation (grass, weeds, grainfields, brush, chaparral, tundra, and forest and woodland); often these fires also involve structures. In addition to the wildfires, several million acres of forest land are intentionally burned each year under controlled conditions to accomplish some silvicultural or other land-use objective or for hazard reduction (**Fig. 1**).

Nature of fire. Fire is a natural phenomenon that reverses the creative process of photosynthesis, which produces all wood fiber and other plant materials. In simple terms, photosynthesis uses solar energy to turn carbon dioxide and water into cellulose (woody fiber) and oxygen: $CO_2 + H_2O + \text{solar energy} \rightarrow \text{cellulose} + O$. When the temperature near woody or other plant material is raised to the kindling point by a lighted match, burning cigarette, or other means, combustion takes place. As the material burns, carbon dioxide and water are released, along with heat which can spread the fire to nearby combustible plant materials. If dead woody or plant material does not get burned, it decays. In decay the same process produces the same end products of carbon dioxide, water, and heat at a much slower pace. The heat of oxidation is usually not noticeable, and the debris of decaying organic material accumulates to form a thick layer, as on the forest floor. During dry seasons this layer may dry out to such an extent as to be a serious potential fire hazard.

Forest fire causes. Most wildfires are caused by human beings, directly or indirectly. In the United

Fig. 1. Controlled fire conditions. (*a*) Closed jack pine (*Pinus banksiana*) cones, which require heat in order to open. (*b*) Prescribed burning after seed tree cutting so that jack pine cones can open for natural regeneration. (*Photographs by W. R. Beaufait*)

States less than 10% of all such fires are caused by lightning, the only truly natural cause. In the West (the 17 Pacific and Rocky Mountain states) lightning is the primary cause, with smoking (cigarettes, matches, and such) the second most frequent. Combined they account for 50 to 75% of all wildfires. In the 13 southern states (Virginia to Texas) the primary cause is incendiary. This combined with smoking and debris burning make up 75% of all wildfires. Miscellaneous causes of wildfires are next in importance in most regions. The other causes of wildfires are machine use and campfires. Machine use includes railroads, logging, sawmills, and other operations using equipment.

Fire behavior. The manner in which fuel ignites, flame develops, and fire spreads and exhibits other phenomena constitutes the field of fire behavior. Factors determining forest fire behavior may be considered under four headings: attributes of the fuel, the atmosphere, topography, and ignition.

Fuel. Live and dead vegetation in the natural forest complex constitutes the fuel for forest fires. The amount of moisture in relation to the heat content of the fuel determines its flammability. Moisture in living vegetation varies with species and with time of year. The moisture content of dead fuels, the more important component of the fuel complex, responds to precipitation, relative humidity, and to a lesser extent temperature. It shows important daily fluctuations.

The rate of combustion and the heat output are also determined by the quantity of fuel, the fuel arrangement, and the thermal and chemical properties of individual fuel particles.

Atmosphere. Major direct effects of the atmosphere on fire behavior are through variations in oxygen supply and in flame angle caused by wind, and the stability of the atmosphere. Secondary effects on combustion rate are through air and fuel temperature, and the relative humidity of the air. SEE ATMOSPHERE; HUMIDITY.

Topography. Heated air adjacent to a slope tends to flow up the slope, creating a chimney effect. Unburned fuels above a fire advancing up a slope are closer to approaching flames because of the angle of the slope. Both of these effects act similarly to wind on flat ground in increasing the rate of fire spread.

Ignition. An igniting agent of sufficient intensity and duration is necessary to start a forest fire. The agent may be human-caused, such as a match or

Fig 2. Characteristic fire behavior. (a) Crown fire. (b) Surface fire. (*U. S. Forest Service*)

lighted cigarette, or natural, such as lightning. Once a fire has started, its spread is by successive ignition of adjacent unburned fuel. This fuel is brought to ignition temperature by heat radiated and convected from the flame front. Generally fuels must be very close to, or even enveloped by, flame or superheated gases in the convection column before igniting. This mechanism results in more or less continuous advancement of a fire. Fire spread may also be caused by spotting, that is, ignition by burning brands carried outside the fire area by wind and turbulence.

Types. A forest fire may burn primarily in the crowns of trees and shrubs—a crown fire (**Fig. 2***a*); primarily in the surface litter and loose debris of the forest floor and small vegetation—a surface fire (Fig. 2*b*); or in the organic material beneath the surface litter—a ground fire. The most common type is a surface fire.

Indexes. The U.S. Forest Service has developed a National Fire Danger Rating System (NFDRS) to provide fire-control personnel with numerical ratings to help them with the tasks of fire-control planning and the suppression of specific fires. The system includes three basic indexes: an occurrence index, a burning index, and a fire load index. Each of these is related to a specific part of the fire-control job. These indexes are used by dispatchers in making decisions on setting up fire-fighting forces, lookout systems, and so forth.

Seasons. Because of annual cycles in precipitation and in growth of vegetation, most sections of the United States have a well-defined fire season during which most forest and wild-land fires occur. This fire season varies widely in duration, from two short seasons in the northeastern states, in spring and fall, to frequently a year-long season in southern California. **Figure 3** shows the normal peak fire seasons for the United States.

Prevention of wildfire. This means keeping all unwanted human-caused wildfires from starting. Actually prevention covers a wide range of activities, and must be patterned to the causes of fires in a particular area. The best tools for prevention are education, elimination of hazards, and fire law enforcement. Risks refer to the presence of people and to their activities, such as cigarette smoking and starting brush fires. Hazards are the various types, conditions, volumes, and locations of fuels, such as grass, brush, and forest fuels.

In areas of intensive use, hazard reduction includes many forestry activities aimed at reducing fuel accumulations in order to reduce the channel of a starting fire or to reduce the severity of one that might be started. These activities include roadside burning, slash disposal, controlled burning of forest areas to reduce fuel accumulations, and some silvicultural practices.

Prevention activities should be conducted in line with a carefully planned and written program. The keystone of such a program is a wildfire prevention plan that includes at least the following elements: (1) basis of the plan (consisting of maps and statistics covering past fires, maps showing fire risks, industrial operations, and hazards, and maps showing signs, radio and television stations, and newspaper offices); (2) summary of objectives, problems, and action to be taken; (3) prevention contact plan; (4) public education; (5) closures and restrictions; (6) industrial operations; (7) reduction of physical hazards; (8) sign-posting plan; (9) prevention training; and (10) legislative needs and law enforcement.

Detection. Although many forest fires are detected and reported by local residents and transient forest users, primary reliance for detection is placed on specialized detection systems. Most fire-control agencies use a combination of lookout towers with trained observers during the fire season and regularly scheduled aerial patrols. Use of aircraft for routine detection patrol has increased greatly, paralleling the increase in aircraft use in other protection activities.

Fig. 3. Normal peak fire seasons in United States.

Fig. 4. Fire fighters rappelling to the scene of a fire.

Infrared scanners developed originally by the military for battlefield applications have been adapted for use in detecting forest fires. Aircraft-mounted detectors are routinely used to detect fires started by intense lightning storms. Such scanners have the capability to detect even campfires from an altitude of 12,000 ft (3.7 km). Other electronic equipment, including television, radar, and sferics (to detect lightning discharges and thus storms), has been used experimentally.

Communication. Rapid and accurate communication is essential not only to the detection network but also to the forces engaged in actual suppression work. Land-line telephones are being rapidly supplanted or supplemented by radios. In many organizations all motorized units are equipped with two-way radios. As the size of portable, self-contained equipment is reduced, more and more supervisory personnel on actual fires are also being equipped.

Presuppression. In spite of careful plans and efforts to prevent wildfires, they do occur. Then they must be detected and reported promptly to the suppression forces responsible. These will be prepared to act if adequate suppression steps have been taken. Aside from prevention, the steps include all the preparation, organization, development, and maintenance of equipment, as well as planning, cooperation, mutual aid arrangements, and training.

Generally, public agencies are responsible for presuppression planning and suppression action. State and federal forestry or forest fire organizations have a clearcut understanding and lines of authority as to which areas are their primary responsibility. Each should have a well-defined organizational structure and a specific plan to prevent fires and to detect and suppress any fires that do occur. This plan includes maps of the type described for a fire-prevention program, an inventory of equipment, and a program of training and a program for securing additional personnel equipment if needed. The program for additional personnel should be established through use of cooperative agreements well before each fire season begins.

Transportation. Emphasis on fast attack of discovered fires has steadily increased over the years. Many fire-control organizations, both urban and forest, divide their protection area into zones of allowable attack times. These are based on times shown by experience as necessary for successful control according to acceptable standards. Location of suppression forces and methods of transportation are planned to meet these objectives.

Because of the great distances involved, forest fire-control organizations have placed special emphasis on increasing the speed and mobility of their forces. Most personnel and equipment arrive at the majority of fires by a combination of ground-transportation methods, including the most elementary of all, walking. Therefore in areas of high value and high fire incidence, an extensive network of roads and trails is usually maintained. The development of reliable, lightweight gasoline engines has made possible the use of trail scooters and motorized equipment carriers. These require trails intermediate in quality between horse and foot trails and the more expensive truck trails.

Fig. 5. Parachutes used for the delivery of fire fighters and materials to fire areas. (a) Two fire fighters descending. (b) Air drop of fire-fighting equipment, showing drop location marker (X). (*U. S. Forest Service*)

In remote areas with relatively low and widely scattered fire incidence, the airplane and helicopter are the primary means of delivering both personnel and material to the scene of a fire. Even in areas with good road and trail networks, it is often cheaper and faster to supply suppression forces by air. Successful parachute jumping by fire fighters, started by the U.S. Forest Service in 1940, demonstrated the feasibility of wartime use of paratroops. Postwar development by the Forest Service of techniques and equipment for delivery of personnel and material by parachute and by helicopters led to increased use of airborne fire fighters in the forests of the western United States (**Figs. 4** and **5**).

Mapping. Specialized heat-sensitive infrared mapping devices are used operationally to map fire perimeters from the air. These are somewhat similar to television systems that are sensitive to radiation in the far infrared rather than to visible light. They have the great advantage of being able to see through the smoke of a fire and locate the regions of active combustion on the ground. The image, which can be photographed, indicates the temperature of the fire in shades from black to white and thus enables fire-control personnel to map the fire edge, determine the intensity of the fire along the perimeter, and locate spot fires outside the main fire at night or when the fire itself is completely obscured by smoke.

Such sophisticated systems of mapping are likely to be applied primarily in the West, where fires may involve extensive areas or the most valuable stands of virgin timber or second growth. For most ground fires that are common in the eastern states, fire maps can be quickly plotted directly on prints of aerial photographs, or made from compass and pacing surveys.

Suppression methods. Fire can be suppressed by robbing it of its fuel or oxygen supply, or enough heat may be removed to stop the chain reaction, and the fire goes out. Combustion may also be suppressed by the addition of small amounts of certain chemicals to the combustion zone.

Fuel removal. One of the most common methods of controlling a forest fire is by creating a fuelless barrier. This may be done by digging a trench to mineral soil ahead of an approaching fire of sufficient width to prevent the fire from crossing (**Fig. 6***a*). Since this may require a line of considerable width (some evidence is available that this width is approximately equal to the square of the height of the flames), it is customary for the unburned fuel between the prepared line and the approaching fire to be intentionally fired, thereby effectively widening the line.

Techniques of constructing fire lines vary with terrain, soil character, and type of vegetation. Organized crews with hand tools, such as axes, shovels, rakes, and other specially constructed tools, are used in

Fig. 6. Land fire suppression methods. (*a*) Digging a trench ahead of an approaching fire. (*b*) Constructing a fire line to stop the advancing fire. (*c*) Bulldozer making fire lane near the edge of the fire. (*d*) Using a tank truck to suppress fire. (*e*) Fighting fire with hose attached to a portable pump. (*U. S. Forest Service*)

Fig. 7. Aerial fire suppression. (a) Mixing and loading fire retardants in preparation for an air drop. (b) A helicopter with a detachable 40-gal (151-liter) tank drops borate slurry on a pinpoint target. (*U. S. Forest Service*)

many areas, especially those too rugged or remote to permit use of mechanized equipment (Fig. 6b). Specially developed motordriven flails, similar to garden-tractor rotary tillers, are sometimes employed, although their usefulness is limited to terrain and soil types on which they can be maneuvered satisfactorily. Bulldozers are used extensively (Fig. 6c), and tractor-drawn plows are standard line-construction equipment in the relatively flat terrain of the southeastern states.

Occasionally, existing roads or previously prepared firebreaks are used as control lines, usually as a line from which a counterfire is set. Natural firebreaks, such as rocky ridges or rivers, are used similarly.

Heat removal. The second major method used in suppressing fires is to remove enough heat to break the chain reaction. Water, with its high specific heat and heat of vaporization, is an ideal substance for this purpose. Long the favorite with urban fire-control organizations, water is becoming more popular with forestry organizations as techniques and equipment for handling it are improved. An extraordinarily large amount of burning material can be extinguished with a small amount of water when it is used with maximum efficiency.

Hand-operated pumps with a 5-gal (14-liter) tank carried on the back are most satisfactory when used on fires in light fuels, for suppressing small spot fires, and for mop-up, the tedious work of extinguishing burning fuel after the fire has been contained within a fireproof boundary.

Gasoline-operated pumps are used extensively wherever water supplies are convenient or road networks permit the use of tank trucks (Fig. 6d). Portable pumps are available that can be carried by one person (Fig. 6e), making hose lays of several thousand feet (1 ft = 0.3 m) or even several miles (1 mi = 1.6 km) feasible. Techniques have been developed for laying hose rapidly from helicopters, cutting the time required to lay a mile of hose from hours to minutes, even seconds. For use in inaccessible regions,

small units including a pump, a 50- or 100-gal (179- or 379-liter) tank, and several hundred feet of hose have been developed that can be delivered by helicopter to the scene of a fire.

Chemicals that inhibit the combustion process are used regularly in the suppression of large forest fires. These are generally prepared in the form of water solutions or slurries, and are dropped from aircraft or applied to fires from ground-based tank trucks. More than 15,000,000 gal (57×10^6 liters) of such fire-retardant chemicals are used annually in the United States.

Although surplus World War II aircraft were originally used in the development of airborne delivery systems (**Fig. 7a**), newer aircraft have permitted more flexible and efficient release systems. Four-engine cargo planes with pressurized tanks permit the delivery of as much as 3000 gal (11,000 liters) of retardant mixture to a fire. The retardant is released at a low altitude, either directly on the burning material at or near the fire edge, or some distance in front of an advancing fire. A single pass may cover an area several yards wide and several hundred yards long. Helicopters are also used, especially in initial attack and mop-up operations (Fig. 7b). While helicopters carry smaller amounts of retardant materials (50 to 100 gal or 179 to 379 liters), their great accuracy makes them excellent for strategic use of expensive materials.

Retardant drops are used primarily to cool down hot spots and help hold a fire pending arrival of ground forces, and to control spot fires outside the main fire perimeter. The air tanker has limited value in attacking the head of a rapidly moving crown fire.

Little direct use is made of the third possibility of removing the oxygen supply to a fire, although water has this effect to some extent and soil is sometimes used to smother flames.

Suppression strategy. The manner in which the various suppression techniques are utilized on a fire is determined by the fire boss, who is comparable to the fire chief in urban organizations. It is the responsibility of the fire boss to determine the strategy appropriate to the particular fire. Depending on the size of the fire, the fire boss may have a few people or a few hundred, and occasionally more than a thousand, to assist in carrying out the suppression strategy.

When a wildfire has been suppressed, it is essential that it be covered by a report. The fire boss should have someone specifically charged with report duties, or make the report personally. Usually there are printed forms available which include at least the following: (1) name of the fire or district number in which the fire occurred, (2) location of the fire, (3) size of the fire, (4) cause of the fire, (5) estimate of damage in dollars, and (6) date and times when the fire started and when it was suppressed or brought under control. See FOREST AND FORESTRY.

Willard S. Bromley

Bibliography. A. A. Brown and K. P. Davis, *Forest Fire: Control and Use*, 1973; T. T. Kozlowski and C. E. Ahlgren, *Fire and Ecosystems*, 1974; W. E. Reifsnyder, *Proceedings of the 10th Annual Tall Timbers Fire Ecology Conference*, 1970; T. Van Nao, *Forest Fire Prevention and Control*, 1982

Forest management

Forest management provides for planning and carrying out the owner's objectives and policies in continuously supplying forest crops and in using the forest and other natural resources. See FOREST RESOURCES.

Objectives and policies. The owner may be a private individual, a private company, or a public agency. Management decisions regarding forests are therefore made by individuals or by people representing the owner's organization. Their needs and expectations of results from a specific course of action determine the objectives and policies established to manage any specific forest area.

The expected results are wide-ranging, from minimum protection and extensive forestry to intensive forest management, and involving use of the forest only for wilderness, wildlife management, or watershed protection, or for combinations of all feasible uses. That choice must be made after a careful review of all the resources concerned and after full consideration of how the people in and out of the forest may be affected. When a decision has been made, a plan of management, or several alternative plans, can be prepared to meet the selected objectives. Policies can be established, but they may have to be modified to meet any limiting factors established by expected costs and returns, by law, or by public needs or opinions.

Management plans. The management of forests and their natural resources require long-term planning. It may take from 30 to 100 years to convert an overstocked, overmature virgin stand of timber to a well-stocked fully productive forest. To establish a new forest on essentially bare land takes at least 20 to 30 years to grow pulpwood and from 40 to 80 years to grow sawlogs. In any case, such long-term plans should be based on adequate inventories and maps of the natural resources, estimates of the current status and growth of those resources, recommendations as to their management practices, and estimates of new returns and benefits.

Inventories and maps. Adequate knowledge of the land areas, the timber resources, and the nontimber resources of any forest should be available to the forest manager.

Maps showing the legal boundaries of the forest and the clear establishment of those boundaries on the ground are essential. Such maps should include, or be supplemented with, maps showing topographic features, major soil types, and possibly some note of the geological formations and characteristics of any rock outcroppings.

Timber estimates should include maps showing the major forest types—by size or age classes. Estimates of the volume of timber by species of trees must be available by compartments or use zones of the forest. Boundaries must be recognized on the ground by such natural features as ridge tops, streams, or roads, or by established survey lines. Compartment areas should, if possible, not exceed the size of what might be harvested in one year of operation. Maps and timber estimates can be derived from forest survey techniques that require sampling only a small percentage of forest area. The actual percent of the area to be covered by strips or plots mechanically distributed over the forest can be calculated by statistical analyses.

Surveys of the nontimber resources require techniques quite different from those used for timber resources. Rangeland or grazing resources may be measured along strips or plots, but the size of the plot and data collected on grasses and plant cover are radically different. The techniques for assessment of wildlife, fisheries, water, and recreational resources are available. They can be used most effectively by professionally trained people. These may be staff specialists in the forest organization, foresters on the staff trained in these fields, or consultants hired specifically to make such surveys. Surveys of nontimber resources on public forests are becoming an essential part of any review of natural resources and of plans for them. They are also being made on some industrial and private forest.

Growth estimates. The current growth or yield of harvestable products annually or periodically must be known to make any decisions as to how much may be harvested annually or periodically. For timber harvesting there should be a progression of tree age or size classes from small to large so that merchantable trees are regularly available for cutting in approximately equal volume. When this is established, a sustained-yield form of management has been achieved. Estimating the current growth of timber and of the nontimber resources is a complex problem. For virgin stands of timber, primarily in the West, current growth may be offset completely by losses from competition and mortality. Even if there were no mortality, the growth on the sound trees would still be abnormally slow. To obtain estimates of growth in such stands, one is forced to make assumptions, or to rely on measurements of previously cut stands, usually established by forest experiment stations.

Similar problems are presented by estimating growth of newly established forests, as in forest tree plantations. Although data from some of the plantations made in the 1920s and 1930s became available, the modern standards of stocking (that is, the spacing of trees) are usually different from those used in the older plantations. Industrial forests are planting seedlings from "super trees" which grow at much faster rates than average seedlings. In spite of these problems, the best possible estimate of the growth of the forest under management must be made to provide a basis for making annual or periodic harvests. Similar studies of the wildlife and fish populations must be made on public forests to see whether these populations are stable, decreasing, or increasing.

Management practices. From a timber management point of view, forest practices hinge materially upon whether the forest is composed of even-aged or uneven-aged groups or stands of trees.

In an even-aged forest stand, the individual trees originated at about the same time and occupy an area large enough to grow under essentially full-light conditions. Such a stand has a noticeable beginning and an end in time. The end is the rotation time in years that it takes for the forest crop to reach the size or condition desired. It is established either naturally or by planting or seeding. Thinnings or other intermediate cuttings may be made during its life (**Figs. 1** and **2**). When these even-aged stands are ready for harvest, the forest should have a relatively even distribution of stands representing the youngest to the oldest age groups. When this distribution includes stands of equal area, or better yet of equal productivity, the annual or periodic harvest can be essentially the same volume, and the cut of the forest can be said to be under regulation. If the annual cut volume is close to the annual growth of the forest as a whole, the forest is said to be managed on a sustained yield basis.

With uneven-aged or all-aged stands, the trees originated at different times, so that the stand includes

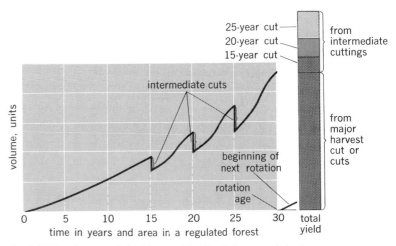

Fig. 1. Lifeline of even-aged stand in a regulated forest of even-aged stands.

trees of varying ages. The age-class distribution may not be perfect, but there is a reasonably good representation of trees from the youngest to the oldest age classes on all or most of the stand areas (**Fig. 3**). Such stands have no beginning or end in point of time. With uneven-aged stands there is no major single harvest cut, nor a guiding rotation. Intermediate and harvest cuts are merged into partial cuttings of the stand which are repeated periodically in cutting cycles. The cutting-cycle length is set to provide sufficient volume to make up an economical cut per acre to justify logging costs and to make a net return. The

Fig. 2. Clear-cut areas of an even-aged stand in Six Rivers National Forest, California.

Fig. 3. Properly thinned uneven-aged loblolly-shortleaf pine stand. (*U. S. Forest Service*)

turn of the cycle is also set to provide for sufficient growth between cuts to replace the volume removed in the last cut of the stand concerned.

Cutting cycle. The organization of a large uneven-aged forest unit for continuous production is diagrammatically shown in **Fig. 4**. A 5-year cutting cycle is assumed, which means that the various stands constituting the forest unit are grouped into five areas of approximately equal productivity, as shown by number in the diagram.

Each year, a harvest cutting is made covering one of these five areas, equal in volume to 5 years of growth, plus or minus whatever changes are considered appropriate to maintain the average amount of reserve growing stock. In Fig. 2, a small increase in the amount of reserve growing stock over the two cycles shown is indicated. The entire forest management unit is cut over every 5 years.

Even-aged management is applied worldwide in commercial timber production considerably more than is uneven-aged management. The reasons are that species control in regeneration, stand and area treat-

ments, and harvest cuts can be more cheaply and effectively applied uniformly over fairly large areas than is possible in all-aged management. In uneven-aged management, cutting is much more dispersed over the total management unit, and uniform areas treatment is less practicable, but there is less of a drain on soil fertility and less likelihood of nonpoint pollution or erosion of the soil. The latter are becoming important considerations from the public's long-term point of view.

Individual trees or groups of trees must be selected and marked for cutting. This requires the skills of foresters or forest technicians trained to apply marking guides or rules to carry out the silvicultural and management objectives.

The management of a wildlife and fish populations and the management of grazing animals also require specific practices to maintain, improve, and increase their numbers if their needs for sustenance can be provided within the current or changed environment.

Net returns and benefits. In developing a forest management plan or alternative plans, the impact on the environment must be considered, and a review of the objectives and policies to be applied may become necessary. Net monetary returns for the long run may be the primary goal of the industrial forest manager. A financial analysis of a plan may show that growing sawtimber for a southeastern pulp mill produces the greatest net return for the capital invested. This may not produce sufficient pulpwood and chips to keep the mill in operation. A shift of objectives and plans may be required. State laws or public opinion may require that the size and location of clear-cut operations be modified to meet their standards. *See* WOOD PRODUCTS.

Forest owners, public or private, may have nonfinancial goals such as the maximum output of game, water, fish, or timber, aside from the net financial returns. The final decision on plans of management will require the plan is adopted and put into action. *See* FOREST AND FORESTRY.

Willard S. Bromley

Bibliography. T. E. Avery and H. E. Burkhart, *Forest Measurements*, 3d ed., 1983; K. P. Davis, *Forest Management*, 2d ed., 1966; W. A. Duerr, *Forest-Resource Management*, 1982; C. D Oliver and B. C. Larson, *Forest Stand Dynamics*, 1990.

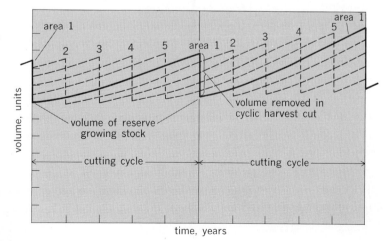

Fig. 4. Lifeline of uneven-aged stand in a regulated forest of uneven-aged stands.

Forest pest control

The techniques and methods used in protecting forests from pests and diseases. In the natural, unmanaged forest, pests are most often of little significance because there are usually many kinds of trees of different ages, which discourages the buildup of pest populations. In many of today's forested areas, however, this natural balance has been changed, and trees of more or less continuous age and species composition are grown in large areas. In such a management procedure, known as monoculture, pest problems take on increased significance.

Fusiform rust (caused by *Cronartium quercuum fusiforme*) is one example. Prior to 1930, fusiform rust was rare in the United States, but since that time it has become a problem among southern pines. The cause of the problem is twofold: increased monoculture in pine management, and the increase in the number of oaks in neighboring stands. The rust requires both oaks and pines as hosts. Fire prevention resulted in an increase in the abundance of oaks in southern forests; natural fires had previously kept oak populations at low levels. This, combined with even-aged pine stands, provided a perfect environment for the rust. When the fungus was accidentally sent to the field on infected pine nursery stock, it proliferated rapidly. It still causes annual losses in excess of $100 million (**Fig. 1**).

Other pests of major consequence occur where major outbreaks were part of a natural cycle in the past. An example of this is spruce budworm (*Choristoneura fumiferana*) on balsam fir in the Lake States. In the past, the firs grew over relatively large continuous areas. When the firs reached a certain age, a budworm outbreak occurred which killed most of the resource; the firs regenerated, and the cycle started over again. But because of the value of the resource, this natural process has been found to be unacceptable by foresters.

A third example is the introduced pest, where the susceptible trees were present and the disease or insect was introduced from abroad. Examples of these are chestnut blight (caused by *Endothia parasitica*), Dutch elm disease (caused by *Ceratocystis ulmi*), white pine blister rust (caused by *Cronartium ribicola*), and the gypsy moth (*Porthetria dispar*). Many of these pests did not cause serious losses in their natural habitat, but resulted in epidemics when introduced into new ones.

Seed and seedling pests. As trees go through their natural developmental process from seed to seedling to mature and finally overmaturity, each stage is subject to attack by a different series of pests.

A variety of insects and fungi attack seeds on the trees. Pests, such as weevils and shieldback pine seedbugs (*Tetyra bipunctata*), attack the seeds directly and can cause complete seed crop losses. Fungi, such as *Fusaria* sp., *Alternaria* sp., and *Diplodia* sp., which are commonly found on the surface of tree seed and may be found inside otherwise healthy seed, can play a major role in the next major problem in the seedling history, called damping-off. These fungi, and others in the soil, invade the seed just prior to or after germination and cause mortality. Birds, squirrels, and other rodents also cause major losses to seed under natural field conditions.

Seedlings grown in a forest tree nursery are subjected to a number of nematodes, insects, and fungi that attack roots, stems, and foliage. It is under these conditions that pests, such as *Lophodermium pinastris* on certain tree species and *Microsphaera alphitoides* on oak, which would not be a problem under field conditions, can cause serious losses.

In the field, seedlings become susceptible to a wider variety of pests. Some of the major pests at this stage are debarking weevils (pales weevil, *Hylobius pales*); rust fungi, such as white pine blister rust (caused by *C. ribicola*); foliage disease, such as brown spot on longleaf pine (caused by *Scirrhia acicola*); scleroderris canker (caused by *Scleroderris lagerbergii*); rodent damage; shoot-boring insects; and root-feeding insects. The most severe problem at this stage, however, is weed competition and drought. The rate of loss varies with the type of problem. For example, drought, rodent damage, and debarking weevils normally cause a rapid loss, while rust fungi, foliage disease, and stem cankers take longer to kill the seedlings and thus distribute the losses over a longer time. Some pests, such as shoot insects, may

Fig. 1. Loblolly pine stand severely damaged by the fusiform rust fungus, *Cronartium quercuum fusiforme*. (*Photograph by Harry Powers*)

not kill the seedling, but do cause stem deformity. The chestnut blight fungus keeps chestnut sprouts from ever reaching the larger stages.

Sapling and mature tree pests. As the seedling becomes a sapling, some of the seedling pests persist and new pests, including sawflies, foliage diseases, canker diseases (such as that caused by *Dothichiza populea* on poplar), borers, and root rots begin to play a major role.

The poletimber stage provides the timber for forest products, but some of the more destructive pests are found in this stage, including bark beetles (**Fig. 2**), borers (**Fig. 3**), rust fungi, root rots, cankers, and decay (**Fig. 4**). Black locust trees can be destroyed by

Fig. 2. Galleries made by bark beetles under the bark of a slash pine tree. (*USDA Forest Service*)

Fig. 3. Rough, distorted bark on a red oak tree caused by oak borers. (*Photograph by Robert L. Anderson*)

the black locust borer (*Megacyllene robiniae*); trees scarred by fire can be infected and ruined by decay fungi for the life of the tree; and larch can be destroyed by a canker disease (caused by *Trichoscyphella willkommii*).

Fig. 4. Decay at the base of a southern hardwood caused by the fungus which produced the conks above the opening. (*Photograph by Robert L. Anderson*)

Trees of sawtimber size are the largest and most valuable, but experience the greatest losses from pests. Vascular wilts (for example, Dutch elm disease and oak wilt), bark beetles (southern pine beetle and mountain pine beetle), root rots (annosus root rot and laminated root rot), hardwood borers (oak borer and black locust borer), defoliators (gypsy moth and spruce budworm), decay (heart rot and butt rot), dwarf mistletoes, and a variety of other pests cause serious damage at this stage.

In some cases, a complex decline is caused by a combination of age, defoliating agents, root diseases, borers, and environmental stresses all working together. Some times, either through lack of continuous management or special use, trees are permitted to become overmature. When this happens, decay, borers, bark beetles, root rots, and other pests work overtime to reduce the number and quality of remaining trees. However, these stands may still be valuable for use other than as lumber.

Loss estimates. Some pests, for example, rust diseases, root rots, hardwood borers, and mistletoes cause about the same economic loss each year. Others such as spruce budworms, pine bark beetles, and most defoliators, result in cyclic losses, where millions of dollars are lost in certain years, with virtually no loss the next year. Still another group of pests, such as gypsy moths, cankerworms, and leafrollers, can cause growth loss and mortality after repeated defoliation, but their primary impact is esthetic. The actual losses caused by these pests are very difficult to measure.

Many pests result in death of the tree with outright loss of wood products or the esthetic value of trees. About 50% of the annual tree mortality in the United States is caused by insects, disease, weather, or animals; the remaining 50% is due to fire and unknown causes, the majority of which are probably pest-related. Certain diseases, such as root diseases, and pests, such as dwarf mistletoes, result in death, but cause a growth loss prior to killing the tree. Fortunately, although the combination of mortality, growth loss, and quality losses result in annual losses in the billions of dollars, there are a number of ways to prevent or control pests and thus minimize their impact.

Integrated pest management. In years past, land managers approached each forest pest individually, but it is now understood that pest problems are often interrelated. Pests frequently aggravate one another's impact due to the compounding stress factors. Therefore, one option is an integrated pest management (IPM) approach.

As defined here, integrated pest management is a strategy that manipulates forest pests to achieve resource management objectives. It is the planned and systematic use of all necessary and appropriate cultural, biological, chemical, and mechanical means to prevent or reduce pest-caused damage and losses to levels that are economically, environmentally, and esthetically acceptable. Key elements in this process include systematic detection and evaluation of forest pests and hazard rating of stands. Given early discovery and evaluation processes, environmentally and economically responsible actions can be combined into an integrated pest management program.

In many cases in the past, managers relied almost exclusively on direct control techniques, such as salvage removal and chemical control. While these approaches provide short-term relief, essentially they

Preventive Guidelines:

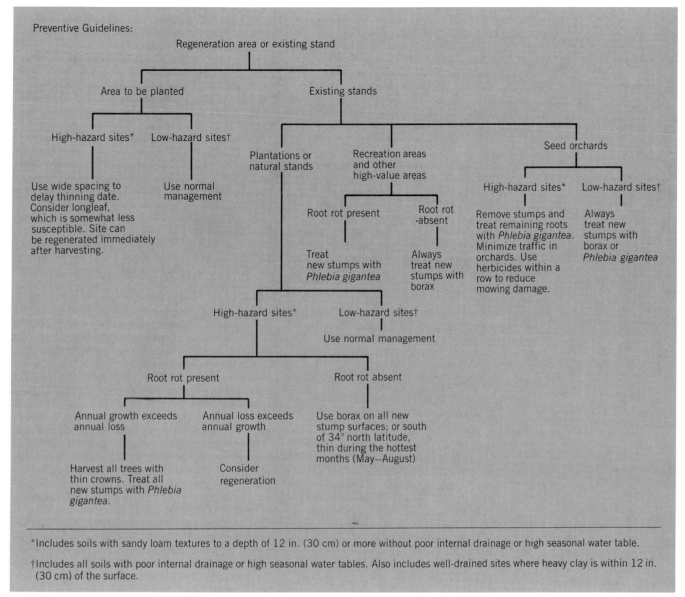

*Includes soils with sandy loam textures to a depth of 12 in. (30 cm) or more without poor internal drainage or high seasonal water table.

†Includes all soils with poor internal drainage or high seasonal water tables. Also includes well-drained sites where heavy clay is within 12 in. (30 cm) of the surface.

Fig. 5. Example of a decision key for annosus root rot in the southeast United States. (*After S. A. Alexander and R. L. Anderson, How to identify and control annosus root rot in the Southeast, USDA Forest Service Forestry Bull. SA-FB/P45, 1982*)

treat the symptom rather than the problem. In contrast, integrated pest management considers the use of these control measures, but emphasizes preventive techniques. One such technique is thinning, which eliminates high-risk trees and increases stand vigor. Genetic resistance of trees serves as the major source of prevention for several pests (such as white pine blister rust and fusiform rust), while some pests (fusiform rust and annosus root rot) can be reduced by altering the stocking or planting density. Delaying planting for 6 to 9 months after cutting will avoid reproduction weevil damage, and delaying thinning during drought periods will discourage the buildup of beetles (*Ips* spp.).

Site, tree species, weather, stocking, age, geographic location, and management objectives all play major roles in integrated pest management processes. With specific information about a site, the manager can determine the current and future hazard and develop preventive management strategies for the life of the stand. Flow charts (**Fig. 5**) are commonly used to

help the resource manager tailor the recommendation to the specific site. Because of the complexity of making such a match, computer models, such as the integrated pest management decision key (IPM-DK), have been developed. The IPM-DK, developed in the southeastern United States for major pests of southern pines and hardwoods, allows the user to call upon the computer, respond to several questions, and get the most current information for a specific pest and host environment listed.

A typical and effective IPM program would be made up of the following items:

1. Frequent detection surveys; most of these are from the air and scheduled to coincide with the activity of the major pests.

2. If a problem is identified during a detection survey, biological evaluations are made to determine the extent of the problem and prescribe direct control measures. This may involve salvage removal, chemicals, burning, or other techniques.

3. Each site is hazard-rated for major pests, includ-

ing both current and future hazards. At this point, steps are being taken to prevent high-hazard situations or reduce the current hazard. These involve the use of preventive techniques, such as thinning, the use of resistant trees, fertilization, and sanitation cutting.

Fortunately, the application of modern systems of integrated pest management such as the foregoing is increasing in scope each year. The need for accelerating such programs will become more apparent as economic losses from pests are more fully appreciated in the future.

Robert L. Anderson

Bibliography. R. L. Anderson, *Forest and Shade Tree Entomology*, 1964; W. T. Johnson and H. Lyon, *Insects That Feed on Trees and Shrubs*, 2d ed., 1988; W. A. Sinclair et al., *Diseases of Trees and Shrubs*, 1987.

Forest resources

Forest resources consist of two separate but closely related parts: the forest land and the trees (timber) on that land. In the United States, forests cover one-third of the total land area of the 50 states, in total, about 736×10^9 acres (1 acre = 0.405 hectare). The fact that 1 of every 3 acres of the United States is tree-covered makes this land and its condition a matter of importance to every citizen. Recognizing this importance, Congress has charged the U.S. Forest Service with the responsibility of making periodic appraisals of the national timber situation, a charge that was substantially increased in scope by the Forest and Rangeland Renewable Resources Planning Act of 1974 and the National Forest Management Act of 1976.

Some 482×10^6 acres, or about two-thirds of the total forest area in the United States, is classified as commercial forest land, that is, forest land capable of producing at least 20 ft³ (1 ft³ = 0.028 m³) of industrial wood per acre per year, and not reserved for uses incompatible with timber production. The 254×10^6 acres of noncommercial forest includes about 25×10^6 acres which meets the growth criteria for commercial timberland but has been set aside for parks, wilderness areas, and such. The remaining 228×10^6 acres is incapable of producing a sustained crop of industrial wood, but is valuable for watershed production, grazing, and recreation use. **Table 1** gives details of the distribution of forest land in the four main regions of the United States.

Most of the noncommercial forests are in public ownership, including approximately 20×10^6 productive forest acres legally withdrawn for such uses as national parks, state parks, and national forest wilderness areas. Another 4.6×10^6 acres, classed as productive-deferred, is under study for possible inclusion in the wilderness system. Of the remaining noncommercial forest, about 107×10^6 acres are in Alaska (part of the Pacific Coast region). Most discussions of forest resources, however, concentrate upon the commercial areas, and these lands are the primary concern of the following discussion.

For many years, changes in United States agriculture led to abandonment of marginal farms, which rapidly reverted to forest. This "new forest" was more than enough to offset those areas lost to highways, pipelines, urban development, and such. In all regions, substantial areas have been taken over by suburban development, highways, reserves, and other nontimber uses, while in the South (where much of the early decline occurred) timberland has been cleared for crop production and for pasture.

Forest types. There are literally hundreds of tree species used for commercial purposes in the United States. The most general distinction made is that between softwoods (the conifers, or conebearing trees, such as pine, fir, and spruce) and hardwoods (the broad-leafed trees, such as maple, birch, oak, hickory, and aspen). Viewed nationally, 51% of United States commercial forest land is occupied by eastern hardwood types. Softwoods of various kinds make up 42%, western hardwoods only 3%; and 4% of the area is unstocked. Oak-hickory stands cover the largest area, accounting for 23% of all commercial timberland. The oak-pine type (14% of the eastern hardwood area) is mostly in the South and is primarily the residual from the cutting of merchantable pine in mixed pine-hardwood forests. During the last few decades many of these stands have been converted to pine by the killing or cutting of hardwoods and, often, by the planting of pine, although little change, percentage-wise, has occurred since 1970.

Of the eastern hardwood forests, 44% are oak-hickory types, containing a large number of species but characterized by the presence of one or more species of oak or hickory. Other important eastern types are the maple-birch-beech (found throughout the New England, Middle Atlantic, and Lakes states regions), the oak-gum-cypress forests (primarily in the Mississippi Delta and other southern river bottoms), and the aspen-birch type of the Lake states (relatively short-

Table 1. Distribution of forest land in the United States

Type of forest land	Area, 10⁶ acres*				
	Total†	Pacific Coast‡	North	South	Rocky Mt.
Commercial forest	482.5	70.5	166.1	188.0	57.8
Noncommercial forest	—	—	—	—	—
Productive reserved	20.7	4.1	6.0	2.0	8.4
Productive deferred	4.6	1.2	0.2	0.1	3.2
Other forest	228.8	138.4	5.3	16.7	68.4
Total noncommercial	254.1	143.7	11.5	18.8	80.0
Total forest land	736.6	214.3	177.7	206.9	137.7

*1 acre = 0.405 hectare.
†Totals may not agree in last figure due to rounding.
‡Pacific Coast includes both Alaska and Hawaii.

Table 2. Summary of net annual growth and removals of growing stock and sawtimber, by species group and region

Section and species group	Growing stock, 10^9 ft^{3*}			Sawtimber, 10^9 bd-ft†		
	Net growth	Removals	Growth-removal ratio	Net growth	Removals	Growth-removal ratio
North						
Softwoods	1.6	0.7	2.3	4.0	2.2	1.8
Hardwoods	4.2	1.9	2.2	9.8	6.2	1.6
South						
Softwoods	6.2	4.5	1.4	24.2	19.0	1.3
Hardwoods	4.5	2.1	2.1	13.3	7.7	1.7
Rocky Mountains						
Softwoods	1.4	0.8	1.7	6.3	4.8	1.3
Hardwoods	0.1	—	28	0.3	—	17.4
Pacific Coast						
Softwoods	2.9	4.0	0.7	15.1	26.9	0.6
Hardwoods	0.5	0.1	4.3	1.6	0.4	3.9
United States						
Softwoods	12.3	10.0	1.2	49.0	50.9	.98
Hardwoods	9.4	4.2	2.2	24.9	14.3	1.7

$^*10^9$ ft^3 = 28,316,846 m^3.
$^\dagger10^9$ bd-ft = 2,359,737 m^3, as nominal recovered lumber.

lived species that followed logging and fires). The bottomland hardwoods (oak-gum-cypress type) were reduced about 20% between 1962 and 1970, primarily by the clearing of forests for agriculture. For many years these forests have supplied much of the quality hardwoods in the United States.

Softwood types dominate the western forests, altogether occupying 83% of the region's commercial forest area. Douglas-fir and ponderosa pine, the principal types, together constitute 45% of the region's commercial timberland. The western softwood types are the principal sources of lumber and plywood in the United States. Nearly all the commercial forest area of coastal Alaska is of the hemlock-Sitka spruce type. Hardwoods, mostly in Washington and Oregon, occupy only 12% of the West's commercial forest area, but have increased substantially since 1962 as the Douglas-fir forests have been cut.

Growth. Growth on these areas has been more than enough to match the harvest since the mid-1960s. This is commendable, but the fact that growth and drain are in approximate balance provides no assurance that all is well. Much of the growth is still on low-quality hardwoods in the East, while about two-thirds of United States demand for the raw materials of the forest is met by the softwood production of the West and South. Potentially the most productive forest land is that of the Pacific Coast states. The North is considerably less well off as far as forest growth rates are concerned.

Growth per acre on forests of the United States has been rising steadily—in all regions and on all ownerships. The increase has been particularly dramatic: since 1952 average per-acre growth increased from 28 to 45 ft^3. This 61% rise is due at least in part to efforts made by American forestry on both public and private lands. But there is still far to go: net growth per acre is far below that possible under intensive management, and only three-fifths of what could be achieved from fully stocked natural stands.

Timber inventory. Only soil productivity exceeds stocking (the number of trees per acre) and the age of the trees in importance as factors determining timber production.

Stocking. The commercial forests contained a truly vast amount of sound wood—792,371 × 10^6 ft^3 at

the beginning of 1977. Only 8.5% of this consisted of trees that were dead, diseased, or in such poor condition they were not commercially useful. Another 1.8% consisted of trees which were dead but still usable for timber. Some 64% of the total volume was in trees sufficiently large to yield at least one sawlog: such trees are called sawtimber. Another 26% was in pole timber—trees ranging from about 5 in. (13 cm) in diameter (breast high) up to sawtimber size. Softwoods accounted for 61% of the total growing stock (pole timber plus sawtimber) and for 64% of the portion in sawtimber sizes, with 69% of the latter in the western states. This distribution highlights an important facet of timber distribution: the western states have only 27% of the commercial forest land and 27% of the total growing stock of the nation. But these western forests have 75% of the important softwood sawtimber, and 69% of the nation's softwood growing stock (**Table 2**). The East, on the other hand, has 93% of the total hardwood growing stock (about equally divided between the North and South) and 91% of the hardwood sawtimber volume.

Age. Age is the other factor that must be considered before the significance of growth (and removals) can be understood. The virgin softwood stands of the West are growing relatively slowly, but as these old stands are replaced with young, vigorous trees, growth on western forests will begin to balance the cut—although almost surely at a reduced level. Harvest of western sawtimber cannot be maintained at present levels unless forest management is greatly intensified. In the East, however, net growth of softwood growing stock exceeds removals, while softwood sawtimber growth is above removals. Here it should be noted that hardwood harvesting is concentrated in high-valued species such as walnut, cherry, gum, yellow birch, and maple, and in trees of large diameter, while much of the growth is in trees of less preferred species. and of small size. Annual growth and removal data are summarized in Table 2.

Ownership. The future condition of forest land in the United States is dependent to a very large extent on the decisions of the people who own these areas. The key factors in understanding the forest situation, therefore, are the forest land ownership pattern and the attitude these owners have toward forest manage-

Table 3. Areas of commercial timberland in the United States by type of ownership and section*

Type of ownership	Total United States		Region			
	Area, 10^3 acres	Proportion, %	North, 10^3 acres	South, 10^3 acres	Rocky Mt., 10^3 acres	Pacific Coast, 10^3 acres
National forests	88,718	18.4	9,831	10,955	36,436	31,497
Bureau of Land Management	5,803	1.2	19	3	1,667	4,113
Other	4,889	1.0	1,120	3,343	75	352
All federal	99,410	20.6	10,970	14,300	38,178	35,962
Native American	6,062	1.3	994	185	2,711	2,172
State	23,415	4.9	12,941	2,519	2,203	5,753
County and municipal	6,834	1.4	5,608	727	75	425
All public	135,722	28.1	30,513	17,731	43,167	44,311
Forest industry	68,782	14.3	17,913	36,245	2,096	12,528
Farm	115,777	24.0	45,993	55,909	8,311	5,564
Miscellaneous private	162,205	33.6	71,722	78,161	4,191	8,130
All private	346,364	71.8	135,628	170,315	14,598	26,223
All ownerships	482,486	100.0	166,141	188,046	57,765	70,534

*1 acre = 0.405 hectare.

ment and hence toward the future of the forest lands they hold.

About 72% of the commercial forest is held in private ownership (346×10^6 acres). The remaining 28% is held by various public owners, with about 18% in national forests, 2% in other federal ownership, 5% in state holdings, 2% under county and municipal control, and slightly over 1% under native-American sovereignty. Among private owners, three major classes can be distinguished: industrial, farm, and a very heterogeneous group labeled miscellaneous. About 14% of the commercial forest land is in the hands of industry, the remainder being divided between farmers (24%) and miscellaneous private owners (34%). **Table 3** gives details about forest ownership, as well as the distribution of privately owned forests, in the four major regions of the United States.

Private owners. Some of the most productive forest land of the United States is in private industrial holdings. Pulp and paper companies lead the forest-based industries, with much of their forest land concentrated in the southern states, where nearly 36×10^6 acres is industrially owned. As forest industries become integrated, it is increasingly difficult to make distinctions between pulp and paper, lumber, and plywood companies, and certainly the distinctions are much less meaningful than in former years.

The miscellaneous private category, which holds 34% of the privately owned forest land, consists of a tremendous variety of individuals and groups, ranging from housewives to mining companies. Relatively few of these owners are holding this land for commercial timber production. Some owners, such as railroad companies or oil corporations, may indeed be interested in producing timber while holding the subsurface mineral rights, but miscellaneous private owners are usually interested in other, nontimber, objectives.

Most farm forests have been cut over several times; and, because farmers are primarily interested in the production of other kinds of crops, they tend to be less concerned with the condition of their woodlands than are other owners. The condition of farm-owned woodlands has been a source of much disappoint-

ment, discussion, and considerable action on the part of public conservation agencies. Whether this situation is of crucial significance to the production of forest products in the United States is a matter of dispute. In past years some professional foresters have argued that these farm woodlands should somehow be made to contribute their full share to the timber supply of the nation. Others, of a more economic persuasion, have argued that, as long as farmers have opportunities for investing time and money in ways that will yield a greater return, they should not be expected to worry about timber production. Farm owners are often unfamiliar with forest practices, usually lack the capital required for long-term investments, and in many cases are simply not interested in growing trees.

When compared with other forest land of the same quality and within the same region, farm woodlot management levels are only slightly, if at all, below that given other ownership categories.

Public owners. Public agencies of several kinds hold large forest areas, the most important being the national forests. These contain 89×10^6 acres of commercial forest land which is managed and administered by the U.S. Forest Service, a bureau of the U.S. Department of Agriculture. The Bureau of Land Management oversees about 6×10^6 acres. Various other agencies, especially those of the armed services, administer about 5×10^6 acres under federal supervision. State ownerships total 23×10^6 acres, and counties and municipalities control another 7×10^6 acres. The remainder, somewhat over 6×10^6 acres, is under native-American sovereignty. Most of the public holdings are managed under multiple-use principles. As on most forest land, wood has always been the principal product of the national forests. With the passage of the 1974 Planning Act and the 1976 National Forest Management Act, the nontimber uses were given increased official attention, and the ongoing debate between those favoring timber production and those primarily concerned with range, water, wildlife, and recreation has been much intensified.

Public holdings now contain 57% of the softwood growing stock but only 18% of the hardwoods. Sixty-two percent of all softwood sawtimber is publicly owned, and most is in national forests. The high concentration of sawtimber in these areas makes many wood-based industries in the United States highly dependent upon government-owned raw material supplies.

World forest resources. Since much of the world's forested area has yet to be surveyed, data concerning volume, species, or even area undoubtedly contain substantial errors. Advances in remote sensing, particularly the information being relayed from satellites, give promise of vast improvement in knowledge of how the world's forests are faring. About 7.5×10^9 acres have a 20% or more tree crown cover—roughly one-third of the world's land surface and about the same average percentage as that for the United States as a whole. Latin America and the tropical regions of Africa and Southeast Asia have most of the hardwood forests, while the softwood areas are concentrated in North America and the Soviet Union.

Latin America has about 43% of the world's hardwood growing stock, and this is nearly half again as much as the hardwood forested area of Africa—the continent next richest in hardwood. Together, Latin America and Africa account for 72% of the world's hardwoods, with Southeast Asia adding another 15%. North America has only 5% of the total. In the important softwood category, however, the Soviet Union and North America come in first and second, and together account for 83% of the world's softwoods. The Soviet Union has by far the largest share—about 2½ times as much as North America. Because of low productivity, great distance from markets, and rugged terrain, much of the softwood in the Soviet Union will be difficult to bring into commercial use.

Forests reflect differences in soil, climate, situation, and past land use and merely listing the forest types of the world would take several pages. Yet there is value in distinguishing very generalized forest types by broad locational patterns (see **illus.**).

Coniferous and temperate mixed forests. In Europe, the Soviet Union, North America, and Japan, the forests are predominantly coniferous, a fact that has been of great significance in shaping the pattern and nature of wood use in the industrialized part of the world. Closely associated with the industrialized nations are the temperate mixed forests, which normally contain a high proportion of conifers along with a few broad-leafed species.

Most of the temperate mixed forests are in use, for these heavily populated areas have well-developed transportation systems. Growth rates in both the coniferous and temperate mixed forests of the North Temperate Zone are similar to those already given for the United States, which is an excellent example of the general region.

Tropical rainforests. These forests are made up exclusively of broad-leafed species and include the bulk of the volume of the world's broad-leafed woods. They are concentrated in and around the Amazon Basin in South America, in western and west-central Africa, and in Southeast Asia. Generally characterized by sparse population and only slight industrial development, these forests have been little used. The fact that they typically contain many species within a small area (as many as a hundred species per acre)

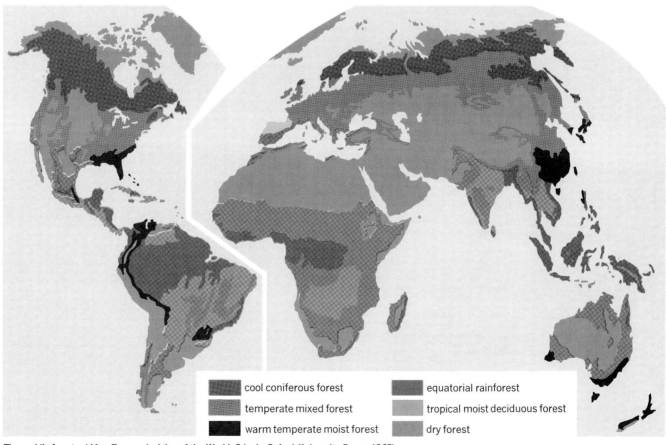

cool coniferous forest

temperate mixed forest

warm temperate moist forest

equatorial rainforest

tropical moist deciduous forest

dry forest

The world's forests. (*After Economic Atlas of the World, 3d ed., Oxford University Press, 1965*)

has also served to limit their use, even though tropical rainforests include some of the most valuable of all woods, such as mahogany, cedar, and greenheart (South America); okoume, obeche, lima, and African mahogany (Africa); and rosewood and teak (Asia).

The rate of growth in the tropics can be very high, and someday it may be possible to obtain a major part of the world's wood fiber needs from the more than 2×10^9 acres of these forests. Today, however, so little is known about many of the species, and so few areas are under any form of systematic management, that little reliance can be placed on these vast areas to satisfy the furture wood needs of humanity. A number of experts believe that tropical rainforests are in danger of extinction.

Savanna. Most of the other forests in the tropics and subtropics are dry, open woodlands, or savannas. These forests contain low volumes per acre, mostly in small sizes, and only a few of the species are of commercial value. Much of Africa (excluding western and west-central Africa) is of this low-yielding type.

Management. The use of measures such as careful soil preparation prior to planting, application of fertilizer, and even irrigation to adapt the environment to high-yielding species can result in an enormous increase in returns from forests. For example, yields of 400–500 ft^3/acre are common with eucalyptus in both South America and Africa, or with poplars in southern Europe. Only slightly smaller yields are obtained from the fast-growing pines under similarly intensive management. The high-yield potential of cultivated forests makes them much more important than their area might indicate.

While fast-growing plantations could add a new component to the world's industrial wood supply, a major threat to virtually all forests in developing nations stems from the pressing need for fuelwood. Expanding populations in Africa, Latin America, and Southeast Asia are destroying forests at a truly alarming rate as increasing numbers seek the means to cook their food and warm their families. There is a very real danger that in some areas the deforestation could lead to ecological changes that would be difficult or impossible to reverse. Forest removal from hill regions and drought-prone areas has far-reaching consequences, since soil and wind erosion and drastic changes in stream flow are almost inevitable. These, in turn, threaten food supplies for major segments of the world's population. *See* FOREST AND FORESTRY; FOREST MANAGEMENT.

G. Robinson Gregory

Bibliography. S. L. Pringle, Tropical moist forests in world demand, supply and trade, *Unasylva*, vol. 28, no. 112–113, 1976; U.S. Forest Service, *An Analysis of the Timber Situation in the United States 1952–2030*, For. Resource Rep. 23, 1982; U.S. Forest Service, *The Nation's Renewable Resources: An Assessment, 1975*, For. Resource Rep. 21, 1977.

Forest soil

The natural medium for growth of roots of trees and associated forest vegetation. The relationship with forest vegetation gives rise to characteristics that distinguish forest soils from soils formed under other vegetation systems. The most obvious feature is the humus layer, or horizon, which reflects the microenvironment imposed by the forest (**Fig. 1**). The humus horizon affects germination of seeds that fall on the

Fig. 1. Soil under an uncut forest is friable and porous, and it is deeply penetrated by roots and infiltrated with organic matter. (*USDA*)

forest floor, influences soil moisture distribution, serves as a reservoir of nutrient elements, influences the susceptibility of forest stands to fire, and represents the energy source for most soil-inhabiting organisms.

The process of humification starts when residues of forest plants and animals fall to the soil surface and are gradually decomposed. The course and extent of decomposition, which determine humus characteristics, depend chiefly on the microclimate of the forest stand, tree species, associated flora and fauna, and the nature of the underlying mineral soil material. Organic matter may accumulate on the soil surface with little or no mixing with mineral material. This form is called mor humus. Mull humus occurs when organic matter is incorporated into the mineral soil and only coarse debris, such as twigs and petioles, remains on the surface (**Fig. 2**). Transitional types combining characteristics of both mor and mull also occur. Mor humus is usually associated with a cool moist microclimate and predominantly coniferous or ericaceous vegetation growing on acidic parent material at higher latitudes or altitudes. In these situations soil fauna are generally small and ineffective in mixing organic matter with mineral soil, and the microflora population is dominated by fungi.

Leaf litter associated with mull soils is usually richer in calcium and other nutrient elements and hence supports a much more diverse population of soil animals and microorganisms than is found in mor humus layers. Metabolic activity of these organisms is stimulated by somewhat higher surface soil temperatures so that litter decomposition proceeds more rapidly. Earthworms, millipedes, and similar animals ingest litter and incorporate it into mineral soil. This process is accompanied by microbial conversion of the organic matter into relatively stable complexes of lignin and protein, which in some cases may be adsorbed on surfaces of clay minerals. These processes darken the upper few centimeters of mineral soil.

Fig. 2. Forest cover returns large quantities of organic matter to the soil each year. The depression in the center shows the depth of litter. (*USDA*)

The importance of soil fauna in organic matter breakdown cannot be overemphasized. Populations may exceed 100 million individuals per square meter of the forest floor and animal biomass is usually inversely related to population. These animals vary greatly in their range of movement. Some are confined to water films at the organic-mineral soil interface, while others may burrow to depths of more than a meter (3.3 ft) in the mineral substratum. Many mull soils are dominated by annelid earthworms which forage over relatively great distances. In contrast, mites and springtails are frequently the dominant soil animals in mor soils. These are generally unable to burrow and thus do not influence mineral soil aggregation the way annelids do. It is generally believed that there is little humification where there is little animal activity and that the mixing and binding activity associated with soil animals cannot be replaced by any other agent in the soil.

Humus-mineral relationships. A definite relationship exists between humus characteristics and the horizons that form deeper in the soil profile. Many of the biochemical reactions responsible for profile development originate in the humus layer, and by-products of these reactions are transmitted downward by percolating water. Mor humus is often associated with pronounced weathering of primary minerals and leaching of the breakdown products, particularly iron, to positions lower in the profile, whereas in mull soils profile transitions may be less distinct. Because of the delicate balances that function in organic matter decomposition, behavior of the humus layer responds rather quickly to changes in the microenvironment that may result from modification of the forest stand by wind damage, fire, or silvicultural operations. By contrast, deeper soil horizons are relatively stable and usually will show little change unless the soils are mechanically disturbed due to cultivation or catastrophic landslides, or when trees are uprooted.

Root relations. The humus layer is the focal point of biological activity in forest soils. In addition to litter-decomposing animals and microorganisms, it contains roots of forest vegetation. Because the supply of moisture and nutrients is generally favorable, nearly all of the absorbing roots of trees and other forest vegetation are located in and immediately below the humus layer. This is especially true in many tropical forests where the absorbing root mat literally rests on the upper surface of the deeply weathered mineral soil. When such a forest is removed, the bulk of the nutrient capital is removed with it, thus leaving the relatively impoverished deeply weathered soil to sustain the succeeding vegetative system.

Portions of the root systems of many trees and other woody plants exhibit root hair modifications called mycorrhizae (**Fig. 3**), which result from invasion of root tissues by certain fungi. The fungus is apparently attracted to soluble carbohydrates and other substances transported from the leaves to the younger portions of the root system where exudation may occur. The roots thus altered are evidently more efficient in absorbing water and solutes to be used by the tree.

This arrangement allows maximum utilization of nutrient elements released by decomposition of organic material, but nonetheless some leaching loss does occur. Such loss is balanced by root-induced weathering of rocks and minerals at deeper extremities of the root system. Forest soil depth is determined by depth of root penetration, which may vary from a few centimeters to many meters. Trees utilize a much larger volume of soil to maintain growth than do agricultural crops.

Classification. Forest soils may be classified in various ways. The classification of the Cooperative Survey of the Soil Conservation Service with Soil Taxonomy is sometimes used, but since this system

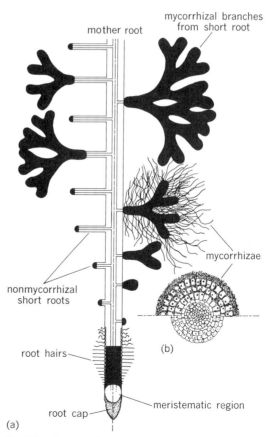

Fig. 3. Development of mycorrhizae on a pine root. Solid areas indicate absorbing surfaces. (*a*) The main axis, a mother root; (*b*) cross section, representing a mycorrhizal root. (*After P. J. Kramer, Plant and Soil Water Relationships, McGraw-Hill, 1949*)

is based on soil features important to agriculture, it usually must be modified for forestry purposes. Forest composition, secondary vegetation, parent material, topography, depth to groundwater, total soil depth, and growth and yield of forest stands all have been used, individually and in various combinations in classifying forest soils. Classifications based on forest productivity have been found to be fairly successful. In such systems, tree growth measured by height, diameter, or volume is related to soil properties, such as texture, structure, aeration, water infiltration, moisture-retention capacity, depth, type and distribution of organic matter, nutrient supply, and other characteristics known to influence growth of the root systems. These relationships are then used to predict potential productivity of understocked or deforested lands with similar soil characteristics. Because of the large areas involved, aerial photographs are frequently used as a mapping base on which forest cover types and soil boundaries are delineated.

Hydrologic cycle relations. In addition to their role in producing cellulose, timber, and other forest benefits, forest soils perform an important regulatory function in the hydrologic cycle. Undisturbed or well-managed forested watersheds are characterized by soils with a high water-infiltration capacity. This capacity is due partly to the extensive network of vertical and lateral channels resulting from decay of previous root systems and partly from the thousands of animal burrows intersecting the soil surface. Such soils are well protected by the litter layer and by secondary vegetation from the destructive energy of falling raindrops that would otherwise cause surface sealing and promote overland flow. Excessive overland flow results in soil erosion and reduction in water quality. Where falling rainwater or meltwater from snow has maximum opportunity to penetrate into the soil, normal drainage channels such as streams and rivers are recharged gradually through subsurface flow, and a steady supply of high-quality water is assured. Under certain types of vegetation, burning the litter may cause vaporized organic compounds to move downward in the soil profile, where they are condensed to form a water-repellent zone. If this condition is severe, as is frequently the case in the chaparral region of California, downward movement of water is retarded. The resulting increase in overland flow usually causes severe soil erosion or even landslides. *SEE HYDROLOGY.*

Nutrient cycling. Much research has been done on the circulation of nutrient elements in forest ecosystems. Movement of chemical elements occurs from minerals in the soil or from atmospheric sources, usually through the root system, into various tissues of forest vegetation. These tissues are utilized by consumer organisms or are ultimately deposited on the forest floor, where decompositon occurs, releasing the elements for reabsorption by root systems. It has been demonstrated that in undisturbed or in well-managed forests there is little nutrient leakage from those ecosystems. When the forest undergoes drastic disturbance as from a fire, from invasion of parasitic insects, or in large-scale clearcutting, loss of nutrients may be substantial and in extreme cases may cause drastic changes in downstream ecosystems. The study of nutrient cycling has elucidated the concept of limiting elements in the growth of forest vegetation. The species composition, and especially growth rate, of natural stands generally adapts to availability of nutrients in the soil. In commercial forestry, however,

the use of plantations is frequently prescribed for more intensive utilization of the productive capacity of the forest site. *SEE BIOGEOCHEMISTRY.*

Intensive forest management. Increasing demands for forest products and benefits coupled with increasing competition from other uses of land indicate that forest management at nearly all levels is likely to become more intensive. Foresters are manipulating the genetic potential of the tree species chosen for planting by using advanced tree breeding and tissue culture techniques. In may cases, highly mechanized methods of site preparation as well as routine applications of chemical fertilizers and herbicides are standard practice. Replacement of mixtures of species with a monoculture is done frequently. Whole-tree harvesting, which removes more organic residue than stem-only harvesting, as well as shorter harvesting rotations are becoming more commonplace. All of these practices increase economic yields from forest products substantially, but they also impose more stress on the productive capacity of the site. Knowledge of forest ecosystems may not be sufficient to determine whether if the productivity of intensively used areas can be sustained. *SEE FOREST MANAGEMENT.*

Air pollution. There is increasing concern that growth of forests in Europe and in parts of North America is being adversely affected by air pollution from combustion of fossil fuels by industry and automobiles. The most important regional air pollutants thought to be involved in growth decline are photochemical oxidants, especially ozone, trace metals such as lead or cadmium, and acidic deposition. Acidic deposition results when pollutants capable of forming acidifying compounds are deposited in the dry state as particulates or in solution or are condensed from vapor in the liquid or frozen state. Deposition may take place initially on the surface of vegetation or the forest floor, and subsequent movement into the mineral soil results from similarly acidified rainfall or meltwater. Many field and laboratory studies have been conducted on the effects of acidic deposition on forest soil characteristics. Generally these studies have shown little evidence that decline of forest growth is solely and directly attributable to changes in the soil. Significant acidification of forest soils has not been observed at current levels of pollution. In some cases, however, the potential for increased leaching losses of growth limiting cations may exist. Increased mobilization of soluble aluminum as Al^{3+} may have adverse effects on terrestrial and especially aquatic ecosystems. These adverse effects appear less likely to occur in those soils originating from geologic materials that are characterized by minerals high in alkali metals and alkaline-earth elements. *SEE ACID RAIN; SOIL ECOLOGY.*

Garth K. Voigt

Bibliography. K. A. Armson, *Forest Soils, Properties and Processes*, 1977; F. H. Bormann and G. E. Likens, *Pattern and Process in a Forested Ecosystem*, 1979; P. Farnum, R. Timmis, and J. L. Kulp, Biotechnology of forest yield, *Science*, 219(4585): 694–702, 1983; J. P. Kimmins, Sustained yield, timber mining and the concept of ecological rotation, a British Columbian view, *For. Chronicle*, 50:27–31, 1974; W. L. Pritchett, *Properties and Management of Forest Soils*, 1979; U.S. Environmental Protection Agency, *The Acidic Deposition Phenomenon and Its Effects*, Critical Assessment Review Papers, vols. 1 (EPA-600/8-83-016AF) and 2 (EPA-600/8-83-016BF), 1983.

Fresh-water ecosystem

An ecosystem is a fundamental unit of study in ecology; fresh water is best defined, in contrast to the oceans, as water that contains a relatively small amount of dissolved chemical compounds. Some studies of fresh-water ecosystems focus on water bodies themselves, while others include the surrounding land that interacts with a lake or stream. *See Ecology*.

Fresh-water ecosystems are often categorized by two basic criteria: water movement and size. In lotic or flowing-water ecosystems the water moves steadily in a uniform direction, while in lentic or standing-water systems the water tends to remain in the same general area for a longer period of time. Size varies dramatically in each category. Lotic systems range from a tiny rivulet dripping off a rock to large rivers such as the Amazon or Mississippi. Lentic systems range from the water borne within a cup formed by small plants or tree holes to very large water bodies such as the Laurentian Great Lakes.

Fresh-water studies consider an interacting array of the geological, physical, and chemical features along with the biota, the organisms that occur in an area. For example, in a lake the presence of a fish species may have a major effect on lake chemistry, while in a river, water flow patterns may determine the types of fishes that are present.

PHYSICAL ENVIRONMENT

Of primary concern in examining the physical environment are light and temperature distribution and the patterns of water movement.

Light. Light is the ultimate source of energy for almost all biological processes. Its quantity and spectral quality have major influences on the distribution of the biota and also play a major role in the thermal structure of lakes. Quantity of light can be measured as the total amount of energy which falls on an area or as the portion of that energy which can fuel photosynthesis. Interactions with the biota and water itself vary significantly with the wavelength of light.

The light that reaches the surface of a lake or stream is controlled by latitude, season, time of day, weather, and the conditions that surround a water body. As light penetrates a water surface, some is reflected into the atmosphere. Light which is not reflected may be scattered within the water, changing its direction; it may be reflected out of the water or it may be absorbed. Longer wavelengths of light (red and orange) are absorbed after passing through only a short distance in water, warming the water surface; shorter wavelengths (green and blue) penetrate deeper. Light penetration is controlled by the nature of water itself and by dissolved and particulate material in a water column. Light is reduced to 1% of the amount at the water surface in depths of less than 3 ft (1 m) in many productive or turbid lakes and rivers, whereas this light level is not reached until below 100 ft (30 m) in Crater Lake, Oregon.

Thermal stratification. Water exhibits a number of unusual thermal properties, including its existence in liquid state at normal earth surface temperatures, a remarkable ability to absorb heat, and a maximum density at 39.09°F (3.94°C), which leads to a complex annual cycle in the temperature structure of fresh-water ecosystems.

As water is warmed at the surface of a lake, it becomes less dense, and resistance develops to mixing with lower layers. Wind blowing over the surface mixes the warmer water into the lower layers to a certain extent, but a distinct surface layer of warmer water usually remains. Eventually a stable condition

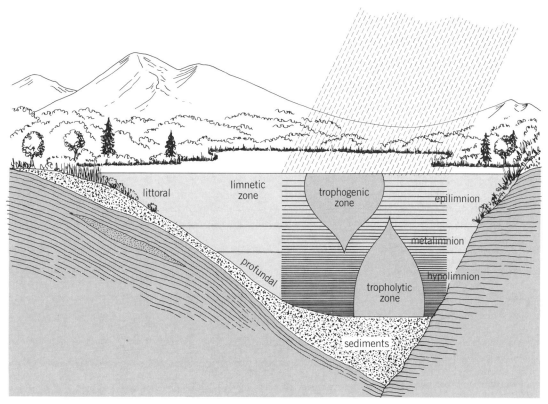

Fig. 1. Some major zones in lakes. (*After G. A. Cole, Textbook of Limnology, 3d ed., C. V. Mosby, 1983*)

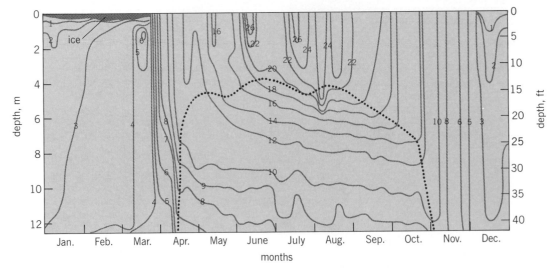

Fig. 2. Characteristic annual distribution of temperature (in °C) in a northern temperate zone lake. The region below the dotted line approximates hypolimnion. °F = (°C × 1.8) + 32°. 1 m = 3.3 ft. (*After R. G. Wetzel, Limnology, 2d ed., Saunders, 1983*)

is reached in which a physically distinct upper layer of water, the epilimnion, is maintained over a deeper, cooler stratum, the hypolimnion (**Fig. 1**). The region of sharp temperature changes between these two layers is called the metalimnion. The characteristic establishment of two layers is of major importance in the chemical cycling within lakes and consequently for the biota.

As the surface waters of a lake cool, the density of epilimnetic waters increases, which decreases their resistance to mixing with the hypolimnion. If cooling continues, the entire water column will mix, an event known as turnover. However, at temperatures below 39.09°F (3.94°C), water again becomes less dense and an inverse thermal gradient is established. Ice and very cold water float above slightly warmer water, maintaining liquid water below ice cover even in lakes in the Antarctic.

Many lakes in the temperate zones undergo two distinct periods of mixing annually, one in the spring and the other in the fall, that separate periods of stratification in the summer and winter (**Fig. 2**). Where winters are moderate, mixing may occur continuously from fall to spring so that lakes exhibit only a period of summer stratification. This occurs even in tropical lakes, despite the relatively constant temperatures. Some shallow lakes do not exhibit stratification as winds are sufficiently strong to mix them completely all year. Lakes also exist that never undergo mixing and are permanently stratified.

In lotic systems there is little temperature stratification with depth. Water movement ensures a relatively constant mixing. However, major changes occur as water moves downstream, with a tendency for an increase in temperature.

Water movement. Water movement is more extensive in lotic than in standing-water ecosystems, but water motion has important effects in both types. Turbulence, the disorderly mixing of water, occurs ubiquitously and affects the distribution of organisms, particles, dissolved substances, and heat. Turbulence increases with the velocity of flowing water, and the amount of material transported by water increases with turbulence. Flowing-water ecosystems are characterized by large fluctuations in the velocity and amount of water.

Aside from surface waves on large lakes, most water movement in lentic systems is not conspicuous. Tides are negligible, being less than a few inches in the largest lakes. Turbulent mixing occurs at a lake surface, within a lake, and at the interface between the epilimnion and the hypolimnion, and controls many lake processes. Large-scale water movements, termed seiches, occur slowly below a lake's surface, and these can be accompanied by large waves within the lake at the metalimnion.

CHEMICAL ENVIRONMENT

For an element, three basic parameters are of importance: the forms in which it occurs, its source, and its concentration in water relative to its biological demand or effect. Most elements are derived from dissolved gases in the atmosphere or from minerals in geological materials surrounding a lake. In some cases the presence of elements is strongly mediated by biological activities. *SEE BIOGEOCHEMISTRY*.

Dissolved and particulate forms. Most elements can occur in a dissolved and a particulate form, and the transitions between them are often accomplished by biological processes. Organisms incorporate dissolved forms into their bodies, forming particles. Bacteria decompose particles, releasing dissolved compounds. Particulate forms tend to sink, causing an accumulation in sediments in lakes and streams. The net effect of element uptake and sinking is a removal of many dissolved elements from epilimnia or upper waters in streams. Removed materials can be returned after decomposition by seasonal turnover in lakes and general mixing in streams.

Oxygen. Oxygen occurs as dissolved O_2 and in combination with other elements resulting from chemical or biological reactions. Dissolved O_2 is only moderately soluble in water, and its solubility decreases as temperature increases. Oxygen enters water primarily from the atmosphere through a combination of diffusion and turbulent mixing. The amount of oxygen in water is often small enough that it can be affected significantly by photosynthesis and respiration.

Respiration by organisms reduces the quantity of oxygen in water. Under some circumstances photosynthesis can also add oxygen to water, although this is not usually an important source. When biological demands for oxygen exceed supply rates, it can be depleted from fresh-water ecosystems (**Fig. 3**). This is usually accomplished by bacteria when large quantities of organic materials are present. Anoxic conditions occur in hypolimnia during summer and under ice cover in winter when lake strata are isolated from the atmosphere. These periods of anoxia are important in releasing from sediments a number of elements (for example, iron, manganese, phosphorus) that are soluble only under reducing conditions. Oxygen depletion may also occur in rivers that receive heavy organic loading. Aside from specialized bacteria, few organisms can occur under anoxic conditions.

Carbon dioxide and pH. Carbon dioxide is fairly soluble in water, dissolving to form carbonic acid which dissociates and releases hydrogen ions. Its chemical species exert a major control on the hydrogen ion concentration of water (the acidity or pH). Carbon dioxide is derived primarily from the atmosphere, with additional sources from plant and animal respiration and carbonate minerals. In ecosystems where carbonate minerals are abundant, the pH is relatively constant and photosynthesis may lead to the precipitation of calcium carbonate from water. Where minerals are poor in carbonates, biological activities can lead to large shifts in dissolved carbon dioxide concentrations and pH.

Acidity is influenced by a number of other ions in water, in addition to carbonate species. Natural pH conditions usually range from 6 to 9, although waters affected by *Sphagnum* moss may exhibit values of 4 or lower. Acidity exerts a controlling influence on the chemistry of many elements. Low pH conditions may also limit the occurrence of organisms.

Phosphorus. Phosphorus occurs primarily as a phosphate ion or in a number of complex organic forms. Some phosphate compounds are only slightly soluble in water, particularly when oxygen is present (Fig. 3). Phosphorus is derived primarily from minerals surrounding fresh-water ecosystems. It is the element which is most commonly in the shortest supply relative to biological demand. Phosphorus is thus a limiting nutrient, and its addition to fresh-water ecosystems through human activities can lead to major problems due to increased growth of aquatic plants.

Nitrogen. Nitrogen occurs in water as N_2, NO_2, NO_3, NH_4, and in diverse organic forms. It may be derived from precipitation and soils, but its availability is usually regulated by bacterial processes. Many bacteria and blue-green algae fix N_2 into an organic form, incorporating it into biotic nutrient cycling. Similarly, most transitions between the varied forms of nitrogen are mediated by bacterial activities (Fig. 3). Nitrogen occurs in relatively short supply relative to biological demand. It may also limit growth in some fresh-water systems, particularly when phosphorus levels have been increased because of human activity.

Other elements. A variety of other elements also help determine the occurrence of fresh-water organisms either directly or by the elements' effects on water chemistry. Trace amounts of metals and vitamins are necessary for plant growth. Other compounds, such as copper, may have adverse affects on organisms when present in very small quantities. Calcium, usually the most abundant cation in fresh water,

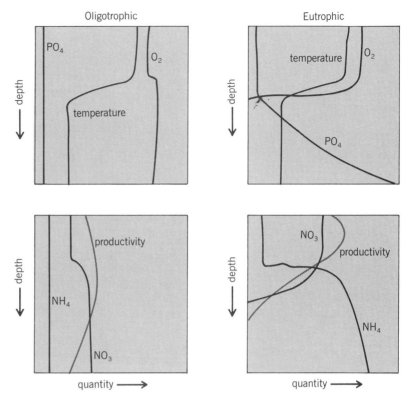

Fig. 3. Characteristic profiles with depth for a number of important limnological variables in an oligotrophic and a eutrophic lake. Temperature distribution is the same in either lake. In the oligotrophic lake, the occurrence of all variables except primary production and temperature is influenced primarily by chemical processes. In the eutrophic lake, biological processes have a major influence on chemical variables. (*After R. G. Wetzel, Limnology, 2d ed., Saunders, 1983*)

rarely is limiting to organisms directly but plays a major role in determining overall water chemistry. Silica may limit the occurrence of diatoms and sponges but has little effect on most organisms.

BIOTA

In addition to taxonomy, fresh-water organisms are classified by the areas in which they occur, the manner in which they move, and the roles that they occupy in trophic webs. Major distinctions are made between organisms that occur in bottom areas and those within the water column, the limnetic zone (Fig. 1).

The occurrence of organisms may be evaluated as the number of individuals, or by the mass or the amount of material produced by organisms in a region. These variables can be evaluated for individual species or for groups of species (for example, producers, herbivores). Production is the most difficult variable to measure, but it provides the greatest information on the role of organisms in an ecosystem. *SEE BIOLOGICAL PRODUCTIVITY; BIOMASS.*

Plankton. Plankton organisms occur in open water and move primarily with general water motion. Their capability for locomotion is limited, although many exhibit some swimming ability. Planktonic communities occur in all lentic ecosystems. In lotic systems they are important only in slow-moving areas.

Phytoplankton (plant plankton) comprise at least eight major taxonomic groups of algae, most of which are microscopic. They exhibit a diversity of forms ranging from one-celled organisms to complex colonies. Many algae have no means of locomotion, while

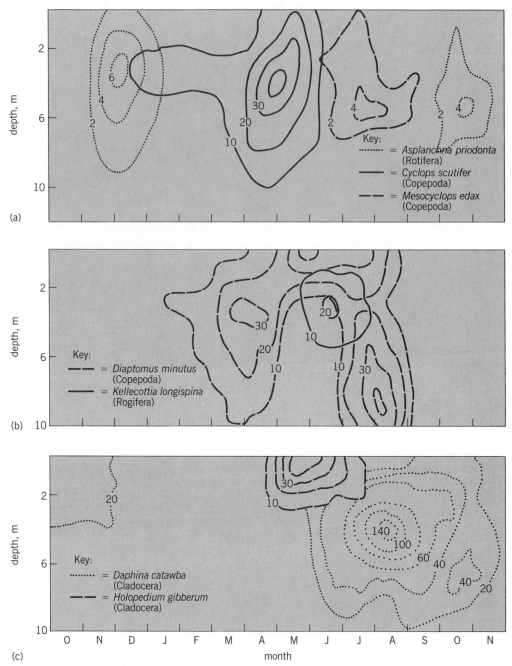

Fig. 4. Distribution of zooplankton production (micrograms of dry mass per liter per month) with depth and time for three functional groups of zooplankton: (a) predators, (b) macroconsumers, and (c) microconsumers, from Mirror Lake, New Hampshire. The data illustrate clear patterns of separation in the occurrence of the zooplankton groups. 1 m = 3.3 ft. (*After S. Eddy and A. C. Hodson, Taxonomic Keys to the Common Animals of the North Central States, Burgess, 1961, and W. T. Edmondson, ed., Freshwater Biology, 2d ed., Wiley, 1959*)

others have flagella or a system for adjusting their buoyancy by using gas vacuoles. Distinct functional differences occur among the major phytoplankton groups. Diatoms generate a boxlike silica structure called a frustule. With sufficiently high levels of dissolved silica, they can exhibit rapid growth rates. Some blue-green algae can fix dissolved nitrogen, and have an important advantage over other algae when nitrogen levels are limited. Some flagellated algae are capable of collecting small particles or dissolved organic compounds, combining heterotrophic nutrition with autotrophy. Some green algae may resist being consumed or digested by planktonic animals, and have an advantage when grazing pressure is high.

Zooplankton (animal plankton) comprise protozoans and three major groups of eukaryotic organisms: Rotifers, Cladocerans, and Copepods (**Fig. 4**). Most are microscopic but some are clearly visible to the naked eye. Three main problems confront these organisms: food procurement, reproduction, and predator avoidance. Many zooplankton species are suspension feeders that strain phytoplankton from water as a food source. In this way they link planktonic primary production to higher trophic levels. Other planktonic animals are predatory, consuming other forms of zooplankton. Predation pressure on zooplankton from fishes and predatory zooplankton can be severe. Fishes generally prey on large-bodied forms, including predatory zooplankton, while invertebrate predators consume smaller animals. The types of predators in a fresh-water ecosystem have a major effect on zooplankton community composition. Many zooplankton populations exhibit strong shifts in body form (for example, spine length, helmet size) as adaptations to avoid predation. Reproductive processes among zooplankton are complex. Rotifers and cladocerans usually reproduce through asexual cloning, allowing rapid population expansion. When they exhibit sexual reproduction, it often leads to the formation of a dormant egg which can survive harsh environmental conditions. Copepods reproduce exclusively through sexual processes but often exhibit a dormant stage in their development. Dormant stages for all forms of zooplankton also facilitate the colonization of new fresh-water habitats. SEE POPULATION ECOLOGY.

Nekton. Animals, such as fishes and swimming insects, that occur in the water column and can control their position independently of water movement are termed nekton. In addition to their importance as a human food source, fishes may affect zooplankton, benthic invertebrates, vegetation, and lake sediments.

Benthos. Benthic organisms are a diverse group associated with the bottoms of lakes and streams. Variation in the types of bottom materials has a major effect on the kinds of organisms that occur in an area.

The phytobenthos ranges from microscopic algae to higher plants. Almost every submerged surface in fresh-water ecosystems is covered with a diverse assemblage of algae. Algae also occur in the interstices below the surface of some sediments. Aquatic macrophytes, which are higher plants, exhibit a number of adaptations to fresh-water habitats. Some species grow completely submerged, while portions of other forms emerge from the water. Some desire nutrients from sediments, and others obtain needed materials from the water column. Some occur in littoral areas, and others in swiftly moving streams.

In the zoobenthos some organisms are sessile, that is, permanently attached to or embedded in the substratum. Other organisms crawl on the sediments or swim just above them. Benthic animals range from microscopic protozoans and crustaceans to large aquatic insects and fishes. Many aquatic insects exhibit complex life cycles in which larval stages occur in water, making use of food resources there. Adults emerge from the water and can move within or among water bodies. This adaptation is well suited for the colonization of new habitats and for lotic systems where upstream movement is limited by water flow. Benthic animals are classified into functional groups based upon the food resources that they use. Collectors make use of fine particulate organic materials suspended in water. Shredders consume coarse pieces of organic material and generate finer materials. Grazers utilize algae growing on surfaces. Predators consume other animals. SEE FOOD WEB.

Bacteria. Bacteria occur throughout fresh-water ecosystems in planktonic and benthic areas and play a major role in biogeochemical cycling. Organisms that take up nutrients in upper water layers are eventually decomposed primarily by bacteria either in the water column or in the sediments. Decomposition releases organically bound nutrients, facilitating continued production. Most bacteria are heterotrophic, using reduced carbon as an energy source; otheers are photosynthetic or derive energy from reduced compounds other than carbon.

INTERACTIONS AMONG ECOSYSTEM COMPONENTS

Ultimately the conditions in a fresh-water ecosystem are controlled by numerous interactions among biotic and abiotic components.

Production. Primary production in a fresh-water ecosystem is controlled by light and nutrient availability. As light diminishes with depth in a column of water, a point is reached where energy for photosynthesis balances respiratory energy demands. This compensation point occurs approximately when light at midday reaches 1% of surface levels. The trophogenic zone occurs above the point where photosynthesis exceeds respiration (Fig. 1). The tropholytic zone, where respiration is greater than photosynthesis, underlies this region. In benthic areas, the region where light is sufficient for plant growth is termed the littoral zone; deeper areas are labeled profundal.

Nutrient availability generally controls the total amount of primary production that occurs in fresh-water ecosystems. Production levels vary substantially among water bodies. One classification scheme for lakes ranks them according to total production, ranging from oligotrophic lakes, where water is clear and production is low, to eutrophic systems, characterized by high nutrient concentrations, high standing algal biomass, high production, low water clarity, and low concentrations of oxygen in the hypolimnion (Fig. 3). Eutrophic conditions are more likely to occur as a lake ages. This aging process, termed eutrophication, occurs naturally but can be greatly accelerated by anthropogenic additions of nutrients. A third major lake category, termed dystrophy, occurs when large amounts of organic materials that are resistant to decomposition wash into a lake basin. These organic materials stain the lake water and have a major influence on water chemistry which results in low production. SEE EUTROPHICATION.

In herbivory and predation, reduced carbon is consumed by other organisms while it is still in a living organism. Alternatively, carbon in the form of detritus, nonliving material, may be used by decomposers. The relative proportion of these two pathways can vary substantially among trophic levels and among ecosystems.

In ecosystem studies, a distinction is made between carbon that is fixed within a unit being studied, called autochthonous carbon, and that which is derived externally, called allochthonous carbon. In some large lakes most of the carbon used by organisms is generated autochthonously within the lake through photosynthesis by phytoplankton in the epilimnion. In some mountain streams which are shaded by forests, little light is available for plant growth and reduced carbon is derived primarily from leaf litter falling into the stream, an allochthonous source. SEE POPULATION ECOLOGY.

Distribution of organisms. Distinct gradients of physical and chemical features occur in fresh-water ecosystems. They result from physical and chemical processes but are also developed by the interactions of the biota with the abiotic environment. Characteristic gradients occur with depth and season; they may occur in both space and time. Many organisms are adapted to only a subset of the conditions in aquatic gradients and are confined in their distribution within an ecosystem.

Primary producers occur only where sufficient light is available for growth. Some plants function optimally when bright light is available, while others are specialized to grow under darker conditions. In eutrophic lakes, dense concentrations of phytoplankton near the water surface limit light penetration, and algae are confined to a much shallower stratum in the water column than in oligotrophic lakes where nutrient availability limits the growth of phytoplankton (Fig. 3). In rivers, suspended particles may limit light and plant growth even when nutrients are abundant.

Plants may control nutrient availability, and in turn nutrients influence plant distribution. Planktonic diatoms deplete silica from the epilimnion, generating conditions that favor the growth of other algae. Similarly, low nitrogen availability favors blue-green algae over other groups. Rooted plants may return nutrients to the water column from sediments or contribute detritus to bottom areas.

Consumer organisms are affected by gradients of food availability as well as by physical and chemical features. For stream invertebrates, shredder groups are dominant in areas where available reduced carbon is derived primarily from terrestrial detritus. When light is available for autochthonous production, grazer groups may be more abundant. Consumers may affect nutrient availability directly by materials that they release and indirectly by their effects on producers. Temperature and reduced oxygen conditions may limit the occurrence of animals in lakes or streams. Species that are adapted to low oxygen, however, may occur only when other organisms are eliminated by oxygen stress.

In lakes, gradients with depth occur in temperature, oxygen, and nutrients. Organisms in phytoplankton, zooplankton, and fish communities are restricted to certain depths by these gradients. Lake organisms may also be distributed along a gradient of distance from shore. In lotic systems, major gradients occur with water flow patterns, primarily along an upstream-downstream axis.

Other gradients, which occur with seasons as temperature changes are accompanied by major shifts in chemical and biological parameters. In lakes, there is often a predictable seasonal succession of chemistry, phytoplankton, and zooplankton (Fig. 4). Changes in epilimnetic chemistry from spring through summer may be as large as those that occur with depth. Assemblages of species are associated with different points in this time gradient. Seasonal changes also have major effects on lotic ecosystems. SEE ECOSYSTEM; LAKE; LIMNOLOGY; RIVER.

Thomas M. Frost

Bibliography. G. A. Cole, *Textbook of Limnology*, 3d ed., 1988; D. Gunnison (ed.), *Microbial Processes in Reservoirs*, 1985; O. T. Lind, *Handbook of Common Methods in Limnology*, 2d ed., 1985; H. Loffler, *Paleolimnology*, 1987; M. Straskraba and A. H. Gnouck, *Freshwater ecosystems: Modelling and simulation*, Develop. Environ. Model. 8, 1985; R. Thomas et al. (eds.), *Ecological Effects of In-Situ Sediment Contaminants*, 1987; W. D. Williams, *Life in Inland Waters*, 1983.

Front

An elongated, sloping zone in the troposphere, within which changes of temperature and wind velocity are large compared to changes outside the zone. Thus the passage of a front at a fixed location is marked by rather sudden changes in temperature and wind and also by rapid variations in other weather elements such as moisture and sky condition.

In its idealized sense, a front can be regarded as a sloping surface of discontinuity separating air masses of different density or temperature. In practice, the temperature change from warm to cold air occurs mainly within a zone of finite width, called a transition or frontal zone. The three-dimensional structure of the frontal zone is illustrated in **Fig. 1**. In typical cases, the zone is about 0.6 mi (1 km) in depth and 60–120 mi (100–200 km) in width, with a slope of approximately 1/100. The cold air lies beneath the warm in the form of a shallow wedge. Temperature contrasts generally are strongest at or near the Earth's surface, the frontal zone usually being narrowest near the ground and becoming wider and more diffuse with height. Frontal zones seldom extend more than several miles above the Earth's surface. There are, however, sharp, narrow fronts of limited extent often present in the middle and upper troposphere, as discussed at the end of this article. With the exception of that section, the following concerns fronts at the Earth's surface.

The surface separating the frontal zone from the adjacent warm air mass is referred to as the frontal surface, and it is the line of intersection of this surface with a second surface, usually horizontal or vertical, that strictly speaking constitutes the front. According to this more precise definition, the front represents a discontinuity in temperature gradient rather than in temperature itself. The boundary on the cold air side is often ill-defined, especially near the Earth's surface, and for this reason is not represented in routine analysis of weather maps. In typical cases about one-third of the temperature difference between the Equator and the pole is contained within the narrow frontal zone, the remainder being distributed within the warm and cold air masses on either side. SEE AIR MASS; WEATHER MAP.

The wind gradient, or shear, like the temperature gradient, is larger within the frontal zone than on either side of it. In well-developed fronts the shift in wind direction often is concentrated along the frontal surface, while a more gradual change in wind speed may occur throughout the frontal zone. An upper-level jet stream normally is situated above a well-defined frontal zone. SEE JET STREAM.

A front moves approximately with the speed of the wind component normal to it. The strength of this component varies with season, location, and individual situation but generally lies in the range of 0–50

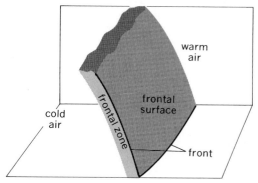

Fig. 1. Schematic diagram of the frontal zone, the angle with Earth's surface much exaggerated.

mi/h (0–80 km/h); 25 mi/h (40 km/h) is a typical frontal speed.

Frontal waves. Many extratropical cyclones (the lows on a weather map) begin as wavelike perturbations of a preexisting frontal surface. Such cyclones are referred to as wave cyclones. The life cycle of the wave cyclone is illustrated in **Fig. 2**. In stage I, prior to the development, the front is gently curved and more or less stationary. In stage II the front undergoes a wavelike deformation, the cold air advancing to the left of the wave crest and the warm air to the right. Simultaneously a center of low pressure and of counterclockwise wind circulation appears at the crest. The portion of the front which marks the leading edge of the cold air is called the cold front. The term warm front is applied to the forward boundary of the warm air. During stage III the wave grows in amplitude and the warm sector narrows. In the final stage the cold front overtakes and merges with the warm front, forming an occluded front. The center of low pressure and of cyclonic rotation is found at the tip of the occluded front, well removed from the warm air source. At this stage the cyclone begins to fill and weaken. *See Storm.*

Many frontal waves are weak, shallow, and fast-moving, appearing more like stage II or III (Fig. 2), rather than progressing to stage IV. Also, cases have been documented in which the occluded structure depicted in panel IV (Fig. 2) forms in a different manner from that described above. In such cases, sometimes referred to as pseudo-occlusions, the low-pressure center is observed to retreat into or form within the cold air, and frontogenesis takes place along a line joining the low center and the tip of the warm sector. Cloud observations from meteorological satellites have provided visual evidence of this process. Since the classical occlusion process, in which the cold front overtakes and merges with the warm front, has never been adequately verified, it is possible that most occlusions form in this other way.

Cloud and precipitation types and patterns bear characteristic relationships to fronts, as depicted in **Fig. 3**. These relationships are determined mainly by

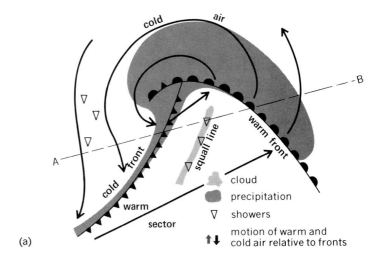

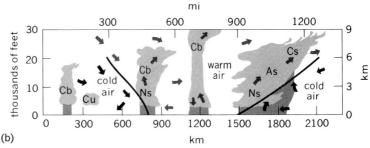

Fig. 3. Relation of cloud types and precipitation to fronts. (*a*) Surface weather map. (*b*) Vertical cross section (along A-B in diagram *a*). Cloud types: Cs, cirrostratus; As, altostratus; Ns, nimbostratus; Cu, cumulus; and Cb, cumulonimbus.

the vertical air motions in the vicinity of the frontal surfaces. Since the motions are not unique but vary somewhat from case to case and, in a given case, with the stage of development, the features of the diagram are subject to considerable variation. In general, though, the motions consist of an upgliding of the warm air above the warm frontal surface, a more restricted and pronounced upthrusting of the warm air by the cold front, and an extensive subsidence of the cold air to the rear of the cold front. Fast-moving cold fronts are characterized by narrow cloud and precipitation systems. Smaller, more intense cells or rainbands usually are embedded within the more extensive regions of warm and cold frontal precipitation. *See Cloud; Cloud physics.*

When potentially unstable air is present in the warm sector, as often occurs in the spring and summer over North America, the main weather activity often breaks out ahead of the cold front. Complexes of cumulonimbus clouds, having horizontal dimensions on the order of 60 mi (100 km) and collective lifetimes of perhaps a day, may be present. Convective precipitation may also occur in the form of elongated lines of cumulonimbus clouds called squall lines, as represented by the tall cumulonimbus in Fig. 3*b*. *See Squall line.*

In the above conceptual model, the movement of the frontal zones associated with the cyclone's evolution is primarily responsible for the cloudiness and precipitation as the warm air flows up and over the warm front and as the cold front wedges under the warm air sector. Thus, the largely mechanical wedge action of the frontal zones produces the vertical motion associated with the clouds. This conceptual

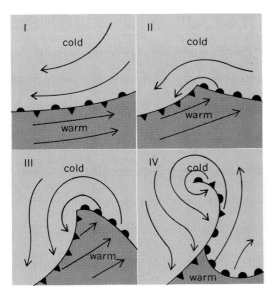

Fig. 2. Life cycle of the wave cyclone, surface projection. Arrows denote airflow. Patterns depicted are for the Northern Hemisphere while their mirror images apply in Southern Hemisphere.

model (known as the polar-front cyclone model) was based on the idea that most cyclones formed on preexisting surface fronts.

Since about 1940, it has been realized that extratropical cyclones often develop in regions where no significant surface frontal zones exist. The development of the cyclones is often more related to the three-dimensional structure of the atmosphere over a large volume than to the location of any frontal zones. More modern conceptual models of cyclone development (which can be referred to as baroclinic-wave models) emphasize the flow of airstreams relative to the evolving cyclone, rather than the distortion of air masses by the moving fronts. Yet the relative distribution of cloudiness and precipitation, as well as the evolution of frontal zones with respect to the cyclone, is still quite similar in these later models to that in the older model discussed above. Thus, Figs. 2 and 3 are consistent with the newer concepts.

Polar front. A front separating air of tropical origin from air of more northerly or polar origin is referred to as a polar front. Frequently only a fraction of the temperature contrast between tropical and polar regions is concentrated within the polar frontal zone, and a second or secondary front appears at higher latitudes. In certain locations such a front is termed an arctic front.

The polar front can also be defined in a climatological sense as a region in which the horizontal temperature gradient tends to be large compared to surrounding areas; within this region frequent formation of sharp frontal zones occurs. This definition applies for the remainder of this section.

In winter the major or polar frontal zones of the Northern Hemisphere extend from the northern Philippines across the Pacific Ocean to the coast of Washington, from the southeastern United States across the Atlantic Ocean to southern England, and from the northern Mediterranean eastward into Asia. An arctic frontal zone is located along the mountain barriers of western Canada and Alaska. In summer the average positions of the polar frontal zones are farther north, the Pacific zone extending from Japan to Washington and the Atlantic zone from New Jersey to the British Isles. In addition to a northward-displaced polar front over Asia, an arctic front lies along the northern shore and continues eastward into Alaska.

The polar frontal zone of the Southern Hemisphere lies near 45°S in summer and slightly poleward of that latitude in winter. Two frontal bands, more pronounced in winter than in summer, spiral into the main zone from subtropical latitudes. These bands, originating east of the Andes and northeast of New Zealand, merge with the main frontal zone after making a quarter circuit of the globe.

Frontogenesis. When extratropical cyclones form in the absence of preexisting fronts, strong frontogenesis (initial formation of a front) can occur in conjunction with the cyclone's development. The formation of a frontal zone requires an increase in the temperature gradient and the development of a wind shift.

The transport of temperature by the horizontal wind field can initiate the frontogenesis process as is shown for two cases in **Fig. 4**. The two wind fields shown would, in the absence of other effects, transport the isotherms in such a way that they would become concentrated along the A-B lines in both cases. (Both of these types of wind fields, or combinations of them,

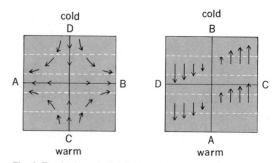

Fig. 4. Two horizontal wind fields which can cause frontogenesis. Broken lines represent isotherms, and heavy arrows show wind directions and speeds (length of arrow shaft is proportional to the speed).

are found in developing extratropical cyclones, and sometimes elsewhere.) Since the temperature gradient is inversely proportional to the spacing of the isotherms, it is clear that frontogenesis would occur along the A-B lines. Vertical air motions will modify this frontogenesis process, but these modifications will be small near the ground where the vertical motion is small. Thus, near the ground the temperature gradients will continue to increase in the frontal zones as long as the horizontal wind field does not change. As the temperature gradient increases, a circulation will develop in the vertical plane through C-D in each case. The thermal wind relation is valid for the component of the horizontal wind which blows parallel to the frontal zone. The thermal wind, which is the change in the geostrophic wind over a specific vertical distance, is directed along the isotherms, and its magnitude is proportional to the temperature gradient. As the frontogenesis process increases the temperature gradient, the thermal wind must also increase. But if the thermal wind increases, the change in the actual wind over a height interval must also increase (since the thermal wind closely approximates the actual wind change with height). This corresponding change in the actual wind component along the front is accomplished through the action of the Coriolis force. A small wind component perpendicular to the front is required if the Coriolis force is to act in this manner. This leads to the circulation in the vertical plane that is shown in **Fig. 5**.

This circulation plays an important role in the frontogenesis process and in determining the frontal structure. The rising motion in the warm air and the sinking motion in the cold air are consistent with observed cloud and precipitation patterns. The circulation helps give the front its characteristic vertical tilt which leaves the relatively cooler air beneath the front. Near

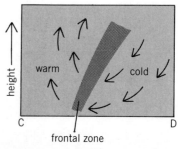

Fig. 5. Circulation in the vertical plane through C-D for both cases of Fig. 4.

the ground the circulation causes a horizontal convergence of mass. This speeds up the frontogenesis process by increasing the rate at which the isotherms move together. The convergence field also carries the momentum lines together in the frontal zone in such a way that a wind shear develops across the front. This wind shear gives rise to the wind shift which is observed with a frontal passage. Eventually the front reaches a quasi-steady state in which the turbulent mixing balances the frontogenesis processes. Other frontogenesis effects are important in some cases, but the mechanism presented above appears to be the predominant one.

Upper-level frontal zones. In addition to and independent of the surface frontal zones described above, elongated sloping zones of strong temperature contrast and wind shear can form in the upper troposphere in conjunction with jet stream intensification. These upper-level frontal zones are characterized by low humdity, air sinking within them. Their development is often accompanied by a downward folding of the tropopause and the incorporation of stratospheric air into the upper portion of the zones. The strong wind shear within these frontal zones often produces severe turbulence, a potentially dangerous situation for jet aircraft, as the zones cannot be detected visually due to a lack of cloudiness in the dry, descending air. Upper-level frontal zones thus are significant (but not the only) sources of clear-air turbulence (CAT).

Stephen E. Mudrick

Bibliography. B. J. Hoskins, The mathematical theory of frontogenesis, *Annu. Rev. Fluid Mech.*, 14:131–151, 1982; S. E. Mudrick, A numerical study of frontogenesis, *J. Atm. Sci.*, 31:869–892, 1974; P. Ray (ed.), *Mesoscale Meteorology and Forecasting*, American Meteorological Society, 1986; J. M. Wallace and P. V. Hobbs, *Atmospheric Science: An Introductory Survey*, 1977.

Frost

The formation of ice on the ground, on plants, or on structures near the Earth's surface as a result of the drop in air temperature to lower than 32°F (0°C) and the presence of water vapor or liquid water in the air. The causes of the cooling, and the types of ice that form, can be quite varied, depending on the existing meteorological factors. Frost can have serious impact, with the main effect being in agriculture, but transportation and other areas are also affected. *See Air Temperature*.

Causes. There are two principal causes of the cooling necessary for frost formation: heat loss by radiation, and the advection of cold air. Other factors that have a significant influence on frost formation are wind, atmospheric humidity, surface wetness, and topography.

Radiational heat loss. The Earth's surface loses heat by long-wave, infrared radiation. At night, when there is no incoming radiation from the Sun, and especially with clear skies, when there is no returned infrared radiation from clouds, the heat loss can lead to rapid cooling of the surface. In turn, the cold surfaces cool the lowest layers of air as well. In the absence of wind to stir the air, a steep gradient of temperature can become established, so that the temperature within inches of the ground may be many

degrees colder than the air several feet above the ground. The depth of this inversion layer increases and the temperature near the surface steadily decreases during the night. *See Temperature inversion*.

Wind tends to cause turbulence and this mixes the coldest air from near the surface with warmer air higher up. Cloudy skies and, to a lesser degree, humidity in the air reduce the rate of heat loss and the risk of frost. Also, conduction of heat from the subsurface soil helps to reduce the loss of heat to some degree. The total amount of cooling that can develop may be calculated by using semiempirical schemes, but the errors in such calculations are fairly large. Furthermore, in hilly terrain the coldest air tends to sink to the lowest elevation, and even small differences in terrain height can lead to substantial differences in temperature. As a result of radiational heat loss, up to 36°F (20°C) cooling during the course of a night is possible.

Heat loss by advection. The movement of cold air, such as that which accompanies the advance of a cold front, is the second major class of situations that can lead to frost formation. In these situations, the air is colder then the ground and, usually, the temperature decreases with altitude. The severity of the drops in temperature can approach those due to radiation cooling, but the most dramatic cooling events are those where both processes contribute. However, fronts are often associated with clouds and usually with winds, so that conditions tend to be contrary to those producing the strongest radiational cooling. *See Front*.

Ice types. While low temperatures themselves might be considered as frost, the most readily notable manifestations and the most serious impacts of frost are in the formation of ice that results from the low temperatures when water is present. The water may be held in the soil or in the plants, or it may come from vapor or droplets in the air.

In order for the water within the surface soil or in the tissues of plants to freeze, a small amount of supercooling is required, typically a few degrees; thus ice formation will not begin (the process is called nucleation) until those temperatures are reached. Nucleation depends on the presence of specific substances. Continued freezing may be limited by the release of latent heat associated with the freezing; in fact, some plants have developed protection against extensive freezing damage by having large internal reservoirs of water. Wind velocity is a crucial factor in this regard, as air motion greatly increases the removal of heat from the plant.

Water vapor from the air deposits on surfaces whose temperature is lower than the ice point corresponding to the ambient humidity. These deposits grow as feathery crystals, known as hoarfrost; the crystals are quite beautiful and can attain a size greater than 0.5 in. (1.3 cm). The formation of hoarfrost is analogous to the formation of dew at temperatures higher than 32°F (0°C). *See Dew point*.

If condensation of droplets takes place in the air (that is, a fog forms) coincident with the cooling of the ground and plants, some fog droplets impinge and freeze onto the objects, forming rime. Rime is much denser than hoarfrost. The total mass (weight) deposited by rime can also be much higher than the deposit of hoarfrost. Occasionally, the two forms of ice form in combination.

If moisture is deposited as liquid water prior to the lowering of temperatures below the freezing point, the water deposit (dew or rain) may subsequently freeze, forming a transparent (black) ice coating known as glaze. Very heavy and damaging glaze can form if rain falls from warmer air aloft into a surface layer of cold air.

Climatology. Frost climatology is widely available for agricultural areas. The dates of first and last frosts for 32, 28, 24, 20°F (0, −2.2, −4.4, −6.7°C), or other sets of temperatures, are usually tabulated, as well as the probabilities of frosts for given calendar days. Tables of the numbers of frost days per year are also available. These data represent the average conditions over many years. Deviations from the average can always be expected. Also, local variations are very important. Other factors, such as humidity or water content in the soil, add further variability to the actual frequency and impact of frosts.

Forecasting and prevention. General advances in the 1- to 2-day synoptic-scale meteorological forecasts are providing improved information for the generation of frost forecasts. As a result, frost warnings of several hours are quite reliable, but forecasts more than a day ahead are still beset with inaccuracies. The incorporation of small-scale local effects places further demands on the forecaster. Good forecasts of frost are of great value to growers who operate expensive frost-protection systems. Prevention measures are decided on the basis of the forecasts and the susceptibility of the plants at that moment. Common techniques of frost prevention are heating of the air with burners, smoke production to reduce radiation heat loss, spraying of the plants with water to utilize the latent heat of freezing as a heat source, and treatments to reduce the temperature threshold for nucleation. The last-mentioned method is experimental, but it has the potential of giving protection down to 24°F (−4.4°C). *See* Agricultural meteorology.

Gabor Vali

Geomorphology

The study of landforms, including the description, classification, origin, development, and history of planetary surface features. Emphasis is placed on the genetic interpretation of the erosional and depositional features of the Earth's surface. However, geomor-phologists also study primary relief elements formed by movements of the Earth's crust, topography on the sea floor and on other planets, and applications of geomorphic information to problems in environmental engineering.

Geomorphologists analyze the landscape, a factor of immense importance to humankind. Their purview includes the structural framework of landscape, weathering and soils, mass movement and hillslopes, fluvial features, eolian features, glacial and periglacial phenomena, coastlines, and karst landscapes. Processes and landforms are analyzed for their adjustment through time, especially the most recent portions of Earth history.

History. Geomorphology emerged as a science in the early nineteenth century with the writings of James Hutton, John Playfair, and Charles Lyell. These men demonstrated that prolonged fluvial erosion is responsible for most of the Earth's valleys. Impetus was given to geomorphology by the exploratory surveys of the nineteenth century, especially those in the western United States. By the end of the nineteenth century, geomorphology had achieved its most important theoretical synthesis through the work of William Morris Davis. He conceived a marvelous deductive scheme of landscape development through the action of geomorphic processes acting on the structure of the bedrock to induce a progressive evolution of landscape stages.

Perhaps the premier geomorphologist was Grove Karl Gilbert. In 1877 he published his report "Geology of the Henry Mountains." This paper introduced the concept of equilibrium to organize tectonic and erosional process studies. Fluvial erosion was magnificently described according to the concept of energy. Gilbert's monograph "Lake Bonneville" was published in 1890 and described the Pleistocene history of the predecessor to the Great Salt Lake (see **Fig. 1**). The monograph is a masterpiece of dynamic analysis. Concepts of force and resistance, equilibrium, and adjustment dominated in Gilbert's study of geomorphology. He later presented a thorough analysis of fluvial sediment transport and the environmental effects of altered fluvial systems. He even made a perceptive study of the surface morphology of the Moon.

Despite Gilbert's example, geomorphologists in the early twentieth century largely worked on landscape

Fig. 1. The great bar of Pleistocene Lake Bonneville at Stockton, Utah. (*After G. K. Gilbert, U.S. Geol. Surv. Monogr. 1, 1890*)

Fig. 2. Surveying large transverse gravel bars created by flooding of the Medina River, Texas, in August 1978.

classification and description according to Davis's theoretical framework. Toward the middle of the twentieth century, alternative theoretical approaches appeared. Especially in France and Germany, climatic geomorphology arose on the premise that distinctive landforms and processes are associated with certain climatic regions. Geomorphology since 1945 has become highly diversified, with many groups specializing in relatively narrow subfields, such as karst geomorphology, coastal processes, glacial and Quaternary geology, and fluvial processes.

Process geomorphology. Modern geomorphologists emphasize basic studies of processes presently

Fig. 3. Streamlined uplands and large sinuous channels in the Chryse Planitia region of Mars. (*National Aeronautics and Space Administration*)

active on the landscape (**Fig. 2**). This work has benefited from new field, laboratory, and analytical techniques, many of which are borrowed from other disciplines. Geomorphologists consider processes from the perspectives of pedology, soil mechanics, sedimentology, geochemistry, hydrology, fluid mechanics, remote sensing, and other sciences. The complexity of geomorphic processes has required this interdisciplinary approach, but it has also led to a theoretical vacuum in the science. At present many geomorphologists are organizing their studies through a form of systems analysis. The landscape is conceived of as a series of elements linked by flows of mass and energy. Process studies measure the inputs, outputs, and transfers for these systems. Although systems analysis is not a true theory, it is compatible with the powerful new tools of computer analysis and remote sensing. Systems analysis provides an organizational framework within which geomorphologists are developing models to predict selected phenomena.

The future. Geomorphology is increasing in importance because of the increased activity of humans as a geomorphic agent. As society evolves to more complexity, it increasingly affects and is threatened by such geomorphic processes as soil erosion, flooding, landsliding, coastal erosion, and sinkhole collapse. Geomorphology plays an essential role in environmental management, providing a broader perspective of landscape dynamics than can be given by standard engineering practice.

The phenomenal achievements of nineteenth-century geomorphology were stimulated by the new frontier of unexplored lands. The new frontier for geomorphology in the late twentieth century lies in the study of other planetary surfaces (**Fig. 3**). Each new planetary exploration has revealed a diversity of processes that stimulates new hypotheses for features on Earth. Geomorphology must now solve the mysteries of meteor craters on the Moon and Mercury, great landslides and flood channels on Mars, phenomenally active volcanism on Io, and ice tectonics on Ganymede. SEE EROSION.

Victor R. Baker

Bibliography. V. R. Baker and S. J. Pyne, G. K. Gilbert and modern geomorphology, *Amer. J. Sci.*, 278:97–123, 1978; A. L. Bloom, *Geomorphology: A Systematic Analysis of Late Cenozoic Landforms*, 1978; A. F. Pitty, *Introduction to Geomorphology*, 1971; D. F. Ritter, *Process Geomorphology*, 1978.

Geosynthetic

Any synthetic material used in geotechnical engineering.

GEOTEXTILE

Geotextiles are used with foundations, soils, rock, earth, or other geotechnical material as an integral part of a manufactured project, structure, or system. These textile products are made of synthetic fibers or yarns, constructed into woven or nonwoven fabrics that weigh from 3 to 30 oz/yd^2 (100 to 1000 g/m^2). Geotextiles are more commonly known by other names, for example, filter fabrics, civil engineering fabrics, support membranes, and erosion control cloth.

Permeable geotextiles perform three basic functions in earth structures: separation (the fabric provides a boundary that segregates materials); reinforcement (the fabric imparts tensile strength to the system, thereby increasing its structural stability); and filtration (the fabric retains soil particles while allowing water to pass through). Such geotextiles can thus be adapted to numerous applications in earthwork construction. The major end-use categories are stabilization (for roads, parking lots, embankments, and other structures built over soft ground); drainage (of subgrades, foundations, embankments, dams, or any earth structure requiring seepage control); erosion control (for shoreline, riverbanks, steep embankments, or other earth slopes to protect against the erosive force of moving water); and sedimentation control (for containment of sediment runoff from unvegetated earth slopes). No one geotextile is suited for all these applications. Each use dictates a specific fabric requirement to resist installation stresses and to perform its function once installed.

Stabilization applications. Soft or low-strength soils on a project site present costly problems in the construction and maintenance of haul roads, storage yards, railroads, and other areas which must support vehicular traffic. Poor soil conditions also cause rapid deterioration of paved and unpaved roads, city streets, and parking lots. Problems are caused by subgrade deformation and intermixing between subgrade soil and aggregate base, resulting in a rutted and unstable surface that impedes or even prohibits traffic flow (**Fig. 1a**).

Geotextiles can eliminate or reduce the effect of these soft-soil problems through separation and reinforcement. When placed over a soft soil, the geotextile provides a support membrane for placement and compaction of aggregate base. The fabric barrier prevents aggregate particles from intruding into the soft soil and prevents soil particles from pumping up into the aggregate layer. As a continuous membrane between soil and aggregate base, the geotextile helps confine the aggregate against lateral and vertical movement. This confinement maintains the density and hence the load-distributing characteristics of the aggregate. The fabric also resists the upward heaving of subgrade between wheel paths. If the subgrade is extremely soft and cannot support vehicle loads, the fabric will act as a reinforcing membrane to assist the subgrade in supporting loads (Fig. 1b and c).

Drainage applications. Soil moisture control through drainage is essential to maintain stability in pavements, foundations, cut slopes, and earth dams.

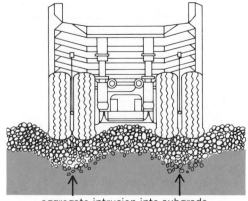

aggregate intrusion into subgrade

(a)

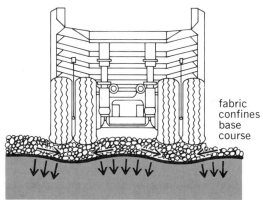

fabric confines base course

fabric resists subgrade heaving

(b)

(c)

Fig. 1. Geotextiles are used to stabilize soils. (a) A rutted and unstable surface results from subgrade deformation and intermixing between subgrade soil and aggregate base. (b) Geotextiles resist rutting through separation and reinforcement (*from Mirafi Fabrics for the Mining Industry, Celanese Fibers Marketing Co.*) (c) A highway base course constructed with geotextile between subgrade and aggregate base (*from Mirafi Family of Construction Fabrics/MPB8, Celanese Fibers Marketing Co.*).

Drainage is accomplished by providing a trench or blanket of porous rock for soil moisture to seep into. A perforated pipe is often installed within the porous rock to collect the moisture and transport it to an outlet. To ensure effective performance and long life, drain structures need a filter to retain soil particles that would clog the drain.

Graded aggregate filters are conventionally used. A properly designed graded aggregate will confine or retain the soil, thus preventing significant particle movement. If, however, the drainage aggregate is too coarse, the voids between rocks at the soil-aggregate interface will be too large for soil particles to bridge across. The resulting lack of soil-particle confinement will result in erosion when water seeps out of the soil, that is, soil piping. (**Fig. 2***a*). SEE GROUNDWATER HYDROLOGY.

The pore structure and permeability of some geotextiles are similar to those of graded aggregate filters. These fabrics can provide the same particle retention at the soil-drain interface while permitting unrestricted flow of water from the adjacent soil. Geotextiles can thus eliminate the need for graded aggregate filters in drains. When drainage fabric is used, no special aggregate gradation is required, because the fabric prevents soil from washing into the drain (Fig. 2*b* and *c*). SEE DAM.

Erosion control applications. Embankments along coastal shorelines and inland waterways are subjected to wave and current action that can cause severe erosion, instability, and even destruction of the earth slope. To protect against erosion, earth slopes have often been covered with armor (riprap, concrete blocks, concrete slabs). Despite the armor covering, erosion can still occur, undermining the armor's foundation. To assure long-term stability and performance, the erosion-control structure must include a barrier that shields the soil surface from scouring. This barrier should be permeable so that any moisture seeping from the soil slope can escape without buildup of hydrostatic pressure. Traditionally, granular filters of specially graded sand, gravel, or stone

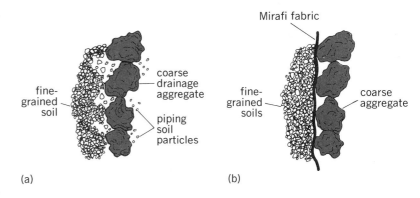

Fig. 2. Geotextiles find wide use for drainage. (*a*) Without a filter, soil particles may wash into and clog the drain. (*b*) Drainage fabric provides retention at the soil-drain interface, while allowing water to pass through (*from Mirafi Fabrics for the Mining Industry, Celanese Fibers Marketing Co.*). (*c*) Drain trench lined with a geotextile and backfilled with coarse aggregate.

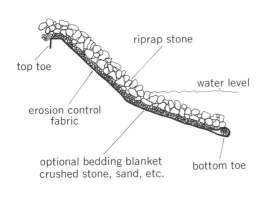

Fig. 3. Slopes along waterways can be protected by geotextiles and armor stone. (*Mirafi Family of Construction Fabrics/ MPB8, Celanese Fibers Marketing Co.*)

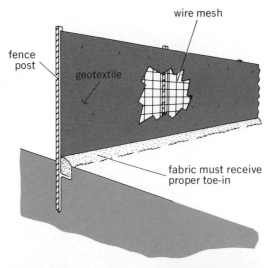

Fig. 4. A silt fence is a fabric-lined fence structure. When lined with a geotextile, it retains sediment runoff, preventing contamination of adjacent waterways. (*Mirafi Fabrics for the Mining Industry, Celanese Fibers Marketing Co.*)

have been used to prevent slope erosion beneath the armor. But granular filters are expensive, particularly when not locally available, and even when properly installed are subject to erosive forces that can wash them away.

Some geotextiles are ideal erosion control barriers. Erosion control fabrics will shield a soil slope from the erosive force of moving water, and they are permeable so that seepage from the earth slope can pass through freely. These fabrics will remain intact, covering the soil slope as long as the armor stone remains above it (**Fig. 3**). *SEE EROSION.*

Sedimentation control. Severe erosion can occur during earthwork construction or mining operations when protective vegetation is removed and soil slopes are left temporarily unprotected. Resultant sediment runoff can create serious downstream damage, for example, contaminated waterways, clogged storm drains, or sediment-covered forests or pastures. Government agencies at the federal and state level have recognized the problems associated with sedimentation, and legislation has been passed requiring the control of sediment runoff from any disturbed land

area. As a result, earthwork contractors and mine operators are faced with the responsibility and cost of controlling sediment runoff from work sites.

Silt fences constructed with geotextiles offer a cost-effective solution to sedimentation control. A silt fence is a fabric-lined structure installed on, or at the base of, an unvegetated slope. It acts as a water-permeable barrier that retains sediment runoff from the slope. The silt fence can be thought of as a temporary impoundment structure that forms a sediment pond aboveground (**Fig. 4**). When installed along the perimeter of a construction site, a silt fence can prevent sediment from leaving the disturbed area. By installing silt fences along stream banks, sediment can be kept from reaching the waterway.

Robert G. Carroll, Jr.

GEOMEMBRANE

A geomembrane is any impermeable membrane used with soils, rock, earth, or other geotechnical material in order to block the migration of fluids. These membranes are usually made of synthetic polymers in sheets ranging from 0.01 to 0.14 in. (0.25 to 3.5 mm) thick. Geomembranes are also known as flexible membrane liners, synthetic liners, liners, or polymeric membranes.

Early liners included clay, bentonite, cement-stabilized sand, and asphalt. Such liners, however, have measurable permeability or tend to crack and fissure when exposed to certain environments and chemicals. Traditional soil liners such as clay are regarded as good barriers if their permeability is 10^{-7} cm/s. Geomembranes, by contrast, have no true permeability if there are no leaks or holes in the membrane, and they possess inherent flexibility to accommodate geotechnical settlement and shifting. Migration through a geomembrane takes place at extremely low levels via chemical diffusion. Effective permeabilities for geomembranes can be calculated from measured diffusion rates, and vary from 10^{-11} to 10^{-13} cm/s, depending on the type of polymeric membrane. Modern geomembranes are commonly made of medium-density polyethylenes that are very nearly high-density polyethylenes (HDPE), several types of low-density polyethylene (LDPE), polyvinyl chloride (PVC), chlorosulfonated polyethylene (a synthetic rubber), ethylene propylene diene monomer (EPDM), and several other materials. Some geomembranes require reinforcement with an internal fabric scrim for added strength, or plasticization with low-molecular-weight additives for greater flexibility.

Applications. Geomembranes are able to contain fluids, thus preventing migration of contaminants or valuable fluid constituents. Since they prevent the dispersal of materials into surrounding regions, geomembranes are often used in conjunction with soil liners, permeable geotextiles, fluid drainage media, and other geotechnical support materials. The major application of geomembranes has been containment of hazardous wastes and prevention of pollution in landfill and surface impoundment construction (see **Fig. 5**). They are also used to a large extent in mining to contain chemical leaching solutions and the precious metals leached out of ore, in aquaculture ponds for improved health of aquatic life and improved harvesting procedures, in decorative pond construction, in water and chemical storage-tank repair and spill containment, in agriculture operations, in canal construction and repair, and in construction of floating covers for odor control, evaporation control, or wastewater treatment through anaerobic digestion.

Basin liners. When geomembranes are used as basin liners, they are often applied in direct contact and on top of soil liners. Such a composite lining system offers extra security for containment because the soil liner backs up the geomembrane. Rolls of geomembrane are deployed downslope, with seams parallel to the slope of the basin. Texture-surface geomembranes have been developed to allow deployment over steep slopes.

Final cover. Final caps form covers over waste impoundments or other containments. In final-cover applications, geomembranes prevent intrusion of precipitation into isolated and contained areas and, in addition, prevent the escape of gases from the containment. Often the surface over which the final cover is applied is unstable or subject to settlement. Seaming can take place on floating barges, if necessary, in the construction of floating covers.

Final covers over landfills are often subject to deformation from differential settling of the subsoils. Geomembranes capable of extreme elongation and flexibility should be selected to accommodate the differential settlement, so that they can be stretched a great distance before tearing and can be bent (flexed) with ease. Textured-surface geomembranes are desirable for final covers because they impart long-term slope stabilities.

Vertical cut-off walls. Geomembranes are hung vertically in repair of tank linings and in construction of vertical barrier walls in soils. They can be used either alone or in conjunction with bentonite slurry trenches to cut off and isolate sections of groundwater in cases of pollution remediation, salt-water intrusion, or dike construction. Geomembrane panels are inserted directly into these cut-off walls to depths of 100 ft (30 m) by using vibratory hammers and sheet pile drivers. The adjacent panels are not joined by heat seaming but are interlocked through prefabricated complementary joint sections; the locking mechanism is engaged as the panels are slid alongside one another into the cut-off wall.

Design and installation. A geomembrane is not intended to provide structural support or load-carrying capacity. Many applications, in waste containment particularly, require maximum durability and longevity, with a lifetime of as much as hundreds of years. Therefore, in addition to selecting materials that are suitably resistant to chemicals and to wear, it is desirable to limit fatigue-inducing tension stresses through good design and installation practice.

Soil subgrades and cover soils must be free of sharp objects such as sticks and angular stones that would introduce puncture stresses on a liner used as a containment barrier. Heavy equipment used to place covering soils over the synthetic liner should be separated from the geomembrane by a suitable thickness of the soil. If necessary, geotextiles are placed above or below a geomembrane in order to increase puncture resistance.

Seaming. Joining adjacent panels of geomembrane is usually accomplished through the application of heat. Some heat seaming (welding) is done in factories during construction of prefabricated panels. However, for most panel installations, some if not all seams must be constructed in the field. Types of welding include extrusion, hot-wedge, and hot-air.

In extrusion welding, a strand of molten polymer is deposited at the edge of the overlapped geomembrane panels, bonding the sheets together. The technique is

Fig. 5. Calabasas solid-waste landfill in Los Angeles County, California, being lined with geomembrane.

similar to arc welding of steel and requires abrading the surface of the sheet prior to deposition of the molten bead.

In hot-wedge seaming (**Fig. 6**), a wedge of hot steel is passed between the overlapped panel edges, followed directly by pressure rollers effecting the seam. The most advanced variation creates two welded tracks separated by an air gap. It allows testing by air pressure at the gap to detect potential leaks in the seam. (**Fig. 7**a).

In the hot-air welding method the sheets are melted by hot air blown between them, and then the molten sheets are pressed together. This welding system is not considered sufficiently consistent for final seaming operations; it is generally used only in conjunction with extrusion welding to keep the panels stationary before application of the extrusion weld.

Fig. 6. Dual-track hot-wedge-welder heat-seaming of adjacent geomembrane panels.

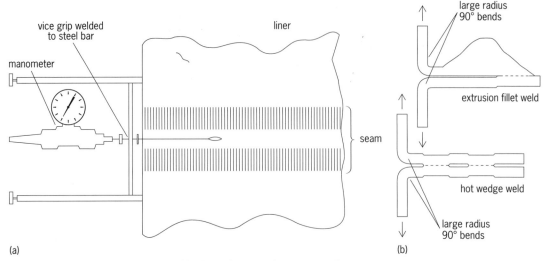

Fig. 7. Schematic diagrams of testing. (a) Nondestructive seam air-pressure test for leaks. (b) Destructive peel testing of both extrusion and dual-track hot-wedge seams to assess quality of welding, showing specimen configuration for peeling apart seams.

Alternatively, solvent-adhesive seams can be effected for certain geomembranes. In solvent-adhesive welding operations the solvent-adhesive mixture is brushed onto panel edges, and various methods are used to press the panel edges together to form the seam.

Testing. Geomembrane seams are tested very carefully to assure that they are free of leaks and adequately joined. Nondestructive testing is used to check the entire seamed distance for leaks, and if any are found they are repaired.

Destructive testing is used to assess the quality of the bonding between panels. It requires that samples of the finished seam be removed and pulled apart in order to observe bonding. True welding is required, as opposed to surface attachments analogous to those in soldered metals. It is important to determine if welds are fully integrated because a mere surface attachment can be disrupted by absorbed chemicals. Samples are pulled apart by bending back the top panel from the overlapped section of the bottom panel in an attempt to peel the surface between the seamed panels (**Fig. 7b**). If true welding has occurred, the resulting tear is through one of the panels as opposed to delamination (peeling). In contrast to nondestructive testing, destructive testing is limited to an interval basis.

Mark Cadwallader; Hal Pastner

Geothermal power

Thermal or electrical power produced from the thermal energy contained in the Earth (geothermal energy). Use of geothermal energy is based thermodynamically on the temperature difference between a mass of subsurface rock and water and a mass of water or air at the Earth's surface. This temperature difference allows production of thermal energy that can be either used directly or converted to mechanical or electrical energy.

CHARACTERISTICS

Temperatures in the Earth in general increase with increasing depth, to 400–1800°F (200–1000°C) at the base of the Earth's crust and to perhaps 6300–8100°F (3500–4500°C) at the center of the Earth. Average conductive geothermal gradients to 6 mi (10 km; the depth of the deepest wells drilled to date) are shown in **Fig. 1** for representative heat-flow provinces of the United States. The heat that produces these gradients comes from two sources: flow of heat from the deep crust and mantle; and thermal energy generated in the upper crust by radioactive decay of isotopes of uranium, thorium, and potassium. The gradients of Fig. 1 represent regions of different conductive heat flow from the mantle or deep crust. Some granitic rocks in the upper crust, however, have abnormally high contents of uranium and thorium and thus produce anomalously great amounts of thermal energy and enhanced flow of heat toward the Earth's surface. Consequently, thermal gradients at shallow levels above these granitic plutons can be somewhat greater than shown on Fig. 1.

The thermal gradients of Fig. 1 are calculated under the assumption that heat moves toward the Earth's surface only by thermal conduction through solid rock. However, thermal energy is also transmitted toward the Earth's surface by movement of molten rock (magma) and by circulation of water through interconnected pores and fractures. These processes are superimposed on the regional conduction-dominated gradients of Fig. 1 and give rise to very high temperatures near the Earth's surface. Areas characterized by such high temperatures are the primary targets for geothermal exploration and development.

Commercial exploration and development of geothermal energy to date have focused on natural geothermal reservoirs—volumes of rock at high temperatures (up to 662°F or 350°C) and with both high porosity (pore space, usually filled with water) and high permeability (ability to transmit fluid). The thermal energy is tapped by drilling wells into the reservoirs. The thermal energy in the rock is transferred by conduction to the fluid, which subsequently flows to the well and then to the Earth's surface.

Natural geothermal reservoirs, however, make up only a small fraction of the upper 6 mi (10 km) of the Earth's crust. The remainder is rock of relatively low permeability whose thermal energy cannot be produced without fracturing the rock artificially by means of explosives or hydrofracturing. Experiments involving artificial fracturing of hot rock have been performed, and extraction of energy by circulation of water through a network of these artificial fractures may someday prove economically feasible.

There are several types of natural geothermal reservoirs. All the reservoirs developed to date for electrical energy are termed hydrothermal convection systems and are characterized by circulation of meteoric (surface) water to depth. The driving force of the convection systems is gravity, effective because of the density difference between cold, downward-moving, recharge water and heated, upward-moving, thermal water. A hydrothermal convection system can be driven either by an underlying young igneous intrusion or by merely deep circulation of water along faults and fractures. Depending on the physical state of the pore fluid, there are two kinds of hydrothermal convection systems: liquid-dominated, in which all the pores and fractures are filled with liquid water that exists at temperatures well above boiling at atmospheric pressure, owing to the pressure of overlying water; and vapor-dominated, in which the larger pores and fractures are filled with steam. Liquid-dominated reservoirs produce either water or a mixture of water and steam, whereas vapor-dominated reservoirs produce only steam, in most cases superheated.

Natural geothermal reservoirs also occur as regional aquifers, such as the Dogger Limestone of the Paris Basin in France and the sandstones of the Pannonian series of central Hungary. In some rapidly subsiding young sedimentary basins such as the northern Gulf of Mexico Basin, porous reservoir sandstones are compartmentalized by growth faults into individual reservoirs that can have fluid pressures exceeding that of a column of water and approaching that of the overlying rock. The pore water is prevented from escaping by the impermeable shale that surrounds the compartmented sandstone. The energy in these geopressured reservoirs consists not only of thermal energy, but also of an equal amount of energy from methane dissolved in the waters plus a small amount of mechanical energy due to the high fluid pressures. *SEE AQUIFER; GROUNDWATER HYDROLOGY.*

USE OF GEOTHERMAL ENERGY

Although geothermal energy is present everywhere beneath the Earth's surface, its use is possible only when certain conditions are met: (1) The energy must be accessible to drilling, usually at depths of less than 2 mi (3 km) but possibly at depths of 4 mi (6–7 km) in particularly favorable environments (such as in the northern Gulf of Mexico Basin of the United States). (2) Pending demonstration of the technology and economics for fracturing and producing energy from rock of low permeability, the reservoir porosity and permeability must be sufficiently high to allow production of large quantities of thermal water. (3) Since a major cost in geothermal development is drilling and since costs per meter increase with increasing depth, the shallower the concentration of geothermal energy the better. (4) Geothermal fluids can be transported economically by pipeline on the Earth's surface only a few tens of kilometers, and thus any generating or direct-use facility must be located at or near the geothermal anomaly.

Direct use. Equally important worldwide is the direct use of geothermal energy, often at reservoir temperatures less than 212°F (100°C). Geothermal energy is used directly in a number of ways: to heat buildings (individual houses, apartment complexes, and even

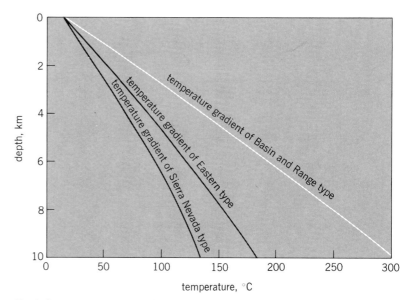

Fig. 1. Calculated average conductive temperature gradients in representative heat-flow provinces of the United States. 1 km = 0.6 mi. °F = (°C × 1.8) + 32. (*After D. E. White and D. L. Williams, eds., Assessment of Geothermal Resources of the United States—1975, USGS Circ. 726, 1975*)

whole communities); to cool buildings (using lithium bromide absorption units); to heat greenhouses and soil; and to provide hot or warm water for domestic use, for product processing (for example, the production of paper), for the culture of shellfish and fish, for swimming pools, and for therapeutic (healing) purposes.   *L. J. Patrick Muffler*

Major localities where geothermal energy is directly used include Iceland (30% of net energy consumption, primarily as domestic heating), the Paris Basin of France (where 140–160°F or 60–70°C water is used in district heating systems for the communities of Melun, Creil, and Villeneuve la Garenne), and the Pannonian Basin of Hungary.

Electric power generation. The use of geothermal energy for electric power generation has become widespread because of several factors. Countries where geothermal resources are prevalent have desired to develop their own resources in contrast to importing fuel for power generation. In countries where many resource alternatives are available for power generation, including geothermal, geothermal has been a preferred resource because it cannot be transported for sale, and the use of geothermal energy enables fossil fuels to be used for higher and better purposes than power generation. Also, geothermal steam has become an attractive power generation alternative because of environmental benefits and because the unit sizes are small (normally less than 100 MW). Moreover, geothermal plants can be built much more rapidly than plants using fossil fuel and nuclear resources, which, for economic purposes, have to be very large in size. Electrical utility systems are also more reliable if their power sources are not concentrated in a small number of large units.

In the United States a law was passed in 1978 that required the output from geothermal power generation projects (and others not based on fossil fuel resources, and cogeneration projects) to be purchased by electrical utilities at the cost that was avoided by the utility as a result of obtaining the power from a geothermal power plant. The legislation is called the Federal Public Utility Regulatory Policies Act (PURPA) and has

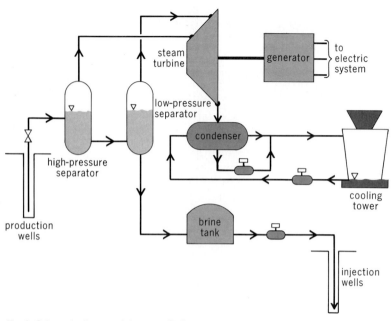

Fig. 2. Schematic diagram of the steam flash process.

created an incentive for the development of geothermal power projects.

The process used for generating power varies in accordance with the characteristics of the geothermal resource. The characteristics that affect the process are the temperature, the suspended and dissolved solids in the resource, and the level of noncondensable gases (primarily carbon dioxide) entrained in the geothermal brine, or steam. Almost all resources discovered to date are of the hydrothermal type (pressurized hot water) which can be produced from a well by two methods. If the temperature of a hydrothermal resource is below 400°F (204°C), a geothermal well can be produced with a pump, which maintains sufficient pressure on the geothermal brine to keep it as pressurized hot water. For hydrothermal resources over 400°F, the more suitable method of production is to flow the wells naturally, yielding a flashing mixture of brine and steam from the wells.

Steam flash process. The most common process is the steam flash process (**Fig. 2**), which incorporates steam separators to take the steam from a flashing geothermal well and passes the steam through a turbine that drives an electric generator. For the greatest efficiency in this process, a double-entry turbine is utilized which enables the most amount of steam available in the production from the geothermal well to be converted to electric power. If the resource has a high level of suspended and dissolved solids, it may be necessary to incorporate scaling control equipment in the steam flash vessel at the front of the plant and solids-settling equipment at the tail end of the plant. This will keep the process equipment from becoming plugged and allows a clean residual brine to be maintained for reinjection into the reservoir. If there are significant amounts of noncondensable gases, it may be necessary to install equipment to eject these gases out of the condenser to keep the back pressure on the system from rising and thereby cutting down on the efficiency of the process.

There are, at present, two resources in operation that have "dry steam," which is produced from the wells directly. These are very easy to convert to electric power and use the above described process without the necessity of the separation and brine injection equipment.

Binary process. A more efficient utilization of the resource can be obtained by using the binary process (**Fig. 3**) on resources with a temperature less than 360°F (180°C). This process is normally used when wells are pumped. The pressurized geothermal brine yields its heat energy to a second fluid in heat exchangers and is reinjected into the reservoir. The second fluid (commonly referred to as the power fluid) has a lower boiling temperature than the geothermal brine and therefore becomes a vapor on the exit of the heat exchangers. It is separately pumped as a liquid before going through the heat exchangers. The vaporized, high-pressure gas then passes through a turbine that drives an electric generator. The vapor exhaust from the turbine is then condensed in conventional condensers and is pumped back through the heat exchangers. There is a distinct environmental advantage to this process since both the geothermal brine and power fluid systems are closed from the atmosphere. Hydrocarbons, such as isobutane and propane, are common power fluids used in this proccess. SEE ELECTRIC POWER GENERATION.
                                          Thomas C. Hinrichs

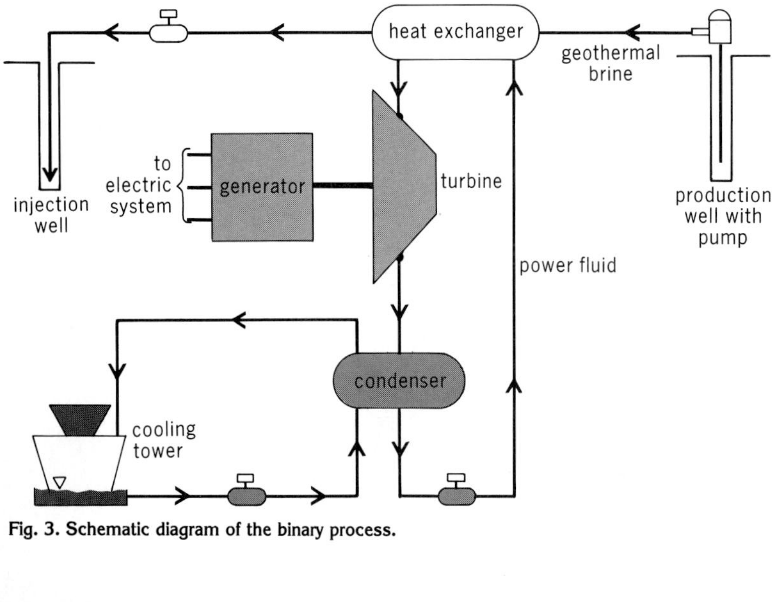

PRODUCTION AND POLLUTION PROBLEMS

The chief problems in producing geothermal power involve mineral deposition, changes in hydrological conditions, and corrosion of equipment. Pollution problems arise in handling geothermal effluents, both water and steam.

Mineral deposition. In some water-dominated fields there may be mineral deposition from boiling geothermal fluid. Silica deposition in wells caused problems in the Salton Sea, California, field; more commonly, calcium carbonate scale formation in wells or in the country rock may limit field developments, for example, in Turkey and the Philippines. Fields with hot waters high in total carbonate are now regarded with suspicion for simple development. In the disposal of hot wastewaters at the surface, silica deposition in flumes and waterways can be troublesome.

Hydrological changes. Extensive production from wells changes the local hydrological conditions. De-

Fig. 3. Schematic diagram of the binary process.

creasing aquifer pressures may cause boiling water in the rocks (leading to changes in well fluid characteristics), encroachment of cool water from the outskirts of the field, or changes in water chemistry through lowered temperatures and gas concentrations. After an extensive withdrawal of hot water from rocks of low strength, localized ground subsidence may occur (up to several meters) and the original natural thermal activity may diminish in intensity. Some changes occur in all fields, and a good understanding of the geology and hydrology of a system is needed so that the well withdrawal rate can be matched to the well's long-term capacity to supply fluid.

Corrosion. Geothermal waters cause an accelerated corrosion of most metal alloys, but this is not a serious utilization problem except, very rarely, in areas where wells tap high-temperature acidic waters (for example, in active volcanic zones.) The usual deep geothermal water is of near-neutral pH. The principal metal corrosion effects to be avoided are sulfide and chloride stress corrosion of certain stainless and high-strength steels and the rapid corrosion of copper-based alloys. Hydrogen sulfide, or its oxidation products, also causes a more rapid degradation than normal of building materials, such as concrete, plastics, and paints.

Pollution. A high noise level can arise from unsilenced discharging wells (up to 120 decibels adjusted), and well discharges may spray saline and silica-containing fluids on vegetation and buildings. Good engineering practice can reduce these effects to acceptable levels.

Because of the lower efficiency of geothermal power stations, they emit more water vapor per unit capacity than fossil-fuel stations. Steam from wellhead silencers and power station cooling towers may cause an increasing tendency for local fog and winter ice formation. Geothermal effluent waters liberated into waterways may cause a thermal pollution problem unless diluted by at least 100:1.

Geothermal power stations may have four major effluent streams. Large volumes of hot saline effluent water are produced in liquid-dominated fields. Impure water vapor rises from the station cooling towers, which also produce a condensate stream containing varying concentrations of ammonia, sulfide, carbonate, and boron. Waste gases flow from the gas extraction pump vent.

Pollutants in geothermal steam. Geothermal steam supplies differ widely in gas content (often 0.1–5%). The gas is predominantly carbon dioxide, hydrogen sulfide, methane, and ammonia. Venting of hydrogen sulfide gas may cause local objections if it is not adequately dispersed, and a major geothermal station near communities with a low tolerance to odor may require a sulfur recovery unit (such as the Stretford process unit). Sulfide dispersal effects on trees and plants appear to be small. The low radon concentrations in steam (3–200 nanocuries/kg or 0.1–7.4 kilobecquerels/kg), when dispersed, are unlikely to be of health significance. The mercury in geothermal stream (often 1–10 microgram/kg) is finally released into the atmosphere, but the concentrations created are unlikely to be hazardous. *See Air pollution.*

Geothermal waters. The compositions of geothermal waters vary widely. Those in recent volcanic areas are commonly dilute (<0.5%) saline solutions, but waters in sedimentary basins or active volcanic areas range upward to concentrated brines. In comparison with surface waters, most geothermal waters contain exceptional concentrations of boron, fluoride, ammonia, silica, hydrogen sulfide, and arsenic. In the common dilute geothermal waters, the concentrations of heavy metals such as iron, manganese, lead, zinc, cadmium, and thallium seldom exceed the levels permissible in drinking waters. However, the concentrated brines may contain appreciable levels of heavy metals (parts per million or greater).

Because of their composition, effluent geothermal waters or condensates may adversely affect potable or irrigation water supplies and aquatic life. Ammonia can increase weed growth in waterways and promote eutrophication, while the entry of boron to irrigation waters may affect sensitive plants such as citrus. Small quantities of metal sulfide precipitates from waters, containing arsenic, antimony, and mercury, can accumulate in stream sediments and cause fish to derive undesirably high (over 0.5 ppm) mercury concentrations. *See Water pollution.*

Reinjection. The problem of surface disposal may be avoided by reinjection of wastewaters or condensates back into the countryside through disposal wells. Steam condensate reinjection has few problems and is practiced in Italy and the United States. The much larger volumes of separated waste hot water (about 55 tons or 50 metric tons per megawatt-electric) from water-dominated fields present a more difficult reinjection situation. Silica and carbonate deposition may cause blockages in rock fissures if appropriate temperature, chemical, and hydrological regimes are not met at the disposal depth. In some cases, chemical processing of brines may be necessary before reinjection. Selective reinjection of water into the thermal system may help to retain aquifer pressures and to extract further heat from the rock. A successful water reinjection system has operated for several years at Ahuachapán, El Salvador.

A. J. Ellis

Bibliography. H. C. H. Armstead, *Geothermal Energy*, 1978; P. D. Blair, T. A. V. Cassel, and R. H. Edelstein, *Geothermal Energy: Prospects for Energy Production*, 1982; R. Bowen, *Geothermal Resources*, 1979; L. Edwards et al. (eds.), *Handbook of Geothermal Energy*, 1982; J. Elder, *Geothermal Systems*, 1981; A. J. Ellis and W. A. J. Mahon, *Chemistry and Geothermal Systems*, 1977; M. A. Grant et al., *Geothermal Reservoir Engineering*, 1983; L. Rybach and L. J. Muffler (eds.), *Geothermal Systems: Principles and Case Histories*, 1981; E. F. Wahl, *Geothermal Energy Utilization*, 1977.

Grassland ecosystem

A biological community that contains few trees or shrubs, is characterized by mixed herbaceous (nonwoody) vegetation cover, and is dominated by grasses or grasslike plants. Grassland ecosystems range from the dense bamboo of the Amazonian tropics to the cool northern steppes of the Soviet Union, and from dry plains in the western United States to Canadian arctic grasslands. Mixtures of trees and grasslands occur as savannas at transition zones with forests, as in the east-central United States, or where rainfall is marginal for trees, such as in south-central Africa and Australia. About 1.2×10^8 mi^2 (4.6×10^7 km^2) of the Earth's surface is covered with grasslands, which make up about 32% of the plant cover of the world. The proportion of original grasslands varies widely among continents with about 44% remaining in Europe and less than 10% in Australia, although the latter has vast expanses of savannas. In North America, grasslands include the Great Plains, which extend from southern Texas into Canada. The European meadows cross the subcontinent, and the Eurasian steppe ranges from Hungary eastward through the Soviet Union to Mongolia; the pampas cover much of the interior of Argentina and Uruguay. Vast and varied savannas and velds can be found in central and southern Africa and throughout much of Australia. SEE SAVANNA.

Most civilizations have developed in grassland and savanna regions, and were it not for the abundance and widespread distribution of grasses, the human population of the world would not have attained its present level. Significant portions of the world's grasslands have been modified by grazing or tillage or have been converted to other uses. The most fertile and productive soils in the world have developed under grassland, and in many cases the natural species have been replaced by cultivated grasses (cereals).

Grasslands occur in regions that are too dry for forests but that have sufficient soil water to support a closed herbaceous plant canopy that is lacking in deserts. Thus, temperate grasslands usually develop in areas with 10–40 in. (25–100 cm) of annual precipitation, although tropical grasslands may receive up to 60 in. (150 cm). Grasslands are found primarily on plains or rolling topography in the interiors of great land masses, and from sea level to elevations of nearly 16,400 ft (5000 m) in the Andes. Because of their continental location they experience large differences in seasonal climate and wide ranges in diurnal conditions. In general, there is at least one dry season during the year, and drought conditions occur periodically. SEE DROUGHT.

Classification. Different kinds of grasslands develop within continents, and their classification is based on similarity of dominant vegetation, presence or absence of specific dominant species, or prevailing climate conditions (see **illus.**). In North America, the tallgrass prairie lies between the eastern deciduous forest and the Central Plains. Annual rainfall is 30–40 in. (75–100 cm), and under optimum conditions the dominant bluestem (*Andropogon*) grass species may exceed a height of 6 ft (2 m). The mixed-grass prairie contains species of the tallgrass prairie and the shortgrass prairie, which dominates farther west. Annual precipitation amounts range from 20 to 30 in. (50 to 75 cm), and the height of the dominant species has a similar range. Shortgrass prairies have precipitation amounts of 10–20 in. (25–50 cm) and are dominated by grasses adapted to dry conditions, such as grama grasses (*Bouteloua*) and buffalo grass (*Buchloe dactyloides*). Desert grasslands have annual rainfalls of 10–18 in. (25–45 cm), which usually fall in summer (July–August) and winter (December–January). Between those wet periods, the desert grasslands are subjected to extreme drought.

Other North American grasslands include the annual grassland in the central valley of California. Originally, these grasslands were dominated by perennial species, but with grazing pressure most of them have been replaced by native and exotic annual species that are more resistant to grazing. Mountain grasslands occupy higher elevations and are frequently mixed in a parklike appearance with trees up to elevations of 8200 ft (2500 m). Shrub steppe grassland vegetation can be found in the northwestern United States and includes many herbaceous grassland species in combination with woody species such as sagebrush (*Artemisia*).

Climate. The climate of grasslands is one of daily and seasonal extremes. Deep winter cold does not preclude grasslands since they occur in some of the coldest regions of the world. However, the success of grasslands in the Mediterranean climate shows that marked summer drought is not prohibitive either. In North America, the rainfall gradient decreases from an annual precipitation of about 40 in. (100 cm) along the eastern border of the tallgrass prairie at the deciduous forest to only about 8 in. (20 cm) in the shortgrass prairies at the foothills of the Rocky Mountains. A similar pattern exists in Europe, with the taller grasses along the northwestern coast and decreasing plant height and rainfall toward the south and east into the plains of Hungary. Growing-season length is determined by temperature in the north latitudes and by available soil moisture in many regions, especially those adjacent to deserts. Plants are frequently subjected to hot and dry weather conditions, which are often exacerbated by windy conditions that increase transpirational water loss from the plant leaves.

Soils. Soils of mesic temperate grasslands are usually deep, about 3 ft (1 m), are neutral to basic, have high amounts of organic matter, contain large amounts of exchangeable bases, and are highly fertile, with well-developed profiles. The soils are rich because rainfall is inadequate for excessive leaching of minerals and because plant roots produce large amounts of organic material. Humus, partially decomposed organic material that may constitute up to 10% of the soil, expands its capability to retain water by as much as 20% and binds soil particles into clumps, increasing the effectiveness of the soil to make nutrients and water available to the plants. With less rainfall, grassland soils are shallow, contain less organic matter, frequently are lighter colored, and may be more basic. Tropical and subtropical soils are highly leached, have lower amounts of organic material because of rapid decomposition and more leaching from higher rainfall, and are frequently red to yellow. Almost all true grasslands soils are classified as Mollisols and Aridisols, although a few from drier climates are Alfisols and some coastal grasslands are Vertisols.

Grassland soils are dry throughout the profile for a portion of the year. If the soil profile is relatively shallow over a rock subsurface or an impervious layer, the total water stored may be too small to support trees even in geographical areas of relatively high rainfall, which accounts for the presence of grasslands in regions whose climate would support forests. Sandy soils reduce loss of water from runoff and increase water storage in the soil profile because of increased percolation. As a result, sandy soils support more vigorous grassland vegetation, or permit tree growth in a relatively arid region, when compared with soils containing higher amounts of silt and clay particles. Because of their dense fibrous root system in the upper layers of the soil, grasses are better adapted than trees to make use of light rainfall showers during the growing season. When compared with forest soils, grassland soils are generally subjected to higher temperatures, greater evaporation, periodic

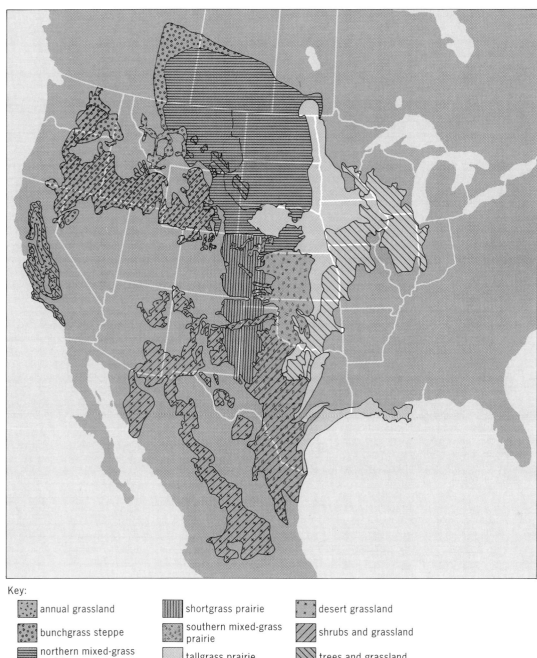

Key:

annual grassland	shortgrass prairie	desert grassland
bunchgrass steppe	southern mixed-grass prairie	shrubs and grassland
northern mixed-grass prairie	tallgrass prairie	trees and grassland

Map of grassland types in central and western North America.

drought, and more transpiration per unit of total plant biomass. *SEE BIOMASS; SOIL.*

Vegetation. Worldwide, there are approximately 600 genera and 7500 species of grasses. Temperate North American dominant grass genera include the bluestems (*Andropogon, Schizachyrium*), grama grasses (*Bouteloua*), switchgrasses (*Panicum*), wheatgrasses (*Agrypyron*), wire grasses (*Artistida*), fescues (*Festuca*), and bluegrasses (*Poa*). However, many other herbaceous grassland species are broad-leaved forbs, which are plants other than grasses, and like most of the grasses, are perennial. Throughout the year, flowering plants bloom in the grasslands with moderate precipitation, and flowers bloom after rainfall in the drier grasslands. The number of plant species in any one grassland is relatively small, usually 50 to 350 species. Dominant species that flower late in the growing season tend to be taller than the early, cool-season species. In general, the dominant species persists from year to year with relatively small changes in biomass production or changes in importance. The subdominant species demonstrate much greater fluctuations from year to year, depending upon the weather conditions and especially in relation to periods of seed germination and growth.

Just as the above-ground canopy is layered, so are the roots below ground. In mesic grasslands, the roots of perennial grasses have rooting depths greater than 5 ft (1.5 m); many forbs have even deeper roots. Usually, however, 75% or more of the root biomass occurs in the top 10 in. (25 cm) of the soil profile.

With increasing aridity and temperature, grasslands

tend to become less diverse in the number of species; they support more warm-season species (which mature late in the growing season); the complexity of the vegetation decreases; the total above-ground and below-ground production decreases; but the ratio of above-ground to below-ground biomass becomes smaller.

Many grassland plant species demonstrate adaptations to minimize damage from grazing. Unlike forbs and woody species, the growing tissues in grasses are at the base of the leaves near the soil surface, so when the leaves are grazed, the meristematic region is protected and can still produce new leaves. Some forbs also have antigrazing mechanisms, such as spines or tough structural material, chemicals that discourage grazing because of taste, supine growth forms so that the leaves stay near the soil surface, or growth flushes of plentiful forage under advantageous environmental conditions so that some of the plants are likely to be ungrazed.

Animal life. There are many more invertebrate species than any other taxonomic group in the grassland ecosystem. For example, more than 1600 different species of insects have been identified from a shortgrass prairie in Colorado. In North America, each prairie state has at least 100 species of grasshopper; Kansas has nearly 300 species. Invertebrate species occur both above and below the soil surface, and depending upon their life cycle, some are found in both locations. Invertebrates play several roles in the ecosystem. For example, many are herbivorous, such as grasshoppers, and eat leaves and stems, whereas others, like cutworms, feed on the roots of plants. Earthworms process organic matter into small fragments that decompose rapidly, scarab beetles process animal dung on the soil surface, flies feed on plants and are pests to cattle, and many species of invertebrates are predaceous and feed on other invertebrates. Soil nematodes, small nonarthropod invertebrates, include forms that are herbivorous, predaceous, or saprophagous, feeding on decaying organic matter. In a South Dakota mixed-grass prairie, $2\text{--}6 \times 10^6$ herbivorous nematode forms were found within a soil sample 3 ft (1 m) square and 8 in. (20 cm) deep. *See Soil Ecology.*

Most of the reptiles and amphibians in grassland ecosystems are predators. For example, lizards and box turtles prey on insects, and snakes prey on rodents and small invertebrates.

Relatively few bird species inhabit the grassland ecosystem, although many more species are found in the flooding pampas of Argentina than in the dry grasslands of the western United States. In North American prairies, perhaps only about a dozen bird species are restricted to the grasslands, and another two dozen are characteristic of but not limited to the grasslands. The small number of species is related to the uniform habitat. Typical groups of birds include hawks, grouse, meadowlarks, longspurs, and sparrows. Their role in the grassland ecosystem involves consumption of seeds, invertebrates, and vertebrates; seed dispersal; and scavenging of dead animals.

Small mammals of the North American grassland include moles, shrews, gophers, ground squirrels, and various species of mice. Among intermediate-size animals are the opossum, fox, coyote, badger, skunk, rabbit, and prairie dog; large animals include the mule deer (*Odocoileus hemionus*), white-tailed deer (*O.*

virginianus), pronghorn (*Antilocapra americana*), and elk (*Cervus canadensis*). The most characteristic large mammal species of the North American grassland is the bison (*Bison bison*), but the $60\text{--}75 \times 10^6$ of these animals were largely eliminated in the late 1800s and are now mostly confined to reserves. Mammals include both ruminant (pronghorns) and nonruminant (prairie dogs) herbivores, omnivores (opossum), and predators (wolves).

Except for large mammals and birds, the animals found in the grassland ecosystem undergo relatively large population variations from year to year. These variations, some of which are cyclical and others more episodic, are not entirely understood and may extend over several years. Many depend upon predator–prey relationships, parasite or disease dynamics, or weather conditions that influence the organisms themselves or the availability of food, water, and shelter. *See Population ecology.*

Microorganisms. Within the grassland ecosystem are enormous numbers of very small organisms, including bacteria, fungi, algae, and viruses. One study found 9×10^6 bacteria in a gram of tallgrass prairie soil; another study found about 6560 ft (2000 m) of fungal hyphae (strands of fungus) in 0.04 oz (1 g) of short-grass prairie soil. From a systems perspective, the hundreds of species of bacteria and fungi are particularly important because they decompose organic material, releasing carbon dioxide and other gases into the atmosphere and making nutrients available for recycling. Bacteria and some algae also capture nitrogen from the atmosphere and fix it into forms available to plants.

System functions. The grassland ecosystem consists of several components. Producers are plants that use the Sun's energy to capture carbon as carbon dioxide from the atmosphere and, with available nutrients from the soils, produce more plant material. Consumers consist of animals and microorganisms that feed upon plant parts (herbivores) and other animals (carnivores). Decomposer microorganisms and invertebrates convert dead organic matter to released carbon dioxide and available nutrients in the soil. The carbon cycle involves the transfer of carbon from the atmosphere into plants, through various animals and microorganisms, and back into the atmosphere. Energy is captured first from the Sun and then cycled through the system as organic material until this organic material is eventually decomposed to carbon dioxide. The nutrients are then released again to the soil. Only about 1% of the total solar radiation is captured by the vegetation. *See Biogeochemistry.*

The amount of vegetation produced depends on the type of grassland and the level of water and nutrients in the soil. In the tallgrass prairie, annual above-ground plant production is 1.6–2.0 oz/ft^2 (500–600 g/m^2), about 1.1 oz/ft^2 (350 g/m^2) in the mixed-grass prairie, 0.5–0.6 oz/ft^2 (150–200 g/m^2) in the short-grass prairie, and as much as 13.1 oz/ft^2 (4000 g/m^2) in tropical grasslands. Total annual primary production is two or more times those amounts, because much of the energy is translocated below ground. *See Biological productivity; Ecological energetics.*

Grasslands have been used for grazing for the last $1.5\text{--}2.0 \times 10^7$ years, probably beginning in the Miocene. For all practical purposes, it can be assumed that grasslands have evolved under the influence of herbivores. In North America, the bison roamed across the landscape, heavily grazing the grassland they traversed. As the bison moved on, however, the rangelands recovered. Where the grassland is grazed heavily, as in prairie dog towns, around waterholes, and in fenced-in livestock pastures, grazing exerts enormous pressure on the vegetation. Because many of the native species are palatable, they are selectively grazed and weedy, less palatable species remain. Moreover, those influences may extend to other components of the grassland ecosystem and increase the vulnerability of the soil to erosion or the susceptibility of the rangeland to insect herbivory or diseases. *See* Ecological succession.

Much of the grassland ecosystem has been burned naturally, probably from fires sparked by lightning. Human inhabitants have also routinely started fires intentionally to remove predators and undesirable insects, to improve the condition of the rangeland, and to reduce cover for predators and enemies; or unintentionally. Thus, grasslands have evolved under the influences of grazing and periodic burning, and the species have adapted to withstand these conditions. If burning or grazing is coupled with drought, however, the grassland will sustain damage that may require long periods of time for recovery by successional processes. Because of the prehistoric and historic burning of prairies, some rangeland management strategies have included periodic fires to remove woody species and old or dead herbaceous vegetation. *See* Agroecosystem; Ecosystem.

Paul G. Risser

Bibliography. J. R. Estes et al., *Grasses and Grasslands: Systematics and Ecology*, 1982; P. G. Risser et al., *The True Prairie Ecosystem*, 1981; Time-Life Book Editors, *Grasslands and Tundra*, 1985.

Greenhouse effect

The effect created by Earth's atmosphere acting as the glass walls and roof of a greenhouse in trapping heat from the sun. The atmosphere is largely transparent to solar radiation, but it strongly absorbs the longer-wavelength (infrared) radiation from the Earth's surface. Much of this long-wave radiation is reemitted down to the surface, with the paradoxical result that the Earth's surface receives more radiation than it would if the atmosphere were not situated between it and the Sun.

The absorption of long-wave radiation is affected by small amounts of water vapor, carbon dioxide, ozone, nitrous oxide, methane, and other minor constituents of air, and by clouds. Clouds absorb, on average, about one-fifth of the solar radiation striking them, but unless they are extremely thin, they are almost completely opaque to infrared radiation. The appearance even of cirrus clouds after a period of clear sky at night is enough to cause the surface air temperature to increase rapidly by several degrees because of long-wave radiation emitted by the cloud. *See* Atmosphere; Atmospheric ozone; Cloud.

The greenhouse effect is most marked at night, and usually keeps the diurnal temperature range below 20°F (11°C). Over regions where the water-vapor content of the air is low, however, the atmosphere is more transparent to infrared radiation, and cool nights may follow hot days.

The effect, described by John Tyndall in 1861, was among the earliest discoveries resulting from the rapid development of quantitative spectroscopy in the 1850s. The greenhouse analogy was attached to the effect at a much later date. Tyndall showed that water vapor was the major contributor to the effect, since its contribution to absorption in a cell of laboratory air was an order-of-magnitude greater than that of carbon dioxide and the remainder of the air.

Although the term greenhouse effect has generally been used for the role of the whole atmosphere (mainly water vapor and clouds) in keeping the surface of the Earth warm, it has been increasingly associated in the twentieth century with the contribution of carbon dioxide, since Svante Arrhenius raised the problem in 1896 of increasing temperature at the Earth's surface due to production of carbon dioxide by industrial combustion of fossil fuel. Arrhenius calculated that a doubling of carbon dioxide would raise the average temperature by about 9°F (5°C). Four decades later G. S. Callendar estimated that the industrial production of carbon dioxide since the 1880s could account for the continual rise in surface temperatures that had been observed thereafter.

The continual rise in surface temperature did not persist after Callendar's papers, despite a continuous increase in atmospheric carbon dioxide, raising the possibility that much of the earlier temperature rise could have been due to fallout of stratospheric dust from the great Krakatoa eruption. Some other uncertainties are the rate of absorption of excess carbon dioxide by the ecosystem and oceans, the rate of production of carbon dioxide by destruction of forests, the cooling effect of increasing aerosols, both anthropogenic and from revived volcanic activity, and feedback effects of water vapor and clouds.

The energy crisis and increasing sophistication of numerical atmospheric circulation models have led to greatly increased interest and investigation of the carbon dioxide greenhouse effect. In 1975 V. Ramanathan pointed out that the greenhouse effect is enhanced by the continued release into the atmosphere of chlorofluorocarbons, even though their combined concentration is less than a part per billion by volume. This is because of the spectral location of several of their absorption bands in the 8–14-micrometer region, where the atmosphere is relatively transparent and blackbody emission at terrestrial temperatures is high.

In contrast, the much more abundant constituent carbon monoxide, which is increasing from automobile exhausts and other combustion processes, does not have absorption bands in spectral regions where it can make a direct significant contribution to the greenhouse effect. It does play an indirect role in enhancing the greenhouse effect, however, by acting as a sink for the hydroxyl radical, which acts as a catalyst in modulating the increase of nitrous oxide from combustion processes and use of chemical fertilizer, and the increase of methane from biogenic and industrial production. *See* Air pollution; Climatic change.

Lewis D. Kaplan

Bibliography. M. C. Barth and J. G. Titus, *Greenhouse Effect and Sea Level Rise*, 1984; W. H. Berger and L. D. Labeyrie (eds.), *Abrupt Climatic Change*, 1987; National Research Council, *Changing Climate*, 1983.

Groundwater hydrology

The occurrence, circulation, distribution, and properties of any liquid water residing beneath the surface of the earth. This article excludes any water molecules which constitute mineral species such as clays. Generally groundwater is that fraction of precipitation which infiltrates the land surface and subsequently moves, in response to various hydrodynamic forces, to reappear once again as seeps or in a more obvious fashion as springs. Most of groundwater discharge is not evident because it occurs through the bottoms of surface water bodies; in fact, large fresh-water springs are relatively common on the ocean bottom off the eastern coast of Florida.

Groundwater can be found, at least in theory, in any geological horizon containing interconnected pore space. Thus a groundwater reservoir (an analogy to an oil reservoir) can be a classical porous medium, such as sand or sandstone; a fractured, relatively impermeable rock, such as granite; or a cavernous geologic horizon, such as certain limestone beds. Groundwater reservoirs which readily yield water to wells are known as aquifers; in contrast, aquitards are formations which do not normally provide adequate water supplies, and aquicludes are considered, for all practical purposes, to be impermeable. These terms are, of course, subjective descriptions; the flow of water which constitutes an economically viable supply depends upon the intended use and the availability of alternative sources.

Equations for flow. Groundwater and its dissolved constituents move according to mathematical relationships derived from the physics of flow through porous media. These relationships are simplest in the case of the saturated flow of a homogeneous fluid in a granular formation. There are a number of governing equations for this family of problems, and many solutions are available for problems of practical importance. There are also equations describing the behavior of dissolved constituents in flowing groundwater. This class of problems has gained prominence because of the recognition of existing and potential instances of groundwater contamination. However, these equations are more difficult to solve, and consequently the simulation of most field situations involving contaminant transport requires the use of large digital computers. When the unsaturated zone must be considered, the governing equations are still available, but there is a paucity of solutions. The major research advances in unsaturated flow can be attributed to soil physicists who are primarily concerned about water movement through the root zone during the irrigation of crops.

Regional flow. Groundwater flow in a regional sense is concerned with movement attributable to gravitational forces. Groundwater moves from points of high potential energy to points of low potential energy. Water in transit from regional topographic highs to regional topographic lows dissipates energy through friction. The flow path may be relatively short or extend for hundreds of miles, depending on the physical system. The generally observed correspondence between changes in the elevation of the surface of the saturated zone and changes in the land topography is maintained because of a continual source of water via precipitation. When precipitation patterns change, the groundwater surface responds ac-

cordingly, rising in wet years and falling in dry years. The topographic lowlands often correspond to areas of groundwater discharge. They may be characterized by springs, wetlands, or surface water bodies such as lakes, rivers, and oceans.

Artesian systems. The water level in a drilled well is a measure of the potential energy of the groundwater it encounters. In a recharge area, where water moves downward under gravitational forces, the fluid potential energy, and therefore the water level in wells, decreases with depth. On the other hand, in a discharge area where groundwater moves toward the surface, the fluid potential increases with depth. This latter situation results in a well water elevation which is higher than that observed for the upper surface of the saturated zone in the vicinity of the well. This phenomenon has been designated an artesian head. In some instances the well-water-level elevation may actually be higher than the land surface elevation. In this situation the groundwater flows naturally from the well, and no pump is required. Such wells are called flowing artesian wells. It has often been observed that the discharge of flowing wells decreases with time. This is a natural consequence of providing a groundwater flow path to the surface which is less energy-dissipating than the original porous medium flow. *See* Artesian systems.

Groundwater mining. It is important to recognize that when groundwater is used consumptively, that is, when it is removed permanently from the hydrologic system, the groundwater reservoir must be affected. The most immediate impact is a lowering of the saturated zone elevation. As the influence of the pumping reaches surface water bodies, water is generally induced from them. The rate of loss from the surface water body will increase until an equilibrium is established between water withdrawn from the well and that entering the aquifer. If no surface water bodies are available, the groundwater surface will fall as long as groundwater is utilized: this is called groundwater mining. Practically speaking, the process is self-limiting, because the cost of pumping groundwater increases as the water levels in the wells decline.

Chemical and physical characteristics. As groundwater moves through a regional flow system, its physical and chemical characteristics are modified by the environments encountered. It dissolves soluble ions, and thereby changes its chemical composition. Thus the chemistry of groundwater can sometimes be used to decipher its complex flow history. During transit through the subsurface, when groundwater encounters elevated rock temperatures, the water is heated. Under certain circumstances, the water may reach the surface as hot springs or geysers. When surface manifestations are absent, hot water and occasionally steam may be tapped by wells to provide a source of energy. High-temperature water can be used to produce electricity; lower-temperature water may heat homes, or may be employed effectively in selected industries. *See* Geothermal power.

Reservoir behavior. To effectively utilize groundwater as a natural resource, it is necessary to be able to forecast the impact of exploitation on water availability. When groundwater is used for water supply, a concern is the potential energy in the aquifer as reflected in the water levels in the producing well or neighboring wells. When a groundwater reservoir which does not readily transmit water is tapped, the energy loss associated with flow to the well can be such that the well must be drilled to prohibitively great depths to provide adequate supplies. On the other hand, in a formation able to transmit fluid easily, water levels may drop because the reservoir is being depleted of water. This is generally encountered in reservoirs of limited areal extent or those in which natural infiltration has been reduced either naturally or through human activities.

Models. To forecast reservoir behavior, some type of model of the groundwater system must be employed. Such models may be statistical or deterministic. When problems involving a change in pumping demand are encountered, deterministic models founded on physical principles are generally employed. They can be physical (scale models of the prototype), electrical (based on the analogy between porous media flow and electric current flow), or mathematical (involving analytical or numerical solutions of the governing physical equations).

Early models focused on forecasting well performance. From the point of view of water supply, it was important to forecast how the water level in the pumping well and neighboring wells would respond to pumping. Analytical solutions to the appropriate governing equations were developed for a number of field situations. The solution for the long-term equilibrium case is known as the Thiem equation. The Theis equation is a similar expression, but expresses transient behavior. These, and related expressions, can be readily modified to accommodate a number of possible hydrologic complications. For example, as mentioned earlier, when a well is located in the vicinity of a stream, the stream will, unless hydraulically disconnected from the aquifer, eventually contribute some of its flow to satisfying the well discharge. On the other extreme, when a well is located near the aquifer boundary, the well water levels will be lower than would be encountered had the well been located away from any such impermeable barrier.

These analytical solutions have, in fact, a dual purpose. It is evident that, given appropriate aquifer parameters, these equations can be used to forecast groundwater reservoir response to pumping. A less evident application involves the determination of the aquifer parameters. This requires a carefully controlled field experiment called a pumping test, which normally involves a central pumping well and a series of nearby observation wells. Analysis of the response of the groundwater system after the cessation of pumping is known as the recovery test. Both the pumping and recovery tests are analyzed by using the analytical formulas discussed above.

Groundwater quality. Problems involving groundwater quantity were once the primary concern of hydrologists; interest is now focused on groundwater quality. Groundwater contamination is a serious problem, particularly in the highly urbanized areas of the United States. Legislation restricting the design and construction of waste-disposal facilities has accelerated and expanded groundwater quality studies. Predictive models which describe the convective and dispersive transport of contaminants have been developed and applied to field situations. Such models can be used to investigate the effectiveness of remedial measures designed to contain or remove contaminated groundwater. SEE WATER POLLUTION.

Applications. Although this discussion has considered the groundwater phenomenon in a rather narrow sense, the same fundamental principles are applicable to a number of related but distinctly different disciplines. Soil mechanics, the study of foundation engineering, relies heavily upon porous flow physics for its governing equations. This is also true of excavation dewatering in construction and mining, drainage problems in agricultural engineering, and reservoir simulation problems in the oil, gas, and geothermal industries. Groundwater hydrology has played a historically important role in the exploitation of water resources in the United States, and continues to contribute to their protection and effective utilization. SEE HYDROLOGY.

George F. Pinder

Access to groundwater resources by wells has enabled the growth of agriculture, population, and commerce throughout the world. The types and uses of

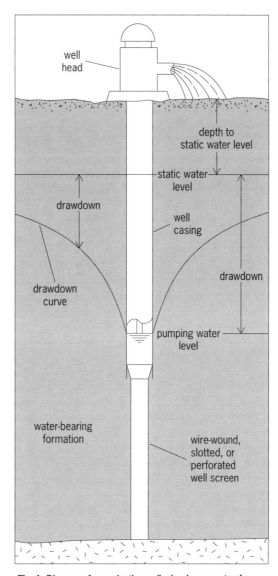

Fig. 1. Diagram of a production well, showing aspects of design that relate to well hydraulic performance. *(After F. G. Driscoll, Groundwater and Wells, 2d ed., Signal Environmental Systems, Johnson Division, 1986)*

wells vary substantially, reflecting the widespread dependence on water supply as well as the efforts to assess and protect the quality and quantity of water for future uses.

Water supply wells. These serve a variety of water needs ranging from those of an individual home or farmstead to those of urban population centers and industries. Water supply wells are usually designed, constructed, and operated in order to maximize the yield of water. The design factors should include both durable materials and pumping strategies that will provide long-term sustained yield from the aquifer. **Figure 1** shows a typical design for a production well, including terms relating to well hydraulic performance. The diameter of these wells may range from 4 to greater than 24 in. (10 to > 61 cm) depending on the aquifer properties and the pump required for lifting the amount of water needed. The well screen interval is normally placed in the most transmissive (or high-water-yeilding) geologic formation available. Above the screen, a well casing made of iron, steel, or a thermoplastic material completes the subsurface portion of the well. Surface completion methods vary; however, the casings are carefully sealed with clay and cement grouting materials to ensure that surface water does not enter the well. In this way, the infiltration of microbial organisms or runoff chemicals from the land surface are prevented from entering the produced water. A pump and water discharge line are contained within the well and are fitted with appropriate valves at the wellhead.

The hydraulics of well operation depicted in Fig. 1 relate to the response of the static water level in the aquifer to pumping. Pumping causes a decline in the water level (drawdown) to the pumping water level. The drawdown curve shown in Fig. 1 depicts the effect of pumping on water levels as a function of radial distance from the well. In certain hydrogeologic settings, the water level in the aquifer may be above the land surface (because the water in the geologic formation is confined or is at higher pressure than overlying formations), and the well may yield water without pumping. Such wells are termed artesian. Once completed, the well would provide water without pumping as long as the pressure differential between the land surface and the screened formation was maintained.

The long-term yield and hydraulic performance of production wells are usually evaluated on the basis of a pumping test, which provides information on the hydraulic properties of the aquifer under pumping conditions. In this type of test, an array of water-level-observation wells are located within the estimated zone of drawdown of the production well. A typical schematic is shown in **Fig. 2**, in which wells no. 1, 2, and 3 are small-diameter observation wells screened in the same formation as the production well. Observation well no. 4 would be used to determine if the clay layer shown between 46 and 50 ft (14 and 15 m) below land surface acts as a confining layer between the upper water-table aquifer and the lower aquifer. Water levels would be collected before pumping of the production well was begun, and then at successive time intervals over several days to weeks as the pumping water levels declined from static (nonpumping) levels. The amount of water in storage in the aquifer and the transmissive properties of the geologic formation can then be determined in order to establish a pumping strategy that would provide long-term yield of water without causing excessive drawdown (so-called mining) of the resource.

Monitoring or observation wells. These wells, also known as piezometers, are often used to permit the observation of water levels and to collect samples of groundwater for microbiological or chemical analyses. They have many similarities to water supply wells in design and construction. The principal difference between monitoring and production wells is that

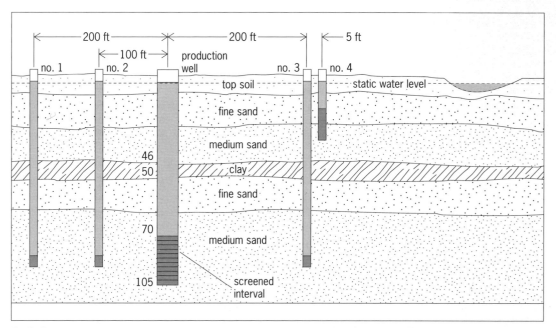

Fig. 2. Geologic section on a line through a test well and observation wells. Numbers along the production well indicate depth in feet. 1 ft = 0.3 m. *(After F. G. Driscoll, Groundwater and Wells, Signal Environmental Systems, Johnson Division, 2d ed., 1986)*

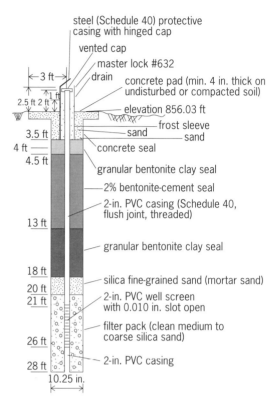

Well number	7H
Start	8/13/87 8:00 a.m.–1:00 p.m.
Finish	8/14/87 10 a.m.–12:00 p.m.
Drilling method	Hollow stem auger

Fig. 3. Design detail for a typical monitoring well. *(After L. Aller, Handbook of Suggested Practices for the Design and Installation of Ground-Water Monitoring Wells, National Water Well Association, 1989)*

monitoring wells are most often screened in discrete formations to provide specific hydrogeologic and chemical information rather than to produce large volumes of water. In general, these wells have diameters from 1 to 4 in. (2.5 to 10 cm), and the screened intervals are of the order 2 to 10 ft (0.6 to 3 m). The construction materials may be similar to those used for water supply wells, but designs often call for the use of stainless steel or chemical-resistant thermoplastics for durability under potentially contaminated subsurface conditions. **Figure 3** depicts the design and construction details for a typical monitoring well. In this case the well has been completed at 21 to 26 ft (6 to 8 m) below land surface with 2-in. (5-cm) polyvinyl chloride (PVC) casing and screen. As seen in the diagram, the precautions to seal the monitoring well bore from surface infiltration with bentonite clay and cement may be far more involved than in the construction of a production well. The need to achieve a proper seal becomes all the more important when surface soils or overlying formations may be contaminated. Percolation of contaminated water down the well bore would otherwise bias the analytical results from the well.

Since monitoring or observation wells are designed to provide depth-discrete information, they are frequently built in nested installations. In this situation, two or more wells are finished at different depth ranges to provide information on vertical hydraulic-head (that is, pressure) differences or concentration distributions of chemical or microbial parameters.

Water sample collection is conducted in monitoring wells by small-diameter submersible pumps, surface pumps (if the static water level is within approximately 18 ft or 5.4 m of land surface), or grab samplers. Water-level measurements are made during sampling events to record water levels relative to a surveyed benchmark for analysis of groundwater flow velocity and direction.

Alternative designs for nested monitoring installations include multilevel sampling arrays that employ discrete sampling ports linked to the wellhead by tubing. In these cases, mechanical samplers or surface pumps are used to retrieve water samples. These types of installations can provide significantly more vertical detail in chemical distributions than nested, conventionally screened monitoring wells. However, their use has been linked mainly to shallow depths (less than 100 ft or 30 m below land surface) because of constraints on the size of the sampling mechanism and the lift capabilities. *SEE* WATER SUPPLY ENGINEERING.

Michael J. Barcelona

Bibliography. L. Aller et al., *Handbook of Suggested Practices for the Design and Location of Ground-Water Monitoring Wells,* 1989; M. J. Barcelona et al. (eds.), *Handbook of Groundwater Protection,* 1988; J. Bear, *Hydraulics of Groundwater,* 1980; S. N. Davis and R. J. M. De Wiest, *Hydrogeology,* 1966; F. G. Driscoll, *Groundwater and Wells,* 2d ed., 1986; R. A. Freeze and W. Back (eds.), *Physical Hydrogeology,* 1983; L. H. Keith (ed.), *Principles of Environmental Sampling,* 1988; D. M. Nielsen (ed.), *Practical Handbook of Ground Water Monitoring,* 1991; J. F. Pickens et al., A multilevel device for ground-water and piezometric monitoring, *Ground Water,* 16(5):322–327, 1978; M. Raghunath, *Ground Water,* 2d ed., 1987; U.S. Environmental Protection Agency, *Ground Water Handbook,* vol. 1: *Ground Water and Contamination,* EPA 625/6-90/016a, and vol. 2: *Methodology,* EPA 625/6-90/016b, 1991; F. van der Leeden, F. L. Troise, and D. K. Todd, *The Water Encyclopedia,* 2d ed., 1990; A. Verruijt, *Groundwater Flow,* 2d ed., 1982.

Hazardous waste

Any solid, liquid, or gaseous waste materials that, if improperly managed or disposed of, may pose substantial hazards to human health and the environment. Every industrial country in the world has had problems with managing hazardous wastes. Improper disposal of these waste streams in the past has created a need for very expensive cleanup operations. Efforts are under way internationally to remedy old problems caused by hazardous waste and to prevent the occurrence of other problems in the future.

Characteristics. A waste is considered hazardous if it exhibits one or more of the following characteristics: ignitability, corrosivity, reactivity, and toxicity. Ignitable wastes can create fires under certain conditions; examples include liquids, such as solvents, that readily catch fire, and friction-sensitive substances. Corrosive wastes include those that are acidic and those that are capable of corroding metal (such as tanks, containers, drums, and barrels). Reactive wastes are unstable under normal conditions. They can create explosions, toxic fumes, gases, or vapors when mixed with water. Toxic wastes are harmful or fatal when ingested or absorbed. When they are disposed of on land, contaminated liquid may drain (leach) from the waste and pollute groundwater. *See GROUNDWATER HYDROLOGY; WATER POLLUTION*.

Sources. Hazardous wastes may arise as by-products of industrial processes (**Table 1**). They may also be generated by households when commercial products are discarded. These include drain openers, oven cleaners, wood and metal cleaners and polishes, pharmaceuticals, oil and fuel additives, grease and rust solvents, herbicides and pesticides, and paint thinners.

According to the U.S. Environmental Protection Agency, about 2.5×10^8 tons (2.3×10^8 metric tons) of hazardous waste are generated annually in the United States. This represents approximately 4% of the total of industrial, agricultural, commercial, and domestic waste generated. Ninety percent of the 2.5×10^8 tons is generated by large facilities that produce more than 500 lb (about 100 kg) per month.

The predominant waste streams generated by in-dustries in the United States are corrosive wastes, spent acids, and alkaline materials used in the chemical, metal-finishing, and petroleum-refining industries. Many of these waste streams contain heavy metals, rendering them toxic. Solvent wastes are generated in large volumes both by manufacturing industries and by a wide range of equipment maintenance industries that generate spent cleaning and degreasing solutions. Reactive wastes come primarily from the chemical industries and the metal-finishing industries. The chemical and primary-metals industries are the major sources of hazardous wastes (**Table 2**).

Waste management hierarchy. There is a growing acceptance throughout the world of the desirability of using waste management hierarchies for solutions to problems of hazardous waste. A typical sequence involves source reduction, recycling, treatment, and disposal (see **illus.**).

Source reduction. This comprises the reduction or elimination of hazardous waste at the source, usually within a process. Source reduction measures include process modifications, feedstock substitutions, improvements in feedstock purity, changes in housekeeping and management practice, increases in the efficiency of equipment, and recycling within a process.

Table 1. Examples of hazardous waste generated by businesses and industries*

Waste generators	Waste type
Chemical manufacturers	Strong acids and bases Spent solvents Reactive wastes
Vehicle maintenance shops	Heavy-metal paint wastes Ignitable wastes Used lead-acid batteries Spent solvents
Printing industry	Heavy-metal solutions Waste inks Spent solvents Spent electroplating wastes Ink sludges containing heavy metals
Leather products manufacturing	Waste toluene and benzene
Paper industry	Paint wastes containing heavy metals Ignitable solvents Strong acids and bases
Construction industry	Ignitable paint wastes Spent solvents Strong acids and bases
Cleaning agents and cosmetics manufacturing	Heavy-metal dusts Ignitable wastes Flammable solvents Strong acids and bases
Furniture and wood manufacturing and refinishing	Ignitable wastes Spent solvents
Metal manufacturing	Paint wastes containing heavy metals Strong acids and bases Cyanide wastes Sludges containing heavy metals

*After Office of Solid Waste, U.S. Environmental Protection Agency, *Solving the Hazardous Waste Problem*: EPA's RCRA Program, EPA/530-SW-86-037, 1986.

Table 2. Industry ranking by hazardous waste generation*

Rank	Industry	Percent of total waste generated
1	Chemical and allied products	47.9
2	Primary metals	18.0
3	Petroleum and coal products	11.8
4	Fabricated metal products	9.6
5	Rubber and plastic products	5.5
6	Miscellaneous manufacturing	2.1
7	Nonelectrical machinery	1.8
8	Transportation equipment	1.1
9	Motor freight transportation	0.8
10	Electric and electronic machinery	0.7
11	Wood preserving	0.7
12	Drum reconditioning	<0.1

*After Congressional Budget Office, *Hazardous Waste Management: Recent Changes and Policy Alternatives*, 1985.

In the United States there is a requirement in the federal environmental regulations that all large hazardous waste generators must have a program at their facility to encourage source reduction and recycling. Other countries such as Austria, Germany, and Denmark have initiated direct subsidies to encourage preferable waste management options.

Recycling. This is the use or reuse of hazardous waste as an effective substitute for a commercial product or as an ingredient or feedstock in an industrial process. It includes the reclamation of useful constituent fractions within a waste material or the removal of contaminants from a waste material to al-low it to be reused.

Treatment. This refers to any method, technique, or process that changes the physical, chemical, or biological character of any hazardous waste so as to neutralize such waste; to recover energy or material resources from the waste; or to render such waste nonhazardous, less hazardous, safer to manage, amenable for recovery, amenable for storage, or reduced in volume.

Disposal. This is the discharge, deposit, injection, dumping, spilling, leaking, or placing of hazardous waste into or on any land or body of water so that the waste or any constituents may enter the air or be discharged into any waters, including groundwater.

Options such as source reduction and recycling are often grouped together and included under the heading of waste minimization, as opposed to treatment and disposal. Minimization techniques offer considerable advantages to the waste generators and to the public, since much waste that would have to be otherwise managed is not created in the first place. The illustration shows a flow chart for utilizing waste minimization techniques.

Treatment technologies. There are various alternative waste treatment technologies, for example, physical treatment, chemical treatment, biological treatment, incineration, and solidification or stabilization treatment. These processes are used to recycle and reuse waste materials, reduce the volume and toxicity of a waste stream, or produce a final residual material that is suitable for disposal. The selection of the most effective technology depends upon the wastes being treated.

Physical treatment. This includes processes that sep-

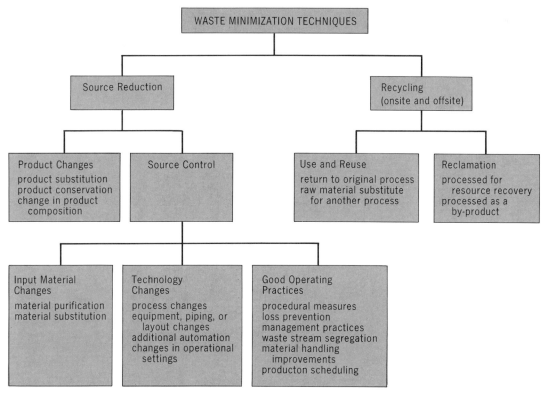

Flow chart for utilizing waste minimization techniques. (*After U.S. Environmental Protection Agency, The EPA Manual for Waste Minimization Opportunity Assessments, EPA/600/Z-88/025, 1989*).

arate components of a waste stream or change the physical form of the waste without altering the chemical structure of the constituent materials. Physical treatment techniques are often used to separate the materials within the waste stream so that they can be reused or detoxified by chemical or biological treatment or destroyed by high-temperature incineration. These processes are very useful for separating hazardous materials from an otherwise nonhazardous waste stream so that they may be treated in a more concentrated form, separating various hazardous components for different treatment processes, and preparing a waste stream for ultimate destruction in a biological or thermal treatment process.

Physical treatment processes are important to most integrated waste treatment systems regardless of the nature of the waste materials or the ultimate technologies used for treatment or destruction. The physical processes that are commonly used in waste treatment operations are as follows:

Screening is a process for removing particles from waste streams, and it is used to protect downstream pretreatment processes.

Sedimentation is a process for removing suspended solid particles from a waste stream. Sedimentation is usually accomplished by providing sufficient time and space in special tanks or holding ponds for settling. Chemical coagulating agents are often added to encourage the settling of fine particles.

Flotation is a process for removing solids from liquids by floating the particles to the surface by using tiny air bubbles. Flotation is useful for removing particles too small to be removed by sedimentation.

Filtration is a process for separating liquids and solids by using various types of porous materials. There are many types of filters designed to achieve various levels of separation.

Centrifugation is a process for separating solid and liquid components of a waste stream by rapidly rotating a mixture of solids and liquids inside a vessel. Centrifugation is most often used to dewater sludges.

Dialysis is a process for separating components in a liquid stream by using a membrane. Components of a liquid stream will diffuse through the membrane if a stream with a greater concentration of the component is on the other side of the membrane. Dialysis is used to extract pure process solutions from mixed waste streams.

Electrodialysis is an extension of dialysis. This process is used to separate the components of an ionic solution by applying an electric current to the solution, which causes ions to move through the dialysis membrane. It is very effective for extracting acids and metal salts from solutions.

Reverse osmosis separates components in a liquid stream by applying external pressure to one side of a membrane so that solvent will flow in the opposite direction. SEE SALINE WATER RECLAMATION.

Ultrafiltration is similar to reverse osmosis, but the separation begins at higher molecular weights. The result is that dissolved components with low molecular weights will pass through the membrane with the bulk liquid while the higher-molecular-weight components become concentrated through the loss of solvent. Ultrafiltration systems can handle much more corrosive fluids than reverse-osmosis units.

Distillation is a process for separating liquids with different boiling points. The mixed-liquid stream is exposed to increasing amounts of heat, and the various components of the mixture are vaporized and recovered. The vapor may be recovered and reboiled several times to effect a complete separation of components.

Solvent extraction is a process for separating liquids by mixing the stream with a solvent which is immiscible with part of the waste but which will extract certain components of the waste stream. The extracted components are then removed from the immiscible solvent for reuse or disposal.

Evaporation is a process for concentrating nonvolatile solids in a solution by boiling off the liquid portion of the waste stream. Evaporation units are often operated under some degree of vacuum to lower the heat required to boil the solution.

Adsorption is a process for removing low concentrations of organic materials on the surface of a porous material, usually activated carbon. The carbon is replaced and regenerated with heat or a suitable solvent when its capacity to attract organic substances is reduced.

Chemical treatment. Chemical treatment processes alter the chemical structure of the constituents of the waste to produce either an innocuous or a less hazardous material. Chemical processes are attractive because they produce minimal air emissions, they can often be carried out on the site of the waste generator, and some processes can be designed and constructed as mobile units. The five chemical treatment operations commonly used in treating wastes are as follows:

Neutralization is a process for reducing the acidity or alkalinity of a waste stream by mixing acids and bases to produce a neutral solution. This has proven to be a viable waste management process.

Precipitation is a process for removing soluble compounds contained in a waste stream. A specific chemical is added to produce a precipitate. This type of treatment is applicable to streams containing heavy metals.

Ion exchange is used to remove from solution ions derived from inorganic materials. The solution is passed over a resin bed, which exchanges ions for the inorganic substances to be removed. When the bed loses its capacity to remove the component, it can be regenerated with a caustic solution.

Dechlorination is a process for stripping chlorine atoms from chlorinated compounds such as polychlorinated biphenyls (PCBs). One of the processes uses a metallic sodium reagent to break the chlorine bond.

Oxidation-reduction is a process for detoxifying toxic wastes in which the chemical bonds are broken by the passage of electrons from one reactant to another.

Biological treatment. Biological waste treatment is a generic term applied to processes that use microorganisms to decompose organic wastes either into water, carbon dioxide, and simple inorganic substances, or into simpler organic substances, such as aldehydes and acids. Typically, the microorganisms used in a biological process are present in the incoming waste. In some instances, microorganisms that were developed to attack specific compounds are injected into a waste stream.

The purpose of a biological treatment system is to control the environment for microorganisms so that their growth and activity are enhanced, and to provide a means for maintaining high concentrations of the microorganisms in contact with the wastes. Since biological treatment systems do not alter or destroy inorganic substances, and high concentrations of such materials can severely inhibit decomposition activity, chemical or physical treatment may be required to extract inorganic materials from a waste stream prior to biological treatment.

There are five principal types of conventional biological treatment. Treatment with activated sludge involves exposing waste to a biological sludge that is continuously extracted from the clarified waste stream and recycled. In the aerated lagoon method, waste is agitated with air in large enclosures to increase oxygen-dependent biological oxidation. In treatment using trickling filters, wastes are allowed to trickle through a bed of rocks coated with microorganisms that alter the waste components by using them as food. Waste stabilization ponds are ponds in which wastes are allowed to decompose over long periods of time, aeration is provided only by wind action. Anaerobic digestion is a method for decomposing organic matter by using anaerobic organisms in closed vessels in the absence of air; methane may be produced in the process.

Incineration and pyrolysis. Incineration and pyrolysis techniques reduce the volume or toxicity of organic wastes by exposing them to high temperatures. When organic chemical wastes are subjected to temperatures of 800–3000°F (430–1700°C), they break down into simpler and less toxic forms. If the wastes are heated in the presence of oxygen, combustion occurs, and the process is known as incineration. Incineration systems are designed to accept specific types of materials; they vary according to feed mechanisms, operating temperatures, equipment design, and other parameters. The main products from complete incineration include water, carbon dioxide, ash, and certain acids and oxides, depending upon the waste in question.

If the wastes are exposed to high temperatures in an oxygen-starved environment, the process is known as pyrolysis. The products of this process are simpler organic compounds, which may be recovered or incinerated, and a char or ash.

Hazardous waste incineration and pyrolysis systems include single-chamber liquid systems, rotary kilns, and fluidized-bed incineration systems. In a single-chamber liquid system a brick-lined combustion chamber contains liquids that are burned in suspension; in addition to being the primary parts of an incineration system, these units are used as afterburners for rotary kilns. A rotary kiln is a versatile large refractory-lined cylinder capable of burning virtually any liquid or solid organic waste, the unit is rotated to improve turbulence in the combustion zone. Fluidized-bed incineration uses a stationary vessel within which solid and liquid wastes are injected into a heated, extremely agitated bed of inert granular material; the process promotes rapid heat exchange and can be designed to scrub off the gases.

Solidification and stabilization. Solidification and stabilization are treatment systems designed to accomplish one or more of the following: improve handling and the physical characteristic of the waste; decrease the surface area across which transfer or loss of contained pollutants can occur; and limit the solubility of, or detoxify, any hazardous constituents contained in the wastes. In solidification these results are obtained primarily, but not exclusively, via the production of a monolithic block of treated waste with high structural integrity. Stabilization techniques limit the solubility or detoxify waste contaminants even though the physical characteristics of the waste may not be changed. Stabilization usually involves the addition of materials that ensure that the hazardous constituents are maintained in their least soluble or least toxic form.

Disposal. Ultimately, after all treatment is completed, there remains an inorganic valueless residue that must be disposed of safely. There are five options for disposing of hazardous waste as follows: (1) Underground injection wells are steel- and concrete-encased shafts placed deep below the surface of the earth into which hazardous wastes are deposited by force and under pressure. Some liquid waste streams are commonly disposed of in underground injection wells. (2) Surface impoundment involves natural or engineered depressions or diked areas that can be used to treat, store, or dispose of hazardous waste. Surface impoundments are often referred to as pits, ponds, lagoons, and basins. (3) Landfills are disposal facilities where hazardous waste is placed in or on land. Properly designed and operated landfills are lined to prevent leakage and contain systems to collect potentially contaminated surface water run-off. Most landfills isolate wastes in discrete cells or trenches, thereby preventing potential contact of incompatible wastes. (4) Land treatment is a disposal process in which hazardous waste is applied onto or incorporated into the soil surface. Natural microbes in the soil break down or immobilize the hazardous constituents. Land treatment facilities are also known as land application or land farming facilities. (5) Waste piles are noncontainerized accumulations of solid, nonflowing hazardous waste. While some are used for final disposal, many waste piles are used for temporary storage until the waste is transferred to its final disposal site.

Of the hazardous waste disposed of on land, nearly 60% is disposed of in underground injection wells, approximately 35% in surface impoundments, 5% in landfills, and less than 1% in waste piles or by land application.

Comprehensive treatment facilities. In the United States, Canada, and many western European countries, there are large facilities capable of treating and disposing of many types of hazardous wastes. These facilities are able to realize economies of scale by incorporating many treatment processes that might not be economical for individual generators. Comprehensive facilities are also able to exploit the synergistic opportunities made possible by having many different types of waste present at a single site. These include using waste acids and alkalies to neutralize one another, waste oxidants to treat cyanides and organic contaminants in water, salts and acids to salt out organic compounds from wastewater, on-site incinerators to dispose of organic vapors generated by other on-site processes, ash and calcium and magnesium oxides to aid in stabilization processes, and combustible solids and liquids to produce blended liquid fuels.

Abandoned disposal sites. There are sites in many countries where hazardous waste has been disposed of improperly and where cleanup operations are needed to restore the sites to their original state. In the United States, some 20,000 such sites have been identified; an estimated 2000 of these require immediate action. Denmark, the Netherlands, and Sweden have also identified sites requiring immediate attention.

Cleaning up abandoned disposal sites involves isolating and containing contaminated material, removal and redeposit of contaminated sediments, and in-place and direct treatment of the hazardous wastes involved. There are five types of treatment technologies for abandoned disposal sites:

> Aqueous waste treatment
> > Activated carbon treatment
> > Biological treatment
> > Filtration
> > Precipitation/flocculation
> > Sedimentation technology
> > Ion exchange and sorptive resin
> > Reverse osmosis
> > Neutralization
> > Gravity separation
> > Air stripping
> > Oxidation
> > Chemical reduction
>
> Solids treatment
> > Solids separation
> > Dewatering
>
> Solidification/stabilization
> > Cement-based solidification
> > Silicate-based process
> > Sorbents
> > Thermoplastic solidification
> > Surface microencapsulation
> > Vitrification
>
> Gaseous waste treatment
> > Flaring
> > Adsorption
>
> Thermal destruction of hazardous wastes
> > Liquid injection
> > Rotary kiln
> > Multiple hearth
> > Fluidized bed
> > Mobile incineration

As the state of the art for remedial technology improves, there is a clear preference for processes that result in the permanent destruction of contaminants rather than the removal and storage of the contaminating materials.

Harry M. Freeman

Bibliography. Center for Hazardous Materials Research, University of Pittsburgh, Applied Research Center, *Hazardous Waste Minimization Manual for Small Quantity Generators*, 1987; H. F. Freeman (ed.), *Standard Handbook of Hazardous Waste Treatment and Disposal*, 1988; R. W. McIlvane, A hazardous waste overview, *Waste Age*, pp. 93–102, June 1988; Office of Solid Waste, U.S. Environmental Protection Agency, *Solving the Hazardous Waste Problem*: *EPA's RCRA Program*, EPA/530-SW-86-037, 1986; S. K. Stoddard, G. Davis, and H. M. Freeman, State of California, Office of the Governor, *Alternatives to the Land Disposal of Hazardous Waste*: *An Assessment for California*, 1981.

Heat balance, terrestrial atmospheric

The (approximate) balance between the average solar radiation received and absorbed by the Earth–atmosphere system and the average Earth–atmosphere radiation emitted back to space. Alternatively, the term terrestrial atmospheric heat balance is increasingly used to mean the disposition, distribution, and transformation of the energy received from the Sun by the Earth and its atmosphere. *See Solar energy.*

An area of 1 cm^2 (0.155 in.^{2}) at the Earth's mean distance from the Sun and perpendicular to the Sun's rays would receive about 139 milliwatts of solar radiation per second if there were no intervening atmosphere. This quantity is known as the solar constant. Since the area of a sphere is four times that of the circle it presents to parallel radiation, the outside of the Earth's atmosphere receives an average of 35 mW/(cm$^2 \cdot$ s) [225 mW/(in.^{2} s^{-1})]. Approximately three-tenths of this radiation is reflected and scattered to space, mostly by clouds. The fraction of insolation returned directly to space is called the albedo. The remaining seven-tenths is absorbed by the Earth, clouds, and atmosphere and acts to raise their temperature and to evaporate water from the oceans and clouds.

The Earth and atmosphere can lose heat to space only by radiation. Since the magnitudes of the temperature changes on the Earth over long periods of time are small compared to the changes that would have occurred had a significant fraction of the solar radiation been retained as a net heat gain, the outward radiation must be equal to the seven-tenths of the solar radiation that is not reflected or scattered directly to space.

Heat balance cycle. The **illustration,** a schematic diagram of the distribution and transformation of the 35 mW/(cm$^2 \cdot$ s) [225 mW/(in.^{2} s^{-1})] of mean incoming solar radiation (taken arbitrarily as 100 units), gives details of the terrestrial atmospheric heat balance. Since 30 units are reflected to space by the clouds, the air, and the Earth's surface, only 70 units provide heat to the Earth and the atmosphere. In the illustration the solar radiation reflected from the surface is not shown separately; it is included in the 30 units of solar radiation returned to space.

Of the 70 available units of solar radiation, about 20 are absorbed by the atmosphere and 50 by the oceans and land. About 20 of these 50 units absorbed at the surface are balanced by the loss of about 6 units of infrared radiation to space and about 14 net units to the atmosphere. These 14 units are the difference between two large quantities, each probably greater than 100 units, namely infrared radiative transfer from surface to atmosphere minus that from atmosphere to surface. The remaining 30 energy units required to complete the surface-to-atmosphere balance are the sum of the estimated fluxes of 6 units of sensible heat and 24 units of latent heat due to evaporation at the surface followed by condensation in the atmosphere.

The 64 units of solar and infrared radiation and sensible and latent heat absorbed by the atmosphere increase its internal energy; and this energy is eventually lost to space as infrared radiation which, together with the 6 units of infrared radiation lost to space by the Earth's surface, closes the heat balance cycle with the 70 units of solar radiation absorbed by the Earth and atmosphere.

Space and time variations. There are, of course, marked geographical deviations from this average picture of the heat balance. In particular, the tropical regions of the Earth receive considerably more solar radiation than is lost by terrestrial radiation to space, and the polar regions considerably less. To maintain

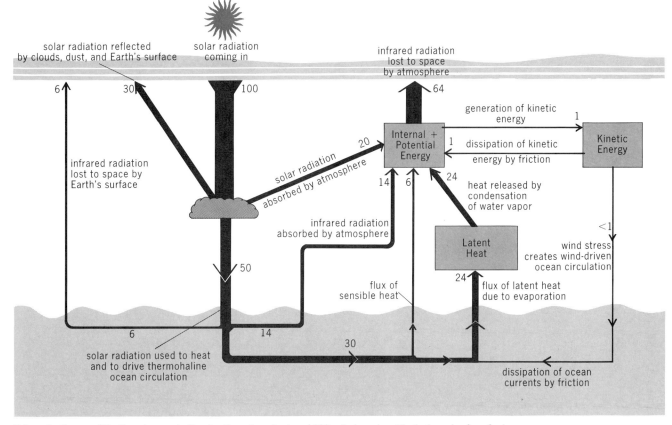

Schematic diagram of the flow of energy in the climatic system. A value of 100 units is assigned to the incoming flux of solar energy. All values represent annual averages for the entire atmosphere. (*After J. J. Peixóto and A. H. Oort, Physics of climate, Rev. Mod. Phys., 56(3):365–429, 1984*)

balance, heat must be transferred from low to high latitudes by the wind systems and, to some extent, by the ocean circulations. The circulations required for this heat transport and other wind systems are provided by the cycle, shown in the upper right part of the illustration, of conversion of internal energy to potential energy by differential heating, to kinetic energy generated by the mass distribution, and back to internal energy by frictional dissipation of the wind and ocean currents. About 1 energy unit of the 100 units coming from the Sun drives the large-, medium-, and small-scale circulations of the atmosphere and oceans. This illustrates both the huge amount of solar energy incident on the Earth and atmosphere, and the relative inefficiency of its utilization by the atmospheric-oceanographic heat engine. Cloud development plays a key role in local departures from heat balance by differential deposition of latent heat and modification of the radiation field. *See* Atmospheric general circulation; Cloud physics; Maritime meteorology; Wind.

Although the overall heat balance does not generally hold locally, it holds approximately for global annual averages; otherwise there would be appreciable changes in terrestrial atmospheric temperatures. Actually, the world meteorological instrumental record does indicate a global surface annual temperature variability of about 0.2°C (0.36°F) superimposed on a 0.5°C (0.9°F) warming over the past century. Departures from global annual balance are also indicated more directly by measurements from satellites of the overall components of the net radiation balance,

namely the insolation, albedo, and infrared emission to space, and their spectral distribution.

The more detailed components of the heat balance, such as the internal heat transfer cycles and the heat exchanges between surface and atmosphere, cannot be determined directly from measurements from space. They are estimated with much greater uncertainty and much less thorough coverage. These estimates are being improved by calculations that use climate models whose parametrizations of physical properties such as cloud, surface, and atmospheric temperature, and the distribution and precipitation of water vapor are tested and tuned with the use of measurements from satellites. A major effort along these lines and including compositional monitoring is taking place, prompted by the possibility that much of the global warming is the result of direct and indirect human introduction of massive amounts of radiatively active greenhouse gases into the atmosphere. *See* Greenhouse effect.

Lewis D. Kaplan

Bibliography. J. P. Peixóto and A. H. Oort, *Physics of Climate*, American Institute of Physics, 1990; J. P. Peixóto and A. H. Oort, Physics of climate, *Rev. Mod. Phys.*, 56(3):365–429, 1984.

Herbicide

Any chemical used to destroy or inhibit plant growth, especially of weeds or other undesirable vegetation. The concepts of modern herbicide technology began

Important herbicides

Common name*	Chemical name	Major uses†
Acetochlor	2-Chloro-N(ethoxymethyl)-6′-ethyl-o-acetotoluidide	Sel. PE corn, soybeans and other crops
Acifluorfen-sodium	Sodium 5-[2-chloro-4-(trifluoromethyl)phenoxy]-2-nitrobenzoate	Sel. POE soybeans
Acrolein	2-Propenal	Aquatic weed control
Alachlor	2-Chloro-2′,6′-diethyl-N-(methoxymethyl) acetanilide	Sel. PE corn, soybeans, and other crops
Ametryn	2-(Ethylamino)-4-(isopropylamino)-6-(methylthio)-s-triazine	Sel. PE and POE pineapple, sugar-cane, bananas
Amitrole	3-Amino-s-triazole	NS weed control in noncrop areas
AMS	Ammonium sulfate	NS POE weed and brush control
Asulam	Methyl sulfanilylcarbamate	Sel. POE sugarcane, range, forests
Atrazine	2-Chloro-4-(ethylamino)-6-(isopropylamino)-s-triazine	Sel. PE or POE corn, sorghum, sug-arcane
Barban	4-Chloro-2-butynyl-m-chlorocarbanilate	Sel. POE cereals and other crops
Benefin	N-Butyl-N-ethyl-α,α,α-trifluoro-2,6-dinitro-p-toluidine	Sel. PE legumes, lettuce, tobacco, turf
Bensulide	O,O-Diisopropyl phosphonodithioate S-ester with N-(2-mercaptoethyl)benzene sulfonamide	Sel. PE turf and vegetables
Bentazon	3-Isopropyl-1H-2,1,3-benzothiadiazin-4-(3H)-1-2,2-dioxide	Sel. POE cereals and legume crops
Benzadox	(Benzamidooxy)acetic acid	Sel. POE sugar beet
Bifenox	Methyl 5-(2,4-dichlorophenoxy)-2-nitrobenzoate	Sel. PE soybean, rice, and other crops
Bromacil	5-Bromo-3-sec-butyl-6-methyluracil	NS PE/POE weed and brush control
Bromoxynil	3,5-Dibromo-4-hydroxybenzonitrile	Sel. POE cereals, flax, turf
Butachlor	N-(Butoxymethyl)2-chloro-2′ 6′-diethylacetanilide	Sel. PE rice, barley
Buthidazole	3-[5-(1,1-Dimethylethyl)-1,3,4-thiadiazol-2-yl]-4-hydroxy-1-methyl-2-imidazolidinone	NS PE/POE weed and brush killer
Butylate	S-Ethyl diisobutylthiocarbamate	Sel. PE corn
Cacodylic acid	Hydroxydimethylarsine oxide	NS POE general weed control and cotton defoliant
CDAA	N,N-Diallyl-2-chloroacetamide	Sel. PE corn and vegetables
Chloramben	3-Amino-2,5-dichlorobenzoic acid	Sel. PE soybeans, vegetables
Chloroxuron	3-[p-(p-Chlorophenoxy) phenyl]-1,1-dimethylurea	Sel. PE/POE soybeans and other crops
Chlorpropham	Isopropyl m-chlorocarbanilate	Sel. PE legume and vegetable crops
Chlorsulfuron	2-Chloro-N-[(4-methoxy-6-methyl-1,3,5-triazin-2-yl)aminocarbonyl]-benzenesulfonamide	Sel. PE/POE cereals; NS PE/POE general weed killer
Cyanazine	2-[[4-Chloro-6-(ethylamino)-s-triazin-2-yl]amino]2-2 methylpropionitrile	Sel. PE corn
Cycloate	S-Ethyl N-ethylthiocyclohexanecarbamate	Sel. PE beets, spinach
Dalapon	2,2-Dichloropropionic acid	Sel. PE/POE sugarcane, tree crops, and other crops
Dazomet	Tetrahydro-3,5-dimethyl-2H-1,3,5-thiadiazine-2-thione	Sel. PE turf, tobacco seedbeds, orna-mentals
DCPA	Dimethyl tetrachloroterephthalate	Sel. PE turf, ornamentals, vegetables
Desmedipham	Ethyl m-hydroxycarbanilate	Sel. POE sugar beet
Diallate	S-(2,3-Dichloroallyl) diisopropylthiocarbamate	Sel. PE sugar beet, cereals, and other crops
Dicamba	3,6-Dichloro-o-anisic acid	Sel. PE/POE corn, cereals, turf
Dichlobenil	2,6-Dichlorobenzonitrile	NS PE ornamentals, tree fruits, aquatic weed control
Dichlorprop	2-(2,4-Dichlorophenoxy) propionic acid	NS brush control
Diclofop-methyl	Methyl 2-[4-(2,4-dichlorophenoxy) phenoxy] propanoate	Sel. POE cereals, soybeans, and other broad-leafed crops
Diethatyl-ethyl	N-Chloroacetyl-N-(2,6-diethylphenyl)-glycine ethyl ester	Sel. PE legumes, vegetables, sugar-beets
Difenzoquat	1,2-Dimethyl-3,5-diphenyl-1H-pyrazolium methyl sulfate	Sel. POE cereals
Dinitramine	N⁴,N⁴-Diethyl-α,α,α-trifluoro-3,5-dinitrotoluene-2,4-diamine	Sel. PE cotton, soybeans, and other crops
Dinoseb	2-sec-Butyl-4,6-dinitrophenol	Sel. PE/POE soybeans, peanuts, and other crops
Diphenamid	N,N-Dimethyl-2,2-diphenylacetamide	Sel. PE turf, peanuts, vegetables, and other crops
Dipropetryn	2,4-Bis(isopropylamino)-6-(ethylthio)-s-triazine	Sel. PE cotton
Diquat	6,7-Dihydrodipyrido[1,2-a:2′,1′-c]pyrazinediium ion	NS POE noncrop land and aquatic weed control
Diuron	3-(3,4-Dichlorophenyl)-1,1-dimethylurea	Sel. PE/POE cotton, sugarcane, ce-reals, tree crops; NS PE/POE gen-eral weed killer
DSMA	Disodium methanearsonate	Sel. POE cotton, turf; NS POE gen-eral weed killer
Endothall	7-Oxabicyclo[2.2.1]heptane 2,3-dicarboxylic acid	Sel. PE sugar beets; aquatic weed killer; cotton defoliant
EPTC	S-Ethyl dipropylthiocarbamate	Sel. PE corn, potatoes, and other crops
Ethalfluralin	N-Ethyl-N-(2-methyl-2-propenyl)-2,6-dinitro-4-(trifluoromethyl)benzeneamine	Sel. PE cotton, beans
Ethofumesate	(±)-2-Ethoxy-2,3-dihydro-3,3-dimethyl-5-benzofuranyl methanesulfonate	Sel. PE/POE sugarbeets
Fenac	(2,3,6-Trichlorophenyl)acetic acid	Sel. PE/POE sugarcane; general weed killer
Fenuron TCA	1,1-Dimethyl-3-phenylurea mono(trichloroacetate)	NS PE/POE general weed and brush killer

Important herbicides (cont.)

Common name*	Chemical name	Major uses†
Flamprop-methyl	Methyl N-benzoyl-N-(3-chloro-4-fluorophenyl)-2-aminopropionate	Sel. POE wheat
Fluazifop-butyl	(±)-Butyl 2-[4-[(5-(trifluoromethyl)-2-pyridinyl)oxy]phenoxy] propanoate	Sel. POE cotton, soybeans, and other broad-leafed crops
Fluchloralin	N-(2-Chloroethyl)-2,6-dinitro-N-propyl-4-(trifluoromethyl) aniline	Sel. PE cotton, soybeans
Fluometuron	1,1-Dimethyl-3-(α,α,α-trifluoro-m-tolyl)urea	Sel. PE/POE cotton, sugarcane
Fluridone	1-Methyl-3-phenyl-5-[3-(trifluoromethyl)phenyl]-4(1H)-pyridinone	Sel. PE cotton; aquatic weed killer
Glyphosate	N-(Phosphonomethyl)-glycine	NS POE general weed killer
Hexazinone	3-Cyclohexyl-6-(dimethyl-amino)-1-methyl-1,3,5-triazine-2,4(1H,3H)-dione	NS PE/POE general weed and brush killer
Ioxynil	4-Hydroxy-3,5-diiodobenzonitrile	Sel. POE cereals
Isopropalin	2,6-Dinitro-N,N-dipropylcumidine	Sel. PE tobacco
Linuron	3-(3,4-Dichlorophenyl)-1-methoxy-1-methylurea	Sel. PE soybean, potatoes, and other crops
MCPA	[(4-Chloro-o-toly)oxy]acetic acid	Sel. POE cereals, legumes, flax
MCPB	4-[(4-Chloro-o-tolyl)oxy]butyric acid	Sel. POE legumes
Mecoprop	2-[(4-Chloro-o-tolyl)oxy]propionic acid	Sel. POE turf
Mefluidide	N-[2,4-dimethyl-5-([(trifluoromethyl)sulfonyl]amino)phenyl]-acetamide	Sel. POE soybeans
Metolachlor	2-Chloro-N-(2-ethyl-6-methylphenyl)-N-(2-methoxy-1-methylethyl)acetamide	Sel. PE corn
Metribuzin	4-Amino-6-tert-butyl-3-(methylthio)-as-triazin-5(4H)-one	Sel. PE soybeans, potatoes, sugarcane
Molinate	S-Ethyl hexahydro-1H-azepine 1-carbothioate	Sel. PE/POE rice
Monuron TCA	3-(p-Chlorophenyl)-1, 1-dimethylurea mono(trichloroacetate)	NS PE/POE general weed killer
MSMA	Monosodium methanearsonate	Sel. POE cotton, turf; NS POE general weed killer
Napropamide	2-(α-Naphthoxy)N,N-diethylpropionamide	Sel. PE tomatoes, tree fruits
Naptalam	N-1-Napthylphthalamic acid	Sel. PE soybean, peanut, and vegetables
Nitrofen	2,4-Dichlorophenyl-p-nitrophenyl ether	Sel. PE/POE vegetables
Norflurazon	4-Chloro-5-(methylamino)-2-(α,α,α-trifluoro-m-tolyl)-3(2H)-pyridazinone	Sel. PE cranberries, cotton, tree fruits
Oryzalin	3,5-Dinitro-N⁴,N⁴-dipropylsulfanilamide	Sel. PE cotton, soybeans
Oxadiazon	2-tert-Butyl-4-(2,4-dichloro-5-isopropoxyphenyl)-Δ²-1,3,4-oxadiazolin-5-one	Sel. PE/POE rice, turf, ornamentals
Oxyfluorfen	2-Chloro-1-(3-ethoxy-4-nitrophenoxy)-4-(trifluoro-methyl)benzene	Sel. PE/POE soybeans, cotton, tree crops
Paraquat	1,1'-Dimethyl-4,4'-bipyridinium ion	NS POE general weed killer
Pebulate	S-Propyl butylethylthiocarbamate	Sel. PE sugar beets, tobacco
Pendimethalin	N-(1-Ethyl)-3,4-dimethyl-2,6-dinitrobenzeneamine	Sel. PE corn, cotton, soybeans
Perfluidone	1,1,1-Trifluoro-N-[2-methyl-4-(phenylsulfonyl)phenyl]methanesulfonamide	Sel PE cotton
Phenmedipham	Methyl m-hydroxycarbanilate m-methylcarbanilate	Sel, POE beets
Picloram	4-Amino-3,5,6-trichloropicolinic acid	NS PE/POE general weed and brush killer
Procyazine	2-[[4-Chloro-6-(cyclopropylamino)-1,3,5-triazine-2-yl]amino]-2-methylpropanenitrile	Sel. PE/POE corn
Prometon	2,4-Bis(isopropylamino)-6-methoxy-s-triazine	NS PE/POE general weed killer
Prometryn	2,4-Bis(isopropylamino)-6-(methylthio)-s-triazine	Sel. PE/POE cotton, celery
Pronamide	3,5-Dichloro(N-1,1-dimethyl-2-propynyl)benzamide	Sel. PE/POE legumes, turf, lettuce
Propachlor	2-Chloro-N-isopropylacetanilide	Sel. PE corn, milo, soybeans
Propanil	3',4'-Dichloropropionanilide	Sel. POE rice
Propazine	2-Chloro-4,6-bis-(isopropylamino)-s-triazine	Sel. PE milo
Propham	Isopropyl carbanilate	Sel. PE forages, lettuce, and other crops
Pyrazon	5-Amino-4-chloro-2-phenyl-3(2H)-pyridazinone	Sel. PE beets
Sethoxydim	2-[1-(Ethoxyimino)butyl]-5-[2-(ethylthio)propyl]-3-hydroxy-2-cyclohexen-1-one	Sel. POE cotton, soybeans, and other broad-leafed crops
Siduron	1-(2-Methylcyclohexyl)-3-phenylurea	Sel. PE turf
Silvex	2-(2,4,5-Trichlorophenoxy)propionic acid	Sel. POE sugarcane, rice, rangeland
Simazine	2-Chloro-4,6-bis-(ethylamino)-s-triazine	Sel. PE corn, forages, and other crops; aquatic weed control
TCA	Trichloroacetic acid	Sel. PE/POE sugar beets, sugarcane, cotton, soybeans
Tebuthiuron	N-[5-(1,1-Dimethyl)-1,3,4-thiadiazol-2-yl]-N,N'-dimethylurea	NS PE/POE general weed killer
Terbacil	3-tert-Butyl-5-chloro-6-methyluracil	Sel. PE sugarcane, tree fruits, and other crops
Terbutryn	2-(tert-Butylamino)-4-(ethylamino)-6-(methylthio)-s-triazine	Sel. PE/POE cereals, milo
Thiobencarb	S[(4-chlorophenyl)methyl]diethylcarbamothioate	Sel. PE/POE rice
Triallate	S-(2,3,3-Trichloroallyl)diisopropylthiocarbamate	Sel. PE cereals
Triclopyr	[(3,5,6-trichloro-2-pyridinyl)oxy] acetic acid	NS general weed and brush killer
Trifluralin	α,α,α-Trifluoro-2,6-dinitro-N,N-dipropyl-p-toluidine	Sel. PE legumes, cotton, and other crops
2,3,6-TBA	2,3,6-Trichlorobenzoic acid	NS PE/POE general weed control
2,4-D	(2,4-Dichlorophenoxy)acetic acid	Sel. POE cereals, milo, corn, and other crops: aquatic and general weed control
2,4-DB	4-(2,4-Dichlorophenoxy)butyric acid	Sel. POE legume crops
2,4,5-T	(2,4,5-Trichlorophenoxy)acetic acid	Sel. POE rice, forage grasses; general weed and brush control
Vernolate	S-Propyl dipropylthiocarbamate	Sel. PE peanuts, soybeans

*Major trade names can be found in *Farm Chemicals Handbook*, Meister Publishing Co., Willoughby, Ohio, 1983.
†Sel. = selective herbicide; NS = nonselective herbicide; PE = preemergence; POE = postemergence.

to develop about 1900 and accelerated rapidly with the discovery of dichlorophenoxyacetic acid (2,4-D) as a growth-regulator-type herbicide in 1944–1945. A few other notable events should be mentioned. During 1896–1908, metal salts and mineral acids were introduced as selective sprays for controlling broadleafed weeds in cereals; during 1915–1925 acid arsenical spray, sodium chlorate, and other chemicals were recognized as herbicides; and in 1933–1934, sodium dinitrocresylate became the first organic selective herbicide to be used in culture of cereals, flax, and peas. Since the introduction of 2,4-D, a wide variety of organic herbicides have been developed and have received wide usage in agriculture, forestry, and other industries. Today, the development of highly specific herbicides that are intended to control specific weed types continues. Modern usage often combines two or more herbicides to provide the desired weed control. Worldwide usage of herbicides continues to increase, making their manufacture and sale a major industry.

The control of weeds by means of herbicides has provided many benefits. Freeing agricultural crops from weed competition results in higher food production, reduced harvesting costs, improved food quality, and lowered processing costs, contributing to an abundant supply of low-cost, high-quality food. Not only are billions of dollars saved through increased production and improved quality, but costs of labor and machinery energy for weed control are reduced, livestock is saved from the effects of poisonous weeds, irrigation costs are reduced, and insect and disease control costs are decreased through the removal of host weeds for the undesirable organisms.

Additional benefits due to appropriate herbicide use result as millions of people are relieved of the suffering caused by allergies to pollens and exposure to poisonous plants. Recreational areas, roadsides, forests, and parks have been freed of noxious weeds, and home lawns have been beautified. Herbicides have reduced storage and labor costs and fire hazards for industrial storage yards and warehouse areas. Modern herbicides even benefit the construction industry, where chemicals applied under asphalt prolong pavement life by preventing weed penetration of the surface.

Classification. There are well over a hundred chemicals in common usage as herbicides. Many of these are available in several formulations or under several trade names. The many materials are conveniently classified according to the properties of the active ingredient as either selective or nonselective. Further subclassification is by method of application, such as preemergence (soil-applied before plant emergence) or postemergence (applied to plant foliage). Additional terminology sometimes applied to describe the mobility of postemergence herbicides in the treated plant is contact (nonmobile) or translocated (mobile—that is, killing plants by systemic action). Thus, glyphosate is a nonselective, postemergence, translocated herbicide.

Selective herbicides are those that kill some members of a plant population with little or no injury to others. An example is alachlor, which can be used to kill grassy and some broad-leafed weeds in corn, soybeans, and other crops.

Nonselective herbicides are those that kill all vegetation to which they are applied. Examples are bromacil, paraquat, or glyphosate, which can be used to keep roadsides, ditch banks, and rights-of-way open

and weed-free. An important use for such chemicals is the destruction of vegetation before seeding in the practice of reduced tillage or no tillage. Some are also used to kill annual grasses in preparation for seeding perennial grasses in pastures. Additional uses are in fire prevention, elimination of highway hazards, destruction of plants that are hosts for insects and plant diseases, and killing of poisonous or allergen-bearing plants.

Preemergence or postemergence application methods derive naturally from the properties of the herbicidal chemical. Some, such as trifluralin, are effective only when applied to the soil and absorbed into the germinating seedling, and therefore are used as preemergence herbicides. Others, such as diquat, exert their herbicidal effect only on contact with plant foliage and are strongly inactivated when placed on contact with soil. These can be applied only as a postemergence herbicide. However, the distinction between pre- and postemergence is not always clearcut. For example, atrazine can exert its herbicidal action either following root absorption from a preemergence application or after leaf absorption from a postemergence treatment, and thus it can be used with either application method. This may be an advantage in high-rainfall areas where a postemergence treatment can be washed off the leaf onto the soil and nevertheless can provide effective weed control.

Herbicidal action. Many factors influence herbicide performance. A few are discussed below.

Soil type and organic matter content. Soils vary widely in composition and in chemical and physical characteristics. The capacity of a soil to fix or adsorb a preemergence herbicide determines how much will be available to seedling plants. For example, a sandy soil normally is not strongly adsorptive. Lower quantities of most herbicides are needed on a highly adsorptive clay soil. A similar response occurs with the organic portion of soil; higher organic matter content usually indicates that more herbicide is bound and a higher treatment rate necessary. For example, cyanazine is used for weed control on corn at the rate of 1.5 lb/acre (1.7 kg/ha) on sandy loam soil of less than 1% organic matter, but 5 lb/acre (5.6 kg/ha) is required on a clay soil of 4% organic matter.

Leaching. This refers to the downward movement of herbicides into the soil. Some preemergence herbicides must be leached into the soil into the immediate vicinity of weed seeds to exert toxic action. Excessive rainfall may leach these chemicals too deeply into the soil, thereby allowing weeds to germinate and grow close to the surface.

Volatilization. Several herbicides in use today will volatilize from the soil surface. To be effective, these herbicides must be mixed with the soil to a depth of 2 to 4 in. (5 to 10 cm). This process is termed soil incorporation. Once the herbicide is in contact with soil particles, volatilization loss is minimized. This procedure is commonly employed with thiocarbamate herbicides such as EPTC and dinitroaniline herbicides such as trifluralin.

Leaf properties. Leaf surfaces are highly variable. Some are much more waxy than others; many are corrugated or ridged; and some are covered with small hairs. These variations cause differences in the retention of postemergence spray droplets and thus influence herbicidal effect. Most grass leaves stand in a relatively vertical position, whereas the broad-leafed plants usually have their leaves arranged in a more horizontal position. This causes broad-leaf plants to intercept a larger quantity of a herbicide spray than grass plants.

Location of growing points. Growing points and buds of most cereal plants are located in a crown, at or below the soil surface. Furthermore, they are wrapped within the mature bases of the older leaves. Hence they may be protected from herbicides applied as sprays. Buds of many broad-leafed weeds are located at the tips of the shoots and in axils of leaves, and are therefore more exposed to herbicide sprays.

Growth habits. Some perennial crops, such as alfalfa, vines, and trees, have a dormant period in winter. At that time a general-contact weed killer may be safely used to get rid of weeds that later would compete with the crop for water and plant nutrients.

Application methods. By arranging spray nozzles to spray low-growing weeds but not the leaves of a taller crop plant, it is possible to provide weed control with a herbicide normally phytotoxic to the crop. This directed spray technique is used to kill young grass in cotton with MSMA or broad-leafed weeds in soybeans with chloroxuron in an oil emulsion. Another example of selective application technology is the use of wiper applicators. This apparatus commonly employs absorbent ropes which draw herbicide solution by capillary action from a reservoir. The equipment is arranged so that the ropes can pass above crop plants and transfer the herbicide solution to weeds taller than the crop by a wiping action. Use of a nonselective translocated herbicide in this recirculating sprayer system will then selectively remove the weeds from the crop. Glyphosate is being used commercially in such systems to remove johnson grass from cotton and soybeans.

Protoplasmic selectivity. Just as some people are immune to the effects of certain diseases while others succumb, so some weed species resist the toxic effects of herbicides whereas others are injured or killed. This results from inherent properties of the protoplasm of the respective species. One example is the use of 2,4-DB or MCPB (the butyric acid analogs of 2,4-D and MCPA) on weeds having β-oxidizing enzymes that are growing in crops (certain legumes) which lack such enzymes. The weeds are killed because the butyric acid compounds are broken down to 2,4-D or MCPA. Another example is the control of a wide variety of weeds in corn by atrazine. Corn contains a compound that conjugates with the atrazine atom, rendering it nontoxic; most weeds lack this compound. A third important example of protoplasmic selectivity is shown by trifluralin, planavin, and a number of other herbicides applied through the soil which inhibit secondary root growth. Used in large seeded crops having vigorous taproots, they kill shallow-rooted weed seedlings; the roots of the crops extend below the shallow layer of topsoil containing the herbicides and the seedlings survive and grow to produce a crop.

Properties. Several factors of the commercial herbicide influence selectivity to crops.

Molecular configuration. Subtle changes in the chemical structure can cause dramatic shifts in herbicide performance. For example, trifluralin and benefin are very similar dinitroaniline herbicides differing only in the location of one methylene group. However, this small difference allows benefin to be used for grass control in lettuce, whereas trifluralin will severely injure lettuce at the rates that are required for weed control.

Herbicide concentration. The action of herbicides on plants is rate-responsive. That is, small quantities of a herbicide applied to a plant may cause no toxicity, or even a slight growth stimulation, whereas larger amounts may result in the death of the plants. It has long been known that 2,4-D applied at low rates cause an increase in respiration rate and cell division, resulting in an apparent growth stimulation. At high application rates, 2,4-D causes more severe changes and the eventual death of the plant.

Formulation. The active herbicidal chemical itself is seldom applied directly to the soil or plants. Because of the nature of the chemicals, it is usually necessary that the commercial product be formulated to facilitate handling and dilution to the appropriate concentration. Two common formulations are emulsifiable concentrates and wettable powders. Emulsifiable concentrates are solutions of the chemical in an organic solvent with emulsifiers added which permit mixing and spraying with water. Wettable powders are a mixture of a finely divided powder, active chemical, and emulsifiers which allow the powder to suspend in water and to be sprayed. An additional ingredient called an adjuvant is sometimes added to the formulation or to the spray tank when the spray solution is mixed. These adjuvants are normally surface-active agents (surfactants) which improve the uniformity of spray coverage on plants and the plant penetration of the herbicide. An example is the addition of surfactant to paraquat spray solutions to improve its nonselective postemergence action on weeds. Another material sometimes added to spray solutions is a nonphytotoxic oil. These oils may be used to improve postemergence action of herbicides such as diuron which normally have limited foliar absorption.

Available herbicides. In the **table**, some of the important herbicides used in the United States are listed alphabetically by the common name approved by the Weed Science Society of America. The chemical name and some major uses of each herbicide are included.

Many of the chemicals listed in the table are used in proprietary mixtures. These normally combine two or more herbicides in a single formulation and are marketed under brand names. Such mixtures are not included in the table. SEE PESTICIDE.

Rodney O. Radke

Bibliography. J. R. Crister, Jr., *Herbicides*, 1978; *Farm Chemicals Handbook*, 1983; *Herbicide Handbook of the Weed Science Society of America*, 5th ed., 1983; P. C. Kearney and D. Kaufman (eds.), *Herbicides: Chemistry, Degradation, and Mode of Action*, 1975–1976; R. D. King, *Farmers Weed Control Handbook*, 1985; G. C. Klingman and F. M. Ashton, *Weed Sciences: Principles and Practices*, 1975; H. A. Roberts (ed.), *Weed Control Handbook: Principles*, 7th ed., 1982; W. T. Thomas, *Agricultural Chemicals: Herbicides 1986-87*, 1986.

Hill and mountain terrain

Land surfaces characterized by roughness and strong relief. The distinction between hills and mountains is usually one of relative size or height, but the terms are loosely and inconsistently used. Because of the prevalence of steep slopes, hill and mountain lands offer many difficulties to human occupancy. Cultivable land is scarce and patchy, and transportation routes are often difficult to construct and maintain. On the other hand, many rough lands, especially those readily accessible to centers of population, attract tourists because of their scenic quality and the opportunities they may afford for outdoor recreation.

High mountain ranges set up major disturbances in the broad pattern of atmospheric circulation, and thus affect climates over extensive areas. More locally, by inducing turbulence or forcing moist air to rise in crossing them, rough lands commonly induce condensation and precipitation that makes them moister than surrounding lowlands. Within the rough country, local differences in elevation and in exposure to sun and wind produce complex patterns of local climatic contrasts. These variations, in turn, are often accompanied by unusual local variety in vegetation and animal life.

Development of rough terrain. Uplift of the Earth's crust is necessary to give mountain and hill lands their distinctive elevation and relief, but most of their characteristic features—peaks, ridges, valleys, and so on—have been carved out of the uplifted masses by streams and glaciers. The upraised portions of the crust may have been formed as broad, warped swells, smaller arched folds or domes, upthrust or tilted blocks, or folded and broken masses of extreme complexity. Some limited areas owe their elevation and certain of their local features to the outpouring of thick sheets of lava or the construction of volcanic cones. Hill lands, with their lesser relief, indicate only lesser uplift, not a fundamentally different course of development.

In some rough lands, for example the Appalachians or the Scottish Highlands, the most intense crustal deformation is known to have occurred hundreds of millions of years ago, while in others, such as the Alps, the Himalayas, or the California Coast Ranges, intense deformation has occurred quite recently. Since mountains can be erosionally destroyed in relatively short spans of geologic time, however, the very existence of mountains and hills indicates that structural deformation, at least simple uplift, has continued in

those areas until recent times. This conclusion is reinforced by the fact that the major cordilleran belts are currently foci of earthquake activity and volcanism.

Distribution pattern of rough land. Hill and mountain terrain occupies about 36% of the Earth's land area. The greater portion of that amount is concentrated in the great cordilleran belts that surround the Pacific Ocean, the Indian Ocean, and the Mediterranean Sea. Additional rough terrain, generally low mountains and hills, occurs outside the cordilleran systems in eastern North and South America, northwestern Europe, Africa, and western Australia. Eurasia is the roughest continent, more than half of its total area and most of its eastern portion being hilly or mountainous. Africa and Australia lack true cordilleran belts; their rough lands occur in patches and interrupted bands that rarely show marked complexity of geologic structure. The broad-scale pattern of crustal disturbance, and hence of rough lands, is related to the relative movements of a worldwide system of immense crustal plates. The intense deformation of the cordilleran belts, for example, occurs where the margins of rigid continental masses are being jammed into the zones where such plates are converging.

Predominant surface character. The features of hill and mountain lands are chiefly valleys and divides produced by sculpturing agents, especially running water and glacier ice. Local peculiarities in the form and pattern of these features reflect the arrangement and character of the rock materials within the upraised crustal mass that is being dissected.

Stream-eroded features. The principal features of most hill and mountain landscapes have been formed by stream erosion together with landslides and slower forms of gravity-induced movements (mass wasting) on the valley sides. The major differences between one rough land and another are in the size, shape, spacing and pattern of the stream valleys and the divides between them. These differences reflect variations in the original form and structure of the uplifted mass and in the ways in which erosion has been produced.

In consequence of uplift, streams have a large range of elevation through which they can cut, and as a result usually possess steep gradients early in their course of development. At this stage they are swift, have great erosive power, and are marked by many rapids and falls. Because of the rapid downcutting, the valleys are characteristically canyonlike with steep walls and narrow floors. At the same early stage, however, divides are likely to be high and continuous, and broad ridge crests common. In hill lands such ridges often provide easier routes of travel than do the valleys. In the Ozark Hills of Missouri, most of the highways and railroads follow such broad ridge crests. In high mountain country the combination of gorgelike valleys and continuous high divides makes crossing unusually difficult. In the Himalayas and the central Andes, and to a lesser degree in the Rocky Mountains of Colorado, the narrow canyons are very difficult of passage, and the divides are so continuously high and steep as to provide no easy pass routes across the ranges.

As erosional development continues, the major streams achieve gentle gradients and their valleys continue to widen. Divides become narrower and deep notches develop at valley heads, with well-defined peaks remaining between them. At this stage, which is represented by much of the Alps and by the

Fig. 1. Head of a glaciated mountain valley ending in a cliff-walled amphitheater, called a cirque, showing a steplike valley bottom with lakes and waterfalls. (*Photograph by Hileman, Glacier National Park*).

Cascade Mountains of Washington, the principal valleys and the relatively low passes at their heads furnish feasible routes across the mountain belts. If other conditions are favorable, the wide valleys may afford significant amounts of cultivable or grazing land, as is true in the Alps. Still further erosion continues the widening of valleys and reduction of divides until the landscape becomes an erosional plain upon which stand only small ranges and groups of mountains or hills. The mountains of New England and many of the mountains and hill groups of the Sahara and of western Africa represent late stages in the erosional sequence.

Glaciated rough terrain. Glacial features of mountain and hill lands may be produced either by the work of local glaciers in the mountain valleys or by overriding glaciers of continental size. Continental glaciation has the general effect of clearing away crags, smoothing summits and spurs, and depositing debris in the valleys. The resulting terrain is less angular than is usual for stream-eroded hills, and the characteristic glacial trademark is the numerous lakes, most of them debris-dammed, a few occupying shallow, eroded basins. Examples of rough lands overridden by ice sheets are the mountains of New England, the Adirondacks, the hills of western New York, the Laurentian Upland of eastern Canada, and the Scandinavian Peninsula.

In contrast, mountains affected by local glaciers are made rougher by the glacial action. The long tongues of ice that move slowly down the valleys are excellent transporters of debris and are able to erode actively on shattered or weathered rock material. Valleys formerly occupied by glaciers are characteristically steep-walled and relatively free of projecting spurs and crags, with numerous broad cliffs, knobs, and shoulders of scoured bedrock. At their heads they generally end in cliff-walled amphitheaters called cirques (**Fig. 1**). The valley bottoms are commonly step-like, with stretches of gentle gradient alternating with abrupt rock-faced risers. Especially in the lower parts of the glaciated sections are abundant deposits of rocky debris dropped by the ice. Sometimes these form well-defined ridges (moraines) that run lengthwise along the valley sides or swing in arcs across the valley floor. Lakes are strung along the streams like beads, most of them dammed by moraines but some occupying eroded basins.

Because of rapid erosion and steepening of valley walls, either that effected directly by the ice or that attendant upon the exposure of the rock surface by continual removal of the products of weathering, glaciated mountains are likely to be unusually rugged and spectacular. This is true not only of such great systems as the Himalayas, the Alps, the Alaskan Range, and the high Andes, but also of such lesser ranges as those of Labrador, the English Lake District, and the Scottish Highlands.

Most of the higher mountains of the world still bear valley glaciers, though these are not as large or as widespread as formerly (**Fig. 2**). Dryness and long, warm summers limit glaciers in the United States to a few large groups on the higher peaks of the Pacific Northwest and numerous small ones in the northern Rockies. *See* Glaciated terrain.

Effects of geologic structure. Form and extent of the elevated areas, pattern of erosional valleys and divides, and, to some extent, sculptured details of slope and crest reflect geologic structure.

Some areas, such as the Ozarks, the western Ap-

Fig. 2. Upper reaches of Susitna Glacier, Alaska, showing cirques and snowfields. The long tongues of glacier ice carry bands of debris scoured from valley walls. (*Photograph by Bradford Washburn*)

palachians, and the coast ranges of Oregon, are simply unwarped areas of roughly homogeneous rocks that have been carved by irregularly branching streams into extensive groups of hills or mountains (**Fig. 3**). Others, like the Black Hills or the ranges of the Wyoming Rockies, are domes or arched folds, deeply eroded to reveal ancient granitic rocks in their cores and upturned younger stratified rocks around their edges. The Sierra Nevada of California is a massive block of the crust that has been uplifted and tilted toward the west so that it now displays a high abrupt eastern face and a long canyon-grooved western slope. The central belt of the Appalachians displays long parallel ridges and valleys that have been hewn by erosion out of a very old structure of parallel wrinkles in the crust. The upturned edges of resistant strata form the ridges; the weaker rocks between have been etched out to form the valleys. The Alps and the Himalayas are eroded from folded and broken structures of incredible complexity involving almost all varieties of rock materials.

Fig. 3. Hills in the western Appalachians, West Virginia. (*Photograph by John L. Rich, Geographical Review*)

Most volcanic mountains, like the Cascades of the northwestern United States or the western Andes of Peru and Bolivia, are actually erosional mountains sculptured from thick accumulations of lava and ash. In these areas however, modern eruptive vents give rise to volcanic cones that range from small cinder heaps to tremendous isolated mountains. The greater cones, such as Fuji, Ararat, Mauna Loa, Rainier, or Shasta, are among the most magnificent features of the Earth's surface.

Edwin H. Hammond

Homeostasis

In living substance, the maintenance of internal constancy and independence of the environment. Homeokinesis, a related concept, is constancy of energy production, enzyme activity, and locomotor activity, even though internal state may vary.

The essence of living substance is that it differs chemically from the surrounding medium and yet maintains a dynamic equilibrium with its environment. Homeostasis occurs in all living cells and in the fluids and organ systems of multicellular organisms. Referring to mammals, the nineteenth-century French physiologist Claude Bernard coined the expression "constancy of the internal environment is the condition of life." The American physiologist W. B. Cannon, who first used the word homeostasis, referred to the systems of checks and balances which maintain internal constancy as "the wisdom of the body."

Patterns of adaptive responses. The cells of multicellular organisms are bathed in fluids which are kept relatively constant in ionic composition, osmotic composition, pH, level of sugar, and organic composition. Two patterns of homeostasis of internal state in the face of environmental change are recognized: (1) An animal may alter a given property with reference to the environment; the property conforms to the medium, and homeostasis consists in cellular adjustment such that metabolism continues in the altered state. For example, in cold-blooded animals the body temperature conforms to that of the environment. In many marine animals and endoparasites the body fluids conform in osmotic concentration with the medium. (2) An amimal may regulate its internal state and maintain internal constancy despite an altered environment. Such regulation is achieved by a series of automatic feedback controls as environmental stress is applied; at some environmental limits, regulation fails and the animal cannot long survive. For example, warm-blooded animals maintain a constant body temperature over a range limited by heat and cold. No aquatic organism could be as dilute as fresh water or as concentrated as some saline lakes and survive. Terrestrial organisms must be protected against desiccation, so regulation of water content and osmotic concentration is essential. Some animals conform over part of an environmental range and regulate in another range. An animal may conform with respect to one parameter (osmotic concentration) and regulate with respect to others (concentration of specific ions).

Two types of homeokinetic response are also distinguished: (1) Capacity adaptations are changes in cellular functions such that an intact animal can maintain normal activity over a range of internal states. (2) Resistance adaptations are changes which permit survival at extremes of some physical parameter. Resistance limits are narrow for intact integrated organisms, less restricted for isolated cells and tissues, and much wider for critical molecules such as proteins (denaturation) and lipids (melting). For example, many poikilothermic animals show little or no regulation of body temperature, but they alter energy-yielding enzyme systems to provide for nearly constant activity over a wide temperature range. Also, these animals can, upon acclimation, increase or diminish resistance to heat or cold. Changes in thermal resistance also occur in some homeotherms (temperature regulators).

Organ system controls. A catalog of the mechanisms of homeostasis would be a textbook of the physiology of organ systems and cells. Homeostatic responses occur in a repeatable sequence, and hierarchical levels of controls and series of checks and balances are recognized. The sequence of responses of a mammal to cold illustrates the principles of sequential reactions and hierarchical controls in homeostasis. First, the stimulation of cold receptors in the skin results in constriction of peripheral blood vessels and erection of hairs. If the body is further chilled, the temperature-sensing portions of spinal cord and hypothalamus are stimulated, shivering begins, and metabolism increases, partly under endocrine control. The first line of defense is insulative; the second is increase in heat production. The sequence of homeostatic responses to a severe injury-type stress varies according to the kind of animal. In mammals, a sequence of nonspecific responses may occur to any one of numerous severe stresses. This consists, according to the severity of the stress, of an initial vascular "shock" reaction and counterreactions in which, under pituitary activation, the adrenal cortex is stimulated, lymphocytes in the blood decrease, and numerous chemical defense reactions are mobilized. In a hierarchy of controls, responses occur first in altered cells and then at several levels of endocrine and nervous system controls.

Another principle is that of checks and balances. The vagus nerves slow the heart and stimulate the intestine, while the sympathetics accelerate the heart and relax the intestine. When motor nerve centers for one set of muscles are active, those for antagonistic muscles are inhibited. Various regions of the brain counterbalance other regions. Another mechanism of homeostasis consists of morphological changes over long periods of time. Arctic birds and mammals tend to have thicker coats of feathers or fur and thicker layers of insulating fat in winter; tadpoles grow larger gills when reared in low-oxygen environments; at high altitudes human beings have increased blood hemoglobin concentration; bone structure varies according to mechanical stress. Animal behavior often compensates for environmental changes. Animals (and some plants) may orient toward or away from sources of heat and currents of water or air; and may move into temperature, salinity, or oxygen concentration favorable for efficient metabolism.

Cellular controls. Many animals, particularly "conforming" ones, compensate biochemically and biophysically for environmental change, with the result that a relative constancy of energy output is maintained. The metabolism of most aquatic poikilotherms acclimated to cold, for example, fish, is higher than that of individuals acclimated to warmth when both are measured at an intermediate temperature. Regulation of enzyme levels is achieved by a variety of controls on protein synthesis and degradation. In addition, enzyme activity can be modified by cofactors, membrane phospholipids, hormones, and ions. A much-used method of homeokinesis is the shift from one metabolic pathway to another, for example, the alternation between aerobic (oxidative) and anaerobic (glycolytic) metabolism according to oxygen availability. Also, numerous enzymes exist in one of several forms, as isozymes, and one form may be favored under given conditions. Changes in phospholipids of cell membrane and of organelles such as mitochondria favor constancy of enzyme activity.

An important aspect of cellular homeostasis is the control of the movement of ions and other substances into and out of cells. The first aggregates which could be called living cells must have been separated from their marine environment by a bounding layer which prevented free interchange of materials. The cells of all plants and animals differ in composition from extracellular fluids. An important mechanism of cellular individuation resides in the cell surface, which has selective permeability and which, in some instances, provides some mechanical rigidity. The cell surface consists of a relatively inert pellicle plus a plasma membrane of protein and lipid; it permits entry and exit of relatively few kinds of organic molecules and varies in its permeability to inorganic ions according to environmental conditions and level of metabolic need. The surface also has some carrier enzymes for active transport. An example of membrane regulation is the high intracellular concentration of potassium relative to extracellular fluids which is nearly universal.

Significance. In all systems of homeostasis and homeokinesis—hierarchies of controls, checks and balances, alternate mechanisms, compensatory reactions, and negative and positive feedback—there are analogies to servo systems. Sensing elements are poised at critical levels, and, when deviation occurs, control mechanisms are brought into action to restore equilibrium either of biological state or of energy output. Homeostatic models have been provided by computer science and cybernetics.

C. Ladd Prosser

Human ecology

The study of the interactions of humans, culture, and environment. This definition is derived in part from the traditional view of ecology as the study of interactions between organisms and their environment, or as the structure and function of ecological systems. Ecology may also be defined as the study of the organization of the biosphere—the interface between the Earth and its atmosphere where biological life exists. The focus of human ecology, therefore, is the interactions of human populations and the Earth's ecosystems which compose the biosphere. Human ecology examines the organization and function of human communities and societies within the biosphere through time and space. *See Biosphere; Ecological communities; Ecosystem.*

Scope. Human ecology is nearly boundless, all-encompassing, and beyond the grasp of any single discipline, including biology. Human ecology draws upon data and theory from other fields for analysis, interpretation, integration, and synthesis. These include geography, anthropology, sociology, and epidemiology. Human ecology was closely identified with environmental health in the past. The words ecology and economics have the same Greek root, *oikos* or dwelling place, and it was a German biologist and contemporary of Darwin, Ernst Haeckel, who first used the term "economy of nature" to define ecology. The common grounds between ecology and economics are such that M. Bates treats the "ecology of man" and the "economy of nature" as inseparable concepts in the study of human ecology.

There is no distinct or readily identifiable body of knowledge which encompasses and precisely delineates human ecology. Although the inquiry into human environment interactions has taken many directions, several underlying concepts have emerged. The unifying concept is that *Homo sapiens*, as a biological entity, is an integral part of the ecosystems in which humans live, but the origin, evolution, and expression of culture renders the interpretation of the relationships of humans to nature profoundly complex and variable through time and space. Although several animals make and use tools, and therefore have "culture," nowhere in the biological world is culture and the use of technology so manifest as in human populations, including those with even the most rudimentary science and technology. Indeed, it is culture that is the most distinguishing characteristic between humans and other animals. Whereas ecology is a branch of biology, human ecology is not. The study of human culture has not been a major concern of traditional biology, and the recognition of the role of culture and particularly cross-cultural differences in ecological affairs is a relatively recent and not entirely widespread phenomenon.

Approaches. Traditional ecology may be treated as autecology (the ecology of individual species) or synecology (the ecology of communities). Some ecologists have taken a synecological approach to the study of *H. sapiens,* which defines human ecology as the "ecology of man, the animal" and applies ecological principles and concepts to human populations in the same manner that they may be applied to other species. Humans are subject to the same fundamental laws of nature as are other animals and are linked with the biosphere through energy flows and biogeochemical cycles. Through intelligence, however, humans are capable of significantly modifying natural environments to their benefit and minimizing the negative impacts of human-induced ecological change. A corollary is that humans can have the opposite effect of degrading the quality and productivity of the environments. *See Biogeochemistry.*

The evolutionary approach to the study of human ecology examines human evolution and adaptation in different environments through time. A principal focus is the evolution of the biological characteristics of *H. sapiens* which have enhanced human dominance over the nonhuman world. These include body size, erect posture, bipedal locomotion, opposable digits, stereoscopic depth perception, cranial capacity, and the period from birth to sexual maturity. This period of infancy and immaturity necessitates the prolonged dependence of progeny on parents. It is during this period that learned behavior, or culture, is transmitted from one generation to another, thereby ensuring the ecological dominance of humans in the biosphere.

Ecology had its origins as a science at about the time that Darwin published the ideas that eventually revolutionized the perception of human relationships to other organisms and to his environments. It is not surprising that ecology, particularly human ecology, and the concepts of evolution are closely linked. N. Levine views ecology as the study of change and adaptation in organisms and in their environments, and defines human ecology on the basis of principles of human evolution. There are physical and biological bases of human adaptation to the environment. There is a cultural basis of adaptation as well, superimposed upon the long and arduous process of evolution.

The subject matter of human ecology based on an evolutionary approach includes the evolution of the physical and chemical environments of the Earth; the principles of human evolution, including the internal as well as the external environments of humans; and the cultural evolution and adaptation of humans.

Environmental relationships. Human ecology, viewed from any perspective, also examines the imbalances or disequilibria extant in contemporary human-environment relationships. These include human disease, food supply (nutritional quality as well as quantity), human population ecology, environmental contamination (particularly by toxic and nuclear wastes), and the misuse and unequal allocation of world resources.

Current ecological problems can be analyzed according to scale. Complete and probable irreversible ecological breakdown has occurred locally in many areas, such as toxic-waste dump sites and the industrial centers of some of the major cities, particularly those in the third world. Regional ecological degradation is increasing in areas affected by acid precipitation and in the remaining tropical forests, which are rapidly disappearing, particularly in Southeast Asia and Central Africa. Incipient global disruption is evident in the greenhouse effect, in which increasing quantities of carbon dioxide in the atmosphere act to trap heat near the surface of the Earth. The ultimate human ecological horror imaginable is the threat of unleasing vast quantities of nuclear material into the northern part of the biosphere and the attendant ''nuclear winter'' in the southern part. SEE ACID RAIN; GREENHOUSE EFFECT.

The magnitude of contemporary environmental problems addressed by human ecology is such that the historical antecedents of human-environment interactions are frequently overlooked. The impact of humans on the landscape has long been a major theme in geography and to a lesser degree in anthropology. G. P. Marsh's classic treatise *Man and Nature, or Physical Geography as Modified by Human Action* was written in 1864 when traditional and religious conceptualizations of humans were being challenged by many, including Darwin. Another milestone was the publication in 1956 of *Man's Role in Changing the Face of the Earth* by various authors.

Although human ecology seeks to understand the influences, past and present, of the biological and physicochemical environments upon humans and culture, the notion of environmental determinism of the early twentieth century is rejected. This view held that the physical environment exerts a dominant influence on the development of civilization and on the origin, evolution, and expression of culture. It is now recognized that environmental restraints on human culture are weak and that these are overcome by a very clever *H. sapiens* through biological adaptability (genetic plasticity and phenotypic variability), by the

fusion of science and technology during the last century, and by the application of that technology.

An important discussion today centers on the separation of humans and culture from nature and the implications of this dichotomy for the long-term enhancement of human life throughout the world. While the perceived separation of humans from nature, particularly in western societies, has received the attention of several scholars, others have been concerned with the reconstruction of past environments and human impacts on them. This has proved to be fruitful in understanding current ecological problems and their historical roots, and forms a focal point of human ecological studies. Research has clearly documented the significant impacts that aboriginal peoples had on their environments and has also demonstrated that substantial ecological change is not confined to modern industrial societies or to the twentieth century.

The origins of the human use of fire, the domestication of plants and animals, and the rise of cities and urbanization have been of principal interest to scholars investigating human-environment interactions from a historical perspective because of their importance to the evolution of the ecological dominance of *H. sapiens*. Also of historical importance are attempts to relate environmental problems to philosophical attitudes and religion.

Human ecology is often perceived as being more than a science; it is a perspective, a way of looking at human relationships with the nonhuman world. It transcends scientific inquiry to become an ethic or a philosophy of human stewardship of the Earth and its creatures. This philosophy is represented by what A. Leopold referred to as the land ethic, wherein the unity and integrity of humans and nature are viewed as essential to human well-being. This ethic has been translated into environmentalism or environmental action. Nevertheless, the distinction remains between human ecology as a science and environmentalism as advocacy. SEE ECOLOGY; ENVIRONMENT.

Howard E. Daugherty

Bibliography. R. J. Borden et al. (eds.), *Human Ecology: A Gathering of Perspectives,* 1986; W. B. Clapham, Jr., *Human Ecosystems,* 1981; M. Eisenbud, *The Human Environment: Past, Present, and Future,* 1983; R. Foley, *Another Unique Species: Patterns in Human Evolutionary Ecology,* 1987; A. H. Hawley, *Human Ecology: A Theoretical Essay,* 1986; T. Ingold, *The Appropriation of Nature: Essays on Human Ecology and Social Relations,* 1987; K. E. Maxwell et al., *Environment of Life,* 4th ed., 1985; J. W. Meeker, *Minding the Earth: Thinly Disguised Essays on Human Ecology,* 1988; E. V. Walter, *Placeways: A Theory of the Human Environment,* 1988.

Humidity

Atmospheric water-vapor content, expressed in any of several measures, especially relative humidity, absolute humidity, humidity mixing ratio, and specific humidity. Quantity of water vapor is also specified indirectly by dew point (or frost point), vapor pressure, and a combination of wet-bulb and dry-bulb (actual) temperatures. SEE DEW POINT.

Relative humidity is the ratio, in percent, of the

moisture actually in the air to the moisture it would hold if it were saturated at the same temperature and pressure. It is a useful index of dryness or dampness for determining evaporation, or absorption of moisture.

Human comfort is dependent on relative humidity on warm days, which are oppressive if relative humidity is high but may be tolerable if it is low. At other than high temperatures, comfort is not much affected by high relative humidity. *See* COMFORT TEMPERATURES.

However, very low relative humidity, which is common indoors during cold weather, can cause drying of skin or throat and adds to the discomfort of respiratory infections. The term indoor relative humidity is sometimes used to specify the relative humidity which outside air will have when heated to a given room temperature, such as 72°F (22°C), without addition of moisture. The indoor relative humidity always has a low value in cold weather and is then a better measure of the drying effect on skin than is outdoor relative humidity. This is even true outdoors because, when air is cold, skin temperature is much higher and may approximate normal room temperature. *See* BIOMETEOROLOGY.

Absolute humidity is the weight of water vapor in a unit volume of air expressed, for example, as grams per cubic meter or grains per cubic foot.

Humidity mixing ratio is the weight of water vapor mixed with unit mass of dry air, usually expressed as grams per kilogram. Specific humidity is the weight per unit mass of moist air and has nearly the same values as mixing ratio.

Dew point is the temperature at which air becomes saturated if cooled without addition of moisture or change of pressure; frost point is similar but with respect to saturation over ice. Vapor pressure is the partial pressure of water vapor in the air. Wet-bulb temperature is the lowest temperature obtainable by whirling or ventilating a thermometer whose bulb is covered with wet cloth. From readings of a psychrometer, an instrument composed of wet- and dry-bulb thermometers and a fan or other means of ventilation, values of all other measures of humidity may be determined from tables.

J. R. Fulks

Bibliography. D. Ahrens, *Meteorology Today: An Introduction to Weather, Climate, and the Environment*, 3d ed., 1988; W. L. Donn, *Meteorology*, 4th ed., 1975; A. Miller and J. C. Thompson, *Elements of Meteorology*, 4th ed., 1983.

Hurricane

A tropical cyclone whose maximum sustained winds reach or exceed a threshold of 74 mi/h (119 km/h). In the western North Pacific Ocean it is known as a typhoon. Many tropical cyclones do not reach this wind strength.

Maximum surface winds in hurricanes range up to about 200 mi/h (320 km/h). However, much greater losses of life and property are attributable to inundation from hurricane tidal surges and riverine or flash flooding than from the direct impact of winds on structures.

Tropical cyclones of hurricane strength occur in low latitudes of all oceans except the South Atlantic

and the eastern South Pacific, where combinations of cooler sea temperatures and prevailing winds whose velocities vary sharply with height prevent the establishment of a central warm core through a deep enough layer to sustain the hurricane wind system. *See* WIND.

Impact. Severe hurricanes are responsible for many of the world's greatest natural disasters. Hurricane Camille in 1969 devastated coastal communities of the central Gulf of Mexico; Hurricane Tracy on Christmas 1974 virtually destroyed the Australian city of Darwin; in 1989, Hurricane Hugo, the most destructive atmosphere event of all times, caused $7 billion damage in the Caribbean Sea and South Carolina; and the Bangladesh hurricane of 1970 killed more than 300,000 people. Lesser hurricanes often inflict years of social disruption and economic devastation in small tropical countries.

In the United States, hurricane damage continues to climb, primarily because of increasing exposure of property as the population continues to migrate to the seashores. At the same time, loss of life has decreased sharply because of more effective warnings which reflect the result of extensive research, more complete storm surveillance, and improved programs of public awareness.

On a global scale, the impact of hurricanes may change in the decades ahead as a consequence of increasing carbon dioxide in the atmosphere which may reduce radiative heat losses from the ground—the greenhouse effect. While the impact of global incidence of hurricanes remains controversial, the most likely change is an increase in the number of hurricanes at higher latitudes, owing to possible increases in sea surface temperatures. However, it will remain difficult to distinguish normal climatic aberrations from changes attributable to greenhouse warming for at least several decades. In some regions, the number of hurricanes could decrease. *See* GREENHOUSE EFFECT.

Structure. The characteristic signature of a hurricane (**Figs. 1** and **2**), as viewed by radar or satellite, is of a central, relatively cloud-free eye encircled by an eye wall of towering cumulonimbus clouds 15–50 mi (25–80 km) wide. A dense cloud deck covers the storm at upper levels, and spiral bands of cumulus

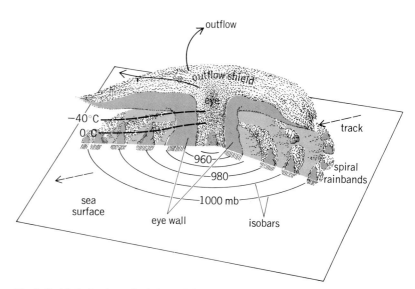

Fig. 1. Model of a hurricane circulation and cloud structure. °F = (°C × 1.8) + 32.

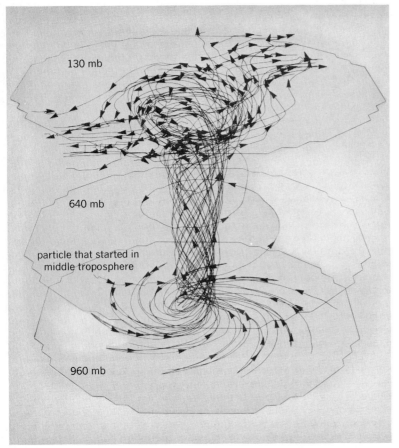

130 mb

640 mb

particle that started in
middle troposphere

960 mb

Fig. 2. Particle trajectories calculated over an 8-day period (90–282 h in 9-h intervals) in an experiment with a three-dimensional model hurricane. All particles start in the lower atmospheric boundary layer except one, which starts in the middle troposphere. 1 mb = 10^2 Pa. (After R. A. Anthes, S. L. Rosenthal, and J. W. Trout, Preliminary results from an asymmetric model of the tropical cyclone, Mon. Weath. Rev., 99:744–758, 1971)

clouds wind inward from the environment to the eye wall.

Near the Earth's surface the hurricane appears as a nearly circular vortex of low pressure, typically 200–400 mi (320–640 km) in diameter. Its dynamic and thermodynamic properties, however, are asymmetrically distributed both at the surface and in upper layers. The cyclonic circulation (counterclockwise in the Northern Hemisphere) extends through most of the troposphere (to an atmospheric depth of about 9 mi or 15 km). In lower layers (up to 2 mi or 3 km), winds spiral inward and accelerate toward lower pressure, reaching peak speeds in a narrow annulus typically 10–20 mi (15–30 km) from the pressure center. Here there is a near balance between the pressure forces acting radially inward and the centrifugal and Coriolis forces acting outward, so that the air, no longer able to move radially, is forced upward, forming and maintaining the cloudy eye wall.

Momentum is transported upward from surface layers, so that wind speeds near the top of the eye wall are almost as strong as peak winds near the surface. Since pressure forces in the relatively warm eye wall must diminish with height, the consequent imbalance of forces causes the air in upper layers to spiral out of the vortex and join environmental circulations, carrying with it a canopy of cloud debris which may extend great distances into the environment. The raging

winds in the eye wall, so closely adjacent to the relative calm within the eye, act as a centrifuge, dragging air from the eye which is replaced from above, the sinking motion therefrom gradually filling the eye with very dry, often cloud-free, warm air—warmer, in fact, than in the moist eye wall.

The spiral bands of cumulus clouds extending from the environment and entwining the eye wall result from complex processes. Some portions of these bands grow tall enough to augment the outflow from the eye wall. SEE CLOUD PHYSICS.

Energy sources and processes. The hurricane draws energy from two main sources, its atmospheric environment and the ocean surface.

In the hurricane vortex, the circulation of mass—inward at low and midlevels, upward and outward aloft—at the rate of some 2.2 million tons (2 metric tons) per second, constitutes an atmospheric heat pump involving the import of angular momentum from the environment. The primary source of fuel for this pump is a combination of the latent heat released by the formation of towering cumulus clouds and heavy precipitation, and the much smaller but crucial flux of sensible heat from the ocean. Since low-level air, flowing from the environment into the storm core, is observed to maintain a nearly constant temperature, an important up-flux of heat energy from the warm ocean surface tends to compensate for the cooling that otherwise would occur during the transit toward lower pressure. Without this oceanic heat source, the pump would be unable to generate and sustain wind speeds of hurricane strength. The loss of this compensating sea-to-air heat flux is the primary reason for rapid decreases in strength usually observed when a hurricane moves over land.

The process by which the tall cumuli in the eye wall maintain the warm, light air in the hurricane core, and in turn the pressure forces that determine the strength of hurricane winds, is not a simple matter of releasing latent heat within the clouds. Latent heat released by cumulus clouds does not directly warm the atmosphere, since most of this heat energy is converted to potential energy as air parcels rise. However, the direct role of the latent heat released is to maintain the buoyancy of the rising cloud air and thus to maintain the vertical circulation of the eye wall. The high temperatures at the storm center are created and maintained by adiabatic compression of descending air.

Since latent heat from atmospheric water vapor is the major fuel for the hurricane heat engine, the efficiency and available fuel supply is dependent upon both the atmospheric and oceanic environment. From a purely thermodynamic point of view, the overall hurricane efficiency is a function of the temperature difference between the ocean surface and the cold upper atmosphere where outflowing air, mixing with a colder environment, is further cooled by long-wave radiation to space. Thus warm tropical oceans provide the best medium for generating and sustaining the most intense hurricanes.

Hurricane intensity is also constrained by the amount of preexisting rotation in the environment. This rotation is normally quantified in terms of angular momentum, a combination of that from the Earth's rotation and that of environmental flow. If there is a store of cyclonic angular momentum and the necessary processes are triggered to set the development in

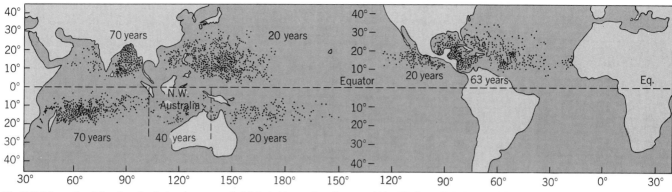

Fig. 3. Points on the globe where tropical cyclones were first detected by weather observers. (*After W. Gray, Global view of the origin of tropical disturbance, Mon. Weath. Rev., 96(10):670, 1968*)

motion, the low-level inflow described earlier carries this momentum toward the vortex center, generating hurricane-force winds in the same manner that rapid spin is achieved when ice skaters bring their arms close to their bodies. Some momentum is lost to friction at the Earth's surface, so that air flowing out of the eye wall returns to the environment with an anticyclonic motion.

The degree of rotation determines the potential for releasing latent heat that can be used to accelerate the winds. In the undisturbed tropics, rotation is very low, so that the latent heat released by daily-observed cumulus clouds and thunderstorms diffuses away, unable to organize a warm core and the consequent pressure drops necessary to produce storm-scale wind systems. Similar amounts of latent heat are released inside hurricanes, but the high rotation ensures that much of this heating is retained locally to lower the pressure.

Formation. An average of about 70 tropical cyclones develops gale or hurricane force somewhere on Earth each year, a figure some 15–20% higher than climatological records indicated before the advent of weather surveillance satellites in the 1960s. The global distribution of tropical cyclone occurrence is shown in **Fig. 3**.

Tropical disturbances, sometimes referred to as seedlings, that breed cyclones of hurricane strength originate mainly in tropical latitudes in the vicinity of the equatorial or monsoonal trough. Some have their origins over continental areas. Seedling disturbances, comprising an agglomeration of convective clouds 180–300 mi (300–500 km) in diameter, often move more than 1200 mi (2000 km) across tropical oceans as benign rainstorms before developing closed circulations and potentially dangerous winds.

A number of well-known factors may influence the development of seedlings. The atmosphere must be able to sustain and consolidate the growth of cumulus clouds to release latent heat and cause pressure falls. Also, ocean temperatures must be high enough to enhance the heat content of environmental air entering the system. It was established in the 1950s that this required an ocean temperature of greater than 79°F (26°C). Because of the need for background rotation, hurricanes rarely form or retain their identity equatorward of 5° latitude (Fig. 3).

The variation of prevailing winds with height also is important. If there is a sufficient change in wind velocity with height, the heat released by convection

and the warming due to subsidence cannot be stored in vertical columns of sufficient height to produce the pressure drop required to sustain hurricane winds. Finally, conditions favorable to development in the low-level flow must be matched by an upper-layer environment that supports outflow from the convective system.

Nevertheless, even when these necessary conditions are satisfied, many seedlings fail to develop. In the North Atlantic, for example, 100 seedlings form each year (more than half emerging from Africa), yet only 9 develop into tropical cyclones. Knowledge of the complex interactions involved is not sufficient to explain this relatively low incidence of hurricanes.

Movement. The observed movement of hurricanes arises from two mechanisms, advection and propagation. Advection occurs when the environment directs an airflow over the hurricane that moves it in a fashion similar to a cork bobbing in a stream. Forecasters call this the steering current, and considerable effort is made to determine it accurately. Although there are many individual differences, the mean flow throughout the middle levels of the troposphere and over a radial band some 300–400 mi (500–650 km) from the center seems to provide the most consistent results.

Dynamically, the hurricane propagates by internal processes that are quite sensitive to the properties of the environment. A full understanding of many of these processes requires in-depth knowledge of fluid dynamics. One illustration, however, can provide an indication of the essential features. Any cyclone is made up of infinitesimally small rotating elements that are measured as vorticity. For a hurricane, maximum combinations of elements, and thus maximum cyclonic vorticity, is found near the center. Air that is stationary relative to the Earth also has cyclonic rotation and vorticity arising from the component of Earth rotation about the local vertical. The Earth's vorticity component increases from zero at the Equator to a cyclonic maximum at each pole. The flow around a hurricane thus brings increasing cyclonic vorticity to the west side, and decreasing cyclonic vorticity on the east side to produce a poleward flow over the tropical cyclone. This effect combined with associated internal rearrangements causes the hurricane to propagate westward and poleward. The magnitude of this propagation is defined by the outer structure of the hurricane; it is largely insensitive to the hurricane intensity.

The propagation velocity is generally about 3–5 mi/h (5–7 km/h) westward and poleward, but it may vary from near zero to over 10 mi/h (16 km/h) for a hurricane of large diameter. By comparison, most tropical cyclones reach hurricane intensity in the steady trade-wind belt where they are advected westward at a speed of 10–20 mi/h (15–30 km/h) As the hurricane approaches the western extremity of a subtropical ridge and begins moving poleward, the steering current first weakens, and then is replaced by westerlies whose speeds often exceed 40 mi/h (65 km/h). Thus cyclone propagation and advection tend to be in the same direction in the tropics but to act oppositely in midlatitudes.

Numerical simulations. Numerical simulation models have become a powerful tool for the study of hurricane dynamics and energetics. These models consist of finite-difference expressions for the system of partial differential equations that govern the dynamics and energetics of the atmosphere. Pioneer experiments with computer models of hurricanes were carried out in the late 1950s. The limited computing capacity restricted hurricane models to be axisymmetric (assuming that hurricanes had no variations in horizontal azimuthal directions). These models were used to study the effects on hurricane intensity of sea-surface temperature, ambient atmospheric temperature and humidity stratification, and various hurricane modification strategies.

By the early 1970s, more advanced computers permitted development of fully three-dimensional models. Figure 2 shows the hurricane circulation obtained with the first of these models. By 1984, some re-

search groups were using three-dimensional numerical models of the hurricane and its environment covering thousands of miles; they used telescoping, or nested, grids to provide fine resolution of mesoscale features near the eye wall, those with finest grid spacing moving with the hurricane. Topics of investigation ranged from the effects of vertical wind shear on hurricane development to the detailed changes of the hurricane's structure as it made landfall. Numerical models have been developed that cover the entire Earth with sufficient resolution to simulate many of the aspects of tropical cyclones. Some sophisticated models use nested grids which allow global integrations of the equations of motion and thermodynamics with coarse resolution while simulating the detailed circulations and cloud systems of tropical cyclones with very high resolution. An operational global model in use at the European Center for Medium Range Weather Forecasting (at Reading, England) uses powerful enough computers with sufficiently small grid spacings to show useful results in anticipating hurricane development and movement without using nested grids.

Prediction. Prediction of the path of the hurricane center as a function of time is the most important aspect of the hurricane forecast. If the track prediction contains major errors, all other aspects of the forecast (intensity, structure, rainfall, and so forth) are of no consequence. Because the high-energy (damage-producing) portion of the storm has small dimensions (60–90 mi or 100–150 km), the forecaster, in landfall situations, must balance the consequences of warning too small an area and missing the landfall, against overwarning a large area and thereby causing unnecessary expensive preparations by the public. The prediction problem is made especially difficult by the sparse coverage of the oceans by conventional surface and upper-air meteorological data. Meteorological satellites provide some data over these regions. Indeed, when storms are well away from landfall, satellites are often the only source of information concerning location of the storm. For the east and Gulf of Mexico coasts of the United States, center fixes are made several times a day by aircraft penetration when the storm is within 36 h of landfall. *See Storm detection.*

An array of objective models is available to the hurricane forecaster for predicting the path of the hurricane. The National Oceanic and Atmospheric Administration's National Hurricane Center in Miami continues to make regular use of at least four models. However, these methods often yield predictive results that differ by a significant amount. The forecaster is then faced with the problem of deciding which is to be given greatest weight in the official forecast.

Forecast models generally fall into three categories. There are statistical models based solely on climatology and persistence. These produce a most probable hurricane track, the only current data required being the initial location of the storm center, past movement of the center, and the calendar date. A second class of statistical models adds, to climatology and persistence, information concerning the large-scale pressure field in which the storm is embedded. The third class of models is based entirely on atmospheric dynamics. These models are similar to, though less sophisticated than, the simulation models described earlier. They differ in that the initial conditions for simulation stud-

Fig. 4. Three-dimensional view of Hurricane Gilbert's eye and cloud system viewed from a weather satellite on September 12, 1988. (*F. H. Hasler, NASA Goddard Laboratory for Atmospheres*)

ies are generally a simplified idealized state of the atmosphere, whereas the dynamical prediction models have initial conditions based on actual observations of the current state of the atmosphere. Generally speaking, the more advanced dynamical models perform better than statistical models for longer-range forecasts (36–48 h), while the statistical models perform better for shorter-period predictions (12–24 h).

Averaged over the Atlantic Ocean, Caribbean Sea, and Gulf of Mexico, the magnitude of the prediction error (length of the line connecting the observed position of the storm center to the predicted position) for the official forecast by the National Hurricane Center is 109, 244, and 377 mi (202, 452, and 698 km), respectively, for forecasts of 24, 48, and 72 h. From the mid-1950s through the 1960s, a decrease of about 10% was observed in the average errors of official forecasts. Since then, however, the principal measure of improvement has been a reduction in standard deviations from the mean, as larger individual errors were significantly reduced.

The notable progress in technology and of data-processing capabilities for meteorological satellites offers great promise for hurricane research and for the design of new dynamically based predictions of both development and movement. **Figure 4**, an example of the observational capabilities of modern satellites, is a three-dimensional view of the cloud systems in Hurricane Gilbert, the most powerful Atlantic hurricane of record, displaying details of cloud structure and implications for both the details of circulation and the thermodynamic properties of the hurricane inner core. Under development is an array of microwave sounders to be installed on weather satellites that will "see through" the clouds to sense the three-dimensional thermal and circulation structure of hurricanes and its interacting environment, and for measuring rainfall distributions. Near the end of the century, satellites are planned which will be able not only to measure the winds throughout the storm core but also to observe the core's thermal structure. Such observations will have a significant impact on the understanding of energetic and dynamic processes which control the degree of development and severity of a hurricane; and they may well provide data for initializing more sophisticated prediction models incorporating far more comprehensive physics than was possible with the previous models. With the increasing archives of satellite data from existing sensors, there are already promising opportunities for prediction research, applying well-known methodologies for principal component analyses (statistical procedures for analyzing data sets) and pattern recognition techniques that could reduce prediction errors for forecasts of 24 h or more, the period most critical for issuance of coast warning. SEE REMOTE SENSING; WEATHER FORECASTING AND PREDICTION.

Greg Holland; Joanne Simpson; Robert Simpson

Bibliography. R. A. Anthes, *Tropical Cyclones: Their Evolution, Structure and Effects*, 1982; R. L. Elsberry (ed.), *A Global View of Tropical Cyclones*, 1988; K. Emmanuel, *Toward a General Theory of Hurricanes*, pp. 371–379, July-August 1987; C. Neumann and J. M. Pelissier, An analysis of Atlantic tropical cyclone forecast errors, 1970–1979, *Mon. Weath. Rev.*, 109:1248–1266, 1981; C. Neumann and J. M. Pelissier, Models for the prediction of tropical cyclone motion over the North Atlantic: An op-eration evaluation, *Mon. Weath. Rev.*, 109:522–538, 1981; R. H. Simpson and H. Riehl, *The Hurricane and Its Impact*, 1981; H. E. Willoughby, J. Clos, and M. Shoreibah, Concentric eyewalls, secondary wind maxima, and the evolution of the hurricane vortex, *J. Atm. Sci.*, 39:395–411, 1982.

Hydrology

The science that treats of the waters of the Earth: their occurrence, circulation, and distribution; their chemical and physical properties; and their reaction with the environment, including their relation to living things. The domain of hydrology embraces the full life history of water on the Earth.

Hydrologic cycle. Water in liquid and solid form covers most of the crust of the Earth. By a complex process powered by gravity and the action of solar energy, an endless exchange of water, in vapor, liquid, and solid forms, takes place between the atmosphere, the oceans, and the crust. Water circulates in the air and in the oceans as well as over and below the surface of land masses. Idealized schematizations of the process are presented in **Figs. 1** and **2**, which show a representation of hydrologic phenomena as they are directly observable, and in an integrated flow pattern which suggests the operation of a global scheme called the hydrologic cycle.

Although the diagram in Fig. 2 appears as an articulated flow pattern, the distribution of water in the planet is uneven. General patterns of circulation are present in the atmosphere, the oceans, and the land masses, but regional features are very irregular and random in their detail. Therefore, while causal relations underlie the overall process, important elements of chance affect local hydrological events. SEE ATMOSPHERIC GENERAL CIRCULATION.

Hydrologic studies. Water is essential for all living things. Its adequate supply is a key factor for urban, agricultural, and industrial development. Water can also be the recipient of pollutants which degrade its quality for all uses, and may be a destructive agent when it inundates valleys and causes death and great damage. The rising of groundwater levels in agricultural lands may cause deterioration of the soils and loss of fertility by waterlogging and increased salinity. Erosion of soil by flowing waters, and ultimate deposition of the sediment in lakes, reservoirs, stream channels, and harbors are also serious problems. Thus, the means whereby natural waters may be captured and controlled are of utmost importance for the development of human economy. The study of hydrology provides the information necessary for determining those means. SEE EROSION; WATER POLLUTION.

Whereas the global linkages of the hydrologic cycle are recognized, the science of hydrology has traditionally circumscribed its direct concern with the detailed study of the portion of the cycle limited by the physical boundaries of the land, and thus excludes specialized investigations of the ocean (which is the subject of the science of oceanography) and the atmosphere (which is the subject of the science of meteorology). SEE METEOROLOGY; OCEANOGRAPHY.

A number of field measurements are performed for hydrologic studies. Among them are the amount and intensity of precipitation; the quantities of water stored as snow and ice, and their changes in time;

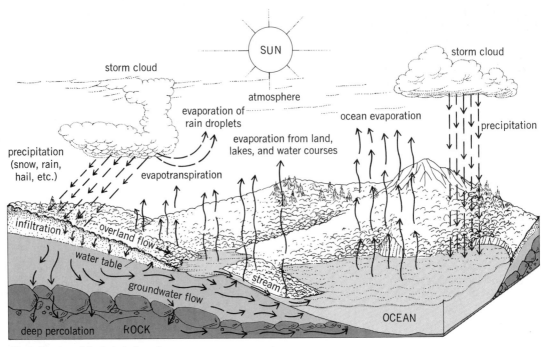

Fig. 1. Diagram of the hydrologic cycle.

discharge of streams; rates and quantities of infiltration into the soil, and movement of soil moisture; rates of production from wells and changes in their water levels as indicators of groundwater storage; dissolved chemical elements and compounds in surface and groundwaters; amounts of water transferred by evaporation and evapotranspiration to the atmosphere from snow, lakes, streams, soils, and vegetation; and sediment lost from the land and transported by streams.

In addition to the making of these measurements by means of specially designed instruments and devices, hydrology is concerned with research on the phenomena and mechanisms involved in all physical and biological components of the hydrogeologic cycle, with the purpose of understanding them sufficiently to permit quantitative predictions and forecasting. The field investigations and measurements not only provide the data whereby the behavior of each component may be evaluated in detail, permitting formulation in quantitative terms, but also give a record of the historical operation of the entire system. Thus, two principal vehicles for hydrological forecasting and prediction become available: (1) a set of elemental processes, whose operations are expressible in mathematical terms, linked to form deterministic models which permit the prediction of hydrologic events for given conditions; and (2) a group of records or time series of measured hydrologic variables, such as precipitation or runoff, which can be analyzed by statistical methods to formulate stochastic models that permit inferences to be made on the future likelihood of hydrologic events.

Surface water. Hydrology, when specifically applied to the solution of problems, such as the estimation of water supplies from streams, flood control and protection, dam and reservoir design and operation, urban drainage, and changes in flow regimes due to modifications introduced by humans, traditionally has been designated as surface-water hydrology. This does not imply that flow barriers are assumed to exist

between surface water and groundwater, but that the primary objective is to evaluate surface flows. Both deterministic and stochastic models are employed.

A variety of deterministic models have been proposed, which differ from each other mainly in the degree of simplification and schematization used to describe the components of the hydrologic cycle and their linkages. The common underlying concept is that the overall process is composed of distinct elements of water storage annd translation, each following specific rules, but all obeying the hydrologic balance equation, expressed, for any finite period of time, as inflow = outflow + change in water storage. Typically, this water accounting is carried out at short intervals of time, both internally for each element and as a whole for the entire catchment, to yield the surface outflows to be expected as a result of changing precipitation rates. Data on relevant physical and vegetative characteristics of the catchment, as well as on factors affecting evaporation and evapotranspiration, are needed for the calculations, which are generally performed on digital computers, except in the simplest models for rough approximations.

Predictions on the fate of chemical and biological species contained naturally in surface waters or introduced as pollutants due to urbanization and industrial and agricultural developments can be made by appropriate coupling of the equations of chemical and biochemical reactions with the storage and translation equations of these models.

Stochastic process models are used for purposes such as drawing inferences on the probabilities of occurrence of future extreme events like floods and droughts, or to simulate possible future flow sequences similar in likelihood to those of the historical record. These inferences and synthetic time series can be used in the planning and design of water resource systems. Research on climatic change is an area of study which will have a profound influence on the interpretation of historical hydrologic data. All conclusions drawn from recorded data will have to be

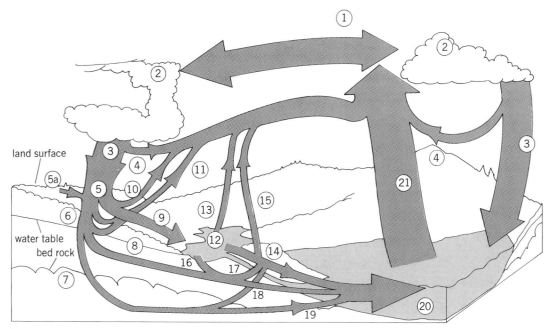

key:
1. Atmospheric water in circulation
2. Formation of storm clouds
3. Precipitation (snow, rain, hail, etc.)
4. Evaporation of precipitation in transit and moisture diffusion
5. Net precipitation on Earth surface
5a. Snow storage and melt
6. Infiltration
7. Deep percolation
8. Groundwater flow and storage
9. Overland flow and depression storage
10. Evporation of intercepted and surface water
11. Evapotranspiration
12. Surface storage in lakes and reservoirs
13. Evaporation from lake surfaces
14. Surface streams
15. Evaporation from streams
16. Groundwater exchange from channel storage (base flow and return)
17. Groundwater exchange from channel storage (base flow and return)
18, 19. Groundwater flow to ocean
20. Storage in the ocean
21. Evaporation from ocean surfaces

Fig. 2. Water flow scheme of the hydrologic cycle.

consistent with the possibility that local hydrologies may or may not remain as observed in the recent past. *See* CLIMATIC CHANGE.

Groundwater. Waters contained in porous formations below the ground are extremely valuable sources of supply. They depend for their long-term availability on replenishment (or recharge) from the surface. Water-bearing layers suitable for economical extraction by means of wells are called aquifers, and operate simultaneously as reservoirs and as flow media. The ability of an aquifer material to store water depends primarily on its porosity, and the ability to permit fluid motion on its permeability or hydraulic conductivity. Because the properties of aquifers vary in space, the flow patterns vary from point to point. These patterns are further altered by the presence of wells, which act as localized sink points. For the rational management of groundwater basins which may contain several nonuniform and nonhomogeneous aquifers, special computer models, based on the equations of flow through porous media, have been developed. Coupled chemical and biochemical reactions can be used for the prediction of water quality in aquifers, and studies can also be undertaken by means of these models for the planning of conjunctive use operations of surface and groundwaters, whereby controlled aquifer recharges and discharges can be combined with regulated surface flows and reservoirs

for optimizing the management of water resources. *See* AQUIFER; GROUNDWATER HYDROLOGY.

Snow management. Snow fields constitute natural reservoirs that accumulate water during the winter and release it during the melting season. The province of snow hydrology is concerned with the study of the conditions of accumulation of snow, the properties of snowpacks as porous media, and the processes of heat and vapor exchange between the atmosphere and the snow as the snowpack evolves and melts under gradually varying conditions of solar radiation. These studies, together with field measurements, permit the formulation of mathematical models for the prediction of snowmelt as a function of time. Accordingly, it becomes possible to plan the operation of surface reservoir systems in combination with expected snowmelt yields for optimal water resource management. In some cases it has been proposed to manage the snowpacks themselves through modification of melt rates by means of vegetative cover, by the change of snow surface exposure angles to solar radiation, or by alteration of the rate of solar energy reflectance, or albedo of the snow, through application of dark inert materials over the surface of the snow. *See* HYDROSPHERE.

J. Amorocho

Bibliography. American Society of Civil Engineers, *Engineering Foundation Conference Proceedings*,

1979, Improved Hydrologic Forecasting: Why and How, 1981; P. P. Bedient et al., *Hydrology and Floodplain Analysis*, 1988; A. D. Feldman (ed.), *Engineering Hydrology*, 1987; G. Fleming, *Computer Simulation Techniques in Hydrology*, 1975; L. B. Leopold, *Water: A Primer*, 1974; R. K. Linsley, Jr., et al., *Hydrology for Engineers*, 3d ed., 1982.

Table 1. Meridional flux of water vapor in the atmosphere

Latitude	Northward flux, 10^{10} g/s
90°N	0
70°N	4
40°N	70
10°N	−61
Equator	45
10°S	71
40°S	−75
70°S	1
90°S	0

Hydrometeorology

The study of the occurrence, movement, and changes in the state of water in the atmosphere. The term is also used in a more restricted sense, especially by hydrologists, to mean the study of the exchange of water between the atmosphere and continental surfaces. This includes the processes of precipitation and direct condensation, and of evaporation and transpiration from natural surfaces. Considerable emphasis is placed on the statistics of precipitation as a function of area and time for given locations or geographic regions.

Water occurs in the atmosphere primarily in vapor or gaseous form. The average amount of vapor present tends to decrease with increasing elevation and latitude and also varies strongly with season and type of surface. Precipitable water, the mass of vapor per unit area contained in a column of air extending from the surface of the Earth to the outer extremity of the atmosphere, varies from almost zero in continental arctic air to about 1.4 oz/in.^{2} (6 g/cm^2) in very humid, tropical air. Its average value over the Northern Hemisphere varies from around 0.46 oz/in.^{2} (2.0 g/cm^2) in January and February to around 0.84 oz/in.^{2} (3.7 g/cm^2) in July. Its average value is around 0.63 oz/in.^{2} (2.8 g/cm^2), an amount equivalent to a column of liquid water slightly greater than 1 in. (2.5 cm) in depth. Close to 50% of this water vapor is contained in the atmosphere's first mile, and about 80% is to be found in the lowest 2 mi (3 km).

Atmospheric water cycle. Although a trivial proportion of the water of the globe is found in the atmosphere at any one instant, the rate of exchange of water between the atmosphere and the continents and oceans is high. The average water molecule remains in the atmosphere only about 10 days, but because of the extreme mobility of the atmosphere it is usually precipitated many hundreds or even thousands of miles from the place at which it entered the atmosphere.

Evaporation from the ocean surface and evaporation and transpiration from the land are the sources of water vapor for the atmosphere. Water vapor is removed from the atmosphere by condensation and subsequent precipitation in the form of rain, snow, sleet, and so on. The amount of water vapor removed by direct condensation at the Earth's surface (dew) is relatively small.

A major feature of the atmospheric water cycle is the meridional net flux of water vapor. The average precipitation exceeds evaporation in a narrow band extending approximately from 10°S to 15°N lat. To balance this, the atmosphere carries water vapor equatorward in the tropics, primarily in the quasi-steady trade winds which have a component of motion equatorward in the moist layers near the Earth's surface. Precipitation also exceeds evaporation in the temperate and polar regions of the two hemispheres,

poleward of about 40° lat. In the middle and higher latitudes, therefore, the atmosphere carries vapor poleward. Here the exchange occurs through the action of cyclones and anticyclones, large-scale eddies of air with axes of spin normal to the Earth's surface.

For the globe as a whole the average amount of evaporation must balance the precipitation. The complete meridional cycle of water vapor is summarized in **Table 1**. This exchange is related to the characteristics of the general circulation of the atmosphere. It seems likely that a similar cycle would be observed even if the Earth were entirely covered by ocean, although details of the cycle, such as the flux across the Equator, would undoubtedly be different.

Complications in the global pattern arise from the existence of land surfaces. Over the continents the only source of water is from precipitation; therefore, the average evapotranspiration (the sum of evaporation and transpiration) cannot exceed precipitation. The flux of vapor from the oceans to the continents through the atmosphere, and its ultimate return to atmosphere or ocean by evaporation, transpiration, or runoff is known as the hydrologic cycle. Its atmospheric phase is closely related to the air mass cycle. In middle latitudes of the Northern Hemisphere, for example, precipitation occurs primarily from maritime air masses moving northward and eastward across the continents. Statistically, precipitation from these air masses substantially exceeds evapotranspiration into them. Conversely, cold and dry air masses tend to move southward and eastward from the interior of the continents out over the oceans. Evapotranspiration into these continental air masses strongly exceeds precipitation, especially during winter months. These facts, together with the extreme mobility of the atmosphere and its associated water vapor, make it likely that only a small percentage of the water evaporated or transpired from a continental surface is reprecipitated over the same continent. SEE ATMOSPHERIC GENERAL CIRCULATION; HYDROLOGY.

Precipitation. Hydrometeorology is particularly concerned with the measurement and analysis of precipitation data. Radar plays an important role in estimating precipitation. By relating the intensity of radar echo to rate of precipitation, it has been possible to obtain a vast amount of detailed information concerning the structure and areal distribution of storms. SEE STORM DETECTION.

Deficiencies in the observational networks over the oceans and over the more sparsely inhabited land areas of the Earth are now being bridged through the

Table 2. Record observed point rainfalls*

Duration	Depth, in. (cm)	Station	Date
1 min	1.23 (3.12)	Unionville, Maryland	July 4, 1956
8 min	4.96 (12.6)	Füssen, Bavaria	May 25, 1920
15 min	7.80 (19.8)	Plumb Point, Jamaica	May 12, 1916
42 min	12.00 (30.5)	Holt, Missouri	June 22, 1947
2 h 45 min	22.00 (55.9)	Near D'Hanis, Texas	May 31, 1935
24 h	73.62 (187)	Cilaos, La Reunion (Indian Ocean)	March 15–16, 1952
1 month	366.14 (930)	Cherrapunji, India	July 1861
12 months	1041.78 (2646.1)	Cherrapunji, India	August 1860 to July 1861

*From R. K. Linsley, M. A. Kohler, and J. L. H. Paulhus, *Hydrology for Engineers*, 2d ed., 1975.

use of meteorological satellite observations. Progress toward the development of methods for estimating rainfall amounts from satellite observations of cloud type and distribution is of particular significance to hydrometeorology.

Precipitation occurs when the air is cooled to saturation. The ascent of air toward lower pressure is the most effective process for causing rapid cooling and condensation. Precipitation may therefore be classified according to the atmospheric process which leads to the required upward motion. Accordingly, there are three basic types of precipitation: (1) Orographic precipitation occurs when a topographic barrier forces air to ascend. The presence of significant relief often leads to large variations in precipitation over relatively short distances. (2) Extratropical cyclonic precipitation is associated with the traveling regions of low pressure of the middle and high latitudes. These storms, which transport sinking cold dry air southward and rising warm moist air northward, account for a major portion of the precipitation of the middle and high latitudes. (3) Air mass precipitation results from disturbances occurring in an essentially homogeneous air mass. This is a common precipitation type over the continents in mid-latitudes during summer. It is the major mechanism for precipitation in the tropics, where disturbances may range from areas of scattered showers to intense hurricanes. In most cases there is evidence for organized lifting of air associated with areas of cyclonic vorticity, that is, areas over which the circulation is counterclockwise in the Northern Hemisphere or clockwise in the Southern Hemisphere.

The availability of data from geosynchronous meteorological satellites, together with surface and upper-air data acquired as part of the Global Atmospheric Research Program (GARP), is leading to significant advances in the understanding of the character and distribution of tropical precipitation. *See* HURRICANE; STORM.

Precipitation may, of course, be in liquid or solid form. In addition to rain and snow there are other forms which often occur, such as hail, snow pellets, sleet, and drizzle. If upward motion occurs uniformly over a wide area measured in tens or hundreds of miles, the associated precipitation is usually of light or moderate intensity and may continue for a considerable period of time. Vertical velocities accompanying such stable precipitation are usually of the order of several centimeters per second. Under other types of meteorological conditions, particularly when the density of the ascending air is less than that of the environment, upward velocities may locally be very large (of the order of several meters per second) and may be accompanied by compensating downdrafts. Such convective precipitation is best illustrated by the thunderstorm. Intensity of precipitation may be extremely high, but areal extent and local duration are comparatively limited. Storms are sometimes observed in which local convective regions are embedded in a matrix of stable precipitation.

Analysis of precipitation data. Precipitation is essentially a process which occurs over an area. However, despite the use of radar, most observations are taken at individual stations. Analyses of such "point" precipitation data are most often concerned with the frequency of intense storms. These data are of particular importance in evaluating local flood hazard, and may be used in such diverse fields as the design of local hydraulic structures, such as culverts or storm sewers, or the analysis of soil erosion. Intense local precipitation of short duration (up to 1 h) is usually associated with thunderstorms. Precipitation may be extremely heavy for a short period, but tends to decrease in intensity as longer intervals are considered. Several record point accumulations of rainfall are shown in **Table 2**.

A typical hydrometeorological problem might involve estimating the likelihood of occurrence of a storm of given intensity and duration over a specified watershed to determine the required spillway capacity of a dam. Such estimates can only be obtained from a careful meteorological and statistical examination of large numbers of storms selected from climatological records.

Evaporation and transpiration. In evaluating the water balance of the atmosphere, the hydrometeorologist must also examine the processes of evaporation and transpiration from various types of natural surfaces, such as open water, snow and ice fields, and land surfaces with and without vegetation. From the point of view of the meteorologist, the problem is one of transfer in the turbulent boundary layer. It is complicated by topographic effects when the natural surface is not homogeneous. In addition the simultaneous heating or cooling of the atmosphere from below has the effect of enhancing or inhibiting the transfer process. Although the problem has been attacked from the theoretical side, empirical relationships are at present of greatest practical utility. *See* METEOROLOGY; MICROMETEOROLOGY.

Eugene M. Rasmusson

Bibliography. R. K. Linsley et al., *Hydrology for Engineers*, 3d ed., 1982; F. K. Lutgens and E. J. Tarbuck, *Atmosphere: An Introduction to Meteorology*, 3d ed., 1986; W. D. Sellers, *Physical Climatol-*

ogy, 1965; World Meteorological Organization, *Compendium of Meteorology: General Hydrology*, vol. 2, pt. 1, 1978.

Hydrosphere

Approximately 74% of the Earth's surface is covered by water, in either the liquid or solid state. These waters, combined with minor contributions from groundwaters, constitute the hydrosphere (1 km^3 = 0.24 mi^3):

World oceans	1.3×10^9 km^3
Fresh-water lakes	1.3×10^5 km^3
Saline lakes and inland seas	1.0×10^5 km^3
Rivers	1.3×10^3 km^3
Soil moisture and vadose water	6.7×10^4 km^3
Groundwater to depth of 4 km (2.5 mi)	8.4×10^6 km^3
Icecaps and glaciers	2.9×10^7 km^3

The oceans account for about 97% of the weight of the hydrosphere, while the amount of ice reflects the Earth's climate, being higher during periods of glaciation. (Water vapor in the atmosphere amounts to 1.3×10^4 km^3 or 3.1×10^3 mi^3.) The circulation of the waters of the hydrosphere results in the weathering of the landmasses. The annual evaporation of 3.5×10^5 km^3 (8.4×10^4 mi^3) from the world oceans and of 7.0×10^4 km^3 (1.7×10^4 mi^3) from land areas results in an annual precipitation of 3.2×10^5 km^3 (7.6×10^4 mi^3) on the world oceans and 1.0×10^5 km^3 (2.4×10^4 mi^3) on land areas. The rainwater falling on the continents, partly taken up by the ground and partly by the streams, acts as an erosive agent before returning to the seas. SEE GROUNDWATER HYDROLOGY; HYDROLOGY; LAKE.

Edward D. Goldberg

The unique chemical properties of water make it an effective solvent for many gases, salts, and organic compounds. Circulation of water and the dissolved material it contains is a highly dynamic process driven by energy from the Sun and the interior of the Earth. Each component has its own geochemical cycle or pathway through the hydrosphere, reflecting the component's relative abundance, chemical properties, and utilization by organisms. The introduction of materials by humans has significantly altered the composition and environmental properties of many natural waters.

Rainwater. Rainwater contains small but measurable concentrations of many elements derived from the dissolution of airborne particulate matter and produced by equilibration of rainwater with atmospheric gases.

Total dissolved solids in rainwater range from over 10 parts per million (ppm) in rain formed in marine air masses to less than 1 ppm in rain precipitated over continental interiors. The major dissolved constituents of rainwater are chloride, sodium, potassium, magnesium, and sulfate (**Table 1**). These salts are derived over oceans and coastal areas from the dissolution of aerosol particles formed during the evaporation of sea spray.

A significant portion of the dissolved sodium, potassium, calcium, and sulfate in rain formed over continental areas is introduced by reaction with land-derived dust particles. Additional sulfate comes from the oxidation of sulfur dioxide, produced by the oxidation of hydrogen sulfide and by the burning of fossil fuels and smelting of sulfide ores, shown in reaction (1).

$$2SO_2 + O_2 + 2H_2O \rightarrow 4H^+ + 2SO_4^{2-} \qquad (1)$$

A map of the average sodium content of rain in the continental United States (**Fig. 1***a*) shows sodium contours subparallel to the coastlines, reflecting mixing of continental air masses with salt-rich marine air. The distribution of sulfate (Fig. 1*b*) is more complex, and reflects significant continental input from dust storms and industrial activity.

Rainwater contains in dissolved state each of the gases present in the lower atmosphere. Carbon dioxide is derived from both biological respiration and the burning of fossil fuels. It reacts with rain to form carbonic acid, as in reaction (2).

$$CO_2 + H_2O \rightarrow H_2CO_3 \qquad (2)$$

The presence of free oxygen and carbon dioxide makes rain both a natural oxidizing agent and an acid. Rain equilibrated with normal atmosphere has a pH of 5.7. More highly acidic rains form in areas where the industrial discharge of carbon dioxide or sulfur dioxide is intense. SEE ACID RAIN.

Rain contains variable trace concentrations of many additional elements and compounds. Some of these, such as heavy metals and radionuclides, are derived from industrial pollution and nuclear testing, respectively. Precipitation of rain is the primary process by which many of these materials are transported from the atmosphere to the continents and oceans.

Soil waters. As rainwater percolates downward and laterally through the soils and surface rocks of the continents, a complex group of reactions occurs.

The release of carbon dioxide and organic acids by bacterial processes increases the chemical reactivity of waters passing through the upper part of the soil zone. Weathering of most carbonate or silicate minerals generally involves acid attack, with carbonic acid (H_2CO_3) dominating [reactions (3) and (4)].

$$CaCO_3 + H_2CO_3 \rightarrow Ca^{2+} + 2HCO_3^- \qquad (3)$$
Calcite

$$2KAl_5Si_7O_{20}(OH)_4 + 2H_2CO_3 + 13H_2O \rightarrow$$
Illite

$$5Al_2Si_2O_5(OH)_4 + 4H_4SiO_4 + 2K^+ + 2HCO_3^- \qquad (4)$$
Kaolinite

Table 1. Chemical composition of average rainwater, river water, and seawater, in parts per million

Constituent	Average rainwater	Average river water	Seawater
Na	1.98	6.3	10,500
K	0.3	2.3	380
Mg	0.27	4.1	1,300
Ca	0.09	15.	400
Cl	3.79	7.8	19,000
SO$_4$	0.58	11.2	2,650
HCO$_3$	0.12	58.4	140
SiO$_2$	—	13.1	6
pH	5.7	—	8.2

The weathering of carbonates and silicates consumes acid and produces a soil water enriched in cations, bicarbonate, and dissolved silica (H_4SiO_4). Dis.solved sulfate is derived from dissolution of sulfate minerals and by reaction between sulfide minerals and dissolved oxygen in soil waters, as in reaction (5).

$$4FeS_2 + 15O_2 + 8H_2O \rightarrow$$

Pyrite

$$2Fe_2O_3 + 8SO_4^{2-} + 16H^+ \qquad (5)$$

Hemalite

Chloride is derived from the weathering of fluid inclusions in silicate minerals and dissolution of halite (NaCl).

The ease with which a particular element can be accommodated in soil waters depends in part on the ionic radius r and charge Z of the cation which it forms (**Fig. 2**). The ratio of Z to r is known as the ionic potential. Large cations with a small charge, such as K^+ and Ca^{2+}, are usually readily accommodated in aqueous solution. In oxidizing environments, elements which form small, highly charged cations, such as S^{6+}, combine with oxygen to form highly soluble and stable anionic complexes (for example, SO_4^{2-}). Cations of intermediate size and charge, however, including Al^{3+} and Fe^{3+}, are only sparingly soluble. These elements are usually incorporated in the solid products of weathering, for example, aluminum in kaolinite in reaction (4) and iron in hematite in reaction (5). In soil waters depleted in free oxygen, the more highly soluble, reduced form of iron, Fe^{2+}, may go into solution. Other elements may also be solublized in the absence of oxygen or in the presence of suitable complexing agents.

River water. River water represents a variable mix of subsurface waters, which enter the river at the groundwater table, and surface runoff. Some of the material in river water is derived from the dissolved sea salts and dust present in rainwater, but most has been introduced through weathering reactions. River waters are higher in bicarbonate and dissolved silica, and the relative abundance of the cations they contain reflects the lithology of the drainage basins from which they are derived (Table 1). Waters draining carbonate terranes are typically enriched in calcium and magnesium [reaction (3)].

Shale terranes, in contrast, will produce waters preferentially enriched in potassium, which is released during weathering of illite [reaction (4)]. The salinity of river waters varies from less than 40 ppm for the Amazon River, which drains a region of exceptionally high rainfall, to over 800 ppm for the Rio Grande, which drains a region of low rainfall and high evaporation. Dissolved organic material is high in tropical streams and rivers, where rates of organic production and decay are high. Organics in many rivers draining the southeastern United States exceed the concentration of dissolved inorganic salts. The composition and salinity of a given river may vary seasonally.

Rivers and streams have been used by humans since earliest history as a source of potable water, a place to discard wastes, and a vehicle for the transportation of goods. The concentrations of many metals and organic compounds deliberately or accidentally introduced as wastes now often exceed natural river levels of these materials. Humans have also introduced compounds such as chlorinated hydrocarbons, which were unknown in the natural environment.

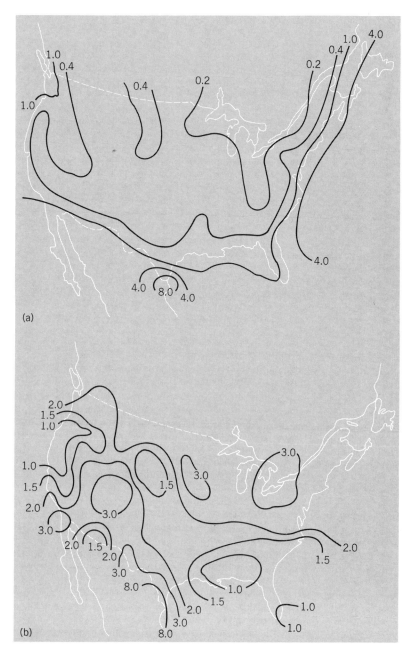

Fig. 1. Dissolved (a) sodium and (b) sulfate in rain (in parts per million) over the continental United States (*After R. M. Garrels and F. T. Mackenzie, Evolution of Sedimentary Rocks, W. W. Norton, 1971*)

Most river water eventually mixes with marine waters in coastal and estuarine areas. The concentrations of most of the major cations and anions in these zones of mixing are not affected by processes other than the physical mixing of fresh and marine waters. Such constituents are said to behave conservatively. Many minor and trace constituents, however, behave nonconservatively, and are preferentially introduced into or removed from aqueous solution by chemical or biological processes occurring in the zone of mixing. Significant quantities of barium, for example, are desorbed from river clays when these particles are transported into marine waters. Humic-metal colloids pres-

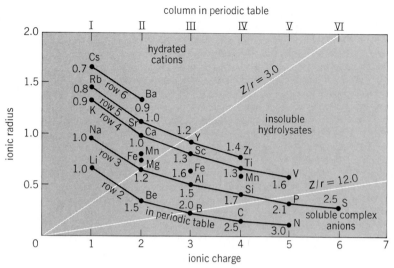

Fig. 2. Accommodation of cations in aqueous solution. (*After H. Blatt, G. Middleton, and R. Murray, Origin of Sedimentary Rocks, Prentice-Hall, 1972*)

ent in river waters are flocculated as they mix with marine waters. The removal of dissolved iron by this process has been extensively documented. Field studies have shown that silica is removed from solution in some river estuaries. However, the question of whether this removal is due to biological uptake, reaction with suspended mineral particles, or both, has not been resolved.

Seawater. The dissolved salt content of open ocean water varies between 32,000 and 37,000 ppm. This range reflects dilution of seawater by rain and concentration by evaporation. Chloride, sodium, sulfate, magnesium, calcium, and potassium ions dominate sea salt (Table 1) and, with the exception of calcium, are present in remarkably constant proportions throughout the oceans. Other elements, such as boron, bromine, and fluorine, also show a constant ratio with chloride, but the chloride ratios of many elements vary significantly.

Most variations in the composition of seawater arise from the removal of elements by organisms that are living in surface seawater and the later release of these elements by the destruction of biologically produced particles which have sunk downward into deeper waters. Exceptions to this general rule are dissolved gases, whose solubility and concentration in surface seawater increase with decreasing temperatures.

Marine plants can live only in surface seawater, where sufficient light is available for photosynthesis. These organisms give off oxygen and extract carbon dioxide and nearly all of the dissolved nitrate and phosphate from seawater to produce organic matter. Some plants, in addition, secrete solid particles of calcium carbonate ($CaCO_3$) or opaline silica ($SiO_2 \cdot nH_2O$). Marine plants are consumed by animals, some of which also extract dissolved calcium, bicarbonate, and silica to make carbonate or opaline shells or tests. During the downward rain of particles produced by plants and animals in surface waters, destruction of organic matter by bacteria and animals releases dissolved nitrogen, phosphorus, and carbon dioxide back into the water column at depth and consumes dissolved oxygen (**Fig. 3**). Ocean waters are

undersaturated with respect to opaline silica, and these particles begin to dissolve, releasing dissolved silica, after the death of their parent organism. Some particles, however, reach the sea floor to accumulate as siliceous oozes. Carbonate particles are stable in surface waters, which are supersaturated, and accumulate readily in shallower areas of the sea floor. Deeper waters are undersaturated because of increased pressure, and below depths of 4000 m (25 mi) the degree of undersaturation is such that carbonate dissolves very rapidly.

Thus, in response to biological processes, nitrogen, phosphorus, and silicon are almost totally depleted in surface waters, and marine plant life can flourish only where upwelling currents renew surface water in these biolimiting elements. Elements which show some lowering in concentration in surface waters are carbon, copper, nickel, and cadmium and the alkaline earths calcium, strontium, barium, and radium. The behavior of strontium, barium, and radium may reflect in part their coprecipitation with calcium in car-

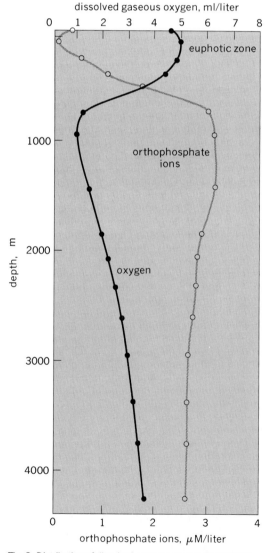

Fig. 3. Distribution of dissolved gaseous oxygen (low values) and nutrient species (high concentrations) of orthophosphate ions at 26°22.′4N and 168°57.′5W in the Pacific Ocean. 1 m = 3.3 ft.

bonate. Dissolved oxygen is unique in that it is produced at the surface and consumed at depth (Fig. 3). Analytical data for many elements are not precise enough to establish patterns of variation in their concentration.

In closed basins on the sea floor, stagnant bottom waters can become totally depleted in dissolved oxygen. In anoxic waters, anaerobic respiration reduces sulfate and forms hydrogen sulfide. Iron and manganese become more soluble and may increase in concentration, while other metals, such as copper, precipitate out as sulfides.

Mass balance. The uniform relative abundance of minerals in recent and ancient marine evaporites has been interpreted to mean that the concentrations of major constituents in seawater have rarely been more than double or less than half their present concentrations during the past 7×10^8 years. As a first approximation, the oceans have behaved as a steady-state system, with the rate of removal of a particular dissolved element being equal to its combined rate of introduction from the continents, atmosphere, and sea floor. The rate of turnover of a particular element in the oceans is reflected in its residence time, which is the average length of time an atom of the element spends in the sea between the time it is introduced and the time it is removed. Residence time may be calculated by dividing the total mass (grams) of the element in the oceans by its rate of input or, if known, rate of output (grams per year). The longest residence times, for sodium, chlorine, or bromine, are on the order of 10^8 years. The shortest residence times, for aluminum, iron, and titanium, are only 10^2 years. The age of the oceans is at least 3.5×10^9 years, and thus is significantly greater than any of these residence times. Seawater does not store indefinitely the dissolved components entering it, but is simply a temporary way station for materials passing through the hydrosphere.

In constructing a geochemical mass balance for the oceans, a reasonable estimate can be made of the rate at which material enters the oceans from the continents and atmosphere. Many of the processes by which elements are removed from seawater are also well understood. Some dissolved silica and calcium and some trace elements, for example, are permanently removed from seawater by biological precipitation of opaline silica and calcium carbonate. Nitrogen, phosphorus, and copper are directly concentrated by organisms in organic matter and can accumulate in this form in marine sediments. Much of the removal of heavy metals, however, is probably by adsorption on organic particles or mineral oxides. All dissolved components are removed to some degree when seawater becomes trapped in the pores of marine sediments during deposition.

Among the least understood processes which regulate the mass balance of the oceans are those which control the removal of elements with very long residence times, such as the major cations Na, K, and Mg. In the early 1960s, it was proposed that the composition of seawater is controlled by thermodynamic equilibrium between the atmosphere, seawater, calcium carbonate, and a suite of silicate mineral phases. This led to the further suggestion that major cations, dissolved silica, and bicarbonate are continuously removed by processes of ''reverse weathering'' in which the above components react with aluminum sil-

icate minerals, brought in as suspended load by rivers, to form illite, chlorite, and montmorillonite. Such a reaction would essentially be the reverse of reaction (4). Field and laboratory studies, however, have failed to identify reverse weathering as a significant process, and it is now believed that silicate reactions with seawater at normal marine temperatures (2–30°C or 36–86°F) are simply too slow to have a major effect on seawater composition. A more probable site for seawater-silicate interaction is thought to be the mid-ocean rise and ridge system, where high temperatures cause the convective circulation of seawater down and up through newly formed basaltic rocks. Reaction rates are rapid at elevated temperatures, and some elements, such as magnesium and alkalies, are removed from seawater, while others, such as aluminum and calcium, are introduced. These submarine processes may play a profound role in the mass balance of the oceans.

Mixing studies. Various aspects of seawater geochemistry provide a means of studying mixing processes in the oceans. The distribution of the stable isotope ^{18}O has been found to be useful in evaluating sources and degree of mixing of deep-water masses. The variations in concentration of the natural radioactive isotopes ^{14}C, ^{32}Si, ^{226}Ra, ^{228}Ra, and ^{222}Rn are used to calculate rates of vertical and lateral transport processes. The distribution of artificial radioisotopes, introduced into surface ocean waters as a result of atmospheric nuclear testing, provides a means of determining mixing processes in the upper ocean. *See* Maritime meteorology; Seawater.

As part of the International Decade of Ocean Exploration in the 1970s, the Geochemical Oceans Sections (GEOSECS) Program was created to obtain high-precision geochemical and hydrographic measurements for the study of circulation and mixing processes in the world oceans.

Surface brines. Evaporation of fresh waters flowing into closed basins on the continents typically produces alkaline brines (**Table 2**, Soap Lake). Calcium and magnesium precipitate out as insoluble carbonates or hydroxysilicates. Sodium and potassium concentrate continuously, and total carbonate and pH increase. Chemical evolution of marine waters during evaporation follows a different course. Gypsum $(CaSO_4 \cdot 2H_2O)$ is the first mineral to precipitate out during continued evaporation, followed by halite (NaCl). Reaction with carbonates to form dolomite $[CaMg(CO_3)_2]$ may remove magnesium (Table 2, Dead Sea).

Table 2. Chemical composition of some saline waters, in parts per million

Constituent	Soap Lake, Washington	Dead Sea	Subsurface brine, Louisiana
Na	12,500	39,700	63,900
K	12,500	7,590	869
Mg	23	42,430	1,070
Ca	4	17,180	9,210
Cl	4,680	219,250	124,000
SO$_4$	6,020	420	153
HCO$_3$	11,270	220	115
CO$_3$	5,130	—	—
SiO$_2$	101	—	16
pH	—	—	6.3

Subsurface waters. Marine waters trapped in the pore spaces of sediments during deposition react with the mineral and organic particles surrounding them and undergo significant changes in composition. Pore waters in organic-rich sediments are quickly depleted in dissolved oxygen, and anaerobic reduction of sulfur destroys dissolved sulfate and produces hydrogen sulfide. Anaerobic reduction of carbon dioxide in the absence of sulfate produces methane. Changes in the relative proportions of dissolved cations occur as a result of diagenetic reactions with silicate minerals. The vertical variation in concentration of dissolved species in sediment pore waters provides valuable information on the nature and rates of diagenetic reactions in fine-grained marine sediments.

With deeper burial, increases in temperature and compaction of sediment produce additional changes in subsurface water composition. Salinity usually increases with depth, and may reach values in excess of 400,000 ppm. High dissolved salt contents reflect solution of evaporites at depth or infiltration of hypersaline waters formed by evaporation in surface environments. Some increases in salinity may be due to membrane filtration. Compacted shales behave as a semipermeable membrane which allows water molecules to escape upward during burial but which retards the migration of cations and anions. The salinity of the residual pore water is thus increased. Some decreases in salinity with depth have been observed which may be due to dehydration of clay minerals at elevated temperatures.

Each sedimentary basin has its own unique suite of subsurface water compositions. As a general rule, however, subsurface waters are enriched in calcium and strontium and depleted in sodium, potassium, magnesium, and sulfate, relative to seawater-chloride ratios (Table 2). Bicarbonate decreases with depth. Some subsurface waters contain abundant dissolved hydrocarbons, introduced during thermal diagenesis of organic matter. Deep-basin waters are introduced back into surface environments by regional groundwater flow or during crustal deformation.

Some subsurface waters are capable of extracting, transporting, and precipitating significant quantities of metals. In areas of igneous activity these waters may be derived in part from magmas or from the circulation of groundwaters. Metals are leached out of the surrounding rocks or contributed by the magma and are transported in aqueous solution. Other ore-forming fluids closely resemble sedimentary brines in composition, and it seems likely that some metals can be introduced into subsurface waters during normal burial diagenesis.

Ice. Ice is a nearly pure solid, and in contrast to the solvent power of liquid water, few foreign ions can be accommodated in its lattice. Ice does contain particulate matter, however, and the change in the composition of these particles with time, as recorded in the successive layers of ice which have accumulated in the polar regions, has provided much information on the progressive input of lead and other materials into the environment by human activity. SEE SEA ICE.

Jeffrey S. Hanor

Bibliography. W. Back and R. Letolle, *Geochemistry of Groundwater*, 1982; J. I. Drever, *Geochemistry of Natural Waters*, 1982; Y. Kitano (ed.), *Geochemistry of Water*, 1975; R. Nace, *Water of the World*, U.S. Geological Survey, 1977; J. D. Riley and G. Skirrow (eds.), *Chemical Oceanography*, 2d ed., vols. 1–9, 1975–1988.

Imhoff tank

A sewage treatment tank named after its developer, Karl Imhoff. Imhoff tanks differ from septic tanks in that digestion takes place in a separate compartment from that in which settlement occurs. The tank was introduced in the United States in 1907 and was widely used as a primary treatment process and also in preceding trickling filters. Developments in mechanized equipment lessened its popularity, but it is still used as a combination unit for settling sewage and digesting sludge. SEE SEPTIC TANK; SEWAGE.

The Imhoff tank is constructed with the flowing-through chamber on top and the digestion chamber on the bottom (see **illus.**). The upper chamber is designed according to the principles of a sedimentation unit. Sludge drops to the bottom of the tank and through a slot along its length into the lower chamber. As digestion takes place, scum is formed by rising sludge in which gas is trapped. The scum chamber, or gas vent, is a third section of the tank located above the lower chamber and beside the upper chamber. As gases escape, sludge from the scum chamber returns to the lower chamber. The slot is so constructed that particles cannot rise through it. A triangle or sidewall deflector below the slot prevents vertical rising of gas-laden sludge. Sludge in the lower chamber settles to the bottom, which is in the form of one or more steep-sloped hoppers. At intervals the sludge can be withdrawn. The overall height of the tank is 30–40 ft (9–12 m), and sludge can be expelled under hydraulic pressure of the water in the upper tank. Large tanks are built with means for reversing flow in the upper chamber, thus making it possible to distribute the settled solids more evenly over the digestion chamber.

Design. Detention period in the upper chamber is usually about 2½ h. The surface settling rate is usually 600 gal/(ft^2)(day) or 24 m^3(m^2)(day). The weir overflow rate is not over 10,000 gal/ft or 125 m^3/m of weir per day. Velocity of flow is held below 1 ft/s or 0.3 m/s. Tanks are dimensioned with a length-width ratio of 5:1–3:1 and with depth to slot about equal to width. Multiple units are built rather than one large tank to carry the entire flow. Two flowing-through chambers can be placed above one digester unit. The digestion chamber is normally designed at 3–5 ft^3 (0.08–0.14 m^3) per capita of connected sewage load. When industrial wastes include large quantities of solids, additional allowance must be made. Ordinarily sludge withdrawals are scheduled twice per year. If these are to be less frequent, an increase in capacity is desirable. Some chambers have been provided with up to 6.5 ft^3 (0.18 m^3) per capita. The scum chamber should have a surface area 25–30% of the horizontal surface of the digestion chamber. Vents should be 24 in (0.6 m) wide. Top freeboard should be at least 2 ft (0.6 m) to contain rising scum. Water under pressure must be available to combat foaming and scum.

Efficiency. The efficiency of Imhoff tanks is equivalent to that of plain sedimentation tanks. Effluents are suitable for treatment on trickling filters. The sludge is dense, and when withdrawn it may have a moisture content of 90–95%. Imhoff sludge has a

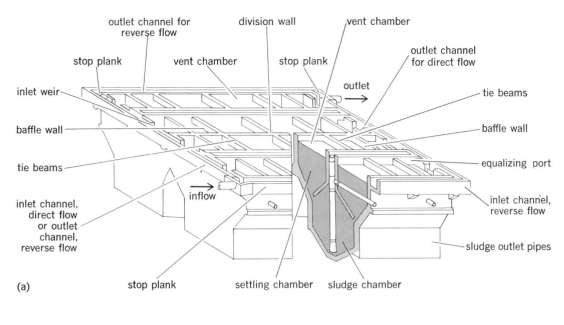

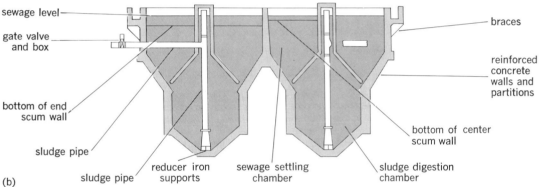

Diagram of typical large Imhoff tank for sewage treatment. (*a*) General arrangement. (*b*) Cross section. (*From H. E. Babbitt and E. R. Baumann,* Sewerage and Sewage Treatment, *8th ed., John Wiley and Sons, 1958*)

characteristic tarlike odor and a black granular appearance. It dries easily and when dry is comparatively odorless. It is an excellent humus but not a fertilizer. Gas vents sometimes give off offensive odors.

William T. Ingram

Indoor air pollution

The presence of gaseous and particulate contaminants in the indoor environment. Most pollution is due to human (anthropomorphic) sources. Natural sources do exist, including plants, animals, and other living organisms, and water sources that release various chemical aerosols. Contamination can occur from infiltration indoors of atmospheric pollutants generated outdoors, and thus the indoor environment is affected by meteorological conditions.

Contamination of the indoor air is considered to be a serious problem because of the amount of time that people spend indoors (65–95%) and the effects of indoor pollutants on humans, pets, and materials. It was not until the twentieth century that serious scientific measurements and studies of air pollution were undertaken. Later developments included investigations of indoor sources and effects. A more recent concern has been the amount of human cancer caused by toxic

material in the air from indoor (and outdoor) pollutant sources and radon. Research involving energy-saving measures, human activities, and consumer products has led to evaluation of the contribution of the indoor environment specifically, as well as of the total air pollution.

Sources. Natural sources are soils and water that release radon progeny, volatile organic compounds, fungi, and such. Chemical releases (emissions) originate from various types of appliances, combustion sources (including those in garages), building materials and water, and living organisms that release allergens (for example, dander from pets). Carbon dioxide (CO_2) is generated by combustion and living organisms. Other sources involve molds, microorganisms (such as bacteria and viruses), insects and arthropods, and pollen from outdoor and indoor plants (see **table**). Human activity has been noted to increase air contamination from all of these sources. Some pollutants are individually generated such as tobacco smoke (environmental tobacco smoke, or ETS) or are generated through use of consumer products. The chemicals in such products can be divided into inorganic and organic, and can be further classified on the basis of their thermal and hygroscopic characteristics. Particles are characterized also by functional size (usually mass-median aerodynamic diameter), den-

Major sources and types of indoor air pollutants

Sources	Pollutants
Combustion with appliances using fossil fuels or wood	Particulate matter Nitrogen oxides Carbon monoxide Carbon dioxide Lead and trace metals Hydrocarbons Volatile organic compounds
Tobacco smoking	Particulate matter Carbon monoxide Carbon dioxide Nitrogen oxides Hydrocarbons Volatile organic compounds Radon progeny
Building and furnishing materials	Hydrocarbons (especially aldehydes) Volatile organic compounds Particulate matter Radon progeny Molds and other allergens
Water reservoirs (fixtures for air conditioning, cleaning, or treating)	Molds Bacilli and other bacteria
Consumer products	Halogenated hydrocarbons Volatile organic compounds Trace metals
Animals (pets and opportunistic dwellers) and plants	Allergens Carbon dioxide
Infiltration	Particulate matter Nitrogen oxides Sulfur oxides Pollen Molds

sity, chemical identity, water content, and affinity for absorption and adsorption. The mass-median aerodynamic diameter is the measurement of size and density of particles (including viable and nonviable organic particles); it is a major characteristic of particles and determines their behavior (dispersal, deposition) and especially their likelihood of inhalation and deposition in different parts of the respiratory system. Sometimes, the gaseous pollutants are further divided into vapor and nonvapor phases and degree of volatility.

Nitrogen oxide (NO_x) pollutants can be produced as gases [nitric oxide (NO) and nitrogen dioxide (NO_2)], as particles [nitrate (NO_3^-)], or in aerosol form [such as nitrous acid (HNO_2)]. Radon progeny are more important when adsorbed on particles, as are aldehydes, other volatile organic compounds, and compounds derived from environmental tobacco smoking; all of these are normally gaseous, but all except radon progeny can occur in the form of particles.

The generation and behavior of pollutants from sources in enclosed environments are also affected by most meteorological factors. Indoor environments are often sealed to the extent that the weather is cold or hot. Infiltration of pollutants is affected also by climate, temperature, humidity, barometric pressure, and wind speed and direction. The small particles and the gases that infiltrate most, that is, NO_2 and volatile organic compounds, are affected by outdoor concentrations, tightness (being sealed, with little air ex-

change), operation of heating and cooling systems, convection currents, full growth (or lack thereof) of local trees and shrubs, and so forth. Indoor environments also possess individual characteristics of ventilation, dispersion, and deposition. Some gases, for example, sulfur dioxide (SO_2) and ozone (O_3), infiltrating the indoor environment are absorbed readily by materials and exist in high concentrations only when the outdoor concentrations are very high. Chemical-physical mass-balance models are used to estimate pollutant concentrations, as are statistical models.

Exposure assessment. Assessments of exposures provide information on the concentration and spatial-temporal distribution of each pollutant, and they are related to relevant spatial-temporal activities of the people assessed. Personal exposure factors include time spent in different indoor environments, activities and behavior, breathing rates, and so forth. These factors indicate that individuals may experience pollution levels very different from those measured at a nearby fixed monitoring station. The pollutant benzene provides a good example (**Fig. 1**). Personal exposure must also take into account the major indoor sources; an example is environmental tobacco smoke that produces particulate matter (**Fig. 2**), leading to concentrations that frequently occur in excess of ambient standards (set by law in the United States).

Biological markers or exposures to pollutants are being developed for a variety of toxic materials in the

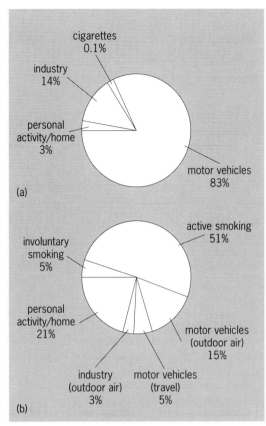

Fig. 1. Benzene as a pollutant. (a) Emissions. (b) Exposures. (*After National Research Council, Human Exposure Assessment for Airborne Pollutants, 1991*)

air. Lead (from indoors and outdoors) has well-established blood assays. These tests have indicated declines in lead in the body (at least that amount circulating in the blood) that parallel the declines in amount of lead in the atmosphere, the amount of lead in gasoline, and the amount of lead in paint and dust that were mandated by law in the United States. Cotinine, a nicotine metabolite, is the current marker used for environmental tobacco smoke.

Indoor monitoring has specific requirements related to the type of pollutants and the enclosed spaces. Monitoring protocols are developed with regard to the availability, practicality, and expense of continuous or integrated sampling methods to measure the pollutant over the time periods of interest. These monitors are either fixed or portable. Personal monitors have been developed for some pollutants. Good surrogate measurements are often utilized to represent more complex exposures (for example, total hydrocarbons for all organics).

Effects. Characterization of the effects of air pollution requires determination of concentration-exposure, exposure-dose (for humans and animals), and exposure/dose-response relationships. These studies have involved humans, animals, and materials.

Humans. Effects experienced by humans include acute and chronic symptoms (morbidity), increases in acute respiratory illness, and declines in lung function, especially in individuals with chronic diseases. There are several indoor pollutants that have similar, and possibly synergistic, effects. Particulate matter, NO_2, and formaldehyde (HCHO) produce irritation of

the eyes and mucous membranes; various types of particulate matter, HCHO, and allergens produce so-called allergic symptoms; NO_2, particulate matter, and HCHO produce changes in pulmonary function; carbon monoxide (CO), NO_2, and HCHO affect cognitive skills; CO, NO, NO_2, nitrates, and methylene chloride (CH_2Cl_2) change carboxyhemoglobin and methemoglobin levels and affect the heart and brain; and radon progeny, especially when associated with tobacco smoke, can promote lung cancer. Lead has been shown to have adverse neurological effects at the concentrations that occurred frequently in the past, especially in infants and children. Benzene has been shown to produce a form of leukemia, and both radon progeny and asbestos have been shown to produce lung cancer in humans. Other types of cancer may occur with exposure to carcinogens found in occupational settings.

Aeroallergens are of great importance, as many people have allergic problems, including asthma. It is likely that aeroallergens and interactive exposures with other pollutants can produce and aggravate these problems. Thus, a large amount of acute disability is related to exposure to indoor pollutants.

Animals. Animal studies have shown effects similar to those found in humans in regard to most of the same pollutants. These studies used mortality, lung pathology, and changes in pulmonary physiology and immunology as criteria. Animal studies of cancer have provided the evidence needed to protect humans from those carcinogens.

Materials. Air pollution produces destruction by corrosion. Economically significant damage has occurred in various metals, both ferrous (iron-based) and nonferrous (copper, silver, nickel, aluminum, and zinc). Extensive damage to rubber, paint and dyes, leather and textiles, and ceramics has been demonstrated.

Controls. For some pollutants, controls used to protect health are based on regulatory law. Control measures include removal of sources or reductions in source emissions. Unfortunately, the experience gained in developing and implementing strategies for the outdoor environment is not very applicable to indoor environments, and new strategies are needed.

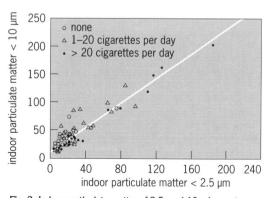

Fig. 2. Indoor particulate matter of 2.5- and 10-micrometer diameter related to the amount of environmental tobacco smoke in Tucson, Arizona. The amount of environmental tobacco smoke was estimated by the number of cigarettes per day smoked indoors. (*After J. J. Quackenboss, M. Krzyzanowski, and M. D. Lebowitz, Exposure assessment approaches to evaluate respiratory health effects of particulate matter and nitrogen dioxide, J. Expos. Anl. Environ. Epidem., 1:83–107, 1991*)

Only a few countries have regulations for indoor pollutants, specifically radon progeny, formaldehyde, and CO_2. Controls should include, where necessary, practices, labeling requirements, building codes, guidelines, and recommendations. Individuals can limit their exposures, especially in residences, by several measures, including avoidance. Governmental agencies can use public health education to help people minimize risks and promote safe indoor environments.

Source removal is the first and most logical form of control. Reductions in source emissions have been achieved for several products through changes in manufacturing process or construction. Reduction of exposure also includes standard direct methods such as ventilation and cleaning as well as good design. SEE AIR POLLUTION; AIR-POLLUTION CONTROL.

Michael D. Lebowitz

Bibliography. Environmental Protection Agency, *Introduction to Indoor Air Quality*, 1991; M. Lippmann (ed.), *Environmental Toxicants*, 1992; T. J. Kneip and J. V. Crable (eds.), *Methods for Biological Monitoring*, 1988; National Research Council, *Human Exposure Assessment for Airborne Pollutants*, 1991; National Research Council, *Indoor Pollutants*, 1981; J. J. Quackenboss, M. Krzyzanowski, and M. D. Lebowitz, Exposure assessment approaches to evaluate respiratory health effects of particulate matter and nitrogen dioxide, *J. Expos. Anl. Environ. Epidem.*, 1:83–107, 1991.

Industrial meteorology

The commercial application of weather information to the operational problems of business, industry, transportation, and agriculture in a manner intended to optimize the operation with respect to the weather factor. The weather information may consist of past weather records, contemporary weather data, predictions of anticipated weather conditions, or an understanding of physical processes which occur in the atmosphere. The operational problems are basically decisions in which weather exerts an influence.

The evolution of applied meteorology from primarily a governmental function to today's mixed economic approach has taken place largely since World War II. In that period there has been a gradual development in the application of meteorological information. Some of the applications are professional meteorologists serving television or radio stations to explain to the public the changes in weather which either have occurred or are about to occur; forecasters working with airline dispatchers to utilize optimum flight paths and to avoid equipment tie-ups during lengthy adverse weather conditions; consultants who help utilities locate future power plant sites with minimal environmental impact; forecasters who advise shipping lines regarding ocean routing paths which avoid storms and decrease by a few hours the travel time for long-distance ocean freight movement; and consultant advisories which help industrial firms in the marketing of weather-sensitive products. In many cases the need for meteorological information is sufficiently important that a complete department within the operational segment of a company is established to serve the needs of that weather-affected firm.

One specialized consulting service involves snowstorm forecasting to aid in keeping city streets, highways, and especially toll roads usable. The city administrator seeks to match the use of worker-power and equipment to the size and duration of the storm. In addition to forecasting the beginning time of the snowstorm, the consultant firm typically makes additional contacts to keep the client advised of the storm's intensity, rate of movement, and total duration. The costs of such weather advisory services are nominal compared with costs of overreacting when only light snow begins, and with street or highway blockage when a little lead time could have been used to enlist supplemental equipment or worker-power.

Several state highway departments use meteorological consulting firms in their decision-making process for segments of highway that are most critical in surface icing conditions. A corollary development has been the installation of networks of surface-temperature and low-level-wind measuring devices from which measurements are collected electronically every few minutes during sensitive storm periods.

Contract research work by professional meteorologists meets a need for intermittent special requirements of governmental agencies. Studies of this type might require the determination of atmospheric airflow frequencies related to the dispersion of air pollution throughout a broad area as it might relate to governmental regulatory policies. A distinct advantage exists when a government agency can meet a nonrecurring need with contract consulting effort.

Along with the advances of communication capacity, use of weather satellite photography, and the expanded international marketing of goods and services, consulting meteorologists within the United States have found a demand for their services among commodity-trading firms. Knowledge of recent past weather or current weather throughout the wheat-growing areas of the world is useful information to wheat users, wheat growers, and speculators in commodity futures who help establish a market value for wheat well in advance of the actual harvest.

Climatological records can be used effectively in developing statistical odds for extreme weather conditions. Climatological records also can be used for postanalyses of sales records of weather-sensitive items. For example, the sales of room air conditioners move up sharply in the months of May and June when early-season extreme hot spells occur throughout the northern areas of the United States. A series of several such hot spells will guarantee a peak sales season for all manufacturers. By contrast, a cold May and June in the same marketing areas will guarantee a carry-over of large numbers of such equipment until the next peak marketing season. Postanalyses of actual daily sequences of weather in a given season can help both the manufacturer and the marketing firms in their planning for subsequent years. An extremely cold season is not likely to be followed a year later with similar low sales.

Meteorological consulting firms range from individual consultants who operate similarly to individual consulting engineers, to large firms having nearly 100 professional meteorologists on their staff. In the United States more than 100 different firms are operational. A high fraction of these firms serve multiple clients as compared with full-time staff members within individual companies. Approximately 10% of the 8000 professional meteorologists in the United States are engaged in some facet of industrial meteorology.

Some measure of the interest in applications of meteorology is indicated by the number of industrial corporate members within the American Meteorological Society. The nearly 160 corporate members include industrial firms, equipment suppliers, utilities, and insurance companies.

Special applications of meteorological knowledge are required in the field of weather modification. Fog dispersal techniques at some commercial airports and field projects to increase winter snowpack on the western slopes of mountain barriers throughout the United States are examples of such use.

Forensic meteorology, the application of atmospheric information to legal cases, requires careful attention to postanalyses of factual information. Since accidents seldom happen in the immediate vicinity of weather observing stations, professional opinions are useful in determining the sequence of weather-affected events that are subject to litigation. Expert-witness testimony is the full-time emphasis of some meteorological consultants and a part-time effort by many consultants.

The National Weather Service recognizes the importance of the role of professional meteorologists serving industry. The Chief of Constituent Affairs and Industrial Meteorology in the National Oceanic and Atmospheric Administration (NOAA) is charged with coordinating the efforts of the governmental data collection service and the many users of such information, whether on a current basis or from the archives of weather records at the National Climatic Center. National Weather Service personnel are encouraged to recognize the needs of private professional practitioners. Industrial meteorologists represent an indispensable part in the government's effort to bring tailored meteorological service to those segments of commerce and industry affected by weather.

The development of weather sensing equipment fitted to the needs of industrial firms, particularly as related to air quality, has led to expanded use of professional personnel who install and maintain such measuring equipment. Weather equipment sales to private industrial firms now exceed sales to governmental agencies.

The location and precise timing of lightning strikes across the entire country have become available on a subscription basis via a private service company. Another private company prepares regional patterns of radar echoes that consolidate the echo patterns portrayed by several individual radar stations operated by NOAA. Several service companies collect specific sets of observed weather data to supply so-called packaged portrayals of weather information to serve many television and radio stations in their respective marketing areas.

In 1968 a nonprofit organization, the National Council of Industrial Meteorologists (NCIM), was formed to further the development and expansion of industrial meteorology.

Annual conferences on industrial meteorology are sponsored by the Committee on Industrial Meteorology of the American Meteorological Society. That society has established a program for the certification of consulting meteorologists who meet rigorous standards of knowledge, experience, and adherence to ethical practice. SEE AGRICULTURAL METEOROLOGY; WEATHER FORECASTING AND PREDICTION.

Loren W. Crow

Bibliography. AMS Bull., vol. 59, no. 8, August 1978; AMS Bull., vol. 70, March 1989; W. J. Maunder, The Value of Weather, 1971; Papers presented at Session 4 of the 56th Annual Meeting of the American Meteorological Society, Philadelphia, January 20, 1976, AMS Bull., 57(11):1318–1342, November 1976; J. A. Taylor (ed.), Weather Forecasting for Agriculture and Industry: A Symposium, 1972.

Insect control, biological

The use of parasitoids, predators, and pathogens to reduce injurious pest insect populations and consequently the damage they cause. Viruses and bacteria are the most commonly used pathogens, but fungi, protozoa, and nematodes may also be important biological control agents.

Ecological foundations. Three ecological assumptions underlie biological control. First, natural enemies are among the prime factors responsible for the regulation, or control, of pest populations. Second, the influence exerted by parasitoids, predators, and pathogens is density-dependent. Density dependence means that the killing power of the natural enemy increases as the prey or host density increases. Conversely, the mortality induced by density-dependent natural enemies decreases as host density increases. Both of these assumptions have become the subject of debate, and scientists have proposed alternative ecological assumptions that do not require density-dependent responses or stable interactions between natural enemy and prey or host. In the dominant, or classical, form of biological control the third assumption is found: when an insect species escapes into a new area without its natural enemies, it reaches outbreak levels and becomes a pest. Biological-control practitioners believe regulation can be reestablished by importing the natural enemies of the pest from its area of origin.

Classical approach. In classical biological control, all efforts are typically directed toward establishing the natural enemies that were left behind in the area of origin. Such an approach demands the verification of the area of origin, foreign exploration for natural enemies in the area of origin, importation of those natural enemies, quarantine, mass rearing, and release of the biological control agents. Quarantine procedures ensure that no natural enemy of the biological control agent selected—including a hyperparasitoid, which is a parasitoid of a parasitoid—is accidentally released. Mass rearing attempts to produce for release the largest number of vigorous and competitive biological control agents possible.

Classical biological control is by far the most frequently used form of biological control, assuming one excludes the use of resistant plant varieties as biological control. The Commonwealth Agricultural Bureau's International Institute of Biological Control has recorded 860 successful establishments of 393 species of parasitoids against 274 pest insects in 99 countries. In 216 cases, parasitoids by themselves or aided by predators achieved complete or satisfactory pest suppression, and an additional 52 cases are considered to have provided a useful reduction.

Conservation. Conservation involves manipulation of the environment in order to favor survival, reproduction, or any other aspect of the natural enemy's biology that affects its function as a biological control agent. Conservation can be undertaken regardless of whether the biological control agent is introduced or native, and generally involves tactics such as maintaining floral food sources, spraying sugar or yeast-sugar solutions for parasitoids and invertebrate predators, or providing nest boxes for vertebrate or invertebrate predators. Modification of agronomic practices or the timing of activities such as tilling or harvest residue destruction is another approach that may enhance the survival of natural enemies. For example, spraying insecticides in strips rather than across entire fields may provide an important degree of protection for natural enemies. Some natural enemies may become established but fail to spread beyond the area of release. That problem often may be solved by redistributing the biological control agent—collecting samples of the agent and releasing them at a distant, appropriate site. SEE INSECTICIDE.

Trends. Aspects of research on and application of biological control may provide new or improved approaches. Successes in the development of pesticide-resistant predatory mites suggest that the improvement of biological control agents through selection, hybridization, or genetic engineering techniques may play an important role. A major strategy for control of pest insects may involve the use of genetic engineering to introduce traits into natural enemies that enhance their performance, or mortality-causing traits of natural enemies, such as insect pathogens, into plants. Corn, tobacco, tomato, potato, and cotton have already been genetically engineered to incorporate the gene that regulates the production of the toxin normally produced by the bacterium *Bacillus thuringiensis*. Insect parasitoids and pathogens such as viruses are also the subject of genetic engineering research, which has attempted to clone and characterize the DNA encoding genes responsible for their toxicity or for characters that determine survival in the environment.

Pedro Barbosa

Bibliography. H. D. Burges, *Microbial Control of Pests and Plant Diseases 1970–1980*, 1981; H. C. Coppel and J. W. Mertins, *Biological Insect Pest Suppression*, 1977; M. A. Hoy and D. C. Herzog, *Biological Control in Agricultural IPM Systems*, 1985; G. C. Papavizas, *Biological Control in Crop Protection*, 1981; R. L. Ridgeway and S. B. Vinson, *Biological Control by Augmentation of Natural Enemies*, 1977; J. Waage and D. Greathead, *Insect Parasitoids*, 1986.

Insecticide

A material used to kill insects and related animals by disruption of vital processes through chemical action. Insecticides may be inorganic or organic chemicals. The principal source is from chemical manufacturing, although a few are derived from plants.

Insecticides are classified according to type of action as stomach poisons, contact poisons, residual poisons, systemic poisons, fumigants, repellents, attractants, insect growth regulators, or pheromones. Many act in more than one way. Stomach poisons are applied to plants so that they will be ingested as insects chew the leaves. Contact poisons are applied in a manner to contact insects directly, and are used principally to control species which obtain food by piercing leaf surfaces and withdrawing liquids. Residual insecticides are applied to surfaces so that insects touching them will pick up lethal dosages. Systemic insecticides are applied to plants or animals and are absorbed and translocated to all parts of the organisms, so that insects feeding upon them will obtain lethal doses. Fumigants are applied as gases, or in a form which will vaporize to a gas, so that they can enter the insects' respiratory systems. Repellents prevent insects from closely approaching their hosts. Attractants induce insects to come to specific locations in preference to normal food sources. Insect growth regulators are generally considered to act through disruption of biochemical systems or processes associated with growth or development, such as control of metamorphosis by the juvenile hormones, regulation of molting by the steroid molting hormones, or regulation of enzymes responsible for synthesis or deposition of chitin. Pheromones are chemicals which are emitted by one sex, usually the female, for perception by the other, and function to enhance mate location and identification; pheromones are generally highly species-specific.

Inorganic insecticides. Prior to 1945, large volumes of lead arsenate, calcium arsenate, paris green (copper acetoarsenite), sodium fluoride, and cryolite (sodium fluoaluminate) were used. The potency of arsenicals is a direct function of the percentage of metallic arsenic contained. Lead arsenate was first used in 1892 and proved effective as a stomach poison against many chewing insects. Calcium arsenate was widely used for the control of cotton pests. Paris green was one of the first stomach poisons and had its greatest utility against the Colorado potato beetle. The amount of available water-soluble arsenic governs the utility of arsenates on growing plants, because this fraction will cause foliage burn. Lead arsenate is safest in this respect, calcium arsenate is intermediate, and paris green is the most harmful. Care must be exercised in the application of these materials to food and feed crops because they are poisonous to humans and animals as well as to insects.

Sodium fluoride has been used to control chewing lice on animals and poultry, but its principal application has been for the control of household insects, especially roaches. It cannot be used on plants because of its extreme phytotoxicity. Cryolite has found some utility in the control of the Mexican bean beetle and flea beetles on vegetable crops because of its low water solubility and lack of phytotoxicity.

The use of inorganic insecticides has declined to almost nil. Domestic production of inorganic arsenicals has apparently ceased, with current uses being supplied from existing stocks and by some limited importation. Probably the largest current uses are as constituents of formulations for wood impregnation and preservation.

Synthetic organic insecticides. After 1945, with the introduction of DDT, organic insecticides began to supplant the arsenicals. There are three major classes: the organochlorines, the organophosphorus insecticides, and the carbamates.

Organochlorines. The first of the chlorinated hydrocarbons to be widely used was DDT, followed by lindane. Since 1968, however, in the United States all nongovernmental and nonprescription uses of DDT have been canceled. Coincidentally, the use of lindane has declined both through the development of resistant strains of insects and through official restriction. Over the years, other chlorinated hydrocarbon insecticides have become available, although a number of these exhibited undesirable characteristics. They include TDE, methoxychlor, Dilan, chlordane, heptachlor, telodrin, aldrin, dieldrin, endrin, toxaphenc, cndosulfone, Kepone, mirex, chlordecone, and Perthane. Registrations for some have been canceled.

The U. S. Environmental Protection Agency (EPA) monitors the risks to human health and the environment of available insecticides and issues registration specifying permitted uses. For example, registrations for all uses of TDE were canceled in 1971 because it is a metabolite of DDT. Most uses of aldrin and dieldrin were canceled by the EPA in 1975, and their legal use is limited to control of subterranean termites. Kepone and mirex were prohibited for all uses in 1976. Most uses of chlordane and heptachlor were canceled in 1978. Toxicity reviews for insecticides are scheduled as needed.

Organophosphorus insecticides. The development of this type of insecticide paralleled that of the chlorinated hydrocarbons. Since 1947, many thousands of organophosphorus compounds have been synthesized in academic and industrial laboratories throughout the world for evaluation as potential insecticides. Parathion and methyl parathion are two examples that have achieved significant use.

A great diversity of activity against insects is found among organophosphorus insecticides. It has been estimated that more than 100,000 different organophosphorus insecticides have been synthesized and evaluated. In general, they are very reactive species and thus readily degrade, having low soil persistence. Unfortunately, many can be quite poisonous to humans and other warm-blooded animals, as well as to insects. A few materials possess the desirable attribute of low mammalian toxicity, however. The gamut of available commercial products includes: azinphosmethyl, bromophos, carbophenothion, chlorpyrifos, crotoxyphos, diazinon, dichlorvos, EPN, ethion, ethoprop, fensulfothion, fonofos, malathion, methidathion, naled, phosmet, sulfotep, stirofos, sulprofos, temephos, terbufos, and trichlorfon.

Schradan was unique among organic insecticides in that it showed systemic properties when applied to plants. Its activity upon direct contact with insects was relatively low, but following spray application to plants, it was absorbed, transported, and altered chemically by enzymatic processes to one or more products which were toxic to pests, such as aphids, which suck juices from plants. Schradan was thus a selective insecticide because it killed pests which fed on fluids from treated plants but did not affect predators which lived on the surfaces and preyed only upon the pests; for example, aphids are the target pests, and ladybird beetles and their larvae which prey upon the aphids are not affected by the insecticide retained within the plant. Unfortunately, schradan was ultimately found to have environmental properties, the risks of which exceeded benefits to the extent that in 1976 all registrations for use in the United States were canceled.

The following materials which exhibit a varied spectrum in degree and breadth of activity have become available commercially for insect control through systemic action following application to plants: acephate, demeton, dimeton methyl, dicrotophos, dimefox, dimethoate, disulfoton, methamidophos, mevinphos, monocrotophos, oxydemetonmethyl, oxymeton methyl, phorate, phosalone, and phosphamidon.

Coumaphos was one of the first products to be discovered which possessed systemic properties. In addition to coumaphos and dimethoate, chemicals useful as animal systemic insecticides include: chlorofenvinphos, chlorothion, crufomate, dialiflor, diaxothion dicapthon, diphos, famphur, fenthion, fenithrothion, menazon, methamiprophos, and ronnel.

Activity of organic phosphate insecticides results from the inhibition of the enzyme cholinesterase, which performs a vital function in the transmission of impulses in the nervous system. Inhibition of some phenyl esterases occurs also. Inhibition results from direct coupling of phosphate with enzyme. Phosphorothionates are moderately active, but become exceedingly potent upon oxidation to phosphates.

Carbamates. These insecticides are relatives of the alkaloid physostigmine. Individual compounds tend to exhibit selective insecticidal activity. The first commercial carbamate insecticide, carbaryl was introduced during the mid-1950s and continues to enjoy broad use not only in the United States but worldwide. The more important products include: aminocarb, bendiocarb, bufencarb, dimetilan, dioxacarb, formetanate, methiocarb, mexacarbate, promecarb, and propoxur.

Considerable success has been achieved in discovering carbamates which exhibit systemic action when applied to plants. The more important products with this property include: aldicarb, carbofuran, methomyl, oxamyl, pirimicarb, and thiofanox.

Carbamates, like organophosphates, are cholinergic. Several not only interfere with cholinesterase, but may also inhibit one or more enzymes known as aliesterases. The binding between carbamate inhibitor and enzyme appears to be much more readily reversible than does that between enzyme and organophosphate inhibitor.

Other types of insecticides. During the mid-1960s, much interest developed in the possibilities of utilizing certain of their own secretions and hormones for control of insects. The secretions, named pheromones, are released by one sex, usually the female, and perceived by the other. All pheromones so far discovered are highly species-specific chemicals whose primary function is to facilitate mate finding and therefore maintenance and propagation of the species. Pheromones are volatile materials, and chemically are frequently unsaturated esters of low-molecular-weight acids in which the molecules tend to lie within a range of 8–20 carbon atoms. The number of unsaturations and the isomerization associated with each are largely responsible for both their specificity and the difficulty of chemical characterization. Attempts to use pheromones to control insects have so far met with limited success. A combination of pheromone and a delivery system has been registered for use against the pink bollworm in cotton. Its performance seems to indicate that the procedure offers considerable promise.

Hormones from insects have been investigated intensively and given careful consideration as potential insect control agents; examples are the molting hormone and the juvenile hormone. The molting hormone is a steroidal molecule which is generally considered too complex and costly for manufacture and use as a pesticide. The juvenile hormone, however, is a more simple aliphatic unsaturated triterpenoid methyl ester. Juvenile hormones II and III have been discovered and identified. The natural hormones have thus far not proved suitable for use in practical pest control. However, some promising synthetic derivatives of the juvenile hormones have been registered, including neotenin, R-20458, hydroprene, and methoprene.

Diflubenzuron, another chemical with a different mode of action, interferes with the action of chitin synthetase, an enzyme necessary for the synthesis of chitin, and as a consequence of that process, disrupts the orderly deposition of that vital element of the exoskeleton. It is registered for the control of the gypsy moth in hardwood forests of the eastern United States. A conditional registration was granted for the use, beginning during the 1979 season, of diflubenzuron for the control and possibly the eradication of the boll weevil from cotton in the United States.

Pyrethrum is one of the oldest insecticides. Because it is highly active and quite safe for humans and animals, extensive effort was made during the period 1910–1945 to determine its chemical structure. The analytical problem was complicated greatly because a number of active principles were ultimately found to be present. Those identified were designated pyrethrins I and II, cinerins I and II, and jasmolins I and II. Efforts began immediately after identification of these natural products to produce chemicals with modified structures through laboratory synthesis. These efforts culminated in the discovery of some of the most active insect control agents yet devised. The first product, allethrin which was only partially synthetic, was introduced commercially during the early 1950s. Subsequent, entirely synthetic products have included: dimethrin, fenothrin, resmethrin, and tetramethrin.

There are two analogs which are highly active with residues on plant surfaces showing significant degrees of persistence. Their structures differ considerably from those of the natural product. Both fenvalerate and permethrin have been granted conditional registrations in the United States for use in the control of pests of cotton.

Insecticides obtained from plants include nicotine, rotenone, pyrethrins, sabadilla, and ryanodine, some of which are the oldest known insecticides. Nicotine was used as a crude extract of tobacco as early as 1763. The alkaloid is obtained from the leaves and stems of *Nicotiana tabacum* and *N. rustica*. It has been used as a contact insecticide, fumigant, and stomach poison and is especially effective against aphids and other soft-bodied insects.

Rotenone is the most active of six related compounds found in a number of plants, including *Derris elliptica, D. malaccensis, Lonchocarpus utilis*, and *L. urucu*. *Derris* is a native of eastern Asia, and *Lonchocarpus* occurs in South America. The highest concentrations of active principles are found in the roots. Rotenone is active against a number of plant-feeding pests and has found its greatest utility where toxic residues are to be avoided. Rotenone is known also as derris or cubé.

The principal sources of pyrethrum are *Chrysanthemum cinerariaefolium* and *C. coccineum*. Pyrethrins, which are purified extracts prepared from flower petals, contain chemically different active ingredients. The pyrethrins find their greatest use in fly sprays, household insecticides, and grain protectants because they are the safest insecticidal materials available.

Synergists. These materials have little or no insecticidal activity, but increase the activity of chemicals with which they are mixed. Piperonyl butoxide, sulfoxide, MGK, propyl isomer, and sesamex are commercially available. These synergists have their greatest utility in mixtures with the pyrethrins. Some have been shown to enhance the activity of insecticides as well.

Insect resistance. The resistance of insects to DDT was first observed in 1947 in the housefly. By the end of 1967, 91 species of insects had been proved to be resistant to DDT, 135 to cyclodienes, 54 to organophosphates, and 20 to other types of insecticides, including the carbamates. By 1975, 203 species were known to be resistant to DDT, 225 to cyclodienes, 147 to organophosphates, 36 to carbamates, and 35 to other insecticides. Since numerous insects are resistant to more than one type of compound, the total number of species involved is 364 worldwide. Almost every country has reported the presence of resistant strains of the housefly.

During 1957 and 1958, many growers of cotton in the Southern states changed from toxaphene and γ-BHC to organic phosphorus chemicals because of the resistance of the cotton boll weevil to chlorinated hydrocarbon insecticides. By 1967, resistant strains of the cotton bollworm and the tobacco budworm had developed and proliferated to the extent that in numerous areas the use of chlorinated hydrocarbon insecticides was of doubtful value. During the same decade, larvae of three species of corn rootworms also developed resistance to three potent chlorinated insecticides—aldrin, dieldrin, and heptachlor—active against a wide spectrum of soil-inhabiting insects. The development of resistance to chlorinated hydrocarbon insecticides among several species of disease-transmitting mosquitoes not only continues to pose a threat to world health, but led a World Health Organization committee to report in 1976 that efforts to cope with vector-borne diseases and to eliminate malaria were being hampered most of all by problems arising from resistance to insecticides.

The need to replace the highly active chlorinated materials stimulated the development and use of organophosphorus and carbamate insecticides. Strains of several species developed which were resistant to widely used organophosphates. One of the notable examples was that of the cotton pest, *Heliothis virescens* (the tobacco budworm), and methyl parathion, for which laboratory tests showed a greater than 100-fold difference between susceptible and resistant strains. The production of cotton in parts of northeastern Mexico was practically abandoned and was seriously threatened in the lower Rio Grande Valley of Texas by the mid-1970s due to difficulties and costs of attempting to control this pest.

Certain of the synthetic pyrethroids have been shown under controlled laboratory conditions to induce the selection of resistant strains of mosquitoes. This knowledge has been obtained prior to their registration and release for large-scale commercial development. Perhaps with this forewarning, these products will be employed in the field in ways that will minimize selection for resistance and thus prolong their usefulness for insect control. The synthetic pyrethroids, like the natural pyrethrins, have a very high unit activity, but differ from the briefly lasting natural products in that they persist for moderate periods of time following application in the field. These two attributes—high activity and persistence—are important factors associated with the selection of resistant strains of insects, regardless of the chemical involved.

Formulation and application. Formulation of insecticides is extremely important in obtaining satisfactory control. Common formulations include dusts, water suspensions, emulsions, and solutions. Accessory agents, including dust carriers, solvents, emulsifiers, wetting and dispersing agents, stickers, deodorants or masking agents, synergists, and antioxidants, may be required to obtain a satisfactory product.

Insecticidal dusts and formulated for application as powders. Toxicant concentration is usually quite low. Water suspensions are usually prepared from wettable powders, which are formulated in a manner similar to dusts except that the insecticide is incorporated at a high concentration and wetting and dispersing agents are included. Emulsifiable concentrates are usually prepared by solution of the chemical in a satisfactory solvent to which an emulsifier is added. They are diluted with water prior to application. Granular formulations are an effective means of applying insecticides to the soil to control insects which feed on the subterranean parts of plants.

Proper timing of insecticide applications is important in obtaining satisfactory control. Dusts are more easily and rapidly applied than are sprays. However, results may be more erratic, and much greater attention must be paid to weather conditions than is required for sprays. Coverage of plants and insects is generally less satisfactory with dusts than with sprays. It is best to make dust applications early in the day while the plants are covered with dew, so that greater amounts of dust will adhere. If prevailing winds are too strong, a considerable proportion of dust will be lost. Spray operations will usually require the use of heavier equipment, however. Whatever the technique used, the application of insecticides should be correlated with the occurrence of the most susceptible or accessible stage in the life cycle of the pest involved. By and large, treatments should be made only when economic damage by a pest appears to be imminent.

Attention has focused sharply on the impact of the highly active synthetic insecticides upon the total environment—humans, domestic animals and fowl, soil-inhabiting microflora and microfauna, and all forms of aquatic life. Effects of these materials upon populations of beneficial insects, particularly parasites and predators of the economic species, have been critically assessed.

The study of insect control by biological means has expanded. The concepts and practices of integrated pest control and pest management involve an insect control strategy that employs ecologically based procedures which rely on multiple interventions with minimal disturbances to the ecosystem.

Among problems associated with insect control are the development of strains of insects resistant to insecticides; the assessment of the significance of small, widely distributed insecticide residues in and upon the environment; the development of better and more re-liable methods for forecasting insect outbreaks; the evolvement of control programs integrating all methods—physical, physiological, chemical, biological, and cultural—for which practicality was demonstrated; the development of equipment and procedures to detect chemicals much below the part-per-million and microgram levels. As a consequence of the provisions of the Federal Insecticide, Fungicide, and Rodenticide Act as amended by the Federal Environmental Pesticide Control Act of 1972, there have been increased efforts to obtain data delineating mammalian toxicology, persistence in the environment, and immediate chronic impact of pesticides upon nontarget invertebrate and vertebrate organisms occupying aquatic, terrestrial, and arboreal segments of the environment.

The registration of pesticides is a detailed, highly technical process. Pesticides must be selected and applied with care. Recommendations as to the product and method of choice for control of any pest problem—weed, insect, or varmint—are best obtained from county or state agricultural extension specialists. Recommendations for pest control and pesticide use can be obtained from each state agricultural experiment station office. In addition, it is necessary to read carefully and to follow explicitly the directions, restrictions, and cautions for use which are on the label attached to the product container. Insecticides are a boon to the production of food, feed, and fiber, and their use must not be abused in the home, garden, farm field, forest, or stream. *See* INSECT CONTROL, BIO-LOGICAL; PESTICIDE.

George F. Ludvik

Bibliography. A. J. Burn et al. (eds.), *Integrated Pest Management*, 1988; R. L. Caswell et al. (eds.), *Pesticide Handbook: Entoma 1981–82*, 1982; H. J. Cottrell (ed.), *Pesticides on Plant Surfaces*, 1987; D. H. Hutson and T. R. Roberts (eds.), *Insecticides*, vol. 5, 1986; *Kirk-Othmer Encyclopedia of Chemical Technology*, 3d ed., vol. 13, 1981; H. Martin and C. R. Worthing, *Pesticide Manual*, 4th ed., 1974; J. J. Menn and M. Boroza (eds.), *Insect Juvenile Hormones*, 1972; *The Merck Index*, 11th ed., 1989; C. L. Metcalf et al., *Destructive and Useful Insects*, 4th ed., 1962; R. L. Metcalf and W. Luckman, *Introduction to Pest Management*, 2d ed., 1982; R. D. O'Brien and I. Yamamoto (eds.), *Biochemical Toxicology of Insecticides*, 1970; U. S. Ramulu, *Chemistry of Insecticides and Fungicides*, 1983; H. H. Shorey and J. T. McKelvey (eds.), *Chemical Control of Insect Behavior*, 1977; T. F. Watson, L. Moore, and G. W. Ware, *Practical Insect Pest Management*, 1976; C. F. Wilkinson (ed.), *Insecticide Biochemistry and Physiology*, 1976.

Island biogeography

The distribution of animals and plants on islands. The most diverse plant and animal biotas in the world are found on islands, which are inhabited by high numbers of endemic species found nowhere else, and unique species that have frequently evolved on islands because of their isolation.

Dispersal of species. Plant species are brought to islands through various dispersal mechanisms. For example, seeds and spores can be carried by the wind, on floating and submerged vegetation and oceanic debris, and in the feathers and digestive tracts of birds that travel long distances. If these seeds or spores are able to germinate, grow, and multiply on the island, the species becomes a permanent inhabitant. *SEE PLANT GEOGRAPHY*.

The immigration of animal species to new islands is more complicated. New species of animals either reach islands as a result of chance events, such as the accidental dispersal of eggs, or they evolve over a long time from other species inhabiting the island. *SEE POPULATION DISPERSAL*.

Unique morphological traits. Both animals and plant species inhabiting islands have evolved unique morphological characteristics caused by isolation over long time periods. The best-known examples of this phenomenon are the biota of the Galápagos Islands, located off the coast of Ecuador. The characteristics exhibited by the plants and animals on these islands inspired Charles Darwin to propose his theories of evolution and natural selection. A closely related group of genera of birds living (with one exception) in the Galápagos is referred to as Darwin's finches because of the observations that Darwin first recorded regarding the morphology of their beaks and talons. These physical characteristics can today be differentiated by studying the food habits of these birds. The isolated habitats of the Galápagos Islands permitted the evolution of many different species of finches. Many other species of plants and other animals have also evolved divergent characteristics because of their isolation on this archipelago.

A wide range of morphological characteristics is found in many island biotas because of the same isolation factors that created the Galápagos biota. For example, a number of birds have evolved flightlessness after millions of years of isolation on islands. Their food and other requirements were fulfilled within the terrestial habitats on these islands, and so their ability to fly was lost. Similarly, the moas, an extinct group of birds once inhabiting New Zealand, evolved their great size range as a result of their isolation on the New Zealand archipelago.

Theory of island biogeography. A variety of habitats is found on oceanic islands, such as coral reefs, mangroves, and volcanoes. The species groups in these habitats have arisen from the interaction of a number of factors, and the theory of island biogeography has been proposed to explain the nature of these interactions.

A relation between the size of an area and the total number of plant and animal species inhabiting the area was discovered in the early twentieth century. Plant ecologists were the first to notice that a relative increase in species number correlates well with an increase in quadrat size. A short time later a similar relation between animal species number and sample size was noted. This relation was later formalized with the introduction of the species–area curve. This allometric relation demonstrated that an incremental increase in the number of species recorded in an area declines for larger areas. An increase in a larger area involves a smaller accrual of species, whereas a similar increase in the size of a smaller area involves a larger accrual.

Subsequently, a unique relationship was documented between the observed number of species and the area of an island. This empirical relation was independently verified by the model of finite species communities and is expressed by the equation $S = CA^z$, where S is the predicted number of species; C is a parameter primarily dependent upon the species diversity of the taxon being considered, the zoogeographic region, and the degree of isolation; a is the area of the island; and z, the slope of the regression line on a log S–log A plot, represents the degree of relation between species number and island area.

The theory of island biogeography is founded on this relationship. The theory presents a group of mathematical models that explain the composition, structure of, and functional processes in biotic communities on oceanic islands. It also proposes that the size and composition of island communities is determined by an equilibrium between species immigration and extinction rates.

Equilibrium model. The theory proposes that the species equilibrium number is attained on islands as a result of the interaction between the immigration of species onto islands and the extinction of species from islands. The number of species inhabiting a given island is defined by a dynamic equilibrium (see **illus.**). A number of variables influence the immigration and extinction rates in the ensemble of species on an island, with a different effect for each taxon or species. In addition, the habitats found on an island are affected by these variables in different ways. The following list describes some of these variables.

1. Islands closer to the species pool (that is, a similar species ensemble on a nearby landmass) will exhibit a reduced species–area effect (that is, the slope of the immigration curve will be increased).

2. The logarithm of the number of species decreases more rapidly with distance on small islands (that is, the extinction rate increases more rapidly with distance on small islands).

3. Clustered islands increase the slope of the immigration curve and thus increase the species equilibrium number even for distant islands.

4. The species–area effect is reduced by the presence of stepping stone islands (that is, islands between an island and the nearest species pool). The presence of stepping stone islands increases the species equilibrium number.

5. A small island with a high biotic turnover rate may exhibit extinction rates that are area-independent. In other words, an increase in area may not affect the species equilibrium number.

The processes, rates, and interactions of immigration and extinction on islands have been studied experimentally. The results suggest that the general processes that are proposed by the theory of island

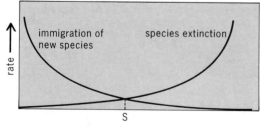

Simplified representation of the relationship of the rates of immigration and extinction processes. The number of species inhabiting an island at equilibrium (S) is located at the intersection of the two curves.

biogeography to regulate the size and composition of insular communities are appropriate, but some specific instances require significant revision.

The theory of island biogeography defines the processes influencing island species communities quantitatively, which represents the essence of the deductive modeling approach: a model is proposed that makes specific predictions about the natural world, and these predictions can be tested against empirical observations; the model can then be refined based on these observations.

Applications to nature reserves. Both theoreticians and conservationists are interested in the possible applications of island biogeographic theory to the design and management of nature reserves. Since national parks and reserves become isolated from the natural habitat by encroaching civilization, the species groups that inhabit these areas will tend to resemble natural communities that are characteristic of islands.

At least two types of isolated species ensembles can be differentiated by species–area relations: the type inhabiting an island, and the type found within a wider expanse of habitat, such as species inhabiting a patch of forest surrounded by grassland. The size and the composition of both type of species may be regulated by the same immigration and extinction processes.

Predictions of species changes in areas recently separated from surrounding natural habitat can be based on the similarity between the above two species ensembles. In nonisolated habitats, the species contained by demarcated areas contiguous with surrounding habitat represent samples from larger communities. These species ensembles are influenced by their interactions with surrounding species populations and thus cannot be characterized as self-contained. On the other hand, species ensembles in areas isolated from surrounding habitat are characterized by independence from contiguous species populations and may have developed an internal integrity lacking in the sample areas. For this reason, a greater species–area relation is observed in the isolated areas; that is, fewer species can maintain viable populations over extended time periods in these areas. Fewer species are found in insular areas than in·sample areas of equal size, and therefore species ensembles in isolated areas are comparatively depauperate.

The encroachment of human civilization will eventually isolate nature reserves and national parks from the surrounding natural habitat. As nature reserves and national parks change from sample areas to islands, their natural communities can be expected to resemble island communities. Since sample continental areas generally contain more species per unit area than islands, newly created reserves might be considered to be supersaturated with species, and the transformation process of reserves to islands may result in species extirpation, that is, the loss of a species from a specific geographic area. (Extirpation differs from extinction in that the latter refers to the loss of a species from the entire planet.) As a reserve becomes more isolated from the surrounding natural habitat, the species ensemble will be slowly reduced and eventually achieve a lower number of species appropriate to the more insular condition. Thus a reduction in species numbers, predicated on a changing species–area relation, is predicted to occur in isolated reserves.

Considerable debate has focused on design and management guidelines for natural reserves based on the species–area relationship and island biogeographic theory. SEE BIOGEOGRAPHY; ECOLOGICAL COMMUNITIES; ECOSYSTEM.

However, theory development and refinement is providing valuable insight into some of the important criteria necessary for the preservation of communities within reserves.

Ronald Miller

Bibliography. R. I. Bowman et al. (eds.), *Patterns of Evolution in Galápagos Organisms*, 1983; S. Carlquist, *Island Biology*, 1974; E. F. Connor and E. O. McCoy, The statistics and biology of the species–area relationship, *Amer. Natural.*, 113:791–833, 1979; R. H. MacArthur and E. O. Wilson, *The Theory of Island Biogeography*, 1967; R. Ornduff, *Islands on Islands*, 1987; F. W. Preston, The canonical distribution of commonness and rarity, pts. 1 and 2, *Ecology*, 43:185–215, 410–432, 1962; M. E. Soule and D. S. Simberloff, What do genetics and ecology tell us about the design of nature reserves?, *Biol. Conserv.*, 35:19–40, 1986; M. Williamson, *Island populations*, 1981.

Jet stream

A relatively narrow, fast-moving wind current flanked by more slowly moving currents. Jet streams are observed principally in the zone of prevailing westerlies above the lower troposphere and in most cases reach maximum intensity, with regard both to speed and to concentration, near the tropopause. At a given time, the position and intensity of the jet stream may significantly influence aircraft operations because of the great speed of the wind at the jet core and the rapid spatial variation of wind speed in its vicinity. Lying in the zone of maximum temperature contrast between cold air masses to the north and warm air masses to the south, the position of the jet stream on a given day usually coincides in part with the regions of greatest storminess in the lower troposphere, though portions of the jet stream occur over regions which are entirely devoid of cloud. The jet stream is often called the polar jet, because of the importance of cold, polar air. The subtropical jet is not associated with surface temperature contrasts, like the polar jet. Maxima in wind speed within the jet stream are called jet streaks.

Characteristics. The specific characteristics of the jet stream depend upon whether the reference is to a single instantaneous flow pattern or to an averaged circulation pattern, such as one averaged with respect to time, or averaged with respect both to time and to longitude.

If the winter circulation pattern on the Northern Hemisphere is averaged with respect to both time and longitude, a westerly jet stream is found at an elevation of about 8 mi (13 km) near latitude (lat) 25°. The speed of the averaged wind at the jet core is about 80 knots (148 km/h). In summer the jet is displaced poleward to a position near lat 41°. It is found at an elevation of about 7 mi (12 km) with a maximum speed of about 30 knots (56 km/h). In both summer and winter a speed equal to one-half the peak value is found approximately 15° of latitude south, 20° of latitude north, 3–6 mi (5–10 km) above, and

3–6 mi (5–10 km) below the location of the jet core itself.

If the winter circulation is averaged only with respect to time, it is found that both the intensity and the latitude of the westerly jet stream vary from one sector of the Northern Hemisphere to another. The most intense portion, with a maximum speed of about 100 knots (185 km/h), lies over the extreme western portion of the North Pacific Ocean at about lat 22°. Lesser maxima of about 85 knots (157 km/h) are found at lat 35° over the east coast of North America, and at lat 21° over the eastern Sahara and over the Arabian Sea. In summer, maxima are found at lat 46° over the Great Lakes region, at lat 40° over the western Mediterranean Sea, and at lat 35° over the central North Pacific Ocean. Peak speeds in these regions range between 40 and 45 knots (74 and 83 km/h). The degree of concentration of these jet streams, as measured by the distance from the core to the position at which the speed is one-half the core speed, is only slightly greater than the degree of concentration of the jet stream averaged with respect to time and longitude. At both seasons at all longitudes the elevation of these jet streams varies between 6.5 and 8.5 mi (11 and 14 km).

Variations. On individual days there is a considerable latitudinal variability of the jet stream, particularly in the western North American and western European sectors. It is principally for this reason that the time-averaged jet stream is not well defined in these regions. There is also a great day-to-day variability in the intensity of the jet stream throughout the hemisphere. On a given winter day, speeds in the jet core may exceed 200 knots (370 km/h) for a distance of several hundred miles along the direction of the wind. Lateral wind shears in the direction normal to the jet stream frequently attain values as high as 100 knots per 300 nautical miles (185 km/h per 556 km) to the right of the direction of the jet stream current and as high as 100 knots per 100 nautical miles (185 km/h per 185 km) to the left. Vertical shears below and above the jet core as often as large as 20 knots per 1000 ft (37 km/h per 305 m). Daily jet streams are predominantly westerly, but northerly, southerly, and even easterly jet streams may occur in middle or high latitudes when ridges and troughs in the normal westerly current are particularly pronounced or when unusually intense cyclones and anticyclones occur at upper levels.

Insufficiency of data on the Southern Hemisphere precludes a detailed description of the jet stream, but it appears that the major characteristics resemble quite closely those of the jet stream on the Northern Hemisphere. The day-to-day variability of the jet stream, however, appears to be less on the Southern Hemisphere.

It appears that an intense jet stream occurs at high latitudes on both hemispheres in the winter stratosphere at elevations above 12 mi (20 km). The data available, however, are insufficient to permit the precise location or detailed description of this phenomenon. SEE AIR MASS; ATMOSPHERE; STORM.

Frederick Sanders; Howard B. Bluestein

Lake

An inland body of water, small to moderately large in size, with its surface exposed to the atmosphere. Most lakes fill depressions below the zone of saturation in the surrounding soil and rock materials. Generically speaking, all bodies of water of this type are lakes, although small lakes usually are called ponds, tarns (in mountains), and less frequently pools or meres. The great majority of lakes have a surface area of less than 100 mi² (259 km²). More than 30 well-known lakes, however, exceed 1500 mi² (3885 km²) in extent, and the largest fresh-water body, Lake Superior, North America, covers 31,180 mi² (80,756 km²; see **table**).

Most lakes are relatively shallow features of the Earth's surface. Even some of the largest lakes have maximum depths of less than 100 ft (30 m; Winnipeg, Canada; Balkash, Soviet Union; Albert, Uganda). A few, however, have maximum depths which approach those of some seas. Lake Baikal in the Soviet Union is about a mile (1.6 km) deep at its deepest point, and Lake Tanganyika, Africa, is approximately 0.9 mi (1.45 km).

Because of their shallowness, lakes in general may be considered evanescent features of the Earth's surface, with a relatively short life in geological time. Every lake basin forms a bed onto which the sediment carried by inflowing streams is deposited. As the sediment accumulates, the storage capacity of the basin is reduced, vegetation encroaches upon the shallow margins, and eventually the lake may disappear. Most lakes also have surface outlets. Except at elevations very near sea level, a stream which flows from such an outlet gradually cuts through the barrier forming the lake basin. As the level of the outlet is lowered, the capacity of the basin is also reduced and the disappearance of the lake assured.

Variations in water character. Lakes differ as to the salt content of the water and as to whether they are intermittent or permanent. Most lakes are composed of fresh water, but some are more salty than the oceans. Generally speaking, a number of water bodies which are called seas are actually salt lakes; examples are the Dead, Caspian, and Aral seas. All salt lakes are found under desert or semiarid climates, where the rate of evaporation is high enough to prevent an outflow and therefore a discharge of salts into the sea. Many lesser arid-region lakes are intermittent, sometimes existing only for a short period after heavy rains and disappearing under intense evaporation. These lakes are called playas in North America, shotts in North Africa, and other names elsewhere. In such regions the surface area and volume of permanent lakes may differ enormously from wet to dry season.

The water of the more permanent salt lakes differs greatly in the degree of salinity and the type of salts dissolved. Compared to typical ocean water (approximately 35 parts per thousand, symbolized ‰), some salt lakes are very salty. Great Salt Lake water has a dissolved solids content about four times that of seawater (150‰) and the Dead Sea about seven times (246‰). Some of the larger salt lakes have a much lower dissolved solids content, as the Aral Sea (11‰) and the Caspian Sea 6‰). The composition of salts depends in part on the geological character of the drainage area discharging into the lake, in part on the age of the lake, and in part on the excess of evaporation over inflow. As saturation is approached, the salts common in surface waters are precipitated in such an order that magnesium chloride and calcium chloride remain in solution after other salts have precipitated.

Dimensions of some major lakes

Lake	Area mi²*	Volume (approx.), 1000 acre-ft†	Shoreline, mi‡	Depth Av. ft§	Depth Max. ft§
Caspian Sea	169,300	71,300	3,730	675	3,080
Superior	31,180	9,700	1,860	475	1,000
Victoria	26,200	2,180	2,130		
Aral Sea	26,233¶	775			
Huron	23,010	3,720	1,680		
Michigan	22,400	4,660			870
Baikal	13,300¶	18,700		2,300	5,000
Tanganyika	12,700	8,100			4,700
Great Bear	11,490¶		1,300		
Great Slave	11,170¶		1,365		
Nyasa	11,000	6,800		900	2,310
Erie	9,940	436			
Winnipeg	9,390¶		1,180		
Ontario	7,540	1,390			
Balkash	7,115				
Ladoga	7,000	745			
Chad	6,500¶				
Maracaibo	4,000¶				
Eyre	3,700¶				
Onega	3,764	264			
Rudolf	3,475¶				
Nicaragua	3,089	87			
Athabaska	3,085				
Titicaca	3,200	575			
Reindeer	2,445				

*1 mi² = 2.6 km².   †1000 acre-ft = 1.2 × 10⁶ m³.   ‡1 mi = 1.6 km.   §1 ft = 0.3 m.   ¶Area fluctuates.

Lakes with fresh waters also differ greatly in the composition of their waters. Because of the balance between inflow and outflow, fresh lake water composition tends to assume the composite dissolved solids characteristics of the waters of the inflowing streams—with the lake's age having very little influence. Lakes with a sluggish inflow, particularly where inflowing waters have much contact with marginal vegetation, tend to have waters with high organic content. This may be observed in small lakes or ponds in a region where drainage moves through a topography of glacial moraines. Lakes formed within drainage areas having a crystalline, metamorphic, or volcanic country rock tend to have low dissolved solids content. Thus Lake Superior, with its major drainage from the Laurentian Shield, has a dissolved solids content of 0.05‰. The water of Grimsel Lake in the high Alps, Switzerland, has a dissolved solids content of only 0.0085‰. Lakes within limestone or dolomitic drainage areas have a pronounced calcium carbonate and magnesium carbonate content. As in all surface water, dissolved gases, notably oxygen, also are present in lake waters. Under a few special situations, as crater lakes in volcanic areas, sulfur or other gases may be present in lake water, influencing color, taste, and chemical reaction of the water. SEE FRESH-WATER ECOSYSTEM; HYDROSPHERE; MEROMICTIC LAKE.

Basin and regional factors. Most lakes are natural, and a large proportion of them lie in depressions of glacial origin. Thus alpine locations and regions with ground moraine or glacially eroded exposures are the sites of many of the world's lakes. The lakes of Switzerland, Minnesota, and Finland are illustrations of these types.

Lakes may be formed in depressions of differing glacial origin: (1) terrain eroded by continental glaciers, with the surface differentially deepened by ice abrasion of rocks of varying hardness and resistance;
(2) valleys eroded differentially by valley glaciers; (3) cirques (glacially eroded valley heads in mountains); (4) lateral moraine barriers; (5) frontal moraine barriers; (6) valley glacier barriers; (7) irregularities in the deposition of glacial drift or ground moraine.

Lakes are particularly important surface features in the peneplaned ancient rocks of the Laurentian Shield and on the Fennoscandian Shield of northern Europe. The lake region of northern North America, which centers on the Laurentian Shield, probably has one-fifth to one-quarter of its surface in lake. Many streams in these areas are interrupted over more than half their total length by lakes. Lakes on the shields as a rule are island-studded and have extremely irregular outlines. The most permanent lakes lie on the shields themselves. Many such lakes on recently ice-scoured shields have fresh hard-rock rims with high resistance to erosion at their outlets. Because of generally low stream gradients and little sediment carried, the abrading and depositing stream actions are slow. As a result, the life of all but the small lakes in these areas probably will be measured in terms of a whole geologic period.

Some lakes in glacially formed depressions, as well as in other basins, may be considered barrier lakes. These glacial lakes are formed on glacial drift behind lateral or frontal moraine barriers. In addition, depressions of sufficient depth to contain a lake may be formed by (1) sediment deposited by streams (alluvium), and also stream-borne vegetative debris, such as tree dams on the distributaries and braided river courses of the lower Mississippi Valley; (2) landslides in mountainous areas; (3) sand dunes; (4) storm beaches and current-borne sediments along the shores of large bodies of water; (5) lava flows; (6) artificial barriers.

A large percentage of lakes is found in either the

glacially formed or barrier-formed depressions. However, a few other types of depressions contain lakes: (1) craters of inactive volcanoes, or calderas (Crater Lake in Oregon is a famous example); (2) depressions of tectonic or structural origin (Great Rift Valley of Africa includes Lake Albert, Lake Tanganyika, and Lake Nyasa); (3) solution cavities in limestone country rock; (4) shallow depressions that cause a dotting of lakes in many parts of the tundra of high latitudes.

Conservation and economic aspects. Lakes created behind manmade barriers are becoming common features and serve multiple purposes. Examples are Lake Mead behind Hoover Dam on the Colorado River, Lake Roosevelt behind Grand Coulee Dam on the Columbia, Kentucky Lake and other lakes of the Tennessee Valley, and Lake Tsimlyanskaya on the Don.

Both natural and constructed lakes are economically significant for their storage of water, regulation of stream flow, adaptability to navigation, and recreational attractiveness. A few salt lakes are significant sources of minerals. Recreational utility, long important in the alpine region of Europe and in Japan, is now a major economic attribute of many American lakes. Economic value is generally increased by location near substantial human settlement. Most of the world's lakes, however, are located in regions where they have only minor economic significance at present. *See* Eutrophication.

Edward A. Ackerman

Bibliography. W. C. Ackermann et al. (eds.), *Man-Made Lakes: Their Problems and Environmental Effects*, 1973; G. W. Bennet, *Management of Lakes and Ponds*, 2d ed., 1970, reprint 1983; S. R. Carpenter (ed.), *Complex Interactions in Lake Communities*, 1988; A. Lerman et al. (eds.), *Lakes: Chemistry, Geology, Physics*, 1978; W. Stumm (ed.), *Chemical Processes in Lakes*, 1985.

Land drainage (agriculture)

The removal of water from the surface of the land and the control of the shallow groundwater table improves the soil as a medium for plant growth. The sources of excess water may be precipitation, snowmelt, irrigation water, overland flow or underground seepage from adjacent areas, artesian flow from deep aquifers, floodwater from channels, or water applied for such special purposes as leaching salts from the soil or for achieving temperature control.

The purpose of agricultural drainage can be summed up as the improvement of soil water conditions to enhance agricultural use of the land. Such enhancement may come about by direct effects on crop growth, by improving the efficiency of farming operations or, under irrigated conditions, by maintaining or establishing a favorable salt regime. Drainage systems are engineering structures that remove water according to the principles of soil physics and hydraulics. The consequences of drainage, however, may also include a change in the quality of the drainage water.

Agricultural drainage is divided into two broad classes: surface and subsurface. Some installations serve both purposes.

Surface drainage. Poor surface drainage conditions exist over large areas of land in the eastern half of the United States and Canada. The condition is caused by the inability of excessive rainfall to move over the ground surface to an outlet or through the soil to a subsurface drainage system. These poor surface drainage conditions are usually associated with soils that have low hydraulic conductivity. Often the soils are very shallow over a barrier such as rock or a very dense clay pan. The impermeable subsoil prevents the water from moving downward and prevents the proper functioning of a subsurface drainage system. Often the land slope is not sufficient to permit the water to flow across the ground surface. In other cases, the areas lack adequate drainage outlets. In order to correct this problem, something must be done to eliminate the depressions and to provide sufficient slope for overland flow. In addition, it is necessary to provide channels to convey the water from the affected area.

The practice of surface drainage may be defined as the diversion or orderly removal of excess water from the land surface by means of improved natural or constructed channels. The channels may have to be supplemented by shaping and grading the land surface so that the water may flow freely into the channel.

In some instances, a subsurface drainage system of pipes is needed in conjunction with surface drains. The effectiveness of the subsurface drains is increased by the removal of the water from the soil surface. As soon as the surface water is removed, the drain pipes can act to lower the water table and to provide a satisfactory environment for the growth of plants. There are essentially five types of surface field drainage systems in common use today: bedding system (**Fig. 1**); random ditch system; interception system; diversion ditch system; and field ditch system. Combinations of two or more systems may be required by circumstances encountered in the field. The choice of a particular system used for surface drainage depends upon the soil type, topography, crops to be grown, and farmer preference.

Subsurface drainage in humid regions. Subsurface drainage is required where a high water table is present. The main purpose of the drainage is to provide a root environment that is suitable for the maximum growth of plants and to sustain yields over long periods of time. One of the main reasons that poor drainage causes a decrease in crop production is the fact that the plant roots have only a limited amount of soil in which to grow. Not only do the plants lack food, but the plant roots suffer from a deficiency of oxygen which is needed for the respiratory processes, as the water that fills the soil pores displaces the air in the soil. Moreover, the water obstructs the gases which are given off by the roots, and some of these gases inhibit plant growth.

The critical need for drainage occurs in the early spring months when the plants are germinating. Lack of drainage retards the normal rise in the soil temperature, decreases plant resistance to disease, and inhibits root development. Poor drainage discourages the growth of aerobic bacteria which are needed to supply nitrogen for crops. Toxic organic and inorganic compounds develop in saturated soils.

The depth of drains in humid regions is largely determined by soil conditions. Drain depths from 24 to 48 in. (60 to 120 cm) are commonly used to control a shallow groundwater table. The spacing of the drains depends upon the soil hydraulic conductivity and the amount of the rainfall that must be removed.

The spacings vary between 33 and 100 ft (10 and 30 m).

A number of drain spacing formulas have been proposed and one of the most successful is S. B. Hooghoudt's formula, Eq. (1), where L = drain spacing

$$L^2 = \frac{4K}{v}(H^2 + 2dH) \qquad (1)$$

(meters), K = hydraulic conductivity (meters/day), v = drainage coefficient, which is the rate of removal

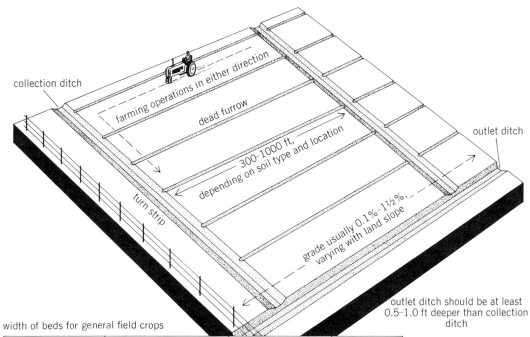

width of beds for general field crops

degree of internal drainage of the soil	width of bed in feet, center to center of dead furrows	number of 3½-ft corn rows with 2 ft. allowed per dead furrow	number of rounds using 2-14 in. plows
very slow	23	6	5
	30	8	6½
	37	10	8
slow	44	12	9½
	51	14	11
fair	58	16	12½
	65	18	14
	72	20	15½
	79	22	17
	86	24	18½
	93	26	20

cross section at end of field showing collection ditch and turn strip

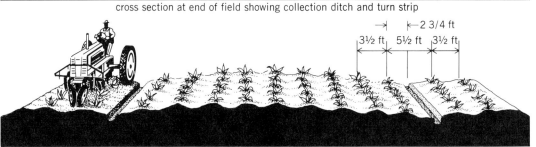

cross section of bed showing crown effect and proper pacing of corn rows

Fig. 1. Surface drainage bedding system. 1 in. = 25 mm; 1 ft = 0.3 m; 1 ft² = 0.09 m². (*USDA*)

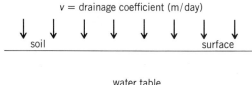

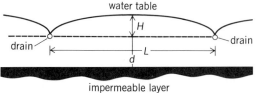

Fig. 2. Hooghoudt's drain spacing formula. Symbols are explained in the text.

of water from the soil that is necessary to protect the crop from damage (meters/day), H = height of water table above the plant through drains (meters), d = distance from the plane through drains to the impermeable layer. Developed for the drainage of land in the Netherlands, the formula is based upon steady-state replenishment of the groundwater. The height of the water table halfway between the drains is calculated as a function of the soil hydraulic conductivity and the rate at which water replenished the groundwater table. The significance of the various parameters involved in the formula are presented in **Fig. 2**.

Drainage coefficients are of the order of 5–10 mm/day in Europe. Somewhat higher values (1–4 cm/day) are used in the United States.

Subsurface drainage in arid regions. Irrigation waters contain substantial quantities of salt, from 6 to 240 lb per 1000 ft³ (0.1 to 4 metric tons per 1000 m³). Irrigation water is applied at rates of 140,000 to 210,000 ft³ per acre per year (10,000 to 15,000 m³ per hectare per year) and hence between 0.05 to 26 tons is added to each acre annually (0.1 to 60 metric tons per hectare). Some of the applied salt precipitates in the soil; a small proportion is used by the plants, and the remainder of the salt must be removed from

the soil by adding an amount of irrigation water in excess of the crop needs.

The output of salt in the drainage water must equal the input of salt in the irrigation water. If precipitation of salts in the soil and plant uptake of salts are ignored, it can be stated that salt input equals salt output.

The leaching requirement (LR) is defined as the fraction of irrigation water that must be drained in order to maintain the salt balance, as in Eq. (2),

$$\text{LR} = \frac{v}{I} \qquad (2)$$

where v represents the drainage coefficient and I the amount of applied irrigation water. The computation of v depends on the salt tolerance of the crop to be grown.

In arid regions, it is necessary to control the groundwater table well below the plant root zone. The plants will extract water from the soil, leaving salt behind. This results in a concentration of salts in the plant root zone; therefore, the water table must be maintained well below the plant root zone so that capillary rise of this salty groundwater into the plant root zone is reduced. The depth of the drains then is determined by capillary rise into the plant root zone. Normally drains in irrigated areas are placed about 6 ft (1.8 m) deep. The spacing between the drains may be determined by Hooghoudt's formula. However, the drainage coefficient is determined by a consideration of the leaching requirement, precipitation of salts in soil from irrigation water, amount of leaching due to winter rainfall, and salt tolerance of crops. Typical drain spacings range from 66 to 330 ft or 20 to 100 m (**Fig. 3**).

In addition to the steady-state formula of Hooghoudt, analyses have been made of the transient water table situation. The U.S. Bureau of Reclamation utilizes this transient water table formula for determining the average depth of water table during the growing season. If according to the bureau's method of anal-

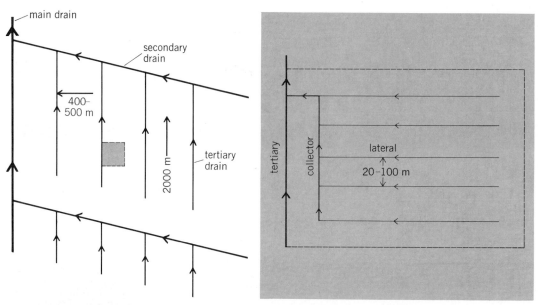

Fig. 3. Typical drainage system for an irrigation project. Shaded box on left is shown in detail on right. 1 m = 3.3 ft.

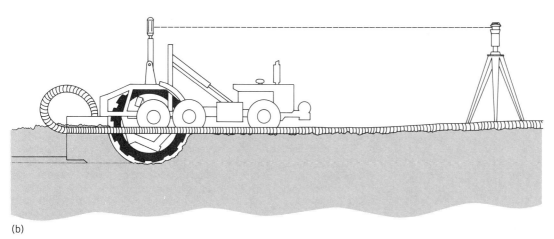

(b)

Fig. 4. Grade control by laser beam.

ysis the water table is rising during the growing season, and continues to rise, the condition indicates a serious drainage problem will occur. The bureau's drainage criteria then are based upon controlling the water table so that it either remains constant or declines over a period. The procedure is called the dynamic equilibrium method.

Construction of drains. The construction of subsurface drains was revolutionized in the years 1976–1979. In the past, a variety of materials such as rocks, clay pipe, concrete pipe, and other materials were used for subsurface drains. With the invention of machines that make perforated corrugated plastic pipe, this pipe largely supplanted the other materials. Corrugated plastic pipe has the advantage of light weight, and it comes in long lengths so the cost of handling is reduced.

Drain pipes either are laid in the bottom of a trench or are pulled into place by a drain plow. The development of laser beams for grade control permits the use of drain plows (called the trenchless method) for installing corrugated plastic tubing (**Fig. 4**).

In unstable soils usually found in arid regions, it is necessary to surround the drain pipe with gravel, sand, synthetic fibers, or organic material in order to prevent fine sands and silts from entering the pipe with the drainage water.

J. N. Luthin

Bibliography. G. R. Bumli (ed.), *Principles of Project Formulation for Irrigation and Drainage Projects*, 1982; E. G. Kruse and C. R. Burdick (eds.), *Environmentally Sound Water and Soil Management*, 1982; J. N. Luthin (ed.), *Drainage Engineering*, rev. ed., 1978; J. Van Schilfgaarde (ed.), *Drainage for Agriculture*, 1974.

Land reclamation

The process by which seriously disturbed land surfaces are stabilized against the hazards of water and wind erosion. A permanent vegetative cover usually provides the most economical means for stabilization. All seriously disturbed land areas are in need of reclamation and should be stabilized and reclaimed as quickly as possible after disturbance. In the United States alone, about 179,200 acres (80,000 hectares) per year are disturbed. Disturbance comes from major construction projects such as interstate highway systems, shopping centers, and housing developments, and from surface mining operations for coal, stone, gravel, gold, phosphate, iron, uranium, and clay. Surface mining for coal is responsible for almost one-half of the total land area disturbed in the United States, another one-fourth is from sand and gravel, and the remainder is from mining of other materials and construction. *SEE EROSION.*

Surface coal mining. During the 1970s and early 1980s, the recovery of coal by surface mining increased dramatically because of reduced cost, safer mining conditions than for deep mining, and the increased emphasis on coal as an energy source. Coal deposits are found in most major countries; approximately 33% of the total world coal reserves is found in the United States, with 37 of the 50 states having known coal deposits, and 13% of the total land area in the United States being underlined by coal (see **illus**.). The amount of these reserves recoverable by surface mining is not known since mining technology is rapidly changing and overburden removal is basically a question of economics.

The coal required to meet the needs of power production cannot be supplied from deep mining. This means that to continue meeting the power requirements demanded by the public, thousands of acres will be added annually to those already disturbed. Federal and state laws require that coal exploration and surface coal mining and reclamation operations be conducted in manners that are compatible with the environment and the economic and social needs of each state. The laws also require that reclamation efforts, including but not limited to back filling, grading, top soil replacement, and revegetation of all land disturbed by surface mining activities, shall occur as contemporaneously as practicable with mining operations. Regulations require immediate precautionary measures to be taken to stabilize these severely disturbed areas to avoid serious pollution of the environment.

Surface mining does create many environmental problems. The chemical and physical properties of the resulting spoil is drastically changed and can create a hostile environment for seed germination and subsequent plant growth. However, many of these environmental problems can be overcome or eliminated by proper planning prior to mining and by proper re-

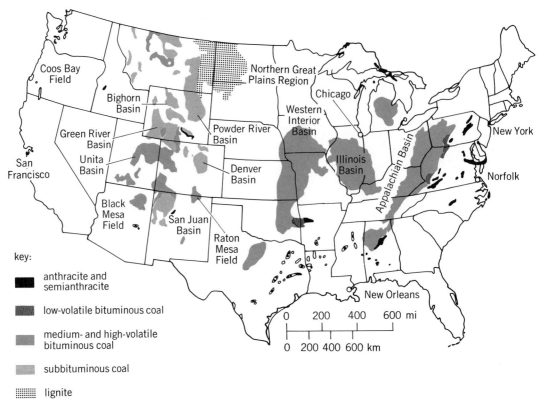

Coal fields of the conterminous United States. (U.S. Department of the Interior, Geological Survey)

moval and replacement of overburden material during mining operations. Federal and state laws further provide for the control of overland water flow by requiring the construction of temporary diversions as well as permanent diversions to handle peak water flow as needed in order to safeguard surrounding areas from environmental damage. Even with the best mining practices, vegetative cover must be established almost immediately, or the denuded areas will be subject to both wind and water erosion that will pollute surrounding streams with sediment. *See Surface mining*.

Humid regions. Coal is surface-mined on land with topography ranging from gentle slopes to rugged mountain terrain. Surface-mined areas in the Appalachian Region sometimes are highly variable, with the chemical and physical properties of spoil material being dramatically different within a few feet. Vegetative cover can be established easily on some areas, but other areas exhibit extremely hostile environments for germinations and seedling growth. Before any intelligent attempt can be made to revegetate these areas, the chemical and physical problems must be identified and corrected.

In most cases, the spoil material is a conglomerate of rock fragments of various sizes mixed with a small amount of soil. The spoil materials may vary in color from very light to almost black. Because of these color differences alone, temperature and soil moisture may constitute serious problems. Temperature variations created by slope and aspect require use of specific plant species. Mulching is usually essential for germination and seedling establishment. Some spoils are almost sterile and usually require applications of many of the nutrient elements necessary for plant growth. Nitrogen, phosphorus, potassium, calcium,

and magnesium deficiencies are major problems on some spoils in the eastern United States, while in other spoils some plant nutrients may be more abundant after mining than before because of weathering of rocks and minerals brought to the surface. Chemical constraints for reclamation in humid areas are low fertility, low pH or high acidity, and toxic concentrations of elements such as aluminum, manganese, and iron. *See Soil chemistry*.

Arid regions. Under arid conditions of the western United States, excessive amounts of sodium and other elements may constitute serious reclamation problems. High-spodic spoils may require applications of surface soil before good vegetative growth can be accomplished. Under arid and semiarid conditions, lack of plant-available soil water is a factor that ultimately limits plant growth on reclaimed land, just as on unmined land. Practices that increase infiltration, reduce evaporation, and increase potential plant growth generally improve the effectiveness of water conservation and use. Environmental problems of major concern under western arid conditions include salinity levels, exchangeable sodium content, nutrient deficiencies (nitrogen and phosphorus), plant toxicities (magnesium, boron, molybdenum), soil compaction, and steepness of slope.

Alpine and arctic areas. Reclamation and rehabilitation of disturbed land areas in alpine and arctic regions constitute a special problem. These areas are found mainly at high elevations in the western states and the Alaskan arctic tundra area. Examples of land disturbance in arctic and alpine areas involve the Alaskan pipeline and discoveries of large deposits of minerals at high elevations in some of the western states, such as the alpine tundra of the Beartooth

Mountain of Montana where chromium and platinum are being surface-mined. Disturbance in the Alaskan areas will continue at an accelerated rate with the advanced drilling technology for gas and oil reserves in the region.

Rehabilitation of these areas is complicated by the short growing season for plants, infertile soils, and the rigorous environments. Use of adapted plant species and better techniques for seeding disturbed areas have shown promise for reclamation in alpine areas. Special research with plant successions and colonization has identified some of the important native species and ecotypes adapted for survival and growth on the modified sites. Some of the greatest problems encountered in reclamation are on areas where total loss of soil has exposed acid-producing pyrites and high concentrations of toxic metals. In some cases, reclamation is aggravated by high winds that remove the exposed soil and sweep away insulating materials, such as snow. *SEE TUNDRA.*

Topsoil replacement. In 1977 the U.S. Congress passed the Federal Strip Mine Law, which requires that topsoil be removed and reapplied on the spoil surface during regrading and reclamation. This practice alone has aided materially in reclamation of surface mine spoil areas throughout the United States. Even when topsoil is reapplied, the surface may contain coarse-textured materials and rock fragments, making it difficult to establish vegetative cover. Many of the eastern mine spoils are derived from sandstone and shales and have a low water-holding capacity. These spoils tend to form crusts and thus create a water-impermeable layer. Practically all of these topsoils have low fertility and thus require extensive fertilization for reclamation and seedling establishment.

Regardless of the location, research indicates that many of the chemical and physical limitations previously associated with mine spoils can be eliminated by replacing the topsoil after mining. In the arid western United States, appreciable quantities of topsoil are often available for spreading over spoil after final grading. As little as 2 in. (5 cm) of soil material placed over spodic spoils under western arid conditions produced yields of native grasses equal to 50–70% of those obtained where as much as 30 in. (76 cm) or more of topsoil was replaced. This research showed that poor physical conditions caused by high sodium content, as well as problems related to nutrient deficiencies, toxicities, and soil-water relationships, were mostly alleviated by replacing topsoil. The situation is somewhat different under high-rainfall conditions, such as found in a mountainous region of the eastern United States. These soils tend to be shallow, extremely acid, infertile, and stony, and have a low water-holding capacity. Even so, replacing the topsoil on the spoil material after final grading has aided materially in the reclamation process. *SEE GROUNDWATER HYDROLOGY.*

Placement of overburden. In the eastern United States, many of the surface soils underlined by coal have very low productivity. With proper placement of overburden during mining, use of better regrading techniques, and proper surface management, many surface mine areas can be more productive after mining than before. Most state laws indicate that selected overburden material may be substituted for, or used as a supplement to, topsoil if it can be demonstrated that the resulting soil media is equal to or more suit-able for sustaining plant growth than the original soil. Some overburden materials contain large amounts of calcium, magnesium, phosphorus, and potassium. If these materials are brought to, or near, the soil surface, weathering may provide a better soil than was there initially.

Use of waste materials. A large number of domestic and industrial waste materials have been tested as amendments on surface mine spoils. These include digested sewage sludges, composted sewage sludge and garbage, tannery waste, bark and fiber mulches, flyash, fluidized-bed combustion waste, and scrubber sludges. Many of these materials contain considerable amounts of essential plant nutrients, but they may also contain some potentially toxic elements. Research has been conducted to determine plant uptake of potentially toxic elements and to evaluate possible risk of disease transmission associated with handling and disposal of these waste materials. Organic waste materials such as composted sewage and garbage and sewage sludges have been utilized effectively without any detrimental effect.

Plant species. A considerable amount of research has been conducted to determine desirable plant species for use on seriously disturbed land areas. Almost any plant species can be grown on these sites if environmental and nutritional requirements are met. Crops tested include most of the agriculturally important grass and legume, horticulture, and forest species. The law requires that herbaceous species such as grasses and legumes be established first. Tree species should be planted with, or after, stabilization with grasses and legumes.

Outlook. The production capacity of many mine spoils is not yet fully known or understood. Management and wise use must be practiced in many surface-mined areas before the full potential of these reclaimed lands is reached. Location and accessibility will determine agricultural, recreational, and industrial or urban development potential. However, because of the federal surface mine laws, future reclaimed areas will have much broader potential use than areas previously mined.

With preplanning and proper reclamation practices, more desirable plant species can be established to control erosion and sediment as well as to offer some economic potential to the landowners. Many reclaimed mined land areas are being successfully utilized for production of forages for livestock and other crops such as small grains and fruit and vegetable crops. The ultimate goal of research in the United States is to ensure that the nation's energy and mineral needs are met in a reasonable, selective, and orderly way without sacrificing food, fiber, quality of life in rural areas, or the quality of the total environment. However, there are no assurances that all surface mine areas will be reclaimed in an acceptable manner and without environmental damage. *SEE ENVIRONMENTAL ENGINEERING; SOIL.*

Orus L. Bennett

Bibliography. W. H. Armiger, J. N. Jones, Jr., and O. L. Bennett, *Revegetation of Land Disturbed by Strip Mining in Appalachia,* ARS-NE-71, 1976; O. L. Bennett, W. H. Armiger, and J. N. Jones, Jr., Revegetation and use of eastern surface mine spoils, in *Land Application of Waste Materials,* Soil Conservation Society of America, 1976; J. N. Jones, Jr., W. H. Armiger, and O. L. Bennett, Forage grasses aid the transition of spoil to soil, *Proceedings of the National Coal Association*, Bituminous Coal Research Conference Exposition, II, Louisville, Kentucky, 1976; T. M. McCalla (ed.), *Land Application of Waste Materials*, Soil Conservation Society of America, 1976; *Proceedings of the Fort Union Coal Field Symposium*, Montana Academy of Science, 1975; Surface Mining Control and Reclamation Act of 1975, H. R. 25, 94th Congress.

Land-use classes

Categories of land resources that provide information about uses and characteristics. In combination with geographic location systems, measurements of the amount of land in use, the amount available for development, and the changes in use over time, decisions about land use can be accurately made. Concerns develop when a certain land quality is required for a specific purpose, such as food production, human living areas, or environmental protection.

Large changes have occurred since the early 1960s concerning land-use classification and natural resource management. Previous concerns were allied to very specific problems such as soil erosion, land availability, desertification, or forest consumption. Technologies and theories now view land-use classification in a larger context and relate it to human use of land-based resources within environmentally acceptable guidelines. Major technological improvements that contributed to these changes include high-resolution films and improved cameras, film processing, lenses, and enlargers. Airplanes, helicopters, and satellites provide platforms for highly developed scanners, return-beam vidicon cameras, radar, lasers, and multispectral retrieval systems. Computerized instrumentation allows merging of numerous sources of data for selected areas of the Earth's surface, including continental or global coverage. Thus, completely new approaches have become feasible, such as the *Land Use Classification System for Use with Remote Sensor Data* prepared by the U.S. Department of the Interior, and previous sources of land-use information have been maintained or enhanced. SEE REMOTE SENSING.

Land is readily classified according to a group of natural characteristics that occur in association. H. E. Conklin developed land classification systems based on soil, climate, topography, and location. Others have preferred to add criteria based on bedrock geology, vegetative cover, subsurface characteristics, landforms, and hydrologic features.

Inventories. Land-use inventories have been encouraged by professional organizations, such as the International Geographical Union. Historically, land-use classification has been based on the concepts of cadastral surveys, which originally included land classification criteria based on quality, quantity, location, and ownership of the land resource. The objective was to provide a basis for equitable taxation. The current objective of land-use classification, however, also includes information for resource management.

Inventories such as the U.S. Department of Agriculture System of Land Capability Classification have centered on the suitability of soils and their limitations for field crop production. The limitations are broadly identified as few, moderate, severe, very severe, impractical to remove, generally too severe for cultivation, very severe limitations for cultivation, or too severe for commercial crop production. Similar major land resource inventories have been developed in Canada, Australia, United States, Netherlands, Denmark, Sweden, England, Switzerland, and other European countries.

Two technologically advanced major inventories, the New York State Land Use and Natural Resource Inventory (LUNR) and the Canada Land Inventory, were developed in the late 1960s for very large areas. The LUNR system provided geographically referenced land-use information on 155 items of information derived primarily from aerial photographs. These can be grouped under the 11 major use headings of agriculture, forest land, water resources, wetlands, residential, commercial and industrial, outdoor recreation, extractive industry, public and semipublic, transportation, and nonproductive uses. Each group is subdivided into 2 to 25 subunits, offering a very detailed classification system for uses of major importance, such as agriculture or residential. Its products included maps, statistical data, computer graphics, and computer printout. The LUNR program sparked activity in land-use classification throughout the United States, and in a few years 32 states developed similar land-use classification systems. The Canada Land Inventory functioned on different concepts, providing highly refined, geographically located in formation on a relatively small number of land-use classification items with computer retrieval capabilities.

Principles. The ideal land-use classification system would provide appropriate identification for all land uses with mutually exclusive units and boundaries clearly defined and easily understood. A thorough description of each unit would describe what the unit contained and why it was placed in its particular classification mode. But natural resources, vegetation, and land patterns influenced by civilization occur in a continuum with transition zones, instead of clearly defined boundaries, between land uses. As a result, generalization of the classification units is required. Because land-based resources are geographically fixed, impurities and mixed units must be included to be comprehensive. The purely theoretical approach may look at vegetative patterns, natural successional systems, and modification of human-impact consequences to maintain the purest possible scientific sequence.

The more common approach is to respond to the request of the sponsor. This usually means forfeiting some of the desired theoretical concepts to maintain cost effectiveness. Steps in this process include: (1) identification of the sponsor's information needs; (2) selection of sources of information; (3) development of a classification system that is comprehensive and provides unique descriptions and discrete assignment; (4) preparation of a geographic referencing system; and (5) selection of appropriate information-retrieval processes.

The classification system should be able to stand alone, independent of other component parts of the inventory project. It should not be dependent on unique talent, special instrumentation, or any one source of information. Classification and inventory decisions do not require computer or other forms or instrument capability; the use of computers is primarily to store, manipulate, and retrieve information.

Technological development. Development of available technologies has enabled many changes to occur in analytical methodologies. There has been rapid proliferation of methods for analysis of the capability of ecological systems to accommodate particular human land-use needs. These have been accompanied by advances in predictive evaluation of regional landscapes, and have thus carried the process into areas of systems modeling.

Methods for land-use capability analysis have progressed from trial-and-error techniques, which were among the early clearly identifiable regional planning methods of the twentieth century, to inventory methods, characterized by systematic inventories of land uses that combine information from natural sciences with engineering classification of soils and aerial photographic interpretations of cultural land-use patterns. Hand-drawn overlay methods came next to address the complex decisions to be handled at a regional level of planning. Finer distinctions between land uses and resources, and better elucidation of relationships between different types of land use were accomplished by hand-drawn overlay methods than by inventory mapping. Subsequently, data classification systems emerged, as information theory and systems analysis were employed as the organizing elements in data classifications. Computer-based planning methods, including computer-aided assessment procedures, later enabled extensive use of quantitative weighting systems and the sophisticated techniques of derived weights and values.

In the early 1900s in North America, soil and physical resource data were often incomplete and were published in literary form and also at different scales which made comparisons of data very difficult. Later the development of inventory methods was made possible by the considerable increase in knowledge about soils, geology, hydrology, and ecology. Innovations in remote sensing, refinements in soil taxonomy, and enhanced cartographic representations added to the greater availability of natural resource and land-use data. With hand-drawn overlay methods, maps of data developed at a common scale and overlaid are employed in various combinations to create a new level of information: composite maps.

Geographic information systems help serve the interest in finer distinctions between land uses and resources, and the attempts at resolution of conflicts by analysis of relationships between categories of land use. These may be found in the United States' state and regional systems, as well as those in western Europe, Canada, and some developing countries. In the computer era, faster data sources have become more comprehensive, leading to more complex site analysis and land-use planning. Highly advanced landscape planning methods have resulted, which include the use of computer-displayed three-dimensional forms.

In the Netherlands, basic material on the natural environment has been collected over a long period of time. Since 1970, such data has been made suitable for use in behalf of national physical planning policy. A national environmental survey begun in 1972 had as its purpose the elaboration of theoretically demonstrated relationships between community and natural environment for practical situations. This survey and a General Ecological Model (GEM) serve to illustrate the Netherlands' commitment to use of the science of landscape ecology in planning.

A. Lieberman; Ernest E. Hardy

Bibliography. J. R. Anderson et al., *A Land Use and Land Cover Classification System for Use with Remote Sensor Data*, U.S. Government Printing Office, Survey Prof. Pap. 964, 1976; J. G. Fabos, *Planning the Total Landscape: A Guide to Intelligent Land Use*, 1979; E. E. Hardy, *The Design of Natural Resource Inventories*, Resource Information Laboratory, New York State Cooperative Extension, 1979; F. J. Marschner, *Boundaries and Records*, Agricultural Research Service, USDA, 1960; Z. Naveh and A. S. Lieberman, *Landscape Ecology, Theory and Application*, 1984; P. J. Trowbridge, *Ecologically Based Regional Planning Methods* (lecture notes for landscape architecture class), Cornell University, 1979.

Land-use planning

Deliberate efforts by governmental bodies to anticipate and to influence the use of land in the interests of avoiding public harm (nuisance) and promoting the public welfare. In the United States, the term land-use planning usually implies public concern with privately owned land, whereas land owned by public agencies (federal, state, or local) is "managed." Land-use planning is closely related to but not synonymous with, planning of other public objectives such as capital facilities, transportation, housing, social services, or economic development. Land-use planning is conducted at various geographic scales ranging from a specific project site (for example, planned unit development), to a municipality (city planning), to a county or substate region (regional planning). Statewide land-use planning has been attempted in Hawaii and in a few other states. Some nations, such as the United Kingdom and France, but not the United States, have formulated national land-use plans.

History. Land-use planning is usually considered a product of rapid urbanization in the twentieth century. Its roots, however, may be traced to antiquity.

Grid patterns. The simplest and most familiar manifestation of land-use planning—the rectangular or grid street plan—has been found by archeologists in the Indian city of Mohenjo-Daro dating back to the third millennium B.C. Rectangularity of streets and building sites was a common characteristic of fortified colonial outposts established by Alexander, by Rome, and in the Middle Ages by English monarchs seeking to stabilize their holdings in France and Wales. In the New World, grid patterns were utilized in French and Spanish fortified settlements such as New Orleans, Saint Augustine, Havana, and Louisburg.

Rectangularity per se reflects the existence of strong centralized control over the founding and layout of new settlements; without such control, each building site would vary and streets would be narrow and crooked as in the typical medieval European city. But the motive and source of control was not always militaristic. Rectangularity was employed by William Penn in the founding of Philadelphia and by most land speculators and developers who laid out new cities in the United States west of the Appalachians during the nineteenth century. In fact, the Federal

Land Survey began in 1785 to divide most land west of the original 13 states into rectangular townships of 36 mi^2 (93 km^2) each of which are further subdivided into 1-mi^2 (2.6-km^2) sections and fractions thereof. This survey has served as an actual plan for both rural and urban land use across the United States heartland; the resulting checkerboard is clearly visible to air travelers crossing the continent on a clear day.

Rectangular land-use planning has several strengths and weaknesses. It is simple to draw on a map. It affords convenience of identification and survey of individual farms or building lots. It also tends to eliminate odd-sized or inaccessible parcels, thereby facilitating the productive use of all available land. On the other hand, it tends to ignore physical irregularity of the land such as hilly terrain, watercourses, wetlands, and areas of unstable soils or seismic risk. The grid pattern has also been widely criticized by modern planners for its monotony and lack of a sense of place.

Baroque designs. An alternative to the grid first appeared in Western Europe in the Renaissance designs for "ideal cities" beginning around 1500 in Italy. These plans combined elaborate geometric fortifications with intricate street systems and architectural motifs based on classical principles. Most of the ideal plans were artistic conceptions, unrelated to the functional realities of actual urban communities. They did, however, influence subsequent city planning of the baroque era which lasted from approximately 1600 until the early twentieth century.

Baroque land-use planning was an extension of baroque architecture. Its characteristics were symmetry, monumentality, formality, and profuse ornamentation. The achetype of the style was the Palace of Versailles whose radiating avenues, statuary, fountains and formal gardens influenced the redevelopment of most European capitals during the eighteenth and nineteenth centuries. The redevelopment of Paris by Baron Haussmann between 1853 and 1870 applied the baroque motif to an entire existing city. Haussmann's Paris in turn influenced the planning of civic improvements in America, most notably in plans prepared by the architect Daniel Burnham for Washington, D.C., and Chicago.

Urban parks and utopias. The nineteenth century contributed two other legacies to twentieth-century land-use planning. One was the concept of the large urban park as best exemplified in the work of the landscape architect Frederick Law Olmsted. Olmsted's achievements included New York's Central Park, Boston's Franklin Park, Philadelphia's Fairmount Park and Golden Gate Park in San Francisco. In contrast to rectangular and baroque traditions, Olmsted's parks emphasized the natural contours and vegetation of the landscape and promoted active recreation and informal relaxation. The juxtaposition of urban and rural settings greatly influenced urban planning policy in this century.

The other legacy was the notion of the "ideal" or model community which took many forms in England and the United States before 1900, for example, the planned worker village at Pullman in Chicago. A crucial link between nineteenth-century idealism and twentieth-century planning practice was the idea of the "garden city" as conceived and publicized by the English reformer Ebenezer Howard.

Current practice. Land-use planning in the United States is normally undertaken by local cities and towns under grants of authority from the state legislature. For unincorporated areas (outside of cities or towns), land-use planning is normally a county function. Planning in most jurisdictions is conducted by voluntary planning boards and commissions selected according to state law. Urban jurisdictions often have full-time planning departments to assist the planning boards; outside planning or engineering consultants also may be used for specific studies. The recommendations of the planning board are advisory in nature; they have no legal effect until adopted into law by the elected legislative body of the city or county. Legal implementation of land-use plans must conform both to relevant state planning and zoning laws and to applicable judicial decisions.

Process. The land-use planning process may conveniently be divided into five stages: formulation of goals, assembly of data, evaluation and interpretation of data, presentation of results, and implementation.

1. Formulation of goals. A land-use plan must be based on explicit objectives for future growth or redevelopment of the community or county. Planning goals may be formulated in several ways, such as surveys of public opinions, public hearings, and studies by experts. Goal formulation usually focuses upon the welfare of the community in question but larger regional needs should also be considered. Local land-use planning is often criticized for being too parochial in the setting of goals.

2. Assembly of data. The planning process requires detailed knowledge of the community—for example, existing land-use patterns, population trends, economic data, and natural resource characteristics. Data may be obtained from a variety of sources such as the U.S. Census, the state, a regional planning agency, or specialized organizations. Smaller jurisdictions may rely for some needs upon house-to-house surveys or "windshield" surveys. Aerial photogrammetry is often used to provide accurate, up to date knowledge of land-use conditions and practices. SEE LAND-USE CLASSES.

3. Evaluation and interpretation of data. This involves translation of raw data into meaningful patterns in light of the formulated goals. Quantitative data are manipulated through conventional statistical techniques to yield significant values and relationships between variables. For example, the need to plan for additional sites for elderly housing should be based upon analysis of projected increase in the elderly population, the available supply of elderly housing, and criteria for the location and scale of new housing projects. This would yield a projection of the number, size, and locations for future elderly housing which must then be correlated with the supply of buildable land within the community.

Computers are often used to assist with the storage, analysis, and presentation of planning data. Data files may be purchased or developed for such diverse planning variables as soil conditions, land values, water resources, political boundaries, and socio-economic characteristics. Such data files may be digitized, that is, assigned spatial coordinates for convenient retrieval and development of computer-generated maps. Software packages are available to permit combination of data sets to solve specific planning problems, for example, to locate optimal sites for important facilities such as power plants, container ports, or hazardous waste disposal sites.

Land-use planning also involves variables that are not readily quantified, such as amenity or compatibility. While efforts are made to assign numerical values to such qualitative data, the need for subjective judgment is unavoidable. The land-use planner thus functions as a humanist as well as a technician.

4. *Presentation of results.* This constitutes the actual preparation of the land-use plan. Normally, this will involve a combination of textual discussion, graphics (maps, photographs, or drawings) and statistical data. The purpose of this task is to communicate the recommendations of the planning body regarding desirable future patterns of land use in the community. The future land-use plan may be one element of a larger comprehensive plan which covers all aspects of public planning in the community. Again, computer graphics may assist in the display of pertinent data and relationships.

5. *Implementation.* The first four stages of the process are advisory in nature. This last stage is legislative and requires action by the appropriate elective body. Land-use zoning is the primary legal tool for effectuating a land-use plan. Other measures include building codes (often adopted on a statewide basis), subdivision regulations, wetland and floodplain regulations, housing codes, and historical preservation restrictions. These are all legal expressions of land-use planning authority and require no compensation to affected property owners. However, if certain land is needed for public use, as for a park or school site, payment of fair market value is required.

Zoning. Zoning is the primary expression of land-use planning in the United States. The first American zoning law was adopted by New York City in 1916. Zoning spread rapidly during the next decade at the urging of urban planning proponents. It was declared to be constitutional by the U.S. Supreme Court in 1926 and thereafter has spread to virtually every American city with the exception of Houston, Texas. Most suburbs and many rural counties also engage in zoning.

Zoning regulates the use of land, the density of residential development, and the bulk of structures. Permissible land use is usually expressed in terms of residential, commercial, or industrial. These are broken down to subcategories, and some zoning laws provide for farm, institutional, or other types of uses. Certain land use already in existence when the zoning law comes into being may legally continue (as a nonconforming use). But land use may not be changed except to an allowed use unless the owner is granted some form of exception under the terms of state law.

Density is regulated through minimum lot sizes and frontage requirements for residential development. Required lot sizes vary from one community to another. Wealthy jurisdictions are often criticized for requiring very large lots (for example, more than a half-acre per house) as a means of curbing the inflow of lower income families. Bulk of structures is controlled through minimum setbacks, side yards, and rear yards, as well as maximum heights.

Zoning in the United States was criticized during the 1970s as an obstacle to social and aesthetic goals such as racial integration and historical preservation. It continues, however, to serve as the dominant

means for effecting land-use plans. SEE *FOREST AND FORESTRY; SOIL CONSERVATION; WATER CONSERVATION.*

Rutherford H. Platt

Bibliography. W. E. Beewer and C. P. Alter, *The Complete Manual of Land Planning and Development*, 1988; L. Benevolo, *The History of the City*, 1980; A. J. Catanese and J. C. Snyder, *Introduction to Urban Planning*, 1979; W. L. Creese, *The Crowning of the American Landscape: Eight Great Spaces and Their Buildings*, 1985; P. Healey et al., *Land Use Planning and the Mediation of Urban Change*, 1989; E. Howard, *Garden Cities of Tomorrow*, 1902; D. A. Krueckeberg, *The American Planner: Biographies and Recollections*, 1983.

Landscape architecture

The art and profession of designing and planning landscapes. Landscape architects are concerned with improving the ways in which people interact with the landscape, as well as with reducing the negative impacts that human use has upon sensitive landscapes. The history of landscape architecture reaches from the gardens and outdoor environments of ancient civilizations to a broad base in environmental design in the twentieth century. Today, landscape architects are involved in such diverse areas as landscape and urban design, community and regional planning, interior and exterior garden design, appropriate and high technology, agricultural and rural land-use planning, parks and recreation, historic site and natural area preservation, landscape restoration and management, research and academic programs, energy and water conservation, and environmental planning. Landscape architects find employment with private landscape architecture, engineering, and planning firms; public agencies, including city, county, and state design, planning, park, and transportation departments; federal agencies, including the U.S. Forest Service, Corps of Engineers, National Park Service, Bureau of Land Management, and Fish and Wildlife Service; and universities and colleges.

Frederick Law Olmstead, the nineteenth-century designer of Central Park in New York City, Yosemite National Park in California, and many gardens and parks throughout the country, is generally considered to be the father of landscape architecture in America. When Olmstead is added to the long list of historical figures associated with the profession, including the eighteenth-century British landscape architect Humphery Repton and the seventeenth-century French landscape architect Andre Le Notre, the form and historical intent of the designed and planned landscape throughout the world can be better understood.

The American Society of Landscape Architects (ASLA) was established in 1899 as the primary informational and lobbying organization for the profession. Over 80% of the states in America have licensure for landscape architects through state consumer, health, and safety regulation boards. There are over 40 accredited college programs in landscape architecture throughout the United States which provide educational training, enabling students to take licensing exams without lengthy apprenticeships. Degrees in landscape architecture are offered at both the bachelor's and master's levels. Many countries have universities with degree programs in landscape architecture, and abundant international employment opportunities exist. There are landscape architects in practice in every country of the world.

The skills required for landscape architecture are concerned with creativity, ecology, social science, horticulture, engineering, and graphics. Landscape architects are generalists in that their educational and professional experience is very broad. Many environmental and cultural factors affect landscape design and planning, and landscape architects have to know how these factors relate. Design process is the main area of specialization for landscape architects, and decision-making related to design process is the fundamental reason why landscape architects are employed. The ability to utilize the information of specialists and to synthesize the information into a usable format remains the essence of the profession. SEE ENVIRONMENTAL ENGINEERING; LAND-USE PLANNING.

Kerry J. Dawson

Bibliography. R. Austin, *Designing the Natural Landscape*, 1984; T. Higuchi, *The Visual and Spatial Structure of Landscapes*, 1988; J. E. Ingels, *Landscaping Principles and Practices*, 3d ed., 1987; T. Turner, *Landscape Planning*, 1987.

Landscape ecology

The study of the ecological effects of spatial patterning of ecosystems. Specifically, landscape ecology examines the development and dynamics of spatial heterogeneity; interactions and exchanges across heterogeneous landscapes; the influences of spatial heterogeneity on biotic and abiotic processes; and the management of spatial heterogeneity. The consideration of spatial patterns distinguishes landscape ecology from traditional ecological studies, which frequently assume a spatially homogeneous system. SEE ECOSYSTEM.

The term landscape commonly refers to the landforms of a region considered together with its associated habitats at scales that range from acres to many square miles. For example, a rural landscape might include the forests, croplands, pastures, rivers, and towns within a region. Landscape ecology studies those large, heterogeneous areas as intact units with emphasis on ecological processes.

The discipline of landscape ecology arose from European traditions of regional geography and vegetation science. Many fields of study, including geography, ecology, landscape architecture, forestry, and regional planning, have contributed to the development of landscape ecology. In Europe, landscape ecology is well integrated into land-use planning and decision making. SEE LAND-USE PLANNING.

Three useful landscape characteristics are structure, function, and change. Structure refers to the spatial patterns or relationships between distinctive ecosystems, that is, the distribution of energy, materials, and species in relation to the sizes, shapes, numbers, kinds, and configurations of components. Function encompasses the interactions between the spatial elements, that is, the flow of energy, materials, and organisms among the component ecosystems. Change refers to alteration in the structure and function of the ecological mosaic through time.

Landscape structure. Vegetation and animal communities, as well as human land uses, are often patchy when observed in the landscape because of the complex interactions between physical, biological, and social forces. Most landscapes have been influenced by humans (such as by forest cutting or agriculture), and so the resulting landscape mosaic is a mixture of natural and artificially managed patches that vary in size, shape, and arrangement. SEE ECOLOGICAL COMMUNITIES.

Patches and matrices. Landscape structure deals with the numbers, kinds, and configuration of landscape elements. A patch is a vegetation community or group of species that is surrounded by a matrix of differing community structure or composition. For example, a meadow may be considered as a patch within a forest matrix, or an isolated woodlot might be a patch within a matrix of agriculture. Patches can result from a variety of mechanisms. Because the environment is heterogeneous and resources are irregularly distributed, species that require different resources tend to form clusters. A small disturbance, such as a contained fire in a grassland or a blowdown of trees in a forest, can create a small patch in a matrix. A large disturbance, such as a hurricane or a very large fire, may miss small areas, which become remnant patches that are relics of the previous community and become embedded in a disturbed matrix. Humans can also create patches, for example, by clearing a forested area for planting.

Patches can be characterized in many ways, including size, shape, and arrangement. The size of landscape patches can influence ecological processes such as water flux and species dynamics. Small patches have a large amount of edge per unit area, limiting the amount of available interior habitat, and so they often have a lower species diversity than large patches. Small patches also may be more vulnerable to disturbances. Size and edge characteristics may be of particular importance for species that require habitat patches of a minimum size or specific arrangement, as is seen in the large patches of old-growth forest needed for survival by the spotted owl *(Strix occidentalis)* in the Pacific Northwest in the United States. Groups of patches may be clustered or dispersed, and may show random, uniform, or aggregated arrangements. Patches also differ in shape and complexity, which may reflect their origins. For example, artificial patches, including woodlots and crop fields, tend to be more regular in shape, whereas natural patches, such as natural forests or wetlands, tend to be more complex.

Corridors and networks. Linear elements that differ from the matrix and span portions of a landscape are called corridors. Line corridors (roads, paths, and hedgerows) are narrow, approximate a continuous edge, and lack interior habitat, but they may serve as movement routes for organisms. Strip corridors, which are wider than line corridors, contain some interior habitat and can support more species. Stream corridors parallel water courses and vary in size with the stream or river.

Corridors both divide and connect a landscape. When corridors intersect and become interconnected, they are termed networks. Corridors generally provide some connectivity between patches in the landscape, connectivity being a measure of the degree of spatial continuity in a corridor. Species survival tends to be higher in patches that have higher connectivity to other patches. Corridors may also provide an efficient migratory pathway for animals. The presence or absence of breaks in a corridor may be a very important factor in determining the effectiveness of its conduit and barrier functions.

Landscape structure may also be characterized by indices that are descriptive of the overall pattern. Indices of dominance, diversity, complexity, richness, evenness, and contagion can be calculated for entire landscapes. For example, a landscape with a high dominance index tends to be strongly influenced by one or two habitats, and a landscape with a high contagion index exhibits a clumped pattern of habitats. Changes in the values of indices may be correlated with changes in species diversity, productivity, or level of disturbance.

Landscape function. Patches in a landscape mosaic are coupled by fluxes of organisms, biotic and abiotic energy, and nutrients. Understanding the relationship between landscape pattern and ecological processes, a primary goal of ecological research on landscapes, is difficult to accomplish because large regions make experimentation and hypothesis testing challenging.

The spread of disturbance across a landscape is an important ecological process that is influenced by spatial heterogeneity. A disturbance is a relatively discrete event in time that disrupts ecosystem, community, or population structure and changes resources, substrate availability, or the physical environment. Disturbances operate in a heterogeneous manner in the landscape: gradients of frequency, severity, and type are often controlled by physical and vegetational features. In some forests, the susceptibility of sites to frequent natural disturbances is controlled by slope position and aspect.

The spatial spread of disturbance may be enhanced or retarded by landscape heterogeneity. In forests of the Pacific Northwest, increased heterogeneity due to checkerboard clear-cutting patterns enhances the susceptibility of old-growth forests to disturbances such as catastrophic windthrow and pest or pathogen invasions (see **illus.**). On a barrier island, the unusually close proximity of different habitats appears to enhance the disturbance effects of ungulate grazers introduced into a mature maritime forest. Landscape heterogeneity may also retard the spread of disturbance. In some coniferous forests, for example, heterogeneity in the spatial patterns of forest by age class tends to retard the spread of fires. Pest outbreaks and erosional problems in agricultural landscapes, on the other hand, are enhanced by homogeneity.

A change in landscape pattern can affect the distribution, movement, and persistence of species—other aspects of landscape function. Connectivity may be important for species persistence. For example, birds and small mammals in agricultural landscapes are found more often near fencerows between woodlots than traveling across open fields, which suggests that well-vegetated fencerows may provide interconnections between patches of suitable habitat. Species in isolated patches may have a lower probability of persistence. Modifications of habitat connectivity or patch sizes can have strong influences on species abundance and movement patterns. For example, road development in wilderness areas disrupts the movement patterns of wild animals such as grizzly bears.

The shape and diversity of patches influence patterns of species abundance. In agricultural landscapes, larger and more heterogeneous forest fragments appear to have more species and bird pairs than small fragments. Revegetation patterns on disturbed areas also differ, depending on whether the adjacent

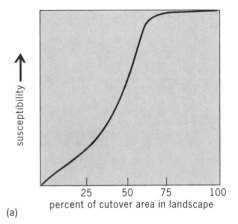

(a)

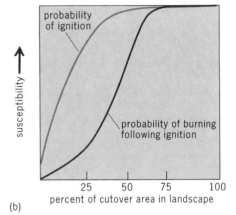

(b)

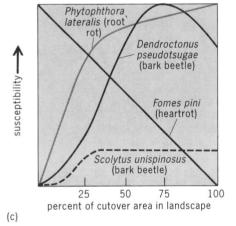

(c)

Predicted changes in the susceptibility to (a) windthrow, (b) wildfire, and (c) selected pests and pathogens of forests in the Douglas-fir region of the Pacific Northwest. (*After J. F. Franklin and R. T. T. Forman, Creating landscape patterns by forest cutting: Ecological consequences and principles, Landsc. Ecol., 1:5–18, 1987*).

boundaries are convex, concave, or straight. Colonizing plants may be more abundant near concave forest boundaries.

The redistribution of matter and nutrients across a heterogeneous landscape is another important landscape function that is influenced by spatial pattern. For example, landscape structure may control the horizontal flow of nutrients or sediment in surface waters of artificially modified landscapes. Riparian forests have been found to reduce sediment and nutrient loads in surface runoff, a process that has important implications for agricultural landscapes because of the large amounts of fertilizer and sediment that can be transported in storm runoff to nearby streams. Nutrients can also be transported by grazing animals across landscapes and between patches. Large animals are important because they typically graze and remove nutrients from patches containing high-quality forage and may transfer these nutrients, through defecation, to other areas.

Spatial heterogeneity may also influence the movement of gases between the atmosphere and the biota. Some patches in a landscape may be a source of carbon dioxide or methane, for example, whereas others may be sinks that assimilate trace gases. The source–sink relationships between soils, microbes, and plants potentially alter gas flux across the landscape. Quantifying these relationships is important for relating land cover to atmospheric processes and climate change.

Landscape change. Like all ecological systems, landscapes are dynamic and change through time, as a result of either natural processes, such as fires and subsequent regrowth in forested landscapes, or human activities, such as forest clearing for agricultural development. Changes in landscape structure and function can be documented by using data from aerial photographs or satellite images, and new technologies, such as remote sensing and geographic information systems, can assist in the study of landscapes. For example, satellites can be used to estimate evapotranspiration, primary production, and other vegetation characteristics over large regions.

Computer simulation modeling also plays an important role in predicting changes in landscape structure or function and the potential consequences of those changes in landscape patterns. Simulations also can identify important hypotheses or assumptions to be tested by collecting data or conducting an experiment in a particular landscape. Because landscape ecology focuses on large areas, and because landscape changes may take place over decades or centuries, modeling will continue to be an important tool in landscape studies. *See Ecological modeling.*

Management considerations. Many land management activities (for example, forestry practices, regional planning, and natural resource development) involve decisions that alter landscape patterns. Ecologists, land managers, and planners have traditionally ignored interactions between the different elements in a landscape and instead have treated each element as a different system. The landscape, like many ecological systems, represents an interface between social and environmental processes, and so a broad-scale perspective that incorporates spatial relationships is a necessary part of land-use planning.

Landscape theory may have direct applications to the management of disturbance-prone landscapes. For example, several studies have suggested that landscape patterns have critical thresholds at which ecological processes change qualitatively, and a threshold level of habitat connectivity may demarcate various processes or phenomena. The number or length of edges in a landscape changes rapidly near the critical threshold, and that change may have important implications for species persistence. Habitat fragmentation may progress with little effect on a population until the critical pathways of connectivity are disrupted. A slight change in habitat connectivity near a critical threshold can have dramatic consequences for the persistence of the population. Similarly, the spread of disturbance across a landscape may be controlled by disturbance frequency when the habitat is below a critical threshold of connectivity, but it may be controlled by disturbance intensity when the habitat is above that threshold. Disturbances can be even more critical when the habitat is an island and species are at risk. *See Island biogeography.*

The long-term maintenance of biological diversity may require an interdisciplinary management strategy that places regional biogeography and landscape patterns above local concerns. Continual tree cutting, for example, may finally threaten a landscape, subjecting it to risks of flooding, erosion, and loss of top soil, even though economic considerations would encourage such clearing. With regional diversity and ecological integrity as the goal, the rarity criterion (for species management) may be most appropriately applied at regional or global scales. *See Biogeography; Ecology; Forest management; Population ecology.*

Monica G. Turner

Bibliography. R. T. T. Forman and M. Godron, *Landscape Ecology*, 1986; Z. Naveh and A. S. Lieberman, *Landscape Ecology*, 1984; P. G. Risser, J. R. Karr, and R. T. T. Forman, *Landscape Ecology, Directions and Approaches*, Ill. Nat. Hist. Surv. Spec. Publ. 2, 1984; M. G. Turner, Landscape ecology: The effect of pattern on process, *Annu. Rev. Ecol. Syst.*, 20:171–197, 1989; M. G. Turner (ed.), *Landscape Heterogeneity and Disturbance*, 1987; D. L. Urban, R. V. O'Neill, and H. H. Shugart, Landscape ecology, *BioScience*, 37:119–127, 1987.

Life zones

Large portions of the Earth's land area which have generally uniform climate and soil and, consequently, a biota showing a high degree of uniformity in species composition and adaptations to environment. Related terms are vegetational formation and biome.

Merriam's zones. Life zones were proposed by A. Humboldt, A. P. DeCandolle, and others who emphasized plants. Around 1900 C. Hart Merriam, then chief of the U.S. Biological Survey, related life zones, as observed in the field, with broad climatic belts across the North American continent designed mainly to order the habitats of America's important animal groups. The first-order differences between the zones, as reflected by their characteristic plants and animals, were related to temperature; moisture and other variables were considered secondary.

Each life zone correlated reasonably well with major crop regions and to some extent with general vegetation types (see **table**). Although later studies led to the development of other, more realistic or detailed systems, Merriam's work provided an important initial stimulus to bioclimatologic work in North America. *See Vegetation and ecosystem mapping.*

Work on San Francisco Mountain in Arizona impressed Merriam with the importance of temperature as a cause of biotic zonation in mountains. Isotherms based on sums of effective temperatures correlated with observed distributions of certain animals and plants led to Merriam's first law, that animals and plants are restricted in northward distribution by the

Characteristics of Merriam's life zones

Zone name	Example	Vegetation	Typical and important plants	Typical and important animals	Typical and important crops
Arctic-alpine	Northern Alaska, Baffin Island	Tundra	Dwarf willow, lichens, heathers	Arctic fox, musk-ox, ptarmigan	None
Hudsonian	Labrador, southern Alaska	Taiga, coniferous forest	Spruce, lichens	Moose, woodland caribou, mountain goat	None
Canadian	Northern Maine, northern Michigan	Coniferous forest	Spruce, fir, aspen, red and jack pine	Lynx, porcupine, Canada jay	Blueberries
Western division					
Humid transition	Northern California coast	Mixed coniferous forest	Redwood, sugar pine, maples	Blacktail deer, Townsend chipmunk, Oregon ruffed grouse	Wheat, oats, apples, pears, Irish potatoes
Arid transition	North Dakota	Conifer, woodland sagebrush	Douglas fir, lodgepole, yellow pine, sage	Mule deer, whitetail, jackrabbit, Columbia ground squirrel	Wheat, oats, corn
Upper Sonoran	Nebraska, southern Idaho	Piñon, savanna, prairie	Junipers, piñons, grama grass, bluestem	Prairie dog, blacktail jackrabbit, sage hen	Wheat, corn, alfalfa, sweet potatoes
Lower Sonoran	Southern Arizona	Desert	Cactus, agave, creosote bush, mesquite	Desert fox, four-toed kangaroo rats, roadrunner	Dates, figs, almonds
Eastern division					
Alleghenian	New England	Mixed conifer and hardwoods	Hemlock, white pine, paper birch	New England cottontail rabbit, wood thrush, bobwhite	Wheat, oats, corn, apples, Irish potatoes
Carolinian	Delaware, Indiana	Deciduous forest	Oaks, hickory, tulip tree, redbud	Opossum, fox, squirrel, cardinal	Corn, grapes, cherries, tobacco, sweet potatoes
Austroriparian	Carolina piedmont, Mississippi	Long-needle conifer forest	Loblolly, slash pine, live oak	Rice rat, woodrat, mocking bird	Tobacco, cotton, peaches, corn
Tropical	Southern Florida	Broadleaf evergreen forest	Palms, mangrove	Armadillo, alligator, roseate spoonbill	Citrus fruit, avocado, banana

sum of the positive temperatures (above 109.4°F or 43°C) during the season of growth and reproduction. The mean temperature for the six hottest weeks of the summer formed the basis for the second law, that plants and animals are restricted in southward distribution by the mean temperature of a brief period covering the hottest part of the year. Merriam's system emphasizes the similarity in biota between arctic and alpine areas and between boreal and montane regions. It was already recognized that latitudinal climatic zones have parallels in altitudinal belts on mountain slopes and that there is some biotic similarity between such areas of similar temperature regime.

In northern North America Merriam's life zones, the Arctic-Alpine, the Hudsonian, and the Canadian, are entirely transcontinental (**Fig. 1** and table). Because of climatic and faunistic differences, the eastern and western parts of most life zones in the United States (the Transition, upper Austral, and lower Austral) had to be recognized separately. The western zones had to be further subdivided into humid coastal subzones and arid inland subzones. The Tropical life zone includes the extreme southern edge of the United States, the Mexican lowlands, and Central America.

Although once widely accepted, Merriam's life zones are little used today because they include too much biotic variation and oversimplify the situation.

However, much of the terminology he proposed persists, especially in North American zoogeographic literature.

Dice's zones. Another approach to life zones in North America is the biotic province concept of L. R. Dice. Each biotic province covers a large and continuous geographic area and is characterized by the occurrence of at least one important ecological association distinct from those of adjacent provinces. Each biotic province is subdivided into biotic districts which are also continuous, but smaller, areas distinguished by ecological differences of lesser extent or importance than those delimiting provinces. Life belts, or vertical subdivisions, also occur within biotic provinces. These are not necessarily continuous but often recur on widely separated mountains within a province where ecological conditions are appropriate.

Boundaries between biotic provinces were largely subjective, supposedly drawn where the dominant associations of the provinces covered approximately equal areas. In practice, however, too few association data including both plants and animals were available, and vegetation generally offered the most satisfactory guide to boundaries. The Dice system recognizes 29 biotic provinces in North America (**Fig. 2**). The two northernmost (Eskimoan and Hudsonian) are transcontinental, reflecting broad, high-latitude climatic belts. Those in the eastern United States (Canadian,

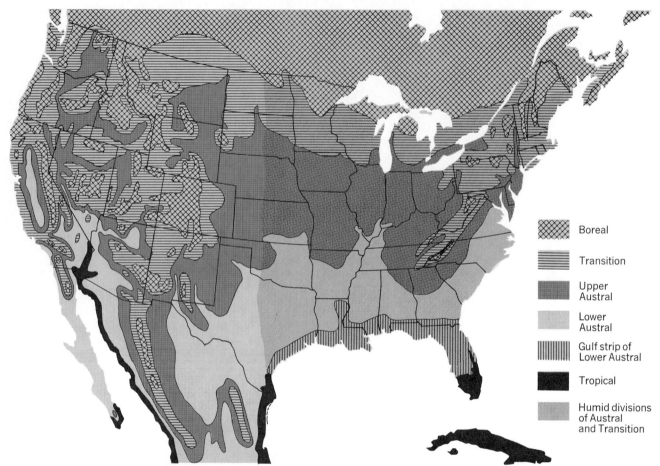

Fig. 1. Life zones of the United States. (*After C. H. Merriam, Life Zones and Crop Zones of the United States, USDA Bull. 10, 1898*)

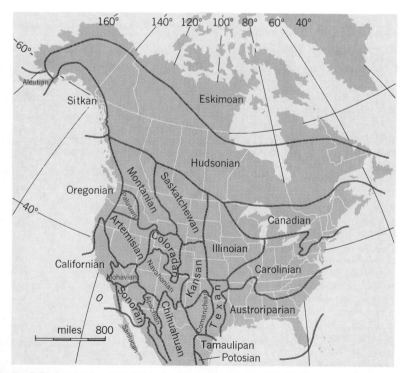

Fig. 2. Biotic provinces of North America (Veracruzian not shown) in the Dice system. 1 mi = 0.6 km. (*After L. R. Dice, The Biotic Provinces of North America, University of Michigan Press, 1943*)

Carolinian, and Austroriparian) reflect both latitudinal temperature change and physiography, whereas province boundaries in the remainder of North America are strongly influenced by physiography.

Holdridge's zones. A life-zone system with boundaries more explicitly defined is that of L. R. Holdridge. These life zones are defined through the effects of the three weighted climatic indexes: mean annual heat, precipitation, and atmospheric moisture. Each axis of the triangle (**Fig. 3**) represents one climatic component, and the three sets of lines parallel to the axes define the life-zone framework. Climatic values which the lines represent progress geometrically. Mean annual biotemperature is computed by summing the monthly mean temperatures from 32°F or 0°C (setting negative winter months equal to 32°F or 0°C when they occur) to about 86°F or 30°C and dividing by 12. Values increase from top to bottom in Fig. 3 and, by extension to either margin, establish equivalent latitudinal regions and altitudinal belts. Precipitation is computed as mean annual precipitation in millimeters and increases from the apex toward the lower right margin of the diagram. The humidity factor is calculated by dividing the value of the mean annual potential evapotranspiration by the mean annual precipitation in millimeters. Values of this ratio increase toward the lower left side of the diagram, signifying a decrease in effective humidity.

Associations of vegetation, animals, climate, physiography, geology, and soils are interrelated in unique

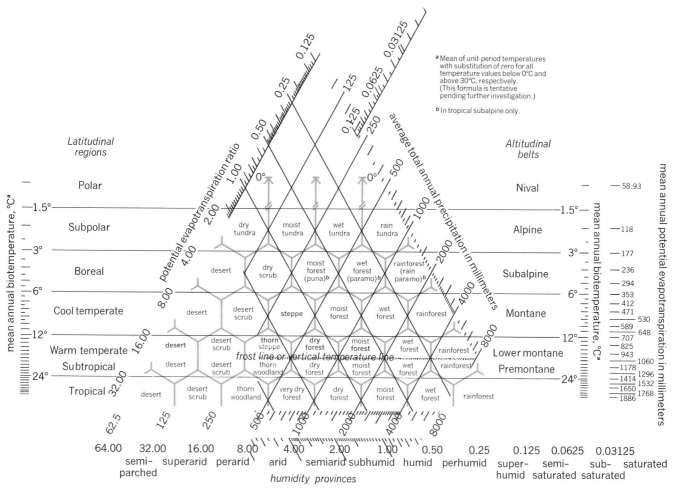

Fig. 3. World life zones. °F = (°C × 1.8) + 32. (*After L. R. Holdridge, Life Zone Ecology, rev. ed., Tropical Science Center, 1967*)

combinations, mostly having distinct physiognomy, in Holdridge's climatic grid. Local investigation should show how well the framework represents the most common life zones of Earth, both north and south of the Equator. The system has been applied with considerable success to the mapping of life zones, primarily in the American tropics. Names of Holdridge's life zones are based on the dominant vegetation of each climatic type; animal life of the zone is supposedly distinctive. SEE ALTITUDINAL VEGETATION ZONES; BIOME; ZOOGEOGRAPHY.

Arthur W. Cooper

Bibliography. W. H. Lewis, *Ecology Field Glossary: A Naturalist's Vocabulary*, 1977; C. H. Merriam, *Life Zones and Crop Zones of the United States*, USDA Bull. 10, 1898; H. Walter, *Vegetation of the Earth*, 1979; J. E. Weaver and F. E. Clements, *Plant Ecology*, 2d ed., 1938.

Limnology

The study of lakes, ponds, rivers, streams, swamps, and reservoirs that make up inland water systems. Each of these inland aquatic environments is physically and chemically connected with its surroundings by meteorologic and hydrogeologic processes (**Fig. 1**). For example, precipitation and runoff, combined with the gradient and watershed characteristics of a river or stream, provide the physicochemical background for the organisms of flowing water (lotic) systems. The frequency and stability of thermal stratification and mixing in standing water (lentic) systems such as lakes, ponds, and reservoirs are determined by the seasonal balance of heating and cooling, the unique temperature-density characteristics of pure water, and the energy of the wind.

Solar energy supply and distribution, physical mixing processes, and nutrients supplied by the surrounding watershed and lake sediments determine how much organic matter is produced by photosynthesis in aquatic environments. That autotrophic production, combined with leaves and other organic matter produced outside the system, supports heterotrophic activities of aquatic communities.

Biogeochemical processes. Food webs are used to illustrate interactions between plants and animals in aquatic communities. The trophic-dynamic approach (**Fig. 2**) traces the energy fixed by photosynthesis through trophic levels from herbivores to top carnivores. The flow of energy and the return of minerals to inorganic nutrient pools maintain internal biogeochemical cycles of aquatic environments. SEE BIOGEOCHEMISTRY; FOOD WEB.

General habitats of aquatic environments. Aquatic organisms may be grouped into categories according

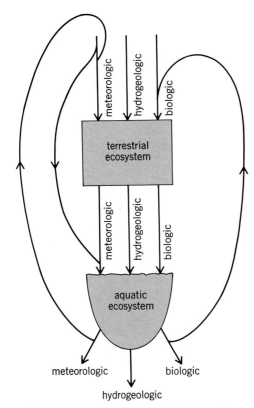

Fig. 1. Diagrammatic model of the functional linkages between terrestrial and aquatic ecosystems. Vectors may be meteorologic, hydrogeologic, or biologic components moving nutrients or energy along the pathway shown.

be occupied by rooted plants and pond weeds (aquatic macrophytes). These plants provide habitats for other plants and animals. The deepest area (profundal zone) is usually bounded by the limnetic zone on the top and the littoral zone on the sides. Benthic organisms such as insects, oligochaetes, and microorganisms may occupy the profundal zone. Free-swimming animals such as fish (nekton) are usually not restricted to any particular zone of a lentic environment. The feeding behavior of fish and other carnivores may influence many food web interactions by removing large herbivores from the food web. The loss of large herbivores alters feeding relationships at the base of the food web, because small herbivores cannot eat large phytoplankton. This cascade of feeding interactions may alter the structure of aquatic communities by permitting the accumulation of large phytoplankton and small herbivores. *SEE PHYTOPLANKTON; ZOOPLANKTON.*

to where they live within a particular system. Generally, habitats of aquatic systems are defined by unique physical conditions. The open water (limnetic zone) of lentic environments is inhabited by microscopic plants (phytoplankton) and animals (zooplankton). Shallows around the edge of the lake that are limited by the depth of light penetration (littoral zone) may

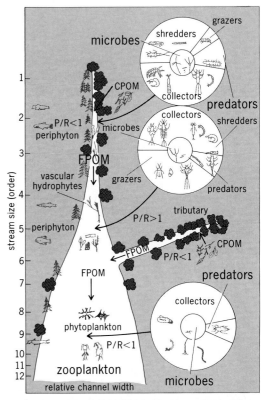

Fig. 3. A proposed relationship between stream size and the progressive shift in structural and functional attributes of lotic communities. Coarse particulate organic material (CPOM) that enters a stream from the watershed is shredded by organisms to form fine particulate organic matter (FPOM). Some organisms collect the fine material, and others graze on autotrophic organisms to sustain the food web of the stream. Production (P) and respiration (R) responses are used to detect changes in autotrophic and heterotrophic processes in the biotic community. (After R. L. Vannote et al., The river continuum concept, Can. J. Fish. Aquat. Sci., 37:130–137, 1980)

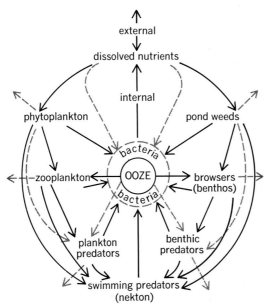

Fig. 2. Diagram of food webs in a lake, showing the interdependence of organisms. Broken lines depict the energy pathways and solid lines the food source.

Lotic environments may also be divided into zones created by water velocity, bottom conditions, and stream gradient. In mountainous areas, rapids and turbulent water zones (riffles) are contrasted with sluggish water zones (pools); each of these habitat may have characteristic organisms. Streams and rivers in valleys and on plains may have many meanders, oxbows, and braids developed by the balance of erosion and deposition of the riverbed. Water movement and sediment characteristics, along with light penetration and oxygen conditions of the river, characterize the habitats of the lotic organisms. When studying the linkage between streams and their terrestrial setting, scientists consider the gradient of physical factors formed by drainage networks. Fluvial geomorphic processes are then integrated with community ecology principles to develop an understanding of functional processes that contribute to mineral cycling and organic matter utilization (**Fig. 3**). *See Fresh-water ecosystem.*

Eutrophication and toxic materials. Aquatic systems with excellent physical conditions for production of organisms and high nutrient levels may show signs of eutrophication. Eutrophic lakes are generally identified by large numbers of phytoplankton and aquatic macrophytes and by low oxygen concentrations in the profundal zone. Eutrophication may be accelerated by poor watershed management, by runoff from overfertilized lands, or by poor septic facilities. *See Eutrophication; Water conservation.*

Organisms of aquatic environments may also be affected by metals such as lead and mercury, or pesticides that enter the aquatic environment from poor watershed management practices. These toxic materials may alter the food webs of aquatic systems by destroying sensitive organisms. Tolerant organisms may concentrate the toxic elements by feeding and absorption in a process called biomagnification; the result is that these organisms acquire levels of toxicity that make them dangerous for human consumption. Lakes and rivers are also influenced by changes in the chemical composition of rain. Acid runoffs cause stress to the biota of aquatic systems in many ways, including direct toxicity of hydrogen ions, disruption of normal food web relations, alterations of behavioral patterns of animals, and modification of biogeochemical cycles. *See Acid rain; Ecology; Hydrology; Lake; River; Water pollution.*

James E. Schindler

Bibliography. S. R. Carpenter and J. F. Kitchell, Consumer control of lake productivity, *BioScience*, 38:764–769, 1988; S. R. Carpenter, J. F. Kitchell, and J. R. Hodgson, Cascading trophic interactions and lake productivity, *BioScience* 35:634–639, 1985; G. A. Cole, *A Textbook of Limnology*, 3d ed., 1983; D. G. Frey (ed.), *Limnology in North America*, 1963; C. Goldman and A. Horne, *Limnology*, 1982; G. E. Hutchinson, *A Treatise on Limnology*, vols. 1–3, 1975; O. T. Lind, *Handbook of Common Methods in Limnology*, 1979; D. W. Schindler et al., Long-term ecosystem stress: The effects of years of experimental acidification on a small lake, *Science*, 228:1395–1401, 1985; R. L. Vannote et al., The river continuum concept, *Can. J. Fish. Aquat. Sci.*, 37:130–137, 1980.

Mangroves, Great Barrier Reef, off northeast Australia. (*a*) Mangroves at northwestern corner of King Island. (*b*) Interior of mangrove swamp, Newton Island. (*c*) Mangroves on north side of Howick Island. (*From J. A. Steers, Salt marshes, Endeavour, 18(70):75–82, 1959*)

Mangrove

A taxonomically diverse assemblage of trees and shrubs that form the dominant plant communities in tidal, saline wetlands along sheltered tropical and subtropical coasts. The development and composition of mangrove communities depend largely on temperature, soil type and salinity, duration and frequency of inundation, accretion of silt, tidal and wave energy, and such fortuitous factors as cyclone or flood frequencies (see **illus.**). Extensive mangrove communities seem to correlate with areas in which the water temperature of the warmest month exceeds 75°F (24°C), and they are absent from waters that never exceed 75°F (24°C) during the year. Intertidal, sheltered, low-energy, muddy sediments are the most suitable habitats for mangrove communities, and under optimal conditions, forests up to 148 ft (45 m) in height can develop, such as those in Ecuador, Thailand, and Malaysia. Where less favorable conditions are found, mangrove communities may reach maturity at heights of only 3 ft (1 m). *See Ecosystem.*

Approximately 58,000 mi² (150,000 km²) of the land in the Americas, Africa, Asia, and Australia is occupied by mangrove communities, which show a great similarity in structure, flora, and function. Plants of the mangrove community belong to many different genera and families, many of which are not closely related to one another phylogenetically. However, they do share a variety of morphological, physiological, and reproductive adaptations that enable them to grow in an unstable, harsh, and salty environment. On the basis of the commonality of those various adaptations, approximately 80 species of plants belonging to about 30 genera in over 20 families are recognized throughout the world as being indigenous to mangroves. About 60 species occur on the east coasts of Africa and Australasia, whereas about 20 species are found in the Western Hemisphere.

At the generic level, *Avicennia* and *Rhizophora* are the dominant plants of mangrove communities throughout the world, with each genus having several closely related species in both hemispheres. At the species level, however, only a few species, such as the portia tree (*Thespesia populnea*), the mangrove fern (*Acrostichum aureum*), and the swamp hibiscus (*Hibiscus tiliaceus*), occur in both hemispheres. Such a present-day distribution can be satisfactorily explained only if the ancestors of the mangroves evolved in the Lower Cretaceous, were dispersed outward from their center of origin in the remnants of the Tethys Sea, and subsequently developed further as two isolated groups following the closure of the Mediterranean Sea as a dispersal route between the Eastern and Western hemispheres.

The mangrove community is often strikingly zoned parallel to the shoreline, with a sequence of different species dominating from open water to the landward margins. These zones are the response of individual species to gradients of inundation frequency, waterlogging, nutrient availability, and soil salt concentrations across the intertidal area, rather than a reflection of ecological succession, as earlier studies had suggested. Not surprisingly, the zonation patterns show some similarity between the Eastern and Western hemispheres. In the Americas and western Africa, *Rhizophora* forms the outermost (seaward) zone, followed by *Avicennia*, then *Laguncularia*, with a sporadic landward fringe of *Conocarpus*. In the Eastern Hemisphere, *Rhizophora* forms the outermost zone, although at some localities *Sonneratia* and *Avicennia* may also be present. *Avicennia* generally forms monospecific stands behind the outer zone, followed by mixed stands of *Bruguiera*, *Heritiera*, and *Xylocarpus*, with a landward zone of *Ceriops* mixed with *Lumnitzera* and *Avicennia*. SEE ECOLOGICAL SUCCESSION.

Most plants of the mangrove community are halophytes, well adapted to salt water and fluctuations of tide level. Many species show modified root structures such as stilt or prop roots, which offer support on the semiliquid or shifting sediments, whereas others have erect root structures (pneumatophores) that facilitate oxygen penetration to the roots in a hypoxic environment. Salt glands, which allow excess salt to be extruded through the leaves, occur in several species; others show a range of physiological mechanisms that either exclude salt from the plants or minimize the damage excess salts can cause by separating the salt from the sensitive enzyme systems of the plant. Several species have well-developed vivipary of their seeds, whereby the hypocotyl develops while the fruit is still attached to the tree. The seedlings are generally buoyant, able to float over long distances in the sea and rapidly establish themselves once stranded in a suitable habitat.

A mangrove may be considered either a sheltered, muddy, intertidal habitat or a forest community; consequently, the mangrove fauna comprises elements dependent on either of these habitats. The sediment surface of mangrove communities abounds with species that have marine affinities, including brightly colored fiddler crabs, mound-building mud lobsters (*Thalassina anomala*), and a variety of mollusks and worms, as well as specialized gobiid fish, whose ability to travel over the mud surface by using their fins has earned them the common name mudskippers. The waterways among the mangroves are important feeding and nursery areas for a variety of juvenile finfish as well as crustaceans such as portunid crabs and penaeid shrimps, all of which are important sources of protein for indigenous populations. Animals with forest affinities that are associated with mangroves include snakes, lizards, deer, tigers, crab-eating monkeys, bats, and many species of birds, including flamingos, ibis, sea eagles, herons, pelicans, and several species of kingfisher.

Economically, mangroves are a major source of timber, poles, thatch, and fuel. The bark of some trees is used for tanning materials, whereas other species have food or medicinal value. In Malaysia, Bangladesh, India, and Thailand, managed forest operations produce commercial timber, fuelwood, charcoal, or woodpulp. Subsistence harvesting of mangrove resources is widespread in Central America and parts of Asia and Africa. Elsewhere, mangroves are gathering areas for honey and fodder. Despite their obvious economic value, mangroves have often been considered wastelands and have been converted to other forms of land use. Gradually, however, opinion has changed, and mangrove communities are now recognized not merely for their economic value but also as living systems of major intrinsic scientific interest. SEE ECOLOGICAL COMMUNITIES; FOREST MANAGEMENT.

Peter Saenger

Bibliography. B. F. Clough (ed.), *Mangrove Ecosystems in Australia: Structure, Function and Management*, 1982; P. Hutchings and P. Saenger, *Ecology of Mangroves*, 1987; P. B. Tomlinson, *The Botany of Mangroves*, 1986.

Marine ecology

An integrative science that studies the basic structural and functional relationships within and among living populations and their physical–chemical environments in marine ecosystems. Although an outgrowth of natural history and the life sciences, marine ecology draws on all the major fields within the biological sciences as well as oceanography, physics, geology, and chemistry. SEE ENVIRONMENT.

Historically, and to some extent today, emphasis within the field has been directed at the gathering and analysis of data and descriptive information about taxonomy, species distributions and abundances, natural history and population biology, and the physical–chemical characteristics of marine environments. However, emphasis has evolved toward understanding the rates and controls on ecological processes that govern both short- and long-term events, including population growth and survival, primary and secondary productivity, and community dynamics and stability.

Marine ecology focuses on specific organisms as well as on particular environments or physical settings. Mangrove forests, salt marshes, seagrasses and seaweeds, and coral reefs form unique ecosystems defined by the dominant biological community. Lagoons, estuaries, bays, and the principal ocean environments of continental shelf, slope, abyssal plain, and mid-oceanic ridges form ecosystems based on physical–geological features. Together, these ecosystems occur in water depths ranging from the intertidal zone to the deepest ocean depths, about 33,000 ft (10,000 m), and encompass temperature extremes of 27°F (−3°C) in the deepest ocean waters to 104°F (40°C) in some tropical lagoons.

Marine environments. Classification of marine environments for ecological purposes is based very generally on two criteria, the dominant community or ecosystem type and the physical–geological setting. Those ecosystems identified by their dominant community type include mangrove forests, coastal salt marshes, submerged seagrasses and seaweeds, and tropical coral reefs. Plankton are a principal component in all marine ecosystems and include organisms ranging in size from bacteria to larval fishes that permanently, or at some stage in their life cycle, reside in the water column. Other communities include benthic (bottom–dwelling) communities in shallow and deep water, occupants of upwelling areas, and the specialized community that inhabits deep-sea hydrothermal vents. Marine environments identified by their physical–geological setting include estuaries, coastal marine and nearshore zones, and open-ocean–deep-sea regions (**Fig. 1**). *See* Ecological communities; Phytoplankton; Zooplankton.

Estuarine ecosystems. An estuary is a semienclosed area or basin with an open outlet to the sea where fresh water from the land mixes with seawater. The ecological consequences of fresh-water input and mixing create strong gradients in physical–chemical characteristics, biological activity and diversity, and the potential for major adverse impacts associated

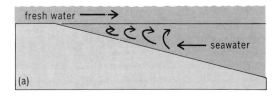
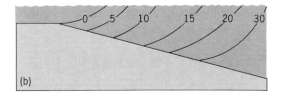
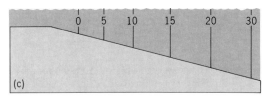

Fig. 2. Salinity structure of the three general types of estuaries found throughout the world. (*a*) Strongly stratified system due to high surface fresh-water inflow. (*b*) Moderated stratified system showing lines of equal salinity in parts per thousand. (*c*) Well-mixed estuary showing vertically homogeneous salinity structure in parts per thousand.

with human activities. Because of the physical forces of tides, wind, waves, and fresh-water input, estuaries are perhaps the most ecologically complex marine environment. They are also the most productive of all marine ecosystems, containing within their physical boundaries many of the principal marine ecosystems defined by community type. *See* Estuarine oceanography.

Salinity, temperature, and submarine irradiance, that is underwater light, determine to a large extent the biological composition of estuarine communities. In estuaries, salinity ranges from nearly fresh-water to oceanic concentrations. The actual salinity structure of estuaries varies both among and within estuaries and is determined by fresh-water inflow, tidal energy, and general estuarine circulation patterns. Estuaries are often classified into three groups, based on salinity structure (**Fig. 2**). The ecological significance of this is that most estuarine populations of plants and animals are physiologically limited by their salinity tolerance range, which restricts their distribution to particular zones. Temperature and submarine light play similarly important ecological roles by limiting or controlling important ecological processes. Temperature extremes generally limit the global distribution of species and seasonally determine the rates of metabolic processes within a given ecosystem. Submarine light plays an equally important role in governing both the rates of photosynthesis and the distribution of photosynthetic organisms. *See* Seawater; Thermocline.

Estuaries are further characterized by their principal ecosystem components, which often form the basic ecological unit of study. Salt marshes, mangroves, seagrasses, plankton, and benthic ecosystems are principal components of estuaries and vary in relative

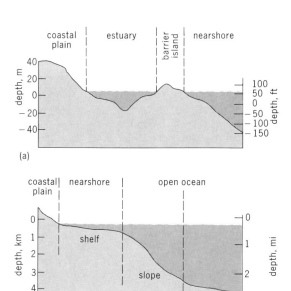

Fig. 1. Cross-sectional profile of (*a*) estuarine and nearshore and (*b*) coastal and open-ocean marine environments. The nearshore region, although not precisely defined, is generally within kilometers of the coastline. 1 m = 3.3 ft.

importance or even occurrence within specific estuaries. Salt marshes and mangroves are ecosystems that are dominated by vascular plants, occur worldwide, and occupy the intertidal zone. Salt marshes have their greatest distribution and abundance in the temperate latitudes, whereas mangroves are restricted to the tropics. Both play important roles in aquatic productivity, trophic structure, and nutrient cycling and serve as natural erosion-control structures. Seagrasses, which are submerged aquatic vascular plants, occur subtidally throughout the world and grow at depths ranging from just below the water surface to more than 30 ft (10 m) in some tropical areas. These plants, evolved from terrestrial ancestors, play many of the same ecological roles as the intertidal salt marsh and mangrove ecosystems, and are limited principally by the availability of submarine light. Planktonic and benthic ecosystems occur in all aquatic systems and for most estuarine environments have the greatest areal extent. Both are important for aquatic productivity and nutrient cycling and support, at least in part, economically valuable fisheries resources. *See Mangrove; Salt marsh*.

Coastal and nearshore ecosystems. Coastal and nearshore marine ecosystems are generally considered to be marine environments bounded by the coastal land margin (seashore) and the continental shelf 300–600 ft (100–200 m) below sea level. The continental shelf, which occupies the greater area of the two and varies in width from a few to several hundred kilometers, is strongly influenced by physical oceanographic processes that govern general patterns of circulation and the energy associated with waves and currents.

Ecologically, the coastal and nearshore zones grade from shallow water depths, influenced by the adjacent landmass and input from coastal rivers and estuaries, to the continental shelf break, where oceanic processes predominate. Biological productivity and species diversity and abundance tend to decrease in an offshore direction as the food web becomes supported only by planktonic production.

Estuarine–nearshore couplings include the advective transport of nutrients and organic matter into nearshore waters, and seasonal migrations of ecologically and economically important species between coastal waters and estuaries. Advective transport contributes organic matter and nutrients, particularly nitrogen, which are thought to augment both primary and secondary production. Net primary production in nearshore waters has often been inadequate to support estimated secondary production, and so riverine and estuarine sources provide organic matter and nutrients. In seasonal migrations, many species of shellfish and finfish that spawn offshore migrate or are transported by water into estuaries during the larval or juvenile stage. There, these species grow and mature and then migrate offshore as adults to complete the cycle.

Among the unique marine ecosystems associated with coastal and nearshore water bodies are seaweed-dominated communities (for example, kelp "forests"), coral reefs, and upwellings. Seaweed communities are distributed worldwide and occupy coastal areas from the intertidal zone to depths exceeding 30 ft (10 m). Green (Chlorophyceae), brown (Phaeophyceae), and red (Rhodophyceae) macroscopic algae dominate seaweed communities and show strong depth-dependent zonation patterns in response to various physical stresses, light requirements, and grazing pressure. Coral reefs are calcium carbonate structures made by reef-building (hermatypic) corals and crustose coralline algae and are best known for their high species diversity and structural complexity. They are limited to the tropical regions and require high light and temperature environments (greater than 68°F or 20°C). Upwelling regions are coastal areas where nutrient-rich bottom waters are moved toward the surface by persistent winds blowing parallel to the coast. As a result of the Coriolis effect and the Ekman spiral, surface water is transported offshore and replaced by bottom or middepth water, leading to a relatively continuous supply of nutrients to enhance primary production. Upwelling regions have historically been areas of economically important fisheries.

Open-ocean–deep-sea environments. Approximately 70% of the Earth's surface is covered by oceans, and more than 80% of the ocean's surface overlies water depths greater than 600 ft (200 m), making open-ocean–deep-sea environments the largest—yet the least ecologically studied and understood—of all marine environments. The major oceans of the world differ in their extent of landmass influence, circulation patterns, and other physical–chemical properties. Other major water bodies included in open-ocean–deep-sea environments are the areas of the oceans that are referred to as seas. A sea is a water body that is smaller than an ocean and has unique physical oceanographic features defined by basin morphology. Because of their circulation patterns and geomorphology, seas are more strongly influenced by the continental landmass and island chain structures than are oceanic environments.

Within the major oceans, as well as seas, various oceanographic environments can be defined. A simple classification would include water column depths receiving sufficient light to support photosynthesis (photic zone); water depths at which light penetration cannot support photosynthesis and which for all ecological purposes are without light (aphotic zone); and the benthos or bottom-dwelling organisms. Occupying the depths between the surface and the average depth of the world's oceans (12,000 ft or 4000 m) are a diverse group of organisms that include microbes, invertebrates, and vertebrates. Classical oceanography defines four depth zones; epipelagic, 0–450 ft (0–150 m), which is variable; mesopelagic, 450–3000 ft (150–1000 m); bathypelagic, 3000–12,000 ft (1000–4000 m); and abyssopelagic, greater than 12,000 ft (4000 m). These depth strata correspond approximately to the depth of sufficient light penetration to support photosynthesis; the zone in which all light is attenuated; the truly aphotic zone; and the deepest oceanic environments. The benthic fauna are classified in a similar manner as continental shelf and slope fauna, ocean basin or abyssal fauna, and fauna unique to the deep ocean basins and trenches.

The open-ocean–deep-sea environments present themselves as both a challenge scientifically and as a world resource that demands cooperative international research and attention. Estuaries and coastal ecosystems, as defined previously, are more localized and lend themselves to regional scientific exploration and understanding. Oceans and seas, on the other hand, are a global resource, crossing all political and national boundaries and requiring international cooperation and participation in ecological studies.

Marine ecological processes. Fundamental to marine ecology is the discovery and understanding of the principles that underlie the organization of marine communities and govern their behavior, such as controls on population growth and stability, quantifying interactions among populations that lead to persistent communities, and coupling of communities to form viable ecosystems. The basis of this organization is the flow of energy and cycling of materials, beginning with the capture of radiant solar energy through the processes of photosynthesis and ending with the remineralization of organic matter and nutrients.

Photosynthesis and autotrophic production. Photosynthesis in seawater is carried out by various marine organisms that range in size from the microscopic, single-celled marine algae to multicellular vascular plants. Conversion of carbon dioxide into simple organic compounds and the subsequent synthesis of algal or vascular plant biomass forms the ultimate base of most food webs in the marine environment (omitted from this discussion are food webs based on chemosynthetic organisms). Because of that relationship, photosynthesis remains the focus of much marine ecological research. *See* FOOD WEB.

The rate of photosynthesis, and thus the growth and primary production of marine plants, is dependent on a number of factors, the more important of which are availability and uptake of nutrients, temperature, and intensity and quality of light. Of these three, the last probably is the single most important in governing primary production and the distribution and abundance of marine plants. Consequently, the optical physics of seawater has been an important component of much research on photosynthesis and autotrophic production in marine environments.

The intensity and spectral quality of light in seawater is a function of incoming solar radiation, surface roughness, dissolved substances, suspended particulates, and water depth. Historically, measures of submarine light were based on photometric standards and units that had been developed for the human eye, such as footcandle, lumen, and lux, which have limited and questionable meaning in a biological context. Both physiologically and ecologically, light in the spectral region termed photosynthetically active radiation (PAR), at about 400–700 nanometers, is important and is measured as irradiance in units of energy flux (joules $\cdot$ m^{-2} $\cdot$ s^{-1}) or photon flux (microeinsteins $\cdot$ m^{-2} $\cdot$ s^{-1}), where one einstein (1 E) equals one mole of quanta or photons (6.02 × 10^{23}). As solar radiation passes through a water column, it is reduced in energy content and changed in spectral quality because of absorption and scattering. The total effect on intensity, termed attenuation, is probably the most common optical property of water reported and is derived according to the exponential decay function expressed in the equation below, where k is the atten-

$$k_{1,2} = \frac{\ln (I_2) - \ln (I_1)}{z_2 - z_1}$$

uation coefficient between depths 1 and 2, I is the irradiance intensity at depths 1 and 2, and z is the depth. Generally, all depths are measured in meters below the water surface, and the attenuation coefficient is expressed in units of per-meter (m^{-1}). PAR attenuation varies considerably depending on water type, with attenuation coefficients of 0.03–0.04 for the clearest open-ocean waters and 3–4 for the most turbid coastal and estuarine waters. PAR attenuation

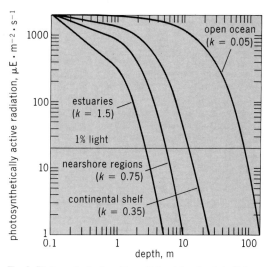

Fig. 3. Photosynthetically active radiation intensity at depth for various values of the attenuation coefficient (k). The intersection of the 1% light level (the limiting light intensity for photosynthesis) with the decay curves marks the depth limit for the photic zone. In these examples, the depth limit ranges from approximately 300 ft (100 m) in the open ocean to 10 ft (3 m) in estuaries. 1 m = 3.3 ft.

determines water depths at which light intensity can support photosynthesis (photic zone) and ranges from a few meters in estuaries and turbid coastal waters to approximately 450–600 ft (150–200 m) in the clearest open-ocean waters (**Fig. 3**).

The relationship between photosynthesis and light intensity varies among the different primary producers in marine environments but can be defined generally by a hyperbolic relationship. Characteristic of this relationship is (1) an initial positive, linear increase in photosynthesis with increasing light; (2) a nonlinear response above a threshold light intensity where photosynthesis does not increase linearly with increasing

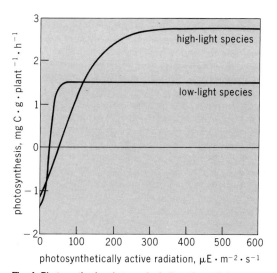

Fig. 4. Photosynthesis–photosynthetically active radiation curves for two marine plants with fundamentally different light relations. The high-light plant, which has a higher P_{max} but requires much more light, is typical of high-light environments such as those of the tropics and shallow water. The low-light plant has a lower P_{max} but requires much less light and photosynthetically saturates more quickly. These plants are typical of more turbid environments or environments where light is limiting for significant portions of the photoperiod.

Areal and total estimates for net primary production in the principal marine environments of the world

Region	Area, 10^6 km²*	Net primary production, g·m⁻²·yr⁻¹	Total net primary production 10^9 t·yr⁻¹	Percent of area	Percent of total net primary production
Open ocean	332	125	41.5	91.9	77.7
Continental shelf	27	300	8.1	7.5	15.2
Estuaries	1.4	1500	2.1	0.4	3.9
Seaweeds and coral	0.6	2500	1.5	0.2	2.6
Upwelling regions	0.4	500	0.2	0.1	0.4
Total	361.4		53.4		

*1 km² = 0.4 mi².

light; and (3) an upper limit to the rate of photosynthesis (P_{max}) at which increasing light has no effect and, if light intensity becomes high enough, may actually reduce or inhibit photosynthesis in some plants. **Figure 4** illustrates the photosynthesis–light relationships for two hypothetical marine plants that differ in these fundamental characteristics.

Autotrophic or primary production is the direct result of the biochemical and physiological processes of photosynthesis, but it is not equal to it, and results from the net positive growth of marine plants. Considering the high attenuation of light in water and the relationships between light intensity and photosynthesis, net autotrophic production is confined to relatively shallow water depths. The major primary producers in marine environments are intertidal salt marshes and mangroves, submerged seagrasses and seaweeds, phytoplankton, benthic and attached microalgae, and—for coral reefs—symbiotic algae (zooxanthellae). These principal autotrophic components of marine ecosystems differ in geographic distribution and abundance, rates of organic matter production, and the food webs they support relative to secondary or heterotrophic production, including fishery yields. Though imprecisely known and highly variable for specific environments, net primary production for the principal marine environments of the world's oceans is summarized in the **table**. On an areal basis, estuaries and nearshore marine ecosystems have the highest annual rates of primary production. From a global perspective, the open oceans are the greatest contributors to total marine primary production because of their overwhelming size.

The two other principal factors that influence photosynthesis and primary production are temperature and nutrient supply. Temperature affects the rate of metabolic reactions, and marine plants show specific optima and tolerance ranges relative to photosynthesis. Nutrients, particularly nitrogen, phosphorus, and silica, are essential for marine plants and influence both the rate of photosynthesis and plant growth. For many phytoplankton-based marine ecosystems, dissolved inorganic nitrogen is considered the principal limiting nutrient for autotrophic production, both in its limiting behavior and in its role in the eutrophication of estuarine and coastal waters.

Food webs and heterotrophic production. The concept of a marine food web and heterotrophic, or secondary, production is based on the view that energy, as well as organic matter and nutrients, is transferred between organisms that occupy different levels in a heirarchical trophic or feeding structure. The complexity and specific interactions among populations within this conceptual framework form the basis of much marine ecological research and are a source of controversy among marine ecologists. What has evolved is that marine food webs and the processes leading to secondary production of marine populations can be divided into plankton-based and detritus-based food webs. They approximate phytoplankton-based systems and macrophyte-based systems.

The classical view of the open-ocean food web involved planktonic algae (diatoms) being grazed by planktonic crustaceans (copepods), which were in turn preyed upon by other invertebrates and fish. Based on size, the final links in the food chain were relatively large organisms, and the classical view dictated that both energy flow and productivity in the oceans were due to these larger populations. To a large extent, this view resulted from the sampling gear and techniques available at the time. This simple, linear food-chain model has been replaced by recognition of the role played by smaller organisms, both autotrophic and heterotrophic, in primary and secondary production, and the cycling of carbon and nutrients. For planktonic food webs, current evidence suggests that primary production is partitioned among groups of variously sized organisms, with small organisms, such as cyanobacteria, playing an equal if not dominant role at times in aquatic productivity. The smaller autotrophs, both through excretion of dissolved organic compounds to provide a substrate for bacterial growth and by direct grazing by protozoa (microflagellates and ciliates), create a microbially based food web in aquatic ecosystems that had once been largely ignored. The consequences of the revised view are that the major portion of autotrophic production and secondary utilization in marine food webs may be controlled, not by the larger organisms typically described as supporting marine food webs (including those leading to the major coastal and oceanic fisheries), but by microscopic populations.

Macrophyte-based food webs, such as those associated with salt marsh, mangrove, and seagrass ecosystems, are not supported by direct grazing of the dominant vascular plant but by the production of detrital matter through plant mortality. The classic example is the detritus-based food webs of coastal salt marsh ecosystems. These ecosystems, which have very high rates of primary production (see table), enter the marine food web as decomposed and fragmented particulate organics. The particulate organics of vascular plant origin support a diverse microbial community that includes bacteria, flagellates, ciliates, and other protozoa. These organisms in turn support higher-level consumers, which include gastropods, mollusks, polychaetes, crustaceans, and fish. The high productivity of estuaries, particularly those in the Mid-Atlantic temperate regions of North America and Europe and the northern coasts of the Gulf of Mexico, results not only from phytoplankton production in the estuaries themselves but also from the contribution of surrounding salt marsh ecosystems.

The highest levels of both primary and secondary production are associated with estuarine and near-shore coastal marine ecosystems. Open-ocean systems are less productive on a per-area basis, and both pelagic (water column) and benthic food webs in deep ocean environments depend on primary production in the overlying water column. For benthic communities, organic matter must reach the bottom by sinking through a deep water column, a process that further reduces its energy content. Thus, in the open ocean, high rates of secondary production, such as fish yields, are associated with areas in which physical–chemical conditions permit and sustain high rates of primary production over long periods of time, as is found in upwelling regions.

Regardless of specific marine environment, microbial processes provide fundamental links in marine food webs that directly or indirectly govern flows of organic matter and nutrients that in turn control ecosystem productivity and stability. *See Biological productivity; Ecology; Ecosystem; Seawater fertility.*

Richard Wetzel

Bibliography. J. W. Day, Jr., et al., *Estuarine Ecology*, 1989; M. L. Dring, *The Biology of Marine Plants*, 1982; J. S. Levinton, *Marine Ecology*, 1982; I. Valiela, *Marine Ecological Processes*, 1984.

Marine fisheries

The harvest of animals and plants from the ocean to provide food and recreation for people, food for animals, and a variety of organic materials for industry. If methods can be devised to harvest smaller organisms not heretofore used because they have been too costly to catch and process, it has been estimated that the world yield could perhaps be increased severalfold. The Soviet Union is said to have developed an acceptable human food product from Antarctic krill, an abundant small shrimplike animal which is the principal food of the blue whale. *See Fishery conservation.*

COMMERCIAL AND RECREATIONAL FISHING

The world marine commercial fish catch grew more than 6% per year from the end of World War II to 1967. In 1969, however, the catch dropped slightly, and in the years following 1967 the average rate of increase was about 1.3% per year. This total was disturbed considerably by the fairly steady growth of the fresh-water fisheries, which grew more rapidly than the marine fisheries, and by the rise and decline of the Peruvian anchovy fishery. Growth in the catch of marine finfishes and invertebrates, minus fresh-water fisheries and Peruvian anchovy, was fairly steady, with perhaps a slight decline after 1976. The growth of world marine fisheries with anchovy removed has been fairly steady since about 1940. Whales are not included in these catches because they are recorded by numbers rather than by weight. Whale fisheries provide whale oil, sperm oil, whale meal, whale livers, vitamin A, whale meat, solubles, and other products.

About 87% of the world fish and shellfish catch comes from the Northern Hemisphere. The increased catch from the Southern Hemisphere was caused mostly by the growth and collapse of the Peruvian anchovy fishery, which was once the largest fishery for a single species in the world. The fishery began in 1956, grew rapidly to a maximum in 1970 (18.5% of the world catch), and dropped thereafter. The Northern Hemisphere contains only about 43% of the total area of ocean, but it includes most of the world's estuaries and continental shelves. It is in these rich and relatively shallow waters that most marine fish and shellfish resources are concentrated.

Over the years, the United States has declined as a world fishing power, but like many popular views about fisheries this is a gross oversimplification. Total domestic fishery production has remained about level for many years, while catches by several other nations have been growing. Americans have obtained increasing amounts of fish and shellfish by imports. The United States consumes more than 12% of world fishery production, and thus is the most attractive fishery market in the world.

The most remarkable fishery development was the climb by Peru from a position of insignificance among fishing nations in the late 1950s to first place by weight landed in the late 1960s. The subsequent decline of this major fishery, based almost entirely on a single species of anchovy, illustrates the inherent instability of most fishery resources. This densely schooling herringlike fish owed its tremendous abundance to the high biological fertility of the Humboldt Current. Fluctuations in anchovy catches are related to fluctuations in the Humboldt Current and also to excessive fishing. Pelagic schooling fishes that feed at relatively low trophic levels, like anchovy, appear to be much more vulnerable to overfishing, and less likely to recover, than demersal species like cod or haddock. *See Seawater fertility.*

Most marine fisheries are located close to coasts. Only a small part of the world catch is taken more than 100 mi (160 km) from shore.

No one knows exactly how many different kinds of marine life are used by people. In official statistics many species are lumped together. Several thousand species are included in the world catch, but a surprisingly small number make up the bulk of the catch. For example, most of the domestic catch in the United States, over 83% by weight, is made up of only 12 kinds of fish and shellfish. Omitting the considerable part of the world marine fishery catch which is unsorted and unidentified, 20 kinds of fish, shellfish, and plants make up about 99% by weight of the world catch. The 10 most important in order of weight are herrings, cods, jacks, ocean perch and redfish, mollusks, mackerels, tunas, crustacea, flounders, and shads.

Changing patterns. Before World War II few fishing crews ventured very far away from their home shores in search of marine fish. There were some notable exceptions, however. Some European fishers had been lured years before to the rich banks of Newfoundland, Nova Scotia, and New England; whaling had begun in the productive waters surrounding Antarctica; the Japanese had started their march across the ocean in search of salmon, tuna, and other species; and the United States tuna fleet was already developing its fishery off Central and South America. But these developments were halted during the war. After the war the need for animal protein stimulated several countries to develop distant water fisheries. In the forefront were Japan and the Soviet Union. These two countries have developed modern, self-sufficient fleets of factory ships, catcher boats, and supply vessels which can and do operate anywhere in the world ocean. Both countries are net exporters of fishery products.

In contrast, the United States fish catch has remained almost static for many years. It rose slightly after the war, reaching an all-time high in 1962. Since 1962 the total catch has dropped slightly. About 2% of the United States commercial catch comes from fresh water. The United States is a net importer of fishery products.

United States fishing industry. The reasons why the United States supplies most of its demand for fishery products by importing, whereas other major fishing nations produce more than they consume, are complicated, and only a brief account can be given here. First, it must be understood that, although there are a few large fishing companies in the United States, most commercial fishing is conducted by a large number of small, independent operators. Most of them are in competition with each other, either to make the catch or to purchase the raw material from the fishing crews. These segments of the industry can be classified in various ways, but the important distinction is between the fishers and the processing-distributing segment of industry.

Problems of fishers. Almost all United States fishers are independent operators. Some are prosperous, but many are struggling to make a living. In many fisheries there are more fishers and units of gear than are necessary to make the catch. They are hemmed in by laws and regulations, many enacted in the name of conservation, but merely increasing the cost of catching fish. The living resources fluctuate widely in abundance from natural causes, and their migration patterns change from time to time. Most fishers in the United States lack the flexibility to shift from one fishery to another in response to these changes. They pay more for boats and gear than do their foreign competitors. Foreign fishers are liberally subsidized in various ways by their governments, and substantial quantities of this subsidized catch are offered in the United States at prices lower than American fishers are willing to accept. Many of the oldest fishery resources in the United States are fully utilized. Others have been overfished, and attempts to rehabilitate them are being made. These obstacles are almost overwhelming to many fishers in the United States.

Legislation. Public Law 94-265 is the Fishery Conservation and Management Act of 1976. This act extended United States fishery jurisdiction to a zone 197 mi (317 km) beyond the territorial sea (that is, 200 mi or 322 km out from the general trend of the coast). It gave preference to United States fishers to harvest the resources of this zone, but if American fishing capacity was not able to take the total allowable catch, the surplus must be allocated to foreign fishers. It also provided that domestic fishers, commercial and recreational, must be regulated so that they will not exceed their share of the quota. This has not been clearly understood by many domestic fishers, who believed that foreign fishing would stop entirely, and that they would be free to fish without restriction.

To administer the act, the law created eight Regional Fishery Management Councils. Each council is composed of the heads of the state agency which administers fisheries in each state, the regional director of the National Marine Fisheries Service for the appropriate region, one member from each state selected from a list submitted by the governor of that state, and an equal number of members, also selected from lists provided by the governor, who can represent any state. In addition, there are four nonvoting members, one from the Department of State, one from the Fish and Wildlife Service in the Department of the Interior, one from the Coast Guard, and one from the interstate Marine Fisheries Commission having jurisdiction in the region. The Mid-Atlantic Council, the largest of the eight councils, has 19 voting members and 4 nonvoting members picked according to this formula.

Regional Fishery Management Councils. The principal functions of the councils are to draw up fishery management plans for each species of fish or shellfish within its region and to recommend licensing of other nations. Only a few fishery management plans (FMPs) are in operation, and for the most part they have had difficulty. The principal problem has been enforcing the laws against domestic fishers. Commercial fishers are ingenious in devising ways in which to circumvent the law, and enforcement agents are having difficulty in carrying out adequate surveillance. Recreational fishers are even more difficult to control because they operate from so many points along the coast and do not have adequate statistics to estimate their share of the catch. The only way in which the catch can be allocated is to calculate the total allowable catch, allocate to recreational fishers the amount they will take based on past records, allocate to commercial fishers that part of the remainder which they are judged able to take, and if any is left over, allocate that to foreign fishers. This is a very poor system, because recreational fishers are known to exaggerate their catches, whereas commercial fishers tend to underreport theirs. This can be corrected only by a better system for gathering statistics, which may be very expensive. The councils have a long way to go before they can be said to be successful. It is beginning to be realized now that the problem was by no means as simple as controlling foreign fisheries.

United States tuna and, to a lesser degree, shrimp fisheries are in a different position. Shrimpers are being closed out of the 200-mi (322-km) zones of Latin American countries. Tuna fishers are exempt from the provisions of PL94-265 and will continue to be regulated through international treaties. The tuna fisheries are in difficulty because more and more nations are moving into the fishery and Americans are taking a smaller proportion of the total catch.

Problems of processor and distributor. These segments of the United States fishing industry do not usually have the same difficulties as the fishers. Those who rely upon a single species, as the now defunct California sardine industry did, are at the mercy of a fluctuating supply of raw material and, when the total catch begins to drop, they are likely to encourage fishers to increase their fishing effort to maintain the total catch at a level that will protect capital investment. Such a policy leads almost inevitably to overfishing and, possibly, destruction of the resource. A reasonable solution is to have alternative resources to turn to as the abundance of a species drops. Unfortunately, however, no two kinds of fish behave exactly alike, and it requires new techniques, and often other types of fishing gear, to catch another kind of fish economically. Thus, while the principal resource is abundant, the industry has no interest in seeking alternate resources, and when the principal resource declines, the capital to develop other fishing methods is hard to find.

Other fish processors in the United States stabilize their supply of raw material by importing partially processed or processed fish in quantity. By diversifying operations and source of supply, the processor or distributor of fish can avoid many economic problems.

Sport fisheries. It is recognized that sport fishing in the United States is big business, and that the recreational fisheries must also be protected. Although the statistics of sport fisheries are inadequate and based upon rather small samples, there is no doubt that they are large. For example, in the section of coast from New York to Virginia inclusive, it is estimated that about three times as many food fishes are taken by recreational fishers as compared to commercial fishers. There is little point in trying to manage such fisheries unless the recreational fisheries also can be controlled.

A considerable industry has developed around the marine sport fisheries. The investment in manufacturing and retailing establishments for tackle, boats, motors, bait, fuel, and all the other necessities of the fisher is large. Operators of marinas, fishing piers, and other establishments in the coastal area may derive all or a considerable part of their income from sport fishing and associated activities.

Fishery management. The objective of modern fishery management has shifted from maintenance of the resource at the level of maximum sustainable yield to aiming for optimum yield. Optimum, in the words of the act, means the amount of fish which will provide the greatest overall benefit to the nation, with particular reference to food production and recreational opportunities; and which is prescribed as such on the basis of the maximum sustainable yield from such fishery, as modified by any relevant economic, social, or ecological factors. This is a very vague definition, which can mean almost anything. Moreover, maximum sustainable yield, as applied to a single fish stock, is no longer recognized as being very meaningful, for fish stocks, predators, competitors, and other environmental variables interact, so that a decline in one may be accompanied by increases in others. This new concept in fishery science requires new research.

A simple model of a fish stock is given in **Fig. 1**. When fishing begins, the catch increases in proportion to fishing effort. But soon there is competition between units of effort for the catch, and the catch increases at an ever-decreasing rate until a maximum is reached. If the intensity of fishing increases beyond that point, the total catch will begin to drop because the capacity of the resource to renew itself has been reduced. The catch per fisher will drop more rapidly than the total catch, for more fishers will be sharing a smaller catch. Actually, the catch per fisher will begin to drop before the point of maximum sustainable yield is reached, for reasons already stated. Economists believe that the amount of fishing effort should be limited to the point of maximum economic yield (MEY), which is reached before the catch reaches a maximum, and which is the point at which a line parallel to the cost line is tangent to the curve. From a conservationist's point of view such a restriction should have advantages, for limiting the catch at a level below the maximum biological yield would provide a safety factor against overfishing. This, however, is such a simple model that it applies to very few, if any, fisheries. The maximum sustainable yield (MSY) usually fluctuates greatly because the environment and other factors are constantly changing and because there are energy transfers from one resource to another as conditions change.

Very few marine fisheries are regulated to maintain the maximum sustainable yield. The classic examples were the Pacific halibut fishery and the fur seal industry on the Pribilof Islands. Both resources had been restored from a condition of overfishing and were producing approximately the maximum sustainable yield. The joint Canadian–United States halibut management program was affected adversely by incidental catches of foreign trawlers fishing for other species. The North American Pacific halibut catch dropped to about one-third of what it was before intensive foreign fisheries developed in the Gulf of Alaska. The fur seal program was also affected by foreign fishing, which removed large numbers of Alaska pollock from the vicinity of the Pribilofs. As a result, the females had to go farther to sea to obtain adequate food, and had to stay out longer, and many pups starved to death. The harvest dropped by about two-thirds in less than 10 years. In the northwest Atlantic a unique development in the mid-1970s was international agreement on a total catch quota for all species combined, which is less than the sum of the quotas for individual major species and stocks. This approach forced the fishing fleets to make major strategy decisions in advance of the fishing season. The plan was designed to relieve pressure on important species, such as haddock and yellowtail flounder, which have been seriously overfished. Management is made difficult by local traditions, natural fluctuations in abundance, difficulty of surveillance and enforcement of laws, and domestic or international disagreements as to the condition of the resource.

International management. With passage of PL 94-265 in the United States and extension of jurisdiction by various means by most other countries, international management of fisheries has become much less important. Tunas are still managed by international agreement because they are highly migratory and could not be managed adequately by individual nations. Yet this is not entirely satisfactory in the United States because some tunas are also important to recreational fishers, whose interests are not being served adequately in the international arena. Some

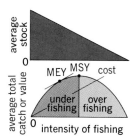

Fig. 1. Relations among fishing intensity, stock size, and average sustainable total catch from a fish population (not to scale).

Regional Fishery Management Councils are proposing that tunas also be included in domestic arrangements. Whales also remain under international control; however, this is under constant attack by extremists who would like to see all marine mammals completely protected from fishing.

Although international fishery management was coming under increasingly severe attack for its inadequacy in dealing with major problems, there is no question that it was more effective, by and large, than domestic control over coastal fisheries. It is significant that the Mid-Atlantic Council, when it began to put fishery management plans into effect, chose a completely domestic species, which never had been subject to foreign fishing, for first attention. It has not been totally successful in managing this sea clam fishery, even though it had an additional simplifying feature in that there is no recreational fishery of any consequence. If this fishery cannot be managed adequately, there is even less chance that there will be success with more complicated fisheries like bluefish, summer flounder or fluke, and other important species.

There is one other possibility: eventually the Law of the Sea Conferences may be able to draft a treaty that will satisfy most countries. This would be preferable, but the chances are not entirely favorable. The Fisheries Conservation and Management Act in the United States foresees this possibility, however, and the act will be modified if and when it occurs. Achievement of a workable fishery management scheme will still be difficult, but in the long run probably will be the most likely route to success.

J. L. McHugh

FISHING TECHNOLOGY

Fishing technology is the rational application of practical experience together with engineering and related natural sciences (such as physics, chemistry, mathematics, biology, and hydrology) to fishing vessels, gears, and operations.

Until the 1930s the technical development of fishing was largely left to the fishers, the ship builders, and the supplying industry. In industrialized countries the overall technical development has had a significant impact on fishing in terms of increased size, power mechanization, range, complexity, and costs. Consequently the traditional trial-and-error approach had to be replaced by systematic research and development. Industrialized countries with important fisheries have, therefore, established specific government- and industry-sponsored research and development capacities, and fishing technology has thus become a fisheries discipline in its own right.

The introduction of engine power to fishing vessels at the end of the last century considerably increased the range and flexibility of fishing operations. It also enabled the development of auxiliary machinery such as winches and haulers to improve efficiency and safety and to reduce hard labor.

Trawling. This mechanization—from which all fishing techniques benefited to various degrees—started a spectacular development of trawling which became one of the most productive fishing methods. In trawling, a conical net bag is towed over the ground (bottom trawling) or through the free water at any depth (midwater trawling) and scoops up the fish in its path. The net is usually towed by a vessel called a trawler; sometimes two vessels are used. Trawlers range from outboard-powered canoes, operating on lakes or in coastal waters, to long-distance factory trawlers that are more than 330 ft (100 m) long and have main engines with more than 5000 hp (3.7 MW) (**Fig. 2**). These are among the most expensive and sophisticated commercial vessels of their size. The most common trawl gear is the otter trawl, for which special shearing devices (otter boards) are used to spread the net opening horizontally. Otter boards range from flat rectangular plates to hydrofoil curved designs up to 129 ft^2 (12 m^2) each. Bottom trawl nets have a mouth opening of up to about 2700 ft^2 (250 m^2) and a total net length of about 260 ft (80 m), and midwater trawl nets of about 22,000 ft^2 (2000 m^2) and 590 ft (180 m), respectively. Commercial bottom trawling goes down to more than 3300 ft (1000 m) depth, and midwater trawling to about 2600 ft (800 m). Towing speed is between about 2.5 and 5 knots (4.5 and 9 km/h).

Aimed trawling. Technical progress in trawlers, trawl gears, and underwater acoustics led during the 1960s to the development of aimed trawling (**Fig. 3**). This involved a horizontal echo sounder or sonar to detect and select suitable fish schools ahead of the trawler, the ship's echo sounder to further assess the depth and quantity of the school and the bottom conditions, and a net sounder to monitor the net depth, the opening height, and the fish in, below, and above the net opening. This combination of echo-sounding (acoustic) devices with modern navigational aids such as gyro compass, sensitive speed log, radar, decca navigator, loran, or even satellite navigation significantly improved the chances of hitting a fish school with the trawl gear and of counteracting escape reactions. Aimed trawling is mainly applied in midwater trawling, but the technology is increasingly also used in bottom trawling.

Integrated trawling systems supplement aimed trawling by adding electronic data processing and computer control of certain parts of the aiming process. A virtually automatic interception of trawl and fish and optimum operational efficiency are achieved

Fig. 2. Example of a long-distance factory trawler (3177 ft or 95 m long, 5000 hp or 3.7 MW) capable of bottom and midwater trawling anywhere in the world. (*Hansetische Hochseefischerei, Germany*)

by computer processing. This processing includes adjustment of course and speed of the trawler and the trawl gear to the position and the movements of selected fish schools, the fixing of sonar to the target, and the adjustment of the trawl winch operation and the towing speed to correct the net depth. Such complex systems are mainly meant for midwater trawling. Other applications are being developed. *SEE SONAR.*

Echo sounding. One of the major problems of fishing is to find the fish when they are not visible at the surface. This was largely solved when, starting in the late 1930s, echo sounding was developed not only to measure the water depth but also to show fish. The principle of echo sounding consists in measuring the time that a sound impulse takes to travel to a target and the reflected echo to come back. Half the total time multiplied by the speed of sound (in water, about 0.9 mi/s or 1500 m/s) gives the distance. The echo strength depends, among other things, on the reflection properties of the target; for example, rocks reflect better than sand or mud and large fish (particularly with swim bladder), or fish schools better than small or single fish. Fish-finding echo sounders need more transmission power and echo amplification than purely navigational echo sounders and also a suitable display, such as a recording or cathode-ray-tube (CRT) presentation for echo discrimination of bottom and various fish sizes and concentrations.

The normal echo sounder, covering the water column below the vessel, is applicable to all fishing methods. Horizontal, or, rather, oblique, echo sounding at various angles between the surface and the bottom forward and around the vessel is also known as sonar (sound navigation and ranging). It mainly serves in midwater trawling and purse seining (see below), for which the advance detection of fish is quite essential. Depending on type and power, the range for fish detection of echo sounders is down to about a 3300-ft (1000-m) depth, and of sonar up to about 9900 ft (3000 m) away from the vessel. The net sounder developed for midwater trawling is an echo sounder with the transducers or sounding units at the net rather than in the ship's bottom (Fig. 3). The connection from net to trawler may be by cable or by an acoustic link (wireless). The more complex multi-net sounder equipment for commercial fisheries includes forward transducers in addition to the down and up transducers, a net filling meter, and a thermometer at the net to check whether the water temperature is according to the preference of the species sought. Scientific multi-net sounder equipment has further transducers across the trawl opening and further aft in the bag, a speed-through-water meter, and a transponder to study gear performance and fish reactions in detail.

Purse seining. In addition to giving all fishers an eye to see under water and paving the way for aimed trawling, the development of underwater acoustics also opened a new dimension to purse seining. This fishing method uses a net which may be 490 to 4900 ft (150 to 1500 m) long and 100 to 660 ft (30 to 200 m) deep which is set in a circle around a fish school and then closed at the bottom like a purse, catching all fish inside. Unless it is done in connection with fish attraction (such as with light), purse seining is completely dependent on finding suitable fish schools. For fish which are not visible at the surface, sonar-guided purse seining is the only solution and quickly led to a very significant expansion of this fishery, which is the largest bulk fish producer in the world.

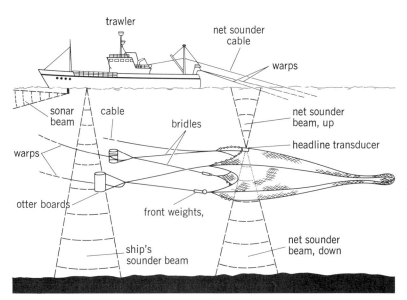

Fig. 3. Typical arrangements of fishing gear and acoustic instrumentation for aimed midwater trawling.

As in aimed trawling, the success of sonar-guided purse seining is largely dependent on the skill of the individual skipper. Consequently, computerized systems have been developed to assist the skipper and also improve the complex tasks of detecting and approaching a fish school, assessing its size and depth, and coordinating the relative movements of vessel and fish school during actual fishing. One such system employs a television screen (**Fig. 4**) to show the situation in the horizontal in relative or true motion as desired. The computer can also link the sonar to a selected school and calculate the depth of the school.

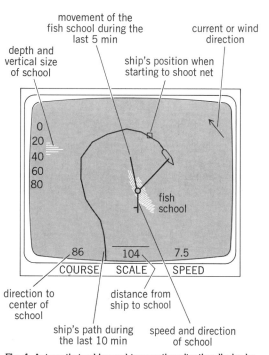

Fig. 4. Automatic tracking and true-motion situation display by a computerintegrated purse-seining system. Course is indicated in degrees, scale in meters, and speed of vessel in knots. Depth scale at left is in meters. 1 m = 3.3 ft. (*SIMRAD AS, Norway*)

Synthetic fibers. Apart from these special developments in trawling and purse seining, the introduction of synthetic materials for yarns, netting, and ropes had an even more general impact on fishing gears and fishing than the introduction of echo sounding, which started at about the same time. The main advantages of synthetics such as polyamide (for example, nylon), polyethylene, and polypropylene are their strong resistance against rotting. Some also have higher breaking strength, elasticity, and abrasion resistance than natural fibers such as cotton, manila, and sisal used hitherto. Higher breaking strength enables the use of thinner yarns, and synthetic monofilaments are almost invisible in water. This can significantly improve the catching efficiency of, for instance, trawls and other bag nets, gill nets, or angling gear. These advantages compensate for the higher price of synthetics which have now almost completely replaced the traditional natural-fiber materials.

Joachim Schärfe

Bibliography. N. G. Benson (ed.), *A Century of Fisheries in North America*, 1970; J. J. Connell (ed.), *Advances in Fish Science and Technology*, 1980; Food and Agriculture Organization, *Yearbook of Fishery Statistics*, annually; J. A. Gulland, *Management of Marine Fisheries*, 1974; T. Laevastu and M. L. Hayes, *Fisheries Oceanography and Ecology*, 1981; National Marine Fisheries Service, *Fisheries of the United States*, annually; B. J. Rothschild (ed.), *Global Fisheries: Perspectives for the 1980s*, 1983.

Marine resources

The oceans, which cover two-thirds of the Earth's surface, contain vast resources of food, energy, and minerals, and are also invaluable in many indirect ways. Capabilities to harvest these resources, and to diminish them, have become so significant that the world's nations have been forced into difficult negotiations toward an internationally accepted legal regime for the oceans, and abiding concerns have been raised about the ocean's ecological status and capacity to serve humankind.

Food. World fisheries expanded steadily from World War II to 1970, particularly the fisheries of Japan and Eastern-bloc countries; some of the annual harvest comes from fish culture in lakes, ponds, and rivers, principally in China and Southeast Asia. The ocean harvest is a very selective one, with 1% of the known oceanic species supplying nine-tenths of the total. It divides into about equal parts for food and industrial products, the latter including meal for livestock feed, fertilizers, and oils. SEE MARINE FISHERIES.

Seafood resources show a distinct geographic pattern, favoring the eastern edge of oceans because of geostrophic upwelling, the high latitudes through seasonal mixing and recycling of nutrients, and the proximity of large rivers.

Unwanted species. Both human preferences and natural factors account for the pause in fisheries expansion. Conservative tastes and dietary preferences prevent the use of many unfamiliar species and of those whose names evoke psychological rejection. Horse mackerel, redfish, spider crabs, and dogfish are examples of undesired food that became highly accepted as Pacific mackerel, ocean perch, Alaska king crab, and grayfish. The marketing of squids, seals, jellyfishes, crabs, and other under- or unexploited species could probably benefit from similar rechristening strategies. Particularly abundant is Antarctic krill, the food of baleen whales; its harvesting and marketing are being explored by the Soviets and Germans. Large populations of sable and lantern fishes in deep water have also attracted fishing effort. Such refocusing measures would counter the domination of ecosystems by left-behind unwanted species.

Species diversity. The California sardine–northern anchovy imbalance seems to be a case in point, except that changes in oceanic conditions—the "climate" in terms of physical and chemical factors—have also been implicated in the ascendancy of the anchovy over the sardine. The study of this fluctuating climate and its effect on species diversity and abundance has been one thrust of oceanographic research.

Competition for resources. It also seems that the insistence on short-term profitability is incompatible with long-term yield and profitability. In whaling, the fleets shifted from the large to the small whales, endangering the survival of most of the cetacean species as well as of the industry. Had the industry been content with a balanced and slightly reduced harvest after the lull of World War II, both the whales and fleets would still thrive. Herring, cod, tuna, and salmon fisheries have also suffered from overcapacity and international competition. In both national and international arenas, means have been sought to regulate the competition for clearly limited and sometimes fragile stocks and to effect a competent management of the living resources and their use.

Mariculture. To help increase the small share that seafood has in world nutrition—less than 20% in animal protein, about 1% in carbohydrates—great effort has been invested in mariculture in the United States and Japan. There exists, of course, much skill in raising of fish and shellfish in fresh and brackish water, and techniques have been developing for thousands of years. The Japanese have been successful in the artificial propagation of the coastal sea bream and yellowtail and the eel and salmon, and also of food and pearl oysters, abalone, and scallops. Mussels are extensively cultured in some bays in Italy and France. Although natural stocks of marine organisms are not overly affected by moderate pollution and do not suffer lasting damage from most oil spills, such events would wipe out the sensitive culture work. Achievement of the goal of large-scale market penetration by the culturing industry requires consideration of its environmental and juridical needs with reference to existing uses.

Energy. The potential for energy from the sea's motion and processes has long been apparent, and designs for wave- and tidal-power devices can be traced back for hundreds of years. Wind was enlisted, of course, by the first sailor. The period from mid-1800 to mid-1900 was particularly fertile for ocean-energy technology and included discovery of the power potential from ocean-thermal gradients. World War II and the period of cheap oil and gas following it pushed many of these ideas aside. With the 1973 Oil Producing and Exporting Countries (OPEC) embargo and recogniton of the limited reserves of fossil fuels, efforts into the use of alternate, renewable energy resources, including the oceanic ones, were redoubled.

Categorizing resources. The categorizing of ocean

energy is somewhat arbitrary. The following are not truly marine: Offshore oil and gas are in principle not different from onshore oil and gas but require greater rigor in exploration and production; about 15% of the world's oil is produced offshore, and extraction capabilities are advancing. Coal deposits, known as extensions of land deposits, are mined under the sea floor in Japan and England. Geothermal resources are known to exist offshore; they are presently not being used, and their prospects are only dimly perceived. Biomass energy in the form of methane from giant kelp is under active investigation. Another extensive energy resource is potentially available in the fissionable and fusible elements contained in seawater; they may provide power for 10^5 and 10^9 years, respectively.

In a strict sense, ocean energy is expressed in the processes of the ocean, such as in the currents, tides, waves, thermal gradients, and the only recently recognized salinity gradients. Solar energy drives them, except the tides, which are fueled by the fossil kinetic energy of the Earth-Moon system. Estimates of the intensities of the processes are given in **Fig. 1**. **Figure 2** shows the size of the resources.

Currents. It is evident that currents constitute the smallest and weakest resource. Low-pressure turbines of 560-ft (170-m) diameter have been proposed for the center of the Gulf Stream, but it is doubtful that ocean currents can be profitably harnessed. A few straits possess fast tidal currents—the Seymour Narrows in British Columbia and the Apolima Straits in Western Samoa, for instance—and offer better prospects.

Tides. Feasible tidal power (see Fig. 2) is limited to a few sites with high tides. Tides now provide the only source of commercial ocean power in the Rance River tidal plant in Brittany, France. It has produced moderate amounts of power in its bank of twenty-four 10-MW turbines, and is still being fine-tuned for greater efficiency. The Soviets have a 400-kW plant near Murmansk, and the Chinese have a number of very small plants.

Waves. Considerable efforts have been directed toward power from waves in England, Japan, Sweden, and the United States. As shown in Fig. 2, wave power is a unique resource in that it could expand under use, because in the open sea the waves could be rebuilt by the winds that cause them.

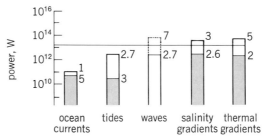

Fig. 2. On the ocean-currents bar, the shading represents the power contained in concentrated currents such as the Gulf Stream. Estimated feasible tidal power is shaded. The dotted extension on "waves" indicates that wind waves are regenerated as they are cropped. "Salinity gradients" includes all gradients in the ocean; the large ones at river mouths are shown by shading. Not shown is the undoubtedly large power if salt deposits are worked against fresh or seawater. On "thermal gradients," the shading indicates the unavoidable Carnot-cycle efficiency. The line at 1.5×10^{13} W is a projected global electricity consumption for the year 2000. (*After G. L. Wick and W. R. Schmitt, Prospects for renewable energy from the sea, Mar. Technol. Soc. J., 11(546):16–21, 1977*)

Salinity gradients. Salinity-gradient energy is present between aqueous solutions of different salinities. Vast amounts of this power are being dissipated in the estuaries of large rivers. Some conversion processes involve semipermeable and ion-selective membranes. One conversion process does not require membranes and is akin to an open-cycle thermal-gradient process. Salinity-gradient energy appears to be the most expensive of the marine options. It does, however, have high intensity and potential, especially when brines and salt deposits are included (see Figs. 1 and 2).

Thermal gradients. Thermal-gradient power, which would use the reservoirs of warm surface water and cold deep water, was first worked on by the French. Georges Claude spent much time and his own money on it in the 1920s, with generally bad luck. The United States government considered it important to its ocean-energy program because, unlike tidal and wave power, it has the capacity for supplying baseload power. It also has a high intensity and potential. Floating tethered units of 100 megawatts electric were projected for locations in the Gulf of Mexico and the Hawaiian Islands. The design as much as possible employs conventional and proved technology, but the continuous operation of a complex system in a corrosive, befouling, and hazardous environment poses a formidable challenge.

Problems. There are some problems common to most marine alternatives. The principal one is transferring the power to shore. Indirect power harvest, such as by tanked or piped hydrogen or by energy-intensive products, from distant units or arrays is often suggested. But the detailed evaluation in the United States' thermal-gradient program pointed to electricity, the highest-value product, to justify the investment and to build up capacity and experience. Other problems pertain to corrosion in saline water, befouling by marine organisms, and deployment in the often violent sea.

Environmental impact. Environmental effects of ocean-energy conversion are generally negligible since the individual sources are large compared with initial demand. Only under extensive conversion would some impacts possibly be felt, such as downstream climatic changes from major ocean-current use, bay and estuarine ecosystem upsets from tidal-

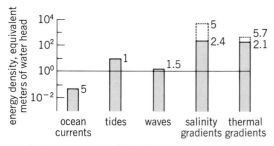

Fig. 1. Intensity or concentration of energy expressed as equivalent head of water. "Ocean currents" shows the driving head of major currents. For tides, the average head of favorable sites is given. For waves, the head represents a spatial and temporal average. The salinity-gradients head is for fresh water versus seawater, the dotted extension for fresh water versus brine (concentrated solution). The thermal-gradients head is for 12°C (68°F), and that for 20°C (54°F) is dotted; both include the Carnot efficiency. (*After G. L. Wick and W. R. Schmitt, Prospects for renewable energy from the sea, Mar. Technol. Soc. J., 11(546):16–21, 1977*)

basin use, possible diminishing of dissolved oxygen from extensive use of waves, and short-circuiting of the ocean's internal heat transfer from thermal-gradient use. Conflicts would also arise with present uses of the sea through hazards to navigation and fisheries operations. Juridical issues still further complicate wide ocean-energy development. Some inadvertent effects may be beneficial, however. Upwelling of nutrients by thermal-gradient plants and the sheltering of organisms by ocean structures could enhance the productivity of fish and invertebrate stocks and their harvest, for instance.

Minerals. Annual production of marine minerals is worth one-tenth that of seafood or offshore oil and one-hundredth that of such nonextractive uses as maritime or military traffic. These minerals fall into two broad categories: geologic ones, or those deposited on or in the seabed; and chemical ones, or those dissolved in seawater.

Geologic resources. Among the deposited resources, the manganese nodules have captured interest in technology development and juridical deliberations, although commercial production has not commenced. Far more important is the dredging of sand and gravel for construction materials. Produced also are aragonite in the Bahamas, monazite off Australia, and diatomaceous earth, while production of diamonds off Namibia was halted in 1971. Southeast Asia produces tin from shallow water, and phosphorite nodule deposits constitute potential fertilizer reserves off Florida and Morocco. Moreover, some hard-rock minerals are won by shaft mining, such as coal off Japan and the British Isles and by drilling such as barytes off Alaska.

Knowledge of the extent of mineral deposits is very scant and spotty. About 0.1% of the United States' continental shelf is surveyed in detail. The shelves of Europe, Southeast Asia, Japan, and South Africa are also explored. Often the surveys belong to private industry, and little is publicly disclosed. If and when shortages and economic prospects stimulate interest, resource surveys and extraction technology progress rapidly, as in the case of oil and gas and the manganese nodules.

The prospects are further enhanced by the work of the United States–operated international Deep Sea Drilling Program, which has drilled and cored more than 500 sites. The resultant insights have revolutionized knowledge of the geologic history and physical dynamics of the sea floor and have advanced understanding of the formation of mineral deposits and ores.

Chemical resources. Among the many elements and compounds dissolved in seawater and taken up by marine organisms, a few have become economically important. Where natural evaporation rates are high, salt and magnesium are won by distillation. Bromine yields to an oxidation-fractionation process. The metals that some marine organisms strongly concentrate—strontium, copper, zinc, nickel, and vanadium—remain unused. Some marine plants are harvested for valuable compounds—a seaweed for agar, kelp for algin, Irish moss for carrageenan. Sponges, pearls, and ambergris are further products elaborated by organisms. Seawater itself is made to yield water for human use, mainly in rich arid countries and on some ships, but large-scale desalination for cities and crops seems to have become the victim of high-energy costs. Rather, the immense tabular icebergs of the Antarctic have been studied as water supplies for arid countries such as Saudi Arabia. One modest-sized Antarctic berg could supply all California with domestic and industrial water and absorb the heat waste of its power plants for a year. SEE SALINE WATER RECLAMATION.

Artifacts. In some sense, past and present artifacts that rest on the bottom of the sea may also be counted as mineral resources. These are often of very high quality in the form of processed ores, trapped oil, finished products and metals, and archeological treasures—coins, jewelry, art objects. Capabilities have grown in archeological, commercial, and military salvage, allowing increasing access to the wrecks of the past.

Passive uses. Often overlooked in resource assessments are nonextractive uses, since they are difficult to quantify. In this category belong such invaluable and indispensable items as inspiration and recreation, commercial and military traffic, and the disposal of waste materials and low-grade heat.

Besides inspiring artists and laymen, the sea has a strong recreational appeal. The crowding on coasts derives in part from the opportunities for sailing, fishing, and water sports, in part from those for trade and defense. Two-thirds of present oil production moves in tankers. Countries use the oceans for cooling water and as a receptacle for liquid and solid wastes: power plants are shore-sited wherever feasible; metropolitan areas discharge wastewater to sea and dump solid materials on a large scale. Such practices have, of course, raised concerns about environmental impact and are now under scrutiny and control; of particular concern is the planned disposal of radioactive wastes in the sub-sea floor.

Conclusions and prospects. The sea is important for intangible and practical ends. It sustains life with its materials and processes. Its organisms satisfy nearly one-fifth of the human demand for animal protein; its content of minerals helps overcome critical shortfalls in terrestrial resources; and it is beginning to yield some of its immense energy flux.

At present the overriding benefit, however, comes from its just being there. It sustains the continents by the spreading of its floor, purifies water and air by the hydrologic cycle, modifies climate zonation by its circulation, inspires humans' vision and carries their trade, and absorbs many of their wastes. It is thus crucial that the sea suffer relatively little from abuse and mismanagement often associated with development and growth, so that it can continue to provide the varied and balanced uses humankind has come to expect from it.

Walter R. Schmitt

Bibliography. A. Brin, *Energy and the Oceans*, 1981; Committee on Merchant Marine and Fisheries, U.S. House of Representatives, *Aquaculture*, 1977; Committee on Science and Technology, U.S. House of Representatives, *Energy from the Ocean*, 1978; J. D. Isaacs, The nature of oceanic life, *Sci. Amer.*, vol. 221, no. 3, 1969; J. D. Isaacs, The sea and man, *Explorers J.*, vol. 46, no. 4, 1968; G. J. Mangone, *The Future of Gas and Oil from the Sea*, 1983; E. Miles and S. Gibbs, *The Management of Marine Regions: The North Pacific*, 1983; National Research Council–National Academy of Sciences, *Priorities for Research in Marine Mining Technology*, 1977; National Research Council–National Academy of Sciences, *Supporting Papers*, *World Food and Nutrition Study*, vol. 1, 1977.

Maritime meteorology

Those aspects of meteorology that occur over, or are influenced by, ocean areas. Maritime meteorology serves the practical needs of surface and air navigation over the oceans. Phenomena such as heavy weather, high seas, tropical storms, fog, ice accretion, sea ice, and icebergs are especially important because they seriously threaten the safety of ships and personnel. The weather and ocean conditions near the air–ocean interface are also influenced by the atmospheric planetary boundary layer, the ocean mixed layer, and ocean fronts and eddies.

Meteorological phenomena. These include heavy weather, tropical storms, fog, ice accretion, and the atmospheric planetary boundary layer.

Heavy weather. Stormy weather at sea outside the tropics is primarily associated with cyclones that form in certain geographical regions where cold, dry air of continental origin and warm, moist air of tropical origin come together during winter (**Fig. 1**). These extratropical storms are especially dangerous to ships at sea because of their relatively high frequency of occurrence and the fact that they can develop extremely rapidly, reaching full force in less than 24 h. A common storm of this type in high latitudes is known as a polar low. Polar lows are relatively small in size (300–500 km or 180–300 mi in diameter) and quite shallow, extending from the sea surface to a height of only 1 or 2 km (0.6 or 1.2 mi). Sudden, explosive storm development (that is, cyclogenesis) is also very common off the east coast of North America in winter. A mature east coast storm is much larger (1000–1500 km or 600–900 mi in diameter) and deeper (8–10 km or 5–6 mi deep or more) than a polar low. Mature extratropical storms that bring most of the heavy weather at sea include gale and hurricane force winds, heavy rains, and high seas.

The fact that such powerful and dangerous marine storms can develop so rapidly presents an especially challenging forecasting problem for meteorologists. The explosive cyclogenesis that occurs off the east coast of North America takes place during winter over the warm Gulf Stream waters east of Cape Cod and south of Nova Scotia. The conditions that are most favorable for such explosive cyclogenesis include a strong, horizontal temperature contrast in the lower atmosphere between the cold continent and the warm Gulf Stream; low vertical stability of the air due to the movement of cold, dry continental air out over the warm water; and the release of latent heat of condensation in the ascent of warm, moist air ahead of the developing storm. Since these conditions are usually prevalent throughout the winter, meteorologists consider the movement of an upper-level (midtropospheric) disturbance over the region favorable for cyclone development to be a key ingredient to triggering the growth of such rapidly developing storms. *See* STORM.

Tropical storms. Cyclones (that is, storms) with very warm, moist air in the center develop in low latitudes over the warmest parts of the tropical oceans (**Fig. 2**). These violent and dangerous storms obtain their energy from the latent heat of condensation that is released in deep, convective rain clouds that form in unstable tropical air. They form when this deep con-

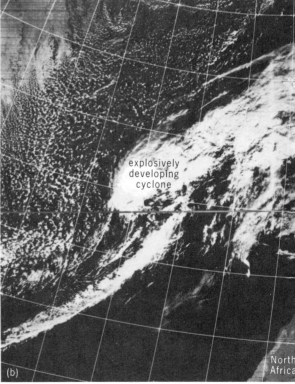

Fig. 1. Cloud patterns in developing extratropical cyclones. (*a*) Photograph (100 mm) taken during a United States space shuttle mission, showing the typical comma-shaped cloud pattern associated with a developing storm off the coast of Nova Scotia (55°N, 50°W). (*b*) Satellite infrared image of a rapidly developing storm in the eastern Atlantic Ocean. The speckled clouds to the northwest of the storm center are seen to originate as thin cloud lines farther upwind to the northwest of the storm (upper left). Such cloud lines are indicative of very cold air that is being drawn into the storm from the northwest by the storm's own cyclonic circulation. (*C. H. Wash, Naval Postgraduate School*)

Fig. 2. Photographs (50 mm) of Hurricane Elena in the Gulf of Mexico on September 1, 1988, taken during a United States space shuttle mission. The low viewing angle and sun angle reveal the different cloud structures and heights in this mature hurricane. (a) Inward-spiraling cloud bands. (b) Close-up of the eye of the storm. (C. H. Wash, Naval Postgraduate School)

vection becomes organized by the inward-spiraling low-level winds associated with an initially weak tropical disturbance. SEE CLOUD PHYSICS.

The winds in a mature tropical storm in the Northern Hemisphere spiral inward and counterclockwise (clockwise in the Southern Hemisphere) in the lower atmosphere and outward and clockwise (counterclockwise in the Southern Hemisphere) aloft. In intense storms, known as hurricanes in the North Atlantic, Gulf of Mexico, and eastern North Pacific, and typhoons in the western North Pacific, the winds can reach 75 m/s (150 knots) or more, with a central calm area or eye roughly 15–70 km (10–40 m) in diameter. These storms generally move from east to west in the trade wind belt, but they occasionally curve poleward into middle latitudes, making forecasting difficult. When a tropical storm moves inland, the source of low-level moisture is greatly reduced, and the storm usually weakens or dissipates—however, not without damage and sometimes loss of life due to the strong winds, heavy rains, and flooding storm tides. With modern technology, tropical storms are easily located and tracked by meteorological satellites. However, their movement can be very difficult to predict because of the strong interaction that occurs between the storm and the larger-scale winds in which the storm is embedded. Also, the reason why so few tropical disturbances actually develop into full-fledged hurricanes is still one of the most important unanswered questions in meteorology. SEE HURRICANE; STORM DETECTION.

Fog. Fog is important to all seagoing activities because it restricts visibility, making navigation (and aircraft operations from navy aircraft carriers) extremely hazardous. Certain types of marine fog can be very thick and persistent. Steam fog is produced when cold air flows over a warmer water surface. Evaporation of the relatively warm water into the overlying, cooler air, followed by condensation into minute liquid droplets, produces the fog. In high

Fig. 3. Sea ice in the marginal ice zone. (a) Relatively small cakes of thin ice near the seaward edge of the marginal ice zone. (b) Much larger and thicker floes farther back from the edge. (P. S. Guest, Naval Postgraduate School)

northern latitudes, steam fog is referred to as arctic sea smoke, and it is very common in the marginal ice zone in winter and early spring (**Fig. 3**). Advection fog occurs when relatively warm, moist air flows over cooler water, cooling the air to saturation. Extensive areas of advection fog can develop when warm air flows poleward over colder water at higher latitudes or when such air flows eastward over the cold, coastal ocean currents that usually exist in midlatitudes off the west coast of continents. Advection fog in such coastal regions is especially pronounced in the summer, when the normally cold ocean currents are made even colder by upwelling of cold water near the coast.

Ice accretion. Ice accretion, which may occur on ships as well as aircraft, not only decreases the efficiency of operation but also may be extremely hazardous, especially to small vessels. The accumulation of ice reduces freeboard and, more importantly, the stability of the ship by making it top-heavy. Ice accretion affects all exposed equipment on ships, including missile launchers and gun systems on navy ships and radar and radio antennas on all ships. Heavy ice accretion can render such equipment completely inoperable. Ice formation occurs primarily from freezing rain and freezing spray from the sea. The most dangerous accumulations of ice develop with freezing spray, which can occur when the air temperature is several degrees or more below freezing. The colder the air and the sea and the stronger the wind, the more rapid is the accumulation of ice. As much as 45 metric tons (50 tons) or more of ice can accumulate in 24 h depending on the size of the ship, which creates a serious hazard to the ship and crew.

Atmospheric planetary boundary layer. Since the atmosphere is semitransparent to incoming solar radiation, about 50% of the Sun's energy passes directly through the atmosphere to be absorbed at the surface. This heat energy is transferred to the atmosphere in the form of sensible and latent heat by conduction and by long-wave radiation, although a large part of the long-wave radiation from the Earth's surface is lost to space and therefore does not affect the atmosphere. The lowest kilometer or so of the atmosphere, in which the air and ocean (or Earth) exchange heat, moisture, and momentum, is known as the atmospheric planetary boundary layer (**Fig. 4**). Except for the lowest millimeter above the sea, the air flow in the atmospheric planetary boundary layer is fully turbulent. This means that the air flow is unsteady, that is, it fluctuates rapidly in space and time; fluid properties mix, that is, they are readily transported from one place to another within the boundary layer; and the forces of inertia dominate those of molecular viscosity. The turbulent nature of the boundary layer greatly increases the vertical transport and the exchange of heat, moisture, and momentum between the atmosphere and the ocean.

As shown schematically in Fig. 4, the atmospheric planetary boundary layer consists of two distinct regions that are of great scientific interest and practical importance to maritime meteorology. In the lowest 50 m (165 ft) or so, in what is called the surface layer, the vertical turbulent transport of heat, moisture, and momentum is essentially constant in the vertical. As a result, the mean temperature, humidity, and horizontal velocity vary approximately logarithmically with height above the sea surface. Above the surface layer, and extending throughout the rest of the bound-

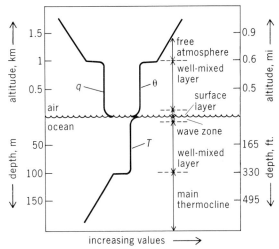

Fig. 4. Schematic drawing of the atmospheric planetary boundary layer and the ocean mixed layer. In the atmosphere, θ is potential temperature (temperature adjusted for the compressibility of the atmosphere), and *q* is specific humidity (ratio of the mass of water vapor to the mass of air in a unit volume of air). In the ocean, *T* is temperature. The quantity θ generally increases with height in the atmosphere, while *T* decreases with depth in the ocean. The wind speed and ocean currents are not shown, but an idealized profile of the winds and currents would tend to follow the θ and *T* lines, respectively.

ary layer, the turbulence is so strong that the mean temperature, moisture, and momentum themselves are well mixed and nearly uniform with height. If the air in the boundary layer is sufficiently moist, clouds (mostly stratocumulus) form in the upper part of the boundary layer, and these clouds sometimes drop to the sea surface as fog. When clouds are present in the boundary layer, both the temperature and the turbulence are affected. Whether the boundary layer is cloudy or not, it usually is capped by a rather thin inversion above which the air is warmer, drier, and much less turbulent. This region above the boundary layer is called the free atmosphere, meaning that the flow there is essentially free of turbulence and largely free from the effects of the underlying surface of the land or ocean. *SEE ATMOSPHERE.*

Oceanic phenomena. These include high seas, sea ice and icebergs, the mixed layer, and fronts and eddies.

High seas. Winds blowing over the sea generate waves and ocean currents. Waves generated by the wind vary in height, length, and period, depending on the wind speed, the length of water over which the wind is blowing in a more or less uniform direction (fetch), and the duration of time the wind has blown. The winds in a mature extratropical cyclone over the ocean can generate waves 10–15 m (33–49 ft) high. Such high seas can cause great damage to ships, harbors, and beaches, and they produce a large amount of ambient noise (sound) in the ocean that hinders naval antisubmarine warfare operations. Because of the importance of high seas to all seagoing activities, oceanographers have developed numerical wave prediction models to forecast the state of the sea. These models include such processes as wave growth, propagation, and dissipation. Their success depends on an accurate analysis and forecast of the surface wind field. Such wave forecasts are used by private companies and government agencies for various purposes, including merchant marine operations, navy tactics and ship maneuvers, refueling at sea, amphibious landing exercises, oil drilling and oil spill operations, and search and rescue. *See Sea state*.

Sea ice and icebergs. Sea ice, formed by the freezing of seawater and floating at the surface of the ocean, is of keen scientific interest and importance to marine meteorology and oceanography. Sea ice plays a key role in air–sea interaction. Since it reflects much of the solar radiation reaching the surface, sea ice greatly reduces the sensible and latent heat exchange between the atmosphere and the ocean, and it severely alters the wind stress acting on the water. At high latitudes, the open and ice-covered regions of the ocean meet in a narrow zone, known as the marginal ice zone (Fig. 3). Environmental parameters of importance in the marginal ice zone include the location, concentration, and thickness of sea ice, and, for naval operations, the small-scale roughness of the top and bottom surfaces of the ice. The ability to predict these parameters depends on a full understanding of how the ocean and the ice exert drag on one another, and how they exchange heat and mass through melting and freezing. Since sea ice rejects most of the salt in the seawater as it freezes, the melting and freezing of sea ice changes the salinity, and hence the density and vertical stability, of the sea immediately below the ice. This, in turn, modifies the dynamic and thermodynamic interaction between the ice and the underlying ocean. In the marginal ice zone, sea ice often drifts, or is episodically forced by the wind, into water that is above freezing, resulting in a rapid melting of the ice. Icebergs, masses of land ice that have broken away from land and are floating on the sea, are of less scientific interest to marine meteorology, but they present a threat to the safety of some ships. They are readily identified and routinely tracked by satellites. *See Sea ice*.

Mixed layer. Over most of the ocean at low and middle latitudes, solar radiation that penetrates the atmosphere is absorbed in the upper ocean, forming a warm, stable, surface layer (Fig. 4). When the wind blows over the surface of the ocean, or when the surface of the ocean is cooled by heat loss to the atmosphere, turbulent motions are generated which mix the warmed and stably stratified surface waters down into the cooler, denser water below. This one-sided mixing process is called entrainment, and it leads to the formation of a well-mixed upper layer in which the temperature is essentially uniform and at the bottom of which there is a sharp temperature drop (density increase). The situation is analogous to the stable inversion that is formed at the top of the atmospheric planetary boundary layer. The only difference is that in the atmospheric boundary layer, active entrainment advances upward from below while in the ocean it works downward from above.

When the winds decrease, turbulence in the upper ocean quickly decays, and active entrainment ceases. The absorption of solar radiation along with lower levels of turbulence then can cause a new mixed layer to form at a shallower depth. Over much of the world's ocean, pronounced deepening and shallowing of the mixed layer takes place over an annual cycle, with warm, shallow mixed layers in summer and cold, deep mixed layers in winter. A less pronounced daily cycle of mixed layer deepening at night and shallowing during the day also occurs. Both of these cycles are greatly modified by episodes of strong winds and high surface-heat losses associated with

tropical and extratropical cyclones over the ocean. Because turbulence in the upper ocean is so strongly dependent on the local atmospheric forcing, the vertical density structure of the upper ocean preserves a fairly accurate record of the wind and weather of the recent past, modified of course by such factors as horizontal and vertical transports within the upper ocean. Fluctuations in the depth of the mixed layer, and in the magnitude of the temperature drop at the base of the mixed layer, are especially important to many tactical naval operations.

Fronts and eddies. Maritime meteorology is concerned about fronts and eddies in the ocean because of their effect on the overlying atmosphere and because they are associated with significant fluctuations in ocean currents, temperature, salinity, and other ocean variables. These fluctuations have horizontal scales of 10–500 km (6–300 mi), vertical scales of 1–2 km (0.6–1.2 mi), and time scales of several days to several weeks or more. Ocean fronts and eddies are commonly referred to as oceanic weather, because of their dynamic and kinematic similarity to atmospheric weather.

Ocean fronts and eddies come in a wide variety of types. The most significant ones are meanders or cutoff eddies (cold and warm core rings) in major ocean current systems such as the north wall of the Gulf Stream or other strong western boundary current systems. Also, there are eddies in the open ocean driven directly by the wind, eddies generated by the interaction of ocean currents with bottom topography, and fronts in the coastal zones caused by upwelling or by cooling of the shallow water on the continental shelf. The meandering of major western boundary currents and the subsequent pinching-off of eddies and rings occur through mixed baroclinic and barotropic instability in the way that midlatitude cyclones develop and occlude in the atmosphere, but the exact mechanisms responsible for these ocean developments are not completely understood. Variations in ocean depth can influence the direction of propagation of preexisting waves and eddies, and cause eddies to be generated locally when water is forced to flow up or down a topographic slope, and they can significantly modify the dynamic stability of major current systems. Oceanic weather associated with upwelling fronts in coastal regions often takes the form of long filaments or dipole (counterrotating) eddies that extend seaward for several hundred kilometers. The origin and dynamics of many of these features are not completely understood, but they are the subject of active research. *See Front*.

Analysis and forecasting. This involves observations and numerical prediction.

Observations. To support the analysis and forecasting of many meteorological and oceanographic elements over the globe, observations are needed from a depth of roughly 1 km (0.6 mi) in the ocean to a height of 30 km (18 mi) in the atmosphere. In addition, the observations must be plentiful enough in space and time to keep track of the major features of interest, that is, tropical and extratropical weather systems in the atmosphere and fronts and eddies in the ocean. Over populated land areas, there is a fairly dense meteorological network; however, over oceans and uninhabited lands, meteorological observations are scarce and expensive to make, except over the major sea lanes and air routes. Direct observations in the ocean, especially below the sea surface, are insufficient to make a synoptic analysis of the ocean except in very limited regions. Fortunately, remotely sensed data from meteorological and oceanographic satellites are helping to fill in some of these gaps in data. Satellite data can provide useful information on the type and height of clouds, the temperature and humidity structure in the atmosphere, wind velocity at cloud level and at the sea surface, the ocean surface temperature, the height of the sea, and the location of sea ice. Although satellite-borne sensors cannot penetrate below the sea surface, the height of the sea can be used to infer useful information about the density structure of the ocean interior. *SEE REMOTE SENSING.*

Numerical prediction. The motion of the atmosphere and the ocean is governed by the laws of fluid dynamics and thermodynamics. These laws can be expressed in terms of mathematical equations that can be put on a computer in the form of a numerical model and used to help analyze the present state of the fluid system and to forecast its future state. This is the science of numerical prediction, and it plays a very central role in marine meteorology and physical oceanography.

The first step in numerical prediction is known as data assimilation. This is the procedure by which observations are combined with the most recent numerical prediction valid at the time that the observations are taken. This combination produces an analysis of the present state of the atmosphere and ocean that is better than can be obtained from the observations alone. Data assimilation with a numerical model increases the value of a piece of data, because it spreads the influence of the data in space and time in a dynamically consistent way.

The second step is the numerical forecast itself, in which the model is integrated forward in time to predict the state of the atmosphere and ocean at a future time. Models of the global atmosphere and world ocean, as well as regional models with higher spatial resolution covering limited geographical areas, are used for this purpose. In meteorology and oceanography the success of numerical prediction depends on collecting sufficient data to keep track of meteorological and oceanographic features of interest (including those in the earliest stages of development), having access to physically complete and accurate numerical models of the atmosphere and ocean, and having computer systems powerful enough to run the models and make timely forecasts. *SEE WEATHER FORECASTING AND PREDICTION.*

Applications. Two important applications of maritime meteorology are ship routing and tactical naval environmental support.

Ship routing. The headway made by a ship transiting the ocean depends to a great extent on the state of the sea, as well as the force of the winds. The larger the waves and the more directly into the waves, or winds, the ship is headed, the slower the headway. Hence, it is clearly desirable to avoid heavy seas and strong winds, not only to avoid damage and possible injuries but also to save time and fuel in ocean crossing. Empirical data collected from ships' logs have enabled researchers to relate ship speed to sea state and, from such relationships, to construct a least-time track for a ship crossing the ocean. This requires an accurate forecast of the weather along all possible routes the ship might take made several weeks in advance. Since this is generally beyond state-of-the-art forecast skill, preliminary ship tracks are recommended based on 5–7-day predictions and climatol-

ogy; and then they are modified, if necessary, as the voyage progresses. Ship routing based on weather and sea conditions has been found to improve the efficiency and reduce the cost of shipping; consequently, it has been widely used for both commercial and naval ships of the United States and other countries.

Tactical naval environmental support. Tactical environmental support refers to describing and predicting those meteorological and oceanographic phenomena that affect the performance of naval weapons systems on time and space scales that are important to tactical naval operations. This aspect of marine meteorology and oceanography is becoming increasingly important to the modern navy because of the increased sophistication and range of naval weapons systems, and the great sensitivity of those systems to variations in the environment. Thus, an accurate knowledge of present and future meteorological and oceanographic conditions can be a significant asset to the operating navy in its conduct of command, control and communication, antisubmarine and electronic warfare, navigation, search and rescue, and many other tactical operations at sea.

The physical environment affects communications and weapon systems primarily by refracting, scattering, and attenuating electromagnetic waves (microwaves, optical, and radio waves) in the atmosphere and acoustic (sound) waves in the ocean. Atmospheric refraction is caused by vertical variations in temperature and humidity, primarily in the lower part of the atmosphere. Such variations can be especially significant in the first few tens of meters above the sea surface and in the sharp transition region between the atmospheric planetary boundary layer and the free atmosphere. As a result, the structure and variability of the atmospheric planetary boundary layer are extremely important to naval meteorology.

An important application of maritime meteorology to naval operations is the prediction of radar (or other electromagnetic or optical) wave propagation in the atmosphere and sound-wave propagation in the ocean. In **Fig. 5***a*, a radar located at the origin has a greater than 90% probability of detecting an object (air target) located within the shaded regions, and a less than 90% probability of detecting the same object in the unshaded regions. In Fig. 5*b*, sound waves leaving the origin travel along the curved lines (acoustic rays) shown (the specific curvature being caused by the vertical profile of the speed of sound shown on the right), producing broad convergence zones near the sea surface at distances of approximately 22,000, 44,000 64,000, and 87,000 m (24,000, 48,000, 70,000, and 95,000 yd). These variations in radar- and sound-wave propagation are due to refraction caused by fluctuations in the atmosphere and ocean.

Sound waves can travel great distances through the ocean, at a speed that depends on the temperature, pressure, and salinity of the water through which the waves are propagating. As a result, variations in these quantities refract sound waves in the ocean in the same way that variations in temperature and humidity refract electromagnetic waves in the atmosphere. Because of refraction, the sound waves emitted from a given location in the ocean will travel along a curved path that depends on the ocean thermal structure. When the waves reach the top or bottom of the ocean, they are reflected into the ocean interior in ways that depend on the properties of the sea surface or sea floor. Because of the variable nature of these environ-

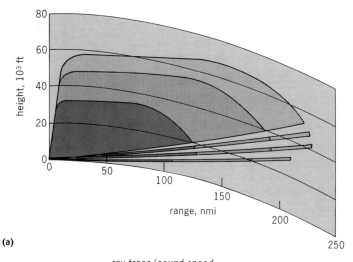

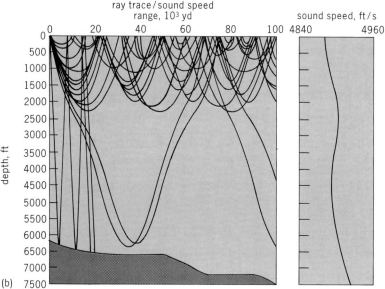

Fig. 5. Prediction of (*a*) radar (or other electromagnetic or optical) wave propagation in the atmosphere and (*b*) sound wave propagation in the ocean. 1 ft = 0.3 m. 1 nautical mile = 1852 m. (*LCDR W. T. "Kim" Curry, U.S. Navy*)

mental factors, acoustic waves leaving a particular sound source will tend to converge into certain areas and diverge from others. The places where sound waves come together because of refraction are called convergence zones, and they represent optimal locations to "listen" for enemy ships. Likewise, places where sound waves tend to diverge from are called shadow zones, and they are good places to "hide" from enemy ships. The location and intensity of convergence zones and shadow zones are strongly affected by ocean fronts and eddies, by fine structure and turbulence in the upper ocean, and by the properties of the sea floor and sea surface. In very high latitudes, the sea ice concentration and the surface wave conditions strongly affect the ambient noise in the ocean, while the roughness of the underside of sea ice is important for acoustic propagation. The application of the science of maritime meteorology and oceanography to naval tactics is a very important aspect of most naval operations at sea. SEE METEOROLOGY; OCEANOGRAPHY.

Robert L. Haney

Bibliography. A. E. Gill, *Atmosphere-Ocean Dynamics*, 1982; G. J. Haltiner and R. T. Williams, *Numerical Prediction and Dynamic Meteorology*, 1980; O. M. Phillips, *The Dynamics of the Upper Ocean*, 2d ed., 1977; A. R. Robinson (ed.), *Eddies in Marine Science*, 1983; R. B. Stull, *An Introduction to Boundary Layer Meteorology*, 1988.

Medical waste

Any solid waste that is generated in the diagnosis, treatment, or immunization of human beings or animals, in research pertaining thereto, or in the production or testing of biologicals. Since the development of disposable medical products in the early 1960s, the issue of medical waste has confronted hospitals and regulators. Previously, reusable products included items such as linen, syringes, and bandages; they were sterilized or disinfected prior to reuse, and the principal waste product was limited to human pathological tissue.

Most hazardous substances are described by their relevant properties, such as corrosive, poison, or flammable. Medical waste was originally defined in terms of its infectious properties, and thus it was called infectious waste. However, given the difficulty of identifying pathogenic organisms in waste that might cause disease, it has become standard practice to define medical waste by types or categories. While definitions differ somewhat under different regulations, in the United States the Centers for Disease Control (CDC) cite four categories of infective wastes that should require special handling and treatment: laboratory cultures and stocks, pathology wastes, blood, and items that possess sharp points such as needles and syringes (sharps). These categories, of necessity, require that the generator of these wastes exercise judgment in identifying the material to be included. For example, a small cotton ball or bandage with minimal amounts of dried blood will probably pose no problems or risk, but a dressing saturated with blood causes greater concern.

The waste category that has generated a great deal of interest is sharps. Needles and syringes, in particular, pose risks, since the instruments can penetrate into the body, increasing the potential for disease transmission. Improper disposal of these items in the past has been the catalyst for increased regulation and tighter management control.

Issues and incidents. In the mid-1980s, various incidents of improper disposal of medical waste received national attention and resulted in the enactment of legislation and regulations for medical waste throughout the United States. Most incidents involved the disposal of needles and syringes in trash dumpsters, in landfills, or in other areas where exposure to the public created a hazard. Other incidents involved waste washing up on coasts and beaches.

The principal risk of exposure to medical waste is the transmission of the hepatitis B virus (HBV), which causes hundreds of hospitalizations annually. While this virus is generally transmitted by occupational exposure (for example, to a health care worker), such incidents have resulted in tighter regulatory controls to minimize the risk of exposure to the general public.

Waste volume and generation. The U.S. Environmental Protection Agency (EPA) estimates that 500,000 tons (450,000 metric tons) of so-called regulated medical waste are generated each year. About

77% of this waste is generated by hospitals. However, hospitals constitute less than 2% of the total number of generators in the United States. The remaining 98% consists of clinics; offices of physicians, dentists, and other licensed practitioners; veterinarian offices; and various in-patient facilities. The fact that hospitals generate a vast majority of the waste has focused regulatory attention on the management of their waste streams; until the mid-1980s other generators were exempted from most of the regulations. However, the incidents of improper disposal revealed that problems were created by these other care providers; consequently most regulations have been extended to apply to any generator of medical waste except households, which are exempted.

Regulations. At the federal level, the Medical Waste Tracking Act (MWTA) established a 2-year demonstration project to be undertaken by the EPA, but this project terminated in 1991. Usually in the United States, requirements for identification, handling, packaging, treatment, storage, and disposal of medical waste are mandated by states and municipalities. This setup allows the various states to address issues on a more specific basis. For example, states with large numbers of rural health facilities may have needs and requirements that are different from those of states having higher and more concentrated population bases with large, centralized health facilities.

Typically, regulations define medical waste by expanding on the list developed by the Centers for Disease Control. Isolation waste from patients with highly communicable diseases is often included in these regulations. For the most part, most standard hospitals do not deal with this type of waste. Many tropical diseases and highly virulent pathogens fall into this category, and such patients are usually cared for at specialized hospitals and treatment centers. Such highly communicable diseases, identified as Biosafety level 4, are caused by those agents listed in Classification 4 in the official classification of etiologic agents of the Centers for Disease Control.

Management. Usually, the regulations mandate that, once identified, medical waste be separated from other waste as close to the source of generation as possible. It is identified by containment in a single, or sometimes double, red bag labeled with the words "Biohazardous Waste" and the international biohazard symbol (see **illus.**). Such waste is stored in an area that can be secured so as to deny access by unauthorized personnel. This area is protected from the elements as well in order to prevent the spread of potentially disease-causing material into the environment.

After separation, the medical waste must be ren-

International biohazard symbol.

dered noninfectious. Various treatment options are available, performed either at the source of generation or by a commercial entity off-site. If the waste is to be transported to an off-site location, a transporation permit must be issued and the vehicle registered with the appropriate regulatory agency. Vehicles used to transport medical waste must be fully enclosed and leakproof or leak-resistant in case the waste container ruptures. Bags containing medical waste should be placed in a rigid container for transport, such as carton, pail, or drum. These containers can be either reusable or disposable; however, before reuse they must be thoroughly disinfected with either chemicals or hot water. The containers and the vehicle must be labeled with the words "Biohazardous Waste" and the international biohazard symbol. Some regulations require that the container as well as the bags also include the identification of the generator of the waste in case tracking the material to a specific source is necessary.

Tracking is also done by using a manifest. Manifest requirements vary somewhat, but a manifest document accompanies the waste in transit from generation to final disposal and identifies the custodian of the waste during transport and treatment. When the generator of the waste transfers custody to a transporter, portions of the manifest document that the transfer has been completed; each party retains a copy. When the waste is transferred from transporter to treatment site, additional portions of the manifest are completed to document that transfer. Upon treatment, disposal-site personnel send a completed copy of the manifest back to the generator, documenting that the amount, type, and source of waste generated was treated in accordance with the generator's instructions and the appropriate regulations. Some regulations mandate that if the generator does not receive a copy of the fully completed manifest within 30 days of shipment, the generator is required to notify the enforcement authorities who regulate medical waste in that particular jurisdiction. This procedure is known as exception reporting.

Treatment. Treatment of medical waste constitutes a method for rendering it noninfectious prior to disposal in a landfill or other solid-waste site. Additionally, some states require that medical waste be rendered "nonrecognizable" or destroyed. This requirement may be for esthetic reasons, as in the case of human pathological waste, or for safety reasons, as in the case of sharps. The treatment technologies currently used for medical waste include incineration, sterilization, chemical disinfection, and microwave, as well as others under development.

Incineration. Incineration has long been the traditional method of disposing of medical waste, dating back to when most of the waste was pathological in nature. Typically, these incinerators were designed to burn pathology wastes, which had a very high moisture content and did not create a great deal of heat in the combustion process. Mortuaries or crematories were often used as alternatives to incinerators at hospitals.

Modern incinerators are highly sophisticated, with air-pollution-control devices used to reduce or eliminate the gases created in the combustion process. These gases result from the high content of plastics in the waste stream, including syringe barrels, suction containers, disposable utensils, and bags containing the waste. Unfortunately, a common perception is that incinerators increase pollution, pose environmental risks, and are not suitable for location at hospitals or in urban areas. These factors have severely reduced public acceptance of incinerators, and as a result other technologies have been developed. SEE AIR-POLLUTION CONTROL.

Sterilization. Steam sterilization has long been used in laboratory settings to sterilize cultures or to prepare samples for analysis or use. Additionally, gas or steam has been used to sterilize surgical instruments and associated items.

In the mid-1970s, the use of steam sterilizers or autoclaves for treating medical waste was begun, largely out of concern over incinerator emissions. Autoclaves, pressure vessels that use a boiler or other source for steam, are used to treat medical waste by hospitals and other generators, as well as by commercial waste-disposal facilities.

Chemical disinfection. Disinfection of medical waste by chemicals is an extension of the long-term hospital practice of applying chemicals to control microorganisms on hard surfaces, such as floors, walls, and tables. Equipment has been developed to use standard chemical agents in a sealed enclosure to treat waste. Often this equipment contains shredders or granulators to render the waste nonrecognizable. Chemical disinfection is growing as a treatment technology for use by generators and commercial entities.

Microwave treatment. Microwave technology combines shredding of the waste material along with exposure to microwaves, which create a moist heat environment for treatment. Waste is sprayed with water upon entering the processor, shredded, and then exposed to the microwaves, which heat the material sufficiently to disinfect it.

Other technologies. Other technologies are being developed that are designed to be environmentally acceptable, including macrowave, plasma-torch, and laser.

Macrowaves, low-frequency electrical waves longer than microwaves, are used to create an internal heat source to disinfect waste. This technology does not require water to create a moist heat environment. The longer wavelengths reduce the requirements for shredding the material, because they penetrate the waste farther than microwaves, thus exposing more of the waste volume.

In plasma-torch technology, gases at elevated temperatures are used to treat the waste. This environment creates a source of heat that can be recovered or generated into electricity.

Laser treatment, a somewhat experimental technology, uses laser-generated heat on the waste. Potential applications include use at the waste-generating site. SEE HAZARDOUS WASTE.

Robert A. Spurgin

Bibliography. Energy and Environmental Research Corporation (Irvine, California), *State of the Art Assessment of Medical Waste Thermal Treatment*, 1990; E. Kunes, The trashing of America, *Omni Mag.*, pp. 40–44, 92–94, 96, February 1988; Office of Technology Assessment, U.S. Congress, *Finding the Rx for Managing Medical Wastes: OTA Special Report on Medical Waste Treatment Methods*, 1990; Office of Technology Assessment, *Issues in Medical Waste Management*, 1988; Office of Technology Assessment, *Medical Waste Treatment Technologies*, 1990; Public Health Service Agency for Toxic Substances and Disease Registry, U.S. Department of Health and Human Services, *The Public Health Implications of Medical Waste: A Report to Congress*, 1991.

Meromictic lake

A lake whose water is permanently stratified and therefore does not circulate completely throughout the basin at any time during the year. Normally lakes in the temperate zone mix completely during the spring and autumn when water temperatures are approximately the same from top to bottom. In meromictic (*mero*, partial; *mixis*, circulation) lakes, there are no periods of overturn or complete mixing because seasonal changes in the thermal gradient either are small or are overridden by the stability of a chemical gradient, or the deeper waters are physically inaccessible to the mixing energy of the wind. Most commonly, the vertical stratification in density is stabilized by a chemical gradient in meromictic lakes.

The upper stratum of water in a meromictic lake is mixed by the wind and is called the mixolimnion. The bottom, denser stratum, which does not mix with the water above, is referred to as the monimolimnion. The transition layer between these strata is called the chemocline (**Fig. 1**).

Of the hundreds of thousands of lakes on the Earth, only about 120 are known to be meromictic; approximately 45 meromictic lakes are reported for North America. In general, meromictic lakes in North America are restricted to sheltered basins that are proportionally very small in relation to depth, basins in arid regions, and isolated basins in fiords. Meromictic lakes frequently contain colored water, which limits penetration of solar radiation. SEE LAKE.

Interest in meromictic lakes is disproportional to their number, not only because they are oddities of nature, but because they offer unique opportunities for limnological research. Research activity on meromictic lakes has been focused on the physiology and behavior of organisms, biogeochemistry, studies of lake history, deep-water circulation, and heat flow through the bottom sediments.

Chemical studies. Relatively few detailed chemical studies have been done on meromictic lakes, particularly on a seasonal basis. The most typical chemical characteristic of meromictic lakes is the absence of dissolved oxygen in the monimolimnion. Large quantities of hydrogen sulfide and ammonia may be associated with this anaerobic condition in deep water. J. Kjensmo proposed that the accumulation of ferrous bicarbonate in the deepest layers of some lakes may have initiated meromixis under certain conditions. Separation of salts from surface water as the water freezes, and then the accumulation of these salts in deeper waters, also has led to meromixis in

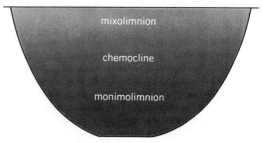

Fig. 1. Cross-sectional diagram of a meromictic lake.

Antarctic lakes. Some human activities have caused meromixis in a few cases. For example, runoff containing salt used for deicing nearby roads can produce permanent stratification in small lakes.

Meromictic lakes are exciting model systems for many important biogeochemical studies. The isolation of the monimolimnetic water makes these studies quite interesting and important. In studies of the biological fractionation of sulfur and carbon isotopes in the monimolimnion of Fayetteville Green Lake, New York, the fractionation factor for sulfur was found to be the highest ever observed.

Sediments from meromictic lakes are among the best for studies of lake history, since there is relatively little disturbance or decomposition of biogenic materials. Such sediments may provide a detailed record of the origin, ecological changes, and development of meromictic lakes and their drainage basins over time. Also, deuterium has been used by several workers in an attempt to unravel the history of meromictic lake water.

Physical studies. Radioactive tracers have been used to show that the monimolimnetic water in a small meromictic lake (Stewart's Dark Lake) in Wisconsin is not stagnant but undergoes significant horizontal movement (**Fig. 2**). While the maximum radial spread was about 16–18 m (52–59 ft) per day, vertical movements were restricted to negligible amounts because of the strong vertical density gradient. A similar pattern of movement was reported in the deep water of a larger meromictic lake (Soap Lake) in Washington. It was determined from these studies that the average horizontal eddy diffusion coefficient is 3.2 cm^2/s (0.50 in.^{2}/s) in the monimolimnion of Soap Lake and 17 cm^2/s (2.6 in.^{2}/s) in Stewart's Dark Lake.

Because vertical mixing is restricted in a meromictic lake, heat from solar radiation may be trapped in the monimolimnion and thereby can produce an anomalous temperature profile. Monimolimnitic water temperatures have been reported as high as 50.5°C (123°F) at a depth of 2 m (7 ft) in shallow Hot Lake, Washington.

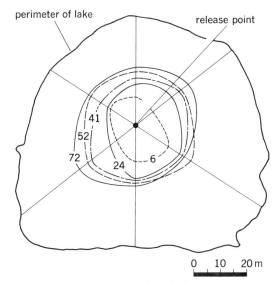

Fig. 2. The outlines show the maximum horizontal displacement of a radiotracer (sodium-24) following its release at the 8-m (26-ft) depth in Stewart's Dark Lake, Wisconsin. 1 m = 3.3 ft. The numbers indicate the hours elapsed after release.

Some meromictic lakes are very convenient for studies of geothermal heat flow because deep-water temperatures may be nearly constant year-round. Studies of terrestrial heat flow have been made in the sediments of Stewart's Dark Lake, Wisconsin, and in Fayetteville Green Lake, New York. Steady-state thermal conditions were found in the sediments of Stewart's Dark Lake, and the total heat flow was calculated to be 2.1×10^{-6} cal/cm^2 s (8.8×10^{-2} W/ m^2). However, about one-half of this flux was attributed to the temperature contrasts between the rim and the central portion of the lake's basin. It was found that the thermal conductivity of the surface sediments in the center of Stewart's Dark Lake was 1.10×10^{-3} cal · cm/(cm^2 · s · °C) [0.46 W · m/(m^2 · °C)], a value substantially lower than that for pure water at the same temperature but consistent with measurements on colloidal gels.

Biological studies. Relatively few kinds of organisms can survive in the rigorous, chemically reduced environment of the monimolimnion. However, anaerobic bacteria and larvae of the phantom midge (*Chaoborus* sp.) are common members of this specialized community. By using sonar, vertical migrations of *Chaoborus* sp. larvae have been observed in meromictic lakes. The sound waves are reflected by small gas bladders on the dorsal surface of the larvae. The migration pattern is similar to that shown by the deep-scattering layers in the sea. The larvae come into the surface waters at night when the light intensity is low and sink into deeper waters during the daylight hours. Biologically significant quantities of chemical nutrients or pollutants can be transported from the deep and relatively inaccessible part of a meromictic lake to the surface and thence to the adjacent terrestrial environment by these organisms. A radiotracer (iodine-131) appeared in flying adult *Chaoborus* sp. along the shoreline of the lake within 20 days after it had been released within the region of the chemocline.

Spectacular degassing events from the deep waters of two tropical meromictic lakes (Lakes Nyos and Monoun) in Cameroon, West Africa, have occurred on occasion during late summer when vertical stability is reduced due to weather conditions and mixing penetrates deeply in the water column. Large releases of carbon dioxide from Lake Monoun (August 15, 1984) and from Lake Nyos (August 21, 1986) killed over 1700 people living near these lakes. SEE BIOGEOCHEMISTRY; FRESH-WATER ECOSYSTEM; LIMNOLOGY.

Gene E. Likens

Bibliography. J. A. Bloomfield (ed.), *The Lakes of New York State*, 3 vols., 1978–1980; G. J. Brunskill et al., Fayetteville Green Lake, New York, I: Physical and chemical limnology, II: Precipitation and sedimentation of calcite in a meromictic lake with laminated sediments, III: The laminated sediments, IV: Interstitial water chemistry of the sediments, V: Studies of primary production and zooplankton in a meromictic marl lake, *Limnol. Oceanogr.*, 14(6):817–873, 1969; E. S. Deevey, N. Nakai, and M. Stuiver, Fractionation of sulfur and carbon isotopes in a meromictic lake, *Science*, 139:407–408, 1963; N. M. Johnson and G. E. Likens, Steady-state thermal gradient in the sediments of a meromictic lake, *J. Geophys. Res.*, 72:3049–3052, 1967; J. H. Judd, Lake stratification caused by runoff from street deicing, *Water Res.*, 4:521–532, 1970; G. W. Kling, Seasonal mixing and catastrophic degassing in tropical lakes, Cameroon, West Africa, *Science*, 237:1022–1024, 1987; K. F. Walker, and G. E. Likens, Meromixis and a reconsidered typology of lake circulation patterns, *Verh. Int. Verein. Limnol.*, 19:442–458, 1975.

Meteorology

A discipline involving the study of the atmosphere and its phenomena. Meteorology and climatology are rooted in different parent disciplines, the former in physics and the latter in physical geography. They have, in effect, become interwoven to form a single discipline known as the atmospheric sciences, which is devoted to the understanding and prediction of the evolution of planetary atmospheres and the broad range of phenomena that occur within them. The atmospheric sciences comprise a number of interrelated subdisciplines. *See* CLIMATOLOGY.

Subdisciplines. Atmospheric dynamics (or dynamic meteorology) is concerned with the analysis and interpretation of the three-dimensional, time-varying, macroscale motion field. It is a branch of fluid dynamics, specialized to deal with atmospheric motion systems on scales ranging from the dimensions of clouds up to the scale of the planet itself. The activity within dynamic meteorology that is focused on the description and interpretation of large-scale (greater than 1000 km or 600 mi) tropospheric motion systems such as extratropical cyclones has traditionally been referred to as synoptic meteorology, and that devoted to mesoscale (10–1000 km or 6–600 mi) weather systems such as severe thunderstorm complexes is referred to as mesometeorology. Both synoptic meteorology and mesometeorology are concerned with phenomena of interest in weather forecasting, the former on the day-to-day time scale and the latter on the time scale of minutes to hours.

The complementary field of atmospheric physics (or physical meteorology) is concerned with a wide range of processes that are capable of altering the physical properties and the chemical composition of air parcels as they move through the atmosphere. It may be viewed as a branch of physics or chemistry, specializing in processes that are of particular importance within planetary atmospheres. Overlapping subfields within atmospheric physics include cloud physics, which is concerned with the origins, morphology, growth, electrification, and the optical and chemical properties of the droplets within clouds; radiative transfer, which is concerned with the absorption, emission, and scattering of solar and terrestrial radiation by aerosols and radiatively active trace gases within planetary atmospheres; atmospheric chemistry, which deals with a wide range of gas-phase and heterogeneous (that is, involving aerosols or cloud droplets) chemical and photochemical reactions on space scales ranging from individual smokestacks to the global ozone layer; and boundary-layer meteorology or micrometeorology, which is concerned with the vertical transfer of water vapor and other trace constituents, as well as heat and momentum across the interface between the atmosphere and the underlying surfaces and their redistribution within the lowest kilometer of the atmosphere by motions on scales too small to resolve explicitly in global models. Aeronomy is concerned with physical processes in the upper atmosphere (above the 50-km or 30-mi level). *See* AT-

MOSPHERIC CHEMISTRY; ATMOSPHERIC ELECTRICITY; ATMOSPHERIC GENERAL CIRCULATION; CLOUD PHYSICS; MICROMETEOROLOGY.

Although atmospheric dynamics and atmospheric physics in some circumstances can be successfully pursued as separate disciplines, important problems such as the development of numerical weather prediction models and the understanding of the global climate system require a synthesis. Physical processes such as radiative transfer and the condensation of water vapor onto cloud droplets are ultimately responsible for the temperature gradients that drive atmospheric motions, and the motion field, in turn, determines the evolving, three-dimensional setting in which the physical processes take place.

The atmospheric sciences cannot be completely isolated from related disciplines. On time scales longer than a month, the evolution of the state of the atmosphere is influenced by dynamic and thermodynamic interactions with the other elements of the climate system, that is, the oceans, the cryosphere, and the terrestrial biosphere. A notable example is the El Niño–Southern Oscillation phenomenon in the equatorial Pacific Ocean, in which changes in the distribution of surface winds force anomalous ocean currents; the currents can alter the distribution of sea-surface temperature, which in turn can alter the distribution of tropical rainfall, thereby inducing further changes in the surface wind field. On a time scale of decades or longer, the cycling of chemical species such as carbon, nitrogen, and sulfur between these same global reservoirs also influences the evolution of the climate system. Human activities represent an increasingly significant atmospheric source of some of the radiatively active trace gases that play a role in regulating the temperature of the Earth. *See* BIOSPHERE; MARITIME METEOROLOGY.

Vertical profiles of pressure and density. The decrease with height in the pressure (p) and density (ρ) in planetary atmospheres is approximately exponential (**Fig. 1**). This behavior is characteristic of atmospheres composed of ideal gases, in which absolute temperature does not vary strongly with height. If it is assumed that the vertical component of the accel-

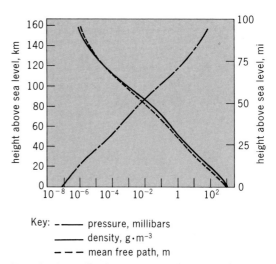

Key: ‒‒‒‒‒ pressure, millibars
        ——— density, g·m⁻³
        ‒ ‒ ‒ mean free path, m

Fig. 1. Vertical profile of pressure , density, and mean free path for typical conditions in the Earth's atmosphere. 1 millibar = 10^2 Pa. 1 m = 3.28 ft. (*After R. C. Weast, ed., CRC Handbook of Chemistry and Physics, 70th ed., CRC Press, 1989*)

eration of the air is small in comparison to gravity (g) and that the weight of a differential layer of unit horizontal cross section and thickness (dz) in the vertical is equal to the difference between the pressure on its upper and lower surfaces, the hydrostatic equation (1)

$$\frac{dp}{dz} = -\rho g \qquad (1)$$

results. This relationship is valid throughout the atmosphere except in the most vigorous convective clouds. Substituting for ρ from the equation of state (2) yields Eq. (3), where R is the gas constant appro-

$$p = \rho R T \qquad (2)$$

$$d(\ln p) = -\frac{g}{RT} dz \qquad (3)$$

priate to the chemical composition of the atmosphere and T is the temperature in kelvins. If T is assumed to be independent of height, this expression can be integrated from a reference level z_0, at which $p = p_0$, to level z and is expressed in the form shown in Eq. (4), where $H \equiv (RT)/g$ is known as the scale height,

$$p = p_0 \exp -\frac{z}{H} \qquad (4)$$

that is, the height over which pressure decreases by a factor of e (the base of natural logarithms). By combining Eqs. (2) and (4), it is readily verified that density exhibits the same functional dependence. The gas constant R is obtained by dividing the universal gas constant $R^* = 8313$ J $\cdot$ kmol^{-1} $\cdot$ K^{-1} by the molecular effective weight μ of the mixture of gases of which the atmosphere is composed. For Earth, up to a level of 120 km (72 mi), $\mu = 28.97$ as explained below, $R = 287$ J $\cdot$ kg^{-1} $\cdot$ K^{-1}, $g = 9.8$ m $\cdot$ s^{-1}, and $T = 240$ K (to within $\pm$ 15%), and so, consistent with the slopes of the pressure and density curves in Fig. 1, $H \cong 7$ km (4 mi). Mean sea-level pressure averaged over the Earth is 1013 millibars (101 kilopascals), and the mean density is on the order of 1.25 kg $\cdot$ m^{-3}. In relating pressure to height in the Earth's atmosphere in the remainder of this section, it is convenient to note that pressure and density drop off by a factor of 10 over a vertical distance of H ln (10) $\cong$ 16 km; and so the 100-mbar (10-kPa) level corresponds to roughly 16 km (10 mi) above sea level, the 10-mbar (1-kPa) level to 32 km (20 mi), the 1.0-mbar (100-Pa) level to 48 km (30 mi), and so forth. Since the pressure at any level is equal to the mass per unit area above that level, divided by g, it follows that 10% of the mass of the Earth's atmosphere lies above the 100-mbar (10-kPa) level, 1% above the 10-mbar (1-kPa) level, and so forth.

Composition of atmosphere. The atmospheres of the planets are believed to have originated from the outgassing of volatile substances [mainly water (H_2O), carbon dioxide (CO_2), and nitrogen compounds] from their interiors. Most of the water vapor condensed out immediately. On Earth (in contrast to Venus and Mars) nearly all the carbon dioxide has dissolved in the oceans and subsequently been incorporated into carbonate deposits in the crust by shell-forming species of plankton. Most of the nitrogen remains in the atmosphere in the form of molecular nitrogen (dinitrogen; N_2). Photosynthesis by plant life that was buried and fossilized before it had time to decay has generated large quantities of molecular oxygen (dioxygen; O_2).

From the surface up to about 100 km (60 mi), macroscale fluid motions keep the atmosphere well mixed, so that the relative proportions of its major gaseous constituents are nearly constant. Nitrogen, oxygen, and argon are the dominant constituents of dry air: they account for roughly 78%, 21%, and 1% of the molecules, respectively (hence the effective molecular weight of 28.97). Important atmospheric trace constituents include water vapor (up to 4% by volume and highly variable in space and time), ozone (O_3; up to 15 parts per million at the 25-km level), and carbon dioxide (approximately 350 ppm in 1990 and increasing at a rate of about 12 ppm per decade). The latter are triatomic species, which exhibit strong absorption bands associated with rotational–vibrational transitions in the infrared part of the electromagnetic spectrum, the implications of which will be discussed below.

At 100 km (60 mi) above the Earth's surface, the mean free path between collisions reaches 1 m (3.3 ft; Fig. 1) and the characteristic time scale for molecular diffusion becomes comparable to the time scale for mixing by macroscale fluid motions. Above this so-called turbopause, the various atmospheric constituents exhibit gravitational settling under the influence of molecular diffusion, the concentration of each species decreasing exponentially, as shown in Eq. (4), with scale height H inversely proportional to its molecular weight, as if it were the only constituent present. At 500 km (300 mi) the atmosphere is composed primarily of atomic oxygen (O), and above 1000 km (600 mi) helium and hydrogen are the dominant species.

Effects of x-ray and ultraviolet radiation. In **Fig. 2** the marked enhancements of the spectrum of solar radiation relative to the blackbody curve at the very short and very long wavelengths are due to the emission from the solar chromosphere and corona. Ultraviolet radiation with wavelengths (λ) shorter than 0.31 micrometer accounts for less than 2% of the energy emitted by the Sun; radiation with $\lambda < 0.24$ μm, less than 0.1%; and x-rays with $\lambda < 0.1$ μm, only about 3 parts in 10^6—yet the radiation in these wave-

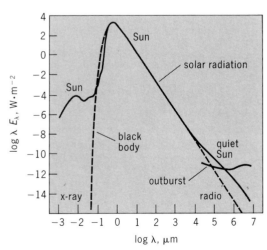

Fig. 2. Spectrum of solar radiation as compared with the spectrum of a blackbody at 5780 K (9934°F). (*After C. W. Allen, Solar radiation, Quart. J. Roy. Meteorol. Soc., 84:311, 1958*)

length bands has profound influences on the structure and composition of the upper atmosphere.

Several types of photochemical reactions occur within the Earth's atmosphere (**Fig. 3**). X-rays with $\lambda < 0.1$ μm are sufficiently energetic to ionize whatever atomic species happen to be present. Peak ion concentrations (about 10^6 cm^{-3}) are observed about 300 km (180 mi) above the Earth's surface. Virtually all the solar radiation in this wavelength band is absorbed before it reaches the 60-km (36-mi) level (the base of the ionosphere), by which time ion concentrations have declined by four orders of magnitude relative to those at 300 km (180 mi).

Ultraviolet radiation with $\lambda < 0.24$ μm is sufficiently energetic to photodissociate molecular oxygen. As a consequence of this reaction, most of the oxygen is in the atomic form at levels above 120 km (72 mi). Radiation at these wavelengths is sufficiently depleted by the time it penetrates to the 20–50-km (12–30-mi) level that it produces only trace amounts of atomic oxygen. At these levels the air is sufficiently dense that atomic oxygen quickly combines with molecular oxygen in three-body reaction (5),

$$O + O_2 + M = O_3 + M \qquad (5)$$

where M represents another molecule, to form ozone. The ozone molecules created in this reaction are dissociated by ultraviolet solar radiation with wavelengths <0.31 μm, as in reaction (6). The resulting

$$O_3 + h\nu = O_2 + O \qquad (6)$$

oxygen atom quickly recombines with O_2 [reaction (5)].

The net result of reactions (5) and (6) is the absorption of a photon of solar radiation with $0.24 < \lambda < 0.31$ μm, and the heating of the other molecules (M) involved in the three-body collision [reaction (5)]. Through this mechanism, the creation of a single odd oxygen molecule can ultimately result in the absorption of millions of photons of ultraviolet radiation which would otherwise be lethal to life on the surface of the planet. The photochemical reactions associated with ozone chemistry are most active in the 30–60-

km (18–36-mi) layer, the so-called ozone layer. Under certain conditions, chlorine radicals created by the photodissociation of anthropogenically produced chlorofluoromethanes at these levels appear to be capable of destroying odd oxygen through catalytic reactions. *See Atmospheric ozone.*

Photoionization and photodissociation are strong heat sources above the 100-km (60-mi) level. Even though only a few parts per million of the solar radiation incident on the top of the atmosphere is absorbed at these levels, the energy input is large because the molecules present at these levels account for less than one-millionth of the mass of the atmosphere. Energy absorption per unit mass increases with height in this layer and, in addition, the molecules become less efficient at disposing of energy by emitting infrared radiation as the frequency of molecular collisions decreases. Hence, above about 80 km (50 mi), temperature increases with height, and the downward flux of heat by down-gradient molecular diffusion plays an important role in the energy balance. This outermost layer of the Earth's atmosphere is known as the thermosphere. Analogous layers are observed in the atmospheres of the other planets. Solar output in the x-ray part of the spectrum varies strongly in response to sunspots and solar flares, whose frequency exhibits a remarkable 11-year cycle. During the active part of the cycle, temperatures in the outer thermosphere reach values of 2000 K (3140°F; compared to about 500 K or 440°F in the quiet sun years), and a significant fraction of the hydrogen atoms attain velocities high enough to allow them to escape from the Earth's gravitational field. Over the lifetime of the solar system, appreciable quantities of hydrogen are believed to have escaped from the Earth's atmosphere, and it has been proposed that the hydrogen atoms in the water outgassed from Venus might have been lost in this manner.

The absorption of ultraviolet radiation by ozone molecules in the 30–60-km (15–36-mi) layer gives rise to a distinct peak in the vertical profile of temperature (**Fig. 4**). It is notable that the atmospheres of Mars and Venus, which lack the oxygen necessary to form an ozone layer, do not exhibit such an intermediate temperature maximum between the surface and the thermosphere. The peak in the temperature profile divides the Earth's middle atmosphere into an upper layer (the mesosphere) and a lower layer (the stratosphere). The temperature maximum corresponds to the stratopause, that is, the top of the stratosphere.

The base of the stratosphere corresponds to a distinct temperature minimum that marks the transition to a lower layer of the atmosphere in which the temperature distribution is maintained by the upward flux of energy from the Earth's surface by macroscale motions. Analogous layers, known as troposphere, are observed on Venus and Mars. The temperature minimum in the Earth's atmosphere corresponds to the tropopause (that is, the top of the troposphere). In the atmospheres of Venus and Mars a deep isothermal (constant-temperature) layer extends from the tropopause to the base of the thermosphere.

Electrical properties. Among the processes that contribute to the production of charged particles in the atmosphere are photoionization of neutral atoms by solar x-rays and ultraviolet rays, and charge separation that takes place when ice particles (or ice and water particles) collide within clouds. The former process gives rise to the ionosphere, which extends

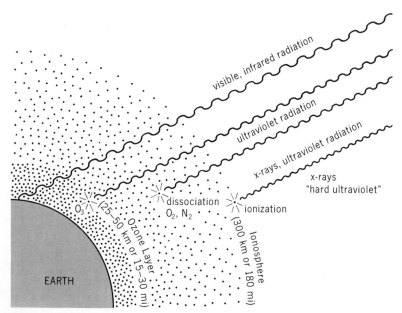

Fig. 3. Schematic representation of the processes responsible for the absorption of solar radiation in the Earth's atmosphere.

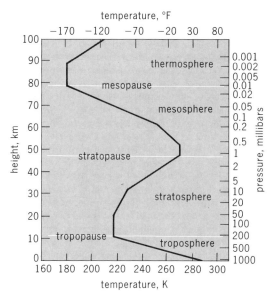

Fig. 4. Typical temperature profile in middle latitudes. 1 millibar = 10^2 Pa. 1 km = 0.6 mi. (*After J. M. Wallace and P. V. Hobbs, The Atmosphere: An Introductory Survey, Academic Press, 1977*)

upward from the 60-km (36-mi) level to the outermost reaches of the atmosphere, and the latter is responsible for maintaining the fair weather electric field, which exists within the lowest few kilometers above the Earth's surface, and the much stronger fields that sometimes exist locally within and near clouds. Although only a minute fraction of the atoms that make up the Earth's atmosphere are electrically charged, their presence accounts for a wide range of geophysical phenomena.

Ion concentrations increase monotonically with height from the base of the ionosphere to a maximum near 300 km (180 mi). The increase with height tends to be concentrated in a series of layers, labeled (in order of increasing height) D, E, and F. The lower layers are present only during the daytime: in the absence of the Sun's ionizing radiation, the charged particles quickly recombine to form neutral particles. Higher in the ionosphere, recombination is slower because the mean free path between collisions is much longer. Collisions between electrons and neutral particles within the D layer are effective at absorbing AM radio waves propagating upward. When the D layer disappears during the night, radio waves are free to propagate into the upper layers of the ionosphere, where they are reflected to the ground, causing interference and sometimes permitting the reception of distant stations.

The fair weather electric field is strongest in the lowest 100 m (330 ft) of the atmosphere, where it averages 120 V/m (36 V/ft) in the vertical: the atmosphere carries a positive charge relative to the Earth's surface. The Earth and its atmosphere may be viewed as a capacitor whose inner conductor is the Earth and whose outer conductor, which encompasses most of the atmosphere, is referred to as the electrosphere. The conductivity within the electrosphere below 60 km (36 mi) is primarily due to the presence of charged particles generated by cosmic rays colliding with air molecules. Relatively few charged particles are generated within the lowest few kilometers of the atmosphere, and they tend to be immobilized by the presence of large, slow-moving particles. This poorly

conducting layer serves as the dielectric of the capacitor. The upward flux of electrons through this "leaky dielectric" would discharge the electrosphere within a matter of minutes were it not continually being recharged by lightning and point discharge currents from the ground within thunderstorms, whose cloud bases carry a strong negative charge relative to the ground because of the charge separation going on within them.

Lapse rates and vertical mixing. The various temperature layers (Fig. 4) have distinctly different dynamical properties, which in turn affect the physical and chemical processes that take place within them. In order to understand why the thermal structure discussed in the previous section is so important, it is necessary to understand the concept of static stability. An idealized air parcel is free to expand and contract in response to the hydrostatic pressure changes [as defined in Eq. (1)] that it encounters as it goes up and down in the atmosphere, and it is thus capable of doing work on its environment as it rises and expands, or having work done on it as it sinks and is compressed; but it is assumed that this air parcel does not exchange heat with its environment. If the parcel does not have any heat source or sink of its own, its temperature will change adiabatically (that is, without the addition or subtraction of heat) as it rises and sinks. The rate of temperature change with height (dT/dz) can be inferred from the first law of thermodynamics, which for an ideal gas can be written in the form shown in Eq. (7), where dq is the differen-

$$dq = c_v \, dT + p \, d\alpha \qquad (7)$$

tial amount of heat added to the parcel, $c_v \, dT$ is the increase in the internal energy of the parcel, $p \, d\alpha$ is the work done by the parcel on the surrounding air as it expands, c_v is the specific heat of air at constant volume (717 J · kg · K^{-1}), and $\alpha = 1/\rho$ is the specific volume of the parcel expressed in m^3 · kg^{-1}. The second term on the right-hand side can be rewritten as $d(p\alpha) - \alpha \, dp$. Substituting from Eq. (2) for $d(p\alpha)$, Eq. (7) can be rewritten as Eq. (8). For an isobaric

$$dq = (c_v + R) \, dT - \alpha \, dp \qquad (8)$$

(constant-pressure) process, $dp = 0$, and therefore the specific heat at constant pressure can be defined by expression (9), which is equal to 717 + 287 =

$$c_p \equiv c_v + R \qquad (9)$$

1004 J · kg^{-1} · K^{-1}. Substituting into Eq. (8) gives Eq. (10), which is the form of the first law more frequently used in atmospheric thermodynamics. The first term on the right-hand side of Eq. (10) is referred

$$dq = c_p \, dT - \alpha \, dp \qquad (10)$$

to as an incremental change in enthalpy or sensible heat. Equation (11) results from setting $dq = 0$ and

$$-\left(\frac{dT}{dz}\right)_{\text{adiabatic}} = \frac{g}{c_p} \qquad (11)$$

substituting for α from Eq. (1), and this is defined as the dry adiabatic lapse rate, that is, the rate at which the temperature of an air parcel that is not saturated with water vapor drops with increasing height under adiabatic conditions. (Note that the minus sign is implicit in the definition of the term lapse rate.) In the Earth's atmosphere, the dry adiabatic lapse rate has a numerical value of 9.8 K · km^{-1}.

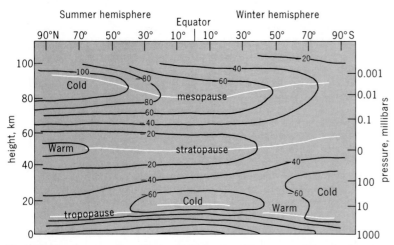

Fig. 5. Meridional cross section of the longitudinally averaged temperature (°C) at the time of the solstices. °F = (°C × 1.8) + 32. 1 millibar = 10^2 Pa. 1 km = 0.6 mi. (*After J. M. Wallace and P. V. Hobbs, The Atmosphere: An Introductory Survey, Academic Press, 1977*)

If the environmental lapse rate is the same as the adiabatic lapse rate, an air parcel forcibly displaced upward or downward from its original level would always remain at the same temperature as its environment, and so it would be neutrally buoyant. However, if the environmental lapse rate is less than the adiabatic lapse rate, a rising air parcel will find itself colder (and therefore more dense) than its environment (and vice versa), and so it will encounter a restoring force that will push it back toward its equilibrium level. The larger the difference in lapse rates, the larger the restoring force for a given vertical displacement. The restoring force per unit vertical displacement can be regarded as a measure of the static stability of the atmosphere at that level. Unstable lapse rates (that is, environmental lapse rates larger than the dry adiabatic value) are only very rarely observed in planetary atmospheres, because free convection produces a strong upward transfer of heat whenever the lapse rate reaches the adiabatic value. An isothermal lapse rate ($dT/dz = 0$) represents quite a stable stratification, and a so-called inversion ($dT/dz > 0$) represents an even stronger one.

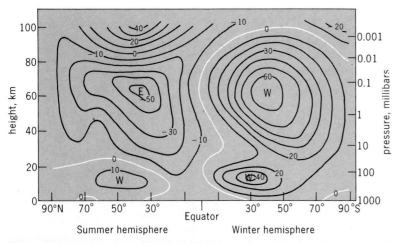

Fig. 6. Meridional cross section of the longitudinally averaged zonal wind (m · s^{-1}) at the time of the solstices. Positive zonal winds denote flow from west (W) to east (E). 1 m/s = 2.2 mi/h. (*After J. M. Wallace and P. V. Hobbs, The Atmosphere: An Introductory Survey, Academic Press, 1977*)

Thus the stratosphere is much more stably stratified than the troposphere (hence the name), and therefore it is a layer in which vertical mixing of trace substances is strongly suppressed. The characteristic residence time of air parcels in the stratosphere (that is, the time elapsed since they were in the troposphere) ranges from a few months just above the base to many years at the stratopause level. Hence, the stratosphere functions as a long-term reservoir for certain types of pollutants, such as debris from nuclear tests, which are quickly cleansed from tropospheric air by processes discussed below. The high static stability of the stratosphere also limits the height to which plumes of rising air in severe thunderstorms or volcanic eruptions can rise before they become negatively buoyant.

Atmospheric motions. The levels and temperatures of the tropopause, stratopause, and mesopause vary with latitude and season (**Fig. 5**). The stratopause is warmest at the summer pole, where the solar heating is strongest, and coolest at the winter pole, which is in darkness. However, the temperature distribution at the mesopause is the reverse of what would be expected on the basis of arguments based on radiative transfer; the summer pole is much colder than the winter pole. An equally strange distribution (from the point of view of radiative transfer) is observed at the tropopause, which is coldest ($-80°C$ or $-112°F$ or less) on the Equator and warmest at the summer pole and at middle latitudes of the winter hemisphere. At these levels the radiative heating is relatively weak, and dynamical processes are capable of driving temperatures far from their radiative equilibrium values. For example, the extreme coldness of the summer mesopause and the equatorial tropopause is maintained by adiabatic expansion associated with large-scale upward motion.

There is a corresponding distribution of the zonal (west-to-east) component of the wind (**Fig. 6**). Wind maxima are observed at the tropopause level (the so-called tropospheric jet streams) and in the mesosphere. The tropospheric jet stream, which is present throughout the year, blows from west to east. It is stronger and somewhat farther equatorward during winter. In the mesosphere the winds blow from the west during winter and from the east during summer. These zonal winds are in thermal wind balance, with the temperature distribution shown in Fig. 6: wherever temperature decreases (increases) with latitude, the zonal wind is becoming more (less) westerly with increasing height. *See JET STREAM.*

Winds in the equatorial lower stratosphere (not shown in Fig. 6) exhibit a remarkable 27-month quasi-periodicity, with alternating periods of remarkably persistent easterly and westerly winds, which appear first near the 10-millibar or 1-kPa (30-km or 18-mi) level and gradually descend, over the course of a year or so, to the 70-millibar or 7-kPa (18-km or 11-mi) level. The peak-to-peak amplitude of the so-called quasibiennial oscillation reaches 45 m · s^{-1} (100 mi/h). The westerly polar vortex in the winter hemisphere is distorted by planetary waves that propagate energy upward from below. In the Northern Hemisphere, these disturbances sometimes become so intense during midwinter that they produce a so-called sudden warming, that is, the disappearance of the cold temperatures normally found over the polar regions at this time of year and the westerly vortex that encircles them.

The tropospheric circulation exhibits a complex array of disturbances on a wide range of space and time scales. Prominent among them are baroclinic waves, whose signature on synoptic charts at the Earth's surface is characterized by migrating extratropical cyclones and anticyclones. Because of the relatively lower static stability at these levels, tropospheric disturbances are characterized by much larger vertical motions than stratospheric disturbances. Lifting is often sufficient to produce widespread condensation of water vapor, which gives rise to clouds and precipitation. *See Wind.*

Temperature at Earth's surface. With the notable exception of Jupiter, which is emitting substantial amounts of energy released by gravitational compression, the individual planets can be regarded as being in radiative equilibrium with the Sun. They intercept $\pi R^2 S$ units of solar radiation, where R is the radius of the planet and S is the solar irradiance, which decreases with distance from the Sun in accordance with the inverse-square law. Of the intercepted solar radiation, the fraction A, defined as the planetary albedo, is reflected to space; the remaining fraction $(1 - A)$ is absorbed by the planet and its atmosphere. An equal amount of radiation is emitted to space by the planet and its atmosphere. The planetary radiation may be expressed as the amount of radiation emitted by a blackbody at the effective temperature T_E of the planet. T_E can be determined from the balance between incoming and outgoing radiation, Eq. (12),

$$(1 - A)\, \pi R^2 S = \sigma T_E^4 (4\pi R^2) \qquad (12)$$

where σ is the Stefan-Boltzmann constant $5.67 \times 10^{-8}\ \mathrm{W \cdot m^{-2} \cdot K^{-4}}$. For the Earth, the solar irradiance S is $1380\ \mathrm{W \cdot m^{-2}}$, $A \approx 0.30$, for which the solution of Eq. (12) yields $T_E = 255\ \mathrm{K}$. It is readily verified that if nothing else changed, $dT_E/T_E = \frac{1}{4}\, dS/S$ so that, for example, a 1% increase in solar irradiance would raise the effective temperature of the Earth by about $0.64\ \mathrm{K}$ ($1.2°\mathrm{F}$). Because of its high planetary albedo (0.78), Venus exhibits an effective temperature of only $227\ \mathrm{K}$ ($-51°\mathrm{F}$) despite the fact that it intercepts more than three times as much solar radiation per unit surface area than the Earth does. The effective temperature of Jupiter, as measured from space, is about $125\ \mathrm{K}$ ($-235°\mathrm{F}$), compared with a value of $105\ \mathrm{K}$ ($-271°\mathrm{F}$) computed from Eq. (12).

The peak wavelength λ_m of planetary radiation can be estimated by applying the Wien displacement law to a blackbody at the effective temperature of the planet [Eq. (13)]. For the Earth, it is readily verified

$$\lambda_m = \frac{2897}{T} \qquad (13)$$

that $\lambda_m \approx 15\ \mu\mathrm{m}$. Normalized blackbody curves for solar and terrestrial radiation are shown in **Fig. 7** on a logarithmic scale. Since the overlap between the two curves is minimal, solar and terrestrial radiation may be treated separately.

The fact that the mean surface temperature of the Earth is about $33\ \mathrm{K}$ ($59°\mathrm{F}$) warmer than the effective temperature is due to the absorption and subsequent

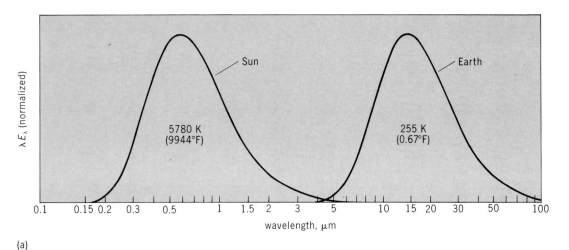

(a)

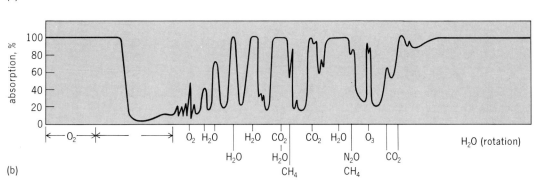

(b)

Fig. 7. Radiation curves. (a) Normalized blackbody spectra representative of the Sun and the Earth plotted on a logarithmic scale. (b) Absorption spectrum for the Earth's atmosphere as a whole. The ordinate denotes the fraction of the radiation incident upon the Earth's atmosphere (either from above or below) that is absorbed during its passage through the atmosphere; the gaseous constituents primarily responsible for the absorption of the radiation at various wavelengths are indicated at the horizontal axis. (*After R. M. Goody, Atmospheric Radiation, Oxford University Press, 1964*)

downward reemission of substantial amounts of terrestrial radiation by water vapor, CO_2, and O_3, and cloud layers, all of which absorb strongly in the infrared (the so-called greenhouse effect). Figure 7b shows position of the absorption bands of the atmosphere's major gaseous constituents in relation to the spectra of solar and terrestrial radiation. The broad spectral window that enables most of the incident solar radiation (apart from that reflected by clouds) to reach the Earth's surface is readily apparent. The main spectral window through which terrestrial radiation escapes to space is in the vicinity of 10 μm. The increasing concentration of CO_2 in the atmosphere due to the burning of fossil fuels is causing its absorption bands to encroach on the long-wavelength end of this window, leading to predictions of a substantial global greenhouse warming. Methane (CH_4), nitrogen oxides (NO_x), and chlorofluorocarbons, whose concentrations are also increasing in the Earth's atmosphere at least partly as a result of human activity, exhibit absorption bands closer to the middle of this window. Hence, even though their concentrations are orders-of-magnitude smaller than that of CO_2, they are also a source of concern. Based on current projections, increases in these constituents over the next 50 years could cause a global warming comparable to that resulting from a doubling of CO_2. SEE GREENHOUSE EFFECT.

The mean surface temperature of the Earth is determined by a rather delicate balance between the globally averaged fluxes of solar and terrestrial radiation, sensible heat, and moisture. The 100 units of incoming radiation shown in **Fig. 8** represents the solar irradiance passing through the Earth's orbit (S) times the cross-sectional area of the Earth (πR^2), divided by the total surface area of the Earth ($4\pi R^2$): hence, it is given by $S/4 = 345$ W · m². The combined effects of the reflection of solar radiation by clouds, air molecules, and the Earth's surface amount to 30 of the 100 units of incoming solar radiation, which accounts for the planetary albedo of 30% alluded to above. Absorption of solar radiation by water-vapor molecules, ozone molecules in the stratosphere, clouds, and

aerosols together amounts to 19% of the incoming solar energy. The remaining 51 units are absorbed at the Earth's surface and eventually are returned to the atmosphere by the processes indicated on the right-hand side of the diagram.

The Earth's surface can be regarded as a blackbody at 288 K (15°C or 59°F), for which the Stefan-Boltzmann law predicts in upward irradiance of 390 W · m⁻², or 113 of the units in Fig. 8. The irradiance of downward infrared radiation emitted by the atmosphere is 92 units, leaving a net upward irradiance of only 21 units, as shown. If the Earth's surface were in radiative equilibrium (in which case it would have to dispose of the full 51 units of solar radiation that it absorbs by a net upward irradiance of infrared radiation), its mean temperature would have to be on the order of 340 K (152°F). The remaining 30 units are transferred to the atmosphere through the fluxes of sensible heat (c_pT) and the latent heat of vaporization of water evaporated at the Earth's surface, which is eventually transferred to the surrounding air molecules when the vapor condenses in clouds. From Fig. 8 it is evident that the effective temperature of the Earth, as viewed from space, is a weighted average of the temperatures of the surface (6/70), the greenhouse gas molecules (38/70), and cloud tops (26/70). The role of water vapor and clouds will be discussed in more detail in the next section.

The estimates presented in Fig. 8 refer to annual and globally averaged quantities. The latitudinal seasonal variation net incoming solar radiation at the top of the atmosphere is shown in **Fig. 9**. The polar night region is shaded. The small deviations from equatorial symmetry are a consequence of the ellipicity of the Earth's orbit: the Earth is closest to the Sun in January. The equator-to-pole heating gradient is very strong in the winter hemisphere, and it disappears or even reverses for about a month centered on the summer solstice. In the annual average, the polar regions absorb only about 30% as much solar radiation per unit area as the equatorial belt when the high reflectivity of the ice and snow and the persistent cloud cover in those regions are taken into account. The

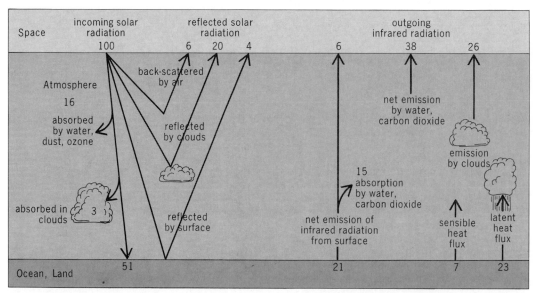

Fig. 8. Annual mean global energy balance of the Earth–atmosphere system. Numbers are given as percentages of the globally averaged solar radiation incident upon the top of the atmosphere. (*After Understanding Climatic Change, U.S. National Academy of Sciences, 1975*)

outgoing infrared radiation through the top of the atmosphere (not shown) is proportional to the fourth power of the local effective temperature T_E at which the radiation is emitted. Annual average surface temperature varies from nearly 300 K (80°F) in the tropics to about 250 K (−10°F) in the polar regions, which would be consistent with a 2:1 ratio of outgoing radiation between Equator and poles. Because cloud tops and water vapor, one of the major gaseous sources of terrestrial radiation, extend to higher levels in the tropical atmosphere than in the polar regions and are therefore relatively colder, the actual ratio is closer to 1.3:1.

Averaged over the entire globe and over the whole year, the net downward solar radiation through the top of the atmosphere must very nearly equal the upward infrared radiation. Since the meridional gradient of the former is stronger, it follows that at low latitudes the incoming solar radiation must exceed the local outgoing infrared radiation, while at higher latitudes the opposite situation must prevail. Hence, the atmosphere and oceans must transport energy poleward from a low-latitude source to a high-latitude sink. This north-south heating gradient, which is much larger in the winter hemisphere than in the summer hemisphere, is the main driving force for large-scale atmospheric motions, the so-called general circulation. Land–sea contrasts (differences in heat capacity, thermal conductivity, reflectivity, and availability of moisture between land and sea and between different types of land surfaces) also contribute to the large observed spatial and temporal variability of the local energy balance. The resulting east-west (zonal) heating gradients drive the monsoon circulations in the tropics and subtropics and the stationary planetary waves at higher latitudes.

The energy balance arguments used in this section should not be interpreted as indicating that the Earth's climate is static. The climate system has, in fact, emerged from a major ice age less than 20,000 years ago, and it has warmed substantially since the 1880s. However, it can be shown that the energy fluxes required to account for the observed changes in the volume of the polar icecaps and the heat storage in the atmosphere and oceans on these time scales are much smaller than the uncertainties in the estimates of the current energy balance in Fig. 8.

Impact of hydrologic cycle. Water in its various phases exerts a profound influence not only upon the biosphere but also upon many aspects the behavior of the atmosphere. It is evident in Fig. 8 that evaporation is an important heat sink for the oceans and vegetated land surfaces, and that condensation of water vapor in clouds is the atmosphere's largest single heat source. Hence, the hydrological cycle transfers massive amounts of heat from the Earth's surface into the atmosphere. On a more local scale, condensation plays a major role in generating the buoyancy and the horizontal temperature gradients that drive hurricanes, explosively deepening extratropical cyclones, and severe thunderstorms. It occurs selectively within rising air parcels, which tend to be warmer than the environmental air at the same level, and it causes them to cool more slowly as they expand than they would under adiabatic conditions. Observed lapse rates in the troposphere rarely exceed this so-called moist adiabatic lapse rate.

Condensation of water vapor within the atmosphere involves a complex array of physical processes. Sub-

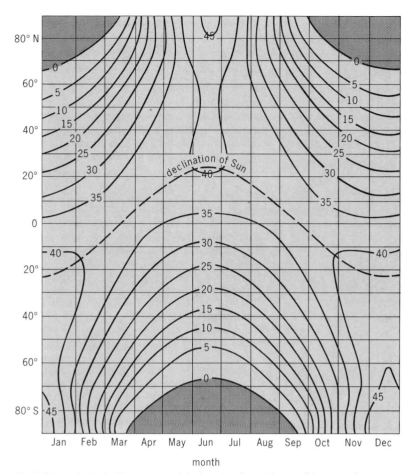

Fig. 9. Solar radiation incident upon a unit horizontal surface at the top of the atmosphere as a function of latitude and calendar date; contours are given in $10^6 \text{ J} \cdot \text{m}^{-2} \cdot \text{day}^{-1}$. (*After R. J. List, ed., Meteorological Tables, 6th ed., Smithsonian Institution, 1951*)

micrometer aerosol particles known as cloud condensation nuclei play an essential role in the initial formation of droplets of liquid water, which subsequently grow by many orders of magnitude on a time scale of minutes to hours, until the speeds at which they fall become large enough to enable them to reach the ground as rain or snow. The principal mechanisms through which this growth occurs involve the coalescence of smaller droplets into larger ones through collisions and the so-called Bergeron mechanism—the freezing of a small fraction of the droplets and their subsequent growth at the expense of the remaining supercooled (below-freezing) liquid droplets through the diffusion of water-vapor molecules from one to the other.

Liquid water droplets and ice particles tend to be concentrated in macroscale clouds, for which a detailed classification scheme has been devised. Among the most common cloud types are extensive, long-lived cloud layers (cirrostratus, altostratus, stratus, stratocumulus), which cool the Earth through their contribution to the planetary albedo and warm it through their contribution to the greenhouse effect (Fig. 8). On balance, upper-tropospheric (cirrostratus) cloud layers, which emit radiation to space at low effective temperatures, tend to warm the Earth; and low cloud layers (stratus, stratocumulus) tend to cool it. Because of this compensation, the phenomenon of cloud–climate feedbacks represents one of the largest sources of uncertainty in projections of future global climate change due to the buildup of greenhouse gases in the atmosphere.

Cloud droplets provide a hospitable environment for certain types of chemical reactions that would not otherwise take place in the atmosphere. Such reactions figure prominently in the destruction of the stratospheric ozone over the polar regions and in the formation of acid rain downstream from industrial sources of sulfur dioxide (SO_2). Scavenging by cloud droplets that subsequently fall out as precipitation is the primary mechanism for cleansing dust, smoke, and other particles from the troposphere. Charge separation by cloud droplets and ice particles within clouds also has implications for the global atmospheric electric field, and it leads to the buildup of the locally strong potential gradients responsible for lightning discharges.

The 23 units of latent heat flux from the Earth's surface in Fig. 8 are based on an observed evaporation rate of about 0.25 cm (0.1 in.) of liquid water per day averaged over the Earth's surface, which must be equal to the average rate of precipitation. The average precipitable water in the atmosphere is on the order of about 2 cm (0.8 in.) of liquid water, and thus the mean residence time for water-vapor molecules in the atmosphere must be on the order of a week. The mass of liquid water and ice present in the atmosphere in the form of cloud droplets is several-orders-of-magnitude smaller than the amount present in the vapor state. In contrast to the tropospheric air, which is often saturated with water vapor, stratospheric air tends to be remarkably dry because it enters the stratosphere by way of the extremely cold equatorial tropopause (Fig. 5), where most of its water vapor is condensed out. Stratospheric cloud layers are observed only in the polar night region where temperatures can drop to $-80°C$ ($-112°F$). SEE CLOUD; HYDROMETEOROLOGY.

Atmospheric prediction. Throughout the atmospheric sciences, prediction is a unifying theme that sets the direction for research and technological development. Prediction on the time scale of minutes to hours is concerned with severe weather events such as tornadoes, hail, and flash floods, which are manifestations of intense mesoscale weather systems, and with urban air-pollution episodes; day-to-day prediction is usually concerned with the more ordinary weather events and changes that attend the passage of synoptic-scale weather systems such as extratropical cyclones; and seasonal prediction is concerned with regional climate anomalies such as drought or recurrent and persistent cold air outbreaks. Prediction on still longer time scales involves issues such as the impact of human activity on the temperature of the Earth, regional climate, the ozone layer, and the chemical makeup of precipitation. SEE CLIMATE MODELING; DROUGHT; TORNADO.

The evolution of the atmospheric sciences from a largely descriptive field prior to World War II to a mature, quantitative physical science discipline is apparent in the development of vastly improved predictive capabilities based upon the numerical integration of specialized versions of the Navier-Stokes equations, which include sophisticated parametrizations of physical processes such as radiative transfer, latent heat release, and microscale motions. The so-called numerical weather prediction models have largely replaced the subjective and statistical prediction methods that were widely used as a basis for day-to-day weather forecasting as recently as the 1950s. The state-of-the-art numerical models exhibit significant skill for forecast intervals as long as about a week.

A distinction is often made between weather prediction, which is largely restricted to the consideration of dynamic and physical processes internal to the atmosphere, and climate prediction, in which interactions between the atmosphere and other elements of the climate system are taken into account. The importance and complexity of these interactions tend to increase with the time scale of the phenomena of interest in the forecast. Weather prediction involves shorter time frames (days to weeks), in which the information contained in the initial conditions is the dominant factor in determining the evolution of the state of the atmosphere; and climate prediction involves longer time frames (seasons and longer), for boundary forcing is the dominant factor in determining the state of the atmosphere.

As in many other systems governed by nonlinear equations, the uncertainties inherent in the definition of the initial state of the atmosphere grow exponentially with time during the forecast until they become as large as typical differences between two arbitrarily chosen states of the atmosphere. Deterministic prediction based solely upon the information contained in the initial conditions is impossible beyond this time frame. The characteristic predictability time of large-scale atmospheric circulation patterns is believed to be on the order of 2 weeks. Prediction on longer time scales such as months or seasons exploits the memory (autocorrelation) and extended predictability of the more slowly varying components of the climate system, which force the atmosphere at its lower boundary. On these longer time scales, prediction is focused on climate anomalies (that is, departures of statistics such as seasonal mean temperature and precipitation from their climatological mean values), which persist or develop in response to the slowly varying boundary forcing. Deterministic prediction of sequences of day-to-day weather changes is not feasible on these extended time scales.

Atmospheric prediction has benefited greatly from major advances in remote sensing. Geostationary and polar orbiting satellites provide continuous surveillance of the global distribution of cloudiness, as viewed with both visible and infrared imagery. These images are used in positioning of features such as cyclones and fronts on synoptic charts. Cloud motion vectors derived from consecutive images provide estimates of winds in regions that have no other data. Passive infrared and microwave sensors aboard satellites also provide information on the distribution of sea-surface temperature, sea state, land-surface vegetation, snow and ice cover, as well as vertical profiles of temperature and moisture in cloud-free regions. Improved ground-based radar imagery and vertical profiling devices provide detailed coverage of convective cells and other significant mesoscale features over land areas. Increasingly sophisticated data assimilation schemes are being developed to incorporate this variety of information into numerical weather prediction models on an operational basis. SEE ATMOSPHERE; CLIMATIC PREDICTION; FRONT; NOWCASTING; WEATHER FORECASTING AND PREDICTION.

John M. Wallace

Bibliography. C. D. Ahrens, *Meteorology Today*, 3d ed., 1988; W. S. Broecker, *How to Build a Habitable Planet*, 1985; R. Goody and J. C. Walker, *Atmospheres*, 1972; F. K. Lutgens and E. J. Tarbuck, *The Atmosphere: An Introduction to Meteorology*, 4th ed.,

1989; V. J. Schaefer and J. Day, *A Field Guide to the Atmosphere*, 1981; J. M. Wallace and P. V. Hobbs, *The Atmosphere: An Introductory Survey*, 1977.

Microbial ecology

The study of interrelationships between microorganisms and their living and nonliving environments. Microbial populations are able to tolerate and to grow under varying environmental conditions, including habitats with extreme environmental conditions such as hot springs and salt lakes. Understanding the environmental factors controlling microbial growth and survival offers insight into the distribution of microorganisms in nature, and many studies in microbial ecology are concerned with examining the adaptive features that permit particular microbial species to function in particular habitats.

Within habitats some microorganisms are autochthonous (indigenous), filling the functional niches of the ecosystem, and others are allochthonous (foreign), surviving in the habitat for a period of time but not filling the ecological niches. Because of their diversity and wide distribution, microorganisms are extremely important in ecological processes. The dynamic interactions between microbial populations and their surroundings and the metabolic activities of microorganisms are essential for supporting productivity and maintaining environmental quality of ecosystems. Microorganisms are crucial for the environmental degradation of liquid and solid wastes and various pollutants and for maintaining the ecological balance of ecosystems—essential for preventing environmental problems such as acid mine drainage and eutrophication. *See Ecosystem; Eutrophication.*

Population interactions. The various interactions among microbial populations and between microbes, plants, and animals provide stability within the biological community of a given habitat and ensure conservation of the available resources and ecological balance. Interactions between microbial populations can have positive or negative effects, either enhancing the ability of populations to survive or limiting population densities. Sometimes they result in the elimination of a population from a habitat.

Commensal relationships, in which one population benefits and the other is unaffected, occur when one population modifies the habitat to the benefit of a second population. For example, one microbial population may produce a growth factor or may oxidize a substrate and form a metabolic product that a second population can use; one microorganism also may grow on the surface of another organism. Synergism or protocooperation between two populations occurs when both populations benefit from a nonobligatory relationship. Synergism enables microbial populations to reach higher densities in the rhizosphere (soil influenced by plant roots) than in root-free soil, and plants exhibit enhanced growth characteristics as a result of interactions with rhizosphere microbes. Mutualism or symbiosis, an obligatory interrelationship between two populations, allows populations to unite, thereby enabling them to occupy habitats that are unfavorable for the existence of either alone. Mutualistic relationships may lead to the evolution of new organisms, such as occurs when a fungus unites with either an alga or cyanobacterium to form a lichen. Some animals rely on microorganisms to degrade cellulosic plant residues; ruminants, such as cattle, establish mutualistic relationships with cellulose-degrading microbial populations from which they derived their nutrition.

Competition for the same resources results in both populations achieving lower densities than would have occurred in the absence of competition, and prevents populations from occupying the same ecological niche. Amensalism, or antagonism, occurs when one population produces a substance inhibitory to another population, such as the production of an antibiotic by a microbe that inhibits the growth of another microbe. In parasitism, the parasite derives its nutritional requirements from the host, and as a result damages the host. Predation involves the consumption of a prey species by a predatory population for nutrition. Many protozoa nondiscriminantly prey or graze upon bacteria, and protozoa and invertebrates similarly graze on algae. *See Population ecology.*

Biogeochemical cycling. The transfer of carbon and energy stored in organic compounds between the organisms in the community forms an integrated feeding structure called a food web. Primary producers that form organic matter are at the base of the food web. In food webs based on phytoplankton, algae and cyanobacteria are the primary food sources; in detrital food webs, microbial biomass produced from growth on dead organic matter serves as the primary food source for grazers, the organisms that feed upon primary producers. Grazers are eaten by predators, which in turn may be preyed upon by larger predators. Microbial decomposition of dead plants and animals and partially digested organic matter in the decay portion of a food web is largely responsible for the conversion of organic matter to carbon dioxide. *See Biomass; Food web.*

Only a few bacterial species are capable of biological nitrogen fixation. In terrestrial habitats, the microbial fixation of atmospheric nitrogen is carried out by free-living bacteria, such as *Azotobacter,* and by bacteria living in symbiotic association with plants, such as *Rhizobium* or *Bradyrhizobium* living in mutualistic association within nodules on the roots of leguminous plants. In aquatic habitats, cyanobacteria, such as *Anabaena* and *Nostoc,* fix atmospheric nitrogen. The incorporation of the bacterial genes controlling nitrogen fixation into agricultural crops through genetic engineering may help improve yields.

Microorganisms also carry out other processes essential for the biogeochemical cycling of nitrogen. In nitrification, chemolithotrophic microorganisms oxidize ammonium to nitrate. In soil, *Nitrosomonas* oxidizes ammonia to nitrite and *Nitrobacter* oxidizes nitrite to nitrate. The conversion of ammonia to nitrate causes leaching of nitrogen from the soil and results in the loss of soil fertility and nitrate contamination of groundwater. Denitrification, the microbial conversion of fixed forms of nitrogen to molecular nitrogen, completes the nitrogen cycle. *See Biogeochemistry.*

Acid mine drainage is a consequence of the metabolism of sulfur- and iron-oxidizing bacteria. When coal mining exposes pyrite ores to atmospheric oxygen, the combination of autoxidation and microbial sulfur and iron oxidation produces large amounts of sulfuric acid. The acid draining from mines kills aquatic life and renders water unsuitable for drinking or for recreation.

Biodegradation of wastes. The biodegradation (microbial decomposition) of waste is a practical application of microbial metabolism for solving ecological problems. Solid wastes are decomposed by microorganisms in landfills and by composting. In landfills, organic matter is decomposed by anaerobic microorganisms. The products of anaerobic microbial metabolism, including methane and fatty acids, move into the surrounding soil, water, and air and cause the landfill to settle. Eventually, decomposition slows, subsidence ceases, and the land is stabilized. Alternatively, the organic portion of solid waste can be biodegraded aerobically by composting, converting noxious organic waste materials into carbon dioxide, water, and a humuslike product.

Liquid waste (sewage) treatment uses microbes to degrade organic matter, thereby reducing the biochemical oxygen demand (BOD). Otherwise, the BOD would cause oxygen depletion and fish kills when the sewage entered receiving waters. In the trickling filter system, sewage is sprayed over a bed of porous material covered with a slimy film of aerobic bacteria, such as *Zoogloea ramigera*, that degrade the organic matter and thus reduce BOD. Similarly, rotating biological contactors use a film of aerobic bacteria to reduce sewage BOD. In the activated sludge process, which uses a suspension of aerobic bacteria, sewage is introduced into an aeration tank, and sludge from a previous run that contains a massive number of microbes is added as an inoculum. Aerobic microbial metabolism results in the complete degradation of most organic compounds in the sewage. Septic tanks and anaerobic sludge digestors rely on anaerobic microbial metabolism for treating sewage.

Because fecal contamination of potable water from untreated or inadequately treated sewage promotes the rapid dissemination of pathogens, chlorination is used for disinfection following sewage treatment and chloramination is used to disinfect municipal water supplies. The degree of fecal contamination of water is monitored by testing for indicator coliform bacteria. Because the coliform bacterium *Escherichia coli* is present in far greater numbers in human fecal material than are enteropathogens, the coliform test can reliably detect potentially dangerous fecal contamination. *See* Sewage treatment.

Biodegradation of environmental pollutants. Human exploitation of fossil fuels and the production of novel synthetic compounds (xenobiotics) such as plastics and pesticides have introduced many compounds into the environment that are difficult for microorganisms to biodegrade. When petroleum spills occur, for example, microorganisms are faced with the task of degrading tons of hydrocarbons with varying chemical structures. Although it cannot work quickly enough to remove coastal oil spills before beaches are coated and plants and animals are killed, microbial biodegradation will eventually degrade petroleum pollutants, preventing the oceans from being completely covered with oil.

The ability of a microorganism to degrade an environmental pollutant is highly dependent on the chemical structure of the pollutant. Often a simple change in the substituents of a pesticide may make the difference between biodegradability and recalcitrance (complete resistance to biodegradation). When xenobiotics are recalcitrant and microorganisms fail in their role of ''biological incinerators,'' environmental pollutants accumulate. Synthetic organic compounds can be designed to eliminate obstacles to biodegradation. For example, some alkyl benzyl sulfonates in laundry detergents and plastics have been synthesized so that they are biodegradable. The environmentally safe use of chemical pesticides depends on microbial biodegradation to prevent persistence and biomagnification of these toxic compounds. When microorganisms fail to degrade the pesticide, serious environmental consequences can result far from the site of application, as seen in the case of dichlorodiphenyltrichloroethane (DDT). Biological control, through the regulated establishment of microbial diseases in pest populations, offers a useful alternative to chemical pesticides. *See* Ecology; Environmental toxicology; Pesticide.

Ronald M. Atlas

Bibliography. M. Alexander (ed.), *Advances in Microbial Ecology,* 5 vols., 1977–1981; R. M. Atlas and R. Bartha, *Microbial Ecology: Fundamentals and Applications,* 1987; R. G. Burns and J. H. Slater (eds.), *Experimental Microbial Ecology,* 1982; R. E. Campbell, *Microbial Ecology,* 1983; C. Edwards, *Microbiology of Extreme Environments,* 1990; J. M. Lynch and J. Hobbie (eds.), *Microorganisms in Action: Concepts and Applications in Microbial Ecology,* 1988.

Micrometeorology

The study of small-scale meteorological processes associated with the interaction of the atmosphere and the Earth's surface. The lower boundary condition for the atmosphere and upper boundary condition for the underlying soil or water are determined by interactions occurring in the lowest atmospheric layers. Momentum, heat, water vapor, various gases, and particulate matter are transported vertically by turbulence in the atmospheric boundary layer and thus establish the environment of plants and animals at the surface. These exchanges are important in supplying energy to the atmosphere, which ultimately determines large-scale weather and climate patterns. Micrometeorology also includes the study of how air pollutants are diffused and transported within the boundary layer and the deposition of pollutants at the surface.

In many situations, atmospheric motions having time scales between 15 min and 1 h are quite weak. This represents a spectral gap that provides justification for distinguishing micrometeorology from other areas of meteorology. Micrometeorology studies phenomena with time scales shorter than the spectral gap (time scales less than 15 min to 1 h and horizontal length scales less than 2 to 10 km or 1 to 6 mi). Processes having time scales longer than the spectral gap are studied by mesoscale meteorology (time scales from 1 hour to 1 day and horizontal length scales from 10 to 2000 km or 6 to 1200 mi), synoptic meteorology (time scales from 1 to 5 days, length scales from 2000 to 8000 km or 1200 to 4800 mi), and global-scale meteorology (time scales longer than 5 days, length scales longer than 8000 km or 4800 mi). Some phenomena studied by micrometeorology are dust devils, mirages, dew and frost formation, evaporation, and cloud streets. *See* Air pollution; Atmosphere.

Atmospheric stability. The behavior of the lowest part of the atmosphere depends strongly on stability. An understanding of stability requires an understanding of the concept of an adiabatic process. An adiabatic process is one in which there is no loss or gain

of heat, no mixing of an air parcel with its surroundings, and no condensation or evaporation of water. An important adiabatic process involves expansion (or contraction) of air as the exterior air pressure decreases (or increases) accompanying rising (or descending) motion of an air parcel with temperature decrease (or increase) by 9.8°C for each kilometer of ascent or descent. A decrease of 9.8°C/km is called the adiabatic lapse rate. Many atmospheric motions are approximately adiabatic.

For any layer in which the air temperature does not decrease as rapidly as the adiabatic lapse rate, an air parcel that is moved adiabatically upward or downward experiences a buoyant force acting on it that tends to cause the air to return to its original level. In this case, buoyancy tends to reduce turbulent mixing, and the atmosphere is said to be stable. An inversion is a very stable situation in which temperature actually increases with height. Whenever the temperature decreases more rapidly with height than the adiabatic lapse rate, any small adiabatic displacement of an air parcel results in a buoyant force that causes the air to move still farther away from its starting level. This is known as a superadiabatic lapse rate. This rate is unstable, meaning that the air will rapidly overturn within this layer. A layer in which temperature decreases at a rate equal to the adiabatic lapse rate is said to be neutral. An air parcel that is adiabatically moved upward or downward in a neutral layer will have no buoyant force acting on it. The neutral case is intermediate between the stable and unstable cases. *See Air temperature.*

Atmospheric turbulence. The air flow near the Earth's surface is nearly always turbulent. Friction causes the wind to be zero at the Earth's surface regardless of the wind speed higher up. The difference in wind speed near the ground and the air above is one manifestation of wind shear. The large wind shear near the ground is one of the main sources of energy for turbulent motions. Away from the surface, buoyancy increases the turbulent energy during unstable situations and decreases the turbulent energy during stable situations. Turbulent flows are highly chaotic, vary rapidly in time and space, and contain motions of many different sizes. Some appreciation for the complexities of turbulent motion can be gained by watching the rapid changes and the many sizes of motion of smoke flow. Even in carefully controlled laboratory studies, a turbulent flow is never exactly the same during any two repetitions of the same experiment. Because it is not possible to predict the exact details of turbulent flow, statistical methods are used. Wind, temperature, humidity, and other properties of the flow are written as an average part plus a fluctuation from the average. This separation, known as Reynold's decomposition, can be used to produce equations that govern turbulent flows. The rates at which quantities such as momentum and heat are transported by turbulent fluctuations are known as Reynold's fluxes or simply fluxes.

Whenever the surface is warmer than the overlying air, an unstable, superadiabatic layer forms near the surface, and buoyant convection produces an upward heat flux that tends to mix the air vertically and enhances turbulent mixing. For surfaces that are cooler than the air, the surface layer is stable, and buoyant forces reduce the amount of vertical mixing. The bulk Richardson number (R_B) is used to quantify the degree of stability of the surface layer, as shown in Eq.

(1), where $g = 9.8$ m · s^{-2} is the acceleration of

$$R_B = 2g \frac{[T_1 - T_2 + 0.0098(z_1 - z_2)](z_1 - z_2)}{(T_1 + T_2)(U_1 - U_2)^2}$$

(1)

gravity, z_1 and z_2 are two heights (meters) at which measurements are made, T_1 and T_2 are the average temperatures in kelvins at the two heights, 0.0098 is the adiabatic lapse rate in °C/m, and U_1 and U_2 are the average wind speeds (m · s^{-1}) at the two heights. For unstable layers $R_B < 0$, for neutral layers $R_B = 0$, and for stable layers $R_B > 0$. When $R_B > 0.25$, the layer is so stable that turbulence can not be sustained and the flow becomes laminar.

Lower atmospheric layers. Several layers can be defined in the lower atmosphere over land. When plants are growing on the surface, the layer from the ground to the plant top is known as the plant canopy. Within this layer, air flow is largely determined by the geometry of the plants. Water-vapor exchange between the plants and the air within the canopy is known as evapotranspiration and is controlled in part by the biology of the plants. Rates of evapotranspiration depend on the photosynthetic and respiration rates of the plants and upon the amount of water within them. Much research is being conducted to determine and test techniques that use satellites for remote sensing of the state of surface plants, the evapotranspiration rate, and the surface heat flux. *See Biometeorology; Remote sensing.*

The surface layer extends from above the canopy to a height of about 10 m (30 ft). Within this layer the transfer rates of momentum, heat, and water vapor are nearly equal to the values they have at the top of the canopy (the surface fluxes of momentum, heat, and vapor). Equations known as diabatic profile equations (Businger-Dyer equations) are used frequently to relate the surface fluxes to the changes of average wind speed, temperature, and humidity with height within the surface layer. When average wind speed, temperature, and humidity are measured at one or more heights, these equations can be used to compute surface flux values.

The atmospheric boundary layer extends upward from the surface. It is the entire layer that is directly influenced by the presence of the Earth's surface. It includes the plant canopy and the surface layer and those higher layers in which turbulent mixing takes place. In stable situations the boundary layer may be only a few tens of meters thick. Under convective conditions it is typically 1 km (0.6 mi) or more thick.

The atmospheric boundary layer undergoes distinctive variations during the course of a day (diurnal cycle). **Figure 1** shows the changes that take place in the temperature of the boundary layer during a typical clear weather day and the following night. In the early morning hours, there is a temperature inversion near the surface caused by nighttime radiative cooling of the surface, and the boundary layer is thin. For the day shown, it extended up to about 200 m (660 ft) at 9 A.M. (Fig. 1*a*). As the Sun warms the surface, convection transfers heat upward into the air, increasing the air temperature and mixing the air vertically, so that by noon on the day shown, the boundary layer extended up to 1200 m (3900 ft). Warming and deepening of the boundary layer continues throughout the day as long as the radiation absorbed by the surface

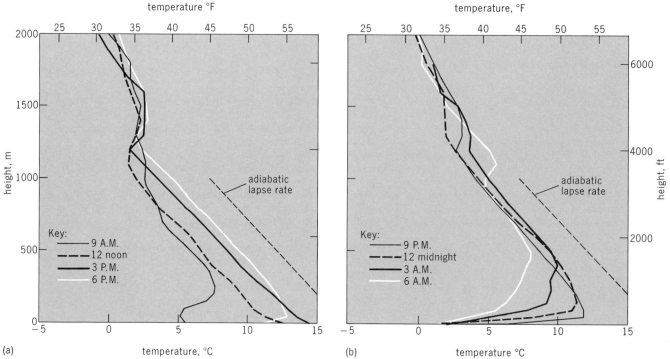

Fig. 1. Soundings of temperature versus height for (a) daytime and (b) nighttime obtained by radiosonde measurements during the Wangara experiment near Hay, New South Wales, Australia, in 1967. Soundings are shown for 9 A.M. through 9 P.M. on day 33 of the experiment and 12 midnight through 6 A.M. on day 34. (*After R. B. Stull, An Introduction to Boundary Layer Meteorology, Kluwer Academic, 1988*)

from the Sun exceeds the losses by long-wave radiation.

Figure 2 shows a typical sounding of air temperature in the middle of the day. Near the surface is an unstable, superadiabatic layer. When surface heating

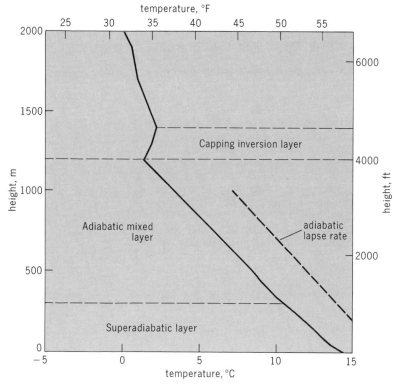

Fig. 2. The 3 P.M. sounding from Fig. 1a showing the layers of the daytime convective boundary layer.

is strong, the temperature at the surface can be several degrees Celsius higher than the air above. This strong temperature gradient can cause mirages. In the middle of the mixed layer the rate of temperature change is close to the adiabatic lapse rate indicating that rapid mixing is taking place. The boundary layer is capped by an inversion layer that limits the extent of vertical mixing and acts like a lid for the convection. During highly convective conditions, such as those shown in Fig. 2, substances are mixed rapidly throughout the boundary layer. These conditions produce rapid dispersion of atmospheric pollutants throughout the boundary layer. Prediction of the height of the inversion is one step in making air-quality forecasts.

Late in the afternoon, solar heating decreases, the surface heat source shuts off, and convection stops. During the night the surface cools because of infrared radiative heat loss, and a layer of cool air forms near the surface, giving a surface inversion as seen in the 6 P.M. sounding of Fig. 1. During the night the air near the surface continues to cool as shown in the 9 P.M. through 6 A.M. soundings (Fig. 1b). The surface inversion is stable and tends to suppress turbulence. When the wind speed is low, there is little wind shear and little turbulent mixing. If surface cooling is very strong, the surface layer may become so stable that the bulk Richardson number exceeds 0.25 and the layer is no longer turbulent. On clear nights when radiative cooling is strong, the surface can reach low temperatures, and a thin layer of cold air can form near the surface. These conditions favor the formation of dew, frost, and possibly crop-damaging hard freezes. When wind speeds are greater, there is more turbulence in the surface layer, warm air is mixed downward toward the surface, and temperature decline in the surface layer during the night will be less extreme. Crops can be protected from frost damage by smudge pots, orchard heaters, and fans. These are used to create turbulent mixing, which warms the air near the surface and thus mitigates crop damage. *See Agricultural meteorology; Frost; Wind.*

Surface energy budget. A classic problem in micrometeorolgy is the study of the balance of heat energy at the surface. Writing a budget for the surface energy fluxes involves consideration of the rates of energy transfer through a horizontal unit area at the surface. The net radiative heat flux downward into any unit area of the Earth's surface (R) is given by Eq. (2), where R is equal to the sum of incoming

$$R = H + E + S \qquad (2)$$

solar radiation, minus the reflected solar radiation, plus the downwelling infrared radiation, minus the upwelling infrared radiation. H is the rate of sensible heat transfer from the soil to the air by convection, and E is the rate of latent heat transfer from the soil to the air. H and E are positive for upward heat transfer, negative for downward. E is the amount of latent heat associated with evaporation or condensation at the surface, or with frost deposition or sublimation if the surface is below freezing. S is the flux of heat downward into the soil by conduction. The law of conservation of energy requires that the quantities R, H, E, and S balance as in Eq. (2).

Ordinarily, during the day the quantities R, H, E, and S are all positive, so that the left-hand side of Eq. (2) represents heat coming into the Earth's surface and the right-hand side represents heat leaving the surface. During nightime, R is generally negative, H and S are generally negative, and E can be either positive of negative. *See Heat balance, terrestrial atmospheric.*

Ocean–atmosphere interactions. Over the two-thirds of the Earth that is covered by ocean, the boundary layer has a somewhat different structure than that occurring over land. When wind speeds are lower than 3 or 4 m·s^{-1} (7 or 9 mi/h), the water surface is aerodynamically smooth, and viscosity and diffusion are the main mechanisms transferring momentum and heat through the first few millimeters above the surface. The transfer of momentum from the air to the water results in generation of waves on the ocean surface. At greater wind speeds, these waves make the surface aerodynamically rough and increase the frictional drag on the air. The transfer of momentum from the air to the water also can produce ocean currents and oceanic coastal upwelling.

The ocean has a much larger heat capacity than does soil, and therefore does not change temperature as rapidly as land does. As a result, the marine atmospheric boundary layer does not exhibit much diurnal variation, and it is seldom as stable or as unstable as the boundary layer over land. An important exception is that the marine boundary layer can be extremely unstable during episodes of outbreaks of cold air, when cold, dry air from over land passes over warm coastal waters. During these episodes, large amounts of heat and moisture enter the air from the ocean. Because of this transfer of heat and moisture, the Atlantic Ocean off eastern North America and the Pacific Ocean off eastern Asia are regions in which many storms are born and grow rapidly. *See Maritime meteorology.*

Research methods. Microscale meteorological features are too small to be observed by the standard national and international weather observing network.

Generally, micrometeorological phenomena must be studied during specific experiments by using instruments that are specially designed for the purpose. Instruments used to study turbulent fluxes must be able to respond to very rapid fluctuations. Special cup anemometers are made from very light materials, and high-quality bearings are used to minimize drag. Other anemometers use the speed of sound waves or measure the temperature of heated wires to measure wind. Tiny thermometers are used, so that time constants are short. Instruments are usually placed on towers, in aircraft, or suspended in packages from tethered balloons. Instruments have been developed that can measure turbulence remotely. Wind speed and boundary-layer convection can be measured with Doppler radar, lidar (light detection and ranging) devices using lasers, and sodar (sound detection and ranging) using sound waves.

Theoretical studies of atmospheric turbulence make extensive use of high-speed digital computers. Because atmospheric turbulent flows have high Reynold's numbers, they have a wide range of sizes and time scales of motion. Even with the fastest modern computers, detailed prediction of only 1 h of boundary-layer turbulence based on the exact equations governing flow would require a time equal to many times the age of the universe to complete. Faced with this obstacle, micrometeorologists have developed approximate techniques based on theoretical and empirical relationships. Higher-order closure techniques use equations that approximate some of the statistics of the flow in terms of simpler quantities and thus obtain a set of equations that can be solved in a reasonable period of time. These models have had good success at reproducing observed behavior of the atmospheric boundary layer.

Large-eddy simulation techniques compute the behavior of the largest features in the flow and use approximations for the smallest features. Even on powerful computers, these techniques require large amounts of time and are thus expensive to use, but they produce very accurate results and are therefore valuable research tools.

Despite the intricate nature of turbulent flow, the rich variety of phenomena involved in micrometeorology, and the detailed computer models available, scientists who make computer weather forecasts are forced to use greatly simplified equations for the boundary layer. These simulate the aspects of the boundary layer that most affect the large-scale weather patterns. Including more detailed boundary-layer equations would be too expensive and time-consuming for routine forecasts. *See Meteorology.*

Steven A. Stage

Bibliography. S. P. S. Arya, *Introduction to Micrometeorology*, 1988; D. A. Haugen (ed.), *Workshop on Micrometeorology*, 1973; T. R. Oke, *Boundary Layer Climates*, 1978; R. B. Stull, *An Introduction to Boundary Layer Meteorology*, 1988; D. A. de Vries and N. H. Afgan (eds.), *Heat and Mass Transfer in the Biosphere*, 1975.

Mineral resources

Mineral deposits, including ore bodies and potential ore, that are presently recoverable and may be so in the future.

Mineral resources can be developed to provide economically valuable commodities. Therefore, extraction and maximum use must be planned for the benefit of the largest number of people. Such a policy is known as conservation, and it is influenced by many economic and political factors. As costs increase, people tend to use less; they retain materials for more essential uses, thus practicing conservation. Governments influence conservation by imposing taxes, by regulating imports and exports and by controlling production and prices, particularly of gas and oil. Many governments control both the price and the sale of all raw materials. A strong sense of awareness of the needs and the values of minerals was created throughout the world by the embargo on petroleum products enforced by the Organization of Petroleum Exporting Countries (OPEC) in 1973–1974. Many underdeveloped countries from which the industrial nations obtain their needed supplies maintain close controls over their mines and oil fields, primarily to regulate production and obtain greater revenues. The worldwide result has been promotion of conservation and curtailment of waste.

Reserves and resources. Reserves represent that fraction of a commodity that can be recovered economically; resources include all of the commodity that exists in the Earth. Traces of copper and iron exist in most rocks, but their recovery is inconceivable. They are resources, but not reserves.

Reserves are classed as proved, probable, possible, and potential. When a company publishes reserve figures, it is usually referring to proved and probable reserves. Proved reserves are those known without doubt; probable reserves are those that are nearly certain but about which a slight doubt exists; possible reserves are those with an even greater degree of uncertainty but about which some favorable information is known; potential reserves are based upon geological reasoning; they represent an educated guess.

At some time in the future, certain resources may become reserves. A change of this type can be brought about by improvements in recovery techniques, either mining or metallurgical, or by improved secondary recovery methods whereby oil and gas are forced to a well and can be pumped to the surface. New methods of extraction and recovery may result in lowering costs enough to make a deposit economical. New uses may also be found for a commodity, and the increased demand may result in an increase in price; or a large deposit may become exhausted, thus forcing production from a lower-grade and higher-cost ore body.

A knowledge of reserves and resources is essential to understanding conservation problems.

Classification of raw materials. For convenience, raw materials are classified as fuels, metals (including ferrous metals, nonferrous metals, light metals, and precious metals), and industrial minerals or nonmetallics. Some metals and minerals, and their major uses, are listed in the **table**.

Many minerals are lost during use and cannot be recovered and recycled. Petroleum in gasoline and natural gas and oil in fuels are dissipated, as are lead and other additives in gasoline. Some metals, for example, iron, steel, copper, brass, and aluminum, are recoverable and may be reused many times. The gold of the ancient Egyptian and Incan treasuries probably still reposes in the vaults of some banks; certainly, it was never destroyed.

Classification of selected metals and minerals and some of their major uses	
Materials	Uses
Fuels	
Bituminous and anthracite coal	Direct fuel, electricity, gas, chemicals
Lignite	Electricity, gas, chemicals
Petroleum	Gasoline, heating, chemicals, plastics
Natural gas	Fuel, chemicals
Uranium	Nuclear power, explosives Metals
Ferrous metals	
Chromium	Alloys, stainless steels, refractories, chemicals
Cobalt	Alloys, permanent magnets, carbides
Columbium (niobium)	Alloys, stainless steels
Iron	Steels, cast iron
Manganese	Scavenger in steelmaking, batteries
Molybdenum	Alloys
Nickel	Alloys, stainless steels, coinage
Tungsten	Alloys
Vanadium	Alloys
Nonferrous metals	
Copper	Electrical conductors, coinage
Lead	Batteries, gasoline, construction
Tin	Tinplate, solder
Zinc	Galvanizing, die casting, chemicals
Light metals	
Aluminum	Transportation, rockets, building materials
Beryllium	Copper alloys, atomic energy field
Magnesium	Building materials, refractories
Titanium	Pigments, construction, acid-resistant plumbing
Zirconium	Alloys, chemicals, refractories
Precious metals	
Gold	Monetary, jewelry, dental, electronics
Platinum metals	Chemistry, catalysts, automotive
Silver	Photography, electronics, jewelry
Industrial	
Asbestos	Insulation, textiles
Boron	Glass, ceramics, propellants
Clays	Ceramics, filters, absorbents
Corundum	Abrasives
Feldspar	Ceramics, fluxes
Fluorspar	Fluxes, refrigerants, acid
Phosphates	Fertilizers, chemicals
Potassium salts	Fertilizers, chemicals
Salt	Chemicals, foods, glass, metallurgy
Sulfur	Fertilizers, acid, metallurgy, paper, foods, textiles

More metals are now being recovered and reused than ever before. As the prices of primary materials increase, scrap becomes increasingly valuable, and conservation is encouraged.

Supplies of minerals. Most of the Earth's surface has been closely examined in the search for useful minerals. Future supplies will depend in large part upon techniques that permit exploration below the surface and in remote and rather inaccessible areas. Exploration is thus becoming increasingly costly and unrewarding. Petroleum is being found in the waters of the continental shelves, at depths and under conditions never before tested, and in remote parts of the Arctic. New techniques are being developed and used. Likewise, greater amounts of hard minerals are being obtained from undeveloped and politically unstable lands. The locations of mineral deposits are fixed by nature; their positions cannot be changed. Competition to obtain the materials needed to sustain industry is growing rapidly; demands are overtaking supplies, and shortages of several commodities can develop within a few years. In order to maintain their economies, the industrial nations must encourage development and conservation of all their resources; they must find substitutes for some resources and must increase recycling. As prices of commodities increase and shortages develop, the standards of living are certain to fall.

After World War II the United States established national stockpiles of minerals in an effort to assure the country of adequate supplies during times of emergency. Over the years the needs of the country have changed, and, likewise, materials in the stockpiles have changed. Efforts to use stockpiles for purposes other than the original purpose have been made, and advocates of price regulation still attempt to buy for the stockpile when prices are low and to sell when they are high. Handling of the national stockpiles clearly influences conservation policies.

Government conservation policies. Many policies of the United States government directly influence conservation and availability of energy and other minerals. The effects of government activities are most clearly evident insofar as oil and gas are concerned. Many state governments have laws that regulate the spacing of oil wells and prevent overpumping. They establish the most effective rate of recovery and ensure maximum life of a field. On the other hand, the Federal government has established price controls that discourage oil exploration in areas where costs are high. Increases in prices charged by OPEC nations for crude oil necessitated both a search for additional oil and conversion to more abundant energy sources such as coal. Government is seeking ways to use energy more efficiently and to develop other sources such as solar power and oil shale. SEE ENERGY SOURCES.

Periodically the government offers blocks of public land for auction and lease. These blocks, thought to contain oil and gas, are bid on by companies or, more commonly, by groups of companies. Legislation passed by the U.S. Congress prohibits large oil companies from making joint bids except with small companies.

The depletion allowance is a tax-exemption policy based upon the rate of depletion of a natural resource and is intended to equate tax policy in the extractive industries with the depreciation allowance permitted manufacturing industries. Producers are allowed to deduct a certain percentage of their gross revenues from the part of their income subject to Federal income tax. Early in 1975 Congress canceled the depletion allowance for the large oil companies, although permitted retention of the allowance for smaller companies and the mining industry. Removal of the depletion allowance reduced capital available for exploration and resulted in an upward pressure on the price of petroleum products.

The political history and legal climate in a country strongly influence private investment in mines and oil fields. Many nations have expropriated raw materials properties, in some places without compensation, and in others with compensation less than the former owners thought reasonable. Such actions greatly discourage private investment, and, as a result, many governments now must finance and operate their own mines and oil fields.

Government policies also influence petroleum and mineral exploration; there is a myriad of regulations and laws concerning environment, right of access, land restoration, and other items. Open-pit or strip mining coal is cheaper, has a much higher recovery, and is safer than underground mining, which results in more than 50% of the coal being left underground. The many government bureaus that issue regulations concerning exploration and development are restrictive. Especially in the energy fields, unsightly strip mines, oil spills offshore, and worries about radioactive leakage have resulted in rigorously enforced regulations. The United States has also withdrawn from exploration of extensive wilderness areas and other tracts of public lands.

Technological changes. Developments in oil well drilling, in enhanced recovery methods, and in mining, milling, and smelting methods all have profound impacts on the availability of raw materials. Oil well drilling is being carried out in the open oceans at depths of 900 ft (270 m) or more, and techniques are available that will enable wells to be drilled to considerably greater depths. Shutoff devices and other safety devices greatly reduce the dangers of oil spills and wellhead fires.

The development of large machines for handling huge tonnages of rock and the use of refined explosives have improved mining methods. Open-pit and strip mines are larger and more efficient than ever before, and lower grades of ore are being recovered. It is common for a mine to produce 50,000 tons (45,000 metric tons) of ore a day, and some yield more than 100,000 tons (90,000 metric tons). Industry is taking advantage of economies of size. Improved methods of transportation, concentration, and smelting permit less costly handling of large tonnages and improve recoveries. Newer smelting methods are cleaner, have as good or better recovery records, and may prove to be less expensive to operate.

Demand and supply problems. A serious problem facing the raw materials industry is the cyclical nature of demands for its products. When economic times are good, the markets are strong; but consumption is greatly curtailed during recessions, and excessive inventories are created. As a result, prices are cyclical and, with some commodities, for example, mercury, are highly volatile. In order to stabilize prices, many countries favor the establishment of cartels and associations. Probably the most effective association of this type is the International Tin Commission, an organization that includes both consumers and producers. A ceiling and a floor price are established: If the market price goes below the floor, the Commission buys tin; if the price goes above the ceiling, the Commission sells. In this way, the price and production of tin are maintained at reasonably stable rates.

Governments that have copper, aluminum, and iron for export have established cartels in these commodities and have made efforts to consolidate controls over rates and prices. Most such cartels aim to increase the price of the commodity and to improve the financial status of the producer at the expense of the consumer. Cartels are usually more successful as industrial needs increase and minerals become difficult to purchase, but whether or not such associations succeed, the prices of raw materials will increase with demand. As a national policy conservation is not only desirable, it is a necessity. SEE CONSERVATION OF RESOURCES.

Charles F. Park, Jr.

Bibliography. P. A. Bailly, *Conversion of Resources to Reserves*, 1975; D. A. Brobst and W. P. Pratt, *United States Mineral Resources*, U.S. Geol. Surv. Prof. Pap. 820, 1973; C. F. Park, Jr., *Earthbound: Minerals, Energy, and Man's Future*, 1975; A. Sutulov, *Minerals in World Affairs*, 1972; U.S. Bureau of Mines, *U.S. Minerals Yearbook*, annually.

Mutagens and carcinogens

A mutagen is a substance or agent that induces heritable change in cells or organisms. A carcinogen is a substance that induces unregulated growth processes in cells or tissues of multicellular animals, leading to the disease called cancer. Although mutagen and carcinogen are not synonymous terms, the ability of a substance to induce mutations and its ability to induce cancer are strongly correlated. Mutagenesis refers to the processes that result in a genetic change, and carcinogenesis (the processes in tumor development) may result from mutagenic events.

Mutagens. A mutation is any change in a cell or in an organism that is transmitted to subsequent generations. Mutations can occur spontaneously or be induced by chemical or physical agents. The cause of mutations is usually some form of damage to deoxyribonucleic acid (DNA) or chromosomes that results in some change that can be seen or measured. However, damage can occur in a segment of DNA that is a noncoding region (that is, no gene product is produced), and thus will not result in a mutation. Mutations may or may not be harmful, depending upon which function is affected. They may occur in either somatic or germ cells. Mutations that occur in germ cells may be transmitted to subsequent generations, whereas mutations in somatic cells are generally of consequence only to the affected individual.

The impact of induced germ cell mutations on humans has been difficult to determine. Germ cell mutations are the basis of inherited human disorders, but there is uncertainty about what types or frequency of mutations are induced by exposure to mutagens. Most mutagens cause specific chemical changes in the informational content of DNA. Among the specific changes are alterations of purine or pyrimidine bases in DNA by rearrangement, deletion, or insertion events. The consequences of such changes can be the loss or altered activities of gene products.

Not all heritable changes result from damage to DNA. For example, in growth and differentiation of normal cells, major changes in gene expression occur and are transmitted to progeny cells through changes in the signals that control genes that are transcribed into ribonucleic acid (RNA). The mechanisms by which differentiation is controlled are not known. It is possible that chemicals and radiation alter these processes. When such an effect is seen in newborns, it is called teratogenic and results in birth defects that are not transmitted to the next generation. However, if the change is transmissible to progeny, it is a mutation, even though it might have arisen from an effect on the way in which the gene is expressed. Thus, chemicals could have somatic effects involving genes

regulating cell growth that could lead to the development of cancer, also without damage to DNA.

Carcinogens. Included in the phenotypic consequences of mutations are changes in gene regulation brought about by changes either in the regulatory region or in proteins involved with coordinated cellular development. Altered proteins may exhibit novel interactions with target substrates and thereby lose the ability to provide a regulatory function for the cell or impose altered functions on associated molecules. Through such a complex series of molecular interactions, changes occur in the growth properties of normal cells leading to transformed cells that are not responsive to normal regulatory controls and can eventually give rise to a visible neoplasm or tumor. While mutagens can give rise to neoplasms by a process similar to that described above, not all mutagens induce cancer and not all mutational events result in tumors. Many DNA changes may occur in genes that do not relate to cellular development or in sequences that do not affect gene function. Such changes are called null mutations. Also, normal cells possess the ability to repair segments of DNA damaged by either ionization, chemical adduction, or other events, thus erasing the damage from the DNA sequence. Alternatively, some chemicals that have the potential to form electrophiles may not be taken up by cells, may not be metabolized to an electrophilic intermediate, or may be rapidly detoxified and excreted from the organism.

On the other hand, there are carcinogens that do not give rise to electrophiles and are believed to induce tumors by mechanisms that do not involve direct DNA interactions and mutation. The mechanisms by which nonmutagenic carcinogens act are not well understood, and the many mechanisms that have been proposed are highly speculative. However, in some cases, nonmutagenic carcinogens may express hormonelike or growth-promoting activities. Hormones have profound effects on the growth and differentiation of cells and tissues through their interactions with DNA that do not involve changes in base sequence. Therefore, it is possible that the carcinogenic effects of some of these chemicals may involve interference with the normal differentiation of somatic cells. Alternatively, such chemicals may affect the way in which the DNA sequence is transcribed into messenger RNA and translated into proteins. There are likely to be a number of diverse mechanisms through which such substances can induce tumors, and different mechanisms may cooperate to produce the phenotypic changes of cancer. For example, it appears that while the induction of a mutation may be necessary to initiate neoplasia, a single mutation may not be sufficient to lead to the development of tumors. Other mutagenic or nonmutational events that involve other actions of carcinogenic chemicals, or events at the cellular or tissue level that occur in a time-dependent fashion, also appear to be necessary for the development of a tumor. One hypothesis is that the action of the chemical results in a general loss of genetic stability, leading to secondary genetic events that appear to be involved in progression to the neoplastic state, including translocation of segments of certain genes or chromosomes.

The identification of certain specific types of genes, termed oncogenes, that appear to be causally involved in the neoplastic process has helped to focus mechanistic studies on carcinogenesis. Oncogenes can be classified into a few functionally different groups, and through DNA transfer experiments specific mutations in some of the genes have been identified and are believed to be critical in tumorigenesis. However, there is also evidence for the existence of tumor suppressor genes or antioncogenes that provide a normal regulatory function. By mutation or other events, the loss of the function of these genes may release cells from normal growth-control processes, allowing them to begin the neoplastic process.

Identifying mutagens and carcinogens. There are a number of methods and systems for identifying chemical mutagens. Because mutagenesis involves several steps and since there may be variation between organisms used for detecting mutagens, an agent may be mutagenic only in some systems. Mutations can be detected at a variety of genetic loci (genes) in very diverse organisms, including bacteria (*Salmonella typhimurium*, *Escherichia coli*), insects (*Drosophila melanogaster*), cultured mammalian cells, and rodents. An important advantage in using cultured cells is that they can be used under conditions designed to specifically select for induced mutants. Spontaneous and induced mutations occur very infrequently, the estimated rate being less than 1 in 10,000 per gene per cell generation. This low mutation rate is probably the result of a combination of factors that include the relative inaccessibility of DNA to damaging agents and the ability of cellular processes to repair damage to DNA. By applying methods that can select for mutations occurring in specific genes, it is possible to use fewer cells to detect mutations, and to be able to generate enough mutants to study quantitative aspects of the mutation process.

Selection methods cannot be used to induce mutations in animals such as mice, and so it is difficult to measure the induction of germ-line mutations because large numbers of animals are required. Effective methods involve exposing male mice to potential mutagens, mating them to normal females, and examining the progeny mice for morphologically visible mutations, for example, hair color or skeletal abnormalities. Progeny also may be examined for altered gene products (such as electrophoretically different enzymes) that do not relate to visible physical changes. By using such laborious methods, it has been possible to study a limited number of chemicals. It appears that not all chemicals that are mutagenic in bacterial or insect systems have the capacity to induce germ cell mutations in rodents. However, it has not been possible to determine the relative predictability of the mouse germ cell mutation assays for humans since there are as yet no agents that have been demonstrated to be human germ cell mutagens. Thus, while it is difficult to directly estimate the potential human health impact of germ cell mutagens, there are many naturally occurring mutations that are the basis of inherited diseases in humans.

Factors that contribute to the difficulty in recognizing substances that may be carcinogenic to humans include the prevalence of cancer (which affects approximately 25% of the United States population); the diversity of types of cancer; the generally late-life onset of most cancers; and the multifactorial nature of the disease process. It is estimated from both epidemiological and experimental data that several steps (which may or may not involve mutations) are required for development of the malignant phenotype. These factors make the clinical recognition of causal factors in human cancer extraordinarily difficult and reduce the certainty of epidemiological methods that attempt to identify risk factors and causal associations. Adding to this uncertainty is the diversity of types and forms of cancers, which suggests different causes for what may be a group of diseases. Furthermore, like the problem of heritable mutations, it is difficult to discriminate between cancers that may be of spontaneous origin and those that may be induced by exogenous substances. With the exception of asbestos and tobacco, the causes of most human cancers are not known.

Because of the difficulty in attempting to identify potential human carcinogens based upon clinical or epidemiological studies, the primary method for identifying potential carcinogens has been tumor induction in laboratory rodents exposed to suspected carcinogens. The typical rodent bioassay involves the exposure of groups of rats and mice to carefully selected doses of chemical or other agents. The doses are minimally toxic, but one dose must be sufficiently high to show evidence of some effect in the animals so that there can be assurance that the animals are being exposed to a potentially biologically active dose of chemical. Exposures for approximately 2 years or more are required to ensure that substances with relatively weak carcinogenic potential can be identified. Although hundreds of chemicals have been evaluated in this manner, there is no scientific consensus on a scheme that would rank the relative potency of various rodent carcinogens. A substance is identified as a carcinogen if it induces significant numbers of tumors at sites at which tumors do not normally occur, or if the substance increases the frequency or changes the pattern of tumors that occur spontaneously. There are, however, uncertainties in quantitatively estimating health risks to humans from tumor data obtained from studying rodents. Most of the organic chemicals that have been identified as carcinogenic in humans are also carcinogenic in rodents, and the sites or types of tumors induced in the rodents are often similar to those seen in humans. However, it has not been possible to validate the rodent bioassay for chemicals that are not carcinogens for humans. Therefore, substances that produce relatively weak carcinogenic effects in rodents are often subject to controversy when efforts are made to extrapolate the results to predict human health hazards.

Because of the problems associated with the use of animals in these bioassays, significant efforts have been mounted to develop alternative cultured-cells or whole-animal short-term assay methods. Cultured-cell methods were developed by using bacteria and other organisms for the identification of mutagens; the most widely used of such assays is the induction of mutations in *Salmonella typhimurium*. This assay system has demonstrated the ability to identify a significant proportion of chemicals that possess electrophilic structures; however, it does not detect all potential mutagens, because some chemicals cannot be adequately metabolized in the assay. Approximately 30% of the substances that are mutagenic in *Salmonella* have been found not to be rodent carcinogens, and another large group of chemicals that are carcinogenic in rodents are not mutagenic in the *Salmonella* assay.

Another assay system is the induction of chromosome damage in bone marrow or white blood cells of rodents exposed to chemicals. Many mutagenic agents (for example, x-radiation) also induce chromosomal damage, and exposure of whole animals, rather than cultured cells, allows chemicals to be appropriately metabolized. In addition, chromosome damage, such as translocation of chromosome segments or changes in chromosome number, are often found in tumor cells. These assays must be characterized for their sensitivity (ability to identify carcinogens) and specificity (ability not to identify noncarcinogens).

Mechanisms of mutagenesis and carcinogenesis. Ionizing radiation was the first agent that was recognized as having the capacity to induce mutations and also to induce cancer. Induction of mutations by ionizing radiation has been recognized to be a product of ionization paths within cells that, when they occur in DNA, cause the breaking of chemical bonds and the alteration of the nucleotide bases. Alterations in properties of cells that occur as a result of exposure to radiation or chemicals are called phenotypic changes; if these changes are the result of DNA alterations and are transmitted to progeny cells, they are mutations. When such mutations affect genes that regulate cellular growth, they may result in cells called transformants, which can give rise to tumors.

Radiation can induce alterations in any segment of DNA, but some of the most important effects occur in genes that are required for survival of cells (injury to one of these genes may kill the cells) or for other important processes such as regulation of cell functions (injury to one of these genes may allow cells to grow uncontrollably). Cancers are disturbances in the growth of cells so that they are no longer under the control of the body. As the altered cells grow, they produce additional cells like themselves, leading to the development of a tumor. Therefore, it was logical to link the capacity of radiation to induce both mutation and cancer. These observations supported the somatic mutation hypothesis of cancer proposed by T. Boveri, which attributed the induction of cancer to mutations induced in normal cells by radiation, chemicals, and other exogenous factors. However, efforts to understand how chemically induced mutations could lead to cancer were unsuccessful until it was recognized that, unlike radiation, many chemicals must undergo a process of enzymatic interaction (metabolism) in cells or tissues. As the cellular enzymes interact with chemicals, they often generate closely related chemical structures that possess mutagenic potential. The chemical basis for induced mutations was found to be the presence of electrophilic groups in the mutagenic chemicals. The **illustration** presents some chemical groups that are structural alerts for potential mutagenicity based primarily on their electrophilic potential. Electrophiles are chemical substituents on molecules that can covalently interact with electron-rich (nucleophilic) donor groups on other chemicals (such as purine or pyrimidine bases in DNA), thereby changing the donor structure. If an electrophilic substituent of a chemical covalently interacts with one or several DNA subunits to form an adduct, the adduct can interfere with the subsequent process of DNA replication, leading to an error in the base sequence subunits of DNA, possibly giving rise to an altered gene product or protein. SEE RADIATION BIOLOGY.

Raymond W. Tennant

Bibliography. J. Ashby and R. W. Tennant, Chemical structure mutagenicity and extent of carcinogenicity as indicators of genotoxic carcinogenesis among 222 chemicals tested in rodents by the U.S. NCI/NTP, *Mutat. Res.*, 204(1):17–115, 1988; D. Grunberger and S. Goff (eds.), *Mechanisms of Cellular Transformation by Carcinogenic Agents*, 1987; L. Hirono (ed.), *Naturally Occurring Carcinogens of Plant Origin; Toxicology, Pathology, and Biochemistry*, 1987; M. M. Moore et al. (eds.), *Mammalian Cell Mutagenesis*, 1988; National Research Council, Committee on Environmental Mutagens, *Identifying and Estimating the Genetic Impact of Chemical Mutagens*, 1983; J. M. Waring and B. A. Ponder (eds.), *Biology of Carcinogenesis*, 1987; R. Weinberg, Oncogenes, anti-oncogenes and the molecular bases of multistep carcinogenesis, *Canc. Res.*, 49:3713–3721, 1989.

Model compound upon which structural alerts to mutagenicity are based. The structural subunits are (*a*) alkyl esters of either phosphonic or sulfonic acids; (*b*) aromatic nitro groups; (*c*) aromatic azo groups (by virtue of their possible reduction to an aromatic amine); (*d*) aromatic ring *N*-oxides; (*e*) aromatic mono- and dialkylamino groups; (*f*) alkyl hydrazines; (*g*) alkyl aldehydes; (*h*) *N*-methylol derivatives; (*i*) monohaloalkenes; (*j*) a large family of nitrogen and sulfur mustards (β-haloethyl); (*k*) *N*-chloramines; (*l*) propiolactones and propiosultones; (*m*) aromatic and aliphatic aziridinyl derivatives; (*n*) both aromatic and aliphatic substituted primary alkyl halides; (*o*) derivatives of urethane (carbamates); (*p*) alkyl *N*-nitrosamines; (*q*) aromatic amines, their *N*-hydroxy derivatives, and the derived esters; (*r*) aliphatic epoxides and aromatic oxides; (*s*) center of Michael reactivities; (conjugate nucleophilic additions); (*t*) halogenated methanes C(X)$_4$, where X = M, F, Cl, Br, or I in any combination. (*After J. Ashby and R. W. Tennant, Chemical structure mutagenicity and extent of carcinogenicity as indicators of genotoxic carcinogenesis among 222 chemicals tested in rodents by the U.S. NCI/NTP, Mutat. Res., 204(1):17–115, 1988*)

Oceanography

The scientific study and exploration of the oceans and seas in all their aspects, including the sediments and rocks beneath the seas; the interaction of sea and atmosphere; the body of seawater in motion and subject to internal and external forces; the living content of the seas and sea floors and the behavior of these organisms; the chemical composition of the water; the physics of the sea and sea floor; the origin of ocean basins and ancient seas; and the formation and interaction of beaches, shores, and estuaries. Hence oceanography, sometimes called the science of the seas, consists of the marine aspects of several disciplines and branches of science: geology, meteorology, biology, chemistry, physics, geophysics, geochemistry, fluid mechanics, and in its more theoretical aspects, applied mathematics. Oceanography is also an environmental science which describes and attempts to explain all processes in the ocean, and the interrelation of the ocean with the solid and gaseous phases of the Earth and with the universe.

OCEAN RESEARCH

Because of the fluid nature of their contents, which permits vertical and horizontal motion and mixing, and because all the waters of the world oceans are in various degrees of communication, it is necessary to study the oceans as a unit. Further unification results from the technological necessity of studying the ocean from ships. Many phases of oceanic research can be carried out in a laboratory, but to study and understand the ocean as a whole, scientists must go out to sea with vessels adapted or built especially for that purpose. Furthermore, data must be obtained from the deepest part of the ocean and, if possible, scientists must go down to the greatest depths to observe and experiment. Another unifying influence is the fact that many oceanic problems are so complex that their geological, biological, and physical aspects must be studied by a team of scientists. Because of the unity of processes operating in the ocean, and because some writers have separated marine biology from oceanography (implying the term oceanography to embrace primarily physical oceanography, bottom relief, and sediments), the term ''oceanology'' is sometimes used as embracing all the science divisions of the marine hydrosphere. As used in this article, the term oceanography applies to the whole of sea science. *SEE HYDROSPHERE.*

Development. The early ocean voyages by Frobisher, Davis, Hudson, Baffin, Bering, Cook, Ross, Parry, Franklin, Amundsen, and Nordenskiold were undertaken primarily for geographical exploration and in search of new navigable routes. Information gathered about the ocean, its currents, sea ice, and other physical and biological phenomena was more or less incidental. Later, the polar expeditions of the Scoresbys, Parry, Markham, Greeley, Nansen, Peary, Scott, and Shackleton were also voyages of geographical discovery, although scientific observations about the sea and its inhabitants were made by some of them. William Scoresby took soundings and observed that discolored water containing living organisms (now known to be diatoms) was related to whale movements. Ross made dredge hauls of bottom-living animals. Nansen contributed to the improvement of plankton nets and suggested the existence of internal waves.

More closely related to the beginning of oceanography as comprehensive study of the seas are the nineteenth-century activities of naturalists Ehrenberg, Humboldt, Hooker, and Örstedt, all of whom contributed to the eventual recognition of plankton life in the sea and its role in the formation of bottom deposits. Charles Darwin's observations on coral reefs and Müller's invention of the plankton net belong to this phase of developing interest in marine science, in which men began to investigate ocean phenomena as biologists, chemists, and physicists rather than as oceanographers. In this group should be included such physicists and mathematicians as Kepler, Vossius, Fournier, Varenius, and Laplace, who provided the background for development of modern theories and investigations of ocean currents and air circulation.

Toward the middle of the nineteenth century a few scientists began to study the oceans as a whole, rather than as an incidental part of an established discipline. Forbes, as a result of his work at sea, first developed a scheme for vertical and horizontal distribution of life in the sea. On the physical side Matthew Fontaine Maury, developing and extending Franklin's earlier work, made comprehensive computations of wind and current data and set up the machinery for international cooperation. His book *Physical Geography of the Sea* has been regarded as the first text in oceanography.

Forbes and Maury were followed by a distinguished group of men whose interest in oceanography led them to make the first truly oceanographic expeditions. Most famous of these was the three-year around-the-world voyage of HMS *Challenger,* which followed earlier explorations of the *Lightning* and *Porcupine.* Instrumental in organizing these was Wyville Thompson, later joined by John Murray. Later in succession were the Norwegian Johan Hjort and the *Michael Sars* North Atlantic exploration; Louis Agassiz; and Albert Honoré Charles, Prince of Monaco, in a series of privately owned yachts named *Hirondelle I* and *II* and *Princess Alice I* and *II.* Other important contributions were made by Michael and G. O. Sars, Björn Helland-Hansen, Carl Chum, Victor Hansen, Otto Petterson, Gustav Ekman, and the vessels *Valdivia,* the Danish *Dana,* the British *Discovery,* the German *National* and *Meteor,* and the Dutch *Ingold, Snellius,* and *Siboga,* the French *Travailleur* and *Talisman,* the Austrian *Pola,* and the North American *Blake, Bache,* and *Albatross.* Among the North American pioneers were Alexander Agassiz, L. F. de Pourtales, and J. D. Dana. Pioneers in modern oceanographic work are M. Kunelsen, Sven Ekman, A. S. Sverdrup, A. Defant, Georg Wüst, Gerhard Schott, and Henry Bigelow.

Modern oceanography relies less upon single explorations than upon the continuous operation of single vessels belonging to permanent institutions, such as *Atlantis II* of the Woods Hole Oceanographic Institution, *Argo* of Scripps Institution of Oceanography, *Vema* of the Lamont Geological Observatory, the French *Calypso,* and the large Soviet vessels *Vitiaz* and *Mikhail Lomonosov.* Single explorations continue to be made, as exemplified by the Swedish *Albatross* and Danish *Galatea.*

The reduction of data and study of collections from earlier expeditions were carried out generally in research institutions, museums, and universities not solely or primarily engaged in oceanography. The first marine laboratories were interested principally in fishery problems or were designed as biological stations to accommodate visiting investigators. Many of the former have extended their activities to cover chemical and physical oceanography during their growth and development. The latter, often active as extensions of university biological departments, are exemplified by the Naples Zoological Station and the Marine Biological Laboratory of Woods Hole. Visitors to such stations contribute greatly to the development of biology, generally in such fields as embryology and physiology.

The number of institutions devoted to organized oceanographic investigations with permanent scientific staffs has gradually grown. At first the requirements of fishery research provided the stimulus in countries adjacent to the North Sea, but in later years laboratories in other countries wholly or mainly devoted to oceanography have grown considerably in number. A few may be mentioned here. In England, among other important institutions, are the National Institute of Oceanography, the Marine Biological Laboratory at Plymouth, and the Fisheries Laboratory at Lowestoft. In the United States are the Woods Hole Oceanographic Institution in Massachusetts, the Scripps Institution of Oceanography in California, the Lamont-Doherty Geological Observatory in New York, the University of Miami Marine Laboratory in Florida, the Texas A. & M. College Department of Oceanography, and the Oceanography Laboratories of the University of Washington at Seattle, the University of Hawaii, and Oregon State University. In Germany oceanographic laboratories are located at Kiel and at Hamburg. In Denmark the Danish Biological Station is at Copenhagen. Other European laboratories include those at Bergen, Norway; Göteborg and Stockholm, Sweden; Helsinki, Finland; and Trieste. Laboratories are located at Tokyo, Japan; Namaimio and Halifax, Canada; and Hawaii. This list is not inclusive and necessarily leaves out a considerable number of important institutions.

Surveys. Oceanographic surveys require careful planning because of high cost. Provision must be made for the proper type of vessel, equipment, and laboratory facilities, adapted to the nature and duration of the survey.

Research ships. Ships of all types and sizes have been gathering information about the oceans since

Fig. 2. Trawl winch used on research vessel *Vema*. (*Lamont-Doherty Geological Observatory*)

earliest times. Vessels of less than 300 tons (270 metric tons) displacement seldom range farther than several hundred miles from land, whereas ships larger than 300 tons (270 metric tons) displacement may work in the open ocean for several months at a time. Research ships of all sizes must be seaworthy and must provide good platforms from which to work (**Fig. 1**). More specifically, a ship must have comfortable quarters, adequate laboratory and deck space for preliminary analyses, plus storage space for equipment, explosives, samples, and scientific data. Machinery, usually in the form of winches and booms, is necessary for handling the complex and often heavy scientific equipment needed to probe the ocean depths (**Fig. 2**).

A number of the larger oceanographic vessels are equipped with general-purpose digital computers, including tapes, disk files, and process-interrupt equipment. The result is that data can be reduced on board for experimental work, and all the operations taking place on the vessel can be centralized, including the satellite navigation equipment. *SEE DIGITAL COMPUTER.*

Standard oceanographic equipment includes collecting bottles (Nansen bottles) for obtaining water samples and thermometers (both reversing thermometers and bathythermographs) for measuring temperatures at all depths. In addition, there are various devices for obtaining samples of ocean bottom sediments and biological specimens. These include heavy coring tubes which punch cylindrical sediment sections out of the bottom, dredges which scrape rock samples from submerged mountains and platforms, plankton nets for collecting very small planktonic organisms, and trawls for collecting large free-swimming organisms at all oceanic depths. Echo sounders provide accurate profiles of the ocean floor.

Specialized equipment for oceanic exploration includes seismographs for measuring the Earth's crustal thickness, magnetometers for measuring terrestrial magnetism, gravimeters for measuring variations in the force of gravity, hydrophotometers for measuring the distribution of light in the sea, heat probes (earth thermometers) for measuring the flow of heat from the Earth's interior, deep-sea cameras to photograph the sea bottom, bioluminescence counters for measur-

Fig. 1. Deep-sea drilling vessel *Glomar Challenger*, equipped with satellite navigation equipment and capable of holding position to within 100 ft (30 m) for several days, using bottom-mounted sonic beacons, tunnel thrusters, and computers.

ing the amount of luminescent light emitted by organisms, salinometers for measuring directly the salinity of seawater, and current meters to clock the speed of ocean currents.

Positioning of a ship is very important for accurate plotting of data and detailed charting of the oceans. Celestial navigation is in wide use now as in the past. Navigational aids such as electronic positioning equipment (loran, shoran, and radar) are increasing the accuracy of positioning to within several tens of yards of the ship's true position. Navigational and radio communications equipment normally is situated near the captain's bridge, but often is duplicated in the scientific laboratories in order that complete communication between the ship's operators, scientists, and other participating ships can be carried on at all times.

Probably the single most important advance in deep-sea oceanography has been the introduction of satellite navigation. Combined with a computer, satellite navigation permits fixes to within several hundred yards while the ship is moving and to within several hundred feet when the ship is located with respect to bottom-mounted beacons, for example, in deep-sea drilling.

Ship's laboratories. Laboratories must be adaptable for a large number of operations. In general they are of two categories, namely, wet and special laboratories. Wet laboratories are provided with an open-drain deck so that surplus ample water can be drained out on deck. Such a laboratory is located near the winches used for running out and retrieving a long string of water-sample bottles (hydrocasts). Adjoining the wet laboratory are special laboratories equipped with benches for measuring chemical properties of the recovered water and for examination of biological and geological samples. Electronics laboratories are either part of, or adjacent to, the special laboratory, depending upon the size of the ship. Here, numerous recording devices, amplifiers, and computers are set up for a variety of purposes, such as measurements of underwater sound, measurement of the Earth's magnetic and gravity fields, and seismic measurements of the Earth's crustal thickness (**Fig. 3**).

Marine technology. The development of nuclear

Fig. 3. Special laboratory aboard research vessel. (*Lamont-Doherty Geological Observatory*)

Fig. 4. Remote-controlled underwater television camera mounted in self-propelled vehicle, which can make visual surveys to depths of 1000 ft (300 m). Self-buoyant unit moves about or hovers at desired depth in currents or tides of several knots. (*Vare Industries, Roselle, New Jersey*)

power plants permits extended voyages without the necessity of refueling. Nuclear power plants, used in conjuction with inertial guidance in the submarines *Nautilus* and *Skate*, made possible the first extended journey under the Arctic ice pack. Uncharted regions of the oceans are within the reach of exploration.

Direct visual observations of the ocean depths are fast becoming a reality, both by crewed submersibles (bathyscaph) and by television cameras. Deep-sea cameras have been developed to the point whereby motion pictures of even the deepest parts of the sea bottom can be taken (**Fig. 4**). However, such observations yield no information about the subsurface material. Major crustal features are determined by seismic measurement. The shallower features of the subbottom structure and deposits were not readily observed until the advent of the subbottom acoustic probe. This device is a very high-energy echo sounder capable of penetrating below the sediment-water interface and yielding a continuous profile of the subbottom strata.

Information as to the physical and chemical makeup of the underlying material, however, is dependent upon penetration and actual recovery. Commonly used coring devices rarely penetrate more than 30–70 ft or 10–20 m (on occasion to about 108 ft or 33 m) below the surface. A new "incremental" coring device has been developed for taking successive 6.6 ft (2-m) sediment cores to depths of possibly 330 ft (100 m) or more.

The most impressive achievement in this area, however, has been in deep-sea drilling. The *Glomar Challenger*, operated by the Global Marine Corporation, was designed primarily for the purpose of taking cores throughout the full column of sediment in midocean. It is capable of handling 24,000 ft (7300 m) of drill string in mid-ocean and drilling through more than 2500 ft (760 m) of sediment, taking 30-ft (9-m) cores in the process. By mid-1969 the vessel had successfully operated at more than 40 sites in both the

Atlantic and Pacific. This operation is sponsored by the National Science Foundation, with scientific guidance supplied by JOIDES (Joint Oceanographic Institutions Deep Earth Sampling), which include the University of Washington; Institute for Marine Sciences, University of Miami; Woods Hole Oceanographic Institution; Lamont-Doherty Geological Observatory of Columbia University; and Scripps Institution of Oceanography. The last-mentioned is the operating institution. Besides incorporating the necessary innovations in drilling and coring, the *Glomar Challenger* is an example of the many important advances in oceanography, such as satellite navigation and positioning.

Oceanographic stations. Work on station consists of sampling and measuring as many marine properties as possible within the limitations of an expedition. Water, sea-bottom, and biological samples are successively collected on the long cables extended to the ocean floor. In some surveys one cable lowering may include samplers for all these items, but this is not the usual procedure. Stations are systematically located at predetermined points along the ship's path. At hydrographic stations, observations of water temperature, salinity, oxygen, and phosphate content are determined upon sample recovery. Seismic stations generally are carried out by two ships, one running a fixed course and dropping explosives while the second remains stationary and records the returning subbottom reflected or refracted sound waves. Biological stations may consist of vertical net hauls or horizontal net tows depressed to sweep the ocean at a fixed depth. Geological stations are usually coring or bottom-dredging operations. Wherever possible the recovered data are given a preliminary reduction aboard ship so that interesting discoveries are not bypassed before sufficient information is obtained. Detailed analyses aboard ship are seldom possible because of the limitations of time, space, and laboratory equipment. Instead, the carefully processed, labeled, and stored material is preserved for intensive study ashore.

Home laboratory. This phase of the work may entail many months of careful examination and detailed analyses. Batteries of sophisticated scientific instruments are often necessary: data computers for reduction of physical oceanography information; spectrographic apparatus consisting of emission units; infrared, ultraviolet, x-ray, and mass spectrometers for chemistry; aquaria, pressure chambers, and chemostats for the biologist; electron microscopes and high-powered optical microscopes for examination of inorganic and organic constituents; radioisotope counters; and numerous standard physical, chemical, geological, and biological instruments. The great variety of measurable major and minor properties is reduced to statistical parameters which may then be integrated, correlated, and charted to increase the knowledge of sea properties and show their relationships. The essentially descriptive properties lead to an understanding of the principles which control the origin, form, and distribution of the observed phenomena. The present knowledge of the oceans is still fragmentary, but the increasing store of information already is being applied to a rapidly expanding number of humanity's everyday problems.

Research problems. Since the middle of the nineteenth century, more and more has been learned about that 71% of the Earth which is covered with seawater. The rate of increase of knowledge is being accelerated by improved tools and methods and increased interest of scientists and engineers. Some of the present and future research problems that are attracting scientists are mentioned below.

One of the oldest and still unsolved problems is the motion of ocean waters, involving surface currents, deep-sea currents, vertical and horizontal turbulent motion, and general circulation. New methods such as distribution of radioactive substances, deep-sea current meters and neutrally buoyant floats, high-precision determination of salt and gas content, and hot-wire anemometers for turbulence studies and current measurements have increased present knowledge considerably. The surface movement of water is wind-produced, and a general theory of the motion has been worked out. The deep-sea currents, which are known to be caused in part by variations in the thermohaline circulation, are still an open problem. Superimposed on these movements is turbulent motion, which ranges over the whole spectrum from large ocean eddies transporting millions of cubic meters of water per second to the tiniest vibrations of water particles. Very little is known about turbulence.

The mixing of water masses and the formation of new water masses cannot yet be completely and adequately described, as many of the thermodynamic parameters are not precisely known. Laboratory experiments and measurements of thermal expansion, saline contraction, and specific heat at constant pressure must be carried out. A further problem is the composition of seawater and the extent to which the ratio among the components is constant. In connection with these problems it has been urged that a library of water samples be established. Improved techniques of measuring sound velocity, electrical conductivity, refractive index, and density must be developed to enable scientists to follow many processes in the ocean. It is therefore necessary to study the small variations of these parameters in the sea. SEE SEAWATER.

The tides in the oceans are rather well known at the surface but are almost completely unknown in the deep sea; also, the influence of land boundaries on deep-sea tides is not yet understood. Further research also must be devoted to the interesting phenomenon of internal waves.

The study of ocean waves is one of the most advanced topics in oceanography, but the energy exchange between atmosphere and sea surface by friction must be studied further. Another problem is that of the heat exchange between ocean and atmosphere, an important link in the heat mechanism which determines the weather and the oceanic circulation.

The climate of the past, in particular that of the last 10^6 years, is best studied in the ocean. Isotopic methods in paleoclimatologic research allow the determination of temperature variations in the ocean with a high degree of accuracy. The rapid growth of geochemistry and the increased sampling of deep-sea sediments through improved techniques have solved some of the problems of deep-sea sedimentation. At the same time a number of new ones have been created, such as: Why is the sediment carpet only about 1000 ft (300 m) thick? What is the mechanism of sediment transport? What is the history of sea water? Of the ocean basin? What is the cause of the ice ages?

The results of the Deep Sea Drilling Project have confirmed the expectations of its most optimistic supporters. It has strikingly confirmed the sea-floor-spreading hypothesis of the development of the ocean basins and the newer concepts of plate tectonics.

The age determination of sediments by radioactivity methods, which was thought impossible 30 years ago, is now used on deep-sea sediments older than 10^7 years. Very little is known about the formation of minerals on the sea floor, the diffusion and adsorption of elements in and on sediments, and the reaction at slow rates in sediments. Certainly microbiological processes on the sea floor are an important factor, as they seem to produce chemical energy in sediments.

In marine biology the systematics and ecology remain the major aspects. It is still the science of the "naturalist." The interest of marine biology is many-sided and not grouped around a few central problems. Ocean life offers to the general biologist the best opportunities to study such complex problems as the structure of communities and the flux of energy through these communities. The zonation of animals on the shore and in the open ocean is not yet fully understood; the cause of patchiness in the distribution must be found. On the other hand, the distribution of species by currents and eddies must be studied, and large-scale experiments on behavior must be carried out. Observation at sea has been neglected to a large extent, and therefore the equilibrium between sea observation and laboratory experiment must be restored. The great advances in genetics, biochemistry, physiology, and microbiology also will advance the study of life in the sea. *See* MARINE ECOLOGY.

Applications of ocean research. Directly and indirectly the ocean is of great importance to humanity. It is valuable as a reservoir of natural resources, an outlet for waste disposal, and a means of transport and communication. The ocean is also important as a harmful agent causing biological, chemical, and mechanical destruction of life and property. In addition to the peaceful exploration of the oceans, there are many military applications of surface and submarine phenomena. In all of these aspects oceanography provides basic information for engineers who seek to increase its benefits and to avoid its harmful effects. *See* MARINE RESOURCES.

Food resources. The food resources of the ocean are potentially greater than those of the land since its larger area receives a proportionately larger amount of solar radiation, the source of living energy. Nevertheless, this potential is only in part realized. Oceanographic studies provide information which can help to increase fishing yields through improved exploratory fishing, economical harvesting methods, fisheries forecasts, processing techniques at sea, and aquaculture.

Fishes are dependent in their distribution upon food organisms and plankton, vertical and horizontal currents which bring nutrients to the plankton, bottom conditions, and physical and chemical characteristics of the water. A knowledge of the relation of food fishes to these environmental conditions and of the distribution of these conditions in the oceans is vital to successful extension of fishing areas. Satisfactory measurements of the basic organic productivity of the sea may become essential in the selection of regions for extended fishery exploration. *See* SEAWATER FERTILITY.

The catching of fishes may be facilitated and new and more efficient methods devised through a knowledge of the reaction of fishes to stimuli and of their habits in general. This knowledge may result in better design of nets and in the use of electrical, sonic, photic, and chemical traps or baits. The harvest also may be increased by using improved methods of locating schools of fish by sonic equipment or other means.

The biology of fishes, their food preferences, their predators, their relation to oceanographic conditions, and the fluctuations in these conditions seasonally and from year to year are important factors in forecasting fluctuations in the fisheries. This information will aid in preventing the economic waste of alternating glut and scarcity, and is essential to good management of fisheries and to sound regulation by conservation agencies.

Other anticipated advances which require further oceanographic study include (1) the improvement of fishing by transplanting the young of existing stocks or by introducing new stocks; (2) farming or cultivation of sea fishes (although this does not seem feasible at present, scientific research has improved the cultivation of oysters and mussels in France and Japan); and (3) the use of planktonic vegetation as a source of food or animal nutrition. *See* FISHERY CONSERVATION; MARINE FISHERIES.

Mineral resources. Although most of the valuable chemical elements in seawater are in very great dilution, the great volume of water of the oceans (about 3×10^8 mi^3 or 8×10^8 km^3) provides a limitless and readily accessible reservoir, if such dilute concentrations can be economically extracted. Magnesium is produced largely from seawater, and bromide also has been extracted commercially. High concentrations of manganese are found in manganese nodules, which are very common on certain areas of the sea floor.

Other elements occur in too great dilution to be extracted by present methods. Possibly a better understanding of the ability of certain marine plants and animals to accumulate and concentrate elements from seawater in their tissues may lead to new methods of recovering these elements.

Energy and water source. Seawater contains deuterium and would be a limitless source of this element in the event of successful nuclear fusion developments. Further oceanographic knowledge and advances in engineering may lead to the increased utilization of tidal energy sources, or of the heat energy available from temperature differences in the ocean. The development of new methods for removing salt from seawater offers promise that the sea may become a practical source for potable water.

Disposal outlet. Because of its large volume, the sea is frequently used for the disposal of chemical wastes, sewage, and garbage. A knowledge of local currents and tides, as well as of the bottom fauna, is essential to avoid pollution of beaches or commercial fishing grounds. Radioactive waste disposal in offshore deeps poses problems of the rate of movement of deep waters and the transfer of radioactive materials through migration and food chains of marine organisms. A problem of rapidly growing concern is oil pollution, which is caused in part by the rapidly expanding exploitation of the continental-shelf-oil resources. There must be considerable development in marine engineering and better ecological understanding if these oil resources are to be fully utilized. A second major cause of oil pollution is the breakup of giant oil tankers. Prevention of such accidents requires improved vessels and more stringent navigation controls.

Traffic and communication. The sea still remains an

important highway; thus the knowledge and forecasting of waves, currents, tides, and weather in relation to navigation are of great practical importance. New developments include the continuous rerouting of ships at sea in order that they may follow the most economic paths in the face of changing weather conditions. A knowledge of submarine topography, geologic processes, and temperature conditions is important for the satisfactory location, operation, and repair of submarine cables. The use of sofar in air-sea rescue operations is based upon submarine acoustics.

Defense requirements. Defense aspects of marine research involve not only the navigation of surface vessels but also undersea craft with special navigational problems related to submarine topography, echo sounding, and the distribution of temperature, density, and other properties. Research in submarine acoustics has improved communication between, and detection of, undersea craft. In spite of these advances natural conditions, such as warm water pockets and subsurface magnetic irregularities, can conceal submarines from conventional means of detection. Investigation of these conditions is essential to any defense against missile-carrying submarines.

Property and life. Damage to docks and ships by marine borers and fouling organisms is controlled by methods that utilize a knowledge of the biology, behavior, and physiology of the destructive organisms, and of the oceanographic conditions which control their distribution. Loss of life caused by the attacks of sharks and other fishes may be reduced through an understanding of their behavior and the development of repellants and other protective devices. The chemical characteristics of seawater pose special problems of corrosion of metals. Beach erosion, wave damage to harbor and offshore structures, the effects of tsunamis and internal waves, and storms cause loss of property and life. Much of this damage may be minimized by the application of oceanographic knowledge to forecasting methods and warning systems. *See Storm surge; Tsunami.*

Indirect benefits of oceanography arise from the application of marine meteorology to weather prediction, not only over the sea areas but also over the land. The study of marine geology and marine ecology aid in the understanding of the character of oil-bearing sedimentary rocks found on land. *See Maritime meteorology.* William A. Nierenberg

Theoretical Oceanography

The basis for theoretical oceanographic studies is the known set of conservation equations for momentum, mass, and energy, supplemented by an equation of state for seawater and a conservation equation for dissolved salts. A general solution to the mathematical system is not possible. The aim of theoreticians is to develop simple mathematical models from the general set to explain observed oceanic features. A model may describe a process, such as the convective overturning of surface waters, or a phenomenon, such as the existence of the Gulf Stream on the western side of the North Atlantic. Whatever the purpose of the model, simplicity is important: the more directly that one can relate a feature to processes that are already understood, the better.

Oceanic flow. Oceanic flows with a horizontal scale of 60 mi (100 km) or more are strongly affected by the rotation of the Earth. Just as a tilted spinning top wobbles laterally instead of falling directly when acted upon by gravity, the rotation of the Earth causes a fluid flow to be deflected from the direction of the applied force. The deflecting (Coriolis) force is proportional to the angular rate of rotation of the Earth and to the sine of the latitude of the position of the fluid. Thus, it is larger at high latitudes than at low.

The effect of rotation is easily incorporated into the conservation equation for momentum. When it is made to play a dominant role, the analysis is simplified because flows that are not affected by the rotation are effectively filtered out of the equations.

Wind effects. Simple theoretical analysis shows that the wind directly affects the surface waters of the ocean only in the top hundred meters or so and that rotation causes the net transport of water in this wind-driven layer to flow to the right of the direction of the wind stress. This indirect circulation in the surface layers induces a deeper flow in the direction of the wind, thereby setting up the wind-drive circulation. The Coriolis force exerts a dominating influence on the structure of the flow, and its variation with latitude gives rise to the Gulf Stream and the other observed western boundary currents.

Thermohaline circulation. Solar heating is most intense at low latitudes, and cooling of surface waters occurs in polar regions. The vertical circulation caused by the generated density differences has a global scale because the dense water that fills the abyssal ocean is formed in only a few polar locations. The rotation of the Earth affects the flow pattern of the deep circulation as well, giving rise to strong currents near coasts and underwater ridges that bound the basins on the west and to a relatively weak flow in the remaining areas. Theories of this thermohaline circulation verify the observation that the waters of the ocean are stably stratified. Light surface waters lie above the thermocline, a layer with a relatively sharp density change, and the abyss is filled with nearly homogeneous, dense water. *See Thermocline.*

Waves. Given the stable stratification of the oceans, theory predicts the existence of a variety of large-scale waves. The periods of gravity waves are limited by rotation to be less than or equal to a day, or more precisely, the period of a Foucault pendulum. Longer-period, planetary waves owe their existence to the variation of the Coriolis force with latitude and to the variable depth of the ocean. These waves have periods ranging from several days to several years. Variable depth also gives rise to waves that are trapped in a layer near the bottom, the depth of the layer depending on stratification, rotation, and the scale of the waves. The periods here range from a few days to a few months. All of these waves can be identified in observational records, and some of the observed, nonwavelike features can be described by combinations of such wave motions.

Instability. Simpler wave studies are valid when the wave speeds are substantially larger than the fluid velocity, a condition that is often violated, especially for long-period waves. In such cases the current velocity must be included in the analysis. The energy associated with the currents then becomes available as a possible source of instability. The waves may grow in amplitude by drawing energy from the kinetic energy of the currents or from the potential energy of the stratification. Both types of instability occur in the ocean, though the more important source of energy seems to be the latter, in which case the basic flow is said to be baroclinically unstable. As the waves grow, they interact with each other and alter the current field from which they draw their energy. Eventually a state of statistically steady equilibrium may be achieved in which the basic flow is altered to the point where it provides enough energy to feed waves whose amplitudes are in equilibrium with the altered mean field.

Turbulence. In more extreme situations the instability may become so intense that it leads to turbulence. In that case traditional analysis breaks down, and a statistical-dynamical approach to the problem is required. The effect of turbulence is often parameterized in terms of properties of the mean field, somewhat in the manner in which the net effect of individual particle motions of a gas is parameterized in kinetic theory as a viscosity coefficient. However, the two situations are very different, and in the present setting that approach gives reasonable results only in some cases.

The latter 1970s saw the development of numerical oceanographic models that can resolve the unstable modes and follow their development as the turbulent regime is approached. The constraints of rotation and stratification help to restrict the structure of the motions essentially to two dimensions so that the problem can be handled with present computing facilities. Eventually the turbulent effects will be parameterized. The role of bottom topography may be important in such a description.

The resolution of the large-scale turbulence problem is especially important in the oceanographic context because the fluctuating turbulent motions are normally much stronger than the velocity of the mean circulation. Hence, good understanding of the latter will require a knowledge of the effects of the former. A similar situation exists in the atmosphere, though the relative intensity of the fluctuations is somewhat smaller there.

Time-averaged circulation. A totally different theoretical approach can be used to determine the time-averaged circulation. Ocean water contains a number of dissolved chemicals, such as oxygen and silicates, which can be looked upon as tracers that indicate the flow from known source regions. Ideally one would like to be able to calculate the flow from the tracer distributions, but it is easy to show that this inverse problem generally does not have a unique solution. So far the most effective attacks on this problem have used a known velocity field, one that satisfies at least the major constraints, in the convective-diffusive equation for the tracer. The calculated distribution is then compared with the observed, and parameters are adjusted until an optimal fit is achieved. A more direct approach is to include the tracer in a numerical model of the circulation.

George Veronis

Bibliography. J. R. Apel, *Principles of Ocean Physics*, 1987; H. Barnes and M. Barnes (eds.), *Oceanography and Marine Biology*, annually; R. A. Davis, Jr., *Oceanography: An Introduction to the Marine Environment*, 1987; M. N. Hill (ed.), *The Sea*, vol. 1, 1982; National Academy of Sciences, *Numerical Models of Ocean Circulation*, 1975; G. L. Pickard and W. J. Emery (eds.), *Descriptive Physical Oceanography*, 4th ed., 1982; R. G. Pirie (ed.), *Oceanography: Contemporary Readings in the Ocean Sciences*, 1977; Scientific American Editors, *The Ocean*, 1969; F. W. Smith and F. A. Kalber (eds.), *Handbook in Marine Science*, 2 vols., 1974; K. Stowe, *Essentials of Ocean Science*, 1988; G. Veronis, Model of world ocean circulation, *J. Mar. Res.*, pt. I, 31:228–288, 1973, pt. III, 36:1–44, 1978.

Open pit mining

The process of extracting beneficial minerals by surface excavations. Open pit mining is a type of surface excavation which often takes the shape of an inverted cone (**Fig. 1**); the shape of the mine opening varies with the shape of the mineral deposit. Other types of surface mining are specific to the type and shape of the mineral deposit. SEE PLACER MINING; SURFACE MINING.

The open pit mine, like any other mining operation, must extract the product minerals at a positive economic benefit. All costs of producing the product, including excavation, beneficiation, processing, reclamation, environmental, and social costs, must be paid for by the sales of the mineral product. A mineral that is in sufficient concentration to meet or exceed these economic constraints is called ore. The terms ore body and ore deposit are used to refer to the natural occurrence of an economic mineral deposit.

Ore bodies occur as the result of natural geologic occurrences. The geologic events that lead to the concentration of a mineral into an ore deposit are generally complex and rare. If those events placed the deposit sufficiently near the surface, open pit mining may be viable.

Material encountered during the mining process that has little or no economic value is called waste or overburden. One important economic criterion for open pit mining is the amount of overlying waste which must be removed to extract the ore. The ratio of the amount of waste to the amount of ore is referred to as the strip ratio. In general, the lower the strip ratio, the more likely an ore body is to be mined by open pit methods.

Mining operations. Modern open pit mining utilizes large mechanical equipment to remove the ore and waste from the open pit excavation. The amount of equipment and its type and size depend on the characteristics of the ore and waste and the required production capacity. In general, there are four basic unit operations common to most open pit mining operations. These are drilling, blasting, loading, and hauling. If the rock types to be excavated are soft enough to permit excavation without blasting, the first two unit operations may not be performed.

The equipment used to accomplish the unit operations works most effectively when applied to a specific set of geometries. These geometric constraints result in the rock being excavated in horizontal slices of equal thickness. A slice is called a bench and may range in height from 10 to 50 ft (3 to 15 m). The specific height of the bench is set, based on the ore body geometry, the distribution of ore and waste, production requirements, and the equipment selected to remove the material. Large base metal mines tend to have benches of 40 or 50 ft (12 or 15 m). Many open pit gold and silver mines have bench heights of 20 ft (6 m) due to the fact that ore and waste are intermixed, requiring better selectivity (less mixing of the ore and waste), and have lower production rates. Mining bench by bench results in the terraced geometry of the pit wall as shown in the background of

Fig. 1. Aerial view of a mature open pit mine. (*Kennecott Copper Corp.*)

Fig. 2; this technique aids in the containment of rock falls.

The total depth of the pit is a function of ore geometry, allowable pit slope angle, and the economic constraints of the strip ratio and the ore quality or grade. Large base metal operations can often exceed 1500 ft (460 m) in depth or may be as shallow as 50 ft (15 m). Slope angles depend on the strength of the rock and the natural fractures or joints in the rock. Overall slope angles may vary from 28 to 55° with 35 to 40° being the more common angles.

Drilling. The primary purpose of drilling is to provide an opening in the rock mass for explosives. Explosives work most efficiently when confined within the rock mass to be blasted. The drilling machine generally sits on top of a bench and bores a vertical hole downward into the bench area to be blasted. The drill should be able to penetrate the full bench height plus 20 to 30% additional depth. The upper limits of the bench height are often set by the effectiveness of the drill. The holes provide a secondary purpose in most metal mining operations in that the cuttings extracted from the hole during the drilling process provide a sample for assaying the grade of the zone near the hole. The results of the assayed drill hole cuttings

are used to delineate the boundaries between ore and waste and between multiple mineral products, if applicable (for example, copper and molybdenum).

The most common form of drilling is rotary drilling where downward pressure is applied to a rotating tricone rotary bit, a type of bit originally developed by the petroleum industry for oil well drilling. The cuttings are removed from the hole by compressed air forced down the hollow drill pipe, past the rotating bit, and up the annulus between the drill pipe and the blast hole wall. The compressed air serves a second function of cooling the bit and bearings. For rotary drilling of harder formations, the tricone surfaces support buttons made of tungsten carbide, an extremely hard, wear-resistant metal.

When hard and abrasive rocks are encountered, rotary percussion drilling is performed with downhole hammers. This type of blast-hole drilling uses impact by a tungsten carbide bit, often in the approximate shape of a chisel. After impact, the bit is mechanically retracted and rotated for another impact. This process occurs very rapidly and is generally powered by compressed air. A downhole hammer is a rotary percussion tool that places the reciprocating hammer or impact mechanism immediately behind the bit. In this way, the drill pipe does not incur the stresses of impact. Compressed air forced down the hollow drill pipe powers and lubricates the tool, cools the bit, and removes the cuttings.

Jet piercing was developed to drill very hard iron ores. The drill hole is made by applying a high-temperature oxygen–fuel oil flame to the rock. The method is being replaced by improved conventional methods.

The drill equipment and air compressor are generally mounted for transport on a truck-type, rubber-tired carrier or a track-type carrier. The track-type carrier is generally more rugged and able to negotiate steeper grades. Rubber-tired carriers are generally used with smaller drills and where more mobility is required in the pit.

Drill hole diameters vary from roughly 3 to 15 in. (7 to 38 cm). The larger mines generally use holes from 6⅝ in. (17 cm) upward in size. Holes of about 12 in. (30 cm) and larger are generally drilled by truck-mounted rotary equipment (Fig. 2). An alternative source to electric power is diesel power for smaller drills or diesel-powered electric for medium- to large-size drills.

Blasting. The process of blasting breaks the rock into manageable sizes so that it can be loaded and moved. While many blasting agents are available, the most common in open pit mining is ANFO (an abbreviation for ammonium nitrate and fuel oil). By itself ammonium nitrate is fairly insensitive and can be handled easily without many of the precautions required for other high explosives. When mixed with roughly 5% diesel fuel, the mixture is a powerful and inexpensive explosive compound. At large mining operations, ammonium nitrate is delivered in bulk in the form of small pellets known as prills, which are stored in bins or silos. A special truck transports the ammonium nitrate to the drill holes, where it is mixed with diesel fuel immediately before being loaded into the drill hole. For small operations, ANFO can be purchased in bags or cartridges.

ANFO cannot be used if the drill holes contain water because the prills are highly soluble and will not detonate if water-soaked. A slurry, which is a mixture of ANFO and one or more additives, can be used to improve water resistance and detonation characteristics. Aluminum is a common additive. A variety of slurry mixtures can be made to fit specific blasting requirements. Other blasting agents, for example, water gel explosives and gelatin dynamites, are available and are used in specialized applications.

Any high explosive must be detonated to achieve

Fig. 2. A truck-mounted, large-diameter, electrically powered rotary drill. (*Kennecott Copper Corp.*)

the desired explosive results. Detonation is provided by caps and boosters. Caps are either electric or non-electric. Nonelectric caps are preferred in open pit mines as they are not sensitive to electric discharges such as lightning. Propagation of the initial detonation from one drill hole to the next is accomplished with a cord or cable known as det cord or primacord, a hollow plastic tubing filled with high explosive. Det cord is used to connect all drill holes which are filled with explosive in a given blast.

It is not efficient to detonate all holes in a blast at once. A timed pattern of drill hole detonation will result in the most efficient breakage of the rock per given weight of explosive. To accomplish this, delays ranging from milliseconds to seconds are used to arrest the detonation of the primacord momentarily.

After blasting is complete, the muck pile or shot rock is surveyed to set ore and waste boundaries based on the assays from the drill hole cuttings. The material is then ready for loading into trucks and haulage out of the mine.

Loading. The blasted rock is loaded onto some conveyance, such as a truck or a train, for transport. Shovels and rubber-tired front end loaders are the most common pieces of loading equipment in open pit mines. Track-mounted cable shovels powered by electricity are widely used in large mining operations (**Fig. 3**). These shovels are classified by the volumetric capacity of the dipper (or loading scoop), with common sizes ranging from 8 to 28 yd^3 (6 to 21 m^3). While smaller sizes are available, they are generally being replaced by front end loaders. Shovels with capacities greater than 28 yd^3 (21 m^3) are available, but

they are either custom-built machines for soft rock waste stripping or oversize dippers on standard shovels for loading low-density materials. Electric cable shovels are high-capital-cost items, but they are extremely reliable and can last 10 to 15 years with proper maintanence. Electric shovels are highly productive and consequently have the lowest operating cost of all loading equipment types.

Rubber-tired front end loaders have become more popular particularly in precious-metals mines in the western United States. Front end loaders for mining applications generally range in size from 3 to 15 yd^3 (2 to 11 m^3) for their loading bucket size (**Fig. 4**). Although both larger and smaller units are available, they are not usually used in open pit mines. Direct diesel power is common for sizes up to 12 yd^3 (9 m^3), with diesel electric more common for larger units. Front loaders do not require trailing power cables and can move from one working area to another rapidly. This mobility is a great benefit where working places are widely separated and the production rate does not require an operating loading unit continuously at each loading area.

Compared to cable shovels, front loaders have lower capital costs but require higher operating costs than shovels of equal capacity. Mining operations with a short mine life or high-mobility requirements are candidates for the application of this type of equipment.

Hydraulic shovels have become more widely applied because of improvements in hydraulic systems and shovel reliability. Hydraulic front shovels generally range in size from 3 to 15 yd^3 (2 to 11 m^3).

Fig. 3. A large (27-yd^3 or 21-m^3) electric cable shovel loading a 170-ton (154-metric-ton) haulage truck. (*Kennecott Copper Corp.*)

Fig. 4. A 13.5-yd³ (10-m³) front end loader putting waste rock onto a 50-ton (45-metric-ton) haul truck. (*Caterpillar Tractor Co.*)

Machines in the 8–12-yd³ (6–9-m³) range fill a gap between large front loaders and small cable shovels. The hydraulic machines are generally diesel-powered, but electric-powered models are also available. Although not as mobile as the front end loader, the hydraulic shovel is more productive per unit of time than the loader.

Two other types of loading equipment used for specific applications in mining are bucketwheel excavators and draglines. Both are used in soft materials that do not require blasting and can be excavated easily. Coal stripping is the most common application of both types of equipment; they are used to remove the overburden above the coal.

Hauling. The broken material is loaded into trucks, trains, conveyors, or combinations of them for transport out of the pit to its destination at the processing plant or the various waste dumps and stockpiles. Truck haulage is the most widely used. In-pit train haulage is used primarily in older pits which have not switched to truck haulage. Direct conveyor haulage from a loading unit is limited to continuous loading systems such as bucketwheel excavators where the material is small and uniform in size so it may be loaded directly onto a belt. Most open pit applications of conveyor haulage require the material to be hauled by truck from the loading unit to an in-pit crusher. The crushed material is placed on a belt for transport out of the mine.

Haul trucks are classified by their payload capacity and vary in size from 20 to 350 tons (18 to 318 metric tons) capacity, with trucks in the 35 to 235 tons (32 to 213 metric tons) capacity range being the most common in open pits. The trucks with capacity less than 35 tons (32 metric tons) are used in very small mines or quarries. The trucks with capacity larger than 235 tons (213 metric tons) are experimental. All trucks are powered by diesel engines. The power supplied by the diesel engine is transferred to the wheels by two methods. The first method is by a mechanical transmission, and in the second method electric power is generated and used to drive electric motors located in the truck wheels. Trucks of 85 tons (77 metric tons) capacity and larger often use the diesel-electric method, and smaller trucks use mechanical drive. There is a range of truck sizes (85 to 150 tons or 77 to 140 metric tons capacity) for which various manufacturers offer mechanical or electric drive trucks.

Truck haulage ramps in the pit commonly range between 7 and 10% grade, depending on equipment size, weather conditions, and location in the pit. Haul roads are kept well graded to assure safe and efficient truck operation at speeds up to 25 mi/h (40 km/h). All trucks require braking systems that can stop the vehicle safely when descending these grades.

To augment truck haulage and help reduce fuel costs, some large mines have installed a trolley assist system to be used with trucks that have electric wheel motors. These are modified trucks that are equipped with pantographs to take electric power from overhead trolley wires instead of from the diesel-alternator system. Such systems are used primarily on relatively permanent haul routes, often on uphill climbs where trucks generally slow down because the diesel engines cannot supply enough power. When not in use, the pantographs are lowered and the trucks operate on power generated by the diesel engine. The system allows the flexibility of truck haulage with the benefit of direct electric power on the more energy-intensive segments of the haul.

Another modification to material haulage has been the placement of a crusher in or near the pit to shorten the truck haul distance. These crushers are either permanent or movable and feed onto a conveyor system that transports the crushed material to its destination. The system is designed so that the conveyors replace the most costly segment of the truck haul, usually an uphill segment. By doing this, electrical energy replaces diesel energy and reduces the cost of transport. For ore, which must be crushed anyway, crushing in the pit represents no increase in cost. Waste material is not normally crushed, and the cost for this portion of the operation must be offset by the reduction in haul costs.

The implementation of a crush-convey system does have some negative aspects which must be balanced against the reduced haul costs. These include the increase in capital costs early in the mine life derived from installation of the system, and the reduction in the flexibility of the mining operation with semipermanent conveyors and crushers installed in the pit (**Fig. 5**). The ore is dumped from the haul trucks into

Fig. 5. An in-pit feeder (left), crusher (center), and conveyor system (right and background). (*Duval Sierrita Mine*)

the feeder which acts as a surge bin and feeds the ore to the crusher at a constant rate. Once the ore has been crushed, it is fed onto the conveyor, which transports the ore out of the pit and to the processing plant. The feeder, crusher, and conveyor are movable and can be relocated in the pit as required by the mining operations.

Waste disposal. Waste material that is generated during the course of mining at most mines must be discarded as economically as possible without jeopardizing future mining activities but while respecting environmental regulations. Two types of waste material are generated at most mining operations: waste rock and overburden from the mine, and tailings—the waste material from the processing plant after treatment of the ore.

The rock, overburden, and soils removed from the pit and not processed are hauled to dumps or storage piles that can be from tens of feet to several hundred feet high, depending on their location and time of existence. These dumps are located as close to the pit as possible without jeopardizing future pit expansion. Waste dumps can be seen on the left side of Fig. 1 extending away from the pit. Lower-grade material that is not being processed but may become valuable is stockpiled for possible processing at some time in the future. These stockpiles must be located so that the material can be conveniently remined and hauled to the processing plant. The soil is often stockpiled for later use in reclaiming the dump and tailings areas.

In large metal mines, tailings are in the form of a slurry which is piped to large ponds. The solids settle out in these ponds, and the water is often reclaimed and pumped back to the plant for use in processing. Some processes result in solid tailings, which can be trucked or conveyed to a disposal site.

More attention is being paid to the long-term effects of the disposal of mine waste material. Precautionary planning and monitoring are actively undertaken at all mining operations in the United States. Precautions include lining of tailings and storage ponds, catchment and control of water runoff from dumps and stockpiles due to rain and snowfall, diverting streams and small waterways around mining properties to avoid contamination of their waters, watering of roads and active mining areas for dust suppression, and continuous monitoring. Air and water are monitored at most mines to comply with government regulations and to protect the air as well as surface and underground water supplies. These environmental practices are slowly being adopted in some mining areas around the world, but in many areas outside the United States no environmental precautions are being taken, primarily because of their high cost.

Once the reserves have been exhausted and mining activity ceases, reclamation of a mining area is required by many states in the United States. Most large coal surface mines have active land reclamation programs. Many planned mining ventures have budgets that include complete or partial land reclamation. This could involve recontouring and revegetating, covering and planting tailings areas, and filling or partial filling of old pits. These measures add to the cost of mining the ore body and will make the lower-grade potential mines uneconomic. As environmental regulations become stricter and more costly in some parts of the world, mining of certain metals will move to areas where sources of these minerals can be mined more economically. SEE LAND RECLAMATION.

Trends in the industry. Computer technology is finding application in the mining industry; computer software is available to assist the mining engineer in ore reserve estimation with the application of geostatistics, mine planning and design, and production and maintenance monitoring and reporting. With the help of high-speed computers the engineering and production staff can evaluate all aspects of the mining activities, which allows a more efficient and economical extraction of the mineral commodity. Computerized truck dispatch systems have been installed at some large mines with fleets greater than 30 trucks. These systems monitor all truck movements, shovel productions and locations, and truck destinations. The computer can instruct the truck drivers to go to specific shovels for loading and to use specific routes to their destinations. Once a particular trip is complete, the computer directs the driver to a specific shovel for the next load. This provides for the best deployment of the truck fleet, minimizing truck-waiting and shovel-waiting time.

The many changes that have occurred in hauling material from its pit source to its destination were prompted in part by the large increases in diesel fuel costs during the 1970s. Both trolley assistance and in-pit crushers with out-of-pit conveyor haulage rely on electrical energy. Where sources of less expensive electrical energy are available, these haulage systems may be viable alternatives to an all–diesel truck haulage system. Their application must be evaluated on a property-by-property basis to determine if the installations are economically feasible.

Herb Welhener; John M. Marek

Bibliography. J. T. Crawford III and W. A. Hustrulid (eds.), *Open Pit Mine Planning and Design,* Society of Mining Engineers of the American Institute of Mining, Metallurgical, and Petroleum Engineers, 1979; A. B. Cummins and I. A. Given (eds.), *SME Mining Engineering Handbook*, Society of Mining Engineers of the American Institute of Mining, Metallurgical, and Petroleum Engineers, 1973; E. P. Pfleider (ed.), *Surface Mining,* American Institute of Mining, Metallurgical, and Petroleum Engineers, 1972.

Permafrost

Perennially frozen ground, occurring wherever the temperature remains below 0°C (32°F) for several years, whether the ground is actually consolidated by ice or not and regardless of the nature of the rock and soil particles of which the earth is composed. Perhaps 25% of the total land area of the Earth contains permafrost; it is continuous in the polar regions and becomes discontinuous and sporadic toward the Equator. During glacial times permafrost extended hundreds of miles south of its present limits in the Northern Hemisphere.

Characteristics. Permafrost is thickest in that part of the continuous zone that has not been glaciated. The maximum reported thickness, about 5300 ft (1600 m), is in northern Yakutia. Average maximum thicknesses are 990–1600 ft (300–500 m) in northern Alaska and Canada and 1300–2000 ft (400–600 m) in northern Siberia. In Alaska and Canada the general range of thickness in the discontinuous zone is 160–490 ft (50–150 m) and in the sporadic zone less than 100 ft (30 m). Discontinuous permafrost in Siberia is generally 660–990 ft (200–300 m).

Temperature of permafrost at the depth of no annual change, about 30–100 ft (10–30 m), crudely approximates mean annual air temperature. It is below 23°F (−5°C) in the continuous zone, between 30 and 23°F (−1 and −5°C) in the discontinuous zone, and above 30°F (−1°C) in the sporadic zone. Temperature gradients vary horizontally and vertically from place to place and from time to time. Deep temperature profiles record past climatic changes and geologic events from several thousand years ago.

Ice is one of the most important components of permafrost, being especially important where it exceeds pore space. Physical properties of permafrost vary widely from those of ice to those of normal rock types and soil. The cold reserve, that is, the number of calories required to bring the material to the melting point and melt the contained ice, is determined largely by moisture content. Ice occurs as individual crystals ranging in size from less than 0.004 in. (0.1 mm) to at least 28 in. (70 cm) in diameter. Aggregates of ice crystals are common in dikes, layers, irregular masses, and ice wedges. These forms are derived in many ways in part when permafrost forms. Ice wedges grow later and characterize fine-grained sediments in continuous permafrost, joining to outline polygons. Microscopic study of thin sections of ice wedges reveals complex structures that change seasonally.

Permafrost develops today where the net heat balance of the surface of the Earth is negative for several years. Much permafrost was formed thousands of years ago but remains in equilibrium with present climates. Permafrost eliminates most groundwater movement, preserves organic remains, restricts or inhibits plant growth, and aids frost action. It is one of the primary factors in engineering and transportation in the polar regions.

Construction engineering problems. The construction of the Alaska Pipe Line to carry oil from Prudhoe Bay to Valdez has been the largest and most difficult project conducted in permafrost regions to date. The hot oil, at a temperature of about 140°F (60°C), requires that special consideration be given to thawing of permafrost and consequent effects on the pipe line itself, as well as adjacent structures. For several short lengths the pipe line had to be buried, and artificial refrigeration is required to maintain the permafrost. The pipe was well insulated to reduce heat flow. About half the pipe line is elevated above the ground because of ice-rich permafrost. So much ice is present in fine-grained materials that liquefaction, flow, and slump would occur on melting. The elevated and insulated pipe dissipates some heat to the air, but with little effect on the ice below ground. However, the vertical supports for the horizontal crossbeams on which the pipe rests are prone to frost heaving in some places. To ensure that they remain securely frozen in place, cooling devices to minimize the thawing effects of the uprights are installed in them. One type is a metal tube filled with a refrigerant that evaporates whenever the ground temperature exceeds the air temperature. The evaporation keeps the ground frozen during warm summers. The devices contain no moving parts and are self-operating.

Buildings and other structures that could thaw ice-rich permafrost are also commonly put on piles, with air spaces separating the structures from the ground. Different kinds of insulation and the incorporation of heat-reflecting colors in road construction minimize thawing of permafrost. However, in places, important roads can be maintained only by eliminating ice-rich permafrost during construction and replacing it with non-frost-susceptible granular aggregate. Because of the disturbance of surface and near-surface water flow by most structures, projects must be well planned to avoid icings, heaving, and erosion, and a variety of new engineering techniques have been developed.

Robert F. Black

Bibliography. S. A. Harris, *The Permafrost Environment*, 1986; K. A. Linnell and C. F. Tedrow, *Soil and Permafrost Survey in the Arctic*, 1988; *Proceedings of the 3d International Conference on Permafrost*, Edmonton, National Research Council of Canada, 1978; A. L. Washburn, *Periglacial Processes and Environments*, 1973; P. J. Williams, *Pipelines and Permafrost: Science in a Cold Climate*, 2d rev. ed., 1988.

Pesticide

A material useful for the mitigation, control, or elimination of plants or animals detrimental to human health or economy. Algicides, defoliants, desiccants, herbicides, plant growth regulators, and fungicides are used to regulate populations of undesirable plants which compete with or parasitize crop or ornamental plants. Attractants, insecticides, miticides, acaricides, molluscicides, nematocides, repellants, and rodenticides are used principally to reduce parasitism and disease transmission in domestic animals, the loss of crop plants, the destruction of processed food, textile, and wood products, and parasitism and disease transmission in humans. These ravages frequently stem from the feeding activities of the pests. Birds, mice, rabbits, rats, insects, mites, ticks, eel worms, slugs, and snails are recognized as pests.

Materials and use. Materials used to control or alleviate disease conditions produced in humans and animals by plants or by animal pests are usually designated as drugs. For example, herbicides are used to control the ragweed plant, while drugs are used to alleviate the symptoms of hay fever produced in humans by ragweed pollen. Similarly, insecticides are used to control malaria mosquitoes, while drugs are used to control the malaria parasites—single-celled animals of the genus *Plasmodium*—transmitted to humans by the mosquito.

Sources. Some pesticides are obtained from plants and minerals. Examples include the insecticides cryolite, a mineral, and nicotine, rotenone, and the pyrethrins which are extracted from plants. A few pesticides are obtained by the mass culture of microorganisms. Two examples are the toxin produced by *Bacillus thuringiensis*, which is active against moth and butterfly larvae, and the so-called milky disease of the Japanese beetle produced by the spores of *B. popilliae*. Most pesticides, however, are products which are chemically manufactured. Two outstanding examples are the insecticide DDT and the herbicide 2,4-D.

Evaluation. The development of new pesticides is time-consuming. The period between initial discovery and introduction is frequently cited as being about 5 years. Numerous scientific skills and disciplines are required to obtain the data necessary to establish the utility of a new pesticide. Effectiveness under a wide variety of climatic and other environmental conditions must be determined, and minimum rates of application established.

Insight must be gained as to the possible side effects on other animals and plants in the environment. Toxicity to laboratory animals must be measured and be related to the hazard which might possibly exist for users and to consumers. Persistence of residues in the environment must be determined. Legal tolerances in processed commodities must be set and directions for use clearly stated. Methods for analysis and detection must be devised. Economical methods of manufacture must be developed. Manufacturing facilities must be built. Sales and education programs must be prepared.

Regulation and restriction. By the mid-1960s, it became apparent that a number of the new pesticides, particularly the insecticide DDT, could be two-edged swords. The benefits stemming from the unmatched ability of DDT to control insect pests could be counterbalanced by adverse effects on other elements of the environment. Detailed reviews of the properties, stability, persistence, and impact upon all facets of the environment were carried out not only with DDT, but with other chlorinated, organic insecticides as well. Concern over the undesirable effects of pesticides culminated in the amendment of the Federal Insecticide, Fungicide, and Rodenticide Act (FIFRA) by Public Law 92-516, the Federal Environmental Pesticide Control Act (FEPCA) of 1972. The purpose behind this strengthening of earlier laws was to prevent exposure of either humans or the environment to unreasonable hazard from pesticides through rigorous registration procedures, to classify pesticides for general or restricted use as a function of acute toxicity, to certify the qualifications of users of restricted pesticides, to identify accurately and label pesticide products, and to ensure proper and safe use of pesticides through enforcement of FIFRA.

Selection and use. Pesticides must be selected and applied with care. Recommendations as to the product and method of choice for control of any pest problem—weed, insect, or varmint—are best obtained from county or state agricultural extension specialists. Recommendations for pest control and pesticide use can be obtained from each state agricultural experiment station office. In addition, it is necessary to follow explicitly the directions, restrictions, and cautions for use on the label of the product container. Insecticides are a boon to the production of food, feed, and fiber, and their use must not be abused in the home, garden, farm, field, forest, or stream.

George F. Ludvik

Persistence. Considerable scientific evidence has been accumulated that documents the deleterious effects on the environment of several of the organic insecticides. Over 800 compounds are used as pesticides and, with increasing technological sophistication, the list can be expected to grow. Until World War II pesticides consisted of inorganic materials containing sulfur, lead, arsenic, or copper, all of which have biocidal properties, or of organic materials extracted from plants such as pyrethrum, nicotine, and rotenone. During World War II a technological revolution began with the introduction of the synthetic organic biocides, particularly DDT.

There is an increasing number of organic biocides. They vary widely in toxicity, in specificity, in persistence, and in the production of undesirable derivatives. The factors that determine how, when, and where a particular pesticide should be used, or whether it should be used at all, are therefore necessarily different for each pesticide. The use of chemicals to achieve a measure of control over the environment has become an integral part of technology, and there are no valid arguments to support the proposition that the use of all of these chemicals should cease.

Some take the view that pests include insects, fungi, weeds, and rodents. Many insects, however, particularly the predatory species that prey upon the insects that damage crops, are clearly not pests. Fungi are essential in the processes that convert dead plant and animal material to the primary substances that can be recycled through living systems. In many ecosystems rodents are also an important link in the recycling process. On the other hand, an increasing number of species traditionally considered desirable are becoming "pests" in local contexts. Thus chemicals are used to destroy otherwise useful vegetation along roadsides or in pine plantations, or vegetation that might provide food and shelter to species undesirable to human populations. The control of any component of the global environment through the use of biocidal chemicals is therefore a problem much more complex than is initially suggested by the connotation of the word pest. The highly toxic chemicals that kill many different species are clearly undesirable in situations in which control over only one or two is sought.

Other pest-control measures. Sophisticated methods of pest control are continually being developed. One technique involves the raising of a large number of insect pests in captivity, sterilizing them with radioactivity, and then releasing them into the environment, where they mate with the wild forms. Very few offspring are subsequently produced. Highly specific synthetic insect hormones are being developed. In an increasing number of pest situations, a natural predator of an insect has been introduced, or conditions are maintained that favor the propagation of the predator. The numbers of the potential pest species are thereby maintained below a critical threshold. An insect control program in which use of insecticides is only one aspect of a strategy based on ecologically sound measures is known as integrated pest management. SEE HERBICIDE; INSECT CONTROL, BIOLOGICAL; INSECTICIDE.

Robert W. Risebrough

Bibliography. B. P. Beirne, *Pest Management*, 1966; A. J. Burn, T. H. Coaker, and P. C. Jepson (eds.), *Integrated Pest Management*, 1988; R. Carson, *Silent Spring*, 25th anniversary ed., 1987; R. L. Caswell et al. (eds.), *Pesticide Handbook—Entoma 1981–82*, 1982; G. P. Georghiou and T. Saito (eds.), *Pest Resistance to Pesticides*, 1983; P. Hurst, N. Dudley, and A. Hay, *The Pesticide Handbook*, 1989; W. W. Kilgore and R. L. Doutt, *Pest Control: Biological, Physical and Selected Chemical Methods*, 1967; H. Martin and C. R. Worthing, *Pest Manual*, 4th ed., 1974; R. L. Metcalf and W. Luckmann, *Introduction to Pest Management*, 2d ed., 1982; G. W. Ware, *The Pesticide Book*, 1989.

Physiological ecology (animal)

The study of biophysical, biochemical, and physiological processes used by animals to cope with factors of their physical environment, or employed during ecological interactions with other organisms. Loosely speaking, animal physiological ecology represents the interface between the fundamental physiological question of how the whole animal works and the fundamental ecological question of how and why the animal lives where it does. The discipline of animal physiological ecology is thus very broadly based, but for the most part it is characterized by highly empirical research that emphasizes physiological function and evolutionary adaptation under natural conditions, and is couched within the framework of intact individual organisms. *See Population ecology.*

Methodology and scope. The methods used by animal physiological ecologists are diverse, but are usually not unique compared to those of general physiology. Physiological ecologists interpret their data, however, in terms of adaptation to the environment and hence ultimately in terms of natural selection and evolution. Since the questions it attempts to answer exist in nature, much of physiological ecology is predicated on studying animals under field conditions or on quantification of the biotic and abiotic environmental factors experienced by animals in their natural habitats.

Measurements in the field are often complex, and results are difficult to analyze because of logistical problems and the lack of control over experimental conditions. Accordingly, hypotheses based on results from field work are often tested in the laboratory under controlled conditions that duplicate the field environment as much as possible. The reverse process is also true—insights and inferences gained in the laboratory may be examined and tested in the field. Because they emphasize whole-animal function and adaptation to natural environments, physiological ecologists not only require competence in physiological techniques, but must also be able to focus on ecological questions and on morphological or behavioral adjustments that animals may use as supplements or substitutes for physiological capacities.

Some of the specific problems commonly addressed by animal physiological ecologists include temperature regulation, energy metabolism and energetics, nutrition, respiratory gas exchange, and water and osmotic balance. These topics are discussed in detail below. However, it is important to remember that these artificial ''categories'' do not represent discrete biological entities, but instead form part of the interacting continuum that includes both the animal and its environment.

Temperature regulation. Organisms consist of complex arrays of interacting molecules that engage in precisely regulated exchanges of energy and materials with their environments. Since the rates of most biochemical reactions are extremely sensitive to temperature, thermal considerations are pervasive factors in biology. Body temperature influences almost all physiological systems and is linked to the characteristics of the environment, so examination of a species' thermal biology offers the physiological ecologist many insights into other aspects of physiology and ecology.

Temperature is a relatively easy parameter to measure and to manipulate experimentally. Animal body temperatures can be determined with simple thermometers, with small thermistor or thermocouple probes, with implanted radiotelemeters, or via noncontact infrared thermography. Responses to different thermal conditions are often quantified by subjecting animals to various temperature regimes in environmental chambers. Because of the high heat capacity of water, the body temperatures of aquatic species are usually tightly coupled to water temperature. Body temperature regulation in terrestrial animals may be strongly influenced by radiation from the Sun and hot ground surfaces and by convective heat transfer (from wind and air turbulence), as well as air temperature. The effects of these factors can be estimated from mathematical equations derived from engineering studies or measured directly in appropriately designed wind tunnels incorporating a source of simulated solar radiation. In all animals, body temperature is the result of a balance between rates of heat gain and heat loss.

Studies of a wide variety of animals have revealed several general patterns by which body temperature is maintained within acceptable limits (**Fig. 1**). Poikilotherms allow their body temperature to fluctuate as

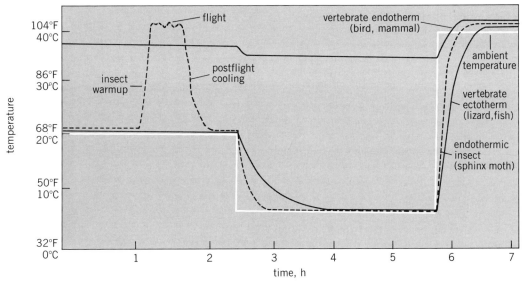

Fig. 1. Relationship between body and ambient temperature in typical vertebrate endotherms (birds, animals), vertebrate ectotherms (lizards, fishes), and endothermic insects (sphinx moths). Note that the body temperature of insects normally closely tracks ambient temperature, but rises rapidly during an endothermic warmup, and stays well above ambient temperature during flight.

environmental conditions change, while homeotherms maintain a relatively constant body temperature despite changes in the external temperature. Homeothermy may be accomplished behaviorally by ectotherms or physiologically by endotherms. Ectotherms, such as reptiles and amphibians, regulate body temperature by selecting appropriate thermal environments (basking in sunlight in order to warm up or seeking shade when overheated). Endotherms, such as birds, mammals, and some insects, are able to produce enough endogenous heat from internal metabolic processes to elevate their body temperature above that of the environment. Overheating in hot environments is countered in some species by evaporation of body water via panting or sweating. Endothermy frees an animal's thermal biology from direct dependence on environmental temperature, but can be very costly in terms of the food energy necessary to keep body temperature high. To avoid this difficulty, some species, such as mammalian hibernators and endothermic insects, are heterotherms—that is, they are endothermic part of the time, but can reduce metabolic heat production and lower body temperature when conservation of food energy supplies is necessary.

Body size has a profound influence on thermal biology. Heat is exchanged with the environment across the body surface, but is stored (and produced by metabolism) within the tissues. As body size increases, the ratio of surface area to tissue volume decreases. As a result, body temperatures in small animals are very tightly linked to thermal conditions in the environment, while large animals are more thermally independent of environmental temperature. Endothermy and stable body temperatures are therefore easier to sustain (and more common) in large animals.

Energy metabolism and energetics. Because they exist as complex and dynamic arrays of molecules that are not at equilibrium with the external environment, organisms can continue to survive and function only by means of continuous expenditure of energy. The sum of all its biochemical energy transformations is an animal's energy metabolism, or metabolic rate. Energy metabolism is an intrinsic factor in all physiological systems and is probably the most useful overall index of animal performance. Knowledge of an animal's rate of energy consumption is relevant to studies at all levels of biological integration from cell function through ecosystem dynamics. Aspects of energy metabolism of particular interest to physiological ecologists include rates of energy consumption under different environmental conditions (temperature, water and food availability, and so on), strategies of energy conservation, the energetic costs of activity, growth, and reproduction, and the effects of body size, phylogeny, and ecological niche on metabolism and energetics.

The details of metabolic processes are exceedingly complex, but total energy metabolism can be measured by a number of methods. Early studies determined metabolic rate from the amount of food consumed and fecal and urinary wastes produced. The primary source of chemical energy for animals is the cellular oxidation of hydrocarbons. Since this process yields heat, measurement of heat production also indicates the rate of energy metabolism. Heat production can be ascertained with direct calorimetry or can be calculated from differences between body and environmental temperatures. Indirect techniques can also be used to estimate energy metabolism. By definition, cellular oxidation reactions consume oxygen; they also produce carbon dioxide as a waste product. Hence, measurements of metabolic rate are often based on determinations of oxygen consumption or carbon dioxide production. All of the methods described above require that test animals be kept under laboratory conditions during measurements, and consequently energy metabolism in natural environments can only be inferred. However, the introduction of isotopic tracers such as doubly labeled water ($^2H_2^{18}O$ or tritium and oxygen-18) has allowed determination of metabolic rate in free-living animals.

Energy metabolism is highly variable within individual animals, among animals of the same species, and between species. In most animals metabolic rate is dependent on body temperature, so that an 18°F (10°C) increase in body temperature is associated with a two- to threefold increase in metabolism. Metabolic rate is also related to body mass, but metabolism does not change in direct proportion to changes in mass. Instead, total energy metabolism appears to vary approximately in proportion to mass$^{0.75}$, and the mass-specific metabolic rate (metabolism per unit mass) decreases markedly with increasing body size. This pattern is observed within taxa ranging from insects to mammals (**Fig. 2**), but its explanation is a matter of disagreement among physiologists.

Despite overall similarity in the slope of the body mass–metabolic rate relationship, there are often profound differences in metabolic rates between major taxonomic groups. These differences are usually related to thermoregulatory strategies and to ecology. For example, over a wide range of body sizes the endothermic birds and mammals (which produce considerable heat in order to maintain elevated body temperatures) have resting metabolic rates five- to tenfold higher than those of ectothermic reptiles and amphibians of similar mass. Metabolic responses to changing environmental temperature are profoundly different in endotherms and ectotherms. As air temperature cools, an ectotherm's metabolism falls rap-

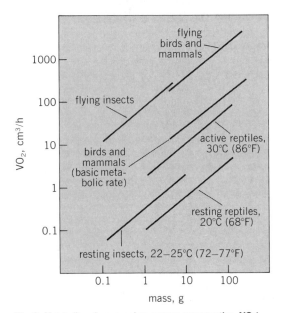

Fig. 2. Metabolism (measured as oxygen consumption, VO_2), body mass, and activity in various vertebrate and invertebrate taxa. Temperatures indicated are body temperatures. A log scale is used for both axes. (*After B. Heinrich, ed., Insect Thermoregulation, Wiley-Interscience, 1981*)

idly as body temperature decreases. In contrast, an endotherm's metabolism increases rapidly as air temperature falls, since more heat production is necessary to keep body temperature constant in the face of increased heat loss rates.

Activity requires increased metabolic expenditures over the amount needed for maintenance of metabolic machinery. A species' capability for activity is its metabolic scope: the difference (usually expressed as a ratio) between minimum and maximum metabolic rates under a given set of conditions. Metabolic scope is usually determined from measurements of oxygen consumption, but results from this method must be interpreted with caution because many animals resort to anaerobic energy sources (such as glycolysis) during brief bouts of intense activity. Typical values of metabolic scope range from 4 to 25 times the minimum metabolism in a wide variety of vertebrates. There is some indication that large species tend to have larger scopes than smaller animals, and scope appears to be correlated with an animal's normal activity pattern—active species tend to have higher scopes than inactive forms. The highest rates of energy metabolism are observed during flight, and flying insects have the largest metabolic scopes yet reported. Oxygen consumption in sphinx moths is more than 100 times greater during flight than at rest.

Energy metabolism in free-living animals in their natural habitats has been studied by means of time budget analysis (behavioral observations of the time spent in various activities coupled with laboratory measurement of the energy costs of those activities), and with doubly labeled water. The latter technique gives a single integrated measurement covering several days, but avoids the need for continuous observation and does not require potentially inaccurate estimates of activity costs. Data suggest that for many animals the daily energy expenditure is roughly two to four times the minimal resting metabolism. Much of the variation in daily energy expenditure is apparently related to ecological and behavioral factors.

Nutrition. Animals need to acquire nutrients from their environments for use as building blocks for maintenance, growth, and reproduction and to provide chemical energy for metabolism. Physiological ecologists are concerned with the kinds and amounts of nutrients animals require, the sources of the nutrients in the foods available in the animal's habitat, the roles and functional characteristics of specialized digestive glands and organs, and the rates and efficiencies of food processing and nutrient extraction in the gut. Techniques commonly employed include field studies of diet preferences and harvesting rates; controlled or artificial diets to determine nutrient requirements; analysis of food, fecal, and urine samples to estimate gain and loss rates for particular nutrients; and the use of isotopic tracers to follow nutrients through the digestive and absorptive processes.

Digestive function is closely correlated with diet. In general, carnivorous animals have more simple digestive systems and are more efficient at extracting nutrients from food than are herbivorous species, especially those that feed on low-quality dry or woody forage. Digestive efficiency (a measure of the amount of ingested chemical energy actually absorbed by the animal) is typically 85–90% in carnivores, but may be less than 40% in herbivores. Vertebrates lack enzymes capable of digesting cellulose, the primary organic constituent of terrestrial plant material. How-ever, many herbivores support large populations of symbiotic microorganisms in specialized regions of the digestive tract, such as outpockets of hindgut or the enlarged and compartmentalized stomach of mammalian ruminants. In these organs microbial fermentation breaks down cellulose into simple compounds (primarily lactic acid and volatile fatty acids) which can be utilized as metabolic energy sources by the host and in addition provide other nutrients such as proteins and vitamins. Nevertheless, digestion of high-cellulose diets is often slow and inefficient, and the rate of nutrient acquisition may be limited by the rate at which food can be processed in the gut, rather than the rate at which the animal can obtain food when foraging. Another problem faced by many herbivores is the presence of toxic compounds in plant materials. Behavioral mechanisms, such as preferences for nontoxic species or for plant parts that have low toxin content, are often important means of reducing toxin intake.

Respiratory gas exchange. Acquisition of oxygen from the environment and elimination of carbon dioxide are essential requirements for all animals. Physiological ecologists study metabolic requirements for gas exchange, energetic costs of respiration, functional characteristics of respiratory organs and gas transport in the blood, and the effects of environmental factors such as temperature, pressure, carbon dioxide concentration, and oxygen availability on respiration.

For most species elimination of carbon dioxide poses few problems. Diffusion can rapidly remove carbon dioxide from the body because concentrations of this gas are low in most environments. Oxygen uptake can, however, be more difficult. For all animals, oxygen uptake is dependent on diffusion from regions of high oxygen concentration (in the external media) into regions of low concentration (in the tissues). Diffusion rates and oxygen concentration vary widely: diffusion of dissolved oxygen in water is hundreds of times slower than in air; oxygen concentration is high in air (about 21% by volume), but is at least 15 times lower in water and may be close to zero in some aquatic systems. The size and design of gas exchange surfaces, energy costs of respiration, and maximum sustainable aerobic metabolic levels are all influenced by these factors. In general, for small animals with large surface/volume ratios and some larger forms with low metabolic activity, diffusion across the skin provides adequate gas exchange. Large active animals require specialized respiratory organs (gills or lungs) and must actively renew the media in contact with these structures by means of ventilation (breathing). Ventilation rates are highly variable but are usually correlated to activity levels and the availability of oxygen. Ventilation can have a high energy cost (up to 30% of the metabolic rate of some fishes is devoted to moving water through the gills), so it is important for animals to maximize oxygen extraction, that is, the proportion of oxygen removed from the respiratory medium.

Gas exchange surfaces of all kinds are thin (for rapid diffusion of oxygen) and, especially in vertebrates, are highly vascularized. A large surface area is usually present, again to facilitate diffusion. The size and complexity of respiratory organs are usually correlated with activity levels—active species have proportionally greater exchange surface than do inactive forms. Large and elaborate exchange organs may also be indicative of low oxygen availability. For example, many species of fishes that inhabit turbid, anaerobic ponds have evolved air-breathing organs to supplement gill respiration.

Once it enters the body, oxygen must be moved to the metabolically active tissues. In small animals simple diffusion is sufficient, but large, active species depend on blood flow to transport oxygen (insects are an exception, in that they move oxygen by diffusion in thin, air-filled tubes called trachae which reach into every body region). Most animals have special oxygen-binding transport molecules which allow blood to hold considerably more oxygen than if it were simply dissolved into the plasma. Blood must efficiently "load" with oxygen at the gas exchange organs and rapidly "unload" oxygen to the respiring tissues. Consequently, the properties of transport molecules must be matched to oxygen availability in the environment and to optimal oxygen concentrations in the tissues. In environments with low oxygen availability (high altitudes, enclosed burrows, hypoxic streams, and so on), transport molecules usually have a high affinity for oxygen and often exist in high concentration in the blood.

Water and osmotic balance. The majority of biochemical reactions occur in aqueous solutions and are sensitive to osmotic conditions. Hence, animals must regulate body water content and the solute compositions of body fluids. Rates of gain and loss of water and solutes must be balanced in order to keep water content and body fluid composition stable. All animals exchange water and solutes with their environments, which necessarily couples the internal and external osmotic conditions to some extent. Nevertheless, precise regulation of body water and solute content occurs even in those species in which the internal osmotic milieu differs greatly from that of the environment.

Measuring water and solute exchange is often difficult because body water is partitioned to some extent into "compartments" (blood, interstitial fluid, intracellular fluid, and so on) and because the exchange pathways are diverse and functionally interconnected. Physiological ecologists are interested in the rates and routes of water and solute exchange, the precision and metabolic costs of osmotic regulation, the ability to tolerate osmotic stresses, and the relationship of these factors to the osmotic environments the animal must face in its natural habitat. Standard investigative techniques include exposing animals to controlled osmotic conditions in the laboratory, manipulation of tissue fluid osmolarity via pharmacological agents or injection of concentrated or dilute solutions, use of isotopic tracers to elucidate exchange pathways and rates, and sampling of natural habitats to determine normal osmotic environments.

In aquatic organisms, water and solutes may enter the body through the skin, the gas exchange organs (gills), the food, or by drinking; routes out of the body include the skin, gills, and the urine and feces. Some species have specialized organs (salt glands) for solute uptake or excretion. Exchange rates through most of these pathways are subject to regulation by the animal, and the importance of particular pathways varies among different species and between habitats. In general, marine vertebrates and many invertebrates are hypotonic (have lower solute concentrations) compared to seawater, and must contend with constant salt influx and loss of body water. In contrast, most fresh-water animals are hypertonic to their environment and are faced with constant water influx and salt loss. Animals in either habitat must work continuously (at some metabolic cost) in order to maintain osmotic homeostasis. Furthermore, while most aquatic animals regulate their water and solute contents, some live in relatively constant osmotic environments (such as the open ocean) while others regularly encounter large and rapid changes in environmental solute concentration (for example, in tidal estuaries). Still other species (mainly marine invertebrates) are osmoconformers that allow their tissue fluid osmolarity to fluctuate with ambient water conditions.

Terrestrial animals are faced with constant desiccation through the skin and respiratory tract, except in extremely humid environments, and some water is unavoidably lost in urine and feces. High temperatures increase the potential for dehydration because the maximum water vapor content of air increases with increasing air temperature. Additional water losses may result from sweating or panting in species that use evaporative cooling as a thermoregulatory mechanism. Water can be gained only through the food, or by drinking or transcutaneous absorption if free water is available (recently it has been demonstrated that some insects can extract significant amounts of water vapor from humid air). To counter water loss to the air, most terrestrial animals have a relatively waterproof skin, and numerous additional adaptations have evolved to reduce water loss through other pathways. For example, mammals from xeric (dry) habitats minimize excretory water losses by producing highly concentrated urine and very dry feces, while birds and reptiles accomplish similar reductions by excreting nitrogenous wastes in an insoluble form (uric acid) that requires very little water for elimination. The physiological ability to withstand harsh osmotic environments is usually correlated with an animal's ecological niche: species from hot, dry environments withstand reduced water availability and desiccation better that do species from cool, moist climates. Behavioral adaptations that conserve body water, such as restricting activity to microhabitats or times of day that minimize osmotic stress, are very important to many terrestrial animals. SEE ECOLOGY; HOMEOSTASIS; PHYSIOLOGICAL ECOLOGY (PLANT).

M. A. Chappell

Bibliography. G. S. Campbell, *An Introduction to Environmental Biophysics*, 1986; R. Eckert, D. Randall, and G. Augustine, *Animal Physiology: Mechanisms and Adaptations*, 3d ed., 1988; D. M. Gates and R. B. Schmerl (eds.), *Perspectives of Biophysical Ecology*, 1975; K. Schmidt-Nielsen, *Animal Physiology: Adaptation and Environment*, 4th ed., 1990.

Physiological ecology (plant)

The study of growth, biological processes, and reproduction within plant populations and ecosystems in natural or controlled environments. The five principal growth forms are unicellular, thallose, and herbaceous forms, and shrubs and trees. Life cycle processes include (1) germination, (2) growth, (3) absorption, internal transfers, and loss of water, gases, and mineral nutrients, (4) photosynthesis and respiration, and (5) production of reproductive structures (flowers, cones, fruits, seeds, and spores). Each process is the result of a complex series of physical and chemical reactions within and between cells. All cellular processes are within the context of the whole plant as governed by the interaction of its genes and its environment through space and time.

Scope. Plant physiological ecology is part of the attempt to answer the question: Why does a plant grow where it does? An answer requires a knowledge of the genetic structure of the population, the physiological processes and their rates, its growth forms, the populational demography including seed sources, and the population's niche in the operation and structure of the ecosystem.

Actual and potential geographic ranges of populations or species seldom coincide. Environments change. Populations evolve, migrate, and become extinct in response to environmental changes. The potential range of a species or a local population depends upon the degree and nature of genetic variation among its individuals, the range of physiological and morphological adaptability within each individual (acclimatization and phenotypic plasticity), and the frequency, extent of occurrence, availability, and stability of suitable environments. These complex variables, operating together determine the kinds and rates of physiological processes, and thus the degree of vegetative and reproductive success of a population within an ecosystem or in the biosphere.

All widespread species are genetically diverse. Within these species, and many others, ecotypes (ecological races) have evolved in response to environmental selection of local populations. Such ecotypes are particularly fitted genetically to the local or regional environment. Often, these ecotypes merge with each other to form a complex biological gradient (ecocline) coinciding with an environmental gradient. Some environmental gradients are simple and repeatable, with expected repeatability and simplicity in their ecoclines. But in broad space, and given enough time, environments exist as complex webs of gradients, and so also do the accompanying ecoclines which thus are displayed as ecoclinal networks.

Ecotypes and ecoclines consist of local populations usually with enough genetic diversity to allow some survival within certain limits of environmental change. Studies of process rates within local populations and ecotypes provide a measure of the environmental tolerance limits of a species. These data allow an understanding of the adaptability of plants and of the evolution of physiological processes. Such information may be obtained in natural environments under field conditions or by experiment in controlled and simulated environments.

Field measurements. The problems which physiological ecology attempts to solve exist in nature, and it is there that the solutions to such problems must begin. Field measurements are difficult because of logistics, and the vagaries of uncontrolled environments and their effects on process rates; but such measurements have the advantage of providing realistic values in an ecosystemic context. Such results should then be tested by experiment under controlled environments in the laboratory or phytotron. It is extremely difficult to work with ecosystems or even most communities under controlled conditions, though in certain ecosystems where plants are small it is possible to collect microcosms or monoliths of vegetation and soil that can be manipulated in the laboratory. Partic-

ular success with this technique has been achieved in the arctic tundra. After going as far as possible by laboratory experiment, one must return to the field to measure and experiment again with more insight and precision than at the start. Such a research strategy not only is possible but is productive of answers.

The rates of most physiological processes can be measured in the field with portable instrument systems. In the past, field measurements were difficult logistically because of size and weight of such systems. Fortunately, as the result of other kinds of research, miniaturization of circuits and the use of solid-state components have helped to solve these problems. Mobile laboratories, with such systems in vans or trailers, make it easier to get laboratory precision in the natural environment of the plant. These field laboratories also include data acquisition systems for the rapid recording and statistical handling of the data.

Since the mid-1970s, as a result of the use of such new equipment by well-trained teams of ecologists and physiologists, there has been considerable growth in knowledge of how plants operate in field environments. The processes most often studied are germination, growth, leaf energy budgets, water movement, mineral nutrition, photosynthesis, respiration, flowering, fruiting, seed production, and dormancy of buds and seeds. Before approaching these processes in detail, it must be stated that the processes themselves are influenced not only by the physical and biological aspects of the environment but by the growth form of the plant. Processes and rates depend to a large extent on whether the plant is herbaceous or woody, a dwarf shrub or tall tree, an annual or a perennial, and upon the configurations of its leaves, stems, and roots.

Germination. Germination times and phenomena can easily be observed in natural populations if one knows young seedling characteristics. Percentage of germination can also be measured by planting known numbers of seeds at known points and marking the seedlings by colored toothpicks or plastic markers as they emerge from the soil surface. Germination can be measured in phytotrons under controlled conditions. Alternating temperatures rather than constant temperatures result in higher germination percentages in many species. Seeds of some species require light for germination; others do not. Seedling survival in communities must also be measured and the environmental stresses on young plants understood.

Growth. Growth of stems or leaves may be measured in terms of height or length, of fresh or dry weight, or of calorific values. Leaf production may be determined by marking each leaf as it emerges with a spot of nontoxic waterproof compound. These leaf counts should be tallied and retallied at daily or weekly intervals. Root growth in the field can be measured by planting or transplanting individual plants or sod blocks into wedge-shaped Plexiglas boxes which are embedded in the natural soil. These boxes can be lifted at frequent time intervals for marking on the Plexiglas the position of each root or rhizome tip.

Leaf energy budgets. The temperature of a leaf is the result of a balance between heat income and heat loss. The measurement of leaf energy budgets involves reflection, absorption, and transmission of visible and infrared radiation from Sun, sky, and ground surface, evaporative heat losses, gains or losses by convection, heat storage, and metabolism. Leaf temperatures may be measured by thermocouples, thermistors, or noncontact infrared thermometers. Temperature of a leaf exposed to bright sun is largely controlled by convection and by transpiration rate (evaporative heat loss); that effect is greater in a large leaf than in a small one. In turn, leaf temperature affects transpiration rate itself and the important metabolic processes of photosynthesis and respiration. All of these energy budget processes are influenced by wind speed, boundary-layer effects, turbulent transfer, and thermal stability of the air.

Water loss and gain. A simple method of measuring transpiration rates and total water loss of whole herbaceous plants or young woody plants is to determine the loss of weight from systems consisting of a plant or sod block having its roots in a sealed container of moist soil. Also, a plant or leaf may be enclosed in a transparent cuvette or chamber and its water vapor losses measured in an airstream by an infrared gas analysis system or a dew-point hygrometer. Transpiration rates of whole trees are difficult to measure directly, but extrapolations may be made from single attached leaves, small branches, or whole tree "seedlings." Stomatal transpiration requires open stomates. Whether or not the stomates are open or closed, and for how long, is best measured by a diffusion porometer. Transpiration rates must be related to leaf surface areas, leaf fresh weight, or soil and plant water potentials.

The ability of a plant to absorb water from the soil is measured by obtaining quantitative data on a gradient in water potential from leaves to roots to soil. Water potential is the difference in free energy or chemical potential (per unit molal volume) between pure water and water in cells and solutions. The potential of pure water is set at zero; the potential of water in cells, in solutions, and in the soil therefore is less than zero and is expressed as a negative number. In rapidly transpiring plants there is a gradient toward decreasing water potential (more negative) from the soil through the roots, stems, and leaves to the air. This causes water to move from the soil through the plant to the atmosphere. All along this gradient, however, there are resistances to the diffusion and flow of water, and these must be considered in all calculations of the movement of water through the plant. A good technique for measuring leaf water potential in the field is to use one of the newer modifications of a Scholander pressure chamber. If this is not available, the Schardokov dye method will work on many leaves, but is relatively slow and somewhat prone to error. More precise measurements are possible in the laboratory with a sensitive thermocouple psychrometer; modifications of this technique are available for field use. Dew-point hygrometry is also available for such field measurement. It has the advantage of not destroying the leaves being measured; thus, the potentials can be measured again later.

Mineral nutrition. Plants require some nutrients in fairly large quantities. These include N, P, S, K, Ca, Mg, and Fe. Other mineral elements, such as Mn, Zn, Cu, Mo, B, and Ce, are needed in only trace amounts. Among these, N is largely made available by microbial fixation in the familiar nitrogen cycle. Others are made available in various ways; soil pH, for example, affects the availability of certain nutrients across the pH scale. Plants and vegetation play a large role in cycling of nutrient elements (and some nonnutrient elements, including pollutants) in the biosphere. The utilization of nutrients in ecosystems can be estimated by analyzing soils, roots, leaves, flowers, and fruits. Fertilization experiments can be done relatively easily in both field and phytotron. Also, the use of isotopes such as ^{15}N as tracers is useful in studying allocation rates and patterns within plants.

Photosynthesis and respiration. These two groups of processes control the gain and loss of carbon by green plants. Physiologists found that several photosynthetic pathways or modes exist. Ecologists were quick to relate these to different groups of species, some closely related and some not. Also, there appear to be some relationships of these pathways to certain kinds of environments. In brief, most plants photosynthesize by the C_3 or reductive pentose phosphate pathway (the Calvin-Benson cycle). Plants of other species, fewer in number, utilize a more complex C_4 pathway (the Hatch-Slack pathway). Leaves of C_4 plants are characterized by a green bundle sheath around each vein. The C_4 process involves 4-carbon acid synthesis in the mesophyll cells. These 4-carbon compounds move to the bundle sheath cells, where they are decomposed into CO_2 and a 3-carbon compound. Thus, CO_2 is very efficiently used in C_4 plants, which results in high productivity.

Many succulent plants in families including the Cactaceae, Crassulaceae, Bromeliaceae, and several others dispay a third method of carbon capture. This photosynthetic mode is crassulacean acid metabolism (CAM). Plants exhibiting CAM have their stomates closed during the day and open at night. Carbon dioxide enters the plant at night through the open stomates and is fixed as malic acid. The stomates close as day comes; malic acid leaves the vacuoles and enters the chloroplasts, where it is decarboxylated in a pathway somewhat similar to that of C_4 plants. The carbon dioxide is converted to carbohydrate through ribulose bisphosphate so that during the daylight hours, with stomates closed, a succulent CAM plant essentially follows the C_3 pathway.

The ecological implications of these three photosynthetic modes have been studied extensively. Most plant species utilize the C_3 pathway; these include plants in all terrestrial climates. The C_4 pathway has evolved more recently, and has evolved independently in many relatively unrelated families, but is most often seen in the grasses and sedges. In the saltbushes (*Atriplex*) some species are C_3 and some are C_4. The C_4 pathway appears to be restricted to regions having warm, often dry, summers, and therefore is more common in the tropics and at low elevations. However, this pathway does occur in plants of the middle latitudes, particularly in grasslands and deserts that have hot or warm summers no matter how cold the winters. It is not known from plants in alpine or arctic conditions, where all plants so far examined have the C_3 pathway. Of course, C_3 plants are not restricted to cool summer environments; some of the principal dominants of hot deserts in North America use the C_3 mode. Creosote bush (*Larrea*), for example, in the Mojave and Sonoran deserts is a C_3 species, as are other common plants there. On the other hand, in the hottest, driest parts of Death Valley, *Tidestromia,* a small, grayish perennial C_4 plant, reaches maximum photosynthesis in full sunlight at leaf temperatures ranging from 115 to 122°F (46 to 50°C) in midsummer.

Plants with CAM are either true succulents or belong to families that are made up primarily of succulents. Cacti are good examples, as are members of the pineapple family. These usually occupy arid or semiarid habitats in warm regions with short daylengths: tropical or subtropical. The advantage of CAM is that the stomates are closed during the hot, dry days, and thus transpiration is reduced in an environment where water is available only occasionally.

Several attributes of C_3 and C_4 plants have ecological significance. Both kinds of plants have dark respiration, as do CAM plants. But C_3 plants also have photorespiration, which occurs only in the bundle sheath cells of C_4 plants and is thus negligible in these latter plants. Dark respiration rates are low compared to photosynthesis, but evidence now exists that photorespiration rates of C_3 plants are two to three times higher than dark respiration rates and that photorespiration can be half as great as the photosynthetic rate. The result is a lower net photosynthesis rate under high light intensities than the net photosynthesis rate in C_4 plants under similar conditions. Photosynthesis is also inhibited at atmospheric O_2 concentrations in C_3 plants but not in C_4 species. Optimum net photosynthesis rates in C_3 plants usually occur from 50 to 77°F (10 to 25°C) but the optimum range in C_4 plants is at higher temperatures, from 86 to 104°F (30 to 40°C).

Another difference between C_3 plants and C_4 plants seems to have great ecological importance. Carbon exists in two stable isotopic forms, ^{12}C and ^{13}C. Carbon dioxide thus exists as $^{12}CO_2$ and $^{13}CO_2$, as well as the radioactive $^{14}CO_2$. Because of the nature of the photosynthetic pathways, C_3 plants discriminate to a greater extent against ^{13}C in assimilation of carbon than do C_4 plants. Therefore, C_4 plants have more ^{13}C in their compounds than do C_3 plants. These stable isotope concentrations are expressed as $\delta^{13}C$ values relative to ^{12}C and ^{13}C values in a standard substance. These δ^{13} values for C_3 plants are in the neighborhood of -28 parts per thousand (compared to the standard), and about -12.5 parts per thousand in C_4 plants. These values are determined by the use of a mass spectrometer. Not only is the $\delta^{13}C$ value of importance in identifying whether or not plants are C_3 or C_4, but the $\delta^{13}C$ value is transmitted into the ecosystem from plant to herbivore. Therefore, analyses of $\delta^{13}C$ in insect predators and also in rumen and fecal material from vertebrate herbivores can reveal which animals or invertebrate predators in an ecosystem prefer C_3 or C_4 plants. The importance of this new ecological tool cannot be overestimated in tropical and temperate zone ecosystems.

Photosynthesis and respiration rates in plants are usually measured in the field by one or both of two systems: an infrared gas analysis system or one using radioactive $^{14}CO_2$. In either system, a plant or leaf is enclosed in a transparent cuvette or chamber which is temperature-controlled. In the gas analyzer system, air with known content of CO_2 is passed through the chamber and then through the infrared analyzer. Decreased CO_2 content is a measure of the net CO_2 exchange or net photosynthesis. With the infrared analyzer system, this can be continuously recorded or calculated and stored by a small computer. It is important to measure flow rate of air through the system and also to measure leaf temperature, temperature of ambient air, humidity, and light intensity and quality. Covering the cuvette with a dark cloth allows mea-surement of dark respiration, which is indicated by an increase in CO_2 content of the controlled airstream.

In the $^{14}CO_2$ method, a plant or leaf is enclosed in a lighted cuvette and exposed to $^{14}CO_2$ of accurately known activity at a given flow rate for a precise period ranging from 30 s to 1 min. The ^{14}C-labeled leaf is then immediately cut, its area is measured, and the leaf is placed in a vial, frozen, and returned to the laboratory for processing and eventual counting in a liquid scintillation counter. Respiration cannot be measured with the $^{14}CO_2$ system. Therefore, this method measures only gross photosynthesis, not net.

By growing plants of the same population or clone under different temperature or light regimes in a phytotron and then measuring their metabolism across a span of temperature or light, it is possible to measure the ability to acclimate physiologically. This can be done with the use of an infrared analysis system. Using this approach to the measurement of photosynthesis and respiration, it has been found that acclimation is under genetic control and that acclimation ecotypes exist in some species.

Total system CO_2 exchange can be measured by using microcosms and an infrared gas analyzer. This can be done in the phytotron with cuvettes over the tops of the natural microcosms; larger cuvettes can be placed over grassland vegetation and soils in the field.

Flowering and fruiting. These processes may be observed and measured in the field and correlated with environmental trends through time. It is particularly important to know whether flower buds are formed in the previous season, what controls their formation, and what governs final development of the flowers. Temperature, photoperiod, and soil moisture are the environmental factors most frequently measured in regard to flowering and fruiting. Within the plant, carbohydrate balance, leaf water potential, and hormonal actions are important. The effects of pollinators and predators also should be measured.

The future. With present data from measurements and experiments in physiological ecology, it is possible to design mathematical models of plant performance in changing environments. Such models can be improved by increased knowledge of physiological processes as they occur under varying field environments in which individual plants and populations are subjected to stress. In this regard, the effects of human-induced changes in the environment, such as increased atmospheric CO_2 and other trace gases, possible increases in ultraviolet-B radiation, radionuclides, air pollutants, acid rain, dust, ash, and heavy metals, need to be studied. These can be done with some success by using ecosystemic microcosms. SEE ACID RAIN; AIR POLLUTION; WATER POLLUTION.

Beyond this, it is possible to carry out "giant" experiments by manipulating whole ecosystems. The results from experiments on an ecosystemic scale provide an integration of the physiological and ecological processes in entire ecosystems. Indeed, this next step has already been taken. In this kind of large-scale research, the techniques of physiological ecology are combined with those of other disciplines to measure ecosystem stress tolerance. From such results, it is possible to construct predictive mathematical models of ecosystemic performance in changing biospheric environments. SEE ECOLOGY; ECOSYSTEM.

W. D. Billings

Bibliography. F. H. Bormann and G. E. Likens, *Pattern and Process in a Forested Ecosystem,* 1985;

A. H. Fitter (ed.), *Environmental Physiology of Plants*, 1988; D. M. Gates and R. B. Schmerl (eds.), *Perspectives of Biophysical Ecology*, 1975; M. Kluge and I. P. Ting, *Crassulacean Acid Metabolism: Analysis of an Ecological Adaptation*, 1978; O. L. Lange et al. (eds.), *Physiological Plant Ecology*, 3 vols., 1981–1983; W. Larcher, *Physiological Plant Ecology*, rev. ed., 1980; G. L. Likens, *Long-Term Studies in Ecology*, 1988; J. D. Terhune, E. M. Caterino, and O. L. Lange, *Plant Response to Stress*, 1987; L. L. Tieszen (ed.), *Vegetation and Production Ecology of an Alaskan Arctic Tundra*, 1979.

Phytoplankton

Mostly autotrophic microscopic algae which inhabit the illuminated surface waters of the sea, estuaries, lakes, and ponds. Many are motile. Some perform diel (diurnal) vertical migrations, others do not. Some nonmotile forms regulate their buoyancy. However, their locomotor abilities are limited, and they are largely transported by horizontal and vertical water motions.

Energy-nutrient cycle. All but a few phytoplankton are autotrophic—they manufacture carbohydrates, proteins, fats, and lipids in the presence of adequate sunlight by using predominantly inorganic compounds. Carbon dioxide, water, inorganic nutrients such as inorganic phosphorus and nitrogen compounds, trace elements, and the Sun's energy are the basic ingredients. This organic matter is used by other trophic levels in the food web for nourishment. The energy in this organic matter ultimately is released as heat in the environment. The inorganic materials associated with this organic matter, on the other hand, are recycled. They are released back into the aquatic environment in inorganic form as a result of metabolic processes at all levels in the food web, and in large part they again become available for reuse by the phytoplankton. Some structural materials, such as the silica in diatoms and silicoflagellates, and carbonates in the scales of certain chrysophytes, are returned to the aquatic environment by chemical dissolution rather than by biological processes. *See Food web.*

Varieties. A great variety of algae make up the phytoplankton. Diatoms (class Bacillariophyceae) are often conspicuous members of marine, estuarine, and fresh-water plankton. Reproducing mostly asexually by mitosis, they can divide rapidly under favorable conditions and produce blooms in a few days' time. Their external siliceous skeleton, termed a frustule, possesses slits, pores, and internal chambers that render them objects of great morphological complexity and beauty which have long attracted the attention of microscopists.

Dinoflagellates (class Dinophyceae) occur in both marine and fresh-water environments and are important primary producers in marine and estuarine environments. Dinoflagellates possess two flagella; one trails posteriorly and provides forward motion, while the other is positioned more or less transversely and often lies in a groove encircling the cell. This flagellum provides a rotary motion; hence the name dino (whirling) flagellate. In some dinoflagellates the cell wall is thin, while in others it consists of a complicated array of rather thick cellulosic plates, the number and arrangement of which are characters used in identifying genera and species.

The dinoflagellates are often conspicuous members of the marine plankton. Some taxa are bioluminescent. Others are one of the causes of red water, often called red tides, although their occurrence is not related to the tides. Depending on the causative species, red water may be an innocuous discoloration of the water, or if *Gymnodinium breve* is dominant, extensive fish mortalities will be experienced. Several species of *Gonyaulax* occur in bloom proportions in inshore marine waters. They contain a toxin which can accumulate in shellfish feeding upon *Gonyaulax* and which is the ultimate cause of paralytic shellfish poisoning in humans.

Coccolithophorids (class Haptophyceae) are also marine primary producers of some importance. They do not occur in fresh water. This class of algae possesses two anterior flagella. A third flagellumlike structure, the haptonema, is located between the two flagella. Calcium-carbonate-impregnated scales, called coccoliths, occur on the surface of these algae, and are sometimes found in great abundance in recent and ancient marine sediments.

Under certain conditions in subtropical and tropical seas, members of the nitrogen-fixing blue-green algal genus *Trichodesmium* (class Cyanophyceae) can occur in sufficient concentrations to strongly discolor the surface of the sea. Other nitrogen-fixing blue-greens commonly occur in great abundance in eutrophic and hypereutrophic freshwater lakes and ponds.

Members of still other algal classes occur in marine and estuarine plankton. Their abundance will vary in different environments at different times, and they may even occasionally dominate the standing crop. Much remains to be learned about the identity, physiology, and ecology of the very small (<8 micrometers) flagellates which commonly occur in almost every marine phytoplankton sample.

Communities. Even though marine and fresh-water phytoplankton communities contain a number of algal classes in common (such as Bacillariophyceae, Chrysophyceae, and Dinophyceae), phytoplankton samples from these two environments will appear quite different. These habitats support different genera and species and groups of higher rank in these classes. Furthermore, fresh-water plankton contains algae belonging to additional algal classes either absent or rarely common in open ocean environments. These include the green algae (class Chlorophyceae), the euglenoid flagellates (class Euglenophyceae), and members of the Prasinophyceae. *See Fresh-water ecosystem; Marine ecology.*

In estuarine environments in which salinities vary from essentially zero to those of the local inshore ocean salinities, a mixture of organisms characteristic of both fresh-water and marine environments will be encountered. In addition, giving the estuarine plankton a somewhat distinctive appearance, some euryhaline planktonic taxa will be present. *See Estuarine oceanography.*

Samples of phytoplankton in shallow areas of the sea, lakes, and estuaries often contain benthic and epiphytic microalgae. These algae become suspended in the water as a result of strong turbulent mixing so often found in shallow aquatic environments, and are called meroplankton to distinguish them from the holoplankton organisms which are truly planktonic.

While phytoplankton community composition reflects some complicated and as yet rather poorly understood series of biotic and abiotic interaction within ecosystems, the chemical composition of water is recognized as an important factor affecting phytoplankton communities. Many of the differences between the marine, estuarine, and fresh-water phytoplankton communities are associated with changes in salinity, major ion concentrations and ratios, pH, nutrients, and quite possibly trace-element concentrations. *SEE ECOSYSTEM.*

Eutrophication. Society's common use of lakes as receptacles for wastes, coupled with nutrient-rich runoff from cultivated fertilized land, has had pronounced biological effects not only on the phytoplankton but on other levels in the food web. Domestic sewage and agricultural runoff are quite rich in inorganic phosphorus, which is generally in short supply in most inland bodies of water. The addition of a nutrient which is limiting phytoplankton production, such as phosphorus, to fresh-water environments increases primary production, alters phytoplankton composition, and can lead to dense algal blooms which adversely affect water quality and esthetic and recreational values. The effects of nutrient enrichment, generally known as eutrophication, have been understood by limnologists since the 1920s–1930s, but the American public became aware of the implication only in the 1960s w``h the widespread use of phosphate detergents a``` `ne associated and accelerated deterioration o`` ``e quality of lakes and ponds. Advanced techn```ues of sewage treatment are now available w`` ``ch remove phosphates sufficiently to greatly ``duce the impact of sewage effluent upon re``` ``ing waters. Important in regulating these cycles are nutrient availability and the presence of a water density gradient, the pycnocline, at some relatively shallow depth (commonly 16.5–165 ft or 5–50 m) below the surface. Above the pycnocline, the location of which is usually well correlated with a zone of rapidly changing water temperature called the thermocline, is a well-mixed region of uniform density and temperature. This layer is called the mixed layer by oceanographers and the epilimnion by limnologists. Within this mixed layer, water motions caused by winds help keep the phytoplankton in suspension within the illuminated surface layer. The pycnocline also greatly reduces the rate of diffusion of nutrients upward into the mixed layer from nutrient-rich deeper waters and thus has a negative effect upon phytoplankton productivity. Any mechanism which introduces nutrients into the mixed layer that are limiting phytoplankton production will enhance primary production. *SEE EUTROPHICATION; LIMNOLOGY; THERMOCLINE; WATER POLLUTION.*

Seasonal cycles. The phytoplankton in aquatic environments which have not been too drastically affected by human activity exhibit rather regular and predictable seasonal cycles. Coastal upwelling and divergences, zones where deeper water rises to the surface, are examples of naturally occurring phenomena which enrich the mixed layer with needed nutrients and greatly increase phytoplankton production. In the ocean these are the sites of the world's most productive fisheries.

In marine and fresh waters in temperate to arctic latitudes, the seasonal cycle of phytoplankton is to a large degree influenced by the pycnocline. During winter months a strong pycnocline is generally not present, and any planktonic plants in the water circulate to considerable depths. Even though nutrient concentrations are high during this period of deep vertical mixing, any phytoplankton present do not spend sufficient time in the illuminated surface layers for photosynthesis to exceed respiration. As spring approaches, incident solar radiation leads to the formation of a pycnocline. Phytoplankton then proliferate, giving rise to the annual spring phytoplankton bloom in which diatoms frequently dominate (thus it is often called the spring diatom bloom). The phytoplankton quickly exhaust the nutrients in the newly formed mixed layer, and throughout the summer phytoplankton concentrations generally remain low due to low mixed-layer nutrient concentrations resulting in part from the restricted upward movement of nutrients through the pycnocline. In the fall, incident solar radiation decreases and the pycnocline deepens. Nutrients or phytoplankton living in the pycnocline are incorporated into the deepening mixed layer, and a fall bloom occurs and then wanes as the pycnocline deepens, and finally disappears.

In the tropical oceans and lakes located near sea level, a permanent thermocline exists, and phytoplankton production remains low but may increase if nutrients are injected into the mixed layer as a result of strong wind mixing or other advective processes.

Fossilization. Under favorable conditions, some phytoplankton are incorporated into the sediments and become part of the fossil record. Diatoms, silicoflagellates, coccoliths, and the cysts of dinoflagellates are frequently sufficiently abundant and well preserved in lake and ocean sediments to permit paleontologists to reconstruct past environmental conditions and changes in environmental conditions through time. These fossilized remains are also used by stratigraphers to determine the age of sediments.

Robert W. Holmes

Bibliography. A. D. Boney, *Phytoplankton*, 1988; G. A. Cole, *Textbook of Limnology*, 3d ed., 1988; I. Morris (ed.), *The Physiological Ecology of Phytoplankton*, 1981; J. E. Raymont, *Plankton and Productivity in the Oceans*, 2 vols., 2d ed., 1980, 1983; C. D. Sandgren (ed.), *Growth and Reproduction Strategies of Freshwater Phytoplankton*, 1989.

Placer mining

The exploitation of placer mineral deposits for their valuable heavy minerals. Placer mineral deposits consist of detrital natural material containing discrete mineral particles. They are formed by chemical and physical weathering of in-place heavy minerals, which are then concentrated through the action of wind or moving water. This concentration can be done through wave and current action in the ocean (beach and offshore placers), glacial action (moraine placers), wind action removing the lighter material (eolian placers), or the action of running water (stream placers). Stream placers are the most important of these deposits because of their common occurrence and their highly efficient concentration mechanisms. Marine placers, primarily beach placers, are the next most economically important, with the potential of offshore placers being the most recent to be recognized and developed.

Minerals that are concentrated in placer deposits are a result of differences in specific gravity and, therefore, the economically important deposits are for minerals with high specific gravities (see **table**).

Precious metals, primarily gold and platinum group metals, have been the most important product from placer mines. Their extremely high specific gravity coupled with their low chemical reactivity means that

Specific gravities of several important placer minerals	
Mineral	Specific gravity
Gold	15–19
Platinum	14–19
Diamond	3.5
Cassiterite (SnO_2)	6.8–7.1
Magnetite (Fe_3O_4)	5.2
Rutile (TiO_2)	4.2
Ilmenite ($FeTiO_3$)	4.7
Monazite ($Ce,La,Y,Th)PO_4$	5.0–5.3
Quartz	2.6
Water	1.0

these minerals are efficiently concentrated in a placer environment and can be effectively recovered in a readily usable form. Historically, placer mines were civilization's first sources of gold and platinum and, until recent times, have continued to yield significant production. Although most modern gold is produced from lode, or "hard rock," deposits, the placer deposits of northern Canada, Alaska, and Siberia represent a virtually untapped source of the metal.

Of more importance than gold are placer diamond deposits. Another important placer mineral is cassiterite, an ore of tin. Additionally, rutile and ilmenite, the principal ores of titanium, are found in commercial quantities only in beach placers. These same types of placers also yield monazite, a source of the rare earths yttrium, lanthanum, cerium, and thorium.

Although the importance of placer gold may have decreased over the years, placer mining still is an important component of modern industrial economy.

Methods. Most placer mining operations involve surface mining methods, although underground methods are sometimes used.

Underground mining. Underground mining of placer deposits is limited to some frozen auriferous gravels in the Arctic and the ancient fossilized gold bearing channels typically found in the "mother lode" country of California and the deep leads (placer gravels) of Australia. These types of deposits are typically worked by sinking a shaft to bedrock and then driving a series of drifts and crosscuts along bedrock to form a room-and-pillar mine. *See Underground mining.*

One unique aspect of drift mining is its application to frozen gravels in the Arctic. The temperature of the gravels ranges between 18 and 22°F (-8 and -5°C) with bedrock temperatures between 8 and 14°F (-13 and -10°C). The gravel contains 10% or more of ice by weight and while frozen provides competent support for the mining method. Rather than a conventional drilling and blasting of the frozen gravels (which are very resistant to this), steam points are driven into the faces and the cohesive ice is melted, allowing the loosened gravel to be loaded without fragmentation.

Surface mining. This proceeds in a manner similar to most strip mining operations. First the overburden is removed, and then the placer ground containing the valuable material is processed. This overburden may consist of material similar to the valuable deposit, such as the barren top section of a stream placer deposit where the gold is concentrated near or on bedrock. The character of the overburden may also be distinct from that of the value-containing deposit, for example, the windblown sands covering the diamond-bearing stream channels in South-West Africa. *See Surface mining.*

In general, overburden is removed in a manner similar to the mining of the valuable material, as by mobile power equipment, dredges, and so on. One method unique to placer mining is the use of high-pressure water to remove the overburden. Hydraulicking involves shooting a stream of water against the overburden bank from a large nozzle (2–10 in. or 5–25 cm in diameter) on a device called a hydraulic monitor or hydraulic giant. This method is commonly used when the overburden contains a high percentage of clay or when it is necessary to strip muck from frozen gravels in arctic areas.

Muck consists of fine windblown material (loess), organic material, and water or ice. Hydraulicking has been the only effective method of removing frozen muck. All other methods require that the muck first be thawed. Common practice in Alaska and Yukon Territory is to thaw with cold water, 50–60°F (10–16°C), pumped into boreholes through ⅜-in.-diameter (10-mm) pipes called sweaters. Cold-water thawing has proven more cost-effective than either steam or hot water.

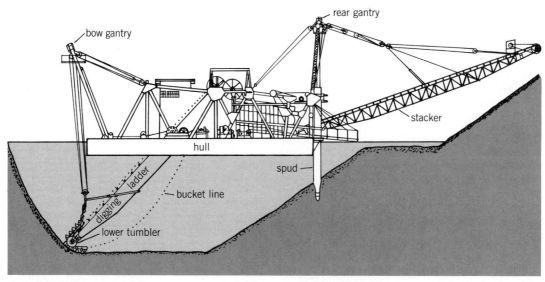

Fig. 1. California bucketline dredge.

Fig. 2. Aerial oblique view upvalley over the site of a placer dredging, in which successive cuts, tailing patterns, and dredge pond are shown. The dredge appears in the left foreground. (*Pacific Aerial Survey, Inc.*)

Techniques. For the actual mining of a placer deposit there are basically four different techniques: hand methods, hydraulic mining, use of mobile power equipment, and dredging.

Hand methods. In this technique, once the mainstay of placer operations, the mined material is shoveled into stockpile for hand washing or directly into a rocker box or "long tom" sluice box. This type of placer mining can be traced back to earliest recorded history, and was still a major factor through the Alaskan gold rush at the turn of the century. While hand mining now accounts for only a small portion of total placer production, it is often the most effective method for sampling prospective placer deposits.

Hydraulic mining. As mentioned above, hydraulic giants (monitors) have often been used to remove overburden. In addition, hydraulic pressure can be used to wash away the actual deposit. The resulting slurry is then channeled through sluices and the valuable material is recovered. Due to environmental regulations regarding water quality standards, the use of hydraulic giants in the United States has practically disappeared. They are still employed in the tin mines of Malaysia and Thailand, primarily for overburden removal prior to dredging. Another variation of hydraulic mining, called ground sluicing, uses water under natural pressure to wash the gravel through the sluices. Here, a stream is diverted and used to wash away the gravel bank. If the stream is first dammed and then released all at once, the process is called booming.

Mobile power equipment. The use of diesel powered equipment such as dozers, scrapers, front-end loaders, and hydraulic excavators has caused a revolution in placer mining technology. Not only does this equipment greatly increase the productivity of the miner for a relatively modest cost (compared to a floating dredge), but the mobility and flexibility of the equipment can be used for overburden removal, mining, and reclamation after mining. As a result, most modern placer mining operations will make use of mobile power equipment either in part or in total.

Dredging. Because of the intimate association of placer deposits and water, many of the more valuable deposits are located below the local water table level. If the water inflow is not severe, pumps can be used to dewater the cut and standard surface mining equipment can be used. However, if the water inflow is significant, such as with a modern beach placer or one located under a flowing river, then mining must be done with equipment that can dig below the waterline. This is called dredging.

There are three types of dredging operations used in placer mining: bucketline dredging, hydraulic dredging, and dragline excavation. The bucketline dredge (**Fig. 1**) is a floating excavator which uses a series of buckets attached to an endless rope. The bucketline travels from the floating dredge down to the lower tumbler at the end of the digging ladder, where it digs into the deposit, is pulled back to the surface, and dumps into the concentrating plant on the dredge. After concentration, a stacker conveyor deposits the waste material behind the dredge.

A cut is made by swinging the bucket ladder from side to side at a constant depth. At the end of each cut, the ladder is lowered and a new cut is begun. This continues until bedrock is reached or the maximum cutting depth is attained. Once a series of cuts has been carried to maximum depth, the dredge is moved forward into the newly extended dredge pond and the process is begun again. In this manner, the dredge moves its pond along in front of it, filling in behind with processed gravel (**Fig. 2**).

The size of the buckets ranges 2–20 ft^3 (0.06–0.60 m^3) each. The average speed of the bucketline is usually 20–24 buckets per minute. This implies that the modern large dredge will produce 10,000–15,000 yd^3 (7600–11,500 m^3) per day. A 20-ft^3 (0.6-m^3) bucket dredge, mining tin in Malaysia, produced nearly 900,000 yd^3 (690,000 m^3) in 1 month digging 150 ft (46 m) below waterline.

Hydraulic dredges are similar to bucketline dredges in that a digging boom is suspended from a floating barge and material is discharged on shore. The principal difference is that, instead of buckets, the excavation is done with a suction pump. A stream of high-pressure water is directed at the digging face near the suction intake to break up the placer material, which is then pumped to the surface. A variation of this process is the cutterhead hydraulic dredge, which uses a rotating cutting head to churn the placer material into suspension. Material mined with hydraulic dredges can be processed onboard the barge, or the slurry can be pumped ashore for processing and disposal.

Hydraulic dredges have found extensive use in off-shore and beach placers where sand is the primary material to be moved. Two cutterhead dredges moving sediments and glacial till in Ontario, Canada, each averaged over 2,000,000 yd^3 (1,500,000 m^3) per month for 3 years. On the other end of the scale, small, 2–4-in.-diameter (5–10-cm) suction dredges are often used in rivers and streams for hand operations and prospecting.

The final type of dredging operation uses a dragline or clamshell excavator to dig below water level (**Fig.**

Fig. 3. Dragline dredge and pond. (*Bucyrus-Erie Co.*)

3). Mined material is usually deposited directly into the concentrating plant, which is either crawler-mounted on the shore or barge-mounted offshore. This type of operation is used on smaller deposits where the capital cost of a large dredge cannot be justified.

Concentration. There are two basic principles used to recover valuable minerals from mined placer material: size classification and gravity separation. These apply to all sizes of operations from the smallest hand mining to the giant bucketline dredges, although in some special cases material adhesion or electromagnetic methods may also be used.

Size classification. This is the screening of the feed to the plant in order to discard oversized material which contains no values. In this manner, the gravity concentrating circuit not only has less material to process but works more efficiently because of the narrowed size range. This technique is effective because valuable placer minerals are discrete grains, separate from the gangue (waste) material and usually fairly small. For example, in a placer gold mining operation where the maximum expected nugget size is ¼ in. (6 mm), all material larger than 1 in. (25 mm) could be discarded without losing any gold. This would eliminate all of the boulders and cobbles as well as a significant amount of gravel.

Classification is usually done wet either over a series of vibrating screens or through a trommel: a long rotating, inclined cylinder with holes in its surface. In a trommel the material is fed into one end with sufficient water to wash the finer sands out through the holes, while the washed oversize is discharged out the other end, usually onto a stacking conveyor.

Gravity concentration. The principle of gravity separation relies on the difference in specific gravity between the valuable minerals and the gangue.

1. Panning. The most simple gravity concentrator is the gold pan. In North America, these pans are flat-bottomed metal or hard plastic, 2–3 in. (5–7.5 cm) deep and 6–18 in. (15–23 cm) in diameter with sloping sides at a 30–40° angle. In some countries a 12–30-in.-diameter (30–75-cm) conical wooden or metal bowl called a batea is used instead of a flat-bottomed pan. In either case the pan filled with the material is immersed in water, shaken to settle the heavy materials, and swirled to wash away the lighter minerals.

The primary use of panning in modern placer mining is in prospecting and sampling. Some use is made of hand panning to separate gold from black sands (magnetite) where mercury amalgamation is not feasible.

2. Sluice boxes. A step up from hand panning, the sluice box is simply a trough with a series of riffles in the bottom. A mixture of placer material and water flows into one end and is washed down the inclined trough, which can vary in width from 12 to 60 in. (30 to 150 cm) and in length from a few feet to several hundred feet.

The riffles, which can consist of rocks, wooden blocks, dowels, or angle irons, produce eddy currents in the flow, allowing the heavy material to settle out while the lighter material is washed away (**Fig. 4**). Plastic outdoor carpeting (artificial turf) is also sometimes used to produce these eddy currents.

Mercury is often used in sluice boxes processing gold. The liquid mercury (specific gravity = 13.6) settles in behind riffles and is not washed away. When it comes in contact with gold, the gold particles

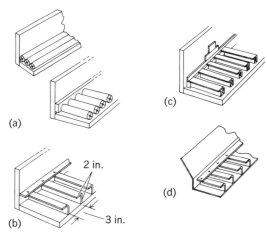

Fig. 4. Types of riffles in partial plan views. (*a*) Pole riffles. (*b*) Hungarian riffle (1 in. = 2.5 cm). (*c*) Oroville Hungarian riffle. (*d*) All-steel sluice. (*After G. J. Young, Elements of Mining, 4th ed., McGraw-Hill, 1946*)

adhere to the mercury, forming an amalgam. During cleanup of the sluice, the amalgam is collected and retorted to separate the gold; the cleaned mercury is recycled.

Undercurrents, often used in conjunction with the primary sluice, are auxiliary sluices which handle specific size fractions of the sluice feed. Screens, gratings, and punch plates within the sluice separate these size fractions and increase the efficiency of the sluicing operation.

Sluices are used to some extent in practically all placer operations. They are efficient, flexible and, because they have no moving parts, very low-cost concentrators.

3. Spinning bowls. Spinning bowls use principles similar to sluices. However, instead of using gravity as the settling force, they use the centrifugal force generated on a rapidly spinning surface. The sized placer material and water is fed into the center of the bowls. The heavy valuable minerals are trapped in baffles similar to riffles, and the lighter material is washed out over the rim. The advantage of the spinners is that a force higher than gravity can be generated, increasing the efficiency of the separation; this force can be easily adjusted through motor speed to "fine-tune" the recovery.

4. Jigs. Another mechanism used to recover heavy minerals, especially on the tin mining dredges in Malaysia, is the jig. A jig is basically a water-filled box into the top of which the slurried placer minerals are fed. A rapid series of upward pulses are generated in the water at the bottom. The heavy minerals sink through these pulses into a hutch at the bottom, while the lighter material is carried out over the edge.

5. Other methods. These include hand picking, especially in diamond processing; adhesion to specially prepared surfaces, as with the grease tables used to collect diamonds; magnetic separation, to separate magnetite and other iron-containing minerals; and other gravity techniques such as spiral classifiers, vibrating tables, and heavy-media separation.

Environmental concerns. The two major environmental problems associated with placer mining are water pollution and land disturbance. Both the mining and the processing of placer minerals require a great deal of water, and, once used, this water contains large amounts of suspended solids. If the water is al-

lowed to run off into the rivers, these solids can have an adverse impact on the downstream environment. In suspension they can harm aquatic habitats, and when settled out can clog waterways and choke off irrigated crops. In 1884, legislation was passed in California banning hydraulic mining because sediments from the Marysville district were inundating crops in the Sacramento River Delta and causing navigational hazards in the San Francisco Bay.

In the United States, environmental laws, such as the Clean Water Act, set limits on the discharge of suspended solids from a mining operation. To operate within these limits, miners use a series of settling ponds downstream from the mine and recycle as much water as possible. *See* ENVIRONMENTAL ENGINEERING; WATER POLLUTION.

Since most placer mining is surface mining, surface disturbance is necessary, especially where dredging operations create vast piles of cobbles as mining progresses. In some arctic or subarctic areas the ground is very sensitive to disturbance. One method of land reclamation is a mining plan which stockpiles top soil (where possible), recontours the spoil (waste) piles, and then returns the land to useful status. This can be done by revegetation to match the original environment, creation of new recreational or agricultural areas or, in urban areas, creation of new industrial sites. These latter alternatives can be extremely beneficial to the local economy, especially in developing nations. *See* LAND RECLAMATION.

Danny L. Taylor

Bibliography. American Institute of Mining, Metallurgical and Petroleum Engineers, *Surface Mining*, 1968; R. S. Lewis and G. B. Clark, *Elements of Mining*, 3d ed., 1964; E. H. Macdonald, *Alluvial Mining: The Geology, Technology and Economics of Placers*, 1983; C. YêKang, *The Combined Use of a Sand Screw, Hydrocyclones, and Gel-Logs to Treat Placer Mine Process Water*, 1988.

Plant geography

The study of the spatial distributions of plants and vegetation and of the environmental relationships which may influence these distributions. Plant geography (or certain aspects of it) is also known as phytogeography, phytochorology, geobotany, geographical botany, or vegetation science.

History. Plant geography arose as a result of the great botanical voyages of the early 1800s, especially those by Alexander von Humboldt, sometimes called the father of plant geography. Early work involved classification of physiognomically and ecologically similar plant types, and so plant geography and plant ecology remained somewhat indistinguishable. Around 1900 the study of vegetation began to split into plant ecology (which focused more on process) and plant geography (including vegetation geography). Two main perspectives had arisen: a historical perspective concerned with migration, dispersal, and the historical development of floras; and an environmental perspective concerned with environmental constraints and ecological relations influencing plant and vegetation distributions.

Floristic plant geography. A flora is the collection of all plant species in an area, or in a period of time, independent of their relative abundances and relationships to one another. The species can be grouped and regrouped into various kinds of floral elements based on some common feature. For example, a genetic element is a group of species with a common evolutionary origin; a migration element has a common route of entry into the territory; a historical element is distinct in terms of some past event; and an ecological element is related to an environmental preference. Aliens, escapes, and very widespread species are given special treatment. An endemic species is restricted to a particular area, which is usually small and of some special interest. The collection of all interacting individuals of a given species, in an area, is called a population.

The idea of area is fundamental to plant geography. An area is the entire region of distribution or occurrence of any species, element, or even an entire flora. The description of areas is the subject of areography, while chorology studies their development. The local distribution within the area as a whole, as that of a swamp shrub, is the topography of that area. Areas are of interest in regard to their general size and shape, the nature of their margin, whether they are continuous or disjunct, and their relationships to other areas. Closely related plants that are mutually exclusive are said to be vicarious (areas containing such plants are also called vicarious). A relict area is one surviving from an earlier and more extensive occurrence. On the basis of areas and their floristic relationships, the Earth's surface is divided into floristic regions (**Fig. 1**), each with a distinctive flora.

Floras and their distribution have been interpreted mainly in terms of their history and ecology. Historical factors, in addition to the evolution of the species themselves, include consideration of theories of shifting continental masses, changing sea levels, and orographic and climatic variations in geologic time, as well as theories of island biogeography, all of which have affected migration and perpetuation of floras. The main ecological factors include the immediate and contemporary roles played by climate (temperature, water availability, wind), soil, animals, and humans. *See* Island biogeography.

Vegetational plant geography. Vegetation, a term of popular origin, refers to the mosaic of plant life found on the landscape. The vegetation of a region has developed from the numerous elements of the local flora but is shaped also by nonfloristic physiological and environmental influences. Vegetation is an organized whole, at a higher level of integration than the separate species, composed of those species and

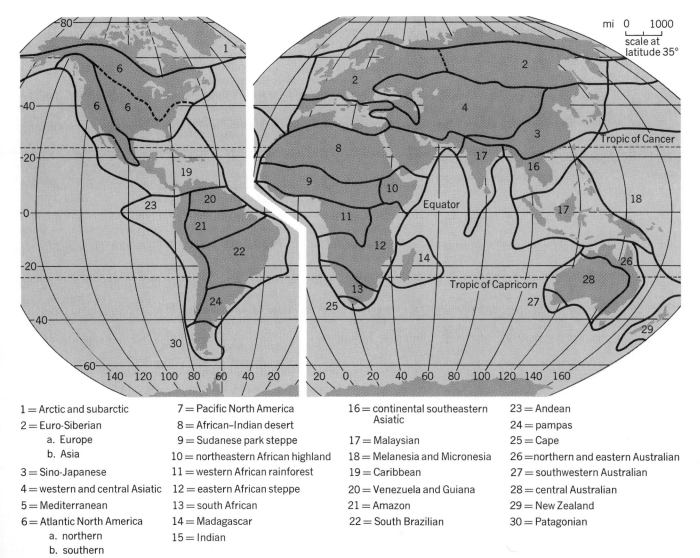

1 = Arctic and subarctic	7 = Pacific North America	16 = continental southeastern Asiatic	23 = Andean
2 = Euro-Siberian	8 = African–Indian desert		24 = pampas
a. Europe	9 = Sudanese park steppe	17 = Malaysian	25 = Cape
b. Asia	10 = northeastern African highland	18 = Melanesia and Micronesia	26 = northern and eastern Australian
3 = Sino-Japanese	11 = western African rainforest	19 = Caribbean	27 = southwestern Australian
4 = western and central Asiatic	12 = eastern African steppe	20 = Venezuela and Guiana	28 = central Australian
5 = Mediterranean	13 = south African	21 = Amazon	29 = New Zealand
6 = Atlantic North America	14 = Madagascar	22 = South Brazilian	30 = Patagonian
a. northern	15 = Indian		
b. southern			

Fig. 1. Floristic regions of world. 1 mi = 1.6 km. (*After R. Good, Geography of Flowering Plants, 3d ed., Longmans, 1964*)

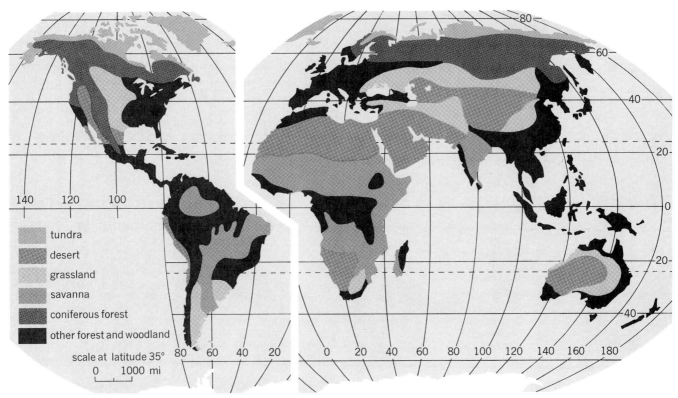

Fig. 2. Map of the world, showing the distribution of physiognomic vegetation types. 1 mi = 1.6 km. (*After R. Good, Geography of Flowering Plants, 3d ed., Longmans, 1964*)

their populations. Vegetation may possess emergent properties not necessarily found in the species themselves. Sometimes vegetation is very weakly integrated, as pioneer plants of an abandoned field. Sometimes it is highly integrated, as in an undisturbed tropical rainforest. Vegetation provides the main structural and functional framework of ecosystems, which have been actively studied since 1950. *SEE ECOSYSTEM.*

Plant communities are an important part of vegetation and are studied in plant ecology and various subfields (such as phytosociology, plant sociology, vegetation science, or phytocoenology). No definition of the plant community has gained universal acceptance. In part, this is because of the high degree of independence of the species themselves. Thus, the community is often only a relative social continuity in nature, bounded by a relative discontinuity, as judged by competent botanists. *SEE ECOLOGICAL COMMUNITIES.*

In looking at vegetation patterns over larger areas, it is the basic physiognomic distinctions between grassland, forest, and desert, with such variants as woodland (open forest), savanna (scattered trees in grassland), and scrubland (dominantly shrubs), which are most often emphasized (**Fig. 2**). These general classes of vegetation structure can be broken down further by reference to leaf types (such as broad or needle) and seasonal habits (such as evergreen or deciduous). Geographic considerations may complete the names of the main vegetation formation types, also called biomes (such as tropical rainforest, boreal coniferous forest, or temperate grasslands). Such natural vegetation regions are most closely related to climatic patterns and secondarily to soil or other environmental factors. *SEE ALTITUDINAL VEGETATION ZONES.*

Vegetational plant geography has emphasized the mapping of such vegetation regions and the interpretation of these in terms of environmental (ecological) influences. Distinction has been made between potential and actual vegetation, the latter becoming more important due to human influence. *SEE VEGETATION AND ECOSYSTEM MAPPING.*

Some plant geographers and other biologists are dissatisfied with these more general approaches and point to the effects of ancient human populations, natural disturbances, and the large-herbivore extinctions and climatic shifts of the Pleistocene on the species composition and dynamics of so-called virgin vegetation. On the other hand, it has been shown that the site occurrence and geographic distributions of plant and vegetation types (that is, above the species level) can be predicted surprisingly well from general climatic and other environmental patterns. Problems occur especially when substrates are unusually young or nutrient-poor and in marginal environments where disturbance can emphasize the stochastic nature of vegetation, permitting one or the other of competing types to gain the upper hand. Unlike floristic botany, where evolution provides a single unifying principle for taxonomic classification, vegetation structure and dynamics have no single dominant influence.

Plant growth forms. Basic plant growth forms (such as broad-leaved trees, stem-succulents, or forbs) have long represented convenient groups of species based on obvious similarities. When these forms are interpreted as ecologically significant adaptations to environmental factors, they are generally called life forms and may be interpreted as basic ecological types. These life forms not only may represent the basic building blocks of vegetation but may also provide a convenient way of describing vegetation structure without having to list each individual species. SEE PLANTS, LIFE FORMS OF.

In general, basic plant types may be seen as groups of plant taxa with similar form and ecological requirements, resulting from similar morphological responses to similar environmental conditions. For example, deciduous leaves are generally ''softer'' and photosynthesize more efficiently in favorable environments. On the other hand, they may lose more water and require more energy and nutrients for their construction (over the plant's lifespan) than ''harder,'' longer-lived evergreen leaves. Similarly, larger plants with larger total leaf area may be vulnerable to greater water loss, but may also have more extensive root systems for more effective water uptake. The vegetation of a particular site will be composed of plants with particular combinations of such form characters which permit the plant to function successfully in a particular environment. When similar morphological or physiognomic responses occur in unrelated taxa in similar but widely separated environments, they may be called convergent characteristics (for example, the occurrence of broad-sclerophyll shrubs in the world's five mediterranean-climate regions).

Research. Work in plant geography has involved a variety of approaches. J. Grime recognized three basic plant ''strategies'' (competitors, stress tolerators, and ruderals), their environmental relationships, and how these may interact. As a result of much work in ecology, there has been an increased emphasis on plant processes and ecophysiology. The focus especially is on plant water and energy budgets throughout the year and how these may influence or limit species distributions. Such work has been carried out, in particular, in nonforest vegetation of grassland, tundra, semidesert, and mediterranean-climate regions. SEE PHYSIOLOGICAL ECOLOGY (PLANT).

The revolutionary discovery of plate tectonics in the twentieth century raised many new questions about past plant migrations and the historical development of taxa and regional floras. The value (and validity) of cladistics and of vicariance theory in the study of plant geographic history has been strongly debated.

As human populations alter or destroy more and more of the world's natural vegetation, problems of species preservation, substitute vegetation, and succession have increased in importance. This is especially true in the tropics, where deforestation is proceeding rapidly. Probably over half the species in tropical rainforests have not yet even been identified. Because nutrients are quickly washed out of tropical rainforest soils, cleared areas can be used for only a few years before they must be abandoned to erosion and much degraded substitute vegetation. Perhaps the greatest current challenge in plant geography is to understand tropical vegetation and succession sufficiently well to design self-sustaining preserves of the great diversity of tropical vegetation. SEE BIOGEOGRAPHY; ECOLOGY; RAINFOREST.

Elgene O. Box

Bibliography. E. O. Box, *Macroclimate and Plant Forms: An Introduction to Predictive Modeling in Phytogeography*, 1981; R. Daubenmire, *Plant Geography, with Special Reference to North America*, 1978; J. P. Grime, *Plant Strategies and Vegetation Processes*, 1979; D. Tilman, *Plant Strategies and* *the Dynamics and Structure of Plant Communities*, 1988.

Plants, life forms of

A term for the vegetative (morphological) form of the plant body. A related term is growth form but a theoretical distinction is often made: life form is thought by some to represent a basic genetic adaptation to environment, whereas growth form carries with it no connotation of adaptation and is a more general term applicable to structural differences.

Life-form systems are based on differences in gross morphological features, and the categories bear no necessary relationship to reproductive structures, which form the basis for taxonomic classification. Features used in establishing life-form classes include deciduous versus evergreen leaves, broad versus needle leaves, size of leaves, degree of protection afforded the perennating tissue, succulence, and duration of life cycle (annual, biennial, or perennial). Thus the garden bean (family Leguminosae) and tomato (Solanaceae) belong to the same life form because each is an annual, finishing its entire life cycle in 1 year, while black locust (Leguminosae) and black walnut (Juglandaceae) are perennial trees with compound, deciduous leaves.

Climate and adaptation factors. There is a clear correlation between life forms and climates. For example, broad-leaved evergreen trees clearly dominate in the hot humid tropics, whereas broadleaved deciduous trees prevail in temperature climates with cold winters and warm summers, and succulent cacti dominate American deserts. Although cacti are virtually absent from African deserts, members of the family Euphorbiaceae have evolved similar succulent life forms. Such adaptations are genetic, having arisen by natural selection. However, since there are no life forms confined only to a specific climate and since it is virtually impossible to prove that a given morphological feature represents an adaptation with survival value, some investigators are content to use life forms only as descriptive tools to portray the form of vegetation in different climates.

Raunkiaer system. Many life-form systems have been developed. Early systems which incorporated many different morphological features were difficult to use because of this inherent complexity. The most successful and widely used system is that of C. Raunkiaer, proposed in 1905; it succeeded where others failed because it was homogeneous and used only a few obvious morphological features representing important adaptations.

Reasoning that it was the perennating buds (the tips of shoots which renew growth after a dormant season, either of cold or drought) which permit a plant to survive in a specific climate, Raunkiaer's classes were based on the degree of protection afforded the bud and the position of the bud relative to the soil surface (see **illus.**). They applied to autotrophic, vascular, self-supporting plants. Raunkiaer's classificatory system is:

> Phanerophytes: bud-bearing shoots in the air, predominantly woody trees and shrubs; subclasses based on height and on presence or absence of bud scales

Chamaephytes: bud within 10 in. (25 cm) of the surface, mostly prostrate or creeping shrubs
Hemicryptophytes: buds at the soil surface, protected by scales, snow, and litter
Cryptophytes: buds underneath the soil surface or under water
Therophytes: annuals, the seed representing the only perennating tissue

Subclasses were established in several categories, and Raunkiaer later incorporated leaf-size classes into the system.

By determining the life forms of a sample of 1000 species from the world's floras, Raunkiaer showed a correlation between the percentage of species in each life-form class present in an area and the climate of the area. The results (see **table**) were expressed as a normal spectrum, and floras of other areas were then compared to this. Raunkiaer concluded that there were four main phytoclimates: phanerophyte-dominated flora of the hot humid tropics, hemicryptophyte-dominated flora in moist to humid temperate areas, therophyte-dominated flora in arid areas, and a chamaephyte-dominated flora of high latitudes and altitudes.

Subsequent studies modified Raunkiaer's views. (1) Phanerophytes dominate, to the virtual exclusion of other life forms, in true tropical rainforest floras, whereas other life forms become proportionately more important in tropical climates with a dry season, as in parts of India. (2) Therophytes are most abundant in arid climates and are prominent in temperate areas with an extended dry season, such as regions with Mediterranean climate (for example, Crete). (3) Other temperate floras have a predominance of hemicryptophytes with the percentage of phanerophytes decreasing from summer-green deciduous forest to grassland. (4) Arctic and alpine tundra are characterized by a flora which is often more than three-quarters chamaephytes and hemicryptophytes, the percentage of chamaephytes increasing with latitude and altitude.

Most life forms are present in every climate, suggesting that life form makes a limited contribution to adaptability. Determination of the life-form composition of a flora is not as meaningful as determination of the quantitative importance of a life form in vegetation within a climatic area. However, differences in evolutionary and land-use history may give rise to floras with quite different spectra, even though there is climatic similarity. Despite these problems, the Raunkiaer system remains widely used for vegetation

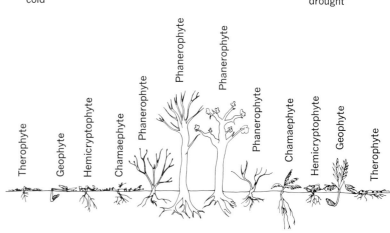

Life forms of plants according to C. Raunkiaer. (*After P. Dansereau, Biogeography: An Ecological Perspective, Ronald Press, 1957*)

description and for suggesting correlations between life forms, microclimate, and forest site index. SEE PLANT GEOGRAPHY.

Mapping systems. There has been interest in developing systems which describe important morpho-

Examples of life-form spectra for floras of different climates						
		Life form*				
Climate and vegetation	Area	Ph	Ch	H	Cr	Th
Normal spectrum	World	46	9	26	6	13
Tropical rainforest	Queensland, Australia	96	2	0	2	0
	Brazil	95	1	3	1	0
Subtropical rainforest (monsoon)	India	63	17	2	5	10
Hot desert	Central Sahara	9	13	15	5	56
Mediterranean	Crete	9	13	27	12	38
Steppe (grassland)	Colorado, United States	0	19	58	8	15
Cool temperate (deciduous forest)	Connecticut, United States	15	2	49	22	12
Arctic tundra	Spitsbergen, Norway	1	22	60	15	2

*Ph = phanerophyte; Ch = chamaephyte; H = hemicryptophyte; Cr = geophyte (cryptophyte); and Th = therophyte.

logic features of plants and which permit mapping and diagramming vegetation. Descriptive systems incorporate essential structural features of plants, such as stem architecture and height; deciduousness; leaf texture, shape, and size; and mechanisms for dispersal. These systems are important in mapping vegetation because structural features generally provide the best criteria for recognition of major vegetation units. SEE ALTITUDINAL VEGETATION ZONES; VEGETATION AND ECOSYSTEM MAPPING.

Arthur W. Cooper

Bibliography. H. C. Bold, *Morphology of Plants and Fungi*, 4th ed., 1980; S. A. Cain, Life forms and phytoclimate, *Bot. Rev.*, 16(1):1–32, 1950; P. Dansereau, *A Universal System for Recording Vegetation*, 1958; R. Daubenmire, *Plant Communities*, 1968; C. Raunkiaer, *The Life Forms of Plants and Statistical Geography*, 1934.

Polychlorinated biphenyls

A generic term for a family of 209 chlorinated isomers of biphenyl. The biphenyl molecule is composed of two six-sided carbon rings connected at one carbon site on each ring. Ten sites remain for chlorine atoms to join the biphenyl molecule. While the rules of nomenclature would indicate that the term polychlorinated biphenyl can refer only to molecules containing more than one chlorine atom, the term has been used to refer to the biphenyl molecule with one to ten chlorine substitutions.

Polychlorinated biphenyls (PCBs) were discovered in the late nineteenth century, were introduced into United States industry on a large scale in 1929, and have been in use since that time in most industrial nations. The qualities that made PCBs attractive to industry were chemical stability, resistance to heat, low flammability, and high dielectric constant. The PCB mixture is a colorless, viscous fluid, is relatively insoluble in water, and can withstand high temperatures without degradation. However, these characteristics are precisely the qualities that make polychlorinated biphenyl persistent in the environment; mono- and dichlorobiphenyl have half-lives in sunlight of about 6 days, but the higher-chlorinated isomers are not readily degraded in the environment.

Uses. The major use of PCBs has been as dielectric fluid in electrical equipment, particularly transformers (including transformers used on railway locomotives and self-propelled cars), capacitors, electromagnets, circuit breakers, voltage regulators, and switches. Electrical equipment containing PCBs is no longer produced in the United States, but in 1981, 40% of all electrical equipment in use in the United States contained PCBs. PCBs have also been used in heat transfer systems and hydraulic systems, and as plasticizers and additives in lubricating and cutting oils.

Environmental distribution. PCBs have been reported in animals, plants, soil, and water all over the world. The fact that PCBs have been detected in the polar ice caps is an indication of the power of atmospheric transport as a major pathway of global contamination. PCBs are also transported through the biosphere in water and attached to sediments. It is not known what quantities of PCBs have been released to the environment, but major sources are industrial and municipal waste disposal, spills and leaks from PCB-containing equipment, and manufacture and handling of PCB mixtures. SEE ATMOSPHERIC GENERAL CIRCULATION; BIOSPHERE.

PCBs have been reported in fishes, eels, and benthic organisms in the waters of the North Sea near the Netherlands. Fish products from United States waters and the Baltic Sea have been found to contain several parts per million of PCB and have been declared unfit for human consumption. PCBs have been found in all organisms analyzed from the North and South Atlantic, even in animals living under 11,000 ft (3400 m) of water. These phenomena are the result of bioaccumulation and biomagnification in the food chain. Uptake of PCBs by plants has also been reported, but it is generally small and does not directly contribute to substantial human contamination. In a few instances, poultry products, cattle, and hogs have been found to contain high concentrations of PCBs after the animals have eaten feed contaminated with PCBs. SEE FOOD WEB.

Following the initial restriction of PCB production in the 1970s, contamination levels dropped rapidly in the Great Lakes. Since 1979, levels in the Great Lakes have ceased to decline, probably because of atmospheric transport, contaminated groundwater, spills and leaks from authorized equipment, continued improper disposal, and the fact that the lower-chlorinated species degraded first, leaving the recalcitrant higher-chlorinated biphenyls. SEE EUTROPHICATION.

PCBs have been detected in human adipose tissues and in the milk of cows and humans. The estimated percentage of the United States population with detectable levels of PCBs was nearly 100% in 1981. The estimated percentage of the United States population with greater than 3 ppm PCBs in their tissue was 2.7% in 1972, and less than 1% in 1981. SEE HUMAN ECOLOGY.

PCBs have also been found as low-level, inadvertently generated contaminants in a wide range of chemical products such as certain paints, inks, plastics, and paper coatings. It has been estimated that fewer than 100,000 lb (45,000 kg) of PCBs are inadvertently generated in chemical processes each year in the United States.

Toxicity. PCBs can enter the body through the lungs, gastrointestinal tract, and skin, circulate throughout the body, and be stored in adipose tissue. Except for occupational contact, human exposure is mainly through food. PCBs can cause chloracne, skin discoloration, liver dysfunction, reproductive effects, development toxicity, and oncogenicity in exposed humans. Some PCBs have the ability to alter reproductive processes in mammals. Prenatal exposure in animals can result in various degrees of developmentally toxic effects. There is concern, based on extrapolation from animal studies, that PCBs may be carcinogenic in humans. The problem is complicated by the presence, in most PCB mixtures, of toxic impurities.

Disposal. Incineration of solid and liquid PCB materials is a common and highly efficient method of destruction. While laboratory tests have demonstrated PCB destruction at about 1470°F (800°C), the commercial incinerators operate at temperatures in excess of 1800°F (1000°C). High-efficiency destruction has been reported in large stationary incinerators and boilers, cement kilns, incinerator ships, and smaller mobile thermal destruction units.

PCB-contaminated fluids have been decontaminated by using chemical reagents to attack the chlorinated molecule. Generally, a metal, such as sodium, is used to remove the chlorine atoms from the biphenyl molecule. Some research has been conducted toward chemical treatment of PCB-contaminated soil by spraying the reagent on soil; the results and environmental consequences are unclear. Microbial degradation of PCB-contaminated soils has been pursued by several investigators, but there is little evidence of commercial-scale success. SEE ECOLOGY; HAZARDOUS WASTE.

Glenn Kuntz

Bibliography. M. Barros et al. (ed.), *PCB Seminar Proceedings,* Organization for Economic Cooperation and Development, 1983; W. Bouchard, PCBs in perspective, *Hazard. Mater. Manag. J.,* 1980; O. Hutzinger et al., *Chemistry of PCBs,* 1974, reprint 1983; A. Leifer et al., *Environmental Transport and Transformation of PCBs,* USEPA 560/5-83-025, 1983; R. Lucas et al., *PCBs in Human Adipose Tissue and Mother's Milk,* USEPA Contract 68-01-5848, 1982; S. Safe, *Polychlorinated Biphenyls (PCBs): Mammalian and Environmental Toxicology,* 1987.

Population dispersal

The process by which groups of living organisms expand the space or range within which they live. Because of their reproductive capacity, all populations have a natural tendency to expand. As increased area supports more individuals, dispersal and reproduction are intimately correlated.

Distinction should be made between dispersal and seasonal migration. Birds, butterflies, salmon, and others migrate regularly without necessarily expanding their geographic range, since they usually return to their original areas or die out.

Dispersal phases. Dispersal consists of several phases: (1) the production of units, that is, of individuals or parts of individuals (disseminules) fit or adapted for dispersal; (2) the transportation of individuals or disseminules to the new habitat; and (3) ecesis, the process of becoming established through germination, rooting, or physiological and psychological adjustment.

Dispersal units. Certain disseminules (propagules or diaspores) may represent various stages of the life cycle of the individual. Many free-living animals do not produce special dispersal structures but rely upon the ability of the entire organism to move about (vagility). Organisms attached to a substratum, such as most plants and certain animals, produce disseminules adapted to certain agents of dispersal. In order to be effective, a disseminule must have the ability to develop into one or more complete individuals. The structures listed in **Table 1** are examples of disseminules. Sperm cells, unfertilized eggs, and pollen grains, although capable of migration, are not true disseminules because they cannot give rise to new individuals.

It is possible to analyze plant communities on the basis of morphological features of the disseminules. By assigning species to dispersal types it is possible to construct dispersal spectra comparable to life form spectra in purpose and usefulness.

Transportation. Individuals or disseminules are transported in five general ways: self-dispersal (autochory), water dispersal (hydrochory), wind dispersal (anemochory), animal dispersal (zoochory), and dispersal by humans (anthropochory).

In active self-dispersal, or autochory, the organism spreads in the course of its normal activities. The flight of starlings resulting in their gradual spread through the United States and the motility of bacteria resulting in gradual spread through the nutrient media are examples. Certain plants possess mechanisms of self-dispersal, such as the auxochores and ballochores listed in **Table 2.** In passive dispersal, one or more agents carry the dispersal unit to a new location. The agents, or vectors, are water currents, wind, animals, and vehicles such as trains, ships, and airplanes.

Table 1. Examples of dispersal stages in life cycle of plants and animals

Environment	Organism	Disseminule	Dispersal by
Sea	Kelp	Zoospore	Currents
	Coral	Planula	Currents
	Sea worm	Trochophore	Currents
	Clam	Trochophore	Currents
	Barnacle	Adult	Driftwood, ships
	Crab	Zoea	Currents
	Sea urchin	Pluteus	Currents
	Fish	Adult	Autochory
	Lamprey	Adult	Fish
Terrestrial	Mushroom	Spore	Wind
	Fern	Spore	Wind
	Pine	Seed	Wind
	Blueberry	Fruit	Birds
	Tumbleweed	Entire plant	Wind
	Insect	Adult	Autochory, wind
	Spider	Young animal	Wind
	Reptiles, birds, mammals	Adult	Autochory
Parasitic	Bacteria	Entire cell	Water, food, air
	Intestinal ameba	Cyst	Water, food, humans
	Malaria parasite	Gamete, sporozoite	Mosquito
	Tapeworm	Egg	Pig
	Blood fluke	Egg, cercaria	Water, snail

Table 2. Plant dispersal types based upon morphological adaptations

Name	Definition	Example
Auxochores	Deposited by parent plant	Walking fern
Cyclochores	Spherical framework	Tumbleweed
Pterochores	Disseminules winged	Maple
Pogonochores	Disseminules plumed	Milkweed
Desmochores	Disseminules sticky or barbed	Cocklebur
Sarcochores	Disseminules fleshy	Cherry
Sporochores	Disseminules minute, light	Fern
Sclerochores	Disseminules without apparent adaptations	Violet
Barochores	Disseminules heavy	Oak
Ballochores	Shot away by parent plant	Touch-me-not

Water dispersal, or hydrochory, is prevalent in all marine and other aquatic populations. Plankton usually contains larval forms of bottom-dwellers (**Fig. 1**). Terrestrial forms associated with shore habitats are commonly dispersed by water. Buoyancy and resistance to salt water are a prerequisite for ocean dispersal. The first invaders of new islands such as Surtsey are often of this type. Transoceanic similarities in floras and faunas have been explained partly by ocean currents.

Wind dispersal, or anemochory, has various effects. It moves rolling disseminules in open deserts and grasslands (cyclochores, **Fig. 2***a*); it deflects falling winged disseminules (pterochores, Fig. 2*b–d*); and it carries lightweight spores and disseminules with plumes for great distances (sporochores and pogonochores, Fig. 2*e* and *h*). Insects, spiders, and other light animals have been found at high altitudes in the atmosphere, together with poplar seeds and other disseminules (Fig. 2*f* and *g*). Thus they may be carried distances of hundreds of miles.

Animal dispersal, or zoochory, is divided into epizoochory (barbed or sticky disseminules, desmo-

chores, **Fig. 3***a–c*) and endozoochory (disseminules eaten and egested by animals). Disseminules adapted to endozoochory are those such as arillate seeds (Fig. 3*d*), common in the tropics, and fruits with a fleshy mesocarp (Fig. 3*f* and *g*). Survival in the digestive tract of animals is a prerequisite. Bright fruit colors are frequent.

Dispersal by humans, or anthropochory, involves purposely dispersed organisms such as domesticated animals and plants and those accidentally transported such as weeds by railroads, beetles in grain shipments, and birds, rats, barnacles, and starfish on ships.

Ecesis. Success in population dispersal depends upon three factors: fitness of the new habitat, fitness of the migrating individuals, and the chance juxtapo-

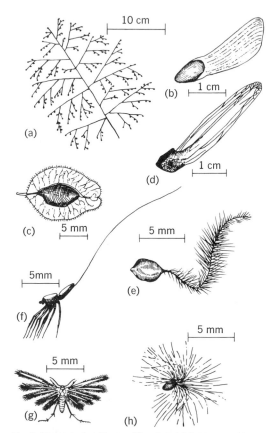

Fig. 2. Disseminules dispersed by wind. (*a*) Panic grass. (*b*) Pine seed. (*c*) Elm samara. (*d*) Tulip tree carpel. (*e*) Clematis carpel. (*f*) Spider. (*g*) Moth. (*h*) Cottonwood.

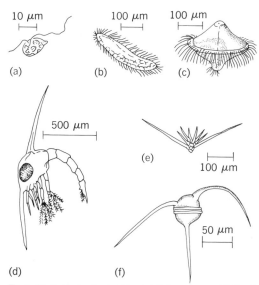

Fig. 1. Disseminules in plankton. (*a*) Kelp zoospore. (*b*) Coral planula. (*c*) Worm trochophore. (*d*) Crab zoea. (*e*) Brittle star pluteus. (*f*) Ceratium tripos.

sition of these two which, in the long run, depends on the number of individuals invading the new habitat. The probability for a new habitat to be favorable is greatest close to the parent population. Spores blown over great distances have less chance of landing in spots suited for germination than have seeds falling close to the parent plant. In wide-range dispersal larger numbers of disseminules are usually necessary than at close range, to insure ecesis.

The fitness of the individuals depends partly upon their genetic makeup. Offspring of organisms that reproduce without sexual union (apomictic), such as aphids, dandelions, and similar organisms, are likely to succeed only in identical habitats. Offspring from self- or cross-fertilizing parents may succeed in a va-

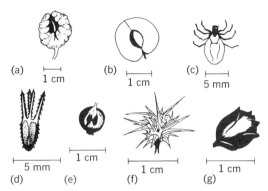

Fig. 3. Disseminules transported by animals. (*a*) Arillate legume seed. (*b*) Cherry. (*c*) Tick. (*d*) Beggar's tick fruit. (*e*) Currant berry. (*f*) Sandbur spikelet. (*g*) Juniper cone.

riety of situations. However, some hybrids which are sexually sterile are known to perpetuate themselves through apomixis. These are usually very successful locally.

Barriers to dispersal. A barrier is any discontinuity in the habitat greater than the maximum distance traveled by organisms in their normal dispersal. Oceans separating terrestrial habitats, continents separating marine habitats, mountain ranges intercepting wind dispersal, and deserts interrupting the continuity of forested land are all effective major barriers. Through the intervention of humans these barriers are broken down in many cases. Since the development of frequent world travel thousands of species have become established on new continents as a result of anthropochory. *See Population dispersion.*

Kornelius Lems / Herbert G. Baker

Bibliography. S. Carlquist, *Island Biology*, 1974; W. George, *Animal Geography*, 1962; P. A. Glick, *The Distribution of Insects, Spiders and Mites in the Air*, USDA Tech. Bull. 673, 1939; R. Hesse, W. C. Allee, and K. P. Schmidt, *Ecological Animal Geography*, 1937; E. J. Salisbury, *The Reproductive Capacity of Plants*, 1942.

Population dispersion

The spatial distribution at any particular moment of the individuals of a species of plant or animal. Under natural conditions organisms are distributed either by active movements, or migrations, or by passive transport by wind, water, or other organisms. The act or process of dissemination is usually termed dispersal, while the resulting pattern of distribution is best referred to as dispersion. Dispersion is a basic characteristic of populations, controlling various features of their structure and organization. It determines population density, that is, the number of individuals per unit of area, or volume, and its reciprocal relationship, mean area, or the average area per individual. It also determines the frequency, or chance of encountering one or more individuals of the population in a particular sample unit of area, or volume. The ecologist therefore studies not only the fluctuations in numbers of individuals in a population but also the changes in their distribution in space. *See Population dispersal.*

Principal types of dispersion. The dispersion pattern of individuals in a population may conform to any one of several broad types, such as random, uniform, or contagious (clumped). Any pattern is relative to the space being examined; a population may appear clumped when a large area is considered, but may prove to be distributed at random with respect to a much smaller area.

Random or haphazard. This implies that the individuals have been distributed by chance. In such a distribution, the probability of finding an individual at any point in the area is the same for all points (**Fig. 1***a*). Hence a truly random pattern will develop only if each individual has had an equal and independent opportunity to establish itself at any given point. In a randomly dispersed population, the relationship between frequency and density can be expressed by Eq. (1), where F is percentage frequency, D is densi-

$$F = 100(1 - e^{-D}) \qquad (1)$$

ty, and e is the base of natural or napierian logarithms. Thus when a series of randomly selected samples is taken from a population whose individuals are dispersed at random, the numbers of samples containing $0, 1, 2, 3, \ldots, n$ individuals conform to the well-known Poisson distribution described by notation (2).

$$e^{-D}, De^{-D}, \frac{D^2}{2!}e^{-D}, \frac{D^3}{3!}e^{-D}, \ldots, \frac{D^n}{n!}e^{-D} \qquad (2)$$

Randomly dispersed populations have the further characteristic that their density, on a plane surface, is related to the distance between individuals within the population, as shown in Eq. (3), where $\bar{r}$ is the mean

$$D = \frac{1}{4\bar{r}^2} \qquad (3)$$

distance between an individual and its nearest neighbor. These mathematical properties of random distributions provide the principal basis for a quantitative study of population dispersion. Examples of approximately random dispersions can be found in the patterns of settlement by free-floating marine larvae and of colonization of bare ground by airborne disseminules of plants. Nevertheless, true randomness appears to be relatively rare in nature, and the majority of populations depart from it either in the direction of uniform spacing of individuals or more often in the direction of aggregation.

Uniform. This type of distribution implies a regularity of distance between and among the individuals of a population (Fig. 1*b*). Perfect uniformity exists when the distance from one individual to its nearest neighbor is the same for all individuals. This is achieved, on a plane surface, only when the individuals are arranged in a hexagonal pattern. Patterns approaching uniformity are most obvious in the dispersion of or-

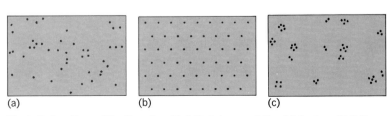

Fig. 1. Basic patterns of the dispersion of individuals in a population. (*a*) Random. (*b*) Uniform. (*c*) Clumped, but groups random. (*After E. P. Odum, Fundamentals of Ecology, Saunders, 1953*)

chard trees and in other artificial plantings, but the tendency to a regular distribution is also found in nature, as for example in the relatively even spacing of trees in forest canopies, the arrangement of shrubs in deserts, and the distribution of territorial animals.

Contagious or clumped. The most frequent type of distribution encountered is contagious or clumped (Fig 1c), indicating the existence of aggregations or groups in the population. Clusters and clones of plants, and families, flocks, and herds of animals are common phenomena. The degree of aggregation may range from loosely connected groups of two or three individuals to a large compact swarm composed of all the members of the local population. Furthermore, the formation of groups introduces a higher order of complexity in the dispersion pattern, since the several aggregations may themselves be distributed at random, evenly, or in clumps. An adequate description of dispersion, therefore, must include not only the determination of the type of distribution, but also an assessment of the extent of aggregation if the latter is present.

Analysis of dispersion. If the type or degree of dispersion is not sufficiently evident upon inspection, it can frequently be ascertained by use of sampling techniques. These are often based on counts of individuals in sample plots or quadrats. Departure from randomness can usually be demonstrated by taking a series of quadrats and testing the numbers of individuals found therein for their conformity to the calculated Poisson distribution which has been described above. The observed values can be compared with the calculated ones by a chi-square test for goodness of fit, and lack of agreement is an indication of nonrandom distribution. If the numbers of quadrats containing zero or few individuals, and of those with many individuals, are greater than expected, the population is clumped; if these values are less than expected, a tendency toward uniformity is indicated. Another measure of departure from randomness is provided by the variance:mean ratio, which is 1.00 in the case of the Poisson (random) distribution. If the ratio of variance to mean is less than 1.00, a regular dispersion is indicated; if the ratio is greater than 1.00, the dispersion is clumped.

In the case of obviously aggregated populations, quadrat data have been tested for their conformity to a number of other dispersion models, such as Neyman's contagious, Thomas' double Poisson, and the negative binomial distributions. However, the results of all procedures based on counts of individuals in quadrats depend upon the size of the quadrat employed. Many nonrandom distributions will seem to be random if sampled with very small or very large quadrats, but will appear clumped if quadrats of medium size are used. Therefore the employment of more than one size of quadrat is recommended.

A measure of aggregation that does not depend on quadrat size of the mean density of individuals per quadrat and that can be applied to patterns consisting of a mosaic of patches with different densities has been developed by Morisita. His index of dispersion is a ratio of the observed probability of drawing two individuals randomly from the same quadrat to the expected probability of the same event for individuals randomly dispersed over the set of quadrats being studied. Index values greater than 1.0 indicate clumping, and values between 0 and 1.0 point to regularity of dispersion.

The fact that plot size may influence the results of quadrat analysis has led to the development of a number of techniques based on plotless sampling. These commonly involve measurement of the distance between a randomly selected individual and its nearest neighbor, or between a randomly selected point and the closest individual. At least four different procedures have been used (**Fig. 2**). The closest-individual method (Fig. 2a) measures the distance from each sampling point to the nearest individual. The nearest-neighbor method (Fig. 2b) measures the distance from each individual to its nearest neighbor. The random-pairs method (Fig. 2c) establishes a base line from each sampling point to the nearest individual, and erects a 90° exclusion angle to either side of this line. The distance from the nearest individual lying outside the exclusion angle to the individual used in the base line is then measured. The point-centered quarter method (Fig. 2d) measures the distance from each sampling point to the nearest individual in each quadrant.

In each of these four methods of plotless sampling, a series of measurements is taken which can be used as a basis for evaluating the pattern of dispersion. In the case of the closest-individual and the nearest-neighbor methods, a population whose members are distributed at random will yield a mean distance value that can be calculated by use of the density-distance equation (3). In an aggregated distribution, the mean observed distance will be less than the one calculated on the assumption of randomness; in a uniform distribution it will be greater. Thus the ratio $\bar{r}_A/\bar{r}_E$, where $\bar{r}_A$ is the actual mean distance obtained from the measured population and $\bar{r}_E$ is the mean distance expected under random conditions, affords a measure of the degree of deviation from randomness.

Students of human geography have used the nearest-neighbor measure as a basis for a highly sophisticated methodology to analyze the dispersion of towns, department stores, and other features of land-use patterns.

Additional information about the spatial relations in

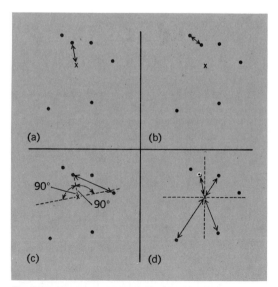

Fig. 2. Distances measured in four methods of plotless sampling. (a) Closest individual. (b) Nearest neighbor. (c) Random pairs, with 180° exclusion angle. (d) Point-centered quarter. The cross represents the sampling point in each case. (*After P. Greig-Smith, Quantitative Plant Ecology, Butterworths, 1957*)

a population can be secured by extending these procedures to measurement of the distance to the second and successive nearest neighbors, or by increasing the number of sectors about any chosen sampling point. However, since all of these methods assume that the individuals are small enough to be treated mathematically as points, they become less accurate when the individuals cover considerable space.

Factors affecting dispersion. The principal factors that determine patterns of population dispersion include (1) the action of environmental agencies of transport, (2) the distribution of soil types and other physical features of the habitat, (3) the influence of temporal changes in weather and climate, (4) the behavior pattern of the population in regard to reproductive processes and dispersal of the young, (5) the intensity of intra- and interspecific competition, and (6) the various social and antisocial forces that may develop among the members of the population. Although in certain cases the dispersion pattern may be due to the overriding effects of one factor, in general populations are subject to the collective and simultaneous action of numerous distributional forces and the dispersion pattern reflects their combined influence. When many small factors act together on the population, a more or less random distribution is to be expected, whereas the domination of a few major factors tends to produce a departure from randomness.

Environmental agencies of transport. The transporting action of air masses, currents of water, and many kinds of animals produces both random and nonrandom types of dispersion. Airborne seeds, spores, and minute animals are often scattered in apparently haphazard fashion, but aggregation may result if the wind holds steadily from one direction. Wave action is frequently the cause of large concentrations of seeds and organisms along the drift line of lake shores. The habits of fruit-eating birds give rise to the clusters of seedling junipers and cherries found beneath such perching sites as trees and fencerows, as well as to the occurrence of isolated individuals far from the original source. Among plants, it seems to be a general principle that aggregation is inversely related to the capacity of the species for seed dispersal.

Physical features of the habitat. Responses of the individuals of the population to variations in the habitat also tend to give rise to local concentrations. Environments are rarely uniform throughout, some portions generally being more suitable for life than others, with the result that population density tends to be correlated directly with the favorability of the habitat. Oriented reactions, either positive or negative, to light intensities, moisture gradients, or to sources of food or shelter, often bring numbers of individuals into a restricted area. In these cases, aggregation results from a species-characteristic response to the environment and need not involve any social reactions to other members of the population. *See Environment.*

Influence of temporal changes. In most species of animal, daily and seasonal changes in weather evoke movements which modify existing patterns of dispersion. Many of these are associated with the disbanding of groups as well as with their formation. Certain birds, bats, and even butterflies, for example, form roosting assemblages at one time of day and disperse at another. Some species tend to be uniformly dispersed during the summer, but flock together in winter. Hence temporal variation in the habitat may often be as effective in determining distribution patterns as spatial variation.

Behavior patterns in reproduction. Factors related to reproductive habits likewise influence the dispersion patterns of both plant and animal populations. Many plants reproduce vegetatively, new individuals arising from parent rootstocks and producing distinct clusters; others spread by means of rhizomes and runners and may thereby achieve a somewhat more random distribution. Among animals, congregations for mating purposes are common, as in frogs and toads and the breeding swarms of many insects. In contrast, the breeding territories of various fishes and birds exhibit a comparatively regular dispersion.

Intensity of competition. Competition for light, water, food, and other resources of the environment tends to produce uniform patterns of distribution. The rather regular spacing of trees in many forests is commonly attributed largely to competition for sunlight, and that of desert plants for soil moisture. Thus a uniform dispersion helps to reduce the intensity of competition, while aggregation increases it. *See Population ecology.*

Social factors. Among many animals the most powerful forces determining the dispersion pattern are social ones. The social habit leads to the formation of groups or societies. Plant ecologists use the term society for various types of minor communities composed of several to many species, but when the word is applied to animals it is best confined to aggregations of individuals of the same species which cooperate in their life activities. Animal societies or social groups range in size from a pair to large bands, herds, or colonies. They can be classified functionally as mating societies (which in turn are monogamous or polygamous, depending on the habits of the species), family societies (one or both parents with their young), feeding societies (such as various flocks of birds or schools of fishes), and as migratory societies, defense societies, and other types. Sociality confers many advantages, including greater efficiency in securing food, conservation of body heat during cold weather, more thorough conditioning of the environment to increase its habitability, increased facilitation of mating, improved detection of, and defense against predators, decreased mortality of the young and a greater life expectancy, and the possibility of division of labor and specialization of activities. Disadvantages include increased competition, more rapid depletion of resources, greater attraction of enemies, and more rapid spread of parasites and disease. Despite these disadvantages, the development and persistence of social groups in a wide variety of animal species is ample evidence of its overall survival value. Some of the advantages of the society are also shared by aggregations that have no social basis. *See Ecological communities.*

Optimal population density. The degree of aggregation which promotes optimum population growth and survival, however, varies according to the species and the circumstances. Groups or organisms often flourish best if neither too few nor too many individuals are present; they have an optimal population density at some intermediate level. The condition of too few individuals, known as undercrowding, may prevent sufficient breeding contacts for a normal rate of reproduction. On the other hand, overcrowding, or too high a density, may result in severe competition and excessive interaction that will reduce fecundity and lower the growth rate of individuals. The concept of an intermediate optimal population density is sometimes known as Allee's principle. SEE POPULATION ECOLOGY.

Francis C. Evans

Bibliography. A. A. Berryman (ed.), *Dynamics of Forest Insect Populations*, 1988; A. A. Berryman (ed.), *Dynamics of Insect Populations: Patterns, Causes, Implications*, 1988; P. Greig-Smith, *Quantitative Plant Ecology,* 3d ed., 1983; A. G. Pakes and R. A. Maller, *Mathematical Ecology of Plant Species Competition*, 1990; E. C. Pielou, *Mathematical Ecology,* 1977; E. C. Pielou, *Population and Community Ecology: Principles and Methods,* 1974.

Population ecology

The study of spatial and temporal patterns in the abundance and distribution of organisms and of the mechanisms that produce those patterns. Species differ dramatically in their average abundance and geographical distributions, and they display a remarkable range of dynamical patterns of abundance over time, including relative constancy, cycles, irregular fluctuations, violent outbreaks, and extinctions. The aims of population ecology are threefold: (1) to elucidate general principles explaining these dynamic patterns; (2) to integrate these principles with mechanistic models and evolutionary interpretations of individual life-history tactics, physiology, and behavior as well as with theories of community and ecosystem dynamics; and (3) to apply these principles to the management and conservation of natural populations.

Definition of a population. A population is the total number of individuals of a given biological species found in one place at one time. In practice, ecologists often deal with density—numbers per unit area for land organisms and numbers per unit volume in aquatic systems—rather than raw numbers, or even weight. What may be described as an individual depends on the kind of organism and the aim of the scientific enquiry. In most animals, the life cycle starts with a fertilized egg, passes through a largely irreversible process of coupled growth and differentiation, and ends in a tightly integrated, unitary, adult organism. Population size can be measured by merely counting adult units and their juvenile prologues. But in most plants and some colonial animals, growth and differentiation proceed in a modular fashion; growth involves the replication of a basic body unit, so that a fertilized egg generates a spatially distributed "population" of connected modules. Modular organisms show tremendous plasticity in size and form, but the connections between modules sometimes break, leading to a dispersed clone of physiologically independent units. For example, one clone of quaking aspen (which spreads by root buds) occupies 200 acres (80 hectares) and is more than 10,000 years old. To a geneticist, this clone constitutes a single huge individual; to an ecologist, each aspen trunk may be considered to be an individual. Modular organisms have an additional dimension of complexity that must be quantified to understand their dynamics. In this article, the population concepts presented apply broadly to both unitary and modular organisms.

There are only four ways a population can change in size: birth, death, immigration, and emigration. If immigration and emigration are negligible, the population is closed, and the difference between birth and death rates drives its dynamics. Terrestrial animals on islands often have closed populations. If immigration and emigration are important, however, the population is open, and its abundance may be substantially influenced by spatially distant events. For example, the number of barnacles that are found on a rocky coastline often reflects the density of setting larvae, which in turn is governed by events in offshore waters. If a population that is under study is found to be highly open, the spatial scale of the study may be too narrowly circumscribed to capture the important mechanisms of population dynamics.

Basic population models. Populations exhibit a great variety of dynamical patterns, ranging from explosive outbreaks, to local extinctions, to regular cycles or relatively constant abundances (see **Fig. 1**). To help describe and explain these patterns, ecologists rely on population models. Simple life cycles and closed populations provide a useful starting point in developing population models. Many temperate-zone insects have one annual generation, and so at any given time all individuals are at the same stage of life. For a population with discrete, nonoverlapping generations, if $N(t)$ is the number of adults censused in generation t, and $R(t)$ is the number of adult offspring in generation $t + 1$ produced per adult in generation t, the number of individuals in the next generation is given by Eq. (1). The quantity $R(t)$ is the growth rate

$$N(t + d) = N(t)R(t) \qquad (1)$$

of the population for generation t. Iterating this discrete time growth model for subsequent generations allows one to project population numbers through time. When d is very small, a limiting form for Eq. (1) is the differential equation (2), where $r(t)$, the in-

$$\frac{dN}{dt} = r(t)N(t) \qquad (2)$$

stantaneous per-capita growth rate, is the difference between per-capita birth and death rates. Equation (2) is literally true only if populations grow continuously with overlapping generations (as is approximately true for some microbes). Constant values for R or r imply exponential growth. If $R > 1$ ($r > 0$), a population grows without bounds; if $R < 1$ ($r < 0$), it declines to extinction. The theoretical framework of population ecology largely consists of elaborations of these basic growth models, including extensions to more complicated life cycles and multiple species.

Exponential growth has a snowballing effect: if the growth rate is constant, then the more individuals there are, the faster the population grows. Even low growth rates eventually lead to populations of enormous sizes. Some natural populations show transient phases of exponential growth, particularly in colonizing episodes: for instance, the collared turtledove invaded Great Britain in 1955 and increased exponentially for nearly a decade. The per-capita rate of growth during exponential growth is called the intrinsic rate of increase, r_0. The value of r_0 quantitatively expresses the interplay of individual traits, such as life history strategies, with the environment.

Exponential growth during colonization often involves expansion across space as well as an increase through time. Equation (2) can be expanded to include immigration and emigration, as given in Eq. (3). When individuals move down spatial density gra-

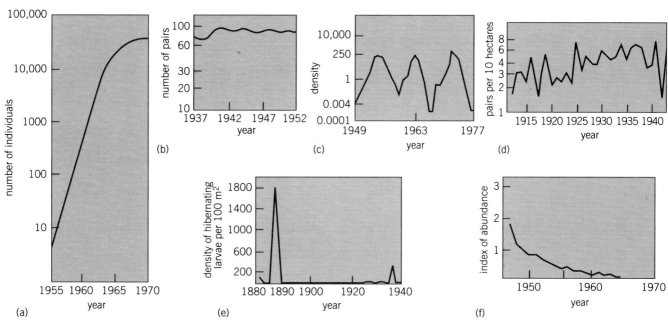

Fig. 1. Graphs of dynamical behaviors showing the diversity of population dynamics. (*a*) Collared dove; a phase of exponential growth. (*b*) Yellow-eyed penguin; steady state. (*c*) Budmoth; regular cycles. (*d*) Songbird; irregular fluctuations. (*e*) *Dendrolimus* moth; outbreaks. (*f*) Blue whale; decline toward extinction.

$$\frac{dN}{dt} = rN + \text{(net change due to dispersal)} \quad (3)$$

dients, which is analogous to chemical diffusion along concentration gradients, their rate of movement is characterized by a diffusion coefficient, D. In a homogeneous environment, this model predicts that the expanding population wave advances at a velocity $2(rD)^{1/2}$, implying a linear expansion in range area with time. Data from a number of colonizing populations show exactly this relationship.

Population heterogeneity. Models such as those given in Eqs. (1) and (2), when interpreted literally, assume that all members of a population are identical. This is rarely true. Birth and death rates typically vary as a function of age, body weight, and genotype. A great deal of work in population ecology is devoted to elucidating age-specific schedules of mortality and fecundity, using these patterns to predict population growth, and interpreting these patterns in the light of evolutionary theory. To study age-structured population dynamics, the number of individuals in each age class must be monitored. The two ingredients needed to project changes in population size and age structure are the mortality schedule or survivorship curve, which describes the fraction of newborns surviving to each age, and the fecundity schedule, which describes the rate of female births per female at each age. It is a formidable task to measure complete fecundity and mortality schedules in natural populations, but if these schedules are given, the geometric growth model of Eq. (1) can be generalized to a matrix model, as in Eq. (4), where $N(t)$ is a vector in which each element

$$N(t + 1) = A(t)N(t) \quad (4)$$

is the number of individuals in an age class, and $A(t)$ is a matrix incorporating the fecundity and mortality schedules. When individuals can be categorized into discrete stages such as body size (for example, number of connected modules in a clonal organism) in addition to age, more general matrices can describe

population growth; the matrix elements are rates of transition between each pair of stages. [The continuous time model of Eq. (2) can be similarly generalized by using partial differential equations.] A fundamental principle of demographic theory is that if these schedules are constant, a population will (with rare exceptions) eventually settle into a stable age distribution in which each age class comprises a constant fraction of the total population. A population in its stable age distribution grows geometrically, as in Eq. (1), at a rate of increase uniquely determined from the mortality and fecundity schedules. A population displaced from its stable age distribution may exhibit transient phases of growth or decline, divergent from its long-term growth pattern.

All populations are genetically variable. If different genotypes have different fecundity or mortality schedules, genetic variation can influence population dynamics. Models that simultaneously incorporate changes in genetic composition and population growth can be quite complex; however, they may be important in describing some populations and are necessary for linking population ecology with evolutionary theory.

Population limitation and regulation. Populations cannot expand exponentially forever. For instance, the growth rate of the collared dove substantially declined in the second decade of its invasion, probably because mortality rates rose or birth rates declined as a result of competition for limited resources such as food or nest sites. Such mechanisms are called negatively density-dependent factors. The notion of density dependence is a specific example of the more general concept of feedback. An alternative hypothesis is that the environment worsened for reasons unrelated to dove density, such as a shift in the weather. Such causes for variation in birth or death rates are called density-independent factors. Ecologists have long disputed the relative importance of density-dependent and density-independent factors in determining population size. The current consensus is that both are important but to differing degrees in different species and environments. For a population to be regulated, it must tend to increase when below a certain size and decrease when above that size. If growth rates vary with time but in a fashion unrelated to density, closed populations will eventually fluctuate to extinction or expand without limit. If a closed population persists over long periods of time, it must be regulated to some degree.

As illustrated below, population regulation by no means implies population stability. In general, a population is stable if it returns to equilibrium following a perturbation. Moreover, many local populations may not be persistent over long periods of time and so may not be regulated in the usual sense. Open populations, by definition coupled by dispersal with other populations, can become reestablished by immigration following a local extinction. The total population of a species may persist, even though no single local population survives, because there is a spreading of risk among an ensemble of local populations (which experience somewhat different environmental conditions) that are loosely coupled by dispersal. SEE POP-ULATION DISPERSAL.

A useful method for considering the interplay of density-dependent and density-independent factors in determining population size is to plot birth and death rates as functions of density (see **Fig. 2**). The carrying capacity K of a population in a given environment is defined to be the largest number of individuals for which the birth rate just matches the death rate. The population decreases above K and increases below K. A given change in density-independent death rates can produce very different changes in population size, depending on the form of the underlying density dependence. If density dependence is weak (Fig. 2b), fluctuations in mortality generate large oscillations in population size; if density dependence is strong (Fig. 2c), the population readily buffers such fluctuations. Density-dependent factors are necessary to regulate populations, but density-independent factors must also be considered to understand fully what limits populations to a given value of K.

Evidence for density dependence. Statistical analyses of time series of population data can suggest density dependence, but it is difficult to demonstrate density dependence conclusively by using such data. Sometimes density dependence can be shown for particular stages in the life cycle, and in general, density dependence may be observed in births, deaths, or dispersal. However, without examining density dependence at each stage in the life cycle, it is difficult to infer the regulatory importance of any single stage. Stronger evidence comes from manipulative experiments in which control populations are compared with artificially enhanced or depressed populations.

Density-dependent population models. The exponential growth model [Eq. (2)] can be modified to include density dependence by expressing r as a function of N. The simplest model that generalizes Eq. (2) is the logistic equation (5), in which per-capita

$$\frac{dN}{dt} = r_0 N \left(1 - \frac{N}{K} \right) \qquad (5)$$

growth rate declines linearly with increasing density. Populations displaced from K converge smoothly back to it, without overshoots. Population growth is maximal when $N = K/2$. This model provides a good fit to some laboratory colonies and captures much of

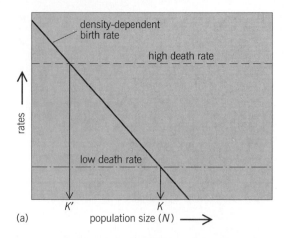

(a)

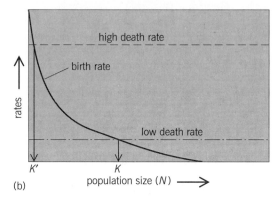

(b)

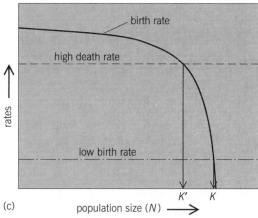

(c)

Fig. 2. Carrying capacity as a reflection of both density dependence and the intensity of density-independent mortality. Births are considered to be purely density-dependent, deaths purely density-independent. The three curves show the effects of (a) an increase in density-independent mortality (a high death rate), (b) weak density dependence, and (c) strong density dependence.

the qualitative behavior of more complex models; it is, however, a somewhat crude first approximation to accurate models of population growth.

The logistics can be improved upon in numerous ways. The simplest method is to use a nonlinear function for the per-capita growth rate. Further refinements in the model can be achieved by incorporating threshold effects and explicitly incorporating submodels that encapsulate the mechanisms of density dependence. At densities far below carrying capacity, there may be an Allee effect—a positive relationship between density and per-capita growth rates. One intriguing possibility that arises in more complex models is that the population may exhibit alternative stable states; the one it actually occupies will depend upon accidents of history. For instance, insects may be regulated at low densities by bird predation, but at a higher threshold density the birds may be satiated and thus no longer regulate insect density; the insect population will then grow until checked by some other factor.

The discrete-time model [Eq. (1)] can be similarly modified to incorporate density dependence by expressing R as a function of N. Analysis of such models has led ecologists to reevaluate their traditional assumptions about the causes of population fluctuations in nature and about the relationship between regulation and stability. For instance, an analog of Eq. (5) is Eq. (6), which, along with similar equa-

$$N(t + 1) = N(t) \exp\left[r\left(1 - \frac{N}{K}\right)\right] \qquad (6)$$

tions, reveals a rich array of dynamical patterns. If $r < 2$, the population equilibrates stably at K; if $2 < r < 2.7$, the population fluctuates cyclically; if $r > 2.7$, the population exhibits chaotic behavior, with cycles of arbitrary periodicity or even aperiodic fluctuations. Such fluctuations intriguingly similar to the fluctuations in real-world data, which in the past were assumed to be produced by random environmental noise. The qualitative properties of the model that trigger pronounced population fluctuations are the time lag implicit in the discrete-time formulation, high growth rates at low densities, and strong density dependence at high densities. This suggests that a potential for complex dynamical behavior exists whenever there are time lags in the feedback between population size and population growth rates. Age structure is a ubiquitous source of time lags in populations, simply because time is required to reach reproductive maturity. Similarly, interactions between two, three, or more species can introduce long time lags, together with strong density dependence. It is an open question whether observed variability in natural populations reflects to any significant extent the complex dynamics latent in deterministic growth models instead of the force of fluctuations in the physical environment.

Mechanisms of density dependence.
Given that density dependence exists, the mechanisms generating it can be used both to predict the consequences of environmental change for population dynamics and to provide insight into systems where experimental manipulations are difficult. Density dependence often arises from competition, which is said to exist when organisms utilize common limiting resources and thereby negatively affect each other. (A resource is limiting if an increase in its supply increases per-capita growth rates.)

There are two principal sorts of competition, interference and exploitative. Interference competition occurs when one individual directly harms another. Interference may be dramatic, as in lethal aggression, or subtle, as when social interactions reduce the time available for gathering resources or increase the risk of predation. A surprising number of animal species are cannibalistic. Large scorpions, for instance, eat with relish their smaller-bodied conspecifics. Because encounter rate increases with increasing population size, cannibalism is likely to be a potent density-dependent factor in scorpion populations. Exploitative competition occurs when one individual consumes a resource such as food that otherwise would have been consumed by another individual. Because exploitative competition is mediated indirectly through a shared resource base, it can be more difficult to demonstrate than interference. In territorial animals, such as many songbirds, less space is available for additional territory holders as population size increases. As a result, competition for space can sharply cap population numbers.

Population regulation and interspecific interactions.
Negative density dependence may arise from interspecific interactions. A schematic classification of interactions between two species comes from considering the positive $(+)$ or negative $(-)$ effect that individuals of one species have on the growth rate of the other. In interspecific competition the interaction is $(-, -)$; in mutualism it is $(+, +)$. Natural enemies, defined broadly to include predators, herbivores, and parasites, are often engaged in $(+, -)$ relations with their prey or hosts. Most species are potential prey to one or more natural enemies; even top-level carnivores may be beset by parasites.

Obviously, competitors and mutualists can dramatically affect the size of a given population and so must be considered when studying population limitation. However, natural enemies are far more likely to be regulatory agents than are either competitors or mutualists. If two species are competing and one increases in density, the other will decrease. This will relax the interspecific competition on the first, which can then increase even more. Hence, competitive loops (and for similar reasons, mutualist loops) tend to produce positive feedback and so will not regulate population growth. By contrast, predator–prey interactions may produce negative density dependence acting across several time scales on both the predator and prey. As prey in one habitat patch become more numerous, predators almost immediately become more active or switch over from other prey types or patches. Predators may also show an intergenerational numerical response to increased prey availability. Because an increase in predator numbers usually decreases prey numbers, this induces delayed density dependence on both the predator and its prey. In host–pathogen systems, these numerical responses may be pronounced, even within a host generation. For example, in tropical trees, seedling mortality from fungal pathogens increases with increasing seedling density, because the rate of spore dispersal increases as the distance between hosts declines. There is mounting evidence that parasites are significant regulatory factors in a wide range of natural populations, including economically important forest insects and game animals.

Several cautionary remarks about natural enemies and density dependence are in order. Predation and intraspecific competition can interact in complex ways. Compensatory responses by prey populations sometimes diminish the impact of enemies. For instance, plants typically produce many more seeds than can possibly become reproductive adults. Predation on some seeds may simply enhance the survivorship of the nonconsumed seeds, leading to no net effect on adult numbers. Conversely, predation can intensify intraspecific competition in mobile animals by restricting them to limited refuges. Generalist natural enemies can greatly depress prey numbers without being important regulatory agents, because by depending on many prey types they are less likely to show a strong numerical response to any one. Indeed, generalist predators may often be destabilizing, driving local prey populations to extinction. Finally, density-dependent responses by natural enemies often involve time lags, setting up the possibility of oscillatory behavior. Host–pathogen systems seem particularly likely candidates for generating strongly cyclic or chaotic dynamics.

Population growth models can incorporate interspecific interactions by taking models such as those in Eqs. (5) and (6) and adding expressions that describe how competitors, mutualists, or natural enemies affect the growth rate of a given species. The dynamics of two or more coupled species is studied in theoretical community ecology, which among other things seeks to understand how the species richness and stability of communities is related to the pattern and strength of interspecific interactions. Analyses of models of interacting species suggest that strong intraspecific density dependence is required for community stability. For two competing species to persist at a stable equilibrium, the negative effect that each species exerts on its own growth must on average exceed the cross-species negative effects. In like manner, predator–prey interactions are most stable when one or both populations experience intraspecific density dependence.

Applied population ecology. In addition to its intrinsic conceptual appeal, population ecology has great practical utility. Control programs for agricultural pests or human diseases ideally attempt to reduce the intrinsic rate of increase of those organisms to very low values. Analyses of the population dynamics of infectious diseases have successfully guided the development of vaccination programs. In the exploitation of renewable resources, such as in forestry or fisheries biology, population models are required in order to devise sensible harvesting strategies that maximize the sustainable yield extracted from exploited populations. Conservation biology is increasingly concerned with the consequences of habitat fragmentation for species preservation. Population models can help characterize minimum viable population sizes below which a species is vulnerable to rapid extinction, and can help guide the development of interventionist policies to save endangered species. Finally, population ecology must be an integral part of any attempt to bring the world's burgeoning human population into harmonious balance with the environment. SEE ECOLOGY; THEORETICAL ECOLOGY.

Robert Holt

Bibliography. M. Begon and M. Mortimer, *Population Ecology: A Unified Study of Animals and Plants*, 2d ed., 1986; B. Ebenman and L. Persson (eds.), *Size-Structured Populations: Ecology and Evolution*, 1989; G. E. Hutchinson, *An Introduction to Population Ecology*, 1978; C. J. Krebs, *Ecology: The Experimental Analysis of Distribution and Abundance*, 1985; I. A. Shilov, *Population Ecology and Ecophysiology*, 1988; M. Williamson, *The Analysis of Biological Populations*, 1972.

Radiation biology

The study of the action of ionizing and nonionizing radiation on biological systems. Ionizing radiation includes highly energetic electromagnetic radiation (x-rays, gamma rays, or cosmic rays) and particulate radiation (alpha particles, beta particles, neutrons, or heavy charged ions). Nonionizing radiation includes ultraviolet radiation, microwaves, and extralow-frequency (ELF) electromagnetic radiation. These two types of radiation have different modes of action on biological material: ionizing radiation is sufficiently energetic to cause ionizations, whereas nonionizing radiation causes molecular excitations. In both cases, the result is that chemical bonds of molecules may be altered, causing mutations, cell death, or other biological changes.

Ionizing radiation originates from external sources (medical x-ray equipment, cathode-ray tubes in television sets or computer video displays) or from internal sources (ingested or inhaled radioisotopes, such as radon-222, strontium-90, and iodine-131), and is either anthropogenic (medical, industrial, or military) or natural (atmospheric or terrestrial).

Nonionizing radiation originates from natural sources (sunlight, Earth's magnetic field, lightning, static electricity, endogenous body currents) and technological sources (computer video displays and television sets, microwave ovens, communications equipment, electric equipment and appliances, and high-voltage transmission lines).

IONIZING RADIATION

The action of ionizing radiation is best described by the three stages (physical, chemical, and biological) that occur as a result of energy release in the biological target material (**Fig. 1**).

Physical stage. All ionizing radiation causes ionizations of atoms in the biological target material. The Compton effect, which predominates at the energies of electromagnetic radiation that are commonly encountered (for example, x-rays or gamma rays), strips orbital electrons from the atoms. These electrons (Compton electrons) travel through the target material, colliding with atoms and thereby releasing packets of energy. About 60 eV of energy is released with each collision, breaking chemical bonds and causing ionizations known as primary ionizations. The typical initial energy of a Compton electron is 200 keV, and so there may be over 3300 primary ionizations from a single Compton electron. For low-energy x-rays, the photoelectric effect predominates, producing photoelectrons that transfer their energy in the same manner as Compton electrons.

The absorbed dose of ionizing radiation is measured as the gray (Gy, 1 joule of energy absorbed by 1 kilogram of material). In general, the amount of absorption of ionizing radiation is greater for target material of high density and high atomic number, and it is independent of the chemical bonds of the target material. Because of the very localized absorption of ionizing radiation as compared to heat energy, an amount of ionizing radiation energy equivalent to 1/100 the heat energy in a cup of coffee will result in a 50% chance that the person absorbing the radiation will die in 30 days.

Neutrons with energies between 10 keV and 10 MeV transfer energy mainly by elastic scattering, that is, billiard-ball-type collisions, of atomic nuclei in the target material. In this process the nucleus is torn free of some or all of the orbital electrons because its velocity is greater than that of the orbital electrons. The recoiling atomic nucleus behaves as a positively charged particle. Because the mass of the neutron is nearly the same as that of the hydrogen atom, hydrogenous materials are most effective for energy transfer. A unit known as the kerma (acronym for kinetic

energy released in material) is used to measure the amount of energy transfer from neutrons and other indirectly ionizing radiation (for example, x-rays and gamma rays). This quantity is frequently equivalent to the absorbed dose of radiation in the material (the gray) because the ranges of the secondary recoiling charged particles are much shorter than the ranges of neutrons, x-rays, or gamma rays.

Chemical stage. Chemical changes in biological molecules are caused by the direct transfer of radiation energy (direct radiation action) or by the production of chemically reactive products from radiolysis of water that diffuse to the biological molecule (indirect radiation action). More than half the biological action of low linear-energy-transfer (LET) ionizing radiation (for example, x-rays and gamma rays) results from indirect radiation action, about 90% of which is due to the action of the hydroxyl radical (OH·). Characteristically, the manifestations of indirect radiation action decrease as the linear energy transfer of the radiation increases. Thus, for high linear-energy-transfer radiation, direct radiation action predominates. Chemicals that react with hydroxyl radicals, rendering them unreactive, provide protection against indirect radiation damage. For example, sulfhydryl compounds (RSH) remove hydroxyl radicals by reaction (1), where R represents an organic

$$2OH· + 2RSH → 2H_2O + RSSR \qquad (1)$$

functional group.

Indirect radiation action is also responsible for the oxygen effect of radiobiology, which describes the increased biological sensitivity when irradiation occurs in the presence of oxygen compared to the absence of oxygen during irradiation. The oxygen must be present during irradiation because of the limited lifetime (less than 1 millisecond) of the chemical species that react with oxygen. The oxygen effect is observed only in biological systems with membranes; the radiosensitivity of viruses and free deoxyribonucleic acid (DNA) is not enhanced by the presence of oxygen. Thus, two types of radiation damage are probable: oxygen-dependent radiation damage, which involves the membrane as the principal target; and oxygen-independent damage, which involves nonmembrane components, including the genome.

The most important biological targets for damage from ionizing radiation are probably the plasma membrane and DNA, because there is only one copy, or a few copies, in the cell; because they serve critical roles for the survival and propagation of cells; and because they are large. The last factor is important because ionizing radiation releases its energy in a random manner; thus the larger the target, the more likely that it will be damaged by radiation.

Membranes are composed of protein (50%) and lipids (50%). Biochemical damage in either of these components can cause membrane damage. Consequences of radiation damage in membranes are changes in ion permeability, with leakage of potassium ions; changes in active transport; and cell lysis.

The initial direct radiation action results in hydrogen abstraction [reaction (2)]. In the presence of oxygen (O_2), reactions (3)–(6) occur. Oxidative decom-

$$RH → R· + H· \qquad (2)$$

$$H· + O_2 → HO_2· \qquad (3)$$

$$R· + HO_2· → ROOH \qquad (4)$$

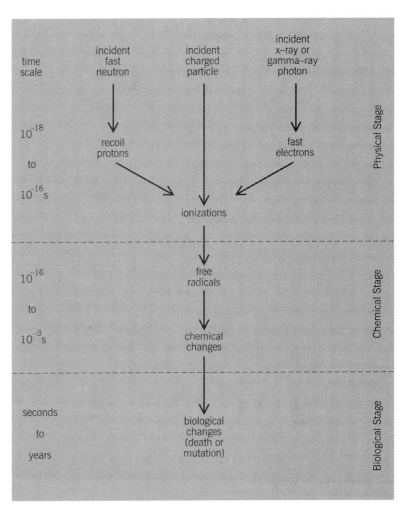

Fig. 1. Diagram of the three stages for the action of ionizing radiation on biological systems. The duration of the physical stage approximates the time required for the ionizing radiation to traverse an atom. During the chemical stage, molecular and thermal equilibrium is achieved. The biological stage involves metabolism of the chemical damage.

$$R· + O_2 → RO_2· \qquad (5)$$

$$RO_2· + H· → ROOH \qquad (6)$$

position products of the organoperoxides (ROOH) accumulate, and overall lipid damage is increased approximately threefold when irradiation occurs in the presence of oxygen. Two sensitive sites for protein damage are the free amino and sulfhydryl groups, as observed by the release of ammonia and hydrogen sulfide gases during irradiation of proteins. Another sensitive site is the imidazole ring of the amino acid histidine. The peptide bond is also subject to attack, which causes breakage of the polypeptide chain and a reduction of the molecular weight of the protein.

Membrane components can be protected by reactions of the initially formed organic radical with sulfhydryl compounds [reaction (7)]. The sulfhydryl

$$R· + RSH → RH + RS· \qquad (7)$$

compound restores the initially damaged membrane component to its original state. This radioprotective reaction does not appear to be important for protection of DNA.

Lesions in DNA that is irradiated in aqueous solution include single-strand breaks, double-strand breaks, base damage, interstrand cross-links, and DNA-protein cross-links. Base damage occurs most in thymine and least in guanine, and the yield of single-strand breaks is about 10 times the yield of double-strand breaks and cross-links. The ratio of the radiosensitivities of thymine in DNA is 1:2:6 when the DNA is in the form of free DNA, active chromatin, and condensed chromatin, respectively. This demonstrates protection of DNA by the proteins of the chromatin against lesions from diffusible water (hydroxyl) radicals. Oxidations of sugars in the DNA backbone and loss of whole nucleotides are the main mechanisms for formation of breaks in strands.

Biological stage. Various biological effects can result from the biological actions of ionizing radiation (**Fig. 2**). Reproductive death is most pronounced in mammalian cells that are actively dividing and in nondifferentiated tissue. Thus, dividing tissues (bone marrow and the germinal cells of the ovary and testis) are radiosensitive, and nondividing tissues (liver, kidney, brain, muscle, cartilage, and connective tissue) are radioresistant in animals exposed to whole-body radiation. Developing embryos are quite radiosensitive, as predicted by this principle. The radiosensitivity of organisms varies greatly, being related to their intrinsic sensitivity to radiobiological damage and to their ability to repair the damage. Radiation doses resulting in 10% survival range form 3 Gy (mouse and human cells), to 60 Gy (most bacteria and the fruit fly), to 130 Gy (cabbage looper), to 600 Gy (viruses), to greater than 1000 Gy (the bacterium *Deinococcus radiodurans*).

Single-break chromosome damage leads to chromosome aberrations in cells irradiated early in the cell cycle (before DNA synthesis has started) and to aberrations in chromatid aberrations in cells irradiated later in the cell cycle (after DNA synthesis). The

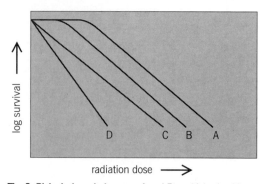

Fig. 3. Biological survival curves. A and B are biphasic with an initial shoulder period followed by exponential inactivation kinetics. C and D are exponential only.

yield of chromosome breaks increases twofold when oxygen is present during irradiation.

Progression through the cell cycle can be delayed, thereby delaying cell division. This effect is more pronounced in cells irradiated later in the cell cycle as compared to earlier in the cell cycle.

Cells lose their reproductive capacity when exposed to ionizing radiation. Mammalian cells are most resistant to this action during the late S phase of the cell cycle, and most sensitive during mitosis. *See* Mitosis.

Repair of biological damage involves repair of damage in the DNA. The kinetics of biological inactivation can be biphasic, with an initial ''shoulder'' period followed by exponential kinetics (**Fig. 3**, A and B), or exponential only (Fig. 3, C and D). Two types of biological repair are involved in the differences in the magnitude of the shoulder region and the slope of the exponential region: the shoulder region arises from the action of Q repair, which diminishes as dose increases, and the value of the exponential slope is affected by the action of P repair, which is not diminished as dose increases. Curves A and B in Fig. 3 exemplify conditions in which the biological system of curve A has a more active Q-repair system than that of curve B while both have the same amount of P repair. Alternatively, the final slope of a curve can be influenced by the intrinsic radiosensitivity of the biological system. Also, the initial shoulder period can result from the necessity that several critical targets must be inactivated before the biological system is inactivated, or several radiation-damaging events (hits) must occur within the same target in order for biological inactivation to occur (Fig. 3, A and B).

The three organ systems that generally contribute to the death of mammals following a single dose of whole-body irradiation are, in decreasing order of radiosensitivity, the hematopoietic system, the gastrointestinal system, and the cerebrovascular system. At very high doses (above 100 Gy), the survival time of the animal is short (from minutes to several days after exposure, depending on the dose), and death results from damage to the cerebrovascular system. At intermediate doses (between 10 and 100 Gy), survival is longer (between 3 and 4 days), and death occurs because of gastrointestinal damage. The longest duration between exposure and death (between 1 week and 1 month) follows radiation doses of 3 to 10 Gy, and arises from failure of the hematopoietic system.

Late somatic effects may take years or decades to appear and include genetic mutations transmitted to subsequent generations, tumor development and car-

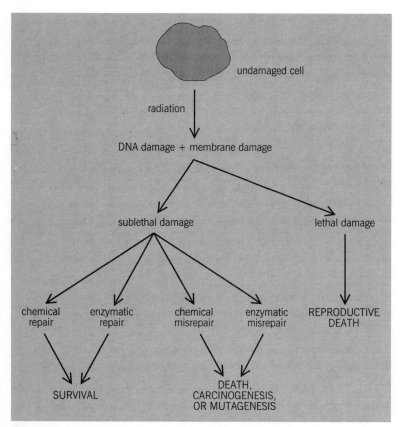

Fig. 2. Possible pathways for cellular response to ionizing radiation.

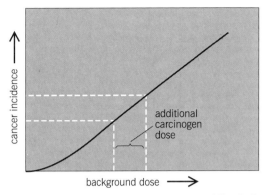

Fig. 4. Additive interaction of carcinogenic agents. (*After A. C. Upton, The question of thresholds for radiation and chemical carcinogenesis, Canc. Invest., 7(3):267–276, 1989***)**

cinogenesis, and shortening of life span. See Muta-gens and carcinogens.

An important and controversial issue concerning ionizing radiation is the question of the existence of a threshold dose, below which no biological effects occur. The most conservative model uses a linear equation to relate the incidence of biological effects with increasing dose. Use of a quadratic equation to describe the dose response predicts the presence of a threshold dose. Because radiation damage is cumulative, and this damage can interact with other chemical agents in causing biological effects such as carcinogenesis, the linear model is favored (**Fig. 4**).

Nonionizing Radiation

Of all the nonionizing radiations, only ultraviolet radiation, microwaves, and high-voltage electromagnetic radiation are considered in the study of radiation biology.

Ultraviolet radiation. This type of radiation is much less penetrating than ionizing radiation. Since it can penetrate only several layers of cells, the effects of ultraviolet (UV) radiation on humans are restricted to the skin and the eyes. Ultraviolet radiation is divided into UV-C (wavelength of 200–280 nanometers), UV-B (280–320 nm), and UV-A (320–400 nm). The most biologically damaging is UV-C, and the least damaging is UV-A, with UV-B having intermediate efficiency of biological action. The solar spectrum at the Earth's surface contains only the UV-B and UV-A radiations. Stratospheric ozone strongly absorbs UV-C radiation and the shorter wavelength portion of UV-B radiation, thus providing some biological protection. Depletion of the ozone layer caused by stratospheric pollution dramatically reduces this protective action, resulting in a decreased atmospheric absorption of UV-B radiation. See Air pollu-tion; Atmospheric ozone.

Biological effects can arise only when absorption of ultraviolet radiation occurs. Absorption is dependent on the chemical bonds of the material, and it is highly specific. Identification of the critical target for biological action has been facilitated by this specific absorption, using a comparison to the action spectrum, that is the relative efficiency for causing biological effects at different wavelengths. The action spectrum for ultraviolet radiation closely matches the absorption spectrum of nucleic acid, at wavelengths between 240 and 300 nm. At wavelengths greater than 320 nm, ultraviolet-mediated damage is oxygen-mediated, because of the interaction of dioxygen (O_2) with photoexcited biological chromophores, whereas below 300 nm, biological damage occurs principally by photochemical damage in DNA. Exposure dose for ultraviolet radiation is measured in units of joules per square meter; it is a measure of the incident energy per unit area impinging on the target material.

Biological responses. Sunburn is a form of erythema produced by overexposure to the UV-B portion of the solar spectrum (which is not transmitted through window glass). A rare but deadly form of skin cancer in humans, malignant melanoma, is induced by exposure to sunlight, with occurrences localized on those regions of the body that are most frequently exposed.

Ultraviolet light can also cause photochemical damage. Cyclobutane pyrimidine dimers are the main photoproduct following exposure to UV-C and UV-B, and they can lead to cell death and precarcinogenic lesions. Other types of dimers are considered to be especially mutagenic. DNA-protein cross-links that are observed after ultraviolet radiation can be lethal.

Repair systems. Survival from ultraviolet irradiation is reduced as the dose of radiation is increased. The shapes of survival curves are similar to those for lethality from ionizing radiation (Fig. 3); they are dependent on the presence or absence of repair systems. The four repair systems that enhance biological survival are discussed below.

Photoreactivation is an enzymatic repair system that enhances biological survival by splitting cyclobutane dimers in the DNA of cells that have been irradiated by ultraviolet light. The process requires light, and the most effective wavelengths are in the blue region of the visible spectrum. The repair system is error-free, and thus it is nonmutagenic. However, the repair must correct the damage before it is copied by DNA replication.

Another system is excision repair. A region of DNA containing bases that have been damaged by ultraviolet radiation is removed enzymatically, followed by synthesis of new DNA to replace the damaged region. There are no errors, and mutant cells that lack this repair system are highly sensitive to ultraviolet radiation. In fact, cells isolated from individuals with the genetic-recessive disease xeroderma pigmentosum lack excision repair. The clinical symptoms of this disease include a high incidence of skin lesions and early death from malignant melanoma. Excision repair operates in the dark. The damage must be corrected before DNA replication copies it. Not all regions of DNA are equally accessible to the action of this repair system, and it has been observed that actively transcribed regions of DNA in mammalian cells are more efficiently repaired than are nontranscribed regions.

Recombination repair is another repair system. DNA that contains damage is replicated, and gaps in the newly synthesized DNA appear opposite to the sites where there is damage in the parental strand. These gaps are filled in by recombining the portion of the undamaged complementary parental strand with the daughter strand containing the gaps. This repair system is essentially error-free; it is sometimes known as postreplicational repair, because it occurs after replication of the damaged region.

The system known as SOS repair is an inducible repair system. It is activated by a reactive intermediate of DNA metabolism in irradiated bacteria. SOS repair is associated with a complex of responsive genes known as *din* (damage-inducible) genes. SOS repair acts by inducing synthesis of an alternative excision repair system, and the recombination repair system, which increases survival. The alternative excision repair system involves removal of a longer segment of DNA containing the damaged region; it is error-prone, which leads to increased mutations. Another manifestation of the SOS response is the induction of DNA replication that can bypass the damaged template region of DNA. Thus this is not actually a repair system, since the original damage remains in the DNA, and can best be thought of as a system for tolerating DNA damage. Survival is increased, because DNA replication is not blocked by the presence of the damage.

Microwaves. Microwaves are electromagnetic radiation in the region from 30 MHz to 300 GHz. They originate from devices such as telecommunications equipment and microwave ovens. Metals reflect microwaves; glass transmits them; and aqueous material absorbs them, accompanied by a rise in temperature of the liquid. The 915- and 2450-MHz bands are used for industrial microwave heating and in microwave ovens. Thermal effects of microwaves occur at exposure rates greater than 10 mW/cm^2 (70 mW/in.^{2}), while nonthermal effects are associated with exposure rates less than 10 mW/cm^2.

Microwave radiation is absorbed unevenly in biological tissue because of the heterogeneity of the dielectric properties of the material. Thus, significant temperature gradients can be established, which may enhance the action of thermal heating from microwaves as compared to that from infrared radiation. Certainly, material with a high water content will have a higher absorption coefficient for microwaves, and thus a greater thermal response to microwave action. Microwave absorption is high in skin, muscle, and internal organs, and lower in bone and fat tissue.

Biological effects. Cultured mammalian cells exposed to microwaves at a high power density show chromosome abnormalities after 15 min of exposure. Progression through the cell cycle is also temporarily interrupted, which interrupts DNA synthesis. Chromosome aberrations in peripheral blood lymphocytes are significantly greater for persons who are occupationally exposed to microwaves.

Microwaves can be lethal when the power intensity and exposure time are sufficient to cause a rise in temperature that exceeds an organism's homeostatic capabilities; this occurs when the temperature rise exceeds approximately 5°C (9°F). For example, cataracts can result from exposure to ultraviolet radiation because the eye is not able to dissipate heat very well since there is not blood circulation. The testicles are at a temperature about 2°C (4°F) below that of body temperature, and spermatogenesis is particularly sensitive to temperature rise. Reversible testicular damage, in the form of reduced spermatogenesis and degeneration of the epithelial lining of the seminiferous tubules, therefore can occur from exposure to microwaves.

There are also some nonthermal effects associated with microwaves. There is significant uncertainty in the actual doses among people exposed as a result of their occupations; this reduces the reliability of the observations of the nonthermal actions of microwaves. However, a list of clinical symptoms includes increased fatigue, periodic or constant headaches, extreme irritability, decreased hearing acuity, and drowsiness during work. Laboratory studies involving exposure of animals to microwaves have produced changes in the electroencephalogram, blood–brain barrier, central nervous system, hematology, and behavior. Cell membrane permeability is also altered.

Exposure limits. It would be desirable to establish limits of exposure to microwaves based on the absorbed dose of microwave energy, similar to the gray unit that is used for ionizing radiation. However, the difficulty associated with measuring the absorbed dose makes this impractical. Therefore, radiation protection standards are based on exposure values instead of the previously used specific absorption rate (SAR, measured as W/kg); exposure dose is measured as W/cm^2. Occupational limits are set at a maximum of 1 mW/cm^2 (7 mW/in.^{2}) for frequencies between 30 and 100 MHz, and 10 mW/cm^2 (70 mW/in.^{2}) for frequencies between 1 and 300 GHz, averaged over a 6-min period. These values are selected to limit the specific absorption rate of the average whole body to 0.4 W/kg (0.2 W/lb), and they take into consideration the variable absorption for microwaves of different frequencies. The maximum acceptable limit for leakage from household microwave ovens is set at 1 mW/cm^2 (7 mW/in.^{2}) or less, measured at a distance of 5 cm (2 in.) from a new oven, and never more than 5 mW/cm^2 measured 5 cm (2 in.) from the oven, during its expected lifetime.

Extremely low-frequency electromagnetic fields. This type of radiation is generated by the electric and magnetic fields associated with high-voltage current in power transmission lines, and also some household and industrial electrical equipment. Biological effects from ELF radiation are the least understood, and the potential consequences are the most controversial. The issue of potential biological damage from this type of radiation has arisen only since the introduction of very high-voltage electric power transmission lines (440 kV and above) and the occurrence of widespread use of various electrical and electronic equipment.

Biological effects. Biological studies on ELF electromagnetic fields have been performed on cells and whole animals; and epidemiological studies have been carried out on populations exposed occupationally. The results share some common features that had not been expected: (1) There is not always a clear dose response; that is, increasing the exposure does not necessarily give rise to an increased biological effect, as is observed commonly for other types of radiation. (2) Some biological effects are seen only at certain frequencies and dose rates. Some of the reported effects are subjective, and may be related to normal physiological adaptation to environmental changes.

In cellular studies, membrane transport of calcium ions by chick brain cells was altered by exposure to ELF electric fields. Chromosome aberrations have not been observed in lymphocytes after long-term exposure to 60-Hz fields of 50 kV/m (15 kV/ft) and 10 gauss (10^{-3} tesla), suggesting that ELF fields whose strengths are less than these are unlikely to cause cancer or mutations; but this does not provide conclusive evidence that such radiation is noncarcinogenic. The major action of ELF electromagnetic radiation is targeted to the cell membrane, and most likely involves changes in membrane activity.

Controlled laboratory studies on developing chick embryos continuously exposed to 60-Hz electric fields up to strengths of 100 kV/m (30 kV/ft) show no effects on the general health, development, mortality, bone growth, malformations, and behavior for embryos that are hatched and followed for 6 weeks of growth. However, rats exposed to 60-Hz electric fields between 2 and 40 kV/m (0.6 and 12 kV/ft) for 21 days had reached nighttime peaks of pineal gland melatonin secretion.

In humans, qualitative biological effects of low-frequency radiation (0 to 300 Hz) include headaches, lethargy, and decreased sex drive. Humans have been noted to perceive the presence of a 60-Hz electric field when the intensity is in the range of 2 to 12 kV/m (0.6 to 3.6 kV/ft), and animals were observed to avoid entering an area where the electric field was greater than 4 kV/m (1.2 kV/ft).

Some epidemiological studies have shown a pattern of increased cancer (leukemias and brain tumors) among individuals occupationally exposed to increased ELF electromagnetic fields. However, the evidence is weak, because no dose dependency has been found; also the evidence is only associative and not of a cause-and-effect relational type. Some studies have reported no link between exposure to ELF fields and cancer.

Exposure limits. Because of the conflicting experimental results on the biological effects of ELF electromagnetic radiation, the guidelines are of an interim nature. Exposure to electric and magnetic fields gives rise to induced current in the human body. Clearly, exposure should be well below values that would lead to acute effects such as heart fibrillation and pain. Measurements show that a current density of 4 mA/m^2 (0.4 mA/ft^2) averaged over the head and trunk regions occurs when an individual is exposed to an electric field of 10 kV/cm (25 kV/in.), or a magnetic field of 500 G (50 milliteslas). The natural current densities in the body are about 10 mA/m^2 (0.9 mA/ft^2). The rationale for setting exposure limits to radiation from ELF electric and magnetic fields is to limit external exposure to no more than the endogenous values.

Studies on humans exposed to a 60-Hz magnetic field of 5 mT combined with a 60-Hz electric field of 20 kV/m (6 kV/ft) for 4 to 6 hours per day over several days revealed no effects on the health or welfare of the volunteer subjects.

The International Radiation Protection Agency (IRPA), in collaboration with the Environmental Health Division of the United Nations World Health Organization (WHO), has established exposure limits to ELF electric and magnetic fields, based upon available knowledge about the endogenous fields, and the biological effects of ELF electric and magnetic fields. Continuous exposure of the general public should not exceed 2 kV/m (0.6 kV/ft) for 50/60-Hz electric fields, and should not exceed 0.1 mT for 50/60-Hz magnetic fields, which includes a safety factor of 5 with regard to the maximum continuous field exposures allowed for industrial safety [10 kV/m (3 kV/ft) and 0.5 mT].

Phillip M. Achey

Bibliography. T. Alper, *Cellular Radiobiology*, 1979; Z. M. Bacq and P. Alexander, *Fundamentals of Radiobiology*, 2d ed., 1961; A. C. Giese, *Living with Our Sun's Ultraviolet Rays*, 1976; W. Harm, *Biological Effects of Ultraviolet Radiation*, 1980; IRPA/INIRC Committee Report, Interim guidelines on limits of exposure to 50/60 Hz electric and magnetic fields, *Health Phys.*, 58:113–122, 1990; D. E. Lea, *Actions of Radiations on Living Cells*, 2d ed., 1955; Special issue on radiation effects on man and animals, *Experientia*, 45:1–114, 1989.

Radiation damage to materials

Harmful changes in the properties of liquids, gases, and solids, caused by interaction with nuclear radiations.

The interaction of radiation with materials often leads to changes in the properties of the irradiated material. These changes are usually considered harmful. For example, a ductile metal may become brittle. However, sometimes the interaction may result in beneficial effects. For example, cross-linking may be induced in polymers by electron irradiation leading to a higher temperature stability than could be obtained otherwise.

Radiation damage is usually associated with materials of construction that must function in an environment of intense high-energy radiation from a nuclear reactor. Materials that are an integral part of the fuel element or cladding and nearby structural components are subject to such intense nuclear radiation that a decrease in the useful lifetime of these components can result.

Radiation damage will also be a factor in thermonuclear reactors. The deuterium-tritium (D-T) fusion in thermonuclear reactors will lead to the production of intense fluxes of 14-MeV neutrons that will cause damage per neutron of magnitude two to four times greater than damage done by 1–2 MeV neutrons in operating reactors. Charged particles from the plasma will be prevented from reaching the containment vessel by magnetic fields, but uncharged particles and neutrons will bombard the containment wall, leading to damage as well as sputtering of the container material surface which not only will cause degradation of the wall but can contaminate the plasma with consequent quenching.

Superconductors are also sensitive to neutron irradiation; hence the magnetic confinement of the plasma may be affected adversely. Damage to electrical insulators will be serious. Electronic components are extremely sensitive to even moderate radiation fields. Transistors malfunction because of defect trapping of charge carriers. Ferroelectrics such as $BaTiO_3$ fail because of induced isotropy; quartz oscillators change frequency and ultimately become amorphous. High-permeability magnetic materials deteriorate because of hardening; thermocouples lose calibration because of transmutation effects. In this latter case, innovations in Johnson noise thermometry promise freedom from radiation damage in the area of temperature measurement. Plastics used for electrical insulation rapidly deteriorate. Radiation damage is thus a challenge to reactor designers, materials engineers, and scientists to find the means to alleviate radiation damage or to develop more radiation-resistant materials.

Damage mechanisms. There are several mechanisms that function on an atomic and nuclear scale to produce radiation damage in a material if the radiation is sufficiently energetic, whether it be electrons, protons, neutrons, x-rays, fission fragments, or other charged particles.

Electronic excitation and ionization. This type of damage is most severe in liquids and organic compounds and appears in a variety of forms such as gassing, decomposition, viscosity changes, and polymerization in liquids. Rapid deterioration of the mechanical properties of plastics takes place either by softening or by embrittlement, while rubber suffers severe elasticity changes at low fluxes. Cross-linking, scission, free-radical formation, and polymerization are the most important reactions.

The alkali halides are also subject to this type of damage since ionization plays a role in causing displated atoms and darkening of transparent crystals due to the formation of color centers.

Transmutation. In an environment of neutrons, transmutation effects may be important. An extreme case is illustrated by reaction (1). The ^{6}Li isotope is

$$^6\text{Li} + n \rightarrow {}^4\text{He} + {}^3\text{H} + 4.8 \text{ MeV} \qquad (1)$$

approximately 7.5% abundant in natural lithium and has a thermal neutron cross section of 950 barns (1 barn = 1×10^{-24} cm^2). Hence, copious quantities of tritium and helium will be formed. (In addition, the kinetic energy of the reaction products creates many defects.) Lithium alloys or compounds are consequently subject to severe radiation damage. On the other hand, reaction (1) is crucial to success of thermonuclear reactors utilizing the D-T reaction since it regenerates the tritium consumed. The lithium or lithium-containing compounds might best be used in the liquid state.

Even materials that have a low cross section such as aluminum can show an appreciable accumulation of impurity atoms from transmutations. The capture cross section of ^{27}Al (100% abundant) is only 0.25 $\times$ 10^{-24} cm^2. Still reaction (2) will yield several percent

$$^{27}\text{Al} + n \rightarrow {}^{28}\text{Al}\xrightarrow{\beta^-}\xrightarrow{2.3 \text{ min}} {}^{28}\text{Si} \qquad (2)$$

of silicon after neutron exposures at fluences of 10^{23} n/cm^2.

The elements boron and europium have very large cross sections and are used in control rods. Damage to the rods is severe in boron-containing materials because of the ^{10}B(n,α) reaction. Europium decay products do not yield any gaseous elements. At high thermal fluences reaction (3) is most important in nickel-

$$^{58}\text{Ni} + n \rightarrow {}^{59}\text{Ni} + n \rightarrow {}^{56}\text{Fe} + \alpha \qquad (3)$$

containing materials. The reaction $(n,n') \rightarrow \alpha$ at 14 MeV takes place in most materials under consideration for structural use. Thus, transmutation effects often can be a problem of great importance.

Displaced atoms. This mechanism is the most important source of radiation damage in nuclear reactors outside the fuel element. It is a consequence of the ability of the energetic neutrons born in the fission process to knock atoms from their equilibrium position in their crystal lattice, displacing them many atomic distances away into interstitial positions and leaving behind vacant lattice sites. The interaction is between the neutron and the nucleus of the atom only, since the neutron carries no charge. The maximum kinetic energy ΔE that can be acquired by a displaced atom is given by Eq. (4), where M is mass of the

$$\Delta E = \frac{4Mm}{(M + m)^2} \cdot E_N \qquad (4)$$

primary knocked-on atom (PKA), m is the mass of the neutron, and E_N is the energy of the neutron.

The energy acquired by each PKA is often high enough to displace additional atoms from their equilibrium position; thus a cascade of vacancies and interstitial atoms is created in the wake of the PKA transit through the matrix material. Collision of the PKA and a neighbor atom takes place within a few atomic spacings or less because the charge on the PKA results in screened coulombic-type repulsive interactions. The original neutron, on the other hand, may travel centimeters between collisions. Thus regions of high disorder are dispersed along the path of the neutron. These disordered regions are created in the order of 10^{-12} s. The energy deposition is so intense in these regions that it may be visualized as a temporary thermal spike.

Not all of the energy transferred is available for displacing atoms. Inelastic energy losses (electronic excitation in metals and alloys, and excitation plus ionization in nonmetals) drain an appreciable fraction of the energy of the knocked-on atom even at low energies, particularly at the beginning of its flight through the matrix material. The greater the initial energy of the PKA, the greater is the inelastic energy loss; however, near the end of its range most of the interactions result in displacements. **Figure 1** is a schematic representation of the various mechanisms of radiation damage that take place in a solid.

A minimum energy is required to displace an atom from its equilibrium position. This energy ranges from 25 to 40 eV for a typical metal such as iron; the mass of the atom and its orientation in the crystal influence this value. When appropriate calculations are made to compensate for the excitation energy loss of the PKA and factor in the minimum energy for displacement, it is found that approximately 500 stable vacancy-interstitial pairs are formed, on the average, for a PKA in iron resulting from a 1-MeV neutron collision. By multiplying this value by the flux of neutrons [10^{14-15} n/(cm^2)(s)] times the exposure time [3×10^7 s/yr] one can easily calculate that in a few

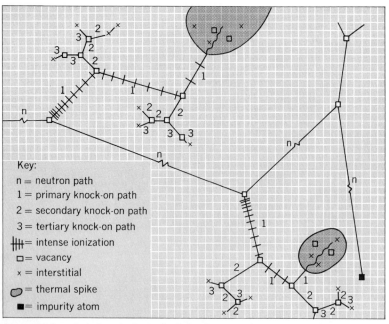

Key:

n = neutron path
1 = primary knock-on path
2 = secondary knock-on path
3 = tertiary knock-on path
||||= intense ionization
□ = vacancy
× = interstitial
⬭ = thermal spike
■ = impurity atom

Fig. 1. The five principal mechanisms of radiation damage are ionization, vacancies, interstitials, impurity atoms, and thermal spikes. Diagram shows how a neutron might give rise to each in copper. Grid-line intersections are equilibrium positions for atoms. (*After D. S. Billington, Nucleonics, 14:54–57, 1956*)

years each atom in the iron will have been displaced several times.

In the regions of high damage created by the PKA, most of the vacancies and interstitials will recombine. However, many of the interstitials, being more mobile than the vacancies, will escape and then may eventually be trapped at grain boundaries, impurity atom sites, or dislocations. Sometimes they will agglomerate to form platelets or interstitial dislocation loops. The vacancies left behind may also be trapped in a similar fashion, or they may agglomerate into clusters called voids.

Effect of fission fragments. The fission reaction in uranium or plutonium yielding the energetic neutrons that subsequently act as a source of radiation damage also creates two fission fragments that carry most of the energy released in the fission process. This energy, approximately 160 MeV, is shared by the two highly charged fragments. In the space of a few micrometers all of this energy is deposited, mostly in the form of heat, but a significant fraction goes into radiation damage of the surrounding fuel. The damage takes the form of swelling and distortion of the fuel. These effects may be so severe that the fuel element must be removed for reprocessing in advance of burn-up expectation, thus affecting the economy of reactor operation. However, fuel elements are meant to be ultimately replaced, so that in many respects the damage is not as serious a problem as damage to structural components of the permanent structure whose replacement would force an extended shutdown or even reconstruction of the reactor.

Damage in cladding. Swelling of the fuel cladding is a potentially severe problem in breeder reactor design. The spacing between fuel elements is minimized to obtain maximum heat transfer and optimum neutron efficiency, so that diminishing the space for heat transfer by swelling would lead to overheating of the fuel element, while increasing the spacing to allow for the swelling would result in lower efficiencies. A possible solution appears to be in the development of low-swelling alloys.

Damage in engineering materials. Most of the engineering properties of materials of interest for reactor design and construction are sensitive to defects in their crystal lattice. The properties of structural materials that are of most significance are yield strength and tensile strength, ductility, creep, hardness, dimensional stability, impact resistance, and thermal conductivity. Metals and alloys are chosen for their fabricability, ductility, reasonable strength at high temperatures, and ability to tolerate static and dynamic stress loads. Refractory oxides are chosen for high-temperature stability and for use as insulators. **Figure 2** shows relative sensitivity of various types of materials to radiation damage. Several factors that enter into susceptibility to radiation damage will be discussed.

Temperature of irradiation. Nuclear irradiations performed at low temperatures (4 K) result in the maximum retention of radiation-produced defects. As the temperature of irradiation is raised, many of the defects are mobile and some annihilation may take place at 0.3 to 0.55 of the absolute melting point T_m. The increased mobility, particularly of vacancies and vacancy agglomerates, may lead to acceleration of solid-state reactions, such as precipitation, short- and long-range ordering, and phase changes. These reactions may lead to undesirable property changes. In the

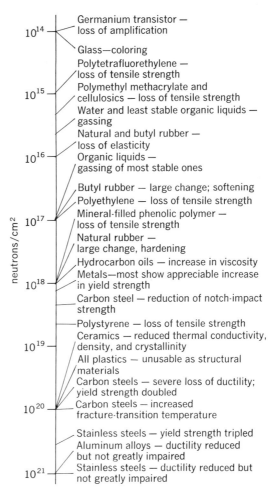

Fig. 2. Sensitivity of engineering materials to radiation. Levels are approximate and subject to variation. Changes are in most cases at least 10%. (*After O. Sisman and J. C. Wilson, Nucleonics, 14:58–65, 1956*)

absence of irradiation many alloys are metastable, but the diffusion rates are so low at this temperature that no significant reaction is observed. The excess vacancies above the equilibrium value of vacancies at a given temperature allow the reaction to proceed as though the temperature were higher. In a narrow temperature region vacancy-controlled diffusion reactions become temperature-independent. When the temperature of irradiation is above $0.55T_m$, most of the defects anneal quickly and the temperature-dependent vacancy concentration becomes overwhelmingly larger than the radiation-induced vacancy concentration. However, in this higher temperature region serious problems may arise from transmutation-produced helium. This gas tends to migrate to grain boundaries and leads to enhanced intergranular fracture, limiting the use of many conventional alloys.

Nuclear properties. Materials of construction with high nuclear-capture cross sections are to be avoided because each neutron that is captured in the structural components is lost for purposes of causing additional fissioning and breeding. The exception is in control rods as discussed earlier. Moderator materials, in particular, need to have low capture cross sections but high scattering cross sections. Low atomic weight is an important feature since moderation of fast neutrons to thermal energies is best done by those elements that maximize the slowing-down process. [See Eq.

(2).] Beryllium and graphite are excellent moderators and have been used extensively in elemental form. Both elements suffer radiation damage, and their use under high-stress conditions is to be avoided.

Fluence. The total integrated exposure to radiation (flux × time) is called fluence. It is most important in determining radiation damage. Rate effects (flux) do not appear to be significant. The threshold fluence for a specific property change induced by radiation is a function of the composition and microstructure. One of the most important examples is the appearance of voids in metals and alloys. This defect does not show up in the microstructure of irradiated metals or alloys until a fluence of 10^{19} n/cm^2 or greater has been achieved. Consequently, there was no way to anticipate its appearance and the pronounced effect in causing swelling in structural components of a reactor. This and other examples point to the importance of lifetime studies to establish the appearance or absence of any unexpected phenomenon during this time.

Lifetime studies in reactors are time-consuming and are virtually impossible if anticipated fluences far exceed the anticipated lifetime of operating test reactors. A technique to overcome this impasse is to use charged-particle accelerators to simulate reactor irradiation conditions. For example, nickel ions can be used to bombard nickel samples. The bombarding ions at 5 to 10 MeV then simulate primary knocked-on atoms directly and create high-density damage in the thickness of a few micrometers. Accelerators are capable of producing beam currents of several $\mu A/cm^2$; hence in time periods of a few hours to a few days ion bombardment is equivalent to years of neutron bombardment. Correlation experiments have established that the type of damage is similar to neutron damage. Moreover, helium can be injected to approximate n,α damage when these reactions do not occur in accelerator bombardments. However, careful experimentation is required to obtain correlation between results obtained on thin samples and thicker, more massive samples used in neutron studies.

Pretreatment and microstructure. Dislocations play a key role in determining the plastic flow properties of metals and alloys such as ductility, elongation, and creep. The yield, ultimate and impact strength properties, and hardness are also expressions of dislocation behavior. If a radiation-produced defect impedes the motion of a dislocation, strengthening and reduced ductility may result. On the other hand, during irradiation, point defects may enhance mobility by promoting dislocation climb over barriers by creating jogs in the dislocation so that it is free to move in a barrier-free area. Moreover, dislocations may act as trapping sites for interstitials and gas atoms, as well as nucleation sites for precipitate formation. Thus the number and disposition of dislocations in the metal alloy may strongly influence its behavior upon irradiation.

Heat treatment prior to irradiation determines the retention of both major alloying components and impurities in solid solution in metastable alloys. It also affects the number and disposition of dislocations. Thus heat treatment is an important variable in determining subsequent radiation behavior.

Impurities and minor alloying elements. The presence of small amounts of impurities may profoundly affect the behavior of engineering alloys in a radiation field. It has been observed that helium concentrations as low as 10^{-9} seriously reduce the high-temperature ductility of a stainless steel. Concentrations of helium greater than 10^{-3} may conceivably be introduced by the n,α reaction in the nickel component of the stainless steel or by boron contamination introduced inadvertently during alloy preparation. The boron also reacts with neutrons via the n,α reaction to produce helium. The addition of a small amount of Ti (0.2%) raises the temperature at which intergranular fracture takes place so that ductility is maintained at operating temperatures.

Small amounts of copper, phosphorus, and nitrogen have a strong influence on the increase in the ductile-brittle transition temperature of pressure vessel steels under irradiation. Normally these carbon steels exhibit brittle failure below room temperature. Under irradiation, with copper content above 0.08% the temperature at which the material fails in a brittle fashion increases. Therefore it is necessary to control the copper content as well as the phosphorus and nitrogen during the manufacture and heat treatment of these steels to keep the transition temperature at a suitably low level. A development of a similar nature has been observed in the swelling of type 316 stainless steel. It has been learned that carefully controlling the concentration of silicon and titanium in these alloys drastically reduces the void swelling. This is an important technical and economic contribution to the fast breeder reactor program.

Beneficial effects. Radiation, under carefully controlled conditions, can be used to alter the course of solid-state reactions that take place in a wide variety of solids. For example, it may be used to promote enhanced diffusion and nucleation, it can speed up both short- and long-range order-disorder reactions, initiate phase changes, stabilize high-temperature phases, induce magnetic property changes, retard diffusionless phase changes, cause re-solution of precipitate particles in some systems while speeding precipitation in other systems, cause lattice parameter changes, and speed up thermal decomposition of chemical compounds. The effect of radiation on these reactions and the other property changes caused by radiation are of great interest and value to research in solid-state physics and metallurgy.

Radiation damage is usually viewed as an unfortunate variable that adds a new dimension to the problem of reactor designers since it places severe restraints on the choice of materials that can be employed in design and construction. In addition, it places restraints on the ease of observation and manipulation because of the radioactivity involved. However, radiation damage is also a valuable research technique that permits materials scientists and engineers to introduce impurities and defects into a solid in a well-controlled fashion.

Douglas S. Billington

Bibliography. American Society for Testing and Materials (ASTM), *Effects of Radiation on Structural Materials*, STP 683, 1979; ASTM, *Irradiation Effects on the Microstructure on Properties of Metals*, STP 611, 1976; ASTM, *Properties of Reactor Structural Alloys After Neutron or Particle Irradiation*, STP 570, 1976; D. S. Billington and J. H. Crawford, Jr., *Radiation Damage in Solids*, 1961; E. E. Bloom et al., Austenitic stainless steels with improved resistance to radiation-induced swelling, *Scripta Met.*, 10:303, 1976; C. J. Borokowski and T. V.

Blalock, A new method of Johnson noise thermometry, *Rev. Sci. Inst.*, 45:151–162, 1974; G. J. Dienes (ed.), *Studies in Radiation Effects in Solids*, 4 vols., 1964–1975; International Atomic Energy Agency, Vienna, *Interaction of Radiation with Condensed Matter*, 2 vols., 1977, 1978; International Atomic Energy Agency, Vienna, *Radiation Damage in Reactor Materials*, 2 vols., 1969; J. F. Kircher and R. E. Bowman (eds.), *Effects of Radiation on Materials and Components*, 1964; C. Lehmann, *Interaction of Radiation with Solids and Elementary Defect Production*, 1977; N. L. Peterson and S. Harkness (eds.), *Radiation Damage in Metals*, 1976; L. E. Steel, *Neutron Irradiation Embrittlement of Reactor Pressure Vessel Steels*, Tech. Publ. 163, International Atomic Energy Agency, Vienna, 1975; Surface effects in controlled fusion, *J. Nucl. Mater.*, 53:1–357, 1974; V. S. Vavilov and N. A. Uklin (eds.), *Radiation Effects in Semiconductors and Semiconducting Devices*, 1977.

Radioactive fallout

The radioactive material which results from a nuclear explosion in the atmosphere. In particular the term radioactive fallout applies to the debris which is deposited on the ground, but common usage has extended its coverage to include airborne material as well.

Nuclear explosion. A nuclear explosion results when the fission of uranium-235 or plutonium-239 proceeds in a rapid and relatively uncontrolled way, as opposed to the controlled fission in a reactor. The energy release of an atomic (fission) bomb is usually expressed in terms of thousands of tons of TNT equivalent, and such explosions may have yields into the range of hundreds of kilotons. Still larger explosions can be produced by using the fission device as a trigger for a fusion reaction to produce a thermonuclear explosion. The yield of such thermonuclear devices can range up to hundreds of thousands of kilotons (hundreds of megatons).

The radioactivity from the explosion is produced by fission products and by activation products. The basic reaction in atomic fission is the splitting of an atom of the fissionable material (uranium or plutonium) into two lighter elements (fission products). These lighter elements are all unstable and emit beta and gamma radiation until they reach a stable state. During the fission reaction a number of neutrons are released, and they can interact with the surrounding materials of the device or of the environment to produce radioactive activation products. The fusion process does not produce fission products but does release neutrons which can add to the activation.

The fissioning of a single atom of uranium or plutonium yields almost 200 megaelectronvolts (MeV) instantaneously, and just over 1.8 oz (50 g) of fissionable material are required to produce a yield of 1 kiloton (5×10^{12} joules). The tremendous energy release produces the explosive shock and temperatures ranging upward from 1.8×10^6 °F (10^6 °C). The device itself and the material immediately surrounding it are vaporized into a fireball which then rises in the atmosphere. The altitude at which the fireball cools sufficiently to stabilize depends very much on the yield of the explosion. In general, an atomic explosion fire-

ball stabilizes as a cloud high in the troposphere, while a thermonuclear fireball tends to break through into the stratosphere and stabilize at altitudes above 16 km (10 mi).

As the fireball cools, the vaporized materials condense to fine particles. If the explosion has taken place high above the Earth, the only material present is that of the device itself, and the fine particulates are carried by the winds and distributed over a wide area before they descend to Earth. Bursts at or near the surface carry large amounts of inert material up with the fireball. A large fraction of the radioactive debris condenses out onto the large inert particles of soil and other material, and many small radioactive particulates attach themselves to the larger inert particles. The larger particles settle rapidly by gravity, and large percentages of the radioactivity may be deposited in a few hours near the site of the explosion. In contrast, the radioactivity from a thermonuclear explosion at high altitude takes months or years to reach the surface. It is also possible to test nuclear explosives deep in the earth. Such underground tests do not produce fallout as long as the explosion is completely contained, and they are not covered by the test ban treaty of 1962.

The first nuclear explosion took place in New Mexico in 1945 and was rapidly followed by the two bombings at Hiroshima and Nagasaki, Japan. Six nations have tested a large number of nuclear and thermonuclear weapons. The United States has tested at its sites in Nevada and the Pacific; the United Kingdom has tested in Australia and Christmas Island. The Soviet Union has several areas, including Novaya Zemlya in the Arctic. Atmospheric testing was heaviest in 1954, 1958, and 1961 and was stopped following negotiation of the test ban treaty. France and China did not sign the treaty, however, and have carried out a number of tests since, France in the Sahara and the South Pacific and China at an inland test site at Lop Nor. India has also carried out one underground test.

Radioactive products. The total fission yield for all tests has been about 200 megatons (10^{18} J), the total explosive yield being over 500 megatons (2.5×10^{18} J). The production of long-lived fission products has been about 20 megacuries (7×10^{17} Bq) of strontium-90 and 30 megacuries (1.1×10^{18} Bq) of cesium-137. **Figure 1** shows the time distribution for strontium-90 fallout in New York City, which may be considered typical of the Northern Hemisphere mid-latitudes. **Figure 2** shows the latitude distribution.

Local fallout. Local fallout is the deposition of large radioactive particles near the site of the explosion. It may present a hazard near the test site or in the case of nuclear warfare. The smaller particulates, which are spread more widely, constitute the worldwide fallout. The radioactivity comes from the isotopes (radionuclides) of perhaps 60 different elements formed in fission, plus a few others formed by activation and any unfissioned uranium or plutonium. Each of the radioactive isotopes produced in the fission process goes through three or four successive radioactive decays before becoming a stable nuclide. The radioactive half-lives of these various fission products range from fractions of a second to about 100 years. The overall beta and gamma radioactivity decays according to the -1.2 power of the activity at

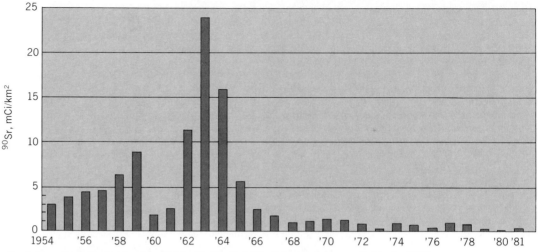

Fig. 1. Time distribution for strontium-90 fallout in New York City. Fallout levels were negligible after 1981.

any time. Thus decay is very rapid at first and then slows down as the short-lived isotopes disappear.

The hazard from local fallout is largely due to the external gamma radiation which a person would receive if this material were deposited near by; fallout shelters are designed to shield survivors of an explosion from this radiation. Actually, the effects of an explosion are so great that a shelter which would resist the shock would shield the occupants from fallout radiation.

In so-called clean nuclear weapons the ratio of explosive force to the amount of fission products produced is high. On this basis, small fission weapons are considered "dirty," although the absolute amount of fission products is much less than with a large clean bomb. It is also possible to increase the radioactivity produced, and thus the fallout, by surrounding the device with a material which is readily activated. Cobalt has been frequently mentioned in this connection.

Tropospheric and stratospheric fallout. As previously mentioned, the large particulates from a nuclear explosion are deposited fairly close to the site. The smaller particles are carried by the winds in the troposphere or stratosphere, generally in the direction of the prevailing westerlies. The debris in the tropo-

sphere circles the Earth in about 2 weeks, while material injected into the stratosphere may travel much faster. The horizontal distribution in the north-south direction is much slower, and it may take several months for radioactivity to cover the Northern Hemisphere, for example, following a test in the tropics. Transfer between the Northern and Southern hemispheres is slight in the troposphere but can take place in the stratosphere. Radioactive debris in the troposphere is brought down to the surface of the Earth mainly in precipitation, with perhaps 10–15% of the total amount brought down by dry deposition. Radioactive material remains about 30 days in the troposphere. The mechanism of transfer from the stratosphere to the troposphere is not fully understood, but it is obvious from measurements that the favored region for deposition is the mid-latitudes (30–50°) of the Northern and Southern hemispheres. Since most of the testing took place in the Northern Hemisphere, the deposition there was about three times as great as in the Southern Hemisphere.

Hazards. Once the fallout has actually been deposited, its fate depends largely on the chemical nature of the radionuclides involved. Since the level of gamma radiation from worldwide fallout is negligible, attention has been paid to those nuclides which might possibly present some hazard when they enter the biosphere. Plants, for example, may be contaminated directly by foliar deposition or indirectly by deposition on the soil that is followed by root uptake. Animals may be contaminated by eating the plants, and humans by eating plant or animal foods. The inhalation of radioactive material is not considered to be a signficant hazard as compared to ingestion.

Based on the various considerations mentioned, the three radionuclides of greatest interest are strontium-90, cesium-137, and iodine-131. Strontium-90 is a beta emitter which follows calcium metabolically and tends to deposit in the bone. The radiation emitted could result in bone cancer or leukemia if the levels were to become sufficiently high. Cesium-137 is distributed throughout soft tissues and emits both beta and gamma radiation. It is considered to be a possible genetic hazard but not as dangerous to the individual as strontium-90. Iodine-131 is relatively short-lived and probably is a hazard only as it appears in tropospheric fallout. It is readily absorbed by cows on pas-

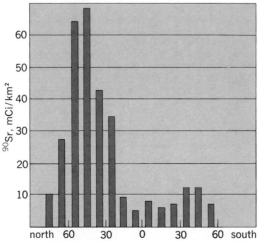

Fig. 2. Latitude distribution of cumulative strontium-90 deposit.

ture and is transferred rapidly to their milk. The iodine in milk in turn is concentrated in the human thyroid and presents a possible high radiation dose, particularly to children, who consume larger amounts of milk and who have smaller thyroids than adults.

Sampling. Radioactive fallout is monitored by many countries. The usual systems involve networks that collect samples of airborne dust, deposition, and milk and other foods. The levels of iodine-131 or cesium-137 can be checked in living individuals by external gamma counting. Strontium-90 on the other hand can be measured only in autopsy specimens of human bone. These national data are also combined and evaluated by the Scientific Committee on the Effects of Atomic Radiation of the United Nations. Their reports are issued at intervals and offer broad reviews and summaries of the available information on levels of fallout and on possible hazards.

The studies of radioactive fallout have also included sampling in the stratosphere by balloons and high-flying aircraft, as well as taking aircraft samples in the troposphere. Very elaborate monitoring systems have been set up, and these have provided considerable scientific information in addition to their original monitoring purposes. The major benefits have been the understanding of stratospheric transfer processes as significant to meteorology and information on the uptake and metabolism of various elements by plants, animals, and humans.

John H. Harley

Bibliography. M. Eisenbud, *Environmental Radioactivity,* 3d ed., 1987; P. L. Fradkin, *Fallout: An American Nuclear Tragedy,* 1989; International Atomic Energy Agency, *Environmental Contamination by Radioactive Materials*, 1969; U.S. Public Health Service, *Radiological Health Data and Reports*, monthly (through 1974).

Radioactive waste management

The treatment and containment of radioactive wastes. These wastes originate almost exclusively in the nuclear fuel cycle and in the nuclear weapons program. Their toxicity requires careful isolation from the biosphere. Their radioactivity is commonly measured in curies (Ci). The curies, chosen to approximate the activity of 1 gram of radium-226 (^{226}Ra), is equal to 3.7×10^{10} becquerels. The becquerel (Bq), the SI unit of activity (radioactive disintegration rate), is the activity of a radionuclide decaying at the rate of one spontaneous nuclear transition per second. Considering its toxicity, the curie is a rather large unit of activity. A more appropriate unit is the microcurie (1 μCi = 10^{-6} Ci), but the nanocurie (1 nCi = 10^{-9} Ci) and picocurie (1 pCi = 10^{-12} Ci) are also frequently used. A common unit of nuclear generating capacity is the gigawatt (electric) [GW(e)], equal to 10^9 watts of electric power, as opposed to thermal power.

Radioactive wastes are classified in four major categories: spent fuel elements and high-level waste (HLW), transuranic (TRU) waste, low-level waste (LLW), and uranium mill tailings. Minor waste categories, such as radioactive gases produced during reactor operation, radioactive emissions resulting from the burning of uranium-containing coal, or contaminated uranium mine water, will not be discussed.

Spent fuel elements arise when uranium is fissioned

in a reactor to generate energy. The fuel elements needed for the production of 1 GW(e)-year of electrical energy contain 40 metric tons (44 short tons) of uranium; the spent fuel contains 1 metric ton (2200 lb) of fission-product nuclides, and also transuranic nuclides such as plutonium and americium produced by neutron capture in uranium nuclei. Spent fuel elements arising in the civilian energy program will not be chemically reprocessed. In the United States, weapons-grade plutonium for nuclear explosives is produced in special reactors. In order to extract this plutonium, the spent fuel must be chemically reprocessed. The resulting high-level waste contains most of the fission products and transuranic elements, including residual plutonium. Transuranic waste, arising mainly during this reprocessing, is now defined as solid material contaminated to greater than 100 nCi/g (3.7×10^6 Bq/kg) with certain alpha-emitting radionuclides. (Prior to 1984, this limit had been set at 10 nCi/g.) Uranium mill tailings are the residues of the chemical extraction of uranium from the ore. Finally, low-level waste is a very broad category of wastes, covering almost every form of radioactive waste not falling into the other categories. **Figures 1** and **2** show a comparison of the radioactivity and the volume of the different waste categories, based on a 1989 Department of Energy projection, assuming no new nuclear plants to be ordered, leading to an installed civilian nuclear generating capacity of 102.5 GW(e) in the year 2000, and 51.6 GW(e) in 2020, as the plants reach the end of their lifetimes [1989: 97.5 GW(e)]. Considerably more radioactivity has been produced in the civilian nuclear energy program than in the weapons program. By the year 2020, the spent fuel is expected to consist of 75,000 metric tons (83,000 short tons) of uranium containing transuranic and fission-product nuclides.

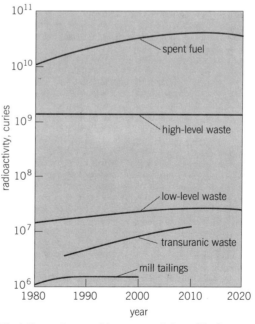

Fig. 1. Past and expected future accumulations of the four major waste categories: high-level waste and spent fuel, transuranic waste from the weapons program, low-level waste, and uranium mill tailings. The radioactivity in the mill tailings is the sum of the radioactivity of all uranium daughters. (*After U.S. Department of Energy, Spent Fuel and Radioactive Waste Inventories, Projections, and Characteristics, Rep. DOE/RW-0006, Rev. 5, Nov. 1989*)

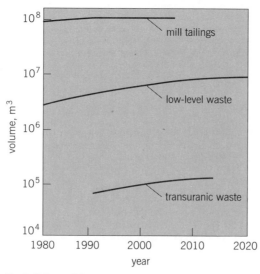

Fig. 2. Volume of the accumulated wastes shown in Fig. 1, except for that of the high-level waste and spent fuel, which is very small (less than 10,000 m³). 1 m³ = 35 ft³.

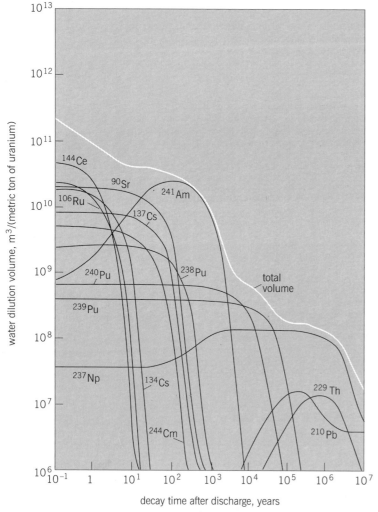

decay time after discharge, years

Fig. 3. Water dilution volume, as explained in the text, of spent fuel containing 1 metric ton (2200 lb) of uranium. The total amount of fuel needed to generate 1 GW(e)-year of electric energy is approximately 40 metric tons. The concentration of some of the transuranics increases for some time, as their parent nuclides decay. 1 m³ = 35 ft³. (*After Board on Radioactive Waste Management, National Research Council, A Study of the Isolation System for Geologic Disposal of Radioactive Wastes, National Academy Press, 1983*)

Since no practical methods exist to detoxify radioactive nuclides, protection against their harmful radiation must rely on their isolation from the biosphere until their radioactivity has decayed. Because each of the waste categories poses different problems, they will be discussed separately. The management of the radioactive wastes that arise during the dismantling of nuclear facilities will also be discussed.

Spent fuel and high-level waste. Most of the existing radioactivity is contained in this waste (Fig. 1). To identify and compare the major contributors to the radiotoxicity of the different nuclides, the water dilution volume is defined as the volume of water required to dilute these nuclides to acceptable concentrations, according to guidelines for occupational exposure, as specified by the International Commission of Radiological Protection (1979). The water dilution volumes for the most important isotopes contained in spent nuclear fuel are shown in **Fig. 3**. (For high-level wastes, a graph like Fig. 3 would be qualitatively similar, except for a reduced contribution by transuranics.) For the first 100 years, the toxicity is dominated by the beta- and gamma-emitting fission products [such as strontium-90 (^{90}Sr) and cesium-137 (^{137}Cs), with half-lives of approximately 30 years]; thereafter, the long-lived, alpha-emitting transuranium elements [for example, plutonium-239 (^{239}Pu), with a half-life of 24,000 years] and their radioactive decay daughters [for example, americium-241 (^{241}Am), with a half-life of 432 years, a daughter of plutonium-241 (^{241}Pu), with a half-life of 13 years] are important. Burial in geologic formations at a depth of 500–1000 m (1600–3200 ft) appears at present the most practical and attractive disposal method, although as of 1990 none of this waste had been disposed of in this way anywhere in the world. Most of the commercial spent fuel is stored in water-cooled basins at the reactor sites. Construction of some interim or emergency storage facilities aboveground for spent fuel has been considered. Such storage would further increase the risks of transportation accidents. The military reprocessed high-level waste is stored in tanks in liquid or solid form. Incorporation of high-level waste into glass blocks suitable for burial is expected to start in the United States in 1992. It is expected that by 2020 only 27% of the existing high-level waste, as measured by its radioactivity, will have been prepared in this form.

Geology as a predictive science is still in its infancy, and many of the parameters entering into model calculations of the long-term retention of the waste in geologic media are questionable. The major single problem is the heating of the waste and its surrounding rock by the radioactive decay heat. This heating can accelerate the penetration of groundwater into the repository, the dissolution of the waste, and its transport to the biosphere. Much effort has been devoted to the development of canisters to encapsulate the spent fuel elements or the glass blocks containing high-level waste, and of improved waste forms and overpacks that promise better resistance to attack by groundwater. The suitability of rock salt, which for 30 years had been widely considered the preferred host rock because of its superior heat dissipative properties and because of its plasticity (which would help to seal cracks), is now questioned because of several shortcomings. The major drawback is that rock salt is a natural resource with a large number of uses. It is impossible to assure that drilling into or through a salt formation housing a nuclear waste repository will never happen. The consequences of such drilling activities add so much to the complexity of predicting the safe containment of the nuclear waste that they seem to outweigh the geophysical advantages that salt might have over other rocks that are not natural resources and not water-soluble.

In the United States, the suitability of a disposal site in tuff, adjacent to the Nevada Nuclear Test Site (Yucca Mountain), has been studied. As planned, this repository could accept all the spent fuel elements, 70,000 metric tons (77,000 short tons), produced up to the year 2020 [used to generate approximately 2000 GW(e)-year of electrical energy]. If approved, the site would not be operational until 2003 at the earliest. *See Tuff*.

Transuranic waste. Although the radioactivity of the transuranic wastes is considerably smaller than that of high-level waste or spent fuel (Fig. 1), the high radiotoxicity and long lifetime of these wastes also require disposal in a geologic repository. Present plans call for disposal in bedded salt at the Waste Isolation Pilot Project (WIPP) in Carlsbad, New Mexico. Suitability for permanent disposal is being tested from 1990 to 1995. During its expected subsequent period of operation, until 2013, the WIPP would accept all transuranic wastes generated up to that time. Waste with less than 100 nCi/g (3.78 Bq/kg) of transuranic elements will be treated as low-level waste.

Uranium mill tailings. Uranium is naturally radioactive, decaying in a series of steps to stable lead. It is currently a rare element, averaging between 0.1 and 0.2% in the mined ore. At the mill, the rock is crushed to fine sand, and the uranium is chemically extracted. The residues, several hundred thousand cubic meters for the annual fuel requirements of a 1-GW(e) reactor, are discharged to the tailings pile (**Fig. 4**). The tailings contain the radioactive daughters of the uranium. The long-lived isotope thorium-230 (^{230}Th, half-life 80,000 years) decays into radium-226 (^{226}Ra, half-life 1600 years), which in turn decays to radon-222 (^{222}Rn, half-life 3.8 days). Radium and radon are known to cause cancer, the former by ingestion, the latter by inhalation. Radon is an inert gas and thus can diffuse out of the mill tailings pile and into the air. It has been estimated by the Environmental Protection Agency that a person living 500 m (1600 ft) away from an unprotected tailings

Fig. 4. Partial view of an operating mill tailings pile (Homestake Mining Company, Milan, New Mexico). The pile measures approximately 1000 m × 1000 m (3000 ft × 3000 ft), is 13 m (42 ft) high on average, and is entirely unprotected. In its 1.7 × 10^7 m^3 (6 × 10^8 ft^3), it contains 8000 Ci (2.9 × 10^{14} Bq) of ^{226}Ra. The extracted uranium was enough to generate 100 GW(e)-year of electric energy in a reactor.

pile containing 280 pCi/g (1 × 10^4 Bq/kg) of ^{226}Ra would have a 30% higher chance of lung cancer from the radon gas it produces than the average person. (The average radium concentration in the existing tailings piles is twice as high, and hence, for these piles, the estimate should be doubled.) Groundwater pollution by radium that has leached from the pile has also been observed around tailings piles, but its health effects are more difficult to estimate, since the migration in the groundwater is difficult to assess and also highly site-specific.

Although the radioactivity contained in the mill tailings is very small relative to that of the high-level waste and spent fuel, it is comparable to that of the transuranic waste (Fig. 1). It is mainly the dilution of the thorium and its daughters in the large volume of the mill tailings (Fig. 2) that reduces the health risks to individuals relative to those posed by the transuranium elements in the transuranic wastes. However, this advantage is offset by the great mobility of the chemically inert radon gas, which emanates into the atmosphere from the unprotected tailings. New mill tailings piles will be built with liners to protect the groundwater, and will be covered with earth and rock to reduce atmospheric release of the radon gas. None of these measures provides protection on the time scales required for the ^{230}Th to decay. Permanent disposal methods, like chemical extraction of the thorium for disposal in a geologic repository, or burial of the tailings in deep mines, are not planned at this time. Because of the enormous volume of the tailings, a permanent disposal—should this be considered necessary—would present serious technical as well as economic problems.

Low-level wastes. By definition, practically everything that does not belong to one of the three categories discussed above is considered low-level waste. This name is misleading because some wastes, though low in transuranic content, may contain very high beta and gamma activity. For example, ion-exchange resins or activated components from reactors, which have radioactivities of hundreds of curies per cubic meter, may even require biological shielding during handling and transport. Of the 130,000 m^3 (4.6 × 10^6 ft^3) of low-level waste generated in 1988, about 70% originated in the weapons program, 20% in the commercial nuclear fuel cycle, 7% in industry, and 3% for research and medical purposes. The radioactivity contained in the last category was very small, less than 1% of the total radioactivity contained in the low-level waste, and is also mostly short-lived. The radioactivity of the wastes generated for medical purposes alone was less than 0.1%.

The current method of low-level waste disposal is shallow-land burial, which is relatively inexpensive but provides less protection than a geologic repository. [Prior to 1970, a total of 10^5 Ci (3.7 × 10^{15} Bq) of low-level waste generated in the United States weapons program was also disposed of by ocean dumping and prior to 1983, 1.3 × 10^6 Ci (4.8 × 10^{16} Bq) was also injected with grout into hydrofractured shale formations underlying the Oak Ridge National Laboratory.] These practices have since been stopped. At present, there are six major Department of Energy shallow-land burial sites and six commercial sites (only three of which are now operating). While sites in arid environments have generally performed in an acceptable manner, those located in humid environments have commonly not performed as hoped, and the fact that three of the four commercial sites in the eastern United States are no longer operating illustrates the problems they have encountered. It also points to the difficulties to be expected in developing new regional low-level waste disposal sites, which are to be located in the humid northeastern United States, as required by law. Besides the very large volume, the nonuniformity of the waste presents formidable problems for low-level waste disposal. Current programs focus on improved waste forms, better site selection criteria, and engineering improvements to the site in order to restrict releases.

Decommissioning of nuclear facilities. At the end of their lifetime, nuclear facilities have to be dismantled (decommissioned) and the accumulated radioactivity disposed of. Nuclear power plants represent the most important category of nuclear facilities, containing the largest amounts of radioactive wastes, and will therefore be discussed here. These wastes can be grouped in three classes: neutron-activated wastes, surface-contaminated wastes, and miscellaneous wastes.

The neutron-activated wastes are mainly confined to the reactor pressure vessel and its internal components, which have been exposed to large neutron fluences during reactor operation. These components contain significant amounts of long-lived nontransuranic radioactive isotopes such as niobium-94 (^{94}Nb, an impurity in the stainless steel), which emits highly penetrating gamma rays and has a half-life of 20,000 years. These wastes are unacceptable for shallow-land disposal as low-level wastes. Disposal in a geologic repository is envisioned. Surface-contaminated and miscellaneous radioactive wastes derive mainly from faulty fuel pin claddings, which allow radioactive material to escape from the fuel. While the surface contamination can be effectively removed from smooth surfaces, such decontamination will inevitably increase the amount of the miscellaneous wastes (solvents, filters, and so forth). SEE DECONTAMINATION OF RADIOACTIVE MATERIALS.

Delaying the dismantling of the facility, in a procedure called safe storage or entombment, allows much of the radioactivity to decay. While this reduces the dismantling cost, it will shift the burden to future generations. For a decommissioning scenario assuming a 2-year wait after shutdown before dismantling and decontaminating the facility, the cumulative volume and radioactivity for the 68 reactors expected to be shut down between 1989 and 2020 has been estimated to be 8.4×10^5 m^3 (3.0×10^7 ft^3) and 3.3×10^7 Ci (1.2×10^{18} Bq), respectively. Of this volume, 0.6% will contain 97% of the radioactivity (mainly the neutron-activated reactor internals). The remainder, containing 1×10^6 Ci (3.7×10^{16} Bq), will be buried in shallow-land disposal sites, where it will constitute by the year 2020 approximately 10% of the accumulated volume and 3% of the accumulated radioactivity (Figs. 1 and 2).

Robert O. Pohl

Bibliography. R. E. Berlin, *Radioactive Waste Management*, 1989; Board on Radioactive Waste Management, National Research Council, *A Study of the Isolation System for Geologic Disposal of Radioactive Wastes*, 1983; B. W. Burton et al., *Overview Assessment of Nuclear Waste Management*, Los Alamos Sci. Lab. Rep. LA-9395-MS, August 1982; R. D. Lipschutz, *Radioactive Waste: Politics, Technology, and Risk*, 1980; A. G. Milnes, *Geology and Rad-*

waste, 1985; U.S. Department of Energy, *Spent Fuel and Radioactive Waste Inventories, Projections, and Characteristics*, Rep. DOE/RW-0006, Rev. 5, November 1989; U.S. Environmental Protection Agency, *Draft Environmental Impact Statement for Standards for the Control of By-product Materials from Uranium Ore Processing* (40 CFR 192), Rep. EPA 520/1-82-022, March 1983.

Radioecology

The study of the fate and effects of radioactive materials in the environment. As a hybrid field of scientific endeavor, it is founded upon, and derives its basic principles from, both of its parent disciplines, that is, basic ecology and radiation biology. Following the discovery of ionizing radiation and radioactive particles in biological studies in the 1940s and 1950s, these phenomena were studied under what were usually controlled laboratory conditions. Soon after, however, a need was demonstrated for a better understanding of the fate and effects of radioactive materials that were being released into the environment following the use or testing of nuclear weapons. This need became an important factor in the emergence of radioecology as a scientific discipline in its own right.

Radiation effects. Because of its early association with nuclear weaponry, radioecology was initially focused on radiation effects, usually under the umbrella of concern for survival under postnuclear attack conditions. Mortality induced by radiation exposure has usually been measured by using some form of lethal dose 50. However, the amount of radiation exposure required to produce mortality under free-living conditions in the field (ecological lethality) may often be substantially less than that required to cause physiological lethality when the organism is held under protected conditions in the laboratory. In the case of young bluebirds (*Sialia sialis*), for example, exposure to radiation levels as low as 800–900 roentgens (R) causes the stunting of wing feather growth, which would reduce the bird's ability to fly and escape predators. Therefore mortality in the field would result from these levels of exposure. When hand-raised and protected from predators in the laboratory, however, exposure to as much as 2500 R would be required to produce 50% mortality.

Similar considerations also apply to sublethal radiation effects, such as perturbations of growth rate, reproduction, and behavior. These responses to radiation stress have consequences for both the individual organism and for the population, community, or ecosystem of which it is a part. When populations or individuals of different species differ in their sensitivities to radiation stress, for example, the species composition of the entire biotic community may be altered as the more radiation-sensitive species are removed or reduced in abundance and are replaced in turn by more resistant species. Such changes have been documented by studies in which natural ecological systems, including grasslands, deserts, and forests, were exposed to varying levels of controlled gamma radiation stress **(Fig. 1)**. SEE POPULATION ECOLOGY.

Techniques of laboratory toxicology are also available for assessing the responses of free-living animals to exposure to low levels of radioactive contamination in natural environments. This approach uses sentinel animals, which are either tamed, imprinted on the in-

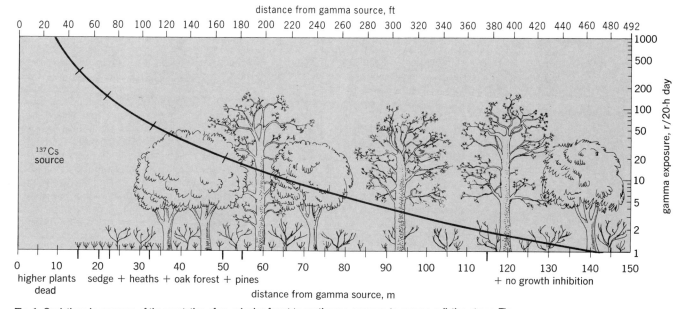

distance from gamma source, ft

gamma exposure, r/20-h day

^{137}Cs source

0   10   20   30   40   50   60   70   80   90   100   110   120   130   140   150

higher plants dead   sedge + heaths + oak forest + pines   + no growth inhibition

distance from gamma source, m

Fig. 1. Gradations in response of the vegetation of an oak-pine forest to continuous exposure to gamma radiation stress. The radiation source was located at the left side of the figure and, as indicated by the curve, exposure levels decreased from left to right with increasing distance from the source. (*After G. M. Woodwell, Radiation and the patterns of nature, Science, 156:461–470, 1967*)

vestigator, or equipped with miniature radio transmitters, to permit their periodic relocation and recapture as they forage freely in the food chains of contaminated habitats. When the animals are brought back to the laboratory, their level of radioisotope uptake can be determined and blood or tissue samples taken for analysis. In this way, even subtle changes in deoxyribonucleic acid (DNA) structure can be evaluated over time. These changes may be suggestive of genetic damage by radiation exposure.

In some cases, assessment of responses to radiation exposures have documented the phenomenon of hormesis, whereby an organism responds to very low-level exposures in the opposite way from which it would respond to higher levels of radiation stress. For example, while growth rates of plants and animals normally decline after high levels of radiation stress, exposure to low levels of radiation may actually result in a stimulation of growth. Moreover, the documentation of such effects may suggest that some physiological processes may be adapted to perform optimally under very low levels of background radiation exposure, such as are provided naturally from cosmic rays and natural sources of radioisotopes in certain rock and soil substrates.

Radionuclide tracers. Because of the ease with which they can be detected and quantified in living organisms and their tissues, radioactive materials are often used as tracers to study the rates and patterns by which biological processes take place under natural conditions. The use of such radioactive tracers in medicine is well known. In the same way, radioactive tracers can also be used to trace food chain pathways or determine the rates at which various processes take place in natural ecological systems (**Fig. 2**). Gamma-emitting isotopes are particularly useful in this regard, since their emissions from deep within the body of a plant or animal allow them to be detected and quantified by sensitive counting equipment without the need for sacrifice and dissection. Other uses of radioactive tracers include tagging adult animals in order

to later identify the particular eggs or young they produce, and using radioactive markers to later relocate and recapture animals that are too small to carry all but the tiniest of radio transmitters.

Although most of these tracer experiments were performed in the past by deliberately introducing a small amount of radioactive tracer into the organism or ecological system to be studied, they now take advantage of naturally tagged environments where trace amounts of various radioactive contaminants were inadvertently released from operating nuclear facilities

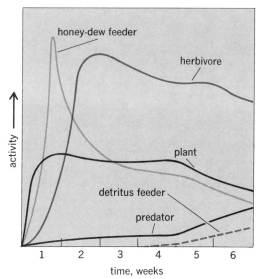

Fig. 2. Varying patterns of uptake of radioactivity by organisms occupying different trophic levels in an old-field ecosystem, following the introduction of radioactive tracers into the plants upon which their food web was based. Animals that suck plant juices and directly consume the vegetation acquired maximum activity levels earlier than did predators and detritus feeders. (*After R. G. Wiegert, E. P. Odum, and J. H. Schnell, Forb-arthropod food chains in a one-year experimental field, Ecology, 48:75–82, 1967*)

such as power or production reactors or waste burial grounds. As long as the amounts of such releases are less than the amounts that could be considered hazardous to health, such low-level contaminated habitats have actually become valuable research sites for conducting studies of functional processes associated with the native flora or fauna of the area.

Radioactive contamination. In some cases, the inadvertent release of radioactive materials into the environment creates concern for the health and well-being of humans and other organisms living in the area. An important component of radioecology, and one that is closely related to the study of radioactive tracers, is concerned with the assessment and prediction of the movement and concentration of these radioactive contaminants in the environment in general, and particularly in food chains that may lead to humans. Primary concern is, of course, focused on agricultural pathways through which radionuclides may enter the human food chain through crop plants or meat, milk, or other products of domestic livestock. Often overlooked, however, is the transfer of radioactive contaminants to humans who may consume fish or wild game as food. In many parts of the world, wild game animals such as deer have been found to have consistently higher concentrations of environmental radioactive contaminants than domestic livestock grazing fertilized pastures in the same region. This phenomenon is most noticeable in regions where natural vegetation has difficulty obtaining sufficient nutrients from the soil and must rely more heavily on "fallout" nutrients distributed by atmospheric processes. In high alpine regions and arctic tundra, for example, the concentration of radioactive contaminants in species such as reindeer may be particularly

severe, as was observed following the nuclear accident of April 1986, in Chernobyl in the Soviet Union. *See Food web.*

The Chernobyl accident was also important because it demonstrated the potential for global transport of radioactive contaminants by both physical forces, such as atmospheric circulation and meteorological factors, and biological vectors such as waterfowl, which might accumulate contaminants at the site of accidental release and then distribute them elsewhere along their migratory journeys. Studies of the migratory habits of these birds suggest that such biological transport of contaminants may not always follow the same patterns and rates as the distribution of contaminants by physical forces. This, in turn, emphasizes the importance of thoroughly understanding all aspects of the basic ecology and natural history of organisms involved in important issues of radioecological study and concern.

Studies in radioecology, when conducted under field conditions, often produce results that are either unexpected or may reverse the conventional wisdom derived from studies conducted under controlled laboratory conditions alone. An example of the latter is the failure of data from some radioecological field studies to support the popular notion of biomagnification, the systematic increase in levels of contaminant concentration in higher levels of food chains. Although some other environmental contaminants such as pesticides or heavy metals may behave in this fashion in natural food webs, such is certainly not always the case in situations documented for radioactive materials **(Fig. 3)**.

Finally, situations where the environmental behavior of radioactive contaminants fail to agree with the predictions of laboratory studies demonstrate how radioecological research can contribute new information about some of the ecological mechanisms responsible for contaminant uptake, cycling, and transport in a more general sense. This information can help to provide a better understanding of the environmental behavior of other forms of contaminants such as pesticides or heavy metals, which, in contrast to radionuclides, are more difficult to detect and measure under natural field conditions. *See Ecology; Environmental radioactivity; Environmental toxicology; Radiation biology.*

I. Lehr Brisbin, Jr.

Bibliography. M. Eisenbud, *Environmental Radioactivity,* 3d ed., 1987; M. Garcia-Leon and G. Madurga (eds.), *Low Level Measurements and Their Application to Environmental Radioactivity,* 1988; E. P. Odum, Feedback between radiation ecology and general ecology, *Health Physics,* vol. 11, 1985; V. Schultz and F. W. Whicker, *Radiological Techniques,* 1982; F. S. Sterrett (ed.), *Environmental Sciences,* 1987; F. W. Whicker and V. Schultz, *Radioecology: Nuclear Energy and the Environment,* 2 vols., 1982.

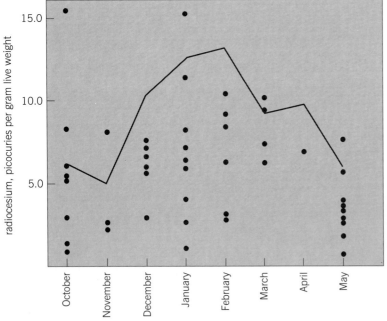

Fig. 3. Monthly changes in levels of radioactive contaminants accumulated by migratory waterfowl wintering on a nuclear-production-reactor cooling reservoir. Contamination levels shown by the strictly herbivorous American coot (*Fulica americana;* curve) nearly always exceeded those shown by other more omnivorous and carnivorous species (solid circles). (*After I. L. Brisbin, Jr., R. A. Geiger, and M. H. Smith, Accumulation and redistribution of radiocaesium by migratory waterfowl inhabiting a reactor cooling reservoir, in Environmental Behavior of Radionuclides Released in the Nuclear Industry, International Atomic Energy Agency, 1973*)

Rainforest

A term used loosely to indicate forests of broad-leaved (dicotyledonous), mainly evergreen trees found in continually moist climates in the tropics, subtropics, and some parts of the temperate zones. Sometimes the term is unjustifiably extended to include other very wet forests such as the Olympic Rain Forest of the state of Washington in which the trees are mostly conifers.

The tropical rainforest includes the vast Amazon forest as well as large areas in western and central Africa, Malaysia, Indonesia, and New Guinea. Estimates of the total world area of rainforest vary from 2 to 3.6×10^6 mi^2 (5.5 to 9.4×10^6 km^2). It is the home of an enormous number of plant and animal species. The trees are of various heights, up to about 150 ft (45 m) or in some places to over 200 ft (60 m), and are arranged in several ill-defined strata. The total biomass, including roots, is larger than in most temperate forests, and is in the range 130–260 tons/acre (48–95 metric tons/hectare), calculated as dry weight. As many as 200 different species of trees 1 ft or more in girth may be found in areas of 4 acres (1.6 hectares). Tropical rainforests, unlike temperate forests of beech or oak, are usually mixed in composition, with no one species forming a large proportion of the whole stand, but in some parts of the tropics there are rainforests dominated by a single species.

Certain structural features are characteristic of tropical rainforests, such as the thin, flangelike buttresses of the larger trees, and flowers and fruit that are produced, as in the cacao (*Theobroma cacao*), on the trunk (cauliflorous) instead of on the branches.

Orchids and other epiphytes and woody vines (lianes) are common. In a rainforest that has not been culled for timber or recently disturbed, the undergrowth is generally rather thin, and visibility is about 60 ft (18 m) or more on the ground (see **illus.**).

In the rainforest, animals of most groups, like plants, show great species diversity. For example, there are several times as many species of birds as in an equal area of North American broad-leaved forest. Insects are far more numerous than other animals, in terms of species and sheer numbers. Interactions between plants and animals are extremely complex, and many very specialized relationships have evolved, such as those between certain types of ants and the trees in whose hollow twigs they live. In the tropical rainforest an unusually large variety of organisms live together in a state of balance, so that it is one of the most stable as well as most complex ecosystems on Earth.

Climatic factors. In typical tropical rainforest climates, there is no winter or severe dry season, and consequently plants can grow and reproduce all year. Nevertheless, many plants are not equally active at all times, leaf production and flowering often taking place at intervals that may be shorter or longer than a year or may be irregular. The behavior of different species, different individuals of the same species, or even different branches of the same tree is often not well synchronized. Rainforest trees seldom show annual growth rings, which makes their age difficult or impossible to determine.

There is little restriction of rainforest animal life by cold or drought, and species that feed on plants can always find food. As a result, groups of animals have evolved, such as hummingbirds, sunbirds, and certain kinds of bats, that depend on flowers being available all year. Rainforest animals have less seasonal breeding habits than those of temperature climates; birds raise several broods every year, but fewer eggs are laid in each clutch.

In tropical regions with a marked dry season the

Tropical rainforest of Brunei (Borneo). Buttressing and cauliflory are characteristic. (*From P. S. Ashton, Ecological Studies on the Mixed Dipterocarp Forests of Brunei State, Oxford Forest. Mem. 25, Clarendon Press, 1964*)

rainforest is replaced by deciduous and semideciduous forests and savannas. In these a considerable proportion of the trees becomes wholly or partly bare of leaves for some part of the year. The transition from the humid rainforest to these deciduous-type trees is usually gradual, and no clear dividing lines can be drawn.

Distribution. The tropical rainforest occupies lowland areas where the annual rainfall is not less than about 80 in. (200 cm) and there are not more than three or four consecutive months with rainfall less than about 4 in. (10 cm). At higher elevations it gives way to montane rainforest, and with increasing latitude it gradually merges into subtropical and temperate rainforests. These other types of rainforest are different in composition, less rich in species, and usually less tall than the lowland forest; features such as buttressing and cauliflory, which are so characteristic of the latter, are absent or less well developed.

Productivity. Rainforest timbers are mostly very hard and are sometimes too dense to float in water. Many, such as the mahoganies (Meliaceae) of Africa and tropical America, provide woods valued for furniture making and veneers. Exploitation of the timber is often difficult because the economically valuable trees are scattered among large numbers of less useful species. In some rainforest localities, wood chip factories have been established so that the entire timber crop can be converted into wood pulp for papermaking, though eucalypts and tropical pines, which are faster-growing than rainforest species, are more suitable for this purpose.

Besides providing timber, rainforests are an increasingly important source of rattans, fibers, drugs, pesticides, and other useful products.

Estimates of the net organic productivity of tropical rainforests vary from about 6 to 10 tons/acre (2.2 to 3.7 metric tons/hectare) per year, which is not much greater than for some temperate forests. The luxuriant appearance of the vegetation is deceptive and does not necessarily indicate a fertile soil. The limited supply of available plant nutrients circulates rapidly between the plants and the superficial layers of the soil. So long as the forest is intact, very little of these nutrients is lost in the drainage water, but when the forest is felled, especially if the trees are subsequently burned, there is a heavy loss of soil fertility. SEE SOIL.

Primary and secondary communities. Rainforests that have never been cleared (virgin forests), or which have been undisturbed long enough to be almost indistinguishable from such forest, are called primary. At the present time these are being replaced by secondary vegetation of various kinds at an ever-increasing rate. Young secondary forests are not so tall as, but are more dense and tangled than, primary rainforests. They are composed mainly of fast-growing, short-lived, soft-wooded trees with fruits or seeds dispersed by wind or animals, enabling them to colonize natural or artificial clearings rapidly. SEE ECOLOGICAL SUCCESSION.

Exploitation. Large areas of tropical rainforest are being felled for lumber or for planting oil palm, rubber, pinetrees, and other industrial crops. More and more areas are also felled by native cultivators to grow manioc, rice, and other food crops under systems of shifting cultivation (slash-and-burn or swidden farming). After one or two harvests a new clearing is made, preferably in primary forest, and secondary forest is allowed to grow on the abandoned land. When the population pressure is heavy, this forest is often cleared again after too short an interval; the soil then deteriorates, especially if the vegetation is grazed and frequently burned. Under such conditions grasses such as *Imperata cylindrica* (alang-alang) invade the secondary forest, which eventually becomes replaced by grassland of little agricultural value, resembling the savannas of less humid climates. SEE SAVANNA.

Because of the rapidly increasing world demand for timber and pulpwood and the needs of fast-growing native populations for food, the tropical rainforest is disappearing rapidly.

The biomass of rainforests stores a substantial amount of carbon. After deforestation this carbon returns to the atmosphere as carbon dioxide (CO_2), contributing to the increase in atmospheric concentration of CO_2, which in turn leads to increased global warming as a result of the greenhouse effect. SEE CLIMATE MODIFICATION; GREENHOUSE EFFECT.

Conservation. Efforts to stop or slow the destruction of tropical rainforests are being made by national and international groups. There is increasing recognition of the importance of rainforests and the need for their conservation, leading to heightened public awareness and increasing public, political, and economic support for conservation efforts. SEE CONSERVATION OF RESOURCES; FOREST ECOSYSTEM.

Paul W. Richards

Bibliography. J. B. Hall and M. D. Swaine, *Distribution and Ecology of Vascular Plants in a Tropical Rain Forest*, 1981; S. Head and R. Heinzman (eds.), *Lessons of the Rainforest,* 1990; C. F. Jordan (ed.), *Amazonian Rain Forests*, 1986; E. G. Leigh, Jr., et al. (eds.), The Ecology of a Tropical Rain Forest, 1983; K. A. Longman, *Tropical Forest and Its Environment*, 2d ed., 1987; P. W. Richards, *The Tropical Rain Forest*, 1975; UNESCO/UNEP/FAO, *Tropical Forest Ecosystems*: *A State of Knowledge Report,* 1979; T. C. Whitmore, *Tropical Rain Forests of the Far East*, 2d ed., 1984.

Recycling technology

Methods for reducing solid waste by reusing discarded materials. Essentially, recycling is a three-part process that uses waste materials to make new products. The three integral phases involve the collection of recyclable materials, manufacture or reprocessing of recyclable materials into new products, and purchase of recycled-content products. Various techniques have been developed to recycle plastics, aluminum, steel cans, paper, and glass, and to convert municipal solid waste into fuel.

PLASTICS

A major barrier to recycling of plastics is lack of separation of plastic from the solid waste stream. Plastic discards represent an estimated 8% by weight and up to 18% by volume of the municipal solid waste generated in the United States. Most of the effort to recycle postconsumer plastic involves high-density polyethylene (HDPE) and polyethylene terephthalate (PET) resins. Plastic waste made of these two resins is more easily identified and separated from other plastic waste as a result of industry standardization of materials for soft drink bottles (polyethylene terephthalate), base cups from these soft drink bottles (high-density polyethylene), and milk bottles (high-density polyethylene).

Plastic available for recycling. Approximately half of plastic waste consists of single-use convenience packaging and containers. Many manufacturers prefer plastic for packaging because it is lightweight, resists breakage and environmental deterioration, and can be processed to suit specific needs. Once plastics are discarded, these attractive physical properties become detriments.

Six resins are used for most commodity plastic products: low-density polyethylene (LDPE), high-density polyethylene, polyethylene terephthalate, polyvinyl chloride (PVC), polypropylene (PP), and polystyrene (PS). These single-resin plastics are considered suitable for recycling because they become pliable when heated and can be remolded.

Plastics are also used with paper and metal as multicomponent films, mostly for packaging. They are more difficult to recycle than single-resin plastic material discards, and can be converted only to mixed-plastic products.

Recycled plastic products. Secondary materials are products recovered from the waste stream and reformulated into new physical forms serving end uses other than those of the original materials. A variety of secondary materials are produced from plastic waste. The outer plastic layer of disposable diapers has been recycled into garbage bags, flower pots, and plastic lumber. Polyethylene terephthalate is currently recycled into scouring pads, fiber fill for jackets, paint brushes, carpet fibers, and other products. Polyethylene terephthalate is also recycled to produce polyol for use in urethane foam and furniture, and unsaturated polyester for boat hulls, pools, auto body parts, and parts for appliances. High-density polyethylene is recycled into base cups for soft drink bottles, flower pots, toys, and pallets. Projects to recycle bottles made from polyvinyl chloride resins have focused on products such as bottles for shampoo and vegetable oil.

Recycling postconsumer polystyrene foam has been targeted in certain pilot projects by industry for reuse as coat hangers, building insulation, office accessories, trash receptacles, and flower pots. As much as 95% of clean preconsumer industrial plastic waste (plastic scrap from an industrial or manufacturing process) is recycled. Companies have also recycled unclean industrial plastic waste for use in inner layers, with virgin resins as outer layers, for products such as multilayer detergent bottles; however, the actual amount of unclean plastic industrial scrap that is recycled is unknown.

Research in recycling of plastics has expanded to include the development of lumber from a mix of all types of postconsumer plastic. Such a mix, commonly called commingled plastics, comprises various plastic resins, pigments, additives used in manufacturing, and nonplastic contaminants. Plastic lumber has a number of advantages over wood, such as resistance to rot, chemicals, water, and insects. Plastic lumber is being used for fence posts, poles, marine pilings and bulkheading, dock surfaces, park benches, landscape timbers, retaining walls, palettes, and parking space bumpers.

Methods and technologies. Postconsumer plastic may be collected in a curbside recycling program or at designated drop-off centers. There are a number of problems associated with the collection of plastic waste: its high volume can burden an existing collection program; the material does not crush easily; and plastics made from different resins may be mixed together.

To assist the public and laborers working in material recovery facilities with identifying different plastics, the Society of the Plastics Industry sponsors a voluntary coding system. The coding system consists of a triangular arrow stamp with a number in the center and letters underneath to identify the resin used in the container. The codes are as follows: 1, PET; 2, HDPE; 3, V (vinyl); 4, LDPE; 5, PP; 6, PS; and 7, other (including multilayer resins).

The collected plastic waste is usually separated manually from the waste stream, and often it is cleaned to remove adhesives or other contaminants. It is sorted further, based on different resins. Mechanical techniques to separate plastics are available, and they can be used to sort plastics based on unique physical or chemical properties. It is anticipated that more sophisticated methods under development will provide better systems for separating plastics made of different resins.

The technologies used to manufacture recycled plastic are virtually the same as those used to manufacture products from virgin plastic resins. The recycled products are melted; for some products, additives or virgin resins are used to improve the properties. The plastic is then extruded into specific products or pellets.

For secondary lumber-type materials made from mixed plastic waste, the technology generally used is known as Extruder Technology 1(ET/1). ET/1 has three main components: an extruder, a molding unit, and an extraction unit. The extruder consists of a short adiabatic screw rotating at a high angular velocity (number of revolutions per minute); it is used for melting the plastic at temperatures of 360–400°F (182–204°C). Plastic with higher melt temperatures, such as polyethylene terephthalate, become encapsulated within the melted plastic. The molding unit consists of linear molds mounted on a turret that rotates through a water cooling tank. The product shrinks within the mold during cooling, and is ejected from the mold by compressed air.

Engineering and environmental issues. A significant problem in plastic recycling is the presence of contaminants such as dirt, glass, metals, chemicals from previous usage, toxics from metallic-based pigments, and other nonplastic materials that are part of or have adhered to the plastic products. The U.S. Food and Drug Administration (FDA) has expressed concern over potential risks in using recycled plastic products in contact with food. Other constraints involve inconsistencies in the amount of different plastic resins in commingled plastic wastes used for recycling, and engineering aspects of recycled plastic products, such as lessened chemical and impact resistance, strength, and stiffness, and the need for additional chemicals to counteract other types of degradation for reprocessing. There may be limitations to the number of times a particular plastic product can be effectively recycled as compared to steel, glass, or aluminum, which can be recycled many times with no loss of their properties and virtually no contamination.

The long-term engineering properties of recycled products are still largely unknown. The many products made from recycled plastic include gimmick toys, penholders, and paper trays; these may appear in the waste stream in a short time.

The recycling of plastics creates a waste stream of its own—contaminated wastewater and air emissions. Many additives used in processing and manufacturing plastics, such as colorants, flame retardants, lubricants, and ultraviolet stabilizers, are toxic and may be present in the waste stream.

Water is commonly used as a coolant in the manufacture of recycled plastic products, and it may become contaminated with residues associated with recycled plastic. Recycled high-density polyethylene can produce odors during processing and severe smoke conditions from blowmolding. The reason may be incomplete cleaning and processing of the plastic resin. Virgin resins exhibit neither odor nor smoke.

Economic and social acceptability. A number of important economic issues must be resolved in order for plastic recycling to be successful. Collection for recycling is taking place on a small scale, compared to the amount of plastic waste being generated. Limited supplies of plastic discards are resulting in the recycling businesses operating at lower capacity, thus hampering profitability.

Markets for recycled single-resin plastics have had more success than mixed-plastic products. The reason may be that bottle return laws lead to better collection of single-resin polyethylene terephthalate beverage containers and to focusing by the plastics industry on recycling technologies for single-resin plastics. Marketing problems that arise with products made from commingled plastics include inconsistency in feedstock, lack of suitable engineering specifications, and unpredictable performance.

An important issue related to the marketability of recycled products is whether such products are, in fact, cheaper than the products they will be replacing. Plastic lumber, for example, is expensive compared to wooden lumber, concrete, and other materials for which it can be substituted. However, product lifetime must also be taken into consideration with the initial cost of a material; the average lifetime of plastic lumber and other products made from commingled plastics is undetermined. Other factors, such as plastic lumber's low maintenance costs, are also significant considerations.

For products made from commingled plastics, marketing problems due to a reduced esthetic appeal may arise: there is a lack of black and very dark colors, and impurities such as bits of paper or metal can be seen within the material.

A notable marketing advantage for recycled plastic products over items made from virgin plastics or other material is that they are appealing from an environmental standpoint to many consumers. Some in the industry argue, however, that this advantage is limited: consumers may not buy recycled products that are more costly than nonrecycled products.

Hopefully, recycling plastics will become a long-term endeavor. It is an essential part of a national waste prevention and waste reduction strategy. Recycling plastic that may otherwise be diverted to landfills, incinerators, or roadside litter is a positive step in reducing the waste stream and should be incorporated in all programs for solid-waste management. Research, engineering specifications, government regulations, and continued interest are necessary for future success of products made from recycled postconsumer plastic.

R. L. Swanson; Vincent T. Breslin; Marci L. Bortman

ALUMINUM

Aluminum recycling is practically as old as the commercial application of the metal itself. The recycling developed rapidly for two reasons: the metal was much more expensive than the traditional metals with which it competed, and remelting aluminum was relatively easy and required only about 5% of the energy it took to make the same amount of metal from ore. While the price of the metal has come down considerably, the energy issue is still valid. Furthermore, concerns about excessive litter caused by discarded cans, hazardous waste products, and lack of landfill space give impetus to the drive to increase recycling of all materials.

Some of the aluminum has passed through the molten phase several times, first as primary metal, then as production scrap, and then as secondary or customer scrap; this processing resulted in an estimated 550,000 metric tons (610,000 tons) of dross and, ultimately, 240,000 metric tons (260,000 tons) of lost metal. A sizable portion of the industry's research and development efforts is aimed at reduction of metal loss during processing in the molten phase (the so-called melt losses).

Dross is a mixture of oxides, contaminants, trapped metal, and gas that floats on top of the molten metal bath in the processing furnaces; it is skimmed off and usually shipped out for recovery of the metal components. Generation of dross has increased significantly, because expansion of recycling efforts has forced the processors to use the more challenging, more dross-generating scrap forms, such as oily machining chips, metal/polymer composites, and used beverage containers. Over the years a specialized industry dedicated to treatment of dross has evolved.

Methods. Aluminum recycling efforts started almost immediately after the invention of the primary metal production process by C. M. Hall and P. L. Heroult in 1888. The rapidly growing primary industry needed an efficient remelting technology for scrap, and in the early 1920s the reverberatory or open-hearth furnace was developed. It consists of a single chamber with a relatively shallow hearth, a large door, and usually a set of two burners firing in a special pattern to maximize initially the convective heat transfer to the pile of cold scrap, pushed in place through the door by way of mobile charging machines. In the later stages of the melting process, radiation becomes the predominant mode of heat transfer. The continued popularity of this type of stationary furnace is due to its simplicity, made possible by the application of the submerged, resealable tap hole. The furnace is designed to handle mostly bulky scrap forms with a high volume–to–surface area ratio, typically the heavy-gage processing scrap generated by the primary producers. With the exception of some baling of lighter-gage scrap forms and scalping chips (produced by smoothing the cast ingots), no special scrap preparation steps are performed.

When the melting is completed, the molten metal bath is skimmed off (to remove dross), gently stirred (to equalize the temperature), and transferred to a holding furnace where the quality of the metal is brought up to specifications prior to casting. Historically, the melting of dirty, low-grade scrap and the reclamation of dross were relegated to secondary processors, which typically use rotary salt furnaces and perform no scrap preparation steps. The rotary salt furnace is essentially a short rotary kiln, gas- or oil-fired from one end with the flue located on the other end. Salt (sodium chloride or a mixture of 50–65% sodium chloride and 50–35% potassium chloride) is charged with the scrap or dross and heated simultaneously. When the mixture starts to melt, there is formed a viscous mass in which the molten metal coalesces are migrates to the lower portion of the fluid bath. The motion created by the rotating drum enhances heat transfer as well as coalescence of the smaller, isolated metal droplets in the salt–oxide mixture.

The metal is tapped through a resealable hole in the drum wall, or through the charged opening by tilting the furnace and decanting first the metal and then the salt cake. The metal is either poured into hot metal crucibles and transported to its final destination or cast in sow molds as remelt scrap ingot. The salt cake, which contains up to 10% aluminum that is difficult to recover, is usually discarded, although environmental concerns are encouraging salt cake treatment for salt recycling and generation of an inert by-product.

Modern recycling started in the early 1960s, when the traditional distribution of roles between primary and secondary industry began to shift. The primary industries started to buy what was considered typical secondary material, namely discarded consumer products (old scrap). The result is that the primary industry recycles more old scrap than the secondary industry. However, there are strong interdependent relationships between primary and secondary producers, the latter often delivering molten metal of acceptable chemical composition ''just in time,'' which requires reliable advanced equipment and control instrumentation.

The second consequence was that more and more scrap went back into the product stream from which it originated, for example, cans into can sheet and pans into cooking utensils, because that is the logical destination for well-segregated, well-prepared scrap. From a simple reuse of metal in a degraded form, the process evolved into a true recycling of metal into its own product. This closed-loop recycling requires strict quality and process control from scrap preparation to postmelt cleaning.

Can recycling technology. **Figure 1** depicts the can manufacturing process for an integrated, state-of-the-art plant for recycling used beverage cans. It demonstrates the close-loop nature of the process and the level of sophistication required for including scrap forms that are badly contaminated in such a high-quality product loop.

Used beverage containers are received from the collection centers as bales of approximately 1.5 m^3 (53 ft^3) and 40 kg (880 lb; the average density is 270 kg/m^3 or 17 lb/ft^3, the lowest density that will allow filling a closed railroad car to capacity. Alternatively, the containers are received as briquettes of a maximum density of 500 kg/m^3 (35 lb/ft^3), which can be stacked on skids (offering storage advantages to the supplier, but some hardship on the equipment of the receiver). In the shredding operation, bales and briquettes are broken apart, and the cans are shredded to ensure that no trapped liquid or extraneous material reaches the melting furnaces and causes damage or

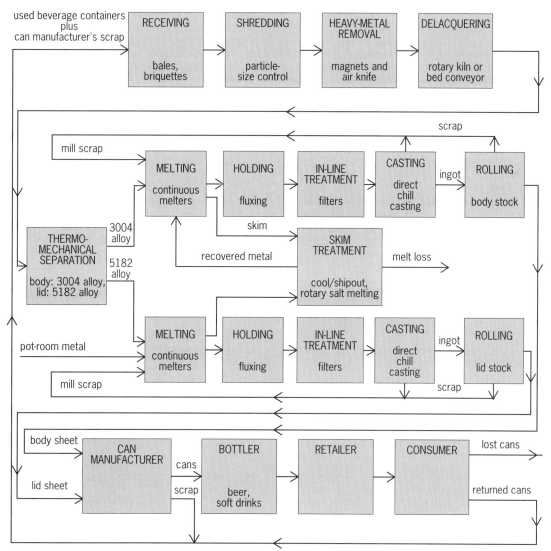

Fig. 1. Flow diagram of closed-loop can manufacturing and recycling.

injuries from molten metal explosion. From the shredder the material passes over a magnetic separator to remove ferrous contaminants and over a set of screens to remove the dirt; and then it passes through an air knife in which the heavy nonferrous and nonmagnetic materials, such as lead, zinc, and stainless steel scrap, drop out while the shredded cans pass on to the delacquering units.

There are two basic thermal delacquering methods. One is based on a relatively long exposure time at a safe temperature, and the other is based on staged temperature increases to just below melting for as short an exposure time as possible. The first method uses a pan conveyor on which a bed of used beverage containers approximately 20 cm (8 in.) deep moves through a chamber held at about 520°C (968°F), with gases that are produced by combustion being diluted with air to provide the proper atmosphere as well as temperature for the delacquering process (part pyrolysis, part combustion). The second method uses a rotary kiln with a sophisticated recirculating system at various entry points for the gases produced by combustion. The temperature in the last stage is near 615°C (1140°F), very close to the temperature at which incipient melting occurs in 5XXX series alloys, the 3–4% magnesium-containing alloys used for the can lids.

The hot, delacquered used beverage containers may then move into the thermomechanical separation chamber, held at a specific temperature and neutral atmosphere, in which a gentle mechanical action breaks up the 5182 alloy lids into small fragments along grain boundaries weakened by the onset of incipient melting. An integrated screening action removes the fragments as soon as they can pass the screen to avoid overfragmentation. This process requires a very narrow operating control capability to avoid melting of entire 5182 alloy particles, which would then cluster with the still-solid 3004 alloy particles from the can body. The screened-out particles of 5182 alloy are transported to the lid stock melters, and the large particles of 3004 alloy continue directly into the body stock melting furnaces.

Continuous melting concept. It is undesirable for low-density scrap to be exposed to the corrosive furnace atmosphere; thus, either the scrap has to be submerged quickly in a heel of superheated molten metal inside the furnace, or molten metal has to be taken out of the furnace for external mixing with the scrap.

The advantage of the latter option is that the inevitable dross (fortunately in much smaller amounts) can be captured outside the furnace as well. The resulting metal stream, cooled down but still molten, can be returned to the furnace for reheating by means of a molten metal pump. In this manner a steady-state condition can be maintained if the heat required for melting a constant mass flow of scrap particles (plus makeup for heat losses) is equal to the net heat input into the furnace.

The key to successful operation of a continuous melt facility is the charge system. The hot delacquered cans need to arrive just in time at a predetermined rate—for example, 10 metric tons (11 tons) per hour—and be submerged in the superheated molten metal stream. Several vortex-inducing methods have been developed to achieve the high rates of ingestion to match the large thermal potential of the more efficient, modern systems. In principle, the circulating molten metal stream is forced to enter a bowl-shaped charge bay tangentially and leave through a duct in the center of the bottom so that the otherwise floating scrap particles are dragged down and submerged in the swirl that is created (**Fig. 2**).

The particles melt in the turbulent stream before it enters the next confined area, the skim bay, where the dross floats to the surface, while the clean molten metal returns through an underpass to the furnace for reheating. Continuous overflow or periodic tapping of limited amounts of metal keeps the metal level at or near optimum for the process.

Continuous dross treatment. Dross floats on molten metal because a considerable amount of gas is trapped in the product. The proportions of gas, metal, and oxide depend on the alloy, the atmosphere, and the mass-flow conditions during the formation. In the case of continuous melting of used beverage containers, the apparent density of freshly formed dross is usually less than 1.3 g/cm^3 (0.75 oz/in.^{3}), while the density of the molten alloy is about 2.3 g/cm^3 (1.3 oz/in.^{3}).

Advantage was taken of this density ratio by designing an in-line continuous dross treatment process in which the dross is continuously manipulated mechanically in a confined zone at the metal bath level. The newly formed dross coming from the charged bay and floating up into the treatment zone constantly lifts the treated, dry, sandlike material to the exit (Fig. 2).

The treatment is based on the principle that a cer-

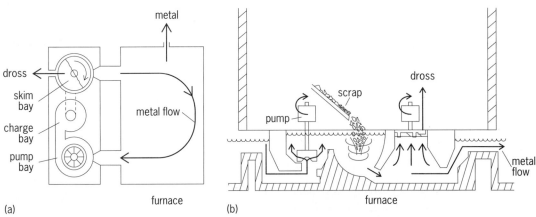

Fig. 2. Diagram of the operation of the advanced continuous scrap melting system. (*a*) Plan view. (*b*) Side view.

tain shear force will tear oxide skins of approximately the same strength simultaneously, so that small neighboring metal droplets can coalesce at the surface of mechanically driven manipulating blades. The blades move the dross mass gradually to the periphery of the cylindrical treatment bay, where the blades have a higher linear velocity and thus increased shear forces. The combined rotary and upward movements result in a steady-state treatment condition, which yields about half of the metal (trapped in the original dross) by letting it rejoin the metal stream, while the metal confined in the fine particles exiting the unit can be recovered in part by conventional salt melting. The 50% direct recovery makes this process economically attractive.

Secondary dross treatment. Traditionally, the primary industry left the metal recovery and disposal of the dross treatment by-product (salt cake) to secondary processors, but environmental considerations have encouraged an industry-wide review of the practices that affect dross formation, handling, and treatment. Essentially, there are two basic approaches for solving the problems associated with hazards in waste streams. The first one eliminates the use of salt in the dross treatment process and instead applies plasma technology using inert gases to achieve high recovery of metals and minimal formation of oxides and other reaction products in essentially the same rotary furnaces that are used for salt-based dross treatment. The process claims a 90% recovery of available metal and a by-product that can be converted into a value-added product by means of a calcining step. The economics of this process have not been entirely elucidated.

The other approach continues the use of salt to promote coalescene of metal droplets in the dross treatment step and adds a treatment process to recover salt from the salt cake. This process consists of a series of crushing and screening steps followed by leaching, filtering, drying, and crystallizing. An evaluation of this process found that with proper material preparation and careful process control, (1) an essentially inert by-product can be obtained, (2) sufficiently improved metal recovery can be achieved through increased salt use in the furnace, and (3) the process is not competitive with landfill costs unless a productive use of the by-product is included.

Both processes will most likely not be economically attractive until landfill costs rise significantly above the levels that obtained in the early 1990s, especially if the metal values left in the dross by the primary producers are reduced as a consequence of improved melting and skimming practices.

Jan H. L. van Linden

STEEL CANS

Steel can recycling involves the collecting, processing, and remelting of steel can scrap in the production of new steel. Steel cans are used as food, beverage, paint, and aerosol containers, as well as other common household containers. Steel beverage cans are often called bimetal cans because of the aluminum lid. Steel food cans are sometimes called tin cans because many of them have a thin coating of tin. Lids and closures found on many nonmetal containers are also made of steel and are generally included in the definition of steel cans.

Need for recycling. Old steel is a necessary ingredient in the production of new steel. This old steel, scrap, is taken from three sources: home scrap, derived from the production of steel; prompt scrap, derived from the manufacture of steel products; and obsolete scrap, derived from steel products that have come to the end of their useful life. Advances in technology have enabled the steel industry to reduce the amount of home scrap and prompt scrap generated. This fact, coupled with the development and use of furnaces that consume greater amounts of steel scrap, has created a demand within the steel industry for more steel scrap.

Available in great supply, steel cans are a resource in the obsolete scrap mix. More than 90% of all metal food containers sold in the United States are made of steel. Millions of steel cans are used by Americans on a daily basis. Despite differences in size, shape, or purpose, all steel cans are easy to process for recycling.

Collection methods. A variety of methods are used to remove steel cans from the solid waste stream, including curbside, drop-off, multimaterial buyback, and commercial/institutional recycling programs. These programs involve the collection and transportation of recyclable materials from consumers to a facility that prepares the materials for reuse.

Curbside recycling programs permit the recycling of steel cans from the home. Residents place selected recyclable material at the curbside on specified days. This material is then collected and delivered to an intermediate processing facility.

Drop-off programs may be used to supplement curbside recycling or may be implemented in areas where curbside recycling is not feasible. Residents in communities with established drop-off programs transport specified recyclable material to a collection site. The collected materials are then delivered to a material recovery facility or to their appropriate end markets. Multimaterial buyback centers, which purchase a variety of recyclable materials directly from consumers, operate in much the same manner.

A large number of restaurants, hotels, and other service-oriented businesses, as well as institutions like hospitals, schools, and military bases, participate in commercial/institutional recycling programs. When they have food service facilities, a great volume of steel food cans is used. Most of the food cans are the larger, one-gallon (454-gram) cans. Because of the sheer number of steel cans, the cans are flattened for efficient storage and easy transportation. The facility usually makes arrangements with a local waste hauler or an independent recycler to have the cans picked up or delivered.

Another means of collecting steel cans is through resource recovery facilities. Unlike the previous four recycling programs, resource recovery facilities require no effort by the users to separate or transport their recyclable materials. Refuse trucks deliver municipal waste to the facility, where steel cans and other steel scrap will be magnetically removed from the municipal solid-waste stream.

Intermediate markets. Intermediate markets (also referred to as material recovery facilities) prepare steel cans and other recyclable materials for transportation to appropriate end markets for subsequent reuse. After the recyclables have been collected from various programs, they are taken to a material recovery facility. There they are loaded onto a conveyor system and are sorted either mechanically or manually. Typically, magnetic sorting equipment is used for cost-effective removal of the steel cans from the other materials. The other materials can then be removed either by hand-picking them off the conveyor belt or by utilizing sophisticated mechanical separation equipment. Once all the materials have been sorted, they are processed according to end-market specifications. Steel cans may be baled, flattened, shredded, or shipped loose, depending on end-market specifications.

Ferrous scrap yards are another intermediate market option for steel cans. Scrap dealers have always recycled a wide array of materials, including steel scrap. Many are now handling retail and wholesale quantities of steel cans received from the sources discussed above. The dealers prepare the steel cans according to end-market specifications, then ship them by truck or rail to end markets.

End markets. End markets, which purchase recyclable material for the production of new material, play a crucial part in the recycling process. Well established for decades, the steel can end markets include iron and steel foundries, detinning companies, and steel mills. Foundries provide essential fabrication of cast and molded parts for industrial and consumer use. Steel can scrap may be part of the 30–40% scrap mix that is used along with the self-generated foundry scrap to produce various iron products. There are more than 2000 iron and steel foundries that could potentially serve as end markets in the United States; several are already doing so.

Detinning companies shred the steel cans, then immerse them in detinning solution, where an electrolytic or chemical process removes the tin from the steel. The recovered steel is sold to steel mills for recycling, and the tin is sold to appropriate end markets. Detinning companies may also act as high-volume processors of steel can scrap by baling or shredding steel cans, then shipping them to steel mills.

Steel mills are the largest consumers of steel scrap. Since the early 1940s, more than 50% of all the steel produced in the United States has been recycled. In recent decades, more than 10^{11} lb (45×10^9 kg) of steel have been recycled by the steel industry annually; the current overall recycling rate is 66%.

Recycled steel and steelmaking. Steel recycling is an integral part of the steelmaking process (**Fig. 3**). The two main types of furnaces employed by domestic steel mills require steel scrap to produce new steel. The basic oxygen furnace uses approximately 25% steel scrap and 75% molten iron created in a blast furnace from iron ore, coke, and limestone. This steelmaking process produces flat-rolled steel, used to make cans, appliances, cars, and other products.

The electric arc furnace, which represents about 40% of the production of steel in the United States, consumes virtually 100% steel scrap in making new steel. It is used to make heavy steel products, such as structural beams, plates, bars, and reinforcing bars.

Because steel cans are remelted in steelmaking furnaces, they can be recycled into a great variety of products. Steel cans may be recycled into steel pipe, refrigerators, or even cars. When that steel product reaches the end of its useful existence, it may be recycled as well. There is no limit to the number of times that steel may be recycled.

Environmental benefits. By recycling steel cans, a number of natural resources are saved for future generations. For example, recycling 1 ton (0.9 metric ton) of steel scrap saves 2500 lb (1100 kg) of iron ore, 1000 lb (450 kg) of coal, and 40 lb (18 kg) of limestone. For every pound of steel recycled, enough energy is conserved to keep a 60-W bulb lit for over 26 h. By diverting steel cans from the solid-waste stream, valuable landfill space is saved.

Steel Can Recycling Institute

PAPER

Paper represents approximately 40% by volume and 28% by weight of what Americans throw away. While some of the more than 50×10^6 tons (45×10^6 metric tons) of paper and paperboard discarded each year is burned to create energy, most is dumped in landfills.

By the year 2010, 80% of the 6500 American landfills available in the early 1990s will be closed. Due to environmental concerns, such as groundwater contamination and lack of available space, few new landfills will open. To ease the pressure on landfills, federal, state, and local governments are encouraging consumers and businesses to recycle paper and other materials.

Sources of waste paper. Postconsumer waste is paper that has been distributed, purchased, printed, or read, or in some other way has served its intended purpose in homes and businesses. Other sources known as mill broke and postindustrial waste consist of scrap paper generated in papermaking and converting (trimming and making unprinted paper products such as envelopes). Virtually all such waste is recycled because it comes from a known source and is essentially contaminant-free. Some of these categories are referred to as preconsumer waste.

Grades of waste paper. The U.S. Department of Commerce has identified five grades of waste paper. (1) Old corrugated containers (OCC) represent nearly half of all waste paper collected for recycling and include used corrugated shipping containers and box clippings. (2) Old newsprint (ONP) is the second most recycled grade of paper and includes old newspapers, overruns, and trimmings. (3) Pulp substitutes are usually directly recycled, since they are derived primarily from clean, industrial converting waste, like envelope and die-cutting clippings and trimmings from sheeting. (4) High-grade deinking, in which ink is removed from the paper during processing, consists of computer printout paper, sorted white office papers, printing plant scrap, and keypunch cards. Pulp substitutes and high-grade deinking grades are in high demand. (5) Mixed grade waste paper is a catch-all category that includes the broadest range of grades, such as mixed office papers, magazines, envelopes, and other collectible paper materials.

Each of these categories comprises different types of paper fibers, making them useful for manufacturing

Fig. 3. Steel scrap being added to a steelmaking furnace.

different types of recycled-content products. Efficiencies in collection and transportation to recycling mills also have an impact on economies of using one grade over another. Community recycling programs have been most successful in recovering newspapers. The commercial sector has done well in collecting corrugated boxes. Although all grades of paper cannot be recycled practically because of their components or use (for example, medical papers and tissue), recycling of all grades needs to be increased to reduce the volume bound for landfills.

Recycled-content products. Recycled paper fibers are used in the manufacture of many recycled-content paper products, such as paperboard, corrugated containers, tissue products, newspapers, and printing and writing paper. Nonpaper products made from recycled waste paper include insulation and packaging materials and molded products such as egg cartons and flowerpots. According to the American Paper Institute, more than 80% of the 600 paper mills in the United States use some amount of recycled fiber, and nearly 200 of these mills rely exclusively on waste paper as a source material.

Collection. This is the crucial first step in recycling. Collection occurs in curbside programs, drop-off centers, paper drives, and commercial collection systems run side by side with waste collection for landfill or incineration. Many factors have an impact on collection programs, including local and state legislation, landfill availability and pricing, proximity to recycling mills, and levels of community commitment and participation.

Reprocessing. One important difference between producing virgin paper and recycled paper is the need to eliminate a wide variety of contaminants and nonfibrous materials from waste paper in order to obtain good clean fibers for papermaking. The most common contaminants are plastic films and coatings, polystyrene foam, metals, glass, dirt or sand, asphalt, and adhesives that do not break down in water. The most common nonfibrous materials used to make the original virgin paper are fillers (like clay and calcium carbonate), starches, latexes, and resins.

Reprocessing begins with sorting waste papers by grade. Next comes pulping, in which waste paper is mixed with water and chemicals in a slusher or pulper to produce a fiber and water slurry. During this stage, the paper is broken down into its fiber state, and large-size contaminants (greater than about 5 mm or 0.2 in.) are separated.

The next stages involve cleaning the fiber and further separating the contaminants to the degree necessary for the specific products being manufactured. These initially include coarse screening and cleaning, in which mechanical processes remove dirt, plastics, metals, and other medium-sized contaminants (usually between 5 and 0.2 mm, or 0.2 and 0.05 in.) from the pulp. This may be followed in some mills by flotation, in which the smaller ink particles remaining in the pulp are removed by foaming. The ink particles are carried to the surface by bubbles and are skimmed off the top of the slurry. Fine screening and cleaning generally follow to remove smaller particles. The smallest particles (30 micrometers or less) are removed in a subsequent washing stage. Finally, the pulp may be bleached, depending on the type and color of paper being produced.

After the pulp is clean, manufacturing processes are similar to those for virgin fiber paper: the pulp is formed on a paper machine, pressed, dried, calendered, coated if necessary, and cut into sheets or wound into rolls for sale.

Purchase of recycled-content products. For recycling to succeed, households and businesses must purchase recycled-content products to close the recycling loop. To accelerate market demand for recovered paper in the United States, all 50 states and the District of Columbia have required their government offices to buy recycled-paper products. More than 100 communities have offical policies that require purchase of recycled paper products, and more than 300 are actually buying those products. In addition, the U.S. Environmental Protection Agency has set guidelines for recycled-paper products purchased by federal agencies and their suppliers.

Because business and industrial concerns in the United States buy almost 85% of all paper produced domestically, they are in a critical position to provide waste paper for recycled-content products and to build demand for those products by buying and using them. Like the government, many businesses are establishing preferential policies for purchasing recycled-content products.

Issues and emerging trends. These involve fiber management, development of standard definitions and labeling practices, and development of programs to support paper recycling.

Fiber management. For recycled paper this can be characterized as harvesting the urban forest. In mills using virgin fiber, fiber management involves stewardship of the company's forest lands and planting programs, purchasing wood fiber from other sources, and subsequently balancing the types of fibers needed for the products produced. In the recycled paper industry, fiber management is more complex. The feedstock must be the right mix of paper grades for the equipment at hand and the right mix of fibers for the products being produced. The importance to the mill of consistent and uniform grades requires that fiber procurement be carefully coordinated with suppliers of fibers: corporations that recycle their waste, community curbside programs, and the many brokers and dealers that serve as intermediaries for buying and selling recycling fibers. To some of the people involved, a stand of trees can look a lot simpler to grade and process than managing the multilayered maze of waste paper.

Definitions and labeling practices. A label stating "recyclable" means the product can be recycled, while the label "recycled" means that a product contains recycled content. Labels can be misleading, however. For example, office paper is technically recyclable, but if collection systems are not in place or are not economical in a given area, the office paper will not find its way into the recycling process. Some so-called recycled papers include a high percentage of virgin materials. In the United States, labeling practices have varied by state and by region.

Prospects. In the United States, the National Recycling Coalition and the National Office Paper Recycling Project are organizations that bring together corporations, governments, and members of the recycling industry with ambitious programs to increase collection of paper waste and purchase of recycled-content products. Public and private initiatives will provide an important impetus for development of the kinds of waste-paper recycling programs required to solve the pressing challenge of diminishing landfills and utilizing resources to their fullest extent.

Jeff Shaw

GLASS

Recycling of glass is an important aspect of solid-waste management. Glass containers are a usual ingredient in community recycling programs; they are 100% recyclable and can be recycled indefinitely. Moreover, the recycling process creates no additional waste or by-products.

In 1991 in the United States, glass containers, which constitute 4% of the solid-waste stream by weight, were recycled at a rate of 31%. This means that nearly one-third of the glass containers available for consumption in the United States were cycled back into glass containers and other useful items such as glasphalt, or were returned as refillable bottles. From 1987 through 1991, glass-container manufacturing plants increased their purchase of cullet (recycled glass) by over 82%, totaling over 2,280,200 tons (2,052,180 metric tons) in 1991. Similarly, since 1980 the number of glass plants has declined by nearly 40%. In 1992, there were 74 glass-container manufacturing plants operating in the United States.

Collection methods. There are three primary methods of collecting glass: drop-off centers, buy-back centers, and curbside collection. Drop-off centers and buy-back centers typically collect less material, but they also have much lower capital and operating costs than curbside programs.

Drop-off centers are one of the simplest forms of glass recovery. These may be mobile collection stations or permanent sites maintained by local municipalities. In some areas, fiberglass domes known as igloos are used as around-the-clock collection points. In other places, a drop-off may be as simple as several 55-gal (208-liter) metal drums, each marked for the color of glass it is to hold.

Buy-back centers purchase glass and other recyclables from people who voluntarily transport the material to the site. The centers serve as a convenient market for recyclers who cannot sell directly to a glass plant.

Comprehensive curbside collection programs are increasingly popular. In 1989 there were approximately 1000 curbside programs nationwide. By 1992 it was estimated that there were 4500 such programs. Curbside collection programs allow residents the opportunity to put their recyclable materials out at the curb, separated from their regular trash, for pick-up. Many programs offer commingled collection, which affords a resident the opportunity to put all recyclable material into one container or bag. Glass is an integral part of these programs. Often aluminum and glass provide the necessary revenue to sustain the community's program. In Pennsylvania, for example, over 96% of the 603 curbside programs collect glass (more than any other material). In New Jersey glass is recycled at a rate of 68%.

Processing specifics. The process of recycling glass is relatively straightforward. Used glass bottles and jars are mixed with silica sand, soda ash, and limestone in a melting furnace at temperatures up to 2800°F (5072°C). The molten glass is poured into a forming machine, where it is blown or pressed into shape. The new containers are gradually cooled, inspected, and shipped to the customer. Before glass can be recycled, however, it must be furnace-ready, that is, sorted by color and free of contaminants.

Color sorting. Sorting of green, amber, and flint (clear) glass containers is essential in order to maintain color consistency during the manufacturing process. Darker brown and green containers are used in many cases to help preserve the shelf life of a food product.

Different chemical agents are used to color glass. For example, chromium salts are generally used to create a green color, selenium salts are used to produce clear bottle glass, and iron oxides impart an amber finish. The coloring properties of these chemicals are so strong that a small amount of miscellaneous colors in a glass batch mix will adversely affect the result. Thus it is critical to deliver color-separated glass to manufacturing facilities in order to avoid costly problems involving equipment and production.

A considerable amount of research is focused on developing automated color-sorting equipment that could be used at glass processing and manufacturing plants. In addition, there is experimentation with the staining of flint glass bottles. The stain would be burned off in the furnace, making it unnecessary to separate by color. It is estimated that of all the glass containers manufactured in the United States, 63.5% are flint, 13.4% are green, and 23.2% are amber.

Beneficiation plants. Cullet must meet a standard of quality similar to that of the raw material it replaces. Contamination from foreign material will result in the cullet being rejected by the plants, as it poses a serious threat to the integrity and purity of the glass packaging being produced. Contaminants include metal caps, lids, stones, dirt, and ceramics. Paper labels do not need to be removed for recycling, as they burn off at high furnace temperatures.

Many glass manufacturers have invested in glass-processing equipment. These beneficiation units remove metals and other contaminants. For example, the New York State Energy Research and Development Authority, with funding and technical assistance support from several private entities including the Glass Packaging Institute, introduced a new glass beneficiation system that can optically sort out ceramics and separate nonferrous metals from the cullet. A nonferrous metal separator is being tested at a recycling facility in Syracuse, New York. This system removes aluminum, lead, and small contaminants, including the rings of residue in bottlenecks. Following this process, the cullet is moved to the optical ceramic sorter, which removes unwanted ceramics by releasing quick jets of air activated by an infrared light that detects the ceramic's opacity. Several other efforts are going on across the country to develop improved methods of processing furnace-ready cullet.

Energy and environment benefits. From a manufacturing standpoint, cullet can reduce wear and tear on furnaces, and maintenance expenses, since it can be melted at a lower temperature than that required to combine virgin materials. This reduced melting point can save as much as 25% of the energy used to make virgin glass, depending on what type of heating is used in the furnace. The energy saved by recycling a single glass bottle is estimated to be the equivalent of lighting a 100-W bulb for 4 h. Similarly, for every soft-drink bottle recycled, enough energy is saved to run a television set for 1½ h.

Glass recycling also has environmental benefits, such as reductions in emissions to the atmosphere. It has been estimated that 27.8 lb of air pollution is produced for every ton of new glass produced (13.9 kg/metric ton), and recycling glass reduces this source of pollution by 14–20%. Recycling a ton of glass saves

1330 lb (599 kg) of sand, 433 lb (195 kg) of soda ash, 433 lb (195 kg) of limestone, and 151 lb (68 kg) of feldspar. Generally costs for cullet are less than for soda ash, which it replaces at a ratio of 3.5 to 1.

End markets. The primary recycling market for container cullet consists of the manufacturers of glass containers. However, over the years difficulties involving color sorting and transportation have spawned new applications for cullet. Thus cullet use in secondary materials has increased. There markets include fiberglass, glasphalt, roadbed, reflective beads, decorative glass, and drainage, which now uses approximately 300,000 tons (270,000 metric tons) of container cullet annually. One of the most visible secondary markets is manufacture of glasphalt, which is a type of asphalt mix that incorporates crushed glass. Glasphalt was developed as an application of commingled cullet. One useful characteristic of glasphalt is its ability to retain heat. Glass acts as an insulating agent, making glasphalt workable under much colder environments. Manufacture of fiberglass, predominantly used in the form of glass wool for thermal and acoustical insulation, is another common secondary market for cullet.   *Natalie U. Roy*

REFUSE-DERIVED FUEL

A refuse-derived fuel (RDF) facility is one in which preprocessing of solid waste takes place to produce a fuel suitable for combustion in a boiler dedicated for this purpose or for use as a supplement in a fossil-fuel-fired boiler. The various types of refuse-derived fuel have been defined as shown in the **table**.

The prime economic driving force for effective resource recovery is the sale and utilization of energy. The reason is that municipal solid waste is composed of approximately 70–75% of combustible materials, with the balance being glass, metal, and dirt. The economic justification for resource recovery plants is developed from a combination of tipping fees (charges for the use of plant disposal facilities) and sale of energy (fuel, steam, or electricity), with a minor contribution from sale of recovered materials. Processes for energy recovery from municipal solid waste are generally subdivided into direct combustion

of as-received refuse (RDF-1), known as mass burning, and processing of as-received refuse to separate and reduce the volume of the combustible portion of the total solid-waste stream (RDF-2 through -7). Advantages claimed for processing of waste to RDF-2 through -7 include production of a more uniform fuel and changes in the form of the fuel such that the resulting material is more storable and transportable.

RDF-1. Combustion of RDF-1 (mass burning) is the most highly developed and commercially proven process available for reducing the volume of municipal solid waste prior to ultimate disposal of the residual material on the land, and also for extracting energy from solid waste. Hundreds of such plants, which incorporate various grate systems and boiler designs, and which differ in details of design, construction, and quality of operation, have been built throughout the world since the mid-1960s. Of the plants built in the United States since 1965, over 90% are still in operation. It is generally agreed that this type of plant currently can be designed and operated with assurance of continuous satisfactory service.

RDF-2. At least two basic types of processes, wet and dry, have been used to produce RDF-2 (so-called coarse refuse-derived fuel). In the dry process, the material may pass through a bag breaker (flail mill, a type of hammer mill, or other device) before being processed by a horizontal or vertical hammer mill to break apart and reduce in size the incoming solid waste to give a more homogeneous product. After the shredding process, which usually produces a nominal particle size of 4–6-in. (10.2–15.2-cm) measured in any direction the material may be subjected to the magnetic recovery of ferrous metal before being combusted. Combustion usually takes place in a dedicated boiler utilizing a spreader stoker. This is the most common type of facility for refuse-derived fuel, other than the mass-burn facility described above.

In the wet process, a hydropulper (an oversized blender) is utilized to produce a solid-waste slurry. A cyclone then separates the light combustible fraction from the heavy fraction that contains glass, metals, and inert materials. Next, the light combustible fraction is dewatered and combusted in a spreader-stoker boiler or fluid-bed furnace. This technology, having been applied in several full-scale facilities, proved not to be cost-effective and is no longer in use.

RDF-3. This fine or fluff refuse-derived fuel is produced by utilizing a horizontal or vertical hammermill to produce a coarse fuel that subsequently is subjected to magnetic separation to remove the ferrous metal. The coarse refuse-derived fuel then is air-classified to separate the lighter combustible fraction from the heavier noncombustible fraction. The light combustible fraction undergoes a second shredding operation to reduce its size to about a nominal 1.5–2-in. (3.8–5.1-cm) particle size. This fine or fluff refuse-derived fuel can be fed into a new or existing suspension-fired boiler, and can either be combusted alone or be cofired, usually with coal. More problems have been encountered in attempts to utilize this technology than with RDF-2, because of the increased equipment required, increased materials handling, and problems related to cofiring two somewhat dissimilar fuels.

RDF-4. This is powdered refuse-derived fuel. It was produced by a proprietary process and installed in an 1800 ton/day (1600 metric ton/day) plant in Bridgeport, Connecticut. In this process, municipal solid waste first passes through a primary trommel, in

Types of refuse-derived fuels*

Classification	Description
RDF-1	Wastes used as a fuel in as-discarded form with only bulky wastes removed
RDF-2	Wastes processed to coarse particle size with or without ferrous metal separation
RDF-3	Combustible waste fraction processed to particle sizes, 95% weight passing 2-in.-square (5-cm-square) mesh screening
RDF-4	Combustible waste fraction processed into powder form, 95% weight passing 10-mesh screening
RDF-5	Combustible waste fraction densified (compressed) into the form of pellets, slugs, cubettes, or briquettes
RDF-6	Combustible waste fraction processed into liquid fuels
RDF-7	Combustible waste fraction processed into gaseous fuel

*From American Society for Testing and Materials, *Thesaurus on Resource Recovery Terminology*, STP832, 1983.

which heavier material is separated from light combustible material. The light combustible material is then reduced in size by shredding, and any ferrous metal present is removed by a magnet. Next, light material is air-classified and conveyed by hot gases to a secondary trommel, in which most of the fine inert material and remaining glass is removed. At the discharge end of the secondary trommel, a chemical embrittling agent (sulfuric acid) is applied to the combustible material. This material is then passed through a ball mill, in which the steel balls are preheated. The combination of heat and the embrittling agent causes the cellulosic material to become a powder under the grinding action of the balls. After several years of trial operation, the process was determined not to be cost-effective and the plant was shut down. It was later replaced with a mass-burn facility.

RDF-5. This densified refuse-derived fuel has been produced sporadically over the years at a number of facilities. This material is produced by processing RDF-3 through an extrusion device under high pressure, with or without binding material added, producing pellets, slugs, cubettes, or briquettes. The material produced, if consistent in size, would be easier to feed with pulverized coal in a spreader-stoker-fired furnace. A number of trial burns have been conducted in the United States over the years. However, use of this material as a fuel has not generally been accepted.

RDF-6 and RDF-7. Production of RDF-6 (liquid fuels) and RDF-7 (gaseous fuels) may be accomplished either through the proper application of heat (pyrolysis or destructive distillation) or through bioconversion processes. The potential use of bioconversion to convert the cellulosic fraction of municipal solid waste to ethanol has been under study for some time. However, research efforts have not led to development of pilot or full-scale plant applications because of practical process problems involving requirements for construction materials, need for sufficient control of feedstock to assure reasonable yields and quality of end product, and cost ineffectiveness. Production of methane gas through bioconversion of primarily cellulosic fractions of municipal solid waste in a digester was accomplished in a pilot-scale facility for a number of years in the 1970s. However, this process was found to have limited applicability, and the pilot plant was closed. No other facilities have been built since.

On the other hand, the use of heat (pyrolysis) to produce liquid or gaseous fuels has been actively investigated (particularly in the 1970s) in laboratory, pilot, and full-scale demonstration installations. One demonstration-scale unit, which was intended to produce pyrolytic oil, was built and carried through start-up operation before being shut down in the late 1970s. Problems arising in the waste preparation process could not be resolved to the extent that the production process for pyrolytic oil could be effectively tested.

Prospects. A number of demonstration and full-scale fuel-gas pyrolysis systems were built and operated between the mid-1970s and the mid-1980s. These installations included a number of facilities in the United States and in Europe. After achieving some varying limited success in operation, all were closed because of an inability to achieve long-term cost-effective operation.

Since the late 1960s some 40 plants incorporating processes to produce and combust RDF-2 through -7 have been built and placed in operation in the United States. These plants have frequently incorporated some related processes of separation and recovery materials. Approximately one-third of these 40 plants have subsequently been shut down. The closed plants utilized wet RDF-2 or RDF-3 through -7 technologies.

Refuse-derived fuel has been burned with and without fossil fuel in new dedicated boilers or in existing boilers that were modified to accept the material. Combustion in the boiler takes place partially in suspension and partially on the boiler grate. Numerous trial burns were conducted during 1970–1985 in large utility-type boiler units. Results were generally satisfactory with respect to combustion conditions, but mixed results have been experienced with respect to plant operation and maintenance conditions. The major problems include periodic explosions in the initial shredding operation; excessive wear and tear on the equipment, resulting in frequent downtime; and difficulties in storage and retrieval of the refuse-derived fuel. The environmental impacts, and the measures needed to mitigate them are similar to those required for RDF-1.

Charles O. Velzy

Bibliography. S. Apotheker, Looking for steel cans, *Resource Recycl.*, 11(2):28–35, 1992; M. J. Coleman (ed.), *Recycling Paper: From Fiber to Finished Product*, vols. 1 and 2, 1990; G. Crawford, Adding steel can recycling to your collection program, *World Wastes*, 34(9):42–46, 1991; Earthworks Group, *The Recyclers Handbook*, 1990; Environmental Protection Agency, *Characterization of Municipal Solid Waste in the United Staes: 1990 Update*, PB90–215112, 1990; Glass Packaging Institute, *Glass Packaging Fact Sheet*, 1992; Glass Packaging Institute, *Glass Recycling: Why? How?*, 1991; J. L. Jones and S. B. Radding (eds)., *Thermal Conversion of Solid Wastes and Biomass*, ACS Sym. Ser. 130, 1980; G. J. Kulik and J. C. Daley, Aluminum dross processing in the 90s, *2d International Symposium: Recycling of Metals and Engineered Materials*, 1990; T. J. Nosker et al., Commingled plastics recycling and environmental concerns, *EPA Meeting on Solid Waste*, San Diego, 1989; Office of Technology Assessment, *Facing America's Trash*, OTA-O-424, 1989; C. J. Philips, *Glass, The Miracle Worker*, 1947; G. A. Smook, *Handbook for Pulp and Paper Technologists*, 1982; Steel Can Recycling Institute, *Recyclable Steel Cans: An Integral Part of Your Curbside Recycling Program*, 1990; Steel Can Recycling Institute, *Steel Cans and Recycling: Today's Environmental Partnership*, 1990; C. G. Thompson, *Recycled Papers: The Essential Guide*, 1992; J. H. L. van Linden, Aluminum recycling: Everybody's business, technological challenges and opportunities, *Light Metals 1990: Proceedings of the Annual Meeting of the Metallurgical Society of AIME*, 1990; C. O. Velzy, Energy from waste incineration, presented at Great Lakes International Solid Waste Management Forum, Lansing, Michigan, March 20, 1990; C. O. Velzy, Incinerator's role in integrated S. W. management, presented at NCSL Conference: Managing SW: Options for State Legislative Action, Breckenridge, Colorado, June 13, 1989; P. S. Vesilind and A. E. Rimer, *Unit Operations in Resource Recovery Engineering*, 1981;

J. S. Viland, A secondary's view of recycling, *Light Metals 1990: Proceedings of the Annual Meeting of the Metallurgical Society of AIME*, 1990; N. J. Weinstein and R. F. Toro, *Thermal Processing of Municipal Solid Waste for Resource and Energy Recovery*, 1976.

Reforestation

The reestablishment of forests on sites denuded of trees. Reforestation has become increasingly important for preventing or reversing environmental degradation and for helping to maximize economic returns on commercially forested lands. Afforestation, establishment of trees where none had been growing, is also important for environmental and economic reasons. Interest in agroforestry, that is, the simultaneous or sequential use of land for traditional agriculture and for trees on the same site, has also been a stimulus to tree planting. Forestation, also termed regeneration, should be planned well in advance whenever possible, because it involves a series of coordinated operations that may include seed collection, timber harvesting, site preparation, seedling production, planting, postplanting care, and follow-up inventories.

PLANTING AND SEEDING

When natural regeneration is not likely to result in a new stand of trees through seedfall or sprouting from stumps or rhizomes, planting or seeding is usually prescribed. Planting is the most common technique by far for establishment of new plantations. It was once common to replant a commercial forest area with a single species—usually the one thought to produce the highest financial return. However, replanting with the same mix of timber or pulpwood species that originally grew on the site has been found to be more ecologically sound and, ultimately, the best economic approach.

Regardless of the regeneration method used, an adequate supply of high-quality seed is essential for success. In artificial regeneration, either by planting or seeding, it is important to know the geographic source as well as the species of seed. Foresters are careful to reforest with genetically diverse propagules that originated from the same ecological zone in which they will be placed so that the resulting trees will be adapted to the sites on which they will be growing. When exotic species or seed sources are to be introduced, foresters conduct small-scale tests called provenance trials before extensive forestation is done. The urgency of recent forecasts of global climate change add another dimension to the problem of matching seed sources and planting sites. Foresters must keep abreast of projected climatic trends and must also consider appropriate changes in species and seed sources. SEE CLIMATIC CHANGE; GREENHOUSE EFFECT.

Most of the developed countries of the world have intensive tree improvement programs in which seeds for reforestation are collected from trees that have been selected for disease resistance or for desirable phenotypic traits such as rapid growth rate and straight stems. The selected trees are marked and left in natural stands or are propagated in special areas called seed orchards. Further refinements include field-testing the progeny of selected parents and intercrossing the best offspring to provide future generations of improved material. Use of rooted cuttings for vegetative propagation of selected trees is common for a few species and is being increasingly used for others. Modern techniques of tissue culture and gene splicing are being studied as means of accelerating genetic improvement of trees.

Ideally, seeds are collected at about the time they ripen naturally—late summer or early fall for most species (**Fig. 1**). Since many species produce good seed crops sporadically, large supplies are usually collected whenever possible and stored for use as needed. Seeds of many species will remain viable at subfreezing temperatures for 5 to 10 years or longer.

Peyton W. Owston

FOREST TREE NURSERY MANAGEMENT

The details of operating either forest tree nurseries or containerized tree-seedling greenhouses vary with species and geographic region, although a number of general principles do apply.

Bare-root seedlings. Site selection, seedbed management, irrigation, soil management, pest control, and lifting and shipping are important factors in successful production of high-quality bare-root seedlings.

Site factors. The selection of a suitable site for a forest tree nursery can be considered the single most important factor in successful production of high-quality bare-root seedlings. The nursery should be located near major planting areas to duplicate as closely

Fig. 1. Specially equipped helicopter used to collect cones from selected tall conifers in natural stands. Seeds are extracted from the cones and used in nurseries to produce seedlings for planting.

as possible the growing season and climatic conditions of the prospective planting sites. A suitable nursery site should be located to minimize extremes of temperature, providing adequate cold-air drainage to alleviate frost damage; sites subjected to strong, drying winds or flooding are unacceptable. Soil depths of 3–5 ft (1–1.5 m) without major textural changes ensure adequate drainage, aeration, and rooting volume. Level sites are acceptable if soils are coarse-textured, but fine-textured soils require a slight slope in one direction for adequate drainage (**Fig. 2**).

Coarse-textured soils, such as loamy sands to sandy loams, which are free of stones, root-restricting layers, and evidence of poor drainage (mottling) are preferred for nurseries; these soils require higher irrigation, fertilizer, and organic matter additions than do fine-textured soils. Soil texture influences a variety of properties, including nutrient retention, erosion, compaction, available moisture, and ease of lifting. Ideal nursery soils should contain 15–25% silt and clay, and 75–85% sand. It is often difficult to control moisture, pH, and nutrients, and to cultivate in soils with more silt and clay. In general, fine-textured soils are also slower to warm in spring and may be prone to frost heaving; seedlings lifted from such soils may be subjected to unacceptable root damage. *SEE SOIL*.

The successful forest tree nursery must be large enough to produce adequate numbers of seedlings for current reforestation needs and to allow needed expansion to meet future demands. In areas such as the southern United States, where 1–0 (1-year-old) plantable seedlings can be produced, 20–50 acres (10–20 hectares) of nursery may be adequate. However, in areas such as the northeastern United States where 2 or more years are needed to produce plantable seedlings, nurseries of 100–200 acres (40–80 ha) may be necessary. Additional acreage is necessary if a rotation of cover crops is used between crops of tree seedlings. Finally, about 20% of a nursery must be devoted to roads, windbreaks, buildings, fences, and watering systems.

Grading and leveling are often necessary to minimize erosion and eliminate depressions that accumulate water; topsoil must be saved and replaced after such operations. Soil maps indicating textures, pH, nutrient levels, and other critical soil properties should be maintained. These detailed maps provide the basis for the planning and record keeping that are vital for a successful nursery operation.

Seedbed preparation and seeding. Seed is often received from a variety of sources, ranging from unregulated collections to genetically improved seed from seed orchards. Every effort must be made to ensure that the seed used is of high quality. Seed orchards provide seed for many commercial species. If these sources of genetically superior seed are not available, seed of local origin from high-quality trees should be used. Seed testing, including sizing and germination capacity and energy, is imperative for adequate seedling production.

Seedbeds, prepared by bed-shaping equipment, are generally 4 ft (1 m) wide, raised, and as long as feasible given area and equipment limitations. Bed surfaces are tilled and cultivated to provide a uniform soil surface for optimum seed germination and seedling growth.

Sowing rates vary depending upon species and seed quality, but generally are designed to produce 25–30 conifer seedlings or 10–20 hardwood seedlings per square foot (0.1 m²) of seedbed. Seedbed density is a critical factor that nursery workers can control to produce high-quality planting stock. Seed is generally planted with a seed drill in rows to aid in density control, lightly pressed into the soil surface with a roller, and covered with sand. Some species are sown in fall, others in spring. Mulching is a common practice to protect beds from frost, erosion, drought, and animal predation.

As seedlings develop, weed competition must be controlled with appropriate combinations of herbicides, cultivation, and hand weeding. Significant advances have been made in chemical weed control, using both pre- and postemergence herbicides that are compatible with the tree species being grown. The proper use of chemical herbicides can eliminate the costly, labor-intensive, hand weeding commonly practiced. *SEE HERBICIDE*.

Root pruning and root wrenching are standard practices on seedlings that are grown for more than 1 year. These techniques are used to achieve more fibrous root systems and to reduce top growth, producing seedlings with more favorable root:shoot ratios. Transplanting is another technique used to produce large seedlings of higher quality than 1-1 seedlings.

Irrigation. In addition to normal precipitation, water is necessary for the production of quality seedlings. Irrigation programs must be flexible to account for variations in climatic conditions, soil, species, and type of seedling being produced. The root zone must be kept moist but not saturated. Adequate aeration is essential, and minimal leaching of nutrients is desirable. Advances in soil-moisture monitoring equipment and the use of soil-moisture characterization curves have contributed to more scientifically sound irrigation practices than those previously used. Small nurseries can effectively monitor irrigation needs by using portable tensiometers, while larger nurseries rely on neutron-scattering devices. The irrigation water must be free of harmful materials such as calcium at high levels, silt or colloids, and weed seeds. Watering during the heat of the day will aid in reducing soil temperatures and consequent heat injury to seedlings.

Soil management. Because of high seedling densities and complete removal of the crop and adhering soil, successful forest tree nursery management ne-

Fig. 2. Seedling beds in a forest tree nursery.

cessitates a sound soil management program. Soil pH should fit the range of requirements of the species being grown. In general, soil reaction should be maintained at about pH 5.2–5.8 for conifers and 5.5–6.5 for hardwoods. Maintenance of these pH values provides a favorable environment for beneficial soil microorganisms, provides optimum availability of nutrient elements, and minimizes toxic conditions. Soil pH can be adjusted by using limestone or sulfur.

An adequate level of organic matter is important in sandy nursery soils to aid in retaining nutrient elements, improving and maintaining soil structure, buffering the soil against acidity changes, providing food for beneficial organisms, and enhancing mycorrhizae development. Soil organic matter can be maintained or enhanced by growing cover crops on the site and incorporating them into the soil. Alternatively, organic matter must be added to the soil in the form of sawdust, peat, animal wastes, sludge, or wood chips. Relatively heavy rates of inorganic fertilizers must be added to nursery soils to replace those constituents lost by leaching, by crop removal, or by fixation in the soil. The fertility needs of nursery soils are best determined by annual chemical analysis of representative samples of soil and seedlings. Minimum fertility recommendations have been developed for most commercial tree species used in forest regeneration programs.

Pest control. Nursery tree seedlings are susceptible to a variety of diseases, insects, and animals. Rodent and bird damage generally occurs during germination and early seedling establishment. Rodents can be controlled by trapping or poisoning, and bird damage is controlled by daily patrols.

Many nursery diseases can be controlled or minimized by maintaining the proper soil environment. Proper maintenance of soil pH below 6.0 minimizes development of most pathogenic fungi. Soil fumigation before planting with compounds such as methyl bromide or eptam is often used to control all soilborne pests. Postemergent fungicidal sprays are also effective. *See* Pesticide.

Lifting and shipping. When seedlings are of suitable size for outplanting, they are mechanically lifted. Trees are graded, counted, and packed in wet peat moss or in polyethylene-lined kraft paper bags for storage or shipment. When necessary, the packed trees can be stored for several months at temperatures of 34–40°F (1–4°C) if adequate moisture and aeration are provided. Roots must be kept cool and moist at all times, including the period immediately before planting at a site.

Containerized seedlings. Large-scale production of greenhouse-grown container stock has become popular. The basic difference between a containerized seedling and a conventional bare-root seedling is the relative lack of root disturbance in the containerized seedling. In general, the same biological principles and knowledge applicable to producing bare-root stock are valid for producing containerized stock. The rooting medium is commonly peat and shredded sphagnum moss mixed with vermiculite. Physical and chemical properties of rooting medium are critical, and optimum levels have been established for many important forest tree species (**Fig. 3**).

Choice of a container is generally dictated by cost and success at outplanting. Some containers are nonbiodegradable plastics or styrofoam from which the seedling are removed in the field before planting.

Fig. 3. Red pine containerized seedling production in a greenhouse.

Other containers are biodegradable paper or peat, and both the seedling and container are planted.

Containers are especially useful for species that are sensitive to root damage or where planting and growing seasons are relatively short. For example, in cool climates several years may be necessary to produce quality bare-root seedlings (2 years before and 1 year after transplanting). Greenhouse production of containerized seedlings, however, requires only a few months.   *E. H. White; David F. Grigal*

Seedling Planting and Establishment

In order to ensure successful reforestation, seedlings must be planted carefully and must be protected from the elements until they are established.

Site preparation. Clearing unwanted vegetation or debris from the site before planting is often necessary. Killing or removing unwanted vegetation facilitates planting and reduces potential competition for site resources such as light and soil moisture. On flat or gently sloping ground, mechanical equipment such as plows and disks is used most often to prepare sites for planting. On slopes steeper than about 35%, controlled burning and the application of herbicides are common practices. However, concern about possible adverse environmental or human health consequences of burning and use of herbicides has resulted in increased efforts to prepare sites by clearing debris during harvesting or by manually clearing areas.

Bare-root planting. Most planting is done by using seedlings that are dug from outdoor nursery beds during the dormant season. After a grading process that removes those that are damaged, unhealthy, or too small to survive, the seedlings are placed in cold storage while being shipped and awaiting planting. They are usually 6–18 in. (15–45 cm) tall with stems 0.12–0.24 in. (3–6 mm) in diameter and root systems 8–10 in. (20–25 cm) long. Dormancy during processing is important because it makes the seedlings more resistant to stresses caused by removing the roots from moist soil. The dormant state also increases the resistance of the seedlings to subfreezing temperatures.

The economic importance of prompt reforestation has led to use of various tests of physiological quality of tree seedlings prior to planting. Knowing the levels of such characteristics as root growth potential, cold hardiness, and desiccation resistance allows foresters to do a better job of planting the seedlings so as to maximize survival and growth.

Timing and technique of planting are important. Even though the remoteness of forest planting sites makes postplanting irrigation unfeasible, seedlings must have well-developed root systems for anchoring and for access to water and nutrients in the soil. It is important that dormant seedlings be planted at a time of year when the soil is moist. Because water loss through transpiration occurs rapidly, roots must have almost immediate access to soil water. Seedlings must also be protected from drying and overheating during planting. Roots must be placed into the ground so that tap roots extend straight down and lateral roots are not mashed tightly together. Also, the seedlings should be planted to the same depth as that at which they had been growing in the nursery, and the soil must be firmed around them to prevent air pockets and easy dislodgment by frost, animals, or wind.

On flat or gently sloping ground, as is found in the southeastern United States, planting is often done by machine. The device used is usually pulled behind a crawler tractor. First, the machine excavates a hole; next, a person riding on the machine places a seedling into the hole; and, finally, the machine closes soil around it. Some machines operate with two planters at a time, and so planting of 10,000 trees a day is possible.

On steep ground or in small areas, seedlings are planted by using a handtool—a shovel, mattock, or any of several specially designed planting tools. A skilled worker can plant 500 or more seedlings a day

Fig. 4. Handtools such as tiling spades are commonly used to plant tree seedlings in mountainous areas. A small supply of seedlings is kept moist in a protective shoulder bag while the main supply is more carefully protected from overheating and drying at a central dispersal point on the site.

(**Fig. 4**). Millions of seedlings are planted this way each year in the mountainous areas of the western United States.

Container planting. Seedlings grown in containers have the same biological requirements as bare-root seedlings and must be handled with care. However, the intact plugs of roots and potting medium provide an added measure of protection from desiccation. The undisturbed root system also permits setting of non-dormant plants if they are handled carefully and placed into relatively moist soil. The small containers commonly used in temperate and boreal regions are 1–2 in. (2.5–5.0 cm) in diameter and 4–8 in. (10–20 cm) deep. They lend themselves to mechanized systems and planting in rocky areas where digging holes for larger bare-root seedlings is extremely difficult.

Plantation care. Although frequent tending of plantations is not always possible, it is common practice to take additional measures after planting to better ensure successful forestation. They include fencing areas, caging individual seedlings, or spraying animal repellent to protect seedlings from damage by wild or domestic animals; shading stems from direct sunlight with cardboard, wood, or plastic cards on the south side of newly planted seedlings; and controlling unwanted vegetation that overtops the seedlings or competes for needed soil moisture. Container seedlings, which are usually smaller than those grown for bare-root planting, often require more intensive follow-up care during the first year or two because of their smaller size.

Another important component of plantation care is the periodic surveying of results to assess the success or failure of a plantation. If problems are detected early, measures such as interplanting can often be taken to mitigate them. SEE CONSERVATION OF RE-SOURCES; FOREST AND FORESTRY.

Peyton W. Owston

Bibliography. K. A. Armson and V. Sadreika, *Forest Tree Nursery Soil Management and Related Practices*, 1979; B. D. Cleary, *Regenerating Oregon's Forests*, 1978; J. Evans, *Plantation Forestry in the Tropics*, 1982; W. L. Pritchett, *Properties and Management of Forest Soils*, 1979; J. B. Scarratt, C. Glerum, and C. A. Plexman (eds.), *Proceedings of the Canadian Containerized Tree Seedling Symposium*, 1982; D. M. Smith, *The Practice of Silviculture*, 8th ed., 1986; USDA Forest Service, *Seeds of Woody Plants in the United States*, 1974.

Remote sensing

The gathering and recording of information about terrain and ocean surfaces without actual contact with the object or area being investigated. Remote terrain sensing is part of the large subject of remote sensing, which deals with the gathering and recording of information on many types of natural phenomena from a distance (see **table**). Remote sensing uses the visual, infrared, and microwave portions of the electromagnetic spectrum (**Fig. 1**).

Humans have always used remote sensing in a primitive form. In ancient times, they climbed a tree or stood on a hill and looked and listened, or sniffed for odors borne on the wind. Although it is possible to sense the environment without the use of instruments, it is not possible to record the sensed information without the aid of instruments referred to as

Some areas of application for remote sensor instruments

Technique	Agriculture and forestry	Geology and planetology	Hydrology	Oceanography	Geography
Visual photography	Soil types, plant vigor, disease	Surface structure, surface features	Drainage patterns	Sea state, erosion, turbidity, hydrography	Cartography, land use, transportation, terrain and vegetation charactersitics, thematic mapping
Multispectral imagery	Same as above	Lithological units, formation boundaries	Soil moisture	Sea color, biological productivity	Same as above
Infrared imagery and spectroscopy	Vegetation extent, soil moisture, conditions	Thermal anomalies, faults	Areas of cooling, soil moisture	Ocean currents, sea-ice type and extent, sea-surface temperature	Thermal activity in urban areas, land use
Radar: imagery, scatterometry, altimetry	Soil characteristics, plant conditions	Surface roughness, structural framework	Soil moisture, runoff slopes	Sea state, tsunami warning	Land-ice type and extent, cartography, geodesy
Passive microwave radiometry and imagery	Thermal state of terrain, soil moisture		Soil moisture, snow, ice extent	Sea state, sea-surface temperature, sea-ice extent	Snow and ice extent

remote sensors. These instruments are a modern refinement of the art of reconnaissance, an early example being the first aerial photograph taken in 1858 from a balloon floating over Paris.

The eye is sensitive only to visible light, a very small portion of the electromagnetic spectrum (Fig. 1). Cameras and electrooptical sensors, operating like the eye, can sense and record in a slightly larger portion of the spectrum. For gathering invisible data, instruments operating in other regions of the spectrum are employed. Remote sensors include devices that are sensitive to force fields, such as gravity-gradient systems, and devices such as antennas that record the reflection or emission of electromagnetic energy.

Both passive electromagnetic sensors (those that rely on natural sources of illumination, such as the Sun) and active ones (those that utilize an artificial source of illumination such as radar) are considered to be remote sensors. Several remote-sensing instruments and their applications are listed in the table.

Terrain Characteristics

Each type of surface material (for example, soils, rocks, vegetation, and ocean waves) absorbs and reflects solar energy in a characteristic manner depending upon its atomic and molecular structure (Fig. 1c). In addition, a certain amount of internal energy is

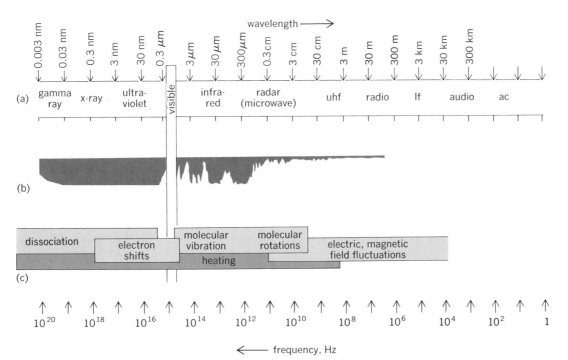

Fig. 1. Characteristics of the electromagnetic energy spectrum which are of significance in remote sensing. (*a*) Regions of electromagnetic spectrum. (*b*) Atmospheric transmission, showing regions through which electromagnetic energy is not transmitted. (*c*) Phenomena detected.

emitted which is partially independent of the solar flux.

The absorbed, reflected, and emitted energy can be detected by remote sensing instruments in terms of characteristic spectral signatures and images. These signatures can usually be correlated with known rock, soil, crop, terrain, or ocean surface features. Chemical composition, surface irregularity, degree of consolidation, and moisture content are among the parameters known to affect the records obtained by electromagnetic remote sensing devices. Selection of the specific parts of the electromagnetic spectrum to be utilized in terrain or ocean sensing is governed largely by the photon energy, frequency, and atmospheric transmission characteristics of the spectrum (Fig. 1).

TYPES OF SENSING

Because remote sensing is a composite term which includes many types of sensing, its meaning can be best understood by describing several of the types. Remote sensing is generally conducted by means of remote sensors installed in aircraft and satellites, and much of the following discussion refers to sensing from such platforms.

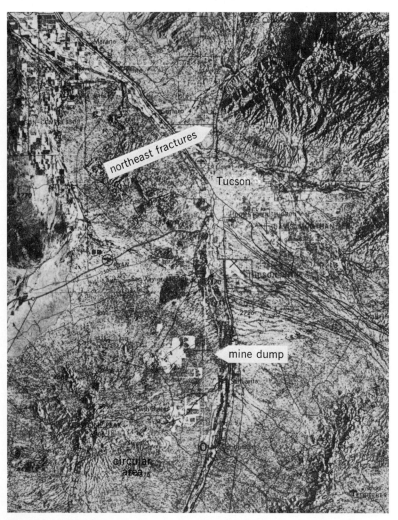

Fig. 2. Space photomap of the Tucson, Arizona, area, using 80-mm-focal-length Hasselblad cameras on the *Apollo 9* flight. The strong northeast-trending fractures in the mountains east of Tucson are apparent. The white patches on the northeast flank of the circular area are open pits and mine dumps, associated with already discovered mineral deposits.

Photography. Photography is probably the most useful remote sensing system because it has the greatest number of known applications, it has been developed to a high degree, and a great number of people are experienced in analyzing terrain photographs. Much of the experience gained over the years from photographs of the terrain taken from aircraft is being drawn upon for use in space.

Conventional. Results of conventional photography experiments carried out in the short-duration crewed spacecraft such as a *Gemini*, *Apollo*, and *Skylab*, and in the long-duration uncrewed spacecraft such as *ERTS*, *Landsat*, *Nimbus*, *NOAA*, and *DMSP*, have vividly shown the applicability of these systems in space. These results indicate that space photography provides valuable data for delineating and identifying various terrain features such as those shown in **Fig. 2**.

The photomap in Fig. 2 was made by rectifying and fitting the photographs to the cultural plate of the existing line map of the area. The result combines all the original photographic detail with the cultural line data important for geographic orientation and location. This combination provides considerably more terrain data than conventional topographic or raised relief maps. A number of major copper deposits occur in this region, and their location is in part controlled by the presence of intense fracturing, as shown on the photomap. Also important is the presence of intrusive rocks, which sometimes show up as circular areas. Fault intersections, intrusive centers, and alteration halos are important clues in the search for new mineral deposits of this copper type. Detailed study of such high-quality spacecraft imagery is very useful for unraveling the structural framework of potential mineral districts.

Multispectral. Multispectral photography can be defined as the isolation of the reflected energy from a surface in a number of given wavelength bands and the recording of each spectral band separately on film. This technique allows the scientist to select the significant bandwidths in which a given area of terrain displays maximum tonal contrast and, hence, increases the effective spectral resolution of the system over conventional black-and-white or color systems.

Because of its spectral selectivity capabilities, the multispectral approach provides a means of collecting a great amount of specific information. In addition, it has less sensitivity to temperature, humidity, and reproduction variables than conventional color photography and retains the high resolution associated with broadband black-and-white mapping film.

Multispectral imagery. An advance in multispectral sensing is the use of multispectral scanning systems which record the spectral reflectance by photoelectric means (rather than by photochemical means as in multispectral photography) simultaneously in several individual wavelengths within the visual and near-infrared portions of the electromagnetic spectrum (0.47–1.11 micrometers). Such instruments have been used in aircraft since the early 1960s and were used in the *Earth Resources Technology Satellite* (*ERTS 1*) and in *Landsat B*.

In the satellite cases, optical energy is sensed by an array of detectors simultaneously in four spectral bands from 0.47 to 1.1 μm. As the optical sensors for the various frequency bands sweep across the underlying terrain in a plane perpendicular to the flight direction of the satellite, they record energy from individual areas on the ground. The size of these individual areas (instantaneous fields of view) is determined by the resolution capability (spot size) of the optical scanner. The smallest individual area distinguished by the scanner is called a picture element or pixel, and a separate spectral reflectance is recorded in analog or digital form for each pixel. A pixel covers about 1 acre (approximately 0.4 hectare, or 4047 m^2) of the Earth's surface in the case of the *Landsat*, with approximately 7.5×10^6 pixels composing each *Landsat* image (115 × 115 mi or 185 × 185 km in area).

Such multispectral scanning systems have a number of advantages over conventional photography: the spectral reflectance values for each pixel can be transmitted electronically to ground receiving stations in near-real time, or stored on magnetic tape in the satellite until it is over a receiving station. When the signal intensities are received on the ground, they can be reconstructed almost instantaneously into the virtual equivalent of conventional aerial photographs (provided the resolution size of the individual pixels is fine enough). In the case of conventional photography, the entire film cassette generally has to be returned physically to the ground, before the film can be developed and studied. Such physical return of film cassettes is not practical for long-duration satellites such as *ERTS* which are continuously recording vast amounts of data.

Computer enhancement of imagery. There are a number of other advantages of multispectral scanning systems. Since they record reflected radiation energy in a number of discrete wavelengths, these radiance values can be used singly or combined by digital computer processing to provide a response optimized for particular terrain features.

One type of such computer enhancement which has proved to be very useful involves the preparation of ratio images. The individual spectral responses are ratioed, picture element by picture element using a computer, and they can also be contrast-stretched to further enhance the spectral differences. Such ratio images are very useful in detecting such items as subtle soil changes (**Fig. 3**) and hydrothermally altered areas (important for mineral exploration), as well as in discriminating most major rock types, and in detecting the nature of the sea floor (**Fig. 4**).

Another advantage of the multispectral scanner is its ability to extend the spectral coverage (beyond the 0.9-μm cutoff available with conventional photographic films) into the infrared wavelengths of the electromagnetic spectrum.

Infrared. Infrared is electromagnetic radiation having wavelengths of 0.7 to about 1400 μm. All materials continuously emit infrared radiation as long as they have a temperature above absolute zero in the Kelvin scale. This radiation involves molecular vibrations as modified by crystal lattice motions of the material. The total amount and the wavelength distribution of the infrared radiation are dependent on two factors: the temperature of the material and its radiating efficiency (called emissivity).

Thermal infrared radiation is mapped by means of infrared scanners similar to the multispectral scanners described previously, but in this case radiated energy is recorded generally in the 8–14-μm portion of the electromagnetic spectrum.

The imagery provided by an infrared scanning system gives information that is not available from ordi-

Fig. 3. Images taken by the earth resources technology satellite over the Mojave Desert of California on October 21, 1972: (*a*) band 4 (0.5–0.6 μm); (*b*) a ratio of band 5 (0.6–0.7 μm) to band 4. Note that the alluvial soils and Middle Butte mining area appear as bright areas on image *b*, while they are difficult to distinguish on image *a*. (*From P. M. Merifeld et al., Enhancement of Geological Features near Mojave, California by Spectral Band Ratioing of ERTS MSS Data, report prepared under U.S. Geological Survey Contract 14-08-0001-13911, 1974*)

nary photography or from multispectral scanners operating in the visual portion of the electromagnetic spectrum. The brightness with which an object appears on an infrared image depends on its radiant

Fig. 4. Ratio image (0.50–0.54 μm)/(0.48–0.52 μm) from the Florida coast, acquired by an airborne multispectral scanner operating in the visible wavelengths. The reflection from the sea surface has been filtered out in the lower image, and the absorption effects of the water column have been removed by means of an algorithm. The residual reflections are from the sea floor and are indicative of surface roughness. (*Environmental Research Institute of Michigan, under contract to the U.S. Navy*)

temperature. The hotter the object, the brighter it will appear on a positive image (**Fig. 5**). Radiant temperature is largely dependent upon chemistry, grain size, surface roughness, and thermal properties of the material. The time of day or night and the season of the year at which the infrared energy is recorded are also important factors, particularly when water or moisture exists in the near-surface terrain materials, since the water has a different thermal inertia relative to rock and soil materials and can therefore appear as a thermal anomaly. Because moisture frequently collects in geologic faults and fractures, infrared images are useful in detecting such features (**Fig. 6**).

Although it is possible to obtain relatively high resolutions (spot sizes of a few feet) from infrared imagers in low-flying aircraft (Fig. 6), it has been more difficult to achieve such fine resolutions from satellite altitudes, partially because of the lower sensing-element sensitivity of infrared scanners (whose sensing elements must be cooled, in contrast to visible spectrum sensors), and partially because there is always a trade-off between field of view (generally large for satellite imagery as compared with aircraft imagery) and resolution. The larger the field of view, the more difficult it is to obtain fine resolution. Despite these restrictions, routine thermal mapping from long-duration satellites is now on the order of 2300–3000 ft (700–900 m) per picture element on the ground (*Nimbus 5* and *NOAA 2* satellites). The multispectral scanner on the short-duration *Skylab* space flight had an 260 ft (80-m) instantaneous field of view and recorded temperature differences of 0.40 K.

In the past, thermal infrared images were generally recorded on photographic film. Videotape records are replacing film as the primary recording medium and permit better imagery to be produced and greater versatility in interpretation of data.

Thermal mapping from satellite altitudes is proving to be useful for a number of purposes, one of which is the mapping of thermal currents in the ocean (**Fig. 7**). Such currents change their position quite frequently; in many cases these changes occur daily or even more frequently. The positions of such thermal boundaries are important for a variety of uses (fishery, naval, and so forth).

Thermal infrared mapping (thermography) from aircraft and satellite altitudes has many other uses also, including the mapping of volcanic activity (Fig. 5) and geothermal sites, location of groundwater discharge into surface and marine waters, and regional pollution monitoring.

Microwave radar. This type of remote sensing utilizes both active and passive sensors. The active sensors such as radar supply their own illumination and record the reflected energy. The passive microwave sensors record the natural radiation. A variety of sensor types are involved. These include imaging radars, radar scatterometers and altimeters, and over-the-horizon radar using large ground-based antenna arrays, as well as passive microwave radiometers and images.

One of the most significant advantages of these instruments is their all-weather capability, both day and night. The active radars also possess a certain amount of foliage-penetration ability which is valuable in jungle terrains (**Fig. 8**). This imagery illustrates the unique capability of side-looking radar airborne to penetrate both cloud cover and dense jungle vegetation and to map the structural fabric of the underlying terrain with considerable detail. It has been demonstrated that radar return amplitude is affected by the

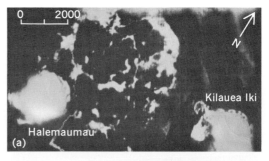

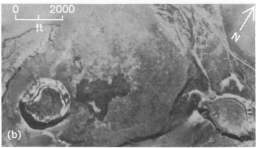

Fig. 5. Infrared imagery of Kilauea Volcano, Hawaii, permits detection of onset of volcanic activity. (*a*) Infrared image. Tonal variation shows distribution of radiant heat; the brighter the tone, the warmer the surface. (*b*) Aerial photograph. Large vent at left and small vent at right are within large crater (caldera). AT-11 mapping camera. 1 ft = 0.3 m. (*U.S. Geological Survey*)

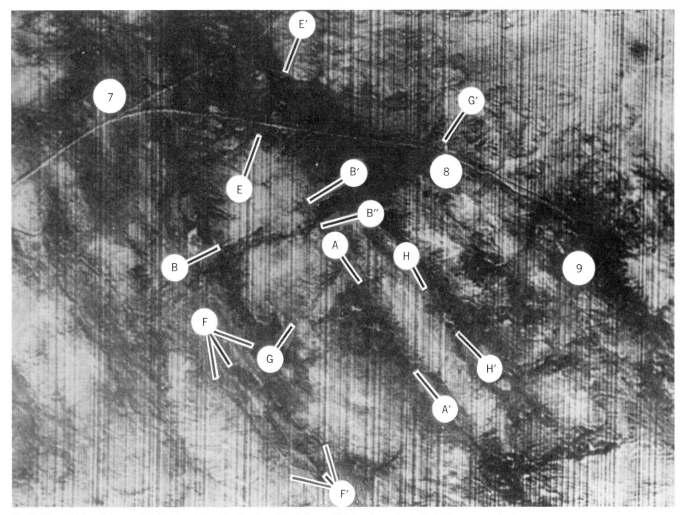

Fig. 6. Thermal infrared image of part of the Goldfields, Nevada, mineral district. Moisture is greater in the fracture zones of this district, which show up as dark bands mainly trending NW-SE (labeled FF′, AA′, HH′). A few less well-developed fractures trend ENE (labeled BB′ and BB″). In this district, commercial mineralization is best developed in fracture zones and in areas where hydrothermal alteration is most intense.

composition of the illuminated area, its moisture content, vegetation extent and type, surface roughness, and even temperature in certain circumstances.

Radar returns are recorded in various forms to aid in their analysis. The forms having primary geoscience interest can be placed in one of the following categories: (1) scattering coefficients, which are a powerful tool in studying the nature of radar return and which have been correlated with different terrain types and directly applied to oceanic surface studies; (2) altimetry data; (3) penetration measurements, which have been utilized for mineral exploration, for example, detection of faults through moisture associated with them; and (4) radar images.

Of these techniques, imagery generally presents the optimum information content for terrestrial geologic purposes, partly because well-developed photographic interpretation techniques are applicable to radar image analysis. These images are especially valuable for delineating various structural phenomena, as shown in Fig. 8.

The image record of the terrain return is affected by the frequency, angle of incidence, and polarization of the radar signal. For example, if the terrain being imaged is covered by vegetation, a K-band (35 GHz) signal records the vegetation, whereas a P-band (0.4 GHz) signal is likely to penetrate the vegetation and thus record a combination of vegetation and soil surface. In general, each frequency band represents a potential source of unique data. The angle of incidence of the incident wave affects the image because of radar shadowing on the backside of protruding objects. The angle of incidence can also show differences because of changes in orientation of the many facets on a surface which affect the return strength. Although information is lost in the shadow region, the extent of the shadow indicates the height of the object and therefore has been useful in emphasizing linear features such as faults and lineations reflecting joint systems.

Although imaging radars have been flown on aircraft for a number of years, it was not until 1978 that the first space-borne radar imagery became available with the launching of *Seasat* on June 28, 1978. This research satellite carried a radar altimeter, a radar scatterometer, a visible and infrared radiometer, and a scanning multichannel microwave radiometer, in addition to a synthetic-aperture radar (SAR) imaging in the L-band (1.275 GHz) with a swath width of 62 mi (100 km). *Seasat* failed in orbit on October 10, 1978, as a result of a massive short circuit in the electrical system. Fortunately, a considerable amount of

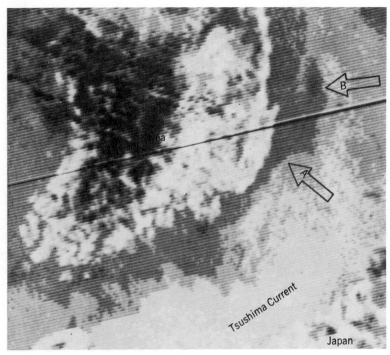

Fig. 7. Thermal infrared image of the Korea Straits, between South Korea and Japan. This image was acquired by the Defense Meteorological Satellite Program (DMSP) on October 13, 1972. DMSP infrared-sensor ground resolution is 2 nautical miles (4 km). The light-gray waters (warm) are part of the Tsushima Current, while the darker gray areas (cool) are the coastal shelf waters. An oceanic "front" forms the boundary between the continental shelf waters and the Tsushima Current. The front turns seaward at A, and a cyclonic eddy is located at B.

data was recorded from several experimental test areas. **Figure 9** is a mosaic of *Seasat* radar imagery taken over the Cape Cod, Massachusetts, area. Internal waves are readily apparent. These are waves with lengths of several hundred meters or more between crests, and they originate below the surface of the ocean due to internal slippage between water layers of different density. The amplitude of the waves is greatest at the density discontinuity. They are generally well developed in coastal waters. Such waves have been noted on a number of the *Seasat* SAR images. The brighter areas on the bottom of Fig. 9 are believed to be due to higher winds in these areas, although no detailed analysis of this image supported by accompanying sea surface truth data has been published. Additional airborne and satellite flights are planned with SAR over controlled test sites because the optimum flight trajectories (azimuths), depression angles, wavelengths (X-, L-band, and so on), and polarizations (HH, HV, and so on) needed for extracting the full data content from the signals received are not fully understood. Although the analysis of oceanographic data returns from SAR are still in their infancy, it is already clear that SAR will yield very valuable information because of its high resolution and all-weather (cloud-penetrating) capability.

High-frequency (hf) radar. Such radars utilize frequencies in the 3-30-MHz portion of the electromagnetic spectrum (median wavelength of about 20 m) and are thus not within the microwave part of the spectrum. The energy is transmitted by ground-based

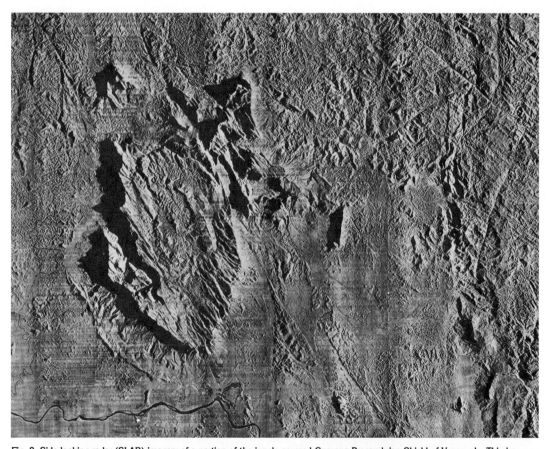

Fig. 8. Side-looking radar (SLAR) imagery of a portion of the jungle-covered Guayana Precambrian Shield of Venezuela. This imagery was acquired by a Goodyear synthetic-aperture X-band (3.12-cm) radar system mounted on board an Aero Service Caravelle aircraft. The flight altitude was 46,000 ft (14,030 m). The east-west dimension of the image mosaic is approximately 104 mi (168 km).

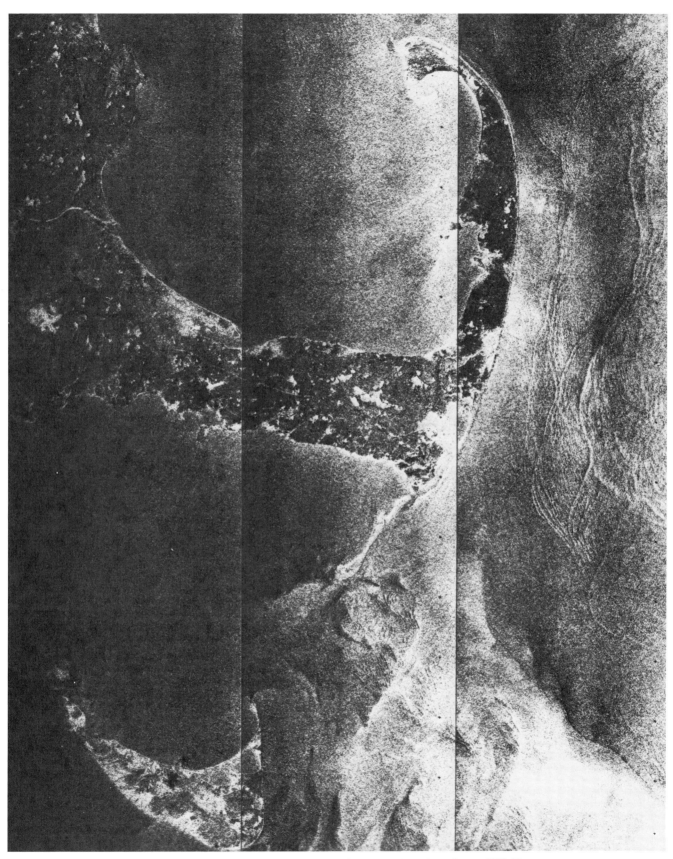

Fig. 9. Mosaic view of part of the Cape Cod, Massachusetts, area acquired by synthetic-aperture radar on board *Seasat*, 1978. The top of the figure is north. Nantucket Island is in the lower left portion of the figure. Internal waves are visible east of Cape Cod. The bright area in the lower part of the figure is believed to be roughened sea due to stronger wind action in this area. (*Johns Hopkins University Applied Physics Laboratory, under contract to the U.S. Navy.*)

antennas in either a sky-wave or surface-wave mode. In the sky-wave mode, the energy is refracted by the various ionospheric layers back down to the Earth's surface some 500–1800 mi (800–3000 km) (on a single-hop basis) away from the hf radar antenna site. The incident waves are reflected from such surface features as sea waves, and the reflections are enhanced when the wavelength of the sea waves is twice the wavelength of the incident radar waves (Bragg reflection effect). In addition, the Doppler principle is applied to determine the component of sea-wave velocities moving toward or away from the radar. Spot sizes observed on the ocean surface by this sky-wave method are now as fine as 9 mi (15 km) in azimuth by 2 mi (3 km) in range, and it is expected that these resolution cells can be reduced by further development work.

In addition to this experimental use of hf radars for remote sensing of sea state, they are being used as telemetry (communication) and direction and range-finding links in conjunction with disposable buoys or drogues. The buoys are used to detect the sea state, surface and subsurface temperature, salinity, and so forth. The information is relayed back to the interrogating site by either sky-wave or surface-wave modes. The surface waves are that portion of the hf wavefront that follows closely along the Earth's surface. Ranges of 60–180 mi (100–300) km or so are possible with this mode, and the buoys can be interrogated and located by low-cost direction-finding loops and commercial battery-powered receivers. The big advantage of these ground-based hf radars is that they can maintain continuous monitoring of an ocean area, while satellite-borne radars can monitor only the areas that they happen to be flying over at the time. In the case of the *Landsat* system, the satellite comes over (revisits) the same area about every 18 days, while in the case of the *Defense Meteorological Satellite Program (DMSP)* craft the frequency of revisits can be up to several times daily, depending upon how many satellites are in orbit at one time. Neither the *Landsat* nor *DMSP* carry all-weather radar systems, however.

Peter C. Badgley

Bibliography. American Society of Photogrammetry, and Remote Sensing Staff and American Congress on Surveying and Mapping, *Remote Sensing*, vol. 1, 1987; A. Chedin (ed.), *Microwave Remote Sensing of the Earth System*, 1989; R. N. Colwell (ed.), *Manual of Remote Sensing*, 2 vols., 2d ed., 1983; A. P. Cracknell and L. W. Hayes, *Introduction to Remote Sensing*, 1990; P. Curran, K. Kondratyev, and V. Kozogerov, *Remote Sensing of Soils and Vegetation*, 1990; G. P. De Loor (ed.), *Radar Remote Sensing of the Atmospheres and the Oceans*, 1984; S. A. Drury, *A Guide to Remote Sensing: Interpreting Images of the Earth*, 1990; Environmental Research Institute of Michigan, *Proceedings of the 14th International Symposium on Remote Sensing of the Environment*, 1980; M. T. Halbouty, *Future Programs and Prospects for Resource Exploration from Space by the Year 2000,* paper presented to the American Astronautics Society, November 1978; M. T. Halbouty, Geologic significance of Landsat data for 15 giant oil and gas fields. *Amer. Ass. Petrol. Geol.*, 64(1):8–36, 1980; Johns Hopkins University Applied Physics Laboratory, *Proceedings of Symposium on Spaceborne Synthetic Aperture Radar for Radio Oceanography*, 1980; R. M. Measures, *Laser Remote Sensing*, 1984; P. Pamploni, *Microwave Radiometry and Remote Sensing Applications*, 1989: J. Vernberg (ed.), *Processes in Marine Remote Sensing*, 1981.

River

A natural, fresh-water surface stream that has considerable volume compared with its smaller tributaries. The tributaries are known as brooks, creeks, branches, or forks. Rivers are usually the main stems and larger tributaries of the drainage systems that convey surface runoff from the land. Rivers flow from headwater areas of small tributaries to their mouths, where they may discharge into the ocean, a major lake, or a desert basin.

Rivers flowing to the ocean drain about 68% of the Earth's land surface. The remainder of the land either is covered by ice or drains to closed basins (common in desert regions). Regions draining to the sea are termed exoreic, while those draining to interior closed basins are endoreic. Areic regions are those which lack surface streams because of low rainfall or lithologic conditions.

Sixteen of the largest rivers (see **table**) account for nearly half of the total world river flow of water. The Amazon River alone carries nearly 20% of all the water annually discharged by the world's rivers. Rivers also carry large loads of sediment. The total sediment load for all the world's rivers averages about 22×10^9 tons (20×10^9 metric tons) brought to the sea each year. Sediment loads for individual rivers vary considerably. The Yellow River of northern China is the most prolific transporter of sediment. Draining an agricultural region of easily eroded loess, this river averages about 2×10^9 tons (1.8×10^9 metric tons) of sediment per year, one-tenth of the world average.

River channels and patterns. The morphological features and the sizes of river channels depend on the supply of water and sediment from upstream. The dependency can be summarized in the proportions below, where Q_w is a measure of mean annual water

$$Q_w \propto \frac{w, d, \lambda}{S}$$

$$Q_s \propto \frac{w, \lambda, S}{d, P}$$

discharge (volume carried by the river per unit time) and Q_s is a measure of the type of sediment given by the proportion of coarse bedload (sand and gravel) to the total load (which includes considerable fine sediment). Q_w and Q_s are the controlling variables, while the other variables are dependent variables. The size of the river channel is indicated by its width w and depth d. Note that larger water discharges produce proportionally larger river channels. The slope or gradient of the river channel S is inversely proportional to the water discharge Q_w but directly proportional to the percentage of coarse load Q_s.

The sinuosity of a river P is the ratio of its channel length to its valley length. A perfectly straight river would have a sinuosity of 1. Such rivers are uncommon. Meandering is the most common river pattern (**Fig. 1**), and meandering rivers develop alternating bends that often have a regular spacing along the valley trend. The spacing of two successive bends is defined as the meander wavelength λ. Note that, like

Characteristics of some of the world's major rivers

River	Average discharge, ft³/s (m³/s)	Drainage area, 10³ mi² (10³ km²)	Average annual sediment load, 10³ tons (10³ metric tons)	Length, mi (km)
Amazon	6,390,000 (181,000)	2770 (7180)	990,000 (900,000)	3899 (6275)
Congo	1,400,000 (39,620)	1420 (3690)	71,300 (64,680)	2901 (4670)
Orinoco	800,000 (22,640)	571 (1480)	93,130 (86,490)	1600 (2570)
Yangtze	770,000 (21,790)	749 (1940)	610,000 (550,000)	3100 (4990)
Brahmaputra	706,000 (19,980)	361 (935)	880,000 (800,000)	1700 (2700)
Mississippi-Missouri	630,000 (17,830)	1240 (3220)	379,000 (344,000)	3890 (6260)
Yenisei	614,000 (17,380)	1000 (2590)	11,600 (10,520)	3550 (5710)
Lena	546,671 (15,480)	1170 (3030)	—	2900 (4600)
Mekong	530,000 (15,000)	350 (910)	206,850 (187,650)	2600 (4180)
Paraná	526,000 (14,890)	1200 (3100)	90,000 (81,650)	2450 (3940)
St. Lawrence	500,000 (14,150)	564 (1460)	4,000 (3,630)	2150 (3460)
Ganges	497,600 (14,090)	451 (1170)	1,800,000 (1,600,000)	1640 (2640)
Irrawaddy	478,900 (13,560)	140 (370)	364,070 (330,280)	1400 (2300)
Ob	440,700 (12,480)	1000 (2590)	15,700 (14,240)	2800 (4500)
Volga	350,000 (9,900)	591 (1530)	20,780 (18,840)	2320 (3740)
Amur	338,000 (9,570)	788 (2040)	—	2900 (4670)

channel width, meander wavelength is directly proportional to both Q_w and Q_s. Sinuosity P is somewhat independent of Q_s, but it depends strongly on the percentage of coarse load Q_s. Highly sinuous streams often transport fine-grained loads and tend to be narrow and deep.

Braided rivers have channels that are divided into anastomosing branches by alluvial islands and bars. They often have steeper gradients, more variable discharges, coarser sediment loads, and lower sinuosity than meandering rivers. The details of river pattern development are more complex than can be presented here. In addition to Q_w and Q_s, important controlling variables include the texture of floodplain and bank sediments, the absolute amount of sediment transported, the channel gradient, the channel stability, and the discharge variability.

River floods. River discharge varies over a broad range, depending on many climatic and geologic factors. The low flows of the river influence water supply and navigation. The high flows are a concern as threats to life and property. However, floods are also beneficial. Indeed, the ancient Egyptian civilization was dependent upon the Nile River floods to provide new soil and moisture for crops.

Floods are a natural consequence of the spectrum of discharges exhibited by a river (**Fig. 2**). Rivers in humid temperate regions often exhibit less variable flood behavior than rivers in semiarid regions of rugged terrain. Floods in the humid regions tend to occur on average once each year. Rarer, larger floods are often no more than one or two times the magnitude of more common annual floods. The semiarid floods, however, are usually very small for common events, such as the average annual flood. However, rare, high-magnitude floods may be catastrophic.

The greatest floods in the geologic record occurred during the Pleistocene about 13,000 years ago in the northwestern United States. Lake Missoula, an ice-dammed lake in western Montana, released several catastrophic floods across the Channeled Scabland region of eastern Washington. The largest of these floods discharged as much as 20×10^6 ft³ (570,000 m³) of water per second. Flow velocities in the Scabland channelways ranged from 33 to 100 ft/s (10 to 30 m/s) for water 100–330 ft (30–100 m) deep. These phenomenal floods created a bizarre landscape of anastomosing channels, abandoned cataracts, streamlined hills, and immense gravel bars. So much water entered the preflood river valleys that they filled to overflowing, and floodwater scoured the divide areas between the valleys.

The Missoula floods were certainly among the most spectacular fluvial phenomena of all time. However, it should be remembered that most rivers do their work very slowly. Rivers are mainly transport agents, removing debris produced by the prolonged action of rainsplash, frost action, and mass movement. The many smaller floods probably accomplish much more of this work of transport than the rare large flood.

Floods are but one attribute of rivers that affect human society. Means of counteracting the vagaries of river flow have concerned engineers for centuries. Today many of the world's rivers are managed to conserve the natural flow for release at times required

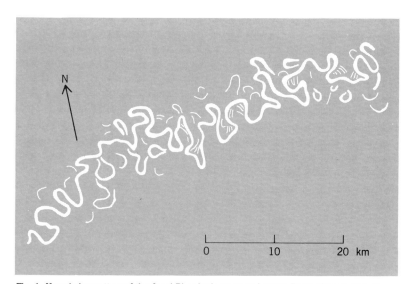

Fig. 1. Meandering pattern of the Juruá River in the western Amazon Basin of Brazil. Note the many abandoned meander loops created by this active river. 1 km = 0.6 mi. (*After V. R. Baker, Adjustment of fluvial systems to climate and source terrain in tropical and subtropical environments, Can. Soc. Petrol. Geol. Mem. 5, pp. 211–230, 1978*)

Fig. 2. Pedernales River near Fredericksburg, Texas, during the flood of August 3, 1978. Note the scour of the stream bank on the right side of this aerial photograph.

by human activity, to confine flood flows to the channel and to planned areas of floodwater storage, and to maintain water quality at optimum levels. *See River engineering*.

Geologic history. Some rivers possess a long heritage related to their location along relatively stable continental cratons or their correspondence to structural lows, such as rift valleys. More commonly, rivers have been disrupted through geologic time by the Earth's active tectonic and erosional processes. The most recent disruptions were caused by the glaciations of the Pleistocene. Many rivers, like the Mississippi, became heavily loaded with coarse glacial debris de-

livered to their headwaters by glaciers. Since the last glacial maximum about 18,000 years ago, most of the world's rivers have adjusted their channel sizes, patterns, and gradients to the new environmental conditions of postglacial time.

In tropical regions the effects of glaciation were indirect. During full-glacial episodes of the Pleistocene, tropical areas of the Amazon and Congo river basins experienced relative aridity. Forests were replaced by savanna and grassland. The greater erosion rates on the land contributed large amounts of coarse sediment to the rivers. Today these regions have returned to their high-rainfall condition. The rivers receive relatively little sediment from interfluves that are stabilized by a dense forest cover. However, it is alarming that human exploitation of the tropical forests is effectively returning the landscape to its glacial condition. This will undoubtedly induce profound changes in many tropical rivers.

Rivers on Mars? Orbital photographs of Mars obtained during the Viking space mission (**Fig. 3**) reveal that the planet possesses a remarkable variety of channeled terrains. Some channels form relatively small networks up to 60 mi (100 km) in length that resemble the dendritic valley systems of the Earth. The most spectacular channels, however, constitute great anastomosing complexes up to 60 mi (100 km) wide that can be traced 1200 mi (2000 km) or more across the planet's surface. These zones are called outflow channels because they appear full-born at localized source regions, usually collapse zones. It has suggested that immense floods of water were released from within the planet, emanating from troughs that receded headward to form the channels. The collapse zones at the heads of the channels mark the last points of fluid release.

The origin of the Martian channels is still somewhat controversial. Nevertheless, it is an exciting thought that rivers may be studied on other planets.

                                                            Victor R. Baker

Bibliography. C. H. Crickmay, *The Work of the River*, 1975; B. R. Davies and K. F. Walker (eds.), *The Ecology of River Systems*, 1986; W. L. Graf, *Fluvial Processes in Dryland Rivers*, 1988; M. Morisawa, *Streams: Their Dynamics and Morphology*, 1968; J. N. Rayner, *Conservation, Equilibrium and Feedback Applied to Atmospheric and Fluvial Processes*, 1972; R. J. Russel, *River Plains and Sea Coasts*, 1967; S. A. Schumm, *The Fluvial System*, 1977; S. A. Schumm, *River Morphology*, 1982; M. M. Smart et al. (eds.), *Ecological Perspectives of the Upper Mississippi River*, 1986; B. A. Whitton (ed.), *Ecology of European Rivers*, 1989.

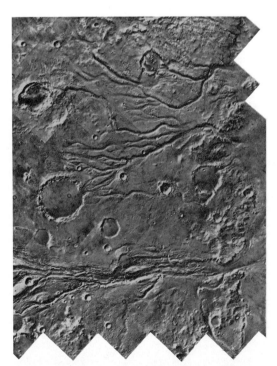

Fig. 3. Large channels in the Chryse Planitis region of Mars. This *Viking* photograph shows a scene about 90 × 120 mi (150 × 200 km). (*NASA*)

River engineering

A branch of civil engineering concerned with the improvement and stabilization of the channels of rivers (particularly channels in erodible alluvium) to better serve the needs of people.

Application. Throughout history, river valleys and river channels have been important to most civilizations. However, the characteristics of some rivers in their natural states have deterred or presented hazards to development of their valleys or beneficial uses of their channels. In many major river systems there is a need to improve channels in order to provide greater flood flow capacity, provide navigable waterways,

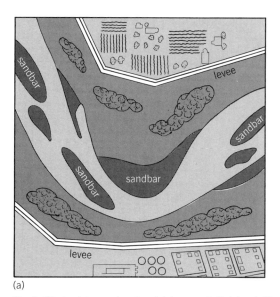
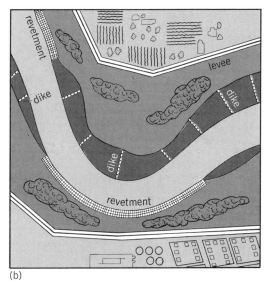

Fig. 1. Effects of river engineering. (*a*) An uncontrolled river (with sharp bends, divided channel, clogging shifting sandbars, and caving banks) threatening flood control levees, cities, and industry and difficult to navigate. (*b*) The same improved and stabilized river, with a single channel of gentle bends and controlled width for easy navigation, and the threat from caving banks removed.

improve water supplies, and stabilize the channels to permit development of adjacent valley areas (**Fig. 1**). This has led to development of extensive and costly river control or management schemes. *See River*.

Channel improvement and stabilization works have been integral parts of river control plans where meandering, shifting channels or inappropriate channel alignments and cross sections are problems. Large-scale channel improvement and stabilization plans have been carried out on many of the world's major rivers. In the United States the most extensive examples of river engineering are found in the Mississippi Basin, along such streams as the Missouri River, the Arkansas River, the Red River, the Atchafalaya River, and the Mississippi River downstream from St. Louis, Missouri. Important objectives of these works are the development of navigable waterways, the improvement of flood flow capacities, and the protection of adjacent flood control levees and valley lands from the disastrous effects of major channel changes. River channel improvement and stabilization works often supplement other types of river management development. *See Dam*.

Potamology. In essence, river engineering works seek to direct or work with the natural processes involved in a stream with erodible bed and banks (**Fig. 2**) to arrive at a stable channel of desired cross section and alignment. It has been recognized that the characteristics of such a stream are governed by complex interrelationships among factors such as the geologic history of the area, the volume and variability of streamflow, stream gradients, erosional characteristics of the contributing area and the channel itself, and the type and amounts of sediment load carried by the stream (both as suspended sediments and as bed load). Even the temperature of the water in the stream has been found to have an effect on the depositional forms in a stream bed and the flow capacity of the

Fig. 2. Caving Mississippi River bank subject to active erosion.

Fig. 3. Constructing stone fill dike on the Lower Mississippi River.

channel. The study of the factors affecting river channels has led to development of a branch of engineering science called potamology, which aims to systematize field and laboratory investigation of river channels and provide rational bases for predictions of the effects on channel characteristics of proposed engineering works. These systematic studies have provided the civil engineer with a much better understanding of the processes involved in river channels. For example, some early channel improvement projects attempted to straighten meandering channels, but the streams would develop new patterns of erosion that would reestablish meander patterns. Now stream improvement projects are planned to continue the general gradients and patterns of sinuosity that are characteristic of the natural streams. SEE STREAM TRANSPORT AND DEPOSITION.

Types of works. A number of types of construction have been developed for use in improving and stabilizing river channels. Each type seeks to achieve one or more of the following objectives: direct improvement of channel geometry by excavation and filling;

armoring of bed or banks of a stream to resist erosion; deflection of river currents from an area subject to undesired erosion; and stilling of river currents in an area of the stream to induce deposition of sediments.

Excavation and filling. Excavation of pilot cutoff channels across meander loops can utilize the erosive forces of river flow to make major changes in stream alignment at relatively low cost. Because of the shorter length of the cutoff channel, as compared with the original around the meander bend, and the consequent steeper hydraulic gradient through the cutoff, the new channel through the cutoff can develop relatively rapidly by erosion. In the 1930s an extensive program of cutoff construction on the Lower Mississippi River shortened the river's length by 152 mi (245 km). Excavation by dredging of shoals or sandbars within a river channel is a commonly used method for improving and maintaining project depths in inland waterways.

Armoring. A great many types of materials and methods of construction have been used to armor river beds and banks to resist erosion, including: planting of willows or other vegetation on banks that are submerged infrequently; mats woven of trunks of willow or similar trees or of sawed timbers sunk in the area to be protected and weighted with stones; dumped or hand-placed rock riprap; gabions (or baskets with covers) made of such materials as wire mesh and filled with stones; asphaltic concrete paving (on upper bank areas); and articulated concrete mats or mattresses. Economy and availability of materials and labor, depths and velocities of water in the areas to be protected, size of those areas, and long-term effectiveness of the protection provided have been factors in the selection among types of erosion protection. High labor costs and scarcity of materials have discouraged use of willow or timber mats in recent decades. Blowouts of impervious asphaltic concrete pavement caused by pressure of water trapped behind the pavement during falling river stages have discouraged the use of that type of bank protection.

There is need to safeguard an erosion protection system against loss of underlying foundation soils caused by pumping action of waves or changes in river stages. To prevent such loss of foundation material, a sand and gravel filter layer or especially prepared filter cloth is often placed between the foundation and the erosion-resistant materials forming the armor layer.

Deflection and stilling of currents. Systems of dikes

Fig. 4. Placing articulated concrete mattress revetment for protection against scour.

are used to deflect currents and to provide stilling action to induce deposition in an area that otherwise would be subject to undesirable erosion (**Fig. 3**). Dikes constructed of one or more lines of timber piles driven into the river bottom with timbers connecting the piles to form a fencelike, permeable structure have been used extensively. Rock or rubble mound dikes formed of quarried stone have been used exclusively in recent years on the Lower Mississippi River. One type of deflection structure consists of structural steel sections welded together to produce a frame resembling a very large version of the jacks with which children play. Lines of these frames connected by steel cables and anchored in place have been used to protect stream areas under heavy erosion attack.

Examples of projects. In nature many reaches of the Missouri River were meandering and unstable with sharp bends and shallow, often divided or braided, low-water channels. Since 1950 the Missouri River, from its junction with the Mississippi River near St. Louis, Missouri, to Sioux City, Iowa, 750 mi (1200 km) upstream, has been transformed into an inland waterway for 9-ft (2.7-m) draft barge navigation. This has been accomplished primarily through the use of pile dikes to contract, deepen, and realign the low-water channel to provide adequate depths and channel geometry suitable for barge navigation.

On the Arkansas River and the Red River in Arkansas and Louisiana, systems of navigation locks and dams provide waterways for barge navigation, but the projects on both rivers also include extensive bank and channel stabilization works.

In nature, the Mississippi River below Cape Girardeau, Missouri, was a wild, ever-changing, unpredictable stream. Throughout the length of the alluvial valley of the Mississippi, from Cape Girardeau to the Gulf of Mexico, numerous ancient oxbow lakes, abandoned river channels, and various types of alluvial deposits mark the past wide meandering of this mighty river as it carried runoff from 41% of what is now the contiguous United States. In 1928 the Mississippi River and Tributaries (MR&T) Project was authorized as a Federal undertaking to provide flood protection and dependable water transportation. The MR&T Project includes such features as extensive levee systems, floodways, and tributary improvements, but one central feature of the basin plan is the improvement and stabilization of the Mississippi River channel. After a half-century of work, dramatic improvement in the river channel has been made, but work to bring this channel under control is still in progress.

As noted above, the channel improvement plan for the MR&T Project included a number of cutoffs to straighten and shorten reaches of the river. Since the cutoffs were made, revetment of banks to provide erosion protection, dikes, and dredging have been the principal means for stabilizing the alignment of the 1000-mi-long (1600-km) channel. The methods of stabilization now in use have evolved over the years, and research and development efforts to improve the methods are continuing. Perhaps the most notable development in the MR&T channel stabilization work has been the articulated concrete mattress revetment currently used for protection against scour (**Figs. 4** and **5**). This type of mattress is composed of concrete blocks 3 in. (76 mm) thick, each block being approximately 14 in. (36 cm) wide by 4 ft (1.2 m) long. Twenty such blocks are cast as a section approximately 4 ft (1.2 m) wide by 25 ft (7.5 m) long held

Fig. 5. Stone upper bank paving used in conjunction with articulated concrete mattress on the subaqueous bank.

together by a noncorrosive wire fabric located at the central plane of each block. By a complex and highly mechanized process, these mat sections are manufactured at several casting fields located at strategic points along the Mississippi, hauled by barge to a sinking plant at the mat-laying locations, assembled into mattresses up to 156 ft (47.5 m) in width (held together by corrosion-resisting cables and wire ties), and launched over the side of the sinking plant to rest on the bottom of the river in the area where revetment protection is needed. Placement of each mattress section starts near the water's edge and, as the mattress is assembled and tied together on the sinking plant, the sinking plant is moved out away from the river bank and the mattress is played out into successively deeper water as much as 600 ft (180 m) from the shore (**Fig. 6**). Each mattress section is tied by wire cables to anchors buried in the river bank at its shoreward end. Mat placement proceeds upstream along the river bank, and each successive mattress overlaps the previously placed downstream mattress.

Prior to placement of the underwater articulated concrete mattress, the river bank is graded to a uniform stable slope from the top of the bank to below the water surface. After mattress placement the graded upper bank is paved with graded riprap.

Dikes are employed extensively in the MR&T channel stabilization work to deflect currents, to trap sand, and to close off back channels at islands and sandbars. Wood piling dikes were used in the past, but to secure more permanence and more immediate effectiveness, dumped quarried-rock dikes have been constructed in recent years.

Excavation of underwater deposits by floating pipe-

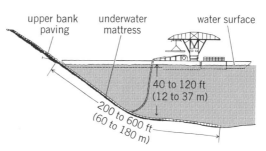

Fig. 6. Cross section of revetment operation.

line dredges is employed in development and maintenance of navigable depths on the Mississippi River. The period of falling river stages following a flood, when reduced current velocities accelerate deposition of sediments, is critical in the maintenance of navigable depths in many sections of the river. As planned dike and revetment construction is completed, it is anticipated that maintenance dredging requirements will lessen.

Homer B. Willis; Staff of the Mississippi River Commission, U.S. Army Corps of Engineers

Bibliography. N. R. Moore, *Improvement of the Lower Mississippi River and Tributaries,* 1972; Office of the President, Mississippi River Commission, *Channel Improvement Feature, Flood Control, Mississippi River and Tributaries Project,* 1977; Public Affairs Office, Mississippi River Commission and U.S. Army Engineer Division, Lower Mississippi Valley, U.S. Army Corps of Engineers, *Flood Control in the Lower Mississippi River Valley,* 1976; U.S. Army Engineer District, Omaha, Corps of Engineers, *Potamology Investigation, Historical Records Research,* 1976; U.S. Army Engineer District, Omaha, Corps of Engineers, *Velocity Trends,* 1971.

Rural sanitation

Those procedures, employed in areas outside incorporated cities and not governed by city ordinances, that act on the human environment for the purpose of maintaining or improving public health. Their purpose is the furtherance of community cleanliness and orderliness for esthetic as well as health values.

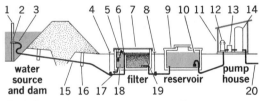

Fig. 1. Farm-pond water-treatment system. The numbers are explained in text.

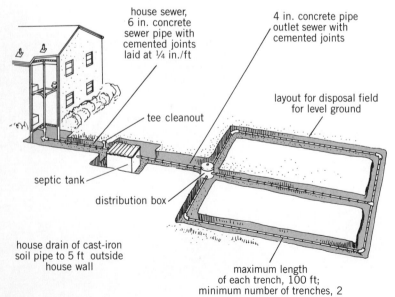

house sewer, 6 in. concrete sewer pipe with cemented joints laid at ¼ in./ft

4 in. concrete pipe outlet sewer with cemented joints

tee cleanout

layout for disposal field for level ground

septic tank

distribution box

house drain of cast-iron soil pipe to 5 ft outside house wall

maximum length of each trench, 100 ft; minimum number of trenches, 2

Fig. 2. Typical family-size sewage-disposal system. 1 in. = 2.5 cm; 1 ft = 0.3 m.

Water. Purification of water supplies since 1900 has helped to prolong human life more than any other public-health measure. Organisms which produce such diseases as typhoid, dysentery, and cholera may survive for a long time in polluted water, and prevention of water contamination is imperative to keep down the spread of diseases. Watertight covers for wells are important means of preventing surface contamination to the water supply in rural areas.

Purification of a surface water supply, such as from a lake or a farm pond, is accomplished by sedimentation, filtering, and chlorination. Sedimentation can be effected in a storage chamber by adding aluminum sulfate, which flocculates the finer particles of soil and other undesirable matter in suspension in the water. Filtering through fine sand removes the flocculated particles. Finally, the water is purified by a chlorine solution at the rate of ½–1 part of chlorine to 10^6 parts of water. The system of treatment for farm-pond water in **Fig. 1** comprises (1) hedge post or pipe; (2) screen suspended from post 3 ft or 90 cm under water; (3) flexible pipe; (4) hand valve; (5) aspirator, or alum feeder; (6) float valve; (7) hinged wood cover; (8) hand valve; (9) reinforced concrete top; (10) foot valve and strainer; (11) insulated pump house; (12) automatic pump; (13) automatic chlorinator; (14) pressure tank; (15) 2-in. or 5-cm iron pipe or plastic pipe muting; (16) concrete cutoff collar; (17) drain when needed; (18) coagulation sedimentation chamber; (19) washed river sand screened through ⅛-in. or 3-mm sieve; and (20) purified water to house, below frost line..

The colon bacillus is the usual indicator of pollution of water supplies by human waste. Chlorine kills such organisms, and therefore it is widely used for purification of water supplies.

Sewage disposal. The problem of safe disposal of sewage becomes more complex as population increases. The old practice of piping sewage to the nearest body of water has proved to be dangerous. Sanitary engineering techniques are now being used in rural areas, as well as in cities, for the disposal of household and human wastes. Where sewage-plant facilities are not available, the most satisfactory method of sewage disposal is by means of the septic tank system (**Fig. 2**). SEE SANITARY ENGINEERING.

The septic tank system makes use of a watertight tank for receiving all sewage. Bacterial action takes place in the septic tank and most of the sewage solids decompose, are given off as gases, or go out into the drainage lines as liquid. The gas and liquid are then released from the top 2 ft (60 cm) of soil without odor or sanitary problems. The solids that do not decompose settle to the bottom of the tank, where they can be easily removed and disposed of safely. Such a sewage-disposal system has made it possible for all farm homes and rural communities to have modern bathroom equipment and sanitary methods of sewage disposal. SEE SEPTIC TANK; SEWAGE DISPOSAL.

Harold E. Stover

Saline water reclamation

The partial or almost complete demineralization of sea and brackish waters, geothermal brines, wastewaters, and industrial effluents to make fresh water suitable for human or animal consumption, diverse industrial uses, irrigation, recreation, or aquifer recharge—broadly referred to as desalination. The min-

Table 1. Typical mineral content of different waters

Type of feed water	Mineral content, ppm
Brackish water	100–5000
Seawater	10,000–45,000*
Geothermal brines	3000–20,000
Industrial effluents	500–5000
Municipal wastewaters	500–5000

*In some locations up to 70,000.

eral content of these waters (**Table 1**) is expressed in units of parts per million (ppm), giving the mineral content in terms of parts by weight of dissolved minerals in a million parts of water or parts per million salinity. The quality requirement for the fresh-water product depends upon its use.

Standards. The U.S. Department of Health, Education and Welfare Public Health Service Drinking Water Standard of 1962 requires that the total dissolved solids of drinking water used on common carriers engaged in interstate commerce should not exceed 500 ppm when other, more suitable supplies are or can be made available.

Water containing several thousand parts per million of dissolved minerals is consumed by humans in many locations without noticeable ill effects, especially where the rate of perspiration is high. Suitable salinities for irrigation waters depend upon the chemistry of the soil and the mineral requirements of the crop, but generally should not exceed about 1200 ppm, particularly if the sodium content is high. Ruminant animals have developed tolerances for salinities up to 12,000 ppm. Industrial water requirements vary greatly from 10 parts per billion (ppb) for pressurized water reactors to about 1 ppm for boiler waters and semiconductor processing, and up to 35,000 ppm or more for some flushing and cooling operations.

Separation processes. A diversity of approaches are used for the separation of water from saline solutions. Thermal processes effect separation by means of phase changes and include distillation and freezing processes. In the membrane processes, one or more suitably designed organic membranes accomplish the separation process. In a single membrane design, reverse osmosis (RO) pressure forces the fresh water through the membrane. In electrodialysis (ED), a system using multiple membranes, direct current leads to formation of pure water and brine streams and drives the salt ions toward the electrodes through charge-selective membranes. There are also chemical processes. In the ion exchange process, substances are added to exchange the ions in the solution or to precipitate the salts. In the solvent extraction process, chemicals with greater affinity for water can remove the wastes from solutions, a system which has not met with commercial success.

There is no optimum or universal process for demineralization of all water streams. Each so-called contaminated or modified water stream must be evaluated for its peculiarities and an optimal process for purification for a specific end use recommended. Among the criteria to be considered are salinity, identity of the ions present, presence of other contaminants, nature of the water, availability, energy costs, quantity, and quality.

The absolute minimum theoretical thermodynamic energy required for separating 10^3 gal (3.8 m³) of

fresh water from seawater is 2.8 kilowatt-hours, but the energy requirement of virtually all processes exceeds this value manyfold. In fact, desalination is an energy-intensive process. Progress in improving water conversion technology and reducing requisite energy for the purpose of desalination has made major strides.

THERMAL PROCESSES

The separation in thermal processes is accomplished by a phase change caused by distillation or freezing.

Distillation methods. These have developed from comparatively simple systems. Distillation was introduced for shipboard use in seventeenth-century England, and finally in 1912 the first land-based unit of the single-effect submerged-tube type was built (**Fig. 1a**). The next generation of equipment consisted of multieffect submerged tube units (Fig. 1b). In the single-effect units water is evaporated and condensed once, while in multieffect units several evaporators or effects are utilized so that the latent heat of evaporation can be captured and reused at lower temperature and pressure, making the process more economical. An insuperable problem of submerged-tube distillation plants was the problem of scale. This was the formation of chemical deposits (scale) on the tubes

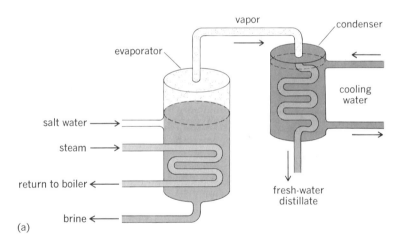

(a)

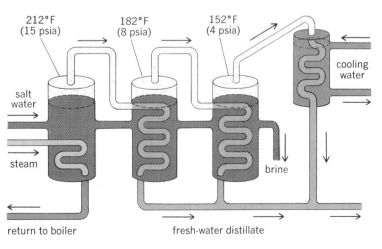

(b)

Fig. 1. Schematics of distillation process. (a) Single effect. (b) Multiple effect. °C = (°F − 32)/1.8; 1 psia = 6.895 kPa.

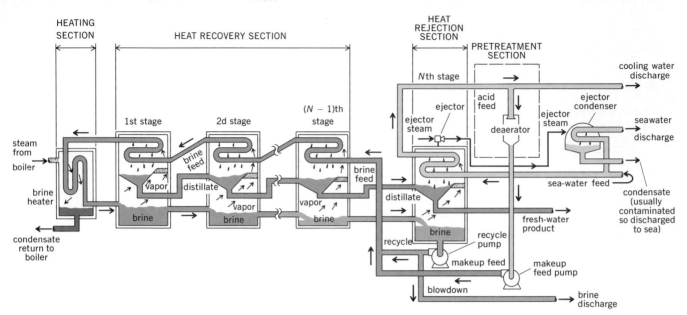

Fig. 2. Simplified flow sheet for multistage flash (MSF) recycle distillation. (*After O. K. Buros, The U.S.A.I.D. Desalination Manual, U.S. Agency for International Development and CH2M Hill International Corporation, August 1980, published by IDEA, 1981*)

(evaporating and heat transfer surfaces) which materially affected plant performance and had to be removed continuously. Both single-effect and multieffect submerged-tube distillers have become obsolete.

Multistage flash. The goal of avoiding the scaling of submerged-tube desalination plants led to the development of the multistage flash (MSF) process, where water is heated up to 480°F (250°C). Polyphosphate, sulfuric acid, or so-called high-temperature additives (Belgard type) are added to the seawater to prevent scaling. Polyphosphate-operated plants have an upper limit of 370°F (190°C); acid and high-temperature additive plants, 480°F (250°C). Both polyphosphate and acid-dosed plants are gradually being phased out; the first because of low thermal efficiencies, and the second, in order to decrease serious corrosion problems. A process modification, which removes the ions responsible for scaling from the water, has demon-

strated operational capabilities approaching 570°F (300°C). In all these units, the seawater is heated by counterflow through the system, recovering the heat of evaporation. The preheated water is given an additional amount of heat at the brine heater to bring it to the requisite temperature for the specific version of the process, and is then made to pass through a number of stages at successively lower temperatures and pressures when the seawater flashes (**Fig. 2**). The condensate from each stage is the product water. This multistage flash process has two versions: the so-called once-through MSF and the MSF with recirculation. The latter is the most widely used distillation process, accounting for over 80% of all land-based desalination plants in the world. Though the process is old, it has proved most reliable. The largest multistage flash complex in the world is in construction in Al Jubail, Saudi Arabia. It will have 2.5×10^8

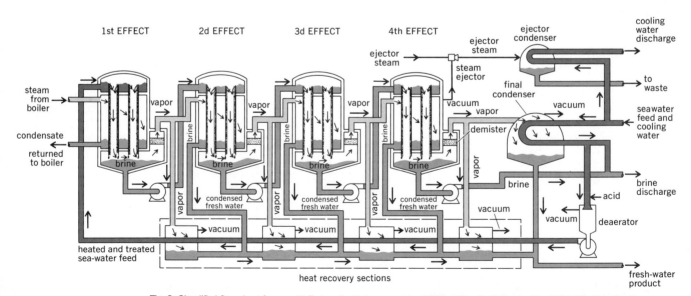

Fig. 3. Simplified flow sheet for a multieffect vertical-tube evaporator (VTE). (*After O. K. Buros, The U.S.A.I.D. Desalination Manual, U.S. Agency for International Development and CH2M Hill International Corporation, August 1980, published by IDEA, 1981*)

gal/day (9.5×10^5 m³/day) capacity. Thus multistage flash plants are expected to be providing distilled water until the year 2000, at least.

Vertical-tube evaporators. In these systems, counterflow preheated seawater, after being brought to boil, is distributed into the top of vertical tubes and allowed to fall as a film down the inside tube wall. Heat transfer through the falling film is excellent. A portion of the seawater evaporates, and this steam vapor is used to heat the outside of the tubes of the following effect, giving up its heat of evaporation as it condenses. The condensate is the product water. While vertical-tube evaporation offers potential for high performance, the process has had only marginal field success (**Fig. 3**).

Horizontal-tube multieffect (HTME) design. Another distillation plant system uses the horizontal-tube multieffect (**Fig. 4***a*) or the multieffect stacked design (Fig. 4*b*). These designs offer exciting future possibilities. Several plants of capacity over 10^6 gal/day (3.8×10^3 m³/day) are in service, and the largest facility of this type, a facility producing 10^7 gal/day (3.8×10^4 m³/day), is under joint United States–Israeli partnership.

Vapor compression (VC). Another distillation process is known as vapor compression. There are two versions: the spray-film vapor compression, usually encountered in smaller-type units of 2.5×10^3 to 3×10^4 gal/day (**Fig. 5**), suitable for facilities such as hotels, industrial plants, and power stations; and vertical-tube vapor compression, which is used for installations in the 10^5 gal/day-and-beyond size (**Fig. 6**). A variety of vapor compression units are found in installations around the world. The key to all these units is the compressor through which the energy is supplied to the system.

Performance ratio. Distillation plants are rated by performance ratio, the number of pounds of water produced for 10^3 Btu (10^6 J). In operational plants the ratios range from 6 to 16, though 20 and higher is considered possible.

Higher performance ratios are obtained at higher capital costs. Vapor compression plants which on the average offer higher performance ratios than multistage flash plants are distinguished by significantly higher operation and maintenance costs.

While the accepted processes predominate, the field itself remains dynamic, and much work directed at developing processes offering better performance and lower cost installations is in progress. Testing and ad-

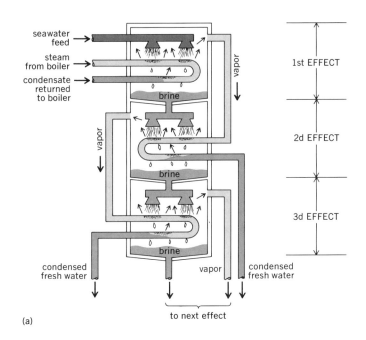

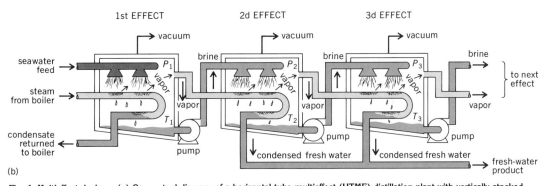

Fig. 4. Multieffect designs. (*a*) Conceptual diagram of a horizontal-tube multieffect (HTME) distillation plant with vertically stacked effects. (*b*) Conceptual diagram of a horizontal-tube multieffect distillation plant. (T = temperature, $T_1 > T_2 > T_3$; P = pressure, $P_1 > P_2 > P_3$). (*After O. K. Buros, The U.S.A.I.D. Desalination Manual, U.S. Agency for International Development and CH2M Hill International Corporation, August 1980, published by IDEA, 1981*)

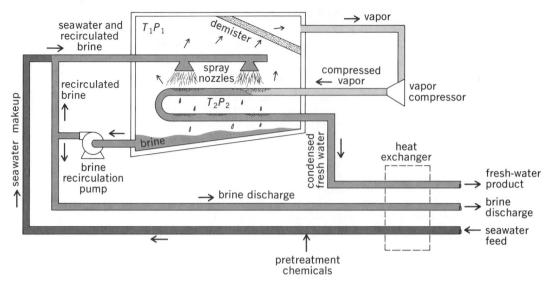

Fig. 5. Simplified flow diagram for an electrically driven spray-film vapor compression process. (T = temperature, $T_2 > T_1$; P = pressure, $P_2 > P_1$). (*After O. K. Buros, The U.S. A.I.D. Desalination Manual, U.S. Aid for International Development and CH2M Hill International Corporation, August 1980, published by IDEA, 1981*)

aptation of new processes are very difficult because water conversion processes with proved performance and reliability are always selected in preference to more efficient but little-known processes.

Dual-purpose plants. The cost of desalination of seawater can be considerably reduced by combining the distillation plant with a power generation plant. This permits the use of waste steam from the power plant in the evaporators. The dual-purpose approach has been successfully applied to fossil-fuel-fired plants and could be adapted to nuclear power plants.

Most of the operational distillation plants around the world are part of fossil-fuel-fired power-water complexes. These provide potable and industrial water and service municipal operations, petrochemical, diverse chemical, pulp and paper, and other processing industries. Nuclear-fueled water plants have been operated on an experimental basis only.

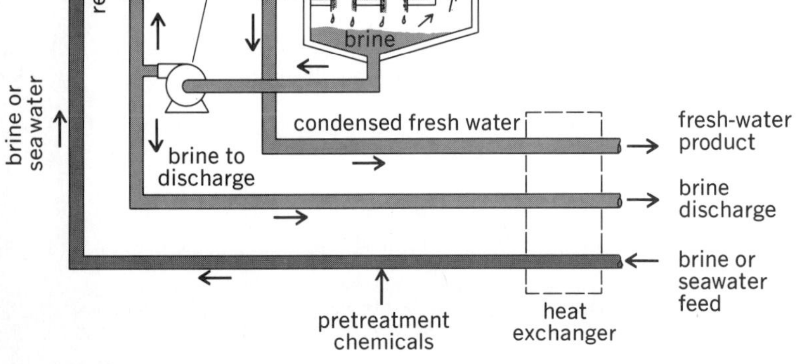

Freezing methods. The alternate thermal-based processes are the freezing processes. In principle, they have a great deal to offer, including lower energy consumption and low-temperature operation, simplifying the material corrosion problems which are integral parts of all distillation processes. Pure ice can be frozen from brine and melted to produce fresh water. However, some of the brine clings to the ice crystals' surfaces or is entrapped within them. A freezing process, then, must involve two operations: one to form the pure ice and the second to separate the ice from the brine. One technique (**Fig. 7**) consists of admitting cold seawater to a chamber under high vacuum in which a portion of the water immediately vaporizes. The evaporation process absorbs heat from the remaining salt water, causing a portion of it to freeze to an ice-brine mixture. This slurry is passed through a separator, where it is washed with a portion of the product water. The water vapor, which has been drawn off from the freezing chamber, is compressed and then brought into contact with the brine-free ice crystals where it condenses, melting the ice. This melted ice is the fresh-water product. Several freezing processes were investigated during the 1970s. In principle at least, freezing processes continue to look attractive, but engineering problems and installation costs have prevented them from becoming commercial. These obstacles may result in applications being limited to solving specialized industrial effluent purification problems. Freeze desalination plants are not available on a commercial basis.

MEMBRANE PROCESSES

Separation of water from saline solutions can be accomplished with the membrane processes of reverse osmosis and electrodialysis.

Reverse osmosis. When pure water and a salt solution are on opposite sides of a semipermeable membrane in a vented container, the pure water diffuses through the membrane and dilutes the salt solution. At equilibrium, the liquid level on the saline-water side of the membrane will be higher than on the fresh-water side. This phenomenon is known as osmosis, and the effective driving force is called osmotic pressure. Its magnitude depends on the characteristics of

Fig. 6. Simplified flow diagram for a vertical-tube vapor compression process.

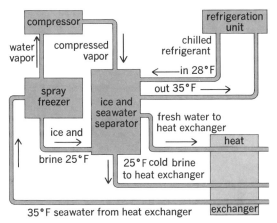

Fig. 7. Freeze-evaporation process. °C = (°F −32)/1.8.

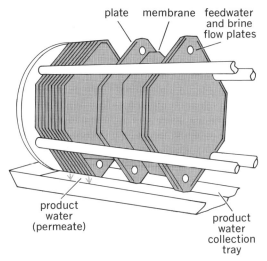

Fig. 8. Construction of a plate and frame membrane.

the product water tube. The most advanced concept, the so-called hollow-fiber configuration (**Fig. 11**), employs a design in which the saline water is on the outside and the product flows in the hollow of the fiber.

Reverse osmosis is employed for brackish waters at pressures of 250–400 psi (1.7–2.8 megapascals) and seawaters at pressures of 800–1200 psi (5.5–8.3 MPa). Successful and cost-effective processing requires that the feed water be limited to water of the type specified by the manufacturer of the membrane assembly, known as the permeator. The quality specifically relates to particulate matter in the feed which could damage the membrane performance. The costs of producing water of such quality can sometimes almost double the processing cost.

The membranes are judged by several criteria including: flux, the quantity of water which can flow through the membrane; salt rejection, the ratio of product salt concentration to that of the feed-water salt concentration as determined by measuring the total dissolved solids in each stream; recovery, the ratio of the product flow to the feed-water flow. There are differences between brackish-water and seawater conversion. In the case of the first, a 45–55% recovery is possible, which can be increased under special provision to 85–90%, while in seawater the recovery factor is only 20–35%.

Both brackish-water and seawater reverse osmosis are firmly established and rapidly growing water conversion processes. The largest seawater reverse osmosis facility, producing 3.5×10^6 gal/day (1.32×10^4 m^3/day), is in Jeddah, Saudi Arabia, while the largest brackish-water reverse osmosis plant (capacity of 4×10^7 gal/day or 1.51×10^5 m^3/day) is in Riyadh, Saudi Arabia.

Electrodialysis. The salts dissolved in saline waters are usually fully ionized, making these waters conductive. When current flows, ions migrate to op-

the membrane, the temperature of the water, and the concentration of the salt solution. By exerting pressure on the salt solution, the osmosis process can be reversed. When the pressure of the salt solution is greater than the osmotic pressure, fresh water diffuses through the membrane in the opposite direction to normal osmotic flow. This is the essence of the reverse osmosis process (RO).

A wide variety of polymeric materials, including polyamides and polyimides, have been brought into the membrane field to replace cellulose acetate, which was used in much of the original development work in the 1950s and 1960s. Most of the dense structure film has been replaced with skinned or asymmetric membranes. There are modified configurations in addition to the original plate configuration (**Fig. 8**). The tubular configuration (**Fig. 9**) has membranes of tubular shape with a diameter of 0.3–1 in. (0.7–2.5 cm) which are placed inside rigid tubes or pipes. These are separated from the membranes by porous supports. The water is pressurized within the pipes and moves through the membranes, the porous supports, and the holes in the rigid supports to be collected from the outer surface. The spiral configuration uses flat sheet membranes, typical of the plate configuration but rolled in spiral modules (**Fig. 10**). The product water flows through the porous material in a spiral path until it contacts and flows through the holes in

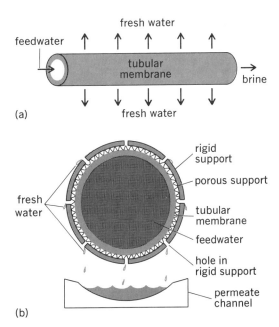

Fig. 9. Construction of a tubular membrane. (*a*) Side view. (*b*) Cross section. (*After O. K. Buros, The U.S.A.I.D. Desalination Manual, U.S. Aid for International Development and CH2M Hill International Corporation, August 1980, published by IDEA, 1981*)

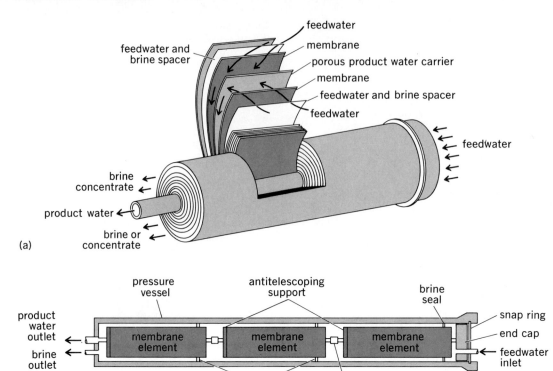

(a)

(b)

Fig. 10. Spiral membrane elements. (*a*) Cutaway view. (*b*) Cross section of pressure vessel with three membrane elements. (*After O.K. Buros, The U.S.A.I.D. Desalination Manual, U.S. Agency for International Development and CH2M Hill International Corporation, August 1980, published by IDEA, 1981*)

positely charged electrodes. If selectively permeable membranes are suitably located in the path of these ions, they can be redistributed into two streams, one containing an increased ion concentration and the other consisting essentially of pure water, the product. This is the essence of electrodialysis, invented around 1940 and developed commercially in the mid-1950s (**Fig. 12**). The essence of the process remained virtually unchanged until the so-called polarity-reversal option was introduced into commercial equipment, an advance which materially enhanced performance. Electrodialysis is an accepted and successful brackish-water process used worldwide. In addition, considerable success in adapting the process to seawater conversion has been reported on a laboratory scale. Some prototype systems are being tested.

CHEMICAL PROCESSES

Of the chemical processes, only the ion exchange has become an integral part of water conversion technology. While it can process higher total-dissolved-solids waters, it is in fact the technique most often recommended for processing of water with total dissolved solids below 500 ppm, as it is economical in that range. It brings such waters down to a very few ppm or even virtually no dissolved solids.

An ion exchanger consists of a porous bed of organic resins that have the ability to exchange ions in the resin through contact with those in the solution to be processed. In the field, both catonic and anionic ion exchangers are used. These can be found placed either in series or in mixed beds. **Figure 13** shows schematically how a cation exchanger replaces the sodium ion with a hydrogen ion, in the process con-

verting the dilute salt solution to a dilute hydrochloric acid solution. When this solution passes through the anion exchanger, the chloride ions are exchanged with the hydroxide ions. The hydrogen and the hydroxide ions then combine to form pure water molecules. A great variety of resins are available, as are commercial systems designed to use these resins and carry out the ion exchange or deionization process. They are very similar in basic design. As a matter of fact, the water softening device used in many homes is a simple ion exchange device. Ion exchange is used most extensively to solve a wide range of water demineralization problems. The resins must be regenerated, and most of them can be regenerated relatively inexpensively with suitable low-cost chemicals such as NaCl or Ca(OH)$_2$.

ENERGY SOURCES AND ECONOMICS

Desalination processes could be fueled by energy derived from sources other than fossil fuels or centrally generated electrical power. Solar energy has been the most prominent of these alternate sources of energy for desalination, but geothermal, wind, and even wave power have become potential contenders as energy costs have increased. In fact, solar distillation, the pioneer method, is perhaps the only quasi-commercialized process using alternate sources, with a wide variety of designs encountered in operational solar stills around the world. A simple unit is shown in **Fig. 14**. Only small amounts of desalinated water, up to a few hundred gallons (100 gal = 0.4 m^3) a day, are being produced using solar energy. A major worldwide effort to increase the use of these alternate energy sources for desalination may increase their im-

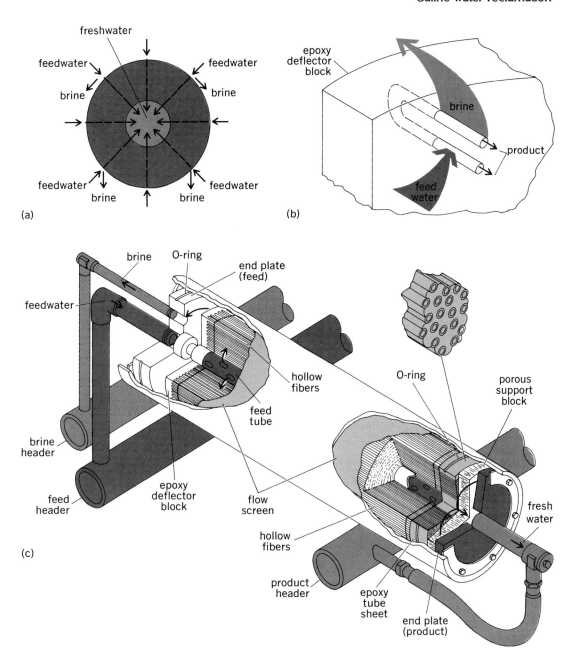

Fig. 11. Hollow-fiber configuration system. (*a*) Cross section of the fiber. (*b*) Cutaway view showing a single winding of the fiber in the deflector block. (*c*) Permeator assembly for hollow-fine-fiber membranes. (*After O.K. Buros, The U.S.A.I.D. Desalination Manual, U.S. Agency for International Development and CH2M Hill International Corporation, August 1980, published by IDEA, 1981*)

portance in the production of desalted water. The most promising approach would use a combination of conventional renewable energy resources. Renewable energy source systems, while having advantages in terms of conservation and replacement of conventional energy sources, will still produce costly water, because these systems are capital-intensive.

There are enormous quantities of fresh water on Earth, but they are poorly distributed and leave large areas of the world essentially water-poor. The tremendous growth of population and industry has led to taxing of available water supplies by overdrafts and pollution, even in locations known to have adequate water resources. Such locales must seriously consider the future of their water reserves. Some resolve their water supply problems by importing water from dis-

tant locations. Alternately, desalination may become desirable in regions poorly supplied with fresh water but containing surplus saline waters. This is a very expensive choice. In the United States, water costs vary depending on location, with an approximately even division between operating expenses and capital costs. **Table 2** shows the component costs of water supplies. These costs are much lower than desalting capital costs alone, desalination or water conversion being the ultimate water treatment. Desalinated water costs, depending on the quality of the raw feed, the specifics of the process used, and its location, can be as high as 10 times greater than treated fresh water. **Table 3** gives the energy requirements for the different desalting processes. In addition, consideration must be given to the costs of heat and pumping. The

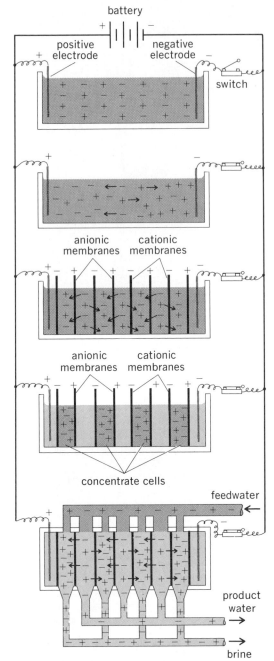

Fig. 12. Movement of ions in the electrodialysis process. (*After O.K. Buros, The U.S.A.I.D. Desalination Manual, U.S. Agency for International Development and CH2M Hill International Corporation, August 1980, published by IDEA, 1981*)

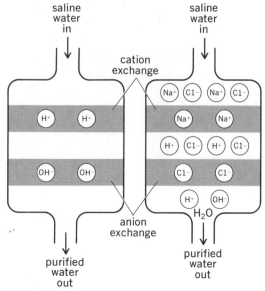

Fig. 13. Ion exchange process.

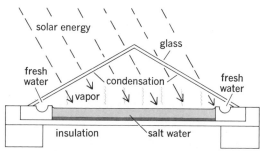

Fig. 14. Simple solar still.

reported overall costs of any process, including that of water conversion, depend very much upon the specific system of cost accounting. In addition to the specific process, the manner in which costs (such as equipment, financing, specific depreciation schemes, and overhead) are charged, plant location, and other related items can profoundly affect the overall cost of water produced. It must be noted that the desalting costs will affect neither the capital and operating costs of the distribution systems nor the business operating costs, which often account for well over half of the delivered costs for water. In many places, water, spe-

Table 2. Component costs of water supply	
Component	Description
Source development and collection	Watersheds, intake facilities at rivers or lakes, reservoirs, wells
Transporation	Pipeline, conduit, or canal with pump stations or tank truck, ship, or barge with terminal facilites
Treatment and/or conversion	Treatment: coagulation, settling, filtration, softening, iron and manganese removal, chlorination, and so on; or desalination: distillation, reverse osmosis, electrodialysis, freeze desalination, and so on
Distribution	Distribution mains, laterals, hydrants, and service connections throughout the community as well as distribution systems, storage tanks, and pumping stations
Business functions	Meter reading, billing, collections, accounting, purchasing, engineering, financing, management, and administration

Table 3. Energy requirements for desalting processes*

Process	Feature	Performance factor, lb water/10³ Btu	Btu/lb water	Pumping energy, kWh/10³ gal
Distillation	Single-effect waste heat	0.95	1053	15–35
Distillation multistage flash	195–214°F (90–102°C)	8	125	8–10
Distillation multistage flash	250–275°F (120–135°C)	12	83	6–8
Distillation multieffect	250–275°F (120–135°C), water only	15	67	4–6
Distillation multieffect (low temperature)	160–175°F (71–79°C)	10	100	4–6
Reverse osmosis	45 kWh/10³ gal	54	18.4	Included
Freezing	50 kWh/10³ gal	49	20.5	Included
Vapor compression	65 kWh/10³ gal	38	26.6	Included
Reverse osmosis	5000 ppm feed, 12 kWh/10³ gal	200	5	Included
Electrodialysis	5000 ppm feed, 12 kWh/10³ gal	200	5	Included

*1 lb water/10³ Btu = 4.30 × 10⁻⁷ kg/J; 1 Btu/lb water = 2326 J/kg; 1 kWh/10³ gal = 9.51 × 10⁵ J/m³.

cifically desalinated water, is subsidized to a great extent, as the population is often unable to pay the true water costs. *See* Water conservation; Water treatment.

Robert Bakish

Bibliography. M. Balaban (ed.), *Desalination* (journal); O. K. Buros, *The U.S.A.I.D. Desalination Manual*, U.S. Agency for International Development and CH2M Hill International Corporation, August 1981; A. H. Khan, *Desalination Processes and Multistage Flash Distillation Practice*, 1985; *Proceedings of Congress Pure Water from the Sea*, European Federation of Chemical Engineers, 1960–   ; *Proceedings of IDEA Desalination Congresses*, International Desalination and Environmental Association, 1976–1979; J. Scott (ed.), *Desalination of Water by Reverse Osmosis*, rev. ed., 1981; K. S. Spiegler and A. D. Laird, *Principles of Desalination*, 2d ed., 1980.

Salt marsh

A maritime habitat characterized by grasses, sedges, and other plants that have adapted to continual, periodic flooding. Salt marshes are found primarily throughout the temperate and subarctic regions.

The tide is the dominating characteristic of a salt marsh. The salinity of the tide defines the plants and animals that can survive in the marsh area. The vertical range of the tide determines flooding depths and thus the height of the vegetation, and the tidal cycle controls how often and how long vegetation is submerged. Two areas are delineated by the tide: the low marsh and the high marsh. The low marsh generally floods and drains twice daily with the rise and fall of the tide; the high marsh, which is at a slightly higher elevation, floods less frequently.

Marsh formation. Salt marshes usually are developed on a sinking coastline, originating as mud flats in the shallow water of sheltered bays, lagoons, and estuaries, or behind sandbars. Where tidal flow is impeded, sediments accumulate with the help of submerged vegetation. Eventually, the surface becomes exposed at low tide, stranding seeds or fragments of plant roots. The first colonizers are *Spartina, Salicornia,* and *Puccinellia;* and with continuing sedimentation, the soil matures and secondary invaders such as *Spartina patens* (salt-meadow hay) and *Distichlis spicata* (salt grass) arrive. The marsh surface then takes on a slope, with the landward edge higher, and finally plant zonation becomes evident (**Figs. 1** and **2**). *See* Estuarine oceanography.

Physiography. The primary physiographic features of salt marshes are creeks and pans. Typically, during the development of mud flats, minor surface irregularities cause water to be deflected into channels. Once channels are formed, scouring takes place, and the constant flooding and ebbing of the tide prevents vegetation from colonizing them. Salt-marsh creeks are an example of a stream bed produced by two conflicting processes—sedimentation and erosion.

In the early stages of marsh development, plant colonization is irregular, and parts of the bare surface, or pans, become surrounded by vegetation. As the

Fig. 1. Plant zonation in a salt marsh, Canary Creek Marsh, Lewes, Delaware: smooth cordgrass (*Spartina alterniflora*) at the left; salt-meadow hay in the middle; and marsh elder (*Iva frutescens*) and groundsel tree (*Baccharis halimifolia*) at the upland edge on the right. (*Courtesy of F. C. Daiber*)

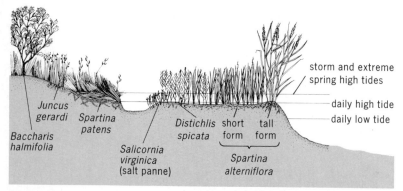

Fig. 2. Salt-marsh profile of the Delaware estuary. Such salt marshes occur primarily in the lower estuary, where they are dominated by smooth cordgrass (*Spartina alterniflora*). The typical profile from creek bank to upland features a levee next to the creek bank that is colonized by the tall form of *Spartina*. Away from the creek bank, the broad expanse of marsh is dominated by short-form *Spartina* intermixed with several subdominant species, including salt-meadow hay (*Spartina patens*) and glasswort (*Salicornia virginica*). (*Courtesy of Karen Grosz*)

marsh surface rises, such bare spots lose their outlets for tidal water. Filled with water, pans prevent the growth of vegetation, but if they are drained, vegetation invades. The so-called rotten spot is an irregularly shaped pan formed by mats of debris deposited by storm tides. This debris, combined with excessive salinity, kills the vegetation below.

Plants. Salt marshes are formed where salinity is high, ranging from 20 to 30 parts per thousand of sodium chloride. Proceeding up the estuary, there is a transitional zone where salinity ranges from 20 to less than 5 ppt. In the upper estuary, where river input dominates, the water has only a trace of salt. This varying salinity produces changes in the marsh—in the kinds of species and also in their number. Typically, the fewest species are found in the salt marsh and the greatest number in the fresh-water tidal marsh.

The salt marshes along the Atlantic shore of the temperate latitudes of North America are dominated by smooth cordgrass (*Spartina alterniflora*) and salt-meadow hay, and at the landward edge by black grass (*Juncus gerardi* or *J. roemarianus*), marsh elder (*Iva frutescens*), and groundsel tree (*Baccharis halimifolia*). The brackish-water marsh is dominated by big cordgrass (*Spartina cynosuroides*) and three-square sedge (*Scirpus americanus*). The fresh-water marsh is dominated by spadder dock (*Nuphar lutem*), pickerelweed (*Pontederia cordata*), broadleaf arrowhead (*Sagittaria latifolia*), and water hemp (*Amaranthus canabinus*).

Animals. Animals—from protozoa to mammals—abound in salt marshes. Just as the plants do, these creatures display a zonation determined by salinity, frequency, and duration of tidal submergence; examples are the ribbed mussel (*Geukensia demissa*), salt-marsh snail (*Melampus bidentatus*), and salt-marsh mosquito (*Aedes sollicitans*). The fauna of a tidal marsh can be placed in three major subdivisions: marine, terrestrial, and marsh species. The marine species, such as the bay anchovy (*Anchoa mitchilli*) and blue crab (*Callinectes sapidus*), have a center of distribution in the estuary. The terrestrial species, such as the meadow vole (*Microtus pennsylvanicus*) and raccoon (*Procyon lotor*), are air breathers; they live on the marsh or at the landward edge and make excursions onto the marsh. The marsh species are unique to the marsh. Most invertebrate species, such as the ribbed mussel, salt-marsh snail, and fiddler crab (*Uca* sp.), are derived from marine ancestors with aquatic larvae; as part of their life cycle, they require two or more adjacent but different ecological communities. Other marsh species include the greenhead fly (*Tabanus nigrovittatus*), mummichog (*Fundulus heteroclitus*), clapper rail (*Rallus longirostris*), seaside sparrow (*Ammospiza maritima*), and, in brackish-water marshes, the muskrat (*Ondatra zibethica*).

The large variety of plants and animals in the marsh leads to an assortment of plant–animal relationships. Direct interactions include trampling of vegetation and feeding, reproductive, and residential activities. Indirect interactions, which become evident some time after the occurrence of plant–animal interplay, include nutrient cycling and seed dispersal. The greater the intensity of interaction, the sooner and the greater the effect.

Productivity. The salt marsh is one of the most productive ecosystems in nature. This productivity is made possible by the involvement of solar energy in the photosynthetic process of higher rooted plants of the marsh and the algae growing on the surface muds. In addition to solar energy, tidal energy repeatedly spreads nutrient-enriched waters over the marsh surface, subsidizing the production process.

Some of this enormous supply of live plant material may be consumed by marsh animals, but the most significant values are realized when the vegetation dies and is decomposed by microorganisms to form detritus. Dissolved organic materials are released, providing an essential energy source for bacteria that mediate wetland biogeochemical cycles (carbon, nitrogen, and sulfur cycles).

Detritus helps form the base of the marsh–estuarine food web. It is fed upon directly by detritivores, small invertebrates and fishes living in the tidal creeks, which are in turn fed upon by coastal fishes such as menhaden (*Brevoortia tyrannus*), croaker (*Micropogonias undulatus*), spot (*Leiostomus xanthurus*), and summer flounder (*Paralichthys dentatus*), which spend a portion of their larval and juvenile stages in tidal creeks or in the adjoining estuary. These fishes then move out of the tidal creeks and estuary into the coastal waters, where they in turn are consumed by larger predators. This sequence represents an important transfer of marsh-derived production to the coastal ocean. SEE *BIOLOGICAL PRODUCTIVITY; FOOD WEB*.

Roles. The salt marsh has two general roles: one is human-based and the other is natural. It has been a source of hordes of biting flies, of pasturage for livestock, and of income from agricultural crops, shellfish, fish, animal pelts, gravel, and clay. It has been ditched, drained, impounded, and filled with trash from human activity, and it has served as a site for homes and factories.

The salt marsh also serves as a sediment sink, a nursery habitat for fishes and crustaceans, a feeding and nesting site for waterfowl and shorebirds, a habitat for numerous unique plants and animals, a nutrient source, a reservoir for storm water, an erosion control mechanism, and a site for esthetic pleasures. An understanding of and an appreciation for the importance of salt marshes has led to federal and state legislation aimed at their protection. SEE *WATER CONSERVATION*.

Franklin C. Daiber

Bibliography. R. H. Chabreck, *Coastal Marshes: Ecology and Wildlife Management*, 1988; V. J. Chapman, *Salt Marshes and Salt Deserts of the World*, 2d suppl. reprint ed., 1974; V. J. Chapman, *Wet Coastal Ecosystems*, 1977; F. C. Daiber, *Animals of the Tidal Marsh*, 1982; F. C. Daiber, *Conservation of Tidal Marshes*, 1986; L. R. Pomeroy and R. G. Wiegert (eds.), *The Ecology of a Salt Marsh*, 1981; D. S. Ranwell, *Ecology of Salt Marshes and Sand Dunes*, 1972.

Savanna

The term savanna was originally used to describe a tropical grassland with more or less scattered dense tree areas. This vegetation type is very abundant in tropical and subtropical areas, primarily because of climatic factors. The modern definition of savanna includes a variety of physiognomically or environmentally similar vegetation types in tropical and extratropical regions.

In the widest sense savanna includes a range of vegetation zones from tropical savannas with vegetation types such as the savanna woodlands to tropical grassland and thornbush. In the extratropical regions it includes the "temperate" and "cold savanna" vegetation types known under such names as taiga, forest tundra, or glades. The physiognomically savannalike extratropical vegetation types differ greatly in environment and species composition.

During the growing season the typical tropical savanna displays a short-to-tall, green-to-silvery shiny cover of bunch grasses, with either single trees or groups of trees widely scattered. This is followed by a rest period of several months during which, because of severe drought, the vegetation appears quite different, with the brown-gray dead grasses bent over and the trees either without leaves or with stiff or wilted gray-green foliage. The heat and drought during this season of the year exert a high selective pressure upon the floral and faunal composition of the savanna.

Floral and faunal composition. The physiognomic similarity of the tropical savannas is underlined by the similarity among certain floristic components. All savannas contain members of the grass family (Gramineae) in the herbaceous layer. Most savannas of the world also have one or more members of the tree family (Leguminosae), particularly of the genus *Acacia*. Also included among the trees are the families Bombacaceae, Bignoniaceae, Palmae, and Dilleniaceae, and the genera *Prosopis* and *Eucalyptus*; these are abundant when they occur. One of the most outstanding savanna trees is *Adansonia digitata* (Bombacaceae), which achieves one of the biggest trunk diameters known for all trees (**Fig. 1**). The grass species, although mostly from the genera *Panicum*, *Paspalum*, and *Andropogon*, include numerous other genera such as *Aristida*, *Eragrostis*, *Schmidtia*, *Trachypogon*, *Axonopus*, *Triodia*, and *Plectrachne*, all of regional importance.

The fauna of the savannas is among the most interesting in the world. Savannas shelter herds of mammals such as the genera *Antelopus*, *Gazellus*, and *Giraffus*, and the African savannas are especially famous for their enormous species diversity, including various members of the Felidae (for example, the lion), and the elephant.

Numerous species of birds are indigenous to the savannas. Among these is the biggest bird, the ostrich

Fig. 1. *Adansonia digitata* of Senegal. (*Courtesy of H. Lieth*)

(*Struthio camelus*), found in Africa. Many birds from extratropical regions migrate into the tropical savannas when the unfavorable season occurs.

Among the lower animals, the ants and termites are most abundant. Termite colonies erect large, conical nests above the ground, which are so prominent in some savannas that they partly dominate the view of the landscape, especially during the dry season.

Environmental conditions. The climate of the tropical savannas is marked by high temperatures with more or less seasonal fluctuations. Temperatures rarely fall below 32°F (0°C). The most characteristic climatic feature, however, is the seasonal rainfall, which usually comes during the 3–5 months of the astronomic summertime. Nearly all savannas are in regions with average annual temperatures from 59 to 77°F (15 to 25°C) and an annual rainfall of 32 in. (81 cm).

The soil under tropical savannas shows a diversity similar to that known from other semiarid regions. Black soils, mostly "chernozem," are common in the moister regions. Hardpans and occasional surface salinities are also found, and lateritic conglomerations occur along the rivers. The soils vary in mineral nutrient level, depending on geologic age, climate, and parent material. Deficiencies of minerals, specifically trace elements, as well as aluminum toxicity, are reported from many grassland areas in the continents of Africa, South America, and Australia. *SEE SOIL.*

Certain savanna areas suffer from severe erosion and no soil can be accumulated. Plant growth in these areas is scarce, often depending on cracks and crevices in the ground material to support tree roots. The herbaceous cover provides only a thin cover for the otherwise rocky surface.

Water is the main limiting environmental factor in the majority of the tropical savannas. Total amount and seasonality of precipitation are unfavorable for tree growth. Additional stresses to forest vegetation are caused by frequent fires, normal activities of animals, excess of salt, or nutrient deficiencies. Wherever a river flows, most of these factors change in favor of tree growth. This explains the existence of extensive gallery forests along the rivers and creeks (**Fig. 2**). The gallery forest is missing only where se-

Fig. 2. Aerial view of savanna with gallery forest north of Guiaba, Brazil. (*Courtesy of H. Lieth*)

vere local floods after storms cause soil erosion and the formation of canyons.

Geographic distribution. Tropical savannas exist between the areas of the tropical forests and deserts; this is most apparent in Africa and Australia. In the New World tropics, different conditions exist because of the circumstances created by the continental relief, and the savannas are situated between tropical forests and mountain ranges. In Madagascar and India there is a combination of both conditions.

The transitional (ecotonal) position of the savannas between forest and grassland or semidesert is the basis for the differences in opinion among authors about the size and geographical distribution of savannas. Most authors include, however, the savanna in East Africa and the belt south of the Sahara, the bush veld in South Africa, the Llanos in northern South America, and some types of scrub vegetation in Australia. Some areas in southern Madagascar, on several tropical islands (in leeward position), in Central America, in southern North America, and in India are usually included. The two latter regions, however, are subtropical. Still other areas included in the savanna concept are the Campo Cerrado and parts of the Chaco in South America; portions of the Miombo in southern Africa; wide portions of northern Africa; south of the Sahara; and wide portions of Madagascar, the Indian peninsula, and Australia. Because of the variations in the savanna concept, it is difficult to give a correct estimate of the total surface area covered by savanna vegetation. The Food and Agriculture Organization (FAO) considers that about one-third of the total land surface is covered by predominantly grassland vegetation. Of this area, one-third can be assumed to be tropical grassland, most of which can be called savanna.

Agricultural practices. Most of the original savanna areas throughout the world are currently farmed. Ranch farming is the predominant type, with sheep being raised in the drier areas and cattle in the moister regions. In the hotter regions zebus are raised, along with several hybrids of zebus and European cattle, which are the preferred stock for this climate. The yield in meat per unit area is low, and even under extensive management it seems to be lower than the meat production of the natural animal herds of the savanna, including antelopes, giraffes, and zebras. Ranch farming does not change the character of the vegetation very much if it is well managed. The adjacent dry woodlands very often resume a physiognomy similar to the natural savannas if good farm management is applied.

Agricultural crops are of many varieties in the savanna areas, where with careful protection and management any crop can be cultivated, provided that enough water is available. Drought-tolerant crops are usually preferred among the perennials.

The majority of human settlements are small in the savanna regions of the world; the hot temperatures during part of or the entire year, together with problems of water supply, limit interest in larger settlements. Settlements are usually found along the rivers, close to the coast, or in the higher elevations. Much of the land is managed by small tribal villages or large plantation or ranch owners, with separate groups of tenants, sharecroppers or employees, or single families. *See Agroecosystem.*

Extratropical types. The main structural character of tropical savannas is the scattered trees standing within a close cover of herbaceous vegetation. This structural character is also found in several extratropical vegetation types, but these differ greatly in the forces that limit a close tree cover, including drought (areas intermediate between steppe or prairie and forest); excess water or water combined with soil that has a shortage of oxygen and nutrients (peatbogs, marshes, or glades); short vegetation periods because of extended cold temperatures below the freezing point; excessive, long snow covers; and low light intensity (forest tundra, taiga, and cold savanna).

An intermediate condition is exhibited by the savannas and everglades of the southeastern United States. The intermittent soaked or dry conditions of a peaty soil, the tropically hot summers and mild winters (with frost periods, however), and the generally low nutrient level of the soil give these areas the characteristics of the cold savannalike vegetation types and the tropical and subtropical types.

The economic potential of the three extratropical savannalike areas also varies greatly. The conditions in the southeastern United States allow orchards, tree plantations, and cattle ranching. Economic considerations control whether a given area should be developed.

Some savanna regions in many parts of the world are the last survival territories for many plant and animal species. This implies the need for conserving some savanna pieces, both tropical and extratropical. Some of the most interesting wildlife sanctuaries are set aside for this reason (such as Serengeti, Tanzania; Ruhung, Sri Lanka; and Krüger National Park, South Africa). *See Forest and forestry; Grassland ecosystem; Taiga; Tundra.*

Helmut Lieth

Bibliography. M. Cole, *The Savannas: Biogeography and Geobotany*, 1986; R. T. Coupland (ed.), *Grassland Ecosystems of the World*, 1979; P. M.

Dansereau, *Biogeography*, 1957; A. Engler and O. Drude (eds.), *Vegetation der Erde*, 15 vols., 1976; L. T. Gutierrez and W. R. Fey, *Ecosystem Succession: A General Hypothesis and a Test Model of a Grassland*, 1980.

Sea ice

Ice formed by the freezing of seawater. Ice in the sea includes sea ice, river ice, and land ice. Land ice is principally icebergs which are prominent in some areas, such as the Ross Sea and Baffin Bay. River ice is carried into the sea during spring breakup and is important only near river mouths. The greatest part, probably 99% of ice in the sea, is sea ice.

Properties. The freezing point temperature and the temperature of maximum density of seawater vary with salinity (**Fig. 1**). When freezing occurs, small flat plates of pure ice freeze out of solution to form a network which entraps brine in layers of cells. As the temperature decreases more water freezes out of the brine cells, further concentrating the remaining brine so that the freezing point of the brine equals the temperature of the surrounding pure ice structure. The brine is a complex solution of many ions. With lowering of temperature below $-8°C$ (18°F), sodium sulfate decahydrate ($Na_2SO_4 \cdot 10H_2O$) and calcium sulfate dihydrate ($CaSO_4 \cdot 2H_2O$) are precipitated. Beginning at $-24°C$ ($-11°F$), sodium chloride dihydrate ($NaCl \cdot 2H_2O$) is precipitated, followed by precipitation of potassium chloride (KCl) and magnesium chloride dodecahydrate ($MgCl \cdot 12H_2O$) at $-34°C$

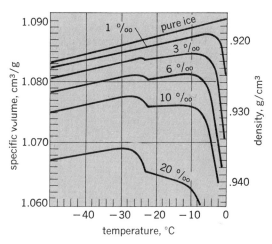

Fig. 3. Specific volume of sea ice for varying salinity and temperature, computed on basis of chemical model. °F = (°C × 1.8) + 32; 1 cm³/g = 1.730 in.³/oz; 1 g/cm³ = 0.578 oz/in.³ (*After D. L. Anderson, based on data in Arctic Sea Ice, NAS-NRC Publ. 598, 1958*)

Fig. 4. Open water in ice field. (*U.S. Navy*)

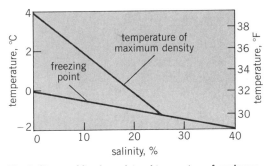

Fig. 1. Change of freezing point and temperature of maximum density with varying salinity of seawater.

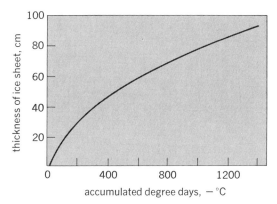

Fig. 2. Growth of undisturbed ice sheet. °F = (°C × 1.8) + 32. 1 cm = 0.4 in.

($-29°F$), and the remaining ions with further lowering of temperature.

The brine cells migrate and change size with changes in temperature and pressure. The general downward migration of brine cells through the ice sheet leads to freshening of the top layers to near zero salinity by late summer. During winter the top surface temperature closely follows the air temperature, whereas the temperature of the underside remains at freezing point, corresponding to the salinity of water in contact. Heat flux up through the ice permits freezing at the underside. In summer freezing can also take place under sea ice in regions where complete melting does not occur. Surface melt water (temperature 0°C or 32°F) runs down through cracks in the ice to spread out underneath and contact the still cold ice masses and underlying colder seawater. Soft slush ice forms with large cells of entrapped seawater which then solidifies the following winter.

The salinity of recently formed sea ice depends on rate of freezing; thus sea ice formed at $-10°C$ (14°F) has a salinity from 4 to 6 parts per thousand (‰), whereas that formed at $-40°C$ ($-40°F$) may have a salinity from 10 to 15‰. Sea ice is a poor conductor

Fig. 5. Pressure ridge formation. (*U.S. Navy*)

of heat and the rate of ice formation drops appreciably after 4–6 in. (10–15 cm) are formed. An undisturbed sheet grows in relation to accumulated degree-days of frost. **Figure 2** shows an empirical relation between ice thickness and the sum of the mean diurnal negative air temperature (degrees Celsius). The thermal conductivity varies greatly with the air bubble content, ranging perhaps between 1.5 and 5.0 × 10⁻³ cal/(cm)(s)(°C) [0.6 and 2.0 J/(m)(s)(°C)].

The specific gravity of sea ice varies between 0.85 and 0.95, depending on the amount of entrapped air bubbles. The specific heat varies greatly because changing temperature involves freezing or melting of ice. Near 0°C (32°F), amounts that freeze or melt at slight change of temperature are large and "specific heat" is anomalous. At low temperatures the value approaches that of pure ice; thus, specific heat for 4‰ saline ice is 4.6 cal/(g) (°C) [19 kJ/(kg)(°C)] at −2°C and 0.6 [2.5] at −14°C; for 8‰ saline ice, 8.8 [37] at −2°C and 0.6 [2.5] at −14°C.

High-saline sea ice may expand when cooled because further freezing out occurs with an increase of specific volume, for example, ice of salinity 8‰ at −2°C expands at a rate of about 93 × 10⁻⁴ cm³/g per degree Celsius decrease in temperature, at −14°C expands 0.1 × 10⁻⁴, but at −20°C contracts 0.4 × 10⁻⁴ per degree Celsius decrease. Change of specific volume with temperature and salinity is shown in **Fig. 3**.

Sea ice is viscoelastic. Its brine content, which is very sensitive to temperature and to air bubble content, causes the elasticity to vary widely. Young's modulus measured by dynamic methods varies from 5.5 × 10¹⁰ dynes/cm² (Pa) during autumn freezing to 7.3 × 10¹⁰ dynes/cm² (Pa) at spring breakup. Static tests give much smaller values, as low as 0.2 × 10¹⁰ dynes/cm² (Pa). The flexural strength varies between 0.5 and 17.3 kg/cm² over salinity range of 7–16‰ and temperatures −2 to −19°C. Acoustic properties are highly variable, depending principally on the size and distribution of entrapped air bubbles.

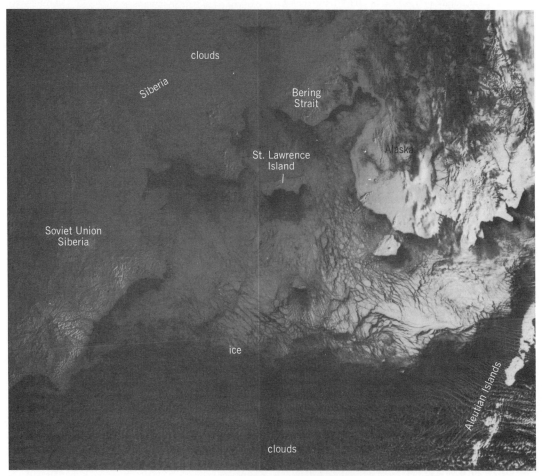

Fig. 6. Enhanced infrared image of Bering Sea by satellite, December 1976. (*Environmental Products Branch, NOAA*)

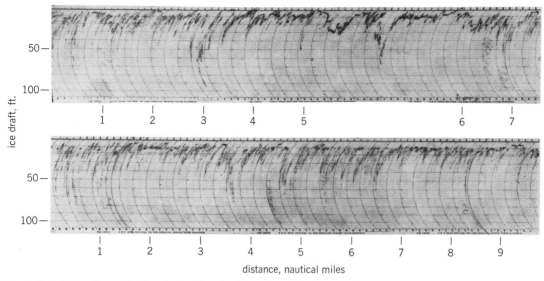

Fig. 7. Underside profile records of sea ice by submarine. Elongation of the distance scale between mile 5 and mile 6 on the upper record is due to the slower speed of the submarine during this portion of the observation. 1 nautical mile = 1.8 km; 1 ft = 0.3 m. (*U.S. Navy*)

Electrical properties vary greatly with frequency because of ionic migration within the brine cells. For example, for sea salinity of 10‰ at $-22°C$, the dielectric coefficient is very large, about 10^6 at 20 Hz, and decreases with increasing frequency to about 10^3 at 10 kHz and to 10, or less, at 50 MHz. The effective electrical conductivity decreases with lowering of temperature, for example, from less than 10^{-3} mho/cm at $-5°C$ to 10^{-6} mho/cm at $-50°C$ (frequency 1 to 10 kHz).

Extent and observation. The sea ice in any locality is commonly a mixture of recently formed ice and old ice which has survived one or more summers. Except in sheltered bays, sea ice is continually in motion because of wind and current. The weaker parts of the sea ice canopy break when overstressed in tension, compression, or shear, pulling apart to form a lead (open water) or piling block on block to form a pressure ridge (**Figs. 4** and **5**). Ridges may form in ice of any thickness, from thin sheets (10 cm or 4 in. in thickness) to heavy blocks (3 m or 10 ft or more in thickness). The ridges may pile 13 m (43 ft) high above and extend 50 m (164 ft) below the sea surface. Massive ridges become grounded in coastal zones. The extent, movement, and type of sea ice are routinely observed by satellite or aircraft-carried sensor systems. **Figure 6** is an infrared photograph of ice covering the Bering Sea. The underside can be observed from a submarine transiting under the sea ice and using a sonar to record the draft profile of the ice canopy (**Fig. 7**).

Waldo Lyon

Bibliography. J. C. Comiso, Sea ice microwave emissivities from satellite passive microwave and infrared observations, *J. Geophys. Res.*, vol. 88, no. C12, September 1983; *Proceedings of the Conference on Sea Ice*, NRC, Iceland, 1972; Symposium on Applied Glaciology, *J. Glaciol.*, vol. 19, no. 81, 1977; Symposium on Remote Sensing in Glaciology, *J. Glaciol.*, vol. 15, no. 73, 1975; P. Wadhams, *Ice Characteristics in the Seasonal Ice Zone, Cold Regions Science and Technology*, vol. 2, 1980.

Sea state

The description of the ocean surface or state of the sea surface with regard to wave action. Wind waves in the sea are of two types: Those still growing under the force of the wind are called sea: those no longer under the influence of the wind that produced them are called swell. Differences between the two types are important in forecasting ocean wave conditions. Properties of sea and swell and their influence upon sea state are described in this article.

Sea. Those waves which are still growing under the force of the wind have irregular, chaotic, and unpredictable forms (**Fig. 1a**). The unconnected wave crests are only two to three times as long as the distance between crests and commonly appear to be traveling in different directions, varying as much as 20° from the dominant direction. As the waves grow, they form regular series of connected troughs and crests with wave lengths commonly ranging from 12 to 35 times the wave heights. Wave heights only rarely exceed 55 ft (17 m). The appearance of the sea surface is termed state of the sea (**Table 1**).

The height of a sea is dependent on the strength of the wind, the duration of time the wind has blown,

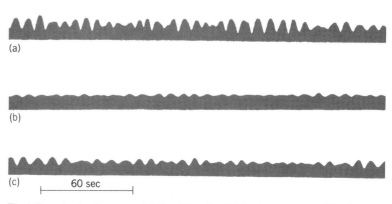

Fig. 1. Records of surface waves. (*a*) Sea, (*b*) swell, and (*c*) in-between waves. (*After W. J. Pierson, Jr., et al., Observing and Forecasting Ocean Waves, H. O. Publ. 603, U.S. Navy Hydrographic Office, 1955*)

Table 1. Sea height code*

Code	Height, ft[†]	Description of sea surface
0	0	Calm, with mirror-smooth surface
1	0–1	Smooth, with small wavelets or ripples with appearance of scales but without crests
2	1–3	Slight, with short pronounced waves or small rollers; crests have glassy appearance
3	3–5	Moderate, with waves or large rollers; scattered whitecaps on wave crests
4	5–8	Rough, with waves with frequent whitecaps; chance of some spray
5	8–12	Very rough, with waves tending to heap up; continuous whitecapping; foam from whitecaps occasionally blown along by wind
6	12–20	High, with waves showing visible increase in height, with extensive whitecaps from which foam is blown in dense streaks
7	20–40	Very high, with waves heaping up with long frothy crests that are breaking continuously ; amount of foam being blown from the crests causes sea surface to take on white appearance and may affect visibility
8	40+	Mountainous, with waves so high that ships close by are lost from view in the wave troughs for a time; wind carries off crests of all waves, and sea is entirely covered with dense streaks of foam; air so filled with foam and spray as to affect visibility seriously
9		Confused, with waves crossing each other from many and unpredictable directions, developing complicated interference pattern that is difficult to describe; applicable to conditions 5–8

*After *Instruction Manual for Oceanographic Observations*, H. O. Publ. 607, 2d ed., U.S. Navy Hydrographic Office, 1955.
[†]1 ft = 0.3 m.

when the components are so poorly defined that it is impossible to separate them, it is reported as confused.

In-between state. Often both sea waves and swell waves, or two or more systems of swell, are present in the same area (Fig. 1c). When waves of one system are superimposed upon those of another, crests may coincide with crests and accentuate wave height, or troughs may coincide with crests and cancel each other to produce flat zones (**Fig. 2**). This phenomenon is known as wave interference, and the wave forms produced are extremely irregular. When wave systems cross each other at a considerable angle, the apparently unrelated peaks and hollows are known as a cross sea.

Breaking waves. The action of strong winds (greater than 12 knots or 6.2 m/s) sometimes causes waves in deeper water to steepen too rapidly. As the height-length ratio becomes too large, the water at the crest moves faster than the crest itself and topples forward to form whitecaps.

Breakers. As waves travel over a gradually shoaling bottom, the motion of the water is restricted and the wave train is telescoped together. The wave length decreases, and the height first decreases slightly until the water depth is about one-sixth the deep-water

Table 2. Swell-condition code*

Code	Description	Height, ft[†]	Length, ft[†]
0	No swell	0	0
	Low swell	1–6	
1	Short or average		0–600
2	Long		600+
	Moderate swell	6–12	
3	Short		0–300
4	Average		300–600
5	Long		600+
	High swell	12+	
6	Short		0–300
7	Average		300–600
8	Long		600+
9	Confused		

*After *Instruction Manual for Oceanographic Observations*, H. O. Publ. 607, 2d ed., U.S. Navy Hydrographic Office, 1955.
[†]1 ft = 0.3 m.

and the fetch (distance of sea surface over which the wind has blown).

Swell. As sea waves move out of the generating area into a region of weaker winds, a calm, or opposing winds, their height decreases as they advance, their crests become rounded, and their surface is smoothed (Fig. 1b). These waves are more regular and more predictable than sea waves and, in a series, tend to show the same form or the same trend in characteristics. Wave lengths generally range from 35 to 200 times wave heights.

The presence of swell indicates that recently there may have been a strong wind, or even a severe storm, hundreds or thousands of miles away. Along the coast of southern California long-period waves are believed to have traveled distances greater than 5000 mi (8000 km) from generating areas in the South Pacific. Swell can usually be felt by the roll of a ship, and, under certain conditions, extremely long and high swells in a glassy sea may cause a ship to take solid water over its bow regularly.

A descriptive classification of swell waves is given in **Table 2**. When swell is obscured by sea waves, or

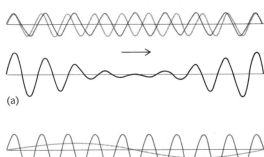
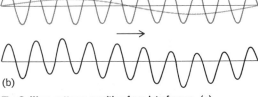

Fig. 2. Wave patterns resulting from interference. (*a*) Interference of waves of equal height and nearly equal length, forming wave groups. (*b*) Interference between short wind waves and long swell. (*After Techniques for Forecasting Wind Waves and Swell, H. O. Publ. 604, U.S. Navy Hydrographic Office, 1951*)

wave length and then rapidly increases until the crest curves over and plunges to the water surface below. Swell coming into a beach usually increases in height before breaking, but wind waves are often so steep that there is little if any increase in height before breaking. For this reason, swell that is obscured by wind waves in deeper water often defines the period of the breakers.

Surf. The zone of breakers, or surf, includes the region of white water between the outermost breaker and the waterline on the beach. If the sea is rough, it may be impossible to differentiate between the surf inshore and the whitecaps in deep water just beyond.

Neil A. Benfer

Bibliography. W. Bascom, *Waves and Beaches: The Dynamics of the Ocean Surface*, rev. updated ed., 1980; R. A. Davis, *Oceanography: An Introduction to the Marine Environment*, 1987; S. Pond and G. L. Pickard. *Introductory Dynamical Oceanography*, 2d ed., 1983.

Seawater

An aqueous solution of salts of a rather constant composition of elements whose presence determines the climate and makes life possible on the Earth and whose boundaries are those of the oceans, the mediterranean seas, and their embayments. The physical, chemical, biological, and geological events in the hydroplane within these boundaries are the studies that are grouped together and known as oceanography. Water is most often found in nature as seawater (about 98%). The rest is found as ice, water vapor, and fresh water. The basic properties of seawater, the distribution of these properties, the interchange of properties between sea and atmosphere or land, the transmission of energy within the sea, and the geochemical laws governing the composition of seawater and sediments are the fundamentals of oceanography. *See Oceanography*.

The discussion of seawater that follows is divided into six sections: (1) physical properties of seawater; (2) interchange of properties between sea and atmosphere; (3) transmission of energy within the sea; (4) composition of seawater; (5) distribution of properties; and (6) sampling and measuring techniques. For further treatment of related aspects of physical character, composition, and constituents *see Hydrosphere; Marine resources; Seawater fertility*.

PHYSICAL PROPERTIES OF SEAWATER

Seawater is basically a concentrated electrolyte solution containing many dissolved salts. The ratio of water molecules to salt molecules is about 100 to 1. Since nearly all the salt exists as electrically conducting ions, the ratio of water molecules to ions is about 50 to 1; consequently, the ions are on the average no farther than about 10^{-7} cm from each other, a distance equivalent to the diameter of about five water molecules. Because pure water has a relatively open structure with tetrahedral coordination, the water molecules by virtue of their electric dipole moment (arising from the separation of the positive and negative charges) can be readily oriented or polarized by an electric field. The polarizability manifests itself in the high dielectric constant of pure water. Since electrostatic attraction between ions is inversely proportional to the dielectric constant, a high dielectric constant facilitates ionization of electrolytes because of the reduced forces between ions of opposite sign.

Salinity effects. In the neighborhood of ions, extremely high electric fields exist (around 100,000 V/cm) and water molecules near them become aligned; water molecules that remain in the vicinity of the ions for a long time constitute a hydration shell, and the ions are said to be solvated. The alignment of water molecules produces local dielectric saturation (that is, no further alignment is possible) around the ions, thereby lowering the dielectric constant of the solution below that of pure water. Details of ion–ion and ion–solvent interactions and their effects on the physical property of solutions are treated in the theory of electrolyte solutions. *See Electrolyte*.

As a consequence of the salts in seawater, its physical properties differ from those of pure water, the difference being closely proportional to the concentration of the salts or the salinity. Salinity measurements (which can be conveniently made by using electrical conductivity apparatus), along with pressure and temperature data, are used to differentiate water masses. In studying the movement of water masses in the oceans and their small- and large-scale circulation patterns, including geostrophic flow, properties such as density, compressibility, thermal expansion coefficients, and specific heats need to be known as functions of temperature, pressure, and salinity.

The large value of the osmotic pressure of seawater is of great significance to biology and desalination by reverse osmosis; for example, at a salinity of 35‰ (parts per thousand) the osmotic pressure relative to

Table 1. Some physical properties of seawater (salinity, 35‰) at sea level

Property	Temperature, °C (°F)			
	0 (32)	10 (50)	20 (68)	30 (86)
Specific volume, cm³/g	0.972664	0.973754	0.975834	0.978729
Isothermal compressibility × 10⁶, bars⁻¹ [× 10¹¹, Pa⁻¹]	46.33	44.03	42.60	41.80
Thermal coefficient of volume expansion × 10⁵, °C⁻¹	5.15	16.68	25.70	33.39
Sound speed, m/s*	1449.08	1489.78	1521.47	1545.47
Electric conductivity × 10³, (ohm-cm)⁻¹	29.04	38.10	47.92	58.35
Molecular viscosity, centipoise	1.89	1.39	1.09	0.87
Specific heat, J/g · °C	3.9865	3.9861	3.9937	4.0011
Optical index of refraction (n − 1.333,338) × 10⁶, λ = 0.5876 µm	6966	6657	6463	6337
Osmotic pressure, bars (1 bar = 10⁵ Pa)	23.4	24.3	25.1	26.0
Molecular thermal conductivity coefficient × 10³, cal/(cm)(s)(°C) [× 10⁵, J/m · s · °C]	1.27 (5.31)	1.31 (5.48)	1.35 (5.64)	1.38 (5.77)

*1 m/s = 3.3 ft/s.

Table 2. Sound attenuation coefficient α in seawater*

Sound frequency, Hz	Attenuation coefficient (α), km^{-1}
100	0.00023
1,000	0.0069
10,000	0.15
100,000	6.3

*Depth ~1200 m (4000 ft), temperature ~4°C (39°F), and salinity = 35‰.

pure water is around 25 atm (2.5 megapascals). Related to osmotic pressure and very important to the formation of ice is the reversal of the freezing point and temperature of maximum density of seawater compared to pure water: the freezing point temperature is lowered to -1.9°C (28.6°F), and the temperature of maximum density is decreased from just below 4°C (39.2°F) for pure water to about -3.5°C (25.7°F) for 35‰ salinity seawater. Some other properties which show significant changes between seawater (salinity 35‰) and pure water at atmospheric pressure are shown in **Tables 1** and **2**. Although the world oceans show a wide range in temperature and salinity, 75% by volume occurs within a range of 0 to 6°C (32 to 43°F) and 34 to 35‰ salinity.

Pressure effects. Since the greatest ocean depths exceed 10,000 m (33,000 ft) and more than 54% of the oceans' area is at pressure above 400 bars (40 MPa), it is necessary to consider the effect of pressure, as well as temperature, on the physical properties of seawater. The pressure corresponding to the maximum ocean depth is about 1100 bars (110 MPa). **Table 3** shows the percent change in some properties at 500 and 1000 bars (50 and 100 MPa), corresponding to depths of about 5000 and 10,000 m (16,000 and 33,000 ft) at 0 and 20°C (32 and 68°F). The usual pressure dependence of viscosity is a consequence of the open structure of water which is altered by pressure, temperature, and solutes.

Sound absorption. Because electromagnetic radiation can propagate in the ocean for only limited distances, sound waves are the principal means of communication in this medium. The attenuation of the intensity of a plane wave (without geometrical spreading losses) is given by Eq. (1), where I_0 is the

$$I = I_0 e^{-2ax} \qquad (1)$$

initial intensity and I is the intensity at a distance of x km. Sound absorption in seawater, shown in Table 2, is considerably greater than in fresh water, about

30 times greater between frequencies of 10 and 100 kHz. This arises from a pressure-dependent chemical reaction involving magnesium sulfate with a relaxation frequency around 100 kHz. At low frequencies (below 10 kHz) the increase in sound absorption above that due to magnesium sulfate is caused by a pH-controlled pressure-dependent boric acid reaction.

F. H. Fisher

Interchange between Sea and Atmosphere

The sea and the atmosphere are fluids in contact with one another, but in different energy states—the liquid and the gaseous. The free surface boundary between them inhibits, but by no means totally prevents, exchange of mass and energy between the two. Almost all interchanges across this boundary occur most effectively when turbulent conditions prevail: a roughened sea surface, large differences in properties between the water and the air, or an unstable air column that facilitates the transport of air volumes from sea surface to high in the atmosphere.

Heat and water vapor. Both heat and water (vapor) tend to migrate across the boundary in the direction from sea to air. Heat is exchanged by three processes: radiation, conduction, and evaporation. The largest net exchange is through evaporation, the process of transferring water from sea to air by vaporization of the water.

Evaporation depends on the difference between the partial pressure of water vapor in the air and the vapor pressure of seawater. Vapor pressure increases with temperature, and partial pressure increases with both temperature and humidity; therefore, the difference will be greatest when the sea (always saturated) is warm and the air is cool and dry. In winter, off east coasts of continents, this condition is most ideally met, and very large quantities of water are absorbed by the air. On the average, 100 g water per square centimeter (2.3 oz per square inch) of ocean surface are evaporated per year.

Since it takes nearly 600 calories (2500 joules) to evaporate 1 g water, the heat lost to each square centimeter of the sea surface averages 150 cal/day (630 J/day). This heat is stored in the atmospheric volume, but is not actually transferred to the air parcels until condensation takes place (releasing the latent heat of vaporization) perhaps 1600 km (1000 mi) away and 1 week later.

Radiation of heat from the water surface to the atmosphere and back again are both large—of the order of 800 cal/(cm^2)(day) [3500 J/(cm^2)(day)]. However, the net flux is out from the sea; it averages about 100 cal/day (420 J/day).

Table 3. Percent change of seawater properties at elevated pressures

Property	500 bars (50 MPa) pressure		1000 bars (100 MPa) pressure	
	0°C (32°F)	20°C (68°F)	0°C (32°F)	30°C (68°F)
Electrical conductivity	6.76	3.88	11.19	6.49
Specific volume	-2.15	-1.99	-4.00	-3.72
Compressibility	-12.26	-11.2	-22.47	-20.61
Thermal expansion coefficient	235.3	19.3	405.1	34.75
Sound speed	5.85	5.66	12.02	11.08
Sound absorption coefficient (above 10 kHz)		-47.0		-65.0
Molecular viscosity	-3.8	-0.3	-4.7	0.5

Conduction usually plays a much smaller role than either of the above; it may transfer heat in either direction, but usually it contributes a small net transfer from sea to air. *See Heat balance, terrestrial atmospheric.*

Momentum. Momentum can be exchanged between these two fluids by a process related to evaporation, that is, migration of molecules of air or water across the boundary, carrying their momentum with them. However, in natural conditions the more effective mechanism is the collision of so-called parcels of the fluids, as distinct from motions of individual molecules. Also, momentum is usually transferred from air to sea, rather than vice versa. Winds whip up waves; these irregular shapes are more easily attached by wind action than is the flat sea surface, and both waves and currents are initiated and maintained by the push and stress of the wind on the water surface. *See Wind stress.*

June G. Pattullo

Isotopic relationships. The isotopic water molecules $H_2^{16}O$, $HD^{16}O$, and $H_2^{18}O$ have different vapor pressures and molecular diffusion coefficients and therefore exchange at different rates between the atmosphere and sea. Variations in the relative proportions of the hydrogen isotope deuterium, D, and oxygen-18 can be measured with high precision using mass spectrometry, and the isotopic fractionation effects can be studied both at sea and in the laboratory. The isotopic vapor pressures have been measured very accurately, and the ratios of the binary molecular diffusion coefficients for HDO-air and $H_2^{18}O$-air to that for $H_2^{16}O$-air have been calculated theoretically and confirmed experimentally. Since the relative transport properties of isotopic molecules are much better known than those of different chemical species, the isotopic variations observed in surface ocean water and atmospheric vapor and in experimental studies on evaporation in small wind tunnels provide a powerful method for the study of the air–sea interface and the molecular and turbulent transport processes controlling the moisture supply to the air.

Precipitation over sea and land varies in isotopic composition because of the effects of fractional condensation of liquid water and variation of the isotopic vapor pressure ratios with temperature. Local equilibrium however, is maintained, and kinetic effects do not occur; the deuterium and oxygen-18 variations in precipitation are linearly correlated, and the concentrations of both heavy isotopes decrease with increasing latitude because of their preferential concentration in the liquid precipitate, which strips them out in lower latitudes. These variations provide a continually varying liquid input into the sea which must be balanced against the direct molecular exchange.

Water vapor over the oceans is never in isotopic equilibrium with surface seawater. The deuterium and oxygen-18 concentrations are always lower than the two-phase equilibrium separation factors given by the vapor-pressure ratios. The deviations from equilibrium are correlated with latitude and go through a maximum in each hemisphere in the trade-winds regions of maximum evaporation to precipitation ratio. The vapor composition relative to surface seawater cannot be understood simply on the basis of multiple equilibrium stage processes in fractional condensation during precipitation, and the isotopic variations reflect the kinetic isotope effects in the molecular exchange of water at the interface.

Two types of kinetic processes affect the isotopic composition of the vapor. There is a fractionation at the interface between liquid and vapor, since the condensation coefficients for the isotopic species are not necessarily the same. (The condensation coefficient may be thought of as the fraction of molecules of a given type striking the liquid surface that actually condense into the liquid structure; conversely, it is also a measure of the probability of a molecule to surmount the energy barrier for evaporation and actually to escape from the liquid.) For such fractionation to occur, the vapor concentration at the liquid–vapor interface must be significantly lower than the equilibrium concentration.

The second kinetic process is molecular diffusion from the interface into the turbulent mixing zone in the atmosphere above the boundary layer. Two types of models have been postulated for the boundary layer. At low wind speeds, it is generally postulated that a true laminar layer exists with a fixed thickness and vapor gradient for a given wind speed, the transport through this layer being by steady-state molecular diffusion. At high wind speeds, above a certain critical velocity, the water surface changes from a smooth surface to a hydrodynamically rough surface. H. U. Sverdrup proposed that small turbulent eddies extend down to the actual liquid surface when it is rough. In such a model the vapor flux into these eddies can be postulated to take place by unsteady-state diffusion. With isotopic measurements it is possible to distinguish between these two models, because in

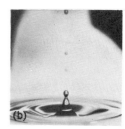

Fig. 1. Collapse of air bubble and formation of jet and droplets. (a) High-speed motion pictures of stages in the process. (b) Oblique view of jet and droplets from bubble 1.0 mm in diameter.

the first case the isotopic fractionation is governed by the ratio of molecular diffusion coefficients, whereas in the unsteady-state process the fractionation is governed by the square root of this ratio. The single-stage enrichments in the two processes thus differ by a factor of 2.

Projection of droplets. Water, salts, organic materials, and a net electric charge are transferred to the air through the ejection of droplets by bubbles bursting at the sea surface. The exchange of these properties between the sea and the atmosphere is of importance in meteorology and geochemistry. Upon evaporation of the water, the droplet residues are carried great distances by winds. These particles become nuclei for cloud-drop and raindrop formations and probably represent a large part of the cyclic salts of geochemistry.

Air bubbles are forced into surface waters of the sea by wave action, impinging raindrops, melting snowflakes, and other means. The larger bubbles rise to the surface, burst, and eject droplets. Many of the smaller bubbles dissolve before reaching the surface. The photomicrograph (**Fig. 1**) shows stages in the collapse of a bubble, and the jet and droplet formations which result. The graph (**Fig. 2**) shows the approximate relationships between the sizes of the bubbles, the sizes of the ejected droplets, and the weight of sea salt in these droplets.

The amounts of water which become airborne as droplets near the sea surface are not known. The best estimates which can be made (from the limited information about the number and size of bubbles in the sea) range from about 2 to 10 g/(m²)(day) during fresh winds.

The average amounts of sea salt which become airborne at considerable altitudes are shown in **Table 4**.

Table 4. Airborne sea salts in relation to wind force

Beaufort wind force	Concentrations,* μg/m³	Flux,* mg/(m²)(day)	Total,† mg/m²
2–3	2.7	0.42	6.0
4–5	9.9	3.9	11.6
6–7	21.3	24.0	21.8

*At about 500 m (1650 ft).
†Integrated through lowest 2000 m (6600 ft).

The total range of observed amounts in individual samples is from about 4×10^{-13} g/ml in a wind of Beaufort force 1 to 10^{-9} g/ml in a wind of force 12. *SEE WIND.*

Parts of marine organisms are seen in droplets ejected from plankton-rich water. The droplets also become coated with organic monolayers when they arise through contaminated surfaces. During moderate winds in oceanic trade-wind areas, organic materials can equal 20 to 30% of the airborne sea salt.

Alfred H. Woodcock

Electrification of the atmosphere. The traditional view states that the net positive space charge usually found in regions of fair weather is maintained by a charge separation process within thunderstorms. However, research has indicated that a charge separation mechanism at the surface of the ocean may contribute significantly to the atmospheric space charge over the oceans. It appears that this mechanism enables the oceans of the world to supply positive charge to the atmosphere at a rate of at least 10% of that supplied to the atmosphere over the oceans by thunderstorms. *SEE ATMOSPHERIC ELECTRICITY.*

The carriers of the charge separated at the ocean surface are the drops that emerge at the collapse of the jet that forms when a bubble breaks at the ocean surface (Fig. 1). Laboratory measurements have shown that the charge on these drops is a function of their size and of the age of the bubble from which they came. For drops in the size range commonly found in the atmosphere over the ocean, the charge per drop is positive and of the order of 10^{-16} coulomb. Measurements made on the windward shore of the island of Hawaii and at sea near Barbados, in the West Indies, show that in whitecaps where many bubbles are bursting, the oceanic charge production is about 4×10^{-11} C/(m²)(s). Since the percent coverage of the sea by whitecaps is roughly proportional to the cube of the wind speed, the oceanic charge production should be a maximum where the winds are the greatest. In each hemisphere this occurs at latitudes of 40–60°.

The normal oceanic fair-weather potential gradient does not have any significant influence on the magnitude of the charge of the drops from the bubble jet, but intense negative thunderstorm potential gradients of the order of 10^4 V/m at the sea surface can, by the process of induction charging, produce a positive charge on the drops that exceeds by many times the positive charge found on the drops in fair weather. Consequently, the normal positive space charge may be increased considerably in regions near oceanic thunderstorms.

Duncan C. Blanchard

Microlayer. The microlayer is the thin zone beneath the surface of the ocean or any free water sur-

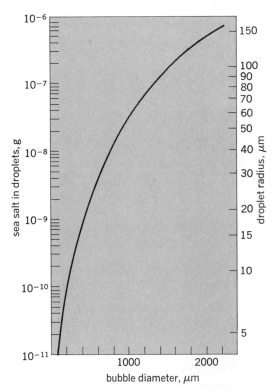

Fig. 2. Approximate relationships between the sizes of the bursting bubbles and the sizes and salt contents of the ejected droplets.

face within which physical processes are modified by proximity to the air–water boundary. It is characterized by suppression of vertical turbulence, a consequent decrease in diffusivity and increase in material, and an increase in kinetic and thermal gradients.

Because the microlayer at a free water surface is at least superficially similar to the boundary layer observed in the tangential flow of any viscous fluid near a rigid surface, it is tempting to identify one with the other. However, in view of the thermohydrodynamic complexity of the free ocean surface, such identification is unwarranted. All that can be described of the nature of the microlayer is gleaned from a few scattered observations. For the most part, these have been measurements of the effect of the microlayer on the flux of heat between water and air. A salinity gradient probably exists at the ocean surface.

A different and striking manifestation of the microlayer can be observed when a gentle breeze blows over calm water. Specks of dust at the surface flow along noticeably faster than those 1 cm (0.4 in.) or so beneath the surface. The strongly developed vertical shear in the wind-driven flow which is thus revealed is possible only because the small eddy stresses in the microlayer permit the motion to remain nearly laminar at a relatively high Reynolds number. The reduction of the shear at higher wind speeds shows that the microlayer is thinner under these conditions.

The development and stability of the microlayer is enhanced by a contaminating film of surface-active agents, which is characteristically present on natural water surfaces. Such films quickly accumulate on any body of water exposed to the air. Even in the laboratory, elaborate precautions are necessary in order to maintain a truly clean water surface.

The origin and composition of such films are complex. However, it can be asserted on thermodynamic grounds that substances will accumulate in a liquid surface if they reduce the surface tension and hence the free energy of the surface. Patches of such film can be observed on the sea under all normal conditions of wind and wave, although they are more strikingly visible at wind speeds under 3 m/s (10 ft/s), when they take the form of long, broad slicks. The most obvious effect of the film is to smooth the smallest ripples, giving the water a shiny appearance. The smoothing results from an altered boundary condition at the interface, substituting a sort of rubber-sheet elasticity for the relatively unrestricted freedom of a clean liquid surface. Such a stabilized surface more nearly approximates a rigid boundary, and therefore the associated microlayer becomes more nearly similar to the familiar boundary layer characterizing flow near a solid surface. Gradients, whether of substance, temperature, or momentum, are thus appreciably enhanced by surface films. In this purely mechanical manner, contaminating films can reduce the convective flux of heat across the air–water boundary independently of any throttling action they may have on the evaporation rate.

The flux of sensible heat across the air–water boundary of the ocean is usually in the upward direction, and hence the microlayer is cooler above than beneath. The sense of the flux results from the circumstance that most of the heating of the ocean is by solar radiation, which penetrates several meters into the sea before being absorbed, whereas heat balance is largely maintained by upward flux of sensible heat from a layer less than a few molecular diameters

deep. This is a form of the well-known greenhouse effect. Thus, on the average, the microlayer is heated from below and cooled from above. The net upward flux is of the order of 150 g-cal/(cm^2)(day) [630 J/(cm^2)(day)], varying with the latitude, the season, and the time of day. The flux is greatest in the tropics, in the autumn, and in the forenoon; least at the poles, in early summer, and in early afternoon.

The importance of the microlayer resides in the fact that most surface measurements are in reality volume measurements of a thin but finitely thick layer. Consequently, the value recorded depends on the method of measurement employed. For many purposes the differences are trivial and are ignored. However, where precision is required, the only way to arrive at a true value of any parameter at the exact surface is to calculate it from theoretical considerations or to estimate it by extrapolating some measured gradient to the boundary. As an example, it may be assumed intuitively that the surface temperature of water must approach the psychrometric, or so-called wet-bulb, temperature of the overlying air as a limit. However, the psychrometric temperature itself varies as the boundary is approached, and therefore cannot be directly measured at the exact surface. Hence, from a physical point of view, the concept of a surface is something of an abstraction which has precise meaning only when referred to a specific parameter.

Gifford C. Ewing

Exchange of gases. The ocean is a potential sink for some gases and has been proposed as a natural source for some others. The flux of gases through the air–sea interface depends not only on the concentration difference across the interface, but also on the transfer coefficient governing the exchange. There are a number of models describing the exchange processes. The most commonly used are the film model, still-surface models, and surface-renewal models. Chemical engineering studies of industrial processes involving the uptake of reactive gases such as ammonia (NH_3), carbon dioxide (CO_2), and sulfur dioxide (SO_2) have indicated that predictions based on the film model are usually remarkably similar to those based on more sophisticated models such as surface-renewal models. For the purpose of discussion and calculation, the film model is preferred because of its relative ease of mathematical formulation. This film model has been used exclusively by oceanographers for the calculations of gas exchange rates. It does provide an adequate first-order approximation to the much more complex processes actually taking place in the ocean.

Film model. A diagram of the film model is shown in **Fig. 3.** A layer of stagnant film of thickness z at the surface of water next to the gas is a major barrier to the transfer of gas. There is no convection in the film, and dissolved gas passes by molecular diffusion only. The water below the film is kept well mixed by agitation. The air above the film is assumed to be homogeneous. The dissolved gas concentration at equilibrium with the atmosphere C_0 ($= \alpha p$, where α is the gas solubility, and p is the partial pressure of the gas in the atmosphere) at the top of the film is assumed to be at equilibrium with the overlying air. The gas flux F that crosses the stagnant film may be expressed as Eq. (2), where C_z is the dissolved gas

$$F = k(C_z - C_0) \qquad (2)$$

concentration in the bulk liquid, and k is the gas

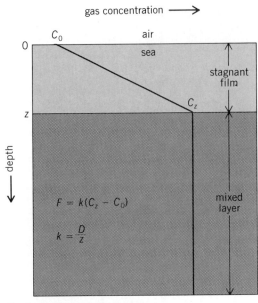

gas concentration ⟶

Fig. 3. Diagram of the film model.

transfer coefficient (or referred to as piston velocity which is equal to D/z, where D is the molecular diffusivity of gas in water). The thickness of the film (and hence the rate of gas exchange) depends on the degree of agitation of sea surface by the wind and wave motion; the higher the state of agitation, the thinner the film and faster the exchange rate.

Radioactive tracers. The techniques used to estimate the rate of gas exchange include the measurements of two radioactive tracer gases. One of these is radon and the other is $^{14}CO_2$. The radon gas is produced within the seawater by the radioactive decay of dissolved radium-226. It has a half-life of 3.85 days. In the open ocean, the radon content in the air is negligible as compared with the radon in the seawater. Hence, the radon in seawater is in part lost to the atmosphere before it undergoes radioactive decay. The magnitude of this loss provides a measurement of the thickness of stagnant film. As part of the Geochemical Section Studies (GEOSECS) program, over 100 stations were occupied in both the Atlantic and the Pacific oceans for the measurements of radon deficiency in the surface ocean. The global mean transfer coefficient k estimated from these GEOSECS data is 2.9 m (9.6 ft) per day (at 20°C or 68°F), which corresponds to a hypothetical stagnant film thickness of about 36 micrometers.

The natural radiocarbon is generated in the atmosphere and transported into the sea as $^{14}CO_2$ through sea–air interface. Before the nuclear bomb test, the atmospheric $^{14}C/^{12}C$ ratio remained nearly constant over the previous 2000 years as documented by the tree ring ^{14}C measurements. The ocean–atmosphere system should have reached steady state, where the rate of radiocarbon decay in the ocean is compensated by the net transport rate of ^{14}C through sea–air interface. Assuming the ratio of $^{14}C/^{12}C$ in the surface mixed layer to that in the atmosphere to be 0.96, the ratio of $^{14}C/^{12}C$ in the mean ocean water to that in the atmosphere to be 0.84, the total CO_2 concentration in the ocean to be 2.3 moles/m³, the mean ocean depth to be 3800 m (12,500 ft), the half-life of radiocarbon to be 5570 years, and the molecular diffusivity of CO_2 to be 1.6×10^{-5} cm²/s, the mean film thickness of the world ocean is calculated to be 30 μm.

Since the nuclear bomb test in the early 1950s, a vast amount of ^{14}C has been produced in the atmosphere. As a result of sea–air gas exchange process, these bomb-produced radiocarbons invade the ocean reservoir. There are enough measurements of ^{14}C in the atmospheric CO_2 since 1954 to provide a complete time history and geographic variation of bomb ^{14}C in the air. By measuring the depth-integrated amount of bomb-produced ^{14}C accumulated by any given portion of the sea, it was possible to determine the average rate of CO_2 invasion occurring from 1960 to 1980. The GEOSECS ^{14}C data in the Atlantic Ocean were used to estimate the mean invasion rate of CO_2 to be 22 moles/(m²)(yr), which corresponds to a film thickness of 25 μm. This value may vary in different sections of the ocean, since the vertical distribution of bomb ^{14}C at any given locality is influenced by the horizontal transportation.

Gas flux. Once the film thickness is known, the transfer coefficient k of various gases of interest can be calculated by applying a proper molecular diffusivity. The flux of gases that passes through the sea–air interface may then be calculated if the atmospheric concentration of the gas, the solubility of the gas in seawater, and the dissolved gas concentration in the seawater are known. The computation of gas flux according to Eq. (2) should be quite straightforward if the gas of interest is not chemically active. For active gases, the chemical enhancement has to be taken into account in the flux calculation. For carbon dioxide, the dissolved CO_2 within the stagnant film reacts with carbonate ion to form two bicarbonate ions. The diffusion of dissolved CO_2 coupled with chemical removal of CO_2 enhances the CO_2 flux across the sea–air interface. The chemical enhancement of CO_2 flux also depends on the thickness of the stagnant film. This has to do with the reaction rate that converts CO_2 to bicarbonate ion (HCO_3^-). The greater the bicarbonate ion content of the water, the greater the reac-

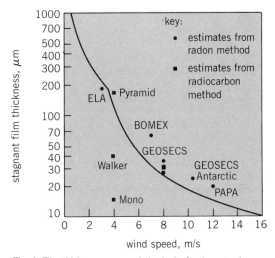

Fig. 4. Film thickness versus wind velocity for the natural systems. The solid line is the curve obtained in the wind tunnel by the Hamburg group, in Germany, with the wind velocity translated to 10 m (33 ft) above the water surface. The slope break in the curve corresponds to the initiation of capillary waves. The locations of the data points are the Geochemical Section Studies program in the Atlantic and Pacific (GEOSECS); the month-long averages obtained off Barbados (BOMEX); an ocean station in the North Pacific (PAPA); an experimental lakes area in Ontario, Canada (ELA); and Pyramid, Walker, and Mono lakes in the Great Basin area. 1 m = 3.3 ft.

tion rate and the thinner the stagnant film thickness at which chemical enhancement becomes important. Fortunately, the global mean ocean film thickness of 30 ± 5 μm fell within the region where the chemical enhancement is negligible. However, this effect cannot be ignored in the continental waters where the film thickness is generally thicker than that in the open ocean and the chemistry of continental waters varies greatly and differently from the seawater.

Wind speed. The relationship between the wind speed and the film thickness in a number of natural systems is shown in **Fig. 4**. The experimental results in the wind tunnel of the Hamburg lab are also given for comparison. Except for Walker and Mono lakes of the Great Basin area, the natural systems follow the trend line predicted by experiment. However, the individual measurements by the radon methods during the GEOSECS program do not show a clear relationship between the wind speed and the gas exchange rate. The gas exchange rates in various parts of the ocean are a complex function of wind history of the area. *See Atmospheric chemistry; Maritime meteorology.*

T.-H. Peng

Composition of Seawater

The concentrations of the various components of seawater are regulated by numerous chemical, physical, and biochemical reactions.

Inorganic regulation of composition. The present-day compositions of seawater (**Table 5**) are controlled both by the makeup of the ultimate source materials and by the large number of reactions, of chemical and physical natures, occurring in the oceans. This section considers the nonbiological regulatory mechanisms, most conveniently defined as those reactions occurring in a sterile ocean.

Interactions between the ions results in the formation of ion pairs, charged and uncharged species, which influence both the chemical and physical properties of seawater. For example, the combination of magnesium and sulfate to form the uncharged ion pair accounts for the marked absorption of sound in seawater. A model accounting for such interactions has been developed for the principal dissolved ions in seawater (**Table 6**).

pH and oxidation potential. The pH of surface seawater varies between 7.8 and 8.3, with lower values occurring at depths. The pH normally goes through a minimum with increasing depth in the ocean, and this depth dependence shows a marked resemblance to the profiles of oxygen.

The oxidation potentials of seawater systems are determined by oxygen concentration in aerobic waters and by hydrogen sulfide concentration in anoxic waters. For 25°C (77°F), 1 atm pressure (10^5 Pa), and pH of 8, the oxidation potential is about 0.75 V for waters containing dissolved oxygen in a state of saturation. In anoxic waters the oxidation potentials can vary from about -0.2 to -0.3 V.

Solubility. Only calcium, among the major cations of seawater, is present in a state of saturation, and such a situation generally occurs only in surface waters. Here its concentration is governed by the solubility of calcium carbonate. Barium concentrations in deep waters can be limited by the precipitation of barium sulfate. The noble gases and dissolved gaseous nitrogen have their marine concentrations determined by the temperature at which their water mass was in

Table 5. Chemical abundances in the marine hydrosphere

Element	Concentration, mg/liter	Element	Concentration, mg/liter
H	108,000	Ag	0.0003
He	0.000007	Cd	0.00011
Li	0.17	In	0.000004
Be	0.0000006	Sn	0.0008
B	4.6	Sb	0.0003
C	28	Te	—
N	15	I	0.06
O	857,000	Xe	0.00005
F	1.2	Cs	0.0003
Ne	0.0001	Ba	0.03
Na	10,500	La	1.2×10^{-5}
Mg	1350	Ce	5.2×10^{-6}
Al	0.01	Pr	2.6×10^{-6}
Si	3.0	Nd	9.2×10^{-6}
P	0.07	Pm	—
S	885	Sm	1.7×10^{-6}
Cl	19,000	Eu	4.6×10^{-7}
A	0.45	Gd	2.4×10^{-6}
K	380	Tb	—
Ca	400	Dy	2.9×10^{-6}
Sc	<0.00004	Ho	8.8×10^{-7}
Ti	0.001	Er	2.4×10^{-6}
V	0.002	Tm	5.2×10^{-7}
Cr	0.00005	Yb	2.0×10^{-6}
Mn	0.002	Lu	4.8×10^{-7}
Fe	0.01	Hf	<0.000008
Co	0.0004	Ta	<0.000003
Ni	0.007	W	0.0001
Cu	0.003	Re	0.0000084
Zn	0.01	Os	—
Ga	0.00003	Ir	—
Ge	0.00006	Pt	—
As	0.003	Au	0.00001
Se	0.00009	Hg	0.0002
Br	65	Tl	<0.00001
Kr	0.0002	Pb	0.00003
Rb	0.12	Bi	0.00002
Sr	8.0	Po	—
Y	0.00001	At	—
Zr	0.00002	Rn	0.6×10^{-15}
Nb	0.00001	Fr	—
Mo	0.01	Ra	1.0×10^{-10}
Tc	—	Ac	—
Ru	0.0000007	Th	0.000001
Rh	—	Pa	2.0×10^{-9}
Pd	—	U	0.003

Table 6. Distribution, in percent, of major cations as ion pairs with sulfate, carbonate, and bicarbonate ions in seawater of chlorinity 19‰ and pH 8.1

Ion	Free ion	Sulfate ion pair	Bicarbonate ion pair	Carbonate ion pair
Ca^{2+}	91	8	1	0.2
Mg^{2+}	87	11	1	0.3
Na^+	99	1.2	0.01	—
K^+	99	1	—	—

Ion	Free ion	Ca ion pair	Mg ion pair	Na ion pair	K ion pair
SO_4^{2-}	54	3	21.5	21	0.5
HCO_3^-	69	4	19	8	—
CO_3^{2-}	9	7	67	17	—

contact with the atmosphere and are in states of saturation or very nearly so.

Authigenic mineral formation. The formation and alteration of minerals on the sea floor apparently are responsible for controlling the concentrations of the major cations sodium (Na^+), potassium (K^+), magnesium (Mg^{2+}), and calcium (Ca^{2+}). Such clay minerals as illite, chlorite, and montmorillonite are presumably synthesized from these dissolved species and the river-transported weathered solids (aluminosilicates, such as kaolinite) as in reaction (3). The silicon

$$Aluminosilicates + SiO_2 + HCO_3^- + cations \rightarrow$$

$$cation\ aluminosilicate + CO_2 + H_2O \qquad (3)$$

dioxide (SiO_2) is introduced in part as diatom frustules. Such a process implies control of the carbon dioxide pressure of the atmosphere.

The formation of ferromanganese minerals, seafloor precipitates of iron and manganese oxides, may govern the concentrations of a suite of trace metals, including zinc, manganese, copper, nickel, and cobalt. These elements are in highly undersaturated states in seawater (**Table 7**) but are highly enriched in these marine ores, the so-called manganese nodules, which range in size from millimeters to about 1 m in the form of coatings and as components of the unconsolidated sediments.

Cation and anion exchange. Cation-exchange reactions between positively charged species in seawater and such minerals as the marine clays and zeolites appear to regulate, at least in part, the amounts of sodium, potassium, and magnesium, as well as other members of the alkali and alkaline-earth metals that are not major participants in mineral formations. High charge and large radius influence favorably the uptake on cation-exchange minerals. It appears, for example, that while 65% of the sodium weathered from the continental rocks resides in the oceans, only 2.5, 0.15, and 0.025% of the total amounts of potassium, rubidium, and cesium ions (ions increasingly larger than sodium) have remained there. Further, magnesium and potassium are depleted in the ocean relative to sodium on the basis of data obtained from igneous rock.

The curious fact that magnesium remains in solution to a much higher degree than potassium is not yet resolved, but may be explained by the ability of such ubiquitous clay minerals as the illites to fix potassium into nonexchangeable or difficultly exchangeable sites.

Similarly, anion-exchange processes may regulate the composition of some of the negatively charged ions in the oceans. For example, the chlorine-bromine ratio in seawater of 300 is displaced to values around 50 in sediments. Such a result may well arise from the replacement of chlorine by bromine in clays; however, the meager amounts of work in this field preclude any unqualified statements.

Physical processes. Superimposed upon these chemical processes are changes in the chemical makeup of seawater by the melting of ice, evaporation, mixing with runoff waters from the continents, and upwelling of deeper waters. The net effects of the first three processes are changes in the absolute concentrations of all of the elements but with no major changes in the relative amounts of the dissolved species.

Changes with time. Changes in the composition of seawater through geologic time reflect not only differences in the extent and types of weathering processes on the Earth's surface but also the relative intensities of the biological and inorganic reactions. The most influential parameter controlling the inorganic processes appears to be the seawater temperature.

Changes in the abyssal temperatures of the oceans from their present values of near 0 to 2.2, 7.0, and 10.4°C (32 to 36, 45, and 50.7°F) in the upper, middle, and lower Tertiary, respectively, have been postulated from studies on the oxygen isotopic composition of the tests of benthic foraminifera. Such temperature increases would of necessity be accompanied by similar ones in the surface and intermediate waters. One obvious effect from the recent cooling of the oceans is an increase in either the calcium and carbonate ions, or both, since the solubility product of calcium carbonate has a negative temperature coefficient. Similarly, the saturated amounts of gases that can dissolve in seawater in equilibrium with the atmosphere increase with decreasing water temperatures.

Edward D. Goldberg

Biological regulation of composition. In the open sea, all the organic matter is produced by the photosynthesis and growth of unicellular planktonic forms. During this growth, all the elements essential for living matter are obtained from the seawater. Some elements are present in great excess, such as the carbon of CO_2, potassium, and sulfur (as sulfate). Other elements—for example, phosphorus, nitrogen, and silicon—are present in such small quantities that plant growth removes virtually all of the supply from the water. During photosynthesis, as these elements are removed from the water, oxygen is released.

Biochemical cycle. The organic matter formed by photosynthesis and growth of the unicellular plants may be largely eaten by the zooplankton, and these in turn form the food for larger organisms. At each step of the food chain a large proportion of the eaten material is digested and excreted, and this, along with dead organisms, is decomposed by bacterial action. The decomposition process removes oxygen from the water and returns to the water those elements previously absorbed by the phytoplankton.

The distribution of oxygen and essential nutrient elements in the sea is modified by the spatial separation of these biological processes. Photosynthesis is limited to the surface layers of the ocean, generally no more than 100 m (330 ft) or so depth, but the decomposition of organic material may take place at any depth. Reflecting this separation of processes, the concentration of nutrient elements in the surface is low, rises to maximum values at intermediate depths (300–800 m or 1000–2600 ft), and decreases slightly to fairly constant values which extend nearly to the bottom. Frequently, a slight increase in the concentra-

Table 7. Observed concentrations of some trace metals in seawater*

Ion	Observed seawater concentration, moles/liter	Limiting compound	Calculated limiting concentration, moles/liter
Mn^{2+}	4×10^{-8}	$MnCO_3$	10^{-3}
Ni^{2+}	4×10^{-8}	$Ni(OH)_2$	10^{-3}
Co^{2+}	7×10^{-9}	$CoCO_3$	3×10^{-7}
Zn^{2+}	2×10^{-7}	$ZnCO_3$	2×10^{-4}
Cu^{2+}	5×10^{-8}	$Cu(OH)_2$	10^{-6}

*Calculated on the basis of their most insoluble compound.

tion of essential elements is observed near the bottom. The oxygen distribution is the opposite of the one just described, with high values at the surface, a minimum value at middepth, and intermediate values in the deep water. The oxygen-minimum–nutrient-maximum level in the ocean is the result of two processes working simultaneously. In part it is formed by the decomposition of organic matter sinking from the surface, and in part it results from the fact that this water was originally at the surface in high latitudes, where it contained organic matter and subsequently cooled, sank, and spread out over the oceans at the appropriate density levels.

Because of the nearly constant composition of marine organisms, the elements required in the formation of organic material vary in a correlated way. Analyses of marine organisms indicate that in their protoplasm the elements carbon, nitrogen, and phosphorus are present in the ratios of 100:15:1 by atoms. In the production of organic matter these elements are removed from the water in these ratios, and during the decomposition of organic matter they are returned to the water in the same ratio. However, since the decomposition of organic material is not an instantaneous process which releases all elements simultaneously, it is not unusual to find different ratios of concentration of these elements in the sea. Particularly in coastal waters and in confined seas the ratio of concentration of nitrogen to phosphorus, for example, may differ widely from the 15:1 ratio of composition within the organisms.

Biochemical circulation. Unlike the major elements in seawater, the concentrations of these nutrients are widely different in different oceans of the world. Pacific Ocean water contains nearly twice the concentration of nitrogen and phosphorus found at the same depth in the North Atlantic, and intermediate concentrations are found in the South Atlantic and Antarctic oceans. The lowest concentrations for any extensive body of water are found in the Mediterranean, where they are only about one-third of those in the North Atlantic.

These variations can be attributed to the ways in which the water circulates in these oceans and to the effect of the biological processes on the distribution of elements. The Mediterranean, for example, receives surface water, already low in nutrients, from the North Atlantic and loses water from a greater depth through the Straits of Gibraltar. While the water is in the Mediterranean, the surface layers are further impoverished by growth of phytoplankton, and the organic material formed sinks to the bottom water and is lost in the deeper outflow. A similar process explains the low nutrient concentrations in the North Atlantic, which receives surface water from the South Atlantic and loses an equivalent volume of water from greater depths.   *Bostwick H. Ketchum*

DISTRIBUTION OF PROPERTIES

The distribution of physical and chemical properties in the ocean is principally the result of (1) radiation (of heat); (2) exchange with the land (of heat, water, and solids such as salts) and with the atmosphere (of water, salt, heat, and dissolved gases); (3) organic processes (photosynthesis, respiration, and decay); and (4) mixing and stirring processes. These processes are largely responsible for the formation of particular water types and ocean water masses.

Horizontal distributions. The general distribution of properties in the oceans shows a marked latitudinal effect which corresponds with radiation income and differences between evaporation and precipitation.

Temperature. Heat is received from the Sun at the sea surface, where parts of it are reflected and radiated back. Equatorward of 30° latitude, the incoming radiation exceeds back radiation and reflection, and poleward it is less. The result is high sea-surface temperature (more than 28°C or 82°F) in equatorial regions and low sea-surface temperatures (less than 1°C or 34°F) in polar regions.

Salinity. Various dissolved solids have entered the sea from the land and have been so mixed that their relative amounts are everywhere nearly constant, yet the total concentration (salinity) varies considerably. In the middle latitudes the evaporation of water exceeds precipitation, and the surface salinity is high; in low and high latitudes precipitation exceeds evaporation, and dilution reduces the surface salinity.

Open ocean surface salinities range from lows of about 32.5‰ in the North Pacific, 34.0‰ in the Antarctic, 35.0‰ in the equatorial Atlantic, 34.0‰ in the equatorial Indian, and 33.5‰ in the equatorial Pacific to highs in the great evaporation centers of the middle latitudes of 35.5‰ and 36.5‰ in the North and South Pacific, 37.0‰ in the North and South Atlantic, and 36.0‰ in the Indian Ocean.

Dissolved oxygen. Dissolved oxygen is both consumed (respiration and decay) and produced (photosynthesis) in the ocean, as well as being exchanged with the atmosphere at the sea surface. Above the thermocline the waters are always near saturation in oxygen content (>7 ml/liter in the cold waters of the high latitudes and <5 ml/liter in the warm equatorial waters).

Density. The density of seawater depends upon its temperature, salinity, and depth (pressure), but can vary horizontally only in the presence of currents, and hence its distribution depends closely upon the current structure. In low and middle latitudes the effect of the high temperature exceeds that of the high salinity, and the surface waters are lighter than those in high latitudes, with values ranging from less than 1.022 g/ml to more than 1.027 g/ml. The density at great depth (10,000 m or 33,000 ft) may exceed 1.065 g/ml. The greatest vertical gradient is associated with the thermocline and the halocline and is therefore very near to the surface. The heavier surface waters from high latitudes move and mix underneath the lighter water at depths that depend upon their density. The difference in surface density is usually not great, since the high-latitude salinity is low, and the waters usually sink only a few hundred meters, forming intermediate water. But in cases where water of high salinity has been carried into high latitudes by the currents and cooled (as in the North Atlantic) or where water of relatively high salinity freezes and gives up part of its water (as on the continental shelf of Antarctica), deep and bottom waters with temperature less than 1°C (34°F) are formed. *SEE THERMOCLINE.*

Vertical distributions. The subsurface distribution of properties is controlled largely by external factors, particularly those which influence surface density, and the type of deep-sea circulation.

Temperature. The thermohaline circulation results in a vertical distribution of temperature such that in low and middle latitudes the deeper waters are colder than the surface waters, and at very high latitudes where surface temperatures are low, the deeper waters are as warm as those at the surface, or warmer. Seasonal cooling in high latitudes may cause the temperature to be at a minimum at some intermediate depth, and the circulation may cause a temperature minimum or maximum at intermediate depths. Over a large part of the Pacific Ocean, where no bottom water is formed, the temperature increases downward from about 400 m (13,000 ft). Since the gradient is not greater than the adiabatic, the water is not unstable.

Density and salinity. Since much of the flow of the ocean is geostrophically balanced, surfaces of constant density slope in various ways with respect to the sea surface and other surfaces of constant pressure, and density varies in the east-west as well as the north-south direction. Mixing and movement of intermediate and deep water along these surfaces cause more complex distributions of other variables. The intermediate waters of the North and South Pacific and of the South Atlantic appear to have salinity minima at intermediate depths in middle and low latitudes, since they originate in the high-latitude regions of low salinity and pass between the high-salinity surface waters of middle latitudes and the bottom waters. In the North Pacific this minimum varies from 33.4 to 34.1‰, and in the South Pacific and South Atlantic from 34.2 to about 34.6‰. In the North Atlantic Ocean there is no intermediate water of low salinity formed, but very saline water (36.5‰) flows in from the Mediterranean at depth and results in a more complicated distribution of salinity than is found in the other oceans. For the temperatures and salinities of the bottom waters, which are more homogeneous than the others, see the later discussion on ocean water masses.

Dissolved oxygen. Where the cold surface waters sink in high latitudes, quantities of oxygen are carried downward. Below the compensation depth, consumption gradually reduces the concentration. The bottom waters of the Atlantic Ocean contain from 5 to 6 ml/liter of dissolved oxygen; the Indian and South Pacific oceans, about 4 ml/liter; and the North Pacific, less than 4 ml/liter. Between these bottom waters and those at the surface, which are saturated, smaller values of oxygen are found ranging from less than 0.10 ml/liter in the eastern tropical Pacific and less than 1.0 ml/liter in the eastern tropical Atlantic to greater than 4 ml/liter in the South Atlantic.

Nutrients. Other properties, such as the nutrients, phosphate and nitrate, have low concentrations in the surface layer, where they are consumed by the plants, and high values at depths, where they are concentrated by the sinking and decay of organisms.

The maximum values of phosphate are found at intermediate depths, usually beneath the layer of minimum oxygen, and vary from less than 1 μg-atom/liter in the North Atlantic to more than 2 μg-atoms/liter in the Antarctic, Indian, and South Pacific, and more than 3.5 μg-atoms/liter in the North Pacific. Surface values vary from less than 0.1 μg-atoms/liter in the North Atlantic and 0.5 μg-atom/liter in the North Pacific to more than 1.5 μg-atom/liter in the Antarctic. Bottom values vary from about 1.0 μg-atoms/liter in the North Atlantic and 2.0 μg-atom/liter in the Antarctic, South Pacific, and Indian oceans to 2.5 μg-atoms/liter in the North Pacific.

Nitrate-nitrogen is present in a ratio of about 8:1 by weight to phosphate-phosphorus.

Silicate has no intermediate maximum but increases monotonically toward the bottom, where the values vary from more than 150 μg-atoms/liter in the North Pacific to less than 40 μg-atoms/liter in the North Atlantic. Surface values are generally less than 10 μg-atoms/liter.

Joseph L. Reid

Carbon dioxide system. When carbon dioxide gas dissolves in seawater, it reacts with the water to form bicarbonate (HCO_3^-) and carbonate (CO_3^{2-}) ions. Thus, its chemical behavior in ocean water differs significantly from other gases such as oxygen, nitrogen, and methane, which do not dissociate into ions. The CO_2 system in seawater can be characterized in terms of the following four measurable chemical quantities: the total amount of CO_2 species dissolved in seawater; the alkalinity, which is a measure of the ionic charge balance in the seawater; the pH; and the partial pressure of CO_2 exerted by the seawater.

Total CO_2 concentration. The total amount of CO_2 dissolved in seawater is the sum of the concentrations of undissociated carbonic acid, H_2CO_3, and the bicarbonate and carbonate ions; the relationships among these species are described by reactions (4) to (6). A

$$H_2O + CO_2(g) \rightarrow H_2CO_3 \qquad (4)$$

$$H_2CO_3 \rightarrow H^+ + HCO_3^- \qquad (5)$$

$$HCO_3^- \rightarrow H^+ + CO_3^{2-} \qquad (6)$$

substantial portion of the bicarbonate and carbonate ions forms metal complexes such as $NaHCO_3^0$, $NaCO_3^-$, $MgHCO_3^+$, $MgCO_3^0$, $CaHCO_3^+$, and $CaCO_3^0$. In normal seawater of pH 8.15 at 25°C (77°F), approximately 31% of the bicarbonate and 91% of the carbonate ions are complexed with Na^+, Mg^{2+} and Ca^{2+} ions. Since knowledge of complex ion speciation in seawater is not complete, a common practice is to express the total dissolved CO_2 species by Eq. (7), where the brackets represent the sum of

$$\Sigma CO_2 = [H_2CO_3] + [HCO_3^-] + [CO_3^{2-}] \qquad (7)$$

the concentrations of both free and complexed ion species. Since H_2CO_3 and CO_2 (aq) molecules are experimentally indistinguishable, both of these are included in the first term. The relationships between the equilibrium concentrations of the species are expressed in terms of the apparent dissociation constants, as shown in Eqs. (8)–(10), where K_0' is the

$$K_0' = \frac{[H_2CO_3]}{pCO_2} \qquad (8)$$

$$K_1' = a_{H^+} \frac{[HCO_3^-]}{[H_2CO_3]} \qquad (9)$$

$$K_2' + a_{H^+} \frac{[CO_3^{2-}]}{[HCO_3^-]} \qquad (10)$$

solubility of CO_2 gas in seawater; pCO_2 the partial pressure of CO_2; a_{H^+} the activity of hydrogen ion; and K_1' and K_2' the first and second apparent dissociation constants of carbonic acid in seawater. The apparent dissociation constants K_1' and K_2' for seawater are respectively 2.5 and 17.5 times greater than the corresponding values in pure water. These differences are attributable not only to the small activity coefficient values that exists in strong electrolyte solutions

($\gamma_{HCO_3^-}$ = 0.68 and γ_{CO_3} = 0.20 for an ionic strength of 0.7 in seawater) but also to the formation of complex ions. In seawater, $[HCO_3^-]$ is the dominant species and accounts for 85–95% of the total dissolved CO_2 concentration, whereas $[H_2CO_3]$ and $[CO_3^{2-}]$ account for 0.3–1.5% and 3–1.5%, respectively.

Alkalinity. This is defined as the difference between the total cationic charge of strong electrolytes, that is, $[Na^+]$ + $[K^+]$ + $2[Ca^{2+}]$ + $2[Mg^{2+}]$, and the total anionic charge, excluding weak acids such as carbonic, boric, phosphoric, and silicic acids, that is, $[Cl^-]$ + $[NO_3^-]$ + $2[SO_4^{2-}]$. In a normal pH range (7.5 to 8.3) for seawater, alkalinity (TA) is expressed by Eq. (11). Since this quantity is commonly deter-

$$TA = [HCO_3^-] + 2[CO_3^{2-}] + [B(OH)_4^-]$$
$$+ [Si(OH)_3^-] + [OH^-] - [H^+] \quad (11)$$

mined by titration method, it is called the titration alkalinity as well as the total alkalinity. The first two terms of the alkalinity expression are the result of the dissociation of carbonic acid, and therefore the sum of these terms is called the carbonate alkalinity. The third term is the borate alkalinity and amounts to 2–5% of the total alkalinity. The fourth through sixth terms are generally small, and the sum of these terms does not exceed 0.25% of the total alkalinity value.

pH. The pH of the open ocean water ranges between 7.7 and 8.3 due mainly to buffering by carbonic and boric acids, and is controlled by the total alkalinity/total CO_2 concentration ratio. The greater the alkalinity and smaller the total CO_2 concentration, the greater is the pH value. Because of this, greater pH values are found in surface waters, which have greater values than deep waters for the alkalinity/total CO_2 concentration ratio.

Partial pressure of CO_2. This is an important quantity for determining the direction and net flux for air–sea CO_2 gas exchange in seawater, since the difference between the partial pressure in surface water and that in the air above it constitutes the chemical driving force for gas exchange. In the oceanic temperature range of 0–30°C (32–86°F), it varies at a rate of about 4% per °C (2.2% per °F) for seawater having a constant alkalinity and total CO_2 concentration. The total CO_2 concentration in seawater affects the CO_2 partial pressure sensitively, and its effect is expressed by Eq. (12) at a constant alkalinity, salin-

$$\gamma = \frac{\Delta pCO_2/pCO_2}{\Delta \Sigma CO_2/\Sigma CO_2}$$
$$= \left(\frac{\partial \ln pCO_2}{\partial \ln \Sigma CO_2}\right)_{TA,S,T} \quad (12)$$

ity, and temperature. This quantity is usually called the Revelle factor or the buffer factor, and is 10 for average surface water, and 15 for deep waters rich in total CO_2. This means that the CO_2 partial pressure is a tenth- to fifteenth-power function of the total CO_2 concentration and implies that a large increase in the atmospheric CO_2 concentration would cause a small increase in the total CO_2 which was dissolved in the surface ocean water.

Variations. The total CO_2 concentration in ocean water ranges from about 1950 to 2400 micro-

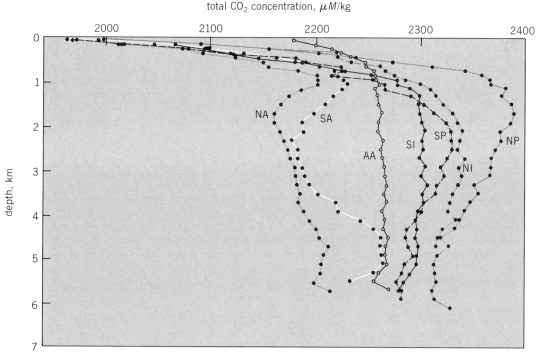

Fig. 5. Vertical distribution of the total CO_2 concentration in various regions of the world oceans: NA = North Atlantic Ocean, from Equator to 40°N; SA = South Atlantic Ocean, from the Equator to 45°S; NP = North Pacific Ocean, north of the Equator; SP = South Pacific Ocean, from the Equator to 45°S; NI = North Indian Ocean, north of the Equator; SI = South Indian Ocean, from the Equator to 45°S; and AA = Antarctic Sea, south of 45°S. The values are normalized to the mean salinity of the world oceans, 34.78‰. The data are from the GEOSECS expeditions in the Atlantic (1972–1973), the Pacific (1973–1974), and the Indian Ocean (1977–1978). 1 km = 0.6 mi. (*After T. Takahashi, W. S. Broecker, and A. E. Bainbridge, The alkalinity and the total CO_2 concentration in the world oceans, in B. Bolin, Carbon Cycle Modelling, SCOPE vol. 16, pp. 159–199, 271–286, John Wiley and Sons, 1981*)

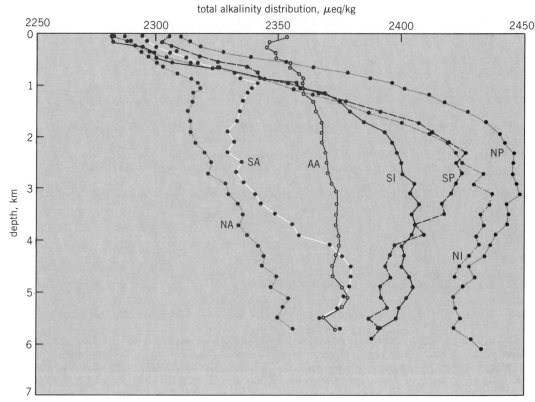

Fig. 6. Vertical distribution of the total alkalinity in various regions of the world oceans: NA = North Atlantic Ocean, from the Equator to 40°N; SA = South Atlantic Ocean, from the Equator to 45°S; NP = North Pacific Ocean, north of the Equator; SP = South Pacific Ocean, from the Equator to 45°S; NI = North Indian Ocean, north of the Equator; SI = South Indian Ocean, from the Equator to 45°S; and AA = Antarctic Sea, south of 45°S. The values are normalized to the mean salinity of the world oceans, 34.78‰. The data are from the GEOSECS expeditions in the Atlantic (1972–1973), the Pacific (1973–1974), and the Indian Ocean (1977–1978). 1 km = 0.6 mi. (*After T. Takahashi, W. S. Broecker, and A. E. Bainbridge, The alkalinity and the total CO_2 concentration in the world oceans, in B. Bolin, Carbon Cycle Modelling, SCOPE vol. 16, pp. 159–199, 271–286, John Wiley and Sons, 1981*)

moles/kg. The lower values are found in surface waters, and the greater values in deep waters. Its vertical distribution in various regions of the world oceans is shown in **Fig. 5**. The total alkalinity in the world oceans varies between 2250 and 2450 microequivalents per kilogram, smaller values being found in surface waters and greater values in deep waters. The alkalinity distribution in various oceanic regions is shown in **Fig. 6**. The lower concentrations found in surface waters are due mainly to the net removal of CO_2 by biological activities and the loss of CO_2 to the atmosphere. The lower alkalinity values in surface waters are attributed mainly to the removal of Ca^{2+} ion by such calcium carbonate–secreting organisms as foraminifera and coccoliths. On the other hand, the greater values of these quantities found in deep waters can be accounted for respectively by CO_2 generation via microbial oxidation of organic debris that sinks through the water column and by the dissolution of calcium carbonate tests deposited on the ocean floor. The observed high alkalinity values in upper waters of the Antarctic region signify a fast vertical circulation rate unique to this region. The regional variations in these quantities are attributed to differences in deep-ocean circulation, to chemical differences in the source waters for various subsurface water masses, and to regional variabilities in the flux and chemical composition of falling organic debris and calcium carbonate tests from the biologically active surface water zone.

The partial pressure of CO_2 in surface water varies from about 130 microatmospheres (13 Pa) to over 500 µatm (50 Pa): about 200 µatm (20 Pa) below and above the current atmospheric value of about 325 µatm (33 Pa). Seawater, which has a CO_2 partial pressure lower than the atmospheric value, is undersaturated with respect to atmospheric CO_2 and absorbs CO_2 from air, whereas that which has a partial pressure higher than the atmospheric value discharges CO_2 into the atmosphere, acting as a CO_2 source. The distribution of the partial pressure of CO_2 in the surface waters of the world oceans is shown in **Fig. 7**. The lowest values are found in the cold Norwegian Sea and Greenland Sea waters in the northern extreme of the Atlantic Ocean. The high values are found in the warm equatorial waters, and values over 500 µatm (50 Pa) have been reported in the coastal upwelling areas. The equatorial high values are due to warm temperatures and to the upwelling of the CO_2-rich subsurface waters in the equatorial belt. Thus, the surface ocean waters in some oceanic regions are significantly out of equilibrium with atmospheric CO_2. The area-weighted global mean value for the CO_2 partial pressure in surface waters is about 10 (±8) µatm [1.0 (±0.8) Pa] lower than the mean atmospheric value, indicating that the oceans are a net CO_2 sink. Using a global mean gas exchange rate of 16 moles $CO_2/(m^2)(yr)$, which has been estimated on the basis of the distribution of radon-222 and carbon-14 in the atmosphere and oceans, the rate for the net

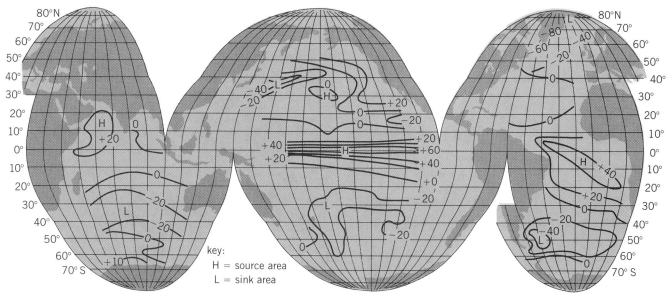

Fig. 7. Distribution of the partial pressure of CO_2 in the surface waters of the world oceans. The values are expressed in terms of the difference between the partial pressure of CO_2 in the surface water and in the atmosphere in microatmospheres (1 μatm = 0.1 Pa). The positive values indicate that the seawater is a CO_2 source, and the negative values indicate that the seawater is a sink for the atmospheric CO_2. The map is based on the data obtained during the GEOSECS expeditions in the Atlantic (1972–1973), the Pacific (1973–1974), and the Indian Ocean (1977–1978).

transfer of CO_2 from air to sea has been estimated to be equivalent to about 50% of the annual industrial CO_2 production rate, 5×10^9 metric tons of carbon per year.

Other dissolved gases. The principal source of the gases dissolved in seawater is the atmosphere, with lesser contributions from in-place processes within the sea, from reactions taking place in the bottom sediments, and from sources beneath the sea such as volcanism. In most cases, the concentration of a given gas depends on a combination of factors, and will usually vary with depth in the ocean, with geographical location, and with time of the year. As a starting point in considering the observed variations in concentration, it is assumed that at one time or another during the Earth's history all parts of the ocean were in contact with the atmosphere long enough for equilibrium between gas and liquid to be attained. Under these conditions, the seawater becomes saturated with the atmospheric gases, and concentrations can then be calculated from Henry's law. Any departures from these predicted saturation values can then be considered to result from chemical, biological, or physical processes within or beneath the sea, and some assessment as to the nature of these processes, and the rates at which they may be occurring, can be made.

Rare gases. Helium, neon, argon, and krypton all exhibit small amounts of supersaturation. Because these gases are chemically inert, the excess amounts of gas have been attributed chiefly to bubble entrapment at the air–sea interface. As the bubbles are carried downward, the increase in hydrostatic pressure results in an increase in partial pressures within the bubble (approximately 10% for each meter that the bubble is carried beneath the surface). This leads to increased amounts of gas going into solution. In the case of helium (He), isotopic analyses have revealed two additional sources of the excess in solution: radiogenic He due to alpha decay of radioactive elements in the sediments, and primordial He escaping from the interior of the Earth. Overall, the extent of

supersaturation for the rare gases is relatively small, seldom exceeding a few percent, and is of significance only insofar as it reveals additional information about the processes responsible.

Nitrogen. Because of its comparative inertness, molecular nitrogen in seawater is relatively constant at its saturation value. Small variations on the order of a few percent have been found, which can be partially explained by physical processes such as bubble entrapment and by fluctuations in temperature and barometric pressure at the time of equilibration. However, other processes are also involved, including both nitrogen fixation (chiefly through organisms occurring in tropical and semitropical waters) and denitrification (reduction of nitrate in anoxic waters). None of these processes significantly affects the overall distribution of dissolved nitrogen.

Oxygen. Dissolved oxygen is of great biological importance, and its distribution has been studied extensively since the early days of oceanography. This distribution is highly variable, being the result of a complex interaction between a number of different processes: exchange of atmospheric O_2 across the air–sea interface, circulation and mixing, in-place photosynthetic production, and oxidation reactions resulting in the consumption of O_2. Dissolution of atmospheric O_2 in the surface waters, followed by mixing processes within the ocean, is responsible for maintaining a supply of free O_2 throughout the depths. Photosynthetic production of O_2 is light-dependent, and is therefore limited to the upper layers of the ocean. In these regions, production may sometimes predominate over consumption, leading to occasional supersaturation and the release of free O_2 into the atmosphere. It has been said that photosynthesis within the ocean is responsible for maintaining the oxygen content of the atmosphere. However, over 99% of the O_2 produced in this manner is also consumed within the ocean, and the amount which escapes into the atmosphere is negligible compared to the quantity of O_2 already there.

At greater depths, oxidation processes involving the decomposition of organic matter take over, and the concentration of dissolved O_2 begins to decrease. Were it not for circulation and mixing processes, this decrease would continue with depth until anoxic conditions such as are found in the bottom waters of the Black Sea resulted. Fortunately, this does not happen; the oxygen concentration usually goes through a minimum with depth, and then increases as the bottom waters are reached. This is because circulation processes are continually replenishing the lower regions of the ocean with dense, cold, oxygen-rich waters which sink near the polar regions and flow along the bottom. Wherever these flows are relatively restricted, the waters become relatively depleted in oxygen.

Trace gases. The occurrence and distribution of trace gases within the ocean [methane (CH_4), hydrogen (H_2), carbon monoxide (CO), and nitrous oxide (N_2O)] are of importance not only for what they may reveal about in-place processes in seawater, but also because of the role which the ocean may play in affecting their mixing ratios in the atmosphere. These gases have several characteristics in common: their distribution in the upper mixed layer is quite variable, their concentrations often exceed equilibrium saturation values, and their depth profiles usually exhibit well-defined subsurface maxima which persist in spite of mixing processes. Although it is generally accepted that these characteristics point toward biological generation, the processes involved are not understood. The types of bacteria which produce CH_4, for example, are obligate anaerobes which require a reducing environment for active growth; the production of this gas in the highly oxygenated waters of the mixed layer remains to be explained. Similarly with H_2; this is known to be an intermediate in the microbial production of CH_4 during anaerobic digestion processes, but how it is produced in the mixed layer, and its possible relation to the presence of CH_4, is not known.

Although supersaturation of CO in the surface waters is widespread, the ocean is a relatively minor source of CO in the atmosphere. Production of CO shows a pronounced diurnal effect, with maximum generation during daylight hours. A number of marine organisms are known to produce CO, but attempts to correlate its observed behavior with biological phenomena have not been successful.

N_2O in the sea seems to be produced by denitrification processes just as it is on land. In certain parts of the ocean, for example, the North Atlantic, supersaturation has been observed, but it is not clear how widespread this may be. Thus, the extent to which the ocean may or may not be a significant source for N_2O in the atmosphere is uncertain.

V. J. Linnenbom

Organic compounds. Several factors are responsible for the distribution of organic compounds in seawater. These include biological production and consumption, geochemical and biological transport processes, and chemically and biochemically controlled transformation reactions. Any organic compound produced by marine macrofauna, zooplankton, phytoplankton, or microorganisms has the potential of being found in seawater. These marine organisms excrete many organic compounds directly into seawater as a mechanism of removal of metabolic wastes and as chemical communicants between organisms. The organic components of the body may also be released into seawater upon death of the organism. These exudates and decomposition products make up one of the most diverse and complex groups of organic compounds found in any environment on Earth.

Sources. In the sea, phytoplankton are the major primary producers of organic carbon from in-place photosynthetic production. Early interest in the chlorophyll molecule as an indicator of phytoplankton standing crop served as a predecessor for the study of other specific classes of organic compounds produced by phytoplankton. These include normal and isoprenoid alkanes, alkenes, polyolefinic carotenoids, and triterpenoid hydrocarbons. Marine organisms also biosynthesize heteroatomic compounds such as low-molecular-weight aldehydes, ketones and halocarbons, amino acids and amino sugars, carbohydrates, urea, acyclic fatty alcohols, tetracyclic steroidal alcohols, xanthophylls, triglycerides, phospholipids, vitamins, fatty acids, and wax esters. While in-place biological production is the major source for these compounds in seawater and sediments, zooplanktonic and bacterial consumption is the major sink. The biota also mediate a large number of transformation reactions of specific organic compounds such as oxidation or reduction, bond formation or cleavage, or inorganic-organic binding reactions. SEE PHYTOPLANKTON.

Distribution. The transport of organic compounds in the sea occurs through biological, physical, or geochemical processes (**Fig. 8**). The movement of organisms both horizontally and with depth in the water column has a major effect on the distribution of biogenic organic matter in the sea. Changes in productivity caused by seasonal fluctuations in water properties, such as temperature, can also be important in controlling organic matter distribution. Since the major algal biomass occurs in the euphotic zone, this is where concentrations of organic carbon are highest. Distributions lower in the water column are modified by the location of bacteria and zooplankton.

Recycling. If all of the organisms existing in the oceans merely excreted their metabolic wastes and then died, allowing their carcasses to pass through the water column, the oceans would contain far larger concentrations of the organic compounds than have been found. The relatively low concentration of organic compounds that have been identified in seawater (parts per billion and lower) shows that most biogenic organic carbon is removed from seawater at a rate comparable with its production. The distribution of biogenic compounds reflects this balance between production and consumption. Consumption of organic matter by phytoplankton or zooplankton does not necessarily lead to complete destruction of organic molecules. The organic compounds can be recycled intact or as a transformed version in the body of the consumer.

Regeneration of organic material in the marine environment takes place primarily in the euphotic zone (upper 100 m or 330 ft). When organic matter escapes mineralization processes in the upper waters, regeneration can also take place deeper in the water column and on the sea floor. However, the recycling process is slower in these areas. It has been demonstrated that in shallow, highly productive areas (<1500 m or 5000 ft), a smaller proportion of the organic matter produced is remineralized in the upper 500 m or 1650 ft, relative to areas of lower productivity. This indi-

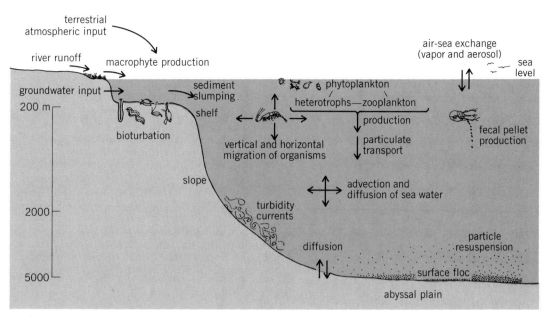

Fig. 8. Schematic showing possible transport processes controlling the distribution of organic compounds in seawater. 1 m = 0.3 ft. (*After E. K. Duursma and R. Dawson, eds., The Organic Chemistry of Seawater, Elsevier, 1980*)

cates that the efficiency of remineralization is lower and increases the probability that labile (and not only resistant) organic material is being transported through the water column. This vertical transport of organic matter in the water column on particulate ma-

terial is considered to be a source of carbon to the benthos.

Transport processes. Other processes are also responsible for transporting organic matter in seawater. Advection and diffusion in water masses are impor-

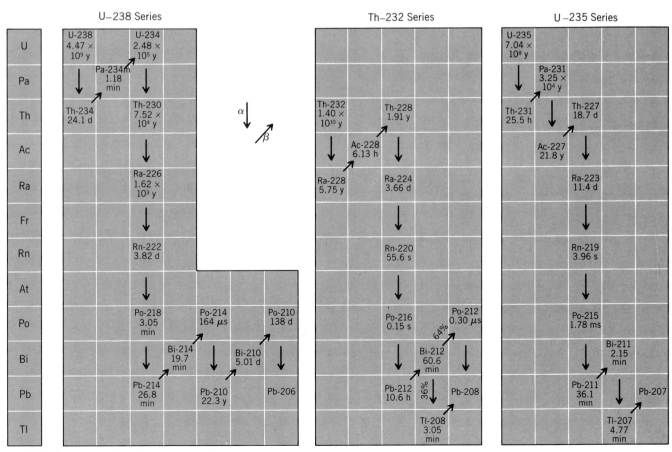

Fig. 9. The three natural radioactive decay series. Minor branches are not illustrated. (a) U-238 series. (b) Th-232 series. (c) U-235 series.

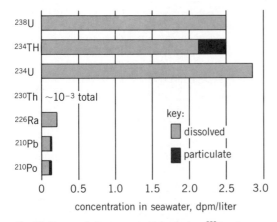

Fig. 10. Representative concentrations of some ^{238}U-series nuclides in seawater illustrating the extent of radioactive disequilibrium (dpm = disintegrations per minute).

tant in controlling the movement of dissolved and small particulate material horizontally as well as vertically in the water column. Bottom currents are capable of moving resuspended sedimentary material across the ocean floor, thus controlling grain size distributions and associated organic matter. Sediments rich in organic compounds from highly productive areas or anoxic basins can serve as sources for organic gases, such as methane, which diffuse into the upper water column and are transported advectively by water masses. Not all of the organic matter delivered to the sediments from the overlying water column is decomposed or diffuses upward. Some of it becomes part of the permanent sedimentary deposit and is slowly transformed to a highly resistant and not easily characterized form of organic matter.

Robert B. Gagosian

Radioactive elements. Distributions of the radioactive elements in seawater are of special interest be-

cause of the information they can yield about rates of oceanic processes. Ocean mixing, sedimentation, biological fixation and release of chemical species, exchange of gases at the air–sea interface, and removal of chemical substances from the deep sea are among the processes that have been studied with these radiotracers. The great versatility arises from the variety of chemical properties and radioactive half-lives represented within the three natural decay series (**Fig. 9**).

Figure 10 illustrates the relative concentrations of the longer-lived members of the uranium-238 (^{238}U) series in seawater. The values shown are typical of deep-ocean water. Somewhat different relationships characterize surface water. Concentrations of radionuclides are ordinarily expressed in activity units: picocuries or disintegrations per minute (1 pCi = 2.22 dpm = 3.7×10^{-2} becquerels). In a system that is closed to migration of uranium and its decay products for a sufficient time, a state of secular equilibrium is approached in which the activities of all members of the decay chain are equal. In the oceanic water column, however, large departures from this condition occur because of transport of decay products into and out of the system. If a steady state is assumed, rates of transport are easily estimated from measurements of the extent of disequilibrium.

Uranium. Uranium occurs in seawater at a concentration of 3.3 micrograms per liter. It is strongly stabilized in solution by formation of $[UO_2(CO_3)_3]^{4-}$. Nuclear recoil effects cause ^{234}U to be more readily leached from solids than is ^{238}U, and a 14% relative excess of ^{234}U is maintained in seawater by transport in rivers and by diffusion across the sediment–seawater interface. Because of its long residence time ($>10^5$ years), uranium is well mixed within the oceans, and there appear to be no significant variations in its concentration or isotopic composition. Thus, the decay products of uranium are generated at a uniform rate throughout the oceans.

Thorium. In contrast to uranium, thorium (Th) is not readily mobilized during weathering, and the concentration of ^{232}Th in surface seawater is very low ($<7 \times 10^{-5}$ μg/liter). Most thorium transport through the oceans occurs in the solid residues of continental weathering, although some mobilization of the element in solution is evidenced by its occurrence in authigenic materials.

Other isotopes of thorium are produced by radioactive precursors dissolved in seawater. The isotopes ^{234}Th, ^{230}Th, and ^{228}Th are often measurably depleted relative to their parents because of adsorption at solid surfaces. An extreme case of depletion is shown by ^{230}Th. Practically the entire oceanic inventory of ^{230}Th is present in the sediment column, where it forms the basis for determining accumulation rates of bottom deposits. A similar behavior is known for protactinium-231 (^{231}Pa), a member of the ^{235}U series, though it appears that somewhat different removal pathways are followed by the two elements.

The input of ^{228}Th to the oceans is governed by the distribution of its parent radium-228 (^{228}Ra). Depletions (^{228}Th/^{228}Ra < 1) have been measured in surface seawater, indicating rapid removal of thorium in this region, presumably by sinking biogenic debris. Similar depletions occur in the case of ^{234}Th (^{234}Th/^{238}U < 1). Both isotopes indicate a residence time of a few months for thorium in the open ocean and faster removal in coastal waters. In the deep ocean, ^{234}Th is in secular equilibrium with its parent

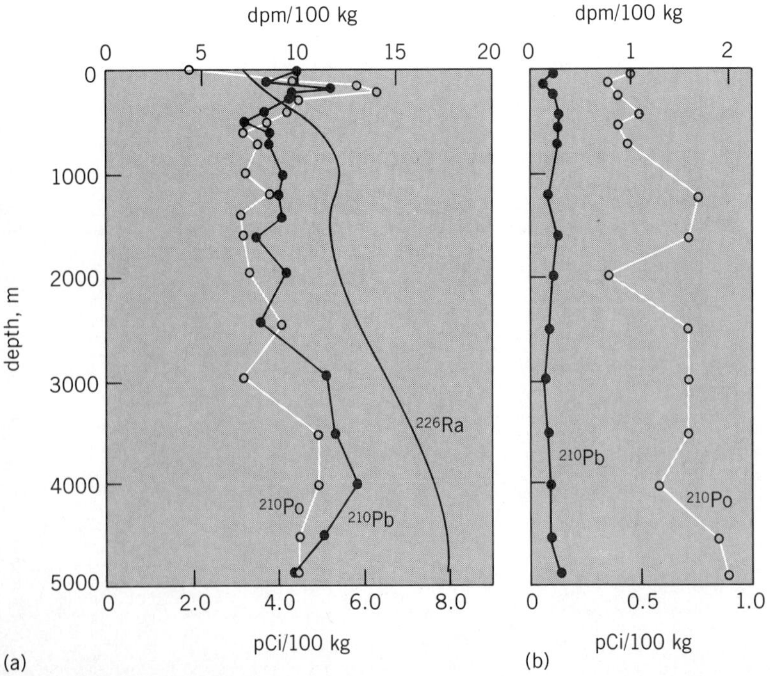

Fig. 11. Distributions of ^{226}Ra, ^{210}Pb, and ^{210}Po at a station in the tropical Atlantic Ocean. 1 m = 3.3 ft. (*a*) Dissolved activity. (*b*) Particulate activity. (*After T. F. Gesell and W. F. Lowder, eds., Natural Radiation Environment III, DOE Rep. CONF-780422, vol. 1, 1980*)

^{238}U, but a larger proportion of it is found in the particulate form. This difference allows rates of particle-solution interaction to be studied. *See Thorium*.

Radium. Two radium isotopes are enriched relative to their parents in seawater, the excess being sustained by diffusion out of the bottom sediments. The half-life of ^{226}Ra is suitable for studies of large-scale ocean circulation. However, the distribution of radium is complicated by biological transport in a cycle similar to that which controls the silicate distribution in the oceans. The highest concentrations of ^{228}Ra are found in surface and bottom waters owing to supply from continental-shelf and abyssal sediments. Because of the short half-life of ^{228}Ra, its distribution is much less affected by biological transport than that of ^{226}Ra. This tracer has potential value in studies of vertical and horizontal mixing within ocean basins.

Radon. Throughout most of the oceanic water column, radon-222 (^{222}Rn) is in secular equilibrium with its parent ^{226}Ra. Within a few hundred meters of the sea floor, however, excess radon derived from the sediment is present. Measurement of the distribution of this excess above the bottom allows vertical mixing rates to be estimated, though complications often result from lateral transport. Surface waters are deficient in ^{222}Rn owing to gas exchange across the air–sea interface. Rates of exchange can be determined from measurements of the radon deficiency, and suitable models allow the results to be applied to other atmospheric gases.

Lead. The nuclide lead-210 (^{210}Pb) is generated within the oceans by decay of ^{226}Ra and its short-lived daughters. In surface waters, excess ^{210}Pb usually occurs (**Fig. 11**) because of input from the atmosphere, where ^{210}Pb is produced by decay of ^{222}Rn derived from the continents. Depletions of ^{210}Pb ranging from 10 to 90% are found in the deep ocean because of adsorption on solid surfaces. The greatest depletions are found at stations close to basin margins and in samples collected close to the sea floor. This suggests that reaction at the sediment–seawater boundary, as well as the flux of sinking particles, is important in governing removal from the deep ocean.

Polonium. The distribution of ^{210}Po in the oceans (Fig. 13) is characterized by depletion in surface waters due to biological uptake and often by subsurface excess sustained by regeneration. The efficiency of regeneration within the water column appears to be quite high (>50%). Within the deep water, ^{210}Po is preferentially partitioned into the particulate form relative to ^{210}Pb, though whole-water samples show the two nuclides to be in secular equilibrium. In this respect the distribution of ^{210}Po resembles that of ^{234}Th.

Michael P. Bacon

Ocean water masses. Ocean water masses are extensive bodies of subsurface ocean water characterized by a relatively constant relationship between temperature and salinity or some other conservative dissolved constituent. The concept was developed to permit identification and tracing of such water bodies. The assumption is made that the characteristic properties of the water mass were acquired in a region of origin, usually at the surface, and were subsequently modified by lateral and vertical mixing. The observed characteristics in place thus depend both on the original properties and on the degree of modification en route to the region where observed.

A water mass is usually defined by means of a characteristic diagram, on which temperature or some

other thermodynamic variable is plotted against an expression for the amount of one component of the mixture. A point on such a diagram defines a water type (representing conditions in the region of origin), and the line between points observes, at least approximately, the property of mixtures; that is, on the line connecting the two points the proportion lying between the point representing one water type and the point for any mixture equals the proportion of the second water type in the mixture. The resulting curve for a vertical water column has been called a characteristic curve, because for a given water mass its shape is invariant, regardless of depth. The existence of such a curve implies continuous renewal of water types, since otherwise mixing would lead to homogeneous water, represented by a point on the diagram.

Temperature–salinity relationships. In oceanography the characteristic diagram of temperature against salinity is usually used in studies of water masses, and the resulting temperature-salinity curve (the *T-S* curve) is used to define a water mass (**Fig. 12**).

In drawing such a curve, data from the upper 100 m (330 ft) are usually omitted because of seasonal variation and local modification in the surface layer, so that strictly speaking, a water mass as defined extends only to within 100 m (330 ft) of the sea surface. Although ideally a water mass is defined by a single *T-S* curve, because of random errors in field measurements and perhaps fine structure in the water mass itself, in practice an envelope of values provides a more useful definition.

On the *T-S* diagram any property which is a function only of temperature and salinity can be represented by the appropriate family of isopleths (such as values at constant pressure of density expressed as σ_t, or thermosteric anomaly, sound speed, and saturation concentration of dissolved gases). Thus, the *T-S* diagram with isopleths can be used to determine values of such temperature–salinity-dependent functions. Since the ocean is inherently stable (that is, density increases monotonically with depth), examination of

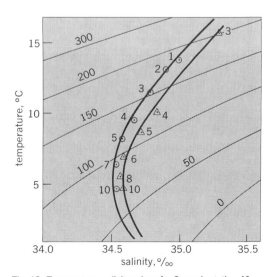

Fig. 12. Temperature–salinity values for Carnegie station 40 (circles) and Dana station 3756 (triangles); see Fig. 14 for locations. Depths of observations in hectometers (100 m). Light black lines represent definition of Pacific equatorial water. Heavy black curves represent specific volume as thermosteric anomaly in centiliters (0.01 liter) per ton. 1 m = 3.3 ft; °F = (°C × 1.8) + 32.

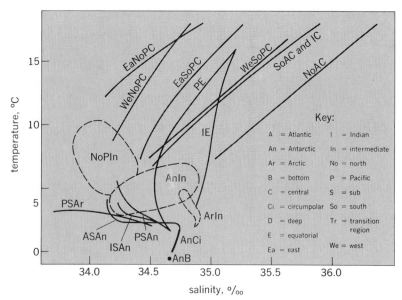

Fig. 13. Temperature-salinity curves for water masses of world ocean. °F = (°C × 1.8) + 32. (*After H. U. Sverdrup, R. H. Fleming, and M. W. Johnson, The Oceans, Prentice-Hall, 1942*)

the slope of a *T-S* curve (on which depth is indicated) relative to the isopleths of density permits an estimate of the vertical distribution of stability. The diagram is often useful for the detection of faulty observations and as a guide to interpolation on neighboring stations. When a uniform series of data is available, it can also be used for the quantitative representation of the frequency distribution of water characteristics.

Water-mass types. The most important and best-established water masses (characterized by *T-S* curves in **Fig. 13**, distribution shown in **Fig. 14**) occur in the upper 1000 m (3300 ft) of the ocean. These are of three general types: (1) polar water, present south of 40°S in all oceans, and north of 40°N in the Pacific; (2) central water, at midlatitudes over most of the world ocean; and (3) equatorial water, in the equatorial zones of the Pacific and Indian oceans.

Polar waters, including the Subarctic, Subantarctic, and Antarctic Circumpolar water masses, are formed at the surface in high latitudes and thus are cold and

have relatively low salinity. Subantarctic water is bounded in the south by the Antarctic Convergence, south of which circumpolar water is found; Subarctic water has no clearcut northern boundary.

The central water masses appear to sink in the regions of the subtropical convergences (35–40°S and N), where during certain seasons of the year horizontal *T-S* relations at the surface are similar to the vertical distributions characteristic of the various water masses. The great differences in their properties are attributed to differences in the amounts of evaporation and precipitation, heating and cooling, atmospheric and oceanic circulation, and the distributions of land and sea in the source regions.

The widespread and well-defined equatorial waters (Fig. 18) separate the central water masses of the Indian and Pacific oceans. These equatorial water masses are apparently formed by subsurface mixing at low latitudes, although the place and manner of their formation are not well known.

Intermediate waters underlie the central water masses in all oceans. Antarctic Intermediate Water sinks as a water type along the Antarctic Convergence; the water mass then formed by subsequent mixing is characterized by a salinity minimum. Arctic Intermediate Water, of little importance in the Atlantic, is widespread in the Pacific and is apparently formed northeast of Japan. Other important intermediate water masses are formed in the Atlantic and Indian oceans by addition of Mediterranean Sea and Red Sea water, respectively. Deep and bottom waters of the world ocean are formed in high latitudes of the North Atlantic, South Atlantic (Weddell Sea), and Indian oceans.

Warren S. Wooster

Bibliography. V. M. Albers (ed.), *Underwater Acoustics*, vol. 2, 1967; B. Bolin (ed.), *The Atmosphere and the Sea in Motion*, 1960; J. D. Burton and R. Chesselet (eds.), *Dynamic Processes in the Chemistry of the Upper Ocean*, 1986; L. Cohen (ed.), *The Ocean Environment*, 1980; R. A. Davis, Jr., *Oceanography: An Introduction to the Marine Environment*, 1987; J. A. De Santo (ed.), *Ocean Acoustics*, 1979; E. K. Duursma and R. Dawson (eds.), *Marine Organic Chemistry: Evolution, Composition, Interactions and Chemistry of Organic Matter in Seawater*, 1981; M. N. Hill (ed.), *The Sea*, 1963, reprint 1982; N. G. Jerlov, *Marine Optics*, 2d rev. ed., 1976; L. E. Kinsler et al., *Fundamentals of Acoustics*, 4th ed., 1991; H. Merkinger (ed.), *Progress in Underwater Acoustics*, 1987; Y. Parsons et al., *A Manual of Chemical and Biological Methods for Seawater Analysis*, 1984; J. P. Riley and G. Skirrow (eds.), *Chemical Oceanography*, vols. 7–9, 1987–1988; R. V. Tait, *Elements of Marine Ecology*, 3d ed., 1981; J. S. Turner, *Buoyancy Effects in Fluids*, 1980.

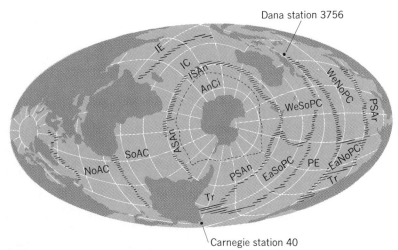

Fig. 14. Distribution of representative water masses of upper 1000 m (3300 ft; symbols as in Fig. 13). Broken line around Antarctica represents Antarctic Convergence. (*After H. U. Sverdrup, R. H. Fleming, and M. W. Johnson, The Oceans, Prentice-Hall, 1942*)

Seawater fertility

A measure of the potential ability of seawater to support life. Fertility is distinguished from productivity, which is the actual production of living material by various trophic levels of the food web. Fertility is a broader and more general description of the biological activity of a region of the sea, while primary production, secondary production, and so on, is a quantitative description of the biological growth at a specified time and place by a certain trophic level. Primary production that uses recently recycled nutrients such as ammonium, urea, or amino acids is called regenerated production to distinguish it from the new production that is dependent on nitrate being transported by mixing or circulation into the upper layer where primary production occurs. New production is organic matter, in the form of fish or sinking organic matter, that can be exported from the ecosystem without damaging the productive capacity of the system.

An example illustrates the difference between fertility and productivity. Waters around Antarctica during the austral summer have dense blooms of diatoms and large swarms of krill, the shrimplike zooplankton that feed on the diatoms and in turn are eaten by whales, seals, fish and penguins. **Figure 1** shows a catch of krill harvested in Antarctic waters, which contain the only unexploited fishery resource that can significantly increase the supply of protein from the sea. In the austral summer, both primary production, the synthesis of organic matter by photosynthesis, and secondary production, the growth of krill, proceed at high rates. In contrast, during the dark and stormy Antarctic winter there is little sunlight for photosynthesis, and winter storms deeply mix the surface waters. Primary and secondary production proceed at undetectably low rates. While productivity of Antarctic waters varies throughout the year from very low to very high, it is correct to refer to the Antarctic as a fertile region because as a region it has the potential to support high levels of biological activity.

Another analogy that clearly illustrates the distinction between fertility and productivity deals with soil. The rich black soil of the Corn Belt in Illinois and Iowa is always fertile, but in winter the actual productivity of the soil is very low because of low temperatures, short day lengths, and snow cover. *SEE BIOLOGICAL PRODUCTIVITY.*

The potential of the sea to support growth of living organisms is determined by the fertilizer elements that marine plants need for growth. Fertilizers, or inorganic nutrients as they are called in oceanography, are required only by the first trophic level in the food web, the primary producers; but the supply of inorganic nutrients is a fertility-regulating process whose effect reaches throughout the food web. When there is an abundant supply to the surface layer of the ocean that is taken up by marine plants and converted into organic matter through photosynthesis, the entire food web is enriched, including zooplankton, fish, birds, whales, benthic invertebrates, protozoa, and bacteria. Since the level of seawater fertility is initially set by the primary producers' response to nutrient conditions, this article is limited to the geographic and temporal variations in nutrients and primary productivity. *SEE FOOD WEB; MARINE FISHERIES.*

Nutrients. The elements needed by marine plants for growth are divided into two categories depending on the quantities required: The major nutrient elements that appear to determine variations in ocean fertility are nitrogen, phosphorus, and silicon. The micronutrients are elements required in extremely small, or trace, quantities including essential metals such as iron, manganese, zinc, cobalt, magnesium, and copper, as well as vitamins and specific organic growth factors such as chelators. Knowledge of the fertility consequences of variations in the distribution of micronutrients is incomplete, but consensus among oceanographers is that the overall pattern of ocean fertility is set by the major fertilizer elements—nitro-

gen, phosphorus, and silicon—and not by micronutrients.

Nitrogen, phosphorus, and silicon are required for plants in relatively large quantities because these elements are building blocks of living material. While the other elements in proteins, carbohydrates, and fats such as carbon, oxygen, or sulfur are necessary to living organisms, seawater contains a large excess of them in proportion to the demands of marine plants in the synthesis of new organic matter. Hence the supply of carbon, sulfur, or oxygen does not determine variations in ocean fertility (**Fig. 2**). Understanding the pattern of fertility requires knowledge of the pat-

Fig. 1. A 17-ton (15-metric-ton) catch of krill harvested in Antarctic waters. (*Photograph by Dr. Gotthilf Hempel*)

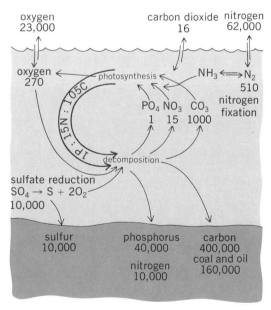

Fig. 2. Biochemical cycle of nutrient elements in the sea. Numbers represent the quantities of elements relative to phosphorus in the ocean and show the excess abundance of carbon and sulfur in comparison with phosphorus and nitrogen. (*After A. C. Redfield, The biological control of chemical factors in the environment, Amer. Sci., 46:205–221, 1958*)

tern of nitrogen, phosphorus, and silicon distribution in the sea.

The nutrient requirement for nitrogen is met in the ocean by forms of fixed inorganic nitrogen such as nitrate, nitrite, or ammonium and by dissolved organic nitrogen species such as urea or amino acids. The nitrate transported across the thermocline into the upper layer supports most of the new primary production in the ocean, while organic nitrogen recycled within the upper layer supports regenerated production (**Fig. 3**). The requirement for phosphorus is met by the phosphate ion and that for silicon by ions of silicate and silicic acid.

Deep waters of the ocean beneath the permanent thermocline contain high concentrations of nitrate, phosphate, and silicate—dissolved inorganic nutrients maintained by a balance of processes. A steady but very small flux of sinking organic particles, especially zooplankton fecal pellets, into the subthermocline water exports material from the upper layer to deep water. In deep water, nitrogen, phosphorus, and silicon are released as the organic matter is decomposed by bacteria and protozoa; the released elements pass from particulate phase back to dissolved phase and are eventually remineralized to the stable terminal oxidation products of nitrate, phosphate, and silicate. In the deep ocean there is no light for photosynthesis, so the abundant inorganic nutrients cannot be taken up by plants; the fertilizer elements accumulate in solution until the nutrient-rich deep water returns to the surface by circulation or mixing. When and where subsurface water is transported to the surface layer, nutrients are brought together with light, and the stage is set for enhanced primary production and greatly increased fertility.

Oceanographers express the atom ratios of inorganic nutrients in seawater in terms of concentrations in microgram-atoms (of N or P) per liter of seawater or the more typical chemical units of micromoles (of nutrient ions) per kilogram of seawater. Since nitrate, phosphate, and silicate are monoatomic ions, the two conventions are quantitatively equal. Deep waters of the Pacific and Indian oceans have a nitrate concentration of about 40 μmol/kg, while Atlantic deep water has half that. Surface waters having a nitrate concentration of more than 10 μmol/kg are highly fertile; those having less than 0.1 μmol/kg are biological deserts. The relative abundances of phosphate and silicate vary in proportion to nitrate.

Primary producers. Two types of marine plants carry out primary production in the ocean: microscopic planktonic algae collectively called phytoplankton, and benthic algae and sea grasses attached to hard and soft substrates in shallow coastal waters.

The benthic and planktonic primary producers are a diverse assemblage of plants adapted to exploit a wide variety of marine niches; however, they have in common two basic requirements for the photosynthetic production of new organic matter: light energy and the essential elements of carbon, hydrogen, nitrogen, oxygen, phosphorus, sulfur, and silicon for the synthesis of new organic molecules. These two requirements are the first-order determinants of photosynthetic growth for all marine plants and, hence, for primary productivity everywhere in the ocean.

Phytoplankton. The term phytoplankton refers to a wide variety of planktonic plants, including diatoms, dinoflagellates, coccolithophorids, microflagellates, blue-green algae, and even ciliates that have endosymbiotic chloroplasts. Diatoms are abundant in the more fertile upwelling and coastal regions of the ocean, and are probably the major group responsible for the new production that provides material to the pelagic food web and to the bottom for consumption by the benthos (see **table**; Fig. 3). Coccolithophorids and microflagellates maintain relatively constant but low levels of productivity in the less fertile offshore provinces of the ocean; in these areas microflagellates may have rapid specific growth rates. That is, the rate of synthesis of new cell material per unit of existing cellular material may be high, but since the biomass of phytoplankton in the offshore provinces is low, the absolute productivity is low when compared with more fertile areas.

Dinoflagellates are a functionally complex group that exploit a variety of marine niches. Some dinoflagellate species are slow-growing and persistent in tropical waters, while other species form concentrated but sporadic so-called red tide aggregations that may be poisonous to both marine life and humans; still others occur with diatoms, during nutrient-rich conditions. However, the niche most often associated with dinoflagellates is intermediate between that occupied by diatoms at the fertile end of the nutrient spectrum and that of coccolithophorids and microflagellates at the nutrient-poor end of the spectrum.

Highly fertile regions of the ocean have been studied frequently because important fisheries are concentrated there. The poisonous red tide dinoflagellate outbreaks have also received considerable study. While diatoms and dinoflagellates are major primary producers where the intensity of production is high, microflagellates and coccolithophorids are important in the large tropical and subtropical offshore province of the ocean where production is low (see table). The offshore province occupies 90% of the ocean area, so that the coccolithophorids and microflagellates make a significant contribution to the global carbon cycle even though they may not support important fisheries. *SEE* PHYTOPLANKTON.

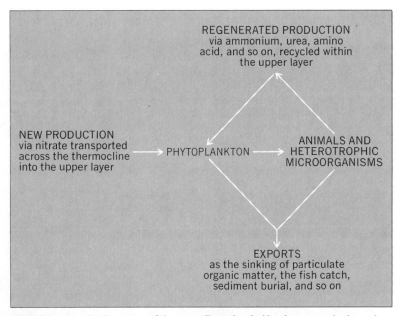

Fig. 3. Primary production system of the ocean, illustrating the idea that new production and regenerated production are driven by nitrogen from qualitatively distinct sources. (*After R. W. Eppley and B. J. Peterson, Particulate organic matter flux and planktonic new production in the deep ocean, Nature, 282:677–680, 1979*)

Primary production and fish production in various provinces of the ocean

Province	Percent of ocean area	Area, mi² (km²)	Average primary production, g C/(m²·yr)	Total primary production, tons/yr (metric tons/yr)	Number of trophic levels	Trophic efficiency, percent	Fish production, tons/yr (metric tons/yr)
Offshore ocean	90.0	125×10^6 (326×10^6)	50	17.9×10^9 (16.3×10^9)	5	10	18×10^5 (16×10^5)
Coastal zone	9.9	14×10^6 (36×10^6)	100	4.0×10^9 (3.6×10^9)	3	15	13×10^7 (12×10^7)
Upwelling areas	0.1	1.4×10^5 (3.6×10^5)	300	0.1×10^9 (0.1×10^9)	1.5	20	13×10^7 (12×10^7)

Benthic plants. An advance in the understanding of ocean fertility has been recognition of the role played by benthic algae and sea grasses. These plants occur in dense stands in shallow waters and carry out primary production at extremely high rates throughout the year. Attached algae and grasses are efficient at nutrient scavenging since they remove dissolved nutrients from many volumes of water as it passes over them. Most of the production by attached algae and sea grasses is not grazed directly by herbivores but becomes detritus, and it is consumed in that form by a wide variety of deposit and suspension feeders. Examples of the important benthic primary producers are brown algae such as *Macrocystis*, *Nereocystis*, *Fucus*, or *Laminaria*, and the sea grasses *Zostera* and *Thallasia*.

Productivity measurement. Productivity is usually expressed as the increase in organic matter per unit area per unit time since light enters the marine environment as an areal function from the surface. This convention makes it possible to compare the productivity of the ocean directly with that of land. The units most frequently used are grams of carbon per square meter (g C/m²). Primary production is measured over short time intervals of 1 day or less, producing data units of g C/(m² · day). For food web considerations these data are converted to annual production as g C/(m² · year), which introduces very large errors because oceanographers have not made daily measurements throughout annual cycles to determine the correct daily-to-annual conversion factors for different marine ecosystems.

Productivity conventionally is expressed in terms of carbon. However, there is no fundamental rationale for choosing carbon over nitrogen, phosphorus, or a cell property like protein. Carbon is convenient, however, because the most precise technique for measuring primary production uses the radioactive isotope of carbon. The excess inorganic carbon in seawater satisfies the requirement of the radioactive isotope of carbon. The excess inorganic carbon in seawater satisfies the requirement of the radiocarbon method that there be no detectable change in the precursor substrate during the measurement. With nitrogen, phosphorus, or silicon, the requirement that there be significant change in the substrate concentration is not often satisfied, so determination of the in-place rate of uptake of these elements is difficult or impossible with isotopic tracers. Conversely, production in terms of nitrogen, silicon, or phosphorus can be accurately measured by following the disappearance of these nutrients from seawater, a technique not possible with carbon.

In fertile areas primary production may be over 1.0 g C/(m² · day), but the sea grasses, kelp, or upwelling phytoplankton can exceed 10.0 g C/(m² · day). It is suspected that these high daily rates of production in fertile areas do not persist for long in the annual cycle, so oceanographers estimate that even highly fertile areas have an annual primary production of only about 300 g C/(m² · year). This crude estimate must suffice until time series studies are done. Provinces of the ocean that are permanently nutrient-poor due to strong thermal stratification have less than 0.1 g C/(m² · day) with little variation throughout the annual cycle. The yearly production is estimated to be 30 to 40 g C/(m² · year). While the coccolithophorids and microflagellates that are the dominant primary producers in this infertile area are important in the global flux of carbon, they are insignificant in the production of fish, as shown in the table.

Patterns of fertility. The regions of the world's oceans differ dramatically in overall fertility. In the richest areas, the water is brown with diatom blooms, fish schools are abundant, birds darken the horizon, and the sediments are fine-grained black mud with a high organic content. In areas of low fertility, the water is blue and clear, fish are rare, and the bottom sediments are well-oxidized carbonate or clay. These extremes exist because the overall pattern of fertility is determined by the processes that transport nutrients to the sunlit upper layer of the ocean where there is energy for photosynthesis.

Upwelling. The fisheries of the world are concentrated in regions of enhanced fertility; it is not generally appreciated that the fertile food-producing areas of the ocean, like on land, are concentrated into a very small proportion of the total area. It has been estimated that 99% of the world's fish catch comes from only 10% surface of the area of the ocean (see table), and of that, 50% comes from the 0.1% ocean area where upwelling carries nutrient-rich water to the surface. Upwelling on the west coasts of the Americas and Africa is a well-known process that enriches fertility, modifies the coastal climate, and has great economic impact because of the large upwelling-based fisheries. However, there are other processes that replenish nutrients to the depleted surface layer, but these processes are not nearly as well known as upwelling.

The annual cycle of heating and cooling of the Earth's surface in temperate and high latitudes drives the transport of nutrients into the upper layer of the ocean. When there is net negative heat flux to the ocean from the atmosphere, the surface water cools, becomes denser and unstable, and subsequently mixes with the underlying water. Mixing replaces nutrient-depleted surface water with nutrient-rich water and sets the stage for high productivity. When the heat flux becomes positive, the now nutrient-rich water is heated, becomes less dense, and forms a stable upper layer separated from the cooler deep water by a thermocline. In the stabilized upper layer, light for photosynthesis is available, and a rapid burst of phytoplankton growth occurs. This brief burst of high primary productivity by the diatom-dominated phytoplankton assemblages is the famous spring bloom of regions such as Long Island Sound, the Gulf of Maine, or the North Sea. The spring bloom in temperate zone seas depletes the upper layer of nitrate, phosphate, and silicate, causing a productivity decrease to a lower maintenance level until the next mixing event replenishes the nutrients.

Estuaries. Studies in lateral estuaries of the Chesapeake Bay and along the coast of Maine show that mixing during the strong tidal flows of the full and new moon generate short blooms in phase with the lunar cycle. In the waters around the British Isles, tidal mixing produces quasistationary blooms where the tidal currents hit subsurface banks or ledges and water mixes upward. Downstream from the wake-generating obstruction, heating restabilizes the upper layer, and blooms of phytoplankton exploit the available nutrients. Wake mixing over topographic features such as Georges Bank, Grand Banks, or Dogger Bank complements seasonal mixing and supports continuously high productivity in a manner analogous to the topographically fixed blooms of upwelling centers. An important portion of the world's fish catch comes from these banks. This yield is made possible by the physical transport of nutrients upward to replace the nitrogen, phosphorus, and silicon removed in the form of organic exports such as harvested fish (Fig. 3). Physical processes drive both the seasonal heat-driven mixing and stabilization and the tidal mixing and stabilization; both processes are important to the continuing fertility of fishing areas such as Georges Bank.

Polar seas. In the polar seas a short burst of high production occurs in midsummer as increased sunlight becomes available for photosynthesis. At that time the water stabilizes slightly from solar heating, and the melting ice packs release fresh water that further stabilizes the surface layer. Phytoplankton blooms in both the Bering and Weddel Seas have some of the highest concentrations of phytoplankton ever recorded in the open ocean, but in both the Arctic and Antarctic the blooms are short-lived and very patchy in distribution. A brief burst of primary production supports a rich food web with large populations of higher-trophic-level organisms such as krill fish and marine mammals. The ecology of these highly fertile polar seas is not well understood. Because the valuable unexploited food resources of the polar areas merit careful management, it is important to have a basic understanding of these ecosystems.

A major difference in the productivity cycle of polar seas is that phytoplankton growth does not proceed to nutrient depletion, and productivity is regulated at the end of the brief summer by the lack of light, deep wind-driven mixing, and low temperatures. Polar and tropical waters are dramatic opposites in regulation of fertility. Polar waters always have an abundance of nutrients, so they are described as being continuously fertile; but there is light limitation of photosynthesis during most of the year. Tropical and subtropical offshore waters are permanently nutrient-depleted; light is never limiting in the upper layer, but the solar heating is so intense that thermal stratification is not broken down in the annual cycle. A biological desert is maintained because the subthermocline nutrient-rich water never mixes or circulates to the upper layer. (Dramatic exceptions to this are coastal and equatorial upwelling and the wake-stream mixing that occurs be-

hind islands and atolls.) In the tropical and subtropical offshore waters that are permanently low in fertility, there is very efficient recycling of nutrients and high turnover rates. That is not true for the regenerated production of tropical and subtropical waters, which explains the fragile nature of tropical and subtropical ecosystems in comparison to the relatively resilient character of higher latitude marine ecosystems.

Richard T. Barber

Size of populations and fluctuations. In temperate waters fish tend to spawn at the same place at a fixed season. The larvae drift in a current from spawning ground to nursery ground, and the adults migrate from the feeding ground to the spawning ground. Adolescents leave the nursery to join the adult stock on the feeding ground. The migration circuit is based on the track of the larval drift, and the population is isolated by its unique time of spawning. Because larvae suffer intense mortality, numbers in the population are perhaps regulated naturally during the period of larval drift.

Methods of measuring the size of marine populations are of three basic kinds. The first is by a census based on samples which together constitute a known fraction either of the whole population, as in the case of sessile species such as shellfish, or of a particular age range, as in the case of fish which have pelagic eggs whose total abundance can be measured by fine-meshed nets hauled vertically through the water column. The second is by marking or tagging, in which a known number of marked individuals are mixed into the population and the ratio of unmarked to marked individuals is subsequently measured from samples. The third is applicable to commercially exploited populations where the total annual catch is known; the mortality rate caused by exploitation is measured, based on the age composition of the populations, thus establishing what fraction of the population the catch is. The last two methods are most generally used.

The largest measured populations are of pelagic fish, particularly of the herring family and related species, Clupeidae. One of these is the Atlantic herring (*Clupea harengus*) which contains on the order of 10^9 mature individuals and ranges over hundreds of miles of the northeast Atlantic.

Populations of bottom-living fish tend to fluctuate slowly over long time periods of 50–75 years. However, those of pelagic fish, like the Atlantic herring, may fluctuate dramatically. If fish spawn at a fixed season, they are vulnerable to climatic change. During long periods there are shifts in wind strength and direction, with consequent delays or advancements in the timing of the production cycle. If the cycle becomes progressively delayed, the fish larvae, hatched at a fixed season, become progressively short of food, and the populations decline with time. Climatic change affects the population during the period of larval drift when isolation is maintained and when numbers are normally regulated.

D. H. Cushing

Biological species and water masses. Biogeographical regions in the ocean are related to the distribution of water masses. Their physical individuality and ecological individuality are derived from partly closed patterns of circulation and from amounts of incident solar radiation characteristic of latitudinal belts. Each region may be described in terms of its temperature-salinity property and of the biological species which are adapted to all or part of the relatively homogeneous physical-chemical environment.

Cosmopolitan species. The discrete distributions of many species are circumscribed by the regions of oceanic convergence bounding principal water masses. Other distributions are limited to current systems. Cosmopolitan species are distributed across several of the temperature-salinity water masses or oceans; their wider specific tolerances reflect adaptations to broadly defined water types. No pelagic distribution is fully understood in terms of the ecology of the species.

A habitat is integrated and maintained by a current system: oceanic gyral, eddy, or current, with associated countercurrents. This precludes species extinction that could occur if a stock were swept downstream into an alien environment. The positions of distribution boundaries may vary locally with seasonal or short-term changes in temperature, available food, transparency of the water, or direction and intensity of currents.

Phytoplankton species are distributed according to temperature tolerances in thermal water masses, but micronutrients (for example, vitamin B_{12}) are essential for growth in certain species. The cells of phytoplankton reproduce asexually and sometimes persist in unfavorable regions as resistant resting spores. New populations may develop in prompt response to local change in temperature or in nutrient content of the water. Such species are less useful in tracing source of water than are longer-lived, sexually reproducing zooplankton species.

Indicator organisms. The indicator organism concept recognizes a distinction between typical and atypical distributions of a species. The orgin of atypical water is indicated by the presumed affinity of the transported organisms with their established centers of distribution.

Zooplankton groups best understood with respect to their oceanic geography are crustaceans such as copepods, and euphausiids, chaetognaths (arrow worms), polychaetous annelids, pteropod mollusks, pelagic tunicates, foraminiferids, and radiolarians. Of these the euphausiids are the strongest diurnal vertical migrants (60–200 ft or 200–700 m). The vertical dimension of euphausiid habitat agrees with the thickness of temperature-salinity water masses, and many species distributions correspond with the positions of the masses. In the Pacific different species, some of which are endemic to their specific waters, occupy the subarctic mass (such as *Thysanoessa longipes*), the transition zone, a mixed mass lying between subarctic and central water in midocean and between subarctic and equatorial water in the California Current (for example, *Nematoscelis difficilis*), the barren North Pacific central (such as *Euphausia hemigibba*) and South Pacific central masses (for example, *E. gibba*), the Pacific equatorial mass (such as *E. diomediae*), a southern transition zone analogous to that of the Northern Hemisphere (represented by *Nematoscelis megalops*), and a circumglobal subantarctic belt south of the subantarctic convergence (such as *E. lucens*).

Epipelagic fishes and other strongly swimming vertebrates are believed to be distributed according to temperature tolerances of the species and availability of food. However, distributions of certain bathypelagic fishes (such as *Chauliodus*) have been related to water mass. See Seawater.

Edward Brinton

Bibliography. R. W. Eppley and B. J. Peterson, Particulate organic matter flux and planktonic new production in the deep ocean, *Nature*, 282:677–680, 1979; A. R. Longhurst (ed.), *Analysis of Marine Eco-systems*, 1980; T. R. Parsons, M. Takahashi, and B. Hargrave, *Biological Oceanographic Processes*, 2d ed., 1977; J. E. G. Raymont, *Plankton and Productivity in the Oceans*, 2d ed., 1980; A. C. Redfield, The biological control of chemical factors in the environment, *Amer. Sci.*, 46:205–221, 1958; J. H. Ryther, Photosynthesis and fish production in the sea, *Science*, 166(3901):72–76, 1969.

Septic tank

A single-story settling tank in which settled sludge is in immediate contact with sewage flowing through the tank while solids are being decomposed by anaerobic bacterial action. Such tanks have limited use in municipal treatment, but are the primary resource for the treatment of sewage from individual residences. Septic tanks are also used by isolated schools and institutions and at small industrial plants.

Home disposal units. Septic tanks have a capacity of approximately 1 day's flow. Since sludge is collected in the same unit, additional capacity is provided for sludge. One formula for sludge storage that has been used is $Q = 17 + 7.5y$, where Q is the volume of sludge and scum in gallons per capita per year, and y is the number of years of service without cleaning. About one-half of a 500-gal (1900-liter) tank is occupied by sludge in 5 years in an ordinary household installation. The majority of states require a minimum capacity of 500 gal (1900 liters) in a single tank. Some states require a second compartment of 300-gal (1100-liters) capacity. Single- and double-compartment tanks are shown in **Figs. 1** and **2**. Such units are buried in the ground and are not serviced until the system gives trouble because of clogging or overflow. Commercial scavenger companies are available in most areas. A tank truck equipped with pumps is brought to the premises, and the tank content is pumped out and taken to a sewer manhole or a treatment plant for disposal. In rural areas the sludge may be buried in an isolated place.

Municipal and institutional units. These hold 12–24 hours' flow, with additional sludge capacity provided. Provision is made for yearly sludge withdrawal. Desirable features are (1) watertight and corrosion-resistant material (concrete and well-protected metal have been used); (2) a vented tank; (3) manhole

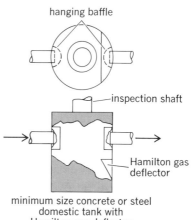

hanging baffle

inspection shaft

Hamilton gas deflector

minimum size concrete or steel domestic tank with Hamilton gas deflector

Fig. 1. Circular household septic tank. (*After H. E. Babbitt and E. R. Baumann, Sewerage and Sewage Treatment, 8th ed., John Wiley and Sons, 1958*)

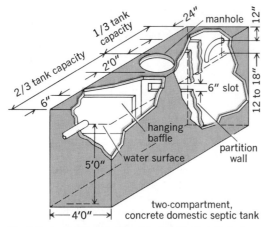

Fig. 2. Two-compartment rectangular household septic tank. 1″ = 2.5 cm; 1′ = 30 cm. (*After H. E. Babbitt and E. R. Baumann, Sewerage and Sewage Treatment, 8th ed., John Wiley and Sons, 1958*)

openings in the roof of the tank to permit inspection; (4) baffles at the inlet and the outlet to a depth below the probable scum line, usually 18–24 in. (46–61 cm) below the water surface; (5) sludge draw-off lines—although seldom used, they should be designed so that they can be rodded or unplugged by some positive mechanism; (6) hoppers or sloped bottoms so that digested sludge can be withdrawn as required; (7) provision for safe handling of septic tank effluent by disposal underground or by chlorination before discharge to a stream, or both.

Tank efficiency. Septic tank effluent is dangerous and odorous. It will contain pathogenic bacteria and sewage solids. Particles of sludge and scum are trapped in the flow and will cause nuisance at the point of discharge unless properly handled. Efficiency in removal of solids is less than that for plain sedimentation. While 60% suspended solids removal is used theoretically, it is seldom obtained in practice. Improvement is noted when tanks are built with two compartments. Shallow tanks give somewhat better results than very deep tanks. *See Sewage treatment.*

William T. Ingram

Bibliography. P. Warshall, *Septic Tank Practices*, 1979.

Sewage

Water-carried wastes, in either solution or suspension, that flow away from a community. Also known as wastewater flows, sewage is the used water supply of the community. It is more than 99.9% pure water and is characterized by its volume or rate of flow, its physical condition, its chemical constituents, and the bacteriological organisms that it contains. Depending on their origin, wastewaters can be classed as sanitary, commercial, industrial, or surface runoff.

The spent water from residences and institutions, carrying body wastes, ablution water, food preparation wastes, laundry wastes, and other waste products of normal living, are classed as domestic or sanitary sewage. Liquid-carried wastes from stores and service establishments serving the immediate community, termed commercial wastes, are included in the sanitary or domestic sewage category if their characteristics are similar to household flows. Wastes that result

from an industrial process or the production or manufacture of goods are classed as industrial wastes. Their flows and strengths are usually more varied, intense, and concentrated than those of sanitary sewage. Surface runoff, also known as storm flow or overland flow, is that portion of precipitation that runs rapidly over the ground surface to a defined channel. Precipitation absorbs gases and particulates from the atmosphere, dissolves and leaches materials from vegetation and soil, suspends matter from the land itself, and carries all these pollutants as wastes in its flow to a collection point. *See Hydrology.*

Wastewaters from all of these sources may carry pathogenic organisms that can transmit disease to humans and other animals; contain organic matter that can cause odor and nuisance problems; hold nutrients that may cause eutrophication of receiving water bodies; and may contain hazardous or toxic materials. Proper collection and safe, nuisance-free disposal of the liquid wastes of a community are legally recognized as a necessity in an urbanized, industrialized society.

In urban areas, wastewaters are generally conveyed away through a series of buried pipes. The inlets, manholes, pipes, and other appurtenances constitute the sewerage system. A system carrying only domestic wastes is known as a sanitary sewer system; if only storm runoff is collected in the drains, it is a storm drainage system; but if both storm water and wastewater are carried in the same sewerage system, the system is known as a combined system. In rural or suburban areas, sanitary sewage from individual buildings may be collected and disposed of on-site through the use of septic tanks and disposal fields.

Sewage flows. The used water supply leaving a community is directly related to the quantity and timed use of water entering that community. To establish values for the engineered design of collection systems, pump stations, and treatment plants, the water consumed within a community must be measured; or it must be evaluated, taking into account climate, extent of industrialization, types of residential districts, socioeconomic status, water cost, water quality, and delivery pressure. Not all water delivered to a community ends up as flow into the sewerage system. Water is lost through public use, fire fighting, street washing, and park and home irrigation, and is consumed in commercial and industrial production and for steam generation and cooling. Average water used in the United States, reported as 166 gal per capita per day [(gpd); 628 liters per capita per day (lpcd)], includes water for residential, mercantile, commercial, public, light and heavy industry, and unaccounted-for losses. Per-capita water use tends to rise with increased community size (**Table 1**). *See Water supply engineering.*

Some of the lost flow is replaced by additions from groundwater infiltration, from inflows and, at times, from private wells and industrial activities. Infiltration is groundwater leakage through poor joints, fittings, and connections into the sewerage system lying below the groundwater level. Inflow is surface water, or directed water entering the sewerage system through manhole covers, illegal roof leaders, foundation and area drains, cooling water discharges, and street washing. *See Groundwater hydrology.*

A community's wastewater flow may be only 60–75% of the average water supply when new sewerage systems with tight joints and no illegal connections

Table 1. Average wastewater flow from various sources*

| Source | Unit | Flow, liters per unit per day[†] | |
		Range	Typical
Residential sources			
Apartment	Person	200–340	260
Hotel, resident	Resident	150–220	190
Individual dwelling			
Average home	Person	190–350	280
Better home	Person	250–400	310
Luxury home	Person	300–550	380
Semimodern home	Person	100–250	200
Summer cottage	Person	100–240	190
Trailer park	Person	120–200	150
Commercial sources			
Airport	Passenger	8–15	10
Automobile service station	Vehicle served	30–50	40
	Employee	35–60	50
Bar	Customer	5–20	8
	Employee	40–60	50
Hotel	Guest	150–220	190
	Employee	30–50	40
Industrial building (excluding industry and cafeteria)	Employee	30–65	55
Laundry (self-service)	Machine	1800–2600	2200
	Wash	180–200	190
Motel	Person	90–150	120
Motel with kitchen	Person	190–220	200
Office	Employee	30–65	55
Restaurant	Meal	8–15	10
Rooming house	Resident	90–190	150
Store, department	Toilet room	1600–2400	2000
	Employee	30–50	40
Shopping center	Parking space	2–8	4
	Employee	30–50	40
	Employee	30–50	40
Institutional sources			
Hospital, medical	Bed	500–950	650
	Employee	20–60	40
Hospital, mental	Bed	300–550	400
	Employee	20–60	40
Prison	Inmate	300–600	450
	Employee	20–60	40
Rest home	Resident	200–450	350
School, day	Employee	20–60	40
With cafeteria, gym, and showers	Student	60–115	80
With cafeteria but no gym and no showers	Student	40–80	60
Without cafeteria, gym, and showers	Student	20–65	40
School, boarding	Student	200–400	280
Recreational sources			
Apartment, resort	Person	200–280	220
Cabin, resort	Person	130–190	160
Cafeteria	Customer	4–10	6
	Employee	30–50	40
Campground (developed)	Person	80–150	120
Cocktail lounge	Seat	50–100	75
Coffee shop	Customer	15–30	20
	Employee	30–50	40
Country club	Member present	250–500	400
	Employee	40–60	50
Day camp (no meals)	Person	40–60	50
Dining hall	Meal served	15–40	30
Dormitory, bunkhouse	Person	75–175	150
Hotel, resort	Person	150–240	200
Laundromat	Machine	1800–2600	2200
Store, resort	Customer	5–20	10
	Employee	30–50	40
Swimming pool	Customer	20–50	40
	Employee	30–50	40
Theater	Seat	10–15	10
Visitor	Visitor	15–30	20

*After Metcalf & Eddy, Inc., and G. Tchobanoglous, *Wastewater Engineering: Treatment, Disposal, and Reuse*, 2d ed., McGraw-Hill, 1979.
[†]1 liter = 0.035 ft^3 or 0.264 gal.

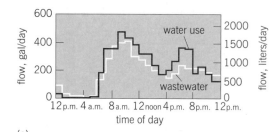

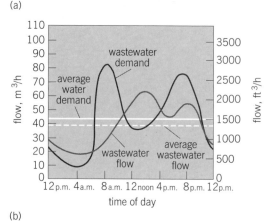

Fig. 1. Comparison of water use and wastewater flows (*a*) for a residential community (*after W. Viessman, Jr., and M. J. Hammer, Water Supply and Pollution Control, 4th ed., Harper & Row, 1985*) and (*b*) for a municipal system (*after S. R. Qasim, Wastewater Treatment Plants: Planning, Design and Operation, Holt, Rinehart and Winston, 1985*).

gravity flow at a collection point is affected by the lag due to areal time of concentration and by available storage volume within the pipes. On any given day the flow is lowest during the night, increasing to peaks at breakfast time and in the evening. In general, the smaller the community, the greater the daily variation from the average. Water use, and hence sewage flow, not only varies with time of day but also varies with time of year. During hot, dry months the flows are greater than during cold, wet periods. Infiltration/inflow varies with rainfall frequency and intensity.

For proper engineering design to safely control and contain all anticipated variations in flow, adequate capacity must be provided within the sewerage system, pumping stations, diversions, treatment plants, and outfalls. To develop practical design flow values, not only the diurnal flow variations but also peak flows must be considered. Peak flows are the maximum flows that may occur over a relatively short period of time, usually time of concentration for storm flows and up to 1 h for other wastewater flows. The total annual flow for a community, divided by 365 days, is termed the average daily flow, and this value is taken as unity. Ranges of ratios of anticipated flow fluctuations as frequently used in wastewater system design are given in **Table 2**.

Peaking factors, combined with infiltration/inflow values, must be analyzed for the total community, as well as for each major district within the community. The smaller and more homogeneous the study area, the more intense the peaking factor. Peaking factors are vital for proper design of pumping stations, treatment plants, and sewerage systems. Many regulatory agencies have set 100 gpd (378 lpcd) as the average daily flow for the design of sewers and plants, with peak flow into sewers at 400 gpd (1500 lpcd) (see **Figs. 2** and **3**).

Storm wastewater. This is the portion of precipitation that, in modern urban environments, must be safely collected and economically removed through a controlled system. Precipitation follows three paths at the Earth's surface. It can be abstracted and evapotranspired back to the atmosphere. In any rainfall occurrence a sum of that storm's water is removed as it initially wets vegetation and the ground, is retained on foliage, is temporarily stored in ground depressions, and is transpired by plants or evaporated from bare surfaces. As more rain falls and overcomes this initial abstraction, a portion of the precipitation infiltrates the soil mantle and percolates downward to the

are installed, and infiltration/inflow is kept to a minimum. However, in time, infiltration/inflow increases; therefore, engineers frequently assume wastewater flows equal to community water supply.

Human activities follow a diurnal pattern; thus fluctuations in water supply and consequently in sewage flows occur according to time of day, day of the week, weather conditions, holidays, and seasons (**Fig. 1**). Size of community, as well as the presence and type of industry, and institutions such as colleges, prisons, or hospitals all affect the quantity and fluctuation of flows. Wastewater peaks are smaller and lag behind water supply peaks within the same community because water supply is a pressure system that is measured at the point of supply (or initial) distribution, whereas wastewater is a gravity system that is usually measured at the treatment plant. Measured

Table 2. Ranges of the ratios of flow fluctuation to average annual value	
Design factor	Ratio
Maximum day in a year	(1.7–2.0) : 1
Maximum hour any day	(1.4–1.8) : 1
Peak hour in year (maximum)	(2.85–3.25) : 1
Minimum day in a year	(.50–.67) : 1
Minimum hour any day	(.35–.50) : 1
Minimum hour in year	(.20–.30) : 1
Daily average during maximum month (late summer)	(1.25–1.40) : 1
Daily average during minimum month (late winter)	(.65–.80) : 1
Daily average during maximum week (dry summer)	(1.30–1.65) : 1

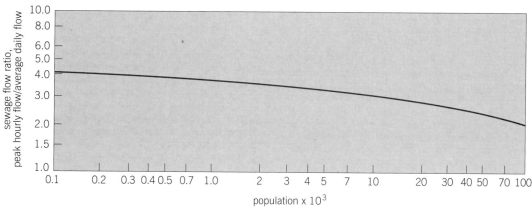

Fig. 2. Ratio of peak to average flow into sewers, based on population. Both axes are log scale. (*After Great Lakes-Upper Mississippi River Board of Sanitary Engineers, Recommended Standards for Sewage Works, Health Education, Inc., Albany, New York, 1978*)

groundwater table. If the rainfall exceeds the rate that can percolate into the ground, this excess water flows overland and is conveyed away as storm water runoff.

For the proper engineering design of storm water drainage systems, the volumes of storm wastewater to be handled must be determined. In the rational method, runoff is related to rainfall through the formula $Q = cIA$, where Q is the peak runoff rate from a drainage area in ft^3/s, c is a dimensionless ratio incorporating all abstractions and losses and is an indication of the portion of the rainfall that can be anticipated to actually run off from the subject drainage area, I is rainfall intensity in in./h based on the time of concentration t_c, and A is the drainage area in acres. If a rainfall with an intensity of 1 in./h falls on a drainage area of 1 acre that is totally impervious ($c = 1.0$), the peak runoff is 1 ft^3/s (28.317 liters/s). Since all the units, in the U.S. Customary System, work out without any conversions, this formula has been called the rational formula. The rational formula is used for urban areas of under 1 mi^2. The rational formula can be used in the International System (SI) with $Q = 2.78 \times cIA$, where Q is in liters/s, I is in mm/h, and A is in hectares. The runoff coefficient c can never be unity, because no surface is totally impervious and there are always abstractive losses. The wide range of runoff coefficients (**Table 3**) demands realistic evaluation of local conditions and use of engineering judgment.

Time of concentration t_c is the total time required for a drop of water to travel from the hydraulically furthest point of the tributary area to the point of collection. The term t_c is composed of two components, inlet flow time t_0 and pipe flow time t_p. Inlet (overland) flow time is the maximum time required for surface water to reach the inlet, and that time is dependent on ground slope, surface texture, and physical distance. Pipe flow time is established by dividing the length of sewer run, from inlet to point of concentration, by the velocity of the wastewater flow within the pipe. The time of concentration is equal to the sum of the two times ($t_0 + t_p$).

Rain gages at various locations in an area measure and record the quantity of precipitation collected per unit time. The rate and quantity of rainfall varies during any one storm and among the gages. Intensity–duration curves are developed by statistical analysis of rainfall data (**Fig. 4**). From accumulated gaged values, over extended time periods, a probability of frequency of occurrence can be developed. The return period is the anticipated average time interval in years between occurrences of a specified magnitude. Rainfall intensity values, correlated with the time of concentration t_c, are obtained from these intensity–duration–frequency curves.

Urban storm water volumes to be collected and carried away are evaluated on a cost-benefit basis. The greater the return period, the greater the probability of a longer time interval between flood damage or hazardous conditions. A larger return period also means larger design flow volumes, greater required capacity of the installed system, and consequently

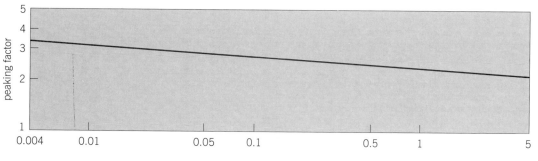

Fig. 3. Peaking factors for facility design. A domestic wastewater flow of 0.004 represents a peaking factor of 3.34; and 5 m^3/s represents a peaking factor of 1.98. 1 m^3/s = 44 gal/day. (*After Metcalf & Eddy, Inc., and G. Tchobanoglous, Wastewater Engineering: Collection and Pumping of Wastewater, McGraw-Hill, 1981*)

Table 3. Recommended runoff coefficients for a specified type of area or surface*

Area or surface	Runoff coefficients[†]
Business	
Downtown	0.70–0.95
Neighborhood	0.50–0.70
Residential	
Single-family	0.30–0.50
Multiunits, detached	0.40–0.60
Multiunits, attached	0.60–0.75
Residential (suburban)	0.25–0.40
Apartment	0.50–0.70
Industrial	
Light	0.50–0.80
Heavy	0.60–0.90
Park, cemetery	0.10–0.25
Playground	0.20–0.35
Railroad yard	0.20–0.35
Unimproved	0.10–0.30
Pavement	
Asphalt and concrete	0.70–0.95
Brick	0.70–0.85
Roof	0.75–0.95
Lawn, sandy soil	
Flat, 2%	0.13–0.17
Average, 2–7%	0.18–0.22
Steep, 7%	0.25–0.35

*After American Iron and Steel Institute, *Modern Sewer Design*, 1980.

[†]The coefficients are applicable for storms of 5–10-year frequencies. Less-frequent, higher-intensity storms require the use of higher coefficients because infiltration and other losses have a proportionally smaller effect on runoff. The coefficients are based on the assumption that the design storm does not occur when the ground surface is frozen.

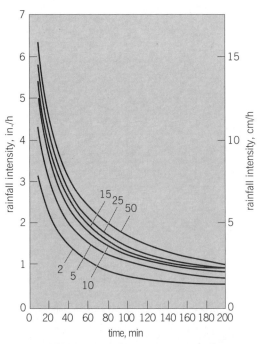

Fig. 4. Rainfall intensity-duration-frequency curves. Frequency (in years) is indicated by numbers on curves. (*After Design of Wastewater and Stormwater Pumping Stations, Manual of Practice no. FD-4, Water Pollution Control Federation, 1981*)

greater construction costs. Engineering judgment must be used to balance construction cost against reduction in future inconvenience, traffic delays, and potential flooding damages. The more serious or costly the anticipated flooding, the greater the justification for the initial higher installed costs. In areas with small structural development, a 5-year return period might be acceptable, while in a highly developed area or a major transportation hub, a more conservative design with a 25-year, or even a 50-year, return might be reasonable.

Design period. This is the time span for which a proposed system or installed infrastructure should be able to function in a safe manner, that is, be capable of providing the desired service without structural failure. The design period is also known as project life expectancy. The U.S. Internal Revenue Service provides estimated life expectancies for many industrial components, with hydraulic items including piping among them. Many nontechnical issues such as legal or regulatory constraints, bonding limitations, politics, or other issues may influence the design periods. Sewerage systems are designed to handle the anticipated peak load that will develop under anticipated population growth within the subject area for a period of 40–50 years. Appurtenances and mechanical equipment are not expected to last that long, and 15–20-year design periods are usual.

Pumping sewage. Pumping facilities become necessary when it is uneconomical or physically impossible to convey sewage or storm water by gravity to the desired point of discharge. Pumps can be installed in deep basements of buildings to raise the wastes to the level of street sewers, or they can be used to overcome cost and construction problems of deep excavation or topographic impediments like crossing a ridge or bypassing a watercourse. Pumping facilities are sited after evaluating topography, subsurface conditions, flooding hazards, and economic feasibility.

Pumping facilities can be factory-assembled or built in place. They can be either wet-pit (**Fig. 5**) or wet-well/dry-well (**Fig. 6**) types. Wet-pit stations are generally employed for small flows up to 700 gal/min (0.044 m³/s). They are usually factory-assembled. The wet-pit stations are automated for routine unattended operation, using pneumatic ejectors, suction lift pumps, vertical wet-pit pumps, or submersible pumps that are nonclogging or self-cleaning. Built-in-place stations, using a separate wet well to receive and store the incoming wastes, have centrifugal pumps installed in an adjacent dry well, and typically handle flows in excess of 1000 gal/min (63 m³/s). Since a pump station is usually installed at a topographic low point, the design must incorporate flood protection and access under all weather conditions. Many states require flood protection for recurrence intervals (return periods) of 25–100 years.

Sewage pumps, even though they are fitted with open impellers designed to pass the large solids anticipated in the flow, must still be protected from clogging. Pumps are additionally protected by grit chambers, comminutors, or bar racks (screens), which must be accessible for service and maintenance. Because organic matter is present in wastewater and decomposes with time, malodorous and hazardous gases frequently develop in pump station wet wells. Proper ventilation, explosion-proof construction, and personnel safety procedures must be adhered to stringently.

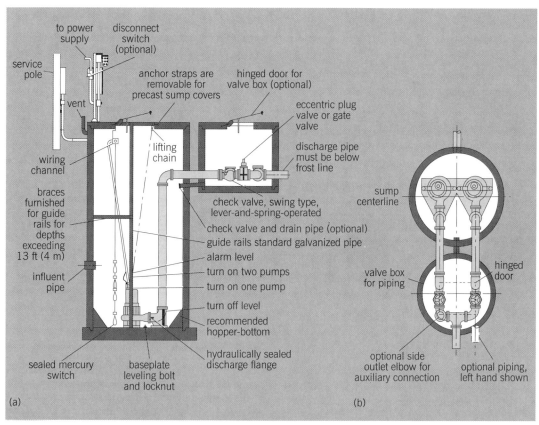

Fig. 5. Wet-pit pumping station with submersible pumps shown (*a*) in section and (*b*) in plan view. (*After Metcalf & Eddy, Inc., and G. Tchobanoglous, Wastewater Engineering: Collection and Pumping of Wastewater, McGraw-Hill, 1981*)

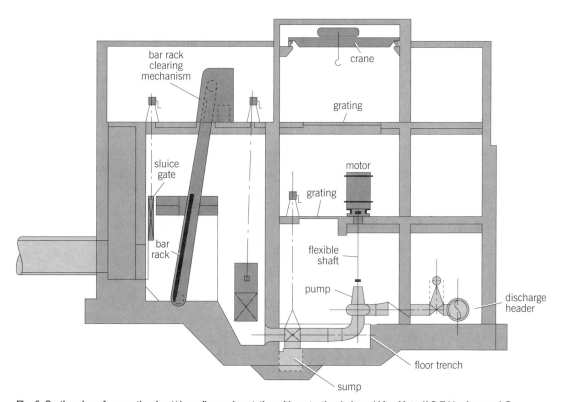

Fig. 6. Section view of conventional wet/dry-well pumping station with protective devices. (*After Metcalf & Eddy, Inc., and G. Tchobanoglous, Wastewater Engineering: Collection and Pumping of Wastewater, McGraw-Hill, 1981*)

Pumping facilities are provided with two or more pumps of the size required to handle the peak anticipated inflow when one pumping unit is out of service. Pumps, with electric drive units set above flood level or otherwise protected, should have dual power sources, either from two separate and distinct electric supplies or through the use of a fuel-fed auxiliary system. Pump stations, particularly unattended ones, must be protected against freezing and should be provided with an alarm system to notify appropriate personnel in the event of any type of power interruption or high-water conditions at the facility. SEE SEWAGE TREATMENT.

Examination. Tests and analysis are employed to establish the characteristics of wastewaters such as composition; condition; and physical, chemical, and biological constituents. Water, as used within a community, undergoes only a slight delay in its passage along the hydrologic cycle. In the modern world, water separated from sewage may eventually be directed into a potable water supply. As such, knowledge about what is being returned to the watercourse and into the immediate environment is essential. Wastewaters contain a myriad of dissolved and suspended materials, including minerals, salts, organic compounds, heavy metals, bacteria, pathogenic organisms, sediments, and toxic substances. It is society's responsibility to return the spent waters to the water-use cycle with safe and acceptable constituents. Tests are used to determine treatability of the waste, amounts of solids and methods to handle these residues, economical amounts of necessary or required additives, and presence of pathogenic organisms, and to establish safe limits for constituents found in effluents that are to be returned to the environment. Technologies and mensuration methods now employed for testing wastes can establish quantities as low as 1 part per trillion (ppt).

Results of chemical laboratory tests are usually expressed in mg/liter or g/m^3. For much smaller values, micrograms (μg)/liter are used. Since wastewater is more than 99.9% water, mg/liter can be interchanged with parts per million (ppm) and μg/liter with parts per billion (ppb). For solids and sludges, where concentrations are greater than 1 kg/liter, percentages are commonly used. Flows are reported in liters/s, m^3/s, or 10^6 gal/day (MGD). In U.S. Customary units, lb/day can be evaluated from the flow rate in MGD $\times$ dose rate in ppm, or mg/liter $\times$ 8.33 lb/gal.

Since any examination is only as useful and as valid as the sample, planning and care must be exercised in selecting the sampling point, the type and frequency of collection, and the actual manner in which the sample is obtained. Sampling may be a single, random sample, known as a grab sample, or it can be a more representative sample that is made up of a repeated number of collections that are composited by either flow or time. All samples collected must be preserved so that there is no significant change in quality between time of sampling and actual testing.

Tests are characterized as physical, chemical, for solids, bioassay, or bacteriological. The physical tests made for turbidity, color, oils, suspended solids, dissolved oxygen, and temperature relate to the esthetic senses. Sewage may be categorized by its dissolved-oxygen content as fresh, stale, or septic. Fresh sewage has a dissolved oxygen content well in excess of

2 mg/liter, is grayish in color, usually is turbid containing visible solids, but has little or no odor. As organic matter undergoes bacterial decomposition, the dissolved oxygen content drops, color darkens, and a musty odor is noted. When all the dissolved oxygen is used up, sewage becomes dark, odors develop, and the waste is septic. Sewage in this last phase is esthetically unacceptable and also more difficult to treat. SEE STREAM POLLUTION; WATER POLLUTION.

Various tests are employed to determine the type and quantity of organics present. Aerobic organisms present in wastewater require dissolved-oxygen and organic matter for growth. As they multiply, they use up the dissolved oxygen but stabilize the organic matter and reduce its putrescibility. By measuring the rate at which these bacteria deplete the dissolved-oxygen during 5 days at 68°F (20°C), the organic strength, reported as the biochemical oxygen demand, is determined. The chemical oxygen demand test uses a strong oxidizing agent instead of bacteria. This quicker method indicates that portion of the organic matter that is susceptible to chemical oxidation. Though both tests provide a measure of oxygen required by organics in wastes, they are different processes producing results that may differ widely and not provide good correlation.

In a small waste sample or where there is a low concentration of organic matter, the organics can be determined by the total organic carbon test. In this test, a known quantity of the sample is injected into a specially designed high-temperature retort. The resulting carbon dioxide produced is automatically read by an infrared analyzer. Still another test for organic content is the total oxygen demand test.

Wastewater solids provide important information about the strength, character, and the quantity of residue that will ultimately have to be disposed of. A measured quantity of a waste that is evaporated to dryness and weighed establishes the total residue. Passing another measured quantity of the same waste through a filter and weighing the trapped residue indicates the suspended solids. Subtracting the weight of the suspended solids from the total residue yields the weight of dissolved solids. Settleable solids are determined by placing a liter of the same waste in an Imhoff cone, letting it stay quiescent for an hour, and measuring what has settled out. Once dry weights of the tested waste have been determined, each sample is burned in a muffle furnace. Organic matter is volatilized, and inert matter or ash remains. The weight loss represents the organic component in each constituent portion of the solids found in that waste (see **Table 4**). SEE SEWAGE SOLIDS.

Many tests are used to evaluate plants involved in pollution control operations and to define the residuals discharged in the effluent. Tests are conducted for pH, alkalinity, residual chlorine, nitrogen in its various forms, and phosphorus. Bioassay tests permit rapid, realistic interactions between minute quantities of difficult-to-detect toxic components on test organisms in their local environment. Bioassays, using fish as test organisms, establish maximum concentrations of toxics, and also provide the means of establishing required dilutions of effluents, so that they will not have significant impact on the local environment.

The sources of most waterborne pathogenic diseases are human and animal fecal discharges. Sewage contains these discharges, but the pathogenic organ-

Table 4. Typical composition of untreated domestic wastewater*

Constituent	Concentration[†]		
	Strong	Medium	Weak
Solids, total	1200	720	350
Dissolved, total	850	500	250
Fixed	525	300	145
Volatile	325	200	105
Suspended, total	350	220	100
Fixed	75	55	20
Volatile	275	165	80
Settleable solids, ml/liter[‡]	20	10	5
Biochemical oxygen demand, 5-day, 68°F (20°C)	400	220	110
Total organic carbon (TOC)	290	160	80
Chemical oxygen demand (COD)	1000	500	250
Nitrogen (total as N)	85	40	20
Organic	35	15	8
Free ammonia	50	25	12
Nitrites	0	0	0
Nitrates	0	0	0
Phosphorus (total as P)	15	8	4
Organic	5	3	1
Inorganic	10	5	3
Chlorides[§]	100	50	30
Alkalinity (as $CaCO_3$)[§]	200	100	50
Grease	150	100	50

*After Metcalf & Eddy, Inc., and G. Tchobanoglous, *Wastewater Engineering: Treatment, Disposal, Reuse*, 2d ed., McGraw-Hill, 1979.
[†]All values except settleable solids are expressed in mg/liter; mg/liter = 0.001 oz/ft^3.
[‡]ml/liter = 11.5 in.^{3}/ft.^{3}
[§]Values should be increased by amount in domestic water supply.

isms are both few in number and difficult to test for. A human voids $2-3 \times 10^{11}$ coliform organisms daily. Since these harmless organisms are hardy, plentiful, and relatively easy to test for, and emanate from the body together with any pathogens, they are used as the index organisms for fecal pollution. Consequently when coliforms are found, it is presumed pathogenic organisms are also present. There are two different bacteriological procedures to determine the number of coliform organisms in a sample. The first method, known as the most probable number, employs the fact that coliform organisms can ferment lactose broth and produce gas. The presence or absence of gas, following 24–48 h of incubation at 95°F (35°C) in multiple fermentation tubes of broth that contain inoculations of serial dilutions of a sample, is noted. A statistical estimate of the probable density of coliforms can be established from the data. Results are recorded as the most probable number of coliforms per 100 ml of sample.

The second procedure, the membrane filter method, is a direct enumeration method; a known volume of sample is passed through a fine-pore membrane that traps the bacteria present on its surface. The filter is then placed in a special petri dish containing requisite nutrients and incubated at 95°F (35°C) for 24 h. Each trapped coliform organism develops into a colony large enough to be identified and counted directly.

Microscopic examinations, frequently performed as a part of evaluation of plant operations, seek particular organisms within the activated sludge floc or in the zoogloea (a gelatinous mass characteristic of bacteria in fixed films). Microscopic and biologic examinations of receiving waters are made for evaluation of water quality. SEE SEWAGE COLLECTION SYSTEMS; SEWAGE DISPOSAL.

Gerald Palevsky

Bibliography. American Public Health Association, American Water Works Association, Water Pollution Control Association Joint Committee, *Standard Methods for the Examination of Water and Wastewater*, 17th ed., 1989; American Water Works Association, *Water Quality and Treatment: A Handbook of Public Water Supplies*, 4th ed, 1990; R. A. Corbitt, *Standard Handbook of Environmental Engineering*, 1990; Metcalf & Eddy, Inc., and G. Tchobanoglous, *Wastewater Engineering: Collection and Pumping of Wastewater*, 1981; Metcalf & Eddy, Inc., G. Tchobanoglous, and F. Burton, *Wastewater Engineering: Treatment, Disposal, and Reuse*, 3d ed., 1990; H. S. Peavy, D. R. Rowe, and G. Tchobanoglous, *Environmental Engineering*, 1985; S. R. Qasim, *Wastewater Treatment Plants: Planning, Design, and Operation*, 1985; W. Viessman, Jr., and M. J. Hammer, *Water Supply and Pollution Control*, 4th ed., 1985.

Sewage collection systems

Configurations of inlets, catch basins, manholes, pipes, drains, mains, holding basins, pump stations, outfalls, controls, and special devices to move wastewaters from points of collection to discharge. Sewage collection systems must be designed and constructed to function without nuisance to the public, with a minimum of maintenance, with maximum safety for workers, without damage due to corrosion or erosion, with all components sized large enough to be capable of adequately serving the community through a justifiable design period with assured durability, and with an economically acceptable cost. The system of pipes and appurtenances is also known as the sewerage system. Wastewaters may be sanitary sewage, industrial wastes, storm runoff, or combined flows.

A sewer is a constructed ditch or channel designed to carry away liquid-conveyed wastes discharged by houses and towns. Modern sewer systems typically are gravity-flow pipelines installed below the ground surface in streets and following the ground slope. The depth of cover over pipelines is controlled by factors such as the location of rock and groundwater, the ability to receive flows from all buildings by gravity, depth to frost line, economics of maintaining gravity flow as compared with pumping, and location and elevation of other existing utilities and infrastructures.

Sewerage systems are designed to carry the liquid wastes smoothly, without deposition, with a minimum of wasted hydraulic energy, and at minimum costs for excavation and construction; they should provide maximum capacity for future populations and flows. Engineered construction, controlled by availability of time, material, personnel, and finances, affects the choice and use of individual components within sewerage systems.

Components. Sewage collection systems include pipes, joints, manholes, house sewers, street inlets, catch basins, inverted siphons, backwater gates, diversions and regulators, outlets, and pumps.

Pipes. Pipes, house sewers, laterals, trunks, mains, and culverts are constructed of various materials to meet diverse design conditions. Sewerage systems are composed of commercially manufactured pipe sec-

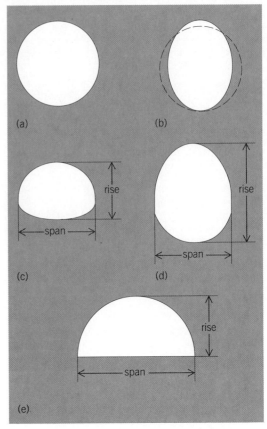

Fig. 1. Various pipe shapes. (*a*) Round. (*b*) Vertically elongated (ellipse). (*c*) Pipe-arch. (*d*) Underpass. (*e*) Arch. (*After American Iron and Steel Institute, Handbook of Steel Drainage and Highway Construction Products, 2d ed., 1971*)

Table 1. Crushing strength of clay and concrete pipe by the three-edge bearing method, lb/linear ft*

Internal diameter, in.[†]	Clay		Nonreinforced concrete			Reinforced concrete ultimate strength				
	Standard	Extra strength	Class I	Class II	Class III	Class I	Class II	Class III	Class IV	Class V
3	—	2000								
4	1200	2000	1500	2000	2400					
6	1200	2000	1500	2000	2400					
8	1400	2200	1500	2000	2400					
10	1600	2400	1600	2000	2400					
12	1800	2600	1800	2250	2600	—	1500	2000	3000	3750
15	2000	2900	2000	2600	2900	—	1875	2500	3750	4690
18	2200	3300	2200	3000	3300	—	2250	3000	4500	5620
21	2400	3850	2400	3300	3850	—	2625	3500	5250	6560
24	2600	4400	2600	3600	4400	—	3000	4000	6000	7500
27	2800	4700	2800	3950	4600	—	3375	4500	6750	8440
30	3300	5000	3000	4300	4750	—	3750	5000	7500	9380
33	3600	5500	3150	4400	4875	—	4125	5500	8250	10,220
36	4000	6000	3300	4500	5000	—	4500	6000	9000	11,250
39	—	6600	—	—	—	—	4825	6500	9750	—
42	—	7000	—	—	—	—	5250	7000	10,500	13,120
48	—	—	—	—	—	—	6000	8000	12,000	15,000
54	—	—	—	—	—	—	6750	9000	13,500	16,880
60	—	—	—	—	—	6000	7500	10,000	15,000	18,750
66	—	—	—	—	—	6600	8250	11,000	16,500	20,620
72	—	—	—	—	—	7200	9000	12,000	18,000	22,500
—	—	—	—	—	—	—	—	—	—	—
108	—	—	—	—	—	10,800	13,500	18,000	27,000	33,750

*1lb/linear ft = 0.0146 kN/m.
[†]1 in. = 2.54 cm.
SOURCE: *Annual Book of ASTM Standards* American Society for Testing and Materials, 1977.

tions joined together; in special circumstances they are constructed in place by using concrete or masonry, or the pipe sections are assembled in place from fabricated component pieces. Pipelines are usually circular, but they can also be elliptical, horseshoe, or arched shapes, boxes, or specially fabricated shapes (**Fig. 1**).

Criteria for choice of system piping include friction factors, size and availability of materials, types of joints, crushing strength, ease of installation, resistance to degradation from corrosion and erosion, and total costs of construction. Vitrified clay, concrete, cast iron, fabricated steel, and plastic are the materials most commonly used for pipes. Standards for uniformity, material quality control, size tolerances, guaranteed strength, and jointing conditions are established by standards organizations and the federal government, as well as industrial, trade, and professional organizations.

Different materials are manufactured in specified diameters, in various standard lengths, and with defined types of ends or joints. The shorter the length of pipe, the more joints are necessary. This can lead to higher labor costs, increased possibility of misalignment, leakage, chance of failure, and lack of durability. Increasing pipe length increases section weight, making pieces heavy, unwieldy, and difficult to place and join in a trench, thus requiring special equipment and, often, more personnel. The choice of pipe frequently depends upon economics, and it may be controlled by construction conditions.

Vitrified clay, generally 4–36 in. (10–91 cm) in diameter, is nonabsorptive and resistant to corrosion, erosion, and scour. It is available in lengths of 1–8 ft (0.3–2.4 m), and it varies in strength with diameter and category (see **Table 1**). Clay pipes with bell-and-spigot joints formerly were used in traditional house drains and street sewer lines.

Cast-iron soil pipe is a bell-and-spigot pipe of limited strength. It is used in plumbing work to carry sanitary wastes from water closets and other fixtures to the street sewer. Soil pipe is often used for house sewers.

Concrete pipe is manufactured in both circular and elliptical shapes that are 4 in.–12 ft (10 cm–3.6 m) in diameter, either plain or reinforced. Various methods, including spinning, casting, and packing, are used in its manufacture. The laying lengths and strength of concrete pipe can be varied and specifically controlled by placing different styles, configurations, and thicknesses of metal reinforcement, as well as by adjusting wall thickness (Table 1). Concrete is subject to corrosion from acids and hydrogen sulfide, and also possibly to scour or erosion where there is excessive velocity and heavy sediment load.

Cast-iron pipe and ductile iron pipe 2–48 in. (5–122 cm) in diameter and with lengths to 20 ft (6 m) and various types of joints provide very tight connections, flexibility, and greater strength than concrete. These pipes, as well as those made of welded steel, are most often used for pipe crossings, in areas of high water, for special load conditions, and for pressure lines. Linings and wrappings are applied inside and out to protect these metal pipes from corrosion.

Fabricated steel pipe is constructed of lightweight corrugated flat sheets that provide strength and flexibility; they can be fabricated into a variety of cross-sectional shapes. Circular, elliptical, partial sections, arches, and pipe arches can be either fabricated in the

shop or erected in the field in sizes up to 25 ft (7.5 m). As the corrugations increase in depth for increased strength and size opening, hydraulic coefficients become lower and flow characteristics change. Corrugated pipes are frequently coated and paved to fill the corrugations in order to increase flow efficiency and reduce erosion and corrosion problems.

Plastic pipe of polyvinyl chloride (PVC), polypropylene, and acrylonitrile butadiene styrene resin (ABS), plastic truss pipe, and other novel materials are being used in sewerage systems. These pipes are very light, are resistant to corrosion, and are available in extended lengths.

Joints. The joints or junctions between two adjacent pipes or between a pipe and an appurtenance must be watertight, possess a degree of flexibility, and have a long life expectancy. Most joints utilize elastomeric O rings that compress between two adjacent pipes to form a tight, yet somewhat flexible, seal. Mortar or grout is used to fill openings or spaces in order to prevent roots from growing into the joints or to prevent soil constituents from interacting with the sealing rings. Corrugated pipe typically uses a band coupling that compresses the O rings set in the corrugated grooves as bolts draw the band tight to the outside of the pipe (**Fig 2.**).

Appurtenances and structures that permit connection to, entry into, or maintenance of sewerage system piping require seals at openings where pipes penetrate these structures. The openings can be grouted closed, or a mechanical compression type of closure may be used (**Fig. 3**).

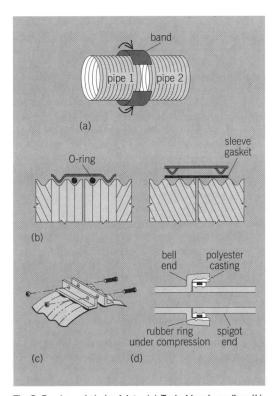

Fig. 2. Band-coupled pipe joints. (*a*) Typical band coupling; (*b*) standard corrugated steel pipe band connectors; (*c*) band angle connector (*after American Iron and Steel Institute, Modern Sewer Design, 1980*). (*d*) Details of an O-ring compression joint for clay, cast iron, and concrete pipes.

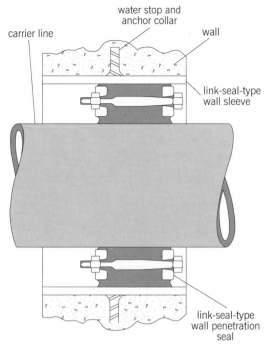

Fig 3. Diagram of a mechanical compression water stop and seal. (*Link Seal, Thunderline Corp., Wayne, Michigan*)

Manholes. Also known as access holes, manholes are openings from the ground surface that are fitted with removable covers and permit personnel to enter, inspect, maintain, and repair the gravity flow system (**Fig. 4**). Manholes are placed at ends of lines and wherever a pipe must be changed in size, elevation, direction, or slope. On straight runs, for up to 24-in. (600-mm) diameter, they are placed no more than 350 ft (100 m) apart to permit mechanical cleaning of the intervening pipe. Spacing increases with diameter. For sewer lines 8–24 in. (20–61 cm) in diameter, manholes 4 ft (1.2 m) in diameter sit directly over the pipe, with the steps of the manhole set into the vertical barrel side. For pipes larger than 24 in. (61 cm), manholes may be offset to the side of the pipe; or larger structures known as junction chambers may be used.

The channel within the bottom of the manhole should provide a smooth passage for the flow entering

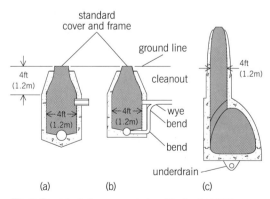

Fig. 4. Some typical sewer manholes with standard 24-in. (61-cm) cover and frame. (*a*) Inside drop. (*b*) Outside drop. (*c*) Unit for a large sewer. (*After R. L. Linsley and J. B. Franzini, Water Resources Engineering, 3d ed., McGraw-Hill., 1979*)

and leaving the structure. The paved invert in the manhole permits transitions from a smaller pipe entry to a larger pipe leaving, and it offers the means to change direction by developing a paved curve. Where the entering line is considerably above the existing pipe, a drop pipe is constructed to permit a smooth transition and yet maintain a clear straight line for ease of cleaning (**Fig. 5**).

Manhole covers, usually in roadway traffic lanes, are generally made of cast iron, set in fabricated frames, and circular in shape so that they cannot fall through the opening when they are lifted for service entry. Covers must lie flat with the pavement, seat well to prevent rattle or movement, be capable of supporting typical traffic loads without damage, and prevent storm water inflow. Covers are frequently provided with special locking devices to prevent removal, vandalism, unauthorized entry, or illegal dumping of wastes into the system.

House sewers. House or building sewers, connections, or service laterals are the small-diameter sewer lines that connect the individual residence or property with the street sewer or lateral (**Fig. 6**). House connections must be made with tight joints, and care must be taken to support the pipe adequately so that subsequent construction does not break the pipe, open joints, or develop pockets in the line. Unused stubs, the openings that have been provided in street sewers for future house sewer connections, must be tightly plugged to control infiltration. Special appurtenances such as flushing manholes, terminal cleanouts, relief overflows, lamp holes, and bypasses are installed in sewerage systems to overcome special topographic or design conditions.

Street inlets. Street inlets are structures that intercept, collect, and transfer storm runoff from street surfaces to the underground storm drain system. Street inlets are located along paved streets and are used to keep pedestrian walkways and crossways relatively free of flowing storm runoff. There are three types: gutter, curb or combined. A gutter inlet has a flat grate at the paved surface that allows flowing storm water to fall through to the inlet structure below. A curb inlet has a vertical opening in the curb and is depressed below the gutter line, allowing water to flow and drop laterally into the inlet structure. A combined inlet has both a gutter and curb opening with the two aligned over the structure. Special designs for areas of very heavy gutter flows, or where gutter flow velocities are very high, use multiple openings, deflector inlets with notches, grooves, or ridges. The outlet line from the inlet to the storm drainline manhole drains the entire structure (**Fig. 7**).

Catch basins. At one time, catch basins were an integral part of combined systems. They existed for storm drainage systems when streets were poorly paved or not maintained and drain lines were not constructed to maintain self-cleaning velocities. Catch basins are constructed with a sump below the outfall line to trap all grit, sand, street sweepings, and other debris within the structure. Catch basins have hatches, covers, or easily removable gutter grates to permit access for periodic maintenance and cleaning of accumulated solids. Special hoods or overflow designs are required on combined systems to prevent sewer gases from venting into the street (**Fig. 8**).

Inverted siphons. An inverted siphon is a depressed or suppressed sewer. The pipe enters the upper end chamber and usually leaves in a number of smaller

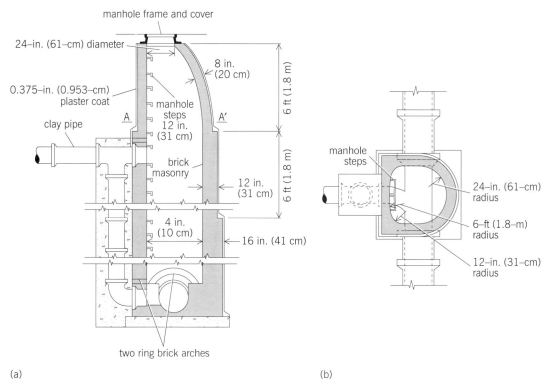

manhole frame and cover

24–in. (61–cm) diameter

0.375–in. (0.953–cm) plaster coat

clay pipe

8 in. (20 cm)

manhole steps 12 in. (31 cm)

brick masonry

6 ft (1.8 m)

6 ft (1.8 m)

12 in. (31 cm)

4 in. (10 cm)

16 in. (41 cm)

two ring brick arches

(a)

manhole steps

24–in. (61–cm) radius

6–ft (1.8–m) radius

12–in. (31–cm) radius

(b)

Fig. 5. Drop manhole detail. (*a*) Vertical section. (*b*) Horizontal section (A-A in part a). (*After National Clay Pipe Institute, Clay Pipe Engineering Manual, 1962*)

lines. The multiple lines pass under the obstruction, structure, or stream with the outlet chamber being at a lower invert elevation so that inflow enters through the inlet and flows out the outlet structure. The section of pipe that is below the hydraulic grade line is always full of liquid, even when there is no flow into the line. The multiple pipes of the inverted siphon are arranged so that as increased flow enters the inlet structure, successive lines are pressed into use, thus maintaining self-cleaning velocities above 3.5 ft/s (1.0 m/s) to prevent clogging.

Backwater gates. Backwater gates are devices that function like check valves to provide unidirectional flow and prevent the reversal of water flow in a line when the water elevation in the receiving water body rises above the pipeline's hydraulic gradient. They are also known as backflow valves, tide gates, or flap valves.

Diversions and regulators. These structures bypass, divert, or dump excess combined flow through use of weirs, of relief siphons, or by float, electrical, or pressure-operated valves and gates. Treatment plants are designed for flows up to three times the volumes of sanitary flows that occur in dry weather but they

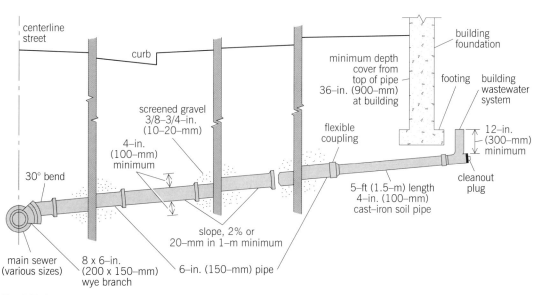

centerline street

curb

30° bend

main sewer (various sizes)

8 x 6–in. (200 x 150–mm) wye branch

6–in. (150–mm) pipe

screened gravel 3/8–3/4–in. (10–20–mm)

4–in. (100–mm) minimum

slope, 2% or 20–mm in 1–m minimum

flexible coupling

minimum depth cover from top of pipe 36–in. (900–mm) at building

5–ft (1.5–m) length 4–in. (100–mm) cast–iron soil pipe

building foundation

footing

building wastewater system

12–in. (300–mm) minimum

cleanout plug

Fig. 6. Typical house sewer connection. (*After Metcalf & Eddy, Inc., and G. Tchobanoglous, Wastewater Engineering: Collection and Pumping of Wastewater, McGraw-Hill, 1981*)

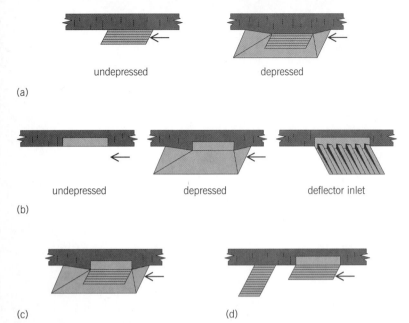

(a)

undepressed   depressed

(b)

undepressed   depressed   deflector inlet

(c)   (d)

Fig. 7. Typical stormwater street inlets. (a) Gutter. (b) Curb. (c) Combination; grate placed directly in front of curb opening and depressed. (d) Multiple; undepressed. (After Joint Committee of American Society of Civil Engineers and Water Pollution Control Federation, Design and Construction of Sanitary and Storm Sewers, ASCE MOP 37, WPCF MOP 9, 1969)

cannot cope with the huge volumes of water delivered by combined sewers during storms. Excess storm flow, above the design flow that is to continue to the treatment plant, is diverted by these structures to relief sewers, to overflows to nearby watercourses, or to holding facilities for later treatment.

Outlets. At the end of any sewerage system—be it from storm water drains, diversion or regulator outlet line, an overflow, or the end of the treatment facility—the treated or untreated flows must be discharged to the environment without causing nuisance, offense, or damage. Outlet structures vary from a single pipe retained by a straight headwall, to flared pipes, structures with special wingwalls, riprapped aprons, or specially constructed devices to dissipate hydraulic energy and prevent erosional damage as water discharges from an outlet and spills over the surface of the land. When the outlet flows are large and velocities high, special devices are used to dissipate energy. They include hydraulic jumps, hydraulic buckets, side channel discharges, and other structures designed specifically for energy dissipation.

Treatment plant outfalls usually discharge below the surface of the receiving water body. Discharges from outfall pipes are generally diffused through a series of manifolded lines fitted with multiple ports. Lines are placed deep enough to allow for good mixing and dilution, prevent so-called water boils, and maintain sufficiently low exit velocities to preclude erosion. They are anchored to prevent undermining or movement by currents or tides, and they are placed in locations where they will not interfere with normal use of the receiving body of water. *SEE EROSION.*

Pumps. Pumping facilities must be included in sewage collection systems when topography or soil conditions preclude typical piping layouts or construction, and where normal gravity flow cannot be employed.

Sewer system design. Sewer design is composed of several phases: initial, preliminary, and final. The initial conceptual phase defines the specific problem with generalized solutions, based on population, area, and financing. Conceptual design addresses broad issues of politics, public policy, probable costs, design period, and phasing of construction. An environmental assessment is necessary. In addition, evaluations should be made of bonded indebtedness, how bonds will be issued, availability of state and federal assistance programs, and preliminary determination regarding tax structures and rates which may be set by the public service commission.

Conceptual design is comprehensive and is based on physical, demographic, economic, and legal information. Projected population distribution and density, dependent upon zoning regulations and economic development within a political subdivision, must be investigated. Topography, rainfall, flood information, soil conditions, groundwater elevations, extent of existing road systems and paving, extent of existing and future infrastructure, and locations for collection, treatment, and outfall must be established. Environmental regulations, regional or multimunicipal systems, intra- and interstate compacts and legal requirements of flood control, flood plain insurance, and final disposal of liquid and solid effluents must all be resolved. *SEE ENVIRONMENTAL ENGINEERING; LAND-USE PLANNING.*

The preliminary design phase uses reliable data to permit development of realistic evaluations of the

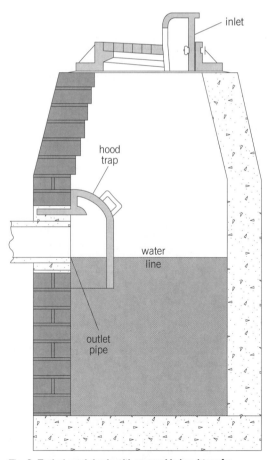

Fig. 8. Typical catch basin with removable hood trap for cleanout. (Neenah Foundry Co., Neenah, Wisconsin)

proposed project. The area to be served and the initial and future quantities of flow to be handled are established, and treatment and discharge points are determined. Tentative pipeline runs are prepared by using topographic maps and aerial photographs to locate major concentrations of buildings, roads, possible easements, streams, and special features. Preliminary sewer lines and grades are approximated, and appurtenances, diversions, pump stations, overflows, treatment plants, and outfalls spotted. Preliminary costs based on projected lengths of pipe, number of manholes, special structures, appurtenances, and approximate excavation are estimated.

Final design is based on refined information of the topography and soil that has been obtained by field surveys and borings. Design flows are established by detailed evaluation of areas and population projections based on demographics. Pipelines and appurtenances are located, sized, and drawn on contract plans. Specifications for construction are prepared, and cost estimates for the designed system are made.

Final construction plans for a sewerage system contain both plan and profile sheets (**Fig. 9**). Plan sheets provide graphical information about the location, dimensions, and clearances of all proposed pipes and appurtenances with respect to topography, legal grades, existing and proposed infrastructure, water mains, overhead power lines, trees, and special situ-ations. The profile sheet, a developmental plan along the centerline of the proposed sewerage system, with stationing and references to the plan sheet, clearly shows initial and final ground elevations; diameter, material, length, and slope of pipes; location of and connections to appurtenances; all control invert elevations; all known belowground infrastructure crossings; clearances and cover over proposed pipe; and special bedding conditions under the pipe.

Additional sheets showing typical details, standard castings, construction limits, trench conditions, and pipe bedding, together with designs of special structures and appurtenances for erosion and sediment control during construction, complete the contract drawings. Specifications defining the quality of material, workmanship of construction, esthetics of finished work, testing of system, and guarantees are an integral portion of the public works contract documents.

The flows established in the design of a sanitary sewer system are dependent upon population. Storm drainage systems are based on rainfall-runoff values coupled with risk evaluation of flood damage. Combined systems are more complex, since they are designed on values derived from both of the above. Combined systems must carry dry weather flows without deposition, must carry limited storm water flow without surcharging treatment facilities, and

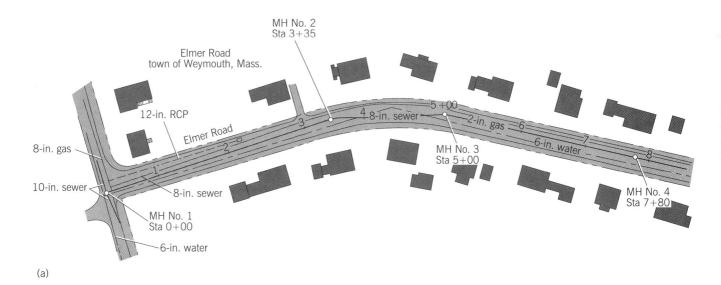

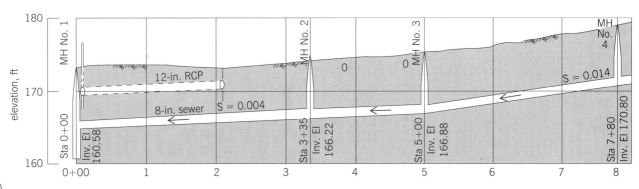

Fig. 9. Typical contract plan and profile sheet for sewer lateral. (*a*) Plan. (*b*) Profile; numbers on horizontal axis refer to sites with same numbers in part *a*. MH = manhole. Sta = Station. Inv. El. = Invert elevation. RCP = reinforced concrete pipe. S = slope in ft/ft or m/m. 1 ft = 0.3 m. 1 in. = 2.54 cm. (*After Metcalf & Eddy, Inc., and G. Tchobanoglous, Wastewater Engineering: Collection and Pumping of Wastewater, McGraw-Hill, 1981*)

must provide for diversion and overflows when heavy storm flows develop.

Pipe flow. Liquid flows from a point of higher energy to a point of lower energy. Energy at a point is made up of position, pressure, and kinetics. Position is elevation above a measured datum; pressure is due to applied external force; and kinetic energy is developed from the velocity of the moving liquid. The difference in energy levels between an upstream and a downstream point is known as the available head.

Within the normal range of sizes used, a pipe section between manholes is a gravity sewer that is an open-channel system. The pipe section between manholes is of a constant size, placed on a continuous slope, with the liquid quantity between manholes assumed constant. Under these conditions, since there is no external pressure, uniform flow exists, and velocity is constant.

The difference in physical elevation between two points along the bottom of the pipe (difference in invert elevation), divided by the horizontal distance between the two points (reach), is the invert slope. Since quantity of flow and pipe size are constant, the depth of flow in the pipe (normal depth) is constant, and the water surface slope, or hydraulic gradient, is parallel to the invert slope. Because the liquid is moving, it develops kinetic energy that is known as the velocity head and is given by Eq. (1), where h_v is the

$$h_v = \frac{V^2}{2g} \qquad (1)$$

velocity head in ft or m, V is velocity in ft/s or m/s, and g is the gravitational acceleration constant. The energy gradient is the theoretical line depicting the total energy in the fluid at every point along the pipe.

Under uniform flow, the energy gradient, the hydraulic gradient, and the bottom of the pipeline are all parallel, and their slopes are identical. **Figure 10** shows a typical hydraulic profile.

Energy is required to move a fluid from one point to another. This energy is used to overcome the resistance or friction of the liquid along the surface of the conduit carrying the flow. The rougher the surface texture, and the more joints or imperfections in alignment, the greater will be the resistance to flow. Energy for flow requires available head, which is the change in elevation, or slope of the energy gradient from manhole to manhole.

An equation used to compute the velocity of uniform flow in an open channel is known as the Manning equation. It provides the formula that is used the most for sewerage system design. The Manning equation (2) relates velocity within a pipe or open channel

$$V = \frac{1.486}{n} \times R^{2/3} \times S^{1/2} \qquad (2a)$$

$$V = \frac{1}{n} \times R^{2/3} \times S^{1/2} \qquad (2b)$$

to slope, to a roughness coefficient that is a measure of the surface friction, and to the hydraulic radius. Here V is velocity in ft/s [Eq. (2a)] or m/s [Eq. (2b)]; n is the coefficient of roughness and is dependent upon the material and finish of the open channel (see **Table 2**); R is the hydraulic radius, obtained by dividing the cross-sectional area of water by the wetted perimeter in the open-channel flow zone (R in pipes flowing full is pipe diameter $\div$ 4); and S is the slope in ft/ft [Eq. (2a)] or m/m [Eq. (2b)].

Sewerage systems should be designed with a velocity high enough to prevent deposition of solids, but

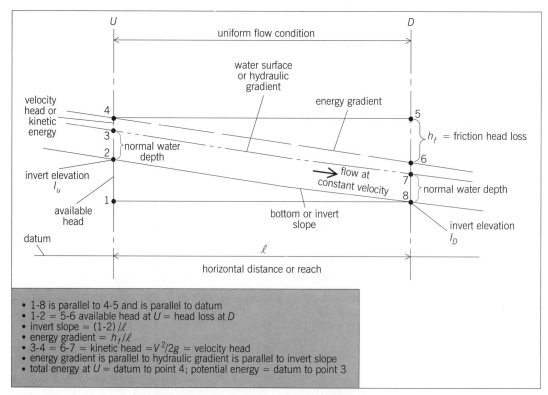

- 1-8 is parallel to 4-5 and is parallel to datum
- 1-2 = 5-6 available head at U = head loss at D
- invert slope = (1-2) $/\ell$
- energy gradient = h_f/ℓ
- 3-4 = 6-7 = kinetic head = $V^2/2g$ = velocity head
- energy gradient is parallel to hydraulic gradient is parallel to invert slope
- total energy at U = datum to point 4; potential energy = datum to point 3

Fig. 10. Hydraulic profile for uniform flow condition, showing values at points U and D.

Table 2. Coefficients of roughness values of *n* for use in the Manning equation

Surface	Best	Good	Fair	Poor
Uncoated cast-iron pipe	0.012	0.013	0.014	0.015
Coated cast-iron pipe	0.011	0.012*	0.013*	
Commercial wrought-iron pipe, black	0.012	0.013	0.014	0.015
Commercial wrought-iron pipe, galvanized	0.013	0.014	0.015	0.017
Smooth brass and glass pipe	0.009	0.010	0.011	0.013
Smooth lockbar and welded O.D. pipe	0.010	0.011*	0.013*	
Riveted and spiral steel pipe	0.013	0.015*	0.017*	
Vitrified sewer pipe	{ 0.010 } { 0.011 }	0.013*	0.015	0.017
Common clay drainage tile	0.011	0.012*	0.014*	0.017
Glazed brickwork	0.011	0.012	0.013*	0.015
Brick in cement mortar; brick sewers	0.012	0.013	0.015*	0.017
Neat cement surfaces	0.010	0.011	0.012	0.013
Cement mortar surfaces	0.011	0.012	0.013*	0.015
Concrete pipe	0.012	0.013	0.015*	0.016
Wood stave pipe	0.010	0.011	0.012	0.013
Plank flumes				
Planed	0.010	0.012*	0.013	0.014
Unplaned	0.011	0.013*	0.014	0.015
With battens	0.012	0.015*	0.016	
Concrete-lined channels	0.012	0.014*	0.016*	0.018
Cement-rubble surface	0.017	0.020	0.025	0.030
Dry-rubble surface	0.025	0.030	0.033	0.035
Dressed-ashlar surface	0.013	0.014	0.015	0.017
Semicircular metal flumes, smooth	0.011	0.012	0.013	0.015
Semicircular metal flumes, corrugated	0.0225	0.025	0.0275	0.030
Canals and ditches				
Earth, straight and uniform	0.017	0.020	0.0225*	0.025
Rock cuts, smooth and uniform	0.025	0.030	0.033*	0.035
Rocks cuts, jagged and irregular	0.035	0.040	0.045	
Winding sluggish canals	0.0225	0.025*	0.0275	0.030
Dredged-earth channels	0.025	0.0275*	0.030	0.033
Canals with rough stony beds, weeds on earth banks	0.025	0.030	0.035*	0.040
Earth bottom, rubble sides	0.028	0.030*	0.033*	0.035
Natural-stream channels				
1. Clean, straight bank, full stage, no rifts or deep pools	0.025	0.0275	0.030	0.033
2. Same as 1, but some weeds and stones	0.030	0.033	0.035	0.040
3. Winding, some pools and shoals, clean	0.033	0.035	0.040	0.045
4. Same as 3, lower stages, more ineffective slope and sections	0.040	0.045	0.050	0.055
5. Same as 3, some weeds and stones	0.035	0.040	0.045	0.050
6. Same as 4, stony sections	0.045	0.050	0.055	0.060
7. Sluggish river reaches, rather weedy or with very deep pools	0.050	0.060	0.070	0.080
8. Very weedy reaches	0.075	0.100	0.125	0.150

*Values commonly used in designing.
SOURCE: Metcalf & Eddy, Inc., and G. Tchobanoglous, *Wastewater Engineering: Collection and Pumping of Wastewater*, McGraw-Hill, 1981.

not so high that the flow causes erosion or excess thrust or movement of pipe or appurtenances (**Table 3**). The basic Manning equation is developed for pipes flowing full; design charts and nomographs are used for sizing pipes. Many regulatory agencies limit maximum flow within pipes to some proportion of full pipe capacity as a safety factor. In addition, inflow to sewerage systems is not a constant; it varies with time and season for volume, depth, and velocity. Since the hydraulic radius *R* is dependent on cross-sectional area and wetted perimeter, and these do not change in a constant or uniform manner, actual flows within the pipes must be determined for these different conditions. Various graphs for determining hydraulic elements for partial flow are available (**Fig. 11**); they are used to determine depths of flow and velocities in sections having different shapes.

Good design of a gravity sewer line attempts to keep the slope of the energy gradient as flat as possible in order to minimize excavation and prevent loss of available energy, which cannot be recovered. Proper calculations for manhole losses must be considered, since wherever pipes change slope, direction, or size within a manhole energy losses occur. A gen-

eral rule of sewerage system construction has been that the soffit (inner top) of the outflow line from a manhole should be at least 0.1 ft (3 cm) lower than the soffits of all lines entering the manhole. This is done to prevent the energy gradient from sloping upward or against the direction of flow, a condition that produces deposition of solids.

When pipe slope is significantly flatter than the overlying ground, insufficient cover over pipes may develop. This is overcome by the use of drop manholes (Figs. 4 and 5). A localized energy loss is sustained as the energy gradient is made rapidly discontinuous. Special designs for inside and outside drop manholes may become necessary to absorb excess turbulence and energy, direct the flows, and prevent scour or erosion from the falling water. Where the pipe is installed on steep grades, with steep slopes and high velocities, special collars, anchorages, thrust blocks, and joint restraints are designed and provided to prevent movement or undermining of the pipe.

Pipe installation. Considerations in installing pipe include trenches, bedding, maintenance, and safety.

Trenches. Sewerage system pipelines must be installed accurately, to proper line and grade. Construc-

Table 3. Minimum slope for gravity flow in sanitary sewers

Size		Slope, m/m*	
mm	in.	n = 0.013	n = 0.015
200	8	0.0033	0.0044
250	10	0.0025	0.0033
300	12	0.0019	0.0026
375	15	0.0014	0.0019
450	18	0.0011	0.0015
525	21	0.0009	0.0012
600	24	0.0008	0.0010
675	27	0.0007†	0.0009
750	30	0.0006†	0.0008†
900	36	0.0004†	0.0006†

*Based on Manning's equation with a minimum velocity of 0.6 m/s. Where practicable, steeper slopes should be used. 1 m = 3.2808 ft.
†The minimum practicable slope for construction is about 0.0008 m/m.
SOURCE: Metcalf & Eddy, Inc., and G. Tchobanoglous, *Wastewater Engineering: Collection and Pumping of Wastewater*, McGraw-Hill, 1981.

tion methods for normal cut and cover, or open-trench excavation, are similar to other types of excavation for general construction. Since sewerage lines are most frequently installed under pavements within the rights of way for roadways, adjacent to existing buildings, with overhead and underground utilities, special care must be exercised to protect work and workers from traffic, cave-ins, flooding, and electrical shock. Professional construction practices and regulations of the Occupational Health and Safety Administration (OSHA) must be followed for shoring, bracing, and dewatering excavations. Spoil, the excavated material from the trench, should be placed on the uphill side to prevent surface water from flowing into the trench; yet it should be placed far enough away from the trench so that it does not add weight and cause a cave-in. If the spoil is of satisfactory material, it may be used for backfilling the trench after the pipe is bedded in place. Trench widths are kept to a minimum to reduce transmitted load to the pipe. If the trench is too narrow, workers cannot work within it, make proper joints, and backfill around the pipe safely. Sheeting, shoring, and bracing, used to maintain stability of the trench excavation and prevent cave-ins, are removed after the pipe is in place and backfilling is under way. Since piping is installed on dry, stable trench bases, dewatering is necessary where groundwater levels are high. Removed water must be disposed of in a safe manner. Pipe must be properly joined with watertight joints, so that a smooth, continuous invert, on the proper slope, with no pockets, depressions, or offsets is developed. Stubs for house sewer connections and manhole openings must be made at proper locations and elevations. Stubs or openings must be sealed to prevent infiltration. Pipe must be properly backfilled to finished grade; the excavation must be paved to provide a safe surface for carrying traffic.

Pipe tunneling and jacking are other construction techniques used for pipe installations. These are generally used to pass under highways, existing embankments, railroads, and streams, or for other special situations. New sewer lines are tested for watertightness, generally with low air pressure, to establish conformance with infiltration and exfiltration limits.

Bedding. Installed sewer lines must be able to withstand the external loads superimposed on them due to dead load from soil backfill and overburden, and from live loads of traffic and impact. The pipe's ability to withstand these loads is based on the crushing strength of the pipe material used, the method of installation, and the type and style of bedding provided. The standard for the crushing strength to which the pipe is manufactured is defined by the laboratory three-edge bearing test (Table 1).

The method of installation is defined as either trench or embankment condition. In the trench condition, pipe is installed in a relatively narrow trench, excavated into firm soil, with trench walls extending above the top of the pipe. Backfill is then placed around and over the pipe and carried up to the final ground surface. An embankment condition occurs when pipe is essentially placed on the existing ground surface or in a very wide trench, with backfill placed over the pipe and carried up to the final ground condition. Bedding, used to reduce stress concentrations and increase pipe support, is the prepared foundation between the bottom of the pipe and the firm trench or support ground surface. The safe support strength or load carrying ability of the pipe is increased with better bedding conditions.

The Marston formula [Eq. (3) for trench condition and Eq. (4) for embankment condition] provides a

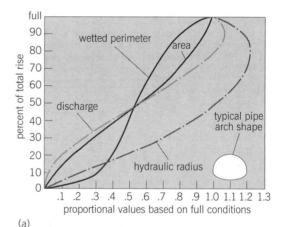

(a)

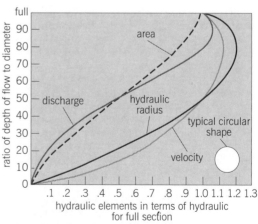

(b)

Fig. 11. Hydraulic element graphs for conditions of partial flow in terms of full section. (a) Pipe-arch section. (b) Circular section. (*After American Iron and Steel Institute, Modern Sewer Design, 1980*)

Table 4. Values of load coefficients C_d for trench condition

Fill material:	Sand and gravel	Saturated topsoil	Clay	Saturated clay
Specific weight, lb/ft³ (kN/m³):	100 (15.7)	100 (15.7)	120 (18.9)	130 (20.4)
Ratio of cover depth to trench width				
1.0	0.84	0.86	0.88	0.90
2.0	1.45	1.50	1.55	1.62
3.0	1.90	2.00	2.10	2.20
4.0	2.22	2.33	2.49	2.65
5.0	2.45	2.60	2.80	3.03
6.0	2.60	2.78	3.04	3.33
7.0	2.75	2.95	3.23	3.57
8.0	2.80	3.03	3.37	3.76
9.0	2.88	3.11	3.48	3.92
10.0	2.92	3.17	3.56	4.04
12.0	2.97	3.24	3.68	4.22
14.0	3.00	3.28	3.75	4.34

SOURCE: R. K. Linsley and J. B. Franzini, *Water Resources Engineering*, 2d ed., McGraw-Hill, 1979.

$$W_d = C_d w B_d^2 \qquad (3)$$
$$W_c = C_c w B_c^2 \qquad (4)$$

value for trench load on a buried pipe. Here W_d or W_c is the vertical dead load of fill in lb/linear ft or kN/m on the buried pipe, w is the unit weight of fill material in lb/ft³ or kN/m³, B_d is the width of the trench in ft or m, measured 1 ft (0.3 m) above the top of the buried pipe, B_c is the outside pipe diameter in ft or m, and C_d or C_c are load coefficients for pipe (**Tables 4** and **5**). As the width of the trench increases, a point is reached where there is no longer a trench and the pipe is in the embankment condition. In this case the smaller value obtained for W_d or W_c controls. In addition to dead loads, vehicular and impact loads must be considered. As the live load is applied to the ground above the pipe, the load is distributed; its intensity decreases with increased depth of cover. Depth of cover is a major concern in sewerage systems to maintain pipeline integrity.

The sum of all loads, multiplied by a safety factor usually taken as 1.5, divided by the rated three-edge crushing strength of the selected pipe, establishes the load factor or type of bedding condition required (Table 1). The combination of pipe material, crushing strength, and bedding is an economic consideration in the design of sewerage systems.

Maintenance. Clogging from accumulations of debris, tree roots, or illegally dumped materials that prevents proper flow of liquid through appurtenances and pipes is the major problem encountered in sewerage systems. Cleaning equipment to remove these obstructions includes cutting or boring tools to cut or rip through roots or balled-up debris and special tools known as pigs to move deposits of sand, grit, or other materials mechanically and hydraulically from the line to a manhole, where orange-peel buckets lift out the deposited materials.

In modern systems, breaks, cracks, spalling of pipe, poor joints, or other defects are inspected through the use of underwater television cameras. Specialized methods of concreting, patching, or even inserting a liner within the pipe have been developed to reduce infiltration, maintain the usefulness of pipes, and reduce the amount of surface excavation needed to make repairs.

Safety. A sewerage system is a confined space where organic matter is undergoing organic decomposition. Hazardous and toxic gases generally exist; in addition, because these areas are belowground, there may be a lack of oxygen. Before personnel can safely enter a manhole, vault, or chamber, the space must be ventilated mechanically for a period of time and then tested for gases.

Entry into the sewerage system is through manholes that have narrow entry hatches or manholes with steps cast into the wall. Care must be exercised that at least two people work together, that the entering person wears a safety harness, and that the steps are safe. As a minimum, OSHA recommendations and regulations should be followed. SEE SEWAGE; SEWAGE DISPOSAL.

Gerald Palevsky

Table 5. Values of load coefficients C_c for embankment condition*

Ratio of cover depth to pipe diameter	C_c
1.0	1.2
2.0	2.8
3.0	4.7
4.0	6.7
6.0	11.0
8.0	16.0

*Rigid pipe, unyielding base, noncohesive backfill.
SOURCE: R. K. Linsley and J. B. Franzini, *Water Resources Engineering*, 2d ed., McGraw-Hill, 1979.

Bibliography. American Concrete Pipe Association, *Concrete Pipe Design Manual*, 1987; American Iron and Steel Institute, *Modern Sewer Design*, 1990; M. J. Hammer, *Water and Wastewater Technology*, 2d ed., 1986; Joint Committee of American Society of Civil Engineers and Water Pollution Control Association, *Design and Construction of Sanitary and Storm Sewers*, ASCE MOP 37 or WPCF MOP 9, 1969; R. K. Linsley and J. B. Franzini, *Water Resources Engineering*, 3d ed., 1977; Metcalf & Eddy, Inc., and G. Tchobanoglous, *Wastewater Engineering: Collection and Pumping of Wastewater*, 1981.

Sewage disposal

The ultimate return of used water to the environment. Disposal points distribute the used water either to aquatic bodies such as oceans, rivers, lakes, ponds, or lagoons or to land by absorption systems, groundwater recharge, and irrigation. Wastewaters must be mixed, diluted, and absorbed so that receiving environments retain their beneficial use, be it for drinking, bathing, recreation, aquaculture, silviculture, irrigation, groundwater recharge, or industry.

Wastewater is treated to remove contaminants or pollutants that affect water quality and use. Discharge to the environment must be accomplished without transmitting diseases, endangering aquatic organisms, impairing the soil, or causing unsightly or malodorous conditions. The type and degree of treatment are dependent upon the absorption capability or dilution capacity at the point of ultimate disposal. *See Sanitary engineering; Sewage; Sewage treatment.*

Water pollution regulations. In the United States, federal and state agencies have established two types of standards. Water quality standards are used to measure an aquatic ecosystem after the discharge has entered and mixed with it. Effluent standards define what is allowed within the wastewaters discharged into the aquatic environment. Water quality standards relate to the esthetics and use of the receiving environment for public water supply, recreation, maintenance of aquatic life and wildlife, or agriculture. The parameters of water quality, which define the physical, chemical, and biological limits, include floating and settleable solids, turbidity, color, temperature, pH, dissolved oxygen, biochemical oxygen demand (BOD), numbers of coliform organisms, toxic materials, heavy metals, and nutrients. Effluent standards specify the allowed biochemical oxygen demand, suspended solids, temperature, pH, heavy metals, certain organic chemicals, pesticides, and nutrients in the discharge.

Discharges into any aquatic system cannot contravene the standards set for the most beneficial use of that water body. Multiple discharges from various sources, different political jurisdictions, diurnal variations in temperatures and flows, location of sampling, and time of sampling complicate efficacy and ease of enforcing water quality standards. Point-source wastewater effluent discharge standards, established for ease of sampling, simplicity of repetitive testing, and clarity for enforcement, are more likely to be used by regulatory agencies. *See Environmental engineering; Water conservation; Water pollution.*

Self-purification. Pollutional constituents, which impact on sight, smell, and esthetic sensibilites, relate to color, pH, turbidity, and dissolved oxygen. Contaminants, which impact on public health and usable water quality, relate to the presence of pathogens, toxic matter, and oxygen-consuming organic substances. The concentration of suspended, colloidal, and dissolved matter, and organics exerting a biochemical oxygen demand within wastewater are reduced by natural processes of settling, oxidation-reduction, dilution, and bleaching. Degradable organics are destroyed within receiving water bodies by bacteriologic and biologic stabilization. The multiplying bacteria are themselves subjected to environmental stresses, predation, and dying, which ultimately reduce their concentration.

Water, in its continuous cycle, exists in various states or forms with different levels of quality. The water molecules themselves remain unchanged. The quantities of pollutants and contaminants associated with the molecules determine water's acceptability or purity. Given sufficient time, water purifies itself. Pollutants and contaminants entering the aquatic system are altered, modified, reduced, and eliminated. New residential communities with greater population, increased industrial activity, and intensified agricultural practices have reduced the distance and hence the time between points of wastewater production and water usage. Wastewater treatment has become imperative in order to maintain a safe, healthy, and viable environment.

There exists a natural balance in the environment. Floatables within sewage discharges rise to the surface upon entering an aquatic ecosystem and ultimately wash ashore to be stabilized by soil bacteria. Heavier suspended solids settle out as benthic deposits that slowly undergo anaerobic decomposition and stabilization. Colloidal and dissolved matter may coagulate and settle, become food for aquatic organisms, or undergo aerobic bacterial attack. The quantities of dissolved oxygen present indicate levels of stream environment viability. Levels of stream dissolved oxygen are dependent on the presence of biodegradable organics and aerobic bacteria. Aerobic bacteria utilize dissolved oxygen as they grow and multiply while feeding on the organic matter that exerts the biochemical oxygen demand. Diffusion at the air–water interface replenishes the diminished dissolved oxygen levels. This complex process is dependent upon biochemical oxygen demand, dilution, temperature, depth of water, turbulence, dissolved oxygen, presence of toxic chemicals, pH, floating scum, and turbidity. A graphic representation known as the oxygen sag curve depicts the summation of oxygen depletion (deoxygenation curve) and oxygen replenishment (reaeration curve). If the point of critical deficit, the lowest point on the oxygen sag curve, does not depress the stream dissolved oxygen below acceptable values, the stream ecology will not be adversely affected. Summer, when temperatures are elevated and stream flow is at its lowest level, is the crucial period for compliance with stream quality standards. *See Soil microbiology; Stream pollution.*

Disposal to lakes and ponds. Factors of mixing, turbulence, dilution, and oxygen transfer affect all aquatic ecosystems. In quiescent, stagnant, nonflowing water bodies, these physical actions are severely curtailed. Deep lakes stratify vertically, as cooler water, with greater density, sinks to the bottom. Summer sunshine warms the surface layer, the epilimnion, and caps the lake, intensifying stratification. Oxygen transfer by both diffusion and wind–wave turbulence maintains a higher concentration of dissolved oxygen in the epilimnion than in the lower strata. In autumn, air temperatures drop; the epilimnion is rapidly cooled, and this surface layer of water becomes heavier and sinks, developing vertical density currents. This rapid change, fall overturn, carries the water laden with dissolved oxygen down, and exposes water with low concentrations of dissolved oxygen to the atmosphere where rapid reaeration occurs. Dissolved oxygen is distributed and the natural process of self-purification can continue through most of the lake depth. Ponds, being shallower, do not stratify; they are usually fully mixed by wind, wave, and local current action.

Disposal of wastewater into lakes and ponds is planned to take full advantage of the local circulation patterns developed by currents, wind action, or waves, and by dispersion and mixing. Outfalls are usually submerged, with many horizontal ports to discharge effluent in spaced, separated locations. Wastewaters, usually warmer than the deeper hypolimnion, tend to develop both horizontal and vertical mixing and dilution as they rise from these dispersed, submerged discharges.

Phosphorus, a major cause of lake eutrophication, is a critical wastewater disposal problem in lakes. Phosphorus enters lakes from septic tank effluents, from agricultural fertilizers and ground runoff, and from wastewater effluents. SEE EUTROPHICATION; FRESH-WATER ECOSYSTEM; LIMNOLOGY.

Lagoons. These are ponds constructed especially for sewage treatment and disposal. Lagoons can remove very high amounts of incoming organic wastes, solids, and bacteria through biological or physical processes. Known by various names, depending on their function, how oxygen is added, and the ultimate method of liquid disposal, the types include oxidation, stabilization, aerobic, anaerobic, facultative, aerated, polishing, concentrating, evaporating, and groundwater-recharge ponds. In all, organic and bacteriological contaminants are reduced and stabilized by facultative aerobic bacteria using the dissolved oxygen obtained from photosynthetic algae and diffusion. Lagoons, with large surface areas providing long detention times, produce outflows that are readily acceptable, after disinfection, to the environment. Lagoons can percolate stabilized sewage for groundwater table recharge, or employ effluent directly for irrigation or silviculture; in arid areas they may rely totally on evaporation. Oxidation ponds are used for aquaculture to grow fish for increased food protein production. SEE GROUNDWATER HYDROLOGY.

Land application. Disposal includes effluent dissipation of individual on-site septic tanks, groundwater recharge, surface or spray distribution for landscape and crop irrigation, or indirect overland flow to surface-water collectors. Design of a wastewater disposal system utilizes site-specific combinations of topography, soil-surface texture and matrix, climate, and plant and crop characteristics. Land disposal requires wastewaters to undergo preapplication treatment to reduce or alter pollutional loads, to prevent clogging of distribution and soil absorption systems, and to prevent malodorous conditions.

Effluent dissipation from on-site septic tanks, using buried leaching drain tiles, relies on the absorbing soil's hydraulic permeability and bacteria to decompose effluent organic matter. If organic matter is being discharged to the soil matrix faster than bacteria can decompose it, the system will clog and fail, causing odors and objectionable flows of liquids on the soil surface.

Crop irrigation by trench, surface distribution, or spray irrigation is used in areas where there is inadequate rainfall. Liquid applied over large land areas at rates up to 4 in. (10 cm) per week is evaporated, transpired, or percolated to groundwater. Most applied nutrients, organic materials, and pollutants are adsorbed on the soil matrix or by the vegetation.

In overland flow, pretreated wastewater spreads over gently sloping, textured soil surfaces with ground cover. Soil must have a relatively low permeability to prevent significant infiltration to the groundwater table. Effluent is dispersed in sheet flow, at low velocities, and through selected vegetation to prevent erosion. Effluent-suspended solids and organic substances are filtered, oxidized, or adsorbed. SEE SEPTIC TANK; SOIL ECOLOGY.

Ocean disposal. Discharge of sewage into estuaries, bays, or oceans relies on large dilution factors and mixing. Effluents discharged through submarine diffusion systems are less dense and warmer than the receiving salt water. Since the wastewater is more buoyant, it rises toward the surface as a wastewater field, with initial dilution and mixing. As tides, littoral currents, waves, and wind cause turbulence, eddy diffusion and dispersion develop. Organic loads, nutrient quantities, dissolved oxygen, and floatable material all affect the initial dilution and dispersion characteristics necessary to prevent unwanted impacts on bathing beaches, recreational facilities, and mariculture in the salt-water environment. Pathogens may affect filter-feeding mollusks; toxic chemicals and sediments may impact on benthic feeders; and fields of upwelling sewage discharges may affect the surface of the salt-water ecosystem. Many variables evolving from paths of tides, density currents, littoral and advective drift, fresh-water flushing rates, dispersion, and vertical stratification provide concerns for safe and proper nearshore discharges into the salt-water environment. SEE ESTUARINE OCEANOGRAPHY; SEWAGE.

Gerald Palevsky

Bibliography. American Water Works Association, *Water Quality and Treatment: A Handbook of Public Water Supplies*, 4th ed.; 1990; Metcalf & Eddy, Inc., G. Tchobanoglous, and F. Burton, *Wastewater Engineering: Treatment, Disposal, and Reuse*, 3d ed., 1990; B. J. Nebel, *Environmental Science*, 2d ed., 1981; G. Tchobanoglous and E. D. Schroeder, *Water Quality*, 1985.

Sewage solids

The accumulated, semiliquid material consisting of suspended, colloidal, and dissolved organic and inorganic matter separated from wastewater during treatment. Sludges are developed as contained pollutants and contaminants are separated by mechanical, hydraulic, biological, or chemical processes. The various classes of solids that are removed and collected must be disposed of in a safe, nuisance-free manner without hazard to health or the environment. Collection, handling, transporting, and disposal of removed solids are difficult and costly, since they are offensive and putrescible, with 92–99.5% water content. Sewage solids must be treated by thickening, chemical conditioning, mechanical dewatering, thermal action, biological stabilization, or digestion to convert putrescible organic matter to relatively inert end products, remove water, and reduce weight and volume.

Types. Sewage solids are classified as screenings, scum, grit, septage, or sewage sludges (see **table**).

Screenings. Large solids, carried by incoming wastewater, are captured mechanically on screens or racks with openings of various sizes. These protective units remove floating debris, including wood, cloth-

Sources of solids and sludge from a conventional wastewater treatment facility*		
Unit operation or process	Type of solids or sludge	Remarks
Screening	Coarse solids	Coarse solids are often comminuted and returned to the wastewater for removal in subsequent treatment facilities.
Grit removal	Grit and scum	Scum-removal facilities are often omitted in grit-removal facilities.
Preaeration	Scum	In some plants, scum-removal facilities are not provided in preaeration tanks.
Primary sedimentation	Primary sludge and scum	The quantities of both sludge and scum depend on the nature of the collection system and whether industrial wastes are discharged to the system.
Aeration tank	Suspended solids	Suspended solids are produced from the conversion of biological oxygen demand (BOD). If wasting is from the aeration tank, flotation thickening is normally used to thicken the waste activated sludge.
Secondary sedimentation	Secondary sludge and scum	Provision for scum removal on secondary settling tanks is now a requirement of the U.S. Environmental Protection Agency.
Sludge-processing facilities	Sludge and ashes	The characteristics and moisture content of the sludge and ashes depend on the operations and processes that are used.

*After Metcalf & Eddy, Inc., G. Tchobanoglous, and F. Burton, *Wastewater Engineering: Treatment, Disposal, and Reuse*, 3d ed., McGraw-Hill, 1990.

ing, cans, rags, paper, rubber and plastic goods, and stringy material that could damage equipment or create problems in plant maintenance and operation. Fine screens, or microstrainers, may be employed at plant outfalls to prevent discharge of esthetically objectionable floating solid matter. Modern, self-cleaning, inclined, rotary-drum or centrifugal screens are being installed to augment or replace grit chambers and primary settling tanks.

Screening volume varies with type of waste flow, season, weather, degree of urban development, and screen opening. Increased use of mechanical cutters and shredding devices has reduced volume of removed screenings. Coarse screenings range from 1.0 to 4.0 $ft^3/10^6$ gal (7.5 to 30 $m^3/10^6$ m^3).

Scum. This is defined as the floating fraction of sewage solids, with specific gravity under 1.0, that, under quiescent conditions, rises to the surface of the wastewater. Primary tank skimmings contain oils, fats, soaps, rubber and plastic hygienic products, cigarette filter tips, paper, and similar materials.

Grit. Heavy suspended solids consisting of sand, cinders, coffee grounds, seeds, small metal objects, and other generally inorganic particles carried in wastewater inflow are collectively known as grit. The amount of grit varies with type of sewer, season, weather, intensity of runoff, condition of streets and sewers, and use of household garbage disposal units. In new, separate sanitary sewers, with proper street sweeping, grit volumes in sanitary sewage are generally less than 4 $ft^3/10^6$ gal (30 $m^3/10^6$ m^3).

Septage. This consists of partially digested material pumped from on-site sanitary wastewater disposal systems. It contains a mixture of grit, scum, and suspended solids, adding to treatment plant sludge. *SEE IMHOFF TANK; SEPTIC TANK.*

Sewage sludge. Sedimentation, subsidence, or clarification of suspended matter from turbid water by gravity occurs when the velocity of that liquid has been reduced below its transport capacity. Transport capacity is controlled by varying flow-through velocity, which causes differential hydraulic subsidence. Thus heavy inorganic solids, grit, can be settled in one chamber while light agglomerated organic particles, sludges, settle in others.

Sludge derives its name from the unit process from which it settles out. Primary sludge, or raw sludge, develops as solids in incoming wastewater settle hy-

draulically. Raw sludge, containing up to 5% solids by weight, is gray, greasy, viscous, unsightly, contains visible fecal solids, scraps of household wastes, and has a disagreeable odor. Use of household garbage grinders can increase primary sludge weight and volumes by 25–40%.

Chemical precipitation may be used to increase the removal of primary solids, to adjust pH for further treatment or to remove nutrients as phosphorus. Chemical dosage is high, producing large volumes of sludge.

Secondary treatment uses aerobic biota to enmesh, coagulate, oxidize, nitrify, and mineralize the unsettled colloidal and dissolved organic matter that remains after primary treatment. Aerobic processes such as trickling filters, rotating biologic disks, or activated sludge utilize microorganisms to reduce organic and nutrient matter, and form sludges of settled biologic floc, which are light tan to dark brown in color, spongy, generally uniform in texture and form, having an earthy odor with solids content up to 1.5% by weight. Anaerobic decomposition will cause these sludges to turn septic rapidly, become dark to black and develop malodorous gases. *SEE WATER TREATMENT.*

Sludge thickening. This process removes water, increases the concentration of solids, reduces weight and volume, and prepares sludges for further treatment and handling. Flotation uses fine air bubbles to entrain and carry solids to the surface for skimming. Gravity thickening allows self-compaction of accumulated sludge, while gentle stirring causes water to separate. Use of a centrifuge compresses sludge against a porous surface that retains solids but allows liquid to pass through. Supernatant, the liquid drawn off from a sludge, is turbid, contains fine solid particles, has a high organic content, is odorous, and is returned to the inflow for retreatment.

Stabilization. When microorganisms multiply rapidly, anoxically, on organic and volatile substances contained within sludges, putrefaction and offensive odors develop. Sludges are stabilized biologically, chemically, or thermally to make them less putrescible and odorous, reduce pathogenic content, reduce weight and volume, and prepare them for final disposal. When stabilized biologically, either aerobic or anaerobic microorganisms reduce organics, volatile matter, and nutrients by converting these to gases, water, and cell tissue. Use of chemicals kills microorganisms, causing biota cells to shrivel and coagulate, releasing and separating water. Thermal processes sterilize (pasteurize) the biota, causing cell destruction, coagulation, and release of water. Chemical and thermal processes generally do not change organic or nutrient levels.

Aerobic stabilization. This allows aerobic microorganisms, during prolonged periods of aeration, to oxidize organic matter within sludge to carbon dioxide, water, ammonia, and nitrates. A humuslike, relatively odor-free and biologically stable mass that has some useful soil conditioning values is developed in some 20 days of controlled operation. The aerobic stabilization process is relatively easy to operate, and it produces a fairly clear supernatant liquor. Drawbacks are high power costs, difficulty with final settling, dewatering, and drying of the sludge, and absence of produced methane gas as a useful by-product.

Anaerobic digestion. Digestion, the most common method of handling sludges in municipal plants, occurs in closed tanks. Anaerobic digestion comprises a series of complex, interrelated biochemical reactions, performed by groups of microorganisms functioning in the absence of free oxygen. Under controlled temperature and pH, the anaerobic microorganisms produce methane gas as they decompose the sludge to a drainable, relatively inert, humic mass.

The digestion process can be envisioned as occurring in discrete, independent steps. In the first stage, acid fermentation, pH drops rapidly as colloidal solids, lipids, dissolved carbonaceous matter and sugars are rapidly converted to organic acids, with evolution of carbon dioxide and hydrogen sulfide. In the second stage, acid regression, pH rises slowly as organic acids formed earlier, and some proteins, are digested to acetate and ammonia compounds. In the third stage, alkaline fermentation or alkaline digestion, proteins, organic acids, and amino compounds are attacked. The pH rises to around neutral (pH 7), with large volumes of gases, predominantly methane, produced. In a properly functioning anaerobic digester the raw sludge is changed from a putrescible mass with over 70% volatile solids and high water content to a more mineralized, easily draining and drying humic mass having an inoffensive tarry odor with less than 50% volatile solids.

The sizing of digestion tanks is a function of raw sludge volumes added, digestion and water separation rates, and the volume of digested sludge draw-off. Sludge digestion occurs at temperatures from 42 to 140°F (5.6 to 60°C), with increased temperatures increasing bacterial action and reducing digestion time. Digestion time is expressed by the days necessary to attain 90% of ultimate gas production (see **illus.**). Thickening sludge prior to its being fed into the digester reduces input sludge volumes, assists in maintaining tank operation at optimum digestion temperatures, and saves space and energy.

The presence of methane gas, as it forms and leaves the mixed sludge liquor, indicates organic stabilization. Gas production at optimum mesophilic temperatures is 12–18 ft³/lb (0.75–1.12 m³/kg) of volatile matter destroyed. Digester gas, 60–70% methane, has a heating value of 600–700 Btu/ft³ (22–26 kJ/m³). The digester gas is generally used at treatment plants as an economical fuel for powering engines and heating digester tanks.

Chemical stabilization. This method uses large dosages of chlorine or lime to render sludges unsuitable

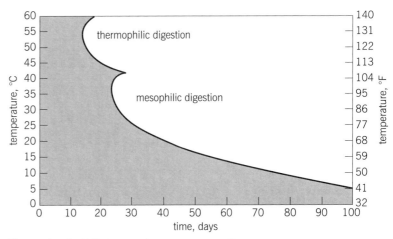

Time required for 90% digestion of sewage sludge at different temperatures. (*After K. Imhoff and G. M. Fair, Sewage Treatment, John Wiley & Sons, 1940, reprint 1946*)

for microorganisms to metabolize the organic substances, to grow or survive. The chemical stabilization process generates large volumes of sludge, often with problems of ultimate disposal.

Thermal processes. These use a variety of heating methods and sludge handling to destroy cell structure and reduce the quantity of moisture. The end solid is relatively dry, sterilized, generally free of offensive odors, and is frequently used as a soil amendment.

Disposal. Materials removed from the wastewater must be disposed of by ultimately returning them to the land, ocean, or atmosphere without damaging the receiving environment. Regulations have prohibited ocean dumping and strict air emission rules have reduced the use of thermal systems. Solids are generally disposed of in landfills, buried, composted, or recycled as soil amendments.

Screenings, after shredding, may be returned to inflow for retreatment or are buried or incinerated. Washed grit is buried or used as fill or cover within landfills.

Digested liquid sludges may, in isolated areas, be spread or plowed under fields, but this is not a generally accepted practice. Wastewater solids may contain pathogenic organisms, but more importantly, higher concentrations of initial pollutants than were in the original wastewater. Disposal of removed solids must neither adversely affect the food chain nor endanger the environment. *SEE FOOD WEB.*

Digested sludge as withdrawn is semiliquid; therefore, for ease of handling, storing, transporting, or landfilling and for increased efficiency in further thermal processing, it must be dewatered or dried. Where adequate area exists, open drying beds can be employed to reduce water content; otherwise centrifuges, belt presses, vacuum filters, thermal or other processes are used. When added to soil, the dried humuslike digested sludge increases the water-holding capacity of the soil, improves texture and tilth, reduces erosion, and provides some nutrient benefit. Digested sludge, an incomplete fertilizer, requires additions of nitrogen, phosphorus, potassium, and even trace elements.

Composting, a natural thermophilic biological process, further reduces pathogens and volatile solids in digested sludge, forming a stable humuslike soil-conditioning material that can be recycled.

Heat drying uses external energy and reduced pressure to reduce moisture content to under 12%. Since drying by heat pasteurizes (sterilizes) the sludge and stops further bacterial action, dried digested sludges can easily be processed mechanically, stored, handled, and applied to land.

Thermal processes, including wet oxidation, pyrolysis, and incineration, require sludges with high content of organic solids that can produce significant heat value. Prestabilization of the sludge with reduction in volatile sludge content is not usually employed. In wet oxidation sludge is mixed with compressed air under high heat to oxidize organic matter. Pyrolysis, a thermal cracking process, converts sludge in reduced oxygen atmospheres to gases, water, and char. In both wet oxidation and pyrolysis, withdrawn supernatant liquors are characterized by high biochemical oxygen demand and solids and are retreated. Incineration is complete combustion and, as practiced in large plants, provides a reduction in volume. Environmental considerations require that air pollution standards be met. Residual ash is usually disposed of in landfills. See Air pollution; Hazardous waste; Sewage; Sewage disposal; Sewage treatment.

Gerald Palevsky

Bibliography. Environmental Protection Agency, *Sludge Treatment and Disposal*, Process Des. Man. EPA 625/1-79-011, Center for Environmental Research Information, Cincinnati, 1979; A. F. Gaudy, Jr., and E. T. Gaudy, *Microbiology for Environmental Scientists and Engineers*, 1980; J. G. Henry and G. W. Heinke, *Environmental Science and Engineering*, 1989; Metcalf & Eddy, Inc., G. Tchobanoglous, and F. Burton, *Wastewater Engineering: Treatment, Disposal, and Reuse*, 3d ed., 1990; H. S. Peavy, D. R. Rowe, and G. Tchobanoglous, *Environmental Engineering*, 1985; T. D. Reynolds, *Unit Operations and Processes in Environmental Engineering*, 1982; P. A. Vesilind, *Treatment and Disposal of Wastewater Sludges*, rev. ed., 1979.

Sewage treatment

Unit processes used to separate, modify, remove, and destroy objectionable, hazardous, and pathogenic substances carried by wastewater in solution or suspension in order to render the water fit and safe for intended uses. Treatment removes unwanted constituents without affecting or altering the water molecules themselves, so that wastewater containing contaminants can be converted to safe drinking water. Stringent water quality and effluent standards have been developed that require reduction of suspended solids (turbidity), biochemical oxygen demand (related to degradable organics), and coliform organisms (indicators of fecal pollution); control of pH as well as the concentration of certain organic chemicals and heavy metals; and use of bioassays to guarantee safety of treated discharges to the environment.

In all cases, the impurities, contaminants, and solids removed from all wastewater treatment processes must ultimately be collected, handled, and disposed of safely, without damage to humans or the environment.

Treatment processes are chosen on the basis of composition, characteristics, and concentration of materials present in solution or suspension. The processes are classified as pretreatment, preliminary, primary, secondary, or tertiary treatment, depending on type, sequence, and method of removal of the harmful and unacceptable constituents. Pretreatment processes equalize flows and loadings, and precondition wastewaters to neutralize or remove toxics and industrial wastes that could adversely affect sewers or inhibit operations of publicly owned treatment works. Preliminary treatment processes are employed to protect plant mechanical equipment; remove extraneous matter such as grit, trash, and debris; reduce odors; and render incoming sewage more amenable to subsequent treatment and handling. Primary treatment employs mechanical and physical unit processes to separate and remove floatables and suspended solids and to prepare wastewater for biological treatment. Secondary treatment utilizes aerobic microorganisms in biological reactors to feed on dissolved and colloidal organic matter. As these microorganisms reduce biochemical oxygen demand and turbidity (suspended solids), they grow, multiply, and form an organic floc, which must be captured and removed in final settling tanks (**Fig. 1**). Tertiary treatment, or advanced treatment, removes specific residual substances, trace organic materials, nutrients, and other constituents that are not removed by biological processes.

On-site sewage treatment for individual homes or small institutions uses septic tanks, which provide separation of solids in a closed, buried unit. Effluent is discharged to subsurface absorption systems. See Imhoff tank; Septic tank; Stream pollution; Water treatment.

Pretreatment. Wastewater, depending on its source, varies in quantity, strength, and composition. Pretreatment, particularly of sewage containing industrial wastes, neutralizes, alters, or removes nonbiologically degradable, toxic, hazardous, and highly corrosive materials before they enter the municipal sewer system. Chemical neutralization brings pH values to the range 6.0–8.0 and provides buffering capacity. Coagulation, flotation, and surface skimming of oils, greases, or other light constituents are enhanced by adding air or chlorine.

In the equalization process, widely varying flows are stored and then discharged more uniformly over longer time periods. Mixing and storing different flow streams neutralizes, dilutes, and dampens both quantities and concentrations, reducing shock loads on receiving systems. Equalization tanks are aerated to mix the sewage, inhibit septicity, increase gas exchange, and prevent sedimentation.

Preliminary treatment. Wastewaters contain sand, cinders, ceramic shards, glass, and other granular inorganic matter that is abrasive, causes wear on pumps and equipment, clogs lines, and occupies tank space. By controlling velocities in grit chambers (**Fig. 2**) at about 1 ft/s (0.3 m/s), dense granular matter [larger than 0.008 in. (0.2 mm)] settles, while materials with low specific gravity remain in suspension within the flow. Settled solids, being removed from the bottom by grit elevators or detritors, are agitated within the incoming flow. Agitation abrades and separates clinging organic matter from the inert solids, and the flowing water carries these removed putrescible substances away, leaving a washed grit that is ready for landfill disposal. See Sewage solids.

Unwanted materials like plastic objects, throwaway sanitary hygiene products, diapers, and towels, and items ranging from string to bed sheets or toothpicks to tree limbs become part of the sewage flow. Screens are provided to protect equipment from impact damage, from stringy material winding around and foul-

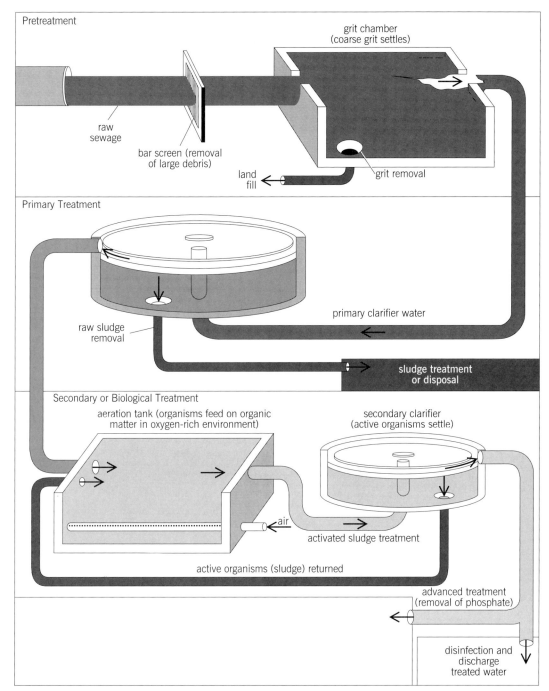

Fig. 1. Schematic diagram of liquid wastewater treatment through the secondary process. (*After B. J. Nebel, Environmental Science: The Way the World Works, 2d ed., Prentice-Hall, 1981*)

ing rotating shafts, or from plastics and rags that clog valves. Bar racks and screens remove such large solids and flotables. Bar racks composed of rigid parallel bars, spaced 0.5–3 in. (12.5–75 mm) apart, held in place by support cross members, are installed within a controlled flow channel to catch this debris. Large, coarse material that is carried in the wastewater impacts the bar rack and is retained on the upstream face, from which it is mechanically removed and collected by traveling rakes.

Screens are formed of wire mesh, screen cloth, or perforated plates, with openings 0.5 in. (12.5 mm) or less. Coarse screens, with openings greater than 0.2 in. (5 mm) are used as pretreatment. Medium screens, 0.01–0.06 in. (0.8–1.5 mm), may be used in lieu of primary treatment. Fine screens, up to 0.003 in. (0.075 mm) openings, are used as final screening before plant discharge.

Disk, drum, band, and other styles of preliminary treatment screens are movable, with only a portion rotating within the flow. As the screen rotates, clean surfaces enter the wastewater, and previously immersed areas are lifted out and cleaned of solids caught on the surface.

Removal, handling, and disposal of screenings from bar racks and coarse screens are generally difficult maintenance problems, with associated odors and esthetically unpleasant conditions. To deal with this situation and to develop a smaller, more uniform sized solid, comminution (shredding) devices are

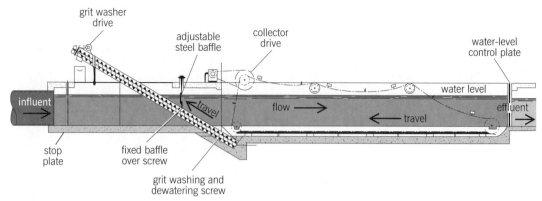

Fig. 2. Diagram showing components of a grit chamber. (*After Joint Committee of Water Pollution Control Federation and American Society of Civil Engineers, Wastewater Treatment Plant Design, MOP 8, 1977*)

used. Solids, trapped and held by the force and flow of liquid on a slotted plate or bars, are cut up or shredded by moving cutters or teeth. The solids, reduced in size, pass through the openings and are carried downstream to further treatment.

Primary treatment. Primary sedimentation, or clarification, is the first process where removal of substantial quantities of suspended solids and materials causing biochemical oxygen demand in wastewater flow occurs. Sedimentation tanks, rectangular or circular, operate on a continuous flow-through basis, yet they maintain relative quiescence to permit suspended solids to settle if the specific gravity is greater than that of water, or to float if the specific gravity is less. Mechanical devices remove the accumulated suspended solids (sludge) from the tank bottom, while floatable materials (skimmings) are taken off the surface. The clarified liquor, known as primary effluent, is discharged over the tank's effluent weirs.

Discrete particles of uniform size, shape, and specific gravity settle according to Stokes' law. Theoretically, if the velocity of a downward-settling particle is greater than the horizontal velocity of the carrying liquid, the particle will be captured and retained within the sedimentation tank. However, empirical values are used because sewage solids vary in shape, size, specific gravity, and concentration, and because the rate and path of settling are affected by temperature, age, density, and wind currents as well as eddies developed by mechanical scrapers and turbulence at influent and outlet structures.

Removal of suspended solids and biochemical oxygen demand is based on surface overflow rate and detention time. The surface overflow rate is expressed in gal/ft^2 (m^3/m^2) of tank surface area per day. Detention time varies from 30 min for minimal removal prior to some types of biological treatment, to 60–90 min (typical values within conventional plants), and longer times if chemical coagulation or nutrient removal is employed (**Fig. 3**).

A solids contact clarifier diverts the incoming wastewater through a layer or blanket of previously settled solids. Suspended solids within incoming sewage contacts the sludge blanket, is agglomerated, and remains trapped within the sludge blanket as the liquid rises and overflows the outlet weirs (**Fig. 4***a*). Although efficient for chemical and special suspensions, and frequently used in water treatment, solids contact clarifiers are used infrequently for biological floc, because extended detention times, particularly when it is warm, leads to septicity, gasification, and odors.

Based on discrete particles, removal of suspended solids is related to available surface area and is independent of tank depth. The use of inclined tubes or plates (lamella) within sedimentation tanks increases the theoretical tank surface area and reduces both the settling time of the particles and the depth at which they come to rest. With highly inclined plates or tubes, there is increased settling efficiency, and solids contact benefits may also be derived, but some problems with biological decomposition remain (Fig. 4*b* and *c*).

Use of chemicals such as lime, alum, chlorine, clays, or polyelectrolytes increases removal of suspended solids from wastewater. These systems produce more sludge and impact on subsequent handling of solids. The added costs for chemicals, feeders, and handling of solids make the use of chemicals less attractive.

Various configurations are employed to reduce velocities at inlet and outlet structures and prevent adverse mixing, currents, short circuiting, or scour. Weir overflow rates are limited to 15,000 gal per day per lineal foot of weir face (186 m^3/m · d).

Static or inclined self-cleaning screens, centrifugal screens, and rotary-drum screens are being used to upgrade overloaded primary units and to replace preliminary and primary units. Removal of suspended solids and biochemical oxygen demand by screens is generally not as complete as by conventional units, but overall costs are lower. Subsequent plant units must be sized to compensate for these differences in removal.

Secondary treatment. Biological organisms, predominantly aerobic bacteria, convert and metabolize dissolved and colloidal matter remaining in wastewater to new cellular material, carbon dioxide, and water. These biological processes use organisms that form either a fixed film (attached growth) or are motile (suspended growth); they convert degradable organics to different, larger forms without significantly reducing total biochemical oxygen demand. Safe discharge to the environment and compliance with effluent standards require that the biota and newly formed cellular material be removed. This is accomplished by provision of secondary settling tanks that function as an integral part of the biological process.

Given adequate detention time, dissolved oxygen, controlled pH, appropriate temperature, absence of any toxic materials or shock loads, these biological processes can reduce biochemical oxygen demand to under 15 mg/liter and suspended solids to under 20 mg/liter. Not all wastewater organics can be fully or adequately degraded in the time available and under

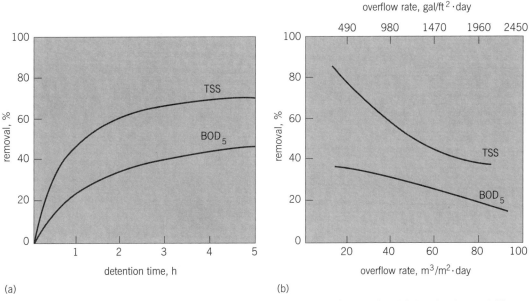

Fig. 3. Removal of suspended solids and biochemical oxygen demand in primary clarifiers at various (a) detention times and (b) overflow rates. (*After S. R. Qasim, Wastewater Treatment Plants, Planning, Design and Operation, CBS College Publishing, Holt, Rinehart and Winston, 1985*)

the constraints found in publicly owned systems.

Fixed-film systems. Trickling filters (**Fig. 5**) contain beds of inert materials, with large surfaces and voids, that support a slime growth. This growth, or attached zoogloeal mass, is composed of algae, fungi, protozoa, rotifera, nematoda, and, most importantly, aerobic bacteria. Wastewater is applied to the surface of a trickling filter having varying depths and made up of volumes of rock, slag, or synthetically formed shapes. The organic materials in this intermittently applied wastewater, flowing over and through the aerobic gelatinous matrix adhering to the support surfaces, undergo biologic coagulation, precipitation, oxidation, and clarification as the flow moves downward to the underdrains. Organisms, in the presence of oxygen, convert the organic substances by various physical, chemical, and enzymatic processes to energy for life, growth, and replication, while giving up carbon dioxide, nitrates, and sulfates to the passing liquid stream.

This reactive zoogloeal mass converts organic matter and trapped particles to a humic mass as long as there is adequate oxygen transfer. If the film becomes too thick, or otherwise so impacted or compacted that oxygen cannot diffuse, portions become anoxic, and the film loses its capability to adhere to the support surface. Applied wastewater physically scours away nonattached portions, rejuvenating the filter by exposing areas for new colonization. Dislodged humic mass, known as the slough-off, is washed through the filter's large voids and conveyed through the underdrains to the secondary settling tank for ultimate capture and disposal.

Trickling filters are classified according to hydraulic and organic loadings and recirculation as standard or low-rate, intermediate, high-rate, and roughing filters. Two-stage operation, the placing of two filters in series, is used for high organic loads. Rotating biological contractors (**Fig. 6**), also known as biodisks, use closely spaced plastic disks on which an aerobic zoogloeal mass grows, mounted on a rotating shaft. The rotating disks, with approximately 40% of their area continually immersed in the tank carrying the wastewater, are intermittently exposed to organics

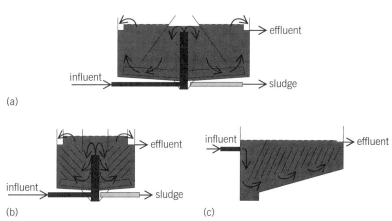

Fig. 4. Diagrams showing solids contact and inclined lamella settlers. (a) Circular settling tank using solids contact with sludge blanket. (b) Inclined lamella within a circular settling tank. (c) Inclined lamella within a rectangular sedimentation tank. (*After S. R. Qasim, Wastewater Treatment Plants, Planning, Design and Operation, CBS College Publishing, Holt, Rinehart and Winston, 1985*)

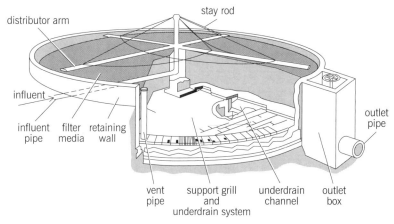

Fig. 5. Diagram of the components of a typical trickling filter. (*After Water Pollution Control Federation, Operation of Wastewater Treatment Plants, MOP 11, 1976*)

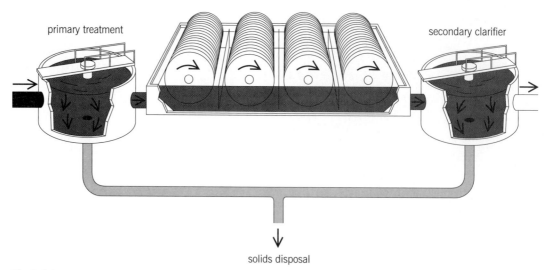

primary treatment

secondary clarifier

solids disposal

Fig. 6. Schematic diagram of a rotating biological contactor. (*After Water Pollution Control Federation, Operation of Wastewater Treatment Plants, MOP 11, 1976*)

and air as they rotate. The relative motion between the rotating disk and the wastewater in the tank scours the attached film. Wastewater throughput carries the slough-off to the secondary settling tank.

Because daily wastewater flows into a publicly owned treatment works are highly variable both in amount of flow and in organic loading, they cause fluctuations in the liquid applications to the trickling filters. Rapid swings in biological density within the attached matrix develop, reducing efficiency. To provide flow and loading uniformity, a portion of the wastewater is recirculated after passing through the filter. This recirculation maintains continuous growth and sloughing, improves operation, increases efficiency, and reduces bed volume. Recirculation rate is the ratio of recycle flow to average daily plant inflow.

Total liquid flow, generally applied through rotating arms over the surface of the bed, intermittently doses each portion and is known as the hydraulic application rate. The average daily dry weight of new organic matter applied to the total bed volume is the organic loading rate. Typical application rates and design data are shown in **Table 1**.

Activated sludge. This is an aerobic suspended-growth process (**Fig. 7**) in which biodegradable organics in wastewater are intimately mixed with a concentrated mass of biota and oxygen within an aeration tank. New microorganisms grow and flocculate as the biotic mass adsorbs, oxidizes, and reduces the organic wastes. As the mixed liquor leaves the aeration tank following several hours of aeration, the biotic mass with the newly formed floc is separated within final settling tanks. A portion of the settled floc, the activated sludge, is returned to the aeration tank to maintain the required concentration of biota, while excess sludge is removed for solids handling and ultimate disposal. Air, required for utilization of dissolved oxygen in metabolism and respiration, is also provided to maintain mixing and prevent sedimentation in the aeration tank.

Modifications of the activated-sludge process relate to how, where, when, and for how long returned activated sludge and oxygen is introduced into the aeration tank and maintained in contact with the mixed liquor. These modifications of conventional activated sludge are known as tapered aeration, step aeration,

Table 1. Typical design information for trickling filters

Parameter	Low-rate filter	Intermediate	High-rate	Roughing
Hydraulic loading (10^6 gal · day)/acre [$m^3/m^2 · d$]	1–4 [1–4]	4–10 [4–10]	10–40 [10–40]	40–200 [40–200]
Organic loading, lb/(10^3 ft^3 · d) [kg/(m^3 · d)]	5–25 [0.08–0.40]	15–30 [0.24–0.48]	25–300 [0.40–4.8]	100+ [1.6+]
Depth, ft (m)	6–8 (1.8–2.4)	5–8 (1.5–2.4)	3–7 (1–2)	6–40 (2–12)
Recirculation ratio (R/I)*	0	0–1	1–3	1–4
Filter media	Rock, slag, etc.	Rock, slag, etc.	Rock, synthetic	Redwood, synthetic
Sloughing	Intermittent	Intermittent	Continuous	Continuous
Filter flies (*Psychoda*)	Many	Some	Few; larvae washed out	Few to none
Dosing intervals	Not more than at 5-min intervals	Continuous up to 60 s maximum	Continuous 10 to 15 s	Continuous
Effluent quality	Usually fully nitrified	Partially nitrified	Limited nitrification	Generally none
BOD removal, %	80–85	50–70	65–80	40–65

*Ratio of return flow from secondary setting tank (R) to average daily inflow (I).
SOURCE: Water Pollution Control Federation, *Operation of Wastewater Treatment Plants*, MOP 11, 1976, and Metcalf & Eddy, Inc., and G. Tchobanoglous, *Wastewater Engineering: Treatment Disposal, and Reuse*, 2d ed., McGraw-Hill, 1979.

extended aeration, contact stabilization, complete mix, and pure oxygen. Mechanical or compressed air systems are used to introduce and maintain dissolved oxygen and mixing. Mechanical systems entrain atmospheric air through brushes, impellers, propellers, or turbines, while compressed air is introduced near the tank bottom through porous diffuser plates, spirally wound tubes, spargers, nozzles, or injection jets (**Fig. 8**).

Depending upon the process used, parameters such as empirical ratios of biodegradable organics (food) to concentration of microorganisms, aeration contact time, concentration of solids in the mixed liquor, and loading criteria for aeration tanks are established to achieve the desired degree of reduction of biochemical oxygen demand. Suspended growth systems, with relatively short detention times, are more sensitive to hydraulic, organic, and toxic shock loads and require greater operational skill and monitoring than fixed-film processes. However, suspended-growth systems occupy much less space and can produce effluents with lower soluble biochemical oxygen demand and suspended solids (**Table 2**).

For the suspended-growth system to operate optimally, the solids in the mixed liquor leaving the aeration tank must be completely separated, settled, and returned to the aeration tank quickly. Final settling tanks, similar in general configurations to primary tanks, generally have lower values of surface overflow rate and are deeper, since both separation and sludge densification of the light, fluffy biofloc must be accomplished.

For industrial wastes and small plants, aerated lagoons, oxidation ponds, and waste-stabilization lagoons are employed for secondary treatment or for final polishing after conventional treatment. Oxidation ponds, with large surface areas, depths less than 5 ft (1.5 m), with loading rates not to exceed 50 lb/acre (56 kg/ha) of biochemical oxygen demand, rely on natural reaeration, diffusion, and photosynthesis. Bacterial and algal actions reduce putrescible organics, converting them to stable algal cells. Although some solids settle and undergo anaerobic decomposition, oxidation ponds can support fish life. Evaporation, screened or filtered settled outflow, maintains liquid levels.

Aerated lagoons are facilities that are intermediate

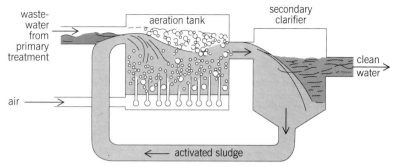

Fig. 7. Schematic diagram of activated sludge treatment. (*After B. J. Nebel, Environmental Science: The Way the World Works, 2d ed., Prentice-Hall, 1981*)

between oxidation ponds and activated sludge, since no sludge is recycled. They are frequently used to pretreat sewage with high organic loads or industrial wastewaters prior to discharge to publicly owned treatment works. Basins are 8–18 ft (2.4–5.5 m) deep, and complete mixing is carried out by using mechanical devices, with detention times of several days. Some solids may settle and undergo anaerobic decomposition. When used as secondary treatment, basins are frequently followed by facultative lagoons, where liquid is retained for up to 20 or more days. The upper portion of a facultative lagoon is maintained aerobic, while the bottom, benthic zone, where solids accumulate, undergoes anaerobic decomposition. Released gases, rising particles, and bacteria are enmeshed, absorbed, destroyed, and converted to algal cells in the upper portion. Effluent may be subject to final mechanical screening, although frequently the effluent evaporates, percolates, or is used for land applications.

Final polishing. Rotating-drum microscreens, with stainless steel or plastic cloth having openings 30 micrometers in diameter, remove solids carried over from biological treatment and provide an effluent that is relatively free of turbidity. Filters are used for polishing of the final effluent as well as for removal of chemical precipitates from advanced treatment systems. Filtration, which is a complex process of screening, adsorption, and sedimentation, is defined and classified by the media, physical force, or application method employed. Flow may be induced by

Table 2. Common design parameters for activated sludge systems

Process modification	Sludge retention time (θ_c), d	F/M,[a] d^{-1}	Aerator loading,[b] kg/m^3·d	MLSS,[c] mg/liter	Aeration[d] period, h	Recirculation ratio (Q_r/Q)
Conventional	5–15	0.2–0.4	0.3–0.6	1500–3000	4–8	0.25–0.5
Tapered aeration	5–15	0.2–0.4	0.3–0.6	1500–3000	4–8	0.25–0.5
Step aeration	5–15	0.2–0.4	0.6–1.0	2000–3500	3–5	0.25–0.75
Complete mix aeration	5–15	0.2–0.6	0.8–2.0	3000–6000	3–5	0.25–1.00
Extended aeration	20–30	0.05–0.15	0.1–0.4	3000–6000	18–36	0.5–2.0
Contact stabilization	5–15	0.2–0.6	1.0–1.2	1000–4000[e] 4000–10000[f]	0.5–1.0[e] 3.0–6.0[f]	0.5–1.0
Pure oxygen	8–20	0.25–1.0	1.6–3.3	6000–8000	2–5	0.25–0.5

[a]The F/M (ratio of food to microorganisms) is kilograms of BOD$_5$ applied per day per kilogram of MLVSS in the aeration basin [lb BOD$_5$/(lb MLVSS · d)]. BOD$_5$ = measure of strength of waste in milligrams per liter. MLSS = mixed-liquor suspended solids in milligrams per liter. MLVSS = mixed-liquor volatile suspended solids, that is, that portion of the solids in the aeration tank that are organic and hence biodegradable. Q_r/Q = ratio of return sludge to average daily plant inflow.
[b]Aerator loading is kilograms of BOD$_5$ applied per day per cubic meter of aeration tank capacity [lb/(10^3 ft^3 · d)].
[c]Generally the ratio of MLVSS to MLSS is 0.75–0.85.
[d]Aeration period is the time in hours that the mixed liquor is in the aeration tank.
[e]Contact tank.
[f]Reaeration or stabilization tank.

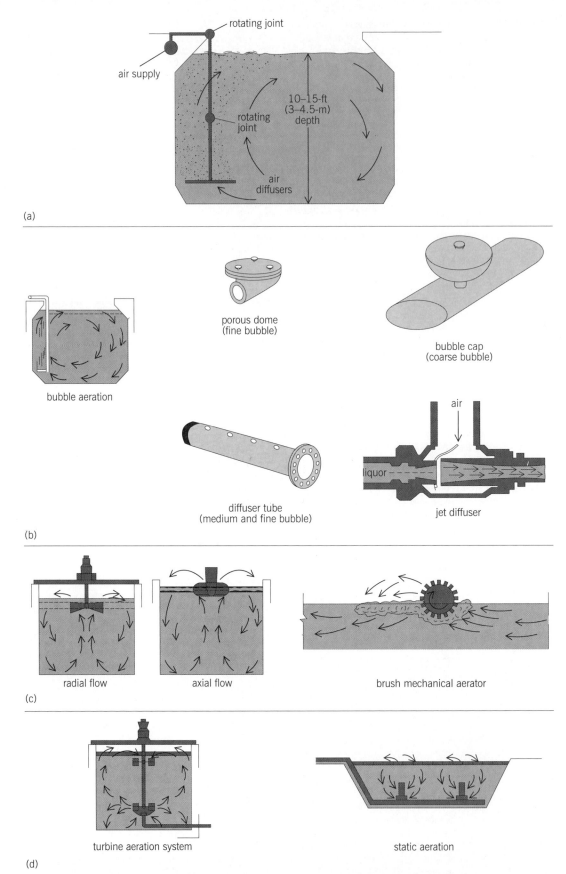

Fig. 8. Aeration systems and devices. (a) Cross section of a typical spiral-flow aeration tank showing the spiral-flow pattern created by aeration along one side (*after W. Viessman, Jr., and M. J. Hammer, Water Supply and Pollution Control, 4th ed., Harper and Row, 1985*). (b) Diffused aeration units, (c) surface aeration systems, (d) below-surface air release (*after W. W. Eckenfelder, Jr., Industrial Water Pollution Control, McGraw-Hill, 1989*).

gravity, pressure, or vacuum; may be applied intermittently or continuously; and may be upflow, downward, or across sand, mixed media, granular carbon, membranes, or diatomaceous earth. Cleaning of filters, usually by backwashing, results in a new wastewater that must be captured, handled, and ultimately disposed of.

Disinfection. This process differs from sterilization in that it kills pathogenic organisms by physical or chemical means without total destruction of all the organisms present. Disinfecting agents should, at low concentrations, be highly selective and toxic to targeted pathogens. They must be stable, noncorrosive, economical, safe to humans and the environment, unaffected by pH or temperature, and long-lasting. None of the available agents or processes meets all or even most of these criteria. Disinfecting agents such as heat, phenols, alcohols, strong acids or alkalies, and halogens cause coagulation and denaturing of cell protein. Soaps and detergents injure cell membranes, change surface tension, or affect permeability. Oxidizing agents such as halogens, hydrogen peroxide, ozone, and heavy metals inhibit or denature enzymes and remove the free sulfhydryl (—SH) group. Direct sunlight, ultraviolet rays, or ionizing radiation destroys pathogens. Thermal processes and moist heat cause protein coagulation. Even though there are some problems with chlorine, it remains the agent most frequently used for wastewater disinfection, since it is relatively inexpensive, readily applied and controlled, and can be monitored by a simple and quick test. *See* Environmental engineering.

Advanced wastewater treatment. This is a treatment process (tertiary or polishing) that goes beyond the biological stage. Advanced wastewater treatment produces high-quality effluent, with reduced targeted toxic chemicals, nutrients, and trace organics. Such systems are a step in the cycle of transforming sewage to drinking water; they are closely related to processes that are used for industrial water treatment and for providing safe drinking water. Most advanced wastewater treatment systems include denitrification and ammonia stripping, carbon adsorption of trace organics, and chemical precipitation.

Nutrient removal of phosphorus and nitrogen is possible by chemical coagulation using lime or by biologic methods. The latter utilize systems having aerobic, anaerobic, and anoxic sequences to nitrify and then dentrify wastewaters. Ammonia can be removed by air stripping, breakpoint chlorination, or ion exchange. Carbon absorption traps refractory organics onto exposed carbon surfaces. Liquid can be passed over carbon in packed columns, or powdered carbon can be added to treated liquid and then filtered out on diatomaceous earth filters, on microstrainers, or by ultrafiltration. Evaporation, distillation, electrodialysis, ultrafiltration, reverse osmosis, freeze drying, freeze-thaw, flotation, and land application are being studied as methods for advanced wastewater treatment to improve the quality of discharged effluents. *See* Sewage; Sewage disposal.

Gerald Palevsky

Bibliography. Joint Committee of the Water Pollution Control Federation and the American Society of Civil Engineers, *Wastewater Treatment Plant Design*, MOP 8, 1977; Metcalf & Eddy, Inc., G. Tchobanoglous, and F. Burton, *Wastewater Engineering: Treatment, Disposal, and Reuse*, 3d ed., 1990; S. R. Qasim, *Wastewater Treatment Plants, Planning, Design and Operations*, 1985; A. M. Thayer, Water treatment chemicals: Tighter rules drive demand, *Chem. Eng. News*, 68(13):17–34, 1990; W. Viessman and M. J. Hammer, *Water Supply and Pollution Control*, 4th ed., 1985; Water Pollution Control Federation, *Operation of Wastewater Treatment Plants*, MOP 11, 1976.

Smog

A mixture of smoke and fog. An analogous term, smaze, means smoke plus haze. Early in the twentieth century the term smog was applied to the pollution cloud that periodically covered London and other parts of the British Isles during the cold season, when both industry and home heating with bituminous coal were producing large quantities of soot, sulfur oxides, and tarry distillates. With high humidities and low winds this mixture led to the formation of extremely stable fogs that sometimes persisted for days. An episode in early December 1952 caused some 4000 excess deaths in London, virtually paralyzed the city because of low visibility, and forced the destruction of a number of prize cattle. This was not a unique episode; it is merely the best documented.

The area around Los Angeles, California, was experiencing a different phenomenon. Frequently dated from the start-up of a World War II butadiene plant, the condition would have occurred in any case. Unlike the London smog, it was characterized by only moderate loss of visibility but intense eye irritation, characteristic damage to vegetation, and rapid deterioration of rubber goods. The initial assumption, however, was that the condition reflected emissions similar to those occurring in London but modified by the drier climate of Los Angeles. It was later demonstrated that the smog in California stemmed not from smoke, moisture, and sulfur dioxide but from the hydrocarbons and nitrogen oxides that occur in auto exhaust and other emissions reacting in the presence of sunlight. To distinguish from the London variety, the phenomenon was called Los Angeles smog; later, when its true ubiquity became apparent, it become known as photochemical smog. In fact, the presence of the basic components of the London smog sufficiently attenuated sunlight to prevent, or at least minimize, the formation of photochemical smog.

The natural processes of the soil and the biosphere have always caused the introduction of large quantities of contaminants into the atmosphere, and processes have evolved to remove them. Most naturally occurring contaminants, such as hydrocarbons from growing plants and nitrogen oxides from soil denitrification, have low concentrations, even though on a global basis their total quantities are enormous—of the order of tens to hundreds of teragrams (millions of metric tons). Geological processes such as volcanism can produce even higher concentrations. To varying degrees, smog in either of its manifestations represents these atmospheric cleaning mechanisms in a state of overload. *See* Atmosphere.

Mechanisms. The most important component of the atmosphere, so far as the removal of trace contaminants is concerned, is the hydroxyl radical (OH), a free radical. In the unpolluted atmosphere, this is formed primarily by the near-ultraviolet photolysis of the traces of stratospheric ozone (O_3) that inevitably leak into the troposphere [reaction (1)]. The result is

$$O_3 + h\nu \rightarrow O_2 + O^* \qquad (1)$$

an oxygen molecule (O_2) and an atom of electronically excited (singlet) oxygen (O^*). The latter then reacts with water vapor (H_2O), as shown in reaction (2).

$$O^* + H_2O \rightarrow 2OH \qquad (2)$$

In addition to its stratospheric source, ozone is formed in the troposphere by the photolysis of nitrogen dioxide (NO_2), but a reaction series rapidly brings the ozone to a steady state in the absence of other species, as in reactions (3)–(5), where M indicates a

$$NO_2 + h\nu \rightarrow NO + O \qquad (3)$$
$$O + O_2 + M \rightarrow O_3 + M \qquad (4)$$
$$NO + O_3 \rightarrow NO_2 + O_2 \qquad (5)$$

third body, usually nitrogen or oxygen.

The presence of other reactive species, however, disturbs the steady state, ultimately resulting in enhanced ozone concentrations, as shown in reactions (6)–(11), where CO is carbon monoxide, H is hydro-

$$CO + OH \rightarrow CO_2 + H \qquad (6)$$

$$H + O_2 + M \rightarrow HO_2 + M \qquad (7)$$

$$HO_2 + NO \rightarrow OH + NO_2 \qquad (8)$$

$$RH + OH \rightarrow R + H_2O \qquad (9)$$

$$R + O_2 + M \rightarrow RO_2 + M \qquad (10)$$

$$RO_2 + NO \rightarrow RO + NO_2 \qquad (11)$$

gen, R is an organic radical, and M is any other molecule that collides with the reacting complex and carries off the energy of the reaction.

The nitrogen dioxide regenerated in these reactions thus reenters the photolytic cycle, and ozone is driven to higher concentrations through reactions (3)–(5). *See Atmospheric ozone.*

In addition to augmented ozone concentrations, an assortment of free radicals are produced. Together with the ozone, these attack organic species, resulting in a cascade of aldehydes, ketones, carboxylic acids, peroxides, and other oxygenated compounds. These processes decrease the size of the organic molecules until the molecules are ultimately converted into carbon dioxide. Similarly, interaction with the nitrogen oxides results in nitro compounds and organic nitrates and nitrites. Of special note are a series of mixed anhydrides of peroxyacids and nitric acid (RCO_2ONO_2), the peroxyacyl nitrates (PANs), which are potent lacrimators and phytotoxic agents. Hydrogen peroxide is also formed.

The hydroxyl radical is a major atmospheric scavenger. In addition to its reactions noted above, it is also primarily responsible for the conversion of sulfur dioxide to sulfuric acid and of nitrogen dioxide to nitric acid, at least by homogeneous reaction (a reaction that occurs within a single phase). In the presence of liquid water (for example, cloud or fog droplets), the high solubility of hydrogen peroxide in water concentrates that species in the aqueous phase, and hetero-

geneous oxidation (a reaction that takes place across a phase boundary) leads to rapid conversion of sulfur dioxide to sulfuric acid, essentially limited only by the rate of solution of the sulfur dioxide from the gaseous phase. The much lower solubility of nitrogen dioxide makes its heterogeneous oxidation far less important. Nitric acid, by contrast, is far more soluble in water, and is a prominent acidifying component of clouds and fogs, as are the carboxylic acids formed in the oxidation of organic compounds. Dienes and alicyclic compounds, among others, cleave to yield difunctional species of sufficiently low vapor pressure to form aerosols, as does sulfuric acid. *See Atmospheric chemistry.*

Meteorology. Air pollution of any kind, other than dust storms, is increased by an increase in the strength of the pollutant sources and by a decrease in the ventilation. In most cases the latter effect predominates, at least in the short run, since adding enough population or industry to double the emissions into the atmosphere takes years in most cases, while the rate of air exchange over a city can change by a factor of 2 or more in minutes to hours. Obviously, the worst situation arises with calm winds, which minimize horizontal air exchange, and a stable atmosphere or temperature inversion, which suppresses vertical mixing. Some cities are partially or completely surrounded by mountains, further restricting air movement. In such circumstances, pollution can become very serious. All of these conditions have been present to some degree in the major smog episodes. *See Temperature inversion.*

Effects. The one effect common to both the London and the Los Angeles types of smog is loss of visibility. In London in 1952 the visibility was effectively zero through the mixture of dense fog and airborne soot. Visibility through photochemical smog is invariably far greater, of the order of a kilometer or more, but it is nevertheless poor enough to be evident. In addition, while the London smog consisted primarily of large droplets of impure water and hence tended to be gray in color, photochemical smog particles are far smaller, with diameters comparable to the wavelength of visible light, resulting in colors ranging from blue to brown, depending on the angle of illumination.

The London smog caused many deaths. While it has not been possible to make a synthetic mixture that duplicates its effects, the evidence suggests that the toxic agents were some rather simple chemicals, such as sulfur dioxide, sulfuric acid, and soot, the last serving to soak up the sulfur dioxide and the sulfuric acid and deliver these compounds deep into the respiratory tract. This proved stressful enough to cause death or serious heart damage in people with cardiorespiratory problems.

On the other hand, there have been no claims of acute episodes of increased mortality from photochemical smog. Its primary impact is on the eyes, leading to lacrimation and irritation. The active substances seem to be organic compounds, including formaldehyde, acrolein, and the peroxyacyl nitrates. On a more chronic basis, the elevated ozone levels are suspected of injuring the surfaces of the lungs, thereby decreasing oxygen exchange. On a still longer-term basis, virtually all air pollution contains tarry combustion products, whether from industry, power generation, or vehicles, that are suspected of playing a role in the induction of cancer.

Both varieties of smog are to some degree toxic to plant life. In 1661 the British diarist J. Evelyn wrote that fruit trees in London rarely bore blossoms. A century later, the editor of his writings noted that the trees could no longer bear leaves. The primary effect here is that of sulfur dioxide, with a lesser impact from sulfuric acid and loss of sunlight. Photochemical smog causes a totally different set of symptoms in plants, including the bronzing of leaves and the development of small necrotic spots in the leaves. These appear to be the results of exposure to, respectively, peroxyacyl nitrates and ozone. In all cases, there are profound differences in plant susceptibility to damage among species, and even between varieties of the same species.

Photochemical smog contains nitric acid, while London-type smog contains sulfuric acid. Thus, both types cause enhanced corrosion of exposed buildings and other structures. In addition, exposed surfaces are soiled by soot, and the necessary cleaning wears away those surfaces. SEE ACID RAIN.

Control. There have been many ingenious suggestions for alleviating smog, such as using fans to increase ventilation, but these have all foundered on the sheer mass of air that would have to be moved. There have also been suggestions for adding substances to photochemical smog that would suppress formation of free radicals. It is known, for instance, that ozone levels may be reduced by adding nitric oxide [reaction (5)]. Diethyl hydroxylamine has been suggested as an agent to remove free radicals. In both cases, however, the ultimate result is the formation of smog at a later time, not its prevention.

The only true preventive measure is a reduction of emissions of the precursors, smoke and sulfur dioxide in London-type smog, and nitrogen oxides and organic compounds in photochemical smog. In the former case, this has meant control of sulfur oxides by use of fuels of lower sulfur content in industry and use of smokeless fuels for home heating. For photochemical smog, the efforts have centered on the reduction of organic emissions by using combustion catalysts in automobile mufflers, decreasing gasoline vapor losses at all stages of distribution, limiting use of volatile solvents, and various other measures. This approach has been relatively ineffective, largely because vegetation emits copious quantities of very reactive organic compounds, such as isoprene. Instead, it will be necessary to undertake the technically more difficult task of reducing nitrogen oxides. These are formed during combustion by the high-temperature reaction of atmospheric nitrogen and oxygen. This reaction can be suppressed by decreasing combustion temperatures, at some cost in efficiency. Furthermore, nitric oxide is thermodynamically unstable at ambient temperatures, although the decomposition is very slow. Catalysts that speed up the reaction have been designed and are used in some automobiles.

A continuing effort is the development of sufficient understanding of the chemistry and meteorology of smog to permit mathematical modeling of its formation and transport. Success in this effort will permit theoretical study of the impact of both new sources and control measures before they are actually implemented, obviating major mistakes and allowing the choice of the least costly strategies. Only modest successes have been achieved, because of the complexity of the problem and the lack of sufficiently complete chemical and meteorological data. SEE AIR POLLUTION; AIR-POLLUTION CONTROL.

James P. Lodge, Jr.

Bibliography. P. Brimblecombe, *The Big Smoke*, 1987; B. J. Finlayson-Pitts and J. N. Pitts, Jr., *Atmospheric Chemistry*, 1986; A. S. Lefohn (ed.), *Ozone: Vegetation Effects*, 1990; E. Meszaros, *Atmospheric Chemistry*, 1981; A. C. Stern (ed.), *Air Pollution*, 3d ed., 8 vols., 1976–1986; M. Treshow (ed.), *Air Pollution and Plant Life*, 1984.

Soil

Finely divided rock-derived material containing an admixture of organic matter and capable of supporting vegetation. Soils are independent natural bodies, each with a unique morphology resulting from a particular combination of climate, living plants and animals, parent rock materials, relief, the groundwaters, and age. Soils support plants, occupy large portions of the Earth's surface, and have shape, area, breadth, width, and depth. Soil, as used here, differs from the term as used by engineers, where the meaning is unconsolidated rock material.

ORIGIN AND CLASSIFICATION

Soil covers most of the land surface as a continuum. Each soil grades into the rock material below and into other soils at its margins, where changes occur in relief, groundwater, vegetation, kinds of rock, or other factors which influence the development of soils. Soils have horizons, or layers, more or less parallel to the surface and differing from those above and below in one or more properties, such as color, texture, structure, consistency, porosity, and reaction (**Fig. 1**). The horizons may be thick or thin. They may be prominent or so weak that they can be detected only in the laboratory. The succession of horizons is called the soil profile. In general, the boundary of soils with the underlying rock or rock material occurs at depths ranging from 1 to 6 ft (0.3 to 1.8 m), though the extremes lie outside this range.

Origin. Soil formation proceeds in stages, but these stages may grade indistinctly from one into another. The first stage is the accumulation of unconsolidated rock fragments, the parent material. Parent material may be accumulated by deposition of rock fragments moved by glaciers, wind, gravity, or water, or it may accumulate more or less in place from physical and chemical weathering of hard rocks.

The second stage is the formation of horizons. This stage may follow or go on simultaneously with the accumulation of parent material. Soil horizons are a result of dominance of one or more processes over others, producing a layer which differs from the layers above and below.

Major processes. The major processes in soils which promote horizon differentiation are gains, losses, transfers, and transformations of organic matter, soluble salts, carbonates, silicate clay minerals, sesquioxides, and silica. Gains consist normally of additions of organic matter, and of oxygen and water through oxidation and hydration, but in some sites slow continuous additions of new mineral materials take place at the surface or soluble materials are de-

Fig. 1. Photograph of a soil profile showing horizons. The dark crescent-shaped spots at the soil surface are the result of plowing. The dark horizon lying 9–18 in. (23–45 cm) below the surface is the principal horizon of accumulation of organic matter that has been washed down from the surface. The thin wavy lines were formed in the same manner.

posited from groundwater. Losses are chiefly of materials dissolved or suspended in water percolating through the profile or running off the surface. Transfers of both mineral and organic materials are common in soils. Water moving through the soil picks up materials in solution or suspension. These materials may be deposited in another horizon if the water is withdrawn by plant roots or evaporation, or if the materials are precipitated as a result of differences in pH (degree of acidity), salt concentration, or other conditions in deeper horizons.

Other processes tend to offset those that promote horizon differentiation. Mixing of the soil occurs as the result of burrowing by rodents and earthworms, overturning of trees, churning of the soil by frost, or shrinking and swelling. On steep slopes the soil may creep or slide downhill with attendant mixing. Plants may withdraw calcium or other ions from deep horizons and return them to the surface in the leaf litter.

Saturation of a horizon with water for long periods makes the iron oxides soluble by reduction from ferric to ferrous forms. The soluble iron can move by diffusion to form hard concretions or splotches of red or brown in a gray matrix. Or if the iron remains, the soil will have shades of blue or green. This process is called gleying, and can be superimposed on any of the others.

The kinds of horizons present and the degree of their differentiation, both in composition and structure, depend on the relative strengths of the processes. In turn, these relative strengths are determined by the way humans use the soil as well as by the natural factors of climate, plants and animals, relief and groundwater, and the period of time during which the processes have been operating.

Composition. In the drier climates where precipitation is appreciably less than the potential for evaporation and transpiration, horizons of soluble salts, including calcium carbonate and gypsum, are often found at the average depth of water penetration.

In humid climates, some materials normally considered insoluble may be gradually removed from the soil or at least from the surface horizons. A part of the removal may be in suspension. The movement of silicate clay minerals is an example. The movement of iron oxides is accelerated by the formation of chelates with the soil organic matter. Silica is removed in appreciable amounts in solution or suspension, though quartz sand is relatively unaffected. In warm humid climates, free iron and aluminum oxides and low-activity silicate clays accumulate in soils, apparently because of low solubility relative to other minerals.

In cool humid climates, solution losses are evident in such minerals as feldspars. Free sesquioxides tend to be removed from the surface horizons and to accumulate in a lower horizon, but mixing by animals and falling trees may counterbalance the downward movement.

Structure. Concurrently with the other processes, distinctive structures are formed in the different horizons. In the surface horizons, where there is a maximum of biotic activity, small animals, roots, and frost action keep mixing the soil material. Aggregates of varying sizes are formed and bound by organic matter, microorganisms, and colloidal material. The aggregates in the immediate surface tend to be loosely packed with many large pores among them. Below this horizon of high biotic activity, the structure is formed chiefly by volume changes due to wetting, drying, freezing, thawing, or shaking of the soil by roots of trees swaying with the wind. Consequently, the sides of any one aggregate, or ped, conform in shape to the sides of adjacent peds.

Water moving through the soil usually follows root channels, wormholes, and ped surfaces. Accordingly, materials that are deposited in a horizon commonly coat the peds. In the horizons that have received clay from an overlying horizon, the peds usually have a coating or varnish of clay making the exterior unlike the interior in appearance. Peds formed by moisture or temperature changes normally have the shapes of plates, prisms, or blocks.

Horizons. Pedologists have developed sets of symbols to identify the various kinds of horizons commonly found in soils. The nomenclature originated in Russia, where the letters A, B, and C were applied to the main horizons of the black soils of the steppes. The letter A designated the dark surface horizon of maximum organic matter accumulation, C the unaltered parent material, and B the intermediate horizon. The usage of the letters A, B, and C spread to western Europe, where the intermediate or B horizon was a horizon of accumulation of free sesquioxides or silicate clays or both. Thus the idea developed that a B horizon is a horizon of accumulation. Some, however, define a B horizon by position between A and C. Subdivisions of the major horizons have been shown by either numbers or letters, for example, Bt or B2. No internationally accepted set of horizon symbols has been developed. In the United States the designations shown in **Fig. 2** have been widely used since about 1935, with minor modifications made in 1962. Lowercase letters were added to numbers in B

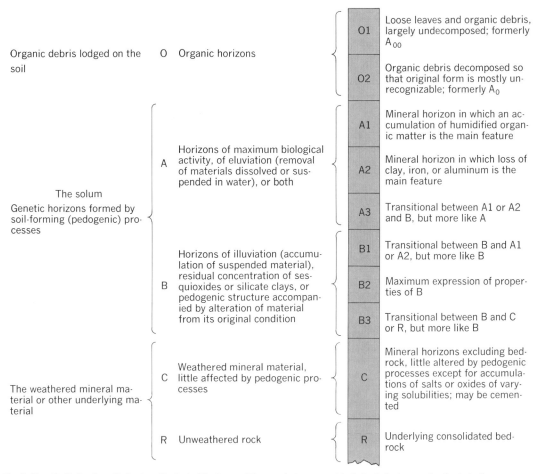

Organic debris lodged on the soil — O Organic horizons

O1 Loose leaves and organic debris, largely undecomposed; formerly A_{00}

O2 Organic debris decomposed so that original form is mostly unrecognizable; formerly A_0

The solum
Genetic horizons formed by soil-forming (pedogenic) processes

A — Horizons of maximum biological activity, of eluviation (removal of materials dissolved or suspended in water), or both

A1 Mineral horizon in which an accumulation of humidified organic matter is the main feature

A2 Mineral horizon in which loss of clay, iron, or aluminum is the main feature

A3 Transitional between A1 or A2 and B, but more like A

B — Horizons of illuviation (accumulation of suspended material), residual concentration of sesquioxides or silicate clays, or pedogenic structure accompanied by alteration of material from its original condition

B1 Transitional between B and A1 or A2, but more like B

B2 Maximum expression of properties of B

B3 Transitional between B and C or R, but more like B

The weathered mineral material or other underlying material

C — Weathered mineral material, little affected by pedogenic processes

C Mineral horizons excluding bedrock, little altered by pedogenic processes except for accumulations of salts or oxides of varying solubilities; may be cemented

R — Unweathered rock

R Underlying consolidated bedrock

Fig. 2. Hypothetical soil profile having all principal horizons. Other symbols are used to indicate features subordinate to those indicated by capital letters and numbers. The more important of these are as follows: ca, as in Cca, accumulations of carbonates; cs, accumulations of calcium sulfate; cn, concretions; g, strong gleying (reduction of iron in presence of groundwater); h, illuvial humus; ir, illuvial iron; m, strong cementation; p, plowing; sa, accumulations of very soluble salts; si, cementation by silica; t, illuvial clay; x, fragipan (a compact zone which is impenetrable by roots).

horizons to indicate the nature of the material that had accumulated. Generally, "h" is used to indicate translocated humus, "t" for translocated clay, and "ir" for translocated iron oxides. Thus, B2t indicates the main horizon of clay accumulation.

Classification. Systems of soil classification are influenced by concepts prevalent at the time a system is developed. Since ancient times, soil has been considered as the natural medium for plant growth. Under this concept, the earliest classifications were based on relative suitability for different crops, such as rice soils, wheat soils, and vineyard soils.

Early American agriculturists thought of soil chiefly as disintegrated rock, and the first comprehensive American classification was based primarily on the nature of the underlying rock.

In the latter part of the nineteenth century, some Russian students noted relations between the steppe and black soils and the forest and gray soils. They developed the concept of soils as independent natural bodies formed by the influence of environmental factors operating on parent materials over time. The early Russian classifications grouped soils at the highest level, according to the degree to which they reflected the climate and vegetation. They had classes of Normal, Abnormal, and Transitional soils, which later became known as Zonal, Intrazonal, and Azonal. Within the Normal or Zonal soils, the Russians distinguished climatic and vegetative zones in which the soils had distinctive colors and other properties in common. These formed classes that were called soil types. Because some soils with similar colors had very different properties that were associated with differences in the vegetation, the nature of the vegetation was sometimes considered in addition to the color to form the soil type name, for example, Gray Forest soil and Gray Desert soil. The Russian concepts of soil types were accepted in other countries as quickly as they became known. In the United States, however, the name soil type had been used for some decades to indicate differences in soil texture, chiefly texture of the surface horizons; so the Russian soil type was called a Great Soil Group.

Many systems of classification have been attempted but none has been found markedly superior; most systems have been modifications of those used in Russia. Two bases for classification have been tried. One basis has been the presumed genesis of the soil; climate and native vegetation were given major emphasis. The other basis has been the observable or measurable properties of the soil. To a considerable extent, of course, these are used in the genetic system to define the great soil groups. The morphologic systems, however, have not used soil genesis as such, but have attempted to use properties that are acquired through soil development.

The principal problem in the morphologic systems has been the selection of the properties to be used. Grouping by color, tried in the earliest systems, produces soil groups of unlike genesis.

The Soil Survey staff of the U.S. Department of Agriculture (USDA) and the land-grant colleges adopted a different classification scheme in 1965. The system differs from earlier systems in that it may be applied to either cultivated or virgin soils. Previous systems have been based on virgin profiles, and cultivated soils were classified on the presumed characteristics or genesis of the virgin soils. The system has six categories, based on both physical and chemical properties. These categories are the order, suborder, great group, subgroup, family, and series, in decreasing rank.

Nomenclature. The names of the taxa or classes in each category are derived from the classic languages in such a manner that the name itself indicates the place of the taxa in the system and usually indicates something of the differentiating properties. The names of the highest category, the order, end in the suffix ''sol,'' preceded by formative elements that suggest the nature of the order. Thus, Aridisol is the name of an order of soils that is characterized by being dry (Latin *arudys*, dry, plus *sol*, soil). A formative element is taken from each order name as the final syllable in the names of all taxa of suborders, great groups, and subgroups in the order. This is the syllable beginning with the vowel that precedes the connecting vowel with ''sol.'' Thus, for Aridisols, the names of the taxa of lower classes end with the syllable ''id,'' as in Argid and Orthid (see **Table 1**).

Suborder names have two syllables, the first suggesting something of the nature of the suborder and the last identifying the order. The formative element ''arg'' in Argid (Latin *argillus*, clay) suggests the horizon of accumulation of clay that defines the suborder.

Great group names have one or more syllables to suggest the nature of the horizons and have the suborder name as an ending. Thus great group names have three or more syllables but can be distinguished from order names because they do not end in ''sol.'' Among the Argids, great groups are Natrargids (Latin *natrium*, sodium) for soils that have high contents of sodium, and Durargids (Latin *durus*, hard) for Argids with a hardpan cemented by silica and called a duripan.

Subgroup names are binomial. The great group name is preceded by an adjective such as ''typic,'' which suggests the type or central concept of the great group, or the name of another great group, suborder, or order converted to an adjective to suggest that the soils are transitional between the two taxa.

Family names consist of several adjectives that describe the texture (sandy, silty, clayey, and so on), the mineralogy (siliceous, carbonatic, and so on), the temperature regime of the soil (thermic, mesic, frigid, and so on), and occasional other properties that are relevant to the use of the soil.

Series names are abstract names, taken from towns or places near where the soil was first identified. Cecil, Tama, and Walla Walla are names of soil series.

Order. In the highest category, 10 orders are recognized. These are distinguished chiefly by differences in kinds and amount of organic matter in the surface horizons, kinds of B horizons resulting from the dominance of various specific processes, evidences of churning through shrinking and swelling, base saturation, and lengths of periods during which the soil is without available moisture. The properties selected to distinguish the orders are reflections of the degree of horizon development and the kinds of horizons present.

Suborder. This category narrows the ranges in soil moisture and temperature regimes, kinds of horizons, and composition, according to which of these is most important. Moisture or temperature or soil properties associated with them are used to define suborders of Alfisols, Mollisols, Oxisols, Ultisols, and Vertisols. Kinds of horizons are used for Aridisols, compositions for Histosols and Spodosols, and combinations for Entisols and Inceptisols.

Great group. The taxa (classes) in this category group soils that have the same kinds of horizons in the same sequence and have similar moisture and temperature regimes. Exceptions to horizon sequences are made for horizons so near the surface that they are apt to be mixed by plowing or lost rapidly by erosion if plowed.

Subgroup. The great groups are subdivided into subgroups that show the central properties of the great group, intergrade subgroups that show properties of more than one great group, and other subgroups for soils with atypical properties that are not characteristic of any great group.

Table 1. Soil orders

Order	Formative element in name	General nature
Alfisols	alf	Soils with gray to brown surface horizons, medium to high base supply, with horizons of clay accumulation; usually moist, but may be dry during summer
Aridisols	id	Soils with pedogenic horizons, low in organic matter, and usually dry
Entisols	ent	Soils without pedogenic horizons
Histosols	ist	Organic soils (peats and mucks)
Inceptisols	ept	Soils that are usually moist, with pedogenic horizons of alteration of parent materials but not of illuviation
Mollisols	oll	Soils with nearly black, organic-rich surface horizons and high base supply
Oxisols	ox	Soils with residual accumulations of inactive clays, free oxides, kaolin, and quartz; mostly tropical
Spodosols	od	Soils with accumulations of amorphous materials in subsurface horizons
Ultisols	ult	Soils that are usually moist, with horizons of clay accumulation and a low supply of bases
Vertisols	ert	Soils with high content of swelling clays and wide deep cracks during some season

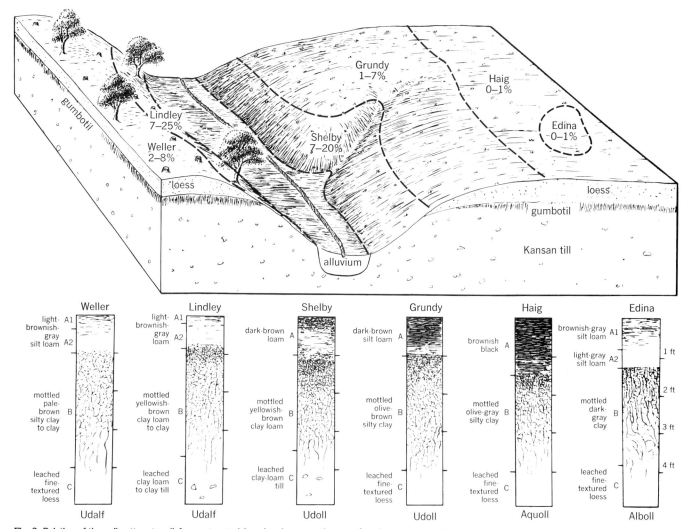

Fig. 3. Relation of the soil pattern to relief, parent material, and native vegetation on a farm in south-central Iowa. The soil slope gradient is expressed as a percentage. 1 ft = 30 cm. (*After R. W. Simonson et al.,* Understanding Iowa Soils, *Brown, 1952*)

Family. The families are defined largely on the basis of physical and mineralogic properties of importance to plant growth.

Series. The soil series is a group of soils having horizons similar in differentiating characteristics and arrangement in the soil profile, except for texture of the surface portion, and developed in a particular type of parent material.

Type. This category of earlier systems of classification has been dropped but is mentioned here because it was used for almost 70 years. The soil types within a series differed primarily in the texture of the plow layer or equivalent horizons in unplowed soils. Cecil clay and Cecil fine sandy loam were types within the Cecil series. The texture of the plow layer is still indicated in published soil surveys if it is relevant to the use of the soil, but it is now considered as one kind of soil phase. Soil surveys are discussed in the next section of this article.

Classifications of soils have been developed in several countries based on other differentia. The principal classifications have been those of the Soviet Union, Germany, France, Canada, Australia, New Zealand, and the United States. Other countries have modified one or the other of these to fit their own conditions. Soil classifications have usually been developed to fit the needs of a government that is concerned with the use of its soils. In this respect soil classification has differed from classifications of other natural objects, such as plants and animals, and there is no international agreement on the subject.

Many practical classifications have been developed on the basis of interpretations of the usefulness of soils for specific purposes. An example is the capability classification, which groups soils according to the number of safe alternative uses, risks of damage, and kinds of problems that are encountered under use.

Surveys. Soil surveys include those researches necessary (1) to determine the important characteristics of soils, (2) to classify them into defined series and other units, (3) to establish and map the boundaries between kinds of soil, and (4) to correlate and predict adaptability of soils to various crops, grasses, and trees; behavior and productivity of soils under different management systems; and yields of adapted crops on soils under defined sets of management practices. Although the primary purpose of soil surveys has been to aid in agricultural interpretations, many other purposes have become important, ranging from suburban planning, rural zoning, and highway location, to tax assessment and location of pipelines and radio transmitters. This has happened because the soil properties important to the growth of plants are also important to its engineering uses.

Soil surveys were first used in the United States in 1898. Over the years the scale of soil maps has been increased from ½ or 1 in. to the mile (8 or 16 mm to the kilometer) to 3 or 4 in. to the mile (47 to 63 mm to the kilometer) for mapping humid farming regions, and up to 8 in. to the mile (126 mm to the kilometer) for maps in irrigated areas. After the advent of aerial photography, planimetric maps were largely discontinued in favor of aerial photographic mosaics. The United States system has been used, with modifications, in many other countries.

Two kinds of soil maps are made. The common map is a detailed soil map, on which soil boundaries are plotted from direct observations throughout the surveyed area. Reconnaissance soil maps are made by plotting soil boundaries from observations which are made at intervals. The maps show soil and other differences that are of significance for present or foreseeable uses.

The units shown on soil maps usually are phases of soil series. The phase is not a category of the classification system. It may be a subdivision of any class of the system according to some feature that is of significance for use and management of the soil, but not in relation to the natural landscape. The presence of loose boulders on the surface of the soil makes little difference in the growth of a forest, but is highly significant if the soil is to be plowed. Phases are most commonly based on slope, erosion, presence of stone or rock, or differences in the rock material below the soil itself. If a legend identifies a phase of a soil series, the soils so designated on a soil map are presumed to lie within the defined range of that phase in the major part of the area involved. Thus, the inclusion of lesser areas of soils having other characteristics is tolerated in the mapping if their presence does not appreciably affect the use of the soil. If there are other soils that do affect the use, inclusions up to 15% of the area are tolerated without being indicated in the name of the soil.

If the pattern of occurrence of two or more series is so intricate that it is impossible to show them separately, a soil complex is mapped, and the legend includes the word "complex," or the names of the series are connected by a hyphen and followed by a textural class name. Thus the phrase Fayette-Dubuque silt loam indicates that the two series occur in one area and that each represents more than 15% of the total area.

In places the significance of the difference between series is so slight that the expense of separating them is unwarranted. In such a case the names of the series are connected by a conjunction, for example, Fayette and Downs silt loam. In this mapping unit, the soils may or may not be associated geographically.

It is possible to make accurate soil maps only because the nature of the soil changes with alterations in climatic and biotic factors, in relief, and in groundwaters, all acting on parent materials over long periods of time. Boundaries between kinds of soil are made where such changes become apparent. On a given farm the kinds of soil usually form a repeating pattern related to the relief (**Fig. 3**).

Because concepts of soil have changed over the years, maps made 50 or more years ago may use the same soil type names as modern maps, but with different meanings.   *Guy D. Smith*

SOIL SUBORDERS

Soil suborders are broad classes at one level in the soil classification system that was adopted in the United States in 1965. A total of 47 suborders form the full set of classes in the second highest category (each category is a set of classes of parallel rank) in the system.

The number of local kinds of soils in a large country is also large. For example, 11,500 soil series have been recognized in soil surveys made in the United States through 1979. On the average, a series consists of six phases, which are the local kinds of soils. This means that approximately 66,000 local kinds have been defined up to the present time in a single large country, though all parts of that country have not been studied.

Despite the myriads of local kinds over the land surface of the Earth, all soils share some characteristics. They can all be related to one another in some way. The relationships are close for some pairs of local kinds and distant for others. The similarities and differences among the thousands of local kinds permit their grouping into sets of progressively broader classes in order to show degrees of kinship.

Though it is impossible for a single mind to retain concepts of 11,500 series or 66,000 phases, the salient features of a few dozen broad classes can be remembered. Consequently, the nature of the 47 suborders is described in this article. The purpose is to provide a general picture of the kinds of soils in the United States and the world. A list of the 47 suborders grouped into the 10 orders is as follows:

Alfisols	Mollisols (*cont.*)
Aqualfs	Aquolls
Boralfs	Borolls
Udalfs	Rendolls
Ustalfs	Udolls
Xeralfs	Ustolls
Aridisols	Xerolls
Argids	Oxisols
Orthids	Aquox
Entisols	Humox
Aquents	Orthox
Arents	Torrox
Fluvents	Ustox
Orthents	Spodosols
Psamments	Aquods
Histosols	Ferrods
Fibrists	Humods
Folists	Orthods
Hemists	Ultisols
Saprists	Aquults
Inceptisols	Humults
Andepts	Udults
Aquepts	Ustults
Ochrepts	Xerults
Plaggepts	Vertisols
Tropepts	Torrerts
Umbrepts	Uderts
Mollisols	Usterts
Albolls	Xererts

The brief individual descriptions of the suborders are arranged in the same sequence as the list.

The broad regional distribution of soils is shown for the world in **Fig. 4**. Each region outlined on the map is identified by the name of the most extensive

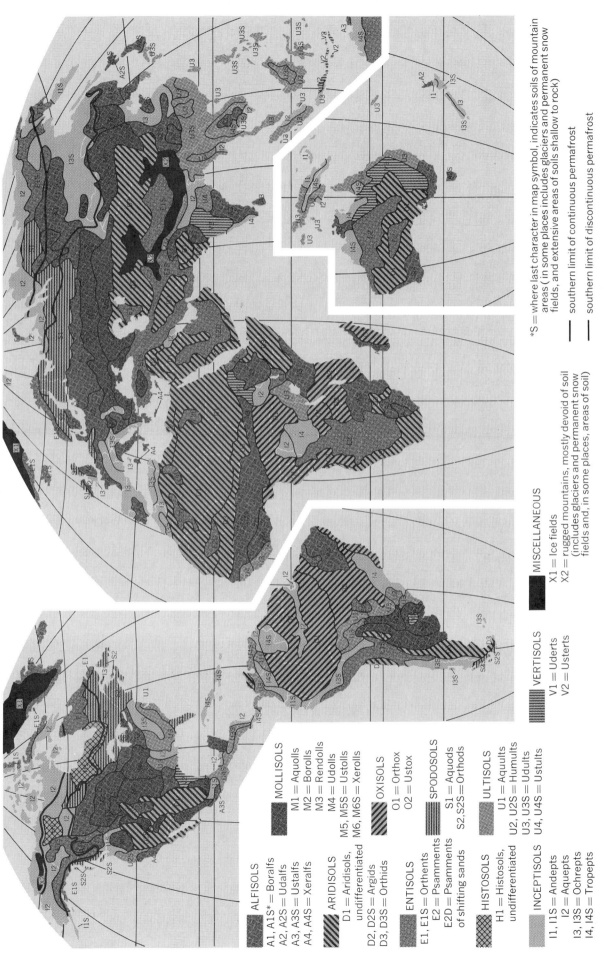

Fig. 4. General soil map of the world. Each region is identified by the name of the most extensive suborder. Other suborders are present in every region and are important in most of them. (*Soil Conservation Service, USDA*)

ALFISOLS

A1, A1S* = Boralfs
A2, A2S = Udalfs
A3, A3S = Ustalfs
A4, A4S = Xeralfs

ARIDISOLS

D1 = Aridisols, undifferentiated
D2, D2S = Argids
D3, D3S = Orthids

ENTISOLS

E1, E1S = Orthents
E2 = Psamments
E2D = Psamments of shifting sands

HISTOSOLS

H1 = Histosols, undifferentiated

INCEPTISOLS

I1, I1S = Andepts
I2 = Aquepts
I3, I3S = Ochrepts
I4, I4S = Tropepts

MOLLISOLS

M1 = Aquolls
M2 = Borolls
M3 = Rendolls
M4 = Udolls
M5, M5S = Ustolls
M6, M6S = Xerolls

OXISOLS

O1 = Orthox
O2 = Ustox

SPODOSOLS

S1 = Aquods
S2, S2S = Orthods

ULTISOLS

U1 = Aquults
U2, U2S = Humults
U3, U3S = Udults
U4, U4S = Ustults

VERTISOLS

V1 = Uderts
V2 = Usterts

MISCELLANEOUS

X1 = Ice fields
X2 = rugged mountains, mostly devoid of soil (includes glaciers and permanent snow fields and, in some places, areas of soil)

*S = where last character in map symbol, indicates soils of mountain areas (in some places includes glaciers and permanent snow fields, and extensive areas of soils shallow to rock)

—— southern limit of continuous permafrost

—— southern limit of discontinuous permafrost

suborder among the component soils. In every region, suborders other than the most extensive one are important.

Alfisols. These soils have A and E horizons that are mostly pale in color and that have lost silicate clay, sesquioxides, and bases such as calcium and magnesium.

The soils have B horizons with accumulations of silicate clay and with moderate to high levels of exchangeable calcium and magnesium. The C horizons are usually lighter in color and lower in clay than the B horizons.

Alfisols are most extensive in humid, temperate regions but range from the edges of the tundra and the desert into the tropics. Mostly, the soils were under forest or savanna vegetation, though some were under prairie. All have been formed on land sufaces that are not old nor yet among the youngest in the world.

Occurring as they do in many parts of the world, these soils are used for a wide variety of crops. Some remain in forest, and those under drier climates are used chiefly for grazing.

Aqualfs. These are the seasonally wet Alfisols. They generally occur in depressions or on rather wide flats in local landscapes. In addition to the general morphology and composition shared with other soils of the order, Aqualfs are marked by gray or mottled colors reflecting their wetness (**Fig. 5**).

Fig. 6. Profile of a Udalf with A and E horizons 12 in. (30 cm) thick over darker B horizon with blocky structure grading into C horizon at a depth of about 4 ft (1.2 m); larger numbers on scale indicate feet. 1 ft = 30 cm. (*Photograph by R. W. Simonson*)

Fig. 5. Profile of an Aqualf with pale A and E horizons about 18 in. (45 cm) thick resting on B horizon high in clay which grades into C horizon at a depth of about 4 ft (1.2 m); numbers on scale indicate feet. 1 ft = 30 cm. (*Photograph by R. W. Simonson*)

Boralfs. These are the well-drained Alfisols of cool or cold regions, such as west-central Canada and the Soviet Union. The soils occur either at high altitudes or in high latitudes, including some frigid zones.

In their morphology and composition, the soils are much like the Udalfs, though colors are more dull on the whole and the surplus of calcium and magnesium a little higher.

Udalfs. These are the well-drained Alfisols of humid, temperate climates. The soils are important in the north-central part of the United States, in western Europe, and in eastern Asia. Udalfs differ from Aqualfs in that B horizons are characteristically brown or yellowish brown and lack marks of wetness. These have higher mean annual temperatures than do the Boralfs and are moist for higher proportions of the year than the Ustalfs and Xeralfs (**Fig. 6**).

Ustalfs. These are well-drained Alfisols occurring in somewhat drier and mostly warmer regions than Udalfs. On the whole, the soils have more reddish B horizons and are a little higher in calcium and magnesium than Udalfs. These soils are intermittently dry during the growing season.

Xeralfs. These are well-drained Alfisols found in regions with rainy winters and dry summers, in what are called mediterranean climates. Like the Ustalfs in nature of B horizons, the soils have A horizons that tend to become massive and hard during the dry season. Some of the soils have duripans [cemented layers at depth of 2 or 3 ft (0.6 or 0.9 m)] that interfere with root growth.

Aridisols. These are major soils of the world's deserts, which form about one-fourth of the land surface. Soils of other orders, especially the Entisols, are also present but less extensive in the deserts.

Formed under low rainfall, Aridisols have been leached little and are therefore high in calcium, magnesium, and other more soluble elements. The low rainfall has also limited growth of plants, mostly shrubs and similar species, so that the soils are low in organic matter and nitrogen. The combined A and B horizons are rarely more and usually less than 1 ft (30 cm) thick. The A horizons are light-colored and usually calcareous. All horizons are neutral or mildly alkaline in reaction.

Most Aridisols in use provide some grazing for nomadic herds. On the other hand, if water and other resources, including adequate skills, are available and climate is favorable, some Aridisols will support a large variety and produce high yields of crops.

Argids. These well-drained Aridisols have B horizons of silicate clay accumulation. The B horizons are characteristically brown or reddish in color and grade into lighter colored C horizons marked by carbonate accumulation. On the whole, these soils occupy the older land surfaces in desert regions (**Fig. 7**).

Orthids. These Aridisols lack B horizons of clay accumulation. Many are free of carbonates in the A and upper B horizons; most are well drained. Common colors are gray or brownish gray with little change from top to bottom of the profile. A few Orthids are fairly high in soluble salts such as sodium sulfate and sodium chloride, whereas others are high in calcium carbonate throughout. More extensive than the Argids, generally, Orthids occupy younger but not the youngest land surfaces in deserts.

Entisols. These soils have few and faint horizons, with reasons for the limited horizonation differing among suborders. Reasons for the practical absence of horizons are indicated for individual suborders.

Entisols occur in all parts of the world and may be found under a wide variety of vegetation. Most, though not all, are on young land surfaces, distributed from the tundra through the tropics and from the deserts to the rainiest climates. Entisols have a wide range in usefulness. Some are highly productive and others are not.

Aquents. These Entisols have been under water until very recent times at the margins of oceans, lakes, or seas. The wetness is reflected in the bluish-gray or greenish-gray colors. Examples are the soils in recently reclaimed polders of the Netherlands. The total extent of Aquents in the world is very small.

Arents. These are Entisols because of severe disturbance of soils formerly classifiable in other orders. The sequence of horizons has been disrupted completely, and remnants of those horizons can be found randomly distributed in the profiles of Arents.

Fluvents. These well-drained Entisols are in recently deposited alluvium. They occur along streams or in fans where the rate of sediment deposition is high. Marks of sedimentation are still evident, and identifiable horizons are lacking, except for slightly darkened surface layers or A horizons. Small bodies of these soils are scattered over all parts of the world.

Orthents. These well-drained Entisols are of medium or fine texture, mostly on strong slopes. The

Fig. 7. Profile of an Argid with pale silty A and E horizons, darker B horizon higher in clay, and calcareous C horizon; profile shown in 20 in. (50 cm) deep; numbers on scale indicate inches. 1 in. = 2.5 cm. (*Photograph by R. W. Simonson*)

soils may have A horizons or slightly darkened surface layers an inch or so thick but otherwise lack evidence of horizonation. Many of the soils are shallow to bedrock.

Psamments. These Entisols are of sandy texture. Like the Orthents, these may have thin A horizons, which grade into thick C horizons. The sandiness is the distinctive character of the suborder (**Fig. 8**).

Histosols. These are wet soils consisting mostly of organic matter, popularly known as peats and mucks. Most have restricted drainage and are saturated with water much of the time. A few are wet but not fully saturated. Widely distributed over the world, these soils may occur in small or large bodies, with the latter occurring chiefly at high latitudes. A large proportion of the total area is idle. Where the climate is favorable, some of the soils have been drained and are producing vegetables and other crops. *SEE WET-LANDS.*

Fibrists. These Histosols consist mainly of recognizable plant residues or sphagnum moss. They are saturated with water most of the year unless drained (**Fig. 9**).

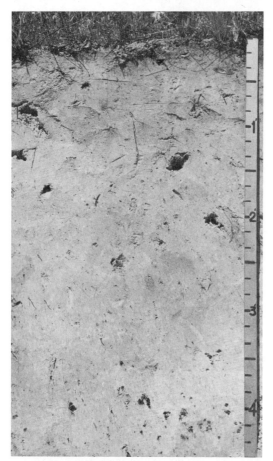

Fig. 8. Profile of a Psamment lacking evident horizons and consisting of sand throughout; numbers on scale indicate feet. 1 ft = 30 cm. (*Photograph by R. W. Simonson*)

Folists. These Histosols consist of forest litter resting on rock or rubble. Drainage is not restricted, but a combination of rainfall, fog, and low temperatures keeps the litter wet.

Hemists. These Histosols consist of partially decayed plant residues. Plant structures have largely been destroyed but an appreciable share of the mass remains as fibers when rubbed vigorously. The soils are saturated with water much of the time unless drained.

Saprists. These Histosols consist of residues in which plant structures have been largely obliterated by decay. A very small part of the mass remains as fibers after vigorous rubbing. The soils are saturated with water much of the time unless drained. Most Saprists in the United States are known as muck.

Inceptisols. These soils have faint to moderate horizonation but lack horizons of accumulation of translocated substances other than carbonates and silica. Two of the suborders have distinct dark A horizons, and most have B horizons formed by losses and transformations without corresponding gains in substances. Thus, the Inceptisols are in some ways intermediate in horizonation between the Entisols and Vertisols on the one hand, and the Alfisols, Mollisols, Spodosols, and Ultisols on the other.

Inceptisols are widely distributed, ranging from the arctic through the tropics and from the margins of the desert into regions of heavy rainfall. They may consequently be found under a wide variety of vegeta-

tion. Usefulness of the soils has as wide a range as does their distribution. Some are highly productive and others are of little or no value.

Andepts. These Inceptisols are formed chiefly in volcanic ash or in regoliths with high components of ash. Mostly, the soils tend to be fluffy. They have thick dark A horizons, rather high levels of acidity, and poorly crystalline clay minerals. The soils are widely distributed but seem to be restricted to regions of fairly recent volcanic activity (**Fig. 10**).

Aquepts. These Inceptisols are wet or have been drained. Like the Aqualfs, the soils have gray or mottled B and C horizons, but they lack silicate clay accumulation in their profiles. The A horizons may be dark and fairly thick or they may be thin, as they are in many of the soils (**Fig. 11**).

Ochrepts. These Inceptisols have pale A horizons, darker B horizons, and lighter colored C horizons. The B horizons lack accumulations of translocated clay, sesquioxides, or humus. The soils are widely distributed, occurring from the margins of the tundra region through the temperate zone but not in the tropics. Ochrepts also occur in the fairly dry regions though not in deserts (**Fig. 12**).

Plaggepts. These Inceptisols have very thick surface horizons of mixed mineral and organic materials

Fig. 9. Profile of a Fibrist with little or no change from the surface to a depth of 5 ft (1.5 m); soil consists of partly decayed plant residues; numbers on scale indicate feet. 1 ft = 30 cm. (*Photograph by R. W. Simonson*)

Fig. 10. Profile of an Andept with thick, dark A horizon, faint B horizon, and lighter C horizon; fine plant roots are numerous; numbers on scale indicate feet. 1 ft = 30 cm. (*Photograph by R. W. Simonson*)

added as manure or as human wastes over long periods of time. For the world as a whole, such soils are of negligible extent, but they are conspicuous where found.

Tropepts. These Inceptisols have moderately dark A horizons with modest additions of organic matter, B horizons with brown or reddish colors, and slightly paler C horizons. The soils are less strongly weathered than the geographically associated Ultisols and Oxisols. In general appearance, the profiles are much like that of the Orthox shown in **Fig. 13**. Tropepts are restricted to tropical regions, largely to those of moderate and high rainfall.

Umbrepts. These Inceptisols have dark A horizons more than 10 in. (25 cm) thick, brown B horizons, and slightly paler C horizons. The soils are strongly acid and the silicate clay minerals are crystalline rather than amorphous as in the Andepts. The Umbrepts occur under cool or temperate climates, are widely distributed, and are of modest extent.

Mollisols. These soils have dark or very dark, friable, thick A horizons high in humus and bases such as calcium and magnesium. Most have lighter colored or browner B horizons that are less friable and about as thick as the A horizons. All but a few have paler C horizons, many of which are calcareous.

Major areas of Mollisols occur in subhumid or semiarid cool and temperate regions. They meet the desert along their drier margins and meet soils such as the Alfisols at their more humid margins. Mollisols were formed under vegetation consisting chiefly of grasses and are thus the major ones of former prairies and steppes. The soils occupy rather young land surfaces.

Though they produce a variety of crops, Mollisols are largely used for cereals. These soils now produce a major share of the world's output of corn and wheat. Topography is generally favorable for the operation of large machinery, and many Mollisols are therefore in large farms. Yields have a wide range, depending on climatic conditions. Wide fluctuations in yield with wet and dry years are normal for the Mollisols marginal to arid regions. On the other hand, yields are consistently high for those under more humid climates.

Albolls. These are Mollisols with dark A horizons, pale E horizons, distinct B horizons marked by clay accumulation, and paler C horizons. The soils are set, especially in the upper part, for some part of the year. Mostly, the soils occur on upland flats and in shallow depressions.

Aquolls. These are wet Mollisols unless they have been drained. Because they were formed under wet conditions, the soils have thick or very thick, nearly black A horizons over gray or mottled B and C hori-

Fig. 11. Profile of an Aquept with thin, dark A horizons, fairly thick, light-gray B horizon, and stone in C horizon beside tape; numbers on scale indicate feet. 1 ft = 30 cm. (*Photograph by R. W. Simonson*)

Fig. 12. Profile of an Ochrept with litter on the surface, dark A horizon 4 in. (10 cm) thick, thin B horizon, and pale C horizon; deeper profile is marked by plant roots and traces of former roots; numbers on scale indicate inches. 1 in. = 2.54 cm. (*Photograph by R. W. Simonson*)

zons. If they have not been drained, the soils may be under water for part of the year, but they are seasonally rather than continually wet (**Fig. 14**).

Borolls. These are Mollisols of cool and cold regions. Most areas are in moderately high latitudes or at high altitudes. The soils have fairly thick, nearly black A horizons, dark grayish-brown B horizons, and paler C horizons that are commonly calcareous. The B horizons of some soils have accumulations of clay. These soils are extensive in western Canada and the Soviet Union.

Rendolls. These are the Mollisols formed in highly calcareous parent materials, regoliths with more than 40% calcium carbonate. The soils may be calcareous to the surface and must have high levels of carbonates within a depth of 20 in. (50 cm). Rendolls do not have horizons of carbonate accumulation. The profiles consist of dark or very dark A horizons grading into pale C horizons. For the most part, Rendolls are restricted to humid, temperate regions.

Udolls. These are Mollisols of humid, temperate and warm regions where maximum rainfall comes during the growing season. The soils have thick, very dark A horizons, brown B horizons, and paler C horizons. Throughout the profile these soils are browner than the Borolls and are not as cold. Udolls lack horizons of accumulation of powdery carbonates. Some

of the soils have B horizons of clay accumulation and others do not. These soils are major ones of the Corn Belt of the United States (**Fig. 15**).

Ustolls. These are the Mollisols of temperate and warm climates with lower rainfall than the Udolls. The soils are therefore dry for an appreciable part of each year, usually more than 90 cumulative days. Horizons and their sequence are much the same as for Udolls except that many Ustolls have accumulations of powdery carbonates at depths of 40 in. (100 cm) or less.

Xerolls. These are Mollisols of regions with rainy winters and dry summers. The nature and sequence of horizons are much like those of the Ustolls. The soils are completely dry for a long period during the summer of each year.

Oxisols. These soils have faint horizonation, though formed in strongly weathered regoliths. The surface layers or A horizons are usually darkened and moderately thick, but there is little evidence of change in the remainder of the profile. Because of the intense or long weathering, the soils consist of resistant minerals such as kaolinite, forms of sesquioxides, and quartz. Weatherable minerals such as feldspars have largely disappeared. Moreover, the clay fraction has limited capacity to retain bases such as calcium and magnesium.

The soils are porous and readily penetrated by water and plant roots. A distinctive feature of Oxisols is the common occurrence of tubular pores about the di-

Fig. 13. Profile of an Orthox with slightly darkened A horizon about 1 ft (30 cm) thick, little further change with depth, and deep penetration by fine plant roots; scale in feet. 1 ft = 30 cm. (*Photograph by R. W. Simonson*)

Fig. 14. Profile of an Aquoll with very thick, dark A horizon, signs of mixing and burrowing by animals at depths between 3 and 3.5 ft (0.9 and 1.1 m), and lighter C horizon at the bottom; the numbers on the scale to the left indicate feet. 1 ft = 30 cm. (*Photograph by R. W. Simonson*)

ameter of ordinary pins extending to depths of 6 ft (1.8 m) or more.

Oxisols are largely restricted to low altitudes in humid portions of the tropics. Any occurring elsewhere seem to be relics of earlier geologic ages. All occupy old land surfaces. Most were formed under forest, with some under savanna vegetation. Regions with Oxisols as major soils are extensive, ranking second in total area only to the Aridisols of deserts.

Most Oxisols remain in forest or savanna and produce little food and fiber. Many regions are sparsely inhabited, with natives depending on shifting cultivation for much of their food. A small proportion of the total area is cultivated with modern technology and is highly productive. Even so, management to ensure sustained high yields is still to be developed for the more strongly weathered Oxisols.

Aquox. These are seasonally wet Oxisols found chiefly in shallow depressions. Because of their wetness, deeper profiles are dominantly gray, with or without mottles and nodules or sheets of iron and aluminum oxides. Total extent is extremely small.

Humox. These are well-drained Oxisols high in organic matter and moist all or nearly all year. Profiles have dark A horizons 1 ft (0.3 m) or so thick over generally reddish B and C horizons. The high amounts of organic matter distinguish Humox from

other suborders of Oxisols, and the soils are also moist much more of the year than are Torrox and Ustox. Humox are believed to be of limited extent, restricted to relatively cool climates and high altitudes for Oxisols.

Orthox. These are well-drained Oxisols moderate to low in organic matter and moist all or nearly all year. Much like Humox in general appearance, Orthox profiles are lower in organic matter. They are moist more of each year than are Torrox and Ustox. Although good data on extent are lacking, Orthox are believed to be extensive at low altitudes in the heart of the humid tropics (Fig. 13).

Torrox. These are well-drained Oxisols low in organic matter and dry most of the year. Profiles resemble those of Orthox except that A horizons are more poorly expressed. The soils are believed to have been formed under more rainy climates of past eras. Total extent of the Torrox seems to be extremely small.

Ustox. These are well-drained Oxisols low to moderate in organic matter and dry for periods of at least 90 cumulative days each year. Profiles resemble those of Orthox, on the whole. Ustox are lower in organic matter than Humox, dry for longer periods each year than Humox and Orthox, and moist for longer periods than Torrox. Good data on extent are lacking but Ustox are believed to be extensive.

Spodosols. These soils have B horizons with accumulations of one or both of organic matter and compounds of aluminum and iron. The accumulated

Fig. 15. Profile of a Udoll with thick, dark A horizon, B horizon gradational in color, and rather pale C horizon; filled former animal burrows in B horizon; numbers on scale indicate feet. 1 ft = 30 cm. (*Photograph by R. W. Simonson*)

Fig. 16. Profile of an Aquod with distinct E horizon, dark B horizon at depth of 18 in. (45 cm), pale C horizon below, and part of buried profile below 4 ft (1.2 m); soil consists of sand; numbers on scale indicate feet. 1 ft = 30 cm. (*Photograph by R. W. Simonson*)

substances are amorphous in nature. They impart red, brown, or black colors to the B horizons, which may have irregular lower boundaries with tongues extending downward a foot or more. If the soil has not been disturbed, the surface layer consists of both fresh and partly decayed litter. This rests on a very pale, leached E horizon overlying a highly contrasting B horizon. The Spodosols formed from sands under boreal coniferous forests have some of the most striking profiles in the world. Mostly, the soils are strongly acid because of the small supplies of bases.

Spodosols are most extensive in humid, cool climates, but some occur at low elevations under tropical and subtropical climates. The soils were largely under forest. The bulk of the Spodosols have been formed in sandy regoliths, with others in loamy regoliths. Land surfaces are fairly young.

Most Spodosols remain in forest, but some are cultivated in both cool and tropical regions. The variety of crops produced is large because of the wide climatic range under which the soils occur. The range in yields is also wide, being dependent on the combination of climatic conditions and prevailing level of technology. Production is modest for most Spodosols under cool climates and simple management. Production is high from some soils cultivated with complex management in tropical climates.

Aquods. These are seasonally wet Spodosols. The soils may be wet most of each year but not all of the time. The B horizons are black or dark brown in color

and some are cemented. Aquods occupy depressional areas or wide flats from which water cannot escape easily (**Fig. 16**).

Ferrods. These are well-drained Spodosols having B horizons of iron accumulation with little organic matter. Appearance of the profile is much like that of Orthods.

Humods. These are well-drained Spodosols having B horizons of humus accumulation, usually black or dark brown in color. Aluminum usually accumulates with the humus but iron is lacking, especially from the upper part of B horizons. Where formed in white or nearly white sands, the soils have striking profiles, as in parts of western Europe.

Orthods. These are well-drained Spodosols having B horizons of humus, aluminum, and iron accumulation. The B horizons are mostly red or reddish in color and are friable. They grade downward into lighter-colored C horizons which are commonly less friable and may be very firm. Orthods form the most extensive suborder among the Spodosols, being widespread in Canada and the Soviet Union.

Ultisols. Like Alfisols, these soils have A and E horizons that have lost silicate clays, sesquioxides, and bases. Most A and E horizons are pale, though not all are. The B horizons have accumulations of silicate clays and low levels of exchangeable calcium and magnesium. The C horizons are usually lighter in color and lower in clay than the B horizons. Combined thickness of the A, E, and B horizons is greater, on the average, for Ultisols than for Alfisols.

Fig. 17. Profile of a Udult with pale A horizon 16 in. (40 cm) thick, darker B horizon higher in clay and iron oxides, and C horizon near bottom; numbers on scale indicate feet. 1 ft = 30 cm. (*Photograph by R. W. Simonson*)

Ultisols are strongly acid throughout their profiles, reflecting the low levels of exchangeable bases.

Ultisols are most extensive under humid, warm-temperate climates but extend through the tropics. They are not found in cold regions. The largest bodies of the soils are in southeastern Asia, nearby islands, and the southeastern United States. The soils were usually under forest but some were covered by savanna vegetation. All were formed in strongly weathered regoliths on old land surfaces.

Many Ultisols remain in forest. Among those producing crops, a majority are used under some method of shifting cultivation. Production is limited in such circumstances. On the other hand, the variety of crops and yields obtained can be large if cultivators are in a position to apply complex technology to Ultisols.

Aquults. These are seasonally wet Ultisols, saturated with water for an important part of the year unless drained. Usually the soils have thin, dark A horizons, but they may be as thick as 20 in. (50 cm). Deeper profiles are gray, with or without red mottles. Aquults occur in depressions or on wide upland flats from which water moves very slowly.

Humults. These are well-drained Ultisols formed under rather high rainfall distributed evenly over the year. The soils are high in organic matter throughout their profiles, and most have darkened A horizons of moderate thickness. Deeper profiles tend to be brown, reddish-brown, or yellowish-brown in color. Humults are common in southeastern Brazil.

Udults. These are well-drained Ultisols of humid, warm-temperate and tropical regions. The soils are low or relatively low in humus and typically have thin, darkened A horizons. The B horizons are yellowish-red, red, brown, or yellowish-brown in color and are fairly thick. Rainfall is high enough and distributed evenly enough over the year so that soils are dry for only short periods. Udults are major soils in the southeastern parts of the United States and Asia (**Fig. 17**), and their total extent is large.

Ustults. These are well-drained Ultisols of warm-temperate and tropical climates with moderate or low rainfall. The soils are like the Udults in general appearance but are dry for appreciable periods each year. Examples of Ustults may be found in northeastern Australia. Total extent of the suborder is appreciably less than that of Udults.

Xerults. These are well-drained Ultisols of regions with warm, dry summers and cool, rainy winters. The soils are like Ustults in appearance but become and remain dry for longer periods in summers. Total extent is small.

Vertisols. These soils have faint horizonation for two main reasons. In the first place, Vertisols are formed in regoliths that are high in clay and therefore resistant to change. In the second place, the clay fraction in the soils has high levels of activity. The soils are therefore subject to marked swelling and shrinking as they wet and dry. Cracks formed as the soils become dry may extend to depths of several feet (about 1 m). Because of the shrinking and swelling of the soils, materials from deeper profiles are forced upward in places so that entire soils are slowly but continually overturned and mixed. Vertisols have therefore been called ''self-swallowing'' and ''soils that plow themselves.''

Some Vertisols have darkened A horizons, whereas others do not. All are low in organic matter and high in bases. Many are calcareous in deeper profiles.

Most are neutral or mildly alkaline in reaction because of goodly supplies of bases.

Vertisols occur in warm-temperate and tropical climates with one or more dry seasons. The soils were under savanna vegetation for the most part with a few in forest. Land surfaces are old or fairly old. Large bodies of Vertisols are found on the Deccan Plateau of India, in the Gezira of Sudan, and in Australia.

Because they are high in active clays, Vertisols are hard to cultivate. The soils therefore remain in savanna in many places, and the savannas are used for grazing or left alone. Large areas of the soils are cultivated, some with simple, bullock-drawn implements and others with large machinery. A wide variety of crops are produced, but yields are generally modest, especially for cultivators dependent on simple technology. The soils will, however, produce crops indefinitely under simple management.

Torrerts. These are Vertisols of arid regions, the driest soils of the order. Because the soils are dry most of the time, cracks that form tend to remain open. The soils do become wet enough at rare intervals to permit cracks to close. Torrerts are of limited extent.

Uderts. These are Vertisols of humid regions; each profile is moist in some part most of each year. The soils do dry out enough to permit formation of cracks once every year, as a rule. Uderts are moist more of each year than other Vertisols. The soils are of moderate extent.

Usterts. These are Vertisols of subhumid and semiarid regions, chiefly under climates with two rainy and two dry seasons each year. Cracks formed during dry seasons are open for at least 90 cumulative days per year. The Usterts are thus intermediate in moisture regimes between Uderts on the wet side and Torrerts on the dry side. Usterts are dry for shorter periods during summer than Xererts. Usterts are extensive,

Fig. 18. Profile of a Ustert with thick, dark A horizon, which is due in part to mixing and churning of soil mass and which grades into the lighter-appearing C horizon; scale in feet. 1 ft = 30 cm. (*Photograph by E. H. Templin*)

represented by large bodies in Australia and India (**Fig. 18**).

Xererts. These are Vertisols of regions with warm, dry summers and cool, rainy winters, the mediterranean climates. Cracks formed as the soils dry out each summer remain open for at least 60 consecutive days. Xererts are higher in moisture than Torrerts and lower than Uderts. They have longer dry periods during warm seasons than Usterts. The soils are of limited extent. *Roy W. Simonson*

ZONALITY

Many soils that are geographically associated on plains have common properties that are the result of formation in similar climates with similar vegetation. Because climate determines the natural vegetation to a large extent and because climate changes gradually with distance on plains, there are vast zones of uplands on which most soils have many common properties. This was first observed in Russia toward the end of the nineteenth century by V. V. Dokuchaev, the father of modern soil science. He also observed that on floodplains and steep slopes and in wet places the soils commonly lacked some or most of the properties of the upland soils. In mountainous areas, climate and vegetation tend to vary with altitude, and here the Russian students observed that many soils at the same altitude had many common properties. This they called vertical zonality in contrast with the lateral zonality of the soils of plains.

Zonal classification. These observations led N. M. Sivirtsev to propose in about 1900 that major kinds of soil could be classified as Zonal if their properties reflected the influence of climate and vegetation, as Azonal if they lacked well-defined horizons, and as Intrazonal if their properties resulted from some local factor such as a shallow groundwater or unusual parent material.

This concept was not accepted for long in Russia. It was adopted in the United States in 1938 as a basis for classifying soil but was dropped in 1965. This was because the Zonal soils as a class could not be defined in terms of their properties and because they had no common properties that were not shared by some Intrazonal and Azonal soils. It was also learned that many of the properties that had been thought to reflect climate were actually the result of differences in age of the soils and of past climates that differed greatly from those of the present.

Zonality of soil distribution is important to students of geography in understanding differences in farming, grazing, and forestry practices in different parts of the world. To a very large extent, zonality is reflected but is not used directly in the soil classification used in the United States. The Entisols include most soils formerly called Azonal. Most of the soils formerly called Intrazonal are included in the orders of Vertisols, Inceptisols, and Histosols and in the aquic suborders such as Aquolls and Aqualfs. Zonal soils are mainly included in the other suborders in this classification.

The soil orders and suborders have been defined largely in terms of the common properties that result from soil formation in similar climates with similar vegetation. Because these properties are important to the native vegetation, they have continuing importance to farming, ranching, and forestry. Also, because the properties are common to most of the soils of a given area, it is possible to make small-scale maps that show the distribution of soil orders and suborders with high accuracy.

Zonal properties. A few examples of zonal properties of soils and their relation to soil use follow. The Mollisols, formerly called Chernozemic soils, are rich in plant nutrients. Their natural ability to supply plant nutrients is the highest of any group of soils, but lack of moisture often limits plant growth. Among the Mollisols, the Udolls are associated with a humid climate and are used largely for corn (maize) and soybean production. Borolls have a cool climate and are used for spring wheat, flax, and other early maturing crops. Ustolls have a dry, warm climate and are used largely for winter wheat and sorghum without irrigation. Yields are erratic on these soils. They are moderately high in moist years, but crop failures are common in dry years. The drier Ustolls are used largely for grazing. Xerolls have a rainless summer, and crops must mature on moisture stored in the cool seasons. Xerolls are used largely for wheat and produce consistent yields.

The Alfisols, formerly a part of the Podzolic soil group, are lower in plant nutrients than Mollisols, particularly nitrogen and calcium, but supported a permanent agriculture before the development of fertilizers. With the use of modern fertilizers, yields of crops are comparable to those obtained on Mollisols. The Udalfs are largely in intensive cultivation and produce high yields of a wide variety of crops. Boralfs, like Borolls, have short growing seasons but have humid climates. They are used largely for small grains or forestry. Ustalfs are warm and dry for long periods. In the United States they are used for grazing, small grains, and irrigated crops. On other continents they are mostly intensively cultivated during the rainy season. Population density on Ustalfs in Africa is very high except in the areas of the tsetse fly. Xeralfs are used largely for wheat production or grazing because of their dry summers.

Ultisols, formerly called Latosolic soils, are warm, intensely leached, and very low in supplies of plant nutrients. Before the use of fertilizers, Ultisols could be farmed for only a few years after clearing and then had to revert to forest for a much longer period to permit the trees to concentrate plant nutrients at the surface in the leaf litter. With the use of fertilizers, Udults produce high yields of cotton, tobacco, maize, and forage. Ustults are dry for long periods but have good moisture supplies during a rainy season, typically during monsoon rains. Forests are deciduous, and cultivation is mostly shifting unless fertilizers are available.

Aridisols, formerly called Desertic soils, are high in some plant nutrients, particularly calcium and potassium, but are too dry to cultivate without irrigation. They are used for grazing to some extent, but large areas are idle. Under irrigation some Aridisols are highly productive, but large areas are unsuited to irrigation or lack sources of water. *Guy D. Smith*

PHYSICAL PROPERTIES

Physical properties of soil have critical importance to growth of plants and to the stability of cultural structures such as roads and buildings. Such properties commonly are considered to be size and size distribution of primary particles and of secondary particles, or aggregates, and the consequent size, distribution, quantity, and continuity of pores; the relative stability of the soil matrix against disruptive forces, both natural and cultural; color and textural properties, which affect absorption and radiation of energy; and the conductivity of the soil for water, gases, and heat. These usually would be considered as fixed properties of the soil matrix, but actually some are not fixed because of influence of water content. The additional property, water content—and its inverse, gas content—ordinarily is transient and is not thought of as a property in the same way as the others. However, water is an important constituent, despite its transient nature, and the degree to which it occupies the pore space generally dominates the dynamic properties of soil. Additionally, the properties listed above suggest a macroscopic homogeneity for soil which it may not necessarily have. In a broad sense, a soil may consist of layers or horizons of roughly homogeneous soil materials of various types that impart dynamic properties which are highly dependent upon the nature of the layering. Thus, a discussion of dynamic soil properties must include a description of the intrinsic properties of small increments as well as properties it imparts to the system.

From a physical point of view it is primarily the dynamic properties of soil which affect plant growth and the strength of soil beneath roads and buildings. While these depend upon the chemical and mineralogical properties of particles, particle coatings, and other factors discussed above, water content usually is the dominant factor. Water content depends upon flow and retention properties, so that the relationship between water content and retentive forces associated with the matrix becomes a key physical property of a soil.

Soil particles and other constituents. Soil is made up of a variety of minerals at various stages of physical and chemical weathering. For descriptive purposes soil mineral particles are divided into size categories (the size being expressed as the diameter of a spherical particle that would fall in a viscous fluid at the same rate as the irregularly shaped soil particle, or the size of the opening in a screen through which the soil particle would barely pass): clay particles less than 0.002 mm in diameter; silt particles 0.002 to 0.02 mm; and gravels larger than 2 mm in diameter. Several different systems of size classification exist, and these size categories often are further subdivided. In addition to mineral particles, organic materials (both decomposed and undecomposed), numerous living organisms, and chemical compounds, such as iron and aluminum oxides, are found in soils. Both water and air also are important components of soil, but being transient in nature they usually are not treated as constituents of the soil matrix.

Texture and textural classification. The mineral composition of a soil with respect to size and size distribution of the primary particles is referred to as soil texture. The textural classification of soil is based upon the relative quantities of clay, silt, and sand found in a sample. The most common textural classification of soils is shown in **Fig. 19**, where descriptive names are given to soil materials with different ranges of particle composition. The names are intended to be suggestive of the physical behavior of soils of different composition. The clay fraction generally is regarded as the active fraction because of its colloidal nature and extremely large surface area per unit mass of particles. More than a dozen types of

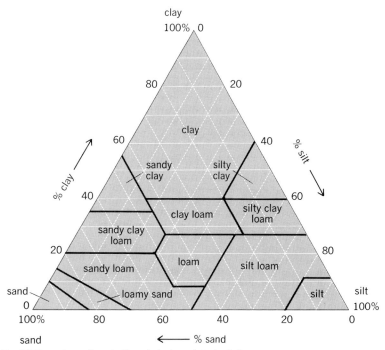

Fig. 19. Percentage of sand, silt, and clay in each textural class.

mineral particles are found in the clay fraction of different soils, each having somewhat different properites, as is discussed elsewhere in this article. However, with respect to soil physical properties, clays may be divided into two major classes, swelling and nonswelling. The nonswelling clays are largely found in areas of high rainfall where chemical weathering has proceeded to a greater degree than in drier areas where swelling clays dominate. The swelling clays generally have a larger surface area (approximately 800 m²/g), with both interlayer and external surfaces, and thus have greater capacity to retain ions by surface adsorption than do nonswelling clays with only external surfaces (approximately 10 to 20 m²/g). Swelling, and the ability of particles to cohere to form granules or aggregates, is affected by the kind of ions on the exchange complex (for example, sodium ions generally lead to deflocculation of clay particles, and calcium ions tend to promote flocculation). Pore size and distribution in soil are materially affected by the degree of flocculation. Silt particles, with considerably smaller surface area and no swelling properties, have little capacity to absorb ions. These particles generally occur in flat shapes, or plates and rods, and often are oriented in the soil so as to form layers with relatively low porosity. Sands and larger particles have irregular shapes and, in the absence of finer soil materials, have large associated pores.

Structure and pore space. Although the mineralogical nature of the clay fraction and the textural classification of the soil are of basic importance to soil physical properties, other factors often have even greater importance. Decomposed organic matter, or humus, and certain inorganic compounds, such as iron and aluminum oxides, form coatings on soil particles, and these, along with some clays, bind soil particles together into granules or aggregates. The size and distribution of such aggregates are major factors in determining pore size and distribution in soil and are important in the physical behavior of soils.

Additionally, fragmented organic materials, undecomposed or only partially so, if present in soil in significant quantity, also can play a major role in determining physical properties. The manner in which mineral soil particles are assembled and maintained in aggregate form, together with quantity, size, and distribution of fragments of partially decomposed organic materials, is referred to as soil structure. Soil structure may develop as a consequence of natural processes such as wetting and drying, freezing and thawing, transport of minerals in moving water and their deposition, or mechanical forces exerted by plant roots or by other biological agents. These processes are discussed elsewhere. Natural structure also may be modified by plowing, cultivation, and mechanical forces associated with cultural activities.

There are two aspects to the evaluation of soil structure which have major practical importance: measurements of pore size and configuration, and assessments of the stability of these characteristics against various natural and cultural forces which act to change the physical arrangement of primary particles and secondary aggregates. Pore size and configuration determine water retention and water and air transport properties of a soil and, in some cases, the ease with which plant roots penetrate and living organisms can move. The equivalent pore size of the largest water-filled pore in a soil sample (that is, the radius of a cylindrical pore which would behave with respect to water retention similarly to the largest water-filled soil pore) may be measured by using the hanging water column apparatus shown in **Fig. 20**, and the equation for capillary rise, $r = 2s/Dgh$, where s is the surface tension of water, D its density, g the acceleration of gravity, and h the height of rise of water in a capillary tube of radius r.

The porous plate apparatus for relating water-filled pore size to the force of removal exerted by the hanging water column (Fig. 20a) is based upon a capillary tube model where soil pores are presumed to be equivalent to small sections of capillary tubes as shown in Fig. 20b. Pores in the porous plate are all considerably smaller than the size of the capillary tube shown in Fig. 20a, so that they remain water-filled as h is varied. More typically, the shape of air-water interfaces is as shown in Fig. 20c, where the radius of curvature, R, is given as a combination of a positive radius r_1 measured axially and a negative radius r_2 at right angles, or $1/R = (1/r_1) + (1/r_2)$. A plot of water content of a soil sample in the hanging column apparatus against the height of the hanging water column characterizes the pore size distribution of the sample. A large change in water content with a small change in hanging water column length indicates a large volume of pores of similar size, whereas a small change in water content with a large change in hanging water column length indicates a relatively small volume associated with pores over a wide size range. More direct evidence of pore size and arrangement may be obtained by microscopic examination.

The second factor which is basic to determining the structural state of soil has to do with soil stability against disruptive forces. The existence of binding forces between clay particles themselves and between clay and other mineral surfaces, together with colloidal organic decomposition products, polysaccharides and polyuronides, and inorganic cementing substances, determines how well a particular geometrical organization of soil particles resists change against disruptive forces. Hence, structural evaluation usually involves both geometrical properties and some indication of how stable a particular arrangement of particles will be against the disruptive forces of a plow, falling raindrops, the weight of an animal, or some other force. Although the nature of the pore space, by implication at least, is a part of any characterization of soil structure, often the measurement involves application of a particular disruptive force and noting the degree to which an existing arrangement is destroyed. A typical measurement of this type involves placing a sample of soil on a nest of size-graded sieve and then moving it up and down in a container of water (or, sometimes, in the air). Following a specified treatment, the quantity of aggregates remaining on each sieve, corrected for the presence of primary particles, is plotted on a graph. From the graph it is possible to devise a rating system which shows how well a given soil has withstood the forces of flowing water. An evaluation technique should utilize the particular type of disruptive force which best simulates the disruptive forces of interest.

Bulk density. An important property which can be used to characterize the structural state of a soil is the bulk density. Where the particle density of soil materials is uniform (often taken as 2.65 g/cm³), it is possible to determine the total pore space fraction of a soil from measurement of the bulk density (mass of dry soil per unit bulk volume) and use of the formula, pore space fraction $= 1 - (D_b/D_p)$, where D_b and D_p are the bulk and particle densities. The presence of organic materials having particle densities differing appreciably from those of the mineral particles introduces some error into such computations. Agricultural soils in the plow depth ordinarily have bulk densities ranging from 1.0 to 1.5 g/cm³ and a pore-space fraction from 0.4 to 0.6, or roughly half particles and half pore space.

Soil horizonation. From some perspectives the physical properties of soil may be presented adequately by a description of the properties of a sample of surface soil. However, horizonation, whether produced by natural or cultural processes, may profoundly affect water flow and retention near the sur-

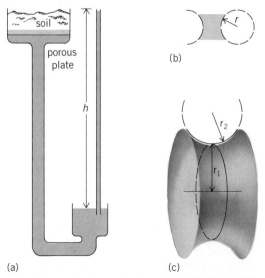

Fig. 20. Measurement of equivalent pore size. (a) Porous plate apparatus. (b) Schematic representations of the air-water interfaces and (c) the particle-water interfaces.

face or within the rooting zone of plants. Such influence is particularly noticeable at boundaries between materials having different pore sizes.

Horizonation may be the result of the method of original deposition, for example, alluvial or loess derived profiles, or it may develop over time as a consequence of differential weathering processes which are different near the soil surface from those at depths beneath. Root growth and development and organic matter decomposition near the surface may promote both the development of aggregates and their stabilization. Also, fine soil particles, silts and clays, may be displaced downward through a profile by moving water, accumulating in layers below. Solutes carried in water also may dissolve minerals, carrying them in the direction of water flow and depositing them as precipitates or leaving them behind as water evaporates.

Horizonation also may occur in soil as a consequence of plowing and cultivation operations. It is not unusual for a plow pan to develop in cultivated soils (**Fig. 21**) as a consequence of the smearing action of an implement surface as it slides through the soil. Decreased porosity at an interface between disturbed and undisturbed soil can profoundly affect water flow and bring about both filtering of fine particles, which may be carried in moving water, and deposition of substances by precipitation. Also, soil may become severely compacted in the surface by vehicle and animal traffic, with a consequent decrease in porosity and increase in hardness.

Forces acting on soil water. Because of the importance of water content upon other soil physical properties, the dynamics of soil water must be understood. Flow of water depends upon forces existing in or applied to the water. In saturated soil the two most important forces are those due to the weight of water which may stand on the soil surface and the pull of gravity upon water within the pores of the soil. Under saturated conditions the hydraulic head is the elevation distance between the water surface above or at the soil surface and the surface of a water table (the elevation at which water would stand in an open pipe extending down into the soil).

Several types of forces act in soil above the water table. Gravity continues to pull downward. But forces independent of gravity exist due to the attraction of solid surfaces for water, the molecular attraction of water molecules for each other, and a force in the air-water interface due to the polar nature of water and consequent unbalanced forces across a plane of organized water molecules which separates a liquid region from a gaseous region. These forces, described as matric forces, are responsible for the phenomenon of capillary rise. In addition to gravity and matric (or capillary) forces, three other types of forces commonly are considered: osmotic forces relating to the attraction between solutes and water, local gas pressure which may exert a force upon air-water interfaces, and overburden forces which arise where substances dissolved or suspended in water add to its density and increase its unit weight. Overburden forces may exist also in saturated soil, but usually such forces are neglected under both saturated and unsaturated conditions. The natures of these five forces differ appreciably, and the direction in which each acts is highly complicated. Hence, it is difficult to apply them quantitatively to soil water. To circumvent this difficulty, the contribution of the various

Fig. 21. Interface between disturbed soil and compact soil produced by the smearing action of a tillage implement as shown by a scanning electron micrograph. Water flow across such an interface is greatly reduced.

forces to the energy state of soil water is considered, thus permitting the addition of the contributions of each type of force. This involves measuring the work required to remove a unit quantity of water, and is known as the potential. Such work depends upon the degree of wetness, so that the energy state is not a linear function of water content. The units of measurement are energy content per unit of liquid volume of water. The commonly used units for potential are the bar, the millibar, and centimeter of water. Above the water table, work is required to remove water, and by convention, potential is negative. The potential at a flat or free air–water interface is taken to be zero.

Practical problems of water flow in unsaturated soil involve mostly the matric and gravity potentials. For flow into roots, because they are semipermeable membranes, additional work must be done by a plant to remove water from those ions which do not readily pass through root membranes. Thus, in dealing with flow of water in soil-plant systems, osmotic potentials also must be considered. However, gravity potential often is small compared to matric and osmotic potentials, and sometimes may be neglected. Matric potential is a function of water content, pore size, and pore size distribution in the soil. As with capillary tubes, small pores hold water tightly, and considerable work must be done to remove it. The capillary rise equation may be used to relate the size of the largest water-filled pores (the size of a cylindrical pore with similar water-retentive properties) to the force required to remove water from wet soil, $h = 2s/(Dgr)$ as described earlier. Such air-water interfaces in small pores are essentially hemispherical so that this radius also approximates the spherical equivalent of the irregularly shaped pore.

Figure 20 illustrates the application of the capillary rise equation to a porous soil system in the wet range. Pores in the porous plate are all small enough to remain water-filled at the elevation of the hanging water column (smaller than the radius of a capillary tube which would raise water to this elevation). The radii of the air-water interfaces in the soil are given by the capillary rise equation. If the elevation h is decreased, larger pores become water-filled; if h is increased, only smaller pores remain water-filled. The elevation is an index of the matric potential, and the potential on a mass basis may be obtained by multiplying by the acceleration of gravity: hg (or if potential is on a volume basis, the value is hDg, where D is the density of water). The pressure in the water just below the interface as given by the equation $p = 2s/r$, and if the radius is taken as negative (the radius of a raindrop is positive and the pressure inside also is positive), the pressure may be seen to be negative or less than the pressure of the atmosphere.

Matric potential in wet soil equals the work done per unit mass or volume to remove water from the air-water interface or against surface tension forces. As the soil becomes drier, larger and larger proportions of the water are associated with particle surfaces, and more work per unit quantity must be done to remove this water, which is tightly held by adsorptive forces in the particle surface. Hence, matric potential may be seen to involve both surface tension and the attraction of particle surfaces for water. Curves showing this relationship over a wide range of water content are obtained experimentally and used to characterize different soils. Several of these for soils of different textural classification are shown in **Fig. 22**. However, since it is the porosity (a characteristic dependent not only upon textural classification but also upon the degree and kind of aggregation) that defines the relationship, different curves can exist for the same basic soil material treated differently.

The water potential–water content curves shown in Fig. 22 are desorption curves obtained in the process of removing water from saturated soil. A slightly different curve would exist for the wetting cycle because filling and emptying of large pores is controlled by the size of entryways rather than the size of the pore

itself. Air is easily trapped in large pores during filling, and water is retained in large pores during drying, until entryways are emptied. This hysteresis phenomenon sometimes complicates use of water potential–water content curves, since it is impossible to determine one from the other without knowledge of the wetting history.

Water movement and retention. Water moves in soil in response to the net force acting. The gradient of the total potential is a force per unit mass if potential is defined as potential energy per unit mass (or a force per unit volume if defined on a volume basis). The flow equation is flux $= -k\lambda$ grad θ, where θ is the total potential, k is the saturated hydraulic conductivity, and λ is a channel-filling factor, which varies from 0 to 1 depending on the water content. If the soil is saturated, this value is unity and the potential term is the sum of the gravity and pressure potentials. The channel-filling factor falls off rapidly as large pores empty, so that the cross section available for liquid flow is greatly reduced. As the soil desaturates, the pressure potential disappears and is replaced by a negative matric potential term. Matric forces are "pulling" rather than "pushing" forces, and water is pulled from regions of high potential into regions of low potential. Liquid water flows through water-filled interstitial space and along surfaces. The air-filled pores contribute nothing to liquid flow. Under such circumstances it may be seen that coarse materials, such as gravels, which would have high conductivity when saturated, would have extremely low conductivity at low water content. Thus water movement in unsaturated soil may be retarded in regions of large pores as well as in regions with fine pores. Aside from the influence of air-filled pores in reducing conductivity, conductivity is also reduced, beyond the amount expected from reduction of flow cross section, as pore size is reduced. The conductivity of capillary tubes varies with the fourth power of the capillary radius (Hagen-Poiseuille equation). On a unit area basis, the variation is with the square of the radius. Hence, with the force term held constant, reducing pore radius by a factor of 2 would reduce flow by a factor of 2^2, or 4.

Movement of water into soil, infiltration, and redistribution of water in soil following water addition both slow down with time as a consequence of changing gradients and reduction of unsaturated hydraulic conductivity as water moves from wet zones into dryer zones. Slow redistribution is of particular importance to consideration of water retention in soil. Water is nearly always moving, downward into dry soil or toward a water table, and upward in response to evaporative forces at the soil surface. Hence, soil has no unique retentive capacity. Water-retentive capacity is a dynamic property and must be defined in the context of change with time. A practical field capacity may be specified as the quantity of water in a defined depth of soil when rate of downward flow, or loss from a designated part of the profile, reduces to a value beyond which any further loss may be regarded as negligible. For agricultural purposes, and depending upon the nature of the profile, this rate would be reached in a period of time ranging from a fraction of a day to 10 or more days. Soil horizon, involving either coarse or fine layers, reduces liquid water flow rates and increases water retention, generally reducing the time required to reach a negligible loss value.

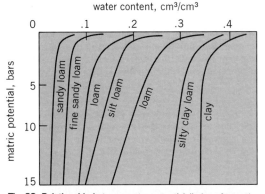

Fig. 22. Relationship between water potential (index of retentive forces) and water content for different soil materials. Wide variations often exist, even for materials in the same textural class. 1 bar = 10^2 kPa; 1 cm^3 = 0.6 in.^{3}

Water vapor is present in the soil air, with high relative humidity existing in soil wet enough to support plant growth (relative humidities of from 98.9 to 100% in the plant growth range). At uniform temperature the sum of matric and osmotic potentials, which affect evaporation, may be equated to relative humidity by the equation: matric + osmotic potential = (RT/M) in (p/p_0), where R is the universal gas constant, T the Kelvin temperature, M the molecular weight of water, and p/p_0 the vapor pressure divided by the vapor pressure of saturated air at the same temperature, or the relative humidity. Where gradients of matric plus osmotic potential exist in soil, vapor pressure gradients also exist, and vapor flow can take place, even when liquid flow is negligibly small. If temperature gradients also exist, appreciable vapor flow can occur because of large vapor density gradients. However, in the absence of temperature gradients, vapor flow over large distances is small in dry soil. Because of low hydraulic conductivity values in dry soil, evaporative water loss from below depths of 25–50 cm (10–20 in.), in the absence of plants, generally is negligibly small, and moist soil, even in deserts, may be found below such depths. Flow of water in dry soil is primarily in vapor form, and the insulation properties of dry soil are high, so that high temperature gradients required for rapid diffusion of vapor do not exist.

Air composition and flow. Gaseous composition of soil air, apart from water vapor discussed above, tends toward the composition of the atmosphere, with somewhat higher concentrations of carbon dioxide and lower concentrations of oxygen due to metabolic processes which utilize oxygen and give off carbon dioxide. Exchange with the atmosphere is most rapid in dry soil having high porosity and least rapid in dense or wet soil. The composition of the soil air affects plant growth and the growth of microorganisms and insects which inhabit the soil. Hence, limited air exchange with the atmosphere often has a marked effect on plant disease and plant growth generally. Oxygen requirements of plant roots vary with different plants, so that plant composition often is dependent upon aeration characteristics of soils.

Solute movement. Physical conditions of soils affect solute movement. Water is necessary in the vicinity of roots to solubilize nutrients contained in clays and other minerals and to form liquid paths through which the nutrients may diffuse and become available for absorption by roots. Also, solutes may be carried in water taken in through roots to form the transpirational stream. SEE PLANT MINERAL NUTRITION; PLANT TRANSLOCATION OF SOLUTES.

Solutes may be carried with moving water downward out of the rooting zone of plants and upward in moving water due to evaporation at the soil surface. In the latter case, transport to the surface and deposition through evaporation of pure water constitute a concentration process leading to high salt concentration in and on the soil surface. SEE ROOT (BOTANY).

Mechanical strength. Single grain soil materials like dry sands have only a limited capability to withstand stress or compressive forces when unconfined. With small amounts of water added, this capability is increased because of surface tension forces in air–water interfaces which tend to hold particles together. Elimination of air–water interfaces by further additions of water, together with lubrication of particle surfaces, reduces the ability to withstand stress. Aggregated soil behaves somewhat in the same fashion except that stabilizing materials such as humus tend to bind particles into aggregates. Soil, particularly when moist, has some tensile strength. However, tensile strength is limited, as may be seen with swelling soils which may shrink and form large cracks upon drying. Compressive strength varies with degree of compaction brought about by animal or vehicle traffic, particularly at critical water contents somewhere between wet and dry. The water content for maximum compaction depends upon textural characteristics and types of clay minerals present. In a like manner an optimum water content generally exists for maximum effectiveness of tillage operations designed to fragment the soil and reduce hardness.

Mechanical strength is an important consideration in agriculture as well as construction engineering. The agriculturalist needs soil which is strong enough to support small plants and trees, yet soft enough to permit easy movement of roots. Additionally, the soil should be sufficiently resistant to the mechanical forces of rain and running water to hold its position. The engineer needs soil with minimum shrink and swell properties and maximum strength over a wide range of water contents.

Soil temperature. Soil temperature depends upon absorption of solar radiation, reradiation from the surface, conductive exchange with the air, heat flow within, and the heat capacity of the soil. Soil color and surface texture influence both absorption and reradiation. Smooth, light-colored materials generally reflect light energy and are poor radiators, while rough, dark materials absorb or reradiate energy best. Thus, rough, dark soils tend to warm faster than smooth, light-colored materials. Organic residues on the soil surface play a major role in determining soil temperature through interception of both incoming and outgoing radiation and reduction in the velocity of air movement at the soil surface. Water content is the major factor involved in both heat transfer and heat retention, increasing both thermal conductivity and thermal capacity. Change of state of soil water—freezing, thawing, and evaporating—involves significant quantities of energy as latent heat. Soil temperature at a given depth and time depends on both heat conductance and storage, and complicated mathematical models are required for its prediction.

Plant growth and biological activity. Growth of plants, microorganisms, and insects in soil all involve establishment of an optimum physical environment. In turn, the presence in soil of organic materials and their decomposition products profoundly affects these physical properties. Broken or partially decomposed organic materials behave somewhat the same as mineral particles, and the decomposed material or humus acts as a binding substance imparting stability to mineral particle arrangements of soil aggregates. From a soil physical point of view, the major factors affecting biological activity are water, temperature, and gas composition. With some exceptions, soil supporting growing plants must have a matric-plus-osmotic potential ranging from about -15 bars (-1.5 megapascals) up to a small fraction of -1 bar (-0.1 MPa). If the soil is too wet, aeration becomes limiting. But, because aeration depends upon the quantity of air-filled pores, which will be different in different soils, it is difficult to specify a definite water potential value which will be limiting. Also, numerous agricultural plants grow best when the water potential is above

−1 bar (−0.1 MPa), even though plants might survive at potentials even below −15 bars (−1.5 MPa).

Soils having mostly fine pores tend to remain wet in the spring and to warm slowly, so that many plants are delayed in growing because of low temperature. Optimum temperature for plants varies widely with species, and temperature thresholds exist for many plants; for example, corn and tomatoes grow poorly or not at all until day-time temperatures are well above 59°F (15°C), and growth is reduced if soil temperature greatly exceeds 86°F (30°C). However, many plants do well in cold soil.

Mechanical properties of soil can restrict root growth. Hard pans or plow pans formed by tillage operations often limit the growth of all but the hardiest of plants. Such pans may reduce the size of the rooting zone. The hardness of the soil also is a factor in plowing and tillage operations. Since soil water content affects hardness, certain tillage operations are timed so as to take advantage of a water content that produces softer soil. If too wet, however, a soil may puddle badly when tilled. Thus an optimum water content for such operations exists. Appreciable attention is being given to no-till or minimum tillage to avoid creating hard soil by excessive traffic compaction and to maintain the protection of plant cover against erosion. Weed control, one of the important functions of tillage, is done chemically when these practices are followed. *See Herbicide.*

Walter H. Gardner

MANAGEMENT

Soil management can be defined simply as the manner in which people use soils to produce food, fiber, and forages. Soil management includes determination and use of many factors and practices, such as land survey maps, cropping systems, organic matter and tilth, soil fertility, salinity, and irrigation. Most often, it is not a single soil that is managed; management is carried out on a field or a portion of a landscape composed of a number of physical and biological features, like climate, vegetation, topography, and drainage. In a true sense, applying soil management strategies involves an integration of a number of factors. Such integration involves a difficult synthesis of many individual characteristics, both measured and observed, to arrive at a meaningful interpretation of how a soil responds to management. In fact, the value of any agricultural soil is determined by how well that soil responds to proper management.

Standards. Meaningful assessment of how soils are responding to a particular management system can be judged only if standards are established. There are two primary standards for judging quality of management: prevention of soil deterioration or degradation, and improving the soil system in ways that result in increased plant production. Examples of deterioration that must be prevented are excessive erosion, fertility depletion, and accumulations of salt within the rooting zone of plants. Examples relating to improving the soil system are conservation of precipitation, irrigation development, reclaiming salt-damaged land, and increased water use efficiency by proper fertilization. *See Agricultural soil and crop practices.*

The two goals are very broad and therefore require the integration of many aspects of science. Incorporation of the basic areas of chemistry, physics, and microbiology into management planning is essential. The sciences of ecology, genetics, and various types of engineering are also essential to modern soil management. Computer modeling will play an increasingly important role in soil management by making simulation models directly available to farm and ranch operators.

Land capability classification. The first step in planning a management system is assessment of the soil and environmental resources. This is accomplished through land classification—more specifically, through land capability classification, which groups land according to properties essential for identifying the opportunities or constraints the land offers for various uses.

Interpretations of land capability classifications are most often based on physical, chemical, and economic considerations. Classification provides assessment of land suitability for agricultural and other uses, identifies adapted crops, estimates yields of crops under defined systems of management, indicates presence of specific soil management problems, and delineates opportunities and limitations of various management practices. Through land capability classification, there usually are identified several alternative management strategies for a given type of land. From this information, analyses can be made to determine which land use or management strategy will be most desirable for both economic and wise land utilization.

The basic requirements for developing a good classification system are soil-survey and soil chemical and physical data; climatic, topographic, and hydrologic data; field and laboratory research data; longtime land-use records; and experience and observations of land response to various uses.

Soil surveys are basic in that they identify soil properties important for determining land-use capability. Surveys provide maps showing the location and boundaries of soils. Soil depth, texture, kinds of minerals, salinity and kinds of salts, and acidity are some properties utilized in determining land capability. The particular set of properties needed for determining land capability is dependent on the particular use.

Land classifications cannot be static because they depend upon interpretation. As technology changes and economic and social conditions change, interpretations change. With basic soil, climatic, and topographic data and maps, however, these interpretations can be revised easily. Combinations of alternative land-use and management strategies, as well as social and economic conditions, do change, but the physical and chemical factors of well-managed land do not change very much.

Land classifications have been developed for specific purposes, for example, tax assessment, sales and credit, soil and water conservation, irrigation potential and management, wildlife suitability, watershed management, recreational uses, industrial uses, or highway construction.

Effective extrapolation of management or use strategies to the land depends on an adequate inventory of basic data and how well an existing classification is chosen or a classification developed that fits the specific need at a given time and place. With appropriate facts and maps, through land classification, predictions can be made about the results of using a specific type of land in a particular way. Then, planning of land use includes the practical combinations of management practices required, and the effects of management on the quality of land resources. Without land classification and appropriate maps, it is difficult to extrapolate experience and research results to the land.

Land capability classification systems have been utilized for many years by the Soil Conservation Service, USDA, and other land resource planning and management agencies. Their utilization is being enhanced greatly through the use of computer data storage and management systems. *See Land-use classes*.

Long-term impacts. Modern soil management practices have a cumulative effect on the soil's future productivity. The foremost management question for the soil manager is whether a given practice or system is causing soil degradation. Many current agricultural problems have developed because managers did not realize the long-term impact of their management techniques. Some practices may appear to be sustainable for periods of time equal to a human lifetime, and yet they could be causing slow soil degradation that will ruin the soil for long-term use. Therefore, long-term plans that identify causes of soil deterioration and avoid it successfully are essential to a nation's future agricultural productivity. For example, proper use of fertilizers and manures can enhance long-term productivity and maintain environmental quality. Poor management choices including fertilizers and manures can actually ruin a soil and damage the environment, almost irreparably. Civilizations have often missed the ''clues'' that a particular system was not sustainable. This has led to loss of their food supply, and with their being conquered eventually or ceasing to exist.

Integrated systems. Soil management involves integration of the type illustrated by the diagram in **Fig. 23**. The resource block includes climate, soil, and plants, these are the natural-resource inputs. Modifications can and will be made on them, but for the most part they are the constants of the system. The agriculturist enters the scheme at this point to impose a management system, which has as its goal the production of food, fiber, or forages. Figure 26 also shows that the cropping system imposed is directly related to the soil, climate, and plant resources. The manager implements a cropping system through choice of crop rotation and tillage system. Choice of tillage system is often conditioned by the rotation chosen.

Erosion control, organic matter conservation, and water conservation are the classical concerns of soil management; they are all highly linked. A change in one or more of these three factors creates feedbacks to the others. For example, control of erosion leads to direct savings in soil organic matter and soil water and thus soil conservation. Furthermore, the control of erosion, which relates to the first goal of preventing soil deterioration, is linked directly to the second goal, namely, improvement of the soil system. Erosion prevention techniques also improve soil water storage by reducing water runoff. Conservation of organic matter may increase water infiltration, which decreases runoff and thus decreases erosion. The other blocks in Fig. 26 represent pest management and irrigation and drainage. They are equally important, but have not been studied to as great an extent as the first three factors. In fact, pest and pesticide management are relatively new concepts in soil management. Soil tillage methods and rotations are intimately involved in pest and pesticide management.

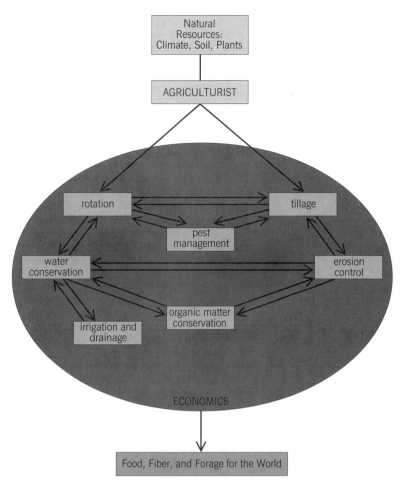

Fig. 23. Diagram showing an integrated system of soil management.

Finally, basic economic principles are involved in all sound soil management systems, as indicated in Fig. 26 by the enclosure of all other factors by economics. This is true in even the most primitive civilizations. If the people cannot live on the food or income produced, the system cannot survive. In more developed nations, quality of management has even influenced the potential value of the land. The ability to cope with the problems of a particular soil eventually determines its economic value to society.

High-quality, efficient management of the natural resources of climate, water, and soil is needed to provide the food and fiber that will sustain life on Earth. Soil management decisions will have an important effect on the future food supply.

G. A. Peterson; W. O. Willis

Salinity

Soluble salt and exchangeable cation concentrations play major roles in determining the pH, physical characteristics, and chemical composition of soils. When a salt dissolves in water, it dissociates or separates into cations and anions. The predominant cations in salt-affected soils are calcium (Ca^{2+}), magnesium (Mg^{2+}), sodium (Na^+), and potassium (K^+); the predominant anions are chloride (Cl^-), sulfate (SO_4^{2-}), carbonate (CO_3^{2-}), and bicarbonate (HCO_3^-).

Clays and organic matter contain negative electrical

charge sites. In salt-affected soils, this charge is satisfied by calcium, magnesium, sodium, and potassium ions. These cations, bound to the exchange sites by the electrical charges, are known as exchangeable cations because they can be removed from the charged surface only by replacement with another cation from the soil solution. *See Soil chemistry.*

Classification. Each soil can be classified as normal, saline, sodic, or saline-sodic, based on its salt content and exchangeable cation ratios.

Normal soils. These soils do not contain sufficient soluble salts to reduce crop yield or sufficient exchangeable sodium to affect soil physical properties adversely. A special technique is employed to measure the salt content of the soil. A saturation paste is made by mixing just enough distilled water with a soil sample to fill the voids without having excess water standing on the surface of a well-mixed sample after 4–16 h. An extract is obtained by removing the solution by vacuum suction through a filter. This saturation paste extract is measured for electrical conductivity (EC_e), which is related to the soluble salt content. For a normal soil the value is less than 4 mmhos/cm. The exchangeable sodium percentage (ESP) of the total exchangeable cations is less than 15. For a normal soil the sodium adsorption ratio (SAR) is less than 13. It is calculated from the concentration, in mmoles/liter, of extract cations, as shown in the equation below. The pH of the saturated

$$SAR = Na^+/(Ca^{2+} + Mg^{2+})^{-1/2}$$

soil paste is less than 8.3. These are defined upper limits, but if salt-sensitive crops were grown on soils with an electrical conductivity of 3.5 mmhos/cm, a significant yield reduction would be expected. Likewise, using a high-volume sprinkler system to irrigate a soil with an exchangeable sodium percentage of 12 could produce serious runoff rates because of low infiltration rates.

Saline soils. These soils contain sufficient soluble salts (electrical conductivity greater than 4 mmhos/cm) in the upper root zone to reduce yields of most cultivated crops and ornamental plants. The exchangeable sodium percentage is less than 15, the sodium absorption ratio is less than 13, and the pH is less than 8.3. The predominant cations are calcium, magnesium, and, in a few cases, potassium. The predominant anions are chloride and sulfate. Water entry and movement through these soils is not inhibited by exchangeable sodium. Osmotic effects and chloride toxicity are the predominant causes of plant growth reduction.

Sodic soils. These soils are lower in soluble salts than saline soils (electrical conductivity less than 4 mmhos/cm). The exchangeable sodium percentage is greater than 15 and the sodium absorption ratio of the saturation paste extract is greater than 13. The pH of the saturation paste extract is greater than 8.5. Bicarbonate, carbonate, and hydroxide (OH^-) ions are the anions that predominate in these soils; they cause calcium to precipitate from solution as calcium carbonate ($CaCO_3$; lime). The combination of high exchangeable sodium percentage and pH, and low electrical conductivity causes the clay and organic matter to disperse, which in turn destroys the soil structure or tilth, causing so-called slick spots. These spots have extremely low rates of water and air exchange. They often have a black, greasy, or oily-looking surface due to the dispersed organic matter; vegetation may be absent because water infiltration is low.

Saline-sodic. These soils are similar to saline soils in that the electrical conductivity is greater than 4 mmhos/cm and the pH is below 8.3. Saline-sodic soils differ from saline soils in that more than 15% of the exchangeable cations is sodium and the saturation-paste sodium absorption ratio is greater than 13. The anions are a mix of bicarbonate, chloride, and sulfate. As long as the electrical conductivity remains above 4 mmhos/cm, infiltration rates and hydraulic conductivities are similar to those of normal or saline soils. Irrigating saline-sodic soils with water having low concentrations will convert them into sodic soils if they do not contain gypsum (a calcium sulfate mineral). This happens as the electrical conductivity decreases without a decrease in the exchangeable sodium percentage, causing the undesirable properties of sodic soils to be expressed. It is not uncommon to have a mix of two or more classes of salt-affected soils within a field. Salt-affected soils tend to be highly variable from one part of a field to another.

Sources. Most soluble salts and exchangeable cations are derived from rock and mineral weathering of the soil parent materials. In high-rainfall, humid, and tropical areas, rain and melting snow leach the salts from the soil as they form. In arid and semiarid areas, the annual evapotranspiration potential is greater than the total annual precipitation, and the salts are not always leached from the soil as they are released. With time, they may accumulate in the root zone at concentration levels that affect plant growth.

Salts often accumulate above shallow water tables as water moves to the soil surface by capillary rise (wicking) and evaporates, leaving the salts on or near the surface. Shallow water tables may occur naturally, induced by irrigating poorly drained areas, by irrigating upslope from lowlands, or by construction activity that blocks natural subsurface lateral drainage.

All natural waters contain dissolved salt. In many arid and semiarid areas, good-quality irrigation water (low in salts and low in sodium) is not available; consequently, water is used that contains more salts or sodium than is desirable. If sufficient water does not move through the soil and leach the salts below the root zone, salts or sodium will accumulate in the soil. It is often stated that under irrigation "hard water makes soft soils and soft water makes hard soils." This implies that irrigation waters containing predominantly calcium and magnesium salts (sodium absorption ratio less than 3 or 4) tend to promote a more friable soil condition than do waters with high concentrations of sodium.

Four conditions must be satisfied in order to remove soluble salts and excess sodium from soils: (1) less salt must be added to the soil than is removed; (2) salts must be leached downward through the soil; (3) water moving upward from shallow water tables must be removed or intercepted to avoid additional salts moving back to the soil surface; and (4) in sodic and saline-sodic soils the exchangeable sodium must be replaced with another cation, preferably calcium, and the sodium leached out. Applications of soil amendments (gypsum, iron sulfate, sulfur, or sulfuric acid) are beneficial only on sodic soils when leaching also occurs and on leaching of saline-sodic soils that do not contain gypsum.

Saline and sodic soils are found primarily in arid and semiarid areas of the world. Exceptions are recently drained coastal areas, salt marshes, and soils formed in depressions from marine deposits where the weathering products are not leached from the soil. Aridisols and Entisols include most salt-affected soils. Low rainfall and unweathered soil materials result in insufficient salts leaching from the root zone. Mollisols, Alfisols, and Vertisols also contain considerable saline and sodic soil areas.

Human activities such as spills or intentional dumping of salts or solutions from drilling-mud ponds, mines, food-processing plants, municipal sewage water, power-plant cooling-tower water, or heavy applications of wood ash can induce saline and sodic conditions in any soil when soluble salts are applied faster than they are leached from the soil.

C. W. Robbins

Effects on plants. Many ions may be essential to plant growth as major or minor nutrients. However, when ion concentrations become too high, plant growth may be adversely affected by either the toxic effect of a specific ion or a general effect of high ion concentrations. Salinity decreases plant growth by a combination of nonspecific ionic effects and by causing a decrease in the water potential of the soil, which is principally an osmotic effect.

The point at which salinity limits plant growth varies; plants are adapted to a wide range of saline environments. The ocean, which has salt concentrations in excess of 35 parts per thousand, is abundant in plant life; over half of the Earth's biomass is marine. Concentrations at which specific ions become harmful to plant growth also vary over several orders of magnitude. For example, boron is toxic to some plants at soil-water concentrations as low as 0.05 mol/m^3, whereas some plants can tolerate chloride concentrations as high as 20 mol/m^3.

Terrestrial plants that are tolerant of high concentrations of soluble salts in their root zones (the area around the root from which a plant extracts water) are known as halophytes. Halophytes can survive and complete their life cycles at optimum salt concentrations of 1.2–30 parts per thousand salt in their rooting medium; they are ecologically competitive only when soil-water salt concentrations are high. Most terrestrial plant species are not adapted to high salt concentrations and may be considered to be glycophytes.

In agriculture, salt is a serious hazard in irrigated areas if growers do not leach their soils properly during irrigation or fail to provide adequate drainage for their crops. High concentrations of salts in groundwaters used for irrigation may also damage crops or reduce yields. As a property of soil or water, salinity acts as an environmental plant stress that may cause leaf damage, reduce growth or, at high concentrations, be lethal. Plant responses to excess salts in their root zones or on their leaf surfaces (from ocean sprays or irrigation) are quantitatively dependent upon salt concentration, time of exposure, and salt composition. Plant sensitivity to salt also varies according to growth stage and with species, varieties, and ecotypes.

Crop salt tolerance. Salt tolerance is the capacity of a plant to endure excess salt in the rooting medium. This ability is quantitative and dependent upon many soil, climatic, and cultural factors. Tolerance assessment may be based upon the ability to survive, to produce high yields, or to withstand adverse growth reductions. In nature, the measure of tolerance may be the ability of a species to survive, reproduce, and compete with other species; whereas in sustenance agriculture, tolerance may be related to both survival and the production of a usable yield for the grower.

However, in commercial agriculture the ability of the crop to withstand salt effects without reducing yields below the economic threshold is the most important consideration. Salt tolerance is described as a function of a threshold salinity at which yield first becomes significantly affected, and then as a linear decrease in yield with each incremental increase in salinity (**Fig. 24**). Soil salinity concentrations are described in terms of the electrical conductivity of a saturated soil paste in units of decisiemens/meter (dS/m). Salt tolerance values may be useful for predicting how one crop may compare with another under similar conditions; however, such assessments are general and relate to growth of the crop after germination and seedling establishment.

Climate and agricultural management practices may reduce or increase the effects of salinity upon plants. Irrigation and management practices that move salts away from, or maintain lower concentrations of salts in, the root zone during growth will reduce salt effects. Seedbeds should be planted and maintained in a manner that allows the irrigation water to move salts past the root zone. If excess salts in the seedbed are not kept low, the resulting reduction in plant stand will decrease yields far more than is predicted by the salt tolerance data. Flood, furrow, drip, and sprinkler irrigations should also be timed and applied in ways that reduce salt accumulation on plant parts or within root zones. Climatic factors such as high temperatures, low humidities, and high wind speed will increase salt damage, whereas factors that reduce transpirational demand will reduce it. Soil type is also an important factor. Light, sandy soils will not accumulate salts as readily and are easier to leach than clay soils.

Genetic variability. Many crops, such as sugarbeet, asparagus, date palm, cotton, and barley, are salt-tolerant and are standard crops in saline areas. Beans, different types of berries, and many fruit trees are very sensitive to salt. Rice, although salt-sensitive, is considered a reclamation crop on saline lands because it has shallow roots and can be grown in flooded fields if water of good quality is available.

Conventional breeding efforts to improve salt tolerance include selection for more tolerant crop varieties through hybridization and selection; hybridization of cultivated species with related, wild salt-tolerant species to increase genetic variability prior to selection; and exploitation of the useful agronomic potential of wild halophytes. The ability of the grower

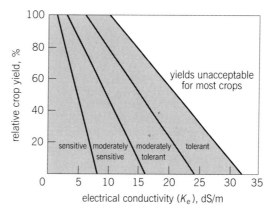

Fig. 24. Typical classifications for the salt tolerance of crops based upon their relative yields under nonsaline conditions in contrast to yields under saline conditions.

to control the effects of salt in the field is of far greater consequence than the salt-tolerance variabilities among cultivars.

Morphological and physiological effects. Salinity reduces plant growth through both osmotic and ionic influences. The osmotic effects are a result of increased solute concentrations at the root–soil water interface, which create lower water potentials. Growth suppression is the result of total electrolyte concentration, soil water content, and soil matrix effects and is manifested in reduced cell enlargement and metabolism. The plant suffers water stress for a short period until it can make some type of osmotic adjustment. Plants usually make this adjustment either by accumulating more salt within their tissues (a halophytic response) or by the organic synthesis of solutes, which increases the osmotic potential of the cytoplasm.

Ionic effects may be both general and specific. General ionic effects are the result of the increased ionic strength of the soil water. Ionic effects may interfere with the normal mechanisms by which plants take up nutrients by changing the surface chemistry near cell walls and membranes. Specific ions may cause damage to metabolic processes or upset nutritional balances. For instance, high sodium concentrations relative to other salts can disrupt root permeability to ions by displacing calcium in the plasma membrane. Additional effects may be caused by upsetting calcium metabolism and nutrition within the cell. At higher sodium-to-calcium ratios, soil structure, tilth, and permeability of the soil to water may be reduced (sodicity).

The specific physiological cause of growth reduction due to salt stress is undoubtedly complex in both the physiological and genetic sense. Salt stress reduces plant growth primarily because it increases the metabolic energy needed to acquire water from the root zone and to make the necessary biochemical and morphological adjustments necessary to maintain growth in a higher ionic environment. *See Soil fertility*.
                                                            Michael Shannon

Erosion

Soil erosion is that physical process by which soil material is carried away by water or by wind. Two categories of erosion are recognized. Geologic erosion is a natural process that takes place independent of human activities; this kind of erosion is always active, wearing away the surface of the Earth. Accelerated erosion occurs when humans disturb the surface of the Earth or quicken the pace of erosion in any way. Accelerated erosion from crop, pasture, range, and forest land poses a problem for the future food and fiber supply of the world. Recognizing and understanding erosion processes and factors that affect them is important for combating erosion. *See Erosion*.

Types. Soil erosion is produced by water or wind. Erosion by water is the result of raindrop action and surface runoff and is recognized in one or a combination of three forms: sheet, rill, and gully erosion. In wind erosion, varying quantities of soil are removed by the force of wind.

Sheet erosion. The removal of a thin layer of soil, more or less uniformly, from the entire surface of an area is known as sheet erosion. It usually occurs on plowed fields that have been recently prepared for seeding, or after the crop is seeded and before a crop canopy covers the soil. Although the depth of soil lost in any one year may not be great, the loss of rich topsoil over a period of years may be serious. In time, if no conservation measures are taken, the entire surface layer of soil may be removed. In most soils, the productive potential of the soil for growing crops decreases as the surface layer erodes. Residue left as a surface mulch from the previous crop is very effective in controlling this type of erosion.

Rill erosion. During heavy rains, runoff water is concentrated in small streamlets or rivulets. As the rate of runoff increases, the water can erode small channels called rills. All traces of the rills are removed by tillage of the land. Erosion of this type can remove large quantities of soil and rapidly reduce soil productivity. If conservation measures are not taken to prevent further loss of soil, the rilling continues year after year until the rich topsoil is gone. Surface mulch use in conjunction with terracing is very effective in controlling this type of erosion.

Gully erosion. This type of erosion occurs where the concentrated runoff is sufficiently large to cut deep channels not crossable with farm machinery. Continued cutting in the same channel deepens the incision. Gullying often develops where there is a water overfall. The stream bed is cut back at the overfall, and the gully lengthens headward or upslope. Once started, gullying may proceed rapidly, particularly in soils that do not possess much strength to resist erosion. Gully erosion requires intensive control measures, such as terracing or the use of waterways, diversion ditches, or check dams or, in extreme cases, grade control structures.

Wind erosion. In the western half of the United States and in many other parts of the world, great quantities of soil are moved by wind. This is particularly so in arid and semiarid areas. Sandy soils are more subject to wind erosion than silt loam or clay loam soils. The latter, however, are easily eroded when climatic conditions cause the soil to break into small aggregates, ranging from 0.004 to 0.02 in. (0.1 to 0.5 mm) in diameter. The coarse particles are usually moved relatively short distances, but the fine dust particles may be carried by strong winds for hundreds or even thousands of miles.

In some areas the coarse, or sand, particles are moved by the wind and deposited over extensive areas as dunes. The dunes move forward in the same direction as the prevailing winds, the particles being moved from the windward side of the dune to the lee side. If dunes become covered with grass or other vegetation, they cease to move. The sandhill region of Nebraska is a good example of such an area. Because of desertification, dunes have ruined much former crop and grazing land in Africa. *See Desertification; Dust storm*.

Factors affecting erosion. The rate and extent of soil erosion depend on such interrelated factors as characteristics of soil, topography, climate, and land use.

Soil factors. Soils vary greatly in physical, mineralogical, and chemical composition. The amounts of sand, silt, clay, and organic matter, and the structure and permeability of soil all affect the susceptibility of soil particles and aggregates to detach from the soil surface. Such detachment is caused chiefly by impacting raindrops, surface runoff, and wind. The particles are then transported downgrade by moving water or wind. Sandy or gravelly soils often have little colloidal material of clay and organic matter to bind particles together, and hence these materials are easily detached by flowing water. However, permeability of these soils is high so water is taken in rapidly, leaving little for carrying the sand or gravel particles. Thus, sand particles are moved chiefly during very intense rain on steep slopes. Soils high in silt are low in binding material and are not highly permeable. These are the most easily detached of all soils by water and are most susceptible to rilling and gullying. High silt soil areas of the world, such as those adjoining the Missouri River of the United States and the Yellow River of China, have suffered intense erosion by water. Sandy soils the world over are very susceptible to erosion by wind and have suffered intense erosion, especially in arid areas with frequent drought, where vegetative cover tends to be reduced or destroyed.

Topography. The amount of total runoff from rainfall increases only slightly with increase in the slope of the land above 1–2%, but the velocity of flowing water greatly increases as slope increases. Since the capacity of moving water to transport soil particles increases in geometric ratio to velocity of flow, the amount of erosion increases greatly with the increase in the slope of the land. Increased slope length adds to the rate and amount of runoff available for detachment and transport of soil material.

Climate. The amount and intensity of rainfall are important factors in determining the erosion that occurs from water in a given region. A region of high rainfall generally has dense natural vegetation which reduces the danger of erosion. Regions of low rainfall and sparse vegetation or fields left bare by plowing are susceptible to erosion when intense rains occur. A rain falling at the rate of 2 in./h (51 mm/h) may cause several times as much erosion as a rainfall of 1 in./h (25 mm/h). Regions where most of the precipitation occurs in the form of mist or gentle rain may undergo little erosion, even though the total rainfall may be high and other conditions conducive to erosion are present.

In some areas of dry climates, strong winds cause soil movement and serious loss of soil. Erosion by wind occurs when velocities at ground level exceed about 12 mi/h (19 km/h). Soils, especially those high in organic matter, which have a loose physical condition produced by freezing and thawing or wetting and drying, or soils that have been smoothed by intense rain, may be moved in great quantities by the wind. Wet soils do not erode readily, but wind dries the soil rapidly so it can erode. Vegetation is much thicker in the more humid areas than in arid areas, and this tends to slow the wind velocity and reduce

erosion. Of course, clean tilled fields erode easily whether they are in humid or arid regions.

In cold climates, frozen soil is not subject to erosion for several months of the year. However, if such areas receive heavy snow, serious erosion may take place if the snow melts rapidly and does not soak into the soil. This happens if the snow melts as the ground gradually thaws; the water moves over the thin, freshly thawed layer of soil, which is especially susceptible to erosion and is easily transported downgrade.

Land use. The type of crops, the system of management, and supporting conservation practices influence the amount and type of erosion. Bare soils, overgrazed uncultivated soils, or land in intertilled row crops permit the greatest amount of erosion. Crops that give complete ground cover throughout the year, such as grass or forests, are most effective in controlling erosion. Small-grain crops, or those that provide a fairly dense cover for only part of the year, are intermediate in their effect on erosion. Many row crops such as corn and soybeans have a period of bare soil after planting that often coincides with the period of most intense rain. **Table 2** gives results of some of the earliest experiments in the United States on differences in land use and the effect on runoff and erosion. These results show that cultivated land, especially without a crop or protective cover of vegetation, is particularly vulnerable to erosion.

In addition, excessive erosion usually occurs where cultivated crops like corn, cotton, soybeans, and tobacco are grown on hilly or sloping land that is subjected to increased runoff. In some areas where row crops have been grown continually, a depth of soil equal to the plow layer has been removed within a lifetime.

Pastures in humid areas usually have a tough continuous sod that prevents or greatly reduces erosion by both wind or water. Natural range cover, if in good condition, is usually effective in controlling erosion, but in areas of limited rainfall, where bunch grasses form most of the cover on rangeland, occasional heavy rain may cause severe erosion of the bare soil exposed between the bunches of grass. Forest lands, with their overhead canopies of trees and surface layers of decaying organic matter, have much greater water intake and much less surface runoff and erosion. Almost all erosion occurring in an undisturbed forest is from channel banks and from material that has slipped into the channel from adjacent steep slopes.

Farmers have learned that leaving a mulch from the previous crop on the soil surface will greatly reduce soil erosion by both wind and water (**Table 3**). Ad-

Table 2. Relative runoff and erosion from soil under different land uses, with mean rainfall of 35.87 in. (91.11 cm)

Land use and treatment	Runoff, %	Tons soil/acre (metric tons/hectare) eroded annually	Years required to lose surface 7 in. (17.8 cm) of soil
Plowed 8 in. (20 cm) deep, no crop; fallowed to keep weeds down	28	36 (80)	28
Plowed 8 in. (20 cm), corn annually	27	18 (40)	56
Plowed 8 in. (20 cm), wheat annually	25	7 (15)	150
Rotation; corn, wheat, red clover	14	2 (5)	437
Bluegrass sod	11	0.3 (0.7)	3547

Table 3. Mulch and tillage effects on soil erosion*

	Soybeans		Corn	
Tillage	Mulch cover, %	Soil loss, Mg/ha†	Mulch cover, %	Soil loss, Mg/ha†
No tillage	26	13	69	2
Chisel (up and down slope)	12	30	25	15
Moldboard plow	1	40	7	22

*After J. V. Mannering and C. R. Fenster, Vegetative water erosion control for agricultural areas, in *Soil Erosion and Sedimentation*, American Society of Agricultural Engineers, 1977.
†Mg = megagrams.

vances in technology of growing crops on soil covered by mulch have made this a promising method of reducing erosion on cropland without reducing crop yield. Reduction in soil loss is a function of percent of residue left on the soil surface. Some other factors also affect this, but it has been shown that percent of surface residue is by far the dominant factor involved. **Figure 25** shows the quantitative reduction in soil loss with each percent increase in residue cover.

Control. There are some fundamental principles that will help control erosion and greatly reduce the damage caused by soil erosion.

Water erosion control. Land should be covered with a growing crop as much as possible. Cover increases intake of water and reduces runoff. The extent of erosion control will be roughly in proportion to the protective cover.

When there is no growing crop, a cover of stubble or crop residue should be retained on the land between crops, at least until the next crop is well started. This can be done by using a system known as conservation tillage, or stubble-mulch farming. It utilizes the idea of preparing a seedbed for a new crop without burying the residue from the previous crop. Tillage tools that work beneath the surface and pulverize the soil without necessarily inverting it, or that till a very narrow strip of soil, are used instead of moldboard plows. This system has been used for many years in regions of low rainfall but is rapidly being adopted in the subhumid and humid areas of the United States.

Water should not be allowed to concentrate and run directly downhill. Terraces with gentle grades that carry the runoff water around the hill at slow velocities are ideal controls. These terraces should empty onto grassed waterways or into underground pipes to prevent the creation of gullies.

Another erosion control technique is to plant crops and till the soil along the contours of the land. On steeper land, other practices such as terraces may be needed to support contour tillage.

Wind erosion control. Wind erosion can be controlled by keeping land covered with sod or planted crops as much of the time as possible. Crop residue should be maintained on the land between crops or at least until the next crop has enough growth to protect the soil from high-velocity winds.

If wind erosion begins on a bare field or where a crop is just getting started, erosion may be stopped temporarily by emergency tillage. An implement with shovels that will throw up clods or chunks of soil to give a rough surface usually gives at least temporary protection. Often, only strips through the field need be so treated to stop erosion on the entire area. Where the soil is sandy and erosion is severe, windbreaks of trees are very effective control.

Moving dunes are very difficult to control. These may require artificial cover or mechanical obstructions on the windward side, followed by vegetative plantings, if rainfall is sufficient to sustain them. Along the shorelines, beach grasses followed by woody plants and forests may be required.

For a discussion of the physical, economic, and social effects of soil erosion *see* Soil conservation.

William C. Moldenhauer

Evaluation. A variety of sophisticated measurement apparatus and techniques have been developed to measure the amount of flowing water (runoff) from experimental plots and in small streams defining small watersheds. As soil is eroded, it is transported as sediment by water flow, so that it is also necessary to measure sediment concentration in the flowing water. The product of sediment concentration (usually expressed as kg sediment/m^3 water) and sediment mixture and flow rate (m^3/s) results in sediment discharge rate (kg/s). The integral of the sediment discharge rate throughout the period of flow or the duration of runoff is the sediment yield from the experimental plot or the area above the point of measurement on a small stream. The same definitions hold for larger streams and rivers. Sediment yield from a plot, a field, or a watershed drained by a stream is the combined result of sediment detachment by raindrop impact and flowing water, sediment transportation by raindrop splash and flowing water, and sediment deposition within the flow.

Data collection. Advances in runoff-measuring

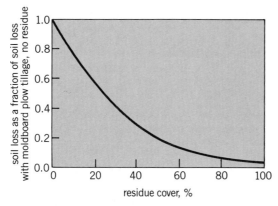

Fig. 25. Ratio of soil loss for a given residue cover to soil loss from conventional tillage vs. residue cover. (*After W. H. Wischmeier, Conservation tillage to control water erosion, Proceedings of a National Tillage Conference, Soil Conservation Society of America, 1973*)

flumes and sediment-concentration samplers have made sediment discharge measurements less expensive and more accurate. Automated determination of sediment concentration has become possible by combining portable sediment samplers with flow-measuring devices such as weirs and flumes. It is also possible to record data automatically from these instruments on site or to transmit them to a remote data-acquisition system.

Since the 1970s, rainfall simulators have become an important means of measuring soil erosion rates under field conditions. By using these techniques, artificial (simulated) rainfall is applied to experimental plots under controlled conditions to measure rates and amounts of rainfall, runoff, and sediment yield from the plots. Computers and automated data-acquisition systems have made these field data collection efforts much more efficient. The development of portable rainfall simulators, portable and automatic data-collection equipment, and portable computers to aid in processing and interpreting the data have led to a significant increase in the ability to conduct soil erosion experiments in the field.

Synthesis and modeling. The increased ability to conduct carefully controlled experiments and to accumulate measurements and data rapidly under a wide variety of soil, climate, and land-use alternatives has provided a stimulus to develop better methods of interpreting, synthesizing, and generalizing research data in order to develop an understanding of the basic physical processes controlling soil erosion. This, in turn, has led to a need to develop a predictive capability. Only by being able to predict the erosional consequences of land uses and management practices will the land managers be able to select the best means of preventing or reducing soil erosion. The predictive capability is essential to erosion control and soil conservation, because alternative management practices are numerous and expensive; in addition, it may take years or decades for the results of a particular practice to exert a measurable influence on soil erosion. Sometimes the effects of a management practice or land-use decision are irreversible.

As scientists begin to understand the physical processes resulting in soil erosion, they are able to begin synthesizing this information in the form of mathematical equations that approximate the physical processes. When the equations for erosion processes—such as raindrop detachment and transportation by splash; runoff and detachment of sediment by flowing water; and transportation and deposition of sediment in the flow—are combined and linked in a logical structure, the result is a mathematical model of erosion. With physical processes as complex as those occurring during erosion, the equations used to describe the processes are in turn complex. Therefore, most modern erosion models are solved or implemented with electronic computers. The result is known as computer simulation models for erosion prediction. SEE SIMULATION.

Modern soil conservation practices are based on the concept of using soil erosion equations and models to predict the likely erosional consequences of a variety of alternative land-use and management practices prior to their implementation or to compare the alternatives with existing land-use practices. Erosion prediction models are now used to evaluate soil erosion. The methodology to evaluate soil erosion includes everything from simple field measurements of the amount of soil lost from a specific location to the use of mathematical models and computers to predict soil erosion at a specific location.

Leonard J. Lane

Bibliography. American Society of Agricultural Engineers, *Optimum Erosion Control at Least Cost: Proceedings of the National Symposium on Conservation Systems*, 1987; P. W. Birkeland, *Soils and Geomorphology*, 1984; C. E. Black (ed.), *Methods of Soil Analysis*, pt. 1, 1965, pt. 2, 1982; A. Blum, *Plant Breeding for Stress Environments*, 1988; N. C. Brady, *The Nature and Properties of Soils*, 10th ed., 1990; E. Bresler, B. L. McNeal, and D. L. Carter, *Saline and Sodic Soils*, 1982; H. E. Dregne, *Soils of Arid Regions*, 1976; H. D. Foth, *Fundamentals of Soil Science*, 7th ed., 1984; H. D. Foth, *Soil Fertility*, 1988; C. T. Haan, H. P. Johnson, and D. L. Brakensiek (eds.), *Hydrologic Modeling of Small Watersheds*, Amer. Soc. Agr. Eng. Monog. 5, 1982; E. H. Isaacs and R. M. Srivastava, *Applied Geostatistics*, 1989; H. Jenny, *The Soil Resource: Origin and Behavior*, Ecological Studies, vol. 37, 1980; R. Lal, *Soil Erosion and Its Control*, 1988; L. J. Lane (ed.), *Erosion on Rangelands—Emerging Technology and Data Base: Proceedings of the Rainfall Simulator Workshop, January 14–15, 1985, Tucson*, 1986; L. Lyles, L. J. Hagan, and E. L. Skidmore, *Soil Conservation: Principles of Erosion by Wind*, Agron. Monogr. 23, American Society of Agronomy, 1983; E. V. Maas, Salt tolerance of plants, *Appl. Agr. Res.*, 1(1):12–26, 1986; National Academy of Sciences, *Soils of the Humid Tropics*, 1972; National Association of Review Appraisers Staff, *Land Classification for Land Uses Management and Valuation*, 1983; K. G. Renard and G. R. Foster, *Soil Conservation: Principles of Erosion by Water*, Agron. Monogr. 23, American Society of Agronomy, 1983; G. Richardson and P. Mueller-Beilschmidt, *Winning with Water: Soil Moisture Monitoring for Efficient Irrigation*, 1988; E. W. Russell, *Soil Conditions and Plant Growth*, 10th ed., 1974; I. Shainberg and J. Shalhevet, *Soil Salinity under Irrigation: Processes and Management*, 1984; M. A. Sprague and G. B. Triplett (eds.), *No-Tillage and Surface Tillage Agriculture: The Tillage Revolution*, 1986; S. J. Stavarek and D. W. Rains, The development of tolerance to mineral stress, *HortScience* 19:377–382, 1984; I. D. Teare and M. M. Peet (eds.), *Crop-Water Relations*, 1982; J. H. Turner (ed.), *Fundamentals of No-Till Farming*, American Association for Vocational Instructional Materials, 1983; U.S. Department of Agriculture, *Soil*, Yearbook of Agriculture, 1957; U.S. Department of Agriculture Soil Conservation Service, *Soil Taxonomy: A Basic System of Soil Classification for Making and Interpreting Soil Surveys*, 1983, reprint 1988.

Soil chemistry

The study of the composition and chemical properties of soil. Soil chemistry involves the detailed investigation of the nature of the solid matter from which soil is constituted and of the chemical processes that occur as a result of the action of hydrological, geological, and biological agents on the solid matter. Because of the broad diversity among soil components and the complexity of soil chemical processes, the application of concepts and methods employed in the

Table 1. Average percentages of the major elements and some microelements in subsurface soil clays and crustal rocks

| Element | Soil order | | | | | | Crustal rocks |
	Alfisol	Inceptisol	Mollisol	Oxisol	Spodosol	Ultisol	
Silicon (Si)	19.20	24.69	23.01	12.43	5.79	16.02	27.72
Aluminum (Al)	12.38	19.61	10.29	19.33	15.86	17.49	8.20
Iron (Fe)	8.04	3.81	6.83	10.83	3.29	11.96	4.10
Calcium (Ca)	0.69	0.00	3.59	0.10	0.29	0.15	4.10
Magnesium (Mg)	1.26	0.40	1.62	0.46	0.15	0.08	2.30
Sodium (Na)	0.18	2.52	0.04	0.00	0.27	0.06	2.30
Potassium (K)	3.63	n.d.	1.20	0.07	0.40	0.22	2.10
Titanium (Ti)	0.40	0.28	0.44	1.32	0.16	0.50	0.56
Manganese (Mn)	0.06	n.d.	0.06	0.08	0.06	0.05	0.10
Phosphorus (P)	0.14	n.d.	0.14	0.27	0.17	0.12	0.10

chemistry of aqueous solutions, of amorphous and crystalline solids, and of solid surfaces is required. For a general discussion of the origin and classification of soils *see Soil*.

Elemental composition. The elemental composition of soil varies over a wide range, permitting only a few general statements to be made. Those soils that contain less than 12–20% organic carbon are termed mineral. (The exact percentage to consider in a specific case depends on drainage characteristics and clay content of the soil.) All other soils are termed organic. Carbon, oxygen, hydrogen, nitrogen, phosphorus, and sulfur are the most important constituents of organic soils and of soil organic matter in general. Carbon, oxygen, and hydrogen are most abundant; the content of nitrogen is often about one-tenth that of carbon, while the content of phosphorus or sulfur is usually less than one-fifth that of nitrogen. The number of organic compounds into which these elements are incorporated in soil is very large, and the elucidation of the chemistry of soil organic matter remains a challenging problem.

Besides oxygen, the most abundant elements found in mineral soils are silicon, aluminum, and iron (**Table 1**). The distribution of chemical elements will vary considerably from soil to soil and, in general, will be different in a specific soil from the distribution of elements in the crustal rocks of the Earth. Often this difference may be understood in terms of pedogenic weathering processes and the chemical reactions that accompany them. Some examples evident in Table 1 are the accumulation of aluminum and iron oxides in the Oxisols and of calcium carbonate in the Mollisols. The most important micro or trace elements in soil are boron, copper, manganese, molybdenum, and zinc, since these elements are essential in the nutrition of green plants. Also important are cobalt, which is essential in animal nutrition, and selenium, cadmium, and nickel, which may accumulate to toxic levels in soil. The average natural distribution of trace elements in soil is not greatly different from that in crustal rocks (**Table 2**). This indicates that the total content of a trace element in soil usually reflects the content of that element in the soil parent material and, generally, that the trace element content of soil often is not affected substantially by pedochemical processes.

The elemental composition of soil varies with depth below the surface because of pedochemical weathering. The principal processes of this type that result in

the removal of chemical elements from a given soil horizon are (1) soluviation (ordinary dissolution in water), (2) cheluviation (complexation by organic or inorganic ligands), (3) reduction (lowering of the oxidation state), and (4) suspension. Soluviation, cheluviation, and reduction include leaching by water into lower horizons; suspension involves removal by erosion or by translocation downward along soil pores. The principal effect of these four processes is the appearance of illuvial horizons in which compounds such as aluminum and iron hydrous oxides, aluminosilicates, or calcium carbonate have been precipitated from solution or deposited from suspension.

Minerals. The minerals in soils are the products of physical, geochemical, and pedochemical weathering. Soil minerals may be either amorphous or crystalline. They may be classified further, approximately, as primary or secondary minerals, depending on whether they are inherited from parent rock or are produced by chemical weathering, respectively.

Primary minerals in soil. The bulk of the primary minerals that occur in soil are found in the silicate minerals, such as the olivines, garnets, pyroxenes, amphiboles, micas, feldspars, and quartz. The feldspars, micas, amphiboles, and pyroxenes commonly are hosts for trace elements that may be released slowly into the soil solution as weathering of these minerals continues. Chemical weathering of the silicate minerals is responsible for producing the most important secondary minerals in soil. The general

Table 2. Average amounts of trace elements commonly found in soils and crustal rocks*

Trace element	Soil, mg/kg	Crustal rocks, mg/kg
Arsenic (As)	7.2	1.5
Boron (B)	33	10
Cadmium (Cd)	0.35	0.11
Cobalt (Co)	9.1	20
Chromium (Cr)	54	100
Copper (Cu)	25	50
Molybdenum (Mo)	0.97	1.5
Nickel (Ni)	19	80
Lead (Pb)	19	14
Selenium (Se)	0.39	0.05
Vanadium (V)	80	160
Zinc (Zn)	60	75

*1 mg = 3.53×10^{-5} oz; 1 kg = 0.45 lb.

scheme of the weathering sequence of the minerals is shown in **Fig. 1**.

Secondary minerals in soil. The important secondary minerals that occur in soil are found in the clay fraction, sometimes in the form of coatings on other minerals. These include aluminum and iron hydrous oxides, carbonates, and aluminosilicates. The term allophane is applied to x-ray amorphous, hydrous aluminosilicates that are characterized by variable composition and a defect-riddled kaolinite structure containing aluminum (Al) in both tetrahedral and octahedral coordination. The significant crystalline aluminosilicates possess a layer structure; they are chlorite, halloysite, kaolinite, illite, montmorillonite (smectite), and vermiculite. These clay minerals are identified in soil by means of the characteristic x-ray diffraction patterns they produce after certain pretreatments, although their positive identification may be difficult if two or more of the minerals are present at once.

The distribution of secondary minerals varies among different soils and changes with depth below the surface of a given soil. However, under a leaching, well-oxidized environment, soil minerals do possess a differential susceptibility to decomposition, transformation, and disappearance from a soil profile. This has made possible the arrangement of the clay-sized soil minerals in the order of increasing resistance to chemical weathering. Those minerals ranked near the top of the following list are present, therefore, in the clay fractions of slightly weathered soils; those minerals near the bottom of the list predominate in extensively weathered soils.

Weathering index	Clay-sized minerals
1	Gypsum, halite
2	Calcite, apatite
3	Olivine, pyroxene
4	Biotite, mafic chlorite
5	Albite, microcline
6	Quartz
7	Muscovite, illite, sericite
8	Vermiculite
9	Montmorillonite, aluminum-chlorite
10	Kaolinite, allophane
11	Gibbsite, boehmite
12	Hematite, goethite
13	Anatase, rutile, zircon

In zonal soils of humid-cool to subhumid-temperate regions, illite is the predominant clay mineral. Mixtures of kaolinite, vermiculite, and interstratified clay minerals are found in humid-temperate regions. In humid-warm regions, kaolinite, halloysite, allophane, gibbsite, and goethite are found. The mineralogical composition of the highly weathered and leached soils of the humid tropics is a subject of active investigation, in part because these soils (the Oxisols and Ultisols) constitute approximately one-third of the world's potentially arable land. The soil minerals are dominated by iron (Fe) and aluminum hydrous oxides, kaolinite, halloysite, and quartz. Weathering residues also are found in thin coatings on clay particle surfaces. Vermiculite and montmorillonite with interlayer aluminum hydroxy polymers are common.

The chemical conditions favoring the genesis of ka-

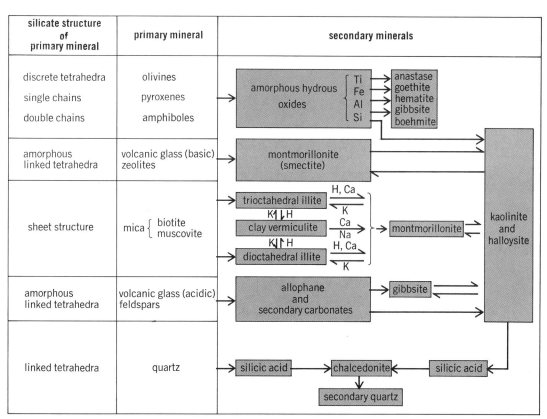

Fig. 1. Scheme of chemical weathering to form secondary minerals from primary silicate minerals. (*After M. Fieldes and L. D. Swinedale, Chemical weathering of silicates in soil formation, J. Sci. Tech. N.Z., 56:140–154, 1954*)

Table 3. Cation exchange capacity (CEC values) in cmol(p⁺)/kg for some soil textural classes and clay mineral compounds

Soil texture	CEC	Soil mineral	CEC
Sand	1–5	Allophane	25–70
Fine sandy loam	5–10	Chlorite	10–40
Loam or silt loam	5–25	Halloysite	5–50
Clay loam	15–30+	Illite	10–40
Clay (mineral soil)	≥25	Kaolinite	3–15
Clay (14% organic)	23	Smectite	80–150
Clay (39% organic)	76	Vermiculite	100–150+
Clay (100% organic)	150–600	Aluminum, iron hydrous oxides	≈4

olinite are the removal of the basic cations and Fe^{2+} by leaching, the addition of hydrogen ion (H^+) in fresh water, and a high aluminum-silicon (Al-Si) molar ratio. Smectite (montmorillonite) is favored by the retention of basic cations (arid conditions or poor drainage) and of silica.

Cation exchange. A portion of the chemical elements in soil is in the form of cations that are not components of inorganic salts but that can be replaced reversibly by the cations of leaching salt solutions or acids. These cations are said to be exchangeable, and their total quantity, usually expressed in units of centimoles of proton charge [cmol(p⁺)] per kilogram of dry soil, is termed the cation exchange capacity (CEC) of the soil. The cation exchange capacity ordinarily is measured by leaching a known amount of soil with a salt solution, such as sodium acetate at pH 8.2, followed by an additional leaching with alcohol to remove the residual salt, then determining the quantity of replacing cation [such as sodium (Na^+)] in the soil. However, this is not a unique procedure, since the quantity of cation remaining after such treatment does not have a unique value characteristic of the soil alone, but depends as well on the concentration, the ionic composition, and the pH of the leaching solution. The cation exchange capacity of a soil generally will vary directly with the amounts of clay and organic matter present and with the distribution of clay minerals (**Table 3**).

Soils which are less weathered because of recent origin, low precipitation, or temperate to cold climate have as exchangeable cations largely calcium (Ca^{2+})

and magnesium (Mg^{2+}). Some soils of dry areas contain significant amounts of exchangeable sodium. Extensively weathered soils, unless formed from basic parent material, have 20–95% of their exchangeable cations as aluminum. Prolonged leaching with fresh water supplies H^+ ions that eventually penetrate and disrupt the structures of soil aluminosilicates, thereby releasing aluminum cations, some of which remain in exchangeable form. The distributions of exchangeable cations for representative soils are shown in **Table 4**.

The chemical equilibrium between exchangeable cations and cations in a leaching solution may be expressed by Eq. (1), where ν is a stoichiometric coef-

$$\nu_A A(ex) + \nu_B B \rightleftharpoons \nu'_A A + \nu'_B B(ex) \qquad (1)$$

ficient, (ex) denotes an exchangeable cation, and A or B refers to a cation species, such as Na^+ or Ca^{2+}. Generally speaking, the equilibrium will shift to the right if cation B has a greater charge or a smaller hydrated radius than cation A. The affinity of a soil for cation species B relative to A may be described formally by the law of mass action, Eq. (2), where K

$$K = \frac{a_{B(ex)}^{\nu'_B}}{a_{A(ex)}^{\nu'_A}} \frac{a_A^{\nu'_A}}{a_B^{\nu_B}} \qquad (2)$$

is an equilibrium constant and a is a thermodynamic activity. Different special cases of Eq. (2) have been developed on the basis of different assumptions about the composition dependence of the exchanger activities. For example, if the activities of the exchangeable cations are set equal to mole fractions and the activity ratio $a_A^{\nu'_A}/a_B^{\nu_B}$ is set equal to its value in the leaching solution, the expression for K is known as Vanselow's equation. The parameter K then is termed a selectivity coefficient and, in principle, may vary with the exchanger composition. If the exchangeable cation activities are set equal to charge fractions raised to a power equal to the cation valence, the expression for K (again a selectivity coefficient) becomes Gapon's equation. Published data on these kinds of special cases demonstrate that selectivity coefficients take on constant values only over a limited range of exchanger soil composition. The development of practicable cation exchange equations with broad applicability remains a challenging problem in soil chemistry.

Isomorphic substitution in clay minerals. One of the most important sources of cation exchange capacity in soils is the negative charge that occurs on 2:1 clay mineral surfaces because of isomorphic substitution.

Table 4. Typical distributions of exchangeable cations in some soil orders*

Soil order (pH value)	CEC, cmol(p⁺)·kg⁻¹	Percentages				
		Calcium (Ca)	Magnesium (Mg)	Sodium (Na)	Potassium (K)	Hydrogen⁺ aluminum (H + Al)
Alfisol (5.4)	38	23	11	0	2	64
Aridisol (6.3)	4	52	26	5	17	0
Entisol (6.4)	5	37	23	<1	6	33
Inceptisol (5.3)	104	6	1	<1	<1	91
Mollisol (6.7)	25	67	12	<1	2	18
Spodosol (3.6)	106	5	6	<1	1	87
Oxisol (4.9)	27	31	8	<1	2	58
Ultisol (3.5)	24	11	3	<1	<1	84

*After R. L. Donahue, R. W. Miller, and J. C. Shickluna, *Soils*, Prentice-Hall, 1983.

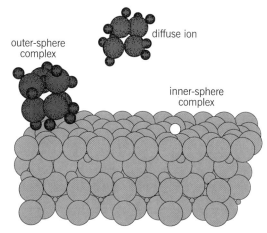

Fig. 2. Three mechanisms of cation adsorption by a clay mineral surface. (*After G. Sposito, The Chemistry of Soils, Oxford University Press, 1989*)

The replacement of Si^{4+} in the tetrahedral sheet by Al^{3+} or of Al^{3+} in the octahedral sheet by Mg^{2+} and Fe^{2+} results in a permanent, negative surface charge on the clay mineral surface that is more or less localized in hexagonal cavities formed by rings of oxygen atoms. This negative charge is balanced either by the formation of surface complexes between the cavities and cations taken from the soil solution or by diffuse swarms of cations remaining free in the soil solution (**Fig. 2**). Extensive isomorphic substitution occurs in the tetrahedral sheet of vermiculite, with the result that K^+ can form inner-sphere surface complexes (**Fig. 3**) stabilized by the fact that this cation does not hydrate easily and fits almost perfectly into the hexagonal cavity in the clay mineral surfaces. On the other hand, isomorphic substitution occurs principally in the octahedral sheet of montmorillonite, and the resultant electrostatic force binding a cation is weaker than for vermiculite because it must act through a greater distance. Cations such as Ca^{2+} which hydrate strongly tend to form outer-sphere surface complexes with the hexagonal cavities in the montmorillonite surface (Fig. 3).

Ionizable hydroxyl groups on clay minerals. At the edges of the structural layers in the crystalline clay minerals and on the surfaces of the amorphous clay minerals, hydroxyl (OH) groups may be found bonded to exposed Si^{4+} or Al^{3+} cations (**Fig. 4**). These hydroxyl groups can act as Brönsted acids, ionizing in aqueous solution when the pH is sufficiently high. Thus a pH-dependent, negative surface charge can develop that will contribute to the cation exchange capacity. The mineral surfaces for which this pH-dependence occurs can form surface complexes with cations, as illustrated in Fig. 4. When this occurs, the complexed cation (for example, H^+, Na^+, or Ca^{2+}) is termed a potential-determining ion for the clay mineral surface, and its degree of surface complexation is governed by its electrochemical potential. The importance of pH-dependent charge versus permanent charge is greater in 1:1 layer silicates than in 2:1 layer silicates. For montmorillonite the pH-dependent cation exchange capacity may be 20% of the total cation exchange capacity; for illite it may be 40%, while for kaolinite and allophane it is essentially 100%.

Ionizable functional groups in organic matter. The organic matter in soil contains two types of functional groups that contribute importantly to the cation exchange capacity: aromatic and aliphatic carboxyls and phenolic hydroxyls. When the pH is greater than 4, these acidic groups ionize in aqueous solution and provide a source of negative charge for metal cation adsorption. The cations of metals in groups I and II (for example, Na^+ and Ca^{2+}) of the periodic table are readily exchangeable after adsorption by soil organic matter, whereas those of the transition metals [for example, Fe^{3+} and copper (Cu^{2+})] often are not. The contribution to the cation exchange capacity from organic functional groups can be large at high pH values.

Anion exchange. The stoichiometric exchange of the anions in soil for those in a leaching salt solution is a phenomenon of relatively small importance in the general scheme of anion reactions with soils. Under acid conditions (pH < 5) exposed hydroxyl groups at the edges of the structural sheets or on the surfaces of clay-sized particles become protonated and thereby

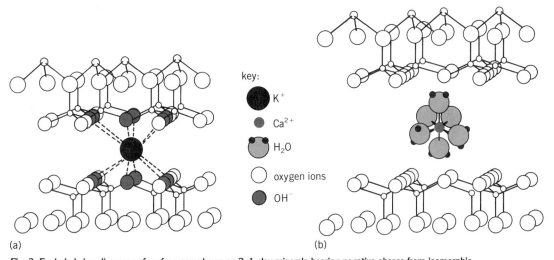

key:
● K^+
● Ca^{2+}
● H_2O
○ oxygen ions
● OH^-

(a)   (b)

Fig. 3. Exploded-view diagrams of surface complexes on 2:1 clay minerals bearing negative charge from isomorphic substitution. (*a*) Inner-sphere surface complex (unhydrated cation): K^+ on vermiculite. The broken lines represent ionic bonds between K^+ and the surrounding oxygen ions. (*b*) Outer-sphere surface complex (hydrated cation): $Ca(H_2O)_6^{2+}$ on montmorillonite. (*After G. Sposito, The Surface Chemistry of Soils, Oxford University Press, 1984*)

Key:

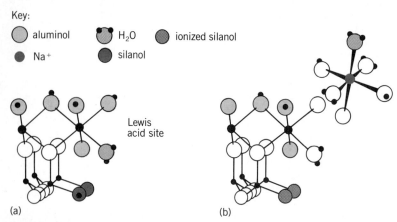

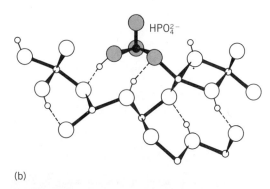

Fig. 4. Kaolinite surface complexes. (*a*) Surface hydroxyl groups bound to Si^{4+} (silanol) and Al^{3+} (aluminol) on kaolinite. (*b*) An outer-sphere surface complex between hydrated Na^+ and an aluminol group. (*After G. Sposito, The Surface Chemistry of Soils, Oxford University Press, 1984*)

acquire a positive charge. The degree of protonation is a sensitive function of pH, the ionic strength of the leaching solution, and the nature of the clay-sized particle. The magnitude of the anion exchange capacity (AEC) usually varies from near 0 at pH 7 for any soil colloid to as much as 50 cmol($-$)/kg of allophanic clay at about pH 4. [cmol(–)/kg means centimoles of negative charge per kilogram.] Smectite and other clay minerals with high, pH-invariant cation exchange capacity values do not adsorb exchangeable anions to any degree. Anion exchange capacity may be measured conveniently by shaking a sample of soil for 1 h in molar sodium chloride (NaCl) at a chosen pH, filtering, and displacing the adsorbed chloride ion (Cl^-). Anion exchange capacity is then the number of cmoles of Cl displaced per kilogram of soil.

Negative anion adsorption. Soils whose cation exchange capacity is approximately independent of pH often display a significant negative adsorption of anions: the concentration of anions in a solution separated from a soil suspension by a membrane permeable to electrolyte is larger than that of the anions in the liquid phase of the suspension. This phenomenon may be understood simply on the basis of the presence of a permanent negative charge on the surface of the solid-phase particles in the suspension. This surface charge attracts cations and repels anions. The principal effects of this repulsion are to reduce the anion exchange capacity and to increase the ease with which anions may be leached from a soil.

Specific anion adsorption and precipitation. Anion exchange in the classic sense applies primarily to halide and nitrate ions. For other ions, in particular, borate, molybdate, sulfate, and orthophosphate, the reaction with the solid matter in soil involves specific adsorption or precipitation. The *o*-phosphate ion, for example, can react with the accessible aluminum hydroxy ions of clay minerals and with hydrous aluminum and iron oxides in soil to form either inner-sphere surface complexes by ligand exchange with OH groups (**Fig. 5**) or x-ray amorphous analogs of the known crystalline aluminum and iron phosphate minerals by precipitation. The nature of the reaction is strongly dependent on pH, the metal cations in solution, the acidity of the added phosphate compound, and the structure of the solid phase with which the phosphate ion reacts. Under conditions of a relatively high pH, low acidity of the added phosphate, or high degree of crystallinity of the solid phase reactant, phosphate ion (PO_4^{3-}) will tend to be ''specifically adsorbed'' by Al or Fe ions at the surface of the solid through ligand exchange. If these conditions are reversed, the combination of PO_4^{3-} with the solid phase may result in a nearly complete destruction of the reactant solid and the formation of an amorphous aluminum or iron phosphate. With either case, the fundamental chemical process is the same. This is an area of active research in soil chemistry.

Soil solution. The solution in the pore space of soil acquires its chemical properties through time-varying inputs and outputs of matter and energy that are mediated by the several parts of the hydrologic cycle and by processes originating in the biosphere (**Fig. 6**). The soil solution thus is a dynamic and open natural water system whose composition reflects the many reactions that can occur simultaneously between an aqueous solution and an assembly of mineral and organic solid phases that varies with both time and space. This type of complexity is not matched normally in any chemical laboratory experiment, but nonetheless must be amenable to analysis in terms of chemical principles. An understanding of the soil solution in terms of chemical properties has proven to be essential to progress in the maintenance of soil fertility and the quality of runoff and drainage waters.

Chemical speciation of macrosolutes. The macrosolute composition of a soil solution will vary depending on pH, pε (negative common logarithm of the electron activity), organic matter content, input of chemical elements from the biosphere (including humans), and effectiveness of leaching. Under conditions of near-

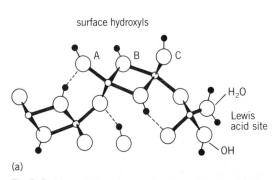

Fig. 5. Surface complexes on the mineral goethite. (*a*) Locations of hydroxyls are shown by A, B, and C, corresponding to OH bound to one, two, or three ions. (*b*) An inner-sphere surface complex between HPO_4^{2-} and Fe^{3+}. The broken lines represent hydrogen bonds. (*After G. Sposito, The Surface Chemistry of Soils, Oxford University Press, 1984*)

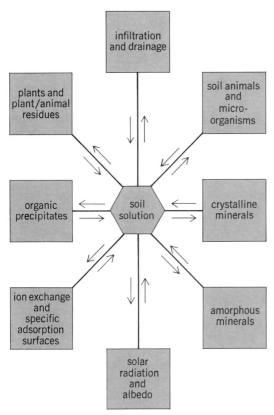

Fig. 6. Factors influencing the chemistry of the soil solution. (*After J. F. Hodgson, Chemistry of the micronutrients in soils, Adv. Agron., 15:119–159, 1963*)

neutral pH, high pϵ, low organic matter content, no solute input from agriculture, and good but not excessive drainage, the expected macrosolutes are Ca^{2+}, K^+, Mg^{2+}, Na^+, Cl^-, biocarbonate ion, (HCO_3^-), silicic acid [$Si(OH)_4$], and sulfate ion (SO_4^{2-}). If the pH is low, H^+ and Al^{3+} should be added to this list; if it is high, carbonate ion (CO_3^{2-}) should be added. If the soil has been fertilized, nitrate ion (NO_3^-) and hydrogen phosphate ion ($H_2PO_4^-$) become important. If the drainage is excessive, Al may be abundant and one or more of the solutes in the original list may be insignificant. If the drainage is poor and, therefore, the pϵ is low, SO_4^{2-} will be replaced by S^{2-} and CO_3^{2-} should be added. If the organic matter content is high, organic solutes become important. Combinations of these different environmental conditions will change the original list of solutes in still other ways (for example, low pϵ and nitrogen fertilizer addition would add NH_4^+ to the list).

The chemical speciation of the macrosolutes (that is, their distribution among the free-ionic, complexed, precipitated, and adsorbed forms) depends on the nature of the solid matter in the soil, the composition of metals and ligands in solution and their concentration, and the pϵ value. Clearly the macrosolutes themselves are interdependent in determining their speciation, and even the three factors just mentioned cannot be considered in complete isolation from one another. Nevertheless, it is possible to make some very broad statements about the macrochemical species to be expected by employing the principle of hard and soft acids and bases. SEE ACID AND BASE.

The macrosolute metal cations are hard acids. This means that they generally tend to form chemical bonds of a simple electrostatic type and, therefore, that their reactivities with any ligand (including a mineral surface) should be predictable on the basis of ionic charge and radius along with their common property of low polarizability. In a soil solution, the macrosolute metal cations will tend to (1) form complexes and sparingly soluble precipitates primarily with oxygen-containing ligands (hard bases), such as H_2O, OH^-, HCO_3^-, CO_3^{2-}, $H_2PO_4^-$, PO_4^{3-}, SO_4^{2-} and nonhydroxylated mineral surfaces; the stabilities of these complexes will tend to increase with the ratio of ionic charge to ionic radius of the metal; usually no reaction will occur with soft or nearly soft bases such as S^{2-} and Cl^-; (2) form complexes with carboxyl groups, but not with organic ligands containing only nitrogen and sulfur electron donors.

These generalizations make it possible to enumerate the probable complexes and precipitates of the macrosolute metals in a soil solution of known composition (including adsorbing surfaces). The exact speciation of the metals then can be calculated if stability constants are available for the expected chemical reactions. Usually a large set of nonlinear equations must be solved on a digital computer and ionic strength corrections must be performed.

Chemical speciation of microsolutes. The important microsolutes in soil include the trace metals, such as Fe, Cu, and Zn, and the trace element oxyanions, such as those formed by arsenic (As), boron (B), molybdenum (Mo), and selenium (Se). The tableau of microsolutes in a given soil solution is more dependent on inputs from the lithosphere and the biosphere (particularly humans) and less on proton or electron activity and hydrologic factors than is the composition of macrosolutes. The trace metals present, for example, usually are derived from the chemical weathering of specific parent rocks, from the application of fertilizers, pesticides, and urban wastes, and from air pollution.

The most general features of the chemical speciation of the microsolutes also may be predicted on the basis of the principle of hard and soft acids and bases. The trace metal cations are soft or nearly soft acids, and the trace element anions are hard or nearly hard bases. The exception to this statement is Fe^{3+}, which is a hard acid. This means that the trace metal cations, except for Fe^{3+}, will tend to form chemical bonds of a covalent type whose strength will depend much more on detailed electronic structural considerations than on cationic size or charge. For the anions, the implication is that they will combine strongly with hard-acid metal cations, just as do other oxygen-containing ligands. Trace metal speciation thus presents a more complicated problem than does that of the macrosolute metals. Generally, the trace metal cations in a soil solution will (1) form complexes and insoluble precipitates more readily with the inorganic ligands Cl^- and S^{2-} and with sites on mineral surfaces that can bind covalently, than with oxyanions; stronger complexes also will form more readily with organic functional groups containing S, P, and N donors than with carboxyl groups; (2) tend to follow the Irving-Williams order in regard to the stabilities of strong complexes: $Mn^{2+} < Fe^{2+} < Co^{2+} < Ni^{2+} < Cu^{2+} > Zn^{2+} > Cd^{2+}$.

These broad predictions imply that trace metal speciation in soil solutions will depend sensitively on the content and type of organic matter, the percentage of kaolinitic and amorphous hydrous oxide minerals, the pH, the pε, and the ionic strength. For example, a low solubility of the micronutrients Cu and Zn should occur for soils high in immobile organic matter (but not too low in pH) or for soil solutions with low pε values. Moreover, the solubilities of the trace metals should increase significantly with an increase in chloride concentration or in organic solutes. Since the complexes formed in these cases would reduce the ionic charge on the soluble trace metal species, a decrease in the affinity of a negative charge adsorbing surface (for example, that of montmorillonite) should also occur (**Fig. 7**). Research has indicated that complex formation also decreases the bioavailability of a trace metal to a plant grown in soil. The uptake of a trace metal by a plant appears to be strongly correlated with the thermodynamic activity of the free metal cation species (**Fig. 8**).

Clay-organic complexes. The clay minerals in soils often are observed to be intimately associated with carbonaceous materials. These materials may be residues from plant or animal decomposition, herbicides or other pesticides, organic polymers and polyelectrolytes, surfactant compounds, or microbial metabolites. The complexes which they form with clay minerals bear importantly on soil fertility, soil structure, soil moisture and aeration characteristics, the biological activity of organic compounds applied or disposed on soil, and the degradation of solid and liquid organic wastes in the soil environment. Generally, the organic component of a naturally occurring clay-organic complex will be of a very complicated nature that defies a conclusive structural determination. Therefore, in order to obtain fundamental information about the mechanisms of bonding between clay minerals and organic matter in soil, a major line of research has involved the study of the reactions of known organic compounds with single types of clay minerals. On the basis of these studies, some important bonding mechanisms have been identified. They are expected to apply to the associations between clay minerals and organic matter in nature whenever the appropriate mineral species and organic functional groups are present.

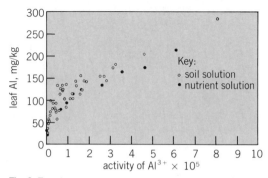

Fig. 8. Experimental relationship between the concentration of Al in the leaves of coffee plants and the thermodynamic activity of the Al^{3+} species in aqueous solution. (*After M. A. Pavan, F. T. Bingham, and P. F. Pratt, Toxicity of aluminum to coffee in Ultisols and Oxisols amended with CaCO₃, MgCO₃, and CaSo₄·2H₂O, Soil Sci. Soc. Amer. J., 46:1201–1207, 1982*)

Bonding mechanisms. The principal mechanisms through which organic compounds may bind to clay minerals have been elucidated largely by spectroscopic and x-ray diffraction studies. They may be classified as follows:

1. Organic cation adsorption can occur, through protonated amine or carbonyl groups, onto any constant-charge clay mineral surface. The protonation of the functional groups may be either a pH effect or an acceptance of a proton that was formerly occupying an exchange site, was associated with a water molecule hydrating a metal cation, or was bound on another adsorbed organic cation. The affinity of an organic cation for a constant-charge surface depends on the molecular weight, the nature of the functional groups present, and the molecular configuration. Steric effects can be particularly significant because of the localized character of exchange sites and the quasirigid hydration envelope built up on a clay mineral surface. The stability of the water structure on a smectite (montmorillonite) surface is, in fact, great enough to require interstratified layers of either adsorbed metal cations or adsorbed organic cations when the clay mineral surfaces are only partially saturated with the organic compound. A mixture of the two types of cation in a single interlayer region disrupts the water structure too much to be stable.

2. Polar organic functional groups can bind to adsorbed cations through simple ion-dipole forces or complex formation involving covalent bonds (inner-sphere surface complex). The ion-dipole mechanism is to be expected, of course, for hard-acid metal cations, such as Ca^{2+} and Al^{3+}, while the formation of covalent bonds is to be expected for soft-acid metal cations, such as Cu^{2+}. As the organic functional groups often would have soft-base character, the strength of binding by this mechanism should be greatest for exchangeable transition metal cations. A sharp exception to this rule could occur with "complexable" Al^{3+} (or Fe^{3+}) in amorphous aluminosilicates that bind organic matter containing large numbers of carboxyl groups.

3. Large organic molecules can bind effectively to

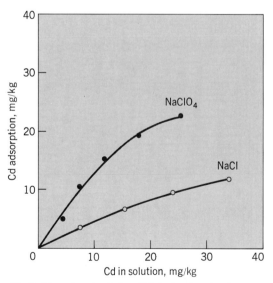

Fig. 7. Adsorption of cadmium (Cd) by the clay mineral montmorillonite at fixed pH and ionic strength (0.05 M) as influenced by chloride complexing. In the sodium chloride (NaCl) system, the amount of adsorption is reduced because of the formation of $CdCl^+$, $CdCl_2^0$, and $CdCl_3^-$, which have smaller positive charges than Cd^{2+}, the only Cd species present in the sodium perchlorate (NaClO₄) system. (*After J. Garcia-Miragaya and A. L. Page, Influence of ionic strength and inorganic complex formation on the sorption of trace amounts of Cd by montmorillonite, Soil Sci. Soc. Amer. J., 40:658–663, 1976*)

a clay mineral surface through hydrogen bonding. This bonding can involve a water bridge from a hydrated exchangeable cation to an oxygen-containing functional group (outer-sphere surface complex), a hydrogen bond from a more acidic functional group adsorbed directly on the clay mineral surface to a less acidic free one containing oxygen, or a direct hydrogen bond to a surface oxygen or hydroxyl plane in the clay mineral. If the exchangeable metal cation is a hard acid, the first type of bond will by far dominate the third type in importance. Direct hydrogen bonds to a plane of surface atoms would be accompanied by weaker dipole-dipole (that is, van der Waals) interactions, in general. This type of binding should be most important when very large organic molecules associate with a clay mineral surface containing relatively few exchange sites.

Catalysis reactions. Clay minerals have been shown often to catalyze reactions involving organic compounds. This catalytic function appears to be connected intimately with the presence of exchangeable metal cations and may be separated into two distinct types. The first type relates to the fact that the water molecules hydrating the exchangeable cations tend to dissociate very readily and, therefore, to endow the clay mineral surface with a pronounced acidity that increases markedly with desiccation. The enhanced proton-donating capability of the clay mineral, which will be greater the harder an acid the exchangeable cation is, serves a catalytic function in, for example, the surface protonation of amines and amino acids.

A second type of catalytic function derives from the formation of inner-sphere organic complexes with the exchangeable cations. The mechanism, which should be more significant the softer an acid the adsorbed metal cation is (again excepting Al^{3+} and Fe^{3+}), appears to play a basic role in, for example, the stabilization of humic compounds against degradation. These and other reactions catalyzed by clay minerals may prove to be very important in understanding how soil organic matter forms and how molecules of biological significance can be synthesized abiotically.

Garrison Sposito

Plant nutrition. Soil chemistry controls availability of plant nutrients within the soil and thus influences plant growth, yield, and nutritional value for human or animal consumption. The nutritional deficiencies or toxicities inherent to the morphology of the soil are known as mineral stress; they often represent a serious constraint for crop production and development. Globally, mineral stress occurs on about 23% of the world's soils. Plant nutritional problems are especially severe on highly weathered soils in tropical or subtropical geographic areas. This occurs because phosphate is made unavailable by iron and aluminum oxides and because the clay minerals often have low cation exchange capacities.

The predominant soil chemical problems on well-aerated soils include acidity, salinity (high salt), and sodicity (high sodium). Important soil chemical processes include dissolution and precipitation of readily soluble minerals. The primary soil chemical problems in waterlogged soils include rapid disappearance of molecular oxygen, denitrification, and increased toxic concentrations of manganese and iron.

Nutrient movement. Soil chemical reactions occur continuously to maintain equilibria between available nutrients in soil solution and those existing as minerals within the soil or on exchange sites located on organic matter or clay minerals. Diffusion gradients (**Fig. 9a**) and mass flow (Fig. 9b) are two primary mechanisms for nutrient movement to plant roots. Phosphorus and potassium move primarily by diffusion, but calcium and magnesium are usually supplied by mass flow. Although root interception (Fig. 9c) occurs, this process does not significantly contribute to plant nutrient accumulation.

Nutrient-specific effects. Carbon, hydrogen, and oxygen are supplied to plants by water and carbon dioxide (CO_2). Provided photosynthesis and transpiration

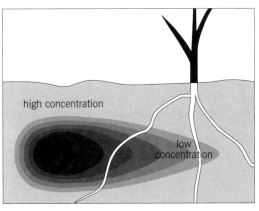

(a)

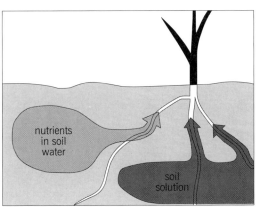

(b)

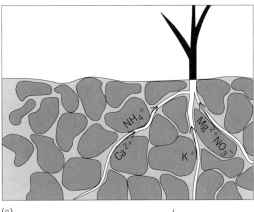

(c)

Fig. 9. Mechanisms of nutrient movement. (*a*) Diffusion; gradient movement. Fertilizer moves from high to low concentration. (*b*) Mass flow; water use controlled. (*c*) Root interception; contact required. NH_4^+ = ammonium ion; Ca^{2+} = calcium ion; K^+ = potassium ion; Mg^{2+} = magnesium ion; NO_3^- = nitrate ion.

are not limited, soil chemistry has very little effect on these nutrients.

Nitrogen (N) is assimilated from soil solution as ammonium (NH_4^+) or nitrate (NO_3^-) ions. Legumes also assimilate nitrogen through symbiotic fixation. The nitrogen cycle is biologically complex, but provided soils are not anaerobic and causing denitrification, soil chemistry has less affect on nitrogen than on a nutrient such as phosphorus (P). One exception is that the balance between NH_4^+ and NO_3^- forms can influence plant availability of nutrients such as magnesium. If NH_4^+ ions interfere with Mg accumulation in plants, then availability of Mg to grazing animals may be inadequate, leading to hypomagnesemia.

Phosphorus concentrations in soil solution are very low when compared with amounts present in organic matter and with amounts in distinct phosphate compounds such as monocalcium phosphate, dicalcium phosphate, octacalcium phosphate, hydroxyapatite, and fluorapatite. Phosphorus also exists as surface films coating soil aggregates and individual particles of sand, silt, and clay.

Phosphorus nutrition of plants is strongly affected by soil chemical conditions, especially soil reaction or pH (**Fig. 10**). Acid soils (pH < 5.0) have reduced availability of phosphorus because relatively insoluble iron and aluminum phosphate compounds are formed. In alkaline soils (pH > 7.0), insoluble calcium phosphate compounds, including octacalcium and hydroxyapatite, can substantially reduce available phosphorus. Primary geographic regions for alkaline phosphorus problems are the semiarid and arid regions, where free calcium carbonate ($CaCO_3$) is often found in the plant root zone. Phosphorus deficiencies associated with acid soil conditions are most prevalent in areas with high rainfall, including the southern United States as well as tropical or subtropical areas.

Potassium is usually the predominant cation in plants, even though calcium is usually the predominant cation in soil. Deficiencies occur on all soils but are most prevalent on sandy soils that are low in organic matter, chalky soils, and soils derived from peat. Excess potassium can exist because of either natural mineral deposits or excessive additions of fertilizer or manure. Maintaining a balance among potassium, calcium, and magnesium is critical, because imbalances can affect plant growth and development, and also can induce hypomagnesemia or grass tetany in cattle grazing forages on those soils.

Unless soils are extremely acidic, they can supply sufficient calcium for optimum plant growth. An exception is soils formed from serpentine minerals. Those soils often have a chemical imbalance between calcium and magnesium, and they have true calcium deficiencies. However, serpentine soils have many other chemical problems, including toxic levels of nickel and other heavy metals, as well as deficiencies of molybdenum.

Soil chemical processes generally supply magnesium in quantities sufficient to meet plant demand. Exceptions and areas where fertilizer response to magnesium may be found include sandy soils with low concentrations of magnesium, acid soils that have been treated with only calcitic limestone, and soils that have very high concentrations of potassium.

Saline and sodic soils. Saline, saline-sodic, and sodic soils are found in arid and semiarid regions where water loss through evaporation exceeds loss through leaching. This results in an accumulation of

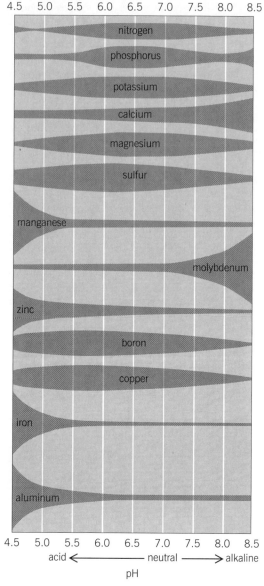

Fig. 10. Relationship of soil pH and plant nutrient availability, which is increased for the major plant nutrients when the soil pH is held between 6.5 and 7.0. Height of the tinted regions represents availability at a given pH level.

soluble salts, precipitated in the surface horizon and attached to cation exchange sites.

Saline soils contain enough chlorides and sulfates of sodium, calcium, and magnesium to interfere with growth of most plants. These are known as white-alkali soils, because the salts often give the soil light color. Saline-sodic soils also contain high amounts of neutral soluble salts and enough sodium to affect most plants seriously. These soils are most difficult to reclaim, because if they are leached with pure water, sodium ions will cause the clays to disperse and completely seal the soil surface. Reclamation must be done by using water with high concentrations of calcium or magnesium. Sodic soils do not contain large amounts of neutral soluble salts but have concentrations of sodium. They often have a very poor physical condition, because sodium disperses the clay particles. They are often known as black-alkali soils, because high concentrations of sodium carbonate (Na_2CO_3) disperse organic matter near the soil surface.

Micronutrients. Plant micronutrients are essential elements found in very low concentrations within plant tissues. These include boron, copper, iron, manganese, molybdenum, and zinc. Soil chemical processes that affect micronutrient availability include formation or dissolution of precipitates that contain these nutrients. Micronutrient availability is significantly influenced by soil pH (Fig. 10). Soil organic matter or microbial and root exudations also affect availability of micronutrients through formation of soluble coordination or chelation compounds. Any soil chemical change that influences formation of these compounds significantly affects micronutrient availability.

Douglas Karlen

Animal nutrition. The transfer of mineral elements from parent rock to plants and animals is an extremely complex process (see **Fig. 11**). Thus it is difficult to establish direct relationships between the physical and chemical properties of soils and animal health. There is, however, evidence that low or high concentrations of certain elements in soils of different origins can be related to the occurrence of conditions of deficiency or toxicity in animals and humans.

Halogens. The classic example of a direct relationship between a dietary deficiency of an element and health is that between iodine and endemic goiter and cretinism in human populations. Low concentrations of dietary iodine result from geologically recent glaciation of soils, distance from salt lakes or oceans (via rainfall), and low annual precipitation. Consequently, hypothyroidism has been common in inland mountain regions, such as the Alps and Himalayas and, in the United States, in the Great Lakes and northwestern

states. Iodine, bromine, and chlorine are enriched mainly in the oceans, while considerable fluoride is derived from weathering of rocks rich in fluoride. Fluorosis (toxicity, indicated by abnormal tooth and bone calcification) has been observed in volcanic regions such as Iceland and, from consumption of subsurface water, in India and Tanzania. Fluorosis in farm animals is also frequently noted in proximity to industrial processes such as production of steel, aluminum, and fertilizer. Halogen levels in the environment are increased by the burning of fossil fuels such as coal and oil. Problems of iodine deficiency have come under control with the introduction of iodized salt. Low-level fluoridation of water supplies is practiced in many countries to prevent dental caries.

Selenium. Concentrations of selenium (Se) in soils reflect those of the parent rock, and there are marked regional differences. Levels of selenium range from 7.8×10^{-7} oz/lb (0.01 mg/kg) in some soils in the Soviet Union, to 7.8×10^{-5} to 5.5×10^{-4} oz/lb (1 to 7 mg/kg) in the central and western United States and Canada, to very high levels of 2.8×10^{-2} to 9.7×10^{-2} oz/lb (360 to 1200 mg/kg) in the upper layers of peat soils formed on glacial lake deposits in seleniferous areas of Ireland. In the United States, low-selenium ecosystems are found in Oregon on acid soils derived from volcanic deposits; concentrations of selenium in forage plants are low (3.9×10^{-6} oz/lb or 0.05 mg/kg), and muscular dystrophy (white muscle disease) occurs in calves and lambs. In contrast, high-selenium ecosystems are characteristic of alkaline soils formed from sedimentary rocks of the Cretaceous period in, for example, South Dakota. In such ecosystems, food crops contain 7.8×10^{-5} to

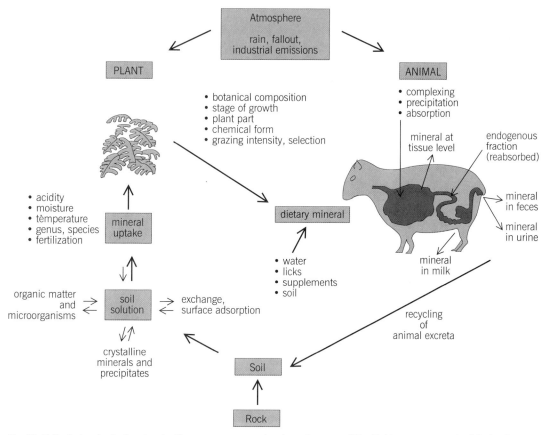

Fig. 11. Soil–plant–animal mineral cycle. Heavy arrows represent major pathways or shifts. Light arrows represent relatively minor pathways.

7.8×10^{-4} oz/lb (1 to 10 mg/kg) of selenium, with concentrations higher than 3.9×10^{-3} oz/lb (50 mg/kg) in accumulator plants, and selenosis used to be common in grazing animals. In California, selenium toxicity in fish and waterbirds has been observed in a reservoir receiving subsurface drainage from irrigated fields in the San Joaquin Valley. The high levels of selenium derive from selenate in alkaline sediments of an alluvial fan.

Areas of selenium deficiency and toxicity occur throughout the world. In China, people living in certain hilly areas of eroded soils suffer from an endemic cardiomyopathy (Keshan disease). Concentrations of selenium in the diet and blood are lower for populations in these areas than for those in other low-selenium countries like New Zealand and Finland. A related disease (Kashin-Beck), characterized by osteoarthropathy in children, occurs in some of the same areas; it is thought to also result from a deficiency in dietary selenium and to be responsive to increased intake of selenium. Another ecological study shows significant correlations between selenium and the distribution of a number of cancers (liver, stomach, and esophagus) in China. Supplementary selenium can be provided in deficient areas in a variety of ways—fertilization, foliar application, oral dosing, treatment with slow-release boluses, direct addition at low levels to the food, or dietary supplementation with cereals grown in high-selenium regions.

Copper and molybdenum. Copper deficiency is manifested in ruminating animals by anemia; nervous disorders; depigmentation of wool, hair, and bone; and disorders of the cardiovascular and reproductive systems. It is usually a conditioned disease, caused by high levels of molybdenum or sulfur in the diet. Copper concentrations in soils vary with parent material, organic matter, clay levels, and soil pH; however, mapping techniques show little relationship between concentrations of copper in soil and plants and deficiency disorders.

Levels of molybdenum are much more variable and are highest in shales, clays, phosphorites, petroleum, and coal. Plant uptake of molybdenum is increased by poor drainage conditions. In England and Northern Ireland, stream sediment analysis has demonstrated that areas of copper deficiency in cattle coincided with geochemically defined areas possessing high molybdenum concentrations, such as outcrops of marine shales. In the United States a copper deficiency in ruminants induced by molybdenum is found in Nevada, Oregon, and California on poorly drained soils derived from high-molybdenum granitic alluvium. Since plant uptake of molybdenum increases with increasing soil pH, improvement of acidic hill soils by liming and reseeding frequently causes an increase in incidence of molybdenum-induced copper deficiency in sheep. A further factor in the soil–plant–animal copper cycle may be increasing sulfate levels found in rainfall and groundwater and interference from soil and plant contamination by industrial emissions. Copper deficiency can be treated by fertilization; by dosing, injection, or provision of copper salts in mineral mixes; and by administration of slow-release copper oxide needles to the animal.

Cobalt. This is one of the best-documented examples of a direct relationship between soil properties and animal health. Cobalt (Co) is required for the synthesis of vitamin B_{12} by rumen microorganisms, and a dietary deficiency results in anorexia, poor growth, anemia, muscle degeneration, and retarded sexual development. Cobalt occurs in soils in association with the manganese oxides, and concentrations are usually higher in fine-textured clays. Regional mapping of cobalt in forage plants in the United States shows the most severe deficiency ($<5.6 \times 10^{-6}$ oz/lb or 0.07 mg/kg) occurring on sandy spodosols on the southeastern Coastal Plain and on leached granitic-derived soils in New England and the Atlantic provinces of Canada. Scottish studies show widespread deficiencies of cobalt on granitic and coarse sandy soils. Cobalt availability increases markedly with poor drainage conditions. Supplementary cobalt can be provided by fertilization or foliar application of the element. Direct treatment of cobalt-deficient animals includes addition of the element to the food or water supply, oral dosing with cobalt sulfate, injection of vitamin B_{12}, and administration of slow-release cobalt ''bullets'' or boluses.

Magnesium. The problem of hypomagnesemic tetany in grazing animals has increased in the United States; in so-called tetany years it causes severe economic losses to farmers. However, the relationship of tetany incidence to soil characteristics is unclear; it is conditioned by such factors as rainfall, temperature, fertilization, and the presence of plant components that reduce availability of magnesium to the animal. Soils developed on sandstones and granites contain less magnesium than those containing dolomites or the basic magnesium silicates, and tetany is more likely to occur on light sandy soils than on heavier classes. Studies in New Zealand cite the importance of the following factors: low exchangeable soil magnesium; high soil potassium; free drainage, supporting rapid growth with high nitrogen concentration and low magnesium concentration; and unfavorable climatic conditions such as high rainfall, high altitude, or low light. Soil fertilization with magnesium sources is effective in increasing concentrations of magnesium in plants, depending on the soil type and the source and level of fertilizer. Foliar dusting with magnesium oxide (MgO) is practiced in Europe to prevent spring tetany. An effective management technique in the United States is the provision of palatable blocks or mixes containing magnesium at critical periods of the year.

Phosphorus. Phosphorus deficiency in grazing animals results in poor growth, abnormal (depraved) appetite, impaired reproduction, and reduced mineralization of bone. But, as for magnesium, a direct relationship to soil plant material and properties is difficult to demonstrate. The main phosphorus-bearing minerals are the apatites, and the soil pool of available phosphorus depends on soil characteristics such as mineral composition, pH, organic matter, clay content, moisture, temperature, and aeration. Phosphorus deficiency in animals is observed when the phosphorus content of plants falls to 0.05–0.15% in the dry matter; such concentrations are often noted in tropical regions. It is maintained that in the United States true soil deficiency of phosphorus occurs on the leached, sandy soils of the Atlantic Coastal Plain and on low-phosphorus parent soils in the north-central and southwest regions; a climate-induced soil deficiency affects uptake of phosphorus by plants in the low-rainfall Great Plains, Basin and Range areas of the west. In the western states, phosphorus nutrition is affected by animal selection behavior involving a diversity of plants. Phosphorus deficiency is frequently prevented by provision of mineral supplements and licks, since phosphorus fertilization may or may not increase plant phosphorus concentrations. Progress has been made, specifically in Australia and in Central and South American countries, in diagnosing phosphorus deficiency states by use of blood analysis and bone biopsy techniques and in relating these to plant composition and phosphorus status of the soil.

R. L. Reid

Bibliography. H. Bohn et al., *Soil Chemistry*, 1985; E. Bresler et al., *Saline and Sodic Soils*, 1982; B. E. Davies (ed.), *Applied Soil Trace Elements*, 1980; D. J. Greenland and M. H. B. Hayes (eds.), *The Chemistry of Soil Constituents*, 1978; D. H. Greenland and M. H. B. Hayes (eds.), *The Chemistry of Soil Processes*. 1981; J. Låg (ed.), *Geomedicine*, 1990; W. Mertz (ed.), *Trace Elements in Human and Animal Nutrition*, vols. 1–2, 5th ed., 1986–1987; R. L. Reid and D. J. Horvath, Soil chemistry and mineral problems in farm livestock: A review, *Anim. Feed Sci. Tech.*, 5:95–167, 1980; E. W. Russell, *Soil Conditions and Plant Growth*, 10th ed., 1974; G. Sposito, *The Chemistry of Soils*, 1989; G. Sposito, *The Surface Chemistry of Soils*, 1984; F. J. Stevenson, *Humus Chemistry: Genesis, Compositions, Reactions*, 1982; W. Stumm and J. J. Morgan, *Aquatic Chemistry*, 1981; B. K. G. Theng (ed.), *Soils with Variable Charge*, 1980; I. Thornton (ed.), *Applied Environmental Geochemistry*, 1983; S. L. Tisdale, W. L. Nelson, and J. B. Beaton, *Soil Fertility and Fertilizers*, 1985.

Soil conservation

The practice of arresting or minimizing artificially accelerated soil deterioration. Its importance has grown because cultivation of soils for agricultural production, deforestation and forest cutting, grazing of natural range, and other disturbances of the natural cover and position of the soil have increased greatly since the middle of the nineteenth century in response to the growth in world population and human technical capacity. Accelerated soil deterioration has been the unfortunate consequence.

Erosion extent and intensity. Accelerated erosion has been known throughout history wherever people have tilled or grazed slopes or semiarid soils. There are many evidences of the physical effects of accelerated erosion in the eastern and central parts of the Mediterranean basin, in Mesopotamia, in China, and elsewhere. Wherever the balance of nature is a delicate one, as on steep slopes in regions of intense rainstorms, or in semiarid regions of high rainfall variability, grazing and cultivation eventually have had to contend with serious or disabling erosion. Irrigation works of the Tigris and Euphrates valleys are thought to have suffered from the sedimentation caused by quickened erosion on the rangelands of upstream areas in ancient times. The hill sections of Israel, Jordan, Syria, central and southern Italy, and Greece experienced serious soil losses from grazing and other land use mismanagement many centuries ago. Accelerated water erosion on the hills of southern China and wind erosion in northwestern China also date far back. Exactly what effects these soil movements may have had on history has been a debated question, but

their impact may have been serious on some cultures, such as those of the Syrian, Israeli, and Jordanian areas, and debilitating on others, as in the case of classical Rome and the China of several centuries ago.

The exact extent of accelerated soil erosion in the world today is not known, particularly as far as the rate of soil movement is concerned. However, it may be safely said that nearly every semiarid area with cultivation or long-continued grazing, every hill land with moderate to dense settlement in humid middle latitude and subtropical climates, and all cultivated or grazed hill lands in the Mediterranean climate areas suffer to some degree from such erosion. Thus recognized problems of erosion are found in such culturally diverse areas as southern China, the Indian plateau, South Australia, the South African native reserves, the Commonwealth of Independent States, Spain, the southeastern and midwestern United States, and Central America.

Within the United States the most critical areas have been the hill lands of the southern Piedmont and the interior Southeast, the Great Plains, the Palouse area hills of the Pacific Northwest, southern California hills, and slope lands of the Midwest. The high-intensity rainstorms of the Southeast and the cyclical droughts of the Plains have predisposed the two larger areas to erosion. The light-textured A horizon formed under the Plains grass cover was particularly susceptible to wind removal, while the high clay content of many southeastern soils predisposed them to water movement. These natural susceptibilities were repeatedly brought into play by agricultural systems which stressed corn, cotton, and tobacco in the Southeast, corn in the Midwest, and intensive grazing and small grains on the Plains, the Palouse, and in California. The open soil surface left in the traditional intertilled cultivation of the Southeast furnished almost ideal conditions for water erosion and at the same time caused heavy nutrient depletion of soils thus cropped. The open fields during seasons between crops have also been susceptible to soil depletion. Open fields have been especially disastrous to maintenance of soil cover during droughts of the Plains. Soil mismanagement thus has been a common practice in parts of the United States where stability of soil cover hangs in delicate balance. *See Erosion.*

Types of soil deterioration. Soil may deteriorate either by physical movement of soil particles from a given site or by depletion of the water-soluble elements in the soil which contribute to the nourishment of crop plants, grasses, trees, and other economically usable vegetation. The physical movement generally is referred to as erosion. Wind, water, glacial ice, animals, and tools in use may be agents of erosion. For purposes of soil conservation, the two most important agents of erosion are wind and water, especially as their effects are intensified by the disturbance of natural cover or soil position. Water erosion always implies the movement of soil downgrade from its original site. Eroded sediments may be deposited relatively close to their original location, or they may be moved all the way to a final resting place on the ocean floor. Wind erosion, on the other hand, may move sediments in any direction, depositing them quite without regard to surface configuration. Both processes, along with erosion by glacial ice, are part of the normal physiographic (or geologic) processes which are continuously acting upon the surface of the

Fig. 1. Erosion of sandstone caused by strong wind and occasional hard rain in an arid region. (*USDA*)

Accelerated erosion may be induced by any land-use practice which denudes the soil surfaces of vegetative cover (**Fig. 2**). If the soil is to be moved by water, it must be on a slope. The cultivation of a corn or a cotton field is a clear example of such a practice. Corn and cotton are row crops; cultivation of any row crop on a slope without soil-conserving practices is an invitation to accelerated erosion. Cultivation of other crops, like the small grains, also may induce accelerated erosion, especially where fields are kept bare between crops to store moisture. Forest cutting, overgrazing, grading for highway use, urban land use, or preparation for other large-scale engineering works also may speed the natural erosion of soil (**Fig. 3**).

Where and when the soil surface is denuded, the movement of soil particles may proceed through splash erosion, sheet erosion, rill erosion, gullying, and wind movement (**Fig. 4**). Splash erosion is the minute displacement of surface particles caused by the impact of falling rain. Sheet erosion is the gradual Earth. The action of both wind and water is vividly illustrated in the scenery of arid regions (**Fig. 1**). Soil conservation is not so much concerned with these normal processes as with the new force given to them by human land-use practices. *See* Land-use planning.

Depletion of soil nutrients obviously is a part of soil erosion. However, such depletion may take place in the absence of any noticeable amount of erosion. The disappearance of naturally stored nitrogen, potash, phosphate, and some trace elements from the soil also affects the usability of the soil for human purposes. The natural fertility of virgin soils always is depleted over time as cultivation continues, but the rate of depletion is highly dependent on management practices. *See* Soil; Soil fertility.

downslope migration of surface particles, partly with the aid of splash, but not in any defined rill or channel. Rills are tiny channels formed where small amounts of water concentrate in flow. Gullies are V- or U-shaped channels of varying depths and sizes. A gully is formed where water concentrates in a rivulet or larger stream during periods of storm. It may be linear or dendritic (branched) in pattern, and with the right slope and soil conditions may reach depths of 50 ft (15 m) or more. Gullying is the most serious form of water erosion because of the sharp physical

Fig. 2. Improper land use. Corn rows planted up and down the slope rather than on the contour. Note better growth of plants in bottom (deeper) soil in foreground as compared to stunted growth of plants on slope. (*USDA*)

Fig. 3. Rill erosion on highway fill. The slopes have been seeded (horizontal lines) with annual lespedeza to bind and stabilize soil. (*USDA*)

the hands of people who had no security in their occupancy, who often were illiterate, and whose terms of tenancy and meager training forced them to concentrate on corn, cotton, and tobacco as crops.

On the Plains and in other susceptible western areas, small-grain monoculture, particularly of wheat, encouraged the exposure of the uncovered soil surface so much of the time that water and wind inevitably took their toll (**Fig. 5**). On rangelands, the high percentage of public range (for whose management little individual responsibility could be felt), lack of knowledge as to the precipitation cycle and range capacity, and the urge to maximize profits every year contributed to a slower but equally sure denudation of cover.

Finally, the United States has experienced extensive erosion in mountain areas because of forest mismanagement. Clearcutting of steep slopes, forest burning for grazing purposes, inadequate fire protection, and shifting cultivation of forest lands have allowed vast quantities of soil to wash out of the slope sites where they could have produced timber and other forest values indefinitely. In the United States

change it causes in the contour of the land, and because of its nearly complete removal of the soil cover in all horizons. On the edges of the more permanent stream channels, bank erosion is another form of soil movement.

Causes of soil mismanagement. One of the chief causes of erosion-inducing agricultural practices in the United States has been ignorance of their consequences. The cultivation methods of the settlers of western European stock who set the pattern of land use in the United States came from a physical environment which was far less susceptible to erosion than North America, because of the mild nature of rainstorms and the prevailing soil textures in Europe. The principal European-sown grains, moreover, were wheat, barley, oats, and rye which covered the soil surface completely as they grew. Corn, cotton, and tobacco, however, were crops unfamiliar to European agriculture. In eastern North America the combination of European cultivation methods and American intertilled crops resulted in generations of soil mismanagement. In later years the Plains environment, with its alternation of drought and plentiful moisture, was also an unfamiliar one to settlers from western Europe.

Conservational methods of land use were slow to develop, and mismanagement was tolerated because of the abundance of land in the eighteenth and nineteenth centuries. One of the cheapest methods of obtaining soil nutrients for crops was to move on to another farm or to another region. Until the twentieth century, land in the United States was cheap, and for a period it could be obtained by merely giving assurance of settlement and cultivation. With low capital investments, many farmers had little stimulus to look upon their land as a vehicle for permanent production. Following the Civil War, tenant cultivators and sharecroppers presented another type of situation in the Southeast, where stimulus toward conservational soil management was lacking. Management of millions of acres of farmland in the Southeast was left in

Fig. 4. Two most serious types of erosion. (*a*) Sheet erosion as a result of downhill straight-row cultivation. Note onions washed completely out of ground. (*b*) Gully erosion destroying rich farmland and threatening highway. (*USDA*)

Fig. 5. Wind erosion. The accumulation of topsoil was blown from the bare field on right. (*USDA*)

the central and southern Appalachian area and the southern part of California have suffered severely in this respect, but all hill or mountain forest areas except the Pacific Northwest have had such losses. *SEE FOREST MANAGEMENT; FOREST RESOURCES.*

Economic and social consequences. Where the geographical incidence of soil erosion has been extensive, the damages have been of the deepest social consequence. Advanced stages of erosion may remove all soil and therefore all capacity for production. More frequently it removes the most productive layers of the soil—those having the highest capacity for retention of moisture, the highest soil nutrient content, and the most ready response to artificial fertilization. Where gullying or dune formation takes place, erosion may make cultivation physically difficult or impossible. Thus, depending on extent, accelerated erosion may affect productivity over a wide area. At its worst, it may cause the total disappearance of productivity, as on the now bare limestone slopes of many Mediterranean mountains. At the other extreme may be the slight depression of crop yields which may follow the progress of sheet erosion over short periods. In the case of forest soil losses, except where the entire soil cover disappears, the effects may not be felt for decades, corresponding to the growth cycle of given tree species. Agriculturally, however, losses are apt to be felt within a matter of a few years.

Moderate to slight erosion cannot be regarded as having serious social consequences, except over many decades. As an income depressant, however, it does prevent a community from reaching full productive potentiality. More severe erosion has led to very damaging social dislocation. For those who choose to remain in an eroding area or who do not have the capacity to move, or for whom migration may be politically impossible, the course of events is fateful. Declining income leads to less means to cope with farming problems, to poor nutrition and poor health, and finally to family existence at the subsistence level. Communities made up of a high proportion of such families do not have the capacity to support public services, even elementary education. Unless the cycle is broken by outside financial and technical assistance or by the discovery of other resources, the end is a subsistence community whose numbers decline as the capacity of the land is further reduced

under the impact of subsistence cultivation. This has been illustrated in the hill and mountain lands of the southeastern United States, in Italy, Greece, Mexico, China, and elsewhere for many millions of farming people. Illiteracy, short life-spans, nutritional and other disease prevalence, poor communications, and isolation from the rest of the world have been the marks of such communities. Where they are politically related to weak national governments, indefinite stagnation and decline may be forecast. Where they are part of a vigorous political system, their rehabilitation can be accomplished only through extensive investment contributed by the nation at large. In the absence of rehabilitation, these communities may constitute a continued financial drain on the nation for social services such as education, public health, roads, and other public needs.

Effects on other resources. Accelerated erosion may have consequences which reach far beyond the lands on which the erosion takes place and the community associated with them. During periods of heavy wind erosion, for example, the dust fall may be of economic importance over a wide area beyond that from which the soil cover has been removed. The most pervasive and widespread effects, however, are those associated with water erosion. Removal of upstream cover changes the regimen of streams below the eroding area. Low flows are likely to be lower and their period longer where upper watersheds are denuded than where normal vegetative cover exists. Whereas flood crests are not necessarily higher in eroding areas, damages may be heightened in the valleys below eroding watersheds because of the increased deposition of sediment of different sizes, the rapid lifting of channels above floodplains, and the choking of irrigation canals.

A long chain of other effects also ensues. Because of the extremes of low water in denuded areas during dry seasons, water transportation is made difficult or impossible without regulation, fish and wildlife support is endangered or disappears, the capacity of streams to carry sewage and other wastes safely may be seriously reduced, recreational values are destroyed, and run-of-the-river hydroelectric generation reaches a very low level. Artificial storage becomes necessary to derive the services from water which are economically possible and needed. But even the possibilities of storage eventually may disappear when

Fig. 6. Ifugao rice terraces, Philippines. (*Philippine Embassy, Washington, D.C.*)

erosion of upper watersheds continues. Reservoirs may be filled with the moving sediment and lose their capacity to reduce flood crests, store flood waters, and augment low flows. For this reason, plans for permanent water regulation in a given river basin must always include watershed treatment where eroding lands are in evidence. *SEE WATER CONSERVATION.*

Conservation measures and technology. Measures of soil management designed to reduce the effects of accelerated erosion have been known in both the

Western world and in the Far East since long before the beginning of the Christian Era. The value of forests for watershed protection was known in China at least 10 centuries ago. The most important of the ancient measures on agricultural lands was terrace construction, although actual physical restoration of soil to original sites also has been practiced. Terrace construction in the Mediterranean countries, China, Japan, and the Philippines represents the most impressive remaking of the face of the Earth before the days of modern earth-moving equipment (**Fig. 6**). Certain land management practices that were soil-conserving have been a part of western European agriculture for centuries, principally those centering on livestock husbandry and crop rotation. Conservational management of the soil was known in colonial Virginia and by Thomas Jefferson and others during the early years of the United States. However, it is principally since 1920 that the technique of soil conservation has been developed for many types of environment in terms of an integrated approach. The measures include farm, range, and forest management practices, and the building of engineered structures on land and in stream channels.

Farm, range, and forest. A first and most important step in conservational management is the determination of land capability—the type of land use and economic production to which a plot is suited by slope, soil type, drainage, precipitation, wind exposure, and other natural attributes. The objective of such determination is to achieve permanent productive use as nearly as possible. The United States Soil Conservation Service has developed one of the more easily understood and widely employed classifications for such determination (**Fig. 7**). In this system, eight

Fig. 7. Land capability classes. Suitable for cultivation: 1, requires good soil management practices only; 2, moderate conservation practices necessary; 3, intensive conservation practices necessary; 4, perennial vegetation—infrequent cultivation. Unsuitable for cultivation (pasture, hay, woodland, and wildlife): 5, no restrictions in use; 6, moderate restrictions in use; 7, severe restrictions in use; 8, best suited for wildlife and recreation. (*USDA*)

classes of land are recognized within United States territory. Four classes represent land suited to cultivation, from the class 1 flat or nearly flat land suited to unrestricted cultivation, to the steeper or eroded class 4 lands which can be cultivated only infrequently. Three additional classes are grazing or forestry land, with varying degrees of restriction on use. The eighth class is suited only to watershed, recreation, or wildlife support. The aim in the United States has been to map all lands from field study of their capabilities, and to adjust land use to the indicated capability as it becomes economically possible for the farm, range, or forest operator to put conservational use into force.

Once the capability of land has been determined, specific measures of management come into play. For class 1 land, few special practices are necessary. After the natural soil nutrient minerals begin to decline under cultivation, the addition of organic or inorganic fertilizers becomes necessary. The return of organic wastes, such as manure, to the soil is also required to maintain favorable texture and optimum moisture-holding capacity. Beyond these measures, little need be added to the normal operation of cultivation.

On class 2, 3, and 4 lands, artificial fertilization will be required, but special measures of conservational management must be added. The physical conservation ideal is the maintenance of such land under cover for as much of the time as possible. This can be done where pasture and forage crops are suited to the farm economy. However, continuous cover often is neither economically desirable nor possible. Consequently, a variety of devices has been invented to minimize the erosional results from tillage and small grain or row crop growth. Tillage itself has become an increasingly important conservational measure since it can affect the relative degree of moisture infiltration and soil grain aggregation, and therefore erosion. Where wind erosion is the danger, straw mulches or row or basin listing (furrowing) may be employed and alternating strips of grass and open-field crops planted. Fields in danger of water erosion are plowed on the contour (not up- and downslope), and if cultivation by lister (a double-moldboard plow) is also employed, water storage capacity of the furrows will be increased. Strip cropping, in which alternate strips of different crops are planted on the contour, may also be employed. Crop rotations that provide for strips of closely planted legumes and perennial grasses alternating with grains such as wheat and barley and with intertilled strips are particularly effective in reducing soil erosion. Fields may also be terraced, and the terraces strip-cropped. The bench terrace, which interrupts the slope of the land by a series of essentially horizontal slices cut into the slope, is used infrequently in the United States in contrast to the broad-base terrace, which imposes comparatively little impediment to cultivation. A broad-base terrace consists of a broad, shallow surface channel, flanked on the downward slope by a low, sloping embankment. If the terrace is constructed with a slight gradient (channel-type or graded terrace), it serves to reduce erosion by conducting excess water off the slope in a controlled manner. If it is constructed on the contour (level or ridge-type terrace), its primary purpose is to conserve moisture. The embankment on the downslope side of a broad-base terrace may be constructed from soil taken from the upper side only (sometimes known as a Nichols terrace) or from both sides (Mangum terrace).

Design of conservational cultivation also includes provision for grass-covered waterways to collect drainage from terraces and carry it into stream courses without erosion. Where suitable conditions of slope and soil permeability are found, shallow retention structures may also be constructed to promote water infiltration. These are of special value where insufficient soil moisture is a problem at times. Additional moisture always encourages more vigorous cover growth.

The measures just described may be considered preventive. There are also measures of rehabilitation where fields already have suffered from erosion and offer possibilities of restoration. Grading with mechanical equipment and the construction of small check dams across former gullies are examples.

For the remaining four classes of land, whose principal uses depend on the continuous maintenance of cover, management is more important than physical conditioning. In some cases, however, water retention structures, check dams, and other physical devices for retarding erosion may be applied on forest lands and rangelands. In the United States such structures are not often found in forest lands, although they have been commonly employed in Japanese forests. In forestry the conservational management objective is one of maximum production of wood and other services while maintaining continuous soil cover. The same is true for grass and other forage plants on managed grazing lands. For rangelands, adjustment of use is particularly difficult, because grazing must be tolerated only to the extent that the range plants still retain sufficient vitality to withstand a period of drought which may arrive at any time.

A last set of erosion-control measures is directed toward minimizing stream bank erosion, which may be large over the length of a long stream. This may be done through revetments, retaining walls, and jetties, which slow down current undercutting banks and hold sand and silt in which soil-binding willows, kudzu, and other vegetation may become established. Sediment detention reservoirs also reduce the erosive power of the current, and catchment basins or flood control storage helps reduce high flows (**Fig. 8**). *See* *Land-use classes; River engineering.*

Conservation agencies and programs. Whereas excellent soil-conserving soil management was maintained for generations by some farmers and farm groups, as in Lancaster County, Pennsylvania, a major amount of the soil conservation activities in the United States is derived from federal government as-

Fig. 8. Stream bank erosion control. Construction of a new conservation pool which will help reduce flooding, retard downstream erosion, and store water. (*USDA*)

sistance. The Soil Conservation Service of the U.S. Department of Agriculture has been a focal agency in spreading knowledge of soil conservation in farmland and rangeland management and aiding in its application. In practice, the local administration of a soil conserving program is within a Soil Conservation District, which usually is coincident with a county, and is organized under state law. The district is the liaison unit between the farmer and public assistance agencies at the state and federal levels. It is managed by a board or committee, generally composed of five members, and usually elected by farmers within the district. Other local public bodies which may have soil-conservation objectives include conservancy districts, wind erosion districts, drainage or irrigation districts, Agricultural Stabilization and Conservation Service County Committees, and Farmers' Home Administration County Committees. In addition, there are private groups with conservational interests, such as the farmers' cooperatives and national farm organizations like the Farm Bureau Federation.

The local districts may be aided technically and financially in their program. Much of the financial aid stems from federal sources, and theoretically it is on a matching fund basis. In actual practice, however, a major part of the expenditures for special soil-conserving programs is from federal funds. Technical aid is provided throughout the nation by the Soil Conservation Service, and also by the U.S. Forest Service for its special fields of forestry and grazing-land management. Technical aid also has been provided by the Agricultural Extension Services and the Land Grant Colleges of the several states. The Tennessee Valley Authority has maintained a program of its own design, with the cooperation of the colleges and the Extension Services. The Soil and Moisture Conservation Operations Office of the Indian Service, U.S. Department of the Interior, likewise has conducted a program limited to specific Indian lands.

Financial assistance for soil conservation measures has been provided by the federal government through the Soil Conservation Service, the Agricultural Stabilization and Conservation Service, the Tennessee Valley Authority, and the Farmers' Home Administration. Assistance has been particularly in the form of loans from the FHA, in low-cost fertilizer from the TVA, and as direct cash outlay from other agencies. Over the years, the program of the Agricultural Stabilization and Conservation Service has been the largest single source of financial aid for these purposes.

The Conservation Reserve Program was enacted through the passage of the Food Security Act of 1985. The basic objective of the program as originally enacted was to encourage American farmers to cease cropping highly erodible soils. Subsequent to its initial enactment, the program was broadened to foster establishment of filter strips having a permanent cover of vegetation adjacent to streams and water bodies. The program is implemented through rental and land-use conversion cost-sharing payments to cooperating farmers.

By the middle 1980s, it was estimated that approximately one-quarter of the utilized cropland in the United States was sufficiently erodible to be eligible for retirement from cropping in the Conservation Reserve Program. The term highly erodible land as used in the program applied to tracts where the potential maximum erosion under cropping would be more than eight times greater than the erosion rate under which long-term crop productivity could be maintained.

Acreage retired from cropping was to be planted to protective grass sod or tree cover. Under the amplified provisions of the Conservation Reserve Program, however, cropland does not need to meet these strict erodibility requirements if it is located within strips from 66 to 99 ft (20 to 30 m) wide flanking stream banks, or flanking water bodies including wetlands in excess of 5 acres (0.4 hectare), and is planted to a permanent vegetation cover.

At the time the Conservation Reserve Program was enacted, it was hoped that up to 4×10^7 highly erodible acres (1.62×10^7) of cropland would be planted to a protective vegetation cover. Within 4 years, contracts covering 3.05×10^7 acres (1.23×10^7 hectares) had been signed, suggesting that the program had been relatively successful, although not fully realized.

In addition to technical and financial aid, the farmers or other land operators of the United States are given valuable indirect assistance through the many research programs, basic and applied, which treat the fields related to soil conservation. The work of the Agricultural Research Service, the Soil Conservation Service, the Tennessee Valley Authority, and the Land Grant Colleges has been especially helpful. Through these works, soil-conserving plans, fertilizers, improved means of physical control, and methods of management have been developed. Through them soil conservation has not only become important but also an increasingly efficient public activity in the United States. *See FOREST AND FORESTRY.*

Edward A. Ackerman; Donald J. Patton

Bibliography. R. L. Donahue, *Our Soils and Their Management*, 5th ed., 1990; S. A. El-Swaify, W. C. Moldenhauer, and A. Lo (eds.), *Soil Erosion and Conservation*, 1985; S. A. Goldman, K. Jackson, and T. Bursztynsky, *Erosion and Sediment Control Handbook*, 1986; E. O. Heady, *Economic Models of Agricultural Land Conservation and Environmental Improvements*, 1990; D. Helms and S. Flader (eds.), *The History of Soil and Water Conservation*, 1985; T. O'Riordan and R. K. Turner (eds.), *Progress in Resource Management and Environmental Planning*, 1983.

Soil ecology

The study of the interactions among soil organisms, and between biotic and abiotic aspects of the soil environment. Soil is made up of a multitude of physical, chemical, and biological entities, with many interactions occurring among them. Soil is a variable mixture of broken and weathered minerals and decaying organic matter. Together with the proper amounts of air and water, it supplies, in part, sustenance for plants as well as mechanical support.

Soil is predominantly a sand-silt-clay matrix, containing living materials (biomass) including microorganisms, roots, and animals, plus dead organic matter, with varying amounts of gases and liquids. Soils, in addition to the three geometric dimensions, are greatly influenced by the fourth dimension, time.

Soils are the result of several factors, including climate, organisms, parent material, and topography (relief), acting through time (**Fig. 1**). These factors affect major processes, such as primary production, decomposition, and nutrient cycling, which lead to the development of ecosystem properties unique to a soil type. Such characteristics as cation-exchange ca-

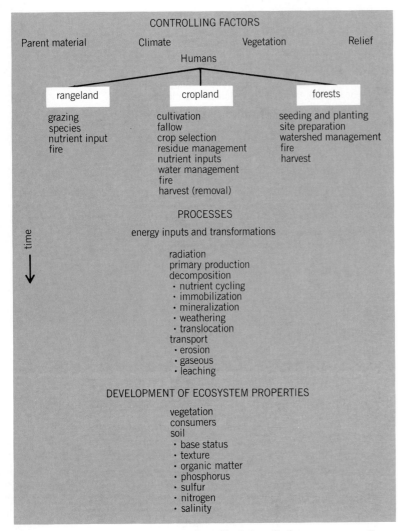

CONTROLLING FACTORS

Parent material   Climate   Vegetation   Relief

Humans

| rangeland | cropland | forests |

grazing
species
nutrient input
fire

cultivation
fallow
crop selection
residue management
nutrient inputs
water management
fire
harvest (removal)

seeding and planting
site preparation
watershed management
fire
harvest

time →

PROCESSES

energy inputs and transformations

radiation
primary production
decomposition
 · nutrient cycling
 · immobilization
 · mineralization
 · weathering
 · translocation
transport
 · erosion
 · gaseous
 · leaching

DEVELOPMENT OF ECOSYSTEM PROPERTIES

vegetation
consumers
soil
 · base status
 · texture
 · organic matter
 · phosphorus
 · sulfur
 · nitrogen
 · salinity

Fig. 1. Factors influencing soil development. Controlling factors affecting processes, over time, influence ecosystem properties. (*From D. C. Coleman, C. P. P. Reid, and C. V. Cole, Biological strategies of nutrient cycling in soil systems, Adv. Ecol. Res., 13:1–55, 1983*)

1–2 cm (0.4–0.8 in.). The continual input of leaf, twig, and root materials, and the algal and cyanobacterial production and turnover make this region prime for biological activity.

The clay fraction in soil, so important to microorganism life and plant activity because of its nutrient content, comprises particles less than 2 micrometers in diameter. Unlike the sand-silt minerals, clays are weathered forms of primary minerals; they are therefore referred to as secondary minerals. Coarse clay particles (0.5 μm) often are derived from quartz and mica; finer clays (0.1 μm) are clay minerals or weathered products of these (such as hydrated ferric, aluminum, titanium, and manganese oxides). The effects of coarse and fine clays on organic matter dynamics have been studied intensively. Labile (that is, rapid turnover) constituents of organic matter may be preferentially adsorbed onto fine clay particles, and thus may be a prime source of energy for the soil microorganisms.

Input of organic matter to soil is one of the major agents of soil structure. The organic matter comes from both living and dead sources (roots, leaves, microorganisms, and fauna). Various physical processes, such as deformation and compression by roots and soil fauna and by freezing-thawing and wetting-drying also have significant influences on soil structure. Plant roots and resistant organic breakdown products (humus) are important in the formation of aggregates. Bacteria, fungi, and their metabolic products are equally important in promoting granulation. The interaction of organic matter and mineral components of soils has a profound influence on cation adsorption capabilities. This property is important to both agrosystem and natural ecosystem management. *See* Agroecosystem; Soil chemistry.

Biological aspects of soil. The biological aspects of soil range from major organic inputs, decomposition by primary decomposers (bacteria, fungi, and actinomycetes), and interactions between microorganisms and fauna (secondary decomposers) which feed on them (Fig. 1).

The detritus decomposition pathway occurs on or within the soil after plant materials (litter, roots, sloughed cells, and soluble compounds) become available through death or senescence. Plant products are used by microorganisms (primary decomposers). These are eaten by the fauna, which thus affect flows of nutrients, particularly nitrogen, phosphorus, and sulfur. The immobilization of nutrients into plants or microorganisms and their subsequent mineralization are critical pathways. These processes are diagrammed in **Fig. 2**, showing flows out from the microorganisms and fauna via mineralization or direct losses into organic pools. The labile inorganic pool is the principal one that permits subsequent microorganism and plant existence. Scarcity of some nutrient often limits production. Most importantly, it is the rates of flux into and out of these labile inorganic pools which enable ecosystems to function successfully. *See* Ecosystem; Systems ecology.

Model of soil interactions. Conceptual models are useful for envisioning ecosystem processes. The array of microorganisms, fauna, and roots all provide organic material belowground, which may move through the underground ecosystem in defined ways (**Fig. 3**). Pathways of organic matter utilization by primary decomposers include bacteria, actinomycetes, or saprophytic fungi. There is considerable grazing by

pacity, texture, structure, and organic matter status are the outcome of these major processes operating as constrained by the controlling factors.

Soil profile. Abiotic and biotic factors lead to certain chemical changes in the top few decimeters (8–10 in.) of soil. In many soils, particularly in more mesic or moist regions of the world, there is a certain amount of leaching and redeposition of nutrients, often accompanied by a distinct color change. Thus, the air-litter surface is at the top of the profile, below are the zones of litter, fermentation, and humification (termed 00, 01, and 02, respectively), and below these is the mineral soil surface, which contains most of the organic matter (A horizon). The B horizon is next, containing deeper-dwelling organisms and somewhat weathered material. This is followed by the C horizon, the unconsolidated mineral material above bedrock.

The work of the soil ecologist is made easier by the fact that the surface 10–15 cm (4–6 in.) of the A horizon has the majority of plant roots, microorganisms, and fauna. A majority of the biological-chemical activities occur in this surface layer; indeed, most of the microorganism- and alga-feeding fauna, such as protozoa and rotifers and tardigrades, are in the top

such bacterial feeders as protozoa, nematodes, tardigrades, and enchytraeids. The final major primary decomposer group are the fungi, a wide array of saprophytic forms and vesicular-arbuscular mycorrhizae which take up nutrients and are mutualistic with the plant roots. The fungal grazers include stylet-bearing nematodes, collembolans, mites, and certain protozoa that are spore grazers. There is a general group of predators such as large predatory mites, nematodes, or centipedes which prey on bacteria-feeders and fungus-feeders and presumably some top predators as well.

While fauna in general account for less than 5% of the total detritus-decomposer respiration and even less biomass (see **table**), their indirect, catalytic role in decomposition is considerably greater in many ecosystems. Such indirect roles include feeding and its effects on microorganism (prey) populations, translocation of nutrients and microorganisms to different locations in the soil profile, and even, in some cases, immobilization of nitrogen and phosphorus in feces or in nests, such as those made by termites.

Earthworms play an important role in mixing and comminuting soil. They ingest large amounts of soil; a single worm such as *Lumbricus terrestris* can ingest several times its own body mass per day in a grassland or pasture. Hence, earthworms have a significant impact on nutrient transformation and availability. In addition to direct ingestion of leaf litter and other organic debris pulled from the soil surface, the earthworms will ingest and generally triturate any small bits of organic matter, including protozoa and nematodes.

Microorganism–fauna interactions. A number of studies have demonstrated the marked effects of protozoa on both bacterial numbers and nutrient dynamics. Protozoa, among the smallest and most abundant soil fauna, feed upon, and promote turnover of, microorganism populations. This has been shown in various natural ecosystems (forest, grassland, marine) as well as cropped-land ecosystems.

Soil incubations (microcosms) have been used to examine the role of some of the soil fauna in decomposition. The microfauna (protozoa) may be as abundant as 10,000–100,000 per gram of soil. Soil mesofauna, such as nematodes, are larger (about 100 times larger than protozoa), and still numerous (100–1000 per gram of soil). Both groups of organisms are voracious feeders on bacteria and fungi, and account for significant effects on nitrogen and phosphorus mineralization in soil (Figs. 2 and 3). Impacts on the primary decomposer populations vary, as noted below.

Several investigators have cultured fungus-feeding nematodes on various species of fungi and have monitored the fungal and nematode populations. Typically, they observed some inhibition of mycelial growth or respiration in cultures with nematodes versus those without nematodes. Grazing at very low nematode population levels actually stimulates the growth of fungi slightly, which is called a grazing-optimization response. The degree of such a grazing-optimization response in natural soil detritus food chains is not known. In several studies, there have been complete shifts of fungal species abundances due to preferential feeding by Collembola (an order of primitive wingless insects) on certain fungal species in aspen woodland and in pine forests.

Spatially, there are three regions where increased populations of microorganisms and fauna occur:

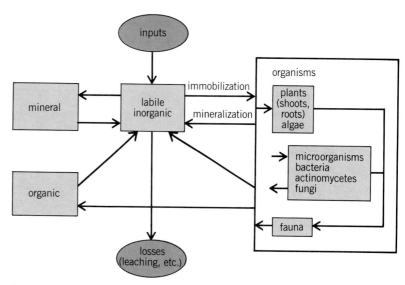

Fig. 2. Generalized nutrient-cycling scheme in soil. The biological activities of immobilization and mineralization are of major importance in ecosystem function. (*From D. C. Coleman, C. P. P. Reid, and C. V. Cole, Biological strategies of nutrient cycling in soil systems, Adv. Ecol. Res., 13:1–55, 1983*)

roots, litter, and aggregates. These regions (or microsites) exist at interfaces, or zones where substrates accumulate. Roots produce exudates such as carbohydrates, amino acids, exfoliates (sloughed cells), and mucigel (in conjunction with microorganism activity) as the roots grow through soil. Microorganisms are more abundant in the rhizosphere (the volume 0.08–0.16 in. or 2–4 mm out from the root surface), and microorganism grazer populations (protozoa, nematodes) also are larger in the rhizosphere region.

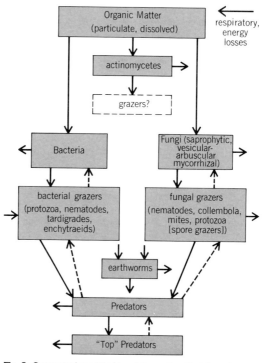

Fig. 3. Conceptual model of breakdown of particulate and soluble organic matter in agroecosystems. Vertical arrows show material flows; horizontal arrows show respiratory energy losses; and broken arrows show information feedback from lower trophic levels.

Numbers of soil organisms in various ecosystems at four different sites*

Trophic group	Aspen poplar, Alberta, Canada	Lodgepole pine, Alberta, Canada	Dryland wheat, Nebraska	Mixed-grass prairies, Nebraska
Bacteria per gram soil	—	—	1.3×10^9	1.2×10^9
Fungi, meters per gram soil[†]	—	—	34	78
Protozoa per gram soil	—	—	37,000	43,000
Microbial biomass carbon, micrograms per gram litter or soil	21,000 (litter)	16,500 (litter)	966 (soil)	1400 (soil)
Nematodes (microbivorous[‡]) per gram soil	—	—	52	74
Collembola (fungal-feeding) per square meter	71,000	22,000	1300	2000
Mites (fungal-feeding and predatory) per square meter	158,000	135,000	900	1200

*1 g = 0.035 oz. 1 m² = 10.7 ft². 1 m = 3.28 ft.
[†]That is, hyphal length is measured in meters.
[‡]Bacterial and fungal feeding.

Several research groups in North America and Europe have investigated the effects of feeding by detrital food-chain organisms on plant growth. By using either protozoa or nematodes in experimental microcosms with growing plant seedlings, significant increases were observed in both plant shoot growth and nitrogen content when bacteria-feeding fauna were present. The fungus–fungus-feeder food chain, however, showed no significant increases in plant growth when compared with the appropriate control treatments, probably because the fungi are very efficient mineralizers of nitrogen.

Selective removal or inhibition of certain target organisms such as fungi, nematodes, and arthropods has been done by using biocides in the field to determine microorganism–fauna interactions. Fungicides, insecticides, and nematicides have been used singly or in combination in field plots in various field sites, and then decomposition has been measured. Compensatory responses of certain decomposers have been observed; with an inhibition of fungi, bacteria become more abundant and active. The bacteria-feeding fauna then multiply, and predators upon them in turn become more active and enhance mineralization processes. *See Soil microbiology.*

Mutualistic interactions in soils. There are several root–microorganism interactions in soil which are mutualistic, that is, beneficial for both organisms. Prominent among these are the mycorrhizal associations between certain fungi and plant roots. Unlike the saprophytic fungi mentioned earlier, these fungi are dependent on the host plant for energy-containing carbon compounds. When the threadlike filaments (hyphae) of these beneficial fungi encounter the growing roots, they penetrate the cortical cells, or the spaces between the cells, and establish metabolic connections with the plant. The fungus receives energy compounds from the host, and there is a beneficial exchange of mineral nutrients. The hyphae grow through the soil, outside the rhizosphere zone that has been depleted of nutrients (primarily inorganic phosphorus and nitrogen), and transport them into the host plant. This mutualism is so beneficial to the plant that mycorrhizal plants can sometimes grow 20 or 30 times more rapidly than otherwise comparable nonmycorrhizal plants. In addition, they may be more resistant to drought and better able to repel disease organisms than nonmycorrhizal plants.

Within certain groups of plants, such as the legume family, including various species of beans, clover, and alfalfa, there is another important group of symbionts. When a legume root grows through soil near the symbiotic bacteria *Rhizobium*, the two future partners initiate production of several compounds, including complex carbohydrate recognition chemicals, called lectins, that allow the root to recognize the bacteria as beneficial rather than pathogenic. The bacteria then invade the root tissue and form a nodule, a swollen structure on the root surface that houses an active population of bacteria, in which nitrogen fixation takes place. By using photosynthetic energy from the plant and a specialized array of enzymes (nitrogenases), the *Rhizobium* bacteria can incorporate (fix) gaseous molecular nitrogen, N_2, breaking its triple covalent bonds and incorporating it into organic compounds, which are then mineralized and made available to the plant. This biological source of nitrogen frees legumes from a dependence on soil-borne sources and allows them to grow vigorously where many other kinds of plants could not thrive without fertilization.

Agroecosystems versus natural ecosystems. There have been several studies of minimum tillage or no-tillage in agricultural systems and how it affects microorganism populations and associated nutrient dynamics.

Soil microorganism and biochemical changes associated with reduced tillage in soybeans and corn have been studied. Differences were found in microorganism populations which convert nitrogenous compounds to nitrate, or produce gaseous nitrous oxide (N_2O) or N_2, related principally to changes in soil water, organic carbon and nitrogen, and pH when the reduced tillage regimes were imposed. There was generally a higher carbon, nitrogen, and water content in the surface soil (0–7.5 cm or 0–3 in.) under no-till, reflected by higher microorganism populations and enzyme activities. These relations were reversed from 7.5–15 cm (3–6 in.) depth in no-till versus conventional tillage, probably because plowing places crop residues at lower depths.

Interestingly, increased numbers of microarthropods and earthworms were found in zero-tilled versus conventional-tilled fields in several locations, such as Georgia and Kentucky, and in Europe. These increases in some faunal groups are probably due more to the effects of tilling on abiotic physical parameters than to increased food availability in no-till.

Systems studies. It seems important to use some integrative properties of ecosystems, particularly those relating to functional groups or guilds, so that groups of organisms that feed on similar types of substrates can be considered. Nematodes and protozoa feeding on bacteria may have a more related role in ecosystem function than various fungus-feeding nematodes and fungus-feeding mites and Collembola, which, in turn, form their own guilds (Fig. 3). A functional understanding of feeding guilds will enable better understanding of the diverse processes that function in the general framework of decomposition, immobilization, and mineralization. These processes are key focal points in determining dynamics of terrestrial ecosystems. *See* ECOLOGY; POPULATION ECOLOGY; SOIL.

David C. Coleman

Bibliography. D. C. Coleman et al., Interactions of organisms at root/soil and litter/soil interfaces in terrestrial ecosystems, *Agric. Ecosys. Environ.*, 24:117–134, 1988; D. C. Coleman, C. P. P. Reid, and C. V. Cole, Biological strategies of nutrient cycling in soil systems, *Adv. Ecol. Res.*, 13:1–55, 1983; E. T. Elliott and D. C. Coleman, Let the soil work for us, *Ecol. Bull.*, 39:23–32, 1988; E. T. Elliott, H. W. Hunt, and D. E. Walter, Detrital foodweb interactions in North American grassland ecosystems, *Agric. Ecosys. Environ.*, 24:41–56, 1988; D. Parkinson, Linkages between resource availability, microorganisms and soil invertebrates, *Agric. Ecosys. Environ.*, 24:21–32, 1988; R. Phillips, and S. Phillips, *No-Tillage Agriculture*, 1984.

Soil fertility

The ability of a soil to supply plant nutrients. Sixteen chemical elements are required for the growth of all plants: carbon, oxygen, and hydrogen (these three are obtained from carbon dioxide and water), plus nitrogen, phosphorus, potassium, calcium, magnesium, sulfur, iron, manganese, zinc, copper, boron, molybdenum, and chlorine. Some plant species also require one or more of the elements cobalt, sodium, vanadium, and silicon.

Nutrient forms in soil. While carbon and oxygen are supplied to plants from carbon dioxide in the air, the other essential elements are supplied primarily by the soil. Of the latter, all except hydrogen from water are called mineral nutrients.

Only part of the 13 essential mineral nutrients in soil are in a chemical form that can be immediately used by plants. The unusable (unavailable) parts, which eventually do become available to plants, are of two kinds: they may be in organic combination (such as nitrogen in soil humus) or in solid inorganic soil particles (such as potassium in soil clays). The time for complete decomposition and dissolution of these compounds varies widely, from days to hundreds of years.

The quantity of the immediately available nutrient is often small. For example, it is common for a soil to contain only 30 lb of available nitrate nitrogen per acre (33 kg/ha) in the top foot (1 ft = 0.3 m) of soil. The same quantity of soil might contain 4000 lb (1800 kg) of unavailable nitrogen in organic compounds (soil humus). As another example, a soil might contain 25,000 lb of total potassium per acre (28,000 kg/ha), with only 300 lb/acre (135 kg/ha) immediately available to crops.

Limits to plant growth. Soils exhibit a variable ability to supply the mineral nutrients needed by plants. This characteristic allows soils to be classified according to their level of fertility. This can vary from a deficiency to a sufficiency, or even toxicity (too much), of one or more nutrients. A serious deficiency of only one essential nutrient can still greatly reduce crop yields. For example, a soil considered fertile in all other ways could have levels of available potassium too low for optimum plant growth. Control of crop growth by the deficient nutrient is known as Liebig's law of the minimum. This law simply states that the plant growth rate is controlled by that mineral nutrient present in the most limiting quantity in the soil (see **Fig. 1**). Modern chemical fertilizers applied to the soil reduce or eliminate nutrient deficiency and ensure that fertility does not limit a soil's potential to produce crops.

Although fertilizers have dramatically increased the soil's potential to produce crops, other variables often control crop production. Both climatic and other soil factors can limit crop yields, as can crop variety, diseases, and insects. Elements of the climate such as insufficient water, temperature stresses (either too hot or too cold), and natural disasters such as wind and hail storms can all lower crop production regardless of a soil's inherent or cultivated fertility. Other undesirable soil conditions such as compacted soil layers or acid soil layers that restrict root growth can also reduce crop yield. *See* CROP MICROMETEOROLOGY.

Influence of crop type. The type of crop grown on a particular soil determines the required soil fertility level. Crops differ greatly in their need for nutrients and their ability to extract them from soils. Also, even if two crops extract a nutrient equally, one crop may use that nutrient more efficiently than the other.

Perhaps the most extreme example of the crop-type influence would be to compare a soil's nitrogen fertility for a legume such as alfalfa with its nitrogen fertility for a grass such as maize. Since alfalfa, through its symbiotic association with *Rhizobium* bacteria, obtains nitrogen from the dinitrogen (N_2) in the air, a severely nitrogen-deficient soil would not limit the growth of alfalfa. The growth of maize would be slowed by insufficient nitrogen, however, since maize

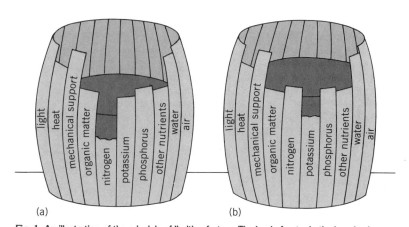

Fig. 1. An illustration of the principle of limiting factors. The level of water in the barrels above represents the level of crop production. (a) Nitrogen is represented as being the factor that is most limiting. Even though the other elements are present in more adequate amounts, crop production can be no higher than that allowed by the nitrogen. (b) When nitrogen is added, the level of crop production is raised until it is controlled by the next most limiting factor, in this case, potassium. (*After N. C. Brady, The Nature and Properties of Soils, 9th ed., Macmillan, 1984*)

depends directly on the uptake of available nitrogen in the soil. *See Soil microbiology*.

Cation exchange and inherent fertility. Several soil properties are important in determining a soil's inherent fertility. One property is the adsorption and storage of nutrients on the surfaces of soil particles. Such adsorption of a number of nutrients is caused by an attraction of positively charged nutrients to negatively charged soil particles (similar to the attraction of the positive and negative poles of two magnets). This adsorption is called cation exchange (adsorbed cations can be exchanged with other cations in solution), and the quantity of nutrient cations a soil can adsorb is called its cation-exchange capacity. A cation is a single atom or a group of two or more atoms combined that has lost one or more of its electrons. Since atoms are made of equal numbers of protons (each has one positive charge) and electrons (each with one negative charge), they have zero charge. Some atoms and molecules lose one or more electrons, resulting in an excess of protons, thereby causing a positive charge. The plant nutrient calcium is a cation with two more protons than electrons, giving it two positive charges (Ca^{2+}). Atoms or groups of atoms having more electrons than protons are negatively charged ions known as anions. *See Soil chemistry*.

The negative charge in soils is associated with clay particles. This negative charge results largely from an imbalance of positive and negative charges from cations and anions within their crystalline structure. The negatively charged clay particle adsorbs enough cations to maintain an overall zero charge balance. The cations adsorbed by clay particles are largely the plant nutrients calcium (Ca^{2+}), magnesium (Mg^{2+}), and potassium (K^+) with lesser amounts of the essential micronutrients manganese (Mn^{2+}), zinc (Zn^{2+}), iron (Fe^{2+} and Fe^{3+}), and copper (Cu^{2+}). Sodium (Na^+) can also be an important adsorbed cation, especially in soils of more arid regions. The cations Ca^{2+}, Mg^{2+}, K^+, and Na^+ are often referred to as a soil's exchangeable bases. The adsorbed cations are in equilibrium with the same cations in the soil water (soil solution). Plant roots absorb most nutrient ions directly from the soil solution. As nutrient cations are taken from the soil solution, exchange reactions resupply the solution with that ion from the soil clays to maintain a nearly constant concentration.

In addition to the exchangeable bases and other nutrient cations, acid cations such as trivalent aluminum, hydroxy-aluminum, and the hydrogen ion are also adsorbed by the soil's negative charges.

Organic matter and cation exchange. Some of the soil's cation-exchange capacity may also arise from organic matter (humus) in the soil. Negative charges of organic matter arise largely from carboxylic and phenolic acid functional groups. Since these functional groups are weak acids, the negative charge from organic matter increases as the soil pH increases, as shown below in equilibrium for a carbox-

$$R-C\underset{OH}{\overset{O}{<}} \rightleftharpoons R-C\underset{O^-}{\overset{O}{<}} + H^+$$

ylic acid. As soil pH increases, hydrogen ion removal from the right side of the equilibrium causes the formation of additional negatively charged carboxyl groups.

The negative charges of soil organic matter can adsorb the same cations as described for the soil clays.

The proportion of cation-exchange capacity arising from mineral clays and from organic matter depends on the proportions of each in the soil and on the kinds of clays. In most mineral soils, the soil clays comprise the greater proportion of cation-exchange capacity. Within the class of mineral soils, those soils with more clay and less sand and silt have the greatest cation-exchange capacity.

The soil cation-exchange sites provide the immediate store of available nutrient cations that can be used by plants. Because of this store of available nutrients, those soils with greater cation-exchange capacities generally provide a greater supply of available nutrients for crop production. However, the fertility level of each plant nutrient must be balanced to the needs of the crop to achieve high productivity.

Soil acidity. The amounts and kinds of acids on the cation-exchange sites can have a substantial influence on a soil's perceived fertility. Soils with a pH of 7 have their exchange sites nearly 100% saturated with the bases Ca^{2+}, Mg^{2+}, K^+, and Na^+. As soil pH's drop below 7, the proportion of the exchange complex saturated with acids begins to increase. Between pH 7 and 5.5, the predominant acid cation is hydroxy-aluminum, which is tightly adsorbed to the clays and causes no reduction in plant growth. At soil pH's around 5.5 and below, the acid cation trivalent aluminum (Al^{3+}), which is toxic to plants, begins to appear on the cation-exchange sites. It and excess manganese (Mn^{+2}) together are the greatest hazards to the growth of healthy crops at low soil pH's. In some cases of extremely low soil pH, insufficient calcium may also limit crop growth, but such cases are rare.

Two factors cause soils to become acid: when crops are harvested, exchangeable bases are removed as part of the crop; and exchangeable bases move with drainage water below the crop's root zone (leaching). Leaching of bases is enhanced when acids are released to the soil from plant roots, from microbial respiration, and from other microbially mediated processes, especially nitrification, the conversion of ammonium nitrogen to nitrate nitrogen. For each ammonium ion converted to nitrate nitrogen, two hydrogen ions are released. Hydrogen ions or aluminum cations resulting from acid decomposition of clays can exchange some of the bases from cation-exchange sites to the soil solution to allow their loss by leaching. Since much of the nitrogen fertilizer supplied to crops contains ammonium nitrogen (this is true of both manure and chemical fertilizers), the addition of high rates of nitrogen enhances soil acidification. Finely ground limestone (calcium carbonate) can be applied to acid soils when needed to neutralize soil acids and to add Ca^{2+} and Mg^{2+}, thereby raising soil pH back to the desirable range for optimum crop production.

Nutrients in soil minerals. While the supply of some plant nutrient cations (especially calcium, magnesium, and potassium) is related to their amounts on a soil's cation-exchange sites, there is often a greater supply of these nutrients within the soil minerals themselves. However, nutrients from soil minerals become available to crops only after the minerals partially dissolve and release the individual ions to the soil solution. Most soil clays contain some potassium and magnesium within their crystalline structures. Feldspars in some soils contain potassium, while other minerals contain supplies of magnesium and calcium. Calcite in some high-pH soils constitutes a large supply of calcium. Other minerals supply many of the micronutrients in soil.

Minerals containing some micronutrients and, especially, the major nutrient phosphorus furnish plant-available forms by slow dissolution. As plant roots absorb these nutrients, more of the soil mineral dissolves in the soil solution. Many micronutrients also have some immediately available forms adsorbed onto the cation-exchange sites, but phosphorus does not since its plant-available forms ($H_2PO_4^-$ and HPO_4^{2-}) are both anions.

Organic matter and nutrient supply. Most of the nitrogen and sulfur in soils are a part of soil organic matter. Soil organic matter can also contain phosphorus and micronutrients, although they are often in soil minerals as well. Soils in the midwestern United States typically contain around 3000 lb of organic nitrogen per acre (3300 kg/ha) in their plow layer. During 1 year, less than 0.5% of the organic nitrogen might be converted to the plant-available ammonium and nitrate forms by soil microorganisms. The amount of total organic sulfur in soil and the amount converted to plant-available sulfur would both be approximately 10% of the nitrogen values. The amounts of mineralization (conversion from organic to available mineral forms) per year are only approximate, since mineralization depends on many factors, some of which are soil temperature, soil moisture, and the quality and quantity of decomposing crop residue. These factors can vary considerably from one location to another and from year to year at a given location.

Soil organic matter, especially the small proportion of soluble organic matter, can increase the supply of micronutrients available to plants by acting as a natural complexing agent. Complexing agents are large organic molecules that can encapsulate some micronutrients. This encapsulation maintains higher levels of that nutrient in the soil solution, increasing its availability for plant uptake.

David E. Kissel

Soil testing. Soil testing is the use of rapid chemical analyses to determine the fertility status of a soil. It is used to identify those nutrients or substances that are present in either insufficient or excessive quantities for optimum plant growth. Analyses are also used to monitor increases or decreases in soil fertility over time. Soil test data are critical for determining rates of commercial fertilizer, animal wastes, and other nutrient sources that maximize profit to farmers that are environmentally responsible. Soil testing is also used by commercial greenhouse operators and by private individuals for lawn and garden management.

The first step for the user is collecting a representative sample from the field or area of interest. This process is of vital importance for the resulting soil tests to be meaningful. Attention must be given to the number of cores collected, the core locations, depth of sampling, time of sampling, and how the samples are handled after collection. The samples are usually submitted to a soil testing laboratory that will perform the tests and normally will provide an interpretation of the results, including fertilizer recommendations.

Most of the laboratory procedures used for evaluating soil fertility involve use of specific chemical solutions to extract a portion of one or more nutrients from the soil. The solutions and procedures are selected from a database of correlation studies that have been conducted previously. These studies determine the correlation of the chemically extracted nutrient with the soil's ability to supply the nutrient to plants.

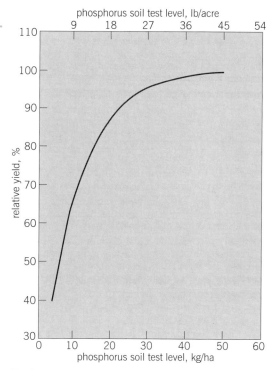

Fig. 2. Relationship between phosphorus soil test level and average relative corn yield or percent sufficiency in Illinois. (*After T. R. Peck et al., eds., Soil Testing: Correlating and Interpreting the Analytical Result, Amer. Soc. Agron. Spec. Publ. 29, 1977*)

The amount of the element present in the soil extract is determined by analytical instruments, which may be as basic as a colorimeter or specific ion electrode or as sophisticated as a plasma spectrophotometer capable of simultaneous multielement analysis.

Indices of the soil nutrient availability are developed from the soil test values obtained from these determinations; they have practical significance only when the interpretation is based on extensive field calibration. In soil test calibration, researchers conduct many experiments across the geographic region of interest and across a range of soil test values. Each experiment includes rates of the nutrient in question such that the optimum rate for the site can be determined. Once a sufficient number of experiments have been performed, the probability of getting a response to application of a nutrient and the average percent sufficiency at a given soil test level can be determined (**Fig. 2**). The same studies are used to estimate the amount of a particular nutrient to apply to give optimum yield at a given soil test level.

The most subjective part of soil testing is the process of deriving specific fertilizer recommendations from soil test values. A multitude of factors can influence this process, including land tenure, supply of capital, fertilizer and crop prices, crop quality effects, crop rotation, and fertilizer placement. Therefore, the recommendations developed are dependent on the assumptions made with respect to these factors. Ideally they are fine-tuned to fit each individual situation. *SEE SOIL.*

Paul Fixen

Bibliography. C. A. Black, *Soil-Plant Relationships*, 2d ed., 1968, reprint 1984; N. C. Brady, *The Nature and Properties of Soils*, 9th ed., 1984; J. R. Brown (ed.), *Soil Testing: Sampling, Correlation,*

Calibration, and Interpretation, 1987; A. L. Page (ed.), *Methods of Soil Analysis,* pt. 2, 2d ed., 1982; T. R. Peck (ed.), *Soil Testing: Correlating and Interpreting the Analytical Results,* 1977; E. W. Russell, *Soil Conditions and Plant Growth,* 10th ed., 1974; S. L. Tisdale and W. L. Nelson, *Soil Fertility and Fertilizers,* 4th ed., 1985; R. L. Westerman (ed.), *Soil Testing and Plant Analysis,* rev. ed., 1990.

Soil microbiology

The study of microorganisms in the soil environment. Since soil serves as the boundary of the terrestrial portion of the Earth's surface, soil microorganisms play an important role in the maintenance of plant and animal life, influencing the fate of both natural and synthetic materials that enter the soil. Traditionally, soil microbiology was directed toward agriculture and forestry, with studies focused on understanding the role of soil microorganisms in maintaining or enhancing plant productivity. However, soil microbiologists have recognized the influence of microorganisms upon the fate of toxic anthropogenic compounds that have been deliberately or unintentionally introduced into soil. The boundaries of soil microbiology have been extended into subsoil environments as a result of concern over the vertical transport of soil-applied pollutants into groundwater supplies. Soil microbiology is a subdiscipline of microbiology that integrates with plant and animal sciences; it also connects with many of the nonbiological sciences such as physics, chemistry, hydrology, engineering, and mathematics.

Soil microorganisms. Soil contains a wide range of microorganisms from all the kingdoms of life. Viruses, prokaryotes (bacteria), and simple eukaryotes [ranging from fungi to plants (algae) and animals (nematodes, protozoa, and "microarthropods")] are all found in great abundance and diversity. Although soils may vary greatly in their physical and chemical characteristics and in their depth, the majority of microorganisms reside in the surface layers; these layers contain most of the organic materials and are influenced by plant and animal life.

Although there are nutritional advantages to residing near or at the soil surface, there are also disadvantages. Climatic variation can result in excessively high temperatures and lack of water, both conditions being detrimental to most microbial life forms. In response, soil microorganisms have adopted two strategies of existence. The zymogenous microflora can respond quickly to the transient appearance of nutrients. Upon exhaustion of the nutrients, their populations die back or return to a dormant state. The autochthonous microflora represent those possessing a slower metabolism; they do not respond rapidly to the transient appearance of introduced nutrients. These microorganisms are believed to utilize more recalcitrant nutrients that the zymogenous microflora are unable to use.

Roles. The sources of nutrients for the majority of microorganisms in soil are the tissues of plants, animals, and microorganisms that either reside in the soil or enter the soil upon death. The tremendous diversity of microbial types results in the decomposition of the complex organic compounds of plant and animal origin into simpler organic molecules that are ultimately processed into simple inorganic compounds such as salts and gases. Since many of these compounds can

be assimilated by plant life, soil microorganisms play a beneficial role in processing nutrients essential for maintenance of life on Earth.

The behavior of each element essential for the growth of organisms can be described conceptually in the form of a cycle, for example, the nitrogen cycle. A major focus in soil microbiology is the study of the role of environmental factors in the cycling of the elements by soil microorganisms. Climatic conditions such as the amount of precipitation and the temperature range influence the rates and characteristics of these cyclic processes. In addition, the physical nature of the soil influences the activity of the soil microorganisms by controlling the availability of oxygen and water and the physical accessibility of the nutrients. Soil chemistry can vary widely, depending on the parent material of the soil, the climate under which the soil developed, and the extent of perturbation by humans. Extremes of acidity and alkalinity, excesses of toxic minerals, or deficiencies in minerals critical for plant growth can influence the rates and characteristics of microorganism-dependent processes. Ultimately, such factors affect the extent to which plant and animal life can colonize the soil and the agricultural or silvicultural productivity of the soil. *See* BIOGEOCHEMISTRY.

Under most natural conditions, nutrient cycles are maintained in equilibrium by the plant, animal, and soil microbial communities. Catastrophic events, natural or anthropogenic, can disrupt the cycles and lead to losses of nutrients from the ecosystem with concomitant loss of surface soil by water and wind erosion. A new period of soil development, critically dependent upon soil microorganisms, must then take place over a period of many years before populations of higher life forms can reach stable equilibrium in the area again.

Types. Some soil microorganisms have received greater attention because of the key roles they play at critical stages in the cycling of elements essential for life. For example, nitrogen is the major limiting factor for plant growth in most soils. Certain soil bacteria can convert nitrogen gas (N_2) into ammonia (NH_3), which is then assimilated into protein. Some of these bacteria can form symbiotic associations within the root systems of leguminous plants (vetch, clover, beans) or with woody shrubs and trees (alder, *Myrica, Ceanothus*). As a result, such plants meet their nitrogen requirements independently of the soil. Nitrifying bacteria use ammonia or nitrite (NO_2^-) as energy sources, resulting in the two compounds being converted to nitrate (NO_3^-), a source of nitrogen favored by most plant species. Denitrifying bacteria can remove nitrate from soil by using it as a substitute for oxygen in respiration. This activity results in the evolution of nitrous oxide (N_2O) and nitrogen gas to the atmosphere.

Filamentous soil microorganisms (actinomycetes) have been studied extensively because they are the source of many antibiotics. Although these organisms grow in a mycelial form and produce spores, they are not fungi, but are prokaryotic in nature since they have neither the cell nucleus nor the cell organelles found in eukaryotes. Certain soil bacteria have been discovered to be incredibly versatile in the kinds of organic compounds from which they can derive energy. Pseudomonads have been isolated that can decompose many of the toxic compounds introduced by humans into natural environments. By developing a better understanding of how these organisms carry out these processes, it is believed that microbiologically based technologies can be developed for restoration of severely contaminated soil environments.

Methods of study. Numerous methods have been developed for studying soil microbiology. Depending upon the objectives, methods have focused on gaining an understanding of the composition of soil microbial communities, on the behavior of specific members within the community, or on the impact and fate of so-called aliens introduced into the community for some beneficial purpose. Parallel with these approaches, methods have been developed to study the characteristics of specific processes carried out by subpopulations within the community.

Microorganisms. Traditionally, soil microorganisms were isolated and enumerated by culture methods. These methods are dependent upon separating microorganisms physically from a soil sample by shaking in an aqueous solution, making appropriate dilutions, and then exposing a given volume of the diluent containing individual cells to nutrients. Upon metabolizing the nutrients, an individual cell can proliferate rather quickly to produce a visible colony containing 1–10 million progeny of the original cell. By varying the composition of the nutrients and other parameters of the growth conditions, such as oxygen, temperature, and pH, conditions can be made sufficiently restrictive so that only specific members of the complex soil community will grow. Such methods have limitations, because no more than one-thousandth of the bacteria in any soil sample can be cultured by conventional methods. As a consequence, understanding of soil microorganisms is still very limited, because it has not been possible to study the majority of them by conventional microbiological methods.

Techniques have been developed for studying the behavior of specific microorganisms in soil without culturing them; these involve removing microorganisms from the optically opaque soil matrix. Subsequently the microbes are visualized with compounds that specifically bind to components of intact cells, for example, deoxyribonucleic acid (DNA). Other staining procedures have been developed that reveal specific members within the soil community. Antibodies, which are proteins produced in the immune system of higher animals to facilitate the removal of foreign microorganisms from within the animal, can be generated to specific soil microorganisms The target of the antibody often lies on the cell surface of the specific microorganism. When molecules of a fluorescent dye are attached to the antibody, the microorganisms to which the antibody is attached can be seen by fluorescence microscopy.

The tools of modern molecular biology have also been applied to soil microbiology. One is known as gene probe. This is either a copy of a particular gene of interest found in a soil microorganism or a copy of a sequence of DNA unique to a specific microorganism or to a group of organisms of special interest. By extracting the DNA from the population of microorganisms resident in a sample of soil and incubating it with the DNA probe, the probe binds to any identical regions of DNA in the natural sample. As a result, the presence and quantity of the gene of interest can be determined, regardless of either the ability to culture or to visualize microscopically the organism in which the gene resides.

Processes. In many soil-microbiology studies, the identity of the specific microorganisms involved is of less interest than the environmental parameters that control the rate and characteristics of the processes they carry out. Procedures that originated in the disciplines of physics, chemistry, and biochemistry are widely used. Subsequently, mathematical procedures are utilized when the goal is to develop a model of the process of interest. As a result, findings from one soil can be compared with those obtained from other soils under different climatic and environmental conditions. *SEE SOIL; SOIL CHEMISTRY; SOIL ECOLOGY.*

Peter J. Bottomley

Bibliography. M. Alexander, *Introduction to Soil Microbiology*, 2d ed., 1977; R. M. Atlas and R. Bartha, *Microbial Ecology*, 2d ed., 1987; C. Edwards, *Microbiology of Extreme Environments*, 1990; M. J. Klug and C. A. Reddy, *Current Perspectives in Microbial Ecology*, 1984; J. M. Lynch, *Soil Biotechnology*, 1983; E. A. Paul and F. E. Clark, *Soil Microbiology and Biochemistry*, 1989; S. A. Waksman, *Principles of Soil Microbiology*, 1927.

Solar energy

The energy transmitted from the Sun. The upper atmosphere of Earth receives about 1.5×10^{21} watt-hours (thermal) of solar radiation annually. This vast amount of energy is more than 23,000 times that used by the human population of this planet, but it is only about one two-billionth of the Sun's massive outpouring—about 3.9×10^{20} MW.

The power density of solar radiation measured just outside Earth's atmosphere and over the entire solar spectrum is called the solar constant. According to the World Meteorological Organization, the most reliable (1981) value for the solar constant is 1370 ± 6 W/m^2. Of this power, 8% is in the ultraviolet wavelengths, 47% in the visible spectrum, and 45% in the infrared region. The solar constant actually is not a true constant, but is subject to a small continuous variation due to the shape of Earth's orbit, amounting to -3.3% from average about July 5, when Earth is at its greatest distance from the Sun, and $+3.4\%$ about January 3, when Earth is closest to the Sun.

Solar radiation is attenuated before reaching Earth's surface by an atmosphere that removes or alters part of the incident energy by reflection, scattering, and absorption. In particular, nearly all ultraviolet radiation and certain wavelengths in the infrared region are removed. However, the solar radiation striking Earth's surface each year is still more than 10,000 times the world's energy use. Radiation scattered by striking gas molecules, water vapor, or dust particles is known as diffuse radiation. Clouds are a particularly important scattering and reflecting agent, capable of reducing direct radiation by as much as 80 to 90%. Because cloud distributions and types are highly variable, these reductions are quite unpredictable. The radiation arriving at the ground directly from the Sun is called direct or beam radiation. Global radiation is all solar radiation incident on the surface, including direct and diffuse. **Figure 1** illustrates the events that affect solar radiation as it passes through Earth's atmosphere.

The amount of atmospheric absorption and scattering of solar radiation is a function of the effective distance (depending on atmospheric thickness and

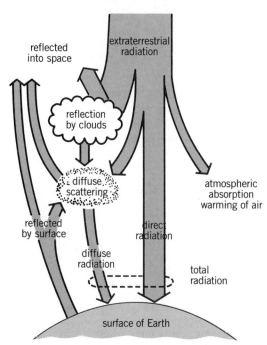

reflected
into space

extraterrestrial
radiation

reflection
by clouds

diffuse
scattering

atmospheric
absorption
warming of air

reflected
by surface

direct
radiation

diffuse
radiation

total
radiation

surface of Earth

Fig. 1. Direct, diffuse, and total solar radiation. (*After W. C. Dickinson and P. N. Cheremisinoff, eds., Solar Energy Technology Handbook, pt. A: Engineering Fundamentals, Marcel Dekker, 1980*)

content) through which the radiation travels. Spectral irradiance is a function of air mass. The term air mass zero is used to represent zero mass of air through which the Sun's rays must pass (the solar intensity outside Earth's atmosphere). Radiation arriving at the surface of Earth can be measured against that reaching the fringes of the atmosphere, where there is no air. The light of the Sun directly overhead at a 90° solar altitude, or zenith, at sea level is said to pass through an air mass of 1, providing an average peak intensity of 1 kW/m^2. The solar declination, the angle between the Earth-Sun line and Earth's equatorial plane, varies as Earth circles the Sun, and this affects the solar radiation (insolation) reaching the ground. Intensity weakens at Sun angles approaching the horizon since the rays have more atmosphere to penetrate. The amount of solar energy incident on a horizontal surface at sea level ranges up to 2400 Btu/ft^2-day (7 kWh/m^2-day). The sites between latitudes 35°N and 35°S receive between 2000 and 3500 h of sunshine per year; higher latitudes receive less.

Solar research and technology development aim at finding the most efficient ways of capturing low-density solar energy and developing systems to convert captured energy to useful purposes. Also of significant potential as power sources are the indirect forms of solar energy: wind, biomass, hydropower, and the tropical ocean surfaces. With the exception of hydropower, these energy resources remain largely untapped. *See* ENERGY SOURCES.

Five major technologies using solar energy are being developed. (1) The heat content of solar radiation is used to provide moderate-temperature heat for space comfort conditioning of buildings, moderate- and high-temperature heat for industrial processes, and high-temperature heat for generating electricity. (2) Photovoltaics convert solar energy directly into electricity. (3) Biomass technologies exploit the

chemical energy produced through photosynthesis (a reaction energized by solar radiation) to produce energy-rich fuels and chemicals and to provide direct heat for many uses. (4) Wind energy systems generate mechanical energy, primarily for conversion to electric power. (5) Finally, a number of ocean energy applications are being pursued; the most advanced is ocean thermal energy conversion, which uses temperature differences between warm ocean surface water and cooler deep water to produce electricity.

SOLAR ENERGY SYSTEMS IN BUILDINGS

Systems employing solar energy are classified as passive or active systems.

Passive systems. Passive solar energy systems use the building itself in combination with solar energy as an energy-saving system. A passive building uses its environment, the features of its site, its structure, and its materials so that it requires much less fuel energy. Passive lighting, usually called daylighting, illuminates the interior of a building as a replacement for or supplement to electric lighting.

Heating systems. Most solar thermal systems consist of three basic parts: a collector, a storage medium, and a distribution system. In a passive solar heating system, the collector is usually the building itself. In direct systems, the Sun's rays enter the building, usually through windows, and heat the room or space in direct sunlight. Excess heat can be vented off or stored in the mass (walls and floor) of the building for later use. The entering solar energy is distributed through a combination of reradiation from the mass and natural convection of warm air between rooms. Indirect heating systems use one or more rooms as a collector, which is combined with a storage mass that separates that room from the rest of the building. The Sun's energy is reradiated and convected into the building after passing through the storage mass, which can store heat during the day for use at night. Popular passive heating systems include greenhouses and sunspaces.

Cooling systems. One type of passive solar cooling occurs when the cycle established in a passive heating system is reversed, allowing the building to radiate heat to the sky at night. As the mass is cooled, it lowers the temperature inside the house. Then, during the daytime, the cool mass helps maintain comfortable conditions in summer without using air conditioning. Sometimes, the radiant cooling process is assisted by placing a storage mass, such as bags of water, on top of the building. The storage mass is covered to prevent heating during the day but is exposed to the night sky.

Another form of passive cooling is natural ventilation, such as is caused by air currents entering through open windows or doors. Ventilation also occurs as heated air rises to the ceiling. If openings are placed near the ceiling of a room and at floor level, warm air will rise and exit through the top openings, drawing cooler air in through the lower openings.

Natural cooling also occurs when a building is shaded during the summer. If shade trees are deciduous (shed their leaves during the winter), they will not interfere with a passive heating system. The house can also be self-shading through the use of overhangs and extended walls.

Daylighting systems. In commercial, institutional, and industrial buildings, the largest energy use is often electric lighting. Daylighting can be used to replace or supplement electric lighting in buildings occupied primarily during the daytime. Windows and other types of apertures allow daylight to enter the building, and special control systems regulate the electric lighting to turn it off when there is sufficient daylight in the building. Unlike other passive systems, daylighting can occur on overcast days because the daylight in the building does not depend on the direct use of the Sun.

It is possible to use a variety of materials to effect passive solar performance, such as antireflective window coatings, insulating window shades and curtains, or modular water walls. Some window coatings carry an electric current that can change window transmittance in response to weather conditions. In addition, there are several chemical compounds that can be incorporated either into window glass or between panes to increase a window's storage or insulating capacity.

Active space conditioning and hot water systems. Solar active space conditioning and hot water systems use mechanical means to collect, store, and distribute solar energy to heat and cool buildings and to heat water for domestic or commercial use. In general, water heating, the simplest system, is characterized by the smallest collector array, the simplest design, and the lowest cost; retrofit can be accomplished easily. Space heating requires a large collector array, has the largest heat storage requirement, and is relatively expensive. Space heating and cooling is the most complex of the solar active systems, requiring the largest collector array, the highest temperatures, and a complicated mechanical process.

Active systems generally encompass four parts: collection (including storage), conversion, distribution, and control (**Fig. 2**).

Collection. Collectors can be flat-plate, evacuated-tube, or concentrating. In most active systems, flat-plate collectors are used in one or more modules. The Sun's radiation is absorbed by the collector and is converted to heat in a liquid (water or glycol) or gas (air) heat-transfer medium. The heat is transported by pumps or fans to the conversion and distribution systems for immediate use or is stored for later use. The heat-transfer medium in liquid systems usually is wa-

ter, which must be protected from freezing in cold climates. An antifreeze can be added to the water, or the collectors can be drained when the outdoor temperature approaches freezing. If an antifreeze is added, a heat exchanger is used to isolate the water in the collectors from the internal building water.

Conversion. For both space heating and cooling and domestic hot water, a conversion system is required to convert the thermal energy to useful heat. The thermal energy may also be converted to mechanical work that can subsequently drive a conventional vapor compression cooling unit. Thermal energy can also be used directly, through absorption refrigeration, for space cooling.

Desiccant cooling for air conditioning uses recirculated, dehumidified air as well as evaporative cooling to produce cool, comfortable air for the building (**Fig. 3**). The desiccant material is regenerated and reused when water is driven off by solar-heated air.

Distribution. The distribution system transports the hot or cold fluid from the conversion system to the point of use in the building. Generally, one distribution system for both the solar system and auxiliary (backup) system is used to reduce duplication.

Control. The control system collects temperature information from inside and outside the building, processes the information, and sends commands as conditions dictate. Temperature sensors provide data to a network of relays or a microprocessor, which processes the data and sends commands to operate either the collection, conversion, or distribution system.

Research has included efforts to improve the cost of collectors by testing lightweight flat-plate collectors using thin-film plastics rather than conventional metal-glass materials, identifying desiccants and other cooling system materials, and collecting data from a network of building sites on performance, reliability, and durability of active solar systems.

SOLAR THERMAL TECHNOLOGY

Solar energy can be converted to useful work or heat by using a collector to absorb solar radiation, allowing much of the Sun's radiant energy to be converted to heat. This heat can be used directly in resi-

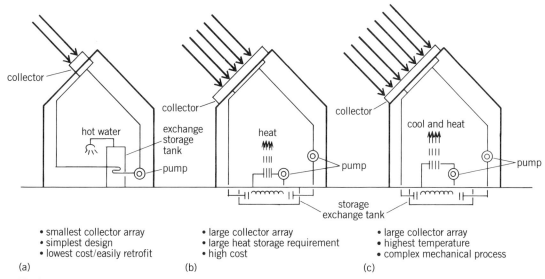

Fig. 2. Building space conditioning and hot water systems. (*a*) Water heating. (*b*) Space heating. (*c*) Space heating and cooling. (*After DOE 5-Year Research Plan for National Active Solar Heating and Cooling Program, U.S. Department of Energy, 1983*)

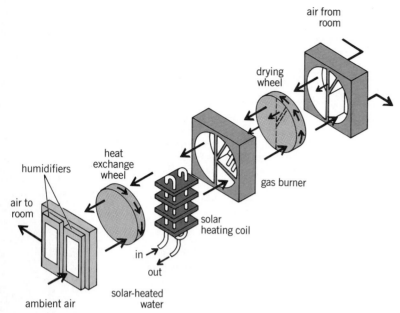

Fig. 3. Desiccant solar cooling system with gas backup in recirculation mode. (*After R. S. Barlow, Analysis of the Adsorption Process and of Desiccant Cooling Systems: A Pseudo-Steady Model for Coupled Heat and Mass Transfer, SERI/TR-631-1330, Solar Energy Research Institute, 1982*)

dential, industrial, and agricultural operations; converted to mechanical or electrical power; or applied in chemical reactions for production of fuels and chemicals.

Collector systems. The collector system contains a concentrator and a receiver. The concentrator redirects and focuses sunlight on the receiver by using mirrors or lenses, and the receiver absorbs solar radiation and converts it to heat. Solar collectors are of two basic classes: nonfocusing and focusing. They are further distinguished on the basis of their concentrator optical properties (**Fig. 4**), and the operating temperature that can be obtained at the receiver (**Table 1**).

Nonfocusing collectors. Nonfocusing collectors are generally kept fixed (nontracking), yielding low-temperature outputs. Two types of this class of collectors are the solar pond and the evacuated-tube collector.

One type of solar collector that could have wide applicability is the salt-gradient solar pond (**Fig. 5**). A thin layer of fresh or low-salinity water covers a deeper layer of water in which a salinity gradient is created (that is, salt concentration increases with depth). The bottom layer is usually at or near salt saturation. Sunlight passing through the water is absorbed and heats the bottom layer. The salt concentration in the deeper water serves to increase the liquid density and thereby prevents the natural convection that would normally mix both the warm lower layers and the cool layers above. The heat is thus trapped and stored at the bottom and can be extracted for use. Care must be taken to prevent the extraction process from upsetting the stability of the layers. Wind effects on the surface tend to cause mixing that is detrimental to pond performance, and floating or suspended debris will reduce the pond's transparency to sunlight.

Several solar ponds have been constructed and are operating around the world. The bottom hot brine, with temperatures near 180°F (82°C), can be used directly or via a heat exchanger to provide low-temperature heat for many industrial applications, for district space heating, or for electricity generation.

Table 1. Typical operating temperatures for solar thermal collectors

Type of collector	Operating temperature range, °F (°C)
Central receiver	400–2500 (200–1400)
Point focus (parabolic dish and Fresnel lens)	550–2500 (300–1400)
Line focus (parabolic trough and Fresnel lens, also multiple reflector)	160–600 (70–320)
Evacuated tube	120–350 (49–177)
Flat-plate	50–160 (10–71)
Solar pond	50–180 (10–82)

The evacuated-tube collector, sometimes incorporated with a reflective backing to provide greater solar concentration, can provide temperatures of up to 300°F (150°C), the temperature required to produce low-grade, industrial process steam.

Focusing collectors. This major class of collectors includes the distributed receiver system and the point-focus central receiver system.

Distributed receiver systems, such as line-focus (for example, parabolic trough) and point-focus (for example, parabolic dish), are commonly considered for remote community-power systems, military applications, individual factory or commercial building systems, or agricultural applications. These collectors must always point toward the Sun and cannot make use of diffuse and reflected light, which can account for a 10 to 20°F (5 to 10°C) temperature rise in flat-plate collectors.

1. Line-focus. The line-focus collector allows the concentrating, mirrored, reflector surface to follow the Sun by rotating about one axis (either east-west or north-south). Radiation is reflected onto an absorber tube (the receiver). The parabolic trough collector

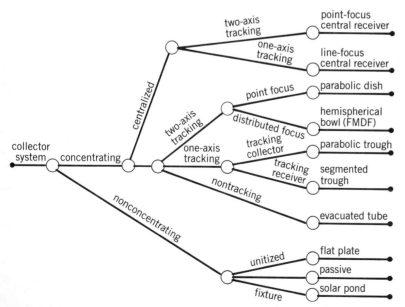

Fig. 4. Solar collector classification based on optical properties. (*After J. P. Thornton, A Comparative Ranking of 0.1-10 MWE Solar Thermal Electric Power Systems, SERI/TR-351-461, Solar Energy Research Institute, 1980*)

(**Fig. 6**) is the most common type of line-focus collector. It offers a wide range of operating temperatures from approximately 160 to 600°F (70 to 320°C). Therefore, it has been used for water heating below 212°F (100°C), steam production at 212 to 600°F (100 to 320°C), and power production at up to 600°F (320°C) using heat-transfer oils.

2. Point-focus. This major class of collectors offers the highest optical and thermal performance of any collector type because of its ability to track the Sun over its full range of diurnal motion and because of the relatively small area of the absorber used in the receiver unit. Parabolic dish–shaped collectors concentrate direct solar radiation to a point at the focus of the parabola. Each dish is a complete power-producing unit (**Fig. 7**), which can function either as an independent system or as part of a group of modules linked to form a larger system. A single parabolic-dish module can achieve fluid temperatures from 550 to 2500°F (300 to 1400°C) and can efficiently produce up to 25 kW of electricity.

The largest subsystem of a parabolic-dish module is the concentrator, a shallow dish with a reflective surface that tracks the Sun to focus sunlight on a receiver. Tracking along two axes ensures maximum solar energy collection during the day. Because the receiver absorbs concentrated solar radiation at very high temperatures (up to 2500°F or 1400°C), the system can be used for high-temperature chemical reactions or the production of steam, electric power, or fuels and chemicals. In many system designs, the engine for thermal-to-mechanical energy conversion is mounted with the receiver at the focus.

3. Central receiver system. The central receiver system concept consists of flat or slightly curved mirrors (heliostats) that rotate about two axes to reflect direct solar radiation onto a tower-mounted receiver. The absorbing surface can be a cylinder (external receiver) or a planar surface contained within a cavity (cavity receiver). Temperatures in excess of 2500°F (1400°C) and more and pressures of 1015 lb/in.^{2} absolute (7 megapascals) can be generated at the receiver. The central receiver–collector concept appears to hold promise for producing solar thermal electric power in capacities from approximately 1 to 100 MWe. **Figure 8** shows the mode of operation of a typical point-focus central receiver system for power generation using conventional steam technology.

Conversion systems. Solar thermal heat can be converted directly to electricity, converted to mechanical and then electrical power, or used in the production of chemicals and fuels via an appropriate thermodynamic engine cycle. Three thermodynamic cycles have been considered for thermal-to-mechanical energy conversion: the Stirling cycle engine with closed-cycle operation; the Brayton cycle engine with either open- or closed-cycle operation; and the conventional Rankine cycle. Key concerns are the achievement of high engine performance and reliability and identification of operating requirements at the interface of the engine and receiver. Thermal energy conversion using parabolic-dish technology can be made at the point of heat generation, or at some distant location by piping heated fluid elsewhere for heat extraction and conversion.

Storage. A solar energy system is normally designed to be able to deliver useful heat for 6 to 10 h a day, depending on the season and weather. Storage capacity in the solar thermal system is one way to increase a plant's operating capacity.

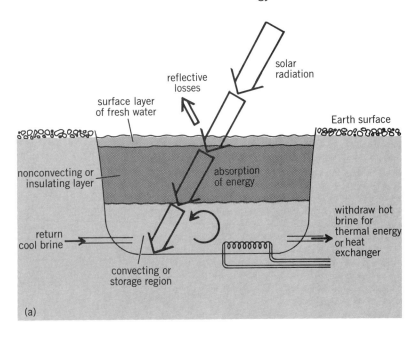

Fig. 5. Salt-gradient solar pond. (*a*) Schematic of the collection process (*after G. Franta et al., Solar Design Workbook, SERI/TR-62-308, Solar Energy Research Institute, 1981*). (*b*) Experimental pond (*Solar Energy Research Institute*).

There are four primary ways to store solar thermal energy: (1) sensible-heat-storage systems, which store thermal energy in materials with good heat-retention qualities; (2) latent-heat-storage systems, which store solar thermal energy in the latent heat of fusion or vaporization of certain materials undergoing a change of phase; (3) chemical energy storage, which uses reversible reactions (for example, the dissociation-association reaction of sulfuric acid and water); and (4) electrical or mechanical storage, particularly through the use of storage batteries (electrical) or compressed air (mechanical).

Applications. Solar thermal systems that are used in electric power applications include the small, distributed power systems (typically 1000 kWe or less) and the large, central power systems of 10,000 kWe or more. Small-power uses include those for remote communities; military applications; and individual factory, commercial building, or agricultural applications. For these categories, the distributed receiver systems are most common. For generating electric

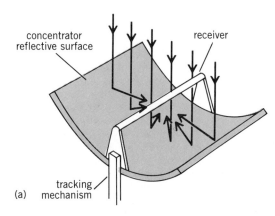

Fig. 6. Parabolic trough system. (*a*) Schematic of the components (*after Jet Propulsion Laboratory, Fact Sheet on Parabolic Trough Systems: A Solar Thermal Concentrating Collector Concept, 5106-22/3, 1982*). (*b*) Typical system (*Solar Energy Research Institute*).

power to distribute through a utility grid or to produce fuels and chemicals, the central receiver power and parabolic-dish systems are the most appropriate.

Industrial process heat is the thermal energy used directly in the preparation and treatment of materials and goods manufactured by industry. Hot water at temperatures between 120 and 200°F (50 and 100°C) can be supplied by directly heating water in the absorber tubes of evacuated-tube-type collectors or linear concentrating collectors. Hot air for industrial drying operations below about 350°F (180°C) can be supplied by collector systems designed to handle air as a circulating fluid or to circulate fluid pumped through an air-liquid heat exchanger. Concentrating solar thermal collector systems, both distributed and centralized, are commonly considered for steam generation at temperatures between 300 and 750°F (150 and 400°C) for use as direct heat in various manufacturing industries. Potential uses also include the production of ammonia in large agricultural fertilizer plants and enhanced oil recovery.

PHOTOVOLTAICS

Photovoltaic systems convert light energy directly to electrical energy. Using one of the most versatile solar technologies, photovoltaic systems can, because of their modularity, be designed for power needs ranging from milliwatts to megawatts. They can be used to provide power for applications as small as a

wristwatch to as large as an entire community. They can be used in centralized systems, such as a generator in a power plant, or in dispersed applications, such as in remote areas not readily accessible to utility grid lines.

Historically, photovoltaic systems have been used where traditional electric power was unavailable or too expensive, providing power for satellites, remote cabins and houses, communication stations, observatories, water pumps, mobile military applications, and even for entire villages. Electricity has been brought to some areas of the world and has replaced fuel- and maintenance-reliant diesel generators. Photovoltaic systems are also used as power sources for hand-held calculators, watches, and portable television sets.

System components. The solar cell, composed principally of semiconductor material, is the basic component of the photovoltaic system. Though many materials and structures are being investigated, most commercial cells use a pure single-crystal silicon wafer that is doped *p*-type (that is, a small amount of an appropriate impurity is added, inducing extra unfilled bonds, or holes, in the wafer). Another impurity is diffused into a shallow region on the top of the wafer, promoting extra unbonded electrons, causing that portion to become *n*-type. A potential barrier, or electric field, is set up at the junction of the electrically different semiconductor layers. When photons strike the cell, they create ion pairs (negatively charged electrons and positively charged holes).

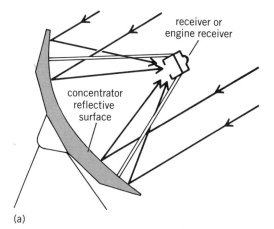

Fig. 7. Point-focus collector. (*a*) Schematic of collection process (*after Jet Propulsion Laboratory, Fact Sheet on Parabolic Dish Systems: A Solar Thermal Concentrating Collector Concept, 5106-22/2, 1982*). (*b*) Typical dish-receiver and engine module (*Jet Propulsion Laboratory*).

These charges move around the silicon lattice structure until they recombine or cross the junction to be used in the photovoltaic process. The potential barrier segregates the ion pairs to opposite ends of the cell. The separated charges set up a potential (voltage), which is used to drive a current (composed of the light-generated electrons) through electrical contacts attached to both faces of the cell and through an external circuit (**Fig. 9**).

The typical crystalline silicon cell produces a characteristic open-circuit voltage of about 0.5 V direct current (dc). The current generated depends on cell efficiency, cell area, and incident sunlight. A typical cell 4 in. (10 cm) in diameter can produce about 1 W of power under conditions where the Sun is directly overhead in a clear sky (one-sun conditions).

For larger voltages or currents, photovoltaic modules are formed by mounting groups of cells together on a rigid plate and interconnecting them in series or parallel. Stringing them in series increases the voltage; connecting them in parallel increases the current (**Fig. 10**). To further increase voltage or current output, modules may be grouped in parallel or strung in series to form photovoltaic arrays. The arrays, in turn, may be interconnected to form array fields. As with cells, series combinations are voltage-additive, and parallel arrangements are current-additive.

Most commercial modules and arrays are based upon flat-plate collectors (which look like windows with cells behind them) that are able to use either direct or diffuse sunlight effectively. They can be mounted on a stationary surface, such as a roof top, and faced in a southerly direction (for systems in the Northern Hemisphere) at an appropriate angle. Concentrating systems, which use lenses or mirrors to focus sunlight on each cell, are also being used. Concentration increases the power produced by each cell. Since such systems require direct sunlight, they must use mechanisms to track the Sun. Also there must be provision for removing heat, since high temperatures can reduce cell output power.

Many electric power applications require alternating-current (ac) electricity. To obtain ac, a power-conditioning system is needed to convert the photovoltaic-generated dc to ac. A typical power-conditioning system consists of an inverter for converting the dc output to ac; filtering circuits to remove harmful or unwanted signals; a logic subsystem to control the on-off cycling of the photovoltaic system; a dc contactor to disconnect the dc source from ac lines during outages; and an isolation transformer to isolate the dc source voltage from the ac line voltage (**Fig. 11**).

When the Sun is not shining, at night or because of inclement weather, no power is generated by photovoltaic collectors. For this reason, and because the photovoltaic system must be able to start up and shut down smoothly and be able to satisfy user needs, a backup or storage system is often required. Systems installed on private residences usually can tie into the local utility grid, using it as an energy receptacle or resource, as conditions warrant. Other options include battery storage, pumped hydroelectric storage, and flywheel energy storage. A diesel engine-generator also can be used.

Efficiencies. Under ideal conditions the theoretical maximum efficiency of a single-crystal silicon cell is about 25%, while the practical maximum efficiency hovers around 22%. Of the factors that combine to limit the efficiency, the most important are due to the

inherent physics of the situation, the interaction between the incident photons and the silicon solar cell. A great percentage of the incident photon radiation is not energetic enough to be absorbed by the cell to

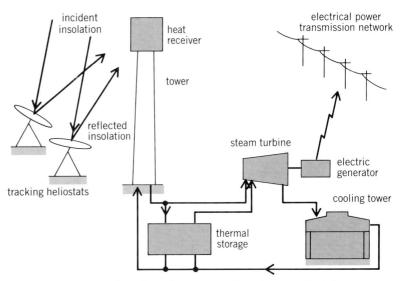

Fig. 8. Typical central receiver collector for power generation using conventional steam technology. (*After F. Krawiec, J. Thorton, and M. Edesess, An Investigation of Learning and Experience Curves, SERI/TR-353-459, Solar Energy Research Institute, 1980*)

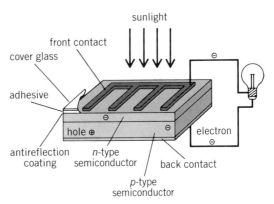

Fig. 9. Typical single-crystal silicon solar cell. (*After G. Cook, SERI Photovoltaic Advanced Research and Development: An Overview, SERI/SP-281-2235, Solar Energy Research Institute, 1984*)

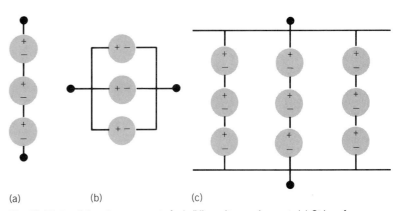

(a)   (b)   (c)

Fig. 10. Photovoltaic cell arrangements for building voltage and current. (a) String of photovoltaic cells (series). (b) Groups of cells (parallel). (c) Group of strings (combination). (*After Renewable Energy Technology Handbook for Military Engineers, SERI/SP-200-1413, Solar Energy Research Institute, 1982*)

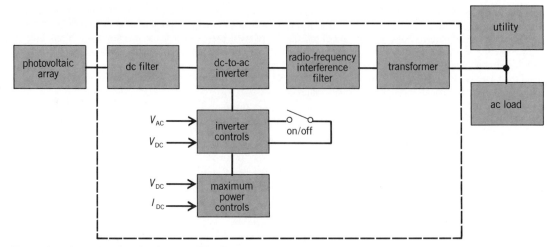

Fig. 11. Transformer isolation of dc from ac. (*After Renewable Energy Technology Handbook for Military Engineers, SERI/SP-200-1413, Solar Energy Research Institute, 1982*)

create electron-hole pairs. An even greater percentage of the radiation is too energetic—the excess photon energy is not used in the conversion process.

By 1984, the efficiency of a typical commercial solar cell made from single-crystal silicon had increased by about a factor of two. Commercial cells became available that can convert from 13 to 15% of the incident radiant energy to electrical energy (at 77°F or 25°C and 1 kW/m² incident radiation). Single-crystal silicon cells have been produced in the laboratory with efficiencies approaching 19% under one-sun conditions, and further improvements are anticipated. Strides have also been made to increase the efficiencies of modules and arrays by decreasing intercell connection resistances and by employing protective circuitry that uses little power. This has resulted in array efficiencies of 12%, nearing the efficiency fig-

ures that some feel are necessary in order for photovoltaic systems to become competitive with conventional energy sources in the central utility market.

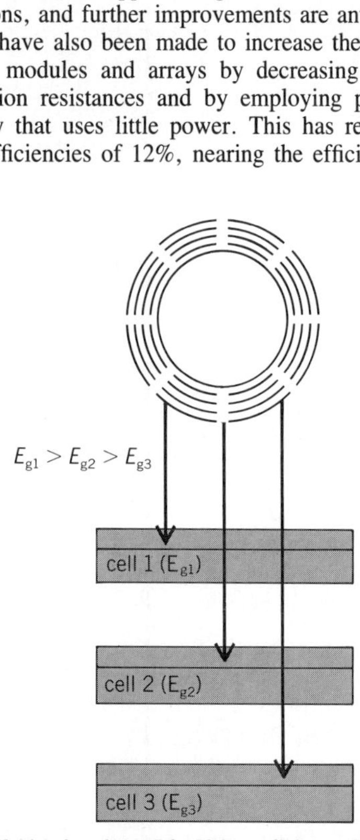

Advances have been made in power conditioning subsystems, another source of power loss for a photovoltaic system. Though commercially available converters in the early 1980s were only about 80% efficient over their broad range of operation, experimental systems have now reached 95% efficiency.

Other photovoltaic materials have energies that more suitably match the Sun's spectrum and thus make more efficient use of it. One of them, single-crystal gallium arsenide, has high efficiency, stability, and the ability to withstand higher operating temperatures than single-crystal silicon. For one-sun conditions, the highest theoretical efficiency of a single-crystal gallium arsenide cell is greater than 27%, and laboratory cells have reached efficiencies as high as 22%. Under sunlight concentrated 150 times, laboratory gallium arsenide cells have reached efficiencies nearing 24%.

For even higher efficiency, there is the multijunction (or stacked) device, a complex structure that uses several different semiconductor materials. Each layer has a junction sensitive to a different portion of the solar radiation spectrum, to make optimal use of all incident radiation. For example, an arrangement using three cells and three junctions—gallium aluminum arsenide, gallium arsenide, and silicon—has a theoretical maximum efficiency greater than 40% (**Fig. 12**).

$$E_{g1} > E_{g2} > E_{g3}$$

cell 1 (E_{g1})

cell 2 (E_{g2})

cell 3 (E_{g3})

Fig. 12. Multiple-junction cell for highest efficiency. Gallium aluminum arsenide cell band gap (E_{g1}) = 1.82 eV. Gallium arsenide cell band gap (E_{g2}) = 1.45 eV. Silicon cell band gap (E_{g3}) = 1.1 eV. (*After G. Cook, SERI Photovoltaic Advanced Research and Development: An Overview, SERI/SP-281-2235, Solar Energy Research Institute, 1984*)

BIOMASS

Biomass is plant and animal material. Biomass energy is solar energy stored in plant and animal matter. Through photosynthesis in plants, energy from the Sun transforms simple elements from air, water, and soil into complex carbohydrates. These carbohydrates can be used directly as fuel (for example, burning wood) or processed into liquids and gases (for example, ethanol or methane). Sources of biomass that can be converted to useful energy include agricultural crops, wastes, and residues; forest wood, waste, and residues; animal wastes; some municipal wastes; aquatic and desert plants; algae; and bacteria. Biomass is a renewable energy resource because it can be harvested periodically and converted to fuel. *SEE BIOMASS*.

Feedstock production. Feedstock for biomass conversion can consist of wood, herbaceous plants, or aquatic plants.

Wood. Wood has been used as a fuel for tens of thousands of years. Woody biomass comes from a variety of sources, ranging from standing forests to wood processing operations. It includes mill and logging residues, timber thinnings, and harvests from well-managed natural stands or from short-rotation, fast-growing plantations. Mill residues are the byproducts of processing operations that include the production of lumber, plywood, pulp and paper, and furniture. Dry mill residues from these operations are the most readily available of all tree biomass. Logging residues (residues left after tree harvest) include tree tops and branches, cull logs, standing dead trees, and stumps.

Wood has a heating value of about 8500 Btu/lb (20 megajoules/kg) when oven-dried compared to gasoline at about 21,000 Btu/lb (48 MJ/kg) and coal at about 13,500 Btu/lb (31 MJ/kg). Moisture dramatically affects the value of wood as a fuel. With a 30% moisture content, wood has a heating value of 5950 Btu/lb (14MJ/kg); at 50% moisture the value is 4250 Btu/lb (10 MJ/kg). There are several methods of reducing moisture in wood to improve its performance as a fuel. Perhaps the simplest is drying, but some faster methods have been developed that apply residual combustion heat to dry the feedstock.

Improved silvicultural practices on harvested forests include overstocking (for example, 1000 stems per acre instead of 600) and improving regrowth from stumps following harvest. Another forestry practice improves production by cultivating fast-growing trees for energy conversion. These trees are selected for their rapid growth, ease of establishment, stump regeneration, and pest and disease resistance. Short-rotation plantations may require intensive cultivation practices similar to those used in agriculture such as irrigation, fertilization, and harvesting operations.

Herbaceous plants. Nonwoody (herbaceous) biomass feedstocks such as grasses and grains show promise as sources of fuel. Some herbaceous plants have both the potential for high yield and the ability to grow on arid and marginal land (**Fig. 13**). Herbaceous feedstock types can include plants intended as fuel for direct combustion to energy and plants grown for their carbohydrate or hydrocarbon content for conversion to liquid and gaseous fuel.

Grasses and legumes can be pressed into pellets for direct burning or gasification, or they can be converted via fermentation to alcohol. Starch and sugar crops also can be converted to energy via fermentation to alcohol. Agricultural residues not used for other purposes such as food or forage can be burned for heat or converted to alcohol.

Numerous plant and seed species are possible candidate crops for oil production. For example, about 2000 species of *Euphorbia* (for example, poinsettia, cassava, or the rubber tree) produce a latex rich in hydrocarbons that can be a substitute for petroleum in almost all its uses. Liquid hydrocarbons that are extracted from *Euphorbia* spp. may be processed into gasoline and similar fuels.

Aquatic plants. Certain aquatic plants can be cultivated on nonarable or nonproductive land. They have exceptional rates of biomass production and provide yields that surpass those of land plants by a factor of four or more. Microalgae have been studied as producers of gaseous (hydrogen) and liquid (oils) fuels. Macroalgae, such as the giant kelp, grow naturally in the open ocean and can be cultivated offshore or on-

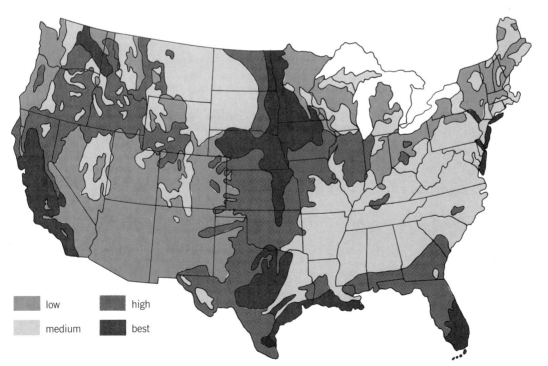

low medium high best

Fig. 13. Potential large-scale productivity of herbaceous biomass with all arable land considered. (*After Solar Energy Research Institute, FY 1982 Biomass Energy Technology Division Annual Technical Progress Report, vol. 1: Executive Summary, SERI/SP-281-2154, Solar Energy Research Institute, 1983*)

Table 2. Projected biomass resources for thermochemical conversion

| Resource | Available quantity, 10^6 dry tons/year (10^6 dry metric tons/year) | | | | | |
| | 1985 | | 1990 | | 2000 | |
	Maximum	Probable	Maximum	Probable	Maximum	Probable
Wood	464 (421)	167 (152)	429 (389)	154 (140)	549* (498)	71 (64)
Surplus agricultural crops[†]	45 (41)	34 (31)	36 (33)	31 (28)	33 (30)	39 (35)
Agricultural residues	220 (200)	115 (104)	240 (218)	123 (112)	278 (252)	110 (100)
Municipal solid waste	92 (83)	69 (63)	99 (90)	77 (70)	116 (105)	89 (81)
Other energy crops	8 (7)	104 (94)	69 (63)	203 (184)	172 (156)	247 (224)
Total	829 (752)	489 (444)	873 (792)	588 (533)	1148 (1041)	556 (504)

*Assumes wood from silvicultural energy farms starting in 1985.
[†]Assumes an aggressive program to establish sorghum as a cash crop that would divert land from corn in 1990 and 2000; data include surplus grain rejected for food processing.

shore in ponds. These species have high growth rates and produce significant amounts of carbohydrates that can be anaerobically digested to methane or fermented to alcohol. Emergent plants, such as cattails and bulrushes, and floating plants, such as water hyacinths, are also highly productive and represent potentially significant feedstock resources for conversion to methane or alcohol.

Conversion to heat and fuel. Liquid and gaseous fuels usually can be transported more easily and efficiently than raw biomass. To be converted to these forms, most biomass must be treated either thermally, chemically, or biologically (**Table 2**). The oldest and simplest method for converting biomass is direct combustion. However, wood is 25 to 50% less efficient as a fuel source than fuel oil, natural gas, or coal. Even dried wood produces lower flame temperatures and requires larger fireboxes and heat transfer surfaces. Converting biomass to heat energy in large boilers is about 70 to 75% efficient, whereas wood can be burned in stoves in homes with efficiency ranges of 50 to 70%.

Gasification. Gasifiers can convert biomass as varied as hardwood chips or animal manure to combustible gases. Most gasifiers are supplied with air to produce a nitrogen-rich low-Btu gas. The oxygen in the air reacts with part of the biomass to produce heat. This heat is then used to produce gas from the remaining biomass. The low-Btu gas is usually used in nearby burners or engines. Conversion efficiencies are generally good, with 60 to 80% of the energy content of the dry biomass transferred to the gas. Use of biomass gasifiers offers flexibility in industrial plant design and provides a way of coupling biomass into existing plants with interchangeability between biomass fuel and conventional fuel (**Table 3**).

Another gasification process uses pure oxygen instead of air to produce synthesis gas (a mixture of carbon monoxide and hydrogen). Methanol, a liquid fuel, can be produced from the synthesis gas by one of several conventional processes. Efficiencies for the overall conversion to methanol are in the range of 40 to 50%. A process for the conversion of methanol to gasoline also is available.

Pyrolysis. Producing charcoal by pyrolysis (breaking complex molecules into simpler ones by heat) has been done for centuries. Wood pyrolysis in general leaves a char that constitutes about 30% (by weight) of the wood and contains about 42% of its heat content. It also yields an oil that carries about 32% of the wood's heat content. The pyrolysis gases that are produced are usually burned to supply the processing plant's energy.

Fermentation. The conversion of sugars and starch to ethanol by fermentation is a well-established technology. Sugar from molasses and cheese whey, and starch from grains or tuberous plants are the most commonly used starting materials. However, most of the recent interest has been in fuel ethanol production involving the use of cornstarch, which is converted to glucose, which is then fermented to ethanol. Ethanol fermentation has traditionally been done with yeast in an 18–48-h batch process that produces 8 to 10% ethanol by volume. With modern techniques, the yield of ethanol is about 79 gallons per bushel of corn (8300 liters/m³); 81% of the manufacturing cost of ethanol is the cost of the starting material.

Biomass with a high fiber content (woody biomass)

Table 3. Evaluation of biomass-gasification technologies

Technology	Advantages	Disadvantages
Pyrolysis	Low operating temperature; simple design; no other reactants required	Can get complex char, tar, and gas mixture; tar removal difficult; heat transfer rate may be limited in some cases
Air gasification	Simple design, only one reactor required; less tar than pyrolysis	Gas diluted with nitrogen (N_2) cannot be used for synthesis; low-Btu gas (LBG) may have a reduced combustion efficiency
Oxygen gasification	Medium-Btu gas (MBG) undiluted with N_2 is suitable for synthesis; can operate at high temperature and pressure if desired	Oxygen plant required, greatly increasing the capital cost at small scales
Steam gasification	MBG undiluted with N_2; no oxygen plant required; catalysts can adjust gas composition in gasifier	MBG is methane-rich; must be steam-reformed for methanol synthesis but is an advantage for synthetic natural gas (SNG) synthesis

is the largest renewable resource available for energy conversion. It is more complex in composition and structure than is starch, and is therefore more difficult to process into potential fuels. Theoretically, the carbohydrates in fibrous biomass can be converted to 100 gallons of ethanol per ton (420 liters/metric ton) of biomass at a 40% net energy conversion compared with 120 gallons/ton (500 liters/metric ton) for corn. One component of woody biomass, lignin, could be chemically removed and used since it has a heating value of about 15,000 Btu/lb (35 MJ/kg) to provide part of the heat needed to convert the carbohydrates to ethanol.

Anaerobic digestion. Anaerobic digestion by bacteria to make methane can use almost any biomass. The technology can be used in a digester of any size, from a small backyard fermenter that uses human waste to the large fermenters that use feedlot waste. Manure is particularly amenable to digestion because of its abundant nutrients, high moisture content, and lack of inhibitors of methane-producing bacteria. The gas produced during digestion is 50 to 70% methane and can be purified, burned as it is, or fed to a natural gas pipeline.

Photosynthetic microorganisms. Some types of microalgae and bacteria have the ability to manufacture energy-rich substances photosynthetically. For example, under appropriate conditions some microalgae will produce increased amounts of oils and lipids that

can be used directly as fuel, and some bacteria will evolve hydrogen that also can be used directly as a fuel. Research concentrates on genetic engineering, artificially maintained production systems, and the basic chemistry and physics of photosynthesis.

WIND ENERGY CONVERSION SYSTEMS

Energy from the wind has been used for centuries to propel ships, to grind grain, and to lift water. Wind turbines extract energy from the wind to perform mechanical work or to generate electricity. Applications to generate electricity are recent and date from about 1930. This discussion concentrates on the production of electricity from wind. *SEE WIND.*

Wind resource. Wind is a source of energy derived primarily from unequal heating of Earth's surface by the Sun. Wind speeds are altered by local terrain and vary significantly by season and day.

Figure 14 shows wind resources as annual average wind power classes based on average wind power density. Average wind power density rather than wind speed is used because it incorporates the combined effect of wind speed, wind speed distribution, and air density.

Since the average wind power density is proportional to the cube of wind speed, location or siting is very important. Wind power of at least 200 W/m² or wind speed 12 mi/h (19 km/h) is considered prereq-

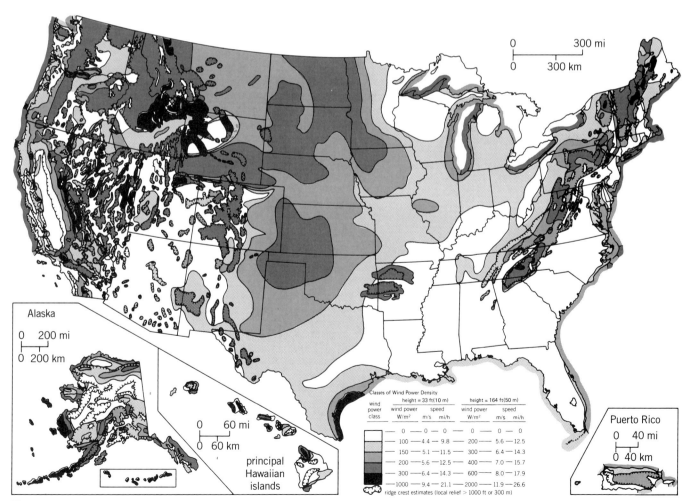

Fig. 14. Wind power in the United States (annual average). (*After Solar Energy Research Institute*)

uisite for additional site evaluation and data gathering. The annual average wind speed is only one consideration. The distribution of wind speed by month, day, and hour is also important, especially in matching power output to power requirements.

The variation of wind speed with height is another important consideration. Generally, wind speed is greater above ground level than it is at the surface due to the frictional effects of Earth's surface.

The output power from a wind turbine can be defined by a power coefficient, C_p, which is a measure of the efficiency with which the rotor extracts power from the wind. The maximum theoretical efficiency, or Betz limit, for a propeller-type rotor is 0.593. Wind turbines available today generally have a C_p between 0.30 and 0.45.

Wind turbine system. The main components of a wind turbine system (**Fig. 15**) are the rotor, generator, tower, and storage devices (or utility interconnection). The rotor consists of blades and a hub that connects the rotor to the turbine system. The blades can spin around a horizontal axis parallel to the ground or around a vertical axis perpendicular to the ground. Both designs are used in commercial and residential applications. Most commercial models are horizontal-axis wind turbines (HAWT). They range in output

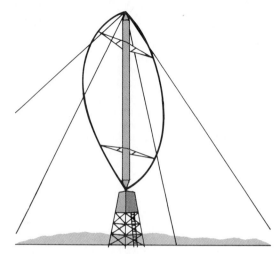

Fig. 16. Darrieus vertical-axis wind turbine. (*After B. H. Bailey, New York State Wind Energy Handbook, New York State Wind Energy Office, 1982*)

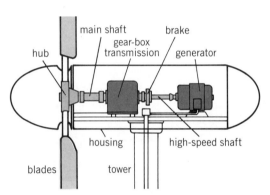

Fig. 15. Main components of a wind turbine. (*After B. H. Bailey, New York State Wind Energy Handbook, New York State Wind Energy Office, 1982*)

from less than 5 kW to 100 kW. The U.S. Department of Energy has tested a large, 2500-kW prototype HAWT, called the MOD-2, for utility applications; and design of a 3200-kW machine, the MOD-5B, has begun. A wind farm is a system in which many turbines are clustered at especially windy sites to generate megawatts of electricity to sell to utilities.

There are three common configurations of vertical-axis wind turbines (VAWT); the most developed is the Darrieus design (**Fig. 16**). They, unlike HAWTs, are omnidirectional—they need not be turned as the wind direction changes. Rotors on HAWTs have many blade configurations (**Fig. 17**). In the familiar farm windmill, the blades constitute most of the area swept by the rotor as it spins about its axis. The farm windmill and the Dutch windmill combine drag and lift for inducing rotation. The rotors on these machines have low speed, but have high torque and are well suited to lifting water or grinding grain.

The blades of high-speed turbines are designed as airfoils. In these, the tip-speed ratio—the ratio of the

speed of the blade tips to the wind speed—can be as high as 15. A high ratio improves efficiency and reduces the size of drive train components. This is important in electricity generation, whereas torque is important to lifting water or grinding grain.

Control of rotor velocity is important to protect the turbine against overspeed in high winds. All wind turbines are designed to start at a certain minimum wind speed and stop when the maximum design speed is reached. Various mechanical, hydraulic, and aerodynamic devices are used to brake the rotor or to turn it out of the wind.

The wind energy captured by the rotor is transmitted by shafts and gears to the generator. Generators can produce either direct current or alternating current; the configurations of wind energy systems using different types of generators are shown in **Fig. 18**.

Wind turbines for residential applications are placed on towers usually at least 80 ft (25 m) tall. Towers are either free-standing or guyed, and either type can be a pole or lattice (truss) structure. Instal-

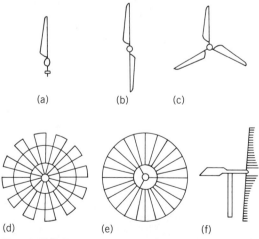

Fig. 17. Some horizontal-axis wind turbine configurations. (*a*) Single-bladed. (*b*) Double-bladed. (*c*) Three-bladed. (*d*) United States farm windmill multibladed. (*e*) Bicycle multibladed. (*f*) Sail wing. (*After Renewable Energy Technology Handbook for Military Engineers, SERI/SP-200-1413, Solar Energy Research Institute, 1982*)

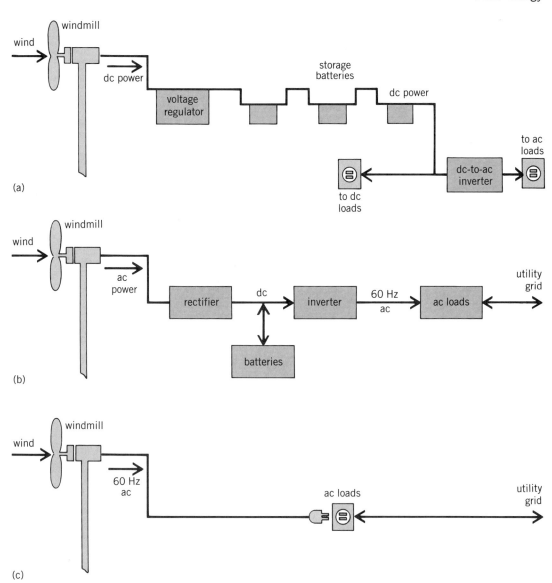

Fig. 18. Possible wind energy system configurations. (*a*) A dc generator windmill. (*b*) Variable-frequency ac generator windmill. (*c*) Induction generator windmill. (*After New York State Wind Energy Handbook, New York State Wind Energy Office, 1982*)

lation can cost as much as 30% of the total price of a small wind system. The cost of a tower can be partially offset by the increased output from higher wind speeds at the higher elevation.

Storage of wind energy can be by battery, pumped-hydro equipment, and other devices. Normally, wind turbines are connected to a utility, which provides backup electricity when needed. Excess electricity can, in turn, be fed into the grid and sold to the utility at a negotiated price.

OCEAN THERMAL ENERGY CONVERSION

Ocean thermal energy conversion uses the temperature difference between surface water heated by the Sun and deep cold water pumped from depths of 2000 to 3000 ft (600 to 900 m). This temperature difference makes it possible to produce electricity from the heat engine concept. Since the ocean acts as an enormous solar energy storage facility with little fluctuation of temperature over time, ocean thermal energy conversion, unlike most other renewable energy tech-

nologies, can provide electricity 24 h a day. In addition, ocean thermal energy conversion plants can be located onshore, mounted on the continental shelf, or placed on moored or floating platforms. Various shapes have been suggested for floating platforms (**Fig. 19**).

Energy content and electricity. A rough estimate of the thermal energy content of the ice-free, mixed layer of the ocean with a temperature difference of 18°F (10°C) is 70 × 10^{20} Btu (75 × 10^{23} joules). Thus, the ocean thermal energy resource is vast, but that suited for ocean thermal energy conversion facilities is only a fraction of this total, although still an enormous amount. Suitable sites are generally limited to an area within 30° north and 25° south of the Equator. With available technology, an annual average temperature difference of 36°F (20°C) or greater between water at the surface and that at a depth not exceeding 4700 ft (1500 m) is required for continuous and efficient operation of an ocean thermal energy conversion plant. Furthermore, the mean temperature difference during the coldest month should exceed

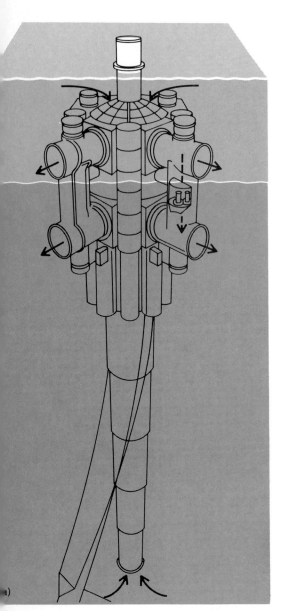

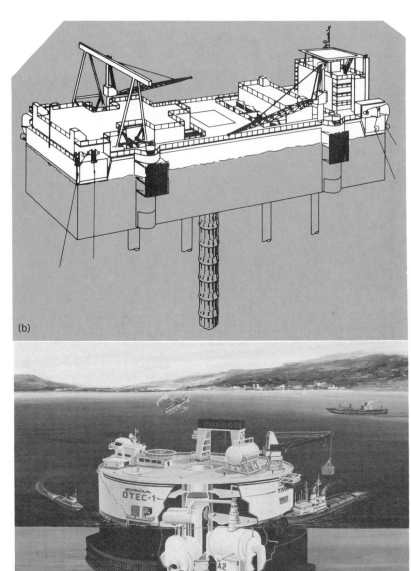

Fig. 19. Platform concepts for ocean thermal energy conversion (OTEC) systems. (*a*) Spar buoy. (*b*) Rectangular barge. (*c*) Cylindrical platform. (*After R. A. Meyers, ed., Handbook of Energy Technology and Economics, John Wiley and Sons, 1983*)

31°F (17°C). If system efficiency is improved, the required temperature difference will be less and a greater ocean area will be suitable for ocean thermal energy conversion use.

The possibility of generating electricity from solar thermal energy collected and stored by the ocean near the Equator was first suggested by A. d'Arsonval in 1881. In 1930, G. Claude built a power plant in Mantazas Bay, Cuba, and converted ocean thermal energy to electricity, using a temperature difference of 25°F (14°C) between the surface and a depth of 2200 ft (700 m) to generate 22 kWe. In 1979, a small closed-cycle test plant produced 50 kWe and a net output of 12 kWe by using ammonia as the working fluid. In 1980, a 1000-kW test bed plant was mounted in a converted U.S. Navy tanker to test heat exchangers.

A 100-kWe, shore-based plant was tested in 1981 by the Japanese for the island republic of Nauru. The Kyushu Electric Company in early 1983 began operating a 50-kWe test plant in Tokunoshima that uses waste heat from a diesel engine to boost the temperature of the warm seawater.

Conversion systems. There are three principal conversion systems for ocean thermal energy: closed Rankine cycle, open Rankine cycle (Claude cycle), and mist or foam-lift cycle. These systems are listed in order of technological development and in inverse order of theoretical energy conversion efficiency. In other words, the least technologically developed system, the lift cycle, theoretically has the highest potential efficiency.

Closed Rankine cycle. In the closed Rankine cycle,

warm seawater is pumped through a heat exchanger to transfer stored thermal energy to a working fluid such as ammonia, which has relatively high vapor pressures at low temperatures (**Fig. 20**). The working fluid is vaporized, and the expanding vapor is used to drive a turbine generator. The vapor is condensed by cold seawater in another heat exchanger to complete the cycle. The major advantage of the closed cycle is that the process of heat exchange and energy conversion is established and familiar. The components can be manufactured with existing technology. The major disadvantage is that in adapting an energy conversion process designed for high temperatures and pressures to a low-temperature heat source, inefficiencies in the conversion process become magnified. The heat exchangers must be large, and a large volume of water must be pumped through them. About half of the total available temperature difference is required to transfer heat in the evaporator and condenser. Since the efficiency is a direct function of the temperature difference that is available after the transfer, the small but inherent drop in temperature through the heat exchange process reduces an already low temperature potential.

Large heat exchanger surfaces and low working temperatures also make the control of slime formation (biofouling) and corrosion very critical. The design, construction, and operation of large closed-Rankine-cycle ocean thermal energy conversion facilities present complex engineering problems even though no technological breakthroughs are needed for any major structural or operating components.

Open Rankine cycle (Claude cycle). Claude showed that the heat exchange process for both evaporation and condensation could be performed by using warm seawater itself as the working fluid. Direct-contact heat exchange eliminates the need for large, costly heat exchangers. The evaporator and direct-contact condenser possibly can be made with inexpensive materials such as polyvinyl chloride and concrete.

In the open-cycle process, steam is generated from warm seawater by flash (very rapid) evaporation in an evacuated chamber. The steam turns a turbine and is condensed by direct contact with cold seawater to complete the cycle. The absence of any barrier between the working fluid and the heating and cooling source makes possible a higher overall system efficiency and lower seawater flow requirement than in the closed-cycle process. Using seawater rather than a substance like ammonia as the working fluid also lessens safety problems. The need for mechanical or chemical measures to control biofouling is also reduced.

The open-cycle process is similar to certain desalination processes, and if a typical closed-cycle surface condenser is used, fresh water can be produced as a by-product at some sacrifice in efficiency. The use of ocean thermal energy conversion facilities for producing fresh water as well as electricity may prove attractive in some locations. SEE SALINE WATER RECLAMATION.

The elimination of volatile working fluids and heat exchangers means that the open-cycle process will function at very low steam pressures. The steam turbine, in turn, must be very large and housed in a correspondingly large vacuum vessel. Present technology is limited to relatively small plants.

Lift cycles. There are several other approaches to the open cycle that involve the conversion of the ther-

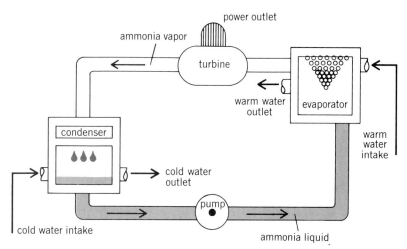

Fig. 20. Closed Rankine (ammonia) cycle. (*After The Ocean Option*, SERI/SP-732-334, *Solar Energy Research Institute, 1980*)

mal gradient into a hydraulic head through the lift of seawater in vertical two-phase flow. The water column created can drive a turbine, as in a hydroelectric dam. An advantage of this approach is that the hydraulic turbine is more compact and less costly than the steam turbine that is required in the Claude system.

Warm seawater is introduced as a mist that is then lifted against gravity by the flow of steam from a low-pressure region to a lower-pressure region. This action is similar to the naturally occurring cycle that converts water evaporated by solar energy to hydropower. In ocean thermal energy conversion lift cycles, an artificial hydrological cycle is created.

Robert L. San Martin

Bibliography. B. Anderson, *Solar Building Architecture,* 1990; J. J. Bartel and P. E. Skvarna, 10 MWe solar thermal central receiver pilot plant, *J. Solar Energy Eng.* 106(1):50–58, February 1984; Biomass Panel of the Energy Research Advisory Board, Review article: Biomass energy, *Solar Energy,* 30(1):1–31, 1983; J. A. Duffie and W. A. Beckman, *Solar Engineering of Thermal Processes,* 1980; F. R. Eldridge, *Wind Machines,* 2d ed., 1980; J. C. C. Fan, Photovoltaic cells, *Kirk-Othmer Encyclopedia of Chemical Technology,* 3d ed., vol. 17, 1982; P. Gipe, Wind in America: The changing landscape, *Solar Age,* 8(10):29–35, October 1983; V. D. Hunt, *Windpower: A Handbook on Wind Energy Conversion Systems,* 1981; Institute of Gas Technology, *Energy from Biomass and Wastes Symposium,* 1989; A. Lavi, Ocean thermal energy conversion: A general introduction, *Energy Int. J.,* 5(6):469–480, June 1980; P. D. Maycock and E. N. Stirewalt, *Photovoltaics,* 1981; R. A. Meyers (ed.), *Handbook of Energy Technology and Economics,* 1983; Y. V. Pleskov, *Solar Energy Conversion,* 1989; T. B. Reed (ed.), *Biomass Gasification: Principles and Technology,* 1981; Solar Energy Research Institute Staff (ed.), *Principles and Concepts for Active Solar Systems,* 1988; Solar Research Institute, Basic Photovoltaic Principles and Methods, 1984; S. Wieder, *An Introduction to Solar Energy for Scientists and Engineers,* 1982, reprint 1990; J. R. Williams, *Design and Installation of Solar Heating and Hot Water Systems,* 1983; H. Yuncu and E. Paykoc (ed.), *Solar Energy Utilization: Fundamentals and Applications,* 1987.

Sonic boom

Strong pressure waves (shock waves) generated by aircraft in supersonic flight and heard along the ground as explosivelike sounds called booms or bangs. Contrary to popular belief, a sonic boom does not occur at only one location at the instant the aircraft exceeds the local speed of sound. Instead, aircraft flying faster than the speed of sound (approximately 1100 ft/s or 330 m/s) generate shock waves that radiate away from and behind the aircraft and are dragged with it as long as it is flying supersonic. Where this trailing shock wave intercepts the ground (**Fig. 1**), it is heard as an impulsive type of sound. In some situations, depending on the shock-wave pattern, an observer may hear two distinct booms or a double boom rather than hear the single sound.

Some factors affecting the sonic boom signal heard on the ground, such as speed, altitude, and route of the aircraft, can be reasonably well controlled. Others, such as meteorological conditions, topography, and ground-level air turbulence, cannot be modified. Consequently, the extent to which sonic booms can be predicted and controlled for known flight profiles and flying conditions is limited by those environmental factors beyond human control. During certain flight conditions, sonic booms much greater in magnitude (superbooms) than those created in straight, level flight may be generated. Sonic booms may be magnified two to three times as the vehicle accelerates from subsonic to supersonic speeds, and as much as two to five times by various flight maneuvers at supersonic speeds.

Typical pressure-time functions or signatures for sonic booms generated by large and small aircraft in supersonic flight are shown in Fig. 1. Because of the N-like shape of the pressure signatures, they are frequently referred to as "N-waves." Aircraft A and B are identical, on the same course flying at the same speed, but differing in altitude. Aircraft B and C differ only in size as represented. The durations of the sonic boom pressure waves Δt are directly related to the length of the aircraft. The range of durations of sonic booms for current military operations and for commercial supersonic transport (SST) operations

varies from about 0.05 s for a fighter aircraft to about 0.5 s for a large commercial supersonic transport. Duration varies only slightly with altitude (compare aircraft A and B in Fig. 1), being shorter and more directly related to aircraft length for lower altitudes where shock waves have less opportunity to disperse. The significant difference between Δt's of the two different-sized aircraft is easily seen.

The loudness of the sonic boom perceived by an observer is a function of, among other things, the initial rise time of the primary shock-wave signature. Signals with a steep or fast rise time have been expected and shown in actual test to sound louder than signals with the same peak overpressure and duration and slower rise times. Sonic booms with fast rise times have much more energy in the frequency bands where the ear is sensitive and, therefore, seem to give louder acoustic signals than the others. A sonic boom with a slower rise time is a more effective stimulus inside buildings. The shaking and rattling of the building and its contents due to the shock wave add to the overall acoustic stimulus caused by the boom and it may be perceived as more intense or more objectionable than a sonic boom of equal intensity heard outdoors.

Intensity. The intensity of the sonic boom, that is, the magnitude of its presure peak ΔP, and the lateral distance from the ground track at which it will be heard are dependent upon the size (lift and drag) of the aircraft and its altitude. Increasing the altitude of the aircraft reduces the magnitude of the overpressure on the ground; however, at the same time it increases the lateral spread or width of the area which is being exposed to the sonic boom. This altitude effect is shown by the two identical aircraft A and B, with the boom at the lower altitude being higher in intensity (ΔP_1 compared to ΔP_2) and with a narrower sonic boom path (40 mi or 64 km as compared to 60 mi or 97 km).

Sonic booms are measured in pounds per square foot (1 lb/ft^2 = 47.88 pascals) or dynes per square centimeter (1 dyne/cm^2 = 0.1 pascal) of overpressure or pressure above the normal atmospheric pressure, or in decibels (dB) of sound pressure level referenced to 20 micropascals. Peak pressure level of the impulsive

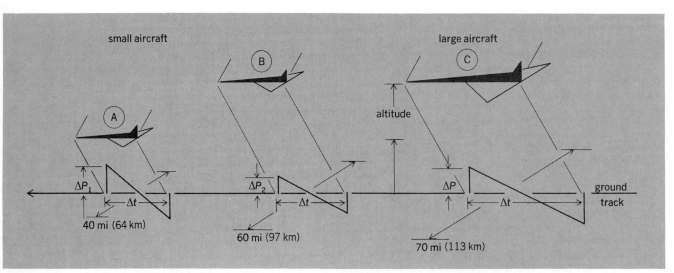

Fig. 1. Duration, intensity, and lateral spread of sonic booms as a function of aircraft size and altitude.

sonic boom in decibels should not be confused with continuous noise levels in decibels. The intensity of sonic booms typically experienced on the ground from aircraft above 30,000 to 40,000 ft (9 to 12 km) is seldom above 2.0 lb/ft^2 (96 Pa) or about 134 dB, and rarely as high as 5.0 lb/ft^2 (239 Pa) or about 142 dB. The maximum sonic booms ever experienced by humans of 120–144 lb/ft^2 (5.75–6.9 kPa) or about 170–171 dB produced by aircraft flying at 50–100 ft (15–30 m) above the ground are about 100 times greater than the usual community sonic boom exposures.

Aircraft altitude is the primary contributor to the magnitude of the sonic boom and is one of the factors most accessible to control measures. Current U.S. Air Force aircraft are restricted from supersonic flight over inhabited areas below an altitude of 30,000 ft (9 km) except for special missions or in the event of emergency.

Maximum nominal overpressures during transoceanic flight of commercial SST-type aircraft are about 2.5 lb/ft^2 (120 Pa) or 136 dB during acceleration, and 1.7 lb/ft^2 (81 Pa) or 133 dB during cruise and descent phases. Minimum altitudes of 50,000–60,000 ft (15–18 km) during cruise produce slightly lower booms of about 1.5 lb/ft^2 (72 Pa) or 132 dB as fuel is consumed and the weight of the aircraft is decreased. It has been determined that these levels of sonic boom are unacceptable to the general population for frequent operations, so that flights over land are not currently permitted.

It appears that there is no possibility to significantly reduce or eliminate the sonic boom from current and next-generation aircraft which fly at supersonic speeds. Longer booms from the larger aircraft may be psychoacoustically no less acceptable assuming a constant magnitude ΔP. No major breakthrough in the reduction of sonic booms appears on the horizon. The most promising approach to minimizing boom exposure is that of regulating flights through operational control. Judicious scheduling of supersonic flights, care in acceleration and maneuver, cruise at high altitudes, and avoidance of population centers are major factors of practical significance. The operational controls and flight regulations necessary to ensure acceptable levels of sonic booms on the ground have not been achieved for present-day aircraft flying over land. Commercial transports are prohibited by law in the United States from supersonic operations over land or over water where the sonic booms may be propagated to impact on land.

Human responses. A scale has been developed in the laboratory which expresses the noisiness or acceptability of sound exposures, and this scale serves as the basis of various criteria and guidelines currently in use for estimating community reaction to aircraft. The level of the noisiness or the perceived noise level (PNL) may be calculated from physical measures of the sound and expressed in units of PN dB. Appropriate psychoacoustical studies have demonstrated, and experience has confirmed, the ranges of acceptability which correspond to the various values along the PN dB scale. Sonic boom exposures have been empirically equated with this well-established noise acceptability scale (PN dB), as demonstrated in **Fig. 2**.

Response of structures. Broken window glass and other minor damage to isolated structures may appear

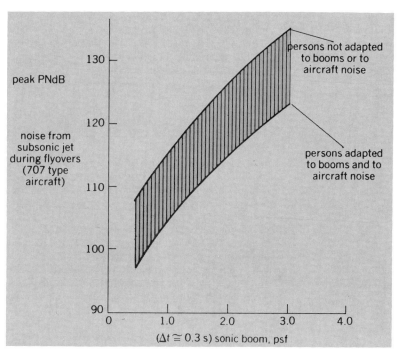

Fig. 2. Sonic boom ($\Delta t \cong 0.3$ s) peak overpressures (psf; 1 psf = 47.88 Pa) judged equal in noisiness or acceptability (PNdB) to noise from subsonic jet aircraft (Boeing 707) during flyovers at altitudes of approximately 400 ft (120 m). (After K. Kryter, P. J. Johnson, and J. R. Young, Psychological Experimentation on Noise from Subsonic Aircraft and Sonic Booms at Edwards Air Force Base, Contract AF 49(638)-1758, Final Report, NSBEO-4-67, SRI International, 1967)

as a result of sonic boom exposures. The types of damage to property most often reported relate to secondary or decorative elements and consist of cracks in brittle surface treatments, such as plaster, tile, window glass, and masonry. Such damage is superficial in nature, is restricted to non-load-bearing members, and thus does not affect the strength of the primary structure. The superficial damage usually reported is, in large measure, associated with stress concentrations in the structure.

Concorde. The only commercial supersonic transport is the Concorde, an aircraft developed and constructed jointly by France and the United Kingdom. Concorde operations began into Dulles International Airport, Washington, D.C., in May 1976 and into Kennedy International Airport, New York, in November 1977. Each of these times represented the beginning of a 12-month demonstration period at the respective airports. During the Kennedy International Airport demonstration period, numerous reports of barely audible booms were received by federal authorities from residents of eastern New England. Low-amplitude secondary pressure disturbances were measured at times along the south shore of Long Island at a level of about 0.8 lb./ft^2 (38 Pa) or 126 dB. Flight controls imposed by the federal government on the operation of the Concorde eliminated its threat of sonic boom exposure to the United States mainland.

Henning E. Von Gierke; Charles W. Nixon

Bibliography. H. H. Hubbard, Sonic booms, *Phys. Today*, 21(2):31–37, February 1968; National Academy of Sciences, *Guidelines for Preparing Environmental Impact Statements on Noise*, 1977; C. W. Nixon, Human response to sonic boom, *J. Aerosp. Med.*, 36:399, 1965; NSBEO, *Sonic Boom Experi-*

ments at Edwards Air Force Base, AD no. 655310, July 27, 1967; L. J. Runyan and E. J. Kane, *Sonic Boom Literature Survey*, DOT Rep. FAA-RD-73-129-1, September 1973; Sonic Boom Symposium, *J. Acoust. Soc. Amer.*, vol. 51, no. 2, pt. 3, 1972, and vol. 39, no. 5, pt. 2, 1966; H. A. Wilson, Sonic boom, *Sci. Amer.*, 206(1):36–43, January 1962.

Spring

A place where groundwater discharges upon the land surface because the natural flow of groundwater to the place exceeds the flow from it. Springs are ephemeral, discharging intermittently, or permanent, discharging constantly.

Springs are usually at mean annual air temperatures. The less the discharge, the more the temperature reflects seasonal temperatures. Spring water usually originates as rain or snow. Meteoric water compositions for the deuterium (D) and oxygen-18 (^{18}O) are given by the empirical equation below,

$$\delta D = 8\delta^{18}O + 10$$

where δ is the isotope composition in parts per thousand referred to standard mean ocean water.

Standard mean ocean water is defined as zero in both ^{18}O and D. Meteoric water from evaporation of seawater is depleted in D and ^{18}O for kinetic reasons and hence the values of δD and $\delta^{18}O$ are negative and increasingly so the farther from the Equator.

Hot springs. Hot-spring water may differ in composition from meteoric water through exchange between the water and rocks. Common minerals consist of component oxides. Oxygen of minerals has more ^{18}O than meteoric water. Upon exchange, the water is enriched in ^{18}O. Most minerals contain little deuterium, so that slight deuterium changes occur. Water in hot rock is buoyant relative to surrounding water and issues as hot springs. Temperatures of the deep water may be estimated. Estimates stem from mineral solubilities with temperature. If saturation with a mineral is assumed and the chemical composition of the water known, a temperature may be calculated. The solubility of quartz, SiO_2, is commonly used for estimating the deep temperatures of hot springs. Common minerals also contain silica, so that temperature estimates are ambiguous. Some hot-spring waters are acid from the oxidation of hydrogen sulfide to sulfate.

Mineral springs. Mineral spring waters have high concentrations of solutes. Mineral springs have long been used for therapy; the study of such use of springs is balneology. Pliny the Younger reported mineral springs in Belgium and Anatolia, which are still in use. Although mineral waters are still valued for therapy in much of the world, in North America such use has declined greatly since the early twentieth century.

Mineral springs have wide ranges in chemistry and temperatures, and hot mineral springs may be classified as hot springs as well as mineral springs. Most mineral springs are high either in sodium chloride or sodium bicarbonate (soda springs) or both; other compositions are found, such as a high percentage of calcium sulfate from the solution of gypsum. The water and the solutes may be of different origins. The stable isotope compositions of the water are the best guides to the sources of the water. For the mineral springs of Europe, the United States, and Asia Minor, deuterium and ^{18}O compositions show that the waters are meteoric.

Carbon dioxide. Carbon dioxide is commonly found dissolved in or issuing through mineral water, and is identifiable by its ^{13}C composition. Carbon of carbonate minerals deposited in oceans is near zero in ^{13}C compared to an international standard, the Peedee belemnite. The carbon of the carbon dioxide in most of the mineral springs of Europe, the United States, and Asia Minor is close to zero in ^{13}C isotope composition. It is inferred that the carbon dioxide results from the breakdown (metamorphism) of the carbonate minerals that are present in rocks of marine sedimentary origin.

Carbon dioxide from mineral springs of volcanic islands of the Atlantic Ocean seems to come from the source of the volcanic rocks, the Earth's mantle, because of the similarity of the isotope compositions of the carbon dioxide in the springs and in carbon dioxide bubbles in volcanic rocks erupted on the deep ocean floor in the -4 to -8 per thousand range. Carbon dioxide from great depth also discharges through springs in the Sierra Nevada, California, and the Alaska peninsula. In mineral springs from the Rocky Mountains, carbon dioxide comes from both very deep sources and the shallower chemical reactions of marine rocks.

A third source of carbon dioxide is organic material. Springs in the Coast Ranges of California, along the Copper River of Alaska, and in New Zealand yield mixtures of carbon dioxide and methane. The carbon dioxide is depleted in carbon-13 and probably comes from the breakdown of organic (woody) materials in the sedimentary rocks.

Salts. Other solutes in the mineral springs are inferred to come from the rocks, but isotope data do not show origins. Salt deposits are sources for solutes in some instances. There are many mineral springs for which there is no possible salt deposit source for the solutes. Chemical compositions may be used to infer the sources of the solutes. Chloride-rich waters in marine sedimentary rocks also contain bromide, iodide, and boron. During metamorphism of the rock the waters may be retained as fluid inclusions or as films along grain boundaries. Flushing of the retained brines may result in the saline springs occasionally found in metamorphic terraines.

Chemical equilibrium. The chemical compositions of spring waters are seldom in chemical equilibrium with the air. Groundwaters whose recharge is through grasslands may contain a thousand times as much CO_2 as would be in equilibrium with air, and those whose recharge is through forests may contain a hundred times as much as would be in equilibrium with air. The high CO_2 content, along with other solutes, makes some spring waters quite nutrient to aquatic plants. If the CO_2-rich groundwater has dissolved calcite, loss of CO_2 in a spring (chiefly by photosynthesis) may cause the calcite to precipitate to make travertine. Groundwater flowing through rocks or sediments containing organic material or reduced minerals such as sulfides loses its dissolved oxygen by oxidizing the organic matter and the sulfides. When the dissolved oxygen is lost, iron enters the groundwater as ferrous ion, Fe^{2+}. The Fe^{2+} is not chemically compatible with air, and springs containing Fe^{2+} lose it as $Fe(OH)_3$ upon oxidation. Thin films of $Fe(OH)_3$ on the water surface are iridescent and resemble oil films. Unlike oil films, the $Fe(OH)_3$ films are brittle and if ruptured do not reform. Accumulations of the iron precipitates may lead to bog iron ores. Sulfate in groundwater may be reduced in the presence of organic matter to H_2S, giving some springs the odor of rotten eggs. SEE GEYSER; GROUNDWATER HYDROLOGY.

Ivan Barnes

Squall line

A line of thunderstorms, near whose advancing edge squalls occur along an extensive front. The thundery region, 12–30 mi (20–50 km) wide and a few hundred to 1250 mi (2000 km) long, moves at a typical speed of 15 m/s (30 knots) for 6–12 h or more and sweeps a broad area. In the United States, severe squall lines are most common in spring and early summer when northward incursions of maritime tropical air east of the Rockies interact with polar front cyclones. Ranking next to hurricanes in casualties and damage caused, squall lines also supply most of the beneficial rainfall in some regions.

A squall line may appear as a continuous wall of cloud, with forerunning sheets of dense cirrus, but severe weather is concentrated in swaths traversed by the numerous active thunderstorms. Their passage is marked by strong gusty winds, usually veering at onset, rapid temperature drop, heavy rain, thunder and lightning, and often hail and tornadoes. Turbulent convective clouds, 6–9 mi (10–15 km) high, present a severe hazard to aircraft, but may be circumnavigated with use of radar.

Formation requires an unstable air mass rich in water vapor in the lowest 0.6–2 mi (1–3 km), such that

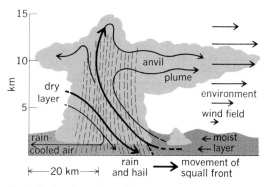

Fig. 2. Section through squall-line-type thunderstorm. Precipitation is represented by numerous broken lines. 1 km = 0.6 mi.

air rising from this layer, with release of heat of condensation, will become appreciably warmer than the surroundings at upper levels. Broad-scale flow patterns vary; **Fig. 1** typifies the most intense outbreaks. In low levels, warm moist air is carried northward from a source such as the Gulf of Mexico. This process, often combined with high-level cooling on approach of a cold upper trough, can rapidly generate an unstable air mass. SEE THUNDERSTORM.

The instability of this air mass can be released by a variety of mechanisms. In the region downstream from an upper-level trough, especially near the jet stream, there is broad-scale gentle ascent which, acting over a period of hours, may suffice; in other cases frontal lifting may set off the convection. Surface heating by insolation is a contributory mechanism; there is a preference for formation in midafternoon although some form at night. By combined thermodynamical and mechanical processes, they often persist while sweeping through a tongue of unstable air, as shown in Fig. 1. Squall lines forming in midafternoon over the Plains States often arrive over the midwestern United States at night. SEE STORM.

Figure 2 shows, in a vertical section, the simplified circulation normal to the squall line. Slanting of the drafts is a result of vertical wind shear in the storm environment. Partially conserving its horizontal momentum, rising air lags the foot of the updraft on the advancing side. In the downdraft, air entering from middle levels has high forward momentum and undercuts the low-level moist layer, continuously regenerating the updraft. Buoyancy due to release of condensation heat drives the updraft, in whose core vertical speeds of 66–132 mi/h (30–60 m/s) are common near tropopause level. Rain falling from the updraft partially evaporates into the downdraft branch, which enters the storm from middle levels where the air is dry, and the evaporatively chilled air sinks, to nourish an expanding layer of dense air in the lower 0.6–1.2 mi (1–2 km) that accounts for the region of higher pressure found beneath and behind squall lines. In a single squall-line thunderstorm about 12 mi (20 km) in diameter, $1–2 \times 10^7$ lb/s (5–10 kilotons/s) of water vapor may be condensed, half being reevaporated within the storm and the remainder reaching the ground as rain or hail.

Chester W. Newton

Bibliography. E. Kessler (ed.), *The Thunderstorm in Human Affairs*, 2d rev. ed., 1988; H. E. Landsberg (ed.), *Advances in Geophysics*, vol. 12, 1967.

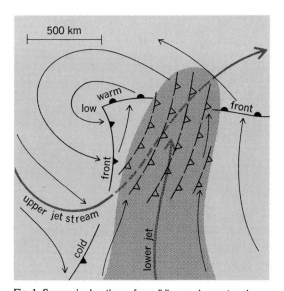

Fig. 1. Successive locations of squall line moving eastward through unstable northern portion of tongue of moist air (dark area) in warm sector of a cyclone. Thin arrows show general flow in low levels; thick arrows, axes of strongest wind at about 0.6 mi (1 km) above ground and at 6–7 mi (10–12 km).

Storm

An atmospheric disturbance involving perturbations of the prevailing pressure and wind fields on scales ranging from tornadoes (0.6 mi or 1 km across) to extratropical cyclones (1.2–1.8 mi or 2–3 km across); also, the associated weather (rain storm, blizzard, and the like). Storms influence human activity in such matters as agriculture, transportation, building construction, water impoundment and flood control, and the generation, transmission, and consumption of electric energy.

The form assumed by a storm depends on the nature of its environment, especially the large-scale flow patterns and the horizontal and vertical variation of temperature; thus the storms most characteristic of a given region vary according to latitude, physiographic features, and season. This article is mainly concerned with extratropical cyclones and anticyclones, the chief disturbances over roughly half the Earth's surface. Their circulations control the embedded smaller-scale storms. Large-scale disturbances of the tropics differ fundamentally from those of extratropical latitudes. *See* Hurricane; Squall line; Thunderstorm; Tornado.

Extratropical cyclones mainly occur poleward of 30° latitude, with peak frequencies in latitudes 55–65°. Those of appreciable intensity form on or near fronts between warm and cold air masses. They tend to evolve in a regular manner, from small, wavelike perturbations (as seen on a sea-level weather map) to deep waves to occluded cyclones. *See* Front; Meteorology; Weather map.

Dynamical processes. The atmosphere is characterized by regions of horizontal convergence and divergence in which there is a net horizontal inflow or outflow of air in a given layer. Regions of appreciable convergence in the lower troposphere are always overlaid by regions of divergence in the upper troposphere. As a requirement of mass conservation and the relative incompressibility of the air, low-level convergence is associated with rising motions in the middle troposphere, and low-level divergence is associated with descending motions (subsidence).

Fields of marked divergence are associated with the wave patterns seen on an upper-level chart [for example, at the 30-kilopascal (300-millibar) level], in the manner shown in **Fig. 1**. The flow curvature indicates a maximum of vorticity (or cyclonic rotation about a vertical axis) in the troughs and minimum vorticity in the ridges. An air parcel moving from trough to ridge would undergo a decrease of vorticity, which by the principle of conservation of angular momentum implies horizontal divergence. In the upper troposphere, where the wind exceeds the speed of movement of the wave pattern, the divergence field is as shown in Fig. 1. To sustain a cyclone, a relative arrangement of upper and lower flow patterns as shown in **Fig. 2** is ideal. This places upper divergence over the region of low-level convergence that occupies the central part and forward side of the cyclone, and upper convergence over the central and forward parts of the anticyclone where there is lower-level divergence.

The upper- and lower-level systems, although broadly linked, move relative to one another. Cyclogenesis commonly occurs when an upper-level trough advances relative to a slow-moving surface front (stages 1 and 2 in **Fig. 3**). The region of divergence

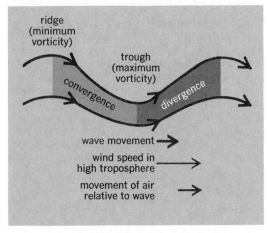

Fig. 1. Convergence and divergence in a wave pattern at a level in the upper troposphere or lower stratosphere. The lengths of arrows indicate the speed and relative motion of wind and wave.

in advance of the trough becomes superposed over the front, inducing a cyclone that develops (stage 3 in Fig. 3) in proportion to the strength of the upper divergence. In a pattern such as Fig. 1, the divergence is strongest if the waves have short lengths and large amplitudes and if the upper-tropospheric winds are strong. For the latter reason, cyclones form mainly in close proximity to the jet stream, that is, in strongly baroclinic regions where there is a large increase of wind with height. *See* Jet stream.

Frontal storms and weather. Weather patterns in cyclones are highly variable, depending on moisture content and thermodynamic stability of air masses drawn into their circulations. Warm and occluded fronts, east of and extending into the cyclone center, are regions of gradual upgliding motions, with widespread clouds and precipitation but usually no pronounced concentration of stormy conditions. Extensive cloudiness also is often present in the warm sector.

Passage of the cold front is marked by a sudden

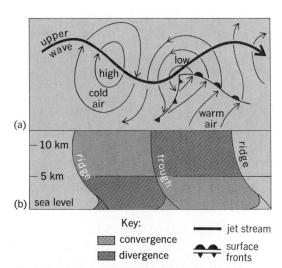

Fig. 2. Air motion associated with a wave pattern. (*a*) Circulation pattern in low levels in relation to upper wave. (*b*) West-east vertical section showing simplified regions of convergence and simplified regions of divergence. 1 km = 0.6 mi.

wind shift, often with the onset of gusty conditions, with a pronounced tendency for clearing because of general subsidence behind the front. Showers may be present in the cold air if it is moist and unstable because of heating from the surface. Thunderstorms, with accompanying squalls and heavy rain, are often set off by sudden lifting of warm, moist air at or near the cold front, and these frequently move eastward into the warm sector. *See Weather.*

Middle-latitude highs or anticyclones. Extratropical cyclones alternate with high-pressure systems or anticyclones, whose circulation is generally opposite to that of the cyclone. The circulations of highs are not so intense as in well-developed cyclones, and winds are weak near their centers. In low levels the air spirals outward from a high; descent in upper levels results in warming and drying aloft.

Anticyclones fall into two main categories, the warm "subtropical" and the cold "polar" highs. The large and deep subtropical highs, centered over the oceans in latitudes 25–40° and separating the easterly trade winds from the westerlies of middle latitudes, are highly persistent.

Cold anticyclones, forming in the source regions of polar and arctic air masses, decrease in intensity with height. Such highs may remain over the region of formation for long periods, with spurts of cold air and minor highs splitting off the main mass, behind each cyclone passing by to the south. Following passage of an intense cyclone in middle latitudes, the main body of the polar high may move southward in a major cold outbreak.

Blizzards are characterized by cold temperatures and blowing snow picked up from the ground by high winds. Blizzards are normally found in the region of a strong pressure gradient between a well-developed arctic high and an intense cyclone. True blizzards are common only in the central plains of North America and Siberia and in Antarctica.

Principal cyclone tracks. Principal tracks for all cyclones of the Northern Hemisphere are shown in **Fig. 4**. In middle latitudes cyclones form most frequently off the continental east coasts and east of the Rocky Mountains.

Movements of cyclones, both extratropical and tropical, are governed by the large-scale hemispheric wave patterns in the upper troposphere. The character of these waves is reflected in part by large circulation systems such as the subtropical highs, and greatest anomalies from the principal cyclone tracks occur when these highs are displaced from the mean positions shown in Fig. 4. Warm highs occasionally extend into high latitudes, blocking the eastward progression suggested by the average tracks and causing cyclones to move from north or south around the warm highs.

Over the Mediterranean, cyclones form frequently in winter but rarely in summer, when this area is occupied by an extension of the Atlantic subtropical high. Both the subtropical highs and the cyclone tracks in middle latitudes shift northward during the warmer months; on west coasts cyclones are infrequent or absent in summer south of latitudes 40–45°. *See Cyclone.*

Mesoscale weather systems. Between the scales of ordinary air turbulence and of cyclones, there exist a variety of circulations over a middle-scale or mesoscale range, loosely defined as from about 6 to a few hundred miles (10 to a few hundred kilometers). Alternatively, these are sometimes referred to as subsynoptic-scale disturbances because their dimensions are so small that they elude adequate description by the ordinary synoptic network of surface weather stations. Thus their detection often depends upon observation by indirect sensing systems.

While cyclones and anticyclones govern general weather conditions over broad areas, mesoscale disturbances superimposed upon the larger circulations often result in great variations of weather conditions over small distances. Even the extensive precipitation shields of cyclones typically have embedded cells and rainbands, with significant changes in rainfall or snowfall rate as they pass overhead. Thus, in terms of short-period, detailed forecasting at a given location, analysis and tracking of mesoscale phenomena are of primary importance. Some are localized owing to their control by physiographical features, while others may migrate over long distances.

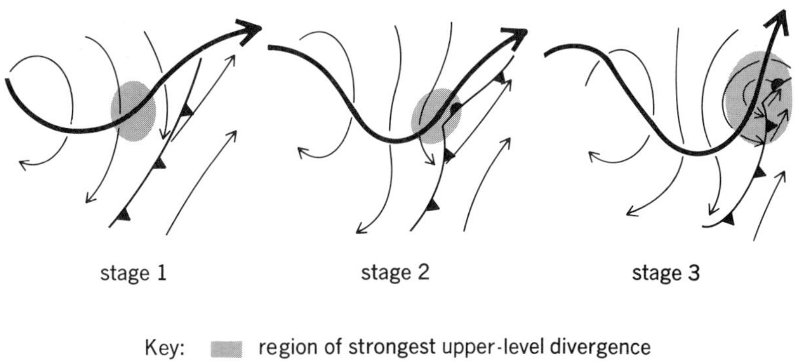
stage 1
stage 2
stage 3
Key: region of strongest upper-level divergence

Fig. 3. Upper-level trough advancing relative to surface front and initiating cyclone.

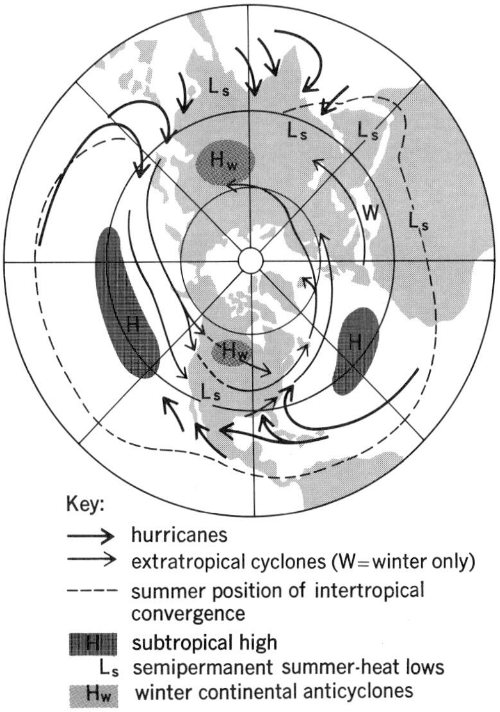
Ls
Hw
W
H
Key:
hurricanes
extratropical cyclones (W=winter only)
summer position of intertropical convergence
H subtropical high
Ls semipermanent summer-heat lows
Hw winter continental anticyclones

Fig. 4. Principal tracks of extratropical cyclones and hurricanes with significantly associated features in the Northern Hemisphere.

Common examples of topographically localized phenomena are sea or lake breezes, mountain valley winds, and mountain waves. Sea breezes and mountain valley winds are ordinarily benign. However, considering that populations and industry tend to cluster in coastal and valley regions, these circulations often exert a dominating influence on the disposition of air pollutants and on local temperature and cloud cover, important because of their effects on human comfort and power consumption. Furthermore, in some regions such as the Florida peninsula, showers and thunderstorms tend to form at the advancing edge of the sea breeze front, a line of convergence between the sea breeze and the air further inland. Another topographically localized phenomenon is the lee wave downwind from mountain ridges, which can cause violent surface winds as well as extreme turbulence hazardous to aircraft. *See Wind*.

In terms of overall damage to crops and structures, as well as injuries and deaths, thunderstorms are the most important class of mesoscale disturbance. Ordinary afternoon thunderstorms are most numerous, but damage is preponderantly caused by a small percentage of exceptionally severe storms that form under special circumstances. Such storms may occur individually or in clusters or linear arrays. They are characterized by organized circulations different from the sporadic cellular forms of ordinary thunderstorms, and often, as individuals or groups, they persist for many hours while migrating over swaths hundreds of kilometers long. Local orography makes certain regions especially prone to thunderstorms and hailstorms. Localized flash floods, which peak in midsummer, account for about half of the overall flood damage in the United States. These are particularly severe when, under special synoptic conditions, thunderstorms remain nearly stationary over a given locality or several heavy rainstorms pass successively over it, resulting in rainfall accumulations upward of 8–12

in. (20–30 cm) on occasion (**Fig. 5**). Thunderstorms move in ways controlled by their interactions with the winds in the troposphere in which they are embedded, and they also interact with one another in complex ways. Thus, while general areas of severe storm potential can be predicted, continuous surveillance of storm evolution by radar, satellite, and other means, and fast communication of observations and warnings, are essential because of the quick changes that occur.

Role in terrestrial energy balance. Air moving poleward on the east side of a cyclone is warmer than air moving equatorward on the west side. Also the poleward-moving air is usually richest in water vapor. Thus both sensible- and latent-heat transfer by disturbances contribute to balancing the net radiative loss in higher latitudes and the net radiative gain in the tropics. Air that rises in a disturbance is generally warmer than the air that sinks (Fig. 2), and latent heat is released in the ascending branches by condensation and precipitation. Hence the disturbance also transfers heat upward, as is required to balance the net radiative loss in the upper part of the atmosphere. *See Atmospheric General Circulation*.

Chester W. Newton

Bibliography. L. J. Battan, *Fundamentals of Meteorology,* 2d ed., 1984; F. Lutgens and E. Tarbuck, *The Atmosphere: An Introduction to Meteorology,* 4th ed., 1989; E. Palmén and C. W. Newton, *Atmospheric Circulation Systems,* 1969; S. Petterssen, *Introduction to Meteorology,* 3d ed., 1968; H. Riehl, *Introduction to the Atmosphere,* 3d ed., 1979.

Storm detection

Any of the methods and techniques used to ascertain the formation of storms. Radars, satellite-borne instruments, and sferics detectors (radio receivers) are used to detect storms and to assess their potential for destruction. In addition, storms can reveal themselves through their creation of pressure variations which travel at the speed of sound and are detectable by microbarographs.

Microbarographs. Certain severe thunderstorms emit an identifiable kind of infrasound, or ultralow-frequency acoustic wave. Traveling at the speed of sound and ducted between the ground and high-temperature layers in the upper atmosphere, these waves are often so powerful that they can be detected by sensitive pressure detectors, known as microbarographs, more than 900 mi (1500 km) from the emitting storm. At such distances, the pressure fluctuations of the waves are only about one-millionth of average atmospheric pressure. It takes 10–60 s for one wave cycle to pass, but the oscillations can last for hours (**Fig. 1**).

Similar storm-related waves travel into the ionospheric F region, 120 mi (200 km) above the Earth. These waves were discovered by looking with a high-frequency radar for a certain kind of oscillation in the radar reflection height. Though there appears to be a causal connection between tornadic storms and ionospheric infrasound, there is no statistical evidence of the warning value of the ionospheric waves. The mechanism causing the emissions is not known, but observations of both ground-level and ionospheric waves have established that only a small fraction of

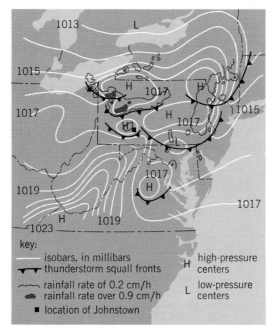

Fig. 5. Mesoscale pressure pattern (millibars; 1 millibar = 100 pascals) and squall-line fronts at 1800 CST, June 19, 1977, associated with a flood at Johnstown, Pennsylvania. 1 cm = 0.4 in.

key:
— isobars, in millibars
▼▼▼ thunderstorm squall fronts
⌒⌒ rainfall rate of 0.2 cm/h
⬤⬤ rainfall rate over 0.9 cm/h
■ location of Johnstown

H high-pressure centers
L low-pressure centers

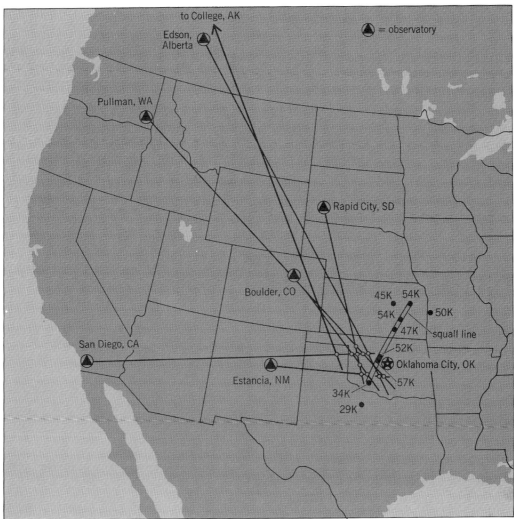

(a)

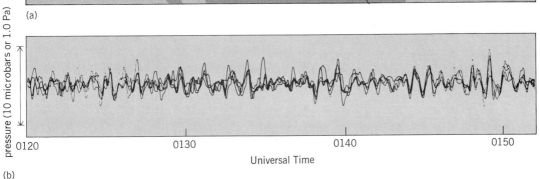

(b)

Fig. 1. Infrasound and microbarograph data during a severe-storm outbreak in Oklahoma. (*a*) Map of the western United States showing the intersecting infrasound bearings measured at seven observatories (the seventh being in College, Alaska). The numbered dots show radar-indicated storm cells whose tops reach the heights shown (K = 10^3 ft or 305 m). The most violent storms often occur at the southern end of a squall line. (*b*) Superimposed pressure records from four microbarographs at Boulder, Colorado, during this event. (*Wave Propagation Laboratory, NOAA*)

all storms emit detectable infrasound, and that most of the emissions appear to come from tornadic storm systems.

In the United States, storm detection exercises have been carried out by using direction-finding arrays of microbarographs for ground-level infrasound. Within a 14-state test area, 65% of the tornadic storms that occurred during the 1973 storm season were considered "detected" by three infrasound observatories, and the storm emissions had enough distinctive char-

acteristics that false-alarm rates were considered acceptable. However, triangulation, when possible, is inaccurate, and even though the waves are often emitted prior to the observed tornadoes, their relatively slow sonic travel speed (600 mi/h or 1000 km/h) diminishes their warning value.

Acoustical detection is thus not being used for storm warning, and its main value lies in storm research.

T. M. Georges

Radar. Radars emit pulses in a beam of electromagnetic radiation at a wavelength (for example, 4 in. or 10 cm) that penetrates storm clouds to provide a three-dimensional, inside view of the storm with the beam's angular resolution of about 1° and a range resolution better than 0.3 mi (0.5 km). Advanced weather radars provide accurate images of both precipitation intensity and radial velocity (that is, the precipitation motion component toward or away from the radar) inside a storm's shield of clouds. Velocity is provided by Doppler radar using the same principle that causes a hearer to sense the change in pitch of a horn on a passing car or train. Precipitation reflects the radar's transmitted pulse and produces change in the microwave pitch proportional to the radial (Dopp-

ler) velocity. There is no Doppler shift for targets moving perpendicular to the radar beam. Doppler weather radars are used by researchers and a few television weather forecasters, but the U.S. National Weather Service will have a network of Doppler radars (NEXRAD) operational in the early 1990s to replace the non-Doppler WSR-57 radar network. The WSR-57 radar generates only maps of precipitation reflectivity, which is proportional to the intensity of rain, snow, or hail.

Contoured reflectivity maps are routinely displayed by radars of the National Weather Service on widely used plan position indicator (PPI) scopes giving range and azimuth to precipitation targets whose reflectivity (intensity) is indicated by a stepped brightness scale

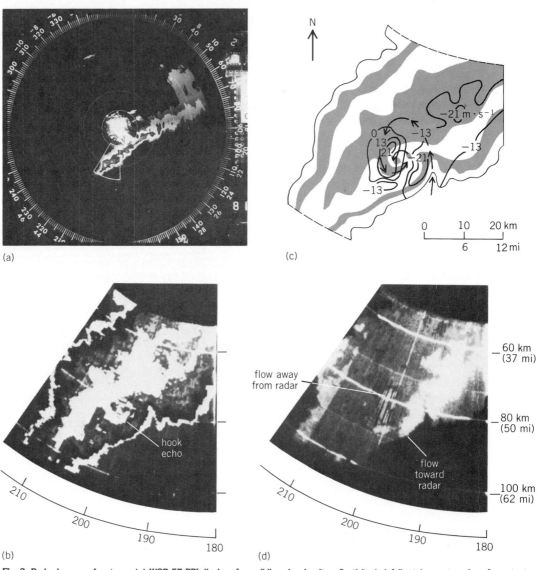

Fig. 2. Radar images of a storm. (a) WSR-57 PPI display of squall line showing its reflectivity (rainfall rate) as categories of constant brightness. Dim brightness area surrounding the squall line corresponds to rainfall rate between 0.05 and 0.30 mm/h (0.002 and 0.012 in./h). Then in sequence to the storm interior: bright, dark, dim, and bright areas are rainfall rates 0.3–1.7, 1.7–9.1, 9.1–48.8, and 48.8–262 mm/h (0.12–0.0068, 0.0068–0.36, 0.036–1.92, and 1.92–10.3 in./h). Circles are range marks spaced 40 km (24 mi) apart. (b, d) Magnifications of area outlined in a to show Doppler radar reflectivity and Doppler velocity signatures of a storm cell. In b, reflectivity pattern from the Doppler radar shows a hook or spiral convergence (see arrows in c) that signifies the presence of a cyclone. In d, isodop pattern shows a tornado cyclone signature. The Doppler signature of the tornado cyclone is between 193–203° and 75–90 km (45–54 mi). Brightness levels are velocity categories: dim (<13 m · s⁻¹), bright (13–21), and brightest (>21). Positive (away) radial velocities are angularly strobed. (c) Schematic overlay of reflectivity and isodop patterns of b and d, showing the coincidence of the reflectivity spiral and radial velocity signature of the cyclone. 1 m · s⁻¹ = 2.24 mi/h. (*NOAA National Severe Storms Laboratory, Norman, Oklahoma*)

(**Fig. 2***a*). While a storm's reflectivity image is valuable for rainfall assessment and severe weather warnings, it rates only fair as a tornado indicator. Highest reflectivity areas often signify hail. Severe storm warnings are primarily based on reflectivity values, on storm top heights, and sometimes on circulatory features (for example, hook echoes) seen in the patterns of reflectivity (Fig. 2*b*). Advances in digital and computer technology have made it practical for a storm's reflectivity image to be presented on a color-coded display with highest reflectivity usually indicated in bright color, making it easier to identify heavy precipitation regions. This technology also allows superposition of a storm's reflectivity image with outlines of city, county, and state boundaries.

Although reflectivity displays are valuable for locating and tracking storms, they do not give as accurate an image of wind hazards (for example, tornadoes, wind shear, and turbulence) as does the display of radial velocity fields mapped by Doppler radar, which can sort from many seemingly severe storm cells the ones that rotate and hence have potential for tornado development. One of the earliest images of a storm's Doppler velocity field was obtained when a pulsed Doppler radar was mated to the plan position indicator. Significant dynamic meteorological events such as tornado cyclones, whose visual sightings are often blocked by rain showers and nightfall, produce telltale signatures in the Doppler velocity field. Such a swirling vortex signature is composed of contours of constant Doppler velocity (isodops) forming a symmetric couplet of closed contours of opposite sign, that is, of velocity toward and away from the radar (Fig. 2*c* and *d*). This pattern portends tornadoes, damaging winds, and hail.

Color displays of Doppler velocity fields, used by researchers and television weather forecasters, show the isodop signatures of wind hazards much better.

The tornadic storm, whose radar images are depicted in Fig. 2, produced a particularly large tornado cyclone, and its reflectivity and isodop signatures are clearly seen. A signature pattern for circularly symmetric convergence of air is similar to the cyclone pattern but is rotated clockwise by 90°. The reflectivity spiral suggests some convergence, as well as rotation, a conclusion supported by the clockwise angular displacement of isodop maxima about the cyclone center with the positive maximum somewhat closer to the radar (Fig. 2*c*).

Experiments have been conducted to assess the improvement in severe storm advisories when Doppler velocity fields are given to forecasters. The probability of detection (POD) of tornadoes with Doppler radar was found to be 0.69 and the false-alarm rate (FAR) 0.25. A weather forecast office, covering the same area with their standard techniques, showed a probability of detection of 0.64 and a false-alarm rate of 0.63. More significant is the Doppler radar detection of tornado cyclones 20 min before tornadoes touch down on the ground, whereas the warning system dependent on visual sightings generally shows a negative lead time. These findings support the concept of a national network of Doppler weather radars. *See* TORNADO.

Hazardous wind shear can be caused by strong downdrafts whose diameters are less than a few kilometers but which produce strong winds diverging out from the region where vertically descending thunderstorm air impacts the ground. These intense but

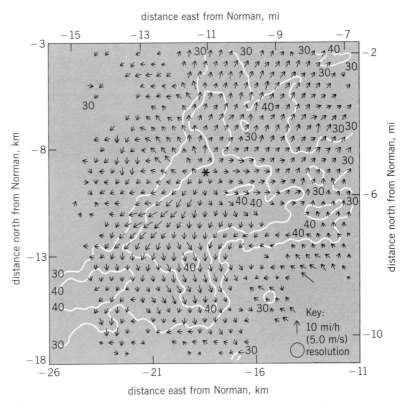

Fig. 3. Horizontal wind field in a downdraft. The height of this plan view is about 1000 ft (300 m) above ground. The length of each arrow gives the wind speed when using the scaled arrow in the key. Circle labeled "resolution" gives the approximate beam width of the radars used. Asterisk indicates location of the downburst.

small-scale downdrafts are called microbursts, and they have been implicated in several airliner crashes. The melting of ice, if present, and the evaporation of water drops embedded in these virtually dry air downdrafts, cool and moisten the air as it descends to the ground, making it heavier and thus accelerating the downward flow. The outrush of air as it deflects from the ground carries precipitation along with the air, causing the base of the precipitation shaft to have a diameter larger than that seen near the cloud base. The horizontal wind field (**Fig. 3**), derived from Doppler velocity fields mapped by two Doppler radars separated by 24 mi (40 km) along a northwest to southwest line, shows a divergent pattern. The divergent flow is centered at a distance 11.5 mi (18.5 km) west and 6.5 mi (9.5 km) south of the Norman, Oklahoma, Doppler radar site. The solid white lines delineate the reflectivity factor of the rainfall which accompanies the divergent flow. The lines marked 30 and 40 represent, under certain assumptions, rainfall rate contours of 0.1 in./h and 0.4 in./h (2 mm/h and 10 mm/h). The circle labeled "resolution" gives the approximate beam width of the radars used to map the fields portrayed in Fig. 3. Headwind to tailwind changes as large as 22 mi/h in 1 mi (12 m/s^{-1} in 1 km) are found in the divergent flow, and this level of shear can be dangerous to aircraft, which are especially vulnerable when they are landing or taking off. This shear is about the average value measured by Doppler radar observing microbursts, which have been defined as divergent flows with a differential Doppler velocity difference of at least 20 mi/h (10 m/s^{-1}) across a distance of between ¼ and 2½ mi (0.4 and 4 km). *See* WIND.

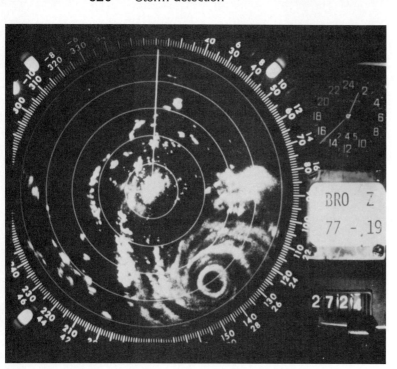

Fig. 4. Radar reflectivity image of a hurricane. (*National Hurricane and Experimental Meteorology Laboratory, NOAA***)**

Hurricanes have spiraling inflow of air like that shown in Fig. 2c for the severe thunderstorm. However, the typical cross section through a hurricane (**Fig. 4**) is an order of magnitude larger than a thunderstorm. Thunderstorms are most common in hurricane outskirts and again near the storm center, or eye, which is clearly revealed and tracked by radar when the storm is within about 200 mi (320 km) of stations which line the Gulf and Atlantic coasts of the United States.

R. J. Doviak

Satellites. The United States maintains two geostationary meteorological satellites approximately 19,300 mi (35,800 km) above the Equator at 75°W (*Geostationary Operational Environmental Satellite-East*) and 135°W (*GOES-West*). These satellites are spin-stabilized, rotating at 100 revolutions per minute, with the spin axis oriented perpendicular to the Earth's equatorial plane. Instruments mounted on the spacecraft sweep west-to-east across the Earth's disk approximately every 0.7 s. These are programmed to step-scan north/south to permit contiguous lines of observations and provide images of the Earth's atmosphere. Each of the *GOES* satellites has been equipped with a visible and infrared spin scan radiometer (VISSR) sensing in the visible with a ½-mi (1-km) resolution, and at 11 micrometers, an infrared "window," with a 2-mi (4-km) resolution. The former provides a photograph of the Earth (during daylight hours), whereas the latter provides an imaged estimate of cloud or surface temperature. The scanline start-stop time and position can be controlled from the ground. In routine operations, images cover from approximately 80°N to 50°S every half hour. However, for storm coverage the interval is routinely reduced to 15 min for viewing the Northern Hemisphere, and it may be reduced to 5 min over a more restricted area.

The principal benefit of *GOES* data has come from a qualitative interpretation of the imagery, particularly when a sequence of pictures is presented in animation. Such a movie highlights the evolution of atmospheric features as a storm develops and dissipates, with a horizontal resolution far better than is available from other data sources with the exception of local radar. In the arena of storm detection, the imagery has been especially effective for severe convective weather outbreaks and for hurricane monitoring.

Important features that guide the forecaster include the following examples. The position of the jet streams aids the dynamic development of the storm. The position is discernible from cirrus cloud streaks and also from cloud shadows. Air mass boundaries on all scales, from major fronts to outflow boundaries from convective complex downdrafts or land-sea breezes can provide surface lifting to trigger convection in an unstable atmosphere. These boundaries are detectable from lines of low-level cumulus clouds. The degree of surface heating can destabilize the atmosphere, leading to enhanced convection. Heating can be estimated from infrared temperature measurements, augmented by observation of the dissipation of fog or the development of low-level cumulus. *SEE AIR MASS; CLOUD; FRONT; JET STREAM.*

An example of half-mile (1-km) imagery for the severe weather outbreak of May 31, 1985, is shown in **Fig. 5**. This storm system over Ohio, Pennsylvania, New York, and Ontario included an outbreak of 42 tornadoes. Figure 5 clearly illustrates the squall line with mature thunderstorms in the north, and new development along the line to the southwest. The drier air behind the front is differentiated from the moist air mass ahead, characterized by low-level cumulus. There is jet streak cirrus, oriented east-west, visible in western central Ohio, suggesting that the principal development will take place to the north. Shadows present below the cirrus anvils in eastern Ohio can be used to estimate cloud altitude, which can be related to the intensity of the convection. Since this imagery is available as frequently as every 5 min, the forecaster has a valuable tool for issuing detailed, short-term warnings that can save lives and property. *SEE SQUALL LINE; THUNDERSTORM.*

Fig. 5. *GOES-East* photograph of frontal squall line on May 31, 1985, at 2200 GMT. Note the sharp moisture transition across the front as revealed by the preceding cloudiness, and the changing characteristics of the convection north versus south of the jet stream indicated by the cirrus from western to central Ohio. (*National Environmental Satellite, Data, and Information Service, NOAA***)**

The *GOES* satellites have made a major contribution to the detection and monitoring of Atlantic and Caribbean hurricanes, which usually develop from weak disturbances traveling in the easterlies across the tropical Atlantic. Using the imagery, forecasters have become highly skilled in interpreting the significant large-scale features of the circulation, together with the apparent organization of the cloud features, to predict the evolution of the storm from disturbance to tropical storm, and finally to hurricane. Significant features include the organization of feeder bands bringing low-level moisture into the storm, and the upper-level, clockwise outflow visible from the cirrus canopy; the size of the storm and the presence of an eye; and the movement of the system relative to the larger-scale flow. *See Hurricane*.

Figure 6 is a visible picture of Hurricane Hugo on September 21, 1989, as it approached the coast of South Carolina. At this time the storm possessed a well-defined eye. The previously mentioned features that are associated with a mature hurricane are readily recognized. Also, the arc of cumulus clouds over the Gulf of Mexico west of Florida should be noted. This feature aids in defining the area of descending air compensating in part for the inflow to the east that is lifted in the storm's core.

Aside from qualitative interpretation, there has always been a quantitative aspect to the *GOES* measurements. This has included wind measurements from animated cloud tracers, precipitation estimates (flash flood warnings) from cloud top temperatures augmented by cloud growth measurements, and short-term hurricane track forecasts based on current storm movement. Improving technology is expanding the quantitative role. Since the launch of *GOES 4* in September 1980, the VISSR Atmospheric Sounder (VAS) has been added, permitting measurements at 11 additional spectral intervals of the infrared. These data are used directly as imagery and also to estimate the vertical distribution of atmospheric parameters (temperature, moisture, wind). The image in **Fig. 7** is composed of measurements at 6.7 μm, representing the emission of thermal energy by water vapor in the atmosphere. High clouds, extending above significant concentrations of water vapor, are also seen, including Hurricane Hugo. Water-vapor imagery reveals details of the circulation not discernible in the visible or infrared window radiation. An example in Fig. 7 is the cold low that is visible over Louisiana. The 6.7-μm imagery has been enthusiastically received by weather forecasters, particularly on the west coast, where it offers guidance on storm systems moving in from the Pacific. It has also proved important in hurricane forecasting, revealing the interaction of the hurricane with the large-scale circulation. The westward retrogression of the cold low in Fig. 7 allowed Hugo to make landfall in South Carolina and to cross the mountains before being swept up in the westerly flow seen approaching the Midwest. Had the hurricane stayed east of the mountains, as initially forecast, more serious flooding would have resulted. Water-vapor imagery is also widely used in severe weather forecasting, because it delineates areas where upper-level dry air (dark in the imagery) overlays warm, moist surface layers, creating potential instability.

The temperature and moisture profiles obtained from the measurements made by the VISSR Atmo-

Fig. 6. *GOES-East* photograph of Hurricane Hugo on September 21, 1989, at 1901 GMT prior to landfall in South Carolina. (***National Environmental Satellite, Data, and Information Service, NOAA***)

spheric Sounder have not yet attained complete operational acceptance, largely because this instrument is considerably more primitive than those flying on the polar orbiting satellites at a lower altitude. However, the VISSR Atmospheric Sounder has been shown to contribute significantly in delineating short-term changes in atmospheric moisture and stability, supplying additional information to the severe weather forecaster. An advanced generation of instruments, for the 1990s, will provide a separate 5-channel imager and 19-channel sounder. These instruments will

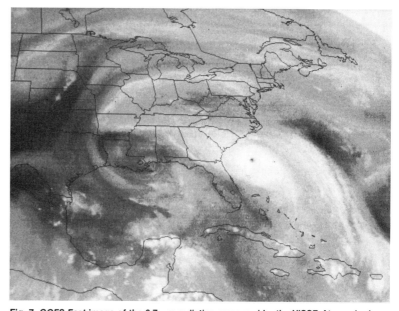

Fig. 7. *GOES-East* image of the 6.7-μm radiation measured by the VISSR Atmospheric Sounder on September 21, 1989, at 2131 GMT. Lighter areas depict middle- and upper-level moisture (or cloud); darker areas delineate dry air aloft and areas of downward motion. An incipient line of thunderstorms is evident over Kansas and Nebraska, associated with the upper level "dry slot" seen there. Note interaction of cold pressure circulation over Louisiana with Hurricane Hugo. (***National Environmental Satellite, Data, and Information Service, NOAA***)

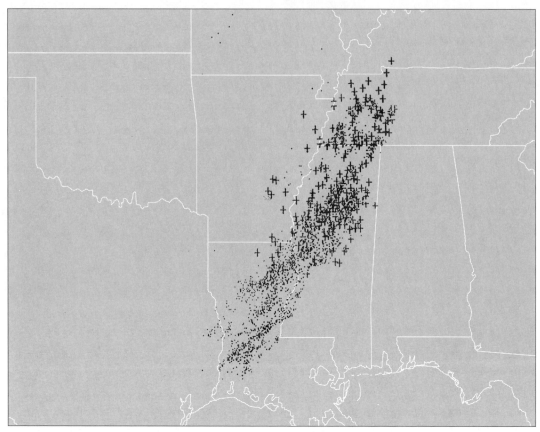

Fig. 8. Display of lightning stroke positions and polarities for a 4-h period during a storm which occurred on November 26, 1988, from 16:08 to 20:08 GMT. Positive strokes (+) [positive charge to earth] and negative strokes (−) [negative charge to earth] are indicated.

be mounted on a three-axis stabilized platform that will permit additional flexibility in areal coverage. Considerably improved capability has been demonstrated in simulation of the future measurements, which should further enhance the utility of the satellite in meeting requirements for storm detection and monitoring.

Christopher M. Hayden

Sferic detectors. Since around 1980, there has been an enormous increase in operating stations and networks devoted to detecting and following storms by using signals (sferics) generated by lightning return strokes. Commercially available equipment for setting up networks, and subscription services for network-processed information have become available in many parts of the world. There are more than 70 lightning direction-finding stations in the United States alone, and networks are operative in Japan, France, Sweden, Germany, and the United Kingdom, among others. Among the prominent users of information about the occurrence of lightning are the electric power distribution industry, the U.S. Weather Service, the Bureau of Land Management, the U.S. Forest Service, television news and weather broadcasters, operators of nuclear reactors, and explosives handlers and fabricators.

Operation of the networks 24 h a day has uncovered a large number of hitherto-unnoticed phenomena that have broadened the view of how thunderstorms originate, develop, and propagate. In addition, hitherto unsuspected, is the systematic appearance of positive lightning strokes to ground associated with a change in storm dynamics. Positive discharges in summer storms appear to be associated with the cessation of vigorous convection, and a possible association of their appearance with the downburst stage (extremely dangerous for aircraft during landing or takeoff operations) has been noted. Network monitoring has also verified that the largest peak currents in lightning are produced by positive strokes.

Real-time monitoring of storm development as indicated by electrical activity complements the satellite visible and infrared imagery. **Figure 8** shows an enlarged portion of the United States map, zooming in on a storm that originated at the Texas-Louisiana border and progressed in an east-northeast direction during the 4-h period shown. From an animated display of the stroke occurrences, it was verified that the positive strokes come primarily at the end of vigorous convection. Note in the figure that there appears to be a latitude cutoff below which no positive discharges occur. This example is only one of many phenomena that have been discovered as a direct result of extensive coverage and 24-h operation of the networks.
SEE STORM; WEATHER FORECASTING AND PREDICTION.

Marx Brook

Bibliography. L. J. Battan, *Fundamentals of Meteorology*, 2d ed., 1984; L. J. Battan, *Radar Observation of the Atmosphere*, rev. ed. 1981; B. Battrick and E. Rolfe (eds.), *Nowcasting II: Mesoscale Observations and Very Short-Range Weather Forecasting*, European Space Agency SP-208, 1984; A. J. Bogush, Jr., *Radar and the Atmosphere*, 1989; Committee of Atmospheric Sciences, National Academy of

Sciences (ed.), *Severe Storms: Prediction, Detection, and Warning*, 1977; R. J. Doviak and D. S. Zrnic, *Doppler Radar and Weather Observations*, 1984; T. T. Fujita, Tornadoes and downbursts in the context of generalized plantetary scales, *J. Atm. Sci.*, 38:1511–1534, 1981; E. P. Krider, A gated wideband magnetic direction finder for lightning return strokes, *J. Appl. Meteorol.*, 15:301–306, 1976; A. C. Lee, An experimental study of the remote location of lightning flashes using a VLF arrival time difference technique, *Quart. J. Roy. Meteorol. Soc.*, 112:203–229, 1986; R. E. Orville and H. Songster, The east coast lightning detection network, *IEEE Trans.*, vol. PWRD-2, July 1987; W. L. Smith, G. S. Wade, and H. M. Woolf, Combined atmospheric sounding/cloud imagery: A new forecasting tool, *Bull. Amer. Meteorol. Soc.*, 66:138–141, 1985; C. S. Velden, Satellite observations of Hurricane Elena (1985) using the VAS 6.7-μm ''water-vapor'' channel, *Bull. Amer. Meteorol. Soc.*, 68:210–215, 1987; J. W. Wilson et al., Microburst wind structure and evaluation of Doppler radar for airport wind shear detection, *J. Clim. Appl. Meteorol.*, 23:898–915, 1984.

Storm surge

A transient, localized disturbance at sea level, resulting from the action of a tropical cyclone, an extratropical cyclone, or a squall over the sea. Storm surges, or storm tides, are not to be confused with tsunamis, or tidal waves, which result from seismic or molar disturbances of the Earth. In the Northern Hemisphere those coastal regions which are particularly vulnerable to storm surges include the periphery of the Gulf of Mexico, the Atlantic Coast of the United States, the Gulf of Bengal, Japan and other islands of the western Pacific which lie in the typhoon belt, and the coastal regions of the North Sea. The surges occurring in the North Sea originate from the actions of large-scale extratropical storms, particularly winter storms. On the eastern coast of the United States, hurricane-induced surges, as well as surges originating from intense winter storms, occur. In the Great Lakes and the Gulf of Mexico, surges resulting from squalls are known to occur; however, hurricane-induced surges pose a more serious threat to the low-lying coastal areas of the Gulf. *See Tsunami.*

The time history of the surge at a given location at shore is represented by the surge hydrograph. This is a time sequence of the difference between the measured tide and the predicted periodic tide (see **illus.**). Maximum surge elevations of 15 ft (5 m) above predicted tide are not uncommon. In the case of hurricane-induced surges, the peak water level seems to depend primarily upon the atmospheric pressure at the hurricane center. However, the horizontal scale, the direction and speed of propagation of the hurricane, and the coastal geometry and bottom topography are important influencing factors in the storm surge behavior. When a hurricane crosses the coast from the sea, the greatest surge alongshore usually occurs to the right of the hurricane path.

A storm surge is essentially a forced inertiogravitational wave of great wave length. This implies that the duration or speed of the storm determines the dynamic augmentation of the water level at shore above that which would occur if the storm were stationary.

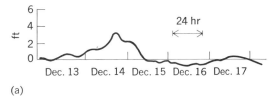

(a)

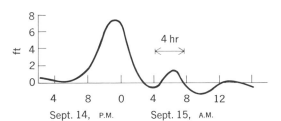

(b)

Surge hydrographs. (*a*) Winter storm of 1954 at Sandy Hook, New Jersey. (*b*) Hurricane of 1944 at Newport, Rhode Island.

Also, the inertial character of surges can explain quasi-periodic resurgences that often follow the primary forced surge.

Robert O. Reid

Bibliography. E. Bishop, *Hurricane*, 1990; J. Erikson, *Violent Storms*, 1988; D. L. Harris, The hurricane surge, *Proceedings of the 6th Conference on Coastal Engineering*, Council on Wave Research, pp. 96–114, 1958; R. H. Simpson and H. Riehl, *The Hurricane and Its Impact*, 1981; U.S. Department of Commerce, *Characteristics of Hurricane Storm Surge*, 1963.

Stormwater runoff

Excess rainwater that flows over the pervious and impervious surfaces of the land, transporting nonpoint-source pollutants into lakes, streams, and rivers. A nonpoint source is stormwater runoff from various land uses such as agriculture, developed land, forest, and landfills. Stormwater runoff can contribute high amounts of sediments, bacteria, nutrients, organic substances, heavy metals, and toxic materials to lakes, reservoirs, streams, and rivers. Rainfall and the resultant runoff and groundwater flow are the major driving forces behind stormwater runoff. The intensity, duration, and timing of rainfall have a direct impact on the magnitude of stormwater runoff and the pollutants therein. Other important factors include land use, land-use activity, soil type, slope, and temperature. *See Groundwater hydrology.*

Stormwater runoff is the primary source of nonpoint-source pollution. The type and magnitude of pollutants carried in stormwater runoff depend on whether the ground is pervious or impervious. Eroded soils from pervious areas usually contain high concentrations of sediments and particulate phosphorus attached to the sediment particles. Stormwater runoff from impervious areas contains pollutants that accumulate on the surface between rainfalls, such as sediments, bacteria, nutrients, litter, animal wastes, organic materials, and sometimes toxic substances.

Sources. Typical sources of stormwater runoff and nonpoint-source pollution include pasture land,

Approximate relationship between unit areal loadings from nonpoint sources*

	Average, kg/(ha)(yr)†			Range, kg/(ha)(yr)†		
	Total nitrogen	Total phosphorus	Total suspended solids	Total nitrogen	Total phosphorus	Total suspended solids
Forest	2.5	0.2	250	1–10	0.005–1	40–400
Range/pasture	5	0.3	400	2–10	0.2–0.6	10–1000
Cropland	10	0.6	1600	1–40	0.03–0.7	300–4000
Developed land	5	0.8	2000	2–20	0.25–5	200–5000
Feedlots	1000	250	—	700–1500	100–400	—

*From Environmental Protection Agency, *Clean Lakes Guidance Manual*, 1980.
†1 kg/ha = 0.89 lb/acre.

cropland, silviculture, residential/urban land, industrial/commerical land, construction activities, animal wastes, mining, roadways, landfills, and streambank erosion.

Unit areal pollutant loadings for various land uses are presented in the **table**. In most instances, there is a wide range of loading values because of physical, chemical, and climatic differences. In general, forest land produces the lowest pollutant loadings; however, when forests are severely cut, forest land can produce high pollutant loads. Pasture land usually produces low pollutant loadings; however, overgrazed pasture land can produce relatively high pollutant loads.

Cropland usually produces high levels of pollutants because of the erosion of highly fertilized soil. The pollutant loadings for cropland have an extremely high range because of the many factors affecting erosion and runoff, including soil type, slope, type of crop, amount of fertilization, and extent of conservation methods.

Stormwater runoff from residential and commercial areas usually contains high levels of pollutants because of the wash-off of pollutants that build up on the surface between rainfalls. In rural areas, residential and commercial runoff consists of eroded soil from unvegetated and poorly vegetated areas. Stormwater runoff from industrial areas contains, in addition to sediments and nutrients, toxic material from industrial processes. Construction activities, unless linked with effective erosion control measures, produce extremely high pollutant loads, especially sediments. In the United States, discharge permits have been required for industrial and municipal wastewater discharges for many years; discharge permits are now required for industrial and municipal stormwater discharges as well.

As shown in the table, animal waste feedlots produce the highest loadings of nitrogen and phosphorus. Thus, a high concentration of animal wastes can produce extremely high levels of both pollutants.

Roads can be a significant pollutant source. A Virginia study indicated that sediment and nutrient loadings to a large water-supply reservoir were directly related to the length and area of roads in each subbasin. Roads can act as conduits to transport sediment and nutrient-laden stormwater runoff directly into streams and lakes. Another source of pollutants is landfills, which can produce both stormwater runoff and contaminated groundwater. Depending on the type, landfills can produce pollutants consisting of sediments, bacteria, nutrients, organic matter, and toxic material. Stormwater runoff from active and inactive mining operations produces low-pH (acid) and toxic runoff that adversely affects stream water quality and biota.

A significant source of stormwater runoff that is often ignored is streambank erosion. Periodic high-water conditions erode the banks of unstable streams. Changing the upstream hydrology by cutting down trees or by building roads and houses causes an increase in stream flow during rain events, resulting in increased streambank erosion. A stream will usually continue to erode until the stream channel has stabilized by enlarging to handle the increased stormwaters. Once a stream has stabilized, streambank erosion decreases significantly.

Impacts on water quality. Pollutants from stormwater runoff usually affect water quality in a manner different from that of point sources such as municipal and industrial treatment-plant discharges. Although stormwater runoff may contribute the same kinds of pollutants as point sources, the pollutants in stormwater runoff are generated in different volumes, combinations, and concentrations during different flow regimes. Pollutants from stormwater runoff are generated during and immediately after storm events, while point sources are generated during dry and wet weather conditions. Pollution incidences, therefore, occur less frequently and for shorter duration for stormwater runoff than for point-source discharges.

Pollutants from stormwater runoff can have short-term and long-term impacts on water quality. Short-term impacts occur during and immediately after a storm event when pollutant concentrations are high and may affect the dissolved oxygen level, the toxicity of the water, or the biota in the water. Long-term impacts occur when the particulate pollutants in stormwater runoff settle to the bottom of the waterway or when the colloidal or soluble pollutants remain in the water column.

Slowly moving bodies of water such as lakes, reservoirs, large rivers, and estuaries are particularly affected adversely by pollutants in stormwater runoff. In a survey conducted by the North American Lake Management Society, all but one of thirty-eight states participating stated that nonpoint sources were seriously affecting lake water quality. Fourteen states with 24,000 lakes reported that more than 75% of lakes were seriously affected by nonpoint-source pollution. Six of the ten Environmental Protection Agency (EPA) Regions reported that nonpoint-source pollution such as stormwater runoff is the principal remaining cause of water quality problems in their region.

Stormwater runoff from agricultural activities such as tillage and animal waste facilities constitutes the most pervasive nonpoint source in every EPA Region. The next two most commonly cited nonpoint-source problems are runoff from urban lands and from mining activities. In developing areas, stormwater runoff from construction activities is a major source of sediments and nutrients.

Sediment, including sand, silt, clay, and organic materials, is the largest contribution by volume to stormwater runoff. Many of the other pollutants are associated with sediments carried in the stormwater runoff.

Monitoring. Control of stormwater runoff is usually a long-term and expensive process. In order to properly allocate financial and technical resources, the first step should be identification and quantification of the nonpoint sources. Once the nonpoint sources are identified and quantified, they can be ranked according to their magnitude and their impact on water quality. This ranking can then be used to develop a prioritized stormwater runoff control program.

In order to quantify stormwater runoff, a wet-weather monitoring program should be performed. Monitoring stations should be located on tributary streams or drainage channels downstream from specific land uses or suspected problem areas. During storm events, multiple water samples and flow measurements should be collected over the complete stream hydrograph as shown in **Fig. 1.** Either stream flow measurements should be made continually over the complete stream hydrograph by using an automated flow recorder, or they should be manually made every time a sample is collected from the stream. Water samples should be collected at intervals over the stream hydrograph either manually or by using an automated water sampler. The multiple samples should be flow-composited to make one flow-proportioned sample; that is, multiple samples should be considered in terms of total volume, and the resulting composite sample would be representative of the flow and conditions of pollutant concentration in the stream hydrograph. Each sample should be analyzed for the constituents of concern, which may include sediments (total suspended solids); total phosphorus and dissolved reactive phosphorus; total nitrogen, ammonia, and nitrate; and other parameters such as biochemical oxygen demand, heavy metals, organic materials, and toxic substances. The total pollutant loading for a particular storm event can be calculated by multiplying the composite concentration by the runoff volume (area of the stream hydrograph;

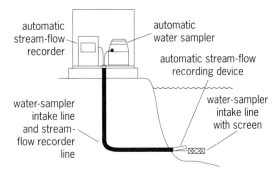

Fig. 2. Diagram of an automated stream-monitoring station used to collect flow and water-quality data.

Fig. 1). Multiple storm events should be monitored to develop a relationship between pollutant loading and runoff volume. The total annual nonpoint-source loading can be calculated by applying this relationship to continuous streamflow records. Dry-weather samples should also be collected periodically to develop base-flow pollutant loadings. Adding dry-weather base-flow loadings and wet-weather nonpoint-source loadings yields the total annual pollutant loading.

Wet-weather monitoring can be performed manually or by installing automated flow-measurement and water-sampling equipment. Manual monitoring requires that samples and flow measurements be collected during and after a rain event by dedicated staff. Automated monitoring is more reliable; it requires an automatic stream-water-level recorder, an automatic discrete water sampler, and a weatherproof enclosure (**Fig. 2**).

Stormwater management. In general, a watershed management program can consist of two approaches to nonpoint sources: source control and regional control. Source controls consist of nonpoint-source controls applied at the source. Regional controls usually consist of regional detention basins that control nonpoint sources downstream of the source.

Source controls consist of structural and nonstructural controls established throughout the watershed. Structural controls include agricultural controls such as grass waterways, diversions, detention basins, and animal waste facilities. They also include erosion control practices for streambank erosion, roadway runoff, and construction activities. Nonstructural practices include natural engineering practices such as erosion control using vegetation. For example, in the eastern United States, streambank erosion can be controlled by planting willow twigs along the shoreline. This practice, which is very inexpensive and can be done by untrained volunteers, results in a dense growth of willow bushes along the streambank.

Source controls are not always feasible because of constraints such as land availability, effectiveness, and cost. In some cases, therefore, regional controls, such as detention basins, should be used alone or in conjunction with source controls. Regional detention basins are sometimes more cost-effective than source controls. SEE EROSION; STREAM POLLUTION; WATER POLLUTION.

Frank Browne

Bibliography. F. X. Browne, *Watershed Management Study of the South Rivanna Watershed,* 1979; Environmental Protection Agency, *Lake and Reservoir Restoration Guidance Manual,* EPA-440/4-90-

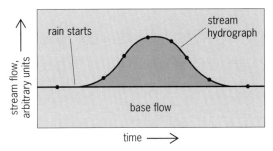

Fig. 1. Typical stream hydrograph showing increase in stream water level during a rain event; data points indicate time intervals at which water samples are collected over the entire stream hydrograph.

006, 1990; Environmental Protection Agency, *Report to Congress: Nonpoint Source Pollution in the U.S.*, Office of Water Program Operations, 1984; North American Lake Management Society, *1983 State Lake Survey*, 1984.

Stream pollution

Biological, or bacteriological, pollution in a stream indicated by the presence of the coliform group of organisms. While nonpathogenic itself, this group is a measure of the potential presence of contaminating organisms. Because of temperature, food supply, and predators, the environment provided by natural bodies of water is not favorable to the growth of pathogenic and coliform organisms. Physical factors, such as flocculation and sedimentation, also help remove bacteria. Any combination of these factors provides the basis for the biological self-purification capacity of natural water bodies.

When subjected to a disinfectant such as chlorine, bacterial die-away is usually defined by Chick's law, which states that the number of organisms destroyed per unit of time is proportional to the number of organisms remaining. This law cannot be directly applied in natural streams because of the variety of factors affecting the removal and death rates in this environment. The die-away is rapid in shallow, turbulent streams of low dilution, and slow in deep, sluggish streams with a high dilution factor. In both cases, higher temperatures increase the rate of removal.

This concentration of many physical characteristics and chemical substances may be calculated directly if the relative volumes of the waste stream and river flow are known. Chlorides and mineral solids fall into this category. Some substances in waste discharges are chemically or biologically unstable, and their rates of decrease can be predicted or measured directly. Sulfites, nitrites, some phenolic compounds, and organic matter are examples of this type of waste.

These simple relationships, however, do not apply to the concentration of dissolved oxygen. This factor depends not only on the relative dilutions but also upon the rate of oxidation of the organic material and the rate of reaeration of the stream.

Nonpolluted natural waters are usually saturated with dissolved oxygen. They may even be supersaturated because of the oxygen released by green water plants under the influence of sunlight. When an organic waste is discharged into a stream, the dissolved oxygen is utilized by the bacteria in their metabolic processes to oxidize the organic matter. The oxygen is replaced by reaeration through the water surface exposed to the atmosphere. This replenishment permits the bacteria to continue the oxidative process in an aerobic environment. In this state, reasonably clean appearance, freedom from odors, and normal animal and plant life are maintained.

An increase in the concentration of organic matter stimulates the growth of bacteria and increases the rates of oxidation and oxygen utilization. If the concentration of the organic pollutant is so great that the bacteria use oxygen more rapidly than it can be replaced, only anaerobic bacteria can survive and the stabilization of organic matter is accomplished in the absence of oxygen. Under these conditions, the water becomes unsightly and malodorous, and the normal flora and fauna are destroyed. Furthermore, anaerobic decomposition proceeds at a slower rate than aerobic. For maintenance of satisfactory conditions, minimal dissolved oxygen concentrations in receiving streams are of primary importance.

Figure 1 shows the effect of municipal sewage and industrial wastes on the oxygen content of a stream. Cooling water, used in some industrial processes, is characterized by high temperatures, which reduce the capacity of water to hold oxygen in solution. Thermal pollution, however, is significant only when large quantities are concentrated in relatively small flows. Municipal sewage requires oxygen for its stabilization by bacteria. Oxygen is utilized more rapidly than it is replaced by reaeration, resulting in the death of the normal aquatic life. Further downstream, as the oxygen demands are satisfied, reaeration replenishes the oxygen supply.

Any organic industrial waste produces a similar pattern in the concentration of dissolved oxygen. Certain chemical wastes have high oxygen demands which may be exerted quickly, producing a sudden drop in the dissolved oxygen content. Other chemical wastes may be toxic or destroy the biological activity in the stream. Strong acids and alkalies make the water corrosive, and dyes, oils, and floating solids render the stream unsightly. Suspended solids, such as mineral tailings, may settle to the bed of the stream, smother purifying microorganisms, and destroy breeding places. Although these latter factors may not deplete the oxygen, the pollutional effects may still be serious.

Deoxygenation. Polluted waters are deprived of oxygen by the exertion of the biochemical oxygen demand (BOD), which is defined as the quantity of oxygen required by the bacteria to oxidize the organic matter. The rate of this reaction is assumed to be pro-

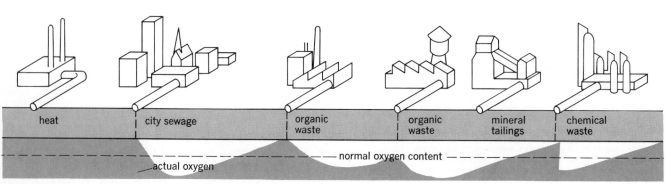

Fig. 1. Variation of oxygen content of polluted stream.

portional to the concentration of the remaining organic matter, measured in terms of oxygen. This reaction may be expressed as Eq. (1), which integrates to give Eq. (2) or Eq. (3), in which L_t is BOD re-

$$\frac{dL}{dt} = -K_1 L \qquad (1)$$

$$L_t = L_0 e^{-K_1 t} \qquad (2)$$

$$y = L_0 (1 - e^{-K_1 t}) \qquad (3)$$

maining at any time t, L_0 is ultimate BOD, y is BOD exerted at end of t, and K_1 is coefficient defining the reaction velocity. The coefficient is a function of temperature given by Eq. (4), in which T is temperature

$$K_T = K_{20} \cdot 1.047^{T-20} \qquad (4)$$

in degrees Celsius, K_T is value of the coefficient at T, and K_{20} is value of the coefficient at 20°C (68°F).

The BOD of a waste is determined by a standard laboratory procedure and is reported in terms of the 5-day value at 20°C (68°F). From a set of BOD values determined for any time sequence, the reaction velocity constant K_1 may be calculated. Knowledge of this coefficient permits determination of the ultimate BOD from the 5-day value in accordance with the above equations. For municipal sewages and many industrial wastes the value of K_1 at 20°C (68°F) is between 0.15 and 0.75 per day. A common value for sewage is 0.4 per day.

The coefficient determined from laboratory BOD data may be significantly different from that calculated for stream BOD data. The determination of the stream rate may be made from a reexpression of Eqs. (1)–(4) in the form of Eq. (5), where L_A is the BOD

$$K_r = \frac{1}{t} \log \frac{L_A}{L_B} \qquad (5)$$

measured at an upstream station, L_B is the BOD at a station downstream from A, and t is the time of flow between the two stations. Values of K_r range from 0.10 to 3.0 per day. The difference between the laboratory rate K_1 and the stream rate K_r is due to the turbulence of the stream flow, biological growths on the stream bed, insufficient nutrients, and inadequate bacteria in the river water. These factors influence the rate of oxidation in the stream as well as the removal of organic matter. Such processes as flocculation, sedimentation, and scour of the organic material in the river affect the removal rate but do not necessarily influence the rate of oxidation and the associated dissolved oxygen concentration. Field surveys are usually required to determine the pollution assimilation capacity of a stream.

When a significant portion of the waste is in the suspended state, settling of the solids in a slow-moving stream is probable. The organic fraction of the sludge deposits decomposes anaerobically, except for the thin surface layer which is subjected to aerobic decomposition due to the dissolved oxygen in the overlying waters. In warm weather, when the anaerobic decomposition proceeds at a more rapid rate, gaseous end products, usually carbon dioxide and methane, rise through the supernatant waters. The evolution of the gas bubbles may raise sludge particles to the water surface. Although this phenomenon may occur while the water contains some dissolved oxygen, the more intense action during the summer usually results in depletion of dissolved oxygen.

Reoxygenation. Water may absorb oxygen from the atmosphere when the oxygen in solution falls below saturation. Dissolved oxygen for receiving waters is also derived from two other sources: that in the receiving water and the waste flow at the point of discharge, and that given off by green plants. The latter source is restricted to daylight hours and the warmer seasons of the year and, therefore, is not usually used in any engineering analysis of stream capacity.

Unpolluted water maintains in solution the maximum quantity of dissolved oxygen. The saturation value is a function of temperature and the concentration of dissolved substances, such as chlorides. When oxygen is removed from solution, the deficiency is made up by the atmospheric oxygen, which is absorbed at the water surface and passes into solution. The rate at which oxygen is absorbed, or the rate of reaeration, is proportional to the degree of undersaturation and may be expressed as in Eq. (6), in which

$$\frac{dD}{dt} = -K_2 D \qquad (6)$$

D is dissolved oxygen deficit, t is time, and K_2 is reaeration coefficient.

The reaeration coefficient depends upon the ratio of the volume to the surface area and the intensity of fluid turbulence. An approximate value of the coefficient may be obtained from Eq. (7), in which D_L is

$$K_2 = \frac{D_L U^{1/2}}{H^{3/2}} \qquad (7)$$

coefficient of molecular diffusion of oxygen in water, U is average velocity of the river flow, and H is average depth of the river section.

The effect of temperature on this coefficient is identical with its effect on the deoxygenation coefficient. A common range of K_2 is from 0.20 to 5.0 per day. Many waste constituents, such as surface-active substances, interfere with the molecular diffusion of oxygen and reduce the value of the reaeration rate from that of pure water. Winds, waves, rapids, and tidal mixing are factors which create circulation and surface renewal and enhance reaeration.

Oxygen balance. The oxygen balance in a stream is determined by the concentration of organic matter and its rate of oxidation, and by the dissolved oxygen concentration and the rate of reaeration. The simultaneous action of deoxygenation and reaeration produces a pattern in the dissolved oxygen concentration known as the dissolved oxygen sag. The differential equation describing the combined action of deoxygenation and reaeration is given in Eq. (8), which states

$$\frac{dD}{dt} = K_1 L - K_2 D \qquad (8)$$

that the rate of change in the dissolved oxygen deficit D is the result of two independent rates. The first is that of oxygen utilization in the oxidation of organic matter. This reaction increases the dissolved oxygen deficit at a rate that is proportional to the concentration of organic matter L. The second rate is that of reaeration, which replenishes the oxygen utilized by the first reaction and decreases the deficit. Integration

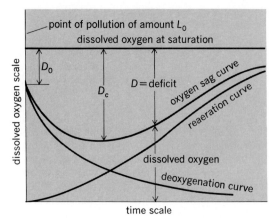

point of pollution of amount L_0
dissolved oxygen at saturation

D_0

D_c

D = deficit

oxygen sag curve

reaeration curve

dissolved oxygen

deoxygenation curve

dissolved oxygen scale

time scale

Fig. 2. Dissolved-oxygen sag curve and its components.

of this equation yields Eq. (9), where L_0 and D_0 are

$$D_t = \frac{K_1 L_0}{K_2 - K_r} (e^{-K_r t} - e^{-K_2 t}) + D_0 e^{-K_2 t} \quad (9)$$

the initial biochemical oxygen demand and the initial dissolved oxygen deficit, respectively, and D_t is the deficit at time t. The proportionality constants K_1 and K_2 represent the coefficients of deaeration and reaeration, respectively, and K_r the coefficient of BOD removal in the stream.

Figure 2 shows a typical dissolved oxygen sag curve resulting from a pollution of amount L_0 at $t = 0$. The sag curve is shown to result from the deoxygenation curve and the reaeration curve. A point of particular significance on the sag curve is that of minimum dissolved oxygen concentration, or maximum deficit. At this location, the rate of change of the deficit is zero, which results in the numerical equality of the opposing rates of deoxygenation and reoxygenation. The balance at this critical point may be written as Eq. (10), where the BOD at the critical

$$K_2 D_c = K_1 L = K_1 L_0 e^{-K_r t_c} \quad (10)$$

point has been replaced by its equivalent at zero time (the location of the waste discharge). The value of the time t_c may be calculated from Eq. (11).

$$t_c = \frac{1}{K_2 - K_r} \log \frac{K_2}{K_r} \left[1 - \frac{D_0(K_2 - K_r)}{K_1 L_0} \right] \quad (11)$$

Allowable pollutional load. The pollutional load L_0 that a stream may absorb is a function of the dissolved oxygen deficit D_c, the coefficients K_1, K_r, and K_2, and the initial deficit D_0. The dissolved oxygen deficit is usually established by water pollution standards of the health agency, and the initial deficit is determined by upstream pollution. The engineering problem is usually associated with the assignment of representative values of the coefficients K_1, K_r, and K_2 for a given flow and temperature condition.

Seasonal temperatures influence the saturation of oxygen and the rates of deaeration and reaeration. Variation in stream flow with the seasons affects the dilution factor. The most critical conditions occur during the summer when the stream runoff is low and the temperatures are high. *See Estuarine oceanography; Fresh-water ecosystem; Sewage disposal; Water pollution.*

Donald J. O'Connor

Stream transport and deposition

The sediment debris load of streams is a natural corollary to the degradation of the landscape by weathering and erosion. Eroded material reaches stream channels through rills and minor tributaries, being carried by the transporting power of running water and by mass movement, that is, by slippage, slides, or creep. The size represented may vary from clay to boulders. At any place in the stream system the material furnished from places upstream either is carried away or, if there is insufficient transporting ability, is accumulated as a depositional feature. The accumulation of deposited debris tends toward increased ease of movement, and this tends eventually to bring into balance the transporting ability of the stream and the debris load to be transported.

Stream loads. Because streams form and adjust their own channels, the debris load to be carried and the ability to carry load tend to reach and maintain a quasi-equilibrium. A reach of stream (part of the course) which attains this equilibrium is considered graded.

Much has been written concerning the concept of the graded stream. At one time absence of waterfalls or other discontinuities of longitudinal profile was considered necessary and, in fact, evidence for the condition of grade. Because much remains to be learned about the mechanics of debris transportation, the criteria for the graded condition may be expected to be extended and revised. In the present state of knowledge, however, it appears acceptable to think of reaches or segments of channel being graded, even when separated by reaches not so adjusted. A graded stream is one in which, over a period of years, slope and channel characteristics are delicately adjusted to provide, with available discharge, the shear forces required for the transportation of the load supplied from the drainage basin.

Two terms which have been useful to geologists and engineers dealing with rivers are competence and capacity. Competence was used by G. K. Gilbert to mean the ability to move debris, and its measure is the maximum size of material which can barely be moved. Capacity of a stream is the total load which it can carry under given conditions and is measured as weight of debris moved per unit of time. The usefulness of these terms has lessened with demand for increasingly quantitative description of stream action. Sampling equipment now in general use measures only the suspended portion of the debris and not that moving close to the streambed. Thus, except in special situations, the carrying capacity of a stream cannot be precisely measured, and available theory allows only an approximation of total load by computation.

The maximum size of debris which can be carried varies, depending on subtle variations of several factors. Thus competence, a highly useful concept, cannot be determined with satisfaction either in the field or by computation. The concepts implied by these terms will gain even greater value and importance as both theory and field measurement techniques improve. The following review of the present status of theory of debris transport will perhaps indicate how the usefulness of these concepts depends greatly on ability to determine quantitative values for them.

Debris transport theory. Debris transport is inextricably associated with the hydromechanics of flow in open channels. It is now known that the introduction of sediment grains into a fluid alters in an important manner many of the hydraulic relationships which applied to a fixed bed. For example, in a movable-bed channel, boundary roughness is not merely the rugosity of the nonmoving bed and banks. Once the particles begin to move, the shear-resisting flow is altered. Particles can assume many different configurations, among which are dunes or ripples or a plane, and these bed forms depend on the transportation process. Thus the resisting shear at the boundary depends on the debris transport itself.

When shear applied by water to a grain bed of uniform-size particles becomes sufficient to move a layer of grains, successive layers do not progressively peel off indefinitely. After some layers are put in motion, an equilibrium is reached. Transport then continues without further degradation. R. A. Bagnold showed by theory and experiment that the grains in transport add a new force normal to the bed which holds the particles exposed at the bed against the stress of the overlying fluid-grain mixture. This force, the dispersive stress between sheared grains, makes a fundamental difference in the stress structure between fixed and movable-bed channels.

Of all the theories put forward to elucidate the physics of sediment transport, the most objectively derived from first principles rather than from empirical data is that of Bagnold. This theory is based on the general idea that work involved in sediment movement comes from the energy expended by the flowing water. The equations are predicated on the idea that only a portion of the total power spent by the water is used for debris transport, that is, that the available power times an efficiency factor equals that part utilized for carrying clastic load.

The formulation most widely used for computing sediment transport is one derived by H. A. Einstein which involves both theory and several empirically derived coefficients. His computational procedure has been simplified by B. R. Colby and C. H. Hembree for application to field problems.

Field measurement. Nearly without exception, the field measurement of sediment in transport is capable of sampling only the suspended part of the load. That which is of size larger than sand and that transported in the 2 in. (5 cm) nearest the bed are not measured. At a few experimental sites it has been possible to measure both the suspended load at a normal river cross section and the total load. In streams carrying material in the sand-size range and smaller, but no gravel, the total load may be measured with the usual suspended-load sampler by creating turbulence sufficient to throw all debris into transit into a condition of suspension for a brief time. Such a procedure was

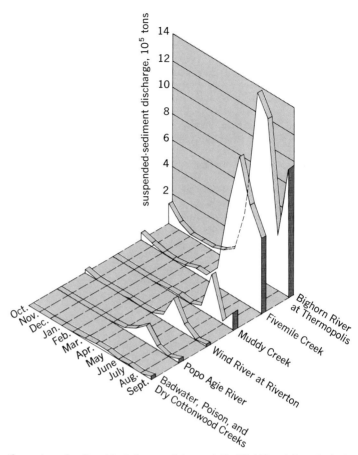

Comparison of sediment loads for several streams in the Wind River drainage basin, in Wyoming, 1950 water year. 1 ton = 0.9 metric ton. (*After B. R. Colby, C. H. Hembree, and F. H. Rainwater, Sedimentation and Chemical Quality of Surface Waters in the Wind River Basin, Wyoming, USGS Water-Supply Pap. 1373, 1956*)

used on the Niobrara River near Cody, Nebraska, by Colby and Hembree, who reported that there the suspended load concentration averaged 51% of the concentration represented by the total sediment load.

In western rivers flowing through alluvial valleys, suspended-load concentrations tend to occur in the range of 100 to 5000 ppm (parts per million). The concentration increases geometrically, not linearly, with increased water discharge. Such concentrations can result in large amounts of sediment in a day, a month, or a year. An example is shown in the **illustration**. A river of moderate size, Bighorn River at Thermopolis, Wyoming, averages 3.6 in. (91 mm) of runoff from the drainage basin of 8080 mi^2 (20,927 km^2). This amounted to 1.36 × 10^6 acre-feet (1.68 × 10^9 m^3) annually during a 41-year period. In the illustration it can be seen that in 1950 about 1.4 × 10^6 tons (1.27 × 10^6 metric tons) of sediment passed Thermopolis during the month of June alone.

In the humid East, sediment concentrations are considerably smaller, but runoff is larger than in the semiarid West. Some average values of suspended sediment contributed from different areas are shown in the **table**.

Luna B. Leopold

Bibliography. R. J. Garde and K. R. Raju, *Mechanics of Sediment Transportation and Alluvial Stream Problems*, 2d ed., 1986; G. V. Middleton and J. B. Southard, *Mechanics of Sediment Movement*, 2d ed.,

Rates of suspended sediment production	
Region	Sediment yield, tons/mi^2-years*
Streams in western United States	1200–1400
Cheyenne Basin, Wyoming	3900
Streams in midwestern United States	240–850

*1 ton/mi^2 = 0.35 metric ton/km^2.

1984; B. W. Nelson (ed.), *Environmental Framework of Coastal Plain Estuaries*, 1973; H. W. Shen (ed.), *Applications of Stochastic Processes to Sediment Transport: Sedimentation Process in Rivers and Coastal Environments*, 1979; D. B. Simons and F. Senturk, *Sediment Transport Technology*, 1990; I. Statham, *Earth Surface Sediment Transport*, 1977; C. R. Thorne, J. C. Bathurst, and R. D. Hey (eds.), *Sediment Transport in Gravel-Bed Rivers*, 1987; E. West, *Equilibrium of Natural Streams*, 1980.

Surface mining

A mining method in which the overburden (earth and rocks) is stripped away completely to reach the underlying coal or other minerals. It has been popularly called strip mining. Surface mining of coal has increased steadily to the point where, in the United States, over 60% of the coal is obtained from such mining activities. Large-scale draglines, shovels, scrapers, front-end loaders, and dozers can reach seams as deep as 1000 ft (305 m) in some open-pit operations, while smaller-size equipment is used effectively in hilly terrain.

Surface mining is safer than underground mining because the miners are not exposed to such potential hazards as roof falls, to explosions caused by methane gas or dust ignitions, and to coal-worker pneumoconiosis (black lung) caused by long-term exposure to respirable coal dust. *See* Underground mining.

Surface mining is also a more productive method of mining coal. Surface mines average 31 tons (28 metric tons) per worker per day, with some of the larger mines achieving 50 to 90 tons (45 to 82 metric tons) per worker per day. In underground mines the overall daily productivity per worker is about 11 tons (10 metric tons).

Stripping methods. There are three general methods of surface mining: contour mining, area mining, and open-pit mining, with variations within each.

Contour mining. This method is practiced commonly in rolling or mountainous terrain where the seams of coal outcrop at the mountain slopes. Mining generally begins by removing the overburden above the coal seam by starting at the outcrop, and proceeding along the hillside.

In the past, the overburden was mostly pushed toward the outslope and allowed to fall downslope. After the exposed coal was loaded out, additional cuts into the hillside were made until the overburden was too high to be removed economically. The final wall (the highwall) was frequently left in place while mining proceeded along the contour. Such contour mining is no longer permitted. Now, the removed overburden (the spoil) must be essentially hauled back into the mined-out pit, the exposed highwall buried, and the mined land returned approximately to the original contour. *See* Land reclamation.

The most popular and environmentally acceptable method of contour mining is haulback mining (**Fig. 1**). In a typical operation, an adjacent hollow is selected and carefully prepared to receive the overburden from the first section cut into the hillside. The first block to be mined is started at the outcrop of the coal seam. Dozers clear the site of brush and trees, stockpile the topsoil, and level the terrain to prepare benches for drilling holes for blasting. The overburden is blasted to cause fragmentation, and the dozers push the earth and blasted rock to a front-end loader, which loads the overburden onto haul trucks for transportation to the hollow-fill area where it will be graded and seeded. Small shovels can be used in place of dozers and front-end loaders for stripping and loading overburden into the haul trucks.

The exposed coal seam is mined by removing the coal from this first pit, using a smaller front-end loader to load the coal onto trucks for transportation away from the site. The coal trucks are frequently

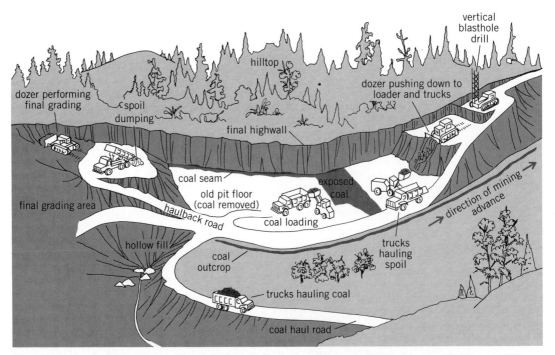

Fig. 1. Single-seam haulback operation. (*After N. P. Chironis, Haulback reclaims naturally, Coal Age, pp. 70–83, July 1977*)

provided by contracted companies that specialize in coal haulage.

The mining then proceeds to an adjacent section, or to the two adjacent sections on either side of the first cut if two pits are to be in simultaneous operation, moving in opposite directions around the hillside. Spoil from the second section (or sections) is hauled back along a road on the bench and is placed in the first pit.

Haulback mining permits the reclamation of the backfilled sections by grading, replacing the topsoil, and seeding with grasses; these operations are performed on a continuous cycle along with the removal of the overburden and coal. Careful planning and synchronization are required so that all equipment for stripping, coal hauling, and land reclamation keeps working without interfering with each other or remaining idle. Problems associated with water-quality control, such as acid-mine drainage, can be minimized by selective replacement of toxic material. Block-cut mining and lateral-movement mining are similar to haulback mining.

Area mining. This method is favored where the terrain is flat or only slightly rolling and where the mine site includes large stretches of land. The first cut, often referred to as a box cut, results in a long pit with a highwall on both sides of the cut. Overburden from the first pit is placed in a convenient hollow or else stored to be available later for filling the final cut.

A second cut is started adjacent to the first cut into which the second cut's overburden is placed. Strip by strip, the mining thus proceeds across the property. This type of mining is usually conducted with giant draglines or shovels (**Fig. 2**).

Mountaintop removal mining adapts area mining to the mountainous region. Instead of mining only the seams near the outcrops, the mountaintop method cuts across a ridge to recover all or considerably more of the coal. Haulback techniques can be applied to avoid spillage of spoil over the outcrops. Overall, the stripping ratio of overburden thickness to coal seam thickness is greater and more material must be removed for each ton of coal mined than with simple contour mining, but because such operations are on a larger scale, the total cost per ton of coal may not be greater and may even be lower. Also the area left on top of the ridge may be useful for home sites, commercial ventures, and airstrips. Regulations in the United States strictly control such deviations from the general requirement that all disturbed mine areas be returned to their approximate original contour wherever possible.

Open pit mining. This method is most often used where the coal beds are extremely thick, as in the subbituminous and lignite (**Fig. 3**) areas of the West and Southwest in the United States, and in the brown-coal areas of the world such as those in Germany.

Open pit mining is also favored where the seams are very deep or steeply sloped, as frequently found in the western United States and in the anthracite regions of Pennsylvania. Open-pit operations generally use the bench-mining approach, in which a series of benches or terraces forms the open pit. Benches are about 200 to 1500 ft (61 to 457 m) wide, depending on how much working room the stripping units need. Each bench gives access to a 30–50-ft (9–15 m) highwall. Side benches are created for hauling the overburden around the pit to the reclamation area. With

Fig 2. Team of draglines, working from spoil side as well as from cast-blasted highwall, strips lower seams from long terraced pit. (*From N. P. Chironis, Blast casting succeeds at multiseam western mine, Coal Age, November 1985*)

proper planning, reclamation can proceed at the same time as mining, so that the pit would seem to move as forward areas are opened and rear areas are restored. SEE OPEN PIT MINING.

Stripping equipment. Machinery used in surface mining includes draglines, shovels, scrapers, front-end loaders, dozers, and bucketwheel excavators.

Draglines. Draglines are the favored stripping tool in the United States because they can handle rocks of various sizes as well as all types of overburden. A dragline uses a huge bucket suspended from a fixed-angle boom and operated by cables. The larger units (**Fig. 4**) have buckets up to 220 yd³ (168 m³) capacity and booms up to 400 ft (122 m) long. The hoist cable raises and lowers the bucket and casts it outward during the machine's pivoting action. The lower cable drags the bucket toward the machine through the material being excavated. A dragline usually operates from the top of the highwall or spoil bank, which gives it greater maneuverability, reach, and dumping radius than a stripping shovel (the dragline's main competitor), which must work from the bottom of the pit.

Draglines have a long service life (typically over 30 years), high productivity, and low operating cost and are not labor-intensive. Some draglines have onboard computer-controlled display screens that inform of the machine's production rate, cycle by cycle as well as hourly. To distribute the huge weight [for example, a 220-yd³ (168-m³) machine weighs about 13,150 tons (12,000 metric tons)], a typical larger unit sits on its own base (tub) while operating, instead of on crawlers as do the smaller draglines. Such tub-sitters "walk" by means of "shoes" that lift the dragline and cam it forward. Large draglines are erected at the site and are costly to be dismantled and moved to a new site. Another type of walking dragline of modular construction, with bolted-together superstructure, can be taken apart, shipped to a new

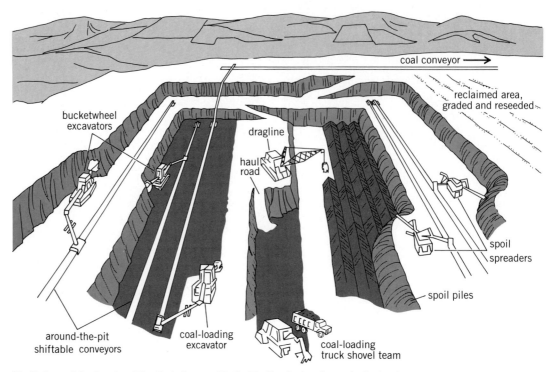

Fig. 3. Open pit lignite mine. (*After D. Jackson and L. Smith, New horizon looms for lignite, Coal Age, pp. 65–101, May 1981*)

site, and reerected more readily then the conventional all-welded units.

Stripping shovels. These shovels are so huge that they need to ride on eight crawlers, are sufficiently tall to be able to operate from the pit floor, and dump their loads of overburden directly onto spoil banks be-hind them. However, while they are being used effectively in some surface mining operations, they are being superseded by draglines and are no longer being manufactured.

Smaller electric and hydraulic shovels are used chiefly to strip and load overburden and coal directly

Fig. 4. Large dragline operating from the top of the highwall.

onto trucks. They are limited to shallower depths of overburden than draglines are, but they are especially effective for stripping partings between coal seams, for preparing benches for draglines, and for truck-shovel mining of multiple-bench open pits. Hydraulic backhoe excavators have long been used in construction, but most of these units are relatively small. Large crawler-mounted hydraulic excavators with front shovels have been developed for coal mining, mostly in removing overburden. Such shovels use diesel-powered hydraulics to power both moving and digging.

Scrapers. These are used to strip topsoil and overburden that needs little or no blasting and to spread the material precisely where it is wanted. They cut into the overburden and load it into their bowl while on the run. The bowl with its cutting edge is lowered for this purpose. When the bowl is filled, it is raised while the machine speeds to the disposal area, where the material is dumped on the run. Some scraper models have a built-in elevating conveyor to assist loading.

Front-end loaders. This equipment can excavate, transport, and load material rapidly. The loads are carried in a front bucket, usually for only a short distance, to a truck, conveyor hopper, or dumping area. For difficult digging conditions, loaders can be equipped with heavy-duty tires, toothed rock-buckets, and counterweights.

Dozers. Also known as bulldozers, these are crawler-mounted tractors that serve as the workhorses of the surface mine. Highly productive for short distances, they clear terrain, rip and remove overburden, level benches for draglines, push scrapers during loading, and level and grade haul roads and spoils for final reclamation. Wheeled dozers are also used for utility work. Special dozer blades with widths up to 48 ft (14 m) and even larger have been used for rapid grading of spoil.

Bucketwheel excavators. These are self-propelled, crawler-mounted units which, unlike draglines and shovels, excavate in a continuous mode by employing a large rotating wheel attached at the end of a long, movable boom. The wheel, resembling a waterwheel, consists of a series of shovellike buckets that, with an upward cutting action, scoop up the overburden and empty it into the machine's conveyor. The conveyor dumps the material directly onto spoil banks, onto moving trains, or onto a series of shiftable conveyors that transport the material around the mine to a spoil area, ready to be graded and reclaimed.

The sizes and types of bucketwheel excavators vary considerably. The huge types (**Fig. 5***a*), originally a German development, have been successful in Europe and in other parts of the world where the overburden is unconsolidated and essentially free of rocks. Such bucketwheel excavators have had only limited success at mine sites in the United States because of the harder ground and the frequency of hard rock and boulders. Smaller bucketwheel excavators (Fig. 5*b*) have been developed that can be used in the farm areas of Illinois and the lignite deposits in the southern United States to remove the upper, softer strata of overburden, leaving the lower levels to draglines or shovel-truck teams.

Augers. These are sometimes used with contour stripping in mountainous regions to recover additional coal that would otherwise be left. Augers operate on

the principle of the drill. After the stripping operation goes to its limit into the hillside and stops because the overburden is too deep to be economically removed, an auger machine is brought to the pit to boreholes into the exposed edge of the coal seam. The augers (the drills) can have diameters as large as 7 ft (2 m), and the machine can drill holes as deep as 200 ft (60 m). Auger machines are equipped with their own conveyors to feed the augered coal to waiting trucks. The augered holes are refilled before the pit is back-filled.

Drilling and blasting equipment. Such machinery is used where necessary to fracture the overburden into pieces that the excavating machines can handle easily. Electrically powered drills produce holes 1 ft (0.3 m) in diameter and larger, usually drilled downward from the surface to points just above the coal seam. The explosive commonly used is an ammonium-nitrate fuel-oil mixture (ANFO). It is either packaged in bags for insertion in the holes or pumped in from explosives trucks. Metallized slurries are sometimes used in wet holes.

Some surface mines use explosive techniques not only to break up the overburden but also to cast it sideways into the previous pit or to the spoil bank. Such explosive casting is performed with the aid of a sequential blasting machine and delay-type blasting caps and primers to set off a powerful, contained charge by having the holes fire sequentially at intervals of milliseconds.

Protecting the environment. Surface mine operations in the United States must meet strict federal and state regulations designed to protect the environment from any form of degradation and to assure that the mined site is restored to acceptable ecological conditions. The mined site must be made at least as productive in some way as it was before mining began. Farms, home sites, parks, wilderness, and recreation areas have been established on lands reclaimed after completion of surface mining. In some cases, because of the selective placement of overburdens, the reclaimed land shows higher pH (less acidic) levels than the original soil, and also better friability, which allows the roots of crop plants to reach deep into the soil and thus better resist the effects of drought.

The Surface Mining Control and Reclamation Act of 1977 established a procedure for regulating surface coal mining and reclamation operations. The regulatory program is administered by the federal Office of Surface Mining. In general, the regulations require separate removal and handling of all upper soil horizons capable of supporting vegetation cover. Topsoil may be redistributed only after the backfilled area has been properly prepared.

All disturbed areas must be returned to their approximate original contours wherever possible. Spoil must be replaced to eliminate all highwalls, spoil piles, and depressions. Final graded slopes may not exceed the premining slopes, and the regulatory authority can require lesser slopes. Highwalls must be eliminated and graded to achieve permissible stability. Cut-and-fill terraces may be used only when approved by the regulating authority.

Mountaintop-removal variances may be allowed if the activity includes the removal of an entire coal seam from the upper fraction of a mountain or hill and the resultant landscape is a plateau. Such a landscape must be designed to meet a postmining land use that will accommodate an industrial, commercial, ag-

Fig. 5. Bucketwheel excavators. (*a*) Largest type, daily capacity 144,000 yd³ (110,000 m³), shown in operation in a German lignite mine. (*b*) Smaller model, shown in operation in a Yugoslavian lignite mine.

ricultural, residential or public facility, including recreational facilities.

During reclamation all disturbed areas must be restored to enhance wherever practical the premining wildlife and fish habitats. Streams and other drainages must be revegetated to provide natural cover along their banks. *See* Mining.

Nicholas P. Chironis

Bibliography. N. P. Chironis (ed.), *Coal Age's New Handbook of Surface Mining*, 1981; N. P. Chironis, Surface mining of coal: Growth through evolution,*Coal Age*, pp. 69–81, June 1986; J. Kirk (ed.), *Western Surface Coal Mining*, 1989; E. S. Lyle, Jr., *Surface Mine Reclamation Manual*, 1986.

Systems ecology

The quantitative and analytical study of ecosystems, with an emphasis on whole-system performance. There is also strong emphasis on applying systems analysis techniques developed in several other fields (notably engineering, computer sciences, operations research, and applied mathematics) to ecological problems. In contrast to the phenomena treated in many ecological studies, research topics in systems ecology frequently concern phenomena that are on large spatial, temporal, or organizational scales. There is also a very strong focus on using mathematical models implemented on computers as analyzable surrogates for ecosystems and on formulating testable hypotheses about ecosystem function with the hope of eventually developing a theory of ecosystems. One of the principal objectives of systems ecologists is to understand how and under what conditions ecosystems change over time.

Origins. Although systems ecology is a relatively young science, many of its concepts have been a part of ecology for many years. A recognition that the interactions among the parts of an ecosystems cause the system as a whole to change in a predictable way over time is incorporated for example, in the ecological concept called succession. F. E. Clements, in papers written in the 1910s and 1920s, formulated several important concepts regarding ecological succession. Many of these ideas are still being debated by ecologists, but most ecologists would agree that the introduction of a dynamic and mechanistic view of ecological processes was Clements's most important contribution. Interestingly, in 1928 Clements cited many case studies as old as 1685 that involved the interactions among vegetation, soil, and the environment to produce evidence for dynamic change in terrestrial ecosystems. *See* Ecological succession.

An important period for the development of concepts that have become central to systems ecology was the decade 1935–1945. Central concepts originating in this period were the ecosystem concept, the trophic-dynamic concept, and compartment models.

Ecosystem concept. In 1935 A. G. Tansley introduced the term ecosystem. Pointing out the dynamic and interactive concept of the system used in physics, he defined the ecosystem as the system resulting from the integration of all living and nonliving factors of the environment. The Soviet ecologist V. N. Sukachev defined a related concept, which was termed the biogeocoenosis, as "any portion of the earth's surface containing a well-defined system of interact-

ing living (vegetation, animals, microorganisms) and dead (lithosphere, atmosphere, hydrosphere) natural components." Biogeocoenosis and ecosystem are used synonymously by modern ecologists.

Trophic-dynamic concept. In 1942 R. H. Lindeman developed the idea that the plants and animals could be grouped according to feeding groups or trophic levels. Lindeman reasoned that grouping the organisms in this way would allow the laws of thermodynamics to be applied to ecosystems. The ecosystems were dynamic in that energy was moving continuously through the trophic levels (producers, herbivores, carnivores) that made up the systems. The amount of energy stored in any one of these trophic levels was the consequence of the balance of material moving into and out of the trophic level. This idea had been anticipated in work done in 1925 by S. A. Graham, who viewed the decomposition and eventual disappearance of rotting logs as a result of the flow

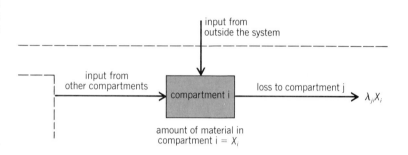

(a)

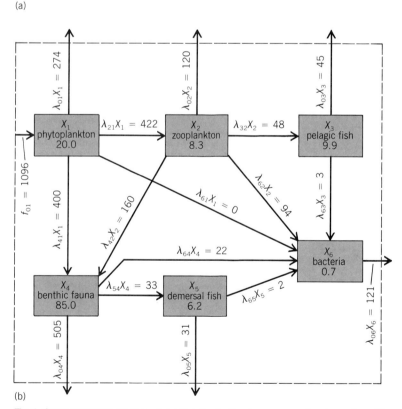

(b)

Fig. 1. Compartment model concept. (a) Notation for flow from a compartment over time. (b) Pathways diagrammed for an ecosystem—the English Channel. Here f_0 is the input to the system and equals 1096 kcal m^{-2} yr^{-1}. The standing crops (the amount of material in each compartment) are in units of kcal m^{-2}. The transfers between compartments ($m_{ji}X_i$) are in units of kcal m^{-2} yr^{-1}. (*From B. C. Patten, ed., Systems Analysis and Simulation in Ecology, vol. 2, Academic Press, 1972*)

of food through the fungi and insects that inhabited the log. The trophic-dynamic concept was an important development in that it emphasized the functional role of plants and animals and in that it treated the flow of material through an ecosystem, both of which are still central topics in systems ecology. *See Food web.*

Compartment models. Physiologists in the 1930s began to study the dynamics of various substances in vertebrates, and conducted experiments in which dyes (and later radioactive tracers) were injected and tracked through the body. Interest in the analysis of these experiments led to the development of a mathematical theory called tracer kinetics or compartment modeling. In tracer theory, the body is divided into a set of mutually exclusive compartments (such as blood, tissue, or bone) and the rate of change of each compartment is expressed as a differential equation. The resultant model can be used to simulate the dynamic change of the compartments over time.

The circulation of material through a system can be viewed as flows between pairs of the compartments that make up the system. In a compartment model, the flow from a compartment over time (**Fig. 1***a*) is taken as a constant proportion of the amount of material in the compartment. In an ecosystem compartment model, the amount of material in a compartment is denoted X_i (for the amount of material in compartment number i). The flow of material from compartment i to compartment j is often denoted $\lambda_{ji}X_i$ (where λ_{ji} is the rate constant for the flow from compartment i to compartment j). Rate constants are dimensioned in units of inverse time, while compartments are usually dimensioned in units of mass or energy. Thus, the product of a rate constant and a compartment are in units of mass (or energy) flows per unit time.

Equations for the change of a compartment over time are formed by collecting the terms for the flows in and out of a compartment in a differential equation for that compartment. The set of such differential equations for all the compartments in an ecosystem is called the system of equations for that system. The system of equations for a given ecosystem is linked internally by common terms among the equations. Such common terms arise because a flow such as $\lambda_{ji}X_i$ would appear as a negative term (for material lost) in the equation for compartment i and also as a positive term (for material gained) in the equation for compartment j. These linkages or pathways correspond to the arrows between boxes in an ecosystem diagram such as Fig. 1*b*. Since a compartment model's formulation accounts for all material in the system, models are said to be constrained by mass balance, meaning that they neither create nor destroy matter (or energy) and that this condition limits to a degree the mathematical form of the system of equations.

A number of properties of compartment models have been studied by mathematicians; such theoretical background has proven to be invaluable to systems ecologists. Many of these derivations are abstract. As an example of one of the properties of compartment-models and of the use of such abstract properties in real systems, the sum of all the losses from a compartment can be determined by adding up all of the rate constants for the compartment i to obtain a value called the turnover rate (constant) for compartment i. The inverse of this rate constant is called the turnover time (T) and is the length of time that the cumulative loss from the compartment will equal the amount of material in the compartment under the condition that its inputs and outputs are in state of balance.

One mathematical attribute of a compartment model is that if the compartment is at a state of equilibrium (inputs = outputs), the compartment turnover time equals the amount of time that is required for 63% of the original material in the compartment to be transferred elsewhere. The practical consequence of this property (and other similar properties) is that one can use the disappearance of a small amount of radioactive material from a compartment to determine the turnover time and turnover rate of parts of ecosystems. This has allowed the development of studies of the large-scale movement of materials through natural environments. These studies have increased the understanding of the way that natural ecosystems process material, and have proven invaluable in the evaluation of the movement of pollutants in the environment.

Ongoing research. In the 1960s and 1970s, systems ecologists were frequently involved in develop-

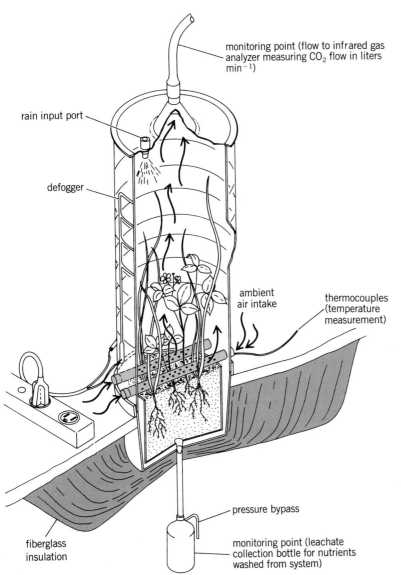

monitoring point (flow to infrared gas analyzer measuring CO_2 flow in liters min^{-1})

rain input port

defogger

ambient air intake

thermocouples (temperature measurement)

fiberglass insulation

pressure bypass

monitoring point (leachate collection bottle for nutrients washed from system)

Fig. 2. Cross section of encased microcosm. The ecosystem-level monitoring points for CO_2 and nutrient export are shown. (*From P. Van Voris et al., Ecology, 61:1352–1360, 1980*)

ment of models that could be used to coordinate multidisciplinary studies and that also could be used to predict the long-term behavior of ecosystems. Probably the most conspicuous case of this sort was in the international research program called the International Biological Programme (IBP), which involved hundreds of ecologists and other scientists working in coordinated studies to compare and contrast the functioning of a range of natural ecosystems. Model development work by systems ecologists in the IBP projects and in similar programs served to identify new research problems; work on these problems, some of which are outlined below, occupies much of the ongoing research of systems ecologists.

Simulation modeling. The use of computer models to predict the behavior of a system over time has developed as a central topic of study in systems ecology. In the construction of a simulation model, the scientific problem is to construct a model that uses diverse information about ecological processes and that can predict ecosystem behavior over time. The hope in developing these models is that the inclusion of the details of the ecological processes will allow the models to predict what ecosystems will do even under conditions that have not been observed. For example, a simulation model of an animal population might incorporate the birth rate of the population as a function of the amount of food, and the temperature and the death rate might be a function of the severity of the winter. Such a model might provide predictions of the change in the population under a range of conditions of food, temperatures, and winter severity—including some combinations of conditions that have not been observed.

The extrapolation of system behavior outside the range of calibration of a model can, however, result in considerable error. In using a simulation model it is important to have an estimate of the degree to which the predictions from a model should be believed. Such model validation procedures involve testing the ability of a model to correctly predict data that was not used in the development of the model (independent data) and to determine from such model tests the domain of applicability, or the set of conditions for which the model appears to have predictive power.

Engineering applications. Ecosystem models can be studied by using a wide range of techniques that originate in the engineering sciences. These applications are often quite practical in their orientation, and include such typical problems as how frequently an ecosystem should be sampled to see change in the system; what the best part of an ecosystem to monitor is in order to detect a pollutant in the system and how the pattern of material released into natural systems affects the concentrations of that material in parts of the ecosystem at later points in time. There is also an interest in designing miniature ecosystems (microcosms) that could be used experimentally to determine properties of larger natural ecosystems (**Fig. 2**).

Ecosystem theory. Theoretical work on ecosystems frequently is based on analysis of ecosystem models to gain insights as to how natural ecosystems function. In part, this emphasis on the use of models has been brought about by the high expense of actually performing experiments on ecosystems. Because of the cost of ecosystem research, there has been an interest in using ''natural experiments'' to substitute for the experimental methods that are normally used to test theory in science. For example, a forest that has been subjected to a wildfire might be studied to test theoretical predictions about disturbances on ecosystems. A model that predicted the response of ecosystems to a change in climate could also be tested to see if it could predict the natural pattern of the vegetation at different altitudes (and different microclimatic conditions) on a large mountain. While these natural experiments are useful, variables are not as well controlled as is the case in most laboratory experiments, and as a result the natural experiments generally do not test the model predictions in an unambiguous way. For this reason, there is an increasing need for experimental work at the ecosystem level. Important theoretical topics deal with the properties of ecosystems that make them resistant to change (system stability problems), the understanding of limits to the productivity of ecosystems, and the determination of single factors that can be used to characterize ecosystems for comparative purposes. Since ecosystem theory is so dependent upon models, there is also an interest in investigating attributes of ecosystems that appear to hold true regardless of which model formulations are used to represent the ecosystem. These ''robust results'' are thought to be less subject to biases inadvertently introduced in the model formulation.

Time and space scale. Space and time scales have proven difficult to incorporate into certain models. For example, it has proven to be difficult to incorporate a detailed model of the processes of photosynthesis in models that grow trees over periods longer than a few years. Photosynthesis (the processes by which plants use light to combine carbon dioxide and water to make sugar) is essential for tree growth, but the mechanisms that control tree growth are usually not explicitly included in models of photosynthesis. Such seemingly paradoxical outcomes have led systems ecologists to become interested in the effect of time and space scales in the manifestation of biological processes at the ecosystem level. One area that has sprung from these investigations is hierarchy theory, which attempts to organize the patterns of time, space, and phenomena in a unified theory. SEE ECOLOGY; ECOLOGY, APPLIED; ECOSYSTEM.

H. H. Shugart

Bibliography. T. P. Burns and M. Higashi (eds.), *Theoretical Studies of Ecosystems*, 1990; *Ecological Modelling* (journal), 20 issues per year; R. L. Kitching, *An Introduction to Ecological Modelling*, 1984; S. A. Levin (ed.), *Applied Mathematical Ecology*, 1989; H. T. Odum, *Systems Ecology*, 1983.

Taiga

A zone of forest vegetation encircling the Northern Hemisphere between the arctic-subarctic tundras in the north and the steppes, hardwood forests, and prairies in the south. The chief characteristic of the taiga is the prevalence of forests dominated by conifers. The taiga varies considerably in tree species from one major geographical region to another, and within regions there are distinct latitudinal subzones. The dominant trees are particular species of spruce, pine, fir, and larch. Other conifers, such as hemlock, white cedar, and juniper, occur locally, and the broad-

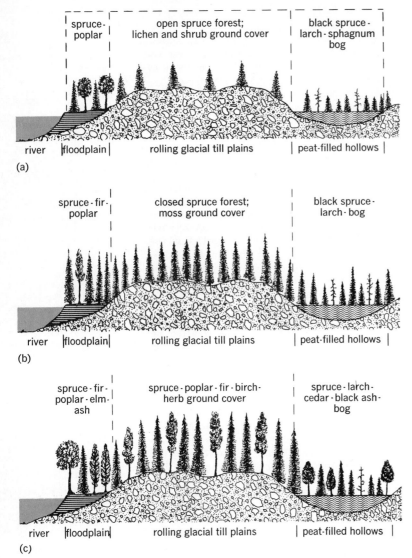

spruce-poplar | open spruce forest; lichen and shrub ground cover | black spruce-larch-sphagnum bog

river | floodplain | rolling glacial till plains | peat-filled hollows

(a)

spruce-fir-poplar | closed spruce forest; moss ground cover | black spruce-larch-bog

river | floodplain | rolling glacial till plains | peat-filled hollows

(b)

spruce-fir-poplar-elm-ash | spruce-poplar-fir-birch-herb ground cover | spruce-larch-cedar-black ash-bog

river | floodplain | rolling glacial till plains | peat-filled hollows

(c)

Schematic profile of the three main subzones of the North American taiga, showing the main forest assemblages on three of the more important landform types. (a) Northern taiga. (b) Middle taiga. (c) Southern taiga.

leaved deciduous trees, birch and poplar, are common associates in the southern taiga regions. Taiga is a Siberian word, equivalent to "boreal forest." SEE FOREST AND FORESTRY; TUNDRA.

Climate. The northern and southern boundaries of the taiga are determined by climatic factors, of which temperature is most important. However, aridity controls the forest-steppe boundary in central Canada and western Siberia. In North America there is a broad coincidence between the northern and southern limits of the taiga and the mean summer and winter positions of the arctic air mass. In the taiga the average temperature in the warmest month, July, is greater than 50°F (10°C), distinguishing it from the forest-tundra and tundra to the north; however, less than four of the summer months have averages above 50°F (10°C), in contrast to the summers of the deciduous forest further south, which are longer and warmer. Taiga winters are long, snowy, and cold—the coldest month has an average temperature below 32°F (0°C). Permafrost occurs in the northern taiga. It is important to note that climate is as significant as vegetation in defining taiga. Thus, many of the world's conifer

forests, such as those of the American Pacific Northwest, are excluded from the taiga by their high precipitation and mild winters.

Subzones. The taiga can be divided into three subzones (see **illus.**) in almost all of the regions which it occupies; these divisions are recognized mainly by the particular structure of the forests rather than by changes in tree composition. These subdivisions are the northern taiga, the middle taiga, and the southern taiga.

Northern taiga. This subzone is characterized on moderately drained uplands by open-canopy forests, dominated in Alaska, Canada, and Europe by spruce and in Siberia by spruce, larch, and pine. The well-spaced trees and low ground vegetation, usually rich lichen carpets and low heathy shrubs, yield a beautiful parkland landscape; this is exemplified best in North America by the taiga of Labrador and Northern Quebec. This subzone is seldom reached by roads and railways, in part because the trees seldom exceed 30 ft (9 m) in height and have limited commercial value. These forests are important as winter range of Barren Ground caribou, but in many parts of the drier interior of North America their area has been decreased by fire, started both by lightning and by humans.

Middle taiga. This subzone is a broad belt of closed-canopy evergreen forests on uplands. The dark, somber continuity is broken only where fires, common in the drier interiors of the continents, have given temporary advantage to the rapid colonizers, pine, paper birch, and aspen poplar. The deeply shaded interior of mature white and black spruce forests in the middle taiga of Alaska and Canada permits the growth of few herbs and shrubs; the ground is mantled by a dense carpet of mosses. Here, as elsewhere in the taiga, depressions are filled by peat bogs, dominated in North America by black spruce and in Eurasia by pine. Everywhere there is a thick carpet of sphagnum moss associated with such heath shrubs as bog cranberry, Labrador tea, and leatherleaf. Alluvial sites bear a well-grown forest yielding merchantable timber, with fir, white spruce, and black poplar as the chief trees.

Southern taiga. This subzone is characterized on moderately drained soils throughout the Northern Hemisphere by well-grown trees (mature specimens up to 95 ft or 29 m) of spruce, fir, pine, birch, and poplar. These trees are represented by different species in North America, Europe, and Siberia. Of the three taiga zones, this has been exploited and disturbed to the greatest extent by humans, and relatively few extensive, mature, and virgin stands remain. In northwestern Europe this subzone has been subject to intensive silviculture for several decades and yields forests rich in timber and pulpwood. In Alaska and Canada the forests have a much shorter history of forest management, but they yield rich resources for the forest industries. SEE FOREST MANAGEMENT.

Fauna. In addition to caribou, the taiga forms the core area for the natural ranges of black bear, moose, wolverine, marten, timber wolf, fox, mink, otter, muskrat, and beaver. The southern fringes of the taiga are used for recreation.

J. C. Ritchie

Bibliography. A. Bryson, *Geographical Bulletin*, vol. 8, 1966; *Good's School Atlas*, 1950; J. P. Kimmins, *Forest Ecology*, 1984; *New Oxford Atlas*, 1975.

Temperature adaptation

The ability of animals to survive and function at widely different temperatures is a result of specific physiological adaptations. Temperature is an all-pervasive attribute of the environment that limits the activity, distribution, and survival of animals. Ocean temperatures range from 28 to 86°F (−2 to 30°C), but considerably warmer temperatures are found near deep-sea hydrothermal vents (up to 662°F or 350°C), backwaters of desert streams (109°F or 43°C), and geothermal springs (194–212°F or 90–100°C). Air temperatures range from −94°F (−70°C) in polar regions to 176°F (80°C) at the desert surface. Although some bacteria and blue-green algae live at temperatures up to 230°F (110°C), life processes are generally restricted to the temperatures between 32 and 113°F (0 and 45°C), and most animals live within an even narrower range. Limits for reproduction and development are generally narrower than those for survival of adults.

Changes in temperature influence biological systems, both by determining the rate of chemical reactions and by specifying equilibria (**Fig. 1**). Because temperature exerts a greater effect upon the percentage of molecules that possess sufficient energy to react (that is, to exceed the activation energy) than upon the average kinetic energy of the system, modest reductions in temperature (for example, from 77 to 59°F or from 25 to 15°C, corresponding to only a 3% reduction in average kinetic energy) produce a marked depression (two- to threefold) in reaction rate. In addition, temperature specifies the equilibria between the formation and disruption of the noncovalent (electrostatic, hydrophobic, and hydrogen-bonding) interactions that stabilize both the higher levels of protein structure and macromolecular aggregations such as biological membranes. Maintenance of an appropriate structural flexibility is a requirement for both enzyme catalysis and membrane function, yet cold temperatures constrain while warm temperatures relax the conformational flexibility of both proteins and membrane lipids, thereby perturbing biological function.

Animals are classified into two broad groups depending on the factors that determine body tempera-

ture. For ectotherms, body temperature is determined by sources of heat external to the body; levels of resting metabolism (and heat production) are low, and mechanisms for retaining heat are limited. Such animals are frequently termed poikilothermic or cold-blooded, because the body temperature often conforms to the temperature of the environment. In contrast, endotherms produce more metabolic heat and possess specialized mechanisms for heat retention. Therefore, body temperature is elevated above ambient temperature; some endotherms (termed homeotherms or warm-blooded animals) maintain a relatively constant body temperature. There is no natural taxonomic division between ecto- and endotherms. Most invertebrates, fish, amphibians, and reptiles are ectotherms, while true homeothermy is restricted to birds and mammals. However, flying insects commonly elevate the temperature of their thoracic musculature prior to and during flight (to 96°F or 36°C), and several species of tuna retain metabolic heat in their locomotory musculature via a vascular countercurrent heat exchanger.

Endotherms. Homeotherms, by defending a constant body temperature, circumvent the problems associated with the maintenance of physiological function under varying body temperatures. The ability to regulate body temperature is dependent upon a suite of physiological adaptations involving the management of heat production, the distribution of heat within the body, and the exchange of heat with the environment (**Fig. 2**). When stressed by cold, homeotherms maintain body temperature by both shivering and nonshivering thermogenesis, that is, the production of heat by processes that do not involve muscle contraction. Both processes are strictly controlled, and the regulated heat production is just sufficient to maintain body temperature. Nonshivering thermogenesis is of particular interest, because the principal site of heat production occurs in brown adipose tissue, a tissue whose sole function is thermogenesis. Brown adipose tissue is a particularly important source of heat in young or cold-acclimated mammals and in arousing hibernators. Conversely, when stressed by heat, homeotherms lose heat to their environment by the evaporation of water from some body surface. In cattle, horses, and humans, high rates of evaporation are accomplished by sweating, whereas in species that do not sweat (dogs and cats), panting occurs. Insulation, in the form of subcutaneous adipose tissue and external pelage, is an adaptation to reduce the cost of thermoregulation in cold environments. Circulatory adaptations permitting the redistribution of blood flow are also important to thermoregulation. When body temperature rises, large volumes of blood are shunted through skin capillaries to increase heat transfer to the environment; conversely, peripheral blood flow is reduced in response to hypothermia in order to curtail heat loss.

Ectotherms. Many ectotherms are essentially isothermal with their environment; even the muscles of actively swimming fish are within 1.8°F (1°C) of the water temperature. Consequently, geographic, seasonal, or diurnal fluctuations in temperature pose particular problems for the maintenance of physiological function in these animals. Yet, although metabolic rates are depressed by acute exposure to cold, many ectotherms (but not all—some ectotherms become torpid at low temperature as a means of conserving energy) remain active in the cold and exhibit similar

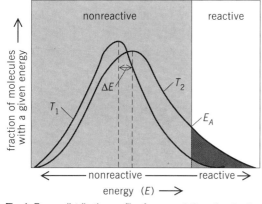

Fig. 1. Energy distribution profiles for a population of molecules at two different temperatures $T_2 > T_1$. The peaks in the two curves represent the average energy contents, and ΔE is the temperature-induced change in average energy content; E_A is the activation energy, and on the right the shaded sections under the two curves show the change in the proportion of molecules with $E > E_A$.

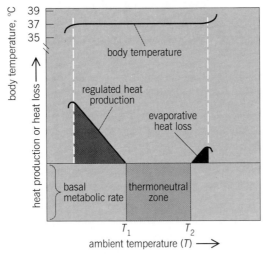

Fig. 2. Relationship between heat production and heat loss as a function of ambient temperature for a homeotherm. Thermoregulation can be achieved at minimal metabolic cost in the thermoneutral zone (defined by T_1 and T_2). Broken lines define the limits of ambient temperature over which a homeotherm can successfully defend (or maintain) its body temperature. $°F = (°C × 1.8) + 32$.

levels of activity at seasonal extremes of temperature. Similarly, arctic and antarctic ectotherms perform as effectively near 32°F (0°C) as tropical species do at 86°F (30°C). Maintenance of similar rates of activity at widely different body temperatures is a clear indication that ectotherms can adapt to temperature extremes. At the cellular level, thermal adaptations are most commonly reflected in the lipid composition of cell membranes and the catalytic properties of enzymes.

Lipid-mediated adaptations. Membranes perform many vital cell functions, including regulating the exchange of material between the cell and its environment; storing energy in the form of transmembrane ion gradients; providing a matrix in which many metabolic processes are organized; and controlling the flow of information between cell and its surroundings by generating intracellular messengers in response to extracellular signals. Yet, the physical properties of phospholipids—the primary structural elements of biological membranes—are markedly temperature-dependent. With cooling, the acyl domain of phospholipids is transformed from a fluid to a gel phase. Such phase transitions significantly perturb membrane function, for in the gel phase the membrane is rigid, passive permeability is reduced, and the activity of membrane-associated enzymes declines. Conversely, at elevated temperatures membranes become hyperfluid and leaky to ions (loss of potassium from muscle cells is a contributing factor in heat death).

Ectotherms overcome these problems by restructuring their membranes so that lipids of appropriate physical properties are matched to the prevailing ambient temperature. As temperature drops, high-melting lipids are replaced by lower-melting ones; consequently, membranes remain fluid at cold temperatures. The melting point of membrane lipids is lowered primarily by increasing the degree of acyl chain unsaturation, which introduces a kink into the acyl chain and prevents close packing at low temperatures. Two metabolic adjustments contribute to this restructuring process: increased activities of acyl

chain desaturases at cold temperatures, and the operation of a deacylation–reacylation cycle, which permits the acyl chain composition to be altered independently of the rest of the phospholipid molecule. In addition, phospholipids with small, as opposed to bulky, head groups also increase in abundance at low temperatures, and the resulting rise in the ratio of conically to cylindrically shaped lipids may offset the direct effects of temperature change upon lipid packing (that is, it may disrupt packing at low temperature). Differences in lipid composition between polar and tropical species resemble those between seasonally adapted individuals of temperature species.

As a consequence of lipid restructuring, membrane fluidity is relatively constant when compared at the respective growth temperatures to which an animal has become adapted, even though varying markedly with acute changes in temperature. This phenomenon is known as homeoviscous adaptation.

Protein-mediated adaptations. In addition to the homeoviscous regulation of membrane fluidity, ectoderms display other adaptations that permit function over a broad temperature range. These range from evolutionarily fixed differences in the structure and function of specific proteins to seasonal adjustments in the rates and patterns of energy metabolism.

Enzyme structure and function vary interspecifically in a manner consistent with the conservation of catalytic rates and regulatory properties at different temperatures. The catalytic efficiency of enzymes is inversely correlated with habitat or cell temperature. For example, lactate dehydrogenase from an antarctic fish produces nearly twice as much product per minute per mole of enzyme as does the homologous enzyme from rabbit muscle when compared at 41°F (5°C). Such increased catalytic efficiencies typical of ectothermic enzymes are a reflection of a lowered activation energy. It has been postulated that differences in catalytic efficiency between homologous enzymes of ectotherms and endotherms reflect varying amounts of weak bond formation between the enzyme and substrate during the activation step of catalysis. The dis-

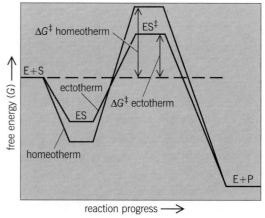

Fig. 3. Energy profiles for the reactions catalyzed by homologous enzymes from an ectotherm and a homeotherm. Note that the activation free-energy barrier is higher for the homeothermic than the ectothermic enzyme because of the tighter binding of substrate by the former. E = free enzyme; S = free substrate; P = free product; ES = enzyme substrate complex, not in the activated state; ES‡ = enzyme substrate complex in the activated state; $\Delta G^‡$ = free energy of activation. (*After P. W. Hochachka and G. N. Somero, Biochemical Adaptation, Princeton University Press, 1984*)

Asia and Europe. The principal plains of Eurasia and the Americas lie on the Atlantic and Arctic sides of the cordilleras, but are in part separated from the Atlantic by lesser areas of rough terrain.

Most of Africa and Australia, together with the eastern uplands of South America and the peninsulas of Arabia and India, show great similarity to one another. They lack true cordilleran belts, and are composed largely of upland plains and tablelands, locally surmounted by groups of hills and mountains, and in many places descending to the sea in rough, dissected escarpments.

Edwin H. Hammond

Terrestrial ecosystem

A community of organisms and their environment that occurs on the land masses of continents and islands. Terrestrial ecosystems are distinguished from aquatic ecosystems by the lower availability of water and the consequent importance of water as a limiting factor. Terrestrial ecosystems are characterized by greater temperature fluctuations on both a diurnal and seasonal basis than occur in aquatic ecosystems in similar climates, because water has a high specific heat, a high heat of vaporization, and a high heat of fusion compared with the atmosphere, all of which tend to ameliorate thermal fluctuations. The availability of light is greater in terrestrial ecosystems than in aquatic ecosystems because the atmosphere is more transparent than water. Gases are more available in terrestrial ecosystems than in aquatic ecosystems. Those gases include carbon dioxide that serves as a substrate for photosynthesis, oxygen that serves as a substrate in aerobic respiration, and nitrogen that serves as a substrate for nitrogen fixation. Terrestrial environments are segmented into a subterranean portion from which most water and ions are obtained, and an atmospheric portion from which gases are obtained and where the physical energy of light is transformed into the organic energy of carbon-carbon bonds through the process of photosynthesis.

Extent. The Earth has an estimated surface area of 197,272,000 mi^2 (510,934,000 km^2) of which about 29%, or 57,200,000 mi^2 (148,100,000 km^2), is occupied by land. About 1,540,000 mi^2 (4,000,000 km^2) of the land surface is occupied by fresh-water ecosystems of lakes, streams, and marshes; so terrestrial ecosystems occupy 55,660,000 mi^2 (144,150,000 km^2), or 28.2%, of Earth's surface.

Earth and the other planets are believed to be about 4.5 billion years old; the earliest fossil life forms are about 3.5 billion years old. The first terrestrial organisms appeared in the Silurian Period, about 425 million years ago. Therefore, terrestrial ecosystems have an age no greater than 9.4% of the total age of the Earth and 12.1% of the duration of life on Earth.

Principal organisms. Although they are comparatively recent in the history of life and occupy a much smaller portion of Earth's surface than marine ecosystems, terrestrial ecosystems have been a major site of adaptive radiation of both plants and animals. Major plant taxa in terrestrial ecosystems are members of the division Magnoliophyta (flowering plants), of which there are about 225,000 species in the class Magnoliopsida (dicots) and 50,000 species in the class Liliopsida (monocots), and the division Pinophyta (conifers), of which there are about 500 species. Members of the division Bryophyta (mosses and liverworts), of which there are about 24,000 species, are also important in some terrestrial ecosystems. Major animal taxa in terrestrial ecosystems include the classes Insecta (insects) with about 900,000 species, Aves (birds) with 8500 species, and Mammalia (mammals) with approximately 4100 species.

Organisms in terrestrial ecosystems have adaptations that allow them to obtain water when the entire body is no longer bathed in that fluid, means of transporting the water from limited sites of acquisition to the rest of the body, and means of preventing the evaporation of water from body surfaces. They also have traits that provide body support in the atmosphere, a much less buoyant medium than water, and other traits that render them capable of withstanding the extremes of temperature, wind, and humidity that characterize terrestrial ecosystems. Finally, the organisms in terrestrial ecosystems have evolved many methods of transporting gametes in environments where fluid flow is much less effective as a transport medium.

Energy and chemical flow. The organisms in terrestrial ecosystems are integrated into a functional unit by specific, dynamic relationships due to the coupled processes of energy and chemical flow. Those relationships can be summarized by schematic diagrams of trophic webs, which place organisms according to their feeding relationships. The base of the food web is occupied by green plants, which are the only organisms capable of utilizing the energy of the Sun and inorganic nutrients obtained from the soil to produce organic molecules. The total living mass present in an ecosystem at any given time is referred to as biomass. The change in biomass through time is referred to as net productivity. Productivity due to the green plants and microorganisms is termed primary productivity while that due to animals is secondary productivity. Productivity will always diminish from stage to stage in the trophic web due to the laws of thermodynamics. This limitation is summarized by the equation $P_g = P_n + R$, where P_g is gross productivity, or total energy entering a trophic level, P_n is the net productivity of that trophic level, and R is the respiratory cost of maintaining that trophic level. For green plants, P_g is the energy initially captured in photosynthesis, R is the cost of maintaining the organisms, and P_n is the energy remaining to produce a biomass increment. Since it is only this biomass increment that is available to higher trophic levels, net productivity must always diminish at progressively higher trophic levels. SEE BIOLOGICAL PRODUCTIVITY; BIOMASS; FOOD WEB.

Terrestrial food webs can be broken into two segments based on the status of the plant material that enters them. Grazing food webs are associated with the consumption of living plant material by herbivores. Detritus food webs are associated with the consumption of dead plant material by detritivores. The relative importance of those two types of food webs varies considerably in different types of terrestrial ecosystems. Grazing food webs are more important in grasslands, where over half of net primary productivity may be consumed by herbivores. Detritus food webs are more important in forests, where less than 5% of net primary productivity may be consumed by herbivores. SEE SOIL ECOLOGY.

Energy flow is unidirectional in ecosystems, with a portion of that energy dissipated at each trophic level.

Area and productivity of the various terrestrial ecosystems*

Type	Area occupied, 10^6 km^2	Mean net primary productivity, g/(m^2)(year)	Total annual productivity, 10^9 tons/year
Tundra	8.0	140	1.1
Desert	42.0	40	1.7
Temperate grassland	9.0	600	5.4
Woodland and shrubland	8.5	700	6.0
Cultivated land	14.0	650	9.1
Boreal forest	12.0	000	9.0
Savanna	15.0	900	13.5
Temperate forest	12.0	1250	14.9
Tropical forest	24.5	2000	49.4

*1 km^2 = 0.386 mi^2; 1 g/m^2 = 0.029 oz/yd^2; 1 ton = 0.9 metric ton.
Source: After R. H. Whittaker, *Communities and Ecosystems*, 2d ed., Macmillan, 1975.

As energy is dissipated, nutrients are released back into the environment. Nutrient flow, therefore, is cyclic. Energy flow and nutrient flow are impossible to separate functionally since they are intimately coupled. Energy flow will depend upon the rate at which nutrients are recycled, and nutrient flow will depend upon the availability of energy. SEE BIOGEOCHEMISTRY; ECOLOGICAL ENERGETICS.

Seasonality. Because of the marked seasonality of most terrestrial ecosystems, due to either temperature fluctuations in temperate locations or rainfall fluctuations in tropical locations, there are corresponding fluctuations in net primary productivity. The plants may sometimes be able to complete their life cycle in a brief time period, as do annual plants in the desert, or they may undergo periods of dormancy, as do deciduous trees in temperate forests. Similarly, animals either may hibernate during unfavorable periods or may migrate to other locations where conditions are more favorable. Many birds, for example, migrate from temperate latitudes during summer to tropical latitudes during winter in the temperate zones. Others may even migrate between the respective summer seasons in north and south temperate zones. Those animals that remain active in terrestrial ecosystems during periods of low primary productivity must have adaptations that allow them to subsist during unfavorable periods, often storing fat during productive periods and depleting those reserves during unfavorable periods.

Types. There is one type of extensive terrestrial ecosystem due solely to human activities and eight types that are natural ecosystems. Those natural ecosystems reflect the variation of precipitation and temperature over Earth's surface (see **table**). The smallest land areas are occupied by tundra and temperate grassland ecosystems, and the largest land area is occupied by tropical forest. The most productive ecosystems are temperate and tropical forests, and the least productive are deserts and tundras. Cultivated lands, which together with grasslands and savannas utilized for grazing are referred to as agroecosystems, are of intermediate extent and productivity. Because of both their areal extent and their high average productivity, tropical forests are the most productive of all terrestrial ecosystems, contributing 45% of total estimated net primary productivity on land. Due to their importance in productivity, tropical forests are believed to play an important role in the global carbon budget. There is increasing concern that deforestation of tropical ecosystems associated with agricultural de-velopment may contribute to increasing atmospheric carbon dioxide concentrations that may lead to climatic change. SEE DESERT; ECOLOGICAL COMMUNITIES; ECOSYSTEM; FOREST AND FORESTRY; GRASSLAND ECOSYSTEM; SAVANNA; TUNDRA.

S. J. McNaughton

Bibliography. W. B. Clapham, Jr., *Natural Ecosystems*, 2d ed., 1983; R. T. T. Forman and M. Godron, *Landscape Ecology*, 1986; E. J. Kormondy, *Concepts of Ecology*, 3d ed., 1984; E. P. Odum, *Basic Ecology*, 1983; R. E. Ricklefs, *Ecology*, 3d ed., 1989.

Terrestrial water

The total inventory of water on the Earth. Water is unevenly distributed over the Earth's surface in oceans, rivers, and lakes. The **table** gives a comparative view of the world's water.

Ocean. The world ocean—139,500,000 mi^2 (361,300,000 km^2) of it—contains 317,000,000 mi^3 (1,321,000,000 km^3) of salt water. The average depth of the ocean basins is about 12,500 ft (3.7 km). If the basins were shallow, seas would spread far onto the continents, and dry land areas would consist chiefly of a few major archipelagoes—high mountain ranges projecting above the sea.

Atmosphere. Considered as a continuous body of fluid, the atmosphere is another kind of ocean. Yet, in view of the total amount of precipitation on land areas in the course of a year, one of the most astonishing world water facts is the very small amount of water in the atmosphere at any given time. The volume of the lower 7 mi (11 km) of the atmosphere—the realm of weather phenomena—is roughly four times the volume of the world ocean. But the atmosphere contains only about 3100 mi^3 (12,900 km^3) of water, chiefly in the form of invisible vapor, some of which is transported overland by air currents. If all vapor were suddenly precipitated from the air onto the Earth's surface, it would form a layer only about 1 in. (25 mm) thick. A heavy rainstorm on a given area may remove only a small percentage of the water from the air mass that passes over. However, some land areas receive more than 400 in. (10 m) of precipitation per year. Several inches of rain can fall during a single storm in a few minutes or hours. Rain-yielding air masses are in motion, and as the water-depleted air moves on, new moisture-laden air takes its place above the area of precipitation.

The source of most atmospheric water is the ocean,

World's estimated water supply*

Location	Surface area, mi² (km²)	Water volume, mi³ (km³)	Percentage of total water
Surface water			
Fresh-water lakes	330,000 (855,000)	30,000 (130,000)	0.009
Saline lakes and inland seas	270,000 (700,000)	25,000 (104,000)	0.008
Average in stream channels	—	300 (1300)	0.0001
Subsurface water			
Vadose water (includes soil moisture)		16,000 (67,000)	0.005
Groundwater within depth of a half mile	50,000,000 (130,000,000)	1,000,000 (4,200,000)	0.31
Groundwater, deep-lying		1,000,000 (4,200,000)	0.31
Other water locations			
Ice caps and glaciers	6,900,000 (18,000,000)	7,000,000 (29,000,000)	2.15
Atmosphere (at sea level)	197,000,000 (510,000,000)	3,100 (12,900)	0.001
World ocean	139,500,000 (361,300,000)	317,000,000 (1,321,000,000)	97.2
TOTALS (rounded)		326,000,000 (1,360,000,000)	100

*1 mi = 1.6 km; 1 mi² = 2.6 km²; 1 mi³ = 4.2 km³.

from which this water is derived by evaporation. Evaporation, vapor transport, and precipitation constitute a major arc of the hydrologic cycle—the continuous movement of water from ocean to atmosphere to land and back to the sea. Rivers return water to the sea along one chord of the arc. In a subterranean arc of the cycle, underground bodies of water discharge some directly into rivers and some directly into the sea. SEE ATMOSPHERE; MARITIME METEOROLOGY.

Rivers. Measurements of only the few principal streams on a continent afford a basis for reasonably accurate estimation of the total runoff item in a continental water balance. The small streams are important locally, but they contribute only minor amounts of the total water discharged. Thus it is possible to estimate the total runoff of all the rivers of the world, even though many of them have not been measured accurately. Sixty-six principal rivers of the world discharge about 3720 mi³ (15,500 km³) of water yearly. The estimated total from all rivers, large and small, measured and unmeasured, is about 9200 mi³ (38,300 km³) yearly (25 mi³ or 105 km³ daily).

Crude estimates have indicated that the total amount of water that is physically present in stream channels throughout the world at a given moment is about 300 mi³ (1300 km³). Evidently, river channels on the average contain only enough water to maintain their flow for about 2 weeks. Some have much more water, others much less, but a 2-week period seems to be a fair average. How, then, do rivers maintain a flow throughout the year, even during rainless periods much longer than 2 weeks? The answer to the question will appear later in the discussion of groundwater. SEE RIVER.

Lakes. After oceans and rivers come lakes, which can be called wide places in rivers. This is certainly true of the many small lakes that are impounded by relatively minor and geologically temporary obstructions across river channels. But no single oversimplified metaphor accurately describes all lakes, which are widely varied in their physical characteristics and the geologic circumstances under which they occur. The handsome little tarn occupying an ice-scooped basin in a glaciated alpine area is radically different from the deep and limpid Crater Lake of Oregon, which fills the crater of a now-extinct volcano. Lake Okeechobee in Florida is totally different from any of the North American Great Lakes, which occupy huge basins formed in a complex manner by glacial exca-

vation at some places, moraine and outwash deposition at others, isostatic subsidence of that whole region of the Earth's crust, and other factors. The Great Lakes of North America, in turn, bear no resemblance to Lake Tanganyika in the great Rift Valley of Africa. Processes that are poorly understood created the rift by literally pulling two sections of the Earth's crust apart, leaving a deep, open gash, part of which is occupied by the lake. And these are only a few examples of wide variations in the nature of lakes.

The Earth's land areas are dotted with hundreds of thousands of lakes. Wisconsin, Minnesota, and Finland contain some tens of thousands each. But these lakes, important though they may be locally, hold only a minor amount of the world supply of fresh surface water, most of which is contained in a relatively few large lakes on three continents (see **illus.**).

Whether a lake contains fresh or salt water makes a considerable difference in its usefulness to humans, and so the Earth's greatest lakes are considered in both of the categories, fresh and salt.

The volume of all the large fresh-water lakes in the world aggregates nearly 30,000 mi³ (130,000 km³),

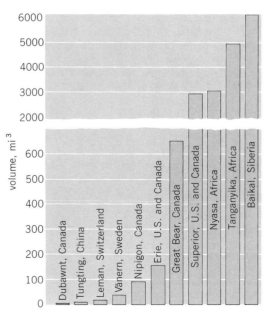

Water volume of lakes. 1 mi³ = 4.2 km³.

and their combined surface area is about 330,000 mi² (855,000 km²). Large is a relative term that requires explanation. For this article, a lake is called large if its contents are 5 mi³ (21 km³) or more. Thus the listing in the illustration includes Dubawnt Lake, Canada (about 6 mi³ or 25 km³), but excludes the Zurichsee of Switzerland (about 1 mi³ or 4 km³). The range of volume among the large lakes is enormous, from a lower limit of 5 mi³ (21 km³) to an upper one of 6300 mi³ (26,300 km³) in Lake Baikal in Asiatic Russia, the largest and deepest single body of fresh water in existence. Some appreciation of its volume may be gained from the realization that Lake Baikal alone contains nearly 300 mi³ (1300 km³) more water than the combined contents of the five North American Great Lakes. The Great Lakes loom large on a map, but their average depth is considerably less than that of Baikal.

Nevertheless, North American lakes are a major element in the Earth's water balance. The Great Lakes, plus other large lakes in North America (chiefly in the continental states and Canada), contain about 7800 mi³ (32,500 km³) of water—26% of all liquid, fresh, surface water in existence.

Similarly, the large lakes of Africa contain 8700 mi³ (36,300 km³), or nearly 29% of the total freshwater supply. Asia's large lakes contain about 6400 mi³ (26,700 km³), or 21% of the total, nearly all of which is in Lake Baikal.

Lakes on these three continents account for roughly 75% of the world's fresh surface water. Large lakes on other continents—Europe, South America, and Australia—have only about 720 mi³ (3000 km³), or roughly 2% of the total. All that remains to fill the hundreds of thousands of rivers and lesser lakes that are found throughout the world is less than one-fourth of the total fresh surface water.

Saline lakes are equivalent in magnitude to freshwater lakes. Their total area is 270,000 mi² (700,000 km²), and their total volume is about 25,000 mi³ (104,000 km³). The distribution, however, is quite different. About 19,240 mi³ (80,200 km³; 75% of the total saline volume) is in the Caspian Sea, and most of the remainder is in Asia. North America's shallow Great Salt Lake is comparatively insignificant with 7 mi³ (29 km³). *See Lake.*

Soil moisture. All these water sources previously discussed are the obvious ones. There is another—soil moisture—that may be the most significant segment of the world's water supply because of the key role played by plants in the food chain. Some plants grow directly in water or marshy ground, but by far the greater mass of vegetation on Earth lives on dry land. This is possible because the land is really dry at just a few places, and often only temporarily. The dust of a dry dirt road may contain up to 15% of water by weight. However, plants cannot grow with so little water because the soil holds small percentages of moisture so tenaciously that plant roots cannot extract it. Aside from desert plants, which store water in their own tissues during infrequent wet periods, land plants flourish only where there is extractable water in the soil. Inasmuch as a quite ordinary tree may withdraw and transpire about 50 gal (190 liters) of water per day, frequent renewals of soil moisture, either by rain or by irrigation, are essential. The average amount of water held as soil moisture at any given time is on the order of 6000 mi³ (25,000 km³) for the world as

a whole—an insignificant percentage of the Earth's total water, but vital to life. Relatively little vegetation receives artificial irrigation, and practically all of it depends on orderly and timely operation of the hydrologic cycle. *See Soil.*

Groundwater. Another little-considered water reservoir has been known to humans for thousands of years. Beneath most land areas of the world there is a zone where the pores of rocks and sediments are completely saturated with water. Hydrologists call this groundwater, and the upper limit of the saturated zone is called the water table. The water table may be right at the land surface, as in a marsh, or it may lie hundreds of feet below the land surface, as in some arid areas. Water in the unsaturated zone above the water table is called vadose water and includes the belt of soil moisture. Water in the intermediate part of this zone has passed through the soil and is percolating downward toward the water table.

The world volume of that part of the vadose water below the belt of soil moisture is probably somewhat more than that of soil moisture—say 10,000 mi³ (42,000 km³). It is highly important because, although it is not extractable by humans, it is potential groundwater recharge and groundwater is extractable. Each influx of water from precipitation on the land surface, followed by percolation through the soil, provides an increment of recharge to the groundwater.

Below the water table, to a depth of half a mile (0.8 km) in land areas of the Earth's crust, there is about 1,000,000 mi³ (4,200,00 km³) of groundwater. An equal if not greater amount is present at a greater depth down to some 10,000–15,000 ft (3.0–4.5 km), but this deeper water circulates sluggishly because the rocks are only slightly permeable. Much of the deep-lying water is not economically recoverable for human use, and a good deal of it is strongly mineralized.

The volume of groundwater in the upper half mile (0.8 km) of the continental crust probably is about 3000 times greater than the volume of water in all rivers at any one time, and nearly 20 times greater than the combined volume of water in all rivers and lakes. Groundwater reservoirs have tremendous importance as equalizers of streamflow. Under natural conditions, most groundwater reservoirs are full to overflowing, and the overflow water provides the base flow of surface streams, enabling them to flow even during long rainless periods and after winter snows have melted. *See Groundwater hydrology.*

Ice caps and glaciers. The next big items on the water-balance sheet are ice caps and glaciers. They may seem unimportant in the water cycle because, although the ice masses alternately shrink or grow a little from time to time, new ice is added about as fast as old ice melts. The polar ice masses, however, have a great influence on weather, and everything that happens in the polar regions indirectly affects everyone throughout the world. Moreover, if a shift in climate led to extensive melting of ice caps, there would be a rise in sea level with important effects in all low-lying coastal areas.

Mountain glaciers, such as those of the Alps in Europe (after which alpine glaciers are named), the Himalayas of Asia, and the Cascades of North America, are like average rivers in some respects. They are important locally, but they contain an insignificant fraction of the world's water. The total volume of all alpine glaciers and small ice caps in the world is only about 50,000 mi^3 (210,000 km^3; comparable to the combined volume of large saline and fresh lakes).

An alpine glacier is one that rises in mountainous uplands and, by plastic deformation, flows along a valley. A continental glacier, or ice cap, is one that is plastered over the landscape, mountain and valley alike. Ice caps tend to flow radially outward from their center of accumulation. Wastage occurs by sublimation from the surface and by melting or calving away around the periphery. Average ice caps, like those on Novaya Zemlya, Iceland, and Ellesmere Land, are analogous to average lakes. They are locally important, but hold an insignificant share of the world's water and only a small part of the total volume of perennial ice.

The Greenland ice cap is an entirely different matter. About 667,000 mi^2 (1,728,000 km^2) in area and averaging nearly 5000 ft (1.5 km) in thickness, the cap has a total volume of about 630,000 mi^3 (2,630,000 km^3). If melted, it would yield enough water to maintain the Mississippi River for somewhat more than 4700 years. Even so, this is less than 10% of the total volume of ice caps and glaciers.

The greatest single item in the water budget of the world, aside from the ocean itself, is the Antarctic ice sheet. Considerable information has been accumulated about Antarctica. Data on the thickness of the ice sheet are relatively scarce, but there is enough information to permit an approximate estimate. The area of the ice sheet is about 6,000,000 mi^2 (15,500,000 km^2), and the total volume, therefore, is 6,000,000–7,000,000 mi^3 (25,000,000–29,000,000 km^3), or some 85% of all existing ice and about 64% of all water outside the oceans.

The hydrologic importance of the continent and its ice may be illustrated briefly. If the Antarctic ice cap were melted at a suitable uniform rate, it could feed the Mississippi River for more than 50,000 years; all rivers in the United States for about 17,000 years; the Amazon River for approximately 5000 years; or all the rivers in the world for about 750 years.

Fresh-water supplies. About 97% of all water in the world is in the oceans. Most of the remainder is frozen on Antarctica and Greenland. Thus, humans must get along with the less than 1% of the world's water that is directly available for fresh-water use. More effective ways of managing it are being sought.

Water is a global concern. The water cycle recognizes no national boundaries. Human population has become so large and human activities so extensive that the water cycle has been affected, certainly on a regional scale and very likely on a global scale. To learn more about the world's water and how to use it, many countries have joined in programs aimed at overcoming on a global scale the critical deficiency in hydrological knowledge. SEE HYDROLOGY; HYDROSPHERE.

Raymond L. Nace

Theoretical ecology

The use of mathematical models to provide a conceptual framework for the analysis of ecological systems. Ecology, the study of the relationship between organisms and their environment, deals with an inherently diverse array of complex systems, rich in idiosyncratic details of natural history. Mathematics is a language that makes it possible to express and think clearly about complex relationships. Thus, mathematical models are considered the essential tools of theoretical ecology. If mathematical ecology is defined as the application of mathematical theory and techniques to ecology, theoretical ecology is the use of such theory and techniques to develop broad conceptual insights into ecological systems.

Tactical versus strategic models. In contrast with other disciplines, ecology is rather diffuse. Theoretical physics, for example, is conceptually unified by the existence of fundamental laws governing all physical systems. Theoretical ecology cannot as yet rely on universal ecological laws, other than those same physical laws and the general notion of evolution by natural selection. Rather than aiming at all-inclusive laws, much theoretical work in ecology has more modest goals, for instance clarifying verbal concepts arising from field studies, or sharpening intuition about the possible reasons for qualitative similarities among disparate systems. A wide spectrum of models is used in ecology, ranging from complex tactical models describing specific empirical systems to simpler strategic models that (while admittedly caricaturizing real systems) can be understood in some depth by virtue of their relative simplicity. The term theoretical ecology usually denotes strategic rather than tactical models.

In addressing practical problems, where quantitative predictions are essential, large-scale computer models that mimic the behavior of particular systems in a detailed manner are often necessary. The very specificity permitting such models to be good descriptors, however, may also make it difficult to draw general conclusions from them, or to see where they fit into broader conceptual schemes. The more abstract models of theoretical ecology can provide guidelines for interpreting the qualitative behavior of complex simulation models. Moreover, there has been a great deal of theoretical work tied closely to applied problems such as pest control, epidemiology, and fisheries management; partly as a result of this development the long-standing division between theoretical ecology and systems or simulation ecology has begun to blur. Instead of trying to incorporate into an applicable model all the details of a system, the aim is to include just enough significant detail to capture its essential behavior, without making the model so complicated that it cannot be understood clearly by a combination of analysis and judicious numerical studies. The diversity of ecological systems is becoming reflected in a corresponding diversity in ecological theories tailored to those systems. SEE ECOLOGY, APPLIED; SYSTEMS ECOLOGY.

Hierarchy of models. The diversity in ecological theories may be categorized in various ways. One obvious way is by the level of organization in the traditional hierarchy of living systems. A given theory may focus on individual organisms, populations, communities, ecosystems, or even the entire biosphere. Particularly rich bodies of theories exist at the organismal, population, and community levels. At the individual level, theoretical models examine the consequences and ultimate evolutionary causes of individual design features, such as leaf size in plants and diet breadth in animals. (A design feature is an organismal trait that can influence rates of death and reproduction, and hence Darwinian fitness.) Such models provide an important link between ecological theory and evolutionary biology. At the population level, theoretical work aims at understanding patterns in distribution and abundance, such as causes for population cycles. Theoretical community ecology is concerned with the factors determining the species composition and functional organization of communities, with a particular emphasis on interspecific interactions such as competition, predation, and mutualism. Theoretical analyses at the ecosystem level attempt to analyze flows of energy and material in entire ecosystems.

Ecological theories at any level may be phenomenological or mechanistic. An example of a phenomenological model is the logistic model of population ecology, which describes how the growth rate of a population declines as the population approaches its carrying capacity, without explaining why this occurs. By contrast, a mechanistic model would incorporate assumptions about the causal processes that depress growth rate near carrying capacity.

Much work in theoretical ecology attempts to bridge these traditional levels by using low-level models as building blocks in constructing higher-level models. For instance, the foraging strategies of individual consumers have been studied by using optimization and game theoretic techniques. Insights gleaned from such studies can be exploited in refining models of resource competition. An advantage for this modeling strategy is that lower-level models are more readily open to experimental evaluation. Many ecosystem ecologists are uneasy with this bottoms-up, reductionist approach. On the one hand they fear that important emergent properties of entire systems may be lost by a myopic concentration on the separate pieces; on the other hand, they note pragmatically that there are just too many lower-level pieces to keep track of in complex ecosystems. A number of top-down approaches to ecosystem theory have been proposed, but it has not been determined which, if any, will provide viable theoretical alternatives to more reductionist theories.

Even firm believers of the reductionist approach admit that complex behaviors arise at higher levels that cannot readily be predicted from the behavior of isolated units at lower levels, and that the causal arrow can point down, as well as up, the hierarchy. The carrying capacity of a population, for instance, reflects not just the life history and foraging strategies of the individuals in the population (these traits themselves being the product of a population process, namely, evolution by natural selection) but also the web of interaction among species in which that population is embedded, as well as ecosystem-level determinants of renewal rates of abiotic resources. *See Ecological communities*.

Ecological theories. Ecological theories may be static or dynamic.

Static. A static theory does not include time as an explicit variable. Static theories describe compactly the structure of large bodies of information; for that reason they have been particularly common in community ecology, which deals typically with complex, multivariate data sets. For instance, considerable attention has been given to describing the structure of food webs. Static models specifying the probability that species pairs are trophically linked have been used with great success to predict statistical properties of food webs. Theoretical ecologists view static models as useful way stations toward the development of dynamic models. *See Food web*.

Dynamic. In a dynamic theory, variables change through time because of forces embodied in the mathematical structure of the theory. The mathematical formalism may be difference equations, in which variables are computed at discrete time intervals, or differential equations, which are appropriate when variables change continuously. The variables themselves may be continuous (such as leaf temperature) or discrete (such as the number of eagles on an island). It is often appropriate to approximate discrete variables with continuous ones, particularly when numbers are large. A model may be deterministic, so that specification of the system's state at one time fixes its states for all future times, or stochastic, such that each state can give rise to an array of future states, each with a specified probability. Stochastic models tend to be quite complex mathematically compared to their deterministic counterparts. However, there are some ecological questions, such as understanding the dynamics of colonizing species, that clearly require stochastic analyses, and others, such as analyzing the coexistence of competing species, where traditional deterministic approaches have been greatly enriched by incorporating the effects of stochastic temporal variation. *See Ecological modeling*.

A particularly important cluster of concepts in theoretical ecology centers around the notions of equilibrium (or steady state) and stability. Although these ideas are formalized in the language of dynamic systems theory, they relate to the earlier notion that there is a balance of nature. For instance, a population is at a point equilibrium when its size does not change over time. (Other possible equilibria include regular cycles and more complicated patterns of numerical fluctuations, which can be produced by time lags and strong nonlinear feedbacks.) For this equilibrium to be stable, the population when pushed away from equilibrium must return to it. The **illustration** shows balls placed on a hilly landscape to illustrate several stability concepts. A ball at position A is not at equilibrium, because it is rolling downhill. Balls at points B through E would all be at equilibrium. But B is a point of unstable equilibrium; once a ball at B moves slightly, it continues to move away from its equilib-

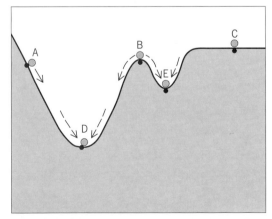

Stability concepts illustrated by balls under the influence of gravity on a hilly landscape. The solid arrow denotes current motion; the broken arrows, motion following small perturbations from the indicated points.

rium position. A ball at C is neutrally stable; if it is moved slightly, it will stay at its new position, neither returning to its old position nor moving farther away. Points D and E are locally stable positions; a ball at either of these points tends to return to its original position (possibly with oscillations) when moved by a small amount, but can be pushed into a new equilibrium position if the perturbation is sufficiently large.

Analyses of equilibrium states and their stability properties permeate theoretical ecology at all levels. For example, at the individual level, the models of evolutionary ecology often lead to functions relating individual fitness to individual traits (such as body size), coupled with the proposition that over evolutionary time (all else being equal) populations evolve toward trait values that maximize fitness (at least locally in a phenotype space), and once a population reaches that state it does not change. The parallel with the balls and landscape in the illustration is strong. More generally, the population stabilizes at the phenotypic value (or combination of phenotypes)—the evolutionarily stable state of the population—such that alternative phenotypes have lower fitness. Likewise, the regulation of population abundance around an equilibrium value is a central feature of many population models. Much of theoretical community ecology has been devoted to elucidating how the destabilizing influence of some interspecific interactions constrains the number of coexisting species and the pattern of their interactions, and how other interactions buffer communities against external perturbations.

Extensions to traditional theories. A model is dynamically insufficient if it leaves out variables that are qualitatively important to the behavior of a system. Extensions to traditional ecological theories are essential if theoretical ecology is to inform attempts to solve important human problems, such as checking the spread of infectious diseases, managing renewable resources, and mitigating the damage of environmental stresses. In modern theoretical ecology, researchers are actively examining three distinct kinds of dynamic insufficiency in the classical models of ecology: the assumption of constant parameters, the omission of key variables, and the aggregation problem.

Constant parameters. Parameters assumed to be constant may in fact be varying with time. For instance, traditional theories about the role of competition in communities concluded that the number of coexisting consumer species must not exceed the number of distinct resource types supporting them. However, work on competition in variable environments has revealed that sometimes a number of consumer species may be sustained by a single, fluctuating resource population. If environmental fluctuations are sufficiently great, the notion of stability in a deterministic landscape (as in the illustration) may be seriously misleading.

Omission of key variables. There may be key variables left out of the models that are involved in feedback relationships with the included variables. An important class of examples, again from community ecology, is the study of indirect interactions. For instance, in a community composed of three species, A, B, and C, if A increases the abundance of B, and B decreases the abundance of C, A indirectly depresses the abundance of C. This indirect effect may exceed any direct effect of A on C. Leaving B out of a model

of the community would lead to a serious misunderstanding of the interaction between A and C.

Aggregation problem. The theoretical variables may aggregate subsidiary variables and thereby obscure crucial facets of the dynamics. Ecology at the ecosystem level, in particular, is plagued by the aggregation problem, but the problem may arise at any level. Most populations, for instance, are internally heterogeneous; models using total numbers may be defined too coarsely. Individuals differ in birth and death rates and in their interactions with other species: this results from differences in genes, age, size, and so forth. Such heterogeneities can crucially affect population dynamics.

Another generic source of heterogeneity in population and community ecology is spatial structuring, which occurs at both large and small scales. Within a generation in a given population, different individuals may reside in different microhabitats and may interact with a limited number of individuals of their own and other species. This can have important consequences for population size and stability. Over several generations, most populations and communities are open to dispersal, receiving immigrants from other populations as well as sending forth emigrants. Understanding the long-term persistence of an ecological system may require an understanding of the dynamics of metapopulations, spatially dispersed open populations coupled by dispersal; this ultimately will require an integration of ecological theory with biogeography and the earth sciences. *See* ECOLOGY; ECOSYSTEM.

Robert Holt

Bibliography. R. May, *Perspectives in Theoretical Ecology*, 1989; R. May (ed.), *Theoretical Ecology: Principles and Applications*, 2d ed., 1981; E. C. Pielou, *Mathematical Ecology*, 1977; J. Roughgarden, *Theory of Population Genetics and Evolutionary Ecology: An Introduction*, rev. ed., 1987.

Thermocline

A layer of seawater in which the temperature decrease with depth is greater than that of the overlying and underlying water. Such layers are semipermanent features of the oceanic temperature structure, and their depth and thickness show marked variation with season, latitude and longitude, and local environmental conditions. Since the three-dimensional temperature structure has a great effect on many oceanic properties, such as the transmission of sound, the study of the nature and behavior of the thermocline is of extreme importance to many oceanographic interests, both economic and military. In general, two major types of thermocline may be identified: the permanent thermocline and the seasonal thermocline. In addition to these types, shallow thermoclines or similar stable layers often occur, owing to diurnal heating of the surface waters.

Permanent thermocline. This feature is so named because its character is virtually unchanged seasonally. In Arctic and Antarctic regions, the water is cold from top to bottom. As this dense water flows south and north, respectively, it sinks beneath warmer water which moves outward from the Equator. This gives rise to the temperature discontinuity known as the permanent thermocline. The cold water flowing slowly through the deep ocean basins exhibits conservative properties throughout all the oceans; however,

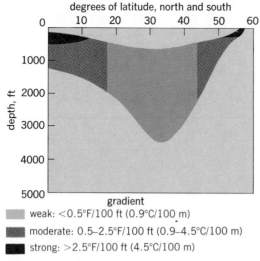

Fig. 1. The permanent thermocline, based on averages for depth, thickness, and gradient within thermocline. 1 ft = 0.3 m.

on top of this dense layer lie a number of shallow layers whose character varies from ocean to ocean. The top of the permanent thermocline is quite shallow at the Equator, reaches maximum depth at mid-latitudes, and becomes shallow again at about 50° latitude. The thermocline disappears between 55 to 60°N or S. In general, as the permanent thermocline deepens, it becomes thicker and the temperature gradient within it decreases. **Figure 1** indicates schematically variations with latitude in the characteristics of the permanent thermocline. *See Seawater.*

Seasonal thermocline. This feature is a summer phenomenon found at shallower water depth than the permanent thermocline in all the world's oceans except those perennially ice-infested. As air temperatures rise above ocean temperatures in the spring season and the sea surface receives more heat than it loses by radiation and convection, the surface water

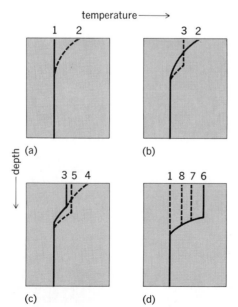

Fig. 2. Formation and breakup of seasonal thermocline. (a) Formation, first stage. (b) Formation, second stage. (c) Formation, third stage. (d) Breakup.

begins to warm so that a negative temperature gradient develops in the first few feet (**Fig. 2**a). (Numbers 1–8 show sequence in development and disappearance of thermocline; profiles show temperature structure.) The surface waters are then mixed by transfer of energy from the wind. Although this mixing serves to lower the surface temperature, the net effect is a downward transport of heat and formation of an isothermal layer whose temperature is warmer than the underlying water (Fig. 2b). A strong temperature gradient, or seasonal thermocline, is thus formed between the isothermal surface layer and water beneath. This process repeats itself (Fig. 2c) until the gradient in the seasonal thermocline becomes so strong that summer winds cannot impart sufficient energy to drive the isothermal layer deeper. From July through September such a surface layer of mixed water underlain by a strong negative temperature gradient is found in most of the ocean. As air temperatures fall in autumn, the water loses heat to the atmosphere by convective and radiative processes, and the surface layer is cooled to the temperature of the water below. The seasonal thermocline breaks up (Fig. 2d), to form again the following spring. Seasonal thermoclines may be affected locally by vertical wind mixing, currents, and heat exchange across the interface between ocean and atmosphere. Further distortions may occur because the density discontinuity associated with thermoclines provides a favorable environment for internal waves. Practically all physical processes occurring in the sea have an effect on thermocline characteristics.

John J. Schule, Jr.

Thunderstorm

A convective storm accompanied by lightning and thunder and a variety of weather such as locally heavy rainshowers, hail, high winds, sudden temperature changes, and occasionally tornadoes. The characteristic cloud is the cumulonimbus or thunderhead, a towering cloud, often with an anvil-shaped top. A host of accessory clouds, some attached and some detached from the main cloud, are often observed in conjunction with cumulonimbus. The height of a cumulonimbus base above the ground ranges from 1000 to over 10,000 ft (300 to 3000 m), depending on the relative humidity of air near the Earth's surface. Tops usually reach 30,000–60,000 ft (9000–18,000 m), with the taller storms occurring in the tropics or during summer in midlatitudes. Thunderstorms travel at speeds from near zero to 70 mi/h (30 m/s). In many tropical and temperate regions, thunderstorms furnish much of the annual rainfall.

Development. Thunderstorms are manifestations of convective overturning of deep layers in the atmosphere and occur in environments in which the decrease of temperature with height (lapse rate) is sufficiently large to be conditionally unstable and the air at low levels is moist. In such an atmosphere, a rising air parcel, given sufficient lift, becomes saturated and cools less rapidly than it would if it remained unsaturated because the released latent heat of condensation partly counteracts the expansional cooling. The rising parcel reaches levels where it is warmer (by perhaps as much as 18°F or 10°C) and less dense than its surroundings, and buoyancy forces accelerate the parcel upward. The convection may be initiated by surface heating or by air flowing over rising terrain or by air ascending in atmospheric disturbances such as fronts. The rising parcel is decelerated and its vertical ascent arrested at altitudes where the lapse rate is stable, and the parcel becomes denser than its environment. The forecasting of thunderstorms thus hinges on the identification of regions where the lapse rate is unstable, low-level air parcels contain adequate moisture, and surface heating or uplift of the air is expected to be sufficient to initiate convection. *See Front*.

Occurrence. Thunderstorms are most frequent in the tropics, and rare poleward of 60° latitude. In the United States, the Florida peninsula has the maximum activity with 60 thunderstorm days (days on which thunder is heard at a given observation station) per year. Thunderstorms occur at all hours of day and night, but are most common during late afternoon because of the diurnal influence of surface heating. The weak nighttime maximum of thunderstorms in the Mississippi Valley of the central United States is still a topic of debate.

Structure. Radar is used to detect thunderstorms at ranges up to 250 mi (400 km) from the observing site. Much of present-day knowledge of thunderstorm structure has been deduced from radar studies, supplemented by visual observations from the ground and satellites, and in-place measurements from aircraft, surface observing stations, and weather balloons.

Thunderstorms occur in isolation, in chaotic patterns over wide areas, in the walls and spiral bands of hurricanes, in clusters within large-scale weather systems, and in squall lines perhaps several hundred miles long. An individual thunderstorm typically covers a surface area of 10–400 mi² (25–1000 km²) and consists of one or more distinct cells, each of which is several miles across, lasts about an hour, and undergoes a characteristic life cycle. In the cumulus or growing stage, a cell consists primarily of updrafts (vertical speeds of 20–90 mi/h or 10–40 m/s) with precipitation suspended aloft; in the mature stage, updrafts and downdrafts coexist and heavy rain falls to the ground; in the dissipating stage, a cell contains weakly subsiding air and only light precipitation. During the mature stage, downdrafts may reach 35 mi/h (15 m/s). The downdraft air is denser than its surroundings due to evaporational cooling, which occurs as clear air is entrained into the cloud from outside, and is forced downward by gravitational pull and by the drag of falling precipitation. The downflowing air spreads outward in all directions as it nears the surface, and forms a cold, gusty wind that is directed away from the precipitation area. This advancing cold air may provide the necessary lift in neighboring warm moist air for the formation of new updraft cells. Intense, narrow downdrafts (sometimes from innocuous-looking cumulonimbi) produce locally damaging, divergent outflow winds as they impact the ground. These small-scale flow features, known as microbursts, contain large wind shears that are extremely hazardous to low-flying aircraft. *See Hurricane; Squall line*.

In an environment where the winds increase and veer with height, and midlevel air is dry enough to provide the potential for strong downdrafts, a thunderstorm may become organized so as to maintain a nearly steady state for hours. In such strong vertical shear of the horizontal wind, the updraft is tilted so that precipitation falls out of the updraft instead of through it, and updraft and downdraft can coexist for several hours in the configuration shown in **Fig. 1**. A long-lived storm in a sheared environment may consist of a single intense cell (supercell) or of many cells with an organized growth of new cells on one side of the storm (generally, the southwest in the Northern Hemisphere) and decay of old cells on the opposite flank. *See Wind*.

Severe storms. Thunderstorms are considered severe when they produce winds greater than 58 mi/h (26 m/s or 50 knots), hail larger than ¾ in. (19 mm) in diameter, or tornadoes. While thunderstorms are generally beneficial because of their needed rains (except for occasional flash floods), severe storms have the capacity of inflicting utter devastation over narrow swaths of the countryside. Severe storms are most frequent in the Great Plains region of the United States, but even there only about 1% of the thunderstorms are severe. Severe storms are most frequently supercell storms which form in environments with high convective instability and moderate-to-large vertical wind shears.

Since severe storms constitute a hazard to aircraft, their internal dynamics has been deduced largely from radar measurements. Doppler radar is specialized to measure the velocity of radar targets parallel to the radar beam, in addition to the intensity of precipitation. Doppler radar studies and analysis of surface pressure falls have shown that large hail, high winds, and tornadoes often develop from a rotating thunderstorm cell known as a mesocyclone (or tornado cyclone, if it spawns at least one tornado). Large hail, high winds, and weak tornadoes may form from nonrotating (on broad scale) multicellular storms, but are less likely. Maximum tangential winds around the typical mesocyclone are roughly 50 mi/h (20 m/s) and are located in a circular band which is 1–6 mi (2–10 km) in radius. A surface pressure deficit of several millibars exists at the mesocyclone center. In one case, a pressure drop of 34 mbar (3.4 kilopascals) was measured. Identification of a mesocyclone signature on radar has been used to issue severe weather warnings. The structure of a supercell storm is shown in **Fig. 2**.

On conventional radar displays, hook-shaped appendages to echoes are also good indications of mesocyclones, but unfortunately a large percentage of tornadic storms never exhibit such a hook. A meso-

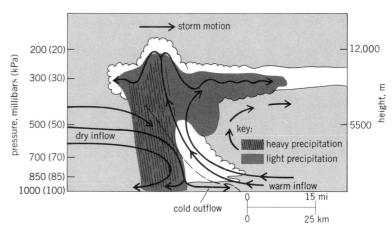

Fig. 1. Cloud boundaries and simplified circulation (arrows denote flow) of a typical mature thunderstorm in winds which blow from left to right and increase with height. Vertical scale has been exaggerated fivefold compared with the horizontal scale. 1 m = 3.3 ft; 1 km = 0.6 mi.

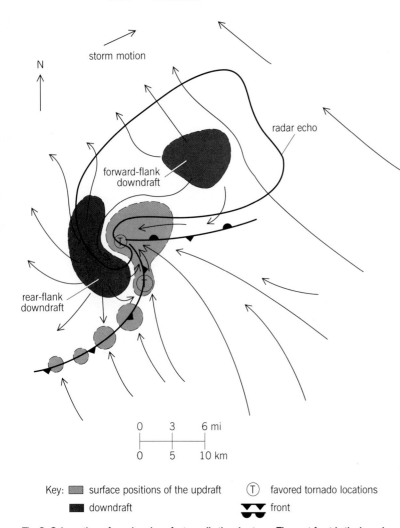

Fig. 2. Schematic surface plan view of a tornadic thunderstorm. The gust front is the boundary between unmodified warm, moist, inflowing air and rain-cooled, outflowing air. Arrows depict flow streamlines relative to the storm. The northern T at the mesocyclone center (wave apex) indicates where a major tornado is most likely. The southern T at the favored place for new mesocycline and tornado development. For storms in the Southern Hemisphere, transpose north and south. (*After R. Davies-Jones, Tornado dynamics, in E. Kessler, ed., Thunderstorm Morphology and Dynamics, 2d ed., University of Oklahoma Press, 1986*)

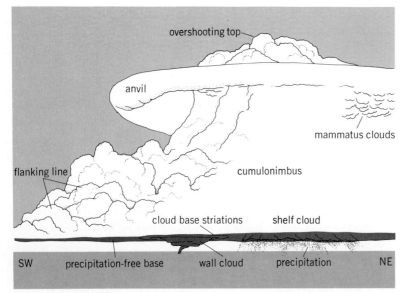

Fig. 3. Composite view of a typical tornado producing cumulonimbus as seen from a southeasterly direction. Horizontal scale is compressed, and all the features shown could not be seen from a single location. (*NOAA picture by C. Doswell and B. Dirham*)

cyclone sometimes is recognizable visually by rotation of a wall cloud, a discrete and distinct lowering of the cumulonimbus base (**Fig. 3**). The wall cloud is often seen visually to be rotating as an entity. The wall cloud is frequently the seat of intense vertical motions at low levels. The rotation of the mesocyclone stems principally from the low-level vertical shear of the horizontal wind present in the environment. An example of this effect is what happens to an initially vertical line drawn by a skywriter; changing wind speed (direction) with height causes the line to turn about a horizontal axis perpendicular (parallel) to the wind. Thus, when the storm-relative winds are roughly constant in speed but veer with height, air parcels flowing into the storm spin about their direction of motion. As the parcels enter the updraft, their spin axes are tipped upward, and so the updraft rotates as a whole. *SEE TORNADO.*

Attempts have been made to modify thunderstorms to increase areal rainfall and suppress hail. The results of such experiments have been inconclusive.

Robert Davies-Jones

Bibliography. D. Atlas (ed.), *Severe Local Storms,* Amer. Meteorol. Soc., Meteorol. Monogr., vol. 5, no. 27, 1963; E. Kessler (ed.), *Instruments and Techniques for Thunderstorm Observation and Analysis,* 2d ed., 1988; E. Kessler (ed.), *The Thunderstorm in Human Affairs,* 2d ed., 1983; E. Kessler (ed.), *Thunderstorm Morphology and Dynamics,* 2d ed., 1986; F. H. Ludlam, *Clouds and Storms,* 1980.

Tornado

A violently rotating, tall, narrow column of air (that is, a vortex), typically about 300 ft (100 m) in diameter, that extends to the ground from a cumulonimbus cloud. The vast majority of tornadoes rotate cyclonically (counterclockwise in the Northern Hemisphere). Of all atmospheric storms, tornadoes are the most violent. *SEE CLOUD.*

Visual appearance. Tornadoes are made visible by a generally sharp-edged, funnel-shaped cloud pendant from the cloud base, and a swirling cloud of dust and debris rising from the ground (**Fig. 1**). The funnel consists of small waterdroplets that form as moist air entering the tornado's partial vacuum expands and cools. The condensation funnel may not extend all the way to the ground and may be obscured by dust. Many condensation funnels exist aloft without tangible signs that the vortex is in contact with the ground; these are known as funnel clouds. Tornado funnels assume various forms: a slender smooth rope, a cone (often truncated by the ground), a thick turbulent black cloud on the ground, or multiple funnels (vortices) that revolve around the axis of the overall tornado.

Many tornadoes evolve as follows: The tornado begins outside the precipitation region as a dust whirl on the ground and a short funnel pendant from a wall cloud on the southwest side of the thunderstorm; it intensifies as the funnel lengthens downward, and attains its greatest power as the funnel reaches its greatest width and is almost vertical; then it shrinks and becomes more tilted, and finally becomes contorted and ropelike as it decays. A downdraft and curtain of rain and large hail gradually spiral from the northeast cyclonically around the tornado, which often ends its life in rain. *SEE THUNDERSTORM.*

Fig. 1. The Cordell, Oklahoma, tornado of May 22, 1981, in its decay stage. (*National Severe Storms Laboratory/ University of Mississippi Tornado Intercept Project*)

Parent storm. Most tornadoes and practically all violent ones develop from a larger-scale circulation, the mesocyclone, which is 2–6 mi (3–9 km) in diameter and forms in a particularly virulent variety of thunderstorm, the supercell. The tornado is located on the edge of the storm's main updraft, close to the downdraft. Some supercells develop up to six mesocyclones and tornadoes repeatedly over great distances at roughly 45-min intervals. Tornadoes associated with supercells are generally of the stronger variety and have larger parent cyclones. Hurricanes during and after landfall may spawn numerous tornadoes from their rainbands. *See Hurricane.*

Damage. The majority of tornadoes are relatively weak and cause only minor damage. However, violent tornadoes demolish houses, sometimes leaving just bare foundations; cut swaths of downed trees through forests; and make heavy missiles out of objects such as roof sections, automobiles, and telephone poles. Engineers have concluded that structural damage is almost always due to wind-associated forces and missiles, not to the sudden reduction in atmospheric pressure. Typically, most debris is ejected out of a tornado along its direction of motion, so that the damage, apart from the characteristic well-defined long narrow path, appears to be from straight-line winds. However, ample signs of the circulation are usually evident in the overall debris distribution of large tornadoes. Multiple-vortex tornadoes that cross fields accumulate soil and vegetation in cycloidal rows, typically 15 cm (6 in.) high and 1.5 m (5 ft) wide, that are visible from the air. The marks are cycloidal because of the circular motion of an individual vortex about the tornado axis combined with the forward motion of the overall tornado. The rows are created by small debris being drawn into the bases of the vortices and left behind in lines of litter in the wakes of the vortices. The individual vortices occur at the locations of the strongest winds, lowest pres-

sure, and most rapid pressure falls. Therefore, multivortex tornadoes passing through cities produce cycloidal swaths of more intense damage. *See Wind.*

Statistics. The typical tornado (described here for the Northern Hemisphere; north/south direction is the opposite for the Southern Hemisphere) is weak and short-lived (1–2 min), moves from the southwest at 15 m/s (30 mi/h), and inflicts damage to an area of about 1 mi × 150 ft (2 km × 50 m). In extreme cases, the length and width of the damage path may exceed 100 mi (150 km) and 2.5 mi (4 km), respectively; the lifetime may be over 1 h; and the translation speed may reach 68 mi/h (30 m/s). The majority of tornadoes (60%) approach from the southwest, and only 4% have a westward component of motion. Tornadoes are categorized by intensity as weak, strong, or violent. Only 2% are violent, 36% are strong (capable of unroofing houses and partially blowing down walls), and 62% are weak.

Climatology. Tornadoes occur most often at latitudes between 20° and 50°, and they are relatively frequent in the United States, Soviet Union, Europe, Japan, India, South Africa, Argentina, New Zealand, and parts of Australia. Violent tornadoes are confined mainly to the United States, east of the Rocky Mountains, and (with less frequency) to the Bangladesh-Assam area. The world's highest frequency, 5–10 tornadoes annually per 10,000 mi^2 (26,000 km^2), occurs in the area known as Tornado Alley, which extends from Texas through Oklahoma and Kansas into Iowa (**Fig. 2**).

In winter in the United States, tornadoes are confined to the southern states, and generally have longer tracks because of stronger steering currents. The tornado belt generally shifts northward with the jet stream and the advance of tropical air through the central states and into the northern states during spring and summer. May is the most active month with 20% of the annual number of tornadoes; January is the least active with only 3%. Tornadoes occur at all hours but are most frequent between 1500 and 1900 local standard time because solar heating of the Earth's surface influences thunderstorm initiation.

Atmospheric conditions. Essentially, there are five atmospheric conditions that set the stage for widespread tornado development: (1) a surface-based layer, at least 3000 ft (1 km) deep, of warm, moist air, overlain by dry air at midlevels; (2) an inversion separating the two layers, preventing deep convection until the potential for explosive overturning is established; (3) rapid decrease of temperature with height above the inversion; (4) a combination of mechanisms, such as surface heating and lifting of the air mass by a front or upper-level disturbance, to eliminate the inversion locally; (5) pronounced vertical wind shear (variation of the horizontal wind with height). Specifically, storm-relative winds in the lowest 6000–9000 ft (2–3 km) should exceed 20 knots (10 m/s) and veer (turn anticyclonically) with height at a rate of more than 10°/1000 ft (30°/km). (Storm-relative wind is the wind measured with respect to a coordinate system that moves with the storm.) Such conditions are prevalent in the vicinity of the jet stream and the low-level jet. Incidentally, the ground-relative winds often are quite similar to the storm-relative winds in strength and directional turning.

The first three conditions above indicate that the atmosphere is in a highly metastable state. There is a strong potential for thunderstorms with intense updrafts and downdrafts. The fourth condition is the ex-

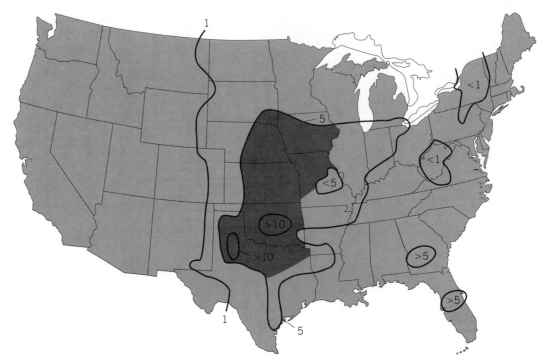

Fig. 2. Map showing average annual number of tornado occurrences per 10,000 mi² (26,000 km²) from National Severe Storms Forecast Center data, 1953–1975. Shaded area shows the approximate location of so-called Tornado Alley. Contour lines indicate the number of tornadoes per 10,000 mi²/year. West of the 1 contour line there is less than 1 per 10,000 mi² per year. (*After R. E. Peterson, ed., Proceedings of the Symposium on Tornadoes: Assessment of Knowledge and Implications for Man, Texas Technical University, 1976*)

istence of a trigger to release the instability and initiate the thunderstorms. The fifth is the ingredient for updraft rotation. *See Air mass; Front; Jet stream; Temperature inversion*.

The reason that the world's worst tornadoes generally occur in the central United States and in Bangladesh-Assam is that both regions are located in the midlatitude belt of westerlies, with warm oceans equatorward and mountains to their west. During the spring, both regions are often in the transition zone between warm and cold air masses, so that they lie beneath the jet stream. Cyclones and upper-level disturbances generally develop in the vicinity of the jet stream and migrate along it. Ahead of cyclones approaching from the west, warm, very moist air flows off the ocean into the region at low levels. At midlevels the air has been dried out by passage over the mountains to the west. Furthermore, the geography of both regions favors the development of low-level jets and associated strong low-level vertical wind shear.

Detection. Microbarographs, radars, satellites, and sferic detectors have all been used to identify potentially tornadic storms. Tornado warnings are issued on the basis of radar observations and reports from trained spotters; such warnings have contributed to a 50% decline in the annual numbers of deaths since 1950. The best detection device is the Doppler radar. Two types of vortex signature appear in Doppler velocity fields, the mesocyclone and tornadic vortex signatures. The tornadic vortex signature is associated with the tornado itself, but generally it is seen only at close range. For large tornadoes, the signatures may be detected aloft 20 min prior to touchdown, allowing warnings to be issued with considerable lead time. Home barometric devices based on detecting rapid pressure falls are inadequate, because only a few seconds warning is provided before the tornado strikes. *See Storm detection*.

Measurements. Winds and pressure deficits in tornadoes are not well known because tornadoes are difficult to intercept and extremely dangerous. Various estimates have been obtained from photogrammetric analyses of tornado movies, engineering analyses of structural failures and missiles generated by the vortex, analyses of the cycloidal marks left by multivortex tornadoes, chance readings from anemometers and microbarographs (when not destroyed) and attempts to introduce probes directly, Doppler radar measurements, and analysis of the size and shape of the funnel cloud. These measurements indicate that the windspeeds in the worst tornadoes probably do not exceed 250–300 mi/h (110–130 m/s). Substantial vertical velocities, up to 180 mi/h (80 m/s), have been documented. Radial inflow velocities may reach 110 mi/h (50 m/s) in narrow bands close to the ground. Surface pressure drops of 20 millibars (2 kilopascals) have been recorded, but the actual drop is undoubtedly underestimated because of sluggish instrument response. Temperature inside a tornado is unknown. *See Air pressure*.

Pressure deficit estimates. The central pressure deficit can be estimated by assuming that the flow, to a crude approximation, is a Rankine's combined vortex; that is, the vertical and radial velocities are zero and the tangential velocity v is given by Eq. (1) for $r > r_c$ and Eq. (2) for $r < r_c$, where r is the radial

$$v = \frac{v_m r_c}{r} \qquad (1)$$

$$v = \frac{v_m r}{r_c} \qquad (2)$$

coordinate, r_c is the radius of the tornado core (or, equivalently, the radius of the maximum winds in the tornado), and v_m is the maximum velocity. The flow consists of a core ($r < r_c$) in solid-body rotation, surrounded by a region where the angular momentum vr is constant. In the radial direction, the inward pressure gradient force balances the outward centrifugal force as in Eq. (3), where p is pressure and ρ is air

$$\frac{\partial p}{\partial r} = \frac{\rho v^2}{r} \qquad (3)$$

density (assumed equal to 1 kg/m³ in estimates below). The central pressure deficit, Δp, is obtained by integrating Eq. (3) from $r = \infty$ to 0 after substituting for v from Eqs. (1) and (2). The result is given by Eq. (4). From Eqs. (1)–(3), it is clear that the largest

$$\Delta p = \rho v_m^2 \qquad (4)$$

pressure gradient is located at the edge of the core. Therefore, for a tornado moving at a speed C, the maximum rate at which the pressure changes at a point is given by Eq. (5). Equations (4) and (5) pre-

$$\left(\frac{\partial p}{\partial t}\right)_{max} = \frac{-C\rho v_m^2}{r_c} \qquad (5)$$

dict a pressure deficit of around 100 mbar (10 kPa) and a maximum rate of pressure change of about 15 mbar/s (1.5 kPa/s) for a tornado with maximum winds of 225 mi/h (100 m/s), a core radius of 300 ft (100 m), and a translation speed of 30 knots (15 m/s). In violent multivortex tornadoes, the pressure at points in the path of the individual vortices undoubtedly changes far more rapidly, because these vortices move at speeds up to 215 mi/h (95 m/s).

Origins of rotation. The basic measure of local spin in a fluid is the vorticity vector, which is the curl or rotation of the wind vector and is aligned parallel to the spin axis in the direction of advance of a right-hand screw. Physically, vorticity is envisioned as twice the angular velocity (rate of spin) that a small spherical parcel of air would have if it were instantaneously solidified without a change in its spin angular momentum. The strong vertical wind shear generally present prior to development of severe storms is associated with horizontal vorticity that is up to 100 times greater than the background vertical vorticity associated with the Earth's rotation and large-scale cyclones. Theory suggests that a thunderstorm updraft could develop a tornado directly from the background vertical vorticity in a few hours. However, tornadoes can be generated more rapidly from background horizontal vorticity. Furthermore, three-dimensional computer models generate storms with rotating updrafts in suitably sheared environments with the Earth's rotation "switched off." Thus, it is widely believed that the mesocyclone forms as a result of the updraft tipping preexisting horizontal vorticity toward the vertical. The updraft rotates as a whole when the vorticity is streamwise (that is, the spin axis is along the flow direction) relative to the storm.

Familiar solid objects with streamwise vorticity are a spiraling American football, a bullet, and an aircraft in a roll. A wind that veers with height with no change in speed has purely streamwise vorticity. This becomes clear after considering how a pencil placed vertically in such a flow would turn. Air parcels with streamwise vorticity that enter the updraft acquire cy-

clonic spin in much the same way as a rolling aircraft that starts a climb. The storm-relative qualifier is necessary, because flow direction depends on motion of the coordinate system. Since the updraft is the agent converting horizontal vorticity into vertical vorticity, clearly the relevant winds are those relative to the storm. Once vertical vorticity has been generated, it can be amplified by the vertical stretching of air parcels in the lower part of the updraft where the flow converges horizontally. This process is analogous to the spinning ice skater. The mechanisms described above produce rotation at midlevels in the storm, which is where it is first observed. The development of rotation at the ground is a more complicated process, involving the storm's downdraft as well as its updraft.

If the environmental winds back (turn cyclonically) instead of veer with height, the vorticity is anti-streamwise, resulting in anticyclonically rotating updrafts. Antistreamwise vorticity is relatively uncommon in storm environments because of biases indirectly associated with the Coriolis force.

A different mechanism applies to small tornadoes and waterspouts that develop in environments with insignificant vertical shear. These tend to develop along wind-shift lines, which become dynamically unstable and roll up into rows of vertical vortices, about 0.6 mi (1 km) in diameter. If one of the vortices happens to be located under the updraft of a cumulus congestus or cumulonimbus cloud, then a tornado may form as a result of the vertical stretching effect. These tornadoes develop when the temperature at low levels decreases strongly with height, and, unlike supercell tornadoes, occur early in the life of the parent cloud.

Energy source. The rate at which kinetic energy is produced in a tornado is estimated to be 10^3 MW in order of magnitude. To explain the high energy density of tornadoes, various exotic energy sources have been postulated in the past, including electrical heating from "rapid-fire" lightning discharges in a confined area. However, it is now believed that the tornado's energy is derived mostly from the buoyant potential energy that is released in the parent cloud by condensing water vapor.

Flow structure. Theory, laboratory simulations, computer models, and analysis of films reveal four

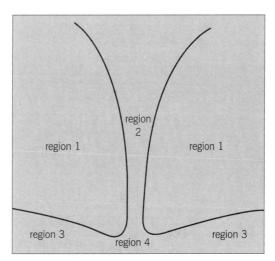

Fig. 3. Different flow regions of a tornado (*After E. Kessler, ed., Thunderstorm Morphology and Dynamics, 2d ed., University of Oklahoma Press, 1986*)

basic flow regions in tornadoes (**Fig. 3**). The first (region 1) is the outer flow away from the ground and the axis of rotation. This region consists of horizontally converging, rising air that approximately conserves its angular momentum. Consequently, the air spins faster as it approaches the axis. The core is region 2. It surrounds the axis, extending outward roughly to the radius of maximum winds. The core is approximately in solid-body rotation. The core flow is generally stable against radial displacements; and so it supports centrifugal waves, which are often seen moving up or down the funnel. This stability also prevents air from region 1 from being entrained into the core. The flow along the axis may be either upward or downward, and there may be stagnation points

(a)

(b)　　　　　　　　　(c)

(d)　　　　　　　　　(e)

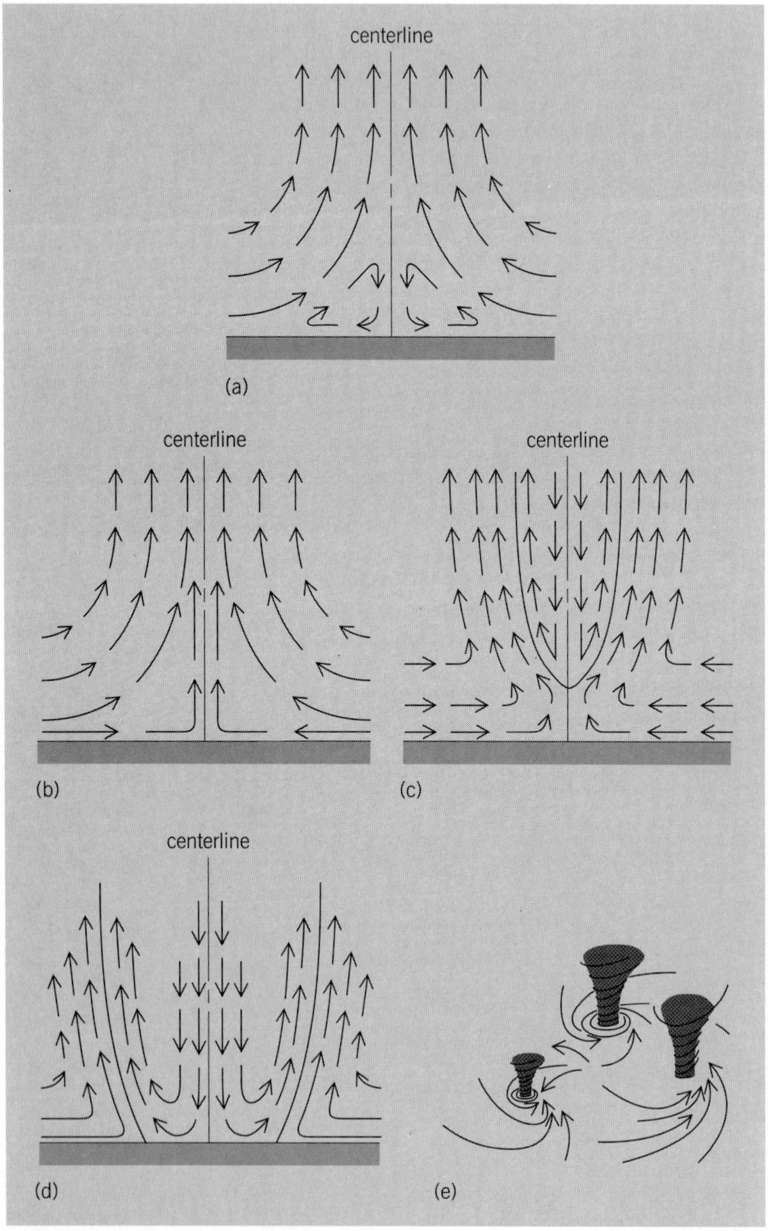

Fig. 4. Effect of increasing swirl ratio on the tornado flow. (a) Weak swirl—no tornado as flow in boundary layer separates and passes around corner region. (b) One-cell tornado (axial updraft). (c) Vortex breakdown (axial downdraft aloft does not reach ground). (d) Two-cell tornado with downdraft impinging on ground (core radius increases rapidly with increasing swirl ratio). (e) Multiple vortices (two to six with increasing swirl ratio). Only the flow in a radial-height cross section is depicted in a–d. (After E. Kessler, ed., *Thunderstorm Morphology and Dynamics*, 2d ed., University of Oklahoma Press, 1986)

aloft separating axial upflow and downflow. In large tornadoes, the axial flow is probably downward all the way to the ground. Interaction with the ground creates a turbulent boundary layer, perhaps a few hundred meters deep, of reduced tangential velocities. In this third region, the outward centrifugal forces no longer can balance the inward pressure gradient forces (as they do in region 1). The resulting net inward force drives a strong radial inflow into region 4, the corner region at the foot of the vortex. Here, conservation of mass dictates a strong updraft into the core, either along the axis or surrounding a central downdraft. Laboratory simulations reveal that vortex structure depends mainly on a single flow parameter, the swirl ratio, which is roughly the ratio of the strengths of the tangential and vertical velocities in the parent updraft. As the swirl ratio increases, the core increases, and the flow changes as shown in **Fig. 4**. Ultimately, transitions occur, first from a single vortex to two, then to three, up to six vortices.

Robert Davies-Jones

Bibliography. E. Kessler (ed.), *Thunderstorm Morphology and Dynamics*, 2d ed., 1986; R. E. Peterson (ed.), *Proceedings of the Symposium on Tornadoes: Assessment of Knowledge and Implications for Man*, Texas Technical University, 1976; P. S. Ray (ed.), *Mesoscale Meteorology and Forecasting*, 1986; J. T. Snow, The tornado, *Sci. Amer.*, 250:86–97, 1984.

Trophic ecology

The study of the feeding relationships of organisms in communities and ecosystems. Trophic links between populations represent flows of organisms, organic energy, and nutrients. Trophic transfers are important in population dynamics, biogeochemistry, and ecosystem energetics. Many influential concepts of community and ecosystem organization have been based on trophic patterns. *See* Biogeochemistry; Ecological energetics.

Food webs. The trophic links among populations in a community can be represented in a food web (**Fig. 1**). In a food web diagram, the arrows most commonly represent potential or inferred feeding relationships. In more elaborate representations, the width of each arrow is correlated to the measured amount of energy or mass transferred from the prey to the predator per unit time.

Most food webs are drawn as heuristic aids to show the main trophic links in a community. Therefore, minor links are omitted, and populations are often combined into functional groups for convenience (for example, the phytoplankton in Fig. 1). The diets of many predators change as the animals grow and develop; therefore, younger, smaller members of the population have quite different diets from those of older, larger individuals. Through growth and development, prey items also change in their vulnerability to particular predators. Many prey and predators undergo seasonal cycles of abundance and activity. Therefore, trophic links in nature are highly variable through time, and published food webs are intended as averages.

The patterns of linkage in food webs have been the subject of numerous theoretical and statistical analyses. The findings of this research remain controversial, in part because of the hidden assumptions made in drawing the webs that are analyzed. However,

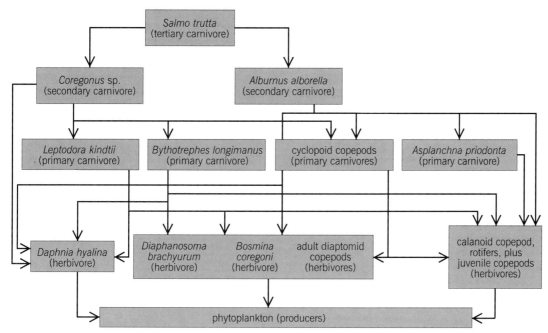

Fig. 1. Diagram of the food web of Lake Maggiore, Italy. Arrows represent potential or inferred feeding relationships. (*After R. DeBernardi, Biotic interactions in freshwater and effects on community structure, Bolletino Zool., 48:353–371, 1981*)

there is keen interest in food web research because of the fundamental importance of trophic links in community and ecosystem ecology. *See Food web*.

Trophic levels. These are functional groups formed by combining organisms that are the same number of trophic links removed from the base of the food web. Generally, the lowest trophic level, primary producers, is made up of green plants that obtain their energy from sunlight. Herbivores (primary consumers) make up the second trophic level, primary carnivores (secondary consumers) make up the third trophic level, and so forth. Decomposers (saprobes) are often viewed as a trophic level that is distinct from consumers of living prey. Combining the organisms into trophic levels collapses the food web into a food chain. Terrestrial food chains have as many as three or four trophic levels, while aquatic food chains have as many as five or six. Food chains are useful, but highly simplified, representations of trophic structure.

In terrestrial communities and ecosystems, the combined numbers, biomasses, or energy contents of the organisms at each tropic level produce a pyramid (**Fig. 2a**). The greatest number, biomass, or energy content occurs at the first (producer) level. Successive decreases occur at each higher trophic level. The energy decrease follows from the laws of thermodynamics, which dictate that some organic energy must be lost at each trophic transfer. Biomass is roughly proportional to energy content. Numbers may decline more than biomass or energy with each successive trophic level, because organisms at higher trophic levels are larger.

In aquatic communities, especially pelagic lakes and oceans, predators generally engulf their prey, and therefore their sizes (and life-spans) are larger at higher trophic levels. The pyramid of numbers has the same orientation as that of terrestrial communities, but the pyramid of biomass is reversed (Fig. 2b). The reverse biomass pyramid is explained by the normal pyramid of production, or energy flow per unit time.

Because lower trophic levels have higher productivity (despite their low biomass), they can support higher biomass at higher trophic levels. At the producer level, a small biomass has high production because the microscopic phytoplankton have very high rates of turnover. The herbivores have lower production but higher biomass than the producers, because the herbivores' birth and death rates are not as fast as those of the producers. Primary carnivores have even slower birth and death rates, and so they sustain greater biomass than the herbivores despite their lower production. *See Biological productivity; Biomass*.

Efficiency of trophic transfer. The ecosystem may be viewed as an energy-transforming system. Efficiencies of trophic transfer determine the transformation of forage energy into consumer energy. Within this framework, efficiency is defined as λ_N/λ_{N-1}, where λ represents the assimilation of energy by the trophic level denoted by the subscript. Efficiencies range from about 1% to more than 30% (with an average of about 10%) for the world's ecosystems.

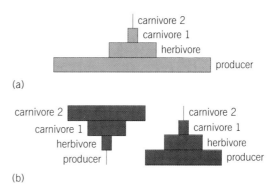

Fig. 2. Trophic levels. (*a*) Typical pyramid for a terrestrial community or ecosystem. The width of each level represents the energy, biomass, or numbers of organisms. (*b*) Reverse biomass pyramid (left) and normal production and numbers pyramids (right) of pelagic lake or ocean ecosystem.

Trophic state. Prior to the theory of an ecosystem as an energy-transforming system, ecologists classified lakes according to trophic state (as indicated by composition and biomass of phytoplankton and benthic insects). For example, oligotrophic lakes have low phytoplankton biomass and deep waters remain oxygenated all year, permitting a rich profundal fauna to flourish. In contrast, eutrophic lakes have high phytoplankton biomass and seasonally anoxic deep waters, restricting the distribution and composition of animal communities in the sediments. More than 30 trophic states were recognized until it was shown that lake ecosystems could pass through several trophic states during typical successional sequences spanning several thousand years. Thus, trophic state is not an immutable property of ecosystems, but a dynamically changing one. A particularly important change in trophic state is the so-called cultural eutrophication of lakes from poor land-use practices or inadequate sewage treatment. *See Eutrophication.*

Perturbations of trophic systems. When perturbation experiments are used to study the linkages in food webs, a relatively small number of the interactions turn out to have especially strong influences on community or ecosystem responses. Food webs based on strong interactions are much simpler than those based on potential feeding relationships or organic energy transfer (for example, Fig. 1), because only a few of the trophic links are highly influential. Strong interactions therefore offer the possiblity of simplifying the analysis of complex food webs. Trophic cascades result from several strong interactions in series. In lakes, for example, increased piscivore densities cause reduced density of planktivores, increased biomass of grazers, and reduced biomass of phytoplankton (Fig. 1). When trophic cascades control the producer trophic level, community changes at high trophic levels feed back to control ecosystem productivity. *See Ecological methods; Ecology; Ecosystem; Population ecology.*

Stephen R. Carpenter

Bibliography. R. Brewer, *The Science of Ecology,* 1988; P. Colinvaux, *Ecology,* 1986; C. J. Krebs, *Ecology,* 3d ed., 1985; R. L. Lindeman, The trophic-dynamic aspect of ecology, *Ecology,* 23, 339–418, 1942; R. T. Paine, Food webs: Linkage, interaction strength, and community infrastructure, *J. Anim. Ecol.,* 49:667–685, 1980.

Tsunami

A radially spreading, long-period gravity-wave system caused by any large-scale impulsive sea-surface disturbance. Being only weakly dissipative in deep water, major tsunamis can produce anomalous destructive wave effects at transoceanic distances. Historically, they rank high on the scale of natural disasters, having been responsible for losses approaching 100,000 lives and uncounted damage to coastal structures and habitations. Because of their uncertainty of origin, infrequency (10 per century), and sporadicity, tsunami forecasting is impossible, but the progressive implementation, since 1946, of the effective International Tsunami Warning System has greatly reduced human casualties. Present efforts, aided by advances in the fields of geomorphology, seismicity, and hydrodynamics, are directed toward an improved understanding of tsunami source mechanisms and the quantitative aspects of transocean propagation and terminal uprush along remote coastlines. These efforts are abetted by ever-increasing coastal utilization for nuclear power plants, oil transfer facilities, and commercial ports, not to mention public recreation. *See Geomorphology.*

Tsunami generation. While minor tsunamis are occasionally produced by volcanic eruptions or submarine landslides, major events are now recognized to be generated by the sudden quasi-unitized dislocations of large fault blocks associated with the crumpling of slowly moving sea-floor crustal plates, where they abut normally against the continental plates. Such sources are predominantly confined to tectonically active ocean margins, the majority of which currently ring the Pacific from Chile to Japan. As opposed to secular creep, tsunami-producing block dislocations are invariably associated with major shallow-focus (<18 mi or 30 km) earthquakes of intensity greater than 7 on the Gutenberg-Richter scale, followed by swarms of aftershocks of lesser intensity that decay in frequency over a week or two. Independent lines of evidence indicate that the aftershock perimeter defines the dislocated area, which is usually elongate, with its major axis parallel to the major fault trend. That only about 20% of large earthquakes fitting the above description produce major tsunamis raises the additional requirement that the dislocations have net vertical displacements, a view supported by seismic fault-plane analyses and confirmed by direct observations in the case of the 1964 Alaskan earthquake. *See Earthquake.*

Because the horizontal block dimensions are characteristically hundreds of miles, any such vertical dislocation (a few yards) immediately and similarly deforms the water surface. The resulting tsunami disperses radially in all directions as a train of waves whose energy is concentrated at wavelengths corresponding to the block dimensions and whose initial heights are determined by the local extent of vertical dislocation.

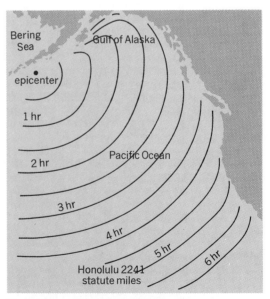

Fig. 1. Advance of tidal wave of April 1, 1946, caused by an earthquake with epicenter southeast of Unimak Island. (*After L. D. Leet and S. Judson, Physical Geology, 2d ed., Prentice-Hall, 1958*)

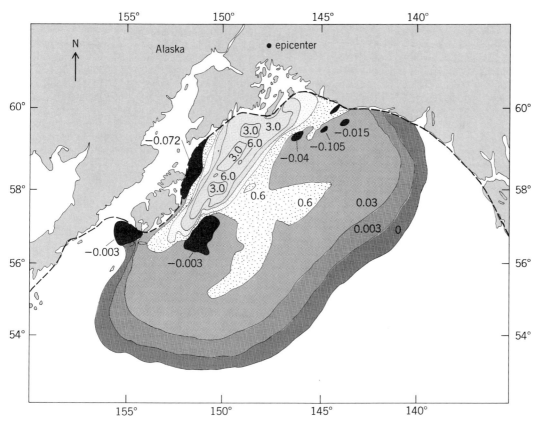

Fig. 2. Computer simulation of tsunami of March 24, 1964, in Gulf of Alaska, 18 min after earthquake. Surface contours in centimeters; wave heights in meters; $t = 1100$ s. 1 cm = 2.5 in., 1 m = 3.3 ft. (*After L.-S. Hwang and D. Divoky, Tsunamis, Underwater J., pp. 207–219, October 1971*)

Deep-sea propagation. Having principal wavelengths much longer than the greatest ocean depths, tsunamis are hydrodynamically categorized as shallow-water waves; to good approximation, their propagation speeds are proportional to the square root of the local water depth (400–500 mi/h or 600–800 km/h in the Pacific). Thus, after determination of the source location by early seismic triangulation, real-time warnings of wave arrival times can be compiled from precalculated travel-time charts (**Fig. 1**).

Because the initial wave energy imparted by the source dislocation is spread ever thinner as the wave pattern expands across the ocean, the average wave height everywhere diminishes with travel distance, amounting to only a few centimeters (virtually undetectable in deep water) halfway around the globe. Beyond this point, energy converges again toward the antipole of the source, and wave heights increase significantly. This convergence accounts, in part, for the severity of coastal effects in Japan from Chilean tsunamis, and conversely. Additionally, azimuthal variations in local wave height are caused by source orientation and eccentricity because, as with a radio antenna, the energy is radiated more efficiently normal to the longer axis. Lastly, further variations of wave height arise from refractive effects associated with regional differences in average water depth.

Coastal effects. After the waves cross the continental margins, the average wave height is greatly enhanced, partly by energy concentration in shallow water, and partly by strong refraction which, like a waveguide, tends to trap and further concentrate energy against the coastline. Ultimately, the shore arrests further progress. Here, the tsunami is characterized by swift currents in bays and harbors, by inundation of low-lying areas as recurrent breaking bores, and by uprush against steep cliffs, where watermarks as high as 60 ft (20 m) above sea level have been observed.

Prediction methods. While most of the above behavior has been predicted qualitatively in theory, the increased accuracy required for engineering design and hazard evaluation has led to the development of numerical modeling on large computers. Taking as input a representative time- and space-dependent source dislocation, as inferred from seismic or observational evidence, and the oceanwide distribution of water depths from bathymetric charts, the computer generates the initial surface disturbance (**Fig. 2**), propagates it across the sea surface, and yields the time history of water motion at any desired location. Where the source motion is known (Alaska, 1964), computer simulations agree quite accurately with observations at places where the linearized equations of motion can be expected to apply. But localized nonlinear effects, such as breaking bores, are more realistically modeled hydrodynamically, using the computer-generated wave field offshore as input.

William G. Van Dorn

Bibliography. W. C. Dudley and M. Lee, *Tsunami!*, 1988; L.-S. Hwang and D. Divoky, Tsunamis, *Underwater J.*, pp. 207–219, October 1971; T. Iwasaki andd K. Ilida (eds.), *Tsunamis: Their Science and Engineering*, 1983; National Academy of Sciences, *Oceanography and Coastal Engineering*, 1972; R. M. Stern, *Tsunami*, 1988.

Tundra

An area supporting some vegetation beyond the northern limit of trees, between the upper limit of trees and the lower limit of perennial snow on mountains, and on the fringes of the Antarctic continent and its neighboring islands. The term is of Lapp or Russian origin, signifying treeless plains of northern regions. Biologists, and particularly plant ecologists, sometimes use the term tundra in the sense of the vegetation of the tundra landscape. Tundra has distinctive characteristics as a kind of landscape and as a biotic community, but these are expressed with great differences according to the geographic region.

Patterns. Characteristically tundra has gentle topographic relief, and the cover consists of perennial plants a few centimeters to a meter or a little more in height. The general appearance during the growing season is that of a grassy sward in the wetter areas, a matted spongy turf on mesic sites, and a thin or

Fig. 1. Fjell-field tundra of the high Arctic. Sedges, mosses, and lichens form a thin and discontinuous sod. Late-persisting snowbanks are withdrawing from surfaces that are lighter in color because they lack many of the common plants, including dark-colored species of lichens. (*W. S. Benninghoff, U.S. Geological Survey*)

Fig. 2. Alpine tundra in French Alps. Altitudinal limit of trees occurs in valley behind building in middle distance. Although similar in vegetation structure to tundra of polar regions, Alpine tundras of lower latitudes are usually richer in vascular plant species than tundras of polar regions, and structure and composition of the vegetation have been modified by pasturing. (*W. S. Benninghoff, U.S. Geological Survey*)

sparsely tufted lawn or lichen heath on dry sites. In winter, snow mantles most of the surface with drifts shaped by topography and surface objects including plants; vegetation patterns are largely determined by protecting drifts and local areas exposed to drying and scouring effects of winter winds. By far, most tundra occurs where the mean annual temperature is below the freezing point of water, and perennial frost (permafrost) accumulates in the ground below the depth of annual thaw and to depths at least as great as 1600 ft (500 m). A substratum of permafrost, preventing downward percolation of water, and the slow decay of water-retaining humus at the soil surface serve to make the tundra surface moister during the thaw season than the precipitation on the area would suggest. Retention of water in the surface soils causes them to be subject to various disturbances during freezing and thawing, as occurs at the beginning and end of, and even during, the growing season. Where the annual thaw reaches depths of less than about 20 in. (50 cm), the soils undergo "swelling," frost heaving, frost cracking, and other processes that result in hummocks, polygonal ridges or cracks, or "soil flows" that slowly creep down slopes. As the soils are under this perennial disturbance, plant communities are unremittingly disrupted and kept actively recolonizing the same area. Thus topography, snow cover, soils, and vegetation interact to produce patterns of intricate complexity when viewed at close range.

Plant species, life-forms, and adaptations. The plants of tundra vegetation are almost exclusively perennial. A large proportion have their perennating buds less than 8 in. (20 cm) above the soil (chamaephytes in the Raunkiaer life-form system), especially among the abundant mosses and lichens. Another large group has the perennating organs at the surface of the soil (hemicryptophytes in the Raunkiaer system). Vegetative reproduction is common—by rhizomes (many of the sedges), stolons (certain grasses and the cloudberry, *Rubus chamaemorus*), or bulbils near the inflorescence (*Polygonum viviparum*, *Poa vivipara*, *Saxifraga hirculis*); thus clone formation is common in plant populations. Apomixis, the short-circuiting of the sexual reproduction process, is found frequently among flowering plants of tundra. Seed is set regularly by agamospermy, for example, in many dandelions (*Taraxacum* sp.), hawkweeds (*Hieracium* sp.), and grasses (*Calamogrostis* sp., *Poa* sp., *Festuca* sp.). The high incidence of apomixis in tundra flowering plants is coincident with high frequency of polyploidy, or multiple sets of chromosomes, in some circumstances a mechanical cause of failure of the union of gametes by the regular sexual process. Asexual reproduction and polyploidy tend to cause minor variations in plant species populations to become fixed to a greater extent than in populations at lower latitudes, and evolution tends to operate more at infraspecific levels without achieving major divergences. Adaptations are more commonly in response to physical factors of the stressful cold environment rather than to biotic factors, such as pollinators or dispersal agents, of the kinds that exert such control in the congenial warm, moist climates.

Soil conditions. Tundra soils are azonal, without distinct horizons, or weakly zonal. Soils on all but very dry and windswept sites tend to accumulate vegetable humus because low temperatures and waterlogging of soils inhibit processes of decay normally carried out by bacteria, fungi, and minute animals. Where permafrost or other impervious layers are several meters or more beneath the surface in soils with some fine-grained materials, leaching produces an Arctic Brown Soil in which there is moderately good drainage and cycling of mineral nutrients. In the greater part of tundra regions not mantled by coarse, rocky "fjell-field" materials (**Fig. 1**), the soils are more of the nature of half-bog or bog soils. These are characterized by heavy accumulations of raw or weakly decayed humus at the surface overlying a waterlogged or perennially frozen mineral horizon that is in a strongly reduced state from lack of aeration. Such boggy tundra soils are notoriously unproductive from the standpoint of cultivated plants, but they are moderately productive from the standpoint of shallowly rooted native plants. In Finland, forest plantations are being made increasingly productive on such soils by means of nutrient feeding to aerial parts. *SEE SOIL*.

Productivity. By reason of its occurrence where the growing season is short and where cloudiness and periods of freezing temperatures can reduce growth during the most favorable season, tundra vegetation has low annual production. Net radiation received at the Earth's surface is less than 20 kg-cal/(cm^2·year) [84 kilojoules/(cm^2 · year)] for all Arctic and Antarctic tundra regions. Assuming a 2-month growing season and 2% efficiency for accumulation of green plant biomass, 1 cm^2 could accumulate biomass equivalent to 66.6 g-cal/year (279 J/year). This best value for tundra is not quite one-half the world average for wheat production and about one-eighth of high-yield wheat production. The tundra ecosystem as a whole runs on a lower energy budget than ecosystems in lower latitudes; in addition, with decomposer and reducer organisms working at lower efficiency in cold, wet soils, litter and humus accumulate, further modifying the site in unfavorable ways. Grazing is one of the promising management techniques (**Fig. 2**) because of its assistance in speeding up the recycling of nutrients and reducing accumulation of raw humus. *SEE BIOMASS; ECOLOGICAL ENERGETICS; ECOSYSTEM*.

Fauna. The Arctic tundras support a considerable variety of animal life. The vertebrate herbivores consist primarily of microtine mammals (notably lemmings), hares, the grouselike ptarmigan, and caribou (or the smaller but similar reindeer of Eurasia). Microtine and hare populations undergo cyclic and wide fluctuations of numbers; these fluctuations affect the dependent populations of predators, the foxes, weasels, hawks, jaegers, and eagles. Alpine tundras generally have fewer kinds of vertebrate animals in a given area because of greater discontinuity of the habitats. Arctic and Alpine tundras have distinctive migrant bird faunas during the nesting season. Tundras of the Aleutian Islands and other oceanic islands are similar to Alpine tundras with respect to individuality of their vertebrate faunas, but the islands support more moorlike matted vegetation over peaty soils under the wetter oceanic climate. Tundras of the Antarctic continent have no vertebrate fauna strictly associated with it. Penguins and other sea birds establish breeding grounds locally on ice-free as well as fringing ice-covered areas. The only connection those birds have with the tundra ecosystem is the contribution of nutrients from the sea through their droppings. All tundras, including even those of the Antarctic, support a considerable variety of invertebrate animals, notably nematode worms, mites, and collembola on

and in the soils, but some other insects as well. Soil surfaces and mosses of moist or wet tundras in the Arctic often teem with nematodes and collembola. Collembola, mites, and spiders have been found above 20,000 ft (6000 km) in the Himalayas along with certain molds, all dependent upon organic debris imported by winds from richer communities at lower altitudes. *SEE TAIGA*.

William S. Benninghoff

Bibliography. Arctic Institute of North America, *Arctic Bibliography*, 16 vols., 1953–1975; M. J. Dunbar, *Ecological Development in Polar Regions*, 1968; P. W. English and J. A. Miller, *World Regional Geography*, 3d ed., 1989; J. D. Ives and R. G. Barry, *Arctic and Alpine Environments*, 1974; M. C. Kellman, *Plant Geography*, 2d ed., 1980; G. A. Llano (ed.), *Antarctic Terrestrial Biology*, American Geophysical Union, Antarctic Research Series, vol. 20, 1972; J. C. F. Tedrow (ed.), *Antarctic Soils and Soil Forming Processes*, American Geophysical Union, Antarctic Research Series, vol. 8, 1966; H. E. Wright, Jr., and W. H. Osburn, *Arctic and Alpine Environments*, 1968.

Underground mining

The extraction of ore from beneath the surface of the ground. Underground mining is also applied to deposits of industrial (nonmetallic) minerals and rocks, and underground or "deep" methods are used in coal mining. Some ores and industrial minerals can be recovered from beneath the surface of the ground by solution mining or in-place leaching using boreholes.

Underground mining involves a larger capital investment and higher production cost per ton of ore than open-pit mining. It is done where mineral deposits are situated beyond the economic depth of open-pit mining; it is generally applied to steeply dipping or thin deposits and to disseminated or massive deposits for which the cost of removing the overburden and the maintaining of a slope angle in adjacent waste rock would be prohibitive. In some situations, the shallower portion of a large orebody will be mined by openpit methods, and the deeper portion will be mined by underground methods. *SEE OPENPIT MINING*.

Underground mine entries are by shaft, adit, incline, or spiral ramp (**Fig. 1**). Development workings, passageways for gaining access to the orebody from stations on individual mine levels, are called drifts if they follow the trend of the mineralization, and crosscuts if they are driven across the mineralization. Workings on successive mine levels are connected by raises, passageways that are driven upward. Winzes are passageways that are sunk downward, generally from a lowermost mine level.

In a fully developed mine with a network of levels, sublevels, and raises for access, haulage, pumping, and ventilation, the ore is mined from excavations referred to as stopes. Pillars of unmined material are left between stopes and other workings for temporary or permanent natural support. In large-scale mining methods and in methods where an orebody and its overlying waste rock are allowed to break and cave under their own weight, the ore is extracted in large collective units called blocks, panels, or slices.

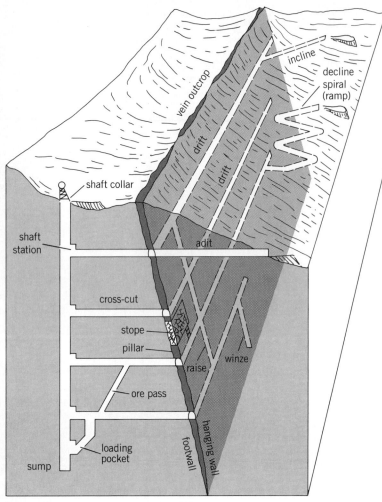

Fig. 1. Underground mining entries and workings.

EXPLORATION

Exploration and development constitute the pre-production stage of underground mining. Exploration, in this context, refers to the delineation of a newly discovered mineral deposit or an extension of a known deposit and to its evaluation as a prospect. During exploration, the deposit is investigated in sufficient detail to estimate its tonnage and grade, its metallurgical recovery characteristics, and its suitability for mining by various methods.

Information on the size, shape, and attitude of a deposit and information for estimating the tonnage and grade of the ore is taken from drill holes and underground exploration workings. Diamond core drilling provides intact samples of ore and rock for assaying and for detailed geologic and geotechnical study; percussion drilling provides chips of material for the recognition of ore and waste boundaries and for additional sampling. Underground exploration workings are used for bulk and detailed sampling, rock mechanics testing, and the siting of machinery for underground drilling.

The tonnage and the grade of the material available in a mineral deposit are interrelated. The cutoff grade is the weakest mineralization that can be mined at a profit. Ore reserves are calculated in respect to the amount of ore in place at potential cutoff grades, the tonnages and average grades in identified blocks of

ore, and the ultimate tonnage and grade of ore that should be available under projected conditions of recovery and wall rock dilution in mining. The suitability of a deposit for mining is determined in testing and evaluation work related to the physical and chemical nature of the ore, hydrologic conditions, and the needs for ground control.

MINE DEVELOPMENT

Where high topographic relief allows for an acceptable tonnage of ore above a horizontal entry site, an adit or blind tunnel is driven as a cross-cut to the deposit or as a drift following the deposit from a portal at a favorable location for the surface plant, drainage facilities, and waste disposal. In situations where the deposit lies below or at a great distance from any portal site for an adit, entry must be made from a shaft collar or from an incline or decline portal. A large mine will commonly have a main multipurpose entry and several more shafts or adits to accommodate personnel, supplies, ventilation, and additional production.

Adits. Access by adit generally provides for relatively low-cost underground mining. The broken ore from above the adit level can be brought to the portal in trains, conveyor belts, and rubber-tired trucks without the need for hoisting, and the workings can be drained without pumping. The driving of an adit is generally less expensive per unit distance of advance than the sinking of a shaft or the driving of an inclined access. In areas of low topographic relief and in the mining of deep orebodies, the sinking of a shaft will, however, often be a more economical approach than the driving and maintaining of a considerably longer incline or adit from a remote part of the site.

Shafts. Production shafts are generally located in stable ground on the footwall side of a dipping deposit rather than in the deposit itself or in the hanging-wall side where protective pillars would be needed to maintain stability as mining progresses. A shaft may be inclined to follow the dip of the deposit and avoid increasingly longer cross-cuts to the ore at greater depth, but vertical shafts are more common because of their lower construction and maintenance cost per unit of depth and their better efficiency for hoisting ore. Shafts are sunk as rectangular or circular openings 15–30 ft (5–9 m) in diameter; they are equipped with a headframe and hoisting system and are lined with timber, steel forms, or concrete for ground support. Smaller shafts 5–15 ft (1.5–5 m) in diameter, generally for escapeways and ventilation, may be bored by mechanical drilling machines.

Inclines. Inclines equipped with hoists, declines for access by rubber-tired equipment, and gently inclined spiral ramps for diesel-powered truck haulage allow for direct access to relatively deep mine levels without having to transfer the ore and materials to hoisting systems.

Development workings. Development workings in the deposit consist of mine levels and sublevels, with drifts in the ore zone or in the more stable rock on the footwall side of the ore zone. Level workings serve as passageways for miners and low-profile equipment and as haulageways. In broken or unstable ground, passageways and haulageways are supported by timber sets and steel beams or arches; further stabilization is given by rock bolts, sometimes in combination with wire mesh, and the walls may be lined with concrete.

The raises that connect levels and sublevels provide for the removal of broken ore (chutes and ore passes), for access by miners, and for ventilation and supply routes.

In conventional mining and in the most common development procedures, headings are advanced in a cyclic sequence of drilling, blasting, mucking (removal of broken rock), and installing ground support. In continuous mining, the cycle is replaced by a single operation in which headings are advanced by powerful machines with teeth that break rock from the face. In situations where the uniformity and texture of the rock and ore permit development by continuous mining, the walls of the resulting passageways are smoother and more stable than would be provided by conventional cyclic operations involving blasting.

The continuous mining procedure of raise boring is relatively well established. Shaft boring is used in the sinking of small-diameter ventilation shafts and escapeways. The driving of mine level development headings by cutting and boring machinery is more common in coal, potash, and salt deposits and in relatively soft sandstones and shales than in hard ore and rock.

Broken rock from development headings is collected at the face by mechanical loading machinery and transferred to the mine haulage system by mobile conveyors or rubber-tired load-haul-dump machines. Haulage beyond the transfer point is done by electric-powered locomotives with trains of cars, by electric- or diesel-powered shuttle cars or trucks, and by conveyor belt systems. In shaft mines, the broken rock is collected in underground storage pockets and loaded into skips for hoisting to the surface.

MINING METHODS

A fundamental condition in the choice of mining method is the strength of the ore and wall rock. Strong ore and rock will permit relatively low-cost methods with naturally supported openings or with a minimum of artificial support. Weaker ore and wall rock will necessitate more costly methods requiring widespread temporary or permanent artificial support. Large deposits with weak ore and weak walls that collapse readily and provide suitably broken material for extraction may be mined by low-cost caving methods. Few mineral deposits are so uniform that a single method can be used without modification in all parts of the mine. Mining to an increasing depth with higher stress conditions and mining from a thicker portion of an orebody into thinner or less uniform portions will especially call for changes in method.

Naturally supported openings. The stopes remain open, essentially by their own strength, during ore extraction. Stability may, however, be maintained to some extent by timbers, rock bolts, and accumulations of broken ore. The workings may collapse with time or may eventually need to be filled with waste material to protect workings in adjacent areas. The methods range from so-called gophering, an unsystematic small-scale practice, to carefully planned and executed systems using limits determined by rock mechanics investigations.

Open stoping. This is used in steeply dipping and thin orebodies with relatively strong ore and wall rock. In overhand methods the ore is stoped upward by miners working on a staging composed of stulls (round timbers) and lagging (planks). With the drilling and blasting of successive small blocks of ore from the back (roof), the broken ore falls to the bottom of the stope and is collected on the haulage level through draw points or chutes. In underhand stoping the ore is mined downward in a series of benches, and the broken ore is scraped or hauled into a raise or ore pass for collection on a lower mine level. The width of an open stope is limited by the strength of the ore and its capability to stand unsupported. Occasional pillars, generally of waste or low-grade zones in a vein, are left for support; stulls may be wedged between the stope walls for stability as well as for access, and rock bolts may also be used to maintain wall stability.

Sublevel stoping. Also referred to as longhole or blasthole stoping, sublevel stoping is practiced in steeply dipping and somewhat wider orebodies with strong ore and strong walls (**Fig. 2**). Sublevel drifts and raises or slots are driven at the ends of a large block of ore so that a series of thinner horizontal slices can be provided. Miners in the sublevels drill patterns of radial holes (ring or fan drilling) or quarrylike parallel holes (slashing). Beginning at the open face of the initial slot, the ore is blasted in successive increments and the broken ore falls directly to the bottom of the stope. A pillar is generally left unmined at the top of the stope in order to support the next major level.

Vertical crater retreat. This is a mining method of sublevel stoping in which large-diameter blastholes are drilled in a parallel pattern between major levels, and the ore is broken from the bottom of the stope in a sequence of localized blasts. All of the drilling, loading, and blasting are done by miners in the upper level, so there is no need for access to the ore from below as the stope progresses upward.

Room-and-pillar mining. This is done in coal seams

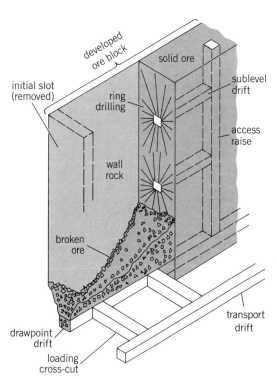

Fig. 2. Sublevel stoping, with ring drilling.

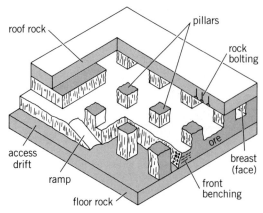

Fig. 3. Room-and-pillar mining; two-stage benching operation.

and in flat-lying or gently dipping ore and industrial mineral deposits (**Fig. 3**). It is a low-cost method of underground mining because fast-moving rubber-tired equipment can operate freely, especially in large rooms and haulageways. Thin-bedded deposits are generally mined in a single stage (pass) by conventional or continuous mining; thicker deposits are mined in a two-stage benching operation. In deposits of considerable thickness, an underground quarrying operation follows the first-stage opening of a development level for sufficient access by open pit-type blasthole drills. Room-and-pillar mining is generally limited to depths on the order of 3000 ft (914 m) in ''hard rock'' mines and to lesser depths in coal mines because of rock bursts and similar manifestations of high-stress concentration on the pillars. Extraction in mining generally amounts to about two-thirds of the ore in a bedded deposit, with the remaining ore being left in pillars; in places where pillars can be ''robbed'' and the roof allowed to settle, extraction can be increased to 90% or more.

Shrinkage stoping. This is an overhand method in which broken ore accumulates in the stope, affording temporary support for the walls and providing a working platform for miners (**Fig. 4**). Shrinkage stoping is most applicable to steeply dipping veins with strong ore that will stand across a span and with relatively strong wall rock that would slough into the stope in places if left completely unsupported. When ore is broken, it has an expansion or swell factor; this

necessitates a periodic drawing (shrinking) of some of the broken ore from the draw points and chutes to allow for continued access to the top of the stope. When all of the ore has been broken except for that left in pillars to protect the adjacent raises and mine levels, the entire content of the stope is drawn. The empty stope may be left open or it may be filled with waste rock, and the pillars may eventually be mined.

Artificially supported openings. In this method, workings are kept open during mining by using waste material, timber, and hydraulic props. After the ore is extracted, the workings are filled to maintain stability or are allowed to cave.

Cut-and-fill stoping. This method is used in steeply dipping orebodies in which the ore has sufficient strength to be self-supporting but the walls are too weak to stand entirely without support (**Fig. 5**). Most cut-and-fill stoping is done overhand, with the drilling and blasting phase similar to that in shrinkage stoping; the broken ore is, however, removed from each new cut or slice along the back, and the floor of the stope is built up of waste material such as sand or mill tailings brought in by pipeline as a water slurry.

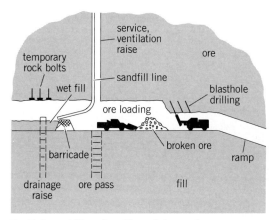

Fig. 5. Cut-and-fill stoping with sand slurry and ramp.

The smooth and compacted fill material provides an especially suitable floor for rubber-tired machinery. Variations in cut-and-fill mining include the ramp-in-stope system, in which load-haul-dump equipment can move rapidly in and out of the stope on an inclined surface of fill material, and the less-mechanized system of resuing in narrow veins. In resuing, ore and waste material are broken separately and the waste material is left to accumulate as fill. One additional system, undercut-and-fill, is applied to bodies of weaker ore. It provides a solid artificial back of reinforced and cemented fill for the mining of successively underlying slices of ore.

Square set stoping. This is a labor-intensive and high-cost method used in situations where the ore is too weak to stand across a wide or long back and the walls are not strong enough to support themselves. A square set, a skeletal box of keyed timbers, is filled and wedged into the available space as each small block of ore is removed by drilling and blasting. Mining continues by overhand or underhand stoping, and the stope becomes a network of interlocked square sets. The sets in the mined portion of the stope are filled with mill tailings or waste rock and pillars are left between mined-out stopes for additional wall support while the remainder of the deposit is being

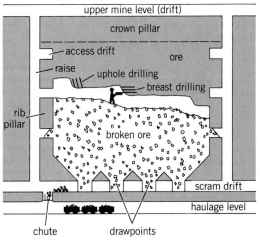

Fig. 4. Shrinkage stoping, longitudinal section.

mined. Because of its high cost, square setting has been superseded in many mines by cut-and-fill, top slicing, and sublevel caving methods.

Longwall mining. This method is applicable to uniform and extensive but relatively thin deposits. Primarily a highly mechanized coal mining method at depths where rock pressures are too high for safe room-and-pillar mining, it has also been used to some extent in potash deposits and in bedded copper, uranium, and iron orebodies. In the South African deep gold mines, a form of longwall mining is used in the thin-bedded ore zones.

In longwall mining, practically all of the coal or ore is recovered except for that left in safety pillars to protect surface structures.

The basic practice is to maintain a temporary opening in a uniform line along a working face and then to allow the roof to cave onto the floor or waste fill (gob) behind the active area. In a typical mechanized longwall coal operation, the roof support units are canopies with hydraulic-powered adjustable legs or chocks that are moved ahead as the coal is shaved into slices by shearing and plowing machinery with integrated conveyor systems. In the mining of South African gold reef deposits, longwall mining is done by drilling and blasting; the active area is kept open by hydraulic props and timber-concrete packs, and the mined-out areas are filled to some extent by waste rock or cemented mill tailings.

Longwall mining systems allow for a high abutment pressure to build up in solid ore or coal in advance of the face, a low-pressure zone to exist in the working area just behind the face, and a normal lithostatic pressure to build up again in the mined-out and caved or gob-filled area as the face is moved ahead.

Top slice stoping. This method is applicable to wide and steeply dipping deposits with weak ore and weak walls, and it is also used in recovering pillars that have been left between filled stopes. It is a relatively expensive and labor-intensive method with a requirement for abundant timber, but it permits nearly total extraction of the ore. Top slicing is ultimately a caving method of mining, but the ore must first be drilled and blasted, and temporary support is needed between the taking of each successive downward slice or horizontal cut of ore. Working begins in drifts and cross-cuts on a mining floor at the top of a raise; after the driving of a series of adjacent cross-cuts so that a slice of sufficient width has been taken, a mat of timber and scrap lumber is laid down on the floor and the supporting timbers are blasted to cave the overlying rock. A new slice is mined laterally from drifts and cross-cuts under the mat, with the mat supported by timber props (stulls). A mat is again laid down, supports are blasted, and subsequent slices are mined beneath the subsiding accumulation of timber mats and waste rock.

Caving methods. These methods are used in large orebodies with relatively weak ore and with weak wallrock that will collapse as the ore is removed. Geologic conditions must permit subsidence, and the ore must be sufficiently jointed or fractured to form fragments small enough to be handled in draw points and raises. Ore recovery in mining is generally quite high, but a certain amount of dilution from waste rock must be accepted.

Sublevel caving. This type is most suited to large and steeply dipping orebodies with weak walls and with ore that has enough stability to maintain sublev-

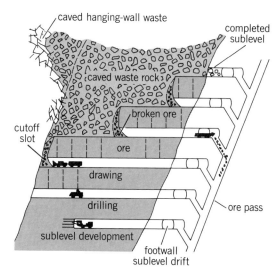

Fig. 6. Sublevel caving, with stages of development and mining.

els (**Fig. 6**). It is similar to sublevel open stoping, but in this method the walls and the back are allowed to collapse. As with top slicing, the ore is mined in downward increments, but here the slices are thicker and they are drilled, blasted, and drawn from levels below the ore. Access drifts are driven on the footwall side of the orebody, sublevel cross-cuts are driven in ore, and fans of blastholes are drilled at intervals in the cross-cuts. A steplike succession of slices is mined in retreat from the hanging wall, with the wall rock collapsing and following the extraction of the ore. As each fan of holes is blasted, the broken ore caves into the sublevel, where it is loaded and transported to the ore pass. Broken waste rock fills the void as the ore is drawn. When an excess of waste rock begins to dilute the broken ore, the drawing is stopped and the next fan of holes is blasted.

Block caving. This is applied to large and relatively uniform bodies in which both ore and waste will cave readily (**Fig. 7**). Production on the order of 50,000–75,000 tons (45,000–68,000 metric tons) per day can be achieved at a very low mining cost, but the capital

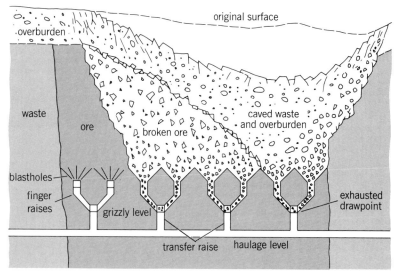

Fig. 7. Block caving, with principal haulage level, driving raises to production (grizzly) levels, and raises to workings.

cost of a block-caving mine is high. A mine is prepared for block-caving operations by establishing a principal haulage level, driving raises to production levels (slusher or grizzly levels), and driving a larger number of raises to workings on an undercut level beneath the orebody or block to be mined. Caving is initiated by drilling and blasting a slice of ore above the undercut level and, if necessary, by excavating narrow stopes at the boundaries of the block. With the drawing of the initially broken ore, the block begins to cave under its own weight. With further drawing, the entire column of ore and overburden rock continues to subside and break upward for as much as 4000 ft (1220 m) to the surface, where a depression forms. The ore, broken and crushed in caving, flows through cone-shaped draw holes and finger raises. The finger raises are carefully monitored at draw points on the grizzly level so that the caving action is kept uniform and salient channels of subsiding waste rock are not allowed to form prematurely. Broken ore collected from finger raises reaches the haulage level through transfer raises. SEE MINING.

William C. Peters

Bibliography. Dravo Corporation (U.S. Bureau of Mines), *Analysis of Large Scale Non-Coal Underground Mining Methods*, 1974; I. A. Given (ed.), *SME Mining Engineering Handbook*, 1973; H. L. Hartman, *Introductory Mining Engineering*, 1987; W. A. Hustrulid (ed.), *Underground Mining Methods Handbook*, 1982; B. Stack, *Handbook of Mining and Tunnelling Equipment*, 1982; K. S. Stout, *Mining Methods and Equipment*, 1980.

Vegetation and ecosystem mapping

The graphic portrayal of spatial distributions of vegetation, ecosystems, or their characteristics. Vegetation is one of the most conspicuous and characteristic features of the landscape and has long been a convenient way to distinguish different regions. Because vegetation provides the basic framework of terrestrial ecosystems, maps of ecosystems and biomes have been mainly vegetation maps. Resources generally must be inventoried and mapped before they can be well managed. Thus, as pressure on the Earth's natural resources grows and as natural ecosystems become increasingly disturbed, degraded, and in some cases replaced completely, the mapping of vegetation and ecosystems, at all scales and by various methods, has become more and more common and important.

Basic approaches and considerations. Probably since classical times, and certainly since the rapid development of mapmaking during the Renaissance, mappers have located vegetation in relation to natural or cultural patterns. Three basic approaches arose for mapping general vegetation patterns: (1) one based on vegetation structure or gross physiognomy, (2) one based on correlated environmental patterns, and (3) a floristic approach based on particular important taxa. The environmental approach provides the least information about the actual vegetation, but succeeds in covering regions where the vegetation is poorly understood. Most earlier and many later vegetation maps involve combinations of the three approaches.

The first world vegetation maps were produced in Europe near the end of the nineteenth century and were inconsistent, since many regions of the world were not well known. As knowledge of more obscure regions increased, however, better maps appeared, for the whole world and for individual continents, countries, or regions. Perhaps the first world vegetation base map free of environmental surrogates was that by A. W. Küchler in 1949. Excellent modern vegetation maps of regions include those of the United States by Küchler (1964), South America by Hueck and Seibert (1972), the Mediterranean and adjacent regions by UNESCO (1969), Western Australia by Beard, and France and India by the French vegetation mapping groups at Toulouse, Grenoble, and Pondicherry (India). In the United States, excellent vegetation maps have also appeared for some states, such as California and Minnesota.

Mapping has expanded since the 1950s to involve other aspects of vegetation and ecosystems as well as new methodologies for map production. Functional processes such as primary production, decomposition rates, and climatic correlates such as evapotranspiration have been estimated for enough sites so that world maps can be attempted. More general structural aspects of ecosystems, such as total standing biomass or potential litter accumulations, are also being estimated and mapped. Such quantitative maps of hitherto poorly known basic processes or accumulations can be quantified geographically to provide first estimates of important aspects of world biogeochemical budgets and resource potentials. Computer-produced maps, often coupled directly with predictive models, remote-sensing capabilities, and other techniques, have also revolutionized vegetation and ecosystem mapping.

Base maps and scales. Maps on a scale of 1:24,000 from the U.S. Geological Survey may be too small for working with plant associations and diverse cultural features; they are widely available, however, and can be enlarged photostatically for field work. U.S. Army Map Service sheets at 1:250,000 are available in a consistent style over wide areas. If maps of these two types have not become too outdated because of land clearing, green forest overlay printing on these maps will provide a first-order distinction between forest/woodland and other kinds of vegetation. Such maps at least can serve to show altitudinal zonation, and may further suggest relations to geologic substrate and soil-type associations if reliable soil maps can be found. SEE GEOMORPHOLOGY.

The mapping of large areas at coarser scales, even with the benefit of the remote-sensing techniques mentioned below, is of varying accuracy for regions with different economic and landscape conditions. A common denominator of mapping at a widely available and acceptable scale convention of 1:1,000,000 has been advocated.

The following outline comprises the legend of the UNESCO Committee on Classification and Mapping (mainly for scales 1:1,000,000 and smaller; larger scale is required for many of the finer subdivisions, however). The legend is only slightly changed from that of H. Ellenberg and D. Mueller-Dombois (1965–1966). A less abbreviated adaptation was published in the "Geographic Index" of Reichle (1970), which is keyed to a map of regions which are coded according to their estimated pre-iron-age carbon mass of vegetation (above and below ground). At the left of the outline is the IBP Index Code for major groups of biomes proposed by the International Biological Program section on Terrestrial Productivity (PT) for indexing projects, sites, and ecosystems.

I. Formation Class
   A. FORMATION SUBCLASS
      1. *Formation Group*
         a. Formation
            1) Subformation

I. Closed Forests (>5 m or 16.5 ft tall, crowns touching in wind—except that immature, cutover and grazed forest types may be shorter or more open without being called scrub or woodland, respectively)
   A. MAINLY EVERGREEN FOREST
     Canopy never without foliage, although individual trees may shed leaves
(Fr). . .   1. *Tropical Rainforest* (= ombrophilous) Little or no bud protection, nor cold or drought resistance; ''drip-tip'' leaves common
(Frd). . .   2. *Tropical and Subtropical Evergreen Seasonal Forest* Some bud protection and noticeable dry-season shedding a-d. Lowland, Submontane, Montane, dry ''Subalpine''
(Fdr). . .   3. *Tropical and Subtropical Semi-Deciduous Forest* Upper canopy mostly drought-deciduous; evergreen trees in canopy layers or understory
(Fr). . .   4. *Subtropical Seasonal Rainforest*
(Fr). . .   5. *Mangrove Forest*
(Fr). . .   6. *Temperate and Subpolar Rainforest*
(Fd). . .   7. *Temperate Evergreen Seasonal Broad-Leaved Forest*
(Fs). . .   8. *Winter-Rain Hard-Broad-Leaved* (Sclerophyll) *Evergreen Forest*
(Fn). . .   9. *Coniferous Evergreen Forests*
         a. Giant evergreen conifers (>50 m or 165 ft tall)
         b. Conifers rounded or flattened
         c. Conifers mostly conical
         d. Conifers cylindro-conical, with short branches
   B. MAINLY DECIDUOUS FORESTS
(Fd). . .   1. *Drought-Deciduous* (Monsoon) *Forest* (tropical, subtropical)
        2. *Cold-Deciduous Forest with Evergreens*
(Fc). . .   a. With evergreen broad-leaved trees and climbers
(Fc). . .   b. With hard-broad-leaved evergreen shrubs
(Fcn). . .   c. With evergreen needle-leaved trees (cool)
(Fcn). . .   d. With evergreen needle-leaved trees (warm)

(Fcn). . .   e. With conifers and/or broad-leaved evergreens
(Fc). . .   3. *Cold-Deciduous (Summergreen) Forests* Evergreens (if any) mostly shrubs, or scattered
         a. Temperate lowland and submontane (''nemoral'')
         b. Montane, boreal and humid-site
         c. Subalpine or subpolar (<20 m or 66 ft; commonly gnarled)
         d. Alluvial, flooded
             1) Occasionally or never
             2) Regularly
         e. Swamp or bog forest
   C. DRY FORESTS (commonly grading to open woodlands)
(Fd). . .   1. *Hard-Leaved Forests*: Some with swollen underground bases (xylopods)
(Fd). . .   2. *Thorn Forests* a, b. Mixed deciduous-evergreen, deciduous
(Ds). . .   3. *Mainly Succulent Forests* (trees and/or shrubs)

II. Open Woodlands (<5 m or 16.5 ft tall, crowns projecting over 30% of surface; may be grassy, grading to savanna)
   A. MAINLY EVERGREEN WOODS
Fs. . .   1. *Evergreen Broad-Leaved Woodlands*
Fn. . .   2. *Evergreen Needle- or Scale-Leaved Woodlands*
         a. Conifers rounded, flattened or irregular (such as pine)
             1) With hard-broad-leaved understory
             2) Without hard-broad-leaved understory
         b. Conifers mostly conical or dense (such as juniper)
         c. Conifers cylindro-conical, or sheared
   B. MAINLY DECIDUOUS WOODLANDS
Fd. . .   1. *Drought-Deciduous Woodlands*
Fcn. . .   2. *Cold-Deciduous Woodland with Evergreens* (see IB2)
Fc. . .   3. *Cold-Deciduous Woodland* (summergreen)
D. . .   C. DRY WOODLANDS (divided as for IC, but sparser)

III. Scrub (mainly 0.5–5 m or 1.65–16.5 ft; thicket or shrubland, with grass)
   A. MAINLY EVERGREEN SCRUB
      1. *Evergreen Broad-Leaved Scrubland or Thickets*
      2. *Evergreen Needle-Leaved and Microphyll Scrub*
   B. MAINLY DECIDUOUS SCRUB
Fd. . .   1. *Drought-Deciduous Scrub with Evergreens*
Fd. . .   2. *Drought-Deciduous Scrub without Evergreens*

TUNDRA

- 1 polar desert
- 2 arctic bogs
- 3 mountains, ice
- 4,4A scrub, meadows

BOREAL bogs + taiga:
spruce-fir (Picea-Abies)
pine-larch (Pinus-Larix)
birch-poplar (Betula-Populus)

NORTHERN parkland
- 5A Alaskan
- 5B Canadian
- 5C Eurasian (including mt.)

MIDDLE woodland
- 6A Yukon
- 6B Canadian
- 6C European
- 6D Siberian (W)
- 6E Siberian (E)
- >6F mt. taiga-tundra

SOUTHERN forest
- 7B mid-Canadian
- 7C Laurentian
- 7D Fennoscandian
- 7E Russian
- 7F Siberian (W)
- 7G Siberian (C)
- 7H Siberian mt. taiga-steppe

OTHER COLD CONIFER

PACIFIC SUBALPINE SNOW WOODS
- 1 Asian Abies, Picea jezoensis
- 2 ± Tsuga diversifolia (Japan)
- 3 Cordilleran Abies, Tsuga

HEMIBOREAL conifer ± deciduous
- 8A Cordilleran Pseudotsuga mix
- 8B Acadian Picea, Abies, Tsuga
- 8C European Picea abies, Pinus
- 8D Asian Abies, Pinus koraiensis

- 9A montane: + Tsuga or meadow
  - 1 Cordilleran Ts. heterophylla
  - 2 S. Himalayan Ts. dumosa
  - 3 E. Himalayan Ts. chinensis
- 9B poplar, larch, birch woodland
  - 1 + spruce-fir transition
  - 2 + grassland transition
  - 3 Pinus + mixes, Quercus

MAIN TEMPERATE (NEMORAL) ZONE

10 COLD-DECIDUOUS AND MIXED FOREST
oak, maple ± linden, beech, etc.
- 10A + northern hardwoods, conifers
- 10B + grassland, streamside woods
- 10C + maritime conifer, moorland
- 10D + Appalachian-Atlantic mixtures
- 10E European Atlantic Quercus robur mix
- 10F central Fagus sylvatica + mixtures
- 10G Asia Minor Fagus orientalis + mts.
- 10H N. Chinese Quercus, Pinus + mixes
- 10J mid Japanese Fagus, Quercus, conifer
- 10K Cordilleran Quercus, no. conifer

SOUTHERN MIXED FOREST AND WOODLAND
oak (partly evergreen), pine, etc.
- 11A + hard-leaved (sclerophyll) and scrub
- 11B + savanna, scrub, grassland mosaic
- 11C + short-leaved pine, and/or juniper
- 11D + long-leaved pines, swamps
- 11E + Castanopsis, conifers
- 11F + Cyclobalanopsis, Cunninghamia
- 11G + Cupressus woodland

OPEN WOODLAND
- 12A + alpine and/or evergreens
- 12B + scrub or desert
- 12C + grassland

GRASSLAND
- 13 tallgrass ± mixed woods
- 14 short and mixed grass
- 15 pampa, cool savanna

DESERTS, EXTRATROPICAL
- 16 northern scrub
- 17 warm-temperate scrub
- 18 saline ephemerals, scrub
- 19 scrub-grass mixtures
- 19A + saxaul, dunes
- 19B + mainly bare dunes
- 20 ephemeral or barren

HIGHLAND-MONTANE COMPLEXES
- 13A forest-meadow-steppe
- 16A desert steppe
- 21 high barrens, grass, puna
- 21A rock or snow vegetation
- 22 alpine meadow, scrub, forest
- 22A paramo, parkland, cloud forest

SPECIAL ECOSYSTEM COMPLEXES
- 28 mangrove shoreline or swamp
- 29 solonchak and desert lowlands
- 30 main alluvial forest-herb complexes
- 31 temperate broad-leaved evergreens
- 32 subtropical seasonal rainforests
- 33 temperate or cool mixed rainforest
- 34 oceanic or giant evergreen forest
- 34A coastal Picea fringe (salt winds)
- 34B other Pseudotsuga-Thuja coast mixes
- 34C Sequoia and conifer mixes
- 34D Southern Hemisphere giant forests

WARM TEMPERATE WOODLAND AND/OR SCRUB
- 35 dry summer—winter rain complex
- 35A sierra mixed forest, grass
- 36 mixed woods ± prairie, pampa
- 37 tall—mixed prairie, scrub
- 38 dry grassland, woodland
- 39 semisucculent halophytes
- 40 semideserts + dry wood
- 41 Chihuahuan
- 42 Jordan—Iranian deserts

SUBTROPICAL TO TROPICAL
TROPICAL BORDER ZONES
- 43 E. Oceanic rainforest
- 44 seasonal rainforest
- 45 dry woodland-savanna
- 46 savanna, scrub-woodland
- 47 semidesert scrub-savanna
- 48 Saharan } continental
  Australian } deserts
- 49 deserts with ocean fog
- 50 Arabian deserts

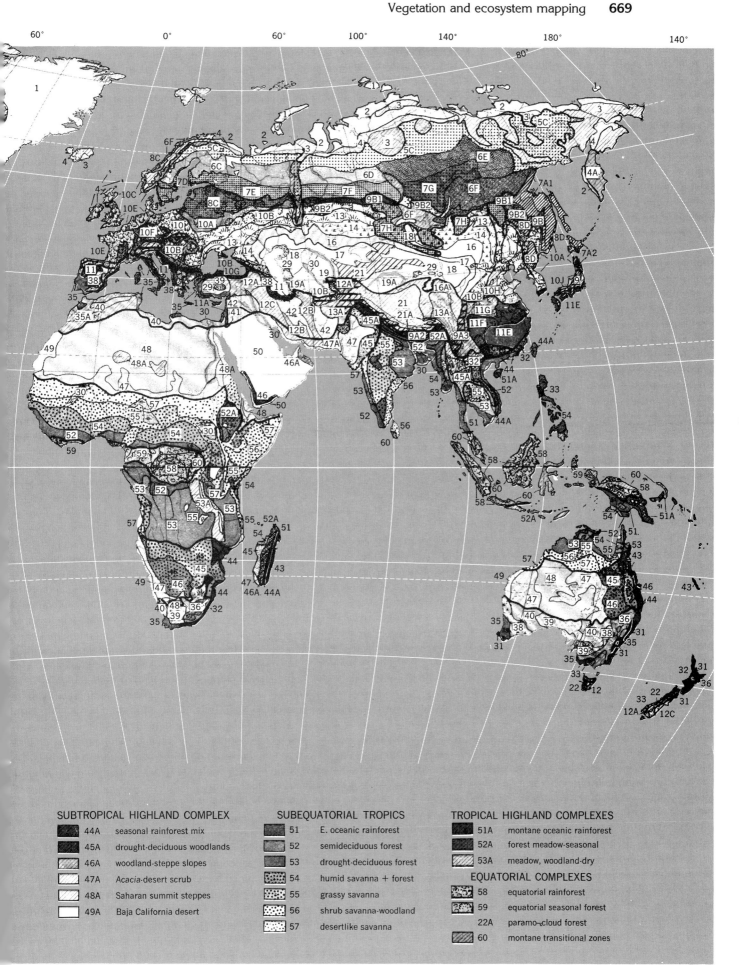

SUBTROPICAL HIGHLAND COMPLEX

	44A	seasonal rainforest mix
	45A	drought-deciduous woodlands
	46A	woodland-steppe slopes
	47A	Acacia-desert scrub
	48A	Saharan summit steppes
	49A	Baja California desert

SUBEQUATORIAL TROPICS

	51	E. oceanic rainforest
	52	semideciduous forest
	53	drought-deciduous forest
	54	humid savanna + forest
	55	grassy savanna
	56	shrub savanna-woodland
	57	desertlike savanna

TROPICAL HIGHLAND COMPLEXES

	51A	montane oceanic rainforest
	52A	forest meadow-seasonal
	53A	meadow, woodland-dry

EQUATORIAL COMPLEXES

	58	equatorial rainforest
	59	equatorial seasonal forest
	22A	paramo-cloud forest
	60	montane transitional zones

Fc. . .   3. *Cold-Deciduous Scrub*
     C. DESERT SHRUBLANDS
Dx. . .   1. *Mainly Evergreen Subdesert*
Dx. . .   2. *Deciduous Subdesert*
       a. Without succulents
Ds. . .   b. With succulents

  IV. Dwarf Scrub and Related Ecosystems
     A. MAINLY EVERGREEN DWARF SCRUB
Th. . .   1. *Evergreen Dwarf Scrub Thickets* (heath)
T. . .   2. *Evergreen Dwarf Shrubland*
Tg. . .   3. *Evergreen Dwarf Scrub–Herb Mixture*
T. . .   B. MAINLY DECIDUOUS DWARF SCRUB
Dx. . .   C. SEMIDESERT DWARF SHRUB
Tt. . .   D. TUNDRAS
       1. *Moss Tundra*
       2. *Lichen Tundra*
Tp. . .   E. MOSSY BOGS
       1. *Raised Bogs* (oceanic, montane, subcontinental)
       2. *Nonraised Bogs*
        a. Blanket bog (oceanic, submontane, montane)
        b. String bogs ("aapa")
        c. Lake bogs
  V. Terrestrial Herbaceous Ecosystems
Gs. . .   A. SAVANNAS AND RELATED GRASSLANDS (tropical, subtropical)
Gp. . .   B. STEPPES AND RELATED GRASSLANDS ("prairie")
       1. *Tall-Grass Prairie* (steppe)
       2. *Mid-Grass (and Mixed) Prairie* (steppe)
       3. *Short-Grass Prairie* (steppe)
       4. *Forb-Rich Meadow Steppes*
     C. MEADOWS, PASTURES AND RELATED GRASSLANDS
Gf. . .   1. *Hay Meadow and/or Grazing Pasture* (below treeline)
Ga. . .   2. *Meadow or Pasture* (above treeline)
Gw. . .   D. SEDGE SWAMPS AND FLUSHES
       1. *Sedge Peat Swamps*
       2. *Flushes* (with seepage water ± lime)
Gr. . .   3. *Reed and Tall Graminoid Swamp*
Gh. . .   E. HERBACEOUS AND SEMIWOODY SALT SWAMPS AND SHORES
       1. *Succulent or Nonsucculent Salt Marsh*
       2. *Salt Meadows* (Marine and Inland)
     F. FORB ECOSYSTEMS
G. . .   1. *Mainly Perennial Forb Complexes*
De. . .   2. *Mainly Ephemeral Forb Complexes*
De. . .   3. *Episodical Forb Complexes*
Ge. . .   G. CROP COMPLEXES, VILLAGES, CITIES

  VI. Deserts and other Sparsely Vegetated Land

D. . .   A. SCARCELY VEGETATED ROCKS AND SCREES
Db. . .   B. SCARCELY VEGETATED SAND
       1. *Presently (or Recently) Active Dunes*
       2. *Bare Migrating Dune*
D. . .   C. DESERT BARRENS

For large countries, wall maps with good color printing can show many details by using patterns and symbols at smaller scales. For the United States, Küchler's 1:3,168,000 map of 116 kinds of "Potential Natural Vegetation" has considerable detail related to patterns of rivers, which are shown on the map, and mountains, which are not shown but are readily recognized by the distribution of montane conifer or meadow types. For the former Soviet Union, an eight-sheet wall map at 1:4,000,000 shows even finer detail for the actual vegetation, with 109 colored mapping units, many of them subdivided by letters and supplemented by symbols for significant species. Coarser scales were required (varying with continent and type of map) in the Soviet Union's "Physical-Geographic Atlas of the World," but there was remarkably little loss of detail.

Colors are generally required for good maps of vegetation types, but process and structural quantities can usually be shown best by black and white shading. Computer-printed maps have limited resolution and in many cases should be redrawn, though some can be adequately sharpened by photographic reduction.

Topographic base maps may be improved to show such features as slope and aspect (direction), as well as altitude, in more detail. Simple, pale contour lines provide this information without distracting from the markings superimposed to represent vegetation or ecosystems. Topographic shading makes relief and drainage stand out more sharply, but may interfere with the biological patterns to be shown.

Data gathering. Two basic approaches to detailed local vegetation analysis are (1) classification, which is usually based on intensively sampled plots, called relevés or quadrats, and (2) ordination, which usually involves some form of gradient or continuum analysis. Ordination is a method for plotting and inferentially ordering sampled vegetation plots in a usually hypothetical environmental space based on the relative similarity or dissimilarity of plots to each other. Both approaches require detailed field sampling and may yield data and patterns which are not easily mapped. More generalized mapping that focuses on vegetation types and other ecological patterns over larger areas requires more extensive data gathering, which can be obtained from aerial photographs and remote sensing.

Aerial photographs. Aerial photography has been used since the 1920s to provide direct images of forests and other visibly distinct vegetation cover, with or without extensive ground checking to provide species recognition and other calibration data. This has been especially useful in countries with large, sparsely populated areas. Large areas are stereoscopically covered from high altitudes for surveys, road and harvest plans, and fire control operations. Also, very fine photographs have been made of statistically selected plots, permitting measurement of shadow and tree height and crown form to provide a basis for estimating tree volume and biomass. *See Forest mapping; Photogrammetry.*

Soil surveys are also made from aerial photographs, such as to estimate soil moisture or to measure areas for which conservation payments are made to individual farmers, but even when land is freshly plowed, there are limits to what can be inferred from the air or from observation of surface soil horizons. Local experience and "ground-truthing" are necessary, but soil variations may still obscure the apparent surface patterns. Ground-truthing involves checking on the ground certain elements of what was seen by aircraft or satellite.

The experienced mapper relies on the "lay of the land" (perhaps perceptibly slight differences in concavity or convexity) and the quality and vigor of vegetation to help fill in the incomplete observations of substrate conditions. The balance of intensive and extensive work and of "calibration" checks and routine extension of the mapped area may depend greatly on available time, money, and competing duties. Administrative considerations tend to favor statistical control and objective measures of unexplained variance within the somewhat arbitrarily grouped mapping units. Yet for the understanding of vegetation, soil, or other terrain variables, which correlate with the whole ecosystem's condition, nonroutine detectivelike insights are needed, as well as the orderly use of what has been guessed, observed, and confirmed. *See Soil conservation.*

Multiband remote sensing. Aircraft or satellite-based sensing methods (using various combinations of wavelengths of electromagnetic radiation reflected differentially from the Earth) may expand the scope of mapping in ways which now can only be guessed. Color photography, especially in the brief periods of changing foliage color at the beginning and end of the growing season, has already made striking improvements in vegetation recognition. Total reflection, especially that involving longer infrared wavelengths, is greater for broad-leaved trees than for conifers. It is hoped that the use of these and other reflectivity differences will allow detection of differences between diseased (hence often drying or dying) trees and healthy trees before the eye or regular film can discriminate. Diagnoses based on infrared photography have also been promising for the relatively uniform conditions of field crops, but more experience will be needed before pest or disease infestations can be detected reliably in wild vegetation and on rough terrain. *See Remote sensing.*

Nonphotographic electronic devices for scanning infrared (thermal) radiation offer more opportunities, including empirical detection of landscape patterns which may then be explained in terms of the microclimatic energy balance. Interference by moisture absorption in certain parts of the infrared spectrum, however, limits some instruments (for example, pistollike bolometers which are used for pointing out "hot spots" of fire or warm microclimate). *See Forest fire control.*

Most promising are scanners which can separate many bands of radiation to take advantage of the proper signature, or wavelength combination, for the cover condition of interest. Complex (and expensive) optical, electronic, and computer processing may then enhance the image. Not even the best engineering methods, however, are always applicable to the full range of natural conditions. For example, orbital characteristics of some satellites may limit their effectiveness, permitting other satellites to sense "greenness," hence vegetation activity, much less expensively than can others.

Map examples. Local detail must be generalized greatly when one attempts an overview of the whole Earth system, as for problems such as biogeochemical cycles and exchange of elements between biosphere and atmosphere.

As a first step, one might focus on environmental characteristics. L. Holdridge's system of life zones, for example, though without seasonal patterns, has been the basis for many maps of potential vegetation, especially in the tropical and subtropical Americas.

In addition to vegetation types, various maps have shown estimated world patterns of annual primary production, based both on generalization from measurements and on prediction from climatic relationships. Omission of animal consumption of vegetation may make the estimates low, but probably will not change the striking geographic pattern shown. Plant respiration, detrital decomposition, and other basic processes have also been mapped by prediction from climatic relationships. These maps probably will be revised only very slowly, since the processes involved are very difficult to monitor or measure directly.

Structural phenomena, on the other hand, are much more difficult to model, because the environmental relations and trade-offs are more complex, but are easier to measure directly and to monitor remotely. J. Olson's map of the inventory of living carbon in actual world vegetation shows great detail and is probably quite accurate. Such maps are generally based on ecosystem types, with boundaries based on vegetation mapping. Values are then assigned to the whole of each mapping unit, based mainly on data collected during and since the International Biological Program, a worldwide scientific research program (1964–1974) that focused on the structure and function of ecosystems. Details of patterns of ecosystem rates and parameters, on the scale of the world vegetation zones and on the more detailed scale showing the accelerating changes due to humans, will then remain a major challenge for future generations of ecologists.

A framework for this ongoing, long-term research on ecosystems is provided by Olson's map (see **illus.**), at intermediate scale. Its working base is Plate 75 (Landscape Types) of the "Physical-Geographic Atlas of the World" (Soviet Union), with a legend which has been simplified in translation. Other details have been changed to aid future matching with the UNESCO legend of ecosystem types. *See Ecology; Ecosystem; Plant geography; Terrestrial ecosystem.*

Elgene O. Box

Bibliography. E. O. Box, *Macroclimate and Plant Forms: An Introduction to Predictive Modeling in Phytogeography*, 1981; D. R. Causton, *An Introduction to Vegetation Analysis*, 1988; D. J. DeLaubenfels, *Mapping the World's Vegetation: Regionalization of Formations and Floras*, 1975; L. R. Holdridge, *Life Zone Ecology*, 1967; C. J. Johannsen and J. L. Sanders, *Remote Sensing for Resource Management*, 1982; A. W. Küchler (ed.), *International Bibliography of Vegetation Maps*, 1965–1968; A. W. Küchler and I. S. Zonneveld, *Vegetation Mapping*, 1988; H. Lieth and R. H. Whittaker (eds.), *Primary Productivity of the Biosphere*, 1975; D. Mueller-Dombois and H. Ellenberg, *Aims and Methods in*

Vegetation Ecology, 1974; J. Olson et al., *Carbon in Live Vegetation of Major World Ecosystems*, 1983; UNESCO, *Vegetation Map of the Mediterranean Zone*, 1969; H. Walter, E. Harnickell, and D. Mueller-Dombois, *Climate-Diagram Maps of the Individual Continents*, 1975.

Water conservation

The protection, development, and efficient management of water resources for beneficial purposes. Water occupies more than 71% of the Earth's surface. Its physical and chemical properties make it essential to life and civilization. Water is combined with carbon dioxide by green plants in the synthesis of carbohydrates, from which all other foods are formed. It is a highly efficient medium for dissolving and transporting nutrients through the soil and throughout the bodies of plants and animals. It can also carry deadly organisms and toxic wastes. Water is a raw material that is indispensable for many domestic and industrial purposes.

UNDERGROUND WATER

Water occurs both underground and on the surface. Usable groundwater in the United States is estimated to be 4.75×10^{10} acre-feet. Annual runoff from the land averages 1.299×10^9 acre-feet (1.602×10^{12} m^3). The volume of groundwater greatly exceeds that of all fresh-water lakes and reservoirs combined. It occurs in several geologic formations (aquifers) and at various depths. Groundwater under pressure is known as artesian water, and it may become available either by natural or artificial flowing wells. Groundwater, if abundant, may maintain streams and springs during extended dry periods. It originates from precipitation of various ages as determined by measurements of the decay of tritium, a radioisotope of hydrogen found in groundwater. The water table is the upper level of saturated groundwater accumulation. It may appear at the surface of the Earth in marshes, swamps, lakes, or streams, or hundreds of feet down. Seeps or springs occur where the contour of the ground intercepts the water table. In seeps the water oozes out, whereas springs have distinct flow. Water tables fluctuate according to the source and extent of recharge areas, the amount and distribution of rainfall, and the rate of extraction. The yield of aquifers depends on the porosity of their materials. The yield represents that portion of water which drains out by gravity and becomes available by pumping. Shallow groundwater (down to 50 ft or 15 m) is trapped by dug or driven wells, but deep sources require drilled wells. The volume of shallow wells may vary greatly in accordance with fluctuations in rainfall and degree of withdrawal. *See GROUNDWATER HYDROLOGY.*

SURFACE WATER

Streams supply most of the water needs of the United States. Lakes, ponds, swamps, and marshes, like reservoirs, represent stored streamflow. The natural lakes in the United States are calculated to contain 1.3×10^{10} acre-feet (1.6×10^{13} m^3). Swamps and other wet lands along river deltas, around the borders of interior lakes, and in coastal regions add millions more to the surface supplies. The oceans and

salty or brackish sounds, bays, bayous, or estuaries represent almost unlimited potential fresh-water sources. Brackish waters are being used increasingly by industry for cooling and flushing. Reservoirs, dammed lakes, farm ponds, and other small impoundments have a combined usable storage of 3×10^8 acre-feet (3.7×10^{11} m^3). The smaller ones furnish water for livestock, irrigation, fire protection, flash-flood protection, fish and waterfowl, and recreation. However, most artificial storage is in reservoirs of over 5000 acre-feet (6.165×10^6 m^3). Lake Mead, located in Arizona and Nevada and formed by Hoover Dam, is the largest (227 mi^2 or 588 km^2) of the 1300 reservoirs, and it contains 10% of the total stored-water capacity, or over 3.1×10^7 acre-feet (3.8×10^{10} m^3). These structures regulate streamflow to provide more dependable supplies during dry periods when natural runoff is low and demands are high. They store excess waters in wet periods, thus mitigating damaging floods. *See DAM.*

Fish, wildlife, and recreation water requirements are nonconsumptive. Clean natural waters and the aquatic environment they create constitute major attractions in undeveloped wilderness areas, national parks, and even in more highly developed agricultural, forest, or suburban localities. However, artificial impoundments, unless properly located, designed, and operated, can destroy or depreciate priceless natural environment.

Water pollution. Streams have traditionally served for waste disposal. Towns and cities, industries, and mines provide thousands of pollution sources. Pollution dilution requires large amounts of water. Treatment at the source is safer and less wasteful than flushing untreated or poorly treated wastes downstream. However, sufficient flows must be released to permit the streams to dilute, assimilate, and carry away the treated effluents. *See WATER POLLUTION.*

Hydrologic cycle. This term refers to the continuous circulation of the Earth's moisture. Because of this characteristic, water is considered a renewable natural resource, but underground water is "mined" when it is pumped out faster than its natural renewal and thus may be like a fund resource. The oceans furnish most of the moisture for evaporation and precipitation. Part of the precipitation evaporates, part is returned directly to the oceans, part runs off quickly into watercourses and lakes, part enters the soil or other porous material where it is retained, and the balance enters deep aquifers where it is stored or flows along impermeable underground layers into streams or springs. Solar radiation provides the energy for the hydrologic cycle. Unequal heating of the Earth's surface creates air currents of varying temperatures and pressures.

Warm air masses carry moisture from the oceans. When these air masses are cooled, their capacity to retain moisture is reduced and precipitation results. The source of the air masses and the pressure and temperature gradients aloft determine the form, intensity, and duration of precipitation. Precipitation may occur as cyclonic or low-pressure storms (mostly a winter phenomenon responsible for widespread rains), as thunderstorms of high intensity and limited area, or as mountain storms wherein warm air dumps its moisture when lifted and cooled in crossing high land barriers (see **illus.**).

Precipitation is characteristically irregular. Generally, the more humid an area and the nearer the ocean, the more evenly distributed is the rainfall. Whatever the annual average, rainfall in arid regions tends to vary widely from year to year and to fall in a few heavy downpours. Large floods and active erosion result from heavy and prolonged rainfall or rapid melt of large volumes of snow. Flash floods often follow local intense thunderstorms.

Runoff depends on depth, porosity, and compactness of the soil and the underlying material, steepness, and configuration of the surface, and character and density of the vegetation. Plant crowns, ground cover, litter, and humus dissipate the force of rainfall, thus reducing its power to compact and dislodge mineral soil particles and seal the surface pores. The quantity of water entering the soil during a given time depends on the rate of rainfall in relation to the size and distribution of the pores in each soil horizon and the thickness of each horizon. Surface runoff follows when rainfall exceeds the rate at which water is absorbed and transmitted downward. Soil water is retained by adhesion against the pull of gravity in the capillary pores of the soil until their capacity is filled. Such water may evaporate or is available for plant use including photosynthesis and transpiration. Excess moisture in the large pores drains slowly into watercourses or wet-weather springs, or enters rock crevices, limestone sinks, and shales, sands, or other permeable materials. *See Hydrology; Soil.*

Land management vitally influences the distribution and character of runoff. Inadequate vegetation or surface organic matter; compaction of farm, ranch, or forest soils by heavy vehicles; frequent crop-harvesting operations; repeated burning; or excessive trampling by livestock, deer, or elk all expose the soil to the destructive energy of rainfall or rapid snowmelt. On such lands little water enters the soil, soil particles are dislodged and quickly washed into watercourses, and gullies may form. *See Land-use planning; Soil conservation.*

Water management problems. These involve economic, social, and intangible values. Efforts to plan and develop river systems for multiple purposes often generate conflicts among different water uses, for example, irrigation versus navigation on the Missouri River, or hydropower versus salmon or trout fisheries, wildlife, national park, wilderness, or historic resources on such rivers as the Columbia, Colorado, and Potomac. Other conflicts stem from actual or threatened dumping of municipal, agricultural (silt), industrial, or acid mine wastes into streams, as occurs upstream from Philadelphia, Pennsylvania; Washington, D.C.; Cumberland, Maryland; and other cities, or from operations of power dams, irrigation projects, or other uses which restrain or divert flows to the extent of destroying fish habitats or impairing recreational or wildlife resources. Another source of conflict is the mining of groundwaters in areas of critically low groundwater supplies.

Water management technology. This involves the application of biological and engineering principles to attain desired goals. Biological methods for growing upland vegetation having low moisture requirements are being studied by the U.S. Forest Service and other agencies. Mechanical methods include the practice of water spreading, which is utilized to desilt floodwaters and to promote the percolation of water into the soil for crop use and groundwater recharge. Water that would be a strong pollutant of streams and lakes may be spread on the land. About 1.03×10^8 acres

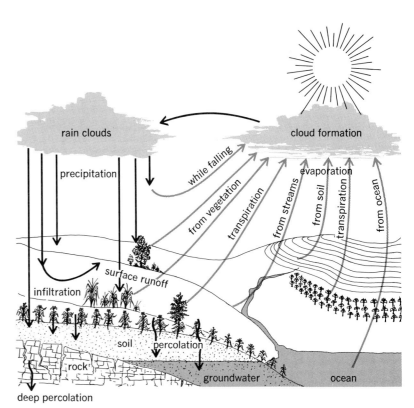

The hydrologic cycle. (*Water, USDA Yearbook, 1955*)

(4.17×10^7 hectares) of wetlands have been drained in 40 states. Drainage has failed, however, where the suitability of soils for such practice was not adequately determined, or where erosion from adjacent slopes of improperly farmed land silted up the drainage structures. In some instances drainage has drastically reduced waterfowl habitat or aggravated downstream flood damages. *See Forest and forestry.*

The avoidance of water waste takes several forms. Recycling has permitted huge savings of water, especially in petroleum plants, chemical factories, and steel mills. In some cases reductions have amounted to 96%. Artificial groundwater recharge is successfully practiced in Long Island, New York, where over 300 injection wells conduct water used in air conditioning to underground storage areas for cooling and reuse. A National Association of Manufacturers survey has reported that many industrial establishments apply some kind of water purification treatment. Flows in pipes can be reduced, warmer water can be used, or several grades can be applied by means of separate pipelines. Metering stimulates more economical use and encourages repair of leaky connections. *See Water treatment.*

Water rights. In the United States early rights to water followed the riparian doctrine, which grants the property owner reasonable use of surface waters flowing past his land unimpaired by upstream landowners. The drier West, however, has favored the appropriation doctrine, which advocates the prior right of the person who first applied the water for beneficial purposes, whether or not his land adjoins the stream. Rights to groundwater are generally governed by the same doctrines. Both doctrines are undergoing intensive study.

State laws generally are designed to protect riparian owners against pollution. States administer the regulatory provisions of their pollution-control laws, develop water quality standards and waste-treatment requirements, and supervise construction and maintenance standards of public service water systems. Some states can also regulate groundwater use to prevent serious overdrafts. Artesian wells may have to be capped, permits may be required for drilling new wells, or reasonable use may have to be demonstrated.

Federal responsibilities consist largely of financial support or other stimulation of state and local water management. Federal legislation permits court action on suits involving interstate streams where states fail to take corrective action following persistent failure of a community or industry to comply with minimum waste-treatment requirements. Federal legislation generally requires that benefits of water development projects equal or exceed the costs. It specifies that certain costs be allocated among local beneficiaries but that most of the expense be assumed by the federal government. In 1955, however, the Presidential Advisory Committee on Water Resources Policy recommended that cost sharing be based on benefits received, and that power, industrial, and municipal water-supply beneficiaries pay full cost. These phases of water resource development present difficult and complex questions, because many imponderables enter into the estimates of probable monetary and social benefits from given projects as well as into the cost allocation aspect.

Watershed control. This approach to planning, development, and management rests on the established interdependence of water, land, and people. Conditions on the land are often directly reflected in the behavior of streamflow and in the accumulation of groundwater. The integrated approach on smaller watersheds is illustrated by projects under the Watershed Protection and Flood Prevention Act of 1954 (Public Law 566) as amended by P. L. 1018 in 1956. This act originally applied to floods on the smaller tributaries whose watersheds largely are agricultural, but more recently the application has been broadened to include mixed farm and residential areas. Damages from such frequent floods equal half the national total from all floods. Coordination of structures and land-use practices is sought to prevent erosion, promote infiltration, and retard high flows. The Soil Conservation and Forest Services of the Department of Agriculture administer the program. The Soil Conservation Service cooperates with other federal and state agencies and operates primarily through the more than 2000 soil conservation districts.

River basins may be large and complex watersheds. For example, the Tennessee River Basin comprises 40,000 mi^2 (103,600 km^2) in contrast to the 390-mi^2 (1010-km^2) upper limit specified in Public Law 1018. Basin projects may involve systems of multipurpose storage reservoirs, intensive programs of watershed protection, and improvement and management of farm, forest, range, and urban lands. They may call for scientific research, industrial development, health and educational programs, and financial arrangements to stimulate local initiative. The most complete development to date is the Tennessee River Basin, where well-planned cooperative activities have encompassed a wide variety of integrated land and water developments, services, and research.

Water conservation organizations. Organizations for meeting water problems take various forms. Local or intrastate drainage, irrigation, water-supply, or flood-control activities may be handled by special districts, soil conservation districts, or multipurpose state conservancy districts with powers to levy assessments. Interstate compacts have served limited functions on a regional level. To date Congress has not given serious consideration to proposals for establishing a special federal agency with powers to review and coordinate the recommendations and activities of development services such as the Corps of Engineers, Bureau of Reclamation, Fish and Wildlife Service, Soil Conservation Service, and Forest Service and to resolve conflicts among agencies and citizen groups. Some national and regional civic groups have studied alternative approaches to the administration of river basin programs.

International agreements. Cooperation in the control, allocation, and utilization of international waters is authorized by treaties with Canada and Mexico. Permanent commissions have been established to deal with specific streams such as the Rio Grande and Colorado, or with boundary waters generally, as provided in the treaty with Canada. The United Nations, through its Technical Assistance Program and through regional commissions, is promoting cooperative studies and developments among underdeveloped nations having common boundaries.   *Bernard Frank*

COASTAL WATERS

Most coastal waters less than 300 ft (100 m) deep were dry land 15,000 years ago. The North Sea was a peat bog, for example, and one could walk from England to France or from Siberia to Alaska. As the glaciers retreated, these exposed continental shelves began to fill with water until they now constitute 10% of the world's ocean area. The average depth of the present continental shelf is 183 ft (60 m), with a width extending 47 mi (75 km) from shore. The salinity of coastal water ranges from 35% (100% ocean water) at the seaward edge of the continental shelf (660 ft or 200 m depth contour) to 0% (100% fresh water) within coastal estuaries and bays at the shoreward edge of the shelf. The annual temperature range of mid-latitude shelf water is 68°F (20°C) off New York and 50°F (10°C) off Oregon, with less temperature change in tropical waters.

Resources. Because of the shallow bottom, compared with the deep ocean of 16,500 ft (5000 m) depth, organic matter is transformed to nutrients and recycled (returned to the water column) faster on the continental shelves. The growth of plants in the sunlit regions of these relatively shallow areas is thus 10 times that of the open ocean, and the rest of the shelf food web is similarly more productive. Approximately 99% of the world's fish catch is taken from these rich shelves. As a result of their accessibility and commercial value, coastal waters have been the object of extensive scientific studies.

Withdrawal of the Wisconsin glacier and buildup of the native Amerindic populations about 10,000 years ago led to simple harvesting of the living resources of the United States continental shelves. Since colonial days, however, this coastal region has been the focus of increased exploitation with little thought given to the impact of these activities. After the discovery of codfish in the New World by Cabot in 1497, a "foreign" fishing fleet was inaugurated by the French in 1502, the Portuguese in 1506, the Spanish in 1540, and the English in 1578; the first ''domestic'' fishery of the United States was initiated by the ill-fated Roanoke colony in 1586. The adjacent human population then grew from a few Indian settlements scattered along the coast to the present east coast megalopolis, housed in an almost continuous urban development from Norfolk, Virginia, to Portland, Maine. By 1970, continued fishing pressure of the foreign and domestic fleets had reduced the fish stocks of the northeast continental shelf to approximately 25% of their virgin biomass. *SEE MARINE FISHERIES*.

Pollutant impacts. At the same time, attempts at waste control in colonial days began as early as 1675 with a proclamation by the governor of New York against dispersal of refuse within the harbor; yet the New York urban effluent expanded until the percent saturation of dissolved oxygen of the harbor halved between 1910 and 1930. The amount of trace metals in the New York Bight Apex sediments now exceeds that of the outer shelf by as much as a hundredfold. Questions about the impact of extended offshore United States jurisdiction of fisheries, construction of ocean sewage outfalls, dredging, beach erosion, and emplacement of pipelines are hotly debated issues in coastal communities that depend on revenue from commercial fishing, tourism, and other forms of recreational activities. As a result of these possibly conflicting uses of the coastal zone, multidisciplinary research on this ecosystem has been intensified over the years by the U.S. Department of Energy (DOE), the National Oceanic and Atmospheric Administration (NOAA), the U.S. Geological Survey (USGS), the Environmental Protection Agency (EPA), the Bureau of Land Management (BLM), and the National Science Foundation (NSF).

People have come to realize that dilution of wastes by marine waters can no longer be considered a simple or permanent removal process within either the open ocean or nearshore waters. The increasing utilization of the continental shelf for oil drilling and transport, siting of nuclear power plants, and various types of planned and inadvertent waste disposal, as well as for food and recreation, requires careful management of human activities in this ecosystem. Nearshore waters are presently subject, of course, to both atmospheric and coastal input of pollutants in the form of heavy metals, synthetic chemicals, petroleum hydrocarbons, radionuclides, and other urban wastes.

However, overfishing is an additional human-induced stress. For example, the sardine fishery collapsed off the California coast, herring stocks are down off the east coast, and the world's largest fishery, for anchovy off Peru, has been reduced to less than 10% of its peak harvest in the late 1960s. Determination of what is the cause and which is the direct effect within a perturbation response of the food web of this highly variable continental shelf ecosystem is a difficult matter. One must be able to specify the consequences of human impact within the context of natural variability; for example, populations of sardines exhibited large fluctuations within the geological record off California before a fishery was initiated.

Furthermore, physical transport of pollutants, their modification by the coastal food web, and demonstration of transfer to humans are sequential problems of increasing complexity on the continental shelf. For example, after 30 years of discharge of mercury into the sea, the origin of the Minimata neurological disease of Japan was finally traced to human consumption of fish and shellfish containing methyl mercuric chloride. The Itai itai disease is now attributed to ingestion of food with high cadmium levels. Discharges of chlorinated hydrocarbons, such as DDT off California, polychlorinated biphenyl (PCB) in both the Hudson River, New York, and within Escambia Bay, Florida, mirex in the Gulf of Mexico, and vinyl chloride in the North Sea, have also led to inhibition of algal photosynthesis, large mortality of shrimp, and reproductive failure of birds and fish.

Oil spills constitute an estimated annual input of 2 $\times$ 10^6 tons of petroleum to the continental shelves with an unresolved ecological impact; another 2 $\times$ 10^6 tons of petrochemicals is added each year from river and sewer runoff. Fission and neutron-activation products of coastal reactors, such as San Onofre (California), Hanford (Washington), and Windscale (United Kingdom), are concentrated in marine food chains with, for example, cesium-137 found in muscle tissue of fish, ruthenium-106 in seaweed, zinc-65 in oysters, and cerium-144 in phytoplankton; their somatic and genetic effects on humans are presumably minimal. Finally, disposal of dissolved and floatable waste material from New York City has been implicated as a possible factor in both shellfish loss off New Jersey and the occasional closure of Long Island beaches.

Simulation models. One approach to quantitatively assess the above pollutant impacts is to construct simulation models of the coastal food web in a systems analysis of the continental shelf. Models of physical transport of pollutants have been the most successful, for example, as in studies of beach fouling by oil. Incorporation of additional biological and chemical terms in a simulation model, however, requires dosage response functions of the natural organisms to each class of pollutants, as well as a quantitative description of the ''normal'' food web interactions of the continental shelf.

Toxicity levels in terms of median lethal concentrations (LC50) of metals, pesticides, biofouling agents (such as chlorine), PCB, and petroleum fractions have been determined only for organisms that can be cultured in the laboratory. The actual form of the pollutant, such as methyl mercuric chloride or chloramine, and its concentration in the marine environment, however, are not always known. Furthermore, the actual contribution of a pollutant to mortality of organisms within a coastal food web is additionally confounded by the lack of understanding of natural mortality. Natural death on the continental shelf is a poorly known process. Nevertheless, there are some clear-cut examples of pollutant impacts on the coastal zone and, in these cases, management decisions are continually being made to correct these situations. *SEE FOOD WEB*.

Sewage. For example, raw sewage contains pathogenic bacteria that cause human diseases such as typhoid, typhus, and hepatitis. These and various gastroenteric diseases may be contracted from eating raw shellfish that live in sewage-polluted waters. Health authorities have closed more than a million acres (4000 km^2) of the best shellfish beds and put segments of the shellfish industry abruptly out of business, with economic losses running to tens of millions of dollars per year. Purification of sewage is thus absolutely necessary for healthy coastal waters. The cost increases as the degree of treatment is intensified, however. Most treatments remove only a fraction of dissolved fertilizing minerals such as nitrates and phosphates. These nutrients from sewage plants over-fertilize coastal waters where the effluent is discharged, and can at times lead to oxygen depletion of bottom waters. The cost of this additional removal of nutrients must now be weighed against their potential damage to the coastal ecosystem. SEE SEWAGE TREATMENT.

Toxic materials. Insecticides also reach coastal waters via runoff from the land, often causing fish kills. Any amount above one-tenth part of insecticide to a million parts of water can be lethal to some fish for most of the following: DDT, parathion, malathion, endrin, dieldrin, toxaphene, lindane, and heptachlor. Contamination of fish eggs by DDT is fatal to a high proportion of young. Insecticides function mainly as paralytic nerve poisons with resulting lack of coordination, erratic behavior, loss of equilibrium, muscle spasms, convulsions, and finally suffocation. Federal and state legislation has all but eliminated DDT from future use in the United States. SEE INSECTICIDE; PESTICIDE.

Other chemical pollutants such as metals, acids, and gases result from industrial activities. Paper and pulp mills discharge wastes that are dangerous to aquatic life because the wastes have a high oxygen demand and deplete oxygen. Other factories discharge lead, copper, zinc, nickel, mercury, cadmium, and cobalt, which are toxic to coastal life in concentrations as low as 0.5 part per million (ppm). Cyanide, sulfide, ammonia, chlorine, fluorine, and their combined compounds are also poisonous. To prevent chemical pollution of the environment, factories are required to remove contaminants from their wastes before discharging them into coastal waters or into local sewage systems.

Oil pollution arises from various sources. Most cases of fish poisoning are from accidental spillage from tankers, storage depots, or wells. However, slow but constant leakage from refineries ruins waterways and is difficult to remedy. Oysters seem unable to breed in the vicinity of refineries. Enclosed ocean regions take longer to recover from oil spills than open coastal areas. Careless handling at plants also results in water pollution by poisonous by-products, such as cresols and phenols that are toxic in amounts of 5–10 ppm. In past years tankers used to pump oil into the water while cleaning their tanks, but this and cleanup procedures after oil spills are being corrected by stronger federal laws.

Thermal pollution. Thermal pollution is caused by the discharge of hot water from power plants or factories and from desalination plants. Power plants are the main source of heated discharges. They are placed at the coast or on bays to secure a ready source of seawater coolant. A large power installation may pump in 10^6 gal/min (63 m^3/s) and discharge it at a temperature approximately 18°F (10°C) above that of the ambient water. Although temperatures of coastal waters range from summer highs of 95°F (35°C) in southern lagoons to winter lows of 30.3°F (−1°C) in northern estuaries, each has a typical pattern of seasonal temperature to which life there has adapted. In a shallow bay with restricted tidal flow, the rise in temperature can cause gross alterations to the natural ecology. Federal standards prohibit heating of coastal waters by more than 0.9°F (0.5°C).

Dredging. Finally, dredging waters to fill wetlands for house lots, parking lots, or industrial sites destroys the marshes that provide sanctuary for waterfowl and for the young of estuarine fishes. As the bay bottom is torn up, the loosened sediments shift about with the current and settle in thick masses on the bottom, suffocating animals and plants. In this way, the marshes are eliminated and the adjoining bays are degraded as aquatic life zones. The northeast Atlantic states have lost 45,000 acres (182 km^2) of coastal wetlands in only 10 years, and San Francisco Bay has been nearly half obliterated by filling. Dredging to remove sand and gravel has the same disruptive effects as dredging for landfill or other purposes, whether the sand and gravel are sold for profit or used to replenish beach sand eroded away by storms. The dredging of boat channels adds to the siltation problem, and disposal of dredge spoils is being regulated in coastal areas.

Management for the future. Human populations have grown to a level where they now can have serious impacts on coastal waters. Past experience suggests that human-induced stress is most likely to lead to species replacement by undesirable forms rather than a decrease in the organic production of the ecosystem. Any societal action must now be considered in the context of what is known about the shelf ecosystem, what management decision is required, what perturbation events are likely to ensue, and what the societal costs are in using renewable and nonrenewable coastal water resources. Prediction of such perturbation events has both immediate and future value to humans in terms of management and conservation options, such as removal of shellfish before depletion of bottom oxygen, the best mode of sewage treatment, preservation of coastal species, and a decrease of toxicant levels within the coastal food web. As one moves from prediction of meteorological events to biological changes of the coastal food web, however, increasing sources of error emerge in the predictions. Since the mid-1800s, humans have introduced more sources of environmental variability to the continental shelf than this coastal ecosystem has encountered during the last 10,000 years. Nevertheless, sufficient information on continental shelf processes is emerging to suggest that specification of management options by delineation of cause and effect within a perturbation response of the coastal zone is a feasible goal.

John J. Walsh

Bibliography. P. E. Black, *Conservation of Water and Related Land Resources*, 2d ed., 1988; F. M. D'Itri, *Wastewater Renovation and Reuse*, 1977; N. T. Kottegoda, *Stochastic Water Resources Technology*, 1980; J. W. Moore, *Balancing the Needs of Water Use,* 1988; National Technical Advisory Committee, *Water Quality Criteria*, Federal Water Pollution Control Administration, 1969; Soil and Water Conservation Society, *Sustainable Agricultural Systems,* 1990.

Water pollution

Any change in natural waters which may impair their further use, caused by the introduction of organic or inorganic substances, or a change in temperature of the water. As human population has expanded with a corresponding expansion in industrial and agricultural activities, the field of water pollution control has increased in importance. In the attack on environmental pollution, higher standards for water cleanliness are being adopted by state and federal governments, as well as by interstate organizations.

Historical developments. Ancient humans joined into groups for protection. Later, they formed communities on watercourses or the seashore. The waterway provided a convenient means of transportation, and fresh waters provided a water supply. The watercourses then became receivers of wastewater along with contaminants. As industries developed, they added their discharges to those of the community. When the concentration of added substances became dangerous to humans or so degraded the water that it was unfit for further use, water pollution control began. With increasing development of land areas, pollution of surface water supplies became more critical because wastewater of an upstream community became part of the water supply of the downstream community.

Serious epidemics of waterborne diseases such as cholera, dysentery, and typhoid fever were caused by underground seepage from privy vaults into town wells. Such direct bacterial infections through water systems can be traced back to the late eighteenth century, even though the germ or bacterium as the cause of disease was not proved for nearly another century. The well-documented epidemic of the Broad Street Pump in London during 1854 resulted from direct leakage from privies into the hand-pumped well which provided the neighborhood water supply. There were 616 deaths from cholera among the users of the well within 40 days.

Eventually, abandoning wells in such populated locations and providing piped water to buildings improved public health. Further, sewers for drainage of wastewater were constructed, but then infections between communities rather than between the residents of a single community became apparent. Modern public health protection is provided by highly refined and well-controlled plants both for the purification of the community water supply and treatment of the wastewater.

Relation to water supply. Water pollution control is closely allied with the water supplies of communities and industries because both generally share the same water resources. There is great similarity in the pipe systems that bring water to each home or business property, and the systems of sewers or drains that subsequently collect the wastewater and conduct it to a treatment facility. Treatment should prepare the flow for return to the environment so that the receiving watercourse will be suitable for beneficial uses such as general recreation, and safe for subsequent use by downstream communities or industries.

The volume of wastewater, the used water that must be disposed of or treated, is a factor to be considered. Depending on the amount of water used for irrigation, the amount lost in pipe leakage, and the extent of water metering, the volume of wastewater may be 70–130% of the water drawn from the supply. In United States cities, wastewater quantities are usually 75–200 gal (284–757 liters) per capita daily. The higher figure applies to large cities with old systems, limited metering, and comparatively cheap water; the lower figure to smaller communities with little leakage and good metering. Probably the average in the United States for areas served by sewers is 125–150 gal (473–568 liters) of wastewater per person per day. Of course, industrial consumption in larger cities increases per capita quantities.

Related scientific disciplines. The field of water-pollution control encompasses a part of the broader field of sanitary or environmental engineering. It includes some aspects of chemistry, hydrology, biology, and bacteriology, in addition to public administration and management. These scientific disciplines evaluate problems and give the civil and sanitary engineer basic data for the designing of structures to solve the problems. The solutions usually require the collection of domestic and industrial wastewaters and treatment before discharge into receiving waters. SEE ENVIRONMENTAL ENGINEERING; HYDROLOGY; SANITARY ENGINEERING.

Self-purification of natural waters. Any natural watercourse contains dissolved gases normally found in air in equilibrium with the atmosphere. In this way fishes and other aquatic life obtain oxygen for their respiration. The amount of oxygen which the water holds at saturation depends on temperature and follows the law of decreased solubility of gases with a temperature increase. Because water temperature is high in the summer, oxygen dissolved in the water is then at a low point for the year.

Degradable or oxidizable substances in wastewaters deplete oxygen through the action of bacteria and related organisms which feed on organic waste materials, using available dissolved oxygen for their respiration. If this activity proceeds at a rate fast enough to depress seriously the oxygen level, the natural fauna of a stream is affected; if the oxygen is entirely used up, a condition of oxygen exhaustion occurs which suffocates aerobic organisms in the stream. Under such conditions the stream is said to be septic and is likely to become offensive to the sight and smell. SEE EUTROPHICATION.

Domestic wastewaters. Domestic wastewaters result from the use of water in dwellings of all types, and include both water after use and the various waste materials added: body wastes, kitchen wastes, household cleaning agents, and laundry soaps and detergents. The solid content of such wastewater is numerically low and amounts to less than 1 weight unit per 1000 weight units of domestic wastewater. Still, the character of these waste materials is such that they cause significant degradation of receiving waters, and they may be a major factor in spreading waterborne diseases, notably typhoid, dysentery, and cholera.

Characteristics of domestic wastewater vary from one community to another and in the same community at different times. Physically, community wastewater usually has the grayish colloidal appearance of dishwater, with floating trash apparent. Chemically, it contains the numerous and complex nitrogen compounds in body wastes, as well as soaps and detergents and the chemicals normally present in the water supply. Biologically, bacteria and other microscopic life abound. Wastewaters from industrial activities may affect all of these characteristics materially.

Industrial wastewaters. In contrast to the general uniformity of substances found in domestic wastewaters, industrial wastewaters show increasing variation as the complexity of industrial processes rises. **Table 1** lists major industrial categories along with the undesirable characteristics of their wastewaters.

Table 1. General nature of industrial wastewaters

Industry	Processes or waste	Effect
Brewery and distillery	Malt and fermented liquors	Organic load
Chemical	General	Stable organics, phenols, inks
Dairy	Milk processing, bottling, butter and cheese making	Acid
Dyeing	Spent dye, sizings, bleach	Color, acid or alkaline
Food processing	Canning and freezing	Organic load
Laundry	Washing	Alkaline
Leather tanning	Leather cleaning and tanning	Organic load, acid and alkaline
Meat packing	Slaughter, preparation	Organic load
Paper	Pulp and paper manufacturing	Organic load, waste wood fibers
Steel	Pickling, plating, and others	Acid
Textile manufacture	Wool scouring, dyeing	Organic load, alkaline

Because biological treatment processes are ordinarily employed in water pollution control plants, large quantities of industrial wastewaters can interfere with the processes as well as with the total load of a treatment plant. The organic matter present in many industrial effluents often equals or exceeds the amount from a community. Accommodations for such an increase in the load of a plant should be provided for in its design.

Discharge directly to watercourses. The industrial revolution in England and Germany and the subsequent similar development in the United States increased problems of water pollution control enormously. The establishment of industries caused great migrations to the cities, the immediate result being a great increase in wastes from both population and industrial activity. For some years discharges were made directly to watercourses, the natural assimilative power of the receiving water being used to a level consistent with the required cleanliness of the watercourse. Early dilution ratios required for this method are shown in **Table 2**. Because of the more rapid absorption of oxygen from the air by a turbulent stream, such a stream has a high rate of reaeration and a low dilution ratio; the converse is true of slow-flowing streams.

Development of treatment methods. With the passage of time, the waste loads imposed on streams exceeded the ability of the receiving water to assimilate them. The first attempts at wastewater treatment were made by providing artificial means for the purification of wastewaters as observed in nature. These forces included sedimentation and exposure to sunlight and atmospheric oxygen, either by agitated contact or by filling the interstices of large stone beds intermittently as a means of oxidation. However, practice soon outstripped theory because the science of bacteriology was only then being born and there were many unknowns about the processes.

In later years testing stations were set up by municipalities and states for experimental work. Notable among these were the Chicago testing station and one established at Lawrence by the state of Massachusetts, a pioneer in the public health movement. From the results of these direct investigations, practices evolved which were gradually explained through the mechanisms of chemistry and biology in the twentieth century.

Thermal pollution. An increasing amount of attention has been given to thermal pollution, the raising of the temperature of a waterway by heat discharged from the cooling system or effluent wastes of an industrial installation. This rise in temperature may sufficiently upset the ecological balance of the waterway to pose a threat to the native life-forms. This problem has been especially noted in the vicinity of nuclear power plants. Thermal pollution may be combated by allowing wastewater to cool before emptying into the waterway. This is often done in large cooling towers.

Current status. Modern water pollution engineers or chemists have a wealth of published information, both theoretical and practical, to assist them. While research necessarily will continue, they can draw on established practices for the solution to almost any problem. A challenging problem has been the handling of radioactive wastes. Reduction in volume, containment, and storage constitute the principal attacks on this problem. Because of the fundamental characteristics of radioactive wastes, the development of other methods seems unlikely. See RADIOACTIVE WASTE MANAGEMENT.

Public desire for complete water pollution control continues, but there is an increasing realization that a solution to the problem is costly. While cities have had little concern about the initial construction cost because of the large federal share, the expenditures for operation fall entirely on the local community. During the life of a project, operating costs may exceed initial construction outlay, and with present rates of increase, may become a major financial burden.

The control of 100% of the organic pollution reaching the watercourses is the goal of many people, but such an ideal cannot be approached, since about one-third of the total is from nonpoint sources. Essentially, this third is from vegetable matter carried by surface drains and direct runoff. To achieve the public health protection which is the primary purpose of collection and treatment of wastewater, proper measures are essential, and should be the principal focus of a program of water pollution control. Such was the original purpose of sewers and drains employed by ancient civilizations, as manifested by the Romans, who gave Venus the title of Goddess of the Sewers, in addition to her other titles associated with health and beauty. The pediment of her lost statue in the Roman Forum identifies her as *Venus Cloacinae*.

Table 2. Dilution ratios for waterways

Type	Stream flow, ft³/(s)(1000 population)*
Sluggish streams	7–10
Average streams	4–7
Swift turbulent streams	2–4

*1 ft³/s = 0.0283 m³/s.

and beauty. The pediment of her lost statue in the Roman Forum identifies her as *Venus Cloacinae*.

However, there are strong manifestations of improved quality in the waters throughout the United States. This is apparent not only in chemical and biological measurements, but in more readily observed effects such as better appearance, eliminated smells, and the return of fish life to watercourses which had become "biological deserts" because of the effects of pollution from municipal and industrial wastewaters. The overall results are living tribute to the cooperative efforts of local citizens and local, state, and federal agencies working together to improve the quality of the nation's waters. A measure of the activity in the field is indicated by the employment of nearly 165,000 in the local wastewater collection and treatment works of the United States.

Federal aid. Because of public demands and the actions of state legislatures and the Congress of the United States, there has been a surge of interest in, and a demand for, firm solutions to water pollution problems. Although the federal government granted aid for construction of municipal treatment plants as an employment relief measure in the 1930s, no comprehensive federal legislation was enacted until 1948. This legislation was supplemented by a major change in 1956, when the United States government again offered grants to municipalities to assist in the construction of water pollution control facilities. These grants were further extended to small communities for the construction of both water and sewer systems.

Since 1965, federal activity in water pollution control has advanced from a minor activity in the Public Health Service, through the Water Pollution Control Administration in the Department of the Interior, to a major activity in the Environmental Protection Agency. In the 1972 act (P. L. 92–500) Congress authorized a massive attack on municipal pollution problems by a grant-in-aid program eclipsing any previous effort. Federal funds for 1973–1986 are given in **Table 3**.

State and federal regulations are constantly increasing in severity. This tendency is expected to continue until the problem of water pollution is brought under complete control. Even then, water quality will be monitored to make certain that actual control is achieved on a day-to-day or even an hour-to-hour basis. *See* Hazardous waste; Septic tank; Sewage; Sewage collection systems; Sewage disposal; Sewage solids; Sewage treatment.

Ralph E. Fuhrman

Bibliography. G. M. Fair et al., *Elements of Water Supply and Wastewater Disposal*, 1971, reprint 1983; R. C. Loehr, *Pollution Control for Agriculture*, 2d ed., 1984; Metcalf and Eddy, Inc., *Wastewater Engineering: Collection and Pumping of Wastewater*, 1981; N. L. Nemerow, *Industrial Water Pollution*, 1978, reprint 1988; Water Pollution Control Federation, *Wastewater Disinfection*, 1986; Water Pollution Control Federation Staff, *Emergency Planning for Municipal Wastewater Facilities*, 1989.

Water supply engineering

A branch of civil engineering concerned with the development of sources of supply, transmission, distribution, and treatment of water. The term is used most frequently in regard to municipal water works, but applies also to water systems for industry, irrigation, and other purposes.

SOURCES OF WATER SUPPLY

Underground waters, rivers, lakes, and reservoirs, the primary sources of fresh water, are replenished by rainfall. Some of this water flows to the sea through surface and underground channels, some is taken up by vegetation, and some is lost by evaporation.

Groundwater. Water obtained from subsurface sources, such as sands and gravels and porous or fractured rocks, is called groundwater. Groundwater flows toward points of discharge in river valleys and, in some areas, along the seacoast. The flow takes place in water-bearing strata known as aquifers. The velocity may be a few feet to several miles per year, depending upon the permeability of the aquifer and the hydraulic gradient or slope. A steep gradient or slope indicates relatively high pressure, or head, forcing the water through the aquifer. When the gradient is flat, the pressure forcing the water is small. When the velocity is extremely low, the water is likely to be highly mineralized; if there is no movement, the water is rarely fit for use. *See* Aquifer; Groundwater hydrology.

Permeability is a measure of the ease with which water flows through an aquifer. Coarse sands and gravels, and limestone with large solution passages, have high permeability. Fine sand, clay, silt, and dense rocks (unless badly fractured) have low permeability.

Water table. In an unconfined stratum the water table is the top or surface of the groundwater. It may be within a few inches of the ground surface or hundreds of feet below. Normally it follows the topography. Aquifers confined between impervious strata may carry water under pressure. If a well is sunk into such an aquifer and the pressure is sufficient, water may be forced to the surface, resulting in an artesian well. The water table elevation and artesian pressure may vary substantially with the seasons,

Table 3. Federal funds for wastewater treatment plant construction, 1973–1984, × 10⁹ dollars

Fiscal year	Authority	Appropriated	Obligated	Outlays
1973	5	2	1.531	0
1974	6	3	1.444	.159
1975	7	4	3.616	.874
1976*	0	9	4.814	2.563
1977†	1.48	1.48	6.664	2.710
1978	4.5	4.5	2.301	2.960
1979	5	4.2	3.9	3.6
1980	5	3.4	4.4	4.3
1981	5	3.2	3.6	3.9
1982	2.4	2.4	‡	2.8
1983	2.4	2.4	3.2	2.9
1984	2.4	2.4	3.0	2.6
1985	2.4	2.4	2.1	2.9
1986	—	0.6§	—	—

*Includes transition quarter, July-September 1976.
†Includes $480 million under Public Works Employment Act.
‡New York City deobligated a large sum, reducing this figure to minus $90 million.
§This was reduced to 0.574 on February 19, 1986, as a result of the Gramm-Rudman Act. Another $1.8 million was planned for fiscal year 1986, provided the Clean Water Act was reauthorized and an appropriation bill was enacted.

depending upon the amount of rainfall recharging the aquifer and the amount of water taken from the aquifer. If pumpage exceeds recharge for an extended period, the aquifer is depleted and the water supply lost. *See Water table*.

Salt-water intrusion. Normally the groundwater flow is toward the sea. This normal flow may be reversed, however, by overpumping and lowering of the water table or artesian pressure in an aquifer. Salt water flowing into the fresh-water aquifer being pumped is called salt-water intrusion.

Springs. Springs occur at the base of sloping ground or in depressions where the surface elevation is below the water table, or below the hydraulic gradient in an artesian aquifer from which the water can escape. Artesian springs are fed through cracks in the overburden or through other natural channels extending from the aquifer under pressure to the surface. *See Spring (hydrology)*.

Wells. Wells are vertical openings, excavated or drilled, from the ground surface to a water-bearing stratum or aquifer. Pumping a well lowers the water level in it, which in turn forces water to flow from the aquifer. Thick, permeable aquifers may yield several million gallons daily with a drawdown (lowering) of only a few feet. Thin aquifers, or impermeable aquifers, may require several times as much drawdown for the same yields, and frequently yield only small supplies.

Dug wells, several feet in diameter, are frequently used to reach shallow aquifers, particularly for small domestic and farm supplies. They furnish small quantities of water, even if the soils penetrated are relatively impervious. Large-capacity dug wells or caisson wells, in coarse sand and gravel, are used frequently for municipal supplies. Drilled wells are sometimes several thousand feet deep.

The portion of a well above the aquifer is lined with concrete, stone, or steel casing, except where the well is through rock that stands without support. The portion of the well in the aquifer is built with open-joint masonry or screens to admit the water into the well. Metal screens, made of perforated sheets or of wire wound around supporting ribs, are used most frequently. The screens are galvanized iron, bronze, or stainless steel, depending upon the corrosiveness of the water and the expected life of the well. Plastic screens are sometimes used.

The distance between wells must be sufficient to avoid harmful interference when the wells are pumped. In general, economical well spacing varies directly with the quantity of water to be pumped, and inversely with the permeability and thickness of the aquifer. It may range from a few feet to a mile or more.

Infiltration galleries are shafts or passages extending horizontally through an aquifer to intercept the groundwater. They are equivalent to a row of closely spaced wells and are most successful in thin aquifers along the shore of rivers, at depths of less than 75 ft (23 m). The galleries are built in open cuts or by tunneling, usually with perforated or porous liners to screen out the aquifer material and to support the overburden.

Ranney wells consist of a center caisson with horizontal, perforated pipes extending radially into the aquifer. They are particularly applicable to the development of thin aquifers at shallow depths.

Specially designed pumps, of small diameter to fit inside well casings, are used in all well installations, except in flowing artesian wells or where the water level in the well is high enough for direct suction lift by a pump on the surface (about 15 ft or 5 m maximum). Well pumps are set some distance below the water level, so that they are submerged even after the drawdown is established. Well-pump settings of 100 ft (30 m) are common, and they may exceed 300 ft (90 m) where the groundwater level is low. Multiple-stage centrifugal pumps are used most generally. They are driven by motors at the surface through vertical shafts, or by waterproof motors attached directly below the pumps. Wells are sometimes pumped by air lift, that is, by injecting compressed air through a pipe to the bottom of the well.

Surface water. Natural sources, such as rivers and lakes, and impounding reservoirs are sources of surface water. *See Dam*.

Water is withdrawn from rivers, lakes, and reservoirs through intakes. The simplest intakes are pipes extending from the shore into deep water, with or without a simple crib and screen over the outer end. Intakes for large municipal supplies may consist of large conduits or tunnels extending to elaborate cribs of wood or masonry containing screens, gates, and operating mechanisms. Intakes in reservoirs are frequently built as integral parts of the dam and may have multiple ports at several levels to permit selection of the best water. The location of intakes in rivers and lakes must take into consideration water quality, depth of water, likelihood of freezing, and possible interference with navigation. Reservoir intakes are usually designed for gravity flow through the dam or its abutments.

Transmission and Distribution

The water from the source must be transmitted to the community or area to be served and distributed to the individual customers.

Transmission mains. The major supply conduits, or feeders, from the source to the distribution system are called mains or aqueducts.

Canals. The oldest and simplest type of aqueducts, especially for transmitting large quantities of water, are canals. Canals are used where they can be built economically to follow the hydraulic gradient or slope of the flowing water. If the soil is suitable, the canals are excavated with sloping sides and are not lined. Otherwise, concrete or asphalt linings are used. Gravity canals are carried across streams or other low places by wooden or steel flumes, or under the streams by pressure pipes known as inverted siphons. *See Canal*.

Tunnels. Used to transmit water through ridges or hills, tunnels may follow the hydraulic grade line and flow by gravity or may be built below the grade line to operate under considerable pressure. Rock tunnels may be lined to prevent the overburden from collapsing, to prevent leakage, or to reduce friction losses by providing a smooth interior.

Pipelines. Pipelines are a common type of transmission main, especially for moderate supplies not requiring large aqueducts or canals. Pipes are of cast iron, ductile iron, steel, reinforced concrete, cement-asbestos, or wood. Pipeline material is determined by cost, durability, ease of installation and maintenance, and resistance to corrosion. The pipeline must be large enough to deliver the required amount of water and strong enough to withstand the maximum gravity or pumping pressure. Pipelines are usually buried in the ground for protection and coolness.

Distribution system. Included in the distribution system are the network of smaller mains branching off from the transmission mains, the house services and meters, the fire hydrants, and the distribution storage reservoirs. The network is composed of transmission or feeder mains, usually 12 in. (30 cm) or more in diameter, and lateral mains along each street, or in some cities along alleys between the streets. The mains are installed in grids so that lateral mains can be fed from both ends where possible. Mains fed from one direction only are called dead ends; they are less reliable and do not furnish as much water for fire protection as do mains with the grid. Valves at intersections of mains permit a leaking or damaged section of pipe to be shut off with minimum interruption of water service to adjacent areas.

House services. The small pipes, usually of iron, copper, or plastic material, extending from the water main in the street to the customer's meter at the curb line or in the cellar are called house services. In many cities each service is metered, and the customer's bill is based on the water actually used.

Fire hydrants. Fire hydrants have a vertical barrel extending to the depth of the water main, a quick-opening valve with an operating nut at the top, and connections threaded to receive a fire hose. Hydrants must be reliable, and they must drain upon closing to prevent freezing.

Distribution reservoirs. These are used to supplement the source of supply and transmission system during peak demands, and to provide water during a temporary failure of the supply system. In small waterworks the reservoirs usually equal at least one day's water consumption; in larger systems the reservoirs are relatively smaller but adequate to meet fire-fighting demands. Ground storage reservoirs, elevated tanks, and standpipes are used for distribution reservoirs.

Ground storage reservoirs, if on high ground, can feed the distribution system by gravity, but otherwise it is necessary to pump water from the reservoir into the distribution system. Circular steel tanks and basins built of earth embankments, concrete, or rock masonry are used. Earth reservoirs are usually lined to prevent leakage and entrance of dirty water. The reservoirs should be covered to protect the water from dust, rubbish, bird dropping, and the growth of algae, but many older reservoirs without covers are in use.

Elevated storage reservoirs are tanks on towers, or high cylindrical standpipes resting on the ground. Storage reservoirs are built high enough so that the reservoir will maintain adequate pressure in the distribution system at all times.

Elevated tanks are usually of steel plate, mounted on steel towers. Wood is sometimes used for industrial and temporary installations. Standpipes are made of steel plate, strong enough to withstand the pressure of the column of water. The required capacity of a standpipe is greater than that of an elevated tank because only the upper portion of a standpipe is sufficiently elevated for normal use.

Distribution-system design. To assure the proper location and size of feeder mains and laterals to meet normal and peak water demands, a distribution system must be expertly designed. As the water flows from the source of supply or distribution reservoir across a city, the water pressure is lowered by the friction in the pipes. The pressures required for adequate service depend upon the height of buildings, need for fire protection, and other factors, but 40 lb/in.^{2} (275 kilopascals) is the minimum for good service. Higher pressures for fire fighting are obtained by booster pumps on fire engines which take water from fire hydrants. In small towns adequate hydrant flows are the controlling factor in determining water-main size; in larger communities the peak demands for air conditioning and lawn sprinkling during the summer months control the size of main needed. The capacity of a distribution system is usually determined by opening fire hydrants and measuring simultaneously the discharge and the pressure drop in the system. The performance of the system when delivering more or less water than during the test can be computed from the pressure drops recorded.

An important factor in the economical operation of municipal water supplies is the quantity of water lost from distribution because of leaky joints, cracked water mains, and services abandoned but not properly shut off. Unaccounted-for water, including unavoidable slippage of customers' meters, may range from 10% in extremely well-managed systems to 30–40% in poor systems. The quantities flowing in feeder mains, the friction losses, and the amount of leakage are frequently measured by means of pitometer surveys. A pitometer is a portable meter that can be inserted in a water main under pressure to measure the velocity of flow, and thus the quantity of flow. *See* FLOW MEASUREMENT.

Pumping stations. Pumps are required wherever the source of supply is not high enough to provide gravity flow and adequate pressure in the distribution system. The pumps may be high or low head depending upon the topography and pressures required. Booster pumps are installed on pipelines to increase the pressure and discharge, and adjacent to ground storage tanks for pumping water into distribution systems. Pumping stations usually include two or more pumps, each of sufficient capacity to meet demands when one unit is down for repairs or maintenance. The station must also include piping and valves arranged so that a break can be isolated quickly without cutting the whole station out of service.

Centrifugal pumps have displaced steam-driven reciprocating pumps in modern practice, although many of the old units continue to give good service. The centrifugal pumps are driven by electric motors, steam turbines, or diesel engines, with gasoline engines frequently used for standby service. The centrifugal pumps that are used most commonly are designed so that the quantity of water delivered decreases as the pumping head or lift increases.

Both horizontal and vertical centrifugal pumps are available in a wide capacity range. In the horizontal type, the pump shaft is horizontal with the driving motor or engine at one end of the pump. Vertical pumps are driven by a vertical-shaft motor directly above the pump or are driven by a horizontal engine through a right-angle gear head.

Automatic control of pumping stations is provided to adjust pump operations to variations in water demand. The controls start and stop pumps of different capacity as required. In the event of mishap or failure of a unit, alarms are sounded. The controls are activated by the water level in a reservoir or tank, by the pressure in a water main, or by the rate of the flow through a meter. A remote control system for pumps is often used, with the signals being transmitted over telephone wires. SEE WATER POLLUTION; WATER TREATMENT.

Richard Hazen

Bibliography. M. A. Al-Layla et al., *Water Supply Engineering Design*, 1977; American Water Works Staff, *Standard Methods for the Examination of Water and Wastewater*, 17th ed., 1989; C. V. Davis and K. E. Sorensen, *Handbook of Applied Hydraulics*, 3d ed., 1968; G. M. Fair et al., *Elements of Water Supply and Waste Water Disposal*, 2d ed., 1971; M. J. Hammer, *Water and Waste Water Technology*, 1975; Nalco Chemical Co., *The Nalco Water Handbook*, 2d ed., 1988; E. W. Steel and T. McGhee, *Water Supply and Sewerage*, 5th ed., 1979; D. Stephenson (ed.), *Water and Wastewater Systems Analysis: Developments in Water Science*, 1988; T. H. Tebbut, *Principles of Water Quality Control*, 1983.

Water table

The upper surface of the zone of saturation in permeable rocks not confined by impermeable rocks. It may also be defined as the surface underground at which the water is at atmospheric pressure. Saturated rock may extend a little above this level, but the water in it is held up above the water table by capillarity and is under less than atmospheric pressure; therefore, it is the lower part of the capillary fringe and is not free to flow into a well by gravity. Below the water table, water is free to move under the influence of gravity. The position of the water table is shown by the level at which water stands in wells penetrating an unconfined water-bearing formation.

Where a well penetrates only impermeable material, there is no water table and the well is dry. But if the well passes through impermeable rock into water-bearing material whose hydrostatic head is higher than the level of the bottom of the impermeable rock, water will rise approximately to the level it would have assumed if the whole column of rock penetrated had been permeable. This is called artesian water, and the surface to which it rises is called the piezometric surface.

The water table is not a level surface but has irregularities that are commonly related to, though less pronounced than, those of the land surface. Also, it is not stationary but fluctuates with the seasons and from year to year. It generally declines during the summer months, when vegetation uses most of the water that falls as precipitation, and rises during the late winter and spring, when the demands of vegetation are low. The water table usually reaches its lowest point after the end of the growing season and its highest point just before the beginning of the growing season. Superimposed on the annual fluctuations are fluctuations of longer period which are controlled by climatic variations. The water table is also affected by withdrawals, as by pumping from wells. SEE GROUND-WATER HYDROLOGY.

Albert N. Sayre / Ray K. Linsley

Bibliography. W. Back (ed.), *Hydrogeology*, 1989; S. N. Davis and R. J. M. DeWiest, *Hydrogedogy*, 1966; L. Huisman and T. N. Olsthorn, *Groundwater Recharge*, 1983.

Water treatment

Physical and chemical processes for making water suitable for human consumption and other purposes. Drinking water must be bacteriologically safe, free from toxic or harmful chemical or substances, and comparatively free of turbidity, color, and taste-producing substances. Excessive hardness and high concentration of dissolved solids are also undesirable, particularly for boiler feed and industrial purposes. The treatment processes of greatest importance are sedimentation, coagulation, filtration, disinfection, softening, and aeration.

Plain sedimentation. Silt, clay, and other fine material settle to the bottom if the water is allowed to stand or flow quietly at low velocities. Sedimentation occurs naturally in reservoirs and is accomplished in treatment plants by basins or settling tanks. The detention time in a settling basin may range from an hour to several days. The water may flow horizontally through the basin, with solids settling to the bottom, or may flow vertically upward at a low velocity so that the particles will settle through the rising water. Settling basins are most effective if shallow, and rarely exceed 10–20 ft (3–6 m) in depth. Plain sedimentation will not remove extremely fine or colloidal material within a reasonable time, and the process is used principally as a preliminary to other treatment methods.

Coagulation. Fine particles and colloidal material are combined into masses by coagulation. These masses, called floc, are large enough to settle in basins and to be caught on the surface of filters. Waters high in organic material and iron may coagulate naturally with gentle mixing. The term is usually applied to chemical coagulation, in which iron or aluminum salts are added to the water to form insoluble hydroxide floc. The floc is a feathery, highly absorbent substance to which color-producing colloids, bacteria, fine particles, and other substances become attached and are removed from the water.

The coagulant dose is a function of the physical and chemical character of the raw water, the adequacy of settling basins and filters, and the degree of purification required. Moderately turbid water coagulates more easily than perfectly clear water, but extremely turbid water requires more coagulant. Coagulation is more effective at higher temperatures. Lime, soda ash, or caustic soda may be required in addition to the coagulant to provide sufficient alkalinity for the formation of floc, and regulation of the pH (hydrogen-ion concentration) is usually desirable for best results. Powdered limestone, clay, bentonite, or silica are sometimes added as coagulant aids to strengthen and weight the floc, and a wide variety of polymers developed in recent years are used for the same purpose.

Filtration. Suspended solids, colloidal material, bacteria, and other organisms are filtered out by passing the water through a bed of sand or pulverized coal, or through a matrix of fibrous material supported on a perforated core. Filtration of turbid or highly colored water usually follows sedimentation or coagulation and sedimentation. Soluble materials such as salts and metals in ionic form are not removed by filtration.

Slow sand filters. Used first in England about 1850, slow sand filters consist of beds of sand 20–48 in. (51–122 cm) deep, through which the water is passed at fairly low rates—2.5–10 $\times$ 10^6 gal/acre (2.4–9.4 $\times$ 10^4 m^3/hectare). The size of beds ranges from a fraction of an acre in small plants to several acres in large plants. An underdrain system of graded gravel and perforated pipes transmits the filtered water from the filters to the point of discharge. The sand is usually fine, ranging from 0.2 to 0.5 mm in diameter. The top of the filter clogs with use, and a thin layer of dirty sand is scraped from the filter periodically to maintain capacity.

Slow sand filters operate satisfactorily with reasonably clear waters but clog rapidly with turbid waters. The filters are covered in cold climates to prevent the formation of ice and to facilitate operation in the winter. In milder climates they are often open. Slow sand filters have a high bacteriological efficiency, but few have been built since the development of water disinfection, because of the large area required, the high construction cost, and the labor needed to clean the filters and to handle the filter sand. Slow sand filters are still used in many English and European cities, but have not been built in the United States since 1950, and few remain in operation.

Rapid sand filters. These operate at rates of 1.25–2.5 $\times$ 10^8 gal/(acre/day) [1.17–2.34 $\times$ 10^6 m^3/(ha/day)], or 25 to 50 times the slow-sand-filter rates. The high rate of operation is made possible by the coagulation and sedimentation ahead of filtration to remove the heaviest part of the load, the use of fairly coarse sand, and facilities for backwashing the filter to keep the bed clean. The filter beds are small, generally ranging from 150 ft^2 (14 m^2) in small plants to 1500 ft^2 (140 m^2) in the largest filter plants. The filters consist of a layer of sand or, occasionally, crushed anthracite coal 18–24 in. (46–62 cm) deep, resting on graded layers of gravel above an underdrain system. The sand is coarse, 0.4–1.0 mm in diameter, depending upon the raw water quality and pretreatment, but the grain size must be fairly uniform to assure proper backwashing. The underdrain system serves both to collect the filtered water and to distribute the wash water under the filters when they are being washed. Several types of underdrains are used, including perforated pipes, perforated false bottoms of concrete, and tile and porous plates.

Filters are backwashed at rates 5–10 times the filtering rate. The wash water passes upward through the sand and out of the filters by way of wash-water gutters and drains. Washing agitates the sand bed and releases the dirt to flow out of the filter with the wash water. The quantity of water used for washing ranges from 1 to 10% of the total output, depending upon the turbidity of the water applied to filters and the efficiency of the filter design. Combination air and water filter washes are popular in Europe, but are not often used in the United States.

Municipal and large-capacity filters for industry usually are built in concrete boxes or in open tanks of wood and steel. The flow through the sand may be caused by gravity, or the water may be forced through the sand under pressure by pumping. Pressure filters can be operated at higher rates than gravity filters, because of the greater head available to force the water through the sand. However, excessive pressure may increase the effluent turbidity, and bacteria may appear in the discharge water. For this reason, and because pressure filters are difficult to inspect and keep in good order, open gravity filters are favored for public water supplies.

Diatomaceous earth filters. Swimming-pool installations and small water supplies frequently use this type of filter. The filters consist of a medium or septum supporting a layer of diatomaceous earth through which the water is passed. A filter layer is built up by the addition of diatomaceous earth to the water. When the pressure loss becomes excessive, filters must be backwashed and a fresh layer of diatomaceous earth applied. Filter rates of 2.5–6 gal/(min/ft^2) [1.7–4.1 $\times$ 10^{-3} m^3/(s/m^2)] are attained.

Disinfection. There are several methods of treatment of water to kill living organisms, particularly pathogenic bacteria; the application of chlorine or chlorine compounds is the most common. Less frequently used methods include the use of ultraviolet light, ozone, or silver ions. Boiling is the favorite household emergency measure.

Chlorination is simple and inexpensive and is practiced almost universally in public water supplies. It is often the sole treatment of clear, uncontaminated waters. In most plants it supplements coagulation and filtration. Chlorination is used also to protect against contamination of water in distribution mains and reservoirs after purification.

Chlorine gas is most economical and easiest to apply in large systems. For small works, calcium hypochlorite or sodium hypochlorite is frequently used. Regardless of which form is used, the dose varies with the water quality and degree of contamination. Clear, uncontaminated water can be disinfected with small doses, usually less than one part per million; contaminated water may require several times as much. The amount of chlorine taken up by organic matter and minerals in water is known as the chlorine demand. For proper disinfection the dose must exceed the demand so that free chlorine remains in the water.

Chlorination alone is not reliable for the treatment of contaminated or turbid water. A sudden increase in the chlorine demand may absorb the full dose and provide no residual chlorine for disinfection, and it cannot be assumed that the chlorine will penetrate particles of organic matter. Chlorine is applied before filtration, after filtration, and sometimes at both times.

Chlorine sometimes causes objectionable tastes or odors in water. This may be due to an excessive chlorine dose, but more frequently it is caused by a combination of chlorine and organic matter, such as algae, in the water. Some algae, relatively unobjectionable in the natural state, produce unbearable tastes after chlorination. In other cases, strong chlorine doses oxidize the organic matter completely and produce odor-free water. Excessive chlorine may be removed by dechlorination with sulfur dioxide. Also, ammonia is often added for taste control to reduce the concentration of free chlorine.

Granular activated carbon. Fine-grain powdered activated carbon has been used for years to reduce objectionable tastes and odors, harmful organic compounds, and heavy metals in public water supplies. Since the capacity of granular activated carbon for this use is great, no special facilities are normally designed for taste and odor control. Rather, the carbon is put on top of the filters or is used as the filter medium.

Granulated activated carbon (GAC) has been proposed by the Environmental Protection Agency (EPA) to eliminate or reduce potentially carcinogenic organic substances in public supplies. The harmful substances, defined as trihalomethanes, are derived from naturally occurring humic and fulvic acids combining with chlorine and bromine. A nationwide survey of chlorinated public water supplies indicated many with trihalomethanes. As a step toward correcting the situation, the EPA has adopted the final regulations to the National Interim Primary Drinking Water Regulations, limiting the maximum concentration of trihalomethanes in systems serving 10,000 persons or more to 0.1 mg per liter (average). Most communities not meeting these limitations have adjusted their disinfection procedures in a manner that decreases the trihalomethanes to acceptable levels. Where such adjustments are found not sufficient, granulated activated carbon facilities are being installed. Facilities have been built at only a few places, and there is little reliable operating and cost data.

Designing the contact chamber to pass water plant effluent through a bed of granulated activated carbon is simple. The real job and cost of the process are in the periodic removal, cleaning, regeneration, and returning of the granulated activated carbon to the contact chambers, and adding new material to make up for losses. Several regeneration furnaces are available, including infrared furnace, stream, and multiple hearths. All of these involve the operation and maintenance of machinery and equipment, and a competent labor force. The frequency of regeneration varies greatly, since it depends not only upon how much trihalomethane must be removed, but upon what other chemicals are present in the water that interfere with trihalomethane removal, and the type of granulated activated carbon used.

With these factors in mind, the overall cost of facilities and operations has been judged to match the cost of conventional water treatment.

Since changes in raw water quality may affect the performance of the granulated activated carbon, some irregularity can be expected. Design, construction, and installation of equipment and monitoring facilities should not be started without reliable, expert advice.

Water softening. The "hardness" of water is due to the presence of calcium and magnesium salts. These salts make washing difficult, waste soap, and cause unpleasant scums and stains in households and laundries. They are especially harmful in boiler feedwater because of their tendency to form scales.

Municipal water softening is common where the natural water has a hardness in excess of 150 parts per million. Two methods are used: (1) The water is treated with lime and soda ash to precipitate the calcium and magnesium as carbonate and hydroxide, after which the water is filtered; (2) the water is passed through a porous cation exchanger which has the ability of substituting sodium ions in the exchange medium for calcium and magnesium in the water. The exchange medium may be a natural sand known as zeolite, or may be manufactured from organic resins. It must be recharged periodically by backwashing with brine.

For high-pressure steam boilers or some other industrial processes, almost complete deionization of water is needed, and treatment includes both cation and anion exchangers. Lime-soda plants are similar to water purification plants, with coagulation, settling, and filtration. Zeolite or cation-exchange plants are usually built of steel tanks with appurtenances for backwashing the media with salt brine. If the water is turbid, filtration ahead of zeolite softening may be required.

Aeration. Aeration is a process of exposing water to air by dividing the water into small drops, by forcing air through the water, or by a combination of both. The first method uses jets, fountains, waterfalls, and riffles; in the second, compressed air is admitted to the bottom of a tank through perforated pipes or porous plates; in the third, drops of water are met by a stream of air produced by a fan.

Aeration is used to add oxygen to water and to remove carbon dioxide, hydrogen sulfide, and taste-producing gases or vapors. Aeration is also used in iron-removal plants to oxidize the iron ahead of the sedimentation or filtration processes. SEE WATER POLLUTION; WATER SUPPLY ENGINEERING.

Richard Hazen

Bibliography. American Water Works Ass. Inc., *A Handbook of Public Water Supplies*, 3d ed., 1971; G. M. Fair and J. C. Geyer, *Water Supply and Waste Water Disposal*, 1954; G. M. Fair, J. C. Geyer, and D. A. Okun, *Water Supply and Wastewater Removal*, 1966; Y. Y. Haimes, J. Kindler, and E. J. Plate (eds.), *The Process of Water Resources Project Planning: A Systems Approach*, 1987; H. E. Hudson, Jr., *Water Clarification Processes, Practical Design, and Evaluation*, 1981; Nalco Chemical Co., *The Nalco Water Handbook,* 2d ed., 1988.

Weather

The state of the atmosphere, as determined by the simultaneous occurrence of several meteorological phenomena at a geographical locality or over broad areas of the Earth. When such a collection of weather elements is part of an interrelated physical structure of the atmosphere, it is termed a weather system, and includes phenomena at all elevations above the ground. More popularly, weather refers to a certain state of the atmosphere as it affects humans' activities on the Earth's surface. In this sense, it is often taken to include such related phenomena as waves at sea and floods on land.

An orderly association of weather elements accompanying a typical weather system of the Northern Hemisphere may be illustrated by a large anticyclone, or high-pressure region. In such a "high," extending over an area of many thousands of square miles, the usually gentle winds circulate clockwise around the high-pressure center. This system often brings fair weather locally, which implies a bright sunny day with few clouds. The temperature may vary widely depending on season and time of day. However, a cyclone or low-pressure region is frequently associated with a dark cloudy sky with driving rain (or snow) and strong winds which circulate counterclockwise about a low-pressure center of the Northern Hemisphere.

A weather element is any individual physical feature of the atmosphere. At a given locality, at least seven such elements may be observed at any one time. These are clouds, precipitation, temperature, humidity, wind, pressure, and visibility. Each principal element is divided into many subtypes. For a discussion of a characteristic local combination of several elements, as they might be observed at a U.S. Weather Bureau station, *SEE WEATHER MAP*.

The various forms of precipitation are included by international agreement among the hydrometeors, which comprise all the visible features in the atmosphere, besides clouds, that are due to water in its various forms. For convenience in processing weather data and information, this definition is made to include some phenomena not due to water, such as dust and smoke. Some of the more common hydrometeors include rain, snow, fog, hail, dew, and frost.

Both a physical (or genetic) and a descriptive classification of clouds and hydrometeors have been devised. The World Meteorological Organization, which among many other activities coordinates the taking of weather observations among the nations of the world, recognizes at least 36 cloud types and 100 classes of hydrometeors.

Certain optical and electrical phenomena have long been observed among weather elements, including lightning, aurora, solar or lunar corona, and halo. *SEE AIR MASS; ATMOSPHERE; ATMOSPHERIC GENERAL CIRCULATION; CLOUD; FRONT; METEOROLOGY; STORM; WIND.*

Philip F. Clapp

Bibliography. L. J. Battan, *Weather*, 2d ed., 1985; H. Dickson, *Climate and Weather*, 1976; F. W. Cole, *Introduction to Meteorology*, 3d ed., 1980; J. Farrand, Jr., *Weather*, 1990; D. Riley and L. Spolton, *World Weather and Climate*, 2d ed., 1982; M. L. Shelton, *Climate and Weather: A Spatial Perspective*, 1988.

Weather forecasting and prediction

Processes for formulating and disseminating information about future weather conditions based upon the collection and analysis of meteorological observations. Weather forecasts may be classified according to the space and time scale of the predicted phenomena. Atmospheric fluctuations with a length of less than 100 m (330 ft) and a period of less than 100 s are considered to be turbulent. Prediction of turbulence extends only to establishing its statistical properties, insofar as these are determined by the thermal and dynamic stability of the air and by the aerodynamic roughness of the underlying surface. The study of atmospheric turbulence is called micrometeorology; it is of importance for understanding the diffusion of air pollutants and other aspects of the climate near the ground. Standard meteorological observations are made with sampling techniques that filter out the influence of turbulence. Common terminology distinguishes among three classes of phenomena with a scale that is larger than the turbulent microscale: the mesoscale, synoptic scale, and planetary scale.

The mesoscale includes all moist convection phenomena, ranging from individual cloud cells up to the convective cloud complexes associated with prefrontal squall lines, tropical storms, and the intertropical convergence zone. Also included among mesoscale phenomena are the sea breeze, mountain valley circulations, and the detailed structure of frontal inversions. Because most mesoscale phenomena have time periods less than 12 h or are located at low latitudes, they are little influenced by the rotation of the Earth. The prediction of mesoscale phenomena is an area of active research. Most forecasting methods depend upon empirical rules or the short-range extrapolation of current observations, particularly those provided by radar and geostationary satellites. Forecasts are usually couched in probabilistic terms to reflect the sporadic character of the phenomena. Since many mesoscale phenomena pose serious threats to life and property, it is the practice to issue advisories of potential occurrence significantly in advance. These "watch" advisories encourage the public to attain a degree of readiness appropriate to the potential hazard. Once the phenomenon is considered to be imminent, the advisory is changed to a "warning," with the expectation that the public will take immediate action to prevent the loss of life.

The next-largest scale of weather events is called the synoptic scale, because the network of meteorological stations making simultaneous, or synoptic, observations serves to define the phenomena. The migratory storm systems of the extratropics are synoptic-scale events, as are the undulating wind currents of the upper-air circulation which accompany the storms. The storms are associated with barometric minima, variously called lows, depressions, or cyclones. The sense of the wind rotation about the storm is counterclockwise in the Northern Hemisphere, but clockwise in the Southern Hemisphere. This effect, called geostrophy, is due to the rotation of the Earth and the relatively long period, 3–7 days, of the storm life cycle. Significant progress has been made in the numerical prediction of synoptic-scale phenomena.

Planetary-scale phenomena are persistent, quasi-stationary perturbations of the global circulation of the air with horizontal dimensions comparable to the radius of the Earth. These dominant features of the general circulation appear to be correlated with the major orographic features of the globe and with the latent and sensible heat sources provided by the oceans. They tend to control the paths followed by the synoptic-scale storms, and to draw upon the synoptic transients for an additional source of heat and momentum. Long-range weather forecasts must account for the slow evolution of the planetary-scale circulations. To the extent that the planetary-scale centers of action can be correctly predicted, the path and frequency of migratory storm systems can be estimated. The problem of long-range forecasting blends into the question of climate variation.

The remainder of this article contains five sections. Under the heading of development, the highlights of the historical emergence of modern weather forecasting techniques are presented. The special problems of long-range forecasting are elaborated in the second section. Sections three and four deal with the techniques of statistical and physical-numerical weather prediction, respectively. In the concluding section, the organization of weather forecast offices and centers is outlined. For further information on the observation and processing of weather data *SEE ATMOSPHERE; MICROMETEOROLOGY.*

Joseph P. Gerrity

DEVELOPMENT

The development of weather forecasting techniques was made possible in the seventeenth century by the invention of instruments that measure key atmospheric parameters. The Italian mathematician Evangelista Torricelli invented the barometer in 1644. This instrument, quantifying atmospheric pressure, soon proved its utility by foretelling storms as its mercury fell. Later, Torricelli's sponsor, Grand Duke Ferdinand II, refining Galileo's observation that air expands and contracts upon heating and cooling, developed the thermometer. Ferdinand used these innovations in establishing the first network of weather observations. An instrument to measure the atmosphere's water vapor content, the hygrometer, was also developed by Ferdinand. The anemometer, measuring wind speed, was invented by the British physicist Robert Hook in 1667. These developments provided for description and physical understanding of the atmospheric motions.

The eighteenth century was marked by Leonhard Euler's articulation of equations of fluid dynamics; these provided a theory of air motions. Joseph Black's discovery after 1760 that heating occurs when water vapor condenses into liquid was important because many weather systems, especially in the tropics, derive their energy from this latent heating. Surface weather observations began to be taken regularly during the eighteenth century. However, organized networks of stations, necessary to document large migratory storms, did not exist until 1820, when H. W. Brandes produced the first weather charts. These maps showing that storms approaching Europe originated in the North Atlantic Ocean helped to define the synoptic method of forecasting.

Synoptic method. The synoptic method of forecasting consists of the simultaneous collection of weather observations, and the plotting and analysis of these data on geographical maps. An experienced analyst, having studied several of these maps in chronological succession, can follow the movement and intensification of weather systems and forecast their positions. This forecasting technique requires the regular and frequent use of large networks of data.   In the United States, James Espey, having been appointed by Congress in 1842 as the first federal government meteorologist, began to produce weather maps routinely; these clearly showed that weather disturbances in midlatitudes move from west to east. By 1860, about 500 stations were regularly telegraphing weather reports to the Smithsonian Institution in Washington, D.C., where weather maps were published. The U.S. Army Signal Service was authorized in 1870 to build a nationwide storm-observing network. Meteorologists in Washington routinely made 24-h forecasts and telegraphed their synopses to railroad stations and post offices across the country. The U.S. Weather Bureau, a civilian agency founded in 1890, was charged with the task of issuing storm advisories. An important nineteenth-century discovery was made by William Redfield, who documented the counterclockwise rotation of winds around Northern Hemisphere cyclones. SEE WEATHER MAP.

The synoptic forecasts during the nineteenth century, while useful, were limited because they were almost exclusively based upon surface observations. Though mountaineering and cloud observations suggested that wind and temperature patterns aloft differed from those at the Earth's surface, no systematic network of upper-air observations existed to allow meteorologists the opportunity to trace these patterns. Teisserenc de Bort, using instrumented varnished paper balloon ascents as high as 9 mi (about 14.5 km), had demonstrated the existence of the stratosphere. This layer of air, generally located above levels from 5.5 to 8 mi (9 to 13 km) and characterized by temperatures remaining constant or increasing with elevation, acts as a cap on much of the world's weather. A cost-effective, trackable, and expendable instrument suspended beneath a rubber balloon (the radiosonde) began to be routinely deployed from a network of stations after World War I. The tracking of the balloon allowed for wind measurements to be taken at various elevations throughout its ascent. Currently, such a network of more than 2000 upper-air stations around the world reports its observations twice daily.

Dynamic method. Soon after 1900, Vilhelm Bjerknes of Norway began a program that involved using the basic laws of hydrodynamics and thermodynamics to define the current state of the atmosphere, and to compute its future state. This concept marked the birth of the dynamic method of forecasting, though its practical application was realized only after 1950, when sufficiently powerful computers became available to produce the necessary calculations efficiently. Bjerknes and his colleagues developed the first conceptual model of the life cycle of a surface cyclone. Careful surface observations showed that cyclonic storms typically formed along fronts, that is, boundaries between cold and warm air masses. The Norwegian model showed that precipitation was associated with active cold and warm fronts, and that this precipitation began to wrap around the cyclone as it intensified. Though subsequent work demonstrated that fronts are not crucial to cyclogenesis, the Norwegian frontal cyclone model is still used in weather map analyses. SEE FRONT.

It was not until the late 1930s that routine aerological observations had a substantial impact on forecasting. Carl-Gustaf Rossby studied the meandering jet stream and proposed a theory to explain the movement of upper-air disturbances, based upon the principle that air parcels conserve their absolute vorticity. Jule Charney, after World War I, developed theories for surface cyclone development and for numerical weather prediction. By the 1950s, Charney and his collaborators succeeded in producing qualitatively reasonable numerical forecasts of the atmosphere. Numerical weather prediction techniques, in addition to being applied to short-range weather prediction, are used in such research studies as air-pollutant transport and the effects of greenhouse gases on global climate change. SEE AIR POLLUTION; GREENHOUSE EFFECT; JET STREAM.

Though numerical forecasts continue to improve, statistical forecast techniques, once used exclusively with observational data available at the time of the forecast, are now used in conjunction with numerical output to predict the weather. Statistical methods, based upon a historical comparison of large samples of numerical model output with actual weather conditions, routinely play a role in the prediction of surface temperatures and precipitation probabilities. SEE DYNAMIC METEOROLOGY.

Advances. The best weather forecasts result from application of the synoptic method to the latest numerical and statistical information. The forecaster has an ever-increasing number of valuable tools with which to work. Numerical forecast models, owing to faster computers, are capable of explicitly resolving mesoscale weather systems. Geostationary satellites allow for continuous tracking of such dangerous weather systems as hurricanes. The increased routine use of Doppler radar, in conjunction with data derived from wind and temperature profiler soundings, promises to give added capability in tracking and forecasting mesoscale weather disturbances. Very high-frequency and ultrahigh-frequency Doppler radars may be used to provide detailed wind soundings. These wind profilers, if located sufficiently close to one another, will allow for the hourly tracking of mesoscale disturbances aloft. Ground- and satellite-based microwave radiometric measurements are being used to construct temperature and moisture soundings of the atmoshpere. The assimilation of such new data at varying times in the numerical model forecast cycle offers the promise of improved prediction. Medium-range forecasts, ranging up to 2 weeks, may be improved from knowledge of forecast skill in relationship to the form of the planetary-scale atmospheric circulation.   *John R. Gyakum*

LONG-RANGE FORECASTING

Long-range forecasts usually extend in some general terms over a month or a season and are issued with only a short lead time before their period begins. Medium-range forecasts overlap the early parts of the longer ranges by commencing where daily weather forecasts leave off, at the sixth day, and continuing to 10 days. The usage "extended forecast," once applied to the several days following a 48-h forecast, has been transferred to open-ended experimental trials beyond the tenth day.

Two or three dozen weather services around the world produce some kind of long-range forecast; far fewer offer medium-range forecasts. The discrepancy reflects an important difference in technique. Medium-range forecasts are built on a direct extension of the output of dynamical models from shorter ranges, adjusted by statistical and subjective methods; thus they require major computing facilities found only in a few forecast centers. On the other hand, the classical empirical techniques of long-range forecasting—statistical and synoptic (chart-based)—benefit from, but do not require, the availability of dynamical model output.

Because its predictability falls off markedly by day 6, daily weather does not enter into medium- and longer-range forecasts. Instead information is given about prevailing conditions: average temperature, total rainfall or rainfall frequency, and perhaps some information on trends or variability during the period. All predictions are referred to the climatic norms for the locality and time of year, whether as numerical deviations from them or as the predicted occurrence of one of a few general climatic categories, for example, light, moderate, or heavy precipitation.

Aside from the normal seasonal changes, the temporal variations of weather from days to years are fundamentally irregular. They are therefore difficult to predict. Not only are exact periodicities missing, but even quasi-periodicities or general preferences for certain time scales of fluctuation are few: some modulations of large-scale energy conversions over 2 or 3 weeks, tropical traveling waves over 5–8 weeks, stratospheric tropical wind reversals over about 26 months (the Quasi-Biennial Oscillation, QBO). Distinct physical phenomena that are understandable and

predictable are scarce. Instead, general interactive processes among the elements of the climatic system—atmosphere, upper ocean, land surface conditions—produce slow changes upon which the dynamics of storms and other daily weather phenomena develop and feed back. One great exception occurs every few years on a nearly global scale: the combined oceanic and atmospheric event, centered on the tropical Pacific basin, known as El Niño–Southern Oscillation (ENSO). Taking a year or two to run its course, El Niño–Southern Oscillation carries implications for seasonal forecasts in many areas, some of them outside the tropics and near-tropics.

Partly because of El Niño–Southern Oscillation and the specifically tropical traveling disturbances, and partly because of the great intensity of rapid storm-related changes peculiar to the middle latitudes, the tropics and the temperate-to-polar zones present quite different long-range forecasting problems.

Standard practices. Within the tropics, statistical forecasts of the Indian Summer Monsoon were begun in the early years of the twentieth century and have become perhaps the most successful of all seasonal forecasts. Taking account of the springtime configuration of pressures aloft over the Indian Ocean and of the phase of the Southern Oscillation (pressure swings between Indonesia and the eastern South Pacific), forecasters can capture more than half the year-to-year variance of all-India summer rainfall.

Elsewhere in the tropics, seasonal drought in Brazil can be related to earlier general circulation patterns over the tropical Atlantic. Drought or rainfall excesses over Indonesia, northern Australia, coastal Peru, and the tropical Pacific islands follow the evolution of El Niño–Southern Oscillation and its variations of sea temperature. Seasonal rainfall in the African Sahel zone just south of the Sahara, which exhibits much longer and more pronounced interannual trends than rainfall elsewhere, is being predicted statistically with some success from worldwide patterns of sea surface temperature.

Outside the tropics, wherever dynamical model output for periods beyond a few days can be had, the practices of medium-range and monthly forecasting are tending to converge and to be separated from seasonal forecasting. In the shorter forecasts, the critical first stage, predicting the broad-scale—even hemispheric—pattern of abnormality of time-averaged wind and pressure aloft, can draw heavily on model output, extended by statistical calculations of persistence and forecasters' judgement on where and how firmly to stabilize the model-generated pattern. Then both statistical regression equations and the selection of cases of analogous upper-level flow from other years can help transform a circulation forecast to one of surface temperature and precipitation.

The seasonal forecast in temperate latitudes also requires first a picture of abnormalities in the flow field aloft. Without the significant guidance of a dynamical model, the forecaster must depend on (1) statistical regressions from the preceding month and from one to four or more preceding seasons, which yield usable indications in a few (often widely separated) locations around the hemisphere; (2) statistical cross-correlations (teleconnections) among these locations; (3) the phase of El Niño—Southern Oscillation (if that is clear-cut); and (4) in some circumstances, anomalies of sea-surface temperatures in the North Pacific Ocean. To convert ideas about circulation anomalies to seasonal prevailing weather, the forecaster chooses a few guiding cases from the analog map file and then turns to the patterns generated by a separate, objective analog selection system. This alternate system points to other years whose corresponding seasons or months resemble the current year most closely in critical patterns of atmospheric large-scale flow and temperature, sea-surface temperature, and phase of El Niño–Southern Oscillation. Discordant indications must then be reconciled. The unavoidable element of subjectivity introduced by so much choosing and adjusting can be reduced by asking several forecasters to produce charts independently and to discuss the differences and to revise if persuaded, and by finally combining the forecasts objectively.

Seasonal midlatitude forecasts produced by this blend of empirical techniques possess severely limited accuracy. On a scale measuring zero for randomness of choice (among three categories) to 100 for perfect choice, they average 7 points for temperature and 4 for precipitation in the United States, with a wide fluctuation from case to case and some seasonal and regional differentials. Monthly temperature forecasts have gradually become 5 points better than this by exploiting the output of continually improving dynamical models: precipitation forecasts have gained 3.

Prediction research. The problems of long-range forecasting have drawn increasing attention and effort from the research community since the late 1970s. Particularly in the United States and the United Kingdom, major computational experiments with 30-day runs on atmospheric general-circulation models create a rich body of data to explore how dynamical predictions decay under varying initial conditions. Statistical methods for correcting, tuning, or adapting model output for practical forecast use continue to be derived. The study of blocking phenomena has enjoyed a renaissance. Blocks are splits in the major band of midlatitude westerlies, diverting storms from their more normal tracks and causing major weather anomalies over a week or two—sometimes in one fixed area, other times in a moving pattern, occasionally in a large part of the middle latitudes. Any major improvements in medium-range and monthly forecasting skill must depend on understanding and predicting them.

Abnormalities in snow cover offer another potential for forcing—perhaps predictably—variations in monthly and seasonal weather. The reaction of the Indian Monsoon to winter snow-cover anomalies many months earlier over central Asia is being examined observationally and by model simulations. Another land surface variable, soil moisture deficit, is being tested computationally as a forcer—or reenforcer—of drought. Sea-temperature anomalies in spring or summer may also be implicated in the formation or intensification of drought. *See Drought.*

The behavior of the biggest models, however, can be almost as hard to understand as that of the atmosphere they mimic. The computational tests of all these lower boundary effects with the very complex models of atmospheric general circulation are being restudied diagnostically by simpler models in the search for clearer physical insight. Particularly for seasonal forecasting, such insights should provide a key to any further improvements in analog or other statistical systems.

The underlying surface not only acts on the atmosphere but also reacts to variations of the atmosphere on seasonal and sometimes monthly time scales. Modeling of the full array of interactions requires conversion of a general-circulation model to a kind of climate model in which separate models of the atmosphere, upper oceans, and the land surface are properly coupled and boundary processes accounted for. The practical applicability of such models to long-range prediction is not assured, but must be tested step by step.

Finally, there has been a revival of the idea of prediction from an extraterrestrial source, solar variability, which was considered a discredited concept. There is evidence that suggests an effect on patterns of winter circulation and temperature from the 11-year solar cycle combined with the stratospheric Quasi-Biennial Oscillation. *See Atmospheric general circulation.*

Predictability research. Prediction by dynamical models suffers from unavoidable errors that grow in part systematically and in part randomly. The systematic errors produce a gradual drift toward a climate model that may differ seriously from the real climate and that may thereby distort long-range forecasts to uselessness if not corrected. Much attention is being given to estimating these errors, seeking their sources in the models, and revising models or correcting their output statistically. Random growth of error, which proceeds most rapidly at the smallest spatial scales, gradually cascades through the working of the model into the very largest scales of motion. The rate at which this happens, which governs the predictability of each scale, is studied in model predictability tests by comparing outcomes from many long runs with slightly differing prescribed initial conditions and noting when those outcomes begin to differ as much as a randomly chosen set. The results imply that only the very largest scales of motion—continental or larger—may be predicted with some skill beyond 10–15 days. This residual predictability seems itself to be variable, perhaps depending on the nature of the particular starting conditions of a forecast. Such regime-dependent predictability is being investigated by the statistical and synoptic analysis of both experimental and operational sets of model-generated predictions.

Simple dynamical systems governed by nonlinear differential equations have been found to display complex, nonperiodic behavior known as chaotic, in which the state variables of the system tend to follow a limited number of somewhat constrained and repetitive trajectories (attractors) in their multidimensional phase space, occasionally flying off from one of them to another. The "regimes" long known to extended forecasters may be examples of attractors in large-scale atmospheric dynamics.

Predictability that goes beyond the limits achievable simply by knowing an initial state—that is, beyond atmospheric predictability—should perhaps be called short-term climate predictability. It would refer to predictions of monthly or seasonal means with a lead time from at least a month to several seasons, and it would arise from the physical forcing action of other parts of the climate system (land, sea, snow and ice cover) on the atmosphere. Most explorations of this type of climate predictability have been carried out by statistical power-spectrum analysis of weather data records, in which the variability of monthly or seasonal means is partitioned into a climate signal and climate noise. The latter is that part of the total variability of monthly or seasonal means due only to the daily weather variations—whose unpredictability after 2 weeks or so has been cited. The climate signal, taken to be potentially predictable, has been found to vary widely by region, weather element, time of year, and length of forecast period.

Probabilistic forecasting. Economic decision making that tries to employ inherently uncertain weather forecasts must also incorporate information about the level of uncertainty, or serious losses may be incurred that could have been avoided by ignoring the forecasts altogether. Long-range forecasts are more uncertain than most; to be useful they require some appropriate announcement of their own uncertainty. After 1982, official forecasts in the United States were presented in an explicitly probabilistic format, where the estimated chances of occurence of the classes of predicted temperature or precipitation are shown as contoured fields on the maps. The probabilities are based primarily on records of past performance, with whatever regional and seasonal variations those records clearly justify, modulated finally by the forecaster's own judgment about the nature and difficulty of the current case.

Three kinds of research may help forecasters sharpen the probability estimates attached to the predictions. Just as in the model predictability tests, the use of ensembles of dynamical model computations from slightly varied initial conditions—rather than of single runs—may allow the model to predict its own skill at various ranges from the rate at which the ensemble members diverge. In addition, successful results of regime predictability studies could easily be applied to model output. Finally, the steadiness of the model forecast may itself provide valid information about likely skill.

Two other benefits would flow from the capacity to predict a model's skill in any given forecast. The length of model run actually applied to the forecast could be adjusted case by case, and the conventional forecast period of 1 month—a financial and organizational planning unit, not a meteorological unit—could be supplemented very usefully by a higher-probability period whose length would itself be part of the prediction.   *Donald L. Gilman*

STATISTICAL WEATHER FORECASTING

Statistical weather forecasting is the prediction of weather by use of data from past weather developments. Examples of statistical predictions may be the nocturnal minimum temperature tomorrow at a particular site and the probability of precipitation within a given county during the next 36 h. In each case the prediction is based on statistical relations obtained from earlier records and intended for a specific location and forecast period. Because of the geographic and atmospheric complexities, extension of these relations to another location or time period tends to produce less accurate forecasts, and a separate treatment usually leads to better success.

The necessity for statistical methods in weather prediction is due largely to a lack of a detailed knowledge of atmospheric processes at any one time. It is presumed that the atmosphere obeys accepted physical laws, under the influence of solar energy, terrain and oceanic effects, and human activities. These laws are the basis for numerical weather predictions of relatively large-scale features of the atmosphere. Because of gaps between observing stations, however,

such predictions, while valuable, have limited accuracy. Consequently, statistical weather predictions based on historical data continue to be useful.

Statistical procedures. Regression methods are frequently employed in prediction. The simplest regression equation is a linear relation between the weather element to be predicted (the predictand) and one or more other weather elements (the predictors). A sample of historical values of these elements is used to develop the equation by the least-squares method. A linear rather than nonlinear equation is preferred, mostly for simplicity. For example, the nocturnal minimum temperature might be represented as a linear function of the observed temperature and wind speed at 8 P.M. on the previous evening, among other possible predictors.

A large sample of historical observations is desirable in developing the equation in order to ensure reliability when it is applied to independent data. Furthermore, practical experience has shown that the most successful regression equations include predictors having known physical relationships with predictands. A useful predictor could be a combination of two or more meteorological observations. Thus, formal knowledge and subjective experience are combined to obtain equations that are objective forecast tools thereafter.

Predictors. The use of a large number of predictors in one equation is not particularly advantageous, in part because correlations among them may result in redundant predictive information. A procedure to overcome this problem is screening regression. Predictors are selected according to their ability to account for the variability of the predictand, and are rendered independent of each other by use of regression techniques that define new predictors in place of original ones. After several repetitions of these two steps, hundreds of potential predictors are usually reduced to a dozen or less.

Regression estimation. To forecast the probability of an event, such as the occurrence of precipitation or freezing temperatures, a technique called regression estimation of event probabilities can be employed. Basically, this relies on a determination of the relative frequencies of the predictand as observed in predefined classes of one or more predictors in the developmental sample. A predictor may be continuous or binary. If it is continuous, the class containing its value is the one used to obtain the predicted probability.

In general, weather predictions from regression equations and other purely statistical methods are not very useful beyond 24 h. However, with the advent of numerical prediction methods that employ hydrodynamical and thermodynamical models to make predictions a day or more ahead, there has been a parallel development of methods that link statistics and dynamics to give more extended forecasts of weather elements than are provided by dynamical models alone.

Model output statistics. An important example of this linkage is the method of model output statistics. A regression equation in this case might predict the value of a weather element by using as predictors values of some elements at the initial time or earlier and values of others that are predicted by the dynamical model. Thus, the predictand and some of the predictors might be concurrent.

This technique has been applied to forecasts of

maximum and minimum daily temperatures, wind speed and direction, precipitation amount, and probabilities of precipitation occurrence, as well as other variables, for intervals up to 48 h. It is the basis for many National Weather Service forecasts. These are supplied to local forecasters, who may improve on them by using additional information and personal experience.

Two disadvantages of the method are that developmental samples are not large because dynamical models have been in operation only for a short period of time, and because the statistical equations must be rederived as the models improve. Nevertheless, the useful range of weather prediction has been increased by this technique.

Other procedures. Procedures other than regression analysis may be employed by the meteorologist. Combinations of chosen predictors may be classified into categories, then a table constructed by choosing, for each category, the average observed value of the predictand as the expected value, or by choosing the observed frequency of occurrence as the probability; or the meteorologist may construct a series of graphs of the predictand against pairs of predictors, to be used in arriving at a forecast.

Applications. In all of these procedures the forecast is obtained by introducing the currently available values of predictors into equations, tables, or graphs. The evaluation of a given statistical method can be made in several ways; an examination of the mean square error of prediction is frequently favored.

By themselves, statistical methods are highly suitable for predicting special local phenomena, such as the occurrence of fog. For preparing prognostic weather maps a day or so in advance, statistical formulas are somewhat useful but are frequently inferior to subjective forecasts. The unification of statistical methods and numerical prediction methods is an attractive alternative here.   *Thomas A. Gleeson*

NUMERICAL WEATHER PREDICTION

Numerical weather prediction is the prediction of weather phenomena by the numerical solution of the equations governing the motion and changes of condition of the atmosphere. More generally, the term applies to any numerical solution or analysis of the atmospheric equations of motion.

The laws of motion of the atmosphere may be expressed as a set of partial differential equations relating the instantaneous rates of change of the meteorological variables to their instantaneous distribution in space. These are developed in dynamic meteorology. A prediction for a finite time interval is obtained by summing the succession of infinitesimal time changes of the meteorological variables, each of which is determined by their distribution at the preceding instant of time. Although this process of integration may be carried out in principle, the nonlinearity of the equations and the complexity and multiplicity of the data make it impossible in practice. Instead, it is necessary to resort to numerical approximation techniques in which successive changes in the variables are calculated for small, but finite, time intervals over a domain spanning part or all of the atmosphere. Even so, the amount of computation is vast, and numerical weather prediction remained only a dream until the advent of the modern high-speed electronic computing machine. These machines are capable of perform-

ing the millions of arithmetic operations involved with a minimum of human labor and in an economically feasible time span. Numerical methods are gradually replacing the earlier, more subjective methods of weather prediction in the government weather services of many countries. This is particularly true in the preparation of prognoses for large areas. The detailed prediction of local weather phenomena has not yet benefited greatly from the use of numerical dynamic methods, as indicated above in the general section on weather forecasting.

There are two major methods of approximating the continuous nonlinear partial differential equations, the finite-difference method and the spectral method. In the finite-difference method, the continuous temporal and spatial derivatives are approximated by differences between values of variables defined at discrete points in time and space. An example of the finite-difference approach is given in the next section.

In the spectral method, the dependent variables (such as pressure, temperature, and wind) are represented by a sum of functions, called basis functions, that have a prescribed structure in space. A common set of basis functions is composed of sines and cosines (Fourier series). The spatial resolution of spectral models is determined by the number of basis functions. Each of the basis functions in the sum has an amplitude which varies in time. The spectral method results in a transformation of the original set of partial differential equations into a set of ordinary differential equations for the time-dependent coefficients, which can be solved by finite-difference equations. After the solutions for the amplitude of the coefficients are obtained for some future time, the values of the variables may be calculated in physical space by summing the contributions from each basis function.

Short-range numerical prediction. By the nature of numerical weather prediction, its accuracy depends on (1) an understanding of the laws of atmospheric behavior, (2) the ability to measure the instantaneous state of the atmosphere, and (3) the accuracy with which the solutions of the continuous equations of motion are approximated by finite-difference means. The greatest success has been achieved in predicting the motion of the large-scale (>1000 mi or 1600 km) pressure systems in the atmosphere for relatively short periods of time (1–3 days). For such space and time scales, the poorly understood energy sources and frictional dissipative forces may be approximated by relatively simple formulations, and rather coarse horizontal resolutions may be used.

The large-scale motions are characterized by their properties of being quasistatic, quasigeostrophic, and horizontally quasinondivergent, as discussed in another article. *SEE METEOROLOGY.*

These properties may be used to simplify the equations of motion by filtering out the motions which have little meteorological importance, such as sound and gravity waves. The resulting equations then become, in some cases, more amenable to numerical treatment.

A simple illustration of the methods employed for numerical weather prediction is given by the following example. Consider a homogeneous, incompressible, frictionless fluid moving over a rotating, gravitating plane in such a manner that the horizontal velocity does not vary with height. For quasistatic flow the equations of motion are Eqs. (1), and the equation of mass conservation is Eq. (2), where u and

$$\frac{\partial u}{\partial t} + u\frac{\partial u}{\partial x} + v\frac{\partial u}{\partial y} = -g\frac{\partial h}{\partial x} + 2\omega v \tag{1}$$

$$\frac{\partial v}{\partial t} + u\frac{\partial v}{\partial x} + v\frac{\partial u}{\partial y} = -g\frac{\partial h}{\partial y} - 2\omega u$$

$$\frac{\partial h}{\partial t} + u\frac{\partial h}{\partial x} + v\frac{\partial h}{\partial y} = -h\left(\frac{\partial u}{\partial x} + \frac{\partial v}{\partial y}\right) \tag{2}$$

v are the velocity components in the directions of the horizontal rectangular coordinates x and y, t is the time, g is the acceleration of gravity, ω is the angular speed of rotation, and h is the height of the free surface of the fluid. Let the variables u, v, and h be defined at the points $x = i\Delta x$, $y = j\Delta x$ ($i = 0, 1, 2, \ldots, I$; $j = 0, 1, 2, \ldots, J$) and at the times $t = k\Delta t$ ($k = 0, 1, 2, \ldots, K$), and denote quantities at these points and times by the subscripts i, j, and k. Derivatives such as $\partial u/\partial t$ and $\partial u/\partial x$ may be approximated by the central difference quotients given by Eqs. (3). In this way Eqs. (4), the finite-

$$\frac{\Delta_k u_{i,j}}{2\Delta t} \equiv \frac{u_{i,j,k+1} - u_{i,j,k-1}}{2\Delta t} \tag{3}$$

$$\frac{\Delta_i u_{j,k}}{2\Delta x} \equiv \frac{u_{i+1,j,k} - u_{i-1,j,k}}{2\Delta x}$$

$$u_{i,j,k+1} = u_{i,j,k-1} - \frac{\Delta t}{\Delta x}(u_{i,j,k}\Delta_i u_{j,k} + v_{i,j,k}\Delta_j u_{i,k}$$
$$+ g\Delta_i h_{j,k}) + 4\omega v_{i,j,k}\Delta t$$

$$v_{i,j,k+1} = v_{i,j,k-1} - \frac{\Delta t}{\Delta x}(u_{i,j,k}\Delta_i v_{j,k} + v_{i,j,k}\Delta_j v_{i,k}$$
$$+ g\Delta_j h_{i,k}) - 4\omega u_{i,j,k}\Delta t \tag{4}$$

$$h_{i,j,k+1} = h_{i,j,k-1} - \frac{\Delta t}{\Delta x}[u_{i,j,k}\Delta_i h_{j,k} + v_{i,j,k}\Delta_j h_{i,k}$$
$$+ h_{i,j,k}(\Delta_i u_{j,k} + \Delta_j v_{i,k})]$$

difference analogs of the continuous equations, are obtained. Equations (4) give u, v, and h at the time $(k + 1)\Delta t$ in terms of u, v, and h at the times $k\Delta t$ and $(k - 1)\Delta t$. It is then possible to calculate u, v, and h at any time by iterative application of the above equations.

It may be shown, however, that the solution of the finite-difference equations will not converge to the solution of the continuous equations unless the criterion $\Delta x/\Delta t > c\sqrt{2}$ is satisfied, where c is the maximum value of the speed of long gravity waves $\sqrt{gh}$. This criterion is known as the Courant-Friedrichs-Lewy (CFL) criterion. Under circumstances comparable to those in the atmosphere, Δt is found to be so small that a 24-h prediction requires some 200 time steps and approximately 1 billion multiplications for an area the size of the Earth's surface. The computing time on a machine with a multiplication speed of 100 microseconds, an addition speed of 10 μs, and a memory access time of 10 μs would be about 30 min. The magnitude of the computational task may be comprehended from the fact that the more accurate atmospheric models being planned will require some 100–1000 times this amount of computation.

A saving of time is accomplished by utilizing the quasi-nondivergent property of the large-scale atmospheric motions. If, in the above example, the horizontal divergence $\partial u/\partial x + \partial v/\partial y$ is set equal to zero, the motion is found to be completely described by the equation for the conservation of the vertical component of absolute vorticity.

The solution of this equation may be obtained in far fewer time steps since gravity wave motions are filtered out by this constraint and the velocity c in the Courant-Friedrichs-Lewy criterion becomes merely the maximum particle velocity instead of the much greater gravity wave speed.

Cloud and precipitation prediction. If, to the standard dynamic variables u, v, w, p, and ρ, a sixth variable, the density of water vapor, is added, it becomes possible to predict clouds and precipitation as well as the air motion. When a parcel of air containing a fixed quantity of water vapor ascends, it expands adiabatically and cools until it becomes saturated. Continued ascent produces clouds and precipitation.

To incorporate these effects into a numerical prediction scheme, Eq. (5), which governs the rate of

$$\frac{dr}{dt} \equiv \frac{\partial r}{\partial t} + u\frac{\partial r}{\partial x} + v\frac{\partial r}{\partial y} + w\frac{\partial r}{\partial z} = S \tag{5}$$

change of specific humidity r, is added. Here S represents a source or sink of moisture. Then it is necessary also to include as a heat source in the thermodynamic energy equation a term which represents the time rate of release of the latent heat of condensation of water vapor. The most successful predictions made by this method are obtained in regions of strong rising motion, whether induced by forced orographic ascent or by horizontal convergence in well-developed depressions. The physics and mechanics of the convective cloud-formation process make the prediction of convective cloud and showery precipitation more difficult.

Large-scale numerical weather prediction. In 1955 the first operational numerical weather prediction model was introduced at the National Meteorological Center (NMC). This simplified barotropic model consisted of only one layer and therefore could model only the temporal variation of the mean vertical structure of the atmosphere. By the late 1960s, the speed of computers had increased sufficiently to permit the development of multilevel (usually about 6–10) models which could resolve, at least in part, the vertical variation of the wind, temperature, and moisture. These multilevel models predicted the fundamental meteorological variables mentioned above for large scales of motion. The characteristic grid size was about 240 mi (400 km) on a side, and the model's domain covered most of the Northern Hemisphere.

The forecast skill of these hemispheric models was limited in part by errors introduced at the artificial boundary of the model which was located near the Equator. Following the development of faster computers with larger memory, it was possible to eliminate this source of error by using models that covered the entire Earth. Global models with horizontal resolutions are fine as 120 mi (200 km) are being used by weather services in several countries.

Numerical calculation of climate. While global models were being implemented for operational weather prediction 1–10 days in advance, similar research models were being developed that could be run for much longer time periods. These general circulation models can be used to simulate the long-term variation of weather, that is, the climate.

The extension of numerical predictions to long time intervals requires a more accurate knowledge of the energy transfer and turbulent dissipative processes within the atmosphere and at the air-earth boundary, as well as greatly augmented computing-machine speeds and capacities. However, predictions of mean conditions over large areas may well become possible before such developments have taken place, for it is has become possible to incorporate into the prediction equations estimates of the energy sources and sinks—estimates which may be inaccurate in detail but correct in the mean. Several mathematical experiments involving such simplified energy sources have yielded predictions of mean circulations that strongly resemble those of the atmosphere.

Such experiments may make it possible to explain the principal features of the Earth's climate, that is, the statistical properties of the weather, well before it becomes possible to predict the daily fluctuations of weather for extended periods. Should these hopes be realized it would then become possible to undertake a rational analysis of paleoclimatic variation and changes induced by artifical means. If the existing climate could be understood from a knowledge of the existing energy sources, atmospheric constituents, and surface characteristics of the Earth, it might also be possible to predict the effects on the climate of natural or artificial modifications in one or more of these elements. SEE CLIMATE MODIFICATION; CLIMATIC CHANGE.

Specialized prediction models. Although the coarse grids in the hemispheric and global models are necessary for economical reasons, they are sources of two major types of forecast error. First, the truncation errors introduced when the continuous differential equations are replaced with approximations of finite resolution cause erroneous behavior of the scales of motion that are resolved by the models. Second, the neglect of scales of motion too small to be resolved by the mesh (for example, thunderstorms) may cause errors in the larger scales of motion. In an effort to simultaneously reduce both of these errors, models with considerably finer meshes have been tested. However, the price of reducing the mesh has been the necessity of covering smaller domains in order to keep the total computational effort within computer capability. Thus the limited-area fine-mesh model (LFM) run at NMC has a mesh length of approximately 72 mi (120 km) on a side, but covers a region only slightly larger than North America. Because the side boundaries of this model lie in meteorologically active regions, the variables on the boundaries must be updated during the forecast. A typical procedure is to interpolate these required future values on the boundary from a coarse-mesh model which is run first. Although simple in concept, there are mathematical problems associated with this method, including overspecification of some variables on the fine mesh. Nevertheless, limited-area models have made significant improvements in the accuracy of short-range numerical forecasts over the United States.

Even the small mesh sizes of the LFM are far too coarse to resolve the detailed structure of many important atmospheric phenomena, including hurricanes, thunderstorms, sea- and land-breeze circulations, mountain waves, and a variety of air-pollution phenomena. Considerable effort has gone into developing specialized research models with appropriate mesh sizes to study these and other small-scale systems. Thus, fully three-dimensional hurricane models with mesh sizes of 12 mi (20 km) simulate many of the features of real hurricanes. On even smaller scales, models with horizontal resolutions of a few hundred meters reproduce many of the observed fea-

tures in the life cycle of thunderstorms and squall lines. It would be entirely misleading, however, to imply that models of these phenomena differ from the large-scale models only in their resolution. In fact, physical processes which are negligible on large scales become important for some of the phenomena on smaller scales. For example, the drag or precipitation on the surrounding air is important in simulating thunderstorms, but not for modeling large scales of motion. Thus the details of precipitation processes, condensation, evaporation, freezing, and melting are incorporated into sophisticated cloud models.

In another class of special models, chemical reactions between trace gases are considered. For example, in models of urban photochemical smog, predictive equations for the concentration of oxides of nitrogen, oxygen, ozone, and reactive hydrocarbons are written. These equations contain transport and diffusion effects by the wind as well as reactions with solar radiation and other gases. Such air-chemistry models become far more complex than atmospheric models as the number of constituent gases and permitted reactions increases.   *Richard A. Anthes*

U.S. FORECAST CENTERS AND OFFICES

Weather forecasts for all parts of the United States are prepared by the National Weather Service (NWS), a part of the National Oceanic and Atmospheric Administration (NOAA). Various phases of the forecast work are performed at National Centers, River Forecast Centers (RFCs), and Weather Service Forecast Offices (WSFOs).

National Meteorological Center. The National Meteorological Center (NMC) manages three national centers and three divisions. They include the National Hurricane Center (NHC) located in Coral Gables, Florida, and the National Severe Storms Forecast Center (NSSFC) located in Kansas City, Missouri. The other four include the Climate Analysis Center, the Meteorological Operations Division, the Development Division, and the Automation Division, all of which are located in Camp Springs, Maryland.

The NMC collects virtually all the meteorological data over the globe and generates analysis and forecast guidance products that are distributed to NWS field offices, private meteorologists, public media, government offices, and the international meteorological community. The World Meteorological Organization (WMO) has designated the NMC as the analysis and forecast arm of the Washington World Meteorological Center, which requires global responsibilities as part of the international effort and cooperation known as the World Weather Watch. To carry out these responsibilities, many NMC products cover the entire globe.

Operations. The centralized preparation of data, analysis, and forecasts is designed to eliminate most requirements for hand charting and independent meteorological analysis in the NWS offices as well as user groups such as airline and private meteorologists (**Fig. 1**). The NMC, through the use of a large computer facility together with numerical forecast methods, provides the NWS and other government agencies with daily forecasts and outlooks to 90 days in advance, as well as specialized forecasts for hurricanes, severe convective weather, aviation, and space vehicle launch and recovery operations. In the course of a day, the NMC receives 25,000 hourly aviation

Fig. 1. Meteorologists in National Meteorological Center Operations Division manually adjust computer-generated surface prognostic charts to reduce errors and interpret areas of weather and cloudiness for guidance of National Weather Service field offices. (*NOAA*)

reports, over 19,000 synoptic land stations reports, 4500 ship and buoy reports, 4300 aircraft reports, and 2500 atmospheric soundings. All available cloud and temperature data derived from weather satellites are integrated into the analysis. The NMC products are received by field offices over an internal communication system. The Center makes 1848 facsimile transmissions daily to user groups outside the NWS.

Meteorological Operations Division. The Meteorological Operations Division is the seat of practical synoptic meteorology within NMC. Incoming data and outgoing products are examined for quality assurance. Numerical guidance is interactively evaluated and adjusted to produce value-added analysis and forecast

products out to 120 h (**Fig. 2**). The division also provides specialized support for the aviation industry and the national space program.

Automation Division. This division operates the NOAA computers and is responsible for the operational job sites that perform the analysis and numerical forecasts and generate the many forms of output needed by the multitude of users.

Development Division. This division develops advanced methods of analysis of atmospheric and oceanic data and numerical modeling to increase the skill in operational weather forecasts. Emphasis is placed on short- and medium-range weather forecasting and marine weather prediction.

Fig. 2. Cathode-ray-tube display system used throughout National Weather Service for forecast preparation and weather watch. (*NOAA*)

Climate Analysis Center. The Climate Analysis Center maintains a continuous watch on short-term climate fluctuations and monitors long-term climate trends. Forecasts from 6 to 10 days and outlooks from 30 to 90 days are produced for a wide variety of government and private users. Research is also conducted on a variety of climate-related topics.

National Severe Storms Forecast Center. The NSSFC is responsible for preparing and transmitting forecasts of areas of expected severe local storms, including tornadoes, damaging thunderstorm winds, and large hail. A long-range outlook is prepared for 1 and 2 days in advance giving the geographic areas that are most likely to have severe thunderstorms or tornadoes. These severe weather outlooks are used for planning purposes by the media, by emergency preparedness groups, and as input to the local forecast programs by NWS offices throughout the contiguous United States. As the possibility of severe thunderstorms increases, the NSSFC severe-storms meteorologist prepares tornado or severe-thunderstorm watches, typically for an area of 25,000 mi^2 (65,000 km^2) and for time periods of 1–7 h in advance. A second group of NSSFC meteorologists monitors weather observations, including pilot reports, weather surveillance radar reports, and satellite imagery depicted on sophisticated interactive computer displays. This group locates areas of potential weather hazards for aircraft in flight and immediately issues advisories, called AIRMETs (aircraft meteorological advisories) and SIGMETs (significant meteorological advisories), to various facilities of the Federal Aviation Administration (FAA) and to airline operations offices. SIGMETs dealing with hazards due to thunderstorms are called convective SIGMETs; these are in-flight hazardous weather warnings that apply to all aircraft. In a typical year, the NSSFC logs 700–900 tornadoes and 6000–8000 severe thunderstorms. Five hundred or so tornado or severe-thunderstorm watches are issued annually along with 10,000–15,000 convective SIGMETs. *See* Storm detection; Thunderstorm; Tornado.

National Hurricane Center. The NHC, located in Miami, Florida, prepares hurricane and tropical storm watches and warnings through bulletins known as advisories for most of the tropical Atlantic Ocean, the Caribbean, the Gulf of Mexico, and the Eastern Pacific. The NHC has been designated by the WMO as the Regional Tropical Cyclone Warning Center for other countries in these areas. Tropical cyclone forecasting services for the Central Pacific are provided by the Central Pacific Hurricane Center located in Honolulu. *See* Hurricane.

River Forecast Centers. There are 13 RFCs, which prepare river, flood, and water-resource forecasts for a total of 3500 locations. Flood forecasts include forecasts for height of the flood crest as well as times when the river is expected to overflow its banks and when it will recede into its banks. At many points along larger streams or rivers, such as the Columbia, Missouri, and Mississippi, daily forecasts of river stage or discharge are routinely prepared for activities such as navigation and water management. Forecasts of seasonal or water-year flow prepared for these river systems and many others are critical elements in operations of dams, navigation systems, and irrigation systems.

Weather Service Forecast Offices. There are 52 WSFOs within the NWS; there are none in Rhode Island, Connecticut, Vermont, and New Hampshire,

Fig. 3. Meteorological technician monitoring weather on National Weather Service long-range radar. (*NOAA*)

while California and Pennsylvania have two and Alaska, Texas, and New York three. Each of these offices provides whatever weather service is required for the geographical areas it serves, utilizing output from the NMC, NSSFC, NHC, and a RFC where appropriate.

Each WSFO provides routine issuances of state and zone forecasts for the public plus terminal and route forecasts for aviation. Other specialized services are handled where there is a need and where resources and workload permit. These include a Warning Coordination and Hazard Awareness Program designed to save lives and mitigate the social and economic impacts of natural disasters; Severe Local Storm Warning Program, where the weather radar is the principal method for monitoring the storms (**Fig. 3**); Winter Weather Warning Service; Coastal Flood Warning Program; Agricultural Weather Service; warnings of low temperatures for winter and spring crops; forecasts for flights from the United States and its possessions to other countries; meteorological support to control and combat air pollution; specialized forecasts and warnings to fire-control agencies; flash flood watches and warnings; tsunami watches and warnings; warnings for high seas, coastal waters, and inland waterways; and offshore marine forecasts for recreational boating and fishing. Forecasts and warnings are transmitted via the NOAA Weather Wire, a dedicated communications satellite broadcast service, and over the NOAA Weather Radio, a continuous weather and river information broadcast on one of three high-band frequencies—162.40, 162.475, or 162.55 MHz.

Weather Service Offices. There are an additional 206 Weather Service Offices (WSO), which represent the third echelon of the system. They issue local forecasts that are adaptations of the zone forecasts. They are important in the warning and observation programs and are generally located in smaller cities.

Frederick Zbar

Bibliography. J. R. Anderson and J. R. Gyakum, A diagnostic study of Pacific Basin Circulation Regimes, *Mon. Weath. Rev.*, 117:2672–2686, 1989; R. Benzi, B. Saltzman, and A. C. Wiin-Nielsen (eds.), *Anomalous Atmospheric Flows and Blocking*, 1986; W. Bonner et al., NMC overviews: Recent progress and future plans, *Weath. Forecast.*, 4:275–443, September 1989; E. S. Epstein, Long-range weather prediction: Limits of predictability and beyond, *Weath. Forecast.*, 3:69–75, 1988; A. Gilchrist, Long-range forecasting, *Quart. J. Roy. Meteorol. Soc.*, 122:567–592, 1986; G. J. Haltiner and R. T. Williams, *Numerical Prediction and Dynamic Meteorology*, 2d ed., 1980; S. Hastenrath, Prediction of Indian monsoon rainfall: Further exploration, *J. Clim.*, 1:298–304, 1988; D. D. Houghton (ed.), *Handbook of Applied Meteorology*, 1985; R. E. Livezey and A. G. Barnston, An operational multifield analog/antianalog prediction system for United States seasonal temperatures, *J. Geophys. Res.*, 93:10,953–10,974, 1988; T. F. Malone, *Compendium of Meteorology*, 1951; G. I. Marchuk, *Numerical Methods in Weather Prediction*, 1973; A. H. Murphy and R. W. Katz, *Probability, Statistics, and Decision Making in the Atmospheric Sciences*, 1985; S. Petterssen, *Introduction to Meteorology*, 3d ed., 1969; S. Petterssen, *Weather Analysis and Forecasting*, 2 vols., 2d ed., 1956; P. Ray (ed.), *Mesoscale Meteorology and Forecasting*, 1986; C. Singer, *A Short History of Scientific Ideas to 1900*, 1959; M. S. Tracton et al., Dynamical extended range forecasting (DERF) at the National Meteorological Center, *Mon. Weath. Rev.*, 117:1605–1635, 1989.

Weather map

A chart that portrays the state of the atmosphere at one or more levels over a wide area. Surface and upper-atmospheric conditions are based on observations at many locations at the same universal time, and the portrayals are therefore known as synoptic maps or charts. Several such maps are used by meteorologists to define a three-dimensional picture of the atmosphere. Successive surface and upper-air maps along with computer-generated forecast maps depict the motion of weather systems and their changes in intensity. SEE ATMOSPHERE.

Maps of the state of the atmosphere along the Earth's surface typically show temperature, dew-point temperature, air pressure, wind direction and speed, amount of cloud cover, visibility, and any significant weather at hundreds of reporting stations. Over land, observations are made at ground level, but pressure is extrapolated to sea level. If this extrapolation were not done, then a pressure analysis would show lower pressure over higher terrain. Surface observations are recorded at hundreds of locations each hour across the United States and are transmitted to the National Meteorological Center (NMC) in Washington, D.C. SEE AIR PRESSURE; DEW POINT.

Surface maps. Surface observations are plotted on a weather map by a computer (**Fig. 1**). Lines of equal sea-level pressure (isobars) are drawn to aid in the positioning of fronts, troughs, and areas of high and low pressure. Fronts represent narrow transition zones in the atmosphere that separate warm and cold air masses, while troughs depict elongated areas of low pressure that may have no significant change in air mass from one side to the other. Often, extratropical cyclones (low-pressure systems) form along frontal boundaries. The map in Fig. 1 shows a surface trough

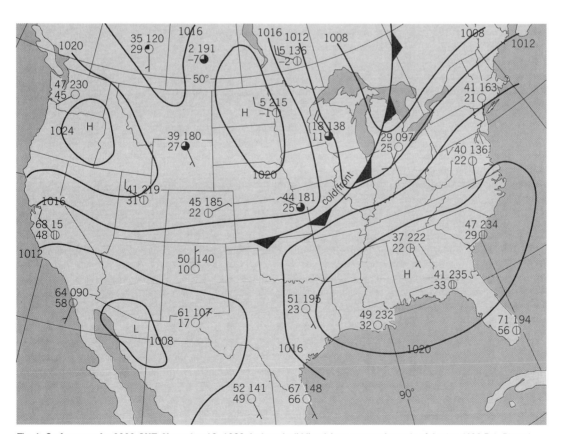

Fig. 1. Surface map for 0000 GMT, November 18, 1989; isobars (solid lines) have contour intervals of 4 mbar (400 Pa). Plotted observations from selected sites record air temperature in °F (upper left), dew-point temperature in °F (lower left), and atmospheric pressure in tenths of millibars (upper right). Circle at the center of each information group represents cloud cover, ranging from completely clear (open cirlce) to completely overcast (solid circle). The flag attached to the center circle indicates the direction from which the wind is blowing. Wind speed (in knots) is represented by the number of barbs attached to the flag: full barb = 10 knots. half barb = 5 knots. 1 knot = 0.5 m/s. °C = (°F − 32)/1.8. H = high-pressure center. L = low-pressure center.

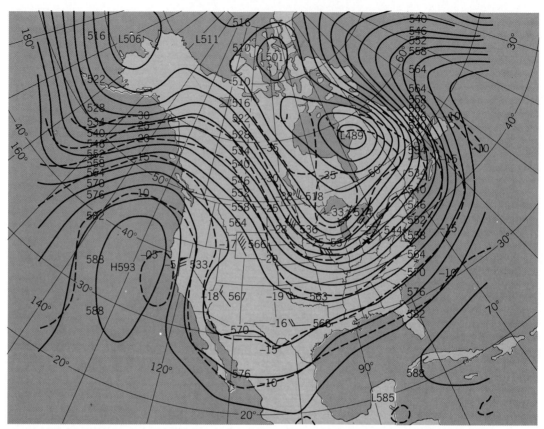

Fig. 2. A 500-mbar (50-kPa) map for 0000 GMT, November 18, 1989; isohypses (solid lines) have contour intervals of 60 m (197 ft), and isotherms (broken lines) have contour intervals of 5°C (9°F). Plotted observations from selected sites record air temperature in °C (west of the wind flag), altitude above sea level for the 500-mbar (50-kPa) surface, along with wind direction (flag) and wind speed (barbs on flag: solid triangle = 50 knots, full barb = 10 knots, and half barb = 5 knots). 1 knot = 0.5 m/s. °F = (°C × 1.8) + 32. H = center of high elevation. L = center of low elevation.

and cold front that extends from the eastern Great Lakes southwest into southern Kansas and is positioned between high-pressure centers located across the northern plains states and in the southeastern United States. Lines of equal temperature (isotherms) and dew-point temperature (isodrosotherms) may also be drawn. *See Air mass; Front*.

Without friction between the Earth's surface and moving air currents just above, surface winds would blow along isobars with low pressure to the left and high pressure to the right when one is facing downstream (geostrophic wind). In response to surface friction, true winds at the surface blow across the isobars from high to low pressure at an angle usually between 20 and 40°. The crossing angle is influenced greatly by the terrain and the speeds of the winds. Wind speed is inversely proportional to the distance between isobars (that is, tightly packed isobars produce stronger winds than widely spaced isobars). *See Wind*.

Upper-atmosphere maps. For the upper atmosphere, weather maps are usually constructed at constant pressure levels of 850, 700, 500, and 200 millibars (85, 70, 50, and 20 kilopascals; **Fig. 2**). Essential data are obtained from radiosondes that are released daily at 0000 and 1200 GMT (Greenwich Mean Time) at nearly 100 locations throughout the United States and Canada. Lines of equal height above sea level (isohypses) and isotherms are usually drawn on the maps. Above the Earth's surface, true wind is approximated by the geostrophic wind. Simi-

lar to conditions at the surface, the wind speed above the surface is inversely proportional to the distance between height contours drawn at fixed intervals. Figure 2 shows the plotted observations at selected locations, detailing strong northwest and west winds across the upper midwest (80 knots or 41 m/s) with temperatures below −25°C (−13°F).

Other maps. Other tools used by meteorologists include vertical cross sections through the atmosphere and thermodynamic diagrams similar to those used in studies of heat engines. Newspapers and television often display animated surface weather maps, radar maps showing the local or national precipitation field, and maps of cloud images over large areas from weather satellites.

Forecast weather maps are based on computer forecasts of the atmosphere into the near future. Numerical weather prediction models start from an initial state of the atmosphere at 0000 or 1200 GMT. By using surface and upper-air observations along with other methods of measurement, the initial state of the atmosphere is inserted into the numerical weather prediction models. The three-dimensional state of the atmosphere is then integrated forward through a series of very small time steps (usually 1–3 min). This process continues until the end of the forecast period is reached. Depending on the needs of the forecaster or researcher and the characteristics of the numerical weather prediction model, forecast periods may range from a few hours up to 10 days. Numerical weather prediction models make millions of calculations at each time step; therefore they require powerful computers to arrive at the end of the forecast period within a reasonable amount of time (usually under 1 h). Operational numerical weather prediction models, used by forecasters across the United States, will be run on class 7 supercomputers at the National Meteorological Center during the 1990s.

The National Meterological Center along with similar centers from key nations in the World Meteorological Organization (WMO) work together to prepare accurate weather maps that cover the entire Earth. This step is essential for improving long-range weather prediction by using numerical weather prediction models and for studying the worldwide transfer and production of kinetic and potential energy in the atmosphere. *See* CLIMATOLOGY; METEOROLOGY; WEATHER FORECASTING AND PREDICTION.

Kenneth C. Crawford; Michael Emlaw

Bibliography. C. Donald Ahrens, *Meteorology Today, An Introduction to Weather, Climate and the Environment*, 1988; G. J. Haltiner, *Numerical Weather Prediction*, 2d ed., 1980; National Weather Service, *NMC Models and Automated Operations*, NWS Tech. Proced. Bull. 355, NOAA, 1985; W. J. Saucier, *Principles of Meteorological Analysis*, 1955.

Weather modification

Human influence on the weather and, ultimately, climate. This can be either intentional, as with cloud seeding to increase precipitation, or unintentional, as with air pollution, which increases aerosol concentrations and reduces sunlight. Weather is considered to be the day-to-day variations of the environment—temperature, cloudiness, relative humidity, windspeed, visibility, and precipitation. Climate, on the other hand, reflects the average and extremes of these variables, changing on a seasonal basis. Weather change may lead to climate change, which is assessed over a period of years. *See* CLIMATIC CHANGE.

Specific processes of weather modification are as follows: (1) Change of precipitation intensity and distribution result from changes in the colloidal stability of clouds. For example, seeding of supercooled water clouds with dry ice (solid carbon dioxide, CO_2) or silver iodide (AgI) leads to ice crystal growth and fallout; layer clouds may dissipate, convective clouds may grow. (2) Radiation change results from changes of aerosol or clouds (deliberately with a smoke screen, or unintentionally with air pollution from combustion), from changes in the gaseous constituents of the atmosphere (as with carbon dioxide from fossil fuel combustion), and from changes in the ability of surfaces to reflect or scatter back sunlight (as replacing farmland by houses.) (3) Change of wind regime results from change in surface roughness and heat input, for example, replacing forests with farmland.

Ice phase and cloud seeding. Water, when present in clouds in the atmosphere as droplets about 10 micrometers in diameter, often supercools—that is, exists as a metastable liquid—to temperatures as low as $-40°F$ ($-40°C$). Random motion of water molecules in the liquid leads to the formation of clusters with an ice configuration; below $-40°F$ ($-40°C$) a cluster can quickly grow to freeze the whole droplet (homogeneous nucleation). The vapor pressure over supercooled water is greater than over ice at the same tem-

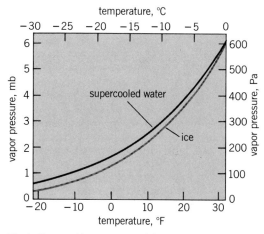

Fig. 1. Change with temperature of the vapor pressure of water vapor in equilibrium with supercooled water and ice.

perature (**Fig. 1**), leading to preferential growth of ice crystals. A small ice crystal introduced into such a supercooled cloud grows to become a visible snow crystal about 1 mm in diameter in a few minutes, and is sufficiently large to fall out as precipitation (**Fig. 2**). Under natural conditions, ice crystals are only rarely found in growing clouds with temperature entirely above 14°F ($-10°C$). Below this temperature, ice crystals are found with increasing frequency as the temperature lowers. Here insoluble impurities (minerals, silver iodide, bacteria) nucleate ice at temperatures as high as -10 to $-5°C$ (14 to 23°F) and with increasing frequency as the temperature lowers to $-40°C$. This is known as homogeneous nucleation.

Aircraft measurements show a wide variation of ice crystal concentrations at a given temperature in different cloud types. Lenticular wave clouds formed near mountains sometimes are ice-free at $-31°F$ ($-35°C$); convective clouds over the ocean sometimes contain more than one crystal per liter of cloudy air just below 14°F ($-10°C$). Within this temperature range, ice crystals are nucleated on solid impurities of about 0.1 μm, having an atomic structure resembling ice (heterogeneous nucleation) carried upward from the Earth's surface—usually minerals such as kaolin-

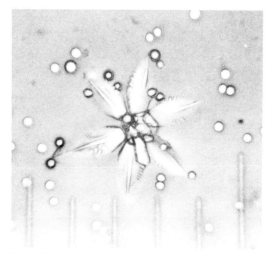

Fig. 2. Replica of cloud droplets and an ice crystal made during an aircraft penetration of a convective cloud in Montana. Each scale division represents 100 micrometers.

ite (clay) or organic materials such as bacteria resulting from leaf decay.

Supercooled clouds may be induced to snow artificially by introduction of ice crystals in sufficient concentrations. This can be achieved in two ways. In the first method cloudy air is cooled locally by dry-ice pellets at $-108°F$ ($-78°C$) dropped from an aircraft. As they fall, they cool air in their wake below $-40°F$ ($-40°C$), where droplets form and freeze. One kilogram of carbon dioxide produces 10^{14} crystals. A similar effect may be achieved by evaporation of liquid propane. The second method involves generating an impurity aerosol (diameter of about 0.05 μm) whose crystallographic structure is similar to ice, such as silver iodide or metaldehyde and dispersing it into the cloud to form ice crystals [1 g AgI gives about 10^{15} ($23°F$ or $-5°C$) to 10^{17} ($5°F$ or $-15°C$) ice crystals].

Such an aerosol may be made by combustion of AgI–acetone solutions with a complexing additive. The aerosol generated at the ground is carried aloft under convective or turbulent conditions. Otherwise, aircraft may carry continuous burners into the cloud, or drop flares containing silver iodate ($AgIO_3$) from above cloud top, to burn as they fall through the cloud. Rockets have also been used to inject an explosive charge containing silver iodide into the cloud.

Historically, several projects employing these techniques have claimed an enhancement of precipitation by 10–15%. Assessment has been based on statistical evaluation of snowfall or rainfall at the ground. Since rainfall (along with most other meteorological quantities) is a highly variable quantity, and the effects produced are usually not large, such statistical tests need to be carried out over many seasons. It is necessary to evaluate whether any apparent rainfall enhancement as a departure from a mean is to be attributed to such variability or to the seeding process itself. Two techniques have been applied: use of an unseeded control area and cross-correlation of measured rainfall, and randomized seeding of one area and correlation of rainfall on seeded and nonseeded days. Each technique has problems of interpretation, since weather patterns producing precipitation change dramatically from day to day. It might seem desirable to acquire for seeding trials as long a data record as practicable; however, too long a data record may lead to complications because of the possibility of changes on a climatic time scale unrelated to the changes being sought.

Physical evaluation of the seeding effectiveness is vital in removing uncertainties of an inadequate statistical base and the wide variability of a small number of precipitation situations. Aircraft penetration of seeded clouds reveals the presence of regions of supercooled water, a prerequisite, and whether or not the seeding aerosol has reached these regions to produce ice crystals in sufficient numbers (about one crystal per liter of air) to give measurable precipitation. Under ideal conditions, rainfall from the melting of snow has been measured by radar techniques and supplemented by rain gage measurements at the ground.

The most striking effects from seeding are observed in a stratiform cloud layer, or a layer of fog at the ground; dry-ice seeding from an aircraft typically produces an ice crystal track some 0.3 mi (0.5 km) wide (**Fig. 3**). This procedure is used for clearing airports of overnight fog; it works well with cloud tempera-

Fig. 3. Cloud dissipation. (a) Three lines in stratocumulus cloud layer 15 min after seeding. (b) Opening in stratocumulus layer 70 min after seeding. (*U.S. Army ECOM, Fort Monmouth, New Jersey*)

tures below about $25°F$ ($-4°C$). It has been suggested that this technique be used for clearing clouds over an urban area to allow sunlight to melt snow on the streets. By contrast, seeding cumulus clouds produces a visible result only rarely. In 1947, workers in Australia succeeded in causing a single cumulus cloud in a large number of such clouds to grow by dry-ice seeding. This was an example of dynamical seeding, resulting when release of latent heat by growth of crystals and freezing of droplets is sufficient to cause additional cloud convection. This is more likely when the cloud contains large quantities of supercooled water ($2–4$ g · m^{-3}), particularly in the form of supercooled raindrops. An effect is more likely when such seeding is timed to enhance the maximum natural updraft. It has been suggested that seeding clusters of clouds leads to an overall increase in rainfall, since more moist air is incorporated into the more vigorously growing region than would occur naturally.

It is evident that ice phase modification is possible only when ice crystals are not provided by natural processes—either by direct nucleation or by fallout or downward mixing of ice crystals from colder regions aloft into supercooled clouds below. A lack of crystals is often the case for ground fog or stratus cloud below a clear sky; also, for a field of developing cumuli. Developing clouds resulting from orographic lift over a mountain range offer similar opportunities implemented in many cloud seeding projects undertaken in the Sierra Nevada (California) and the Rocky Mountains. Statistical evaluation of several studies of convective cloud modification has found inconclusive results (Colorado, Florida, Switzerland), and it is evident that the possibilities of seeding for enhanced rainfall are less obvious than had first been thought. The pattern of subsequent weather modification attempts has involved searching for situations with regions having large amounts of supercooled water which persist for several hours, seeding in a controlled way, and evaluating the effect produced both by aircraft and by radar. *See Cloud physics.*

Hail modification. Efforts have also been made to reduce hail by similar seeding techniques. This could be accomplished by freezing every droplet in a cloud so that hailstones no longer grow, a technique that would require an unrealistic amount of seeding aerosol and would present serious distribution problems. An alternative and more realistic approach would reduce the sizes of all hailstones so that they are less than a few millimeters in diameter on falling to the ground. This would minimize crop damage. It has been suggested that hail modification can be achieved by seeding the hail-forming part of the cloud so that a given amount of cloud water is distributed over a larger number of smaller stones. Careful control of induced ice concentrations in different parts of the supercooled liquid water cloud would be required, depending on the natural hailstone concentration. This is well beyond available technology.

Hurricane modification. It has been suggested that hurricanes might be seeded, either to reduce their maximum wind strength or to change their direction of motion. However, research has revealed that large quantities of ice are often present naturally. Thus systematic large-scale seeding would not be effective. Regions of supercooled water do exist asymmetrically around the eye, offering the possibility of "leading" the hurricane in a different direction by selective seeding in one quadrant. *See Hurricane.*

Warm cloud modification. Coalescence precipitation occurs by the collision and coalescence of droplets of diameter greater than 30 μm formed by con-

Fig. 4. Convective cloud forming over a forest fire.

densation with slower-moving, smaller droplets. Continuing coalescence eventually results in raindrops several millimeters in diameter. Such larger drops form on occasional large hygroscopic nuclei of NaCl or $(NH_4)_2SO_4$ or by special mixing and evaporation mechanisms. This process produces rain not only in clouds whose temperature lies entirely above the freezing point ("warm" clouds) but sometimes also occurs in supercooled clouds. It is evident that many clouds fail to rain at all, and it has been suggested that the larger cloud droplets are not present in sufficient numbers and that seeding with larger droplets might initiate precipitation. Hygroscopic materials—such as sodium chloride (NaCl)—have been dispersed in airborne trails to test such hypotheses, without obvious succes. The inverse process—of producing many small droplets by additional nuclei from com-

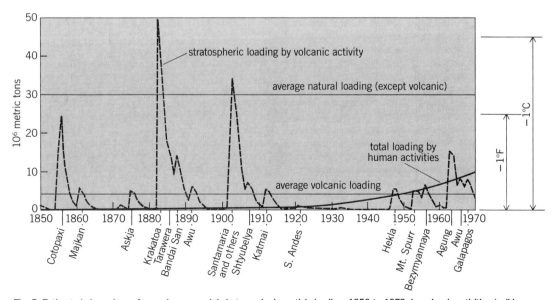

Fig. 5. Estimated chronology of annual average global atmospheric particle loading, 1850 to 1972, by volcanic activities (solid curve), and by all natural sources other than volcanic (assumed constant at 3×10^7 metric tons, broken curve). Estimated calibration of volcanic loading curve in terms of planetary temperature influence is shown at right. 1 metric ton = 1.1 ton. (*After S. F. Singer, ed., The Changing Global Environment, Ridel, 1975*)

bustion such as agricultural burning—has also been suggested as leading to a rainfall decrease; this hypothesis is also unproven. Attempts to clear warm fog by high-pressure, high-volume fire-fighting sprays similar in size to 0.08-in. (2-mm) raindrops have shown some measure of success, doubling the visibility over a region of a few hundred yards.

The use of sound—as shock waves from explosives carried aloft on balloons or by ringing church bells—characterized nineteenth-century efforts in rainmaking and hail dissipation. It appears to have had only psychological value, and has been shown to be quite ineffective in causing significant changes in the cloud, either by nucleating ice crystals or by causing droplet coalescence.

Heating effects. Somewhat greater cloudiness and precipitation exists near cities, which act as "heat islands" and give enhanced convective activity and deeper clouds later in the afternoon. The effect has been found both in Chicago and St. Louis; it results from an increase in the amount of sunlight absorbed by roads and buildings and changes of surface wind flow. More dramatic effects occur over natural extended heat sources such as forest fires and also volcanoes (**Fig. 4**). Under certain conditions, setting a prairie fire will produce a thunderstorm which will extinguish the fire; this skill was practiced only in past times.

Radiation modification. Particulates produced by forest fires and by fossil fuel combustion in industrial society pass into the air and are efficiently removed during natural precipitation processes. These particles influence the radiation balance and may be responsible for reducing sunlight and local visibility. The effect may be present on a worldwide basis; particulates have a half-life before removal of about 1 week, and can be carried considerable distances during this time. The overall result is a decrease in direct sunlight, which is somewhat compensated for by an increase in diffuse radiation scattered from other directions. The net result is a decrease in surface radiation available for photosynthesis by about 5%. The atmosphere above is heated by comparable amounts, and calculations show that this heat is lost to space more rapidly than if it were absorbed at the surface; the net result is a slight atmospheric cooling. Average anthropogenic particle loading is around 20% of natural loading, and each is substantially less than peaks resulting from major volcanic eruptions (**Fig. 5**). It has been suggested that a large effect could result from smoke produced by widespread nuclear war—the nuclear winter. This would lead to cooling the Earth's surface and heating aloft. Contrails from high-level aircraft give a similar effect, increasing high-level cloudiness in well-traveled parts of the globe. The worldwide effect does not appear to be important.

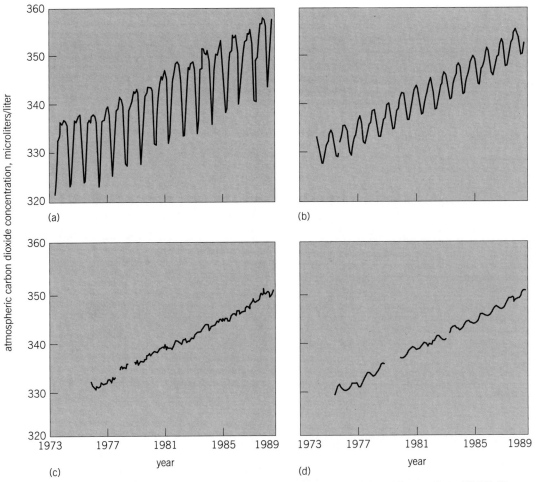

Fig. 6. Seasonal cycles of atmospheric concentrations at various locations during 1973–1989. (a) Barrow, Alaska; 71.3°N. (b) Mauna Loa, Hawaii; 19.5°N. (c) American Samoa; 14.3°N. (d) South Pole; 90°S. (*After W. M. Post et al., The global carbon cycle, Amer. Sci., 78:310–326, 1990*)

Greenhouse effect. In addition to particulate emissions, fossil fuel combustion increases atmospheric content of carbon dioxide, about 50–75% of the emissions remaining in the atmosphere, the remainder being absorbed by the oceans and contributing to enhanced photosynthesis. Carbon dioxide has increased by 15% since 1850, with further increases projected until fossil fuel becomes exhausted in the twenty-first century (**Fig. 6**). Other gases (for example, methane produced by rice paddies) may have a smaller but similar effect. There is a suggestion that the recent upward tendency in the Earth's temperature may be an indication of this effect (**Fig. 7**). Calculations confirm that increased carbon dioxide would lead to an atmospheric warming, but this would be at least in part offset by the radiational cooling from particles and additional cloud formation. Such calculations are not sufficiently precise to predict the overall effect with confidence. SEE GREENHOUSE EFFECT.

Ozone hole. Ozone (O_3) is normally produced at altitudes between 12 and 30 mi (20 and 50 km) in the atmosphere by ultraviolet light absorption by ordinary atmospheric oxygen. The ozone absorbs further ultraviolet radiation at these levels, providing a shield to such radiation, which has harmful biological effects at the Earth's surface.

Measurements of ozone over Antarctica in the late 1980s showed systematic wintertime decreases at 6–12 mi (10–20 km). This has been attributed to the use of manufactured fluorocarbon compounds, which are used in refrigerators, in aerosol sprays, and in the manufacture of foamed insulation. These gases are unreactive in the lower atmosphere; however, at high altitudes they become dissociated and react with ozone, particularly in the presence of ice and nitrogen oxides from combustion processes, leading to a reduction in ozone concentration. If ozone depletion extends to the sunlit regions of the globe, there will be an enhanced risk of skin cancer in humans. An extensive fleet of supersonic transport aircraft in midstratosphere could lead to enhanced ozone loss in these regions. SEE ATMOSPHERIC OZONE.

Acid rain. Sulfur is a trace component of the atmosphere, being part of the biological cycle of plants and animals. Emissions of sulfur dioxide (SO_2), particularly from fossil fuel combustion and ore refining and reduction processes, add about half as much again on a worldwide basis. Problems arise from very high concentrations of sulfur dioxide produced in industrial areas such as the northeast United States and the Ruhr Valley in Europe. These gases eventually react to form sulfate ions (SO_4^{2-}), a process enhanced by the presence of nitrogen oxides from automobile exhausts. The reactions take place in cloud droplets, which are removed during winter frontal precipitation and summer convective showers, to be deposited as acid precipitation often hundreds of miles downwind of the source. Rain is always slightly acidic (pH 5.7) because of the absorption of atmospheric carbon dioxide. The effect of pollution is to increase this acidity; values in the range pH 2–3 have been measured. It has been suggested that this leads to damage in specific types of vegetation (some pines and conifers) growing in soils which lack buffering capacity, and to kills of fish in acidic spring runoff. Low-pH fogs have occasionally been observed in the Los Angeles Basin. Freezing on trees of acid fog containing nitrate (NO_3) and sulfate (SO_4) ions may lead to enhanced acidity and damage at temperatures a few degrees below freezing. The actual extent of the effects is subject to disagreement because of uncertain measurement techniques of earlier years and lack of systematic observations of tree damage from natural causes over a long time period. SEE ACID RAIN.

John Hallett

Bibliography. B. Bolin et al., *The Greenhouse Effect, Climatic Change, and Ecosystems,* 1986; A. S. Dennis, *Weather Modification by Cloud Seeding,* International Geophysics Series, vol. 24, 1980; R. A. Dirks, Progress in weather modification research 1979–1982, *Rev. Geophys. Space Phys.,* 21:1065–1076; D. H. Miller, *Energy at the Surface of the Earth,* International Geophysics Series, vol. 27, 1981; S. F. Singer, *The Changing Global Environment,* 1975; C. Spence, *The Rainmakers: American Pluviculture to World War II,* 1980; World Meteorological Organization and United Nations Environmental Program, *Developing Policies for Responding to Climatic Change,* April 1988.

Wetlands

Wet flatlands, where mesophytic vegetation is areally more important than open water, and which are commonly developed in filled lakes, glacial pits, and potholes (**Fig. 1**), or in poorly drained coastal plains or floodplains. The term swamp is usually applied to a wetland where trees and shrubs are an important part of the vegetative association, and the term bog implies lack of solid foundation. Some bogs consist of a thick zone of vegetation floating on water.

Unique plant associations characterize wetlands in various climates and exhibit marked zonation characteristics around the edge in response to different thicknesses of the saturated zone above the firm base of soil material. Coastal marshes covered with vegetation adapted to saline water are common on all continents. Presumably many of these had their origin in recent inundation due to post-Pleistocene rise in sea level.

The total area covered by these physiographic features is not accurately known, but particularly in glaciated regions many hundreds of square miles are covered by marsh. SEE MANGROVE.

Luna B. Leopold

In the United States, wetlands are defined by legislation. Section 404 of the Clean Water Act (1977) defines wetlands as areas that are inundated or saturated by surface water or groundwater at a frequency

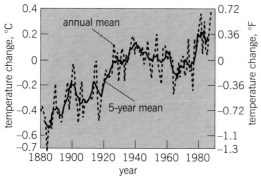

Fig. 7. Global temperature changes, 1880–1987. (*After R. A. Kerr, The Weather in the Wake of El Niño, Science, 242:883, 1988*)

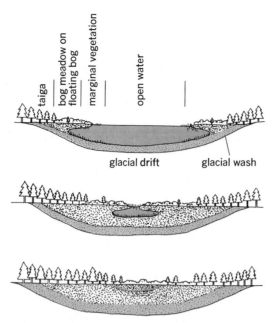

Fig. 1. Cross-sectional diagram representing the progressive filling by vegetation of a pit lake in recently glaciated terrain.

and duration sufficient to support, and under normal circumstances do support, a prevalence of vegetation typically adapted for life in saturated soil conditions. This legislation also states that wetlands generally include swamps, marshes, bogs, and similar areas.

Delineation of wetlands. The surface soils of all wetlands are saturated with water for periods that are long enough for the soil oxygen to be depleted for a part of the growing season. Hence, wetlands occur only where geological formations or variations in topography impede drainage or permit surface flooding for extended periods. Saturation with water usually gives the soils chemical and visual characteristics that are indicative of wetland conditions. The presence of wetlands soils is also indicated by the occurrence of plants that can live in anaerobic soil by transporting oxygen to their roots internally, by respiring anaerobically, or by adapting to seasonal soil saturation.

Generalizing about wetlands hydrology is difficult, because the hydrology of each wetland is unique. Hydrology is especially complex where soil saturation is maintained by subterranean flow of water. This condition is common in lakes in the northern Midwest and in the sandy flatwoods of Florida. A flatwood is

Fig. 2. Swamp forest with cypress and swamp tupelo that is flooded much of the year.

a nearly level zone in a forest, not clearly defined, that contains imperfectly drained acid soils.

Wetland types. These types include swamps, riverbottom terraces, coastal plain wetlands, and constructed wetlands.

Swamps. These are flooded for long periods and frequently support stands of cypress and water tupelo. This type of swamp forest is shown in **Fig. 2**; it has been logged repeatedly and regenerates naturally from the residual stand of trees. Black willow and certain other species can reproduce vegetatively in standing water under some conditions, but not even the most hydric forest species can regenerate from seed in standing water. The characteristic vegetation of deep swamps arises by regeneration from seed, which can occur only when mineral soil is exposed for a 2–3-month period during the growing season. Thus, natural regeneration in swamps depends on the occurence of periodic droughts. SEE DROUGHT.

As sediment gradually fills swamps, they are invaded by mesic species, with hydric species being replaced. Filling and replacement of species can take from less than 10 years to several hundred years and is a normal geologic succession. Artificial alteration of hydrology can accelerate or retard the filling of swamps with sediment. Road construction and water control projects often alter the hydrology of swamps. When such projects result in deeper flooding, tree stands are harmed and natural regeneration does not occur. Improved drainage promotes invasion by species less tolerant to flooding. Forestry activities that do not alter hydrology have no adverse effect on the function of swamps. It is not feasible to convert deep swamps to agriculture. SEE ECOLOGICAL SUCCESSION; HYDROLOGY.

Riverbottom terraces. These are better drained than cypress-tupelo swamps; they support ashes, oaks, hickories, maples, sweetgum, persimmon, and other mesic species. Generally, ecological succession is slower on riverbottom terraces than in swamps, and is not substantially impacted by sedimentation. Fire has little impact on terrace vegetation because the terraces are moist and terrace forest communities do not carry fire well. Riverbottom terraces have enormous value for wildlife and species diversity as well as for productive agriculture and forestry.

Coastal plain wetlands. These wetlands occupy large areas in the South and Southeast. They vary in function and vegetation according to hydrology and nutrient supply. In pre-Columbian times, much of the flatwoods portion of this area was in loblolly, slash, and longleaf pine forests that were maintained in a subclimax state by periodic fire. Sites that did not burn supported swamp tupelo, cypress, and many of the broadleafed hardwood species common on moist river bottoms.

Constructed wetlands. These are created by intentionally restricting drainage to develop hydric or partially hydric environments. Constructed wetlands include greentree reservoirs (mesic woodland in which normal drainage is blocked during the dormant season) and wetlands that function as water purification systems.

Greentree reservoirs attract waterfowl and are used as a substitute for altered waterfowl habitat. Unless the hydrology of greentree reservoirs is managed carefully, however, tree productivity declines and other functions of the wetland are lost.

The use of constructed wetlands to remove contaminants from wastewater is relatively new. The hydrology of a constructed wetland that removes nitrates from sewage-treatment-plant effluents or heavy metals from mining wastewater must prevent both escape of contaminants from the wetland and accumulation of excessive levels of toxic materials. Constructed wetlands may be stocked with plants that will absorb toxic materials, combine them with organic matter, and render the chemicals inert, or may be created on soils that will hold the pollutants. SEE LAND RECLAMATION.

Introduction of nutrient-rich effluents into wetlands systems can result in the rapid breakdown of peat under extreme reducing conditions and in the production of large quantities of methane, a greenhouse gas. Technology for dealing with this problem is not yet available.

Loss of wetlands. Many fresh-water wetlands are transitory. Sedimentation tends to raise the level of the soil surface and to drain wetlands, especially in river floodplains. The accumulation of organic matter can alter the hydrology of wetlands; this process is common in peat bogs in the north-central states. Ground fire can reverse the accumulation of organic matter; this process occurs often in swamps and on cypress domes on the Atlantic Coastal Plain. Hence, the ecological functions and value of wetland areas can change over time.

Fresh-water wetlands are also lost as a result of subsidence of the land elevation of sea level. Subsidence and salt-water intrusion has caused significant losses of wetlands near the Mississippi River delta in recent years.

About 55–60% of the pre-Columbian wetlands in the United States have been altered by agriculture or destroyed by development. This loss has had a severely adverse impact on migratory waterfowl and other wildlife. Most prairie wetlands of the Midwest and northern Midwest have been converted to agriculture. Previously, these sites consisted of glacial till covered with tall-grass prairie that was maintained by fire. Except in the northern plains states, almost all of this wetland type has been converted to extremely productive agricultural land. The surviving prairie wetland sites are important to migratory waterfowl and for groundwater recharge.

The construction of dams, levees, and other water-control structures has had a profound impact on wetlands, particularly in river bottoms. The impact of public-works projects on wetlands has come under increased scrutiny in recent years. Agriculture and the development of tillable land have affected very large areas of wetlands. Most convertible wetland areas have already been brought under the plow, however, and conversion to agriculture has almost ceased. In some instances, agricultural land has reverted to forested wetlands or has been replanted to forests.

Many riverbottom wetland areas have been converted to agriculture during the last 75–100 years. This process has affected very large acreages in the Mississippi, Ohio, and Missouri river valleys.

Coastal plain wetlands have been less affected by conversion to agriculture. They are small, scattered, and hard to drain, and their soils are infertile. Many of these areas have been altered, however, by the construction of roads, water-control structures, and utility corridors and, to a lesser extent, by intensive forestry practices. In pre-Columbian times, much of the coastal plain flatwoods was in southern pine for-

Fig. 3 Managed forest wetland with planted pine trees on a southeastern flatwoods site. Note the minor drainage in the foreground.

ests that were maintained by periodic fire. Development of the coastal plain has led to the control of fire, and hardwoods have invaded much of the original pine-grass savanna. Many of the remaining wetlands are privately owned and are managed primarily for timber production (**Fig. 3**). Some of the silvicultural practices employed in flatwoods areas are controversial. However, these practices are normally exempt from regulation under the Clean Water Act. Urban encroachment, which is quickly replacing agriculture as a threat to wetlands, is regulated by this act.

Legislation in the United States. Concern over loss of fresh-water wetlands has prompted states and the federal government to pass legislation to protect and manage these areas for the benefit of society. The most significant federal laws are the Clean Water Act of 1977 and the Food Security Act of 1985. States have passed or are in the process of adopting legislation to address wetlands protection issues of local concern.

William H. McKee, Jr.

Bibliography. Federal Interagency Committee for Wetland Delineation, *Federal Manual for Identifying and Delineating Jurisdictional Wetlands*, 1989; D. D. Hook et al. (eds.), *The Ecology and Management of Wetlands*, vols. 1 and 2, 1988; D. D. Hook and R. Lee, *Proceedings: Symposium on the Forested Wetlands of the Southern United States*, U.S. Department of Agriculture, Forest Service, Gen. Tech. Rep. SE-50, 1988; W. J. Mitsch and J. G. Gosselink, *Wetlands*, 1986.

Wind

The motion of air relative to the Earth's surface. The term usually refers to horizontal air motion, as distinguished from vertical motion, and to air motion averaged over a chosen period of 1–3 min. Micrometeorological circulations (air motion over periods of the order of a few seconds) and others small enough in extent to be obscured by this averaging are thereby eliminated. The choice of the 1- to 3-min interval has proven suitable for the study of the hour-to-hour and day-to-day changes in the atmospheric circulation pattern, and the larger-scale aspects of the atmospheric general circulation.

The direct effects of wind near the surface of the Earth are manifested by soil erosion, the character of vegetation, damage to structures, and the production of waves on water surfaces. At higher levels wind directly affects aircraft, missile and rocket operations, and dispersion of industrial pollutants, radioactive products of nuclear explosions, dust, volcanic debris, and other material. Directly or indirectly, wind is responsible for the production and transport of clouds and precipitation and for the transport of cold and warm air masses from one region to another. *SEE AT-MOSPHERIC GENERAL CIRCULATION*.

Cyclonic and anticyclonic circulation. Each is a portion of the pattern of airflow within which the streamlines (which indicate the pattern of wind direction at any instant) are curved so as to indicate rotation of air about some central point of the cyclone or anticyclone. The rotation is considered cyclonic if it is in the same sense as the rotation of the surface of the Earth about the local vertical, and is considered anticyclonic if in the opposite sense. Thus, in a cyclonic circulation, the streamlines indicate counterclockwise (clockwise for anticylonic) rotation of air about a central point on the Northern Hemisphere or clockwise (counterclockwise for anticyclonic) rotation about a point on the Southern Hemisphere. When the streamlines close completely about the central point, the pattern is denoted respectively a cyclone or an anticyclone. Since the gradient wind represents a good approximation to the actual wind, the center of a cyclone tends strongly to be a point of minimum atmospheric pressure on a horizontal surface. Thus the terms cyclone, low-pressure area, or low are often used to denote essentially the same phenomenon. In accord with the requirements of the gradient wind relationship, the center of an anticyclone tends to coincide with a point of maximum pressure on a horizontal surface, and the terms anticyclone, high-pressure area, or high are often used interchangeably.

Cyclones and anticyclones are numerous in the lower troposphere at all latitudes. At higher levels the occurrence of cyclones and anticyclones tends to be restricted to subpolar and subtropical latitudes, respectively. In middle latitudes the flow aloft is mainly westerly, but the streamlines exhibit wavelike oscillations connecting adjacent regions of anticyclonic circulation (ridges) and of cyclonic circulation (troughs).

Although the atmosphere is never in a completely undisturbed state, it is customary to refer to cyclonic and anticyclonic circulations specifically as atmospheric disturbances. Cyclones, anticyclones, ridges, and troughs are intimately associated with the production and transport of clouds and precipitation, and hence convey a connotation of disturbed meteorological conditions.

A more rigorous definition of circulation is often employed, in which the circulation C over an arbitrary area bounded by the closed curve S is given by Eq. (1),

$$C = \oint v_t \, dS \qquad (1)$$

where the integration is taken completely around the boundary of the area. Here v refers to the wind at a point on the boundary, the subscript t denotes the component of this wind parallel to the boundary, and dS is a line element of the boundary. The component v_t is considered positive or negative according to whether it represents cyclonic or anticyclonic circulation along the boundary S. In this context, the circulation may be positive (cyclonic) or negative (anticyclonic) even when the streamlines within the area are straight, since

the distribution of wind speed affects the value of C. *SEE ATMOSPHERE; CLOUD; STORM*.

Convergent or divergent patterns. These are said to occur in areas in which the (horizontal) wind flow and distribution of air density is such as to produce a net accumulation or depletion, respectively, of mass of air. Rigorously, the mean horizontal mass divergence D over an arbitrary area A bounded by the closed curve S is given by Eq. (2), where the integra-

$$D = \frac{1}{A} \oint \rho v_n \, dS \qquad (2)$$

tion is taken completely around the boundary of the area. Here ρ is the density of air, v refers to the wind at a point on the boundary, and the subscript n denotes the component of this wind perpendicular to the boundary, and dS is an element of the boundary. The component v_n is taken positive when it is directed outward across the boundary and negative when it is directed inward. Convergence is thus synonymous with negative divergence. If spatial variations of density are neglected, the analogous concept of velocity divergence and convergence applies.

The horizontal mass divergence or convergence is intimately related to the vertical component of motion. For example, since local temporal rates of change of air density are relatively small, there must be a net vertical export of mass from a volume in which horizontal mass convergence is taking place. Only thus can the total mass of air within the volume remain approximately constant. In particular, if the lower surface of this volume coincides with a level ground surface, upward motion must occur across the upper surface of this volume. Similarly, there must be downward motion immediately above such a region of horizontal mass divergence.

The horizontal mass divergence or convergence is closely related to the circulation. In a convergent wind pattern the circulation of the air tends to become more cyclonic; in a divergent wind pattern the circulation of the air tends to become more anticyclonic.

Regions which lie in the path of an approaching cyclone are characterized by a convergent wind pattern in the lower troposphere and by upward vertical motion throughout most of the troposphere. Since the upward motion tends to produce condensation of water vapor in the rising air current, abundant cloudiness and precipitation typically occur in this region. Conversely, the area in advance of an anticyclone is characterized by a divergent wind pattern in the lower troposphere and by downward vertical motion throughout most of the troposphere. In such a region, clouds and precipitation tend to be scarce or entirely lacking.

A convergent surface wind field is typical of fronts. As the warm and cold currents impinge at the front, the warm air tends to rise over the cold air, producing the typical frontal band of cloudiness and precipitation. *SEE FRONT*.

Zonal surface winds. Such patterns result from a longitudinal averaging of the surface circulation. This averaging typically reveals a zone of weak variable winds near the Equator (the doldrums) flanked by northeasterly trade winds in the Northern Hemisphere and southeasterly trade winds in the Southern Hemisphere, extending poleward in each instance to about latitude 30°. The doldrum belt, particularly at places and times at which it is so narrow that the trade winds from the two hemispheres impinge upon it quite sharply, is designated the intertropical convergence zone, or ITCZ. The resulting convergent wind field is associated with abundant cloudiness and locally heavy rainfall. A westerly average of zonal surface winds prevails poleward of the trade wind belts and dominates the middle latitudes of both hemispheres. The westerlies are separated from the trade winds by the subtropical high-pressure belt, which occurs between latitudes 30 and 35° (the horse latitudes), and are bounded on the poleward side in each hemisphere between latitudes 55 and 60° by the subpolar trough of low pressure. Numerous cyclones and anticyclones progress eastward in the zone of prevailing westerlies, producing the abrupt day-to-day changes of wind, temperature, and weather which typify these regions. Poleward of the subpolar low-pressure troughs, polar easterlies are observed.

The position and intensity of the zonal surface wind systems vary systematically from season to season and irregularly from week to week. In general the systems are most intense and are displaced toward the Equator in a given hemisphere during winter. In this season the subtropical easterlies and prevailing westerlies attain mean speeds of about 15 knots (7.7 m/s), while the polar easterlies are somewhat weaker. In summer the systems are displaced toward the pole by 5 to 10° of latitude and weaken to about one-half their winter strength.

When the pattern of wind circulation is averaged with respect to time instead of longitude, striking differences between the Northern and Southern hemispheres are found. On the Southern Hemisphere, variations from longitude to longitude are relatively small due to the predominance of ocean, and the averaged pattern is described quite well in terms of the zonal surface wind belts. On the Northern Hemisphere there are large differences from longitude to longitude because of the ocean-continent contrast. In winter, for example, the subpolar trough is mainly manifested in two prominent low centers, the Icelandic low and the Aleutian low. The subtropical ridge line is drawn northward in effect over the continents and is seen as a powerful and extensive high-pressure area over Asia and as a relatively weak area of high pressure over North America. In summer the Aleutian and Icelandic lows are weak or entirely absent, while extensive areas of low pressure over the southern portions of Asia and western North America interrupt the subtropical high-pressure belt. *See Climatology.*

Upper air circulation. Longitudinal averaging indicates a predominance of westerly winds. These westerlies typically increase with elevation and culminate in the average jet stream, which is found in lower middle latitudes near the tropopause at elevations between 35,000 and 40,000 ft (10.7 and 12.2 km). The subtropical ridge line aloft is found equatorward of its surface counterpart and easterlies occur at upper levels over the equatorward portions of the trade wind belts. In high latitudes, weak westerlies aloft are found over the surface polar easterlies. Seasonal and irregular fluctuations of the circulation aloft are similar to those which characterize the surface winds. *See Jet stream.*

Variation of wind with height. The rate of change of the wind vector with respect to height is called the wind shear. When the wind direction changes in a clockwise sense with increasing height, the wind is said to be veering with height. For example, if a southerly wind at the surface becomes southwesterly a kilometer above the ground, and westerly in the midtroposphere, the wind veers with height. If the geostrophic wind veers with height, then as a consequence of hydrostatic balance, there is warm advection, that is, warmer air is being blown toward colder air. Veering with height often occurs east of surface cyclones, and west of surface anticyclones in midlatitudes. When the wind direction changes in a counterclockwise sense with increasing height, the wind is said to be backing with height. For example, if a northerly wind at the surface becomes northwesterly a kilometer above the ground, and westerly in the midtroposphere, the wind backs with height. If the geostrophic wind backs with height, then there is cold advection, that is, colder air is being blown toward warmer air. Backing with height often occurs east of surface anticyclones and west of surface cyclones.

The winds may also veer with height as a result of surface friction. Typically, at the surface there is a component of wind across isobars from higher to lower pressure, while above the surface the wind tends to blow parallel to the isobars.

The variation of wind speed and direction with height has a significant impact on the type of thunderstorms which can form. Severe thunderstorms and tornadoes often form when the winds veer and increase in strength with height. *See Thunderstorm; Tornado.*

The expressions veering and backing are used also to describe the change of wind direction with respect to time. For example, north of the track of a low in the Northern Hemisphere the winds back with respect to time, while south of the track of a low the winds veer with time.

Minor terrestrial winds. In this category are circulations of relatively small scale, attributable indirectly to the character of the Earth's surface. One example, the land and sea breeze, is a circulation driven by pronounced heating or cooling of a given area in comparison with little heating or cooling in a horizontally adjacent area. During the day, air rises over the strongly heated land and is replaced by a horizontal breeze from the relatively cool sea. At night, air sinks over the cool land and spreads out over the now relatively warm sea.

Another example is formed by the mountain and valley winds. These result from cooling and heating, respectively, of the mountain slopes relative to the horizontally adjacent free air above the valley floor. During the day, air flows up from the valley along the strongly heated mountain slopes, but at night, air flows down the relatively cold mountain slopes toward the valley bottom. A similar type of descending current of cooled air is often observed along the sloping surface of a glacier. This night-time air drainage, under proper topographical circumstances, can lead to the accumulation of a pool of extremely cold air in nearby valley bottoms.

Local winds. These commonly represent modifications by local topography of a circulation of large scale. They are often capricious and violent in nature and are sometimes characterized by extremely low relative humidity. Examples are the mistral which blows down the Rhone Valley in the south of France, the bora which blows down the gorges leading to the coast of the Adriatic Sea, the foehn winds which blow down the Alpine valleys, the williwaws which are characteristic of the fiords of the Alaskan coast and the Aleutian Islands, and the chinook which is observed on the eastern slopes of the Rocky Mountains. Local names are also given in some instances to currents of somewhat larger scale which are less directly related to topography. Examples of this type of wind are the norther, which represents the rapid flow of cold air from Canada down the plains east of the Rockies and along the east coast of Mexico into Central America; the nor' easter of New England, which is part of the wind circulation about intense cyclones centered offshore along the Middle Atlantic coastal states; and the sirocco, a southerly wind current from the Sahara which is common on the coast of North Africa and sometimes crosses the Mediterranean Sea.

Frederick Sanders; Howard Bluestein

Bibliography. J. A. Dutton, *The Ceaseless Wind: An Introduction to the Theory of Atmospheric Motion,* 1976, reprint 1986; R. Holton, *An Introduction to Dynamic Meteorology,* 2d ed., 1979; J. M. Wallace and P. V. Hobbs, *Atmospheric Sciences: An Introductory Survey,* 1977.

Zoogeography

The subdivision of the science of biogeography that is concerned with the detailed description of the distribution of animals and how their past distribution has produced present-day patterns. Scientists in this field attempt to formulate theories that explain the present distributions as elucidated by geography, physiography, climate, ecological correlates (especially vegetation), geological history, the canons of evolutionary theory, and an understanding of the evolutionary relationships of the particular animals under study. Zoogeographical theories are then tested by new data from all germane fields to amplify, verify, or falsify the constructs. In this sense, zoogeography is an integrative science that synthesizes data from other disciplines to apply to the realities of animal distribution.

Realities. The field of zoogeography is based upon five observations and two conclusions. The observations are as follows. (1) Each species and higher group of animals has a discrete nonrandom distribution in space and time (for example, the gorilla occurs only in two forest areas in Africa). (2) Different geographical regions have an assemblage of distinctive animals that coexist (for example, the fauna of Africa south of the Sahara with its monkeys, pigs, and antelopes is totally different from the fauna of Australia with its platypuses, kangaroos, and wombats). (3) These differences (and similarities) cannot be explained by the amount of distance between the regions or by the area of the region alone [for example, the fauna of Europe and eastern Asia is strikingly similar although separated by 6900 mi (11,500 km) of land, while the faunas of Borneo and New Guinea are extremely different although separated by a tenth of that distance across land and water]. (4) Faunas strikingly different from those found today previously occurred in all geographical regions (for example, dinosaurs existed over much of the world in the Cretaceous). (5) Faunas resembling those found today or their antecedents previously occurred, sometimes at sites far distant from their current range (for example, the subtropical-warm temperate fauna of Eocene Wyoming, including many fresh-water fishes, salamander, and turtle groups, is now restricted to the southeastern United States).

The conclusions are as follows. (1) There are recognizable recurrent patterns of animal distribution. (2) These patterns represent faunas composed of species and higher groups that have evolved through time in association with one another.

Approaches. Two rather different approaches have dominated the study of zoogeography since the beginning of the nineteenth century: ecological and historical. Ecological zoogeography attempts to explain current distribution patterns principally in terms of the ecological requirements of animals, with particular emphasis on environmental parameters, physiological tolerances, ecological roles, and adaptations. The space and time scales in this approach are narrow, and emphasis is upon the statics and dynamics of current or very recent events.

Historical zoogeography recognizes that each major geographical area has a different assemblage of species, that certain systematic groups of organisms tend to cluster geographically, and that the interaction of geography, climate, and evolutionary processes over a long time span is responsible for the patterns or general tracks. Emphasis in this approach is upon the statics and dynamics of major geographical and geological events ranging across vast areas and substantial time intervals of up to millions of years. The approach is based on concordant evolutionary association of diverse groups through time.

Ecological zoogeography is the study of animal distributions in terms of their environments; historical zoogeography is the study of animal distributions in terms of evolutionary history.

Ecological zoogeography. Ecological zoogeography is rooted within the discoveries of nineteenth-century plant ecologists and physiologists. They found that under similar conditions of temperature and moisture, terrestrial plants develop similar growth forms, regardless of their evolutionary relationships, to produce one of the following vegetation forms: forest, woodland, savanna, grassland, or scrub. Subsequently it was demonstrated that these units showed differentiation associated with major soil types and broad latitudinal climatic regions. Each of these main kinds of vegetation is called a formation type (such as tropical lowland evergreen forest), and its geographical subdivisions are formations (such as South American tropical lowland evergreen forest; African tropical lowland evergreen forest).

Later investigators realized that within each formation a series of animals had evolved to undertake homologous ecological functions in the dynamics of the community, so that the concept of biome-type (vegetation and associated animals) was developed. The biome-type is a series of major geographical climatic regions characterized by similar ecological adaptations in plants and animals. For example, the grassland biome-type may be typified by the comparisons in the **table**. The biome-types are distinctive from the zoological point of view in that ecological equivalents (such as top predator) in the different biomes are usually from phylogenetically nonrelated stocks. M. D. F. Udvardy provides the best recent summary of the general distribution of world terrestrial biomes.

The concept of biomes is a method of generalizing the distribution of animals by major environments on a latitudinal basis. The ecological zoogeographer is also interested in vertical (altitudinal and bathymetric) zonation as a feature of animal distribution. The idea of zonation is based upon the recognition that there

Comparison of three grassland biomes			
Ecological roles	North American	African	Australian
Top predator	Wolf (dog)	Lion (cat)	Tasmanian wolf (marsupial)
Large herbivore	Bison (cattle)	Zebra (horse)	Red kangaroo (marsupial)
Small predator-scavenger	Coyote (dog)	Hyena (hyena)	Tasmanian devil (marsupial)

are ecoclinal gradients in the parameters of the environment (especially temperature) with an increase in altitude or in ocean depth. The composition of species distributions along these ecoclines, because of differences in ecological requirements, produces recognizable and characteristic life zones. As an example, **Fig. 1** shows the principal life zones in the ocean. These zones are divided into two groups: benthos or substrate zones and pelagic or free-swimming zones. Altitudinal life zones on land have been similarly described, most recently and completely by L. R. Holdridge. *See* BIOME; *LIFE ZONES*.

Historical zoogeography. This approach has its origins in systematic biology. Workers in this field recognized very early in the nineteenth century that different geographical regions support different faunas and that representatives of these faunas occur in a wide variety of environments (for example, apes and monkeys in Africa in rainforest to desert environments). In addition, they noted that different systematic groups tend to cluster geographically (kangaroos in Australia and anteaters in South America). With the development of the canons of evolutionary theory later in the century, a framework for understanding the evolution of faunas through time became the backbone of historical zoogeography.

The raw data of historical zoogeography are the distributions or tracks of individual species of animals in space (geographical ecology) and time. Because each species has its own set of peculiar ecological requirements and its own unique evolutionary history, each has a discrete nonrandom ecogeographical distribution. As a consequence, no species is universally present, and many species have small or unique tracks. The first level of generalization in zoogeography is based on the recognition that, in spite of the unique nature of individual species distributions, many tracks are concordant or show a common pattern. Determination of patterns involving the coincident distribution of species or monophyletic groups (genera, families, and so on) of species (generalized tracks) is the fundamental step in zoogeographical analysis.

The second level of generalization in this process is to cluster the strongly recurrent generalized tracks involving extensive geographical areas, whose components are then regarded as the major modern faunas. A third level of generalization attempts to tentatively identify the historical source units (ancestral faunas) that have contributed to the modern patterns.

Zoogeographical patterns. The early workers in zoogeography, especially P. Sclater in 1858 (birds) and A. Wallace in 1876, developed a system for classifying major patterns of terrestrial distributions, which in modified form (**Fig. 2**) is still applicable today. This system reflects the long-term isolation of major parts of the Earth's surface and the consequent divergent evolution of the fauna in each isolate. In some cases, subsequent reconnections of formerly isolated areas have blurred the distinctiveness of the core faunas in an area of transition. The major units in this system are called biogeographic realms; a se-

ries of biogeographic provinces form subdivisions within the larger divisions.

The eight recognized realms (which correspond to what were called zoogeographic regions in the Sclater-Wallace system and by many subsequent authors), with the number of provinces recognized for each realm indicated in parentheses are briefly characterized below. These units are based primarily on comparisons for the best-known animal groups. For this reason the several classes of vertebrates are used to characterize the realms below, although terrestrial and fresh-water invertebrates follow similar patterns but are less well known.

Nearctic Realm (22). North America, north of the edge of the Mexican-Guatemala highlands, although many workers would place the boundary with the Neotropical Realm at the edge of the Mexican plateau, west of the Isthmus of Tehuantepec. In terms of vegetation the northern areas support transcontinental zones of tundra and needle-leaf coniferous forests (taiga). The eastern portion of the continent to the south of the taiga zone was originally covered with broadleaf deciduous forests, and the central region by extensive grasslands. Coniferous forests predominate along the northwest coast and in the Rocky Mountains, Sierra Nevada, and upper regions of the Sierra Madre of Mexico. Much of the southwestern United States and adjacent Mexico are covered by oak savannas, scrub, and desertic vegetation. In terms of the fauna, a great many groups and species are shared with the Palearctic (that is, they have a holarctic distribution), and in more southern areas with the Neotropical Realm.

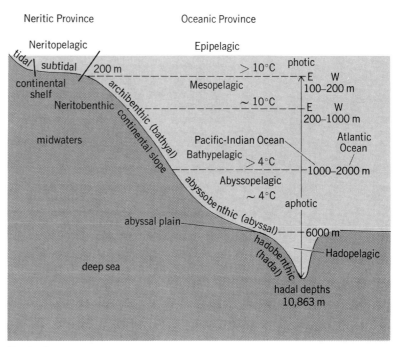

Fig. 1. Life zones in the sea. 1 m = 3.3 ft; °F = (°C × 1.8) + 32.

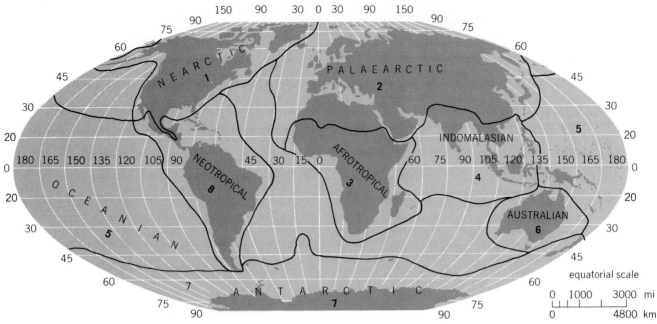

Fig. 2. Terrestrial biogeographic realms of the world. (*After M. D. F. Udvardy, A classification of the biogeographical provinces of the world, Int. Union Conserv. Nat. Occas. Pap., 18:1–49, 1975*)

Distinctive vertebrate groups of the Nearctic include bowfin, gar-pike, bullhead catfishes, panfish, and basses; hellbenders, mud puppies, amphiumas and sirens, the bell-frog (*Ascaphus*), spadefoot toads, snapping turtles, the land tortoises (*Gopherus*), the Gila monster and its ally the Mexican beaded lizard (*Heloderma*), the night lizards, fence lizards and their allies, glass lizards, worm lizard (*Rhineura*), rattlesnakes, and alligator; flycatchers, vireos, orioles, hummingbirds (all shared with tropical America); racoons, pocket gophers (also tropical), and pronghorn. Many characteristic birds and mammals (woodpeckers, wood warblers, tanagers, pikas, flying squirrels, beaver, jaguar, and cougar) belong to wide-ranging groups, with endemic species in the New World.

Palearctic Realm (44). The Eurasian land mass from southern China and the southern slopes of the Himalaya Mountains northward and westward from the Indus Valley to include the Arabian Peninsula and northern Africa. As with the Nearctic Realm, transcontinental zones of tundra and taiga occur in the northernmost areas. Broadleaf deciduous forest originally occurred over much of western (Europe) and eastern (China) portions of the realm, and the central areas of the land mass were steppe, grassland, or desert. Scrub-to-desert vegetation is typical of the Mediterranean area east to the Indus. The Palearctic fauna is a peculiar mixture of widespread groups with strong affinities to the Nearctic and others from the Old World tropics. For this reason, there is very little endemism at the major group level, and the distinctive groups are ones with a major radiation of species in the Palearctic. Distinctive vertebrate groups include a vast radiation of cyprinid fishes and numerous salmonids; many salamanders, lacertid lizards, slowworms, vipers; warblers, hedge sparrows (endemic); dormice, jerboas, the two-humped camel, and pandas.

Africotropical Realm (29). Africa south of the Sahara Desert and Madagascar. The realm is mostly tropical with broadleaf evergreen forests along the margins of the Gulf of Guinea and inland through the Congo Basin and on the eastern coast of Madagascar. Deserts cover the Kalahari, Namib, and the Somali Coast. Much of the rest of the continent was originally covered by tropical broadleaf deciduous forests which degraded to scrub-forest or savanna-grassland under human use. Montane evergreen forest occurs on the mountains of east Africa.

Although the realm shares many groups with tropical Asia and the Palearctic, it has one of the most easily recognizable faunas. Distinctive vertebrate groups for the continent include bichirs (lungfishes); caecilians, clawed frogs (*Xenopus*), reed frogs; sideneck turtles, chameleons, monitor lizards, sungazers, pythons, cobras, vipers, crocodiles; ostrich, secretary bird, hammerhead, touracos, mousebirds, helmet shrikes; otter shrew, golden mole, elephant shrews, monkeys, chimpanzees, gorilla, hyenas, aardvark, hyraxes, hippopotamuses, and spring haas. There are many genera and species of big game: the cats, rhinoceroses, buffalo, antelope, and pigs are African endemics. Madagascar lacks many important Continental groups but has a unique radiation of microhylid and reed frogs, specialized iguanids and boas, the endemic elephant birds (now extinct), flightless mesoenatids, endemic rollers, philapittas, and vangas; tenrecs, and lemurs, unique endemic mammals.

Indomalasian Realm (27). The Asian land mass from the west margin of the Indus Valley and south of the Himalaya Mountains and southern China and adjacent islands including Taiwan, the Philippines, and the Lesser Sundas. Most of the realm originally supported tropical forests with evergreen forests in western peninsular India, much of Burma, southeast Asia, southern China, the Malay Peninsula, and the Indo-Malayan Archipelago. Deciduous vegetation covered most of India and some areas of southeast Asia. Most of the latter has been converted to human use and degraded into scrub, grassland, or desert.

Distinctive groups of the Indo-Malayan include a high diversity of cyprinid fishes, loaches, labyrinth fishes; caecilians, rhacophorid tree frogs, microhylids; many endemic emydid turtles; gavial; pythons, pipesnakes, cobras, sea snakes, pit vipers. pheasants, fairy bluebirds and leaf birds; hairy hedgehog, flying lemur, and spiny dormice. Endemics include monkeys, gibbons, orangutan, tarsiers, an elephant, a tapir, two rhinoceroses, and many antelopes.

Oceanian Realm (7). The Pacific islands of Melanesia, Micronesia, Polynesia, Hawaii, New Caledonia, and New Guinea. These islands are covered with tropical vegetation and show strong affinities with the Indo-Malayan unit. Many workers include New Guinea in the Australian Realm because of its great similarity in vertebrates to the latter. The remaining islands have a high degree of endemism, very few distinctive major groups, and a depauperate vertebrate fauna. There are no truly fresh-water fishes, frogs occur only on the islands near New Guinea and on the Fijis, snakes occur naturally only as far east as Fiji, while geckos and skinks range over the entire area and native flightless mammals occur only out to the Solomons.

Australian Realm (13). For these purposes, Australia and Tasmania, although many zoogeographers would include New Guinea and adjacent islands to the Solomons. Most of Australia is covered by grasslands, scrub, and desert, with temperate forests along the eastern and southeastern lowlands (including Tasmania) and tropical forests in the northwest. The Australian Realm has a unique fauna including these distinctive groups: an endemic lungfish, an osteoglossid (other fresh-water fishes are all marine-derived), myobatrachid frogs, pelodryadid tree frogs, side-neck turtles, a vast radiation of geckos and agamid lizards, pygopodids, pythons, many elapid snakes; cassowaries, emus, megapodes, owlet frogmouths, lyrebirds, scrubbirds, flowerpeckers, honey-eaters, bell magpies, magpie larks, bower birds, and birds of paradise; spiny anteater, platypus, marsupials—Tasmanian wolf, Tasmanian devil, anteater, bandicoots, Australian opossums, koala, wombats, kangaroos, wallabies, and wallaroos.

Antarctic Realm (4). The Antarctic continent, New Zealand, and the subantarctic islands. New Zealand has extensive temperate forests of mixed evergreen and deciduous trees over much of the North and South islands, with grassland predominating on parts of South Island. The subantarctic islands are relatively barren with vegetation primarily of grasses, sedges, and annual composites. The Antarctic continent is covered by ice and snow. Only New Zealand is of interest here because of its depauperate but unique fauna. It has no truly fresh-water fishes. A single amphibian, the frog *Leiopelma*, and the tuatara (*Sphenodon*), the only survivor of a Cretaceous order of reptiles, occur there. There are no turtles or snakes (except marine ones), but several endemic genera and species of geckos and skinks. Unique birds include the extinct moas, kiwis, an extinct flightless goose, flightless rails, a flightless parrot, and a predatory parrot (the kea). Native land mammals are two bats.

Neotropical Realm (47). Lowland Mexico, Central America, South America, and the Antilles. Evergreen forests predominate along the Atlantic slope of Mexico, Central America, Panama, northwestern South America, and the Amazon Basin. Extensive deciduous forests formerly covered the lowlands of western Mexico and Central America, the Greater Antilles, and much of southern Brazil. Grassland and scrub vegetation cover extensive areas in central South

America south of the Amazon Basin, while desert conditions occur along the west coast of Chile-Peru. The high mountains of Central America, the Andes, and the planaltino of Peru-Bolivia support a wide variety of montane vegetation. Temperate rainforest occurs in southern Chile, while steppe conditions prevail over the Patagonian region of southern Argentina and extreme southern Chile.

It is no wonder that, with this diversity of habitats, the Neotropical Realm has the richest fauna of any region. The fresh-water fish fauna is extremely diverse, but represented by rather primitive stocks, characins, gymnotid eels, several endemic catfish families as well as endemic osteoglossids, a lungfish, and synbranchid eels; distinctive are caecilians, Surinam toads, and leptodactylid and microhylid frogs; reptiles are side-neck turtles, caimans, many iguanid and microterid lizards, boas, coral snakes, and pit vipers; birds include rheas, tinamous, New World vultures, screamers, cracids, the hoatzin, seriamas, trumpeters, the limpkin, the sun bittern, seed snipes, potoos, motmots, hummingbirds, puffbirds, jacamars, toucans, manakins, and cotingas; distinctive mammals are phalangers, armadillos, anteaters, sloths, tapirs, peccaries, porcupines, capybara, paca, agouti, marmosets, and New World monkeys.

A similar biogeographical scheme has been established for marine areas; J. C. Briggs has provided an up-to-date summary of the system.

Zoogeographical dynamics. The early workers in zoogeography concentrated their effort on the description of patterns of animal distribution and the clustering of patterns into large units of distribution by major environment or major fauna. These static approaches, while useful in phrasing and structuring data, have proved inadequate for understanding scientific zoogeography since they address only the first of four key elements: (1) recognizing common patterns of distribution; (2) analyzing these patterns to determine common ecological or evolutionary processes that produced the patterns; (3) using the patterns and processes as a prediction of patterns for as yet unstudied groups and (4) for as yet undiscovered geographical and evolutionary events.

The static approach ultimately had a stultifying effect on the development of zoogeography, since by the middle of the twentieth century descriptive and narrative zoogeography had run out of new ideas. Fortunately since the 1960s the science has been revitalized by a resurgence of interest in the dynamics of animal distribution. This interest has led to the development of two major new theories of zoogeographical explanation, one ecological (the dynamic equilibrium theory) and one historical (the vicariance theory). The development of the latter theory has forced a reexamination of the previously dominant historical zoogeographical explanation (the dispersion theory), most effectively expounded earlier in the century by W. D. Matthew and G. G. Simpson.

Dynamic equilibrium theory. This theory of zoogeography was developed during the 1960s primarily by R. H. MacArthur and E. O. Wilson. It originally was aimed at developing predictive mathematical models that would explain the differences in numbers of species on islands of differing sizes and differing distances from the closest mainland source areas. Since almost all habitats on the mainland are patchy in distribution as well (meadows, lakes, mountaintops, and so forth), the theory can also be applied to any discontinuous (insular) segments of the same environment type.

The central axiom of the theory is that the fauna of any disjunct ecological area is a dynamic equilibrium between immigration of new species into the area and extinction of species already present. Species number is thus constant over ecological time, while evolution will act gradually over geological time to increase the equilibrium number of species. From this base it is possible to construct equilibrium models that predict the interactions of distance from the source area, areal extent of the disjunct area, and immigration versus extinction (**Fig. 3**). Data from well-known insular faunas supported the value of these models. Subsequently, controlled defaunization experiments on small islands and study of the immigration process through time confirmed the predictive power of the theory.

Several conclusions may be derived from these models and have been confirmed in the field: (1) Distant disjunct areas will have fewer species than those close to a source area. (2) Small disjunct areas will have fewer species than large ones. (3) Distant disjunct areas take longer to reach equilibria when originally sterile or defaunated than do those close to the source area. (4) The smaller the area and the closer the area source to the area, the higher the turnover rate (change in species composition). The essential insight of equilibrium theory is that local extinctions and immigrations are relatively frequent events. Development of more complex equilibrium models and extension of the approach to other areas of zoogeography are actively under way and promise to produce exciting new views of distribution events.

Dynamic historical biogeography. This field is currently undergoing a major revolution of thought stimulated by new knowledge of global tectonics based on the now generally accepted theory of continental drift as outlined by R. S. Dietz and J. C. Holden. Simply

stated, theorists now believe that the major continents were formerly welded together as a supercontinent (Pangaea) that began to rift apart in the Triassic, about 190 million years before present. By the Early Jurassic, northern (Laurasia) and southern (Gondwanaland) land masses had drifted apart. During the Cretaceous these masses fragmented further, and in the Cenozoic several southern segments became attached to the northern continents (Africa to Eurasia, India to Eurasia, and South America to North America).

Previously, historical zoogeography had been dominated by the ideas of Matthew and Simpson, who believed in the permanency of the ocean basins and continents. These authors developed the idea that major groups originated on the northern continents and dispersed southward. P. J. Darlington developed a slightly different point of view and suggested that major groups arose in the Asian tropics and dispersed elsewhere on the continental masses across land bridges or marine barriers by island hopping. According to these kinds of ideas, the present-day distribution of lungfishes (tropical Africa, South America, and Australia) involved origin in the Old World (Asia?) and immigration across land bridges or by island hopping to the southern landmasses.

A group of zoogeographers, L. Croziat, G. Nelson, and D. E. Rosen, much influenced by the role of continental drift in geography, have developed and extended some ideas originally put forward by Croziat into a new theoretical construct. This theory focuses not on the dispersion of organisms from centers of origin, but on the idea that current zoogeographical patterns are the result of the fragmentation of previously continuous tracks by major physiographical change. Thus the present distribution of lungfishes is the result of the fragmentation of a previously continuous track by the breakup of Gondwanaland in the Cretaceous Period.

Essentially, this last development creates a contro-

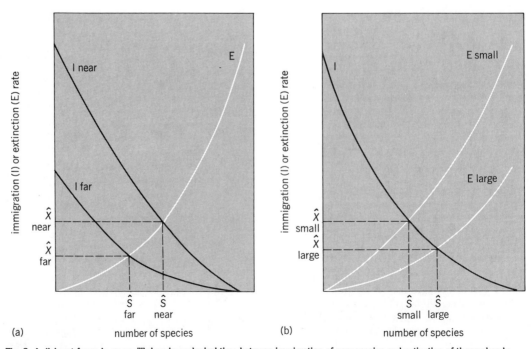

(a)   number of species   (b)   number of species

Fig. 3. A disjunct fauna is an equilibrium in ecological time between immigration of new species and extinction of those already present. (a) Distance effect; a near island has large equilibrium number of species ($\hat{S}$) and turnover rate ($\hat{X}$). (b) Area effect; a large island has larger $\hat{S}$ and smaller $\hat{X}$. (After D. S. Simberloff, Equilibrium theory of island biogeography and ecology, Ann. Rev. Ecol. Syst., 5:161–182, 1974)

versial dichotomy in zoogeographical thought. One view emphasizes the active movement (dispersal) of animals as the principal agent responsible for patterns; the other regards dispersion as unimportant and emphasizes the movement and fragmentation of the land masses and the relative immobility of animals as responsible for patterns. The latter position is called the vicariance theory, in distinction to the dispersion theory. An active, ongoing, vigorous interchange of ideas, with serious reexamination and critique of both schools, is the present theme of zoogeography.

The essential features of the dispersion and vicariance theories are as follows.

Dispersion theory: (1) A monophyletic group arises at a center of origin. (2) Each group disperses from this center. (3) Substantial numbers of monophyletic groups followed the same dispersal route at about the same time to contribute to the composition of a modern fauna. (4) A generalized track corresponds to a dispersion route. (5) Each modern fauna represents an assemblage derived from one to several historical source units. (6) Direction of dispersal may be deduced from tracks, evolutionary relations, and past geodynamic and climatic history. (7) Climate or physiographical change provides the major impetus or opportunity for dispersal. (8) Faunas were shaped by dispersion across barriers and subsequent evolution in isolation. (9) Dispersion is the key to explaining modern patterns: related groups separated by barriers have dispersed across them.

Vicariance theory: (1) Vicariants (allopatric species) arise after barriers separate parts of a formerly continuous population. (2) Substantial numbers of monophyletic groups are simultaneously affected by the same vicariating events (geographical barrier formation). (3) A generalized track estimates the faunal composition and geographical distribution of an ancestral biota before it subdivided (vicariated) into descendant faunas. (4) Each generalized track represents a historical source unit. (5) Sympatry of generalized tracks reflects geographical overlap of different faunas due to dispersal. (6) The primary vicariating events are changes in world geography (geodynamics) that subdivided ancestral faunas. (7) Faunas evolve in isolation after barriers arise. (8) Vicariance is of primary significance in understanding modern patterns: related groups separated by barriers were fragmented by the appearance of the barriers.

J. Savage has presented a critique of vicariance theory and provides a dispersal-vicariance model that combines the best explanatory features of both approaches. SEE ECOLOGY.

Jay M. Savage

Bibliography. H. G. Andrewartha and L. C. Birch, *The Ecological Web: More on the Distribution and Abundance of Animals,* 1986; J. C. Briggs, *Biogeography and Plate Tectonics,* 1987; J. H. Brown and A. C. Gibson, *Biogeography,* 2d ed., 1991; P. J. Darlington, *Zoogeography: The Geographical Distribution of Animals,* 1957; R. S. Dietz and J. C. Holden, The breakup of Pangaea, *Sci. Amer.,* 223(4):30–41, 1970; J. W. Hedgepeth, Classification of marine environments, *Mem. Geol. Soc. Amer.,* 67(1):17–27, 1957; G. Nelson and N. Platnik, *Systematics and Biogeography,* 1981; G. Nelson and D. E. Rosen, *Vicariance Biogeography,* 1981; J. M. Savage, The enigma of the Central American herpetofauna, *Ann. Missouri Bot. Gard.,* 69(3):444–556, 1983; D. S. Simberloff, Equilibrium theory of island biogeography and ecology, *Annu. Rev. Ecol. Syst.,* 5:161–182, 1974; G. G. Simpson, *The Geography of Evolution,* 1965.

Zooplankton

Animals that inhabit the water column of oceans and lakes, and lack the means to counteract transport currents. Zooplankton inhabit all layers of these water bodies to the deepest depths sampled, and constitute a major link between primary production and higher trophic levels in aquatic ecosystems. Many zooplankton are capable of strong swimming movements and may vertically migrate tens to hundreds of meters. Even these good swimmers, however, lack the ability to maintain their position against the movement of large water masses.

Zooplankton can be divided into various operational categories. Size is a common basis of classification, but is primarily related to the collection of plankton (by towed nets of various mesh sizes), and thus is not always related to biologically meaningful criteria. A commonly accepted size classification scheme includes the groupings: picoplankton (<2 micrometers), nanoplankton (2–20 µm), microplankton (20–200 µm), mesoplankton (0.2–20 mm), macroplankton (20–200 mm), and megaplankton (>200 mm). A classification based on biological criteria divides these animals into meroplankton and holoplankton. Meroplanktonic forms spend part of their life cycles on the bottom, and include larvae of benthic worms, mollusks, crustaceans, echinoderms, coral, and even insects, as well as the eggs and larvae of many fishes. Holoplankton spend essentially their whole existence in the water column. Examples are chaetognaths, pteropods, larvaceans, siphonophores, and many copepods.

Systematic composition. Nearly every major taxonomic group of animals has either meroplanktonic or holoplanktonic members. Some of the more common zooplankton groups are described below.

Protozoa are vital to planktonic systems. New methods of sampling and preservation reveal that soft-bodied ameba, nonphotosynthetic flagellates, and ciliates constitute the largest proportion of the microzooplankton. The best-known planktonic protozoa, however, are the ameboid Foraminifera and Radiolaria and the ciliated Tintinnida that have hard skeletons. The skeletons of foraminiferans and radiolarians form an important part of the deep-sea sediments. Foraminiferan fossils aid in identifying the geologic age of the layers and are used as markers in oil exploration.

The phylum Cnidaria contains a number of groups which are important in the marine plankton, including scyphozoans, the true jellyfish. Both scyphozoans and the colonial siphonophores are carnivores with tentacles bearing stinging nematocysts. They are found at all depths in the ocean but are most common in the upper waters. Cnidaria are rare in fresh water.

The ctenophores, or comb jellies, were once grouped with Cnidaria but are now treated separately because they lack nematocysts. All are exclusively carnivorous and are important predators of many zooplankton, especially copepods.

Rotifers probably arose in fresh water; only a few species are marine. About a hundred species are holoplanktonic. Most rotifers feed on bacteria, detritus, and algae, although some are predators of protozoa and other rotifers. Rotifers exhibit parthenogenesis under favorable conditions, and sexual reproduction as a response to certain environmental stresses. Cyclomorphosis (seasonal changes in morphology within a species) is common among rotifers.

Chaetognatha is a carnivorous marine group with worldwide distribution. They are mostly holoplanktonic and are found at all depths, although a given species may be restricted to certain water masses and depths. The elongate body is transparent with lateral fins and is usually less than 3 cm in length.

Veliger larvae of many benthic mollusks are frequently seen in coastal plankton. There are also marine gastropods, including heteropods and pteropods, which are adapted to a holoplanktonic life style. Another group represented in shallow marine waters by larvae is Polychaeta. This annelid class also contains a few holoplanktonic families.

Copepods are almost always the most numerous members of the macrozooplankton community in marine systems, and are important in fresh water as well. They often migrate to deeper water in daytime and move toward the surface at night, swimming by using the first antennae and the thoracic appendages. Most use other appendages with hairlike setules to filter phytoplankton and detritus from the water, but some also feed on larger particles, including smaller zooplankton.

Cladocera usually outnumber copepods in fresh water and occasionally are abundant in coastal marine waters. Their occurrence tends to be seasonal, with a resting egg formed between periods of rapid parthenogenic reproduction. Cyclomorphosis is common. Phytoplankton, the primary food source, is filtered from water passing through appendages within a bivalved carapace. The enlarged second antennae are the primary swimming appendages.

Euphausids are found worldwide at all depths, although individual species have more limited distribution. Some species, especially cold-water forms, demonstrate swarming behavior; in high latitudes they are the major food source of baleen whales. The most important food of polar euphausids appears to be diatoms, while carnivorous species are more common in warmer waters.

Tunicates are all marine. Many are benthic and produce planktonic larvae, but two classes, Appendicularia and Thaliasia, are holoplanktonic. Appendicularia are neotenic and build a mucous house which acts as a filter to capture small food particles. The Thaliacea, including salps and doliolids, are also filter feeders.

Adaptations. A problem faced by all plankton is to maintain position in the water column. Flattened bodies and numerous lateral spines or plumose setae which increase surface-to-volume ratios are common in various zooplankters. This increases resistance to the passage of water and thus slows sinking. Positive buoyancy mechanisms, such as oil droplets, gas-filled floats, or regulation of ionic balance by replacement of heavy ions with lighter ones, are other adaptations to a floating existence.

Life in open water exposes zooplankton to heavy predation by visual predators, especially fishes. Many zooplankters are nearly transparent, which affords them some protection. Others, such as fresh-water mites, have conspicuous coloration to advertise their noxious taste, so that visual predators learn to avoid them. In the blue light that penetrates to deep water, reddish hues appear black and thus invisible; it is not surprising that many bathypelagic zooplankton are red. Tactile predation by other zooplankton appears to be a major cause of cyclomorphosis in rotifers and cladocerans. The changes in morphology reduce predation.

Communities. Zooplankton, like all organisms, have a range of environmental conditions to which they are adapted. The optimum environment for one species may be barely tolerable to another. Physical and chemical boundary conditions, including turbulence, light, temperature, and salinity gradients, are important in determining species makeup of a zooplankton community. For example, plankton on the two sides of the Gulf Stream or within the upper and lower waters of a lake differ considerably. Some zooplankton have such clear-cut ecological demands that the presence of particular species can indicate the origin of the water mass. Narrow temperature tolerances limit some taxa to tropical or polar waters or to certain periods of the year in temperate zones. Differential salinity tolerances are reflected by changes in the composition of a community as estuaries become increasingly brackish downstream.

Biological parameters (for example, food availability, predation, and reproductive and social behavior) also structure zooplankton communities. Presence of fishes which feed selectively on larger zooplankters can limit the species composition to smaller-bodied animals. Lakes without size-selective vertebrate predators usually have a higher proportion of larger invertebrate plankton.

Seasonal breeding of holoplanktonic organisms and entrance of larval meroplankton into the water column play a large part in changing community composition. Food supply, temperature, and other factors interact to determine seasonal breeding patterns in zooplankton. Increasing light or temperature in temperate and boreal areas leads to spring phytoplankton blooms, when many zooplankters release their young. Other groups have maximum abundances in summer or during a secondary peak of primary production in the fall. *See Ecological communities.*

Vertical migration. Most major zooplankton groups have at least some species which display diel (diurnal) migrations, which usually consist of downward movement during the day and upward movement at night. The distance traveled can be hundreds of meters. The same species may display the classical day-down, night-up movement in one area and display no migratory behavior in another location. The sex and age of the zooplankton, as well as the season, can affect their vertical position in the water column and the degree of migration observed.

Diurnal light variation is the most likely mechanism triggering vertical migration. Many planktonic animals are positively phototactic at low light intensities and negatively phototactic at high intensities. Although the general consensus is that light is a major stimulus for migration, there are many explanations for its purpose. Zooplankton may sink to depths where illumination is insufficient for detection by visual predators in daytime, while at night, when visual predators do not hunt, zooplankton can return to the surface to feed on phytoplankton. Another explanation is that zooplankton remain in deeper, colder water during the day to reduce their metabolism, which is energetically advantageous, returning to the surface at night to feed. This advantage gained by remaining in colder water must exceed that expended in migration and lost due to lack of continuous feeding at the surface. Differential migration by ecologically similar species could also reduce competition for resources. It is unlikely that a single factor can explain all vertical migration; the above factors and others probably interact, or are important at different times.

Planktonic food web. The classic description of the trophic dynamics of plankton is a food chain consisting of algae grazed by crustacean zooplankton which are in turn ingested by fishes. This abstraction may hold true in upwelling areas, but it masks the complexity of most natural food webs. Zooplankton frequently assume different feeding habits as they grow from larval to adult form. They may ingest bacteria or phytoplankton at one stage of their life cycle and become raptorial feeders later. Other zooplankton are primarily herbivorous but can opportunistically become carnivorous. Zooplankton apparently can track changes in the particle-size spectrum of phytoplankton and graze the most abundant size classes. Some phytoplankton are noxious and are avoided by grazers, while others are ingested but not digested.

The importance of understanding the trophic ecology of zooplankton becomes evident when the link to commercial fisheries is considered. Zooplankton are a major food of fishes and a feasible direct source of protein to humans. Soviet and Japanese fishing crews harvest and package Antarctic euphausids (krill) in huge factory ships. Direct exploitation of other planktonic groups is possible if they can be detected in high concentrations. However, exploitation of zooplankton should await a thorough knowledge of their ecology and position in food webs. Repercussions of the uncontrolled harvesting of these animals must be expected—a lesson learned from the collapse of other fisheries in the past. *See Ecology; Ecosystem; Food web; Fresh-water ecosystem; Phytoplankton.*

Robert W. Sanders

Bibliography. P. Bougis, *Marine Plankton Ecology*, 1976; J. A. Downing and F. H. Rigler (eds.), *A Manual on Methods for the Assessment of Secondary Productivity in Fresh Waters*, 2d ed., 1984; W. C. Kerfoot (ed.), *Evolution and Ecology of Zooplankton Communities*, 1980; J. E. Raymont, *Plankton and Productivity in the Oceans*, vol. 2: *Zooplankton*, 1979; K. A. Steidinger and L. M. Walker, *Marine Plankton Life Cycle Strategies*, 1984; Z. Zheng, *Marine Planktology*, 1988.

Contributors

Contributors

A

Achey, Prof. Phillip M. *Institute of Food and Agricultural Sciences, University of Florida.*

Ackerman, Dr. Edward A. *Deceased; formerly, Carnegie Institution, Washington, D.C.*

Allen, Dr. Lawrence H., Jr. *Department of Soil Sciences, University of Florida.*

Amorocho, Dr. Jaime. *Department of Civil Engineering, University of California, Davis.*

Anderson, Dr. Robert L. *Forest Insect and Disease Management, USDA Forest Service, Asheville, North Carolina.*

Anthes, Prof. Richard A. *National Center for Atmospheric Research, Boulder, Colorado.*

Armstrong, Dr. Richard L. *Institute of Arctic and Alpine Research, University of Colorado.*

Atlas, Dr. Ronald M. *Department of Biology, University of Louisville.*

Avallone, Prof. Eugene A. *Formerly, Department of Mechanical Engineering, City University of New York.*

B

Bacon, Dr. Michael P. *Department of Chemistry, Woods Hole Oceanographic Institution, Woods Hole, Massachusetts.*

Badgley, Dr. Peter C. *Earth Science Division, Office of the Naval Reserve, Arlington, Virginia.*

Baker, Dr. Herbert G. *Department of Botany, University of California, Berkeley.*

Baker, Dr. Victor R. *Department of Geosciences, University of Arizona.*

Bakish, Dr. Robert. *Department of Engineering Technology, Fairleigh Dickinson University.*

Barber, Richard T. *Duke University Marine Laboratory, Beaufort, North Carolina.*

Barbosa, Dr. Pedro. *Department of Entomology, College of Life Sciences, University of Maryland.*

Barcelona, Dr. Michael J. *Director, Institute for Water Sciences, Western Michigan University.*

Barker, Dr. Joseph W. *Retired; formerly, Chairperson of the Board, Research Corporation, New York, New York.*

Barnes, Dr. Ivan. *Department of Physics, U.S. Geological Survey, Water Resources Division, Menlo Park, California.*

Benfer, Neil A. *Retired; formerly, Scientific Editor, National Oceanic and Atmospheric Administration.*

Bennett, Dr. Orus L. *GRC Panels Unlimited, Leeds, Alabama.*

Benninghoff, Dr. William S. *Department of Botany, University of Michigan.*

Berkofsky, Prof. Louis. *Institute for Desert Research, Ben Gurion University of the Negev, Beersheba, Israel.*

Berner, Dr. Elizabeth K. *Department of Geology and Geophysics, Yale University.*

Berner, Dr. Robert A. *Department of Geology and Geophysics, Yale University.*

Billings, Dr. W. D. *Department of Botany, Duke University.*

Billington, Dr. Douglas S. *Senior Staff Advisor for Materials Science, Metals and Ceramics Division, Oak Ridge National Laboratory, Oak Ridge, Tennessee.*

Billinton, Dr. R. *Head, Department of Electrical Engineering, University of Saskatchewan, Saskatoon, Canada.*

Bjerknes, Dr. Jacob. *Deceased; formerly, Professor Emeritus, Department of Meteorology, University of California, Los Angeles.*

Black, Dr. Robert F. *Department of Geology, University of Connecticut.*

Blanchard, Duncan C. *Senior Research Associate, Atmospheric Sciences Research Center, State University of New York, Albany.*

Blondel, Dr. Jacques. *Centre Louis Emberger, Montpellier, France.*

Bluestein, Prof. Howard B. *Department of Meteorology, University of Oklahoma.*

Bortman, Dr. Marci L. *Waste Management Institute, Marine Sciences Research Center, State University of New York, Stony Brook.*

Bose, Prof. Anjan. *Department of Electrical and Computer Engineering, Arizona State University.*

Bottomley, Dr. Peter J. *Department of Microbiology, Oregon State University.*

Box, Dr. Elgene O. *Department of Geography, University of Georgia.*

Breslin, Dr. Vincent T. *Waste Management Institute, Marine Sciences Research Center, State University of New York, Stony Brook.*

Bromley, Willard S. *Consulting Forester and Association Consultant, New Rochelle, New York.*

Brook, Dr. Marx. *Department of Physics, New Mexico Institute of Mining and Technology.*

Browne, Dr. Frank. *F. X. Browne, Inc., Lansdale, Pennsylvania.*

Bryan, Robert J. *La Habra, California.*

Burke, Dr. Kevin C. *Department of Geosciences, University of Houston.*

C

Cadwallader, Mark. *Director of Research and Technical Development, Gundle Lining Systems, Inc., Houston, Texas.*

Campbell, Dr. John S. *Department of Biological Sciences, University of Lethbridge, Alberta, Canada.*

Canter, Dr. L. W. *Sun Company Professor of Ground Water Hydrology and Director, Environmental and Ground Water Institute, University of Oklahoma.*

Carpenter, Dr. Stephen, R. *Department of Biological Sciences, University of Notre Dame.*

Carroll, Robert G., Jr. *Manager of Technical Development, Mirafi, Inc., Charlotte, North Carolina.*

Chappell, Dr. M. A. *University of California, Riverside.*

Chen, Dr. Mo-Shing. *Department of Electrical Engineering, University of Texas, Arlington.*

Chironis, Nicholas P. *Senior Editor, "Coal Age," McGraw-Hill, Inc., New York, New York.*

Clapp, Philip F. *National Weather Service, National Oceanic and Atmospheric Administration, Washington, D.C.*

Coleman, Dr. David C. *Department of Entomology, University of Georgia.*

Cooper, Dr. Arthur W. *Department of Botany, North Carolina State University.*

Court, Dr. Arnold. *Retired; formerly, Department of Climatology, California State University.*

Crafts, Dr. Alden S. *Professor Emeritus, Department of Botany, University of California, Davis.*

Crocker, Prof. Malcolm J. *Chairperson, Department of Mechanical Engineering, Auburn University.*

Crow, Loren W. *President, Loren W. Crow, Consultants, Inc., Certified Consulting Meteorologist, Denver, Colorado.*

D

Daiber, Dr. Franklin C. *College of Marine Studies, University of Delaware.*

Daugherty, Prof. Howard E. *Environmental Studies, York University, Toronto, Ontario, Canada.*

Davies-Jones, Dr. Robert P. *Meteorologist, National Severe Storms Laboratory, U.S. Department of Commerce, National Oceanic and Atmospheric Administration, Environmental Research Laboratories, Norman, Oklahoma.*

Dawson, Prof. Kerry J. *Environmental Horticulture, University of California, Davis.*

Day, Prof. Frank P., Jr. *Associate Professor and Director, Department of Biological Science, Old Dominion University.*

Deland, Dr. Raymond J. *Retired; formerly, Department of Meteorology and Oceanography, New York University.*

Doviak, Dr. R. J. *Senior Engineer, Doppler Radar and Storm Electricity, National Severe Storms Laboratory, Norman, Oklahoma.*

Dyer, Dr. K. R. *Institute of Oceanographic Sciences, Somerset, England.*

E

Easterbrook, Don J. *Department of Geology, Western Washington University, Bellingham.*

Eisenbud, Dr. Merrill. *Institute of Environmental Medicine, New York University Medical Center.*

Ellis, Dr. A. J. *Director, Chemistry Division, Department of Scientific and Industrial Research, Petone, New Zealand.*

Evans, Prof. Francis C. *Division of Biological Sciences, University of Michigan.*

Ewing, Dr. Gifford C. *Woods Hole Oceanographic Institution, Woods Hole, Massachusetts.*

F

Ffwocs-Williams, Prof. John E. *Department of Engineering, University of Cambridge, England.*

Fisher, Dr. F. H. *Marine Physical Laboratory, Scripps Institution of Oceanography, University of California, San Diego.*

Fixen, Dr. Paul E. *North Central Director, Potash and Phosphate Institute, Brookings, South Dakota.*

Fox, Dr. William K. *Standard Havens Research Corporation, Kansas City, Missouri.*

Frank, Dr. Bernard. *Deceased; formerly, Professor of Watershed Management, Colorado State University.*

Fravel, Maris T. *Bechtel Power Corporation, Ann Arbor Power Division, Ann Arbor, Michigan.*

Freeman, Harry M. *Chief, Waste Minimization Branch, Risk Reduction Engineering Laboratory, U.S. Environmental Protection Agency, Cincinnati, Ohio.*

Frost, Dr. Thomas M. *Center for Limnology, University of Wisconsin.*

Fuhrman, Dr. Ralph E. *Civil and Environmental Engineer, Washington, D.C.*

Fulks, J. R. *Retired; formerly, National Weather Service, Chicago, Illinois.*

G

Gagosian, Dr. Robert B. *Department of Chemistry, Woods Hole Oceanographic Institution, Woods Hole, Massachusetts.*

Gardner, Dr. Walter H. *Department of Agronomy and Soils, Washington State University.*

Georges, Dr. T. M. *Environmental Research Laboratories, National Oceanic and Atmospheric Administration, Boulder, Colorado.*

Gerrity, Dr. Joseph P. *National Meteorological Center, National Oceanic and Atmospheric Administration, Camp Springs, Maryland.*

Gilbert, Dr. Ronnie J. *Aquaculture and Fisheries, College of Agriculture, University of Georgia.*

Gilman, Dr. Donald L. *Formerly, Chief, Prediction Branch, Climate Analysis Center, National Weather Service, National Oceanic and Atmospheric Administration, Washington, D.C.*

Glasscock, Dwight L. *Deceased; formerly, Harza Engineering Company, Chicago, Illinois.*

Gleeson, Dr. Thomas A. *Department of Meteorology, Florida State University.*

Goldberg, Dr. Edward D. *Scripps Institution of Oceanography, La Jolla, California.*

Golley, Dr. Frank B. *Institute of Ecology, University of Georgia.*

Gregory, Dr. G. Robinson. *Department of Forestry, School of Natural Resources, University of Michigan.*

Grigal, Prof. David F. *Department of Soil Science, University of Minnesota.*

Gyakum, Dr. John R. *Department of Meteorology, McGill University, Montreal, Quebec, Canada.*

H

Hallet, Dr. John. *Director, Atmospheric Ice Physics Laboratory, Desert Research Institute, Atmospheric Sciences Center, University of Nevada.*

Hammond, Prof. Edwin H. *Department of Geography, University of Tennessee.*

Haney, Dr. Robert L. *Department of Meteorology, Naval Postgraduate School, Monterey, California.*

Hanna, Dr. Steven R. *Environmental Research and Technology, Concord, Massachusetts.*

Hanor, Jeffrey S. *Department of Geology, Louisiana State University.*

Hardy, Dr. Ernest E. *Department of Natural Resources, Cornell University.*

Harley, Dr. John H. *Department of Environmental Medicine, New York University.*

Harris, Prof. Richard W. *Department of Environmental Horticulture, University of California, Davis.*

Hartmann, Dr. Dennis L. *Department of Atmospheric Sciences, University of Washington, Seattle.*

Harwell, Dr. Christine C. *Global Environment Program, Center for Environmental Research, Cornell University.*

Harwell, Dr. Mark. *Global Environment Program, Center for Environmental Research, Cornell University.*

Hasler, Dr. Arthur D. *Laboratory of Limnology, University of Wisconsin.*

Hatfield, Dr. Jerry L. *Laboratory Director, U.S. Department of Agriculture, Agricultural Reserve Service, National Soil Tilth Laboratory, Ames, Iowa.*

Hayden, Dr. Christopher M. *U.S. Department of Commerce, National Oceanic and Atmospheric Administration, National Environmental, Satellite, Data and Information Service, Madison, Wisconsin.*

Hayes, William C. *Editor in Chief, "Electrical World," McGraw-Hill, Inc., New York, New York.*

Hazel, Prof. Jeffrey R. *Department of Zoology, Arizona State University.*

Hazen, Richard. *Hazen and Sawyer, Consulting Engineers, New York, New York.*

Hicks, Dr. Bruce B. *Atmospheric Turbulence and Diffusion Division, National Oceanic and Atmospheric Administration, Oak Ridge, Tennessee.*

Hinrichs, Thomas C. *Vice President, Magma Power, San Diego, California.*

Holland, Dr. Greg. *Bureau of Meteorology Research Center, Melbourne, Australia.*

Holmes, Dr. Robert W. *Department of Biological Sciences, University of California, Santa Barbara.*

Holt, Dr. Robert D. *Museum of Natural History, University of Kansas.*

Horn, Dr. David J. *Department of Entomology, Ohio State University.*

Humphreys, Dr. William F. *Western Australian Museum, Perth, Western Australia.*

I

Ingram, William T. *Consulting Engineer, Whitestone, New York.*

K

Kaplan, Dr. Lewis D. *Atmospheric and Environmental Research, Inc., Cambridge, Massachusetts.*

Karlen, Dr. Douglas L. *Soil Scientist, National Tilth Soil Laboratory, U.S. Department of Agriculture, Agricultural Research Service, Ames, Iowa.*

Keller, Prof. Walter D. *Department of Geology, University of Missouri.*

Kessler, Prof. Edwin. *Formerly, Director, National Severe Storms Laboratory, Norman, Oklahoma.*

Ketchum, Dr. Bostwick H. *Woods Hole Oceanographic Institution, Woods Hole, Massachusetts.*

Kissel, Dr. David E. *Department of Agronomy, Kansas State University.*

Kuntz, Glenn. *Regional Director, ETI of North America, Inc., Washington, D.C.*

Kutzbach, Prof. John E. *Department of Meteorology, University of Wisconsin.*

L

Lamb, Dr. Dennis. *Department of Meteorology, Pennsylvania State University.*

Landsberg, Dr. H. E. *Deceased; formerly, Institute for Physical Science and Technology, University of Maryland.*

Lane, Dr. Leonard J. *U.S. Department of Agriculture, Agricultural Research Service, Tucson, Arizona.*

Lapple, Charles E. *Consultant, Fluid and Particle Technology, Air Pollution and Chemical Engineering, Los Altos, California.*

Lebowitz, Dr. Michael D. *Professor of Medicine and Associate Center Director, Respiratory Sciences Center, University of Arizona.*

Lems, Dr. Kornelius. *Deceased; formerly, Associate Professor and Chairperson, Department of Biological Sciences, Goucher College.*

Leopold, Dr. Luna B. *Department of Geology and Geophysics, University of California, Berkeley.*

Lesins, Dr. Glen. *School of Meteorology, University of Oklahoma.*

Lewis, Dr. George W. *Head, Aquaculture and Fisheries, Collge of Agriculture, Extension Fisheries Specialists, University of Georgia.*

Lieberman, Prof. A. *Landscape Architecture, Cornell University.*

Lieth, Dr. Helmut. *Department of Botany, University of North Carolina.*

Likens, Prof. Gene E. *Institute of Ecosystem Studies, New York Botanical Garden, Millbrook.*

Linnenbom, Dr. V. J. *Naval Research Laboratory, Washington, D.C.*

Linsley, Prof. Ray K. *Department of Civil Engineering, Stanford University.*

Lodge, Dr. James P., Jr. *Consultant, Boulder, Colorado.*

Ludlam, Prof. Frank H. *Deceased; formerly, Department of Meteorology, Imperial College, London, England.*

Ludvik, Dr. George F. *Insecticide Application Research, Agricultural Research and Development Department, Monsanto Company, St. Louis, Missouri.*

Luthin, Prof. James N. *Department of Civil Engineering, University of California, Davis.*

Lyon, Dr. Waldo. *Arctic Submarine Laboratory, Naval Ocean Systems Center, San Diego, California.*

M

McHugh, Dr. J. L. *Marine Sciences Research Center, State University of New York, Stony Brook.*

McKee, Dr. William H., Jr. *Research Soil Scientist, Southeastern Forest Experiment Station, U.S. Department of Agriculture, Charleston, South Carolina.*

McNaughton, Prof. Samuel J. *Department of Biology, Syracuse University.*

Marek, John M. *Independent Mining Consultants, Inc., Tucson, Arizona.*

Mason, Dr. Basil John. *Programme Director, Centre for Environmental Technology, Imperial College of Science and Technology, London, England.*

Miller, Dr. Ronald. *Ecological Consultant, The World Bank, Washington, D.C.*

Mitchell, Prof. Rodger. *Department of Zoology, Ohio State University.*

Mitterer, Dr. Richard M. *Department of Geosciences, University of Texas, Dallas.*

Moldenhauer, Dr. William C. *National Soil Erosion Laboratory, U.S. Department of Agriculture, Agricultural Research Service, Purdue University.*

Morgan, Dr. Karl Z. *Neely Professor, School of Nuclear Engineering, Georgia Institute of Technology.*

Mudrick, Prof. Stephen E. *Department of Atmospheric Science, University of Missouri.*

Muffler, Dr. L. J. Patrick. *Geologist, Branch of Field Geochemistry and Petrology, U.S. Geological Survey, Department of the Interior, Menlo Park, California.*

N

Nace, Dr. Raymond L. *Retired; formerly, U.S. Geological Survey, Department of the Interior, Raleigh, North Carolina.*

Namias, Jerome. *Scripps Institution of Oceanography, La Jolla, California.*

Newton, Dr. Chester W. *National Center for Atmospheric Research, Boulder, Colorado.*

Nierenberg, Prof. William A. *Director, Scripps Institute of Oceanography, University of California, San Diego.*

Nixon, Dr. Charles W. *Consultant, Kettering, Ohio.*

North, Dr. Gerald R. *Director, Climate System Research Program, Department of Meteorology, Texas A & M University.*

O

O'Connor, Dr. Donald J. *Environmental Engineering and Science Program, Manhattan College, Bronx, New York.*

Oris, Dr. James T. *Department of Zoology, Miami University, Oxford, Ohio.*

Owen, Dr. Denis F. *Department of Biology, Oxford Polytechnic.*

Owston, Dr. Peyton W. *Project Leader, Reforestation Systems in the Pacific Northwest Research Station, U.S. Department of Agriculture, Corvallis, Oregon.*

P

Paine, Dr. Robert. *Department of Zoology, University of Washington.*

Palevsky, Dr. Gerald. *Environmental Engineering: Consulting·Design·Research, New Hyde Park, New York.*

Park, Prof. Charles F., Jr. *Department of Applied and Earth Sciences, Stanford University.*

Pastner, Hal. *Vice President, Gundle Lining Systems, Inc., Houston, Texas.*

Patton, Dr. Donald J. *Department of Geography, Florida State University.*

Pattullo, June G. *Deceased; formerly, Department of Oceanography, Oregon State University.*

Peng, Dr. T.-H. *Lamont-Doherty Geological Observatory, Columbia University, Palisades, New York.*

Peters, Dr. William C. *Professor Emeritus, Mining and Geological Engineering, University of Arizona.*

Peterson, Prof. G. A. *Department of Agronomy, Colorado State University.*

Pinder, Dr. George F. *Department of Civil and Geological Engineering, Princeton University.*

Pionke, Dr. Harry B. *Northeast Watershed Research Center, U.S. Department of Agriculture, University Park, Pennsylvania.*

Platt, Prof. Rutherford H. *Department of Geology, University of Massachusetts.*

Pohl, Prof. Robert O. *Laboratory of Atomic and Solid State Physics, Cornell University.*

Prendiville, Paul W. *Senior Vice-President, Camp, Dresser and McKee, Inc., Environmental Engineers, Scientists, Planners, & Management Consultants, Boston, Massachusetts.*

Priester, Gayle B. *Consulting Engineer, Baltimore, Maryland.*

Prinn, Prof. Ronald G. *Department of Meteorology, Massachusetts Institute of Technology.*

Prospero, Dr. Joseph M. *Department of Marine and Atmospheric Chemistry, University of Miami.*

Prosser, Dr. C. Ladd. *Department of Physiology, University of Illinois.*

R

Radke, Dr. Rodney O. *Agricultural Product Research Laboratory, Monsanto Co., St. Louis, Missouri.*

Randerson, Dr. Peter. *Department of Applied Biology, University of Wales Institute of Science and Technology, Cardiff.*

Rasmusson, Dr. Eugene M. *Geophysical Fluid Dynamics Laboratory, Environmental Science Services Administration, Princeton, New Jersey.*

Reddoch, Dr. Thomas W. *Electrotek Concepts Inc., Knoxville, Tennessee.*

Reichle, Dr. David E. *Manager, Head, Environmental Science Division, Oak Ridge National Laboratory, Oak Ridge, Tennessee.*

Reid, Joseph L. *Scripps Institution of Oceanography, La Jolla, California.*

Reid, Dr. R. L. *Division of Animal and Veterinary Sciences, College of Agriculture and Forestry, Agricultural and Forestry Experiment Station, West Virginia University.*

Richards, Dr. Paul W. *School of Plant Biology, University College of North Wales, Bangor.*

Risser, Dr. Paul G. *Vice President for Research, University of New Mexico.*

Ritchie, Dr. J. C. *Department of Biology, York University, Toronto, Ontario, Canada.*

Robbins, Dr. C. W. *Agricultural Research Service, U.S. Department of Agriculture, Kimberly, Ohio.*

Roy, Natalie. *Director of Recycling and Legislative Affairs, Glass Packaging Institute, Washington, D.C.*

S

Saenger, Dr. Peter. *Centre for Coastal Management, University of New England, Northern Rivers, Lismore, Australia.*

Sanders, Dr. Fredrick. *Department of Meteorology, Massachusetts Institute of Technology.*

Sanders, Dr. Robert W. *Department of Zoology, University of Georgia.*

San Martin, Robert L. *Deputy Assistant Secretary for Renewable Energy, Department of Energy, Washington, D.C.*

Savage, Dr. Jay M. *Department of Biology, University of Miami.*

Sayre, Dr. Albert N. *Deceased; formerly, Consulting Groundwater Geologist, Behre Dolbear and Company.*

Scharfe, Dr. Joachim. *Fisheries Technology Service, Fishery Industries Division, Food and Agriculture Organization of the United Nations, Rome, Italy.*

Schindler, Dr. James E. *Department of Biological Sciences, College of Sciences, Clemson University.*

Schmitt, Walter R. *Scripps Institution of Oceanography, La Jolla, California.*

Schnabel, Dr. Ronald R. *Soil Scientist, U.S. Department of Agriculture, Agricultural Research Service, Northeast Watershed Research Center, University Park, Pennsylvania.*

Scholz, Christopher H. *Lamont-Doherty Geological Observatory, Palisades, New York.*

Schule, John J., Jr. *Acting Director, Department of Marine Science, U.S. Naval Oceanographic Office.*

Sekhar, Natarajan. *Manager, General Electric Environmental Services, Inc., Lebanon, Pennsylvania.*

Seliskar, Dr. Denise M. *Associate Research Scientist, College of Marine Studies, University of Delaware.*

Sellers, Prof. W. D. *Department of Atmospheric Sciences, University of Arizona.*

Shannon, Dr. Michael C. *Research Geneticist, U.S. Department of Agriculture, Agricultural Research Service, Salinity Laboratory, Riverside, California.*

Shaw, Jeff. *Manager, 3M Paper Technology Center, St. Paul, Minnesota.*

Shugart, Dr. H. H. *Department of Environmental Sciences, University of Virginia.*

Simberloff, Prof. Daniel. *Department of Biological Science, Florida State University.*

Simonson, Dr. Roy W. *Retired; formerly, Director, Soil Classification and Correlation, U.S. Department of Agriculture, Hyattsville, Maryland.*

Simpson, Dr. Joanne. *Head, Severe Storms Branch, Goddard Space Flight Center, National Aeronautics and Space Administration, Greenbelt, Maryland.*

Simpson, Dr. Robert H. *Retired; formerly, Director, Ex-*

perimental Meteorology Laboratory, National Weather Service, Miami, Florida.

Smith, Dr. Guy D. *Geological Institute, Krisgslann, Ghent, Belgium.*

Sorensen, Dr. Robert M. *Coastal Engineering Research Center, Department of the Army, Fort Belvoir, Virginia.*

Southwood, Prof. T. R. E. *Department of Zoology, Oxford University, England.*

Sposito, Dr. Garrison. *College of Natural Resources, Department of Plant and Soil Biology, University of California, Berkeley.*

Spurgin, Robert A. *President, Spurgin & Associates, Irvine, California.*

Staff of the Mississippi River Commission, U.S. Army Corps of Engineers.

Stage, Dr. Steven A. *Department of Meteorology, Florida State University.*

Starr, Dr. Eugene C. *Bonneville Power Administration, U.S. Department of the Interior, Portland, Oregon.*

Stover, Dr. Harold E. *Retired; formerly, Professor and Extension Agricultural Engineer, Kansas State University.*

Swanson, Dr. R. Lawrence. *Director, Waste Management Institute, Marine Sciences Research Center, State University of New York, Stony Brook.*

T

Taylor, Dr. Danny L. *Chairperson, Department of Mining Engineering, Mackay School of Mines, University of Nevada.*

Tennant, Dr. Raymond W. *Chief, Cellular and Genetic Toxicology Branch, Department of Health and Human Resources, National Institutes of Health, National Institute of Environmental Health Sciences, Research Triangle Park, North Carolina.*

Turner, Dr. Monica G. *Environmental Sciences Division, Oak Ridge National Laboratory, Oak Ridge, Tennessee.*

V

Vali, Dr. Gabor. *Department of Atmospheric Science, University of Wyoming.*

Van Dorn, Dr. William G. *Scripps Institution of Oceanography, University of California, San Diego.*

van Linden, Dr. J. H. L. *Alcoa Laboratories, Aluminum Company of America, Alcoa Center, Pennsylvania.*

Velzy, Charles O. *Retired; formerly, Charles R. Velzy Associates, Inc., Valhalla, New York.*

Veronis, Dr. George. *Head, Department of Geology, Yale University.*

Voigt, Dr. Garth K. *Acting Dean, School of Forestry and Environmental Studies, Yale University.*

Von Gierke, Dr. Henning E. *Consultant, Yellow Springs, Ohio.*

Vonnegut, Dr. Bernard. *Retired; formerly, Department of Atmospheric Science, State University of New York, Albany.*

W

Wallace, Dr. John M. *Department of Atmospheric Sciences, University of Washington, Seattle.*

Walsh, John J. *Brookhaven National Laboratories, Upton, New York.*

Walz, Arthur H., Jr. *United States Committee on Large Dams, Corps of Engineers, Washington, D.C.*

Welhener, Herb. *Principal Mining Engineer, Independent Mining Consultants, Inc., Tucson, Arizona.*

Wetzel, Dr. Richard. *College of William and Mary, Virginia Institute of Marine Science, School of Marine Science, Gloucester Point, Virginia.*

White, Dr. E. H. *College of Environmental Science and Forestry, State University of New York, Syracuse.*

Wiegert, Dr. Richard G. *Department of Zoology, Franklin College of Arts and Sciences, University of Georgia.*

Willett, Prof. Hurd C. *Department of Meteorology, Massachusetts Institute of Technology.*

Willis, Homer B. *Consultant, Bethesda, Maryland.*

Willis, Dr. W. O. *Deceased; formerly, Department of Agronomy, Colorado State University.*

Woodcock, Dr. Alfred H. *Oceanography and Meteorology, Institute of Geophysics, University of Hawaii.*

Wooster, Dr. Warren S. *Department of Fisheries, University of Washington, Seattle.*

Index

Index

Asterisks indicate page references to article titles.